ENCYCLOPEDIA OF AMERICAN HISTORY

ADVISERS

Dean Albertson, University of Massachusetts

Richard Ellis, University of Virginia

Louis Filler, Antioch College

Lloyd Gardner, Rutgers University

J. Joseph Huthmacher, University of Delaware

John M. Murrin, Princeton University

Warren Susman, Rutgers University

Alan Trachtenberg, Yale University

Irwin Unger, New York University

CONTRIBUTORS

Dean Albertson, University of Massachusetts

Robert G. Albion, Harvard University

Edward Alvey, Jr., Mary Washington College of the University of Virginia

Thomas Archdeacon, University of Wisconsin

Sheldon Avery, Johns Hopkins University

Norman Barka, College of William and Mary

Paul Boyer, University of Massachusetts

John D. Buenker, University of Wisconsin, Parkside

Michael Burlingame, Connecticut College

John C. Burnham, Ohio State University

Dan T. Carter, University of Maryland

Robert W. Cherny, California State University, San Francisco

Seddie Cogswell, California State University, San Francisco

Richard Collin, Louisiana State University, New Orleans

Michael H. Ebner, City College of The City University of New York

Richard Ellis, University of Virginia

Louis Filler, Antioch College

David F. Forte, Skidmore College

Joe B. Frantz, University of Texas, Austin

Arrell M. Gibson, University of Oklahoma

Myron Goldfinger, Pratt Institute

Martin Gruberg, University of Wisconsin, Oshkosh

George C. Herring, Jr., University of Kentucky

Michael F. Holt, Yale University

Philip C. Homes, Franconia College

Ari Hoogenboom, Brooklyn College of The City University of New York

Reginald Horsman, University of Wisconsin, Milwaukee

Akira Iriye, University of Chicago

Peter d'A. Jones, University of Illinois, Chicago Circle

Allen F. Kifer, Skidmore College

Alexander W. Knott, University of Northern Colorado

Marvin Koenigsberg, Brooklyn College of The City University of New York

George Lankevich, Bronx Community College of The City University of New York

Lewis Leary, University of North Carolina, Chapel Hill

Erwin L. Levine, Skidmore College

Dennis S. McNally, University of Massachusetts

Douglas T. Miller, Michigan State University

Jack Murphy, University of Massachusetts

John M. Murrin, Princeton University

Marion Nowak, Michigan State University

Roger L. Nichols, University of Arizona

C. Herman Pritchett, University of California, Santa Barbara

Ronald Radosh, Queensborough Community College of The City University of New York

Alan Rich, *New York* Magazine

Jean Scarpaci, Towson State College

Aaron M. Shatzman, Washington University

Robert F. Smith, Skidmore College

Murray S. Stedman, Jr., Temple University

Merle L. Steir, Sculptor and Designer

Carl Ubbelohde, Case Western Reserve University

Paul P. Van Riper, Texas A & M University

William Veeder, University of Chicago

A. Munroe Wade, Westminster Choir College

William D. Wagoner, Louisiana State University

Robin W. Winks, Yale University

Nancy Woloch, Hebrew Union College

ENCYCLOPEDIA OF
AMERICAN HISTORY

The Dushkin Publishing Group, Inc.
Guilford, Connecticut

Library of Congress Catalog Card Number: 73-85201

Manufactured in the United States of America
First Printing

Cover Illustration: *A View of Mount Vernon,* artist unknown. Courtesy of National Gallery of Art, Gift of Edgar William and Bernice Chrysler Garbisch.

PREFACE

An understanding of the tools of a discipline is essential to understanding the discipline—its development, accomplishments, and problems. Our goal has been to answer specific questions about American History as clearly and as concisely as possible. For maximum utility—because the editors insisted that you should be able to find the information you want in the first place you look it up— we adopted the short-entry, alphabetical form. More than 1,000 relatively short articles—arranged alphabetically and tied together by a system of direct cross references and item guides—form the basis of the book's easily accessed information. Because of this interweaving structure, almost any article in the encyclopedia can serve as the point of entry for a systematic study of the entire field.

Authority

All the articles in the encyclopedia were prepared by authorities working in their own specialties. Articles of 250 or more words in length bear the signature and affiliation of the contributor. Most of the shorter, unsigned pieces were prepared by the same authorities who wrote the longer pieces.

Preparing an encyclopedia of this length is as much a problem of deciding what to leave out as of what to include. The advisers and contributors were involved in a process of assembling an enormous body of information and, at the same time, of paring it down to essentials. We have sought to be of most value to nonprofessional readers, and this goal guided our decisions about how best to present the information. An examination of the Bibliography at the end of this volume will show that many of our authors have made important professional contributions in their own areas of specialization, but for this book each was asked, first, to approach our articles from the viewpoint of the nonprofessional's information needs. Each contributor was also asked to ensure that every article would be as complete as possible within the limitations of the space available. Thus, we sought to provide the best presentation of information possible within the limits of our chosen length.

Organization of the Encyclopedia

This encyclopedia is fully comprehensive. It was constructed topically first and then arranged alphabetically for ease of access. This organization has enabled us to include a number of guidance functions as integrated parts of the information system.

Cross references are of two kinds. *See* references, which appear as individual entries in the alphabetical sequence, take the place of a separate index and send you directly to the location of the information you want. *See also* references at the end of an article direct you to carefully selected supplementary articles.

Subject maps show in a single display the interrelationships among the articles in each of 12 major areas of American History. These subject maps allow you to see at once the encyclopedia's full coverage of the area you're exploring. The maps appear in the book under the following headings:

American Wars	Frontier in American History
Blacks in the United States	Indians
Business Regulation and Industrialization	Labor Movement
Civil War and Reconstruction	New Deal and Depression
Constitution	Revolutionary War Era
Exploration and Colonization	Slavery and Emancipation

Item guides point out specific relationships between individual articles in the book and lead in a meaningful sequence from one article to another. They accompany more than 20 key articles in this edition.

Consult references at the end of an article are numerically keyed to a classified bibliography at the back of the volume. All of the bibliography titles have been selected by the authors of the encyclopedia articles as suggestions for further reading.

Illustrations are used functionally in the encyclopedia. The computer-composed format permits the inclusion of photographs, cartoons, drawings, maps, and charts wherever the editors considered them valuable.

Reader's Response

For historians, the type and accuracy of the information available to them are critical considerations. The editors of this encyclopedia have faced the same problems in trying to meet your needs. Evaluating the quality and usefulness of information and deciding what to include are always demanding tasks. For the editors of this book that task is never completed. The revision for the next edition is already under way. Now, however, we hope to add a new level of information to the book: your opinion of it—for you can become involved in the life of this encyclopedia. We urge you to let us know what you missed in the book, what you think could be done better, what was done well, and what more might be done. We're looking forward to hearing from you.

The Publishers

ENCYCLOPEDIA OF AMERICAN HISTORY

ABERNATHY, RALPH (DAVID) (1926–), prominent black civil rights leader and president of the Southern Christian Leadership Conference (SCLC) (1968–1973). Abernathy, a Baptist minister with a degree in sociology, assumed leadership of SCLC following the murder of Dr. Martin Luther King, Jr.

A native of Linden, Ala., Rev. Abernathy formulated his own programs but adhered basically to King's nonviolent philosophy. He led the massive Poor Peoples' March on Washington in May 1968 and a demonstration at the Republican National Convention at Miami the same year. He was arrested in Atlanta for blocking emergency garbage pickups in support of striking sanitation workers and was jailed a year later (1969) on charges of inciting Charleston, S.C., hospital workers to riot. Overall, he is a leader in the effort to raise the standard of living of the nation's poor blacks and to regain the confidence of young activists disillusioned with nonviolence.

See also Blacks in the Unites States; Civil Rights Movement.

ABOLITIONISM, the movement to end slavery in the United States. This movement should be distinguished from *antislavery,* which involved an attitude of distaste or regret that slavery existed. Some slaveholders abhorred the institution, and a few freed their own slaves. Some were even willing to see the spread of slavery retarded in colonial land grants and, later, the Western domain of the United States. However, they were unwilling to declare slavery a sin or to take aggressive steps to undermine the institution.

Thomas Jefferson. During the early stages of abolitionism, most expected that it would flourish in the South because slavery very easily rooted itself in the plantation system. Jefferson was an exception among Virginia leaders in that he sought a gradual end to enslavement. Although he was principally concerned with what slavery did to his ethnic peers, he was a kind master and intended that emancipation aid blacks as well as whites. His outstanding achievement in the field was the Northwest Ordinance, which became law in 1787. It stipulated that slavery be outlawed in the western domain north of the Ohio River.

Early Abolitionists. Before the Missouri crisis of 1820, there were antislavery groups in the Border States and farther south. The greatest of the early abolitionists was Benjamin Lundy. About 1815 he began a propaganda and organizing campaign that took him through the upper South, as well as Ohio and Maryland, and as far as Texas and Canada. One of his objects was to colonize blacks both in this country and overseas, where they could display their talents and so speed up emancipation.

William Lloyd Garrison. On a trip north, Lundy met a young journalist and reformer, Garrison, who joined Lundy in editing his journal, *The Genius of Universal Emancipation,* in 1829. The young man quickly caused trouble by denouncing a Northern shipper in the slave trade. Garrison was jailed for libel and was not released until Arthur Tappan, a New York businessman and abolitionist, paid his fine. Garrison settled in Boston, where on Jan. 1, 1831, he began publishing The *Liberator.* This was the first "immediatist" publication in the country. Garrison did not expect that slavery could be ended "immediately," but he and his little New England Anti-Slavery Society argued that moral people should act and talk as though it should be.

American Anti-Slavery Society. By 1833 a number of abolitionists in the North believed interest in the country was high enough to warrant organizing a national society. A meeting convened in Philadelphia set the American Anti-Slavery Society on its way. Emerging antislavery leaders included John Greenleaf Whittier, William Jay (son of John Jay, former Chief Justice of the Supreme Court), and James G. Birney, a distinguished Alabaman, formerly a colonizationist. Outstanding in the 1830s was Theodore D. Weld, whose eloquence and organizational abilities helped establish many abolitionist societies. Weld also brought together abolitionist ministers to agitate throughout the Midwest.

The period following organization of the national society was one of violence against abolitionist speakers. A high point of antiabolitionist resentment was the shooting to death of Rev. Elijah P. Lovejoy in 1837. He had left St. Louis because of the hatred inspired by his newspaper *The Observer* and had moved across the Mississippi River to Alton, Ill. In the process he had lost three printing presses to mobs. During his fourth effort to issue his paper, he was killed by rioters. Abolitionists everywhere mourned him as a martyr to free speech. The following year in Philadelphia, Pennsylvania Hall, built to serve abolitionists and reform movements, was burned to the ground by arsonists during dedication ceremonies. By then, however, abolitionists had largely won their fight to be heard.

Abolitionist Causes. The movement opposing slavery was limited by "states' rights." All privileges not specifically given to the federal government were ceded to the states and citizens. Abolitionists had to concentrate on stirring sympathy in the North and petitioning Congress on national issues. Accordingly, they opposed the entrance of the Texas Territory into the Union because it might add six to eight slave states. They also sought to influence their state legislatures to aid free blacks and fugitive slaves. They protested because the post office refused to guarantee the safety of abolitionist publications. They petitioned to end slavery in the District of Columbia, which they

Black civil rights leader Ralph Abernathy dramatizes needs of poor by bringing rally to Wall Street financial district in New York City.

ABOLITIONISM — Item Guide

The article on ABOLITIONISM covers the history of the events and people in the movement to end SLAVERY. Early national leaders, such as THOMAS JEFFERSON, had been concerned with slavery, and its extension was limited by such measures as the NORTHWEST ORDINANCE (1787) and the MISSOURI COMPROMISE (1820).

WILLIAM LLOYD GARRISON, emerged during the late 1820s as the most prominent abolitionist and was active in the AMERICAN ANTI-SLAVERY SOCIETY. Other early leaders were poet JOHN GREENLEAF WHITTIER, JAMES G. BIRNEY, THEODORE D. WELD, and ex-President JOHN QUINCY ADAMS.

Disagreements among abolitionists led to the diffusion of their energies among several organizations, including the AMERICAN AND FOREIGN ANTI-SLAVERY SOCIETY and, in politics, the LIBERTY PARTY, the FREE-SOIL PARTY, which nominated ex-President MARTIN VAN BUREN (1848), and the REPUBLICAN PARTY. Free blacks, such as FREDERICK DOUGLASS and UNDERGROUND RAILROAD conductor HARRIET TUBMAN actively participated in EMANCIPATION MOVEMENTS and opposed the FUGITIVE SLAVE ACTS.

The demands of abolitionists, such as CHARLES SUMNER, became more strident in the 1850s. After ABRAHAM LINCOLN's election in 1860, the Civil War broke out, leading eventually to the EMANCIPATION PROCLAMATION and slavery's abolition by the Thirteenth Amendment (AMENDMENTS, CONSTITUTIONAL).

insisted ought to honor Northern principles because it was national property.

Dissension Among Abolitionists. The movement to end slavery was but one of many reform movements of the era. Spirited women demanded additional rights, which Garrisonians honored but moderates deplored. Lewis Tappan believed that to force women speakers on American audiences would lose abolitionists the broader public they desired. Garrison also opposed engagement in politics, since it would require compromises with conservatives. Such differences in outlook reached their peak in the 1840 annual meeting of the American Anti-Slavery Society in New York. Garrisonians forced on the meeting Abby Kelley, one of their number, as head of a committee. The moderates left to organize their own American and Foreign Anti-Slavery Society. Thereafter, both the new and old societies diminished in influence.

Liberty Party. Some of the moderates sought to create an abolitionist party. Their Liberty Party of 1840 offered James G. Birney for president. With little organization (Birney himself was in England at the time), the party received only 7,053 votes and was ridiculed by Garrisonians for having sold its moral purity in vain. Four years later, however, with Birney again the Liberty Party candidate, his 15,814 votes in New York State destroyed Henry Clay's bid for the presidency. Many abolitionists were dismayed since the Liberty Party's vote had helped elect James K. Polk, a dedicated proslavery leader.

Abolition and Free Soil. Southerners were no longer defensive about their slavery system. With John C. Calhoun as their leading spokesman, they now pronounced it a "Positive Good" and demanded protection for their property. Many Northerners not sympathetic to abolitionism began to fear for the future of the Western domain. If slavery could expand into it, it would put free men interested in working the soil in competition with slave labor. With the Democratic Party now committed to defense of its proslavery members, Free Soilers among them began to look elsewhere for political strength. In 1848 the Free Soil Party gave its nomination to ex-President Martin Van Buren, with political abolitionists joining his effort. He received about .25 million votes against a combined Whig-Democratic 2.5 million. The Liberty Party, led by the abolitionist and philanthropist Gerrit Smith, received only 2,733.

Abolitionism during the 1850s. Politically, the moral abolitionists were uninfluential. The political abolitionists were increasingly forced to modify their program in order to gain votes. The Republican Party, which succeeded a disintegrated Whig Party, was essentially a Free Soil party. It became more conservative as the decade progressed. However, it depended increasingly on abolitionist slogans and the tried agitators with many years of experience.

Fugitive Slaves. It was in the fight to aid fugitive slaves that the abolitionists made their greatest contribution during the 1850s. They worked continuously with such ardent black activists as Frederick Douglass and Harriet Tubman. They rescued fugitives out of the hands of federal marshals, wrote eloquent pamphlets detailing the wrongs against fugitives, and warned the North that its own civil rights were bound up with those of the pursued runaways. The abolitionists involved themselves in court cases, "underground railroad" operations, and other activities that increasingly won the sympathy and cooperation of the Northern public.

Charles Sumner, a Free Soiler, won a seat in the U.S. Senate and Lincoln the presidency, while Garrison received increased admiration for his steadfast abolitionist doctrine. With the passage of the Thirteenth Amendment to the Constitution in 1865, outlawing slavery, the abolitionist movement passed into history.

Consult (III) Dumond, 1961.
—Louis Filler, *Antioch College*

ABORTION AND BIRTH CONTROL LAWS have been controversial issues in recent times. A century ago, the dissemination of birth control information was prohibited by the Comstock Law of 1873, under which the U.S. Post Office could deny mailing privileges for birth control information and devices. Through the efforts of pioneers such as Margaret Sanger, the dissemination of birth control information to physicians was legalized in 1937. In 1965 the Supreme Court, in *Griswold v. Connecticut*, declared laws regulating birth control unconstitutional on the grounds that they infringed on the right to marital privacy.

Legislation in the states varies as to whether birth control information and devices can be made available to minors, but there has been a trend toward liberalization of such laws. In 1967, Title IV of the federal Social Security Act was amended to require local welfare agencies to provide contraception to recipients without regard to marital status, age, or whether or not they were already parents.

Until the twentieth century, abortion was a medically hazardous procedure. There was no legislation regulating abortion in the United States until 1827, when Illinois passed a law prohibiting it in the early months of pregnancy. A statute passed by the New York legislature in 1829, prohibiting abortion except for preservation of the mother's life, became the standard regulation in most states. By the early twentieth century, therapeutic abortions could be done fairly safely in hospitals. Demand for abortion rose in the 1960s with evidence that rubella (German measles) and drugs (such as thalidomide) could cause fetal

Abolitionist Henry Ward Beecher (1813–1887), a minister, advocated disobedience of Fugitive Slave Act.

deformities. Decisions as to whether an abortion was legal—that is, necessary to preserve the mother's life—were made by boards of doctors. Under these arrangements, therapeutic abortions became available to women who could secure medical certification that childbirth endangered their lives or psychiatric certification that childbirth made them suicidal. Meanwhile, thousands of other women resorted to illegal abortions.

Reform Proposals. In 1962 the American Law Institute (ALI) recommended, in its proposal for a Model Penal Code, that abortion be permitted (1) when the mother's mental or physical health was in jeopardy, (2) when there was significant risk of fetal deformity, and (3) in cases of rape or incest. In 1967 the American Medical Association reversed its opposition to abortion and supported the ALI recommendation. The same year, Colorado became the first state to liberalize its abortion laws according to the new guidelines, and several other states followed—sometimes with slight variations from the ALI model. In 1968 and 1969, reform proposals were put forth in more than 35 state legislatures, and by 1972, 16 states and the District of Columbia had changed their abortion laws.

Reformed abortion laws, following the ALI model, increased the number of legal abortions in many states but did not stem the tide of illegal ones. Pressure groups for abortion reform urged the more effective measure of abortion law repeal. In 1970, abortion laws were repealed in Hawaii, Alaska, and New York, where, after a long battle, a 140-year old abortion law was discarded and abortion-on-demand became available. Not all legal changes were progressive, however: in 1972, Connecticut passed a restrictive abortion law that returned to the nineteenth-century formula. Nor have illegal abortions been ended. It was estimated that in 1972 at least 2,500 illegal abortions were performed every day.

Controversy over abortion often centers on whether a fetus, before the twentieth week of pregnancy, is a living human being, as asserted by the leadership of the Roman Catholic Church. Since 1869, church leaders have stated the belief that life begins at the moment of conception. Feminist and other pressure groups argue for a woman's right to control her own body. There are no abortion laws that force a woman to undergo abortion against her will.

Restrictive abortion laws have been challenged in the federal courts to determine their constitutionality. It has been contended that the right to have an abortion is protected by the Ninth Amendment, since at the time that amendment was adopted, in 1791, women enjoyed such a liberty under common law. This view was upheld in 1973 in a landmark Supreme Court decision, *Jane Roe v. Henry Wade,* which ruled that abortions could be barred only during the last 10 weeks of pregnancy.

See also Jane Roe v. Henry Wade (1973); Sanger, Margaret; Women's Liberation.
 —Nancy Woloch, *Hebrew Union College*

ABRAMS v. U.S., Supreme Court decision upholding the Sedition Act. See Espionage Act (1917).

ABSTRACT EXPRESSIONISM, dominant painting style in the post-World War II era. See Painting.

ABZUG, BELLA (1920-   ), lawyer and Democratic congresswoman, known as an advocate of equal rights for women. A graduate of Hunter College and Columbia Law School, Abzug was admitted to the New York Bar in 1947. In the 1960s, she was active in the peace movement, the "Dump Johnson" movement, women's groups, and the New Democratic Coalition. In 1970 she was elected to Congress from New York City and, after a redistricting controversy and a primary fight, was reelected in 1972.

Consult (VIII) Abzug, 1972.

ACADIA. *See* French Colonies.

ACCULTURATION, process by which immigrants adapt to the cultural traits of a new society. Immigrants who arrive in a new country individually usually learn the language rapidly and are easily absorbed into a new community, whereas immigrants who arrive in groups tend to isolate themselves and retain their language and cultural practices for several generations and may, in fact, never become acculturated.

See also Assimilation; Ethnic Group; Immigration.

ACHESON, DEAN (GOODERHAM) (1893-1971), American diplomat and Secretary of State. He was born in Middletown, Conn., and graduated from Yale University and Harvard Law School. He served in the Navy in World War I and then was private secretary to Supreme Court Justice Louis Brandeis. In 1921 he began to practice law in Washington, D.C., a career he followed, except for 6 months in the Treasury Department, until he entered the State Department in 1941. He served first as Assistant Secretary of State, and in 1945–1947 as Undersecretary, helping to outline the Marshall Plan and the Truman Doctrine. He was made Secretary of State by President Truman in 1949.

As the principal shaper of foreign policy under Truman, Acheson was a strong supporter of the North Atlantic Treaty Organization

Flamboyant and outspoken Bella Abzug took the struggle for women's equal rights to Congress.

Lawyer and presidential adviser Dean Acheson served as secretary of state (1949–1953) during the height of the Cold War.

John Adams, 2nd President of the United States (1797–1801).

John Quincy Adams, son of John Adams and 6th President of the United States (1825–1829).

(NATO) as well as of UN military involvement in Korea. A controversial figure because of his Cold War policy for the containment of communism, Acheson was often criticized by members of both parties. This criticism came to a head when Truman removed Douglas MacArthur as Commander of the UN forces in Korea.

Acheson retired in 1953 and returned to a lucrative private practice, although he continued to serve subsequent presidents in an advisory capacity. Acheson wrote several books, including *Power and Diplomacy* (1958) and *Present at the Creation* (1969).

Consult (VIII) Graebner, 1961.

ADAMS, JOHN (1735–1826), 2nd President of the United States (1797–1801). He was born in Braintree (now Quincy), Mass., on Oct. 19, 1735, graduated from Harvard in 1755, and in the years before the Revolution practiced law in Boston. He served as a delegate from Massachusetts to the First Continental Congress and became prominent in the second as a leading advocate of independence. In 1778 he went to Europe as a diplomat and along with Benjamin Franklin and John Jay was chiefly responsible for the establishment of peace with Britain and American independence in 1783. After the war he became the first U.S. envoy to Britain, but he had a frustrating mission owing to British resentment and their reluctance to establish formal diplomatic relations.

From 1789 to 1797 Adams served as the first U.S. vice-president, and when American political parties came into being in the 1790s he became one of the leaders of the new Federalist Party. In the election of 1796, Adams, the Federalist candidate for president, narrowly defeated Jefferson by 71 to 68 electoral votes.

Presidency. Adams became president at a time of quickly deteriorating relations with France. The French resented the Federalist accord with Britain and the signing of Jay's Treaty with that country in 1794, and they began to attack American shipping. The whole Adams Administration was dominated by this collapse of the French alliance. Adams tried to secure peace by sending a special mission to France in late 1797, but this effort failed amid the bitter recriminations of the XYZ Affair. From 1798 to 1800 the United States and France engaged in a quasi-war highlighted by clashes at sea. Adams was anxious to avoid outright war, and he resisted those in his own party who pressed him to take all possible military action. Against their wishes he sent a peace mission to France that brought the conflict to an end in 1800.

In the election of 1800, Adams had to face dissension within his own party and also the bitter opposition of the Democratic-Republicans, who were infuriated by the Alien and Sedition Acts issued in 1798. In a close

race, an alliance of Thomas Jefferson from Virginia and Aaron Burr from New York defeated Adams. As president Adams would not subordinate his own judgment to party allegiance. After 1801 he went into retirement and died in Braintree on July 4, 1826.

See also Alien and Sedition Acts; Continental Congress, Second; Jay's Treaty; Paris, Treaty of; XYZ Affair.

Consult (III) Kurtz, 1957; Smith, 1962.
—Reginald Horsman, *University of Wisconsin, Milwaukee*

ADAMS, JOHN QUINCY (1767–1848), 6th President of the United States (1825–1829). The son of President John Adams, John Quincy was born in Braintree (now Quincy), Mass., on July 11, 1767. He became a lawyer and in the 1790s served as Minister to the Netherlands and to Prussia. He was elected to the Senate as a Federalist from Massachusetts in 1803, but in the controversies with England he followed an independent course and eventually left the Federalist Party. Before the War of 1812 he was appointed Minister to Russia, and he played an important role in the negotiations at Ghent that ended the War of 1812.

When James Monroe became president in 1817, Adams was appointed secretary of state. He is commonly regarded as one of the most able men in American history to have held that office. By the Adams-Onís Treaty of 1819 he acquired the Floridas and Spanish claims to the Oregon region, and in 1823 he was the guiding force behind the presidential statements that became known as the Monroe Doctrine. Adams had a vision of a United States spanning the North American continent, with a sphere of influence extending throughout South America.

In the presidential race of 1824, Adams received powerful support from New England but ran second to Andrew Jackson in a four-man race. Because no candidate had an absolute majority, the election was thrown into the House of Representatives. Adams was elected after Henry Clay, the fourth-place candidate, gave him his support. Clay became Secretary of State in the Adams Administration, and the opposition raised the cry of "corrupt bargain" to attack the Adams-Clay alliance. Adams further infuriated his opponents with an inaugural speech calling for extensive governmental support of internal improvements. Andrew Jackson was able to weld together a powerful opposition that eventually emerged as the Democratic Party. Adams could accomplish little as president because he faced bitter opposition in Congress. In the election of 1828, Jackson defeated him.

From 1831 to 1848 the ex-President had a distinguished career in the House of Representatives, throwing his strong influence behind opposition to the expansion of slavery.

He died in Washington, D.C., on February 23, 1848.

See also Adams-Onís Treaty; Ghent, Treaty of; Monroe Doctrine.

Consult (III) Bemis, 1949; Bemis 1956.

—Reginald Horsman, *University of Wisconsin, Milwaukee*

ADAMS, SAM(UEL) (1722-1803), Revolutionary War patriot who was a second cousin of John Adams. Sam Adams was an able political organizer and one of the earliest advocates of American independence. He served in the Massachusetts legislature (1765-1774), helped organize the Sons of Liberty, and in general enjoyed remarkable influence over the Boston citizenry. He drafted the Massachusetts Circular Letter, which enunciated the American position in terms thought seditious by royal authorities, and helped form the Non-Importation Association of 1768, which resisted the Townshend Acts.

Adams' major contribution to the coming of independence may have been keeping the controversy between Britain and the colonies alive in the years immediately after the repeal of the Townshend Acts in 1770. He was responsible for the establishment of the Boston Committee of Correspondence in 1772 and the development of a network of similar groups throughout the colonies. A nemesis of Massachusetts executives, Adams embarrassed Thomas Hutchinson by publishing some politically indiscreet letters that the lieutenant governor had sent to England. Adams was an instigator of the Boston Tea Party, and, when England responded with the punitive Coercive Acts, he called for a continental congress.

A delegate to the Continental Congress (1774-1781), Adams urged separation from Britain and signed the Declaration of Independence. As a delegate to the Massachusetts ratifying convention, he initially opposed but then supported the proposed U.S. Constitution. Adams served as governor of Massachusetts from 1793 to 1797.

See also Boston Tea Party (1773); Committees of Correspondence; Continental Congress, Second; Declaration of Independence; Hutchinson Letters.

Consult (II) Miller, 1936.

—Thomas Archdeacon, *University of Wisconsin*

ADAMS FAMILY. Henry Adams (1583-1646) brought his family of nine children to Massachusetts from England in 1636, but until Samuel (1722-1803), member of the Continental Congress and governor of Massachusetts, the most exalted Adams' progeny was a village pastor in New Hampshire. "Deacon" John (1691-1761), the father of the first Adams president, was a farmer, shoemaker, and village selectman. His son, John (1735-1826), and Samuel Adams, who

were second cousins, became signers of the Declaration of Independence.

Of John's three sons, one, John Quincy (1767-1848), became president; the other two dissolved in drink. John Quincy also had three sons, one of whom, Charles Francis (1807-1886), entered politics. With the revival of antislavery sentiment in 1858, Charles Francis, a Republican, moved into the national political scene. He was elected to Congress from his father's old district and was reelected in 1860. Charles Francis also ran for vice-president on the Free Soil ticket with Martin Van Buren in 1848 and narrowly missed a presidential nomination. During the Civil War, he served as Minister to Britain.

Henry Brooks (1838-1918), one of Charles Francis' six children, went to Washington as his father's secretary and served him in this capacity in London. On his return to the United States, Henry began to develop as a historian and as the author of articles attacking the Grant Administration, Congress, political rings, monetary policies, and the railroads. He led an exciting, well-traveled life, exploring the Orient, Europe, and the Pacific islands. A prolific writer, Henry, in his later years produced his two masterpieces, *Mont-Saint-Michel and Chartres* (1904) and *The Education of Henry Adams* (1907).

Henry was the last nationally famous Adams, although later generations have produced a historian, a secretary of the navy, and business leaders. The Adamses of the eighteenth and nineteenth centuries were industrious intellectuals who built an impressive record of achievement and a political dynasty without abundant financial means. Of course, some of the family fared less well, but the Adamses, for a century and a half, were prominently involved in the political fabric of the country.

See also Adams, John; Adams, John Quincy; Adams, Sam.

ADAMS-ONÍS TREATY (1819) , an agreement between the United States and Spain to resolve territorial claims in North America.

After 1815 the United States wished to obtain Spanish East Florida and set the whole boundary between United States and Spanish possessions. Discussions began in 1817 between American Secretary of State John Quincy Adams and Spanish Minister Luis de Onís. In 1818, Andrew Jackson invaded East Florida in the course of waging a campaign against the Seminole Indians, but Adams used the invasion as another means of persuading the Spanish that they should cede the Floridas.

The Adams-Onís Treaty was signed on Feb. 22, 1819, but it did not take effect until 1821. Spain ceded both East and West Florida (which was already occupied) to the United States, and the American government agreed to

Sam Adams, revolutionary Massachusetts patriot, was a leader of the Boston Tea Party (1773).

pay up to $5 million of the claims of U.S. citizens against the Spanish. The southern boundary of the Louisiana Purchase was so established that it left Texas in the hands of Spain, but the United States gained a major concession on the Pacific Coast. Spain surrendered any claim to the area north of California, which opened the region for contention between the United States, Russia, and Britain.

See also Mexican War; Seminole Wars.

ADDAMS, JANE (1860–1935), pioneer settlement worker, social reformer, suffragist, and pacifist who became the most prominent American woman of her day. In 1889, with her friend Ellen Gates Starr, Addams bought an old mansion in the Chicago slums and established Hull House, which became the foremost settlement establishment in the nation. She assembled there a dedicated group of women social workers and sponsored civic improvements for the surrounding immigrant community. Hull House also became a political pressure group in Chicago, supporting such measures as child labor laws, compulsory school attendance, juvenile courts, and political reform.

Jane Addams' social convictions led her to Progressive politics, women's suffrage, and pacifism. In 1912 she seconded Theodore Roosevelt's nomination at the Progressive Party convention and campaigned for him. Convinced that women's suffrage would help to end social problems such as prostitution, she served as first vice-president of the National American Woman Suffrage Association (1911–1914). As a pacifist, she became, in 1915, chairman of the Woman's Peace Party and president of the International Congress of Women at the Hague. In 1919 she became president of the International League for Peace and Freedom, and in 1931 she was corecipient of the Nobel Peace Prize.

An active lecturer and author, she published many articles and books, including *Democracy and Social Ethics* (1902), *The Newer Ideals of Peace* (1907), *The Spirit of Youth and the City Streets* (1909), and *Peace and Bread in Time of War* (1922).

See also Suffrage, Women's.
Consult (VI) Addams, 1966.
—Nancy Woloch, *Hebrew Union College*

ADJUSTED COMPENSATION ACT. *See* Soldiers Bonus Act (1924).

ADMINISTRATION OF JUSTICE ACT, special legislation for crown officials; one of the Coercive Acts. *See* Coercive Acts (1774).

ADMINISTRATIVE PROCEDURE ACT. *See* Freedom of Information Act (1967).

AFL. *See* American Federation of Labor.

Social reformer Jane Addams founded Chicago's Hull House to help relieve slum conditions.

Vice-President Spiro Agnew, noted for his headline-making speeches, gestures during a 1972 campaign address.

AGNEW, SPIRO (THEODORE) (1918-   ), 39th Vice-President of the United States. He was born in Baltimore, the son of a Greek immigrant who shortened his surname from Anagnostopoulos. He attended Johns Hopkins University and received his law degree from the University of Baltimore in 1947. During World War II, Agnew served in the Army.

Agnew became active in Republican politics in the late 1950s. He was elected Baltimore county executive in 1962 and in 1966 governor of Maryland. During his term in office he was responsible for a strong antipollution law, the first open-housing law in the South, a graduated income tax, and repeal of the state's antimiscegenation law.

Agnew was elected vice-president on the Republican ticket headed by Richard M. Nixon in 1968 and 1972. In his role of presiding officer over the Senate his tie-breaking vote ensured passage of Nixon's antiballistic missile program. He made several worldwide trips as the President's representative, including one to Africa in 1971, in which he unfavorably compared American blacks with African leaders.

In 1969, Agnew gained wide attention when he charged that those opposed to the Vietnam War were "an effete corps of impudent snobs" and when he criticized the press and television for presenting news in a biased fashion. With these charges Agnew became popular with conservatives and was a popular speaker at Republican fund-raising dinners.

See also Nixon, Richard M.
Consult (VIII) Witcover, 1972.

AGRICULTURAL ADJUSTMENT ACT (1933), New Deal legislation, the major purpose of which was to balance farm production and consumption in order to raise agricultural prices to provide farmers with a "parity" of purchasing power measured against a period just prior to World War I. It established the Agricultural Adjustment Administration (AAA). All its features had been discussed publicly before, yet the AAA seemed innovative and in some respects shocking to contemporaries. In its first year, crops and animals were destroyed to bring about the desired balance. In subsequent years penalties were imposed for overproduction, and subsidies were paid for cutting back production. The program was financed by a tax on the processor, who passed the extra cost on to the consumer. Under the AAA's Commodity Credit Corporation, producers could borrow money on the crop and hold it off the market until prices rose.

AAA was a boon to the land-owning farmer, but tenants and sharecroppers did not fare so well, many being forced out of employment by the program. In 1936, the AAA was outlawed by the Supreme Court in *United States v. Butler,* the majority holding that the taxing power of Congress could not be used to regulate agriculture. In 1938 a second AAA was set up to replace the earlier one; it was written as a soil conservation bill to circumvent the Court's objections. The AAA became the basis for continuing farm support programs after the New Deal era.

See also Bankhead-Jones Farm Tenant Act (1937); New Deal; Resettlement Administration.

Consult (VI) Conrad, 1965.

—Allen Kifer, *Skidmore College*

AGRICULTURAL MARKETING ACT (1929), carefully thought-out improvement that President Hoover had promised in place of the McNary-Haugen Bill. The 1929 act created the Federal Farm Board (FFB) with $500 million to purchase commodities from farmers' producer cooperatives, thus stabilizing the prices of major farm products, especially cotton and wheat, at a high level. The FFB was then to hold its purchases until the market turned favorable and under normal seasonal changes of the 1920s would have succeeded and even made a profit.

In the aftermath of the panic market conditions of 1929, however, the FFB surpluses were additional depressing factors in the market, and the scheme became unworkable. A product of Hoover's vision for "normal" times, the FFB became merely a forerunner of more direct government aid to farmers under the New Deal.

See also McNary-Haugen Bill.

AGRICULTURE, DEPARTMENT OF, cabinet-level executive department established in 1862 in response to pressure from farmer organizations for a separate federal bureau to provide agricultural research and education.

The 1929 Depression spurred social and economic legislation including price supports; farm credit; crop insurance; soil, water, and forest conservation; and rural electrification that were administered by the department. Following World War II, advances in agricultural technology created farm surpluses and led to falling prices in the 1950s. The department expanded markets with shipments to underdeveloped nations and domestic programs such as food stamps and lunches and milk for schools. The department inspects meat and poultry, establishes standards for every major agricultural commodity, regulates pesticides, and sponsors consumer education programs.

AIR FORCE, U.S. established officially by the National Security Act of 1947. The Air Force is part of the Department of Defense and is commanded by the Air Force Chief of Staff, who is a member of the Joint Chiefs of Staff.

The Air Force began as the Aeronautical Division of the Army Signal Corps in 1907. During World War I, the Corps had 740 planes and had 1,200 men stationed in France. The Air Service was created by Congress in May 1918, and it became the Air Corps in 1926. In 1935, the air forces became the General Headquarters Air Force and then, during World War II, the Army Air Forces. The Air Force has also participated in the fighting in Korea, Vietnam, Laos, and Cambodia.

AIRPLANES. *See* Aviation.

ALABAMA, the 22nd state, admitted to the Union on Dec. 14, 1819. It was first settled by the French at Mobile in 1702. Control passed to the British in 1763 and to the United States as part of the Territory of Mississippi in 1798. Andrew Jackson's defeat of the Creek Indians in 1814 secured it for new settlers, and in 1817 Alabama became a territory. It joined the Confederacy during the Civil War. The state legislature is bicameral; the capital is Montgomery. The population in 1970 was 3,444,165.

See also Creek War.

ALABAMA CLAIMS, American demands that Britain pay for the damage wrought during the Civil War by the British-built Confederate ships *Alabama, Florida,* and *Shenandoah.* Secretary of State Seward asserted that the claims amounted to $15 million, but the Senate also included indirect damages of more than $2 billion because British aid to the Confederates had prolonged the war.

An agreement in 1869 to arbitrate the claims was rejected by the Senate, but through the work of Canadian finance minister Sir John Rose and Secretary of the Treasury Hamilton Fish the Treaty of Washington, agreeing to submit the claims to a tribunal of arbitration. was signed on May 8, 1871. The tribunal met in Geneva in December 1871, and on Sept. 14, 1872 it awarded the United States $15.5 million in damages; the indirect claims were ruled out. This agreement was important to Anglo-American friendship; before the treaty, relations were at such a low point that Senator Charles Sumner tried to claim Canada as payment of the claims.

ALAMO, scene of a heroic stand by Americans in 1836, during Texas' war for independence. A group of fortified mission buildings in San Antonio, the Alamo was defended from Feb. 23 until March 6 by 200 Americans under the command of Colonel W. B. Travis and Colonel James Bowie. They were besieged by about 3,000 Mexicans led by General Santa Anna.

When the Mexicans finally penetrated the fort, the defenders fought hand to hand until all were dead. Among the last killed were Davy Crockett, Travis, and Bowie. News of the massacre stiffened Texan resistance, and "Remember the Alamo" became the Texans' rally-

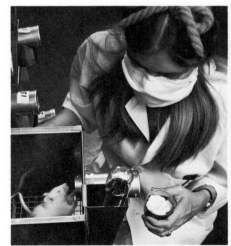

Nutrition scientist conducts liver experiment on a rat in Department of Agriculture laboratory.

"THE BIG THING."

Thomas Nast cartoon satirizes U.S. purchase of Alaska by Secretary of State Seward. Seward tries to placate President Johnson, then battling Congress.

JOIN, or DIE.

Albany Congress (1754) tried to develop common colonial policy on the eve of the French and Indian War.

ing cry as they went on to defeat the Mexican army and capture Santa Anna at San Jacinto on April 21.

See also Crockett, Davy; San Jacinto, Battle of; Texas.

ALASKA, the 49th state, admitted to the Union on Jan. 3, 1959. It is the largest state. Alaska was first explored by Vitus Bering in 1741, and the first white settlement was established at Kodiak Island in 1784 by Russian fur trappers. In 1799 Russia chartered the Russian-American Company, a fur monopoly that governed until the United States purchased Alaska from the Russians in 1867 for $7.2 million. The discovery of gold in 1880 in the panhandle and in 1896 in the Yukon brought American settlers. Alaska became a territory in 1912. The state legislature is bicameral; the capital is Juneau. The population in 1970 was 302,873, the smallest in the nation.

See also Alaska Purchase (1867).

ALASKA PURCHASE (1867), the deal made by Secretary of State William H. Seward in which the United States bought Alaska from Russia for $7.2 million. The Russian minister to the United States offered Alaska to Seward in March 1867. As an expansionist, Seward accepted, but then the Russian minister had to use $200,000 of the purchase price to push the bill through the hostile House of Representatives.

Seward was anxious to eliminate Russian influence from the Western Hemisphere; in addition, he hoped that the U.S. presence in Alaska would have a pincer-like effect in eliminating Britain from Canada. The American public, however, viewed Alaska as an Arctic wasteland, and Alaska was dubbed Seward's Folly and Seward's Icebox until gold was discovered.

ALBANY CONGRESS (1754), intercolonial congress, called on the crown's order to discuss relations with the Iroquois. Since armed conflict with New France seemed likely, the possible defection of the Iroquois from their traditional English alliance greatly worried London and thoughtful colonists. Delegates from seven colonies (New Hampshire, Massachusetts, Rhode Island, Connecticut, New York, Pennsylvania, and Maryland) eventually participated in the Congress, which finally assembled in Albany, N.Y., in June, just as hostilities were erupting near the Ohio River.

The Congress eloquently supported Iroquois grievances and urged the crown to take direct control of relations with all border tribes rather than permit any colony to embroil the others in a major war. The Congress also approved a plan of union. It called for a crown-appointed military executive who would serve as commander in chief and carry out the laws

of the "Grand Council," which was to consist of delegates elected by the member assemblies. The Grand Council would have broad powers to negotiate treaties with the Indians, to regulate westward settlement, to erect forts, and to levy soldiers.

Only Massachusetts, which had borne the heaviest burden in three previous French wars, came close to ratifying the plan. By late 1754 it had met rejection everywhere. Individual colonies feared surrender of their autonomy to their provincial neighbors. Britain, which briefly considered a similar scheme, chose to send troops instead. The plan failed because no society affected by it was willing to assume the risks it involved.

See also Iroquois Confederacy; New York.

ALBEE, EDWARD (FRANKLIN) (1928-), American playwright who became a leading author of the new drama of the absurd. He is noted for his satirical attacks on conformity, hypocrisy, and the rigidity of American life. He deftly mixes realism with fantasy and employs cleverly contrived incriminatory-recriminatory dialogue that is particularly evident in his first three-act play, Who's Afraid of Virginia Woolf? (1962).

Albee was born in Washington, D.C., and grew up in the New York area. He left college to concentrate on writing and soon had four one-act plays produced. They are The Zoo Story (1959), The Death of Bessie Smith (1960), The Sandbox (1960), and The American Dream (1961). Albee describes his grotesque comedy as "a stand against the fiction that everything in this slipping land of ours is peachy-keen." In 1965 Albee's Tiny Alice, an obscure symbolic drama, was produced. For A Delicate Balance, produced in 1967, Albee was awarded the Pulitzer Prize. All Over (1971) was a failure.

See also Theater.

ALDRICH, NELSON W(INTHROP), United States Senator (1881-1910). See Aldrich-Vreeland Currency Act (1908); Payne-Aldrich Tariff Act (1909).

ALDRICH-VREELAND CURRENCY ACT (1908), legislation passed as a stopgap emergency measure by Congress after the financial panic of 1907. The U.S. currency supply was inflexible and sometimes inadequate, and this act allowed national banks to issue circulating notes based on securities other than federal bonds.

More importantly, it set up the National Monetary Commission, chaired by Senator Nelson W. Aldrich (1841-1915), the act's chief sponsor, who was a conservative Rhode Island Republican and who represented Eastern manufacturers and long opposed progressive reforms within his party. Aldrich's commission made a comprehensive study of the nation's banking and monetary needs and issued more than 20 volumes. Out of its work came the centralized Federal Reserve System in 1913.

See also Payne-Aldrich Tariff Act (1909).

Consult (V) Studenski and Krooss, 1963.

ALGER, HORATIO (1832-1899), most widely read author of his century, published more than 100 novels, which sold an estimated 200 million copies. A Harvard graduate (1852), he became a minister but was unhappy in the pulpit. He found his true vocation writing boys' novels that preached honesty, integrity, self-reliance, and the ultimate triumph of goodness. Deeply committed to aiding New York City's exploited newsboys, Alger recognized the forces reshaping American cities. His volumes stressed social mobility and enterprise and gave millions of readers their first knowledge of urban life. His philosophy that wealth came inevitably to the virtuous suited the age, although most Alger heroes attained success as much by luck as by their sterling qualities.

ALI, MUHAMMAD (1942-), former world heavyweight boxing champion. Born Cassius Clay in Louisville, Ky., he won an Olympic gold medal in 1960 and then turned professional. He won the heavyweight crown in 1964 from Sonny Liston, and before his defeat by Joe Frazier in 1971, Ali had won 31 consecutive bouts. Ali, who changed his name when he became a Black Muslim, made headlines in his fight to refuse the draft, a battle he successfully carried to the Supreme Court.

Considered a black folk hero, Ali preaches a philosophy of black pride, clean living, and racial separation. He has tried his hand at acting and speaking, and his ability to make up poems and deliver extemporaneous speeches has given him a reputation as a charming, ebullient showman.

ALIEN AND SEDITION ACTS, four acts passed in June and July 1798 with the object of curbing criticism of the Federalist Party and of the government at a time when war with France seemed likely. Because a number of the most articulate critics of the government were from Britain and France, three of the acts dealt specifically with aliens. The Naturalization Act made it necessary for an immigrant to live in the United States for 14 rather than 5 years before he could obtain citizenship; the Alien Act empowered the president to deport aliens if he decided that they were dangerous to the peace and safety of the United States; and the Alien Enemies Act provided for the deportation or imprisonment of subjects of opposing powers in time of war. These acts placed great power in the hands of the executive.

The most controversial measure was the Sedition Act. Section 1 provided for the prosecution of conspiracies against governmental

measures. Section 2, which caused the biggest uproar, provided for the prosecution of those who wrote or published "false, scandalous and malicious" writings against the U.S. government. Under its terms a number of prosecutions were undertaken against newspaper editors and publishers, some of whom were imprisoned.

The Alien and Sedition Acts helped to consolidate opposition against the Federalists, led to the Virginia and Kentucky resolutions of James Madison and Thomas Jefferson, and contributed to the Federalist defeat in the election of 1800. Only the Alien Enemies Act continued in force past 1802.

See also Virginia and Kentucky Resolutions (1798).

ALIEN ENEMIES ACT (1798), one of the Alien and Sedition Acts. *See* Alien and Sedition Acts.

ALLEN, ETHAN, Revolutionary War leader. *See* Revolutionary War Battles.

ALLIANCE FOR PROGRESS (Span., *Alianza para Progreso*), economic assistance program for Latin America. The program, proposed by President John Kennedy in 1961, was joined by 20 member states of the Organization of American States for a period of 10 years and was to have a total investment of $100 billion. The major part of the financial burden was to be borne by the Latin American states. The Agency for International Development administered U.S. aid.

Delegates met in Punta del Este, Uruguay, in August 1961 and ratified the charter, agreeing that major goals were free schooling, literacy for 50 million Latin Americans, elimination of malaria, land and tax reform, public housing programs, and good drinking water. The United States promised at least $1.1 billion direct aid for each program for 10 years plus aid from other sources. After a promising start, the program soon bogged down, and goals were not met. A 1971 report, however, revealed that economic growth in Latin America was just short of the alliance's goal of 2.5 percent.

ALLIANCE OF 1778, United States-French treaties. *See* French Alliance.

ALLSTON, WASHINGTON (1779-1843), painter who was a major influence in introducing the romantic style to America. He was born on a South Carolina plantation. His 5-year visit to Europe, begun in 1803, brought him in contact with the leading figures of the European romantic movement, such as Samuel Taylor Coleridge, with whom he spent much of his stay in Rome. His first paintings date from 1800, but his major work dates from 1804 with *The Deluge, Rising of a Thunderstorm at Sea,* and *Italian Landscape* (1805). Although he agreed

"Frank observed the accident and sprang quickly to his help." Horatio Alger's heroes, such as Frank Fowler, often started up ladder of success through fortuitous circumstances.

Heavyweight boxer Muhammed Ali won and lost championship while opposing military draft and advocating Black Muslim ideals.

CONSTITUTIONAL AMENDMENTS — Item Guide

The entry on AMENDMENTS, CONSTITUTIONAL, summarizes the amendments to the CONSTITUTION OF THE UNITED STATES, where they are reprinted and which has a Subject Map. The first 10 amendments, the BILL OF RIGHTS, were developed at the CONSTITUTIONAL CONVENTION (1787), partly through the efforts of JAMES MADISON.

Amendment XII set new procedures in the ELECTORAL COLLEGE for selecting the PRESIDENT and VICE-PRESIDENT OF THE UNITED STATES, whose functions were further defined in XXII and XXV.

The Civil War amendments (XIII, XIV, and XV) met the goal of ABOLITIONISM, ended SLAVERY and gave legal equality to BLACKS IN THE UNITED STATES. Amendment XVI established the INCOME TAX, while XVII dealt with election to the SENATE. XVIII established PROHIBITION, which was repealed by XXI.

SUFFRAGE, WOMEN'S was legalized by XIX, but further demands for sexual equality, a goal of WOMEN'S LIBERATION, led to proposal of XXVII, called the Equal Rights Amendment.

FOUR METHODS OF AMENDING THE CONSTITUTION

Methods of Proposal	Methods of Ratification
By two-thirds vote in both houses of Congress	By legislatures in three-fourths of the states
or	or
By national constitutional convention called by Congress on request of two-thirds of state legislatures	By conventions in three-fourths of the states

with most American artists in Europe that the way to succeed in American art was to imitate European styles, Allston's paintings mirrored the much wilder aspects of nature found in America rather than resembling the historical paintings then coming into vogue in Europe.

He returned to America in 1808, married the sister of William Ellery Channing, and settled in the Boston area. Boston seemed dreary after Europe and once again he traveled to England, this time with the painter and inventor Samuel F. B. Morse as his pupil. Allston's success in London did not still his longing for America, and he again returned to Boston in 1818.

See also Morse, Samuel F. B.; Painting.

AMANA SOCIETY. *See* Utopian Communities.

AMENDMENTS, CONSTITUTIONAL, changes in the wordings of or additions to the U.S. Constitution according to an explicit procedure outlined in the Constitution itself (Article V).

History. The Articles of Confederation, which governed the nation from 1781 to 1789, required the assent of all 13 states to pass amendments. The framers of the 1787 Constitution realized it would be impossible to obtain unanimous approval. Thus they decided that the new Constitution would only need the ratification of three-quarters of the states. They also included a complicated procedure in the Constitution to make future amendment difficult.

Procedure. To amend the Constitution, two-thirds of both houses of Congress must recommend to the states the exact wording of the proposed amendment. The amendment must then be approved by three-fourths of the states. Article V gives Congress the power to decide whether state legislatures must approve the amendment or whether special state conventions must do so. Congress also has the right to set a specific time period for ratification; otherwise the amendment becomes void. The president has no veto power in the amending process. As an alternate procedure, two-thirds of the state legislatures may petition Congress to call a national convention to propose amendments, but this has never been done. However, if this procedure were followed, the rest of the ratification process would be the same as outlined above, except when Congress specifies a different process by special legislation.

Summary of Amendments. The first 10 amendments (the Bill of Rights) were ratified by the states with the Constitution in 1791; Amendment XI (1795) forbade a citizen of one state to sue the government of another state, and Amendment XII (1804) established separate ballots for the president and vice-president in the electoral college. Amendments XIII (1861), XIV (1868), and XV (1870) were known as the Civil War amendments and declared people of all races constitutionally equal before national and state law.

There were two amendments in 1913: Amendment XVI gave Congress the right to enact individual income tax legislation, and Amendment XVII changed the selection process of U.S. senators from election by state legislatures to a direct election by the people of the states. Amendment XVIII (1919) enabled Congress to establish the prohibition of liquor traffic in the United States. Amendment XIX (1920), passed after years of lobbying by women's groups and their supporters, gave women the right to vote. In 1933 there were also two amendments: Amendment XX changed the inauguration dates for the president and vice-president and established annual congressional sessions beginning each January; Amendment XXI repealed Amendment XVIII (it has been the only amendment ratified by state conventions, not state legislatures).

Amendment XXII (1951) prohibited any person from serving as president for more than two elected terms; Amendment XXIII (1961) gave the people of the District of Columbia the right to vote for presidential electors; and Amendment XXIV (1964) prohibited the use of a poll tax to prevent anyone from voting for a federal office. Amendment XXV (1967) established a procedure to fill the vice-presidency in the event of a vacancy and also stated that the vice-president should become acting president in the event that the president could not carry out his duties. Amendment XXVI (1971) lowered the voting age in all the states to 18. Amendment XXVII, which prohibits discrimination based on sex by any law or action of any government—federal, state, or local—went to the states for ratification in March 1972.

See also Bill of Rights; Constitution of the United States.
—Erwin L. Levine, *Skidmore College*

AMERICAN AND FOREIGN ANTI-SLAVERY SOCIETY, abolitionist organization founded in 1840 by Lewis Tappan, William Jay, Theodore Weld, and others. It was, however, largely the personal mouthpiece of Lewis Tappan, a businessman and reformer.

Lewis Tappan supported the efforts of political abolitionists to create a popular following, and he maintained valuable correspondence with British abolitionist sympathizers. He helped establish two abolitionist journals, *The Independent* in New York and the *National Era* in Washington, as well as the American Missionary Association, an abolitionist religious body that helped found Berea College in Kentucky.

See also Abolitionism; American Anti-Slavery Society.
Consult (III) Wyatt-Brown, 1969.

AMERICAN ANTI-SLAVERY SOCIETY, abolitionist group in which William Lloyd Garrison was a leading figure. In 1831, Garrison adopted an "immediatist" position on abolition, demanding that slavery end immediately rather than gradually. The excitement "immediatism" caused in the South, plus the antislavery work of men such as Arthur and Lewis Tappan, Theodore D. Weld, John Greenleaf Whittier, and James G. Birney, created a demand for a national society, which was founded in Philadelphia in 1833. Garrison received no special status in it, and his followers were identified with him rather than with the national society.

The society, with headquarters in New York, first launched a propaganda campaign of leaflets and pamphlets that reached many Northerners. They also resulted in Southern protests, only partially substantiated, that these writings were also intended to reach slaves. More important was the organization, notably under Weld, of a number of eloquent ministers who fanned over the countryside to urge Northerners to join the antislavery crusade, which often resulted in the organization of local antislavery societies. By 1838 the society claimed some 250,000 members, but hopes for societies in the Southern and Border states were never realized.

The growth of the society roused ambitions to abolitionize the nation. Leaders such as Birney and Tappan were disturbed by Garrison's extremism, and Tappan and others left to set up the American and Foreign Anti-Slavery Society in 1840. Although Garrison was left with control of the older society, both organizations took second place in public importance, first to the Liberty Party, then to the Free Soil and Republican parties.

See also Abolitionism; American and Foreign Anti-Slavery Society; Garrison, William Lloyd; Weld, Theodore.
Consult (IV) Filler, 1960.
—Louis Filler, *Antioch College*

AMERICAN COLONIZATION SOCIETY, group that advocated African colonization of American blacks. *See* Liberia.

AMERICAN EQUAL RIGHTS ASSOCIATION, post-Civil War suffrage organization. *See* Suffrage, Women's.

AMERICAN EXPEDITIONARY FORCE (AEF), United States force sent to Europe to fight for the Allies in World War I. It was led by General John J. Pershing, who went to Europe ahead of it and estimated the need for about 3 million men. The "doughboys," as the Americans were called, began to arrive in June 1917, and by the war's end about 2 million Americans had served in Europe. The AEF fought chiefly in eastern France, taking part in such famous battles as Chateau-Thierry and Belleau Wood, the Marne, and the Meuse-Argonne offensive, which ended the campaigns. The intervention of the AEF was decisive in the war.

See also Pershing, John J.; World War I.
Consult (VI) Stallings, 1963.

AMERICAN FEDERATION OF LABOR (AFL), labor group founded in 1886 in Columbus, Ohio, by Samuel Gompers and Adolph Strasser out of the belief that labor unity, essential in order to counter the economic power of large business enterprises, could be achieved only through a national federation of trade unions. From an original membership of 25 unions representing 150,000 workers, the AFL by 1904 claimed 1.7 million members, or 80 percent of organized labor.

Under Gompers' leadership the AFL rejected the social utopian schemes of its predecessors and committed itself to improve the immediate condition of its members. Emphasizing the concepts of craft exclusiveness and job control, the organization paid very little attention to the plight of unskilled workers. As a result only a small proportion of the total labor force was organized—4.5 percent in 1900 and less than 20 percent by 1920. In 1955, President George Meany presided over the merger of the AFL with the Congress of Industrial Organizations.

See also American Federation of Labor–Congress of Industrial Organizations; Gompers, Samuel; Labor Movement; Meany, George.
Consult (VIII) Brooks, 1964.

AMERICAN FEDERATION OF LABOR-CONGRESS OF INDUSTRIAL ORGANIZATIONS (AFL-CIO), labor group that resulted from the merger of the nation's two largest labor organizations in December 1955. Traditional antagonisms and philosophical differences between the craft and industrial proponents of union organization, which had marred labor history, were mitigated with recognition of equality between craft and industrial unions. George Meany, president of the AFL, was elected president of the new organization, and Walter Reuther, president of the CIO, was named vice-president in charge of the industrial union department. The new federation consisted of 60,000 local unions representing more than 15 million members.

See also American Federation of Labor; Congress of Industrial Organizations; Labor Movement; Meany, George; Reuther, Walter.

AMERICAN FUR COMPANY, fur trading company established in 1808 by John Jacob Astor. *See* Astor, John Jacob; Fur Trade.

AMERICAN INDEPENDENT PARTY. *See* Political Parties; Wallace, George C.

From humble beginnings organized labor has reached a position of power and affluence. AFL-CIO leader George Meany *(center right)* presides at executive council meeting.

AMERICAN PROTECTIVE ASSOCIATION (APA), secret anti-Catholic society founded in Clinton, Iowa, by Henry F. Bowers in 1887. The APA grew slowly and steadily in the Midwest until the Panic of 1893 brought home to nativists the economic rivalry of second-generation immigrants. This, in addition to antagonism toward urban Catholics and the political instability following the 1892 elections, widened its appeal. By 1896, APA supposedly had I million members across the country, particularly in the large cities and in the Midwest. A strong Republican organization at its height, the APA began to decline in power after a split over support of William McKinley for the presidency, and by 1911 it was virtually ineffective.
See also Immigration; Nativist Movements.

AMERICAN RAILWAY UNION (ARU) had a major role in the Pullman Strike. *See* Debs, Eugene; Pullman Strike (1894); Railroad Unions.

AMERICAN SYSTEM, Henry Clay's program for the U.S. economy. *See* Clay, Henry; Tariffs.

AMERICAN WARS. There are numerous articles on the wars in which Americans have participated and on the men who fought in them. During the colonial period the battlegrounds in North America were adjuncts of great-power struggles in Europe, and the colonists fought on their home soil. In the modern era, as the United States became a great power, the emphasis shifted to foreign conflicts. The accompanying subject map illustrates the encyclopedia's coverage of America at war.

AMERICAN WOMAN SUFFRAGE ASSOCIATION, influential nineteenth-century women's group. *See* Suffrage, Women's.

AMISH. *See* Colonial Religion.

AMISTAD CASE (1839–1841), a revolt involving about 50 black slaves, led by an African named Cinque, who seized the Spanish vessel carrying them from Cuba. The slaves wanted to return to Africa but were deceived by whites on board into entering American waters, where the ship was taken by the U.S. Navy. The slaves, charged with piracy, were arraigned for trial in New Haven, Conn. Government agents sought to satisfy the Spanish ambassador by having the defendants placed in his keeping, inevitably to be returned to slavery. The slaves were helped by abolitionists who worked to publicize their plight and by former President John Quincy Adams, who also entered the case on the blacks' behalf.

The combination of publicity and legal actions resulted in a Supreme Court decision in 1841 that released them from custody, which was a signal victory for the abolitionist cause. One of the defendants, a cabin boy named Antonio, although ruled subject to slavery, was helped by abolitionists to escape. Cinque later returned to Africa and became a slave dealer.
Consult (IX) Bemis, 1956.

AMNESTY ACT (1872), legislation in effect repealing Section 3 of the Fourteenth Amendment, which barred from officeholding (both state and national) certain groups of Confederates. The Amnesty Act left only about 500 Confederates still under the ban. The General Amnesty Act, as it was officially called, did not deal with the right to vote.

AMNESTY PROCLAMATIONS (1863, 1865). On Dec. 8, 1863, President Lincoln offered pardon to Confederates who swore an oath of allegiance to the U.S. Constitution and to the Union and who agreed to abide by all federal laws regarding slavery. Confederate civil and diplomatic officials and high-ranking military officers, plus those who had left certain categories of federal posts to aid the Confederacy, were excluded.

President Johnson issued an amnesty proclamation on May 29, 1865, that embodied Lincoln's principles but added eight new categories of exceptions, one of which included wealthy Confederates (all whose taxable property was worth more than $20,000). Johnson specified that persons in the excepted classes might win pardon and amnesty if they appealed directly to him.
Consult (IV) Dorris, 1953.

ANARCHISM, a social, economic, and political philosophy with some following among American workers from 1875 to 1920. Anarchist theory was derived in large part from the concepts of Mikhail Bakunin, a Russian. Proclaiming the undesirability of all government and favoring control of industry by the workers, the movement in the late 1870s and 1880s was strongest among foreign-born workers. Anarchist leaders sometimes advocated violence and were blamed for the Haymarket Square bombing of 1886. Anarchist concepts were prominent in the principles of the Industrial Workers of the World, founded in 1905. Foreign-born anarchist leaders were early targets of the Red Scare of 1919–1920, and several hundred were deported. The Sacco-Vanzetti case was the most prominent example of anti-anarchist feelings.
See also Haymarket Massacre; Industrial Workers of the World; Sacco-Vanzetti Case.

ANDERSON, MARIAN (1902–   ), leading concert contralto and one of the best-known black singers of the twentieth century, she was born and educated in Philadelphia. As a concert artist, she scored her first great success in 1935 by singing a group of black spirituals at the end

AMERICAN WARS

DOMESTIC WARS

Indian
INDIAN WARS, COLONIAL
    PEQUOT WAR (1637)
    KING PHILIP'S WAR (1675-1676)
    SCHENECTADY RAID (1690)
    TUSCARORA WAR (1711-1713)
    PONTIAC'S REBELLION (1763)
    LORD DUNMORE'S WAR (1774)
TECUMSEH
SEMINOLE WARS
    ANDREW JACKSON
BLACK HAWK WAR
INDIAN WARS, WESTERN
    GEORGE A. CUSTER
INDIAN POLICY

Struggle For Empire
ANGLO-DUTCH WARS
ALBANY CONGRESS (1754)
EDWARD BRADDOCK
FRENCH AND INDIAN WAR (1754-1763)
KING GEORGE'S WAR (1744-1748)
KING WILLIAM'S WAR (1689-1697)
QUEEN ANNE'S WAR (1702-1713)

REVOLUTIONARY WAR   (see Subject Map)

CIVIL WAR   (see Subject Map)

> The Subject Maps in the Encyclopedia illustrate the coverage of particular aspects of American History, showing the interrelationships among the articles in twelve critical areas of study. Entries in capital letters, except for titles, are subjects for which there are separate articles in the Encyclopedia.
>
> The Subject Maps are arranged alphabetically in the Encyclopedia under the following titles:
>
> American Wars
> Blacks in the United States
> Business Regulation and Industrialization
> Civil War and Reconstruction
> Constitution of the United States
> Exploration and Colonization
> Frontier in American History
> Indians
> Labor Movement
> New Deal and Depression
> Revolutionary War Era
> Slavery and Emancipation

INTERNATIONAL WARS

The New Nation
BARBARY COAST WARS
CHESAPEAKE AND LEONARD (1807)
WAR OF 1812
    WAR HAWKS
    LAKE ERIE, BATTLE OF
    NEW ORLEANS, BATTLE OF
    GHENT, TREATY OF
CAROLINE AFFAIR (1838)
AROOSTOOK WAR (1838-1839)
FILIBUSTERING EXPEDITIONS

Westward Expansion
ALAMO
SAN JACINTO, BATTLE OF
STEPHEN F. AUSTIN
SAM HOUSTON
BEAR FLAG REVOLT
MEXICAN WAR (1846-1848)
    WINFIELD SCOTT
    ZACHARY TAYLOR
MANIFEST DESTINY

Foreign Commitments
OPEN DOOR POLICY
    RUSSO-JAPANESE WAR (1905)
    PORTSMOUTH PEACE CONFERENCE (1905)

GLOBAL CONFLICT

SPANISH-AMERICAN WAR (1898)
    TELLER RESOLUTION
    GEORGE DEWEY
    PLATT AMENDMENT

World War I
WORLD WAR I: CAUSES
    LUSITANIA, SINKING OF
WORLD WAR I BATTLES
    AMERICAN EXPEDITIONARY
        FORCE
    JOHN J. PERSHING
WOODROW WILSON
    FOURTEEN POINTS
VERSAILLES, TREATY OF

Cold War
MARSHALL PLAN
NORTH ATLANTIC TREATY
    ORGANIZATION
TRUMAN DOCTRINE
EISENHOWER DOCTRINE
    JOHN FOSTER DULLES
IRON CURTAIN
SOUTHEAST ASIA TREATY
    ORGANIZATION
DISARMAMENT
STRATEGIC ARMS LIMITATION TALKS

World War II
WORLD WAR II
GEORGE C. MARSHALL
WILLIAM D. LEAHY
PEARL HARBOR
CHESTER W. NIMITZ
BULL HALSEY
DOUGLAS MacARTHUR
D-DAY
DWIGHT D. EISENHOWER
OMAR BRADLEY
GEORGE S. PATTON, JR.
ATOM BOMB

Diplomacy
FRANKLIN D. ROOSEVELT
WINSTON S. CHURCHILL
JOSEPH STALIN
CASABLANCA CONFERENCE
TEHERAN CONFERENCE
YALTA CONFERENCE
POTSDAM CONFERENCE

Korea
KOREAN WAR
UNITED NATIONS
DOUGLAS MacARTHUR
HARRY S TRUMAN
MATTHEW B. RIDGWAY
DWIGHT D. EISENHOWER

Vietnam
VIETNAM WAR
GULF OF TONKIN RESOLUTION
LYNDON B. JOHNSON
ROBERT S. McNAMARA
WILLIAM C. WESTMORELAND
RICHARD M. NIXON

Marian Anderson sings at Lincoln Memorial (1939) after she had been denied permission to perform in Constitution Hall in Washington, D.C. She later became first black to sing at Metropolitan Opera.

of a recital at Salzburg, Austria. By 1941, under the expert management of Sol Hurok, Marian Anderson became one of the highest-paid concert artists in the United States.

One of many notable events in her career was the controversy that raged in 1939, when the Daughters of the American Revolution (DAR) refused her permission to sing in Constitution Hall in Washington, D.C. Public protest grew to such proportions that Eleanor Roosevelt withdrew her membership in the DAR, and the White House made arrangements for the great contralto to sing in an open-air concert on Easter morning on the steps of the Lincoln Memorial. More than 75,000 people were in attendance.

In 1955 she was the first black person to appear with the Metropolitan Opera Company in New York. In 1958, she served as an alternate delegate to the United Nations, and she also traveled as a goodwill ambassador.

ANDROS, SIR EDMUND (1637–1714), English proprietary governor of New York (1674–1680), royal governor of the Dominion of New England (1686–1689), and lieutenant governor of Virginia (1692–1698). A royalist, he made the army his career after the restoration of Charles II in 1660 and won the support of the Duke of York, who in 1674 made him proprietary governor of New York, which had just been recovered from the Dutch. Andros severely disciplined the leading Dutch families and forced them to pledge uncompromising allegiance to English rule. He never won the support of the English settlers, but he took pride in preserving peace and encouraging prosperity in New York at a time when King Philip's War devastated New England and Bacon's Rebellion convulsed Virginia. After an abortive attempt to impose his rule on East Jersey, Andros was recalled, but when the Duke of York became King James II, Andros' career revived.

In 1686 he became royal governor of the Dominion of New England, a government that eventually absorbed all colonies as far south as New Jersey. In effect he applied within the wider sphere the same policies that had not worked in New York. In April 1689 the Boston militia overthrew his regime. When he returned to London, he successfully defended his conduct and thus earned an appointment as lieutenant governor of Virginia (1692). He proved quite capable of working with the House of Burgesses and got along well with the larger planters. Eventually, however, he antagonized a powerful Anglican official in the colony, lost his London support, and was recalled in 1698 to live out his remaining years in obscurity.

See also New York.

—John M. Murrin, *Princeton University*

ANGLICAN CHURCH. *See* Colonial Religion.

ANGLICAN SOCIETY FOR THE PROPAGATION OF THE GOSPEL, group that established colonial schools. *See* Pauper Schools.

ANGLO-DUTCH WARS (1652–1654, 1665–1667, 1672–1674). Determined to challenge Dutch maritime supremacy, England, generally the aggressor, fought three wars with the United Provinces of the Netherlands in the third quarter of the seventeenth century and emerged from these contests as the most serious oceanic competitor of the Dutch. Among other advantages, England won back control of most trade with its own colonies.

In North America the wars had a disruptive influence. Connecticut and Rhode Island generally favored hostilities against the colony of New Netherland, only to be restrained by Massachusetts and Plymouth. The English conquest of New Netherland, by which it became New York in 1664, helped trigger the second of these conflicts. But the Dutch reconquered the colony in 1673 and held it until the peace, by which it was returned to the English. In the last two wars, Virginia probably suffered more from Dutch depredations than any other colony. Dutch raiders wrecked the tobacco fleet in each war, stimulated higher taxation for largely futile defensive efforts, and contributed significantly to the discontent that later erupted in Bacon's Rebellion.

See also Bacon's Rebellion; New York.

ANNAPOLIS CONVENTION (1786), meeting on the inadequacies of the Articles of Confederation, which led to the Constitutional Convention of 1787. After commissioners from Virginia and Maryland met in March 1785 at George Washington's home, Mount Vernon, and successfully negotiated mutual problems concerning navigation of Chesapeake Bay and the Potomac River, the Virginia legislature in January 1786 asked all the states to attend a convention at Annapolis. Nine states accepted but only five—New York, New Jersey, Delaware, Pennsylvania, and Virginia—actually sent representatives. John Dickinson of Delaware was elected chairman when the convention opened on September 11.

Attendance was too sparse to hope to resolve any of the common problems, but the 12 delegates decided on September 13 to issue an address to the states. Alexander Hamilton of New York drafted the report, which called upon all the states to send delegates to a new convention in Philadelphia on the second Monday in May 1787 to discuss all matters necessary "to render the constitution of the Federal Government adequate to the exigencies of the Union."

The Congress took the proposal under consideration and referred it to committee on October 11. On Feb. 21, 1787, the Congress approved the calling of a convention "for the sole and express purpose of revising the Articles of Confederation and reporting to Congress and the several legislatures such alterations and provisions therein." Even before the Congress acted, Delaware, North Carolina, New Jersey, Pennsylvania, and Virginia had named delegates to the proposed convention, and the other states, except Rhode Island, followed suit.

ANTHONY, SUSAN B. (1820–1906), social reformer who achieved world fame as a crusader for women's rights. From a Quaker family in upper New York State, Anthony was educated at a Friends' Seminary. After working as a teacher, headmistress, and manager of her family farm, she became interested in temperance reform, and in 1852, organized the Women's State Temperance Society of New York. In 1850 she met women's rights leader Elizabeth Cady Stanton, with whom she embarked on a lifetime collaboration. Active in the women's cause in New York State, Anthony also became an abolitionist lecturer and New York agent for William Lloyd Garrison's American Anti-Slavery Society.

During the Civil War, Anthony organized the Women's National Loyal League, petitioned for slave emancipation, and supported black suffrage. After the war, when the Fourteenth Amendment gave suffrage to black men, she turned her attention to winning the ballot for women. In 1866 and 1867 she unsuccessfully petitioned both Congress and New York State for women's suffrage. She also became interested in labor problems and organized a Working Women's Association in New York City.

Suffrage Activities. In 1869, she joined Stanton in forming the National Woman Suffrage Association. In 1872, Anthony voted in the presidential election, for which she was arrested, indicted, tried, convicted, and fined, although she refused to pay. With Stanton and Matilda Joslyn Gage, she published the *History of Woman Suffrage,* which began appearing in 1881, and in 1890 she became vice-president of the National American Woman Suffrage Association, serving as president from 1892 to 1900.

See also Stanton, Elizabeth Cady; Suffrage, Women's.

—Nancy Woloch, *Hebrew Union College.*

ANTIETAM, OR SHARPSBURG (Sept. 17, 1862), fiercely fought battle that led to Robert E. Lee's withdrawal from Maryland. *See* Civil War Battles.

ANTI-FEDERALISM, the movement of opponents of the proposed U.S. Constitution to prevent its ratification. Leading Anti-Federalists included Richard Henry Lee and Patrick Henry of Virginia, George Clinton of New York, and

Elbridge Gerry of Massachusetts. Lee's *The Federal Farmer* carried many of the Anti-Federalists' arguments.

The Constitution was attacked on the grounds that it gave the central government, and especially the president, too much power; that the offices were founded on oligarchical principles; that civil liberties were threatened; and that the country was too large for submission and obedience to federal laws. It was also criticized as a threat to states' rights, its institutions unrepresentative, and amendments impossible.

Opposition to the Constitution came generally from the back country and agricultural sections. Coastal and urban sections tended to support it. Despite the vigorous efforts of the Anti-Federalists, the necessary nine states had ratified the new Constitution by June 1788.

See also Federalism; Lee, Richard Henry. *Consult* (III) Rossiter, 1953.

ANTI-SALOON LEAGUE, "federated church in action against the saloon," founded in Washington, D.C., in 1895 that played a major role in the adoption of the Eighteenth Amendment (Prohibition). Essentially a coalition of existing temperance groups, the League was closely connected with major Protestant churches. At its height, the League had affiliates in every state, employed 1,500 full-time workers, had over 50,000 speakers, and its newsletter, *The American Issue,* carried an annual circulation of 16 million. Although looking toward the total prohibition of alcholic beverages, it prudently concentrated its efforts on closing down saloons through the adoption of "local option" laws, and 31 states had adopted such legislation by 1913. The League endorsed candidates committed to its goals and campaigned effectively for their election.

ANTISLAVERY. *See* Abolitionism.

ANTISLAVERY SOCIETIES. *See* American and Foreign Anti-Slavery Society; American Anti-Slavery Society.

ANTITRUST CASES, federal cases against large business trusts in the late nineteenth and early twentieth centuries. The prosecutions were conducted under the provisions of the Sherman Antitrust Act of 1890, which barred any joint action by businessmen "in restraint of trade" and made it a criminal offense to attempt to monopolize interstate commerce. The act expressed a traditional American hostility to monopoly and "privilege." In practice, however, it was difficult to define phrases like "restraint of trade" and "monopoly," and the matter was left to the courts, which were pro-business. Little was done to check monopolies under the act in the first few years.

Susan B. Anthony (1820–1906), one of the leaders in the fight for women's suffrage, started career as an abolitionist and temperance advocate.

Antitrust cartoon shows trusts continuing their activities despite adverse court decisions.

Church in Lancaster, Mass., built in 1816–1817, shows architectural style of Charles Bulfinch.

Interrelationship of pillars, roadway, and web of steel cables in the Brooklyn Bridge made it a landmark of nineteenth-century architecture.

For example, in 1895 in *United States v. E. C. Knight and Co.* the Supreme Court threw out the government's case against the sugar trust, although it was clear that the sugar kings intended to monopolize about 98 percent of all American refining. The Court narrowed its jurisdiction to interstate "commerce" (not "manufacturing"). The majority decision went even further, by giving implicit recognition to the right of one corporation to hold the stock of another corporation. As a result, not only was the antitrust movement set back, but a new wave of mergers took place, using the now acceptable "holding company" format.

Trust Busting. Mergers reached a new climax at the turn of the century, exemplified by the formation of the U.S. Steel Corporation, the first billion dollar trust. Theodore Roosevelt attacked trust abuses in his annual message of 1901 and promised a trust-busting campaign. Congress passed the Expedition Act in 1903 to speed up antitrust cases in circuit courts, and the Bureau of Corporations was created inside the Commerce Department. In *Northern Securities Co. v. United States* (1904), Northern Securities being a railroad combination, the Court reversed its decision of 1895. It definitely extended its jurisdiction to monopolies created by property transfer and invalidated the formation of Northern Securities.

In 1905 the beef trust was attacked in *Swift and Co. v. United States* which gave the phrase "interstate commerce" wider scope. Two big cases in 1911 were the dissolution of the Rockefeller trust (*United States v. Standard Oil Co.*) and *United States v. American Tobacco Co.* In both these cases, however, the Court introduced a new interpretive device, a distinction between "reasonable" and "unreasonable" mergers. The Sherman Antitrust Act was strictly limited to "unreasonable" trusts, which was in line with President Theodore Roosevelt's earlier distinction between "good" and "bad" trusts. In 1914, President Woodrow Wilson, who disliked trusts altogether, introduced the Clayton Antitrust Act, to strengthen the hands of the trustbusters.

See also Clayton Antitrust Act (1914); Sherman Antitrust Act (1890); Trusts; *United States v. E. C. Knight and Co.*

Consult (V) Thorelli, 1955.

—Peter d'A. Jones, *University of Illinois, Chicago Circle.*

APACHE WARS. *See* Indian Wars, Western.

APOLLO SPACE FLIGHTS. *See* Space Exploration.

APPOMATTOX COURTHOUSE SURRENDER, the surrender on Sunday, April 9, 1865, of Gen. Robert E. Lee to Gen. Ulysses S. Grant at the village of Appomattox Courthouse, Va. The terms were that all Confederate officers and men (numbering about 26,000) were to be released after pledging to fight no longer against the United States; that arms, artillery, and public property were to be turned over, with the exception of officers' sidearms, private horse, and baggage; and that cavalrymen who owned their mounts might retain them. Dressed in a mud-spattered uniform, Grant showed no signs of gloating or exultation. The dignified Lee, who wore an immaculate uniform and bore himself calmly, was quite touched by Grant's generosity and consideration.

See also Civil War Battles.

ARCHAEOLOGY. *See* Historical Archaeology.

ARCHITECTURE. American architecture has always been an aggressive, adaptive, and changing architecture, distinguished by such outstanding innovations as the suspension bridge and the skyscraper. It has been sadly unique in the mass destruction of buildings and the endless monotonous sprawl of the suburban single-family house or the urban apartment block. It has produced the biggest and the best structures and the most sophisticated building technology, and it has also produced the most substandard housing and rampant ecological waste of the technologically superior countries. Perhaps the finest achievements of American architecture lie in the integrity and sophistication of early indigenous structures such as the pueblo villages of the Southwest, forerunners of modern mass building.

Pioneer Period. The European settlers of the seventeenth century continued the tradition of a natural architecture by building simplistic yet noble structures of locally available materials to provide shelter and protection. The saltbox wooden houses of New England and the log cabin of the Midwest attest to the basic development of an economical system derived from previous building skills and methods of Western European construction. In some instances, the early settlers learned and adapted techniques from the Indians. In other instances settlers brought their ethnic and regional experiences and incorporated elements of design from the home country into this new architecture.

This early pioneer architecture of improvisation and temporary building, of an architecture by the people rather than by professionals, extended itself well through the eighteenth and nineteenth centuries as the original states expanded. However, as the new communities survived and then prospered, the plans designed by professionals became more complex, their buildings became more substantial in size and structure, and their walls and windows, doors and roofs were embellished with decoration, usually traditionally inspired or copied.

Early National. The most distinguished

early American architects were Thomas Jefferson and Charles Bulfinch. Jefferson's work showed great respect for classical geometry yet expressed a clarity of plan and a human scale of considerable sensitivity as in his design for the estate at Monticello (1771-1772) and, considerably later, the University of Virginia at Charlottesville (1817-1826), designed with Benjamin Latrobe. Bulfinch, a student of French and Italian classical architecture, designed numerous public buildings in New England, including the Massachusetts State House (1800), and private homes such as the Harrison Gray Otis House.

This early classicism extended through the early and middle nineteenth century with such outstanding buildings as the Bank of Philadelphia (1799-1801) by Benjamin Latrobe and the Tennessee state capitol (1845-1854) at Nashville by William Strickland. Both projects contain the familiar columnar entrance with triangular architrave above, developed from the Greek Parthenon, which became the standard classical bank, library, and public building design of that era.

While the classical revival was still popular, a new style, the Gothic revival, began appearing in American architecture. The books of Andrew Jackson Downing helped popularize this trend, which reached its height after the Civil War in Victorian Gothic architecture.

Late Nineteenth Century. The late nineteenth century saw the breakthrough of some very creative American architecture. Cast iron and steel were developed into shapes suitable for use as lightweight and strong building structural systems, which enabled buildings to become taller and horizontal spans longer. One of the first mass-produced systems was patented by James Bogardus in 1849, who expanded upon an earlier English invention of semiprefabricated cast iron buildings. Bogardus built many such structures in Baltimore and New York City in the 1850s and 1860s.

Perhaps a more dramatic achievement was the construction of the Brooklyn Bridge in New York City (1867-1883) by John A. and Washington A. Roebling. It was the world's first large suspension bridge, made possible only by the development of the steel cable. The dramatic contrast among the solidarity of the heavy masonry supports, the lightweight mesh of steel cable supports, and horizontal roadway has never been surpassed as powerful architecture.

During the same period a new architecture with its roots in Romanesque design was being developed for primarily commercial buildings in the Chicago area, which was destroyed by the great fire of 1871. Henry Hobson Richardson, not a structural innovator, used interior cast iron columns and ties but dealt primarily with heavy masonry perimeter walls articulated into rich and powerful external forms expressive of the spirit of commerce and industry in America, as seen in his finest achievement, the Marshall Field Wholesale Store in Chicago (1885-1887). In contrast to Richardson's clarity and smooth and easy associations of form, the highly creative Frank Furness was designing rugged masonry architectural monuments such as the library at the University of Pennsylvania in Philadelphia in 1880-1891.

The early development of the skyscraper took place in Chicago with the designs of such outstanding architects as William Le Baron Jenney, Burnham and Root, and Adler and Sullivan. Louis Sullivan's Carson-Pirie-Scott Department Store (1899-1904), an outstanding achievement of the period, reached a high level of clarity, order, and scale and of vertical and horizontal interaction.

Twentieth Century. The turn of the century saw the rise and development of the great American architect, Frank Lloyd Wright, whose prolific body of work of over 60 years included the most significant works of twentieth-century architecture and led the way to the formulation of modern architecture. His work was characterized by daring spatial designs and bold experiments in mechanical and structural systems and material exploration, including the Robie House (1909), a revolutionary statement of that time, and Falling Water (1936), a complex massing of bold concrete cantilevers, rugged stone walls, and large glass areas. Perhaps his greatest design was the controversial Guggenheim Museum (1946-1959) in New York City, a spiraling three-dimensional mass of concrete in space.

During Wright's lifetime the development and refinement of the skyscraper occurred, including the Philadelphia Savings Fund Society building in Philadelphia (1932) and in New York City the Rockefeller Center complex (1931-1939), the Lever House Office Building (1950-1952), and the elegant bronze and glass Seagram Building (1956-1958) by Mies Van Der Rohe and Philip Johnson. In addition, engineer and philosopher R. Buckminster Fuller developed the lightweight structural space-frame and geodesic dome, conceived in the 1930s and finally built at Expo Montreal in 1967.

In the 1950s two major architects produced outstanding buildings of great influence. Louis I. Kahn, whose creative works have inspired new directions in modern architecture, designed the Richards Medical Laboratory (1957-1961) at the University of Pennsylvania, an ordered complex of brick and concrete towers with crisp articulations of form and bold and honest expressions of detail. Paul Rudolph in 1962-1963 designed the Arts and Architecture Building at Yale University, an interlocking design of planes and masses in space about a multileveled interior column.

New York City's Seagram Building set a new standard for skyscrapers.

Architecture in America appears to be developing in three directions. First there is the Post-Corbu types of dynamic geometric massing, a refinement and development of the work of Swiss architect Le Corbusier. Secondly, there is an architecture of contradiction and complexity as developed by architect Robert Venturi. The third and possibly the most significant direction is systems building, a development of the repetitive form for mass productivity.

Although Americans are a creative and inventive people, they have always been extremely cautious and slow to mass produce innovations because of insecurities and traditional ties. For instance, although the kitchen and the bath have been completely transformed and although air conditioning and plastics have been introduced, the average American still demands and applies the decor of the past to his residences and his public buildings. The fresh and dynamic design approaches are still well in the minority, and mass planning, productivity, and mobility appear to be the future.

See also Bulfinch, Charles; Sullivan, Louis; Wright, Frank Lloyd.

Consult (VIII) Kaufman, 1970; Manson, 1958; Moholy Nagy, 1957; Scully, 1969.

—Myron Goldfinger (AIA), *Pratt Institute*

ARIZONA, the 48th state, admitted on Feb. 14, 1912. It was explored by Spain in 1539 and colonized by Spanish missionaries around 1598. The United States gained Arizona after the Mexican War by the Treaty of Guadalupe-Hidalgo (1848) and through the Gadsden Purchase (1853). Arizona was granted territorial status in 1863. The state legislature is bicameral; the capital is Phoenix. The population in 1970 was 1,772,482.

See also Gadsden Purchase (1853).

ARKANSAS, the 25th state, admitted to the Union on June 15, 1836. First settled by the French in 1685, the area was transferred to Spain in 1762 and then regained by France. Arkansas became U.S. territory as part of the Louisiana Purchase (1803) and was included as part of the Louisiana Territory from 1812 until 1819, when it acquired territorial status on its own. Arkansas seceded during the Civil War. The state legislature is bicameral; the capital is Little Rock. Its population in 1970 was 1,923,-295.

ARMORY SHOW, the international exposition of modern art held in 1913 at the 69th Regiment Armory in New York City. This show, organized by the Association of American Painters and Sculptors, was significant for its introduction of modern art—Fauvism, Cubism, Futurism, and various forms of Expressionism—to the American public on a large scale. Although the works shown shocked both the public and the critics, the exhibition provided an important stimulus for modern American painting, sculpture, and art criticism.

See also Painting.

ARMOUR, PHILLIP DANFORTH (1832-1901), meat packer and entrepreneur. He accumulated a fortune of several million dollars in pork trading near the end of the Civil War, joined his brother's grain commission house in Chicago, and added a pork packing plant that took the name of Armour & Co. He became president of the firm in 1875 and was an important promoter of change in the industry. His firm was among the first to conduct in-plant slaughtering operations, and it was a leader in achieving economies of operation through the development of marketable by-products made from carcass "wastes."

The successful development of refrigerated railroad cars made possible vertical integration in the industry, and Armour responded to the new opportunities by purchasing his own railroad cars, creating a national distribution and marketing system, and moving into European markets. By 1909 Armour & Co. was the eighth largest industrial firm in the United States, measured in terms of total assets. Armour's business activities also extended to banking and the grain markets. One of the numerous beneficiaries of his fortune was the Armour Institute of Technology, which he founded in 1893.

ARMSTRONG, (DANIEL) LOUIS (1900-1971), jazz trumpeter, usually called "Satchmo," who was one of the first forces in American jazz as well as one of the first jazz soloists to achieve world-wide recognition. His musical career began in the streets of New Orleans, where he sang for pennies with other poor black children. By the late 1920s, after working with established bands and organizing a group of his own, Satchmo had achieved a classic synthesis of instrumental virtuosity and melodic and rhythmic inventiveness, demonstrated in his Hot Five and Hot Seven recordings. His style was a major influence on a generation of trumpeters, such as Red Allen, Buck Clayton, and Roy Eldridge, as well as other instrumentalists of the 1920s and 1930s.

Armstrong's career gradually expanded to include, along with personal appearances and recordings, performances on television, in jazz festivals at home and abroad, and in such films as *The Glenn Miller Story* and *High Society*. In the decade before his death, although criticized for his silence on civil rights issues during the black equality movement, he made two goodwill tours, one to Africa and the second to other parts of the world.

ARMY, U.S., officially established under the

Department of War on August 7, 1789. The Department of the Army was not created until 1947. The Army is part of the Department of Defense and is commanded by the Chief of Staff, a member of the Joint Chiefs of Staff.

The Continental Army was established in 1775 by the Second Continental Congress, with George Washington as its first leader. After the Revolutionary War, the Army received little federal support because of fears that a standing Army could be used to achieve political ends. This resulted in an inadequate Army in the War of 1812, but the Army that fought in the Mexican War (1846–1848) was greatly improved.

During World War I a military draft increased the Army to 4 million. More than 1.2 million U.S. Army troops fought for 47 days in the Meuse-Argonne offensive (1918). One of the largest Army offensives in World War II was its participation in the Allied invasion of Normandy. During and after World War II the Army fulfilled its manpower needs by use of the draft. The Army subsequently fought in Korea and Vietnam. In 1973, the draft was ended and a volunteer army reinstituted.

See also articles on important wars and military leaders.

ARMY APPROPRIATIONS BILL (1901), legislation to which the Platt Amendment was attached. *See* Platt Amendment.

ARMY LEAGUE. *See* Preparedness Movement (1915–1916).

ARMY-McCARTHY HEARINGS, public Senate hearings on alleged Communist influence in the U.S. Army. *See* McCarthy, Joseph R.

ARNOLD, BENEDICT (1741–1801), American military leader, whose defection to the British in the Revolutionary War made his name synonymous with treason. Originally a merchant, he convinced Massachusetts authorities to appoint him a colonel after the clash at Lexington. In 1775 he cooperated with Ethan Allen in the reduction of Fort Ticonderoga, N.Y. and then joined in an ill-fated expedition against Quebec.

Promoted to brigadier general in January 1776, Arnold took command of American forces on Lake Champlain and halted an invasion from Canada by brilliant tactics in naval engagements near Valcour Island in October. Much to Arnold's chagrin, Congress in February 1777 promoted five officers junior to him. After Arnold daringly attacked a British force near Danbury, Conn., in April, Congress made him a major general but did not restore his seniority. He submitted his resignation, but Washington asked him to help in operations against General Burgoyne's invasion of New

York. Arnold played a prominent role at Saratoga, where he was badly wounded, and Congress finally granted him seniority. He then took command of Philadelphia, which the British had evacuated in May 1778.

Treason. In April 1779, Arnold married Peggy Shippen, the daughter of Pennsylvania's former chief justice, and in May he offered his services to the British. In 1780, Arnold took command of the garrison at West Point, N.Y., and made arrangements through British Major John André to turn the fort over to the British for £20,000. The capture of André betrayed the plot, but Arnold escaped. The British made Arnold a brigadier general, and he led raids in Virginia and Connecticut. Arnold did not distinguish himself and left for London in 1781. He spent the rest of his life in British territory.

See also Revolutionary War Battles.
Consult (II) Wallace, 1953.
—Thomas Archdeacon, *University of Wisconsin*

AROOSTOOK WAR (1838–1839), undeclared, bloodless war that threatened Anglo-American relations. The northern boundary between Maine and New Brunswick had been a source of Anglo-American dispute since the Revolution. This issue came to a head in the winter of 1838–1839, when Canadian and American lumberjacks began moving into the Aroostook River region. Before actual fighting broke out, President Van Buren dispatched Gen. Winfield Scott to the troubled area, and in March 1839 Scott persuaded the Maine and Canadian authorities to withdraw their forces until the boundary could be set by diplomatic negotiation. The question was settled by the Webster-Ashburton Treaty (1842).

See also Webster-Ashburton Treaty (1842).

ARTHUR, CHESTER A(LAN) (1829–1886), 21st President of the United States (1881–1885). Born in Fairfield, Vt., on Oct. 5, 1829, he entered New York politics and served as New York quartermaster during the Civil War. Arthur supported Roscoe Conkling during New York Republicans' factional disputes, and so it was a Stalwart victory when President Grant appointed him customs collector of New York (1871). With many patronage positions at his disposal, Arthur appointed competent men, but he also believed in rewarding party loyalty. When President Hayes attempted to destroy Conkling's New York organization, Arthur was removed in 1877 for being politically active.

Arthur remained powerful in his party, and when Republican nominee James Garfield offered the vice-presidency to the Stalwarts in 1880, Arthur proved his independence from Conkling by accepting. Partly due to his efforts, the Republicans carried both state and nation, but patronage battles erupted again in 1881.

Chester A. Arthur *(right)*, 21st President of the United States (1881–1885).

Arthur's position was almost untenable when, after Garfield's assassination, he became president (Sept. 19, 1881).

Presidency. A competent executive, Arthur prosecuted the Star Route frauds, vetoed Chinese immigration restrictions, tried to reduce "pork barrel" legislation, authorized a modern Navy, and cut national indebtedness. He shocked both Stalwarts and reformers by demanding civil service reform and signing the Pendleton Act (1883). However, because reformers never forgot his past and his Stalwart friends considered him a traitor, he was denied renomination in 1884. He died in New York City on Nov. 18, 1886.

See also Conkling, Roscoe; Pendleton Act (1883); Stalwarts and Half-Breeds; Star Routes.

Consult (V) Howe, 1957; Josephson, 1938.

—George Lankevich, *Bronx Community College of The City University of New York*

ARTICLES OF CONFEDERATION, the first constitution of the United States. As part of his resolution of June 7, 1776, in favor of independence, Richard Henry Lee proposed that a plan of confederation be devised. On June 12 the Second Continental Congress appointed John Dickinson and others to undertake the task, and on July 12 the committee presented their "Articles of Confederation and Perpetual Union" to the delegates.

The apportionment of representation and taxation became the focus of the long debate over the Articles. The larger states wanted representation to be proportional to population, and the smaller—fearful of an overbearing central government—preferred that each state have an equal vote. States with valuable lands sought to have taxation assessed according to population, and states with poorer lands favored use of the value of improved lands as the appropriation measure. On Oct. 7, 1777, the Congress decided that each state would have one vote and on October 14 that the value of surveyed lands would be the basis of taxation. On November 15 the Congress adopted the Articles and two days later submitted them to the states for approval.

Arguments over the disposition of Western lands delayed full ratification almost 4 years. States with fixed western boundaries objected to a provision, inserted by the states with Western claims, that barred Congress from interfering with the lands of the states. In 1781, Virginia finally ceded its claim to the Old Northwest to Congress, and on March 1, 1781, Maryland became the final state to ratify the Articles.

Government Under The Articles. The Articles served as the frame of government of the United States until replaced by the Federal Constitution in 1789. The Articles had serious defects, especially the inability of the central government to regulate trade or to force states to obey its edicts, but they also incorporated a series of features thought to be democratic. The Articles reserved all powers and rights not expressly given to the central government to the states, provided for annual election of national representatives by the state legislatures, and forbade any man to serve as a congressman for more than three of any six consecutive years.

Congress did not have the power to tax but could borrow money, issue paper currency, and fix the value of coins. Congress had sole authority to conduct diplomatic negotiations, to make war and peace, and to appoint officers serving the United States above the rank of colonel. In addition, Congress could fix weights and measures, establish and operate a post office, and handle affairs with Indians.

See also Constitution of the United States; Continental Congress, Second.

Consult (II) Jensen, 1940.

—Thomas Archdeacon, *University of Wisconsin*

ASHCAN SCHOOL, realistic school of painting concerned with urban life. *See* Painting.

ASHWANDER v. TVA (1936), Supreme Court decision upholding the right of the federal government to build Tennessee Valley Authority projects. *See* Brandeis, Louis D.

ASSASSINATION. A wide range of U.S. political officials—from presidents and cabinet members to local judges and tax collectors—have been targets of assassination attempts, as have other prominent public figures such as leaders of protest movements and candidates for office. Motives for assassination have included gaining revenge for a real or imagined wrong, earning fame or a reward, and removing a political enemy or group from office.

Although four presidents have been struck down (Lincoln, Garfield, McKinley, and Kennedy) and four others (Jackson, both Roosevelts, and Truman) escaped death by assassin, it was not until 1965 that it became a federal crime to kill, kidnap, or assault a president, vice-president, president-elect, or acting president. Previously, however, it was against the law to threaten the life of a president. The most recent attempt on the life of a presidential candidate was the 1972 shooting of George Wallace.

Consult (VIII) Havens, 1970.

ASSIMILATION, the merging of immigrants from one distinct cultural group into the cultural patterns and habits of their new country. Assimilation presents difficult problems for both the immigrants, who want to retain their

NOTABLE ASSASSINATIONS IN THE UNITED STATES

Name	Date of Death
Abraham Lincoln, President of the United States	April 15, 1865
James Garfield, President of the United States	Sept. 19, 1881
Carter H. Harrison, Mayor of Chicago	Oct. 28, 1893
William Goebel, Governor of Kentucky	Feb. 3, 1900
William McKinley, President of the United States	Sept. 14, 1901
Frank Steunenberg, ex-Governor of Idaho	Dec. 30, 1905
Anton Cermak, Mayor of Chicago	March 6, 1933
Huey Long, U.S. Senator from Louisiana	Sept. 10, 1935
Medgar Evers, Mississippi NAACP leader	June 12, 1963
John F. Kennedy, President of the United States	Nov. 22, 1963
Malcolm X, Black nationalist leader	Feb. 21, 1965
George Lincoln Rockwell, American Nazi leader	Aug. 26, 1967
Martin Luther King, Civil rights leader	April 4, 1968
Robert F. Kennedy, U.S. Senator from New York	June 6, 1968

traditions, and the societies into which they move. Established communities resist, sometimes violently, what they consider threats to their traditions and style of life.

See also Acculturation; Ethnic Group; Immigration.

ASTOR, JOHN JACOB (1763-1848), American fur trader, merchant, and real estate speculator. Born in Waldorf, Germany, he came to New York City in April 1784 and began work at a small fur store. Within two years he had his own fur and musical instruments business. By 1800 his fortune was $.25 million, made by trading furs on the western frontier and as far north as Montreal, where he had to work through the powerful British North West Fur Company. Astor also imported necessities from Europe for the U.S. market, such as cutlery, ammunition, and dry goods. He bought New York real estate and in 1800 he began trading with China.

Astor was a tough and shrewd competitor, with his eye always on the main chance. With the Louisiana Purchase (1803) and explorations of Lewis and Clark (from 1804), he looked to the Far West. His American Fur Company (1808), organized with a capital of $1 million, was created to avoid having to deal with the North West Fur Company. Astor aimed at exerting a monopoly on the U.S. fur trade and keeping out the Canadians.

He negotiated with Russian traders. The first U.S. settlement on the Northwest Pacific Coast was his fur center, Astoria, built in 1811 at the mouth of the Columbia River in Oregon. In the War of 1812 he lost Astoria to the North West Fur Company, but throughout the conflict Astor traded with the British in the Great Lakes region, and in 1813 he lent the U.S. government $2 million. In the 1840s Astoria was used as a major argument by the United States for its right to the Oregon Territory.

After the War of 1812, Astor rapidly assumed monopoly control of all U.S. fur trading. He bought up rivals and took over the entire upper Missouri valley. His friendships at high government levels helped—he knew Thomas Jefferson well and was a personal friend of James Monroe—and he was tough with the Indians and with small traders. Astor did not go to the places he traded with but lived mainly in New York or Europe, so he never came in contact with the thousands of frontiersmen and little people who worked for him. In this he was a model capitalist, who treated his workers like commodities. The bulk of his fortune was made in shrewd land and property purchases in Manhattan. Astor realized that the transportation revolution would make New York a great city, and he bought the land when it was cheap.

Astor retired from fur trading in 1834 and devoted himself to the loan business and New York real estate. On his death he was said to be worth between $20 million and $30 million. The fortune was left mainly in family hands and still exists. Before he died Astor said, "Could I begin life again, knowing what I now know, . . .I would buy every foot of land on the island of Manhattan!"

See also Fur Trade.

Consult (III) Porter, 1931.

—Peter d'A. Jones, *University of Illinois, Chicago Circle*

ASTRONAUTS. *See* Space Exploration.

ATCHISON, TOPEKA AND SANTE FE. *See* Railroads.

ATLANTA EXPOSITION SPEECH (1895), address given by Booker T. Washington on the position of blacks in America. *See* Washington, Booker T.

ATLANTIC CHARTER, joint declaration by the United States and Britain after the meeting of President Roosevelt and Prime Minister Churchill (their first of World War II) at sea off Newfoundland in August 1941. The United States was still avowedly neutral, but its policy was clearly one of assisting the enemies of Germany, Italy, and Japan. The charter declared the two nations' adherence to certain principles such as freedom of thought, freedom from fear and want, economic cooperation, self-determination, and armament reduction, and they disavowed any interest in territorial aggrandizement. It was later signed by many other countries and provided justification for their, as well as for America's, participation in the war.

Consult (VII) Wilson, 1969.

ATOM BOMB, weapon that explodes because of the fission of uranium-235 or plutonium and the resultant chain reaction. The bomb's unique features are the superintense heat of the explosion and high amounts of fatal radiation.

Serious work to develop an atom bomb began in 1939, when Albert Einstein, Enrico Fermi, and Leo Szilard warned President Roosevelt that Germany might be working to develop its own A-bomb. Roosevelt established the Office of Scientific Research and Development in May 1941, and the top-secret Manhattan Project to develop the bomb was soon under way. By Dec. 2, 1942, Fermi and his associates had already succeeded in producing the first self-sustaining nuclear chain reaction. The design and construction of a transportable bomb were achieved at Los Alamos, N.M., under the direction of J. Robert Oppenheimer. The first atom bomb was exploded at nearby Alamogordo on July 16, 1945, and had the force of 20,000 tons of TNT.

Mushroom cloud rises above Alamagordo, N.M., as world's first atom bomb explodes.

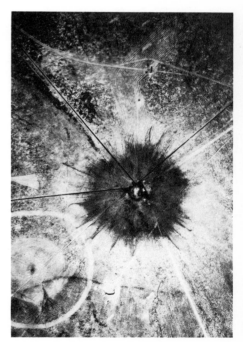

Bare blast site after detonation of first atom bomb on July 16, 1945.

The first atom bomb used in warfare was dropped on Hiroshima, Japan, on August 6, 1945, in an attempt to end World War II; 75,000 people were killed. It was a U-235 type, 14 feet long, 5 feet in diameter, weighed 10,000 pounds, and was fused to explode at 1,850 feet over the city. The second bomb, dropped on Nagasaki, was a plutonium-type bomb. After the war, attempts were made to control the spread and use of atomic weapons. Atmospheric testing was partially banned in the 1960s, and nuclear arms were limited in the 1970s.

See also Manhattan Project; Oppenheimer, J. Robert.

ATOMIC ENERGY. For most people the atomic age opened with the dropping of the first bombs in 1945. Subsequent years have seen evidence of both the peaceful and the lethal uses to which the unleashing of the atom's power can be put. American atomic scientists feared that control of atomic energy by the military might be authoritarian, militaristic, and harmful to the spirit of free scientific inquiry. They succeeded in 1946 in placing atomic research and development, which had been fostered during the war by the military, under a civilian Atomic Energy Commission.

By 1954 Congress had moved to encourage private development of electricity from atomic power. The nation and the world were in a race to solve a growing energy crisis. There would still be considerable governmental underwriting of the cost of research, especially at the major national laboratories of Argonne and Brookhaven. A 1964 act provided for private ownership of nuclear fuels by the power industry.

Meanwhile the arms race continued, and efforts were made to achieve weapons control both through limitation of membership in the nuclear club and by agreements to stabilize deterrence systems (thereby ending the escalation of weaponry).

See also Atom Bomb; Disarmament; Strategic Arms Limitation Talks.

Consult (VIII) Lewis and Wilson, 1971.

ATTUCKS, CRISPUS, mulatto killed in the Boston Massacre. *See* Boston Massacre (1770).

AUDUBON, JOHN JAMES (1785–1851), naturalist and artist famous for his paintings of birds. He was born in Santo Domingo, the illegitimate son of a French sea captain, who adopted him and took him to France. By age 15 he had begun his life's work with a study of French birds. In 1803 he moved to the United States, and while living on his father's estate in Pennsylvania he made the first experimental banding of a wild bird in America in April 1804.

Audubon continued to pursue his ornithological studies and his art, but neither offered any financial support. He turned to storekeeping, but his career as a merchant ended with bankruptcy in 1819. After briefly working as a taxidermist for the Western Museum in Cincinnati, he determined to publish his now considerable collection of wild bird drawings. He was unable to find an American publisher but found subscribers for his work and also a master engraver, Robert Havell, Jr., in Britain. The monumental *Birds of America* was published beginning in 1827 and continuing through 1838. *The Ornithological Biography,* the companion text to the handcolored plates in *Birds of America,* was published between 1831 and 1839.

Audubon returned to the United States with a solid reputation in Europe as a pioneer naturalist and artist. He continued his work in the West and South as well as in Canada. With his sons and friends he produced a popular edition of *Birds of America* and a new book, the *Viva-parous Quadrupeds of North America.*

—Richard Collin, *Louisiana State University, New Orleans*

AUSTIN, STEPHEN F(ULLER) (1793–1836), pioneer settler of Texas. His story really begins with his father Moses, who in 1798 established the town of Potosi, Mo. In 1821, Moses received a grant from Spanish authorities in Texas to settle 300 families, only to die three months later leaving a huge task for his 27-year-old son. Stephen proceeded at once to San Antonio, where he sought authorization from the Mexicans to carry on his father's colonial enterprise. In a law signed on Jan. 3, 1823, incoming families were offered grants of more than 4,600 acres, and a system was established to oversee colonization. Altogether Austin contracted to settle a total of 1,700 additional families about 50 miles west of modern Houston.

As grievances against Mexico mounted, the Texans held conventions in October 1832 and again on April 1, 1833, calling for reform by Mexico. At the latter his followers elected Austin to deliver their petitions to Mexico City. But in January 1834 he was arrested for allegedly trying to incite insurrection in Texas and was imprisoned in Mexico City until 1835.

He was back in Texas when an exchange of shots between Texans and Mexicans occurred at Gonzales on Oct. 1, 1835. Austin was elected to command volunteers against the Mexican army at San Antonio. In November he was chosen as a commissioner to the United States, which again took him out of Texas from January 1836 until the following June; by that time Texas had declared its independence of Mexico and had set up an ostensibly independent republic.

Back in the new republic, Austin reluctantly agreed to run against Sam Houston for

Scientists search for peaceful uses for nuclear fission in Atomic Energy Commission laboratory.

AUDUBON

the presidency, but he was no match for the military hero of San Jacinto. Houston appointed him secretary of state, and he died in that office.

See also Houston, Sam; Texas.
Consult (III) Barker, 1968.
—Joe B. Frantz, *University of Texas at Austin*

AUSTRIAN SUCCESSION, WAR OF THE. *See* King George's War (1744–1748).

AUTOMATION. *See* Mass Production.

AUTOMOBILE. Following the first long-distance European and American motor car races in 1895, it became obvious that the automobile would replace the horse. By 1899, 30 American manufacturers had turned out 2,500 vehicles. At first autos were playthings of the rich, but with the introduction of mass production methods, especially by Henry Ford in 1910, the motor car became increasingly available to many Americans.

During the 1920s the number of cars increased dramatically because of the growth of highways, the success of motor trucks during World War I, and the availability of money. By 1929 there were 24 million cars, and the replacement market was already far bigger than sales to first-time owners; most Americans who could afford a car had one. The enterprise was so vast that small manufacturers could not survive, and increasingly in the twentieth century innovations in design and production decreased as manufacturing required more and more capital. In the early 1970s there were well over 100 million cars, trucks, and buses on the roads of the United States.

The most obvious impact of the automobile was economic. The petroleum, rubber, glass, and to some extent steel and chemical industries became the creatures and dependents of automobile production, especially beginning in the 1920s. A remarkable part of American wealth in the twentieth century went into not only the autos but also the highways and related service industries. Because of the importance of capital investment in economic growth, the automobile in the twentieth century became virtually the basis of American abundance.

But in one sense the automobile was an anachronism: it emphasized individualism with independent choice in a mass society. Cars cut people loose from dependence upon rails, overhead wires, and someone else's schedule. Interurban and finally long-distance passenger traffic was largely diverted to individually owned and operated vehicles. This mobility greatly increased the growth of suburban areas, and it kept rural ideals alive long after the country was essentially urban in character. The importance of his auto to an individual American was indicative of the place of the car in American culture. A survey in the 1930s, for example, showed that hard-pressed Depression era citizens who did not need the transportation nevertheless gave up the family bathtub before surrendering the family car. In the 1960s the perception of the automobile changed when exhaust emissions, junk disposal problems, fears about safety, freeway sprawl, and urban congestion showed motor vehicles to be a major social problem.

See also Ford, Henry; Highway System; Mass Production.
Consult (VIII) Rae 1971.
—John C. Burnham, *Ohio State University*

AVIATION. Two Americans, Orville and Wilbur Wright, flew the world's first successful airplane in 1903, but their achievement was preceded by centuries of experimentation, including work by the ancient Chinese and Leonardo da Vinci. These were heavier-than-air machines that failed because they lacked a powerful engine; human muscle power was entirely inadequate, and bird flight could not be copied.

Experiments with lighter-than-air craft were more successful. Much was learned about flight from the use of balloons and gliders. Free-flying balloons were hard to control, but soon the powered airship, using steam engines, developed and later the internal combustion gasoline engine. Count Ferdinand von Zeppelin (1838–1917) perfected in 1900 the rigid-framed, sausage-shaped dirigible, with passenger gondola beneath. These German airships dominated the scene with scheduled passenger flights until 1937, when the crash of the giant *Hindenburg* abruptly ended the era.

The Wrights. Meanwhile the Wrights, owners of a bicycle store in Dayton, Ohio, had made detailed mathematical studies and were familiar with the existing scientific literature and previous experiments with heavier-than-air machines. They knew of the work of S. P. Langley (1834–1906), of the Smithsonian Institution, who had launched a pilotless airplane in 1896. Their own biplane owed much to the box kite in design. The Wrights "Flyer," a tailless, twin-propeller biplane was powered by a 12-horsepower gasoline engine of their own making.

On December 17, 1903, Orville Wright achieved the first successful, repeatable, level take-off flight and landing at Kitty Hawk, N.C. In a 12-second flight he traveled 100 feet at an airspeed of 35 miles per hour and a height of 10 feet. The longest of that day's four flights was that of his brother Wilbur, who covered 852 feet in 59 seconds. Two years later there was a final breakthrough when Wilbur flew 24 miles in 38 minutes with total control—banking, turning, climbing, and circling at will. Control

Model T Ford helped revolutionize U.S. transportation. This 1909 model was one of more than 15 million built (1908–1927).

Charles Lindbergh's *Spirit of St. Louis* hangs in Smithsonian Institution in Washington, D.C.

was exercised through movable parts connected by wiring: rudder, ailerons, and elevator flaps on the wings. The necessary theory behind this achievement had been outlined in 1809–1810 by the English scientist Sir George Cayley (1773–1857), the "father of aerodynamics." Despite slow public response in the United States, the Wrights received an army contract for planes in 1909.

Between the Wars. Thereafter the aviation industry developed rapidly, with many companies and countless barnstorming stunt pilots before World War I. Glenn H. Curtiss (1878–1930) created world airspeed records and built planes, including a seaplane in 1912. The first Atlantic crossing was made via Newfoundland in 1919. Airpower was used in World War I, and great advances came in the 1920s. Airmail service began, North America was crossed nonstop, and the globe was circled. Charles Lindbergh's much-publicized solo flight of 1927 from New York to Paris in a Ryan monoplane was technically of less importance than other achievements. In 1938 Howard R. Hughes went around the globe in a flying time of 3 days, 19 hours.

Modern Developments. World War II brought massive advances in aviation, including the helicopter, the beginnings of jet power, missiles, and rockets. Jets doubled and tripled airspeeds to supersonic rates in the 1950s and were soon adapted to commercial passenger use. Meanwhile C. S. Cockerell in England invented the "Hovercraft," which travels on a cushion of air (1953). American and Soviet competition in space research brought moon flights by rockets in the late 1960s.

See also Lindbergh, Charles; Space Exploration; Wright, Wilbur and Orville.

Consult (VIII) Singer, 1958; American Heritage, 1962.

—Peter d'A. Jones, *University of Illinois, Chicago Circle*

AXIS ALLIANCE, alliance among Germany, Italy, and Japan formed in September 1940. It brought together the two major opponents of the postwar structure of peace—Germany and Japan—who were trying to establish their own systems of international relations. They had initially been interested in allying themselves against the Soviet Union, but after the Nazi-Soviet nonaggression pact of 1939, Britain, France, and eventually the United States became targets of the possible German-Japanese coalition.

The impetus for the alliance was provided by the German successes in Western Europe in early 1940, which convinced Japan to take advantage of the situation to expand into European colonies in Asia. Germany pledged support in case Japan attacked the British, French, or Dutch possessions in Asia. It was

Cartoon of "Three Horsemen" of Axis Alliance draws parallel between them and Bible's Four Horsemen of the Apocalypse, three of which were War, Famine, and Death.

felt, falsely, that the alliance would prevent U.S. intervention in Asian and European affairs.

Consult (VII) Schroeder, 1958.

BABBITT, novel by Sinclair Lewis about the emptiness of middle-class life. *See* Lewis, Sinclair.

BACKUS, ISAAC (1724–1806), religious leader and historian. A native of Norwich, Conn., he was influenced by leaders of the Great Awakening such as Eleazar Wheelock, James Davenport, and George Whitefield. He belonged to the Norwich church from 1742 until 1746, when he withdrew with a small Separatist group calling itself the New Light Church.

For the period 1746 to 1756, Backus is considered a Separatist in New England Congregationalism. He traveled through Massachusetts and Connecticut preaching religious freedom and, although he never attended a college or religious seminary, was ordained as a minister in April 1748. He was made pastor of a Baptist church in Middleborough, R.I., in 1756.

After becoming a Baptist, Backus was actively involved in expressing Baptist protests against the existing system of control in the church. He wrote several treatises voicing his opinions on religion and the ministry but is best known for his *History of New England with Particular Reference to the Domination of Christians called Baptists.* The documentary evidence in these volumes is a valuable source of New England history through the eighteenth century, particularly in matters pertaining to the church and religion and their relationship to civil government.

See also Great Awakening; Whitefield, George.

BACON'S REBELLION (1676), rebellion against the Virginia government by youthful and wealthy Nathaniel Bacon (1647–1676), which revealed the weakness of the governor and the existence of bitter tensions between large planters and poor whites. When hostilities erupted with the powerful Susquehannock Indians in 1675–1676, Governor Sir William Berkeley hoped to maintain peaceful relations with the smaller dependent tribes surrounding the settled portion of Virginia. Frontiersmen, led by Bacon, demanded an aggressive policy and refused to distinguish between hostile and neutral Indians.

Bacon raised a force of volunteers in April 1676 and was arrested on Berkeley's orders in June, when he appeared in Jamestown. Bacon was released, but he returned with several hundred armed followers to extract at gunpoint from the governor and legislators a commission as general of volunteers. Berkeley then tried to raise a force against him, but the government collapsed, and Bacon took control of the colony outside the eastern shore. After Bacon died in October, Berkeley reconquered the colony and summarily executed 22 Baconians.

On balance, Bacon's Rebellion was a hostile outburst against Indians and encouraged few political reforms. If anything, it discredited a reform program already registering major gains in the House of Burgesses. Only after the American Revolution would Jeffersonians and other Virginians begin to interpret Bacon as a kindred spirit, an early apostle of American liberty.

See also Virginia.
Consult (I) Smith, 1959; Washburn, 1957.
—John M. Murrin, *Princeton University*

BAD AXE, BATTLE OF (1832), battle in which Indians were badly defeated. *See* Black Hawk War.

BAEZ, JOAN (1941–), folk singer and antiwar leader. Her first fame came at the Newport Folk Festival in 1959, and thereafter her records, sung in an "achingly pure soprano," often made the top ten on the folk charts. But her reputation was equally the result of her resistance to the Vietnam War and other "radical" causes—she was twice arrested and jailed, and her husband, David Harris, chose prison over induction into the armed services. A familiar figure at major peace demonstrations during the 1960s, she financed the Institute for Study of Nonviolence in Palo Alto, Cal. As much as her clear voice, her uncompromising integrity endeared her to many people in the 1960s.

BALDWIN, JAMES (1924–), novelist and essayist who expressed the depths of frustration experienced by blacks in American society. He was born in New York City, the son of a Baptist minister and the eldest of nine children. Baldwin turned to writing after an early career as a boy preacher in Harlem storefront churches. His first novel, *Go Tell It on the Mountain* (1953), received favorable criticism. With his first collection of essays, *Notes of a Native Son* (1955), Baldwin again won critical acclaim but did not reach a wide general audience. This was followed in 1958 by *Giovanni's Room,* set in Paris. It was his second collection of essays, *Nobody Knows My Name* (1960), that brought him into the literary spotlight and established him as a major voice in American literature.

His third novel, *Another Country* (1962), was followed by *The Fire Next Time* (1963), which became an immediate best seller and is regarded as one of the most brilliant essays of black protest. Baldwin also had two of his plays produced in New York: *Blues for Mister Charlie* (1964) and *The Amen Corner* (written in 1953, produced in 1965). *Tell Me How Long the Train's Been Gone* (1968) was regarded by the

author as his first "grown-up" novel, but it generated little enthusiasm.

BALLINGER-PINCHOT CONTROVERSY (1910), political controversy in which Secretary of the Interior Ballinger was accused of helping private interest acquire public lands. *See* Pinchot, Gifford.

BALTIMORE, LORDS, proprietors of colonial Maryland. *See* Calvert Family.

BALTIMORE AND OHIO RAILROAD. *See* Railroads.

BANCROFT, GEORGE (1800–1891), scholar and diplomat called "the father of American history" for his life work, the monumental *History of the United States* in 10 volumes (1834–1876). After graduating from Harvard in 1817 Bancroft took his Ph.D at the University of Gottingen, Germany, in 1820.

His *History* began with the colonizing process, and the first three volumes appeared in 1834, 1837, and 1841. Bancroft's work was permeated with the spirit of Jacksonian Democracy, a bias that led him into practical politics in the Democratic Party. Mixing history and politics, Bancroft was defeated in his attempt to become governor of Massachusetts in 1844, although he was influential in winning the presidential nomination for James K. Polk. As secretary of the navy (1845–1846) under Polk, he established the Naval Academy at Annapolis and directed early American naval actions in the first stages of the Mexican War. While also serving as acting secretary of war he gave the order that sent Zachary Taylor into Mexico, precipitating the Mexican War.

As U.S. ambassador to Britain (1846–1849) and Germany (1867–1874), Bancroft devoted his spare time to historical research in foreign sources. The six volumes covering the American Revolution appeared between 1852 and 1866. He wrote President Andrew Johnson's "First Annual Message" in 1865 and in 1874 published his tenth and final volume of the *History.* By 1876 a revised edition in six volumes appeared, and in 1883–1885 he thoroughly revised the entire work, softening some of the more patriotic and florid passages.

BANKHEAD-JONES FARM TENANT ACT (1937), New Deal legislation indicating congressional approval for the complex of agricultural programs gathered together by presidential order in 1935 under the Resettlement Administration (RA). Like the RA, which it superseded, its purpose was to assist farm laborers who did not own the land they worked—tenants, sharecroppers, and migrants. A report in early 1937 publicized what a num-

Joan Baez *(standing, center)* participates in anti–Vietnam War demonstration at Army Induction Center in Oakland, Cal.

James Baldwin emerged as a major novelist in the 1960s and also wrote for the theater.

ber of New Dealers had known all along—that a growing minority of those who worked the land were not owners and that more and more farm families were being forced off the land. The Farm Security Administration (FSA), created by Bankhead-Jones, established nearly 100 camps for migratory families and supervised more than 100 homestead communities for displaced tenants and croppers. Funds of more than $1 billion were made available in the form of short-term rehabilitation loans and long-range farm-purchase loans to farm families.

See also New Deal; Resettlement Administration.

Consult (VI) Baldwin, 1968.

BANKING ACT (1933). See Glass-Steagall Act (1933).

BANK OF AUGUSTA v. EARLE (1839), an important Supreme Court case that affirmed the right of a company chartered in one state to do business in another, under the general legal principle of "comity" among nations (courtesy and respect for one another's laws). Without the clear decision by Chief Justice Roger B. Taney, economic life would have been difficult in the United States in this period of rapid growth.

An Alabama citizen (Earle) had refused to honor the bill of exchange (like a check) of the Bank of Augusta, Georgia, because he claimed a "foreign," out-of-state corporation could not make legal contracts in Alabama. Taney, in deciding in favor of the bank, rejected this anarchic states' rights doctrine by pointing out that nations always respect one another's commercial laws, try to uphold contracts, and do business. Taney affirmed Alabama's right to exclude any "foreign" company from its state borders, but it must do so specifically. Otherwise, the law would assume what he called the "silent acquiescence" of Alabama in that corporation's right to trade.

See also Taney, Roger B.

BANK OF THE UNITED STATES, FIRST (1791-1811), national bank that was designed by Alexander Hamilton as the keystone of his economic program to make the federal government strong and to establish national credit. In 1791 the young nation was short of capital for investment, and its currency was a maze. Hamilton wanted a central bank, chartered by the federal government, that could act as the government's financial agent, hold government funds, collect taxes, regulate a dependable coinage, borrow money, and spend funds. Opponents of Hamilton's Bank feared that its charter would give too much power to wealthy men and that scarce investment funds would be diverted away from farming to be spent on new industrial or speculative activities. In addi-

tion, they thought that such a powerful bank would charge high interest rates and be controlled for the benefit of a few rich men and foreigners.

Thomas Jefferson used constitutional arguments in an attempt to stop the Bank. He told President Washington that the federal government was not given the power by the Constitution to create a central bank. Hamilton denied this. His broader view of the Constitution claimed that the government had authority to create any agency to help it do its job properly. Only three Southerners in Congress supported the Bank, and only one Northerner opposed its chartering in February 1791.

Effect of the Bank. The Bank was a great success. Its interest rate was kept down to 6 percent, and its bank notes were accepted as legal tender for payment of government bills; the notes were stable and came into general business use. The First Bank was a large factor in early national economic growth. It helped to gather capital, improved the flow of funds for business, and gave the United States good credit abroad. When the charter ran out in 1811, however, the jealousy of many smaller commercial banks, chartered by the individual states, prevented Congress from renewing it.

See also Hamilton, Alexander.

Consult (III) Jones, 1965.

—Peter d'A. Jones, University of Illinois, Chicago Circle

BANK OF THE UNITED STATES, SECOND (1816-1836), national bank created by federal charter in 1816 with the support of the young nationalists such as Henry Clay and, at that time, John C. Calhoun. The need for a new central bank had been made clear by the way the government financed the War of 1812—with low, ineffective taxation and high-interest loans. The government overborrowed, and the private, state-chartered banks flooded the nation with paper notes, causing extreme inflation. As more bank notes were issued, their value declined, and in the crisis of 1814 all banks had to suspend payments—refuse to give hard cash for paper bills.

The Second Bank, chartered after much debate, was structured like the First, but it had more funds ($35 million, compared with $10 million in 1791). The federal government owned 20 percent of the Bank's stock and named 5 of the 25 directors. Because the Second Bank's notes were acceptable as currency by the federal government and could be exchanged for hard cash at any time, all the state commercial banks had to make their notes sound enough to be exchanged also. They did not like the central bank's authority over them, but in 1819 the Supreme Court validated the Second Bank in the case of McCulloch v. Maryland.

Conflict with Jackson. The Bank helped stabilize economic growth. It raised capital in the East, lending it in the West, where it was needed; promoted a reliable national currency; and gave the government economical loans. However, President Andrew Jackson disliked the Bank and had a rooted distrust of monied experts and a fear of "monopoly" and "privilege." A personal feud developed between Jackson and Nicholas Biddle, the Bank's powerful director. Biddle asked to have the charter renewed in 1832—an unwise idea because 1832 was an election year and the charter did not run out until 1836. Jackson made the "Bank War" the major issue of his reelection and, once he got his mandate, vetoed the Bank's rechartering.

Jackson went on to harass the Bank after 1832. He withdrew all federal funds from it and deposited them instead in "pet banks," selected state-chartered banks. Without the federal funds to use for investment and loans and without the large volume of federal business, the Second Bank died. The United States (unlike other modernizing nations such as Britain and France) did not introduce central banking again until the Federal Reserve was created in 1913. So, after 1836, the American economy grew to great-power status without an adequate banking structure.

See also Bank of the United States, First; Bank War (1832–1834); Biddle, Nicholas; Jackson, Andrew; McCulloch v. Maryland (1819).

Consult (III) Remini, 1968.

—Peter d'A. Jones, *University of Illinois, Chicago Circle*

BANK WAR (1832–1834), the major political controversy of the Jacksonian era. The charter of the Second Bank of the United States was to expire in 1836, but its president, Nicholas Biddle, was persuaded by Henry Clay, Daniel Webster, and others to seek a congressional bill to recharter it in 1832. The bill was passed, but President Jackson vetoed it, denouncing the Bank as unconstitutional and undemocratic.

The Bank question became the chief issue of the 1832 election, and Jackson interpreted his reelection as an endorsement by the people of his anti-Bank policy. While waiting for the Bank's charter to expire, Jackson decided to further weaken that institution by removing federal deposits. His Secretary of the Treasury, Roger B. Taney, ordered the deposits removed, and the government deposited these funds in "pet" state banks.

Traditionally the Bank War has been seen as a triumph of democracy over aristocracy, although economic historians blamed it for triggering the Panic of 1837. More recent writers have criticized both these theses. The Bank War is now viewed as a psychological issue with the Bank serving as a scapegoat for various frustrations bred by rapid change. International finance, and not Jacksonian banking policy, is now seen as the cause of the Panic of 1837, however. Jackson's actions in the war, however, did increase executive power.

See also Bank of the United States, Second; Biddle, Nicholas.

BAPTISTS. *See* Colonial Religion.

BARBARY COAST WARS (to 1815), conflicts between the United States and the states of North Africa. At the time of the American Revolution these coastal states had long been a menace to shipping in the Mediterranean. Corsairs from Algiers, Morocco, Tripoli, and Tunis captured ships and enslaved their crews. American shipping was particularly vulnerable after 1783 because the United States had no regular navy and American merchant ships could no longer depend on British naval power for protection. Although peaceful relations were established with Morocco in 1787, the United States paid tribute money to avoid depredations by the other powers.

A major crisis broke out in 1801, when Tripoli declared war on the United States. The war lasted until 1805 and was mainly fought by American naval forces off North Africa. In the last stages of the war William Eaton led a land expedition against Tripoli. After this expedition captured Derna, Tripoli agreed to make peace, but the United States had to pay ransom for the prisoners in Tripolitan hands. Some danger from the corsairs continued, but in 1815 the United States declared war on Algiers. A naval expedition quickly forced the Algerians to make peace and to pay reparations.

BARBED WIRE, fencing first patented (1867) in New York by William D. Hunt but perfected and marketed (1874) by J. F. Glidden of Illinois in response to the acute problems of fencing prairie land where timber was scarce and other forms of fencing proved unsatisfactory. Its impact was especially profound on the Great Plains, where it brought an end to the open-range cattle industry. In 1874, 10,000 pounds of the wire were sold; in 1880, sales totaled 80.5 million pounds.

BARNARD, HENRY (1811–1900), influential educator who worked for free education. *See* Education.

BARNBURNERS, name given to radical Democrats, especially in New York in the 1840s. The conservative wing of their party accused them of being willing to burn down their political "barn" in order to get rid of rats—undesirable persons and policies—in the party. The Barnburners appeared in 1844 as followers of ex-President Martin Van Buren and with him in 1848 joined the Free-Soil Party, which nomi-

Bank War pitted President Jackson against Nicholas Biddle (the Devil), President of the Second Bank of the United States.

nated him unsuccessfully for president. By 1852, Van Buren and his Barnburners were back once again in the Democratic Party fold, but many later left to join the Republicans.

See also Free-Soil Party; Van Buren, Martin.

BARNUM, P(HINEAS) T(AYLOR) (1810–1891), promoter whose name is synonymous with American entrepreneurship and showmanship. The first of many triumphs occurred in 1835, when he exhibited a slave, Joyce Heth, who Barnum claimed was George Washington's nurse and 161 years old. Barnum's unique ability to fathom public taste for humbug was well served by his acquisition in 1842 of the American Museum. There were live animals, temperance lectures, stuffed animals, curios, and paintings that Barnum advertised as a National Portrait Gallery. The admission-paying patron could also see a family of trained fleas, the first American Punch and Judy show, a woolly horse, a bearded lady, and a dwarf. Barnum's American Museum established his fame and fortune within a year and became one of New York's popular tourist attractions.

In 1850, Barnum sponsored the American tour of the Swedish singer Jenny Lind. In this combination of showmanship and culture Barnum succeeded both artistically and financially. While the success of Jenny Lind's tour was still fresh, Barnum in 1854 sponsored "Barnum's Great Asiatic Caravan, Museum, and Menagerie," a huge array of exotic foreign animals led by 10 Ceylonese elephants in a mammoth parade up Broadway. This was the forerunner of Barnum's circus, which first went on the road in 1871 and became one of the most popular entertainments in America. In 1881, Barnum joined with James A. Bailey to produce "The Greatest Show on Earth."

Consult (V) Wallace, 1959.
—Richard Collin, *Louisiana State University, New Orleans*

BARUCH, BERNARD M(ANNES) (1870–1965), financier and government planner. After graduating from the College of the City of New York (1889), Baruch began a highly successful Wall Street career in speculation and finance, eventually as a member of the New York Stock Exchange.

In 1916 he became a member of the advisory commission of the Council of National Defense and chairman of the council's committee on raw materials, minerals, and metals. In March 1918 President Wilson named him chairman of the War Industries Board, created to increase production and act as a clearing house for the wartime economy. In this powerful position, Baruch played a central role in the government's mobilization and supervision of American industry—a role that not only helped determine the outcome of

World War I but also prefigured some of the policies of the early New Deal era. In 1919 he attended the Versailles Peace Conference as a member of an economic planning section. Subsequently, he unsuccessfully urged President Wilson to compromise with his Sentate opponents to bring about America's entry into the League of Nations.

Baruch next entered public life in 1942 as head of a presidential fact-finding committee to study the critical shortage of rubber. A year later he became an adviser to James F. Byrnes, War Mobilization Director. In 1946 he was appointed by President Truman as the U.S. representative to the UN Atomic Energy Commission. That June, he proposed to the United Nations the so-called Baruch Plan (rejected by the Soviet Union), which would have placed all nuclear knowledge, materials, and manufacturing facilities under international supervision and control. He was the author of *A Philosophy for Our Times* (1954) and *Baruch: My Own Story* (1957).

See also War Industries Board.
Consult (VI) Baruch, 1957.
—Paul S. Boyer, *University of Massachusetts*

BATTLE OF . . . *See* second part of name.

BEAR FLAG REVOLT, a rising of American settlers in California's Sacramento Valley on June 14, 1846, during the war with Mexico. The uprising followed a period of tension among the settlers, who feared that Mexican authorities would expel them from the region. In May the Americans had sought the help of the soldier and explorer John C. Frémont, who encouraged them to revolt because he believed this would be "the first step in the conquest of California."

On June 10 a group of Sacramento Valley settlers seized Sonoma and proclaimed the independence of the American settlement under the standard of the Republic of California—a flag showing a grizzly bear facing a red star. The Republic of California lasted only until early July, when U.S. forces occupied California and substituted the American flag for the bear and red star.

See also California; Frémont, John C.
Consult (III) Billington, 1960.

BEAT GENERATION, collective name for group that rejected the materialistic values of post-World War II society. While the Cold War and McCarthyism had stifled most tendencies toward political or cultural deviation, traditional cultural ties did not hold for all. As a result, the 1957 publication of Jack Kerouac's *On The Road* was merely a delayed signpost for public awareness of cultural changes in progress.

The Beats were a mixed group of writers (Kerouac and William Burroughs), poets (Allen

P. T. Barnum exploited unusual people, such as the Quaker Giant and Giantess and the midget Tom Thumb, during his legendary show-business career.

Financier Bernard Baruch relaxes at his "office," a bench in New York City's Central Park.

Ginsberg and Gregory Corso), and societal deviants (addict Herbert Huncke and car thief Neal Cassady) who were united only by their distaste for politics and bourgeois respectability. Their goal was beatitude—true beatness, and they should not be confused with "beatniks," their later synthetic imitators. Culturally, they were important challengers to the established culture, artists who created alternatives in life style and vision.

BEATLES, English group that revolutionized rock music. In the late 1950s, four students from Liverpool, England, John Lennon, Paul McCartney, George Harrison, and Paul Best, formed a rock music group. In 1961 they were discovered by Brian Epstein, who introduced them to British television and recording. Best was replaced by drummer Ringo Starr, and by the end of 1963 they were stars in England yet scarcely known in America. Then, in January 1964 came "I Want to Hold Your Hand," followed by their February Carnegie Hall appearance and television debut on the Ed Sullivan Show. For the next five years, the Beatles dominated American record sales while also making successful films. In 1970, the Beatles disbanded, and each of them began recording music under his own name.

BEAUREGARD, P(IERRE) G. T. (1818–1893), Confederate general. Born near New Orleans, Beauregard graduated from West Point in 1838. In 1861 he cast his lot with the Confederacy and was given command of Charleston, from which he launched the assault on Fort Sumter (April 1861).

At the First Battle of Bull Run (July 1861), he led his army to a smashing victory. Promoted to major general and transferred to the west, he attacked General Grant's forces at Shiloh, Tenn. (April 1862) and nearly won. Put in charge of defending the South Carolina and Georgia coasts, he repelled a Union assault on Charleston (August-September 1863). The following spring he took part in the defense of Richmond. He also helped Robert E. Lee during the siege of Petersburg. Beauregard closed the war with Joseph E. Johnston's army in North Carolina. After the war he became a wealthy businessman.

A small, vigorous man, Beauregard cut a glamorous figure and was renowned for his dapper appearance, social poise, and self-confidence (which bordered on vanity). He frequently quarreled with Jefferson Davis and thus hurt his own career, which was marked more by dash than success.

See also Civil War Battles.
Consult (IV) Williams, 1955.

BEECHER, HENRY WARD (1813–1887), one of the most influential American clergymen. He was the son of Lyman Beecher, a liberal Presbyterian clergyman, and brother of Harriet Beecher Stowe. Henry graduated from Amherst College in 1834 and attended Lane Theological Seminary in Cincinnati. An unconventional clergyman, he began preaching independently in 1837. Beecher's preaching was colored by showmanship because he believed it necessary to reach his audience emotionally. When called to the pastorate of the Congregationalist Plymouth Church in Brooklyn, N.Y., Beecher had his well-planned sermons printed in advance in widely circulated pamphlets.

He firmly believed that slavery was wrong but concluded that the Constitution forbade its abolition in the slave states. Therefore, Beecher concentrated his efforts on preventing slavery from extending to the territories. He felt that if slavery were limited to the South, it would die out as an institution. Beecher supported Frémont in 1856 and Lincoln in 1860, and he fiercely defended the Civil War on a lecture tour through England in 1863.

Beecher's influence reached beyond the pulpit with his editorials in *The Independent* (1861-1864) and with his own publication, *The Christian Union* (1870-1881). He called for women's suffrage and civil service reform; he felt that change came about both by evolution and by miracles. His liberal Christianity stressed love and joy. Accused of adultery by a member of his church, Beecher was cleared by a divided jury in the sensational Beecher-Tilton case and was later independently exonerated by the Council of Congregational Churches. He continued as pastor at the Plymouth Church until his death.

—Richard Collin, *Louisiana State University, New Orleans*

BELL, ALEXANDER GRAHAM (1847-1922), scientist, inventor of the telephone, and teacher of the deaf. Born in Scotland, he was the son of Alexander Melville Bell, a distinguished scientist whose work in phonetics led to a system of visible speech. He worked as his father's assistant for several years. In 1871 he came to the United States to give instruction in the visible speech method.

His work in acoustics and telegraphy convinced him that the human voice could be transmitted electrically. He conceived the correct theoretical principle of the telephone in 1874 and in his Boston laboratory on March 10, 1876, achieved the first successful electrical transmission of intelligible sound: "Mr. Watson, come here; I want you." On April 3, 1877, he demonstrated the practical application of his discovery by conducting a telephone conversation between Boston and New York, and three months later the Bell Telephone Company was organized. The first telephone patent had been allowed on March 3, 1877, and although numerous inventors challenged his

Beatles had great influence on rock music of the 1960s.

Alexander Graham Bell, inventor of the telephone, when he was almost 70.

Irving Berlin wrote some of the most popular American songs, including "God Bless America."

Communist Cold War blockade of Berlin was thwarted by U.S. airlift that ferried supplies to the isolated city.

patents, the Supreme Court eventually upheld all his claims.

While leaving the further development of the telephone to others, Bell continued his work in related fields. His other inventions include the photophone, a device for transmitting sound by light; the telephone probe, for detecting metal objects in the human body; and the telephonic telegraph receiver. He advanced Edison's work on the phonograph and solved the problem of stability of balance in flying machines.

See also Edison, Thomas A.; Inventions. *Consult* (V) Burlingame, 1964; Bruce, 1973.

—Seddie Cogswell, *California State University, San Francisco*

BELLEAU WOOD, BATTLE OF (June 6–July 1, 1918), first major engagement of U.S. troops in World War I. *See* World War I Battles.

BENJAMIN, JUDAH P(HILIP) (1811–1884), key cabinet member of the Confederacy. A wealthy New Orleans lawyer and sugar planter, he won a seat in the U.S. Senate (1852) as a conservative Whig. He effectively advocated Southern interests and supported secession after Abraham Lincoln's election.

He resigned from the Senate (February 1861) and was named attorney general of the Confederacy. In September 1861 he took charge of the War Department. Southerners, enraged at several defeats in February 1862, unjustly blamed them on Benjamin and howled for his resignation. His friend Jefferson Davis, however, responded by making Benjamin secretary of state. In vain Benjamin tried to get England and France to intervene in the war. A hard-headed realist, he realized by 1864 that drastic measures had to be taken to reinforce the army, and he urged that slaves be recruited and then emancipated. The Confederacy ultimately took his advice (March 1865).

After the war Benjamin became a famous lawyer in England. Of all the men who served in the Confederate cabinet, he was probably the most brilliant and certainly knew best how to get along with Davis.

Consult (IV) Meade, 1943.

BERLE, ADOLF A., JR., member of the Brains Trust. *See* Brains Trust.

BERLIN, IRVING (1888–   ), American composer who wrote more than 1,000 songs. He is more notable for having written both the lyrics and music to his songs and was largely responsible for the evolution of the popular song from ragtime to jazz.

He was born Israel Baline in Russia and taken as an infant to the United States, where he grew up on New York's Lower East Side. He

worked as a singing waiter, introducing some of his own songs, such as "Alexander's Ragtime Band" (1911), his first great success. A "soldier show" in 1918, called *Yip, Yip Yaphank,* led to musical comedy. Between such shows as *As Thousands Cheer* (1933) and *Louisiana Purchase* (1940), most of Berlin's work was done for films. His greatest stage success was *Annie Get Your Gun* (1946).

In film and on stage, Berlin's gift for simple, fresh melody won him immediate popularity. Among his best-known songs are "Oh, How I Hate to Get Up in the Morning," "White Christmas," "God Bless America," and "There's No Business Like Show Business."

BERLIN BLOCKADE (1948), one of the most dramatic episodes in the Cold War. Berlin, administered by four occupying powers, was a noncommunist island in an East German sea. On June 24, 1948, as the culmination of disagreements between communists and noncommunists, the communists imposed a blockade: all road and rail access routes between Berlin and West Germany were closed. The siege lasted 11 months as the Russians sought to force Western abandonment of the city to Soviet rule. This aim was thwarted by a massive airlift of basic necessities and by the tenacity of the West Berlin population: about 1,000 planes a day conducted 277,728 flights to carry supplies to feed and heat a city of more than 2 million people. A Soviet veto prevented the UN Security Council from declaring the USSR guilty of endangering world peace. However, the Soviet Union was unwilling to risk war for its goal and eventually lifted the blockade.

Consult (VIII) Davidson, 1958.

BERNSTEIN, LEONARD (1918–   ), American composer, conductor, and pianist. He was born in Lawrence, Mass., and educated at Harvard and the Curtis Institute of Music. Bernstein studied composition with Walter Piston, piano with Isabelle Vengerova, and conducting with Fritz Reiner.

Bernstein composed numerous symphonic works, including the *Jeremiah Symphony* (1944), *Age of Anxiety* (1949), and *Chichester Psalms* (1965), as well as song cycles, chamber music, ballets—*Fancy Free* (1944)—and several musicals, including *Wonderful Town* (1953) and *West Side Story* (1957). His *Mass* (1971), a striking theater piece for singers, players, and dancers, was commissioned for the opening of the Kennedy Center for the Performing Arts, in Washington, D.C.

Leonard Bernstein was a soloist and conductor with many orchestras in the United States and abroad. He won praise from critics and the public at 25, when conductor Bruno Walter fell ill and Bernstein, his young protégé, was summoned unexpectedly to conduct the New York Philharmonic. In 1958 Bernstein became that orchestra's musical director, appearing with the orchestra on several international tours before he retired in 1969 to concentrate on composing. He has also given televised lecture-concerts for young people.

BESSEMER STEEL PROCESS (1856), a way to manufacture steel in large quantities. Steel is better than iron for most purposes, less brittle, and stronger. Growing demand for better metal arose from the railroads, the construction industries, and the machine-tool and other mechanical trades. Before Bessemer, steel was made by the expensive crucible method, which produced only a small amount at a time.

Bessemer's converter was a huge, semi-enclosed cauldron-like vessel, cone-shaped at the top. Through pipes at the base, air was forced through the molten iron in the cauldron, burning out the carbon and silicon impurities. Since steel is iron with a specific, lower carbon content, the necessary amount of ferromanganese (containing carbon) could then be added to turn the contents into steel. The result of Bessemer's technique was that inexpensive steel replaced iron in a great variety of uses. Structural steel made possible such developments as the skyscraper and improved bridges.

Sir Henry Bessemer (1813-1898) utilized the converter in Sheffield, England. He was preceded in the discovery by an American inventor, William D. Kelly (1811-1888), in 1851, but it was Bessemer's converter that came into general use. A later method was the Siemens process (1866), in which a mixture of hot air and coal gas are blown over the molten iron in a large shallow bath (the open-hearth process). Both the converter and the open-hearth were soon adopted to great advantage in the American iron and steel industry of the nineteenth century.

BIBLE COMMONWEALTH, belief that a society could be created that would use the Bible as its fundamental law. *See* Massachusetts.

BIDDLE, NICHOLAS (1786-1844), banker and author; president of the Second Bank of the United States, 1822-1836. Biddle was born in Philadelphia and died there. He rose to be a dominating force in the literary and financial circles of the city but ended as a tragic, broken figure. Biddle, a brilliant cultured man who graduated from Princeton at 15, lived two careers. One was literary. After living abroad as secretary to the American embassies in Paris and London, where he worked for James Monroe, he returned to Philadelphia to edit a magazine. With Paul Allen he edited the famous version of Lewis and Clark's journals (2 volumes, 1814). Biddle also served briefly in Congress (1810) and in the Pennsylvania senate (1814-1818).

Monroe, now president, made his former secretary one of the five government directors of the Second Bank of the United States in 1816, and he was elected president of the bank in 1822. As a conservative financier, Biddle believed in fiscal responsibility and tried to give the country a sound currency and cheap commercial loans. His leadership of the bank was very firm—enemies called him "Tsar Nicholas," and he was hated by small bankers and local businessmen, especially in the South and West, whence President Andrew Jackson derived his political strength in the 1830s. In the feud with Jackson that began in 1832, Biddle acted unwisely in demanding a rechartering of the Bank four years early. He also failed to grasp the political climate of the day and the popular forces behind Jackson. Biddle was hated for his very success in making the Bank a major supplier of loans, buyer of stock, and real estate investor. He wanted to create a genuine central bank with control over the nation's money market.

After Jackson's veto of the charter renewal, Biddle kept the bank going for its last four years and in 1836 gained a state charter from Pennsylvania. "Biddle's Bank" collapsed finally in 1841, although he had retired from it in 1839. His personal fortune was wiped out, and he was tried as a criminal but released. He died a failure.

See also Bank of the United States, Second; Bank War (1832-1834); Jackson, Andrew.
Consult (III) Govan, 1959.
—Peter d'A. Jones, *University of Illinois, Chicago Circle*

BILL OF RIGHTS, the first 10 amendments to the U.S. Constitution. During the debates in the state ratifying conventions over the adoption of the Constitution, many people expressed concern about the lack of restraints placed on the powers of the national government, particularly in regard to the rights of individuals. Americans, drawing on the heritage of England's Magna Charta, were used to having a specific listing—Bill of Rights—indicating those areas in which the government could not interfere. At first the Constitution's most ardent supporters denied that such a need existed, but when it became clear that the lack of guarantees was jeopardizing ratification, they quickly agreed to the additions. Under James Madison's leadership, Congress and the state legislatures adopted these 10 amendments in 1791.

Content. These amendments deny the federal government the right to pass laws or take action to establish religion or to abridge freedom of speech, the press, or the right to assemble. They guarantee the right to bear arms and limit the government's power to quarter troops in private homes, and they restrain the government from unreasonable

THE BILL OF RIGHTS

First Amendment
Congress shall make no law respecting an establishment of religion, or prohibiting the free exercise thereof; or abridging the freedom of speech, or of the press; or the right of the people peaceably to assemble, and to petition the Government for a redress of grievances.

Second Amendment
A well regulated Militia, being necessary to the security of a free State, the right of the people to keep and bear Arms, shall not be infringed.

Third Amendment
No soldier shall, in time of peace be quartered in any house, without the consent of the Owner, nor in time of war, but in a manner to be prescribed by law.

Fourth Amendment
The right of the people to be secure in their persons, houses, papers, and effects, against unreasonable searches and seizures, shall not be violated, and no Warrants shall issue, but upon probable cause, supported by Oath or affirmation, and particularly describing the place to be searched, and the persons or things to be seized.

Fifth Amendment
No person shall be held to answer for a capital, or otherwise infamous crime, unless on a presentment or indictment of a Grand Jury, except in cases arising in the land or naval forces, or in the Militia, when in actual service in time of War or public danger; nor shall any person be subject for the same offence to be twice put in jeopardy of life or limb; nor shall be compelled in any criminal case to be a witness against himself, nor be deprived of life, liberty, or property, without due process of law; nor shall private property be taken for public use, without just compensation.

Sixth Amendment
In all criminal prosecutions, the accused shall enjoy the right to a speedy and public trial, by an impartial jury of the State and district wherein the crime shall have been committed, which district shall have been previously ascertained by law, and to be informed of the nature and cause of the accusation; to be confronted with the witnesses against him; to have compulsory process for obtaining witnesses in his favor, and to have the Assistance of Counsel for his defence.

Seventh Amendment

In Suits at common law, where the value in controversy shall exceed twenty dollars, the right of trial by jury shall be preserved, and no fact tried by a jury, shall be otherwise re-examined in any Court of the United States, than according to the rules of the common law.

Eighth Amendment

Excessive bail shall not be required nor excessive fines imposed, nor cruel and unusual punishments inflicted.

Ninth Amendment

The enumeration in the Constitution, of certain rights, shall not be construed to deny or disparage others retained by the people.

Tenth Amendment

The powers not delegated to the United States by the Constitution, nor prohibited by it to the States, are reserved to the States respectively, ·or to the people.

searches and seizures. They assure the people their legal rights under the common law system, including the prohibition of double jeopardy for the same offense, the right not to be compelled to testify against oneself, and due process of law before one's life, liberty, or property can be taken. Finally, the unenumerated rights of the people are protected, while those powers not delegated to the federal government are reserved to the states.

See also Amendments, Constitutional; Constitution of the United States; Magna Charta.

Consult (III) Brant, 1967.
—Richard E. Ellis, *University of Virginia*

BIRNEY, JAMES G. (1792-1857), abolitionist and presidential candidate. A slave owner and a distinguished Alabama lawyer, he became a reformer and abolitionist after a religious conversion. His first cause was the Liberian colonization plan. Frustrated to discover that many slave owners wanted to send free blacks, rather than slaves, as missionaries and settlers to Liberia and feeling the effects of Southern antagonism, Birney retreated first to Kentucky, then to Cincinnati, Ohio, where he published *The Philanthropist.* He later worked with the American Anti-Slavery Society in New York. In 1840 he was the Liberty Party's candidate for president and received only a few thousand votes. Four years later, however, his candidacy won enough support in New York to ruin Henry Clay's bid for the presidency.

A severe accident in 1845 removed Birney from national affairs. He was embittered by what he perceived as unmovable American white racism and returned to colonization as his remedy. In a pamphlet published in 1852, he urged blacks to go to Africa.

See also American Anti-Slavery Society; Liberia; Liberty Party; Presidential Elections.

BIRTH CONTROL LAWS. *See* Abortion and Birth Control Laws.

BLACK, HUGO (LAFAYETTE) (1886-1971), associate justice on the Supreme Court (1937-1971), who pursued a judicial career marked by the absolute defense of civil rights as literally defined in the Bill of Rights and the Constitution.

Black was born in Alabama and practiced law before his election to the Senate in 1924. During his Senate career, Black sponsored what became the Fair Labor Standards Act of 1938. He also supported President Roosevelt's plan to add six justices to the Supreme Court, which became known as the "court-packing" plan.

In 1937, Black, an ardent New Dealer, was appointed by Roosevelt to the Supreme Court, where he developed a coherent philosophy of constitutional law that made him one of the most significant and influential figures in American judicial history. Black repeatedly advocated the application of the entire Bill of Rights to the states through the Fourteenth Amendment and held that First Amendment freedoms of speech, press, and religious liberty were "absolutes." His views have never been wholly accepted by a majority of the Court, and his position resulted in occasional intellectual confrontations with those who held that individual rights should be weighed against the need for governmental authority.

BLACK CODES, legislation passed in the South in 1865-1866 to regulate the status of the recently freed slaves. The end of the Civil War overthrew the Slave Codes, which had defined a slave's legal position and had distinguished it from that of free blacks. But Southern states sought to control their freedmen with Black Codes, which regulated apprentices, vagrants, and employees through rigid penal laws and which had the effect of keeping blacks on the land. The laws varied in severity from state to state but had the overall effect of convincing Radical Republicans that the former Confederate states should be supervised more strictly. Although the codes were overthrown by federal authorities, the end of Reconstruction in 1877 resulted in the reestablishment of white supremacy and renewed efforts to abrogate blacks' civil rights.

Consult (IV) Wilson, 1968.

BLACK FRIDAY (Sept. 24, 1869), a day of stock market panic resulting from Jay Gould and James Fisk's attempt to control America's available gold supply. Businessmen needed gold to satisfy contracts, and those who achieved a corner could sell gold at enormous profit as long as the government refrained from marketing its own bullion. The conspirators enlisted Treasury officials and President Grant's brother-in-law into their scheme and believed the Administration would not sell. On Black Friday the New York Exchange panicked as gold rose precipitously. The price dropped as quickly when Grant ordered the sale of $4 million in gold and broke the corner. Hundreds of people were ruined, Gould and Fisk escaped unscathed, and the Administration's reputation was severely compromised.

See also Gould, Jay.

BLACK HAWK WAR, the last Indian conflict in the Old Northwest. It occurred during the summer of 1832, when Black Hawk, an elderly Sac warrior, led 1,000 men, women, and children of the Sac and Fox tribes east across the Mississippi River into Illinois. These Indians had been forced west of that river in late 1831 as a result of the Indian removal policy. Black Hawk promised a peaceful return to their former homes, so in April 1832 the Indians reentered Illinois. State leaders denounced this "invasion" and asked the army for aid. When the Indians realized they could not live in peace, they tried to flee west but without success. In August 1832 the soldiers and militiamen overtook the exhausted Indians at the Mississippi, and in the Battle of Bad Axe they killed all but 150 of them. This American ruthlessness frightened other tribes in the area, and within less than a decade most of them migrated westward.

See also Indian Policy; Northwest Territory.

Consult (III) Nichols, 1965; Prucha, 1969.

BLACK HILLS GOLD RUSH. *See* Gold Rushes.

BLACK MUSLIMS, members of the Nation of Islam, a religious black nationalist organization in the United States. Members believe that they are descendants of an ancient lost tribe of Muslims, and they hold some of the beliefs of orthodox Islam. Many tenets of the group reflect the members' view of the problems of black people in America. Members give up their "slave names"—for example, the heavyweight boxer Cassius Clay took the name Muhammad Ali when he joined the Muslims. Members are taught to keep apart from whites. The group has a dedicated, puritanical tone, denouncing lying, gluttony, drinking, and use of narcotics.

The Black Muslim movement was founded in Detroit in 1930 by Wali Farad, who was succeeded as leader by Elijah Muhammad in 1934. After World War II the Muslims grew with the help of Malcolm X, and more than 70 mosques or temples were built around the country. In addition to mosques, the Muslims, who have their headquarters in Chicago, maintain their own schools, stores, farms, and a newspaper, *Muhammad Speaks.* Elijah Muhammad has focused on the aim of building a black Islam nation, using the slogan "Build black, buy black."

See also Malcolm X.

Consult (IX) Lincoln, 1961.

BLACK PANTHERS, militant black organization. In October 1966 two black students from Merritt College in Oakland, Cal., Bobby Seale and Huey P. Newton, purchased guns and drafted the 10-point self-defense program. In 1967 they opened their first store-front headquarters in Oakland and began monitoring police in the black ghetto and recruiting members. They called for complete equality for black people, including demands for black exemption from military service, the freeing of all imprisoned blacks, and the calling of all-black juries for blacks accused of crime. Seale and Newton were soon joined by Eldridge Cleaver, who started the Black Panther newspaper.

Between 1968 and 1971 the Panthers (never more than 2,000 strong) established headquarters across the nation, claiming they were armed and would defend themselves if attacked. The police systematically harassed the Panthers, killing a score of them and jailing their leaders (including Seale and Newton, who were eventually exonerated). In 1972 the Panthers discontinued their armed-defense tactics and moved into black community-development programs, with Seale running for mayor of Oakland in 1973.

See also Cleaver, Eldridge.

Consult (VIII) Major, 1971; Seale, 1970.

BLACK RENAISSANCE. *See* Harlem Renaissance.

BLACKS IN THE UNITED STATES. The first blacks were introduced in 1619 by Dutch traders who left 19 of them with Virginia purchasers, but these blacks did not then have the status of slaves, because there were no laws designed to perpetuate servitude. Blacks were thus part of the labor supply of the new English colonies and as such were exposed to the many social options that also faced Indians and white indentured servants. There were recorded cases of blacks who worked their way out of servitude and, indeed, owned slaves of their own. On the other hand, the stigma of color generally distinguished blacks from other laborers. In the late decades of the seventeenth century slavery grew as an institution, especially in the South, due to legal decisions and ordinances intended to define the condition of blacks as slave or free. Nevertheless, slavery appeared to have little future because it did not flourish in the North, because indentured servants seemed superior workers with better incentives for labor, and because opportunities for freedom were furnished by a limitless frontier.

Pre-Civil War Conditions. The invention of the cotton gin in 1793 made slavery profitable and resulted in a more determined effort to reinforce it as an institution. Slavery produced unnumbered tragedies of cruelty, unpaid labor, the tearing apart of slave families by sale as property, and the restriction of personal and social opportunities for free Negroes.

Although most blacks north of the Mason-Dixon line were technically free, they suffered discrimination and limited scope for advancement. However, they created such notable leaders as the wealthy Philadelphia sailmaker James Forten and Richard Allen, who founded the African Methodist Episcopal Church. Most blacks were limited to low-paying jobs and humble housing and educational possibilities. A field early opened to black males was the merchant marine and the navy.

Black Panther Eldridge Cleaver ran for president in 1968.

Young black girls were able to learn a trade at Tuskegee Institute in late nineteenth century.

BLACKS IN THE UNITED STATES

SLAVERY (see also Subject Map)

Slavery
TRIANGULAR TRADE
PLANTATION SYSTEM
COTTON GIN
FUGITIVE SLAVE ACTS
MISSOURI COMPROMISE (1820)
COMPROMISE OF 1850
KANSAS-NEBRASKA ACT (1854)
DRED SCOTT DECISION (1857)

Slave Uprisings
SLAVE REVOLTS, COLONIAL
GABRIEL'S SLAVE PLOT (1800)
VESEY SLAVE UPRISING (1822)
NAT TURNER'S REVOLT (1831)
    VIRGINIA CONVENTION

EMANCIPATION MOVEMENTS

EMANCIPATION MOVEMENTS
ABOLITIONISM
AMERICAN ANTI-SLAVERY SOCIETY
AMERICAN AND FOREIGN ANTI-SLAVERY
    SOCIETY
LIBERIA
UNDERGROUND RAILROAD
    HARRIET TUBMAN

Leaders
WILLIAM LLOYD GARRISON
FREDERICK DOUGLASS
JOHN GREENLEAF WHITTIER
JAMES G. BLAINE
THEODORE DWIGHT WELD
THEODORE PARKER
JOHN BROWN

Politics
LIBERTY PARTY
FREE-SOIL PARTY
REPUBLICAN PARTY

STRUGGLE FOR EQUALITY

Freedom
ABRAHAM LINCOLN
EMANCIPATION PROCLAMATION (1863)
AMENDMENTS, CONSTITUTIONAL
RECONSTRUCTION
    BLACK CODES
    FREEDMAN'S BUREAU
    CIVIL RIGHTS ACTS (1866–1875)
        CIVIL RIGHTS CASES (1883)
    RECONSTRUCTION ACTS (1867–1868)
    ENFORCEMENT ACTS (1870–1871)
RADICAL REPUBLICANS

Early Leaders
GEORGE WASHINGTON CARVER
W. E. B. DU BOIS
MARCUS GARVEY
BOOKER T. WASHINGTON
    TUSKEGEE INSTITUTE

CIVIL RIGHTS

Groups
CIVIL RIGHTS MOVEMENT
BLACK MUSLIMS
CONGRESS OF RACIAL EQUALITY
NATIONAL ASSOCIATION FOR THE
    ADVANCEMENT OF COLORED PEOPLE
STUDENT NONVIOLENT
    COORDINATING COMMITTEE

Arts and Letters
MARIAN ANDERSON
LOUIS ARMSTRONG
JAMES BALDWIN
DUKE ELLINGTON
HARLEM RENAISSANCE
LANGSTON HUGHES
MAHALIA JACKSON
LEONTYNE PRICE
RICHARD WRIGHT

Leaders
RALPH ABERNATHY
RALPH BUNCHE
STOKELY CARMICHAEL
KENNETH CLARK
ELDRIDGE CLEAVER
BENJAMIN O. DAVIS, JR.
JESSE JACKSON
MARTIN LUTHER KING, JR.
MALCOLM X
A. PHILIP RANDOLPH
JACKIE ROBINSON
WHITNEY MOORE YOUNG, JR.

Desegregation
PLESSY V. FERGUSON (1896)
    MELVILLE W. FULLER
BROWN V. BOARD OF EDUCATION
    OF TOPEKA (1954)
    EARL WARREN
CIVIL RIGHTS ACTS (1957, 1960, 1964)

The Subject Maps in the Encyclopedia illustrate the coverage of particular aspects of American History, showing the interrelationships among the articles in twelve critical areas of study. Entries in capital letters, except for titles, are subjects for which there are separate articles in the Encyclopedia.

The Subject Maps are arranged alphabetically in the Encyclopedia under the following titles:

American Wars
Blacks in the United States
Business Regulation and Industrialization
Civil War and Reconstruction
Constitution of the United States
Exploration and Colonization
Frontier in American History
Indians
Labor Movement
New Deal and Depression
Revolutionary War Era
Slavery and Emancipation

Outstanding black businessmen, clergymen, and others organized conventions to discuss ways to strengthen their ties with white society. Some opposed forcible colonization outside the country. Others saw hope in Liberia as a new homeland. Blacks also cooperated with abolitionists and philanthropists who organized schools for black children, sought to aid fugitive slaves from the South, and worked to advance abolitionist ideals.

Post-Civil War Conditions. The Civil War resulted in the Constitution's Thirteenth Amendment, outlawing slavery, which was also undermined by new industry that made chattel (property) ownership in human beings uneconomical. Southern whites first tried to control the freed slaves through Black Codes, which made them readily liable to prison if they transgressed rigid contracts or otherwise could not satisfy discriminating regulations. The Black Codes were overthrown by Reconstruction governments, but such informal terrorist organizations as the Ku Klux Klan continued to frustrate blacks. The Freedmen's Bureau attempted to help former slaves adjust to freedom but too often was merely an agency of the Republican Party in the South, mainly interested in blacks as voters. When Reconstruction was overthrown in 1877, new segregation and disciplinary laws were enacted, depriving most blacks of voting privileges and civil rights.

Southern blacks continued to struggle for education and influence, aided by philanthropic individuals and funds. Hampton Institute and Tuskegee Institute were outstanding in their role of building a black leadership for the new time. Booker T. Washington, a former slave, founded the latter institution and forged a program accommodating Negro ambitions to those of the white supremacists.

Situation in the North. People in the North showed generally less interest in and appreciation of black rights and ambitions. The Republican Party continued to befriend blacks and offered some federal jobs and other patronage. However, the growing cities and industries, labor unions, and educational establishments were relatively slow to further the status of black leaders and communities. A notorious tactic of unprogressive industrialists was to use black workers as strikebreakers. Unions frequently rejected blacks for training and membership.

Black educators, artists, scientists, and others emerged, sometimes attaining national fame, as with George Washington Carver and Paul Lawrence Dunbar. Their dissatisfaction brought on the Niagara Movement in 1905, led by W. E. B. Du Bois. It challenged Washington's leadership and demanded a militant program. With the help of white intellectuals and others, the National Association for the Advancement of Colored People was founded in 1909 and began its long campaign of protest, political

organization, and agitation against riots and discrimination. The National Urban League was founded in 1910.

Since World War I. World War I created new suppressions and also new opportunities for blacks in the military service and in the Northern cities to which many Southern Negroes were drawn by industrial openings. Outstanding blacks in many fields achieved national and even international status. For example, the Harlem renaissance produced a brilliant array of artists in the 1920s.

The Depression of the 1930s often struck harder at white communities with high expectations of affluence than at poorer black communities that appreciated New Deal benefits. In the process, blacks tended to give up their traditional loyalty to the Republican Party and turn to Democrats. Much of the same cycle of war, affluence, and depression followed the New Deal era, progressively raising the expectations of blacks in all fields. During the 1960s white and black activists operating in the North and South created dramas and confrontations that brought on new conditions and laws and new debates on equality.

Consult (IX) Butcher, 1956; Foner, 1972; Frazier, 1957; Meier, 1963; Myrdal, 1962.
—Louis Filler, *Antioch College*

BLACK STAR LINE, shipping line founded by Marcus Garvey to generate capital for black economic projects. *See* Garvey, Marcus.

BLADENSBURG, BATTLE OF (1814), American defeat that preceded the burning of Washington, D.C. *See* War of 1812.

BLAINE, JAMES G(ILLESPIE) (1830–1893), senator and secretary of state. Born in Pennsylvania, he lived in Kentucky and Philadelphia before moving in 1854 to Augusta, Maine, his wife's home, where he bought an interest in the *Kennebec Journal.*

A Republican, he was elected to the state legislature in 1858 and served three terms. In 1862 he was elected to the House of Representatives, where he served as speaker (1869–1875). In 1876 he was appointed to fill a Senate vacancy and was then elected to a full term. During his years in Congress, Blaine was a supporter of Lincoln and the abolition of slavery.

In 1876, Blaine, accused of dishonesty by political opponents, made an unsuccessful bid for the Republican nomination for president. In 1880, he was defeated for the nomination by James A. Garfield, who, when elected, appointed Blaine secretary of state. After Garfield's death in 1881, Blaine resigned. In 1884, Blaine won the Republican nomination but lost the election to Grover Cleveland.

Blaine supported Benjamin Harrison for the presidency in 1888 and was rewarded with

From the 1960s black leaders such as Stokely Carmichael demanded equal rights and economic opportunities—the era of asking had ended.

"And for you good voters, a copy of my Labor Day 'work ethic' speech!" Blacks protesting their inability to gain admittance to unionized trades often cite lack of government support for their efforts.

Entrepreneur Blanche Calloway (*right*) discusses marketing strategy for her company's line of cosmetics for blacks.

a second appointment as secretary of state. During his tenure (1889–1892), he was deeply involved with United States–Latin American and Anglo-American relations. He was a spokesman for the construction of a canal across the Isthmus of Panama and worked hard to strengthen the position of the United States on the Atlantic and Pacific.

See also Presidential Elections.

BLAND-ALLISON ACT (1878), act of Congress that provided for the purchase of silver by the secretary of the treasury and its coinage into silver dollars. The bill was introduced into the House by Richard Bland (Missouri) and passed in 1877 in a form that would provide for the unlimited coinage of silver in a 16 to 1 ratio—that is, there would be 16 times as much silver in the silver dollar as there was gold in the gold dollar. The bill was supported by the silver miners, by the inflationists (including greenback paper currency advocates), and by Western farmers. However, the Bland bill was opposed by bankers because the remonetization of silver would amount to debt repudiation.

A compromise was reached in the Senate with Iowa senator William Allison's substitution of limited for unlimited coinage at an amount that would not lessen the value of gold. However, the act had no inflationary effect, since the Treasury always bought the minimum amount of silver. As a result, the price of silver continued to fall, and its ratio to gold at the end of the 12 years that the act was in effect was 20 to 1.

See also Free Silver; Sherman Silver Purchase Act (1890).

BLEEDING KANSAS (1854–1856). Few episodes in the 1850s more aptly symbolize the causes of the Civil War than the tangled history of Bleeding Kansas. The debacle began in 1854, when Senator Stephen Douglas of Illinois introduced the Kansas-Nebraska Act to organize the unsettled territory west of Illinois and beyond Missouri and Iowa. To gain Southern support, Douglas backed the repeal of the Missouri Compromise, thus making it theoretically possible for Kansas to become a slave state; there was little doubt Nebraska would enter the Union free. It would then be left to the people who settled Kansas to decide whether or not they wanted slavery, a doctrine known as popular sovereignty. At the same time, he reassured Northerners that the neutral forces of climate and geography would form an effective bar to the growth of slavery in the West.

But Douglas had underestimated the explosive potential of the issue. Missouri slave owners temporarily crossed into Kansas in 1854 and outvoted the settlers who opposed slavery, thus permitting the enactment of the Lecompton Constitution, which guaranteed slavery in Kansas. As antislavery settlers poured into the state, however, they formed a rival government, and sporadic fighting and bloodshed erupted. Angry and emotional debate in Congress on the issue further exacerbated sectional animosity.

Although the ineffectual Franklin Pierce finally restored an uneasy peace in 1856, his support for the Lecompton Constitution convinced many Northerners that the Democratic Party was a tool of Southern slavery interests. Although James Buchanan won a narrow victory in the election of 1856, the issue of Bleeding Kansas had given a boost to the Republican Party, crippled the Democratic Party, and exposed the increasing sectionalism that culminated in the Civil War 4 years later.

See also Douglas, Stephen; Kansas-Nebraska Act (1854); Pierce, Franklin.

Consult (IV) Nevins, 1947; Rawley, 1969.

—Dan T. Carter, *University of Maryland*

BLYDEN, EDWARD WILMOT, early colonizer of Liberia. *See* Liberia.

BOARD OF TRADE (1696–1782), the most important British agency in the government of colonies. Established by William III in 1696 to forestall a direct parliamentary attempt to administer the colonies, the Board possessed broad advisory powers but no real patronage, budget, or policy-making capacity. In its early years it attracted able men such as John Locke and pursued energetic policies of colonial reform. But lacking the power to implement its own suggestions, it settled quickly into a less ambitious routine that, in practice, gave individual colonial governors considerable flexibility between about 1710 and 1750.

Reinvigorated under Lord Halifax after 1748, it began to espouse major reforms of colonial administration. Most of these ideas were old, but in the 1760s Parliament finally took them seriously. The Board generally pursued a hard line toward the colonies after 1763. With the collapse of Lord North's ministry after the British surrender at Yorktown, the Board was abolished.

Consult (I) Steele, 1968.

BOONE, DANIEL (1734–1820), the most famous of all American frontiersmen, important for his part in the exploration and settlement of Kentucky during the 1760s and 1770s. Born in 1734 in Pennsylvania, he grew to manhood in western North Carolina, where he worked as a farmer, teamster, and hunter. During the French and Indian War he met John Finley, a fur trader who had traveled in Kentucky. In 1769, Boone, Finley, and several companions passed through the Cumberland Gap and entered Kentucky to explore and hunt. When Boone returned to North Carolina in 1771, he

Daniel Boone, the epitome of the hardy frontiersman, led settlers into Kentucky region.

probably knew more about the region than any other white man in America.

Indian resistance to white encroachments brought about Lord Dunmore's War in 1774, and when that conflict ended, the Shawnee had been defeated and Kentucky opened for settlement. Richard Henderson, the land speculator who organized the Transylvania Company and who had financed Boone's earlier explorations in Kentucky, now hired him to cut a road through the Cumberland Gap to the Kentucky River. In March 1775, Boone and his crew started work, and soon the Wilderness Road pointed toward the new land. Henderson followed with settlers in a few weeks, and they built the village of Boonesborough along the Kentucky River.

Henderson's company failed, but the Wilderness Road lay open to the continuing flow of pioneers. In mid-1778, Boone escaped from 6 months of captivity among the Shawnee just in time to help defend Boonesborough from attack. For another decade or so he remained in Kentucky, but when he lost all his land claims there and in West Virginia because of inadequate care with the paperwork, the embittered explorer moved to central Missouri, where he died in September 1820.

See also Frontier in American History; Land Companies; Lord Dunmore's War.

Consult (II) Bakeless, 1965; Kincaid, 1949.

—Roger L. Nichols, *University of Arizona*

BORAH, WILLIAM E. (1865-1940), U.S. senator. He studied law and was admitted to the bar in 1889. In 1907, he was elected senator from Idaho as a Republican. In the same year he gained prominence as a special prosecutor in the trial of IWW leader William D. Haywood and others.

As an isolationist, Borah is best known as the leader of the "irreconcilables" against President Woodrow Wilson and U.S. entry into the League of Nations. His stand not only helped block U.S. entry into the League but also into the World Court. As chairman of the Senate Foreign Affairs Committee (1924-1933), he favored recognition of the Russian Soviet government. The "Lion of Idaho" continued his lively opposition during Franklin D. Roosevelt's Administration with his disapproval of the New Deal.

BORDER STATES, the slave states that were adjacent to the North—Delaware, Maryland, Virginia, Kentucky, and Missouri. When the Civil War erupted, they were pulled to the North by economic ties and to the South by social inclination. The Border States sent men to both armies, with ideological divisions sometimes pitting brother against brother. On a larger scale, the split within Virginia was so sharp that the western part of the state broke away to form West Virginia, while the eastern part became the only Border State to secede from the Union. Abraham Lincoln's major goal, once war began, was to prevent the disaffection of the Border States, and his Emancipation Proclamation (1863) specifically excluded them from its conditions.

BOSTON ASSOCIATES, group of Massachusetts investors centered around Francis Cabot Lowell (1775-1817). A Boston textile manufacturer, he built the first American factory to include both spinning and weaving machinery in the same plant at Waltham, Mass., in 1814. The Associates sank about $600,000 into this integrated Waltham System in the first 6 years. Management was unified, and eventually all processes were combined from the arrival of raw cotton to the output of finished dyed cloth. A single marketing agency sold the textiles.

The labor force under the Waltham System consisted of New England farm girls, driven off the farms by the decline of agriculture in the region due to the growth of Midwestern farms. The girls were housed in specially built dormitories near the factory and were carefully chaperoned and regulated in their personal lives, a system that was first introduced in the town of Lowell.

Waltham was a huge financial success, and the Associates succeeded in competing with the imports of English textiles because they wisely specialized in making the coarse, standardized, tough fabrics needed by American farm and frontier families. Distinguished New England names such as the Jacksons and Appletons, as well as the Lowells, were among the Associates.

Consult (III) Taylor, 1968.

BOSTON MASSACRE (1770), violent clash between British soldiers and Boston workers. Frequent encounters between citizens and soldiers followed the arrival of two regiments of British troops in Boston on Oct. 1, 1768. A riot erupted on March 5, 1770, when workers taunted a redcoat and that evening a mob near the State House abused a detachment of guards under Captain Thomas Preston. In the confusion the troops fired a musket volley into the crowd. Five civilians, including the mulatto Crispus Attucks, were killed.

When Boston authorities tried Preston and six soldiers for murder, patriot lawyers John Adams and Josiah Quincy, who disapproved of the mob's actions, served as defense counsels. The jury acquitted Preston and four soldiers and allowed two men convicted of manslaughter to escape with minor punishment. Nevertheless, radicals took advantage of

Paul Revere engraving shows British soldiers shooting unarmed civilians in Boston Massacre, which fired Anglo-American hostility.

the tragedy, and Samuel Adams convinced Lieutenant Governor Thomas Hutchinson to remove the troops from the city.

BOSTON PORT BILL, the Coercive Act that closed the port of Boston. *See* Coercive Acts (1774).

BOSTON TEA PARTY (1773), protest by American partiots against British tea taxes. Parliament's Tea Act of 1773 authorized the East India Company to consign its tea cargo directly to favored merchants in America. The measure also remitted all taxes on the exported tea except for the Townshend duties to be collected upon arrival in the colonies. Americans objected to paying the Townshend duties and to the threat of monopoly.

Under pressure, most consignees resigned, but the favored Boston merchants refused to quit. When the tea ships began arriving in Boston in November 1773, Governor Hutchinson insisted that the taxes be paid to England before the ships returned. Confronted with an impossible situation, Boston patriots on Dec. 16, 1773, boarded the tea ships and dumped the cargoes in the harbor, an action that led to the Coercive Acts.

See also Coercive Acts (1774); Townshend Acts (1767).

BOXER REBELLION (1900), revolt by Chinese protesting foreign influence in China. *See* Open Door Policy.

BRADDOCK, EDWARD (1695-1755), British general. A career soldier, he was promoted to major general in 1754 and ordered to North America to stop French expansion south from Canada. Braddock had been in the army 45 years, but he lacked combat experience. He raised a force of 1,400 British regulars and 1,100 Virginia and Maryland militiamen to attack the French at Fort Duquesne, near the present site of Pittsburgh.

On July 9, 1775, about 900 French and Indians hidden behind trees surrounded and decimated Braddock's larger force, which he had imprudently arranged in the strict formations of European warfare. In the Battle of the Wilderness the attackers lost only 43 men; the British casualties included 63 out of 83 officers and 914 out of 1,373 soldiers. Braddock himself was killed in the battle, and his aide-de-camp, Lt. Col. George Washington of Virginia, prevented discovery of the body by burying it in the road over which the British retreated.

BRADFORD, WILLIAM (1590-1657), most famous governor of Plymouth Colony. Bradford was born in Yorkshire, England, and as a boy joined the Separatist congregation at William Brewster's house (1606). He went with the

Separatists to Holland and became a member of the church at Leyden in 1609. Bradford sailed with the Pilgrim Fathers on the *Mayflower* in 1620 and was elected governor of Plymouth Colony after the death of Governor John Carver in 1621. Bradford was intensely religious and struggled throughout his life to keep the colony pious and strict in its Puritan faith. After 1621, he was governor for most of the rest of his life, being reelected 30 times.

William Bradford was one of the best educated and ablest of the Pilgrim Fathers, and his manuscript *History of Plymouth Plantation* (written between about 1630 and 1651) is the chief single source on what happened there. For many years, his word was law. His leadership helped to save the colony from famine, disease, Indian hostility, the pressures from the growing Massachusetts Bay Colony, and inner dissensions. He negotiated with the merchants who had underwritten the colony for greater freedom and self-government, and the "Bradford patent" (finally delivered in January 1630) gave the people of Plymouth clear title to the lands they had settled without authority since 1620 and a large measure of self-government. In 1636 Bradford also helped to draw up a new body of laws for the colony. Although he struggled for the independence of New Plymouth, under his regime the colony did cooperate with other settlements in the Pequot War and in the New England Confederation.

Bradford died in May 1657 a very disappointed man. His early dreams of building a pious community of religious folk, bound together in the harmonious worship of God, had not been realized. Piety declined, and secular ideas crept in. Bradford had opposed giving religious tolerance to Anglicans or Quakers but could not stem the tide of change.

See also New England Confederation; Plymouth.

Consult (I) Bradford, 1952; Langdon, 1966.

—Peter d'A. Jones, *University of Illinois, Chicago Circle*

BRADLEY, OMAR (NELSON) (1893-), U.S. Army general. Born in Clark, Mo., on Feb. 12, 1893, he graduated from West Point in 1915. During his early years in the army he taught at West Point and served on the general staff, of which he became assistant secretary in 1939.

After the United States entered World War II, Bradley served as field aide to General Eisenhower in North Africa and succeeded Gen. George Patton as commander of II Corps in North Africa. In 1944 he led the First Army in the invasion of Normandy and then was made commander of the 12th Army Group, which played a vital role in the defeat of Germany. Bradley returned to the United States and in 1945 was appointed Veteran Affairs Adminis-

Directed by Sam Adams, Boston patriots dressed as Indians dumped British tea into Boston Harbor in December 1773.

General Omar Bradley points out German rocket-launching site in northern France to General Eisenhower in July 1944.

trator. He succeeded Eisenhower as Army chief of staff in 1948, and in 1949 he was made the first chairman of the Joint Chiefs of Staff. He served a second two-year term and was made a five-star general in 1950. Bradley retired in 1953 and became chairman of the board of the Bulova Watch Company.

See also World War II.

Consult (VIII) Bradley, 1951.

BRAINS TRUST, group of unofficial advisers to Franklin Roosevelt, many of them recruited from the faculty of Columbia University. Raymond Moley, who believed in close cooperation between government and the business community, headed the group and recruited new talent. Other important members were Adolf A. Berle, Jr., and Rexford G. Tugwell. Berle was less inclined than Moley to permit business to dominate in the partnership and at times suggested the inevitability of public ownership. Tugwell, from a variety of posts in agricultural agencies, advocated extensive public planning throughout the economy. All three made important contributions to the New Deal before 1935.

Consult (VI) Schlesinger, 1959.

BRANDEIS, LOUIS D. (1856–1941), served as associate justice of the U.S. Supreme Court from 1916, when he was appointed by President Wilson, until 1939. Born in Louisville, Ky., Brandeis was educated in public schools, in the severe academic discipline of Dresden, Germany, and at Harvard Law School. He gained recognition for his expertise in litigation when he undertook the practice of law in Boston. Brandeis disdained the traditional lawyer's brief, which was filled with narrow procedural points. Instead, he filled his legal presentations with social and economic arguments. "The Brandeis brief" became the label given to his type of argumentation. While he was a lawyer, he became an ardent Zionist.

Once on the Court, Brandeis immediately became associated with Justice Oliver Wendell Holmes, Jr., for his advocacy of judicial restraint. Brandeis believed that legislative regulations in the economic sphere were necessary, but he held that the judicial branch had to remain aloof from them (*Truax v. Corrigan,* 1921, dissenting). The thorough scholar, Brandeis' opinions were filled with cross references and footnotes, for the man never shook himself of the importance of the facts involved in any social or legal issue.

Brandeis is also associated with Holmes in the formulation of the "clear and present danger" test in regard to laws restricting speech and press, although, if anything, Brandeis was more emphatic in his defense of the First Amendment freedoms (*Whitney v. California,* 1927). Nonetheless, Brandeis is still generally placed in the tradition of judicial restraint. He consistently argued for a limited role in judicial decision making (*Ashwander v. TVA,* 1936), and he was a dedicated defender of federalism.

Consult (VI) Bickel, 1967; Frankfurter, 1932; Lief, 1936; Mason, 1933, 1956.

—David Forte, *Skidmore College*

BRANDYWINE CREEK (SEPT. 11, 1777), American defeat that led to British occupation of Philadelphia. *See* Revolutionary War Battles.

BRECKINRIDGE, JOHN C(ABELL) (1821–1875), Vice-President of the United States and Confederate general. He was born near Lexington, Ky., and practiced law in Kentucky and then in Iowa. He returned to Lexington and began his political career as a Democrat in the Kentucky legislature.

In 1851 he was elected to the House of Representatives, where he served until his election as vice-president under James Buchanan in 1856. In 1859, while still vice-president, he was elected to the Senate. In 1860 he was chosen as the presidential candidate of the Southern wing of the Democrats, in part because he felt that slavery could not be excluded from any territory. In the race against Abraham Lincoln he carried 11 states and received 72 electoral votes.

In March 1861, Breckenridge took his Senate seat, but he was expelled as a traitor after he joined the Confederate Army as a brigadier general. He fought in numerous battles, including Shiloh, Baton Rouge, Chickamauga, New Market, and Shenandoah and rose to the rank of major general. Appointed Confederate secretary of war by Jefferson Davis in 1865, Breckinridge was forced to flee to Europe at the close of the war. He returned to the United States in 1869 and practiced law in Lexington until his death.

BREED'S HILL, BATTLE OF. *See* Bunker Hill, Battle of (1775).

BRETTON WOODS CONFERENCE, international conference on postwar monetary and financial problems attended by representatives of 44 nations and held at Bretton Woods, N.H., July 1-22, 1944. Chaired by Treasury Secretary Henry Morgenthau, Jr., and convened to prevent a repetition after World War II of the ruinous fiscal wars of the 1930s, the conference adopted proposals drafted by Harry Dexter White of the United States and John Maynard Keynes of Britain. The Bretton Woods program called for the establishment of an International Monetary Fund (IMF) of $8.8 billion to help stabilize international currencies and an International Bank for Reconstruction and Development (World Bank), capitalized at $9.1 billion, to lend money to member nations for

Louis D. Brandeis, Associate Justice of the Supreme Court, was noted for dissenting opinions.

long-term capital improvements. The Bretton Woods IMF proposals were ratified by the U.S. Senate on July 18, 1945. The IMF and the World Bank, both located in Washington, D.C., went into operation in 1947.

BRITAIN, BATTLE OF (AUGUST–SEPTEMBER 1940), air battle in which Britain successfully resisted German attempts to bomb it into submission. *See* World War II.

BRITISH ORDERS IN COUNCIL (1807). *See* Orders In Council.

BROOK FARM, utopian settlement founded in April 1841. Brook Farm Institute of Agriculture and Education was located on a 200-acre site near Roxbury, Mass. It was motivated by two philosophical beliefs, transcendentalism and French Fourierism. Its leading organizing spirit was George Ripley (1807–1880), a literary critic, Unitarian clergyman, editor, and reformer. Ripley was part of the Concord literary group dominated by Ralph Waldo Emerson and William Ellery Channing. Ripley defended Emerson, translated German philosophers, helped found the Transcendental Club, helped edit *The Dial* along with Margaret Fuller, and then became head of Brook Farm.

The farm was a communal cooperative society in which members shared both manual and intellectual labors. Brook Farm became a Fourier phalanx in 1844, when Ripley, believing stronger organization was necessary, wrote a new constitution establishing primary departments of agricultural, mechanical, and domestic arts. The efficient mechanical plant was destroyed by fire in 1846 and—unable to pay the promised 5-percent return on investment—the community dissolved in 1847. Ripley became literary editor of the New York *Tribune* in 1849 and worked for more than 20 years to pay off Brook Farm's debts.

See also Emerson, Ralph Waldo; Transcendentalism; Utopian Communities.

BROTHERHOOD OF SLEEPING CAR PORTERS, labor union. *See* Randolph, A. Philip.

BROWN, JOHN (1800–1859), controversial abolitionist leader. Born in Connecticut, he had a long, unsuccessful career as a businessman but no public image until 1856, when he entered into the Kansas struggle to prevent the territory from being taken over by proslavery settlers.

In 1856, during the Kansas fighting, he and a small number of followers brutally murdered five slavery proponents. The "Pottawatomie massacre" was attacked by Southern sympathizers but defended in the Northern press. Thereafter, Brown became an advocate of stronger action against slavery and gained

A PREMATURE MOVEMENT.
John Brown's raid on Harper's Ferry, Va., in 1859 failed to trigger the slave rebellion he envisioned.

funds and support by visits to many Northern towns and influential individuals.

Although Brown made repeated efforts to raise troops as well as funds, by 1859 he was able to muster no more than 16 white and 5 black men to join him in an effort to capture the federal arsenal at Harpers Ferry, Va., the arms of which would presumably serve embattled slaves. The blacks of the town did not respond to the opportunity, and Brown himself was strangely slow to escape enclosing troops and militia. It has been conjectured that Brown saw his act as symbolic rather than practical. After some bloodshed, he surrendered to Col. Robert E. Lee and at his trial for treason spoke against slavery with an eloquence that moved Northerners and horrified Southerners, who held his "fanaticism" typical of Northern opinion. He was hanged in Charlestown (now in West Virginia) on Dec. 2, 1859. The Civil War enshrined Brown as an antislavery martyr in the North.

See also Abolitionism; Bleeding Kansas. *Consult* (IV) Abels, 1971; Oates, 1970.
—Louis Filler, *Antioch College*

BROWN UNIVERSITY. *See* Colonial Colleges.

BROWN v. BOARD OF EDUCATION OF TOPEKA (1954), one of a series of cases in which several black children contested state laws permitting or requiring the establishment of separate school facilities based on race.

History. These cases were first argued in 1952, but following the death of Chief Justice Frederick M. Vinson and his replacement by Earl Warren, the Court asked for reargument. In a unanimous opinion written by the new Chief Justice, the Court held that all state laws segregating children in public schools because of their race were invalid by virtue of the equal protection of the law clause of the Fourteenth Amendment to the Constitution. Warren chose to base his opinion on contemporary sociological evidence. He did not assert that the Fourteenth Amendment was, since its ratification, designed to outlaw such discrimination. Rather, he stated, "To separate (blacks) from others of similar age and qualifications solely because of their race generates a feeling of inferiority as to their status in a community that may affect their hearts and minds in a way unlikely ever to be undone." In *Plessy v. Ferguson* (1896), which this decision overruled, the majority said that separation did not imply inferiority. In this case, Warren said that it did.

Analysis. Warren not only suggested that legally required separation was unconstitutional, he also stated that separation by any means was unconstitutional. This has led the Supreme Court into the difficult issue of deciding whether or not de facto segregation is as unconstitutional as de jure segregation and whether the Constitution not only prohibits the legal separation of the races but also requires their social intermingling.

The decision in this case eventually brought about vast social changes in the South and, after Congress had entered the field through numerous civil rights acts, in the rest of the nation as well.

See also Civil Rights Acts; Education; Plessy v. Ferguson.

—David Forte, *Skidmore College*

BRYAN, WILLIAM JENNINGS (1860-1925), political leader and three-time Democratic presidential nominee. He was born in Illinois, moved to Lincoln, Nebraska, and was twice elected to Congress (1890 and 1892).

In Congress, Bryan was a prominent advocate of the free coinage of silver and continued in this cause after 1894, speaking throughout the country. At the presidential nominating convention of 1896 his "Cross of Gold" speech electrified the delegates and gave him the presidential nomination. Also nominated by the Populists and Silver Republicans, Bryan carried his silver crusade to the nation in a far-reaching speaking tour, the first time a major-party presidential candidate had gone so directly to the people. Defeated by William McKinley, Bryan nonetheless forged a strong personal following, especially among the Democrats and Populists of the West and South.

In 1900, Bryan made imperialism, silver, and the danger of trusts the major issues of his second bid for the presidency. His third unsuccessful try for the presidency came in 1908. In the 1912 Democratic convention, Bryan was one of the major forces behind the nomination of Woodrow Wilson.

Made secretary of state by Wilson, Bryan worked conscientiously with Democratic congressmen for the passage of many progressive reforms and also sought to put his own pacifism into effect among nations. With the outbreak of World War I, Bryan sought to avoid any U.S. involvement, preferring to resign as secretary of state rather than take the strong attitude toward Germany desired by Wilson. After the war, Bryan continued to promote progressive reforms. He also spoke in support of Protestant fundamentalism, especially to oppose the teaching of Darwinian theories of evolution. His last public appearance was as special counsel to the prosecution in the 1925 trial of John Scopes, a Tennessee schoolteacher charged with violating that state's antievolution law.

Never a deep or original thinker, Bryan's great strength was his faith in, and identification with, the people. To him, his campaign watchword "Shall the People Rule?" was much more than a mere slogan. He gloried in being designated "The Great Commoner." Blessed

with a magnificent voice and an engaging smile, he built a strong following by clothing the sentiments of the common people in eloquence.

See also Free Silver; Fundamentalism; McKinley, William; Populists; Scopes Trial (1925).

Consult (V) Coletta, 1964-1969; Glad, 1960; Levine, 1965.

—Robert W. Cherny, *California State University, San Francisco*

BRYANT, WILLIAM CULLEN (1794-1878), lawyer, influential editor and publisher, and romantic poet. Born in Cummington, Mass., Bryant's life spanned the growing years of the new nation. At the time of his death in 1878, Bryant was editor of the *New York Evening Post,* a position he had held since 1829. Bryant's poetry is best known for its lyrical celebration of nature. His first published poem was a Federalist satire, "The Embargo; or Sketches of the Times, a Satire by a Youth of Thirteen" (1808). The first draft of his best-known poem, "Thanatopsis," was written in 1811 and ultimately published in the *North American Review* in 1817.

He abandoned a law career when he moved to New York in 1825. There he devoted his time to literary work, including the editorship of several literary journals, and became associated with the Knickerbocker School. Bryant's principal career, however, started when he became assistant editor of the *Post.* As the *Post's* editor, Bryant became an important catalyst of public opinion. He was a Jacksonian until the sectional crisis caused him to leave the Democrats in 1848 for the Free-Soil Party. In 1856 he became a leader in the new Republican Party, favoring emancipation of the slaves. During the Civil War Bryant called for a vigorous war policy toward the South. After the war, however, he favored conciliatory policies toward it.

See also Knickerbocker School.

BUCHANAN, JAMES (1791-1868), 15th President of the United States (1857-1861). He was born near Mercersburg, Pa., on April 23, 1791, and began his career as a Lancaster, Pa., lawyer in 1812. He experienced an uninterrupted series of political successes during the next 44 years, climaxed by his election as president in 1856.

Buchanan began his political career as a Federalist, but he joined ranks with the Democratic Party in the 1820s, serving as congressman, minister to Russia, senator, and finally secretary of state (1845-1849) under James K. Polk. Although he was a contender for the Democratic presidential nomination in 1852, the Democrats named the less prominent Franklin Pierce. As minister to England from

William Jennings Bryan, Democratic presidential candidate, speaks during the campaign of 1900.

James Buchanan, 15th President of the United States (1857-1861), could not resolve the nation's crises before the Civil War.

William Buckley, articulate conservative spokesman.

Ralph Bunche received Nobel Peace Prize for his efforts in halting Arab-Israeli war in 1948.

1853 to 1856, Buchanan was removed from the increasingly bitter debate over slavery and thus became an ideal compromise Democratic candidate in 1856.

Presidency. Although Buchanan won the election by successfully straddling the slavery issue, he was soon embroiled in the troublesome consequences of the Dred Scott decision (1857) and in the Kansas struggle. Although he claimed to be impartial, Buchanan's strict constructionist position on the Constitution and his support for the proslavery forces in Kansas made him increasingly unacceptable to most non-Southerners. He was bypassed by the Democrats in 1860, when Republican Abraham Lincoln won the election.

Following the election, South Carolina seceded, and only after two months of vacillation did Buchanan reluctantly move to reinforce Fort Sumter in Charleston harbor. But he retreated from this position in the face of South Carolina's military resistance, and he spent his remaining two months in office pleading ineffectually for the compromise that was no longer possible. When Lincoln's inauguration triggered the secession of the remainder of the South, Buchanan pledged his support for military action against the seceding states, but he is primarily remembered for his feckless leadership between November 1860 and March 1861. He died near Lancaster, Pa., on June 1, 1868.

See also Bleeding Kansas; Dred Scott Decision; Secession.

Consult (IV) Klein, 1962.

—Dan T. Carter, *University of Maryland*

BUCKLEY, WILLIAM F(RANK), JR. (1925-   ), American editor, writer, and politician known for his conservative views. He was born in New York City, one of 10 children of a wealthy father. He studied in Mexico and England, served in World War II, and graduated from Yale with honors in 1950.

Buckley was thrust into national prominence in 1951 with the appearance of his first book, *Man and God at Yale,* an indictment of the university for its liberal political philosophy. In 1955 he founded the *National Review,* a magazine that promoted his conservative views of economic individualism and Roman Catholicism. In the first issue, Buckley stated his desire to repeal many of the foreign policy decisions and social legislation of the preceding 20 years.

Known for his quick wit and intelligence, he frequently debates many of the nation's best-known liberals and hosts his own television program, *Firing Line.* In 1965 he ran unsuccessfully for mayor of New York as a Conservative. His brother James was elected to the Senate from New York as a Conservative in 1970.

Consult (VIII) Buckley, 1972.

BUENA VISTA, BATTLE OF (1847), victory of Americans under Zachary Taylor over Mexicans commanded by Santa Anna. *See* Mexican War (1846–1848).

BUENOS AIRES CONFERENCE (1936). *See* Latin American Conferences.

BULFINCH, CHARLES (1763-1844), one of America's first important architects. Born in Boston to a wealthy family, he went on a European tour after graduating from Harvard in 1781. In Europe he followed Jefferson's suggestion and studied French and Italian classical architecture. On his return to America he began to design public buildings. His commissions included the old Hollis Street Church in Boston, churches in Taunton and Pittsfield, the State House at Hartford, Conn. (1792), and the Massachusetts State House on Beacon Hill (1800). Bulfinch's use of the styles made famous in England by the Adam brothers influenced other American architects such as Samuel McIntyre and Asher Benjamin and helped make the Federal style popular throughout New England.

Bulfinch was a Boston selectman for nearly 25 years, and as chairman of the selectmen (1799–1817) he was influential in planning and refurbishing much of old Boston. The additions of Faneuil Hall, the Boyleston Market, the almshouse, India Wharf, Franklin Crescent, and the design of the Boston Common as a public park were part of his dual responsibilities as government official and architect. He was also commissioned to do the Massachusetts General Hospital (1817–1820) and the State Capitol in Augusta, Maine (1828–1831).

Bulfinch succeeded Benjamin Latrobe as architect of the Capitol in Washington, D.C., in 1817, assuming the responsibility for completing work already designed. He conceived the western front of the Capitol.

See also Architecture.

—Richard Collin, *Louisiana State University, New Orleans*

BULGE, BATTLE OF THE (DECEMBER 1944), resulted from last German counteroffensive and prolonged the war. *See* World War II.

BULL MOOSE PARTY. *See* Progressive Party.

BULL RUN, BATTLES OF (FIRST, JULY 21, 1861; SECOND, AUGUST 29-30, 1862), Confederate victories. *See* Civil War Battles.

BUNCHE, RALPH (JOHNSON) (1904-1971), American political scientist and 1950 Nobel Peace Prize winner. He was born in Detroit, the grandson of a slave. He graduated from UCLA in 1927 and received his M.A. (1928) and Ph.D. (1934) from Harvard. Bunche taught at Howard University and then worked as chief assistant to Swedish sociologist Gunnar Myrdal from 1938 to 1940.

After serving in the Office of Strategic Services during most of World War II, Bunche joined the State Department in 1944. In 1946 he became director of the United Nations trusteeship division, which he had been active in organizing. Bunche won the Nobel Peace Prize in 1950 for his successful mediation of the Arab-Israeli conflict in 1949. He was appointed professor of government at Harvard in 1950, when he also became UN undersecretary for special political affairs. In 1954 he was named undersecretary without portfolio. In 1960, Bunche was made UN special representative when UN troops were sent to the Congo to try to restore order.

BUNKER HILL, BATTLE OF (1775), clash at the beginning of the Revolutionary War, later considered a moral victory by the colonists. After the engagement at Lexington and Concord in April 1775, American soldiers surrounded Boston, where 6,500 British troops were garrisoned. Hoping to break the siege, Governor Thomas Gage, the British commander in chief, determined to occupy strategically located Dorchester Heights. In order to undermine Gage's plan, the rebels sent Col. William Prescott to fortify Bunker Hill on the Charlestown Neck on the evening of June 16, 1775. Prescott, unfortunately, concentrated his men on less easily defended Breed's Hill.

The next afternoon, June 17, on Gage's orders, Maj. Gen. William Howe's 2,500 troops attacked the 2,000 American defenders. Twice the patriots repelled charges, but the colonials, lacking ammunition, retreated in the face of the third assault. The Americans lost 140 dead, including Dr. Joseph Warren, the president of the Massachusetts Provincial Congress. The English counted 226 dead and gave up hopes of taking Dorchester Heights.

See also Revolutionary War Battles.

BURGER, WARREN EARL (1907–   ), 14th Chief Justice of the Supreme Court, appointed in 1969 by President Nixon, who wanted a "law and order" jurist with "strict constructionist" views.

Born in St. Paul, Minn., he developed a successful law practice there and also taught law. A lifelong Republican, Burger supported his friend Harold Stassen in Stassen's bid for the presidential nomination in 1952 but, in the end, helped to swing the Minnesota delegation to Dwight Eisenhower. In 1953, he was appointed assistant attorney general by President Eisenhower and in 1956 was named to the U.S. Court of Appeals for the District of Columbia. Burger made a reputation as a conservative judge in a generally liberal appellate court. He often felt that efforts to achieve reform through the judiciary were too progressive.

When Burger was appointed to the Supreme Court in 1969, conservatives foresaw a reversal of the liberal balance on the court and the creation of a moderate, nonactivist majority for the first time since the mid-1950s. Burger indicated that the Supreme Court was not the place for the type of liberal judicial reform practiced by the Warren Court, although he displayed some liberal feelings and a certain activism off the bench.

BURR, AARON (1756–1836), Vice-President of the United States who killed Alexander Hamilton in a duel. He was born in New Jersey and graduated from the College of New Jersey (Princeton) in 1772. He fought in the Revolution and then became a lawyer in New York. In the 1780s, Burr entered state politics, where he became a rival of Alexander Hamilton. He was appointed New York attorney general in 1789, and from 1791 to 1797 he was a senator from New York. In the presidential election of 1800 he ran on the Democratic-Republican ticket with Thomas Jefferson. The presidential and vice-presidential candidates were not yet separated in voting, and Jefferson and Burr tied in electoral votes. For a time the Federalists in the House attempted to embarrass the Democratic-Republicans by voting for Burr, but Hamilton threw his influence to the side of Jefferson, who became president.

As vice-president, Burr quickly lost the confidence of the Democratic-Republican leaders, and in the 1804 presidential campaign he was dropped in favor of George Clinton. In July 1804, Burr's long rivalry with Alexander Hamilton came to a head when he challenged Hamilton to a duel and killed him. In the following years Burr went West and took the leadership in a strange conspiracy, either to separate the Western states from the union or possibly to invade Mexico—his goals changed according to the listener. The whole affair ended ingloriously when Burr was arrested and tried for treason in 1807. He was acquitted by Chief Justice John Marshall. Most of the rest of his life was spent practicing law in New York City.

See also Hamilton, Alexander; Presidential Elections.

Consult (III) Abernethy, 1954; Schachner, 1937.

—Reginald Horsman, *University of Wisconsin, Milwaukee*

BUSINESS REGULATION. U.S. business regulation is an old practice with its roots in the colonial period, when the British regulated both trade and industry and the colonies further regulated business within their borders. Although the American Revolution swept away British legislation, regulation persisted. In the early nineteenth century, states not only used corporation charters to regulate service, safety, and rates of transportation companies but also

Battle of Bunker's Hill.

Battle of Bunker Hill in June 1775 demonstrated patriots' willingness to fight seasoned British troops.

Boom Town

Critics charge that government legislation benefits, rather than regulates, big business interests.

Handing Down Historical Decision

Harry F. Byrd, influential and conservative senator from Virginia.

frequently subsidized economic interests and participated in economic enterprises. The strictly regulatory activities of the central government, however, were limited to foreign commerce, the merchant marine, immigration, and laws regulating interstate steamboat operations (1838, 1852).

With a national economy emerging by the Civil War, the federal government played a larger role in both supporting and regulating the economy. Regulation, in contrast to support, came with the Interstate Commerce Act (1887) and the Sherman Antitrust Act (1890). The Sherman Act—a token measure for farmers and small businessmen—was ineffective. It declared "every contract, combination in the form of trust or otherwise, or conspiracy, in restraint of trade . . . illegal." The courts, however, were to define what was illegal; so when the Supreme Court ruled in *U.S. v. E. C. Knight Co.* (1895) that the sugar trust, controlling 98 percent of the sugar refined and sold in the United States, was not restraining trade, the Sherman Act was rendered useless.

Early Twentieth Century. Unlike his predecessors, President Theodore Roosevelt (1901–1909) moved to regulate business. His Administration instituted 44 antitrust suits; established the Department of Commerce and Labor, including a Bureau of Corporations with power to investigate and report (1903); strengthened the Interstate Commerce Act through the Elkins Act (1903) and the Hepburn Act (1906); and protected the consumer through the Pure Food and Drug Act (1906) and the Meat Inspection Act (1906). During William Howard Taft's Administration (1909–1913) an additional 90 antitrust suits were instituted, and the Mann-Elkins Act (1910) further expanded the jurisdiction of the Interstate Commerce Commission.

Progressive legislation and wartime mobilization made Woodrow Wilson's Administration (1913–1921) active in business regulation. The Federal Reserve Act (1913) and the Federal Trade Commission Act (1914) were passed, and the Clayton Antitrust Act (1914) attempted to strengthen the Sherman Act. During World War I the War Industries Board controlled the economy.

New Deal Legislation. The federal government retreated from wartime control in the 1920s, but with the crash of 1929, the Great Depression, and Franklin Roosevelt's New Deal, government regulation of business increased. The early New Deal's major attempt to regulate the economy was the National Industrial Recovery Act (1933, declared unconstitutional 1935), which set up codes of fair competition within each industry to be administered by a National Recovery Administration (NRA) and to be enforced by law. The NRA was a long step toward a planned economy, but businessmen did most of the planning.

The New Deal also regulated business through the Emergency Banking Act (1933), establishing the Federal Deposit Insurance Corporation and forcing commercial banks to give up their investment affiliates; the Banking Act (1935), increasing the president's power over the Federal Reserve Board; and the Federal Securities Act (1933) and the Securities Exchange Act (1934), regulating the securities market. The Communications Act (1934), the Motor Carrier Act (1935), the Public Utility Holding Company Act (1935), and the Civil Aeronautics Act (1938) imposed new regulations on broad areas of business. In 1938 the Temporary National Economic Committee began to investigate the growth of monopolies and the concentration of economic power, but because its final report (1941) came amid preparations for World War II, its recommendations to curb concentration were not enacted.

Postwar Regulation. During World War II the War Production Board and the Office of Price Administration mobilized and regulated the economy. With the return of peace, controls were lifted, and the country embarked simultaneously on a postwar inflationary spiral and an economic boom.

During the postwar years, the climate for big business has been favorable despite temporary policies such as the Nixon Administration's wage and price controls. Added to the government's power to regulate business is the fact that enormous spending makes the federal government the nation's leading consumer. Government contract decisions determine the survival of corporations and the economic health of cities and states. Yet during recent decades, while federal power over business has grown with the federal budget, government economic policies have fostered rather than hindered the spectacular development of oligopolies.

Consult (VI) Cochran, 1957; Cochran and Miller, 1961.

—Ari Hoogenboom, *Brooklyn College of The City University of New York*

BYRD FAMILY. William Byrd (1652–1704) was one of the founders of Virginia gentry society. Born in London, Byrd emigrated to Virginia and became a typical seventeenth-century colonial entrepreneur with interests in Indian and slave trades, warehouses, tobacco, and land. His son, William (1674–1744), was educated in England but returned to America to administer his father's estate. He was elected to the Virginia House of Burgesses, served as boundary commissioner to North Carolina, and laid out the town of Richmond. William owned the largest library (4,000 volumes) in the colonies and was one of the leading literary figures of his era.

Harry Flood Byrd (1887–1966) and his brother Admiral Richard Evelyn Byrd (1888–1957) were direct descendants of the

BUSINESS REGULATION AND INDUSTRIALIZATION

BUSINESS REGULATION ──────────────────────────── INDUSTRIALIZATION

Pre-Civil War
EMBARGO ACTS (1807–1809)
DARTMOUTH COLLEGE V. WOODWARD (1819)
CHARLES RIVER BRIDGE V. WARREN BRIDGE (1837)
BANK OF AUGUSTA V. EARLE (1839)

Antitrust Era
SHERMAN ANTITRUST ACT (1890)
    UNITED STATES V. E. C. KNIGHT CO. (1895)
RAILROAD LEGISLATION
ANTITRUST CASES
    THEODORE ROOSEVELT
    WILLIAM HOWARD TAFT
CLAYTON ANTITRUST ACT (1914)
INTERSTATE COMMERCE COMMISSION
    ELKINS ACT (1903)
    HEPBURN ACT (1906)
    PURE FOOD AND DRUG ACT (1906)
    MANN-ELKINS ACT (1910)
    FEDERAL TRADE COMMISSION
FEDERAL RESERVE ACT (1913)
WAR INDUSTRIES BOARD

New Deal and Depression (see Subject Map)
NATIONAL INDUSTRIAL RECOVERY ACT (1933)
    NATIONAL RECOVERY ADMINISTRATION
GLASS-STEAGALL ACT (1933)
SECURITIES EXCHANGE ACT (1934)
COMMUNICATIONS ACT (1934)

World War II
PRICE ADMINISTRATION, OFFICE OF
WAR PRODUCTION BOARD

TARIFFS
TARIFF OF 1828
SMOOT-HAWLEY TARIFF

Functions
INVENTIONS
    AUTOMOBILE
    AVIATION
    COMPUTERS
    SEWING MACHINE
    MCCORMICK REAPER
BOSTON ASSOCIATES
SUFFOLK SYSTEM
BESSEMER STEEL PROCESS (1856)
TRUSTS
    POOLS
    HOLDING COMPANIES
RAILROADS
    CRÉDIT MOBILIER
FREE ENTERPRISE
FREE TRADE
MASS PRODUCTION

Inventors
ALEXANDER GRAHAM BELL
THOMAS A. EDISON
JOHN ERICCSON
ROBERT FULTON
ELIAS HOWE
GEORGE WESTINGHOUSE
ELI WHITNEY
WILBUR AND ORVILLE WRIGHT

Leaders
PHILIP ARMOUR
ANDREW CARNEGIE
SAMUEL COLT
JAMES B. DUKE
HENRY FORD
HENRY CLAY FRICK
JAY GOULD
JAMES J. HILL
J. PIERPONT MORGAN
JOHN D. ROCKEFELLER
CORNELIUS VANDERBILT

The Subject Maps in the Encyclopedia illustrate the coverage of particular aspects of American History, showing the interrelationships among the articles in twelve critical areas of study. Entries in capital letters, except for titles, are subjects for which there are separate articles in the Encyclopedia.

The Subject Maps are arranged alphabetically in the Encyclopedia under the following titles:

American Wars
Blacks in the United States
Business Regulation and Industrialization
Civil War and Reconstruction
Constitution of the United States
Exploration and Colonization
Frontier in American History
Indians
Labor Movement
New Deal and Depression
Revolutionary War Era
Slavery and Emancipation

PRESIDENTIAL CABINET

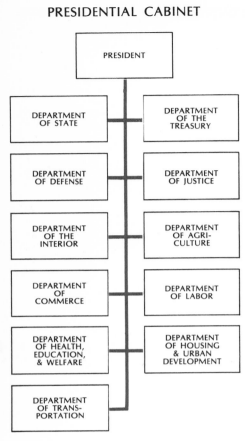

early Byrds. Harry Flood Byrd, a U.S. senator (1933–1965), became Virginia's foremost political leader in the twentieth century. Chairman of the Senate Finance Committee (1955–1965), he was known as the "watchdog of the Treasury." He was an outspoken critic of expanding federal power, especially in regard to welfare. In 1965, Byrd resigned his Senate seat, and in 1966 his son Harry, Jr. (1914–), was elected to that seat as an Independent.

Admiral Richard E. Byrd, naval officer and polar explorer, led five expeditions to Antarctica and was the first man to fly over both the North and South poles. He was named by President Franklin Roosevelt to command the U.S. Antarctic Service Expedition of 1939–1941, and in 1947 he led the largest Antarctic expedition in history.

CABINET, term commonly used to denote the heads (secretaries) of the 11 executive departments of the United States (state; treasury; defense; justice; interior; agriculture; commerce; labor; health, education, and welfare; housing and urban development; and transportation). The meeting of all the secretaries to advise and consult with the president is known as a cabinet meeting. The president may, at his discretion, name other government officials (such as the UN ambassador) as cabinet-level officers. The cabinet has no legal or constitutional function, being rooted rather in custom and usage of the presidents.

The heads of the executive departments are appointed by the president but are subject to Senate confirmation. Traditionally, the secretaries of the departments serve at the president's pleasure. The secretaries have two primary functions. They preside over the work of their departments, and present the views of the hierarchy of their departments to one another and to the president. For the most part cabinet secretaries are political appointees with views generally in line with those of the president.

History. Presidents have used their cabinets differently. Dwight D. Eisenhower often used the cabinet as a fully developed body of advisers on a wide range of governmental policies. John F. Kennedy and Lyndon B. Johnson made little use of the cabinet as a collective body of advisers, preferring to deal more personally with individual secretaries and their departments. As the executive branch itself has grown in other areas and as certain departments have become more individually important, the cabinet has fallen into relative disuse.

CABLE, GEORGE WASHINGTON (1844–1925), author and reformer. A native of New Orleans, Cable served in the Confederate Army with distinction and after the Civil War was both a businessman and a writer.

His first stories immediately established his reputation. His fine ear for Creole speech

astounded and delighted readers, especially in the North. Cable stood forth as one of the great local color authors who were capturing rural speech and outlooks that were rapidly being destroyed by the increasingly urban environments and ways of life. As long as Cable put his attitudes into fictional form he could not be sharply criticized. However, his series of essays in *The Silent South* (1885), denouncing the white supremacy that followed the failure of Reconstruction, roused much bitterness from ardent Southerners.

Cable's crusade for a more humane social and civil establishment in the South was insufficiently supported, so he left to take up residence in Northampton, Mass. In *The Negro Question* (1888) and *The Southern Struggle for Pure Government* (1890) he maintained his involvement with the South, but the comfort and acceptance of Northern life led him to write romances that revealed good will and charm rather than penetration.

CABOT, JOHN AND SEBASTIAN, Italian navigators in the service of England. *See* Exploration and Discovery.

CALHOUN, JOHN C(ALDWELL) (1782–1850), political leader who was the leading spokesman of the planter elite of South Carolina and the chief tactician of Southern secession. The son of Scotch-Irish pioneers from the hill country of South Carolina, Calhoun graduated from Yale (1804), studied law, and was admitted to the South Carolina bar in 1807. The following year he was elected to the state legislature; from 1811 to 1817 he served in the U.S. Congress, where he became a leader of the war hawks and a supporter of nationalistic legislation after the War of 1812. During James Monroe's two terms as president (1817–1825), Calhoun had a distinguished record as secretary of war.

In 1824 and again in 1828 he was elected vice-president, serving under John Quincy Adams and then under Andrew Jackson. Shrewd, intelligent, and ambitious, Calhoun seemed headed for the presidency as Jackson's chosen successor. This possibility was dashed, however, when he broke with Jackson over nullification and the Peggy Eaton affair. Calhoun resigned from the vice-presidency in 1832 and was immediately chosen by the South Carolina legislature to serve in the U.S. Senate. Except for a brief period as President Tyler's secretary of state, when he secured the annexation of Texas (1844–1845), Calhoun remained in the Senate until his death.

Political Tactics. In the late 1820s, Calhoun had switched from a nationalist to a states' rights position. Beginning with *The South Carolina Exposition and Protest* (1828) and ending with the posthumously published *Discourse on the Constitution,* Calhoun labored to devise a system whereby the minority South could be guaranteed protection against the majority North and West. He proposed a variety of schemes including sectional referendums and a dual executive (North and South), each armed with a veto.

He was an original thinker who dealt with the difficult problem of minority rights in a majoritarian democracy; yet most of Calhoun's theories were obstructionist, aiming at upholding slavery and the rights of the small slaveholding class. Although he died a decade before the Civil War, he was the chief intellectual architect of Southern secession.

See also Eaton Affair; Nullification; War Hawks.

Consult (III) Capers, 1960; Wiltse, 1944-1949.

—Douglas Miller, *Michigan State University*

CALIFORNIA, the 31st state, admitted to the Union on Sept. 9, 1850. Spanish sailors entered San Diego Bay in 1542; in 1579, it was explored by Sir Francis Drake. The first Spanish settlement was made in 1769; the first American wagon train reached California in 1826. Andrew Jackson, recognizing the San Francisco area as a gateway to trade with the Far East, tried to purchase it as early as 1835. American settlers began coming in large numbers as early as 1841. In 1846 the Bear Flag Revolt helped overthrow Mexican rule, and in 1848 Mexico officially ceded the area to the United States.

The discovery of gold in 1849 brought an onrush of settlers, and it was admitted as a state under the Compromise of 1850. The capital is Sacramento; the legislature is bicameral. The population in 1970 was 19,953,134.

See also Bear Flag Revolt; Compromise of 1850; Gold Rushes.

CALIFORNIA GOLD RUSH. *See* Gold Rushes.

CALVERT FAMILY, lords proprietor of Maryland. Sir George Calvert (1580-1632), later first Lord Baltimore, was a civil servant under Charles I and an investor in the Virginia Company who had to resign his office when he converted to Roman Catholicism. Determined to find an overseas refuge for persecuted English and Irish Catholics, he eventually turned to the Chesapeake Bay region despite the heated opposition of prominent Virginians. Contemplating a feudal regime for the colony, he secured a proprietary charter for "Maryland" from Charles I, only to die before it was issued.

His son Cecilius (1605-1675), also a Catholic, took over the project, funded the colony in 1634, and successfully retained control despite the Puritan Revolution in England and a sequence of civil wars and rebellions in the colony, where Protestants increasingly outnumbered Catholics. His son Charles

(1637-1715) lost the power to govern the colony during the Glorious Revolution (1688-1689) but retained full title to the land.

When the fourth and fifth Lords Baltimore emerged as Anglicans, the government was restored to them in 1716. In the next half-century the family converted Maryland into one of the world's most lucrative pieces of real estate. Frederick, sixth and last Lord Baltimore, was a peculiarly degenerate man who apparently lacked the imagination to spend all his wealth. His death in 1771 without legitimate heirs initiated a succession of sordid intrigues to gain control of his estate. The tangle had not yet been resolved when American independence came.

See also Maryland; Roman Catholics.

Consult (I) Barker, 1940.

—John M. Murrin, *Princeton University*

CAMDEN, BATTLE OF (1780), British victory that led to the invasion of North Carolina. *See* Revolutionary War Battles.

CANADA. *See* French Colonies.

CANALS. Following the completion of the Erie Canal by New York State in 1825, a canal mania swept the nation. States in the Midwest and upper South—Ohio, Indiana, Illinois, Maryland, Virginia, and Pennsylvania—joined the canal race, trying to catch up with the New England states and New York, which had begun building earlier. Cities and states competed with one another politically and economically, and legislatures encouraged canal building so much that heavy speculation took place.

Later canals were rarely as successful as the Erie. Philadelphia was linked to Pittsburgh and hooked into a canal system from the Atlantic Coast to the Delaware and Ohio rivers. Through the Chesapeake and Ohio Canal, built in 1828-1850, the Potomac was also linked to the Ohio by a cooperative scheme between Maryland and Virginia—a rare example of noncompetition in these frantic years. To get Pennsylvania's coal into New York City, New Jersey built the Morris Canal, connecting Jersey City and the Delaware River. New York was also joined to Philadelphia by an inland water system when New Jersey finished the Delaware and Raritan Canal. In Canada the Welland Canal, completed in 1833, was built around Niagara Falls to connect Lake Erie and Lake Ontario. It was replaced in 1932 by the Welland Ship Canal.

In the Midwest, the Illinois River was joined to Lake Michigan and to the upper Mississippi water system. America's longest canal—the Wabash and Erie—built between 1832 and 1856, opened up the northern Indiana region. It linked Evansville, in southwestern Indiana on the Ohio River, with Toledo on

John C. Calhoun, apostle of states' rights and nullification, in early Matthew Brady photograph.

Sault Ste. Marie Canal, connecting Lake Huron and Lake Superior, facilitated trade on the Great Lakes.

Joseph G. Cannon's dictatorial tactics as Speaker of the House led to revolt that ended his control of Rules Committee.

Industrialist Andrew Carnegie built fortune in steel and devoted later life to philanthropy.

Lake Erie by crossing Indiana diagonally before entering Ohio. It was more than 450 miles long, and it lost money. Many state governments lost money on their canals, and in the Panic of 1837 they defaulted on their foreign debts.

Role of Canals. Canals had certain disadvantages and were always too slow for much passenger traffic—if safer than the muddy roads and trails of the period. Canals were subject to climatic conditions, especially ice and snow, of which there was plenty in the Northeast and Midwest. Yet, they were greatly superior to the mule train or the wagon for the movement of heavy, bulky cargoes such as grain, flour, barreled pork, cotton, iron ore, and coal that did not require speed.

They helped to open up wildernesses into thriving farmlands, and they stimulated the growth of Western cities such as Cincinnati, Buffalo, Toledo, and Cleveland. The ports of the Great Lakes owed their growth to canals. However, railroads came close behind them, and their period of rapid growth was over by 1850, at which time the United States had about 3,700 miles of waterways.

See also Erie Canal.
Consult (III) Taylor, 1968.
—Peter d'A. Jones, *University of Illinois, Chicago Circle*

CANNON, JOSEPH G(URNEY) (1836–1926), powerful speaker of the U.S. House of Representatives. An Illinois lawyer, he served (1873–1891) in the House of Representatives, where he earned a reputation as a profane speaker, hard drinker, and demon poker player. Cannon was one of the most conservative members of the House, railing regularly against "class and social legislation."

Defeated for reelection in 1890, Cannon regained his seat in 1892 and in 1902 was elected speaker of the House. By his control of the Rules Committee, "Uncle Joe" became a virtual dictator over the legislative process. After an abortive attempt in 1909, a coalition of Insurgents and Democrats led a successful revolt in 1910 that expanded the membership of the Rules Committee from 5 to 15, had them elected rather than appointed, and specifically barred the speaker from service. Although the effort to remove Cannon as speaker failed, he was defeated for reelection in the Progressive surge of 1912. Returned to office in 1914, he served until his retirement in 1923.
Consult (V) Bolles, 1951.

CARDOZO, BENJAMIN (NATHAN) (1870–1938), lawyer and jurist of distinction whose liberal but balanced judgments profoundly influenced the Supreme Court in its consideration of New Deal legislation. A descendant of colonial settlers who were Sephardic Jews, he was born in New York City. His private tutor was Horatio Alger. Cardozo was educated at

Columbia University and admitted to the bar in 1891. For 22 years his practice of specialized law was unknown except to members of his profession, who esteemed him for his learning, sensitivity, and tolerance. He was elected to the New York Supreme Court in 1913, and he had an outstanding career there and on the state appeals court.

When Justice Oliver Wendell Holmes retired from the Supreme Court in 1932, President Hoover appointed Cardozo his successor. During his tenure of less than 6 years the Court dealt with the controversial legislation of the New Deal. He wrote 150 opinions notable for their legal reasoning and skill in adapting traditional principles to changing social values. In addition to his frequently cited judicial writings, he wrote *The Nature of the Judicial Process* (1921) and related works.

Cardozo held that the intent of historical law, not its form, should guide justice through successive generations. Government of a modern industrial society by a constitution written for an agrarian land invited legal conflicts that could only be resolved by the flexible application of law to the problems of new generations. He thought that the value of the Constitution lay in its intrinsic generality and that the function of the judiciary was to apply established principles to current trends.

CAREY ACT (1894) authorized federal land grants to the states. *See* National Reclamation Act (1902).

CARMICHAEL, STOKELY (1941–), a leader of the black power movement. He was born in Port-of-Spain, Trinidad, and educated at Howard University (1964). In 1960 he headed south, where he participated in Congress of Racial Equality (CORE) activities and became a leader of the Student Nonviolent Coordinating Committee (SNCC).

Carmichael left SNCC because the organization did not agree with his militant philosophy. From 1967 through 1969, he was an important voice in the Black Panthers and then emerged as a Pan-Africanist in exile in Guinea. In late 1972, Carmichael returned to the United States with his wife, singer Miriam Makeba, to seek black unity.

CARNEGIE, ANDREW (1835–1919), American industrialist and philanthropist. The son of a Scottish weaver, he emigrated with his impoverished parents to America in 1848. Self-educated, he worked in various jobs before Thomas Scott hired him as personal telegrapher and secretary in 1853. As Scott rose in the hierarchy of the Pennsylvania Railroad, Carnegie did also, and in 1860 he became superintendent of its Pittsburgh division.

Carnegie resigned in 1865 to concentrate on selling steel bridges for his Keystone

Bridge Co. He founded Union Iron Mills (1868) and in 1873, after a trip to England, decided to concentrate on production of Bessemer steel. He convinced railroads to buy steel rails, and by 1879 his company produced 75 percent of all American steel. His income eventually rose above $25 million annually. Always innovative, he adopted the open-hearth technique and acquired much of the Mesabi iron range during the 1890s.

In 1901, Carnegie decided to retire and devote his efforts to philanthropy, selling his company for almost $500 million to the combine that was creating U.S. Steel. In *Wealth* (1889) and the *Gospel of Wealth* (1900), Carnegie had claimed that rich men must use their money for public benefit. Accordingly, he endowed more than 2,500 libraries, gave away organs, donated public buildings, and created foundations that have distributed more than $350 million. He managed to dispose of 90 percent of his fortune before he died.

Consult (V) Wall, 1970.
—George Lankevich, *Bronx Community College of The City University of New York*

CAROLINA. *See* North Carolina; South Carolina.

CAROLINE AFFAIR (1837–1838). In 1837 a rebellion against British rule was crushed in Canada, but the remaining rebels took refuge on Navy Island on the Canadian side of the Niagara River. Anti-British Americans supported the rebels, and a small, American-owned steamboat, the *Caroline,* was chartered to supply the rebel forces. On Dec. 29, 1837, Canadian militiamen crossed the river to the American side, boarded the *Caroline,* and burned her, killing one American, Amos Durfee.

The affair triggered a patriotic uproar but cooler heads prevailed in Washington, D.C., and London. President Van Buren proclaimed American neutrality (Jan. 5, 1838) and sent Gen. Winfield Scott to the troubled area. The Canadian rebels were persuaded to surrender their arms to the U.S. militia on Jan. 13, 1838. Anglo-American tensions eased some, although they flared again on May 29, when some Americans burned a Canadian steamer on the American side of the St. Lawrence River, and in 1840–1841, when a Canadian was tried in New York State for the murder of Durfee. Not until the Webster-Ashburton Treaty (1842) were British-American relations normalized.

CARPETBAGGERS, Northerners who moved to the South during Reconstruction. The term had severe pejorative overtones, indicating a class of low-born, poor (all that they owned could be carried in a carpetbag), greedy, uneducated, unscrupulous adventurers and exploiters who flocked like vultures to feed on the carcass of the defeated Confederacy.

CARTERET FAMILY. Sir George Carteret (1610–1680), prominent in England after the Restoration of Charles II (1660), became in 1663 one of the eight proprietors of the Carolinas. Through John Carteret (1690–1763)—Earl Granville—who maintained his Carolina holdings, the family retained its influence in the colonies until the mideighteenth century. In 1664, Sir George and Lord Berkeley were assigned the lands between the Hudson and Delaware rivers, which were named New Jersey. After the death of Sir George, his widow sold his holdings in the colony to William Penn and a group of Quakers.

Philip Carteret (1639–1682), the first colonial governor of New Jersey, was appointed by Sir George, his distant cousin. Philip arrived in the colony in 1665 and presided over the first legislative assembly in 1668. After a rebellion in 1676, the province was divided, and Philip became the governor of East Jersey. Despite some controversy concerning his authority, he governed East Jersey until his death.

CARTIER, JACQUES, French explorer of Canada. *See* Exploration and Discovery; French Colonies.

CARVER, GEORGE WASHINGTON (1861–1943), former slave who became a leading agricultural scientist of his day and world famous as the discoverer of hundreds of industrial and commercial uses of the peanut.

Born a slave in Missouri during the Civil War, Carver did not begin college until age 30, but he graduated with honors in 1894 from Iowa State University, a leading center for agricultural science. In 1896 he accepted an invitation from Booker T. Washington to join the faculty at Tuskegee Institute in Alabama. Washington, with his organizational genius, and Carver, with his genius for agricultural innovation and research, combined to solidify Tuskegee's reputation as America's outstanding black vocational college.

In his own view, Carver's most significant contribution to Tuskegee and Southern blacks was his "moveable school," an agricultural clinic that introduced farmers to the importance of crop rotation, nitrate-fixing legumes, and modern fertilizers. Carver was also one of the few Southern scientists (black or white) who championed the "chemurgic movement," which stressed the importance of developing chemical and industrial uses of farm products. He developed hundreds of uses for soybeans, cowpeas, sweet potatoes, and, especially, peanuts.

Carver's work on the peanut was prompted in part by the spread of the boll weevil, a pest that devastated the South's cot-

Burning of the *Caroline,* a U.S. ship, by Canadian militia in 1837 heightened anti-British feelings in United States.

George Washington Carver's agricultural experiments helped diversify Southern agriculture.

ton fields. In 1915, when farmers overproduced peanuts as a substitute for cotton, Carver literally tore the peanut apart while discovering its use in more than 300 commercial and industrial forms, including soap, cooking oil, butter, flour, cosmetics, paper, dyes, soil conditioners, adhesives, and plastics. Not all these proved commercially successful, but the peanut became the sixth most important U.S. agricultural product and helped Southern farmers escape their dependence on cotton. Carver left his estate to the establishment of the George W. Carver Foundation at Tuskegee.

Consult (IX) Bontemps, 1954; Elliott, 1966; Holt, 1943.
—Sheldon Avery, *The Johns Hopkins University*

CASABLANCA CONFERENCE, Anglo-American conference on World War II strategy held in Casablanca, Morocco, on Jan. 14-25, 1943. President Roosevelt and Prime Minister Churchill agreed to continue the Mediterranean offensive with a landing in Sicily and to postpone the invasion of France until 1944. They also planned a three-pronged drive against Japanese-held islands in the Pacific and an Anglo-American-Chinese campaign in Burma. The most significant and controversial decision reached at Casablanca, however, was the announcement that the United States and Britain would accept nothing less than the "unconditional surrender" of Germany and Japan.

CASH CROPS. *See* Plantation System.

CATHER, WILLA (1876-1947), American author. *See* Literature.

CATHOLICS. *See* Roman Catholics.

CATO CONSPIRACY, slave uprising. On Sept. 9, 1739, about 20 slaves killed 2 warehouse guards at Stono, S.C., 20 miles southwest of Charleston, and stole firearms and ammunition. Heading south toward St. Augustine, the blacks killed all the whites they encountered except an innkeeper named Wallace who was "kind to his Slaves." As the deadly procession continued, about 60 slaves joined the original rebels, who marched "with Colours displayed and two Drums beating."

White authorities acted quickly to restore order. Guards were posted at roads and ferries, and the militia was dispatched. About 10 hours after the insurrection began, a detachment of 80 militiamen encountered the blacks resting 10 miles south of Stono. The better-equipped militiamen initially shot 14 slaves and during the subsequent pursuit killed 20 more and took 40 prisoners, some of whom were later executed. In all about 50 blacks and 25 whites died as a result of the conspiracy.

See also Slave Revolts, Colonial.

CATONSVILLE NINE, a group of nine Catholic priests led by Father Daniel Berrigan and his brother Philip. In an emotional trial, they were convicted of the napalm burning of 378 draft records in Catonsville, Md., in 1969. Most of the defendants received 3-year sentences for interfering with the Selective Service. The group was essentially protesting against the Vietnam War, maltreatment of U.S. blacks, and the exploitation of the poor in Latin America.

CATTLE FRONTIER. *See* Frontier in American History.

CENTRAL INTELLIGENCE AGENCY (CIA), organization that coordinates the intelligence activities of various governmental agencies of the United States as a means of strengthening national security. The CIA is administered by a director and deputy director appointed by the president with Senate approval. Created by the National Security Act of 1947, the CIA is technically under the authority of the National Security Council (NSC), to which it reports. Nevertheless, the CIA may act semiautonomously in investigating matters pertaining to the national interest. Information obtained from these investigations is used to advise the NSC in its policy-making functions.

Adverse public opinion about the activities of the CIA was generated by revelations in the late 1960s of the agency's involvement in foreign aid programs, its alleged role in deposing the Diem regime in South Vietnam, and subsidies paid to student organizations. In 1973 the agency's image was tarnished by its participation in domestic political affairs.

See also National Security Acts (1947, 1949).

CENTRAL PACIFIC RAILROAD. *See* Railroads.

CENTRAL TREATY ORGANIZATION (CENTO), mutual defense organization among Turkey, Iran, Pakistan, and Britain formed in 1955 by the Baghdad Pact to provide a northern tier of defense against Communist penetration of the Middle East. Although the United States is not a member, it has been closely associated with CENTO.

CENTO functions through a council of ministers who meet once a year, deputy ministers who meet every two weeks, and a permanent secretariat. There are also military and economic committees. The organization has no military command structure, and no combat troops have been assigned to it. In the 1965 and 1971 wars between Pakistan and India, the CENTO member received little more than verbal support from its allies.

CERRO GORDO, BATTLE OF (1847), rout of Santa Anna's troops by Americans under Gen. Winfield Scott. *See* Mexican War.

CHAMBERS, WHITTAKER, former Communist who accused Alger Hiss of treason. *See* Hiss-Chambers Case.

CHAMPLAIN, SAMUEL DE (1567–1635), French explorer known as the Father of Canada. The son of a navy captain, he fought with the army before making a voyage to the West Indies in 1601. After writing a description of his journey, he sailed for Canada in 1603 and explored the upper St. Lawrence River. He was convinced of the need for exploration and colonization and joined the expedition of Pierre de Monts in 1604. Subsequently, Champlain visited Nova Scotia and investigated the Maine coast.

On July 3, 1608, Champlain founded a trading post at what is now Quebec, and in 1609 he again visited the St. Lawrence region and actively aided the Algonkians and Hurons against the Iroquois. At that time Champlain traveled up the Richelieu River to Lake Champlain, which he explored. He was made commandant of New France in 1612. During a Huron expedition in 1615, he spent the winter with them and wrote the first account of their life style.

In pursuit of his desire to establish a Christian settlement for Frenchmen and Indians, Champlain often visited France to request aid. Partially to propagandize his cause, he published his most important work, *Voyages,* in 1632. When Quebec fell to the British in 1629, Champlain was sent to England as a prisoner. When New France returned to French hands, Champlain returned and died in Quebec. He was one of the most successful colonizers, but he made a serious mistake in alienating the powerful Iroquois tribe, which allied itself with the British.

See also French Colonies.
Consult (I) Bishop, 1948.

CHANCELLORSVILLE (MAY 2, 1863), Confederate victory marred by the death of Stonewall Jackson. *See* Civil War Battles.

CHANNING, WILLIAM ELLERY (1780–1842), one of the founders of Unitarianism. Channing, born in Newport, R.I., graduated from Harvard in 1796 and became the minister of the Federal Street Church in Boston in 1803, a pastorate he held until his death.

He broke with Calvinist theology mainly over the Calvinist doctrine of the depravity of man. Channing insisted that the Scriptures showed that man was capable of dignity and reason; he preached a gospel of the love and goodness of both God and man and rejected the image of an angry, jealous God. The Unitarian controversy began about 1815. Channing was reluctant to make a formal break with the orthodox Calvinists or to lead a new religious group, but in 1819 he set forth what were to become the basic beliefs of the new Unitar-ians. In 1820 he formed the Berry Street Conference of Liberal Ministers, the precursor of the American Unitarian Association, founded in 1825.

By this time Channing had become not only an influential religious leader but a significant literary figure as well. He directly influenced many of the New England writers, including Ralph Waldo Emerson, and helped pave the way for the popularity of the Transcendental movement. He also became a leading social critic, advocating adult education and urging Americans not to imitate European culture. He vociferously opposed slavery yet even more vigorously opposed the idea of civil war.

See also Transcendentalism; Unitarianism.

CHAPLIN, CHARLIE (CHARLES SPENCER) (1889–), British actor, director, producer, writer, and composer who became a world-famous comedian through his American-produced movies. He was born in London and appeared at an early age in London music halls. In 1913, while on tour in the United States with a pantomime troupe, he attracted the attention of Mack Sennett, for whom he turned out more than 35 one-reel movie comedies with the Keystone Company (1914–1915). Later, he signed contracts with other companies and developed the famous lovable "little tramp" with the trick derby, minute mustache, baggy trousers, oversized shoes, and awkward walk.

In 1923 he founded United Artists with D. W. Griffith, Douglas Fairbanks, Sr., and Mary Pickford. Chaplin composed his own background music for some of his notable films, including *The Gold Rush, The Kid, The Circus, City Lights, Modern Times, The Great Dictator* (the first film in which he spoke), and *Limelight.*

Chaplin, still an English subject in spite of his many years in Hollywood, moved to Switzerland in 1952 because of tax difficulties with the U.S. government brought on by politics. His controversial film, *A King in New York* (1957), made in England, was not shown in the United States. In the spring of 1972 Chaplin, with his wife Oona O'Neill Chaplin, returned to America to receive a variety of long-deserved accolades, including a tribute at Lincoln Center and a special Oscar.

CHAPULTEPEC, BATTLE OF (1847), American victory that preceded capture of Mexico City. *See* Mexican War.

CHARLES RIVER BRIDGE v. WARREN BRIDGE (1837), major Supreme Court decision on contracts. In 1785, Massachusetts had chartered the Charles River Bridge Company to span the river and connect Boston to Charlestown. The company was eventually allowed to collect tolls for

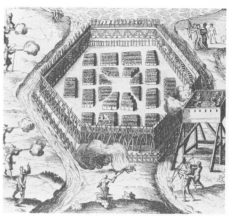

French under Samuel de Champlain and Indian allies attack Onondaga Indian village in 1615.

Charlie Chaplin, with Jackie Coogan in *The Kid.*

Salmon P. Chase, Chief Justice of the Supreme Court during the difficult years after the Civil War.

Farm workers were unionized by Caesar Chavez, who organized boycotts to support their demands.

a period of 70 years. However, in 1828 a later legislature chartered a second company to build a parallel bridge, which would be free. The Charles River Bridge company sued for breach of contract, and the case was appealed to the Supreme Court.

Two issues important to the growth of American society were at odds. The first involved the sanctity of contracts, without which, as Chief Justice John Marshall had said in the Dartmouth College case of 1819, economic growth was not possible ("If business is to prosper, men must have assurance that contracts will be enforced"). The second point was that old monopolies might damage the public welfare.

Since the original contract of 1785 the country had undergone an economic revolution—canals, railroads, and many new businesses had sprung up, and the population had boomed. If new enterprises were to be hamstrung by privileges granted decades before, economic growth would be retarded. In addition, the Jacksonian spirit of democracy was opposed to monopoly. So Chief Justice Taney decided against the Charles River Bridge Company and in favor of the free bridge, the latest charter, economic growth, and the consuming public. His decision significantly modified Marshall's Dartmouth College decision.

See also Dartmouth College v. Woodward (1819); Taney, Roger B.

CHASE, SALMON P(ORTLAND) (1808–1873),

5th Chief Justice of the Supreme Court. He also served as a senator from Ohio and as its governor, as secretary of the treasury, and was a leading Republican antislavery figure.

Born in New Hampshire, he was admitted to the bar in 1829 and began a legal practice in Cincinnati in 1830. He was also active in the abolitionist movement and defended fugitive slaves. In 1848 Chase moved onto the national political scene when he was elected to the Senate.

On the death of Chief Justice Taney in 1864, Lincoln appointed Chase, who had recently been his treasury secretary (1861–1864). In 1868, during Reconstruction, Chase presided fairly over the impeachment trial of President Johnson. Chase was against quick reopening of federal courts in the South and favored some aspects of Radical Reconstruction. Two of the major decisions of his Court were *Ex Parte Milligan* (1866) and the *Slaughterhouse Cases* (1873).

Having first sought the presidency in 1856, Chase tried again unsuccessfully in 1868 and in 1872. Swayed by flattery, despite his strict religious and moral convictions, and ambitious for the presidency, the talented Chase was difficult and self-righteous.

See also Ex Parte Milligan (1866); Slaughterhouse Cases (1873).

CHATTANOOGA (NOV. 23–25, 1863), battle that led to final Confederate withdrawal from Tennessee. *See* Civil War Battles.

CHAVEZ, CESAR (ESTRADA) (1927–), labor leader who heads the United Farm Workers Organization Committee of the AFL-CIO, which he founded in 1962. The unionist was born near Yuma, Arizona, the son of a poor farmer. When he was 10, the family began to follow the harvest as migrant workers.

Chavez became interested in improving the conditions of migrant workers and gradually emerged as a charismatic leader of the drive to found a farm workers' union. He first came to wide public attention in 1965, when he called a strike of grape pickers in the San Joaquin Valley, California, that eventually won union contracts with many of the major wine processors.

After being bedridden for a year with a back ailment, Chavez began touring the country early in 1969 to broaden support for his cause. His campaign led to organizing migrant farm workers in other areas, notably the citrus fruit and lettuce industries.

CHECKS AND BALANCES. *See* Separation of Powers.

CHEROKEE NATION v. GEORGIA (1831). During the early nineteenth century, the federal and state governments made extensive efforts to eject Indian tribes from settled areas. By 1827 the Cherokee, a tribe in Georgia that had adapted to white civilization, were the last tribe in full strength in the East.

Since 1791 various treaties had recognized the Cherokee as a nation. In the summer of 1827, Cherokee delegates met at New Echota, Ga., to formalize this status with a written constitution. The U.S. Constitution, however, forbade creating a new state within an existing state without the latter's consent. Georgia quickly urged the federal government to remove the Cherokee Nation, which would yield all tribal possessions to Georgia, and Congress offered the Indians various inducements to agree to move.

The insult of such allowances, brutal state legislation, Andrew Jackson's inaugural address urging Indian removal, and the 1830 Indian Removal Act led the Cherokees to file for an injunction that would prevent Georgia from enforcing its laws within Cherokee territory. Although the Supreme Court was sympathetic to the Indian request, it ruled that the Cherokees did not have the status of a foreign nation and that their right to the land was only through occupancy.

Later, in *Worcester v. Georgia* (1832), Chief Justice John Marshall declared that Georgia had no right to molest the Cherokees. However, President Jackson defied the Court by refusing to restrain Georgia from harassing the Indians. In 1835 a minority of Cherokees were bribed to sign a treaty surrendering all lands. They were then driven west in a forced march known as the "Trail of Tears," during which a quarter of the Cherokees died.

—Marion Nowak, *Michigan State University*

CHESAPEAKE AND LEOPARD (1807), ships involved in an Anglo-American maritime controversy. In the spring of 1807 a number of British seamen deserted from the ships off Chesapeake Bay, and several of them enlisted on American vessels. When the *Chesapeake,* an American frigate, sailed on June 22, 1807, it was hailed by the British frigate *Leopard* and asked to hand over the British deserters on board. The American commander, Captain James Barron, refused, and the *Leopard* first fired across her bow and then into her, killing 3 Americans and wounding 18. The British seized 4 men, but it was subsequently discovered that only 1 was a deserter. The other 3 were Americans, 2 of them blacks. When the *Chesapeake* returned to port, there was a general demand for war. President Jefferson, however, decided against recommending war and at the end of the year attempted to change the policies of the European powers by economic pressures.

CHESAPEAKE AND OHIO CANAL. See Canals.

CHEYENNE-ARAPAHO WAR (1861–1864), conflict caused by movement of miners into Colorado. *See* Indian Wars, Western.

CHICAGO SEVEN, group of seven defendants, including Abbie Hoffman, who were charged with conspiracy to incite a riot at the 1968 Democratic National Convention. During the sensational, widely publicized trial Judge Julius Hoffman also convicted the seven defendants and two defense lawyers of contempt. Eventually, however, all the defendants were acquitted of charges that they conspired to incite a riot and spent a short time in prison on the contempt charge. However, the jury found five of the defendants guilty of crossing state lines with intent to incite a riot. These convictions were dissipated in a variety of appeals.

See also Hoffman, Abbie.

CHICANOS, word first used to describe refugees from the Mexican Revolution of 1910 who fled to the United States. The term fell into disuse until spring 1969, when, during a Youth Liberation Conference in Denver, Rodolfo Gonzales, director of the barrio Crusade for Justice, suggested it as a description for Mexican-American militants. To further Chicano indentification, Gonzales proposed their use of "pochismos"—a barrio slang—and adherence to a nationalistic conception of "La Raza!"—the race.

CHIEF JOSEPH, Nez Percé Indian leader who led an epic defensive retreat from U.S. forces. *See* Indian Wars, Western.

CHINESE EXCLUSION. Following the acquisition of California by the United States, there was a large influx of Chinese into the state. The immigrants, who had the right to emigrate but not to become citizens because of an 1868 treaty, were welcomed at first as cheap labor. During the next 10 years much anti-Chinese sentiment developed in California, and a ban on Chinese immigration was suggested.

In a treaty of 1880, China allowed the United States some right to restrict but not prohibit Chinese immigration. The Chinese Exclusion Act of 1882 finally banned immigration of Chinese laborers for a decade. In 1894 another treaty with the Chinese restricted immigration for 10 years, after which Congress continued the exclusion unilaterally until 1924. Since 1924, Congress has enacted much immigration legislation, including the McCarran-Walter Act of 1952 and the Immigration and Nationality Act of 1965, both of which allow a certain number of Asians to emigrate to the United States each year.

See also Immigration.

CHIPPEWA, BATTLE OF (1814), battle in which Americans under Gen. Winfield Scott defeated a superior British force. *See* War of 1812.

CHISHOLM, SHIRLEY (1924–   ), Democratic congresswoman known as an advocate of women's rights and civil rights. Born in Brooklyn, she graduated from Brooklyn College and Columbia University. A teacher, nursery school director, and educational consultant, Chisholm worked on child care centers and also became active in Brooklyn reform politics. She served as a member of the New York State Assembly from 1964 to 1968, when she was elected to Congress from Brooklyn.

In Congress, Chisholm refused to be seated on the Agriculture Committee, citing the lack of agriculture in her district, and was appointed instead to the Education and Labor Committee. She cosponsored the Equal Rights Amendment, as well as legislation to repeal the draft and establish a volunteer army and to give fuller tax benefits to the unmarried. She also supported congressional reform, withdrawal from Southeast Asia, a minimum annual income, and day care and voted against all appropriations for the military. In 1972, Chisholm became the first black and the first woman to contend in the primaries for the Democratic presidential nomination, running on the slogan "Unbought and Unbossed."

Consult (IX) Chisholm, 1971.

CHISHOLM v. GEORGIA (1793), one of the earliest important decisions of the Supreme Court. Some South Carolina citizens, the heirs

Anti-Chinese prejudice in the West led to outbreaks of violence, as in Denver, and Chinese exclusion treaties that severely restricted Chinese immigration.

Shirley Chisholm, characterizing herself as "unbought and unbossed," supported black rights and equal opportunity for women as a congresswoman.

Winston Churchill paces the deck of H.M.S. *Prince of Wales* shortly after he and President Roosevelt had worked out the Atlantic Charter in 1941.

Enrollees in the Civilian Conservation Corps, a New Deal program to employ young men, gather outside their mountain barracks.

of Alexander Chisholm, sued the state of Georgia in the federal courts in order to secure compensation for confiscated property. The Court, under Chief Justice John Jay, held that Chisholm could bring such a suit and that it was constitutional for a state to be sued by a citizen of another state. Georgia refused to comply with the Court's decision, and this early Court attempt to enhance federal power was negated by the Eleventh Amendment (1798), which specifically prohibited this type of suit.

See also Amendments, Constitutional.

CHOUTEAU, R. A., AND PIERRE, important Western fur traders. See Fur Trade.

CHRISTIAN SCIENCE, doctrine that relies on spiritual healing. See Eddy, Mary Baker.

CHURCHILL, WINSTON S(PENCER) (1874–1965), British prime minister who played a major role in World War II. A member of England's social and intellectual elite, he was defeated for Parliament in his first attempt in 1899 but was victorious in 1900 owing to his exploits in the Boer War. He became critical of his own Conservative Party and switched to the Liberals, joining the new Liberal government as junior minister in 1905 and rising to become the first lord of the admiralty during World War I.

In the early 1920s Churchill saw British politics in terms of socialism versus antisocialism; he felt that antisocialists must unite to face the peril from the left. In the general election of 1922, he was defeated, and by 1924 he was ready to rejoin the Conservative Party. He was made chancellor of the exchequer, but his intransigent opposition to dominion status for India and to coalition government led to his exclusion from office.

Throughout the 1930s, Churchill warned against the dangers of Nazi Germany. Finally, in May 1940, after the parliamentary debate on the Norway campaign, Neville Chamberlain resigned, and Churchill was named prime minister. His "finest hour" was the period from 1940 through 1945, when he was the leader, spokesman, and symbol of the British war effort. He cultivated a special relationship with the United States and President Roosevelt.

The Conservatives lost the election of 1945, but Churchill continued as head of the party. He opposed the policies of the USSR and called for a united Europe as well as for cooperation among the English-speaking peoples and a summit conference of world powers. In 1951, he again became prime minister. Churchill relinquished the post in 1955, but he continued to serve in the House of Commons until 1964.

Consult (VII) Churchill, 1966–1971.
—Martin Gruberg, University of Wisconsin, Oshkosh

CHURUBUSCO, BATTLE OF (1847), American victory during advance on Mexico City. See Mexican War.

CIO. See Congress of Industrial Organizations.

CITIZEN GENET AFFAIR (1793), controversy surrounding the actions of Edmond Charles Genêt (1763–1834), French minister to the United States. When he arrived in the United States in April 1793, Genêt was received enthusiastically. He misinterpreted this friendship and thought he could act as though the United States were an active participant in the war in Europe.

For a time Genêt was the center of plans to use the United States as a base for anti-British and anti-Spanish operations. He acted quickly to fit out privateers that would sail from American ports to attack British shipping, and he contacted Western leaders with a view to organizing an expedition to attack Spanish New Orleans. These acts alienated even pro-French leaders such as Secretary of State Thomas Jefferson, and, when the American government decided that Genêt was going beyond them to appeal to the American people, it asked the French to recall him. Fearing that it would be unsafe to return to revolutionary France, Genêt asked for asylum in the United States, became an American citizen, and spent the rest of his life in America.

CITY. In contrast to the long history of city development in Europe, the American transformation from village to city took place in an unusually short period of time. In the 1770s, 4 percent of the colonies' population lived in urban areas; today 70 percent of Americans are urban dwellers.

Early History. From the original five port towns of the seventeenth century—Boston, Newport, Charleston, Philadelphia, and New York—there arose by the time of the American Revolution an urban influence that was completely disproportionate to the small numbers of people that lived in these towns. Focal point for the Revolution, the city gave the New World an intellectual, economic, and political identity. Movement to cities intensified in the first half of the nineteenth century. Chicago in 1830 had 40 people, yet 25 years later it was a city of 60,000.

The Industrial Revolution. After the Civil War, rivalry among cities erupted and formed an inherent part of the city dynamic. The winners of the rivalry, such as New York, created great wealth for their businessmen. For the losers there was bankruptcy, depression, and large-scale emigration. From that time on, city administrations set their tax rates to attract business and financed the construction of educational, recreational, and cultural facilities, largely in response to competing attractions from neighboring cities.

Industrialization, with its technology and division of labor, brought fundamental changes in preindustrial city characteristics. Population increased, often as much as 1,000 percent, and modern transportation increased the commuting radius as much as 100 times. This mobility and density led to the breakdown of the demarcation between city and country as urban areas developed amidst open spaces. City politics became linked with vast obligations and opportunities concerning material production and services, and residential areas developed at considerable distances from work areas. As occupational techniques changed and became more sophisticated, upward social mobility for the industrial worker led to a constant movement of both skilled and unskilled workers. By the start of the twentieth century fusion began among several large cities requiring common facilities such as electric power and highway transportation, and thus the idea of the region as a unit of planning emerged.

With the need for more labor came immigrant migration. The majority of the 8 million people who came to the United States between 1880 and 1910 were South and East European Catholics and Jews. The cities, particularly on the East Coast, became chopped up into institutional preserves, which led to Irish politics, Italian unionism, Jewish commercialism and professionalism, and so on.

Black Influx, White Exodus. Beginning with World War I there was another major migration, the internal migration of the blacks from the Southern rural settings to the Northern cities. Blacks often moved into areas that had been ghettos. By World War II this movement had increased. At the end of the war the stage was set for the situation that has continued to the present.

By the early 1950s the white immigrants had been succeeded by their first- and second-generation descendants, who were sufficiently secure financially to think about realizing their prewar dream of a privately owned home. Aided by a federal program that encouraged home building, the exodus from the city began. Within a 10-year period New York saw 1 million of its white middle class move to nearby suburban areas. The blacks, in an accelerated migration from the South, arrived in the cities to find the obstacles of racial prejudice, poverty, and blocked opportunities. The blacks' frustrations resulted, by the mid-1960s, in rebellion and riot in numerous cities, and this violence in turn spurred the middle-class whites' determination to leave the inner cities. The middle class was afraid and lacked confidence in the city's future.

Decline. By the early 1970s, the city's prospects were bleak; revenues were lost as the middle class and both large and small businesses moved to suburban areas, removing the city's financial lifeline. Crime increased and city services, financially starved, began to decline drastically. Erratic financial aid from the federal government often failed to halt the process.

Black political control, coercion, good intentions, city planning—all tried to stem the tide of the exodus but with few encouraging results. Some cities, such as New York and San Francisco with their commanding business and cultural enterprises, might suffer considerably but are not likely to collapse. Scores of smaller cities are in danger of becoming the setting for monolithic ghettos, abandoned to the poor, with the greater society making symbolic gestures of concern.

By 1971, 12 million more Americans lived in the suburbs than in the cities. In both psychology and population density the suburb is becoming an extension of the city. The inner city of the poor, the outer city (older suburbs) of the aspiring lower middle class (black and white), and the suburb itself now together make up the urban experience in America.

Consult (VIII) Callow, 1969; Gans, 1968; Gist and Fava, 1964; Green, 1965.

—Marvin D. Koenigsberg, *Brooklyn College of The City University of New York*

CIVILIAN CONSERVATION CORPS (CCC), agency created during the Hundred Days (1933) to provide work relief for young men. President Roosevelt, who had established a similar program in New York while governor, took a personal interest in the program, viewing it both as a means of getting urban youth out into the healthy countryside and as a means of providing labor for conservation work. The CCC was unique among federal agencies in that several executive departments shared in its administration.

Dispersed throughout the country in 1,500 camps, uniformed enrollees undertook a multitude of forest projects. Although nearly 3 million young men served during the 8 years of CCC's existence, it could not fully meet the needs of unemployed youth. In 1935 the National Youth Administration (NYA) was set up to provide training and work relief for students, young women, minorities, and others not adequately served by the CCC.

See also Hundred Days; New Deal.
Consult (VI) Salmond, 1967.

CIVILIAN PRODUCTION BOARD. *See* War Production Board (WPB).

CIVIL RIGHTS ACTS (1866, 1875). Congress passed two Civil Rights Acts during Reconstruction. The first, adopted on April 9, 1866, declared that all persons born in the United States, save Indians not taxed, were citizens of the United States. This overturned the Dred

Cincinnati's growth over half a century demonstrates the development of American cities. In 1789 there were only a few log cabins on the edge of the forest.

By 1802 the area was cleared, and new settlers were pouring into bustling Cincinnati.

An established city in 1841, Cincinnati filled the horizon and had bridges across the Ohio River.

"Well, ain't dat interestin'."

Justus in The Minneapolis Star

Attempts to control filibusters against civil rights measures have been frequently circumvented.

Judicial rulings against school segregation helped end segregation in other spheres.

Scott decision (1857) denying black Americans citizenship. The act further provided that all U.S. citizens, black and white, had equal legal and property rights. Thus Congress sought to counteract Southern Black Codes. President Johnson vetoed the bill because he thought it violated the states' rights and was too favorable toward blacks, but Congress overrode the veto.

Congress went much further in the Civil Rights Act of 1875, which forbade racial discrimination in hotels, public transportation, theaters, and other places of public amusement. It also provided that no one could be denied the right to sit on federal or state juries on account of race, color, or previous condition of servitude. In 1883 the Supreme Court struck down this statute.

See also Black Codes; Civil Rights Cases (1883); Reconstruction (1865–1877).

Consult (IV) Cox and Cox, 1963.

CIVIL RIGHTS ACTS (1957, 1960, 1964). The Civil Rights Act of 1957 established a Civil Rights Commission to investigate violations of citizens' voting rights based on race, color, national origin, or religion. The act of 1960 enabled the courts to appoint federal referees to protect black voting rights and made it a federal offense to obstruct court orders by threat of violence. These Civil Rights Acts, the first ones enacted since the post-Civil War era, were intended to protect the rights of black voters in federal elections.

The Civil Rights Act of 1964, on its way to enactment before President Kennedy's death and signed by President Johnson, was more comprehensive. It prohibited discrimination in the application of voting laws, in the use of federal funds (which could be withheld from public schools that continued segregation), and in public facilities such as hotels, restaurants, and playgrounds. It also established the Equal Employment Opportunities Commission (EEOC) to prevent discrimination in employment; Title VII prohibited discrimination in employment according to race or sex. The provision on sex was added in an attempt to kill the bill, but when it passed, had unforeseen consequences. The EEOC was inundated by complaints of sex discrimination and eventually took action to prevent it, as in its August 1968 ruling to prevent segregation of employment advertisements by sex.

See also Civil Rights Acts (1866, 1875).

CIVIL RIGHTS CASES (1883), five different cases in which blacks complained that their rights under the Civil Rights Act of 1875 had been violated in public places. The Supreme Court ruled against them, holding that the Fourteenth Amendment did not empower Congress to pass such legislation as the Civil Rights Act. Only discrimination by the state, not by private individuals, could be outlawed by Congress. Moreover, Congress could enact remedial legislation, not legislation designed to meet prospective ills. This decision effectively foreclosed for a long while federal action to protect blacks from discrimination by private individuals.

See also Civil Rights Acts (1866, 1875).

CIVIL RIGHTS MOVEMENT. The 350-year attempt to obtain equal rights for black Americans is the aspect of civil rights most familiar to Americans. Many other groups, including religious and political minorities, criminals, labor unions, the military, other ethnic minorities, and women, have often been an unrecognized part of the American attempt to define and preserve civil rights for all citizens.

Beginnings. The beginnings of the modern civil rights movement are directly traceable to the Civil War and Reconstruction periods. The omission from the Declaration of Independence of guarantees of freedom for slaves and the inclusion in the Constitution of recognition of slavery had to wait for the adoption of the Thirteenth Amendment after the Civil War to begin the period of redress. The Civil Rights Act of 1866 was the first federal legislation to attempt to give blacks equal rights under the law. The legislation was the forerunner of the Fourteenth Amendment, which guaranteed equal protection under the law to all citizens and granted citizenship to exslaves. Other legislation of the period made earnest efforts to secure equal rights for blacks. These attempts included the Civil Rights Act of 1875; the Enforcement Act of 1871; and the Fifteenth Amendment, which granted equal voting rights.

None of these measures was able to secure the goal of equal justice under the law for black Americans. A combination of conservative judicial opinions—as exemplified by the *Plessy v. Ferguson* decision (1896), which resulted in the legal doctrine of "separate but equal"—and the social failure of Americans to accept the validity of equal rights and opportunities for blacks, brought an end to an era of reform in civil rights.

Twentieth Century. *Brown v. Board of Education of Topeka* (1954) reversed the "separate but equal" doctrine and helped initiate new legislation, court decisions, and a changing climate of public opinion that broadened civil rights for black Americans. It also helped create a demand for expansion of equal rights and opportunities from other minorities. In 1957, Martin Luther King, Jr., achieved overnight fame when he led a black boycott of the Montgomery, Ala. bus system. King and his organizational vehicle, the Southern Christian Leadership Conference, challenged the leadership of the older civil rights groups such as the National Association for the Advancement of Colored People (NAACP) and the Urban

League in the new fight for civil rights. Congress, in its first major attempt at civil rights legislation since the act of 1875, passed the Civil Rights Act of 1957. Although generally considered weak in its ultimate impact, the act attempted to reinforce the voting-rights guarantees of the Fifteenth Amendment and provided for the establishment of a Civil Rights Commission and a Civil Rights Division in the Department of Justice. A stronger but still ineffective Civil Rights Act was passed in 1960. Its influence was less important than the effect of the newer organizations such as the Student Nonviolent Coordinating Committee (SNCC) and the Congress of Racial Equality (CORE) on the American conscience.

The Civil Rights Act of 1964 dealt largely with the granting of equal rights in public accommodations. The Voting Rights Act of 1965 was a forceful bill serving to effectively supplement the voting-rights guarantees of the Fifteenth Amendment. It was modeled on, and more radical than, the Enforcement Act of 1871, and it increased the opportunities of blacks to participate in the electoral process in the South.

Following the violence set off by the assassination of Martin Luther King in 1968, a new civil rights act was signed by the President that guaranteed fair housing opportunities for all citizens. The bill was made almost unnecessary by a ruling of the Supreme Court 2 months later. However, the issue of school busing was not resolved, and black militancy seemed to be almost dwarfed by other social issues. The new militancy of Mexican-Americans and American Indians, a growing national concern over environmental problems, and the demands of women's rights groups all combined, at least temporarily, to make the question of civil rights for blacks a less prominent issue.

See also Blacks in the United States; Brown v. Board of Education of Topeka (1954); Civil Rights Acts (1957, 1960, 1964); King, Martin Luther, Jr.; Plessy v. Ferguson (1896).

—David C. Geliebter, *formerly, Deputy Director, New Jersey Division of Civil Rights*

CIVIL SERVICE, the term applied to the body of employees working for a government. In the United States, employees of publicly owned business-type enterprises are included; elected officials, judges, and the military are excluded.

President Washington and the Federalists realized the need for an efficient, incorruptible, and permanent group of federal officials. This goal was not difficult, because the national civil service in 1800 consisted of only about 3,000 people. With the expansion of the government and the development of political parties, public offices became political plums. The spoils system, under which partisan service outweighed technical qualifications for ap-

pointment to office, began in a small way under Jefferson and came to a climax in the period from Jackson through Lincoln. This patronage system came under attack during the post-Civil War scandals.

The Pendleton Act. The attacks on patronage resulted in a reform of the federal civil service through the Pendleton Act (Civil Service Reform Act of 1883), which has also provided the model for state and local services. It accomplished three main goals. First, it established a merit system characterized by competitive examinations for entrance into the public service, partisan neutrality while in office, and, in return for giving up civic rights of partisanship, relative security of tenure.

Second, the Pendleton Act permitted the president to extend the system to most federal employees and established the U.S. Civil Service Commission. Successive presidents expanded the merit system from the 15 percent covered directly by the act to the present 95 percent or more. Except for 1,500 or so top offices, appointments to which are viewed as the function of the president and his political party, old-fashioned spoils appointments have vanished from the federal service.

The Pendleton Act also set in motion for the bulk of the civil service a type of personnel system known as an open system, which is unique in the modern world. An open personnel system is characterized by considerable movement back and forth from government into private enterprise and vice versa (lateral entry). In providing for entrance into the civil service at any age by means of examinations as practical as possible, the Pendleton Act initiated and supported such a system. Most other countries have developed closed career systems similar to the U.S. military, where one enters early and remains for a lifetime career.

State and Local Employees. Nearly one-seventh of the people in the total civilian labor force of about 85 million are public employees. Most of the larger state and local jurisdictions are operating under merit and open system principles. Progress toward the elimination of patronage has been slowest in the smaller local governments.

See also Pendleton Act (1883); Spoils System.

CIVIL SERVICE REFORM ACT OF 1883, alternate name for Pendleton Act. *See* Pendleton Act (1883).

CIVIL WAR: CAUSES. One month before his assassination, Abraham Lincoln cogently analyzed the causes of the war: "One eighth of the whole population (in 1861) was colored slaves, not distributed generally over the Union, but localized in the southern part of it. These slaves constituted a peculiar and powerful interest. All knew that this interest was somehow the cause of the war. To strengthen, perpetuate,

CIVIL RIGHTS MOVEMENT — Item Guide

The article on CIVIL RIGHTS MOVEMENT covers the struggle for equality by American blacks. The roles of blacks are discussed in BLACKS IN THE UNITED STATES and SLAVERY, both of which have Subject Maps. The early efforts of women to obtain equality is covered in SUFFRAGE, WOMEN'S, and there is an Item Guide on WOMEN'S RIGHTS.

After the Civil War, legal attempts to ensure equality took the form of AMENDMENTS, CONSTITUTIONAL and CIVIL RIGHTS ACTS (1866–1875), overturning the DRED SCOTT DECISION (1857). RECONSTRUCTION, outlined in the Subject Map accompanying CIVIL WAR: CAUSES, tried to counteract the BLACK CODES and to suppress the KU KLUX KLAN.

Civil rights received legal setbacks in the Supreme Court decisions in the CIVIL RIGHTS CASES (1883) and PLESSY v. FERGUSON (1896), but the latter was finally reversed in BROWN v. BOARD OF EDUCATION OF TOPEKA (1954). Later CIVIL RIGHTS ACTS (1957, 1960, 1964) aimed at protecting rights of black voters.

Early black leaders such as GEORGE WASHINGTON CARVER and W. E. B. Du BOIS were succeeded later in the twentieth century by A. PHILIP RANDOLPH, WHITNEY YOUNG, MARTIN LUTHER KING, JR., and RALPH ABERNATHY, who worked through such organizations as NATIONAL ASSOCIATION FOR THE ADVANCEMENT OF COLORED PEOPLE, CONGRESS OF RACIAL EQUALITY, and STUDENT NONVIOLENT COORDINATING COMMITTEE.

and extend this interest was the object (of the South) . . . , while the (North) . . . claimed no right to do more than to restrict the territorial enlargement of it."

Modern scholars have grappled with Lincoln's "somehow" and reached the following conclusions. The white South clung to slavery because it was profitable, because it was thought to be the only system of racial adjustment that could effectively keep the blacks controlled and subordinant, and because it formed the basis of a distinct civilization and way of life. Some Northerners opposed the expansion of slavery because they found the "peculiar institution" morally repugnant; others disliked slaveholders more than slavery and sought to check their power; still others simply did not want blacks (free or slave) moving into the Western territories.

If the issue of slavery was the basic cause of the Civil War, several other factors exacerbated tensions between North and South. Conflicting economic interests played an important role. The North wanted to promote industrialization and homesteading by having the federal government adopt protective tariffs, support internal improvements, and give small farmers free homesteads in the West. These proposals were anathema to the South, which did not want to industrialize. High tariffs would raise the prices of foreign imports, which the South relied upon heavily, while only protecting Northern interests. Similarly, internal improvements would be funded by the national treasury, to which the South contributed, but would only benefit the North.

Sectionalism bred further ill will. White Southerners, proud of their distinct civilization and eager to retain their considerable power in the national government, viewed Northern civilization with contempt and growing Northern political power with alarm. By the same token, Northerners tended to regard the South as a brutal, benighted, reactionary region that had unfairly dominated the nation and that must be curbed.

Possibly the war could have been averted if the United States had enjoyed wise, statesmanlike leadership in the prewar era. Unfortunately, presidents such as Franklin Pierce and James Buchanan, congressional leaders such as Stephen A. Douglas, and Supreme Court justices such as Roger B. Taney simply did not provide it.

Consult (IV) Pressley, 1965; Rawley, 1969; Stampp, 1965.

—Michael Burlingame, *Connecticut College*

CIVIL WAR BATTLES. Upon Lincoln's election as president (Nov. 6, 1860), the states of the lower South seceded from the Union, established the Confederacy (February 1861), and seized U.S. military installations within their borders. Fort Sumter in Charleston harbor, however, was beyond their reach and so it was blockaded. When Lincoln tried to send provisions, South Carolina forces under P. G. T. Beauregard opened fire on the fort, which surrendered on April 14. The next day Lincoln called for 75,000 militia to put down the insurrection. The upper South promptly seceded.

Twenty-two Northern states, with a population of about 22 million, faced 11 Confederate states, with 6 million free citizens and 3.5 million slaves. The U.S. Army had a mere 16,000 officers and men; the Confederate army by May was twice as large.

The first major battle of the war came on July 21, 1861, when Irvin McDowell's 28,500 Federal troops attacked an army under Beauregard at Bull Run, Va. The timely arrival of Joseph E. Johnston allowed Beauregard to repulse the assault and drive the routed enemy back to Washington. McDowell was replaced by George B. McClellan, who spent 6 months organizing and training the Union army.

Meanwhile in the West, Missouri was saved for the Union after a bitter struggle. Albert Sidney Johnston established a Confederate cordon that prevented river movements southward on the Mississippi, Tennessee, and Cumberland rivers. In February 1862, Gen. Ulysses Grant broke this line by seizing Fort Henry on the Tennessee and Fort Donelson on the Cumberland. He followed up these remarkable victories by taking Nashville.

The East: 1862. At this time Lincoln was trying to goad the unaggressive McClellan into action. Instead of attacking the Confederates head on, McClellan decided to ship his troops down Chesapeake Bay and assault Richmond, the Confederate capital, from the east. A major obstacle to this plan was the Confederate ironclad ram *Merrimack,* which encountered the *Monitor,* a small Union ironclad that looked like a cheesebox on a raft, on March 9, 1862. In a battle that made wooden warships obsolete, these unique ships fought furiously until the *Merrimack* finally limped back to Norfolk for repairs.

Two weeks later McClellan began moving his 100,000-man army to the Virginia peninsula (between the York and James rivers). Lincoln insisted that adequate forces be left behind to protect Washington, especially after Stonewall Jackson rashly attacked a Union army in the Shenandoah Valley on March 23. In May and June, Jackson conducted a brilliant campaign in the valley, using his 18,000 men to stymie 70,000 Union troops. In 48 days Jackson marched 676 miles, fought five battles, and severely disrupted the Union drive on Richmond.

During the Valley Campaign, McClellan, ever cautious, crawled slowly up the peninsula, finally coming within sight of Richmond by late May. Confederate commander Joseph E.

Ulysses S. Grant, Union commander in chief from March 1864, in Matthew Brady portrait.

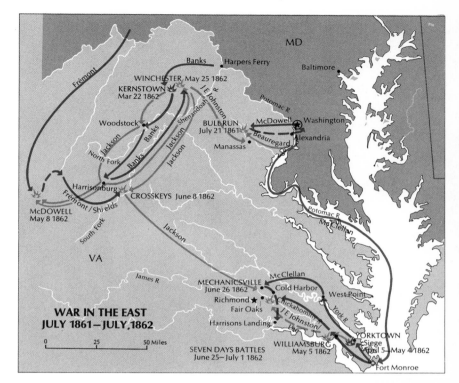

THE CIVIL WAR

→ Union advances
⇠ Union retreats
→ Confederate advances
⇠ Confederate retreats
↓ Union victories
■ Union states
↓ Confederate victories
■ Confederate states

WAR IN THE EAST
JULY 1861 – JULY 1862

0   25   50 Miles

MD

Baltimore

Banks • Harpers Ferry

WINCHESTER May 25 1862
KERNSTOWN Mar 22 1862
J E Johnston

Woodstock
BULL RUN July 21 1861
McDowell • Washington
Beauregard • Alexandria
Manassas

North Fork • Jackson • Banks • Shenandoah R • Jackson

Potomac R

Harrisonburg
CROSSKEYS June 8 1862
Fremont / Shields

McDOWELL May 8 1862
South Fork
Jackson

Potomac R
McClellan

VA

James R

MECHANICSVILLE June 26 1862
McClellan
Cold Harbor
West Point
Richmond ★
Chickahominy R
Fair Oaks
J E Johnston
York R
Harrisons Landing
Lee

SEVEN DAYS BATTLES June 25 – July 1 1862
WILLIAMSBURG May 5 1862
YORKTOWN Siege April 5 – May 4 1862
Fort Monroe

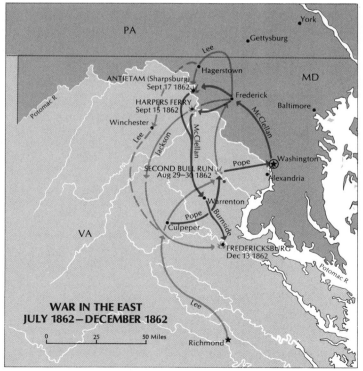

PA

• York
• Gettysburg

Lee

Hagerstown
ANTIETAM (Sharpsburg) Sept 17 1862
MD
Frederick
Baltimore

HARPERS FERRY Sept 15 1862
Winchester
Lee
Jackson
McClellan
McClellan

SECOND BULL RUN Aug 29–30 1862
Pope • Washington
Alexandria

Warrenton
Pope
Burnside
Culpeper

FREDERICKSBURG Dec 13 1862

Potomac R

VA

Lee

Richmond ★

WAR IN THE EAST
JULY 1862 – DECEMBER 1862

0   25   50 Miles

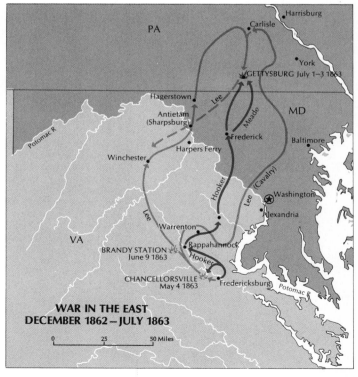

PA
Harrisburg
Carlisle

Hagerstown
Lee
GETTYSBURG July 1–3 1863
• York

Antietam (Sharpsburg)
MD
Frederick
Meade
Baltimore

Harpers Ferry
Winchester
Hooker
Lee (Cavalry)
Washington
Alexandria

Warrenton
Lee
Rappahannock R
BRANDY STATION June 9 1863
Hooker
CHANCELLORSVILLE May 4 1863
Fredericksburg

Potomac R

VA

WAR IN THE EAST
DECEMBER 1862 – JULY 1863

0   25   50 Miles

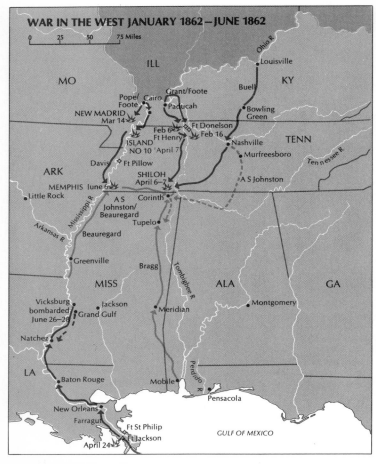

WAR IN THE WEST JANUARY 1862—JUNE 1862

0   25   50   75 Miles

MO

ILL

Louisville

Ohio R.

KY

Pope/Foote
Cairo
Grant/Foote
Paducah
Buell
Bowling Green
NEW MADRID
Mar 14
Feb 6
Ft Henry
Ft Donelson
Feb 16
Nashville
TENN
ISLAND NO 10 April 7
Davis
Ft Pillow
Murfreesboro
Tennessee R.
A S Johnston
ARK
SHILOH
April 6—7
A S Johnston
Little Rock
MEMPHIS June 6
Corinth
Davis
Beauregard
Beauregard
A S Johnston/Beauregard
Tupelo
Arkansas R.
Mississippi R.
Greenville
Bragg
Tombigbee R.
MISS
ALA
GA
Vicksburg bombarded June 26–28
Jackson
Meridian
Montgomery
Grand Gulf
Natchez
LA
Baton Rouge
Mobile
Perdido R.
New Orleans
Pensacola
Farragut
Ft St Philip
Ft Jackson
April 24
GULF OF MEXICO

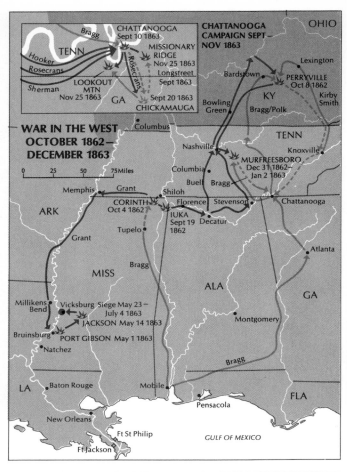

CHATTANOOGA CAMPAIGN SEPT—NOV 1863

Bragg
CHATTANOOGA
Sept 10 1863
TENN
MISSIONARY RIDGE
Nov 25 1863
Hooker
Rosecrans
Rosecrans
Longstreet
Sept 1863
Sherman
LOOKOUT MTN
Nov 25 1863
GA
Sept 20 1863
CHICKAMAUGA

OHIO

Lexington
Bardstown
PERRYVILLE
Oct 8 1862
KY
Kirby Smith
Bowling Green
Bragg/Polk

WAR IN THE WEST OCTOBER 1862—DECEMBER 1863

0   25   50   75 Miles

Columbus
Nashville
TENN
Knoxville
Columbia
MURFREESBORO
Dec 31 1862—Jan 2 1863
Memphis
Grant
Shiloh
Buell
Bragg
ARK
CORINTH
Oct 4 1862
Florence
Stevenson
Chattanooga
IUKA
Sept 19 1862
Decatur
Grant
Tupelo
Bragg
Atlanta
MISS
ALA
GA
Millikens Bend
Vicksburg Siege May 23—July 4 1863
JACKSON May 14 1863
Bruinsburg
PORT GIBSON May 1 1863
Montgomery
Natchez
Bragg
LA
Baton Rouge
Mobile
FLA
New Orleans
Pensacola
Ft St Philip
Ft Jackson
GULF OF MEXICO

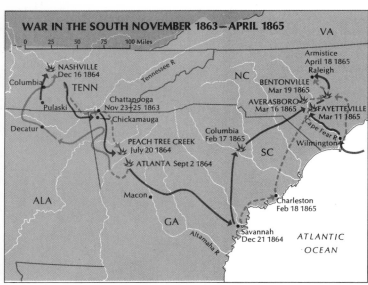

WAR IN THE SOUTH NOVEMBER 1863—APRIL 1865

0   25   50   75   100 Miles

VA
Columbia
NASHVILLE
Dec 16 1864
Tennessee R.
NC
Armistice April 18 1865
Raleigh
TENN
BENTONVILLE
Mar 19 1865
Pulaski
Chattanooga
Nov 23–25 1863
AVERASBORO
Mar 16 1865
FAYETTEVILLE
Mar 11 1865
Decatur
Chickamauga
PEACH TREE CREEK
July 20 1864
Columbia
Feb 17 1865
Cape Fear R.
Wilmington
SC
ATLANTA Sept 2 1864
ALA
Macon
Charleston
Feb 18 1865
GA
Altamaha R.
Savannah
Dec 21 1864
ATLANTIC OCEAN

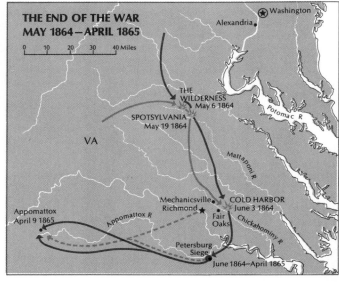

THE END OF THE WAR MAY 1864—APRIL 1865

Washington
Alexandria

0   10   20   30   40 Miles

THE WILDERNESS
May 6 1864
Potomac R.
SPOTSYLVANIA
May 19 1864
VA
Mattaponi R.
Mechanicsville
Richmond
COLD HARBOR
June 3 1864
Appomattox
April 9 1865
Fair Oaks
Chickahominy R.
Appomattox R.
Petersburg Siege
June 1864–April 1865

Johnston attacked on May 31 but was forced to withdraw with nothing gained. During this fight (the Battle of Seven Pines, or Fair Oaks) Johnston received a serious wound and was replaced by Robert E. Lee. With Jackson reinforcing his army, the new commander began the Seven Days' Campaign (June 25–July 1), and, after furious engagements at Gaines' Mill, Savage's Station, White Oak Swamp, and Malvern Hill, McClellan abandoned his scheme. Although suffering more casualties than his opponent, Lee had successfully repelled a significant threat.

Lee then decided to take the initiative before McClellan could reunite with the rest of the Union army under John Pope. The Confederate commander sent Stonewall Jackson's corps north on a rapid flanking march, and when Pope turned to concentrate on Jackson, Lee advanced with the main army and smashed the Federals at the Second Battle of Bull Run (August 29–30).

Lee then crossed the Potomac, hoping by a successful invasion of the North to induce Britain and France to recognize and aid the Confederacy. McClellan, with the Army of the Potomac, followed Lee's advance into Maryland. After preliminary fighting at South Mountain (September 14) and Harpers Ferry (September 14–15), the two armies clashed in one of the bloodiest days of the war (September 17) at Antietam, or Sharpsburg. It was a tactical victory and a strategic setback for the South, for Lee felt compelled to abandon the invasion and retire across the Potomac. McClellan's reluctance to pursue exasperated Lincoln, who removed him from command (November 7).

The new Union commander, Ambrose E. Burnside, soon advanced toward Richmond and clashed with Lee's army near Fredericksburg. Burnside hurled his men against impregnable Confederate lines and suffered a crushing defeat (December 13).

The West: 1862. The Union cause in the West fared better in 1862. After capturing Forts Henry and Donelson, Grant drove the Confederates all the way to Mississippi. On April 6, however, A. S. Johnston caught Grant unaware at Shiloh, Tenn. (Pittsburgh Landing) and inflicted heavy casualties. The arrival of reinforcements permitted Grant to repel the attack, and the Confederates retired to Corinth, Miss. Johnston was killed at Shiloh, and Beauregard took over his command. At the same time a Northern amphibious force seized Island No. 10, an important Confederate fortress in the Mississippi River (April 7). In the Gulf of Mexico, David G. Farragut's fleet moved against New Orleans, seizing the South's largest port on April 25. Farther up the Mississippi a Union flotilla captured Memphis (June 6). These victories had almost opened the Mississippi River; the only important river fortress in Confederate hands was Vicksburg, which Far-

ragut tried vainly to reduce in June and July and which Grant failed to capture with land forces in November and December.

In the Kentucky-Tennessee theater Confederate Braxton Bragg dueled with Union forces under Don Carlos Buell from July to December 1862. Bragg invaded Kentucky and by the end of August controlled most of the state. At the Battle of Perryville (October 8), Buell fought his opponent to a draw. Remarkably, Bragg then withdrew to Tennessee. Buell's failure to pursue led to his replacement (October 24) by W. S. Rosecrans, who also dallied. Finally, on December 31, the armies clashed at Murfreesboro (Stone's River), and once again the outcome was a deadlock, but Bragg's withdrawal made it a strategic victory for the North.

The East: 1863. The year 1863 promised to be more auspicious for the Union army in the East. Lincoln replaced the inept Burnside with Joseph Hooker, who in April led the Army of the Potomac, 110,000 strong, against Lee's force of 60,000 encamped near Fredericksburg. Although well conceived, the offensive was thwarted when Stonewall Jackson took 26,000 men around Hooker's army and crushed the Union right at Chancellorsville (May 2). Heavy fighting continued over the next 4 days and ended with Hooker's withdrawal. This extraordinary victory was marred by the death of Jackson.

Lee then launched his second invasion of the North, moving up the Shenandoah Valley and into Pennsylvania. The Army of the Potomac gave pursuit and engaged Lee at Gettysburg. For three fateful days (July 1–3) the armies struggled, and, after the collapse of Pickett's charge against the Union center, Lee retreated across the Potomac.

The West: 1863. In the West the Federals resumed their attempt to seize Vicksburg. Completely changing his earlier plans, Grant in May shifted his forces from the west to the east side of the river, skillfully split two Confederate armies, and captured Vicksburg after a siege (July 4). The Mississippi River was now open and the Confederacy split. Combined with Lee's defeat at Gettysburg, this triumph marked a decisive turning point in the war—the Confederacy's chances waned rapidly.

Meanwhile, in Tennessee, the dilatory Rosecrans sat immobile until June, when he finally moved against Bragg and through skillful maneuvering forced the Confederates to fall back all the way through Tennessee into Georgia. At Chickamauga, however, Bragg turned on his pursuers and thrashed them (September 19–20). Rosecrans retreated to Chattanooga, where Bragg promptly besieged him, but by late October the Federals managed to lift the siege. A month later at the Battle of Chattanooga, Grant, now in charge of the West, threw 60,000 men against Bragg's well-protected positions on Lookout Mountain and

Union officers convene at Massaponax Church, Va., for council of war during 1864 campaign.

Phil Sheridan rides to the front to rally his troops at Cedar Creek, Va., on Oct. 19, 1864.

CIVIL WAR AND RECONSTRUCTION

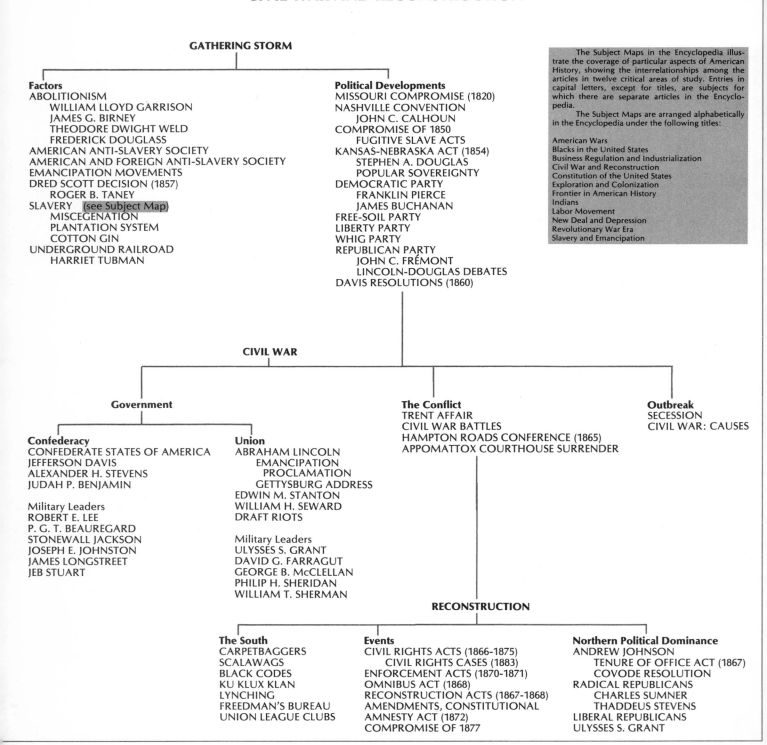

GATHERING STORM

Factors
ABOLITIONISM
    WILLIAM LLOYD GARRISON
    JAMES G. BIRNEY
    THEODORE DWIGHT WELD
    FREDERICK DOUGLASS
AMERICAN ANTI-SLAVERY SOCIETY
AMERICAN AND FOREIGN ANTI-SLAVERY SOCIETY
EMANCIPATION MOVEMENTS
DRED SCOTT DECISION (1857)
    ROGER B. TANEY
SLAVERY (see Subject Map)
    MISCEGENATION
    PLANTATION SYSTEM
    COTTON GIN
UNDERGROUND RAILROAD
    HARRIET TUBMAN

Political Developments
MISSOURI COMPROMISE (1820)
NASHVILLE CONVENTION
    JOHN C. CALHOUN
COMPROMISE OF 1850
    FUGITIVE SLAVE ACTS
KANSAS-NEBRASKA ACT (1854)
    STEPHEN A. DOUGLAS
    POPULAR SOVEREIGNTY
DEMOCRATIC PARTY
    FRANKLIN PIERCE
    JAMES BUCHANAN
FREE-SOIL PARTY
LIBERTY PARTY
WHIG PARTY
REPUBLICAN PARTY
    JOHN C. FRÉMONT
    LINCOLN-DOUGLAS DEBATES
DAVIS RESOLUTIONS (1860)

> The Subject Maps in the Encyclopedia illustrate the coverage of particular aspects of American History, showing the interrelationships among the articles in twelve critical areas of study. Entries in capital letters, except for titles, are subjects for which there are separate articles in the Encyclopedia.
>
> The Subject Maps are arranged alphabetically in the Encyclopedia under the following titles:
>
> American Wars
> Blacks in the United States
> Business Regulation and Industrialization
> Civil War and Reconstruction
> Constitution of the United States
> Exploration and Colonization
> Frontier in American History
> Indians
> Labor Movement
> New Deal and Depression
> Revolutionary War Era
> Slavery and Emancipation

CIVIL WAR

Government

Confederacy
CONFEDERATE STATES OF AMERICA
JEFFERSON DAVIS
ALEXANDER H. STEVENS
JUDAH P. BENJAMIN

Military Leaders
ROBERT E. LEE
P. G. T. BEAUREGARD
STONEWALL JACKSON
JOSEPH E. JOHNSTON
JAMES LONGSTREET
JEB STUART

Union
ABRAHAM LINCOLN
    EMANCIPATION
      PROCLAMATION
    GETTYSBURG ADDRESS
EDWIN M. STANTON
WILLIAM H. SEWARD
DRAFT RIOTS

Military Leaders
ULYSSES S. GRANT
DAVID G. FARRAGUT
GEORGE B. McCLELLAN
PHILIP H. SHERIDAN
WILLIAM T. SHERMAN

The Conflict
TRENT AFFAIR
CIVIL WAR BATTLES
HAMPTON ROADS CONFERENCE (1865)
APPOMATTOX COURTHOUSE SURRENDER

Outbreak
SECESSION
CIVIL WAR: CAUSES

RECONSTRUCTION

The South
CARPETBAGGERS
SCALAWAGS
BLACK CODES
KU KLUX KLAN
LYNCHING
FREEDMAN'S BUREAU
UNION LEAGUE CLUBS

Events
CIVIL RIGHTS ACTS (1866-1875)
    CIVIL RIGHTS CASES (1883)
ENFORCEMENT ACTS (1870-1871)
OMNIBUS ACT (1868)
RECONSTRUCTION ACTS (1867-1868)
AMENDMENTS, CONSTITUTIONAL
AMNESTY ACT (1872)
COMPROMISE OF 1877

Northern Political Dominance
ANDREW JOHNSON
    TENURE OF OFFICE ACT (1867)
    COVODE RESOLUTION
RADICAL REPUBLICANS
    CHARLES SUMNER
    THADDEUS STEVENS
LIBERAL REPUBLICANS
ULYSSES S. GRANT

Missionary Ridge and conquered both (November 23-25). By early December, Tennessee was fully in Northern hands.

The East: 1864. In 1864 the tide of battle swung heavily in favor of the Union. Grant became general in chief of all Union armies on March 10 and inaugurated a campaign of unremitting pressure on all fronts, allowing the North to utilize fully its superior resources. With the Army of the Potomac he marched south in May seeking to destroy Lee's army. Simultaneously Grant dispatched an army down the Shenandoah Valley and ordered Benjamin Butler's army to proceed toward Richmond.

While Grant was entangled in the Wilderness, a huge network of second-growth thickets just south of the Rappahannock River, Lee attacked and on May 5-6 inflicted heavy losses. Undeterred, Grant pressed on, slipping past Lee's right. The Confederates concentrated at Spotsylvania Courthouse, where another bloody battle (May 8-21) cost Grant many more men. Meanwhile the Union cavalry under Philip Sheridan clashed with Jeb Stuart's horsemen at Yellow Tavern (May 11), a battle that checked Sheridan's advance toward Richmond but cost the life of Stuart. At Cold Harbor, Grant tried desperately to split Lee's army but failed after costly assaults (June 1-12). Undaunted, Grant kept hammering away, besieging Petersburg after a bloody battle (June 15-18) but failing to take it. Lee then sent Jubal Early's corps down the Shenandoah Valley sweeping the ineptly commanded Union forces before him; by July 11 he had reached the suburbs of Washington. Grant ordered Sheridan to take charge of the army near Washington, destroy Early, and then devastate the valley. With more than 40,000 men Sheridan ably executed these commands, whipping Early at Winchester (September 19) and Fisher's Hill (September 22) while laying waste the Shenandoah. In the climactic battle of this campaign (Cedar Creek, October 19), Early almost defeated the Federals, but Sheridan rushed to the front and turned near disaster into victory. The valley was no longer a Confederate corridor or a granary to feed Lee's army.

The West: 1864. In the West, Sherman proved as tenacious as Grant and as destructive as Sheridan. Advancing into Georgia (May 7) with 100,000 troops, he executed a series of turning movements that drove the Army of Tennessee to Atlanta. There on July 22 the Confederates vainly assaulted the Union left (Battle of Atlanta). Sherman then swept around the city, cut its rail ties, and forced John B. Hood's army to evacuate it (September 1). Sherman soon resolved to drive through Georgia to destroy its productive capacities and demoralize Southern resistance. He began on November 16 and cut a 50-mile-wide swath of scorched earth to Savannah, which he captured on December 21.

War's End: 1865. While Sherman devastated the Carolinas (February–March 1865), Grant applied more and more pressure on the Petersburg front. At the Battle of Five Forks (April 1), Sheridan defeated Pickett and exposed the entire Confederate right. Grant immediately launched a full-scale assault on Petersburg and forced Lee to abandon it and Richmond. On April 9, Lee surrendered to Grant at Appomattox Courthouse. Two weeks later J. E. Johnston, commanding the last Confederate army, capitulated to Sherman.

The Naval War. The Union navy played a critical role in achieving final victory, not only on the rivers but also on the high seas. In May 1861, Lincoln declared a blockade of the South. By 1863 the blockade was seriously strangling the Confederate economy, although specially constructed speedy blockade runners managed to slip through the net, especially at Charleston, which held out against Union attacks until February 1865. The blockade runners' favorite port in the Gulf of Mexico was Mobile, Ala., which Admiral David Farragut took in August 1864. Another chink in the blockading fleet's armor was Wilmington, N.C., through which vital supplies passed. Its capture in January 1865 made the blockade fully effective.

The Union navy had another difficult task, the suppression of Confederate commerce raiders. The C.S.S. *Florida* ravaged Northern shipping along the Atlantic coast until it was captured in October 1864. More troublesome was the *Alabama*, which captured 65 Federal merchantmen between August 1862 and June 1864, when it was sunk off Cherbourg, France. The Confederates' *Shenandoah* was never caught and managed to destroy the U.S. whaling fleet before learning in August 1865 that the war was over. After the war, in the case of the Alabama claims, America argued that Britain had not been diligent enough as a neutral in preventing the building of these raiders in her shipyards, and an international tribunal awarded damages to the United States.

Casualties. No war has cost so many American lives or involved such a huge percentage of the population. About 2 million men served in the Federal forces, while 750,000 fought for the Confederacy. In the course of 10,455 military actions more than 1 million of these men became casualties. The Confederacy suffered 94,000 battle deaths, with another 164,000 killed by disease and 194,000 wounded. Union losses were even higher: 110,000 battle deaths, 225,000 deaths by disease, and 275,000 wounded.

Consult (V) Basler, 1967; Catton, 1961-1965; Nevins, 1947-1971.

—Michael Burlingame, *Connecticut College*

Partially burned and severely shelled, the Confederate capital of Richmond was abandoned in April 1865.

U.S. flag rises over Fort Sumter, S.C., where the first shots of the war had been fired, on April 14, 1865.

George Rogers Clark fought the British in the West during the Revolutionary War.

A power in Congress for more than 40 years, Henry Clay helped frame the Missouri Compromise and the Compromise of 1850.

CIVIL WAR PENSIONS, a volatile political issue that affected presidential elections. *See* Dependent Pension Acts (1887, 1890).

CIVIL WORKS ADMINISTRATION (CWA), established by President Roosevelt to provide emergency work relief during the winter of 1933-1934. It was a stopgap program urged on Roosevelt by Harry Hopkins to supplement the Federal Emergency Relief Administration and the Public Works Administration, both of which were hindered by the need for long-term planning and by complex federal-state-local financial and administrative arrangements. CWA, financed entirely by federal funds and administered by Hopkins, spent nearly $1 billion and at its peak provided more than 4 million jobs. Like other work relief programs, it concentrated on civic improvements. After 1934 this kind of direct federal assistance was abandoned by Roosevelt in the face of criticism from local politicians and conservatives in Congress.

See also Federal Emergency Relief Act (1933); Public Works Administration.

Consult (VI) Mitchell, 1947.

CLARK, GEORGE ROGERS (1752-1818), Revolutionary War leader from Virginia who in 1777 devised a plan to seize Kaskaskia on the Mississippi River in Illinois. The possessor of this outpost, which was founded by the French, could influence the Indians of the Northwest, dominate the Mississippi and Ohio rivers, and threaten the supply line of the British garrison at Detroit.

Governor Patrick Henry of Virginia endorsed the idea, and the legislature outfitted an expedition. On June 26, 1778, Clark set out with 200 men down the Ohio River to Fort Massac and then, to maintain surprise, traveled overland 150 miles to Kaskaskia. Clark captured Kaskaskia without firing a shot and won the cooperation of the French inhabitants, who went to Vincennes on the Wabash River and convinced the settlers there to give allegiance to Virginia.

When Lt. Gov. Henry Hamilton of Canada recaptured Vincennes on December 17, Clark immediately attacked again. Clark arrived near Vincennes on Feb. 23, 1779, and after he tomahawked five Indian prisoners as proof of his seriousness, the Indians defected from Hamilton, who surrendered the town on February 25. Unable to gather enough men and material to march on Detroit, Clark spent the remainder of the war fighting Tory and Indian raiders. After the war, Clark had a checkered career that included service as a general in the French army. He moved in 1809 to Louisville, Ky., where he died.

See also Revolutionary War Battles.

Consult (II) Bakeless, 1957.

CLARK, KENNETH B(ANCROFT) (1914-   ), educator, psychologist, and civil rights leader. He was born in the Panama Canal Zone, graduated from Howard University in 1933, and received his Ph.D. from Columbia in 1940. In 1942 he began teaching psychology at City College in New York. In 1946—with his wife, Dr. Mamie Phipps Clark, also a psychologist—he opened the Northside Center for Child Development, a guidance center for emotionally disturbed children.

Studies of the schools led Clark to the conclusion that segregation is bad for all children, black and white. His testimony on the damage done by prejudice was cited in the 1954 Supreme Court decision that declared segregation in public schools unconstitutional.

Clark was a leader in the social service agency Harlem Youth Opportunities Unlimited (HARYOU). In 1967 he founded the Metropolitan Applied Research Center (MARC), a social research organization to "alleviate desperation in ghettos in northern cities not helped by federal court decisions or civil rights legislation."

Clark served on the New York State Board of Regents—the only black member. He has written several books, including *Dark Ghetto* (1965), a summation of the experiences of men and women in the slums.

CLAY, HENRY (1777-1852), American statesman. Born in Virginia, he studied law in Richmond and began his practice in Lexington, Ky. He was a legislator in Kentucky from 1803 to 1806 and then entered national politics by filling an unexpired term in the U.S. Senate (1806-1807). He returned to the Kentucky legislature (1807-1809) and then filled another unexpired Senate term (1809-1810). From 1811 to 1825 he was a U.S. congressman who played an instrumental role as a war hawk before the War of 1812 and served as speaker of the House (1811-1820 and 1823-1825).

Throughout his career, Clay longed for the presidency. He ran in 1824 and, although coming in a poor fourth, he was instrumental in throwing the election to John Quincy Adams when the vote went to the House. Adams rewarded Clay by appointing him secretary of state (1825-1829), which prompted charges of a "corrupt bargain."

In the 1824 campaign, Clay had first put forth his "American System," based on a protective tariff to stimulate industry, a national bank to facilitate credit and exchange, and federally funded internal improvements to aid trade and commerce. This "American System" became the major platform of the Whig Party after its emergence in the early 1830s. In 1832 and again in 1844, Clay was the unsuccessful Whig candidate for president, losing to Andrew Jackson and James K. Polk, respectively. From 1831 to 1842 and from 1849 to 1852, Clay again served in the Senate.

Clay's conciliatory, compromising approach to statesmanship was to earn him the nickname "The Great Pacificator." He framed the Missouri Compromise (1820), sponsored the Compromise Tariff of 1833, and helped arrange the Compromise of 1850.

See also Compromise of 1850; Missouri Compromise (1820); Presidential Elections.

Consult (III) Eaton, 1957; Van Deusen, 1937.

—Douglas Miller, *Michigan State University*

CLAYTON ANTITRUST ACT (1914), antitrust measure that, with the Federal Trade Commission Act (1914), formed the heart of President Woodrow Wilson's "New Freedom" reform campaign. Wilson sought to strengthen the antitrust movement and to block loopholes in the Sherman Antitrust Act. In 1913 the House's Pujo Committee had disclosed extensive interlocking and the holding of multiple directorships among banks, insurance houses, and corporations—a new type of hidden merger movement.

The Clayton Act barred these interlocking directorates, although in practice it was not very effective. It also prohibited other techniques not mentioned by the Sherman Act, including price fixing and holding stock in competing firms. Samuel Gompers, the leader of the American Federation of Labor, called the Clayton Act a "charter of freedom" for labor because the act specifically exempted trade unions from the restraint of trade clauses. Previously, the Sherman Antitrust Act had been used by the courts against trade unions.

See also Federal Trade Commission; Sherman Antitrust Act (1890); Trusts.

Consult (V) Jones, 1965.

CLAYTON-BULWER TREATY (1850) settled British-American disputes over a possible trans-Isthmian canal in Central America. Both Britain, the world's major maritime power, and the United States, which wanted faster oceanic communication with rapidly growing California, feared the other country would monopolize the route. Americans were especially anxious for a settlement, for by 1850 Britain had occupied areas on the east coast of Central America.

Negotiated by Sir Henry Bulwer and John M. Clayton, Secretary of State under President Taylor, and ratified on July 4, 1850, the treaty provided that the two countries would jointly control and protect any canal and that neither would "occupy, or fortify, or colonize, or assume, or exercize any dominion over" any part of Central America. The British initially rejected American assertions that this last provision was retroactive and refused to withdraw from their possessions, but eventually they acquiesced. The treaty governed Anglo-American relations in the area until the Hay-Pauncefote Treaty of 1901.

See also Hay-Pauncefote Treaty (1901); Panama Canal.

Consult (III) Nevins, 1947.

CLEAR AND PRESENT DANGER, standard against which espionage and sedition cases were measured. *See* Brandeis, Louis D.; Espionage Act (1917); Holmes, Oliver Wendell, Jr.

CLEAVER, ELDRIDGE (1935-   ), author, revolutionary, and social critic who is the product of both the black ghetto and the California penal system. Born in Arkansas, Cleaver was convicted of possessing marijuana at 18 and, in 1954, began a 12-year cycle of prison terms at Soledad, Folsom, and San Quentin. While in prison, Cleaver obtained a high school diploma, converted to the Black Muslim faith, and began to write. His most famous work, *Soul on Ice* (1968), is a collection of impassioned love letters and brilliant essays probing the depths and conundrums of the modern black psyche.

Cleaver's fiery, grating moods and evocative imagery stamp him as a revolutionary voice in the black world as well as a unique literary stylist. As such, after his release from prison, he became a staff writer for *Ramparts* magazine and a much publicized lecturer on college campuses, where he sought to inspire black students. In 1968, Cleaver became the minister of information for the Black Panther Party and was nominated as the presidential candidate of the Peace and Freedom Party.

In 1969, Cleaver left the United States secretly to avoid a prison sentence for parole violation and for alleged involvement in a shoot-out with Oakland, Cal. police. Cleaver and his family, and other Black Panthers, subsequently settled in Algeria.

See also Black Panthers.

CLEMENS, SAMUEL LANGHORNE, American writer better known under pen name of Mark Twain. *See* Twain, Mark.

CLEVELAND, (STEPHEN) GROVER (1837–1908), 22nd and 24th President of the United States (1885-1889, 1893-1897). A self-educated man, Cleveland became an attorney (1859). Long active in local Democratic politics, he became reform mayor of Buffalo (1881) and governor of New York (1882). Cleveland's honest administration led him to repudiate Tammany Hall, and his "enemies" were one reason he obtained the Democratic presidential nomination in 1884. After a dirty campaign, ultimately decided by only a few votes in New York, Cleveland was elected.

Presidency. Cleveland's first term pleased conservatives by advocating sound money and reducing inflation. He forced re-

Black militant Eldridge Cleaver announces support for Palestinian Arabs against Israel in news conference in Algeria.

peal of the Tenure of Office Act, under which President Johnson had been impeached, and withdrew land for conservation purposes. He attempted to curb party patronage, lost political support from veterans by vetoing private pensions and the Dependent Pension Act, and alienated businessmen by suggesting a lower tariff. All these led to his defeat by Benjamin Harrison in 1888.

In 1892, Cleveland remained the logical Democrat to run against the excesses of Harrison's "Billion Dollar Congress." His reputation for honesty and an accommodation with Tammany Hall won the election, but he had to face the depression of 1893. Insisting on sound money, Cleveland led repeal of the Sherman Silver Purchase Act and negotiated three loans that saved the gold standard. The Wilson Tariff reduced tariff rates and authorized an income tax. Cleveland survived a secret operation for cancer of the jaw in the midst of all this, but his problems were hardly over. Coxey's Army marched in 1894, and the President had to use antitrust injunctions to end the Pullman Strike. In foreign affairs he was criticized for withdrawing the annexation of Hawaii (1893) and intervening in the boundary dispute between Britain and Venezuela (1895).

Cleveland's policies were repudiated by the Democrats in 1896, when they nominated William Jennings Bryan on a free silver platform. He moved to "Westland," near Princeton, where he wrote, and played the role of elder statesman until his death on June 24, 1908.

See also Coxey's Army; Harrison, Benjamin; Presidential Elections; Pullman Strike; Sherman Silver Purchase Act (1890).

Consult (V) Merrill, 1957; Nevins, 1932.
—George Lankevich, *Bronx Community College of The City University of New York*

CLINTON, DE WITT (1769-1828), reform governor of New York. Born in New York to a distinguished family—his father was a Revolutionary War general, and his uncle George Clinton was governor and vice-president—De Witt Clinton entered politics as a Jeffersonian Republican. However, in temperament and ideas he was closer to the Federalists. He rose fast owing to family connections and his own brilliance and leadership qualities. He served as a state senator (1798-1802) and as a successful mayor of New York City (1803-1815). Clinton ran for the presidency in 1812 on an antiwar ticket with strong Federalist support, but he was defeated by James Madison.

Clinton then gave up national ambitions and devoted the rest of his life to New York State, where he took the lead in a variety of reforms. He was governor from 1817 to 1821 and from 1825 to 1828. He is best remembered for his courageous sponsoring of the Erie Canal

DeWitt Clinton, Governor of New York, who was primarily responsible for completion of the Erie Canal.

against bitter criticism and opposition (it was called "Clinton's Big Ditch"). Clinton also sponsored the Champlain-Hudson Canal, and he fought for free public education. He favored the education of women when such a stand was radical, and he was sympathetic toward minorities such as blacks, Indians, and the poor. Public health measures, the abolition of imprisonment for debt, the elimination of harsh punishments for minor offenses, the abolition of slavery in New York, and wider civil rights for Catholics were some of the reforms Clinton supported. It was an amazing record for the period, yet he also found time to pursue and encourage cultural and scientific interests.

See also Erie Canal; Presidential Elections.

—Peter d'A. Jones, *University of Illinois, Chicago Circle*

CLINTON, GEORGE (1739-1812), a Revolutionary War leader and important politician of the early national period. Clinton participated in the capture of Montreal (1760) during the French and Indian War. Elected to the New York Provincial Assembly in 1768, he served until 1775, when he became a member of the Second Continental Congress.

During the Revolutionary War he was an extreme advocate of the patriot side and was appointed a brigadier general. He was not very successful as a military figure, and he returned to state politics, winning the gubernatorial election of 1777. This caused considerable consternation among New York's ruling class because as John Jay noted, "Clinton's family and connections do not entitle him to so distinguished a pre-eminence."

So popular were his skillful handling of financial matters and his demagogic hostility to loyalists that he was reelected governor for seven successive terms until 1795, when he declined to run. During the 1780s he was a vigorous opponent of most attempts to increase the powers of the central government, and he led the opposition in New York to the adoption of the Constitution.

As the powers of the state governments declined during the 1790s, Clinton increasingly turned his attention to national politics, supporting the party of Thomas Jefferson. He became vice-president in 1804 and an insurgent candidate for the presidency in 1808, but when this failed he again accepted the vice-presidency. He died near the end of his second term, shortly after casting the deciding vote against rechartering the First Bank of the United States.

See also New York; Vice-Presidents of the United States.

Consult (III) Spaulding, 1938.
—Richard E. Ellis, *University of Virginia*

CLOTURE, or closure, rule to limit debate. In 1917, during hectic arguments about American entry into World War I, the Senate adopted the cloture rule to limit debate. The rule was passed after filibusters (long speeches to delay the passage of legislation) had prevented a vote on President Wilson's bill to arm U.S. merchant ships.

Cloture was adopted on March 8, 1917, and was amended in 1949 and 1959. It requires a petition signed by one-sixth of the Senate and a subsequent vote of two-thirds of the senators present to end debate. The Senate has rarely agreed to adopt cloture, although it did so in 1965, but the threat of its adoption has often ended debate. The House of Representatives has a 5-minute limitation on each speaker, but members publish their speeches in full.

COAST GUARD, U.S. Officially established on Jan. 28, 1915, it operates as part of the Navy during war and at other times is a part of the Department of Transportation. The Coast Guard is headed by a commandant.

The Coast Guard was established in 1790 under the Treasury Department—as the Revenue Marine—to combat smugglers. It subsequently became the Revenue Cutter Service. Revenue cutters captured enemy ships in the War of 1812 and were a vital part of the Southern blockade during the Civil War. In 1915, the Revenue Cutter Service was combined with the Lifesaving Service to form the Coast Guard. An aviation division was added in 1916. During World War I, the Coast Guard convoyed troop transports and cargo ships across the North Atlantic. During World War II, the Coast Guard participated in rescue operations and manned landing craft. It has been under the Transportation Department since 1967.

COERCIVE ACTS (1774), British legislation designed to punish the colonies after the Boston Tea Party (1773), which shocked even members of Parliament sympathetic to the colonies. Consequently, in the spring of 1774 Parliament passed three measures designed to punish Massachusetts and intimidate the other colonies.

The Boston Port Bill (March 31) closed the port of Boston and moved the customs house to Salem, where food, fuel, and military stores were allowed to enter Massachusetts. The Administration of Justice Act (May 20) provided that royal colonial officials accused of committing capital offenses in executing their duties could be tried in England rather than Massachusetts. The Massachusetts Government Act (May 20) made the province's council and judiciary appointive rather than elective, authorized the governor to limit town meetings to as few as one a year, and gave him

control of their agendas. The Coercive, or Intolerable, Acts angered Americans and led to the calling of the First Continental Congress.

See also Boston Tea Party; Continental Congress, First (1774).

COLDEN, CADWALLADER (1688-1776), American colonial official and scholar. A Scot, Colden came to America in 1710, landing in Philadelphia and soon becoming a prosperous businessman. In 1718 he moved to New York City and 2 years later was appointed surveyor general of the province. He became a member of the governor's council in 1721 and was lieutenant governor of New York (1761-1765). He was acting governor during the Stamp Act riots in 1765 and was, at this time, burned in effigy for his refusal to oppose the act.

Colden's scholarly interests included the study of botany, mathematics, medicine, and philosophy. He corresponded with the Swedish botanist Linnaeus as well as with Benjamin Franklin and England's Samuel Johnson. He wrote several scientific treatises and made particularly valuable contributions to the study and classification of American flora and fauna.

COLE, THOMAS (1801-1848), the moving spirit of the Hudson River School of painting. He was born in England in 1801 and emigrated to America in 1819, where he began work as an engraver in his father's wallpaper factory at Steubenville, Ohio. Cole worked his way eastward by painting portraits for a living and, after studying at the Pennsylvania Academy in 1825, began painting landscapes that captured the vast spaces of the American wilderness. When Cole established his studio in New York City in 1827, he was the acknowledged leader of a group of American romantic painters who drew their inspiration from the countryside along the Hudson River.

His European tour in 1829 brought him into contact with most of Europe's leading artists, and on his return to America he continued to execute monumental paintings. However, his later *The Course of Empire* and *The Architect's Dream* were less involved with nature and more in the style of the fashionable historical painting current in Europe.

See also Hudson River School; Painting.

COLLEGE OF NEW JERSEY (Princeton University). *See* Colonial Colleges.

COLLEGES, COLONIAL. *See* Colonial Colleges.

COLLIER ACT, New Deal legislation designed to help Indians to regroup. *See* Indian Policy.

COLONIAL AGRICULTURE. Most Europeans who came to America wanted to own land, a fact that influenced the land practices and regulations in the colonies. To encourage settlers to remain and to attract other immigrants to its colony, the Virginia Company in 1619 introduced the headright system, by which any person who transported himself to Virginia and remained 3 years was given 50 acres. Headrights were originally intended to populate the wilderness.

During the seventeenth century, however, they became the means of amassing large tracts of land because the practice evolved whereby an individual could claim 50 acres for each dependent or servant he brought to America. The headright system spread to all the Southern colonies, as well as Pennsylvania and New Jersey. In the South, it made possible the acquisition of the vast plantations that produced single cash crops such as tobacco, indigo, and rice.

New England. In New England the Puritan ideal of a community of believers strongly influenced the pattern of settlement. The Puritans vested authority over unsettled lands in the general court, which made grants of 36-square-mile townships to groups of men called proprietors, who often had already gathered a church. Each proprietor received a house lot and parcels of arable, meadow, and wooded lands in various sections of the township. Such land distribution caused farms in New England to be small, compact, and best suited to subsistence agriculture.

Freehold and Quitrents. With few exceptions—most notably New York's Hudson Valley, where manor lords held vast acreages and tenants worked the lands—settlers in the English colonies were able to obtain freehold land grants; that is, they held an inheritable interest in their lands extending for an indefinite time. Most colonists thus owned their lands outright and were free to sell or otherwise dispose of them. But a few remnants of feudalism did influence land tenure in the colonies until the time of the Revolution.

Throughout the colonial period New Hampshire, New York, Pennsylvania, Maryland, and the Carolinas exacted quitrents. The quitrent was a fixed annual rent or land tax that "quit," or freed, the freeholder from feudal obligations to his lord, who was often the proprietor of the colony. Quitrents varied from nominal obligations to fairly stringent taxes. They were unpopular and difficult to collect.

Primogeniture and Entail. Primogeniture and entail were other feudal practices that crossed the Atlantic. Primogeniture, whereby only the eldest son could inherit his father's freehold, prevailed in Rhode Island, the Middle colonies (except Pennsylvania), and the South. In New England all children shared in their fathers' estate, but in Massachusetts and in Pennsylvania, where estates were also divided, the eldest son received a double portion. Entail prevented the holder of an estate from disposing of any part of it and limited

interest in the land to a lifetime. Entail was used to prevent the division of the large manors and plantations in the Southern and Middle colonies.

See also Patroonships; Plantation System.

Consult (I) Morris, 1930.
—Thomas Archdeacon, *University of Wisconsin*

COLONIAL ARCHAEOLOGY. *See* Historical Archaeology.

COLONIAL COLLEGES. Most of the colleges in colonial America were supported by religious denominations and designed to train ministers. Two of the nine colleges dated from the seventeenth century: Harvard in Massachusetts and William and Mary in Virginia. During their first decade in the New World, Massachusetts Puritans (Congregationalists) recognized the importance of educating their own clergy. In 1636 the provincial legislature appropriated £400 for a college in Newtowne (later Cambridge). Two years later the Reverend John Harvard bequeathed his library and some money to the school, which then was named in his honor. Anglicans in Virginia had long planned a college but did not open William and Mary at Williamsburg until 1693. In 1701, Connecticut chartered a Puritan-supported college, which was permanently located at New Haven in 1716 and two years later was named Yale College to honor Elihu Yale, a major benefactor.

Most of the other colleges originated during the Great Awakening, when other denominations saw the need to educate clergymen. Presbyterians began the College of New Jersey in 1746, first at Elizabeth, then Newark, and in 1756 permanently at Princeton; its name was changed to Princeton University in 1896. Baptists founded Rhode Island College at Providence in 1764 (renamed Brown University in 1804); the Dutch Reformed began instruction at Queen's College (changed to Rutgers in 1825) at New Brunswick, N.J., in 1766. Although under Anglican control, King's College in New York City, dating from 1754, was officially nonsectarian; it became Columbia College in 1784.

The only fully nonsectarian colonial college was Benjamin Franklin's Academy. Opened in 1751, it became "the College and Academy of Philadelphia" in 1755 and in 1791 formed the nucleus of the University of Pennsylvania. Dartmouth, a Congregational school at Hanover, N.H., chartered in 1769, was the last college established before the Revolution.

See also Education.

Consult (I) Cremin, 1970.
—Carl Ubbelohde, *Case Western Reserve University*

COLONIAL RELIGION. Religion, with conversion of the Indians to Christianity as one of the

Harvard College in colonial times.

inducements, motivated much of the exploration and settlement of colonial America. England, a Protestant Christian nation, viewed colonization in North America as a way of directly challenging Roman Catholic Spain and France.

Anglicans and Congregationalists. Some of the English colonies were designed as, or became, havens of refuge where particular sects or denominations might escape persecution for their religious beliefs. The Church of England (Anglican) was "established"—that is, it received revenues from the public treasury—in Virginia soon after the Jamestown settlement. Anglicanism was also "established" in both North and South Carolina, Georgia, Maryland, and the lower counties of New York. American Anglicans were under the jurisdiction of the Bishop of London, who appointed commissaries to supervise the colonial churches. After 1698 the venerable Society for the Propagation of the Gospel in Foreign Parts (SPG) dispersed missionary funds to enlarge Anglican activities.

Dissenters from the Anglican church settled much of New England. The Puritans, whether Separatists such as the Plymouth Colony Pilgrims or Nonconformists such as the Massachusetts settlers, all believed that the Church of England required reformation in doctrine and practice. Puritans followed John Calvin's teachings, including emphasis on predestination and the concept of the elect. Most Puritans believed that each congregation was competent to govern itself; hence their later designation as Congregationalists. The Congregational churches were "established" in Massachusetts, Connecticut, and New Hampshire. They had more members than any other denomination in America at the time of the Revolution.

Roman Catholics were attracted to Maryland, where the Calverts (lords proprietor) worked to establish a refuge for them. In 1649, in the famous Maryland Act of Toleration, all Trinitarian Christians—Catholics and Protestants—were accorded equal religious freedoms. However, during England's Glorious Revolution (1689) the Protestant majority seized control of the colony, the Anglican church was "established" in 1702, and Maryland then joined most of the other American provinces in legislating restrictions or prohibitions (voting, officeholding, public worship, educational opportunities) on Catholics. Rhode Island and Pennsylvania were exceptions, Pennsylvania being the only province where the Catholic mass could be publicly performed.

Under the tolerant proprietor William Penn, the Quakers (members of the Society of Friends) in Pennsylvania extended religious freedoms to all settlers. Quakers, who also settled in western New Jersey, saw their "Holy Experiment" in Pennsylvania attract large numbers of Germans, Scotch-Irish, and other eighteenth-century immigrants seeking religious freedom and economic opportunities. The Germans included the "plain people"—Mennonites, Amish, Schwenkfeldians, and Dunkards (German Baptists); the Moravians or United Brethren in Bethlehem (with other settlements in Georgia and North Carolina); and the "church people"—German Reformed (Calvinists) and Lutherans (the latter organized their churches in a synod in 1748). The Scotch-Irish Presbyterians (Calvinists) had initiated their first synod in 1718, while the Dutch Reformed churches (principally in New York), which were Calvinist in theology and Presbyterian in structure, organized a synod in 1747.

Other colonial Protestant churches included the Baptists and the Methodists. The earliest Baptists were followers of Roger Williams in Rhode Island. Opposed to infant baptism, they also championed separation of church and state, a belief reflected in Rhode Island's religious toleration. Later, Welsh and other immigrant groups spread Baptist teachings in the Middle and Southern provinces. The Methodists appeared late in the colonial era. Like John Wesley's system in England, American Methodism originated as a movement within the Anglican churches.

The Jews formed the largest non-Christian religious group in the colonies, although they probably numbered no more than 2,000 at the time of the American Revolution. They lived mostly in seaport towns such as Newport, R.I., New York City, and Charleston, S.C. Like Catholics, they generally were disqualified by law from voting or officeholding.

Despite restrictions against Jews and Catholics and despite the favored position of the "established" Anglican and Congregational churches, a broad toleration of all Trinitarian Protestants developed within American colonial society. This probably resulted more from necessity than from conviction—no denomination was powerful enough to exert its will against other sects. However, toleration also was aided by liberalizing trends during the eighteenth century that emphasized man's role and choice in religious matters. For a few men, such belief extended as far as the deistic principles that negated much of the older, more orthodox Protestant faith.

Great Awakening. From 1725 to the eve of the Revolution a series of revivals known as the Great Awakening was directed toward halting the liberal, more rational influences in colonial Protestantism. Notable leaders of the Great Awakening included Jonathan Edwards, the highly intellectual Congregational minister in Massachusetts whose revivals in Northampton began the New England Awakening, and the popular English evangelist George Whitefield. The Awakening also was preached by

Quaker meeting during colonial era. Courtesy, Museum of Fine Arts, Boston.

Columbus lands in the West Indies on Oct. 12, 1492.

Meteorologist of Commerce Department's National Oceanic and Atmospheric Administration launches radio-sonde to collect upper-air observations at sea.

unlettered laymen, who became itinerant clergymen traveling from place to place with their exhortations to return to older, more "narrow" religious beliefs.

The Great Awakening proved to be disruptive in some aspects. Congregational and Presbyterian congregations often were divided between New Side or New Light (the Awakened) and Old Side or Old Light (opponents of the Awakening). The Anglican churches drew new converts from those who opposed the emotionalism or the more orthodox theology of the Awakening. On the other hand, Baptists and Methodists recruited many members from among the newly converted people.

See also Congregationalists; Great Awakening; Presbyterians; Puritanism; Quakers; Roman Catholics.

Consult (I) Sweet, 1942.
—Carl Ubbelohde, *Case Western Reserve University*

COLORADO, the 38th state, joined the Union on Aug. 1, 1876. Early sixteenth-century Spanish gold hunters were the first white men to cross the area. Spain and France claimed the area in the eighteenth century, and it was included in the Louisiana Purchase (1803). The remainder of what is now Colorado was acquired from Mexico in 1848 and from Texas in 1850. The first American explorer to enter Colorado was Zebulon Pike in 1806–1807. The discovery of gold in 1858 attracted settlers, hastening territorial recognition, which came in 1861.

The state legislature is bicameral; the capital is Denver. Its population in 1970 was 2,207,259.

COLT, SAMUEL (1814–1862), American inventor famous for the invention of the six-shooter revolver, accepted by the U.S. Army in 1847 but first patented in 1836. The revolver was ideal for mounted warfare, and the Colt became the standard weapon on the Great Plains.

His invention of the Colt revolver sometimes overshadows his great contribution to the technique of the mass production of large quantities of complex components. Aided by a brilliant engineer, Elisha Root (1808–1865), Colt in the years 1849–1854 applied the principle of interchangeable manufacture of standardized components to all stages of production of the Colt revolver. His armory at Hartford, Conn., became a showplace of modern industrial techniques, and the Colt revolver was successfully shown in London at the Exhibition of 1851. Later, Colt invented submarine telegraph cable and a submarine battery for the defense of harbors.

See also Mass Production.

COLUMBIA COLLEGE. *See* Colonial Colleges.

COLUMBUS, CHRISTOPHER (1451?–1506), ex-plorer of the New World. Born in Genoa, he became a leader in that great port's merchant marine. His fame came from his decision to reach the East (Asia) by going west instead of around Africa as the Portuguese were doing. Using an ancient but faulty formula, he felt that traveling 3,000 miles would get him to Asia. The irony is that sailing those 3,000 miles led him to discover America, but he died still thinking that he had reached the Far East, and the words *Indians* and *West Indies* preserve that error.

Columbus persuaded Queen Isabella of Spain to finance his venture and name him "Admiral of the Ocean Sea." He made four voyages—August 1492–March 1493, September 1493–June 1496, May 1498–October 1500, and April 1502–November 1504. The first voyage was his most successful. He landed on a Bahamian island and took possession of it for Spain; then he visited Cuba and Hispaniola. On his return, the Pope, a Spaniard, granted Spain all new discoveries to the west.

Then Columbus' fortune suddenly changed. He was a magnificent navigator but a poor governor of the turbulent colony on Santo Domingo. He had various misfortunes on his last two voyages, and at the close of his third he was actually sent home in chains. After his last voyage he lived in Spain in financial comfort and political obscurity. His discoveries gave Spain centuries of wealth and power.

See also Exploration and Discovery.
Consult (I) Morison, 1971.
—Robert G. Albion, *Harvard University*

COMECON, or Council for Mutual Economic Assistance, founded in January 1949 in Moscow as an intergovernmental organization to weld the separate national economies of the Soviet bloc countries into a commonwealth based on international cooperation and the division of labor. It was a response to the Marshall Plan but not so successful as the European Economic Community. The COMECON countries stressed central planning, and their common objective was one international plan for the entire Soviet bloc.

There is a permanent secretariat located in Moscow as well as a number of permanent and ad hoc commissions. Much of the overall planning has been geared to the policies and needs of the USSR. Soviet leaders, especially since the Hungarian uprising of 1956, have wished to tie East Europe firmly to the USSR and to keep the satellite economies fairly prosperous and thereby guarantee the passive cooperation of the people.

COMINFORM, or the Bureau of Information of the Communist and Workers' Parties, agency of the Soviet and Soviet-controlled Communist parties of Europe formed in 1947. It represented an attempt by Moscow to reimpose the rigid discipline of the prewar Communist Third

International (Comintern), a worldwide organization of Communist parties that existed from 1919 to 1943. The Cominform encouraged anti-Americanism in Italy and France and attacked Socialists in Britain, France, Germany, and Austria for betraying the cause of socialism by not resisting the Marshall Plan.

After Stalin's death in 1953 the Cominform gradually declined. Following Nikita Khrushchev's denunciation of Stalin's faults before the Twentieth Soviet Party Congress in 1956 and the regime's effort to accommodate Marshal Tito of Yugoslavia, the Cominform was officially dissolved.

COMMERCE, DEPARTMENT OF, executive department that administers a great variety of programs and divisions concerned with domestic and international commercial affairs. Among the numerous functions are collection, analysis, and dissemination of statistical information (Bureau of the Census, Office of Business Economics); extension of knowledge of oceans, earth, and atmosphere (Environmental Science Service Administration, including the U.S. Weather Bureau); maintenance of the merchant marine; issuance of patents and registration of trademarks. It was part of the Department of Commerce and Labor from 1903 to 1913, when it became a separate cabinet department.

COMMERCE AND LABOR, DEPARTMENT OF, federal executive department (1903–1913) that combined the functions of the modern departments of Commerce and of Labor. *See* Commerce, Department of; Labor, Department of.

COMMITTEES OF CORRESPONDENCE, colonial groups that organized to protest British policies. Alarmed by news that Parliament was going to guarantee salaries to Massachusetts' governor and judiciary and thus free them from local control, the Boston town meeting, at the suggestion of Samuel Adams, authorized on Nov. 2, 1772, the establishment of a committee of 21 to state the rights of the province's citizens and to communicate Boston's sentiments to other Massachusetts communities. Other colonies quickly followed suit. On March 12, 1773, Virginia appointed an 11-man committee of correspondence, and by February 1774 all colonies except North Carolina and Pennsylvania had established similar groups.

COMMON SENSE (1776), pamphlet by Thomas Paine urging American Independence. *See* Paine, Thomas.

COMMODITY CREDIT CORPORATION, arm of the AAA. *See* Agricultural Adjustment Act (1933).

COMMUNICATIONS ACT (1934), legislation establishing the Federal Communications Commission, an independent regulatory board on the pattern of the Interstate Commerce Commission (1887) to oversee the telegraph, cable, and radio broadcasting industries. Along with the Motor Carrier Act (1935), the Air Mail Act (1935), and the establishment of the Civil Aeronautics Authority (1938), this law further extended federal regulation over industries directly affecting the public interest.

See also National Industrial Recovery Act (1933).

COMMUNIST CONTROL ACT (1954) exempts the Communist Party from the rights accorded other legally constituted bodies or political parties and subjects Communists to the penalties of the Internal Security Act. Membership in a Communist organization is determined, subject to court appeal, by the Subversive Activities Control Board. Considered unconstitutional by some, the act has not been strictly enforced or tested in the courts, but it has helped keep the Communist Party off the ballot in most states.

See also Internal Security Act.

COMPROMISE OF 1850, a major attempt to end the sectional disputes that threatened the Union. It had once been hoped that the Missouri Compromise of 1820 had resolved these disputes, but starting in 1831 the country had been aroused by the rise of an aggressive abolitionism that stirred opinion in the North against slaveholders and inspired retaliation in the South. Northern antislavery partisans aided fugitive slaves, fought court actions to prevent slaveholders from gaining security in possession of their slave property, and sought to prevent the spread of slavery to the West.

Senator Henry Clay brought together a number of proposals intended to satisfy both North and South. After lengthy debate in the Senate and numerous changes, a series of acts known as the Compromise of 1850 was passed in September 1850. The compromise endorsed California's admission as a free state, organized New Mexico and Utah as territories that could enter the Union with or without slavery, and abolished the slave trade (but not slavery) in Washington, D.C. Most fateful was the compromise's fugitive slave provision, which attempted by strong federal action to end the abolitionist practice of aiding runaway slaves. Attempted enforcement of the Fugitive Slave Act roused the entire North against it and accentuated sectional differences. Although some stated that the new compromise did not abrogate the Missouri Compromise, which limited the spread of slavery, others held that it did. This debate became academic in 1854, when the Kansas-Nebraska Act specifically repealed the Missouri Compromise.

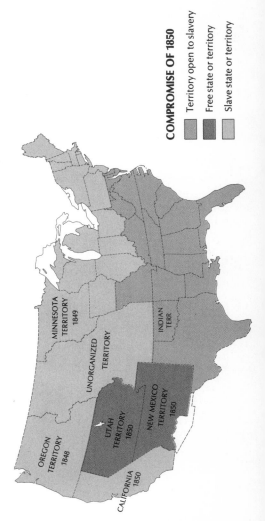

COMPROMISE OF 1850

Territory open to slavery

Free state or territory

Slave state or territory

MINNESOTA TERRITORY 1849

INDIAN TERR

UNORGANIZED TERRITORY

OREGON TERRITORY 1848

UTAH TERRITORY 1850

NEW MEXICO TERRITORY 1850

CALIFORNIA 1850

Computers have made retrieval, tabulation, and analysis of information infinitely faster and have revolutionized business techniques.

CONFEDERATE STATES OF AMERICA
— Item Guide

The article on the CONFEDERATE STATES OF AMERICA discusses the form of government established by the secessionist states in 1861, and the problems it encountered.

Factors leading to the creation of the Confederacy include DAVIS RESOLUTIONS; CIVIL WAR: CAUSES, where there is a Subject Map; NULLIFICATION, a doctrine developed by JOHN C. CALHOUN; SECESSION; and SLAVERY.

There are entries on the major civilian Confederate leaders — JUDAH P. BENJAMIN, JEFFERSON DAVIS, and ALEXANDER H. STEPHENS. Military campaigns are discussed in CIVIL WAR BATTLES and APPOMATTOX COURTHOUSE SURRENDER, and there are entries on the diplomatic maneuvers of the TRENT AFFAIR and the HAMPTON ROADS CONFERENCE (1865). Confederate generals who have entries include P. G. T. BEAUREGARD, STONEWALL JACKSON, JOSEPH E. JOHNSTON, ROBERT E. LEE, JAMES LONGSTREET, and JEB STUART. The South's defeat led to RECONSTRUCTION.

See also Clay, Henry; Fugitive Slave Acts; Kansas-Nebraska Act (1854); Missouri Compromise (1820).

Consult (IV) Hamilton, 1964; Rozwenc, 1957.

—Louis Filler, *Antioch College*

COMPROMISE OF 1877, political compromise that followed the disputed election of 1876. Although Samuel J. Tilden, Democratic presidential nominee, won a popular vote majority, his Republican opponent, Rutherford B. Hayes, protested that irregularities had marred the balloting in three states. If Hayes were to receive all the electoral votes of those states, he would have 185 electoral votes to Tilden's 184.

To settle the issue, Congress on Jan. 29, 1877, established an electoral commission made up of five U.S. representatives, five senators, and five Supreme Court justices. Seven of these were Democrats and eight Republicans. Voting along straight party lines, the commission awarded the disputed states to Hayes. Incensed Southern Democrats threatened to filibuster the official counting of the ballots to prevent Hayes from assuming office with full legal title.

To avert such a deadlock, Republican and Democratic leaders informally agreed on the Compromise of 1877. In return for the Democrats dropping the filibuster, Hayes would withdraw all Federal troops from the South (where they helped prop up Radical governments in South Carolina, Louisiana, and Florida); a prominent Southern ex-Whig would be appointed to the cabinet; and Hayes would favor Southern appeals for federal funding of internal improvement projects in the South. The first two conditions were quickly met, but funds for improvements were not appropriated.

See also Hayes, Rutherford B.; Presidential Elections; Reconstruction (1865–1877).

Consult (V) Woodward, 1966.

—Michael Burlingame, *Connecticut College*

COMPUTERS. The development of high-speed computers with miniaturized circuitry to perform calculations and process data has changed the business, occupational, and living habits of hundreds of millions of people and has had a profound influence on science, government, warfare, and industry. Only machines can handle the mass of complex data in our era of information explosion fast enough to allow timely action based on understanding of the facts. Computers have been used for weather forecasting, digesting of census and tax information, processing election returns, maintaining inventories, programming and detecting missiles, keeping criminal files, communications, teaching, and medical diagnosis.

Computer simulation of processes that actually occur in the world makes possible the study of the behavior of voters under the impact of election campaigns, of combatants in international diplomacy and warfare, and of audiences subjected to propaganda. Computers can plot electoral districts that are compact, contiguous, and composed of equal numbers of inhabitants, and they can also trace the business cycle and aid in economic forecasting.

COMSTOCK LAW (1873). *See* Abortion and Birth Control Laws.

CONCORD. *See* Lexington and Concord (1775).

CONFEDERATE STATES OF AMERICA. On Feb. 4, 1861, delegates from the six states that had seceded from the Union (South Carolina, Georgia, Mississippi, Alabama, Florida, and Louisiana) gathered in Montgomery, Ala., to form a new government. They elected a president (Jefferson Davis) and vice-president (Alexander H. Stephens) on February 9, and a month later adopted a permanent constitution, which was based on the U.S. Constitution. There were several important differences, however: the president's term was 6 years, and he could serve only once; state sovereignty and slavery were recognized; and protective tariffs and general appropriations for internal improvements were prohibited. After Lincoln's call for volunteers to suppress the insurrection (April 15), four more states joined the Confederacy—Virginia, North Carolina, Arkansas, and Tennessee. Texas had been admitted on March 2.

The Confederacy suffered from internal weaknesses. The deep-rooted spirit of states' rights hampered the central government, and President Davis' lack of a coherent strategy undermined military effectiveness. Confederate finances, crippled by traditional agrarian hostility toward taxation, were chaotic. Thus, in almost every sphere the rampant individualism of the Old South militated against the discipline and organization necessary to wage modern war. Devotion to slavery also contributed significantly to the defeat of the Confederacy because European powers were reluctant to help a nation they considered a slave empire.

Consult (IV) Eaton, 1954; Wiley and Milhollen, 1964.

—Michael Burlingame, *Connecticut College*

CONFEDERATION, ARTICLES OF. *See* Articles of Confederation.

CONFEDERATION CONGRESS, name often given to the Congress that met between 1781, when the Articles of Confederation were ratified, and 1789, when the Constitution was ratified. *See* Continental Congress, Second.

CONFESSIONS OF NAT TURNER, THE, novel by William Styron on the celebrated slave revolt. *See* Nat Turner's Revolt (1831).

CONGREGATIONALISTS, the largest and most influential religious body in colonial America and an offshoot of the Puritan movement in England. Its leaders, including John Cotton of Boston, Thomas Hooker of Hartford, and John Davenport of New Haven, actively molded early church government in New England and were well known for their views on many political as well as religious issues.

The first Congregationalist church in Plymouth, Mass. (1620) was made up of English Separatists. Puritans in Massachusetts Bay and later in Connecticut and New Hampshire formed more Congregational churches to worship God and study His Word as revealed in the Bible. As the Congregational membership grew, disputes arose over matters of church government and discipline. Attempts were made by the Massachusetts leaders to enforce certain Presbyterian measures. These were rejected in Massachusetts, but accepted in Connecticut as the Saybrook Platform (1708).

The Great Awakening in the 1740s temporarily revived New England Congregationalism and added thousands of new members. However, the revival produced disagreements about doctrine that divided Congregationalists into several groups. Most of these groups joined the Presbyterians, with the result that Congregationalists eventually became a relatively small religious body. The Congregationalists' high regard for education and the need for ministers led to the founding of several colleges, including Harvard, Yale, Williams, Amherst, and Oberlin.

See also Colonial Religion; Great Awakening; Pilgrims; Puritanism.
Consult (I) Olmstead, 1961.

CONGRESS OF INDUSTRIAL ORGANIZATIONS (CIO), labor group that had its beginning at the 1935 American Federation of Labor convention over the question of whether the nonunion mass production industries should be organized along craft (horizontal) or industrial (vertical) lines. When the craft position won out, John L. Lewis, head of the United Mine Workers, led the formation of the Committee for Industrial Organization. In 1937 the dissident unions were expelled from the AFL, and in the following year they reorganized as the CIO. Introducing the sit-down strike as a means of preventing continued plant operations with scab labor, the CIO achieved spectacular success in organizing such industries as steel, automobiles, rubber, textiles, and shipbuilding. In 1955 the CIO merged with the AFL.

See also American Federation of Labor-Congress of Industrial Organizations; Lewis, John L.
Consult (VIII) Preis, 1964.

CONGRESS OF RACIAL EQUALITY (CORE), civil rights organization founded in 1942 by James Farmer and a group of students at the University of Chicago. CORE, broadly based with a reputed membership of 180,000, at its height (including whites), pioneered such techniques as the sit-in, first used in a Chicago restaurant in 1943, and freedom rides. In 1961, CORE made headlines when freedom riders testing integration of bus facilities were attacked by mobs in Birmingham and Montgomery, Ala.

In the mid-1960s, CORE began an intensive drive for voter registration and desegregation. In the late 1960s the organization made a gradual switch to black nationalism, which was costly in terms of membership.

CONKLING, ROSCOE (1829–1888), New York politician, leader of the Stalwart faction of the Republican Party. Originally a Whig, Conkling became a War Republican serving first in the House and, after 1867, as a senator from New York. An advocate of harsh measures toward the South, Conkling helped to draft the Fourteenth Amendment.

His heartfelt admiration for President Grant was rewarded with federal patronage that enabled him to rule his state party. When President Hayes removed Chester Arthur as customs collector in New York in 1877, Conkling condemned Hayes, and in 1880 he led an attempt to draft Grant for a third term. Disputes over James A. Garfield's patronage policies resurfaced in 1881, and Conkling dramatically resigned from the Senate. The New York legislature ended his political career by refusing to return him to his seat.

A successful lawyer, Conkling often appeared before the Supreme Court, notably in the San Mateo case (1882). He argued that the word *person* in the Fourteenth Amendment had been chosen by the drafting committee in order to extend due process protection to legal persons, meaning corporations, as well as to citizens. That argument, accepted by the Court in 1886, became the prime defense of corporate property rights.

See also Arthur, Chester A.; Hayes, Rutherford B.; Stalwarts and Half-Breeds.
Consult (V) Josephson, 1938.

CONNECTICUT, a southern New England colony and state settled mainly as an offshoot of the Massachusetts Bay and Plymouth colonies. A Dutchman, Adriaen Block, located the Connecticut River in 1614, and in 1633 the Dutch built a small fort at what is now Hartford to forestall British colonization. The Puritans were

Roscoe Conkling, leader of the Stalwart faction of the Republican Party.

already in the region, and they built another fort at nearby Windsor. Edward Winslow from Plymouth Colony explored the area in 1632, and when a group of Puritan nobles in England was deeded lands at the mouth of the Connecticut River, they sent John Winthrop, Jr., there. Winthrop established the town of Saybrook in 1635, the same year in which two groups emigrated from Massachusetts.

Initially, Connecticut was administered by commissioners appointed by Massachusetts Bay, although from the start the franchise was broader—unlike Massachusetts, franchise was not based on church membership. By 1639, Connecticut was independent minded enough to establish its autonomy, and the Fundamental Orders were drawn up, mainly by Rev. Thomas Hooker and John Haynes. The orders were not democratic, because they were based on Hooker's belief that, although the people were fit to choose, only the church elders were fit to govern.

Hooker, a Puritan leader from England who had moved to Hartford in 1636 from Massachusetts, was the virtual ruler of Connecticut, although in form the governorship was always a one-year appointment. Haynes was Connecticut's first governor under the orders and held that post for alternate years until his death in 1654. The eloquent, dominating Hooker shaped the colony in its early years. His *Survey of the Summe of Church Discipline* (1648) summarized the major Congregationalist beliefs and practices of the day. By 1654 no Dutch settlements were left in the area.

While Connecticut was being settled, a colony was created at New Haven. Led by John Davenport and Theophilus Eaton, men from Massachusetts settled at New Haven in 1638. The New Haven Colony was strictly a Bible commonwealth with Old Testament rules such as no trial by jury. Hemmed in by the Dutch on the west and Connecticut on the north and east, New Haven could not easily expand. With the restoration of the monarchy in England in 1660, John Winthrop, Jr., went to London to secure a charter for Connecticut. This charter of 1662 included New Haven, which resisted assimilation for a year or so.

Connecticut was a charter colony after 1662. When Governor Edmund Andros of New York tried to consolidate the northern colonies into the Dominion of New England in 1686–1687, the charter of Connecticut was hidden from him, allegedly in the famous Charter Oak, a tree that fell in 1856. Andros never found the charter, but he dissolved Connecticut's government. The Whig Revolution of 1688 in England restored the charter form, under which the colony continued to elect its governors until the Revolution.

Connecticut played a large role in the framing of the U.S. Constitution through its delegate Oliver Ellsworth, the Hartford lawyer

Conservation acts have aimed at preserving and protecting natural resources such as forests.

who helped to push through the Connecticut Compromise, which saved the Constitutional Convention (1787) from foundering. The compromise created the bicameral legislature, consisting of Senate and House of Representatives, a device by which the voice of the smaller states was given weight. Connecticut was the fifth state to ratify the Constitution (Jan. 9, 1788).

The capital is Hartford; the legislature is bicameral. The population in 1970 was 3,032,-217.

See also Connecticut Compromise; Constitutional Convention (1787); Ellsworth, Oliver.

Consult (I) Savelle and Middlekauff, 1964.

—Peter d'A. Jones, *University of Illinois, Chicago Circle*

CONNECTICUT COMPROMISE provided the solution at the Constitutional Convention (1787) between the large and small states over representation to the national legislature. It was proposed by Oliver Ellsworth of Connecticut. The large states wanted representation to the new Congress to be based on population or wealth (the Virginia Plan). The small states wanted equal representation for each state regardless of size (New Jersey Plan).

Ellsworth's plan provided for representation to the lower house (the House of Representatives) on the basis of population and for equal representation of each state in the upper house (the Senate); this compromise was incorporated into the new Constitution. Not only was the Connecticut Compromise important in breaking the deadlock between the two groups of states, but, coming at a low ebb in the Philadelphia proceedings, it also provided a valuable impetus for the effort needed to complete the Constitution.

See also Constitutional Convention (1787); Ellsworth, Oliver; New Jersey Plan; Virginia Plan.

Consult (III) Warren, 1967.

CONSCIOUSNESS RAISING, effort to reorient women's conception of themselves. *See* Women's Liberation.

CONSERVATION ACTS, legislation to reclaim land, conserve forests, and protect wildlife. The first major act was the Forest Reserve Act (1891), which authorized the creation of forest reserves. This was followed by the Carey Act (1894), giving the president the authority to grant certain states up to 1 million acres for reclamation and settlement, with any funds received from sales to be used for reclaiming other state lands. During President Harrison's Administration 13 million acres were set aside, including the Yellowstone Park Timberland Reserve, the first U.S. forest reserve.

Under Theodore Roosevelt, conservation received increased support from legislation that included the National Reclamation Act (1902), also known as the Newlands Act, which was designed to finance irrigation in arid Western states. Parks continued to increase, and President Wilson established the National Park Service in 1916 to administer them. During the New Deal era such agencies as the Civilian Conservation Corps were engaged in conservation projects.

The culmination of efforts of conservationists throughout the postwar period was the Wilderness Preservation Act of 1964, which established a national wilderness preservation system. The legislation was opposed by various Western-state economic interests who objected that it would prevent development of the land and its resources.

The next year Congress passed the Water Quality Act of 1965 and the Highway Beautification Act. The latter, an effort to improve the landscaping of interstate and primary highways with state controls on billboards and junkyards, was passed with much fanfare, but Congress lost interest and very meager funds were provided to carry through on the promise. In 1968 a National Wild and Scenic Rivers Bill was enacted to preserve sections of selected rivers in their free-flowing unspoiled condition and to protect their water quality and other conservation values, and it was followed by supplementary pollution legislation.

Consult (VIII) Nash, 1970; Udall, 1963.
—Martin Gruberg, *University of Wisconsin, Oshkosh*

CONSTITUTIONAL CONVENTION (1787), also known as the Federal Convention, prepared the U.S. Constitution. The meeting was called in response to the widely recognized need for the creation of a stronger national government, and it was instructed by the Continental Congress to propose amendments to the Articles of Confederation. The delegates met in Philadelphia between May 25 and September 17, and every state except Rhode Island was represented. Altogether, 55 delegates appeared, although not all stayed to the end. Thomas Jefferson and John Adams were on diplomatic missions in Europe at the time, and conspicuous for their absence were Patrick Henry, George Clinton, Samuel Adams, and John Hancock.

Nonetheless, the assemblage represented a striking array of talent. It included George Washington, James Madison, George Mason, Edmund Randolph, and George Wythe of Virginia; Benjamin Franklin, Robert Morris, Gouverneur Morris, and James Wilson of Pennsylvania; William Paterson of New Jersey; Alexander Hamilton of New York; Luther Martin of Maryland; Roger Sherman and Oliver Ellsworth of Connecticut; John Rutledge, Charles Cotesworth Pinckney, and Charles Pinckney of South Carolina; and Elbridge Gerry and Rufus King of Massachusetts.

Shortly after deliberations began, the delegates agreed that it was impossible to amend the Articles of Confederation, and they decided to erect a new and more powerful central government in its place. Although there were some differences among the delegates, particularly on the questions of representation, taxation, and slavery, they were compromised. The Constitution, however, did not go into effect until it was ratified by the required nine states in 1788.

See also Connecticut Compromise; New Jersey Plan; Virginia Plan.
Consult (III) Bowen, 1966; Warren, 1967.
—Richard E. Ellis, *University of Virginia*

CONSTITUTION OF THE UNITED STATES, the basic document by which the United States is governed. America's constitution actually extends beyond this single document and includes the whole scheme of traditions, conventions, and formal and informal rules by which the Constitution has been interpreted since its adoption.

Purpose. The underlying premise of the U.S. Constitution is the belief that the powers of the government should be limited. The main source of this belief is to be found in the political philosophy and experience of America's Revolutionary generation. The movement for independence had revealed the dissatisfaction of that generation with the vagueness of Britain's unwritten constitution, which they believed had allowed Parliament to arrogate to itself so much power that it endangered individual liberty. To effectively prevent this from occurring in their newly established country the Founding Fathers felt it necessary to create a written document that would formally establish the government and be the supreme law by which all the other laws and actions of the state and federal governments could be measured.

Content. Written at the Constitutional Convention during the summer of 1787 and ratified the following winter, the U.S. Constitution organizes the basic political institutions of the country. It divides the powers of governing between the national government and the states in a system known as federalism. It describes the way different members of the federal government are to be elected or appointed and their terms of office. It separates the functions of the legislative, executive, and judicial branches in such a way as to check and balance one against the other. It limits the powers of the government by means of a Bill of Rights that protects individual liberties so as to achieve a proper balance between freedom and authority. And it provides a workable

THE CONSTITUTION OF THE UNITED STATES

We the People of the United States, in Order to form a more perfect Union, establish Justice, insure domestic Tranquillity, provide for the common defence, promote the general Welfare, and secure the Blessings of Liberty to ourselves and our Posterity, do ordain and establish this Constitution for the United States of America.

ARTICLE. I.

SECTION. 1. All legislative Powers herein granted shall be vested in a Congress of the United States, which shall consist of a Senate and House of Representatives.

SECTION. 2. The House of Representatives shall be composed of Members chosen every second Year by the People of the several States, and the Electors in each State shall have the Qualifications requisite for Electors of the most numerous Branch of the State Legislature.

No Person shall be a Representative who shall not have attained to the age of twenty five Years, and been seven Years a Citizen of the United States, and who shall not, when elected, be an Inhabitant of that State in which he shall be chosen.

Representatives and direct Taxes shall be apportioned among the several States which may be included within this Union, according to their respective Numbers, which shall be determined by adding to the whole Number of free Persons, including those bound to Service for a Term of Years, and excluding Indians not taxed, three fifths of all other Persons. The actual Enumeration shall be made within three Years after the first Meeting of the Congress of the United States, and within every subsequent Term of ten Years, in such Manner as they shall by Law direct. The Number of Representatives shall not exceed one for every thirty Thousand, but each State shall have at Least one Representative; and until such enumeration shall be made, the State of New Hampshire shall be entitled to chuse three, Massachusetts eight, Rhode-Island and Providence Plantations one, Connecticut five, New-York six, New Jersey four, Pennsylvania eight, Delaware one, Maryland six, Virginia ten, North Carolina five, South Carolina five, and Georgia three.

When vacancies happen in the Representation from any State, the Executive Authority thereof shall issue Writs of Election to fill such Vacancies.

The House of Representatives shall chuse their Speaker and other Officers; and shall have the sole Power of Impeachment.

SECTION. 3. The Senate of the United States shall be composed of two Senators from each State, chosen by the Legislature thereof, for six Years; and each Senator shall have one Vote.

Immediately after they shall be assembled in Consequence of the first Election, they shall be divided as equally as may be into three Classes. The Seats of the Senators of the first Class shall be vacated at the Expiration of the second Year, of the second Class at the Expiration of the fourth Year, and of the third Class at the Expiration of the sixth Year, so that one third may be chosen every second Year; and if Vacancies happen by Resignation, or otherwise, during the Recess of the Legislature of any State, the Executive thereof may make temporary Appointments until the next Meeting of the Legislature, which shall then fill such Vacancies.

No Person shall be a Senator who shall not have attained to the Age of thirty Years, and been nine Years a Citizen of the United States, and who shall not, when elected, be an Inhabitant of that State for which he shall be chosen.

The Vice President of the United States shall be President of the Senate, but shall have no Vote, unless they be equally divided.

The Senate shall chuse their other Officers, and also a President pro tempore, in the Absence of the Vice President, or when he shall exercise the Office of President of the United States.

The Senate shall have the sole Power to try all Impeachments. When sitting for that Purpose, they shall be on Oath or Affirmation. When the President of the United States is tried the Chief Justice shall preside: And no Person shall be convicted without the Concurrence of two thirds of the Members present.

Judgment in Cases of Impeachment shall not extend further than to removal from Office, and disqualification to hold and enjoy any Office of honor, Trust or Profit under the United States: but the Party convicted shall nevertheless be liable and subject to Indictment, Trial, Judgment and Punishment, according to Law.

SECTION. 4. The Times, Places and Manner of holding Elections for Senators and Representatives, shall be prescribed in each State by the Legislature thereof; but the Congress may at any time by Law make or alter such Regulations, except as to the Places of chusing Senators.

The Congress shall assemble at least once in every Year, and such Meeting shall be on the first Monday in December, unless they shall by Law appoint a different Day.

SECTION 5. Each House shall be the Judge of the Elections, Returns and Qualifications of its own Members, and a Majority of each shall constitute a Quorum to do Business; but a smaller Number may adjourn from day to day, and may be authorized to compel the Attendance of absent Members, in such Manner, and under such Penalties as each House may provide.

Each House may determine the Rules of its Proceedings, punish its Members for disorderly Behaviour, and, with the Concurrence of two thirds, expel a Member.

Each House shall keep a Journal of its Proceedings, and from time to time publish the same, excepting such Parts as may in their Judgment require Secrecy; and the Yeas and Nays of the Members of either House on any question shall, at the Desire of one fifth of those Present, be entered on the Journal.

Neither House, during the Session of Congress, shall, without the Consent of the other, adjourn for more than three days, nor to any other Place than that in which the two Houses shall be sitting.

SECTION. 6. The Senators and Representatives shall receive a Compensation for their Services, to be ascertained by Law, and paid out of the Treasury of the United States. They shall in all Cases, except Treason, Felony and Breach of the Peace, be privileged from Arrest during their Attendance at the Session of their respective Houses, and in going to and returning from the same; and for any Speech or Debate in either House, they shall not be questioned in any other Place.

No Senator or Representative shall, during the Time for which he was elected, be appointed to any civil Office under the Authority of the United States, which shall have been created, or the Emoluments whereof shall have been encreased during such time; and no Person holding any Office under the United States, shall be a Member of either House during his Continuance in Office.

SECTION. 7. All Bills for raising Revenue shall originate in the House of Representatives; but the Senate may propose or concur with amendments as on other Bills.

Every Bill which shall have passed the House of Representatives and the Senate, shall, before it become a Law, be presented to the President of the United States; If he approve he shall sign it, but if not he shall return it, with his Objections to that House in which it shall have originated, who shall enter the Objections at large on their Journal, and proceed to reconsider it. If after such Reconsideration two thirds of that House shall agree to pass the Bill, it shall be sent, together with the Objections, to the other House, by which it shall likewise be reconsidered, and if approved by two thirds of that House, it shall become a Law. But in all such Cases the Votes of both Houses shall be determined by yeas and Nays, and the Names of the Persons voting for and against the Bill shall be entered on the Journal of each House respectively. If any Bill shall not be returned by the President within ten Days (Sundays excepted) after it shall have been presented to him, the Same shall be a Law, in like Manner as if he had signed it, unless the Congress by their Adjournment prevent its Return, in which Case it shall not be a Law.

Every Order, Resolution, or Vote to which the Concurrence of the Senate and House of Representatives may be necessary (except on a question of Adjournment) shall be presented to the President of the United States; and before the Same shall take Effect, shall be approved by him, or being disapproved by him, shall be repassed by two thirds of the Senate and House of Representatives, according to the Rules and Limitations prescribed in the Case of a Bill.

SECTION. 8. The Congress shall have Power To lay and collect Taxes, Duties, Imposts and Excises, to pay the Debts and provide for the common Defence and general Welfare of the United States; but all Duties, Imposts and Excises shall be uniform throughout the United States;

To borrow Money on the credit of the United States;

To regulate Commerce with foreign Nations, and among the several States, and with the Indian Tribes;

To establish an uniform Rule of Naturalization, and uniform Laws on the subject of Bankruptcies throughout the United States;

To coin Money, regulate the Value thereof, and of foreign Coin, and fix the Standard of Weights and Measures;

To provide for the Punishment of counterfeiting the Securities and current Coin of the United States;

To establish Post Offices and post Roads;

To promote the Progress of Science and useful Arts, by securing for limited Times to Authors and Inventors the exclusive Right to their respective Writings and Discoveries;

To constitute Tribunals inferior to the supreme Court;

To define and punish Piracies and Felonies committed on the high Seas, and Offences against the Law of Nations;

To declare War, grant Letters of Marque and Reprisal, and make Rules concerning Captures on Land and Water;

To raise and support Armies, but no Appropriation of Money to that Use shall be for a longer Term than two Years;

To provide and maintain a Navy;

To make Rules for the Government and Regulation of the land and naval Forces;

To provide for calling forth the Militia to execute the Laws of the Union, suppress Insurrections and repel Invasions;

To provide for organizing, arming, and disciplining, the Militia, and for governing such Part of them as may be employed in the Service of the United States, reserving to the States respectively, the Appointment of the Officers, and the Authority of training the Militia according to the discipline prescribed by Congress;

To exercise exclusive Legislation in all Cases whatsoever, over such District (not exceeding ten Miles square) as may, by Cession of Particular States, and the Acceptance of Congress, become the Seat of the Government of the United States, and to exercise like Authority over all Places purchased by the Consent of the Legislature of the State in which the Same shall be, for the Erection of Forts, Magazines, Arsenals, dock-Yards, and other needful Buildings;—And

To make all Laws which shall be necessary and proper for carrying into Execution the foregoing Powers, and all other Powers vested by this Constitution in the Government of the United States, or in any Department or Officer thereof.

SECTION. 9. The Migration or Importation of such Persons as any of the States now existing shall think proper to admit, shall not be prohibited by the Congress prior to the Year one thousand eight hundred and eight, but a Tax or duty may be imposed on such Importation, not exceeding ten dollars for each Person.

The Privilege of the Writ of Habeas Corpus shall not be suspended, unless when in Cases of Rebellion or Invasion the public Safety may require it.

No Bill of Attainder or ex post facto Law shall be passed.

No Capitation, or other direct, Tax shall be laid, unless in Proportion to the Census or Enumeration herein before directed to be taken.

No Tax or Duty shall be laid on Articles exported from any State.

No Preference shall be given by any Regulation of Commerce or Revenue to the Ports of one State over those of another; nor shall Vessels bound to, or from, one State, be obliged to enter, clear or pay Duties in another.

No Money shall be drawn from the Treasury, but in Consequence of Appropriations made by Law; and a regular Statement and Account of the Receipts and Expenditures of all public Money shall be published from time to time.

No Title of Nobility shall be granted by the United States: And no Person holding any Office of Profit or Trust under them, shall, without the Consent of the Congress, accept of any present Emolument, Office, or Title, of any kind whatever, from any King, Prince, or foreign State.

SECTION. 10. No State shall enter into any Treaty, Alliance, or Confederation; grant Letters of Marque and Reprisal; coin Money; emit Bills of Credit; make any Thing but gold and silver Coin a Tender in Payment of Debts; pass any Bill of Attainder, ex post facto Law, or Law impairing the Obligation of Contracts, or grant any Title of Nobility.

No State shall, without the Consent of the Congress, lay any Imposts or Duties on Imports or Exports, except what may be absolutely necessary for executing its inspection Laws: and the net Produce of all Duties and Imposts, laid by any State on Imports or Exports, shall be for the Use of the Treasury of the United States; and all such Laws shall be subject to the Revision and Controul of the Congress.

No State shall, without the Consent of Congress, lay any Duty of Tonnage, keep Troops, or Ships of War in time of Peace, enter into any Agreement or Compact with another State, or with a foreign Power, or engage in War, unless actually invaded, or in such imminent Danger as will not admit of delay.

ARTICLE. II.

SECTION. 1. The executive Power shall be vested in a President of the United States of America. He shall hold his Office during the Term of four Years, and, together with the Vice President, chosen for the same Term, be elected, as follows

Each State shall appoint, in such Manner as the Legislature thereof may direct, a Number of Electors, equal to the whole Number of Senators and Representatives to which the State may be entitled in the Congress: but no Senator or Representative, or Person holding an Office of Trust or Profit under the United States, shall be appointed an Elector.

The Electors shall meet in their respective States, and vote by Ballot for two Persons, of whom one at least shall not be an Inhabitant of the same State with themselves. And they shall make a List of all the Persons voted for, and of the Number of Votes for each; which List they shall sign and certify, and transmit sealed to the Seat of the Government of the United States, directed to the President of the Senate. The President of the Senate shall, in the Presence of the Senate and House of Representatives, open all the Certificates, and the Votes shall then be counted. The Person having the greatest Number of Votes shall be the President, if such Number be a Majority of the whole Number of Electors appointed; and if there be more than one who have such Majority, and have an equal Number of Votes, then the House of Representatives shall immediately chuse by Ballot one of them for President; and if no Person have a Majority, then from the five highest on the List the said House shall in like Manner chuse the President. But in chusing the President, the Votes shall be taken by States, the Representation from each State having one Vote; a quorum for this Purpose shall consist of a Member or Members from two thirds of the States, and a Majority of all the States shall be necessary to a Choice. In every Case, after the Choice of the President, the Person having the greatest Number of Votes of the Electors shall be the Vice President. But if there should remain two or more who have equal Votes, the Senate shall chuse from them by Ballot the Vice President.

The Congress may determine the Time of chusing the Electors, and the Day on which they shall give their Votes; which Day shall be the same throughout the United States.

No Person except a natural born Citizen, or a Citizen of the United States, at the time of the Adoption of this Constitution, shall be eligible to the Office of President; neither shall any person be eligible to that Office who shall not have attained to the Age of thirty five Years, and been fourteen Years a Resident within the United States.

In Case of the Removal of the President from Office, or of his Death, Resignation, or Inability to discharge the Powers and Duties of the said Office, the Same shall devolve on the Vice President, and the Congress may by Law provide for the Case of Removal, Death, Resignation or Inability, both of the President and Vice President, declaring what Officer shall then act as President, and such Officer shall act accordingly, until the Disability be removed, or a President shall be elected.

The President shall, at stated Times, receive for his Services, a Compensation, which shall neither be encreased nor diminished during the Period for which he shall have been elected, and he shall not receive within that period any other Emolument from the United States, or any of them.

Before he enter on the Execution of his Office, he shall take the following Oath or Affirmation:—"I do solemnly swear (or affirm) that I will faithfully execute the Office of President of the United States, and will to the best of my Ability, preserve, protect and defend the Constitution of the United States."

SECTION. 2. The President shall be Commander in Chief of the Army and Navy of the United States, and of the Militia of the several States, when called into the actual Service of the United States; he may require the Opinion, in writing, of the principal Officer in each of the executive Departments, upon any Subject relating to the Duties of their respective Offices, and he shall have Power to grant Reprieves and Pardons for Offences against the United States, except in Cases of Impeachment.

He shall have Power, by and with the Advice and Consent of the Senate, to make Treaties, provided two thirds of the Senators present concur; and he shall nominate, and by and with the Advice and Consent of the Senate, shall appoint Ambassadors, other public Ministers and Consuls, Judges of the supreme Court, and all other Officers of the United States, whose Appointments are not herein otherwise provided for, and which shall be established by Law: but the Congress may by Law vest the Appointment of such inferior Officers, as they think proper, in the President alone, in the Courts of Law, or in the Heads of Departments.

The President shall have Power to fill up all Vacancies that may happen during the Recess of the Senate, by granting Commissions which shall expire at the End of their next Session.

SECTION. 3. He shall from time to time give to the Congress Information of the State of the Union, and recommend to their Consideration such Measures as he shall judge necessary and expedient; he may, on extraordinary Occasions, convene both Houses, or either of them, and in Case of Disagreement between them, with Respect to the Time of Adjournment, he may adjourn them to such Time as he shall think proper; he shall receive Ambassadors and other public Ministers; he shall take Care that the Laws be faithfully executed, and shall Commission all the Officers of the United States.

SECTION. 4. The President, Vice President and all civil Officers of the United States, shall be removed from Office on Impeachment for, and Conviction of, Treason, Bribery, or other high Crimes and Misdemeanors.

ARTICLE. III.

SECTION. 1. The judicial Power of the United States, shall be vested in one supreme Court, and in such inferior Courts as the Congress may from time to time ordain and establish. The Judges, both of the supreme and inferior Courts, shall hold their Offices during good Behaviour, and shall, at stated Times, receive for their Services, a Compensation, which shall not be diminished during their Continuance in Office.

SECTION. 2. The judicial Power shall extend to all Cases, in Law and Equity, arising under this Constitution, the Laws of the United States, and Treaties made, or which shall be made, under their Authority;—to all Cases affecting Ambassadors, other public Ministers and Consuls;—to all Cases of admiralty and maritime Jurisdiction;—to Controversies to which the United States shall be a Party;—to Controversies between two or more States;—between a State and Citizens of another State;—between Citizens of different States;—between Citizens of the same State claiming Lands under Grants of different States, and between a State, or the Citizens thereof, and foreign States, Citizens or Subjects.

In all Cases affecting Ambassadors, other public Ministers and Consuls, and those in which a State shall be Party, the supreme Court shall have original Jurisdiction. In all the other Cases before mentioned, the supreme Court shall have appellate Jurisdiction, both as to Law and Fact, with such Exceptions, and under such Regulations as the Congress shall make.

The Trial of all Crimes, except in Cases of Impeachment, shall be by Jury; and such Trial shall be held in the State where the said Crimes shall have been committed; but when not committed within any State, the Trial shall be at such Place or Places as the Congress may by Law have directed.

SECTION. 3. Treason against the United States, shall consist only in levying War against them, or in adhering to their Enemies, giving them Aid and Comfort. No Person shall be convicted of Treason unless on the Testimony of two Witnesses to the same overt Act, or on Confession in open Court.

The Congress shall have Power to declare the Punishment of Treason, but no Attainder of Treason shall work Corruption of Blood, or Forfeiture except during the Life of the Person attainted.

ARTICLE. IV.

SECTION. 1. Full Faith and Credit shall be given in each State to the public Acts, Records, and judicial Proceedings of every other State. And the Congress may by general Laws prescribe the Manner in which such Acts, Record and Proceedings shall be proved, and the Effect thereof.

SECTION. 2. The Citizens of each State shall be entitled to all Privileges and Immunities of Citizens in the several States.

A Person charged in any State with Treason, Felony, or other Crime, who shall flee from Justice, and be found in another State, shall on Demand of the executive Authority of the State from which he fled, be delivered up, to be removed to the State having Jurisdiction of the Crime.

No Person held to Service or Labour in one State, under the Laws thereof, escaping into another, shall, in Consequence of any Law or Regulation therein, be discharged from such Service or Labour, but shall be delivered up on Claim of the Party to whom such Service or Labour may be due.

SECTION. 3. New States may be admitted by the Congress into this Union; but no new State shall be formed or erected within the Jurisdiction of any other State; nor any State be formed by the Junction of two or more States, or Parts of States, without the Consent of the Legislatures of the States concerned as well as of the Congress.

The Congress shall have Power to dispose of and make all needful Rules and Regulations respecting the Territory or other Property belonging to the United States; and nothing in this Constitution shall be so construed as to Prejudice any Claims of the United States, or of any particular State.

SECTION. 4. The United States shall guarantee to every State in this Union a Republican Form of Government, and shall protect each of them against Invasion; and on Application of the Legislature, or of the Executive (when the Legislature cannot be convened) against domestic Violence.

ARTICLE. V.

The Congress, whenever two thirds of both Houses shall deem it necessary, shall propose Amendments to this Constitution, or, on the Application of the Legislature of two thirds of the several States, shall call a Convention for proposing Amendments, which, in either Case, shall be valid to all Intents and Purposes, as Part of this Constitution, when ratified by the Legislatures of three fourths of the several States, or by Conventions in three fourths thereof, as the one or the other Mode of Ratification may be proposed by the Congress; Provided that no Amendment which may be made prior to the Year One thousand eight hundred and eight shall in any Manner affect the first and fourth Clauses in the Ninth Section of the first Article; and that no State, without its Consent, shall be deprived of its equal Suffrage in the Senate.

ARTICLE. VI.

All Debts contracted and Engagements entered into, before the Adoption of this Constitution, shall be as valid against the United States under this Constitution, as under the Confederation.

This Constitution, and the Laws of the United States which shall be made in Pursuance thereof; and all Treaties made, or which shall be made, under the Authority of the United States, shall be the supreme Law of the Land; and the Judges in every State shall be bound thereby, any Thing in the Constitution or Laws of any State to the Contrary notwithstanding.

The Senators and Representatives before mentioned, and the Members of the several State Legislatures, and all executive and judicial Officers, both of the United States and of the several States, shall be bound by Oath or Affirmation, to support this Constitution; but no religious Test shall ever be required as a Qualification to any Office or public Trust under the United States.

ARTICLE. VII.

The Ratification of the Conventions of nine States, shall be sufficient for the Establishment of this Constitution between the States so ratifying the Same.

done in Convention by the Unanimous Consent of the States present the Seventeenth Day of September in the Year of our Lord one thousand seven hundred and Eighty seven and of the Independence of the United States of America the Twelfth In witness whereof We have hereunto subscribed our Names,

Go. WASHINGTON—Presidt.
and deputy from Virginia

New Hampshire	JOHN LANGDON
	NICHOLAS GILMAN
Massachusetts	NATHANIEL GORHAM
	RUFUS KING
Connecticut	Wm. SAML JOHNSON
	ROGER SHERMAN
New York . . .	ALEXANDER HAMILTON
New Jersey	WIL: LIVINGSTON
	DAVID BREARLEY.
	Wm. PATERSON.
	JONA: DAYTON
Pennsylvania	B FRANKLIN
	THOMAS MIFFLIN
	ROBt MORRIS
	GEO. CLYMER
	THOs. FITZSIMONS
	JARED INGERSOLL
	JAMES WILSON
	GOUV MORRIS
Delaware	GEO: READ
	GUNNING BEDFORD jun
	JOHN DICKINSON
	RICHARD BASSETT
	JACO: BROOM

Maryland	{ JAMES McHENRY
	{ DAN OF St THOs. JENIFER
	{ DANL CARROLL
Virginia	{ JOHN BLAIR—
	{ JAMES MADISON Jr.
North Carolina	{ Wm. BLOUNT
	{ RICHd. DOBBS SPAIGHT.
	{ HU WILLIAMSON
South Carolina	{ J. RUTLEDGE
	{ CHARLES COTESWORTH
	{ PINCKNEY
	{ CHARLES PINCKNEY
	{ PIERCE BUTLER
Georgia	{ WILLIAM FEW
	{ ABR BALDWIN

RATIFICATION OF THE CONSTITUTION

State	Date of ratification
Delaware	Dec 7, 1787
Pennsylvania	Dec 12, 1787
New Jersey	Dec 19, 1787
Georgia	Jan 2, 1788
Connecticut	Jan 9, 1788
Massachusetts	Feb 6, 1788
Maryland	Apr 28, 1788
South Carolina	May 23, 1788
New Hampshire	June 21, 1788
Virginia	Jun 25, 1788
New York	Jun 26, 1788
Rhode Island	May 29, 1790
North Carolina	Nov 21, 1789

In Convention Monday, September 17th 1787.

Present

The States of

New Hampshire, Massachusetts, Connecticut, Mr. Hamilton from New York, New Jersey, Pennsylvania, Delaware, Maryland, Virginia, North Carolina, South Carolina and Georgia.

Resolved,

That the preceeding Constitution be laid before the United States in Congress assembled, and that it is the Opinion of this Convention, that it should afterwards be submitted to a Convention of Delegates, chosen in each State by the People thereof, under the Recommendation of its Legislature, for their Assent and Ratification; and that each Convention assenting to, and ratifying the Same, should give Notice thereof to the United States in Congress assembled. Resolved, That it is the Opinion of this Convention, that as soon as the Conventions of nine States shall have ratified this Constitution, the United States in Congress assembled should fix a Day on which Electors should be appointed by the States which shall have ratified the same, and a Day on which the Electors should assemble to vote for the President, and the Time and Place for commencing Proceedings under this Constitution. That after such Publication the Electors should be appointed, and the Senators and Representatives elected: That the Electors should meet on the Day fixed for the Election of the President, and should transmit their Votes certified, signed, sealed and directed, as the Constitution requires, to the Secretary of the United States in Congress assembled, that the Senators and Representatives should convene at the Time and Place assigned; that the Senators should appoint a President of the Senate, for the sole Purpose of receiving, opening and counting the Votes for President; and, that after he shall be chosen, the Congress, together with the President, should, without Delay, proceed to execute this Constitution.

By the Unanimous Order of the Convention

Go. WASHINGTON—Presidt.

W. JACKSON Secretary.

ARTICLES IN ADDITION TO, AND AMENDMENT OF, THE CONSTITUTION OF THE UNITED STATES OF AMERICA, PROPOSED BY CONGRESS, AND RATIFIED BY THE SEVERAL STATES, PURSUANT TO THE FIFTH ARTICLE OF THE ORIGINAL CONSTITUTION.

AMENDMENT I.

Congress shall make no law respecting an establishment of religion, or prohibiting the free exercise thereof; or abridging the freedom of speech, or of the press; or the right of the people peaceably to assemble, and to petition the Government for a redress of grievances.

AMENDMENT II.

A well regulated Militia, being necessary to the security of a free State, the right of the people to keep and bear Arms, shall not be infringed.

AMENDMENT III.

No Soldier shall, in time of peace be quartered in any house, without the consent of the Owner, nor in time of war, but in a manner to be prescribed by law.

AMENDMENT IV.

The right of the people to be secure in their persons, houses, papers, and effects, against unreasonable searches and seizures, shall not be violated, and no Warrants shall issue, but upon probable cause, supported by Oath or affirmation, and particularly describing the place to be searched, and the persons or things to be seized.

AMENDMENT V.

No person shall be held to answer for a capital, or otherwise infamous crime, unless on a presentment or indictment of a Grand Jury, except in cases arising in the land or naval forces, or in the Militia, when in actual service in time of War or public danger; nor shall any person be subject for the same offence to be twice put in jeopardy of life or limb; nor shall be compelled in any criminal case to be a witness against himself, nor be deprived of life, liberty, or property, without due process of law; nor shall private property be taken for public use, without just compensation.

AMENDMENT VI.

In all criminal prosecutions, the accused shall enjoy the right to a speedy and public trial, by an impartial jury of the State and district wherein the crime shall have been committed, which district shall have been previously ascertained by law, and to be informed of the nature and cause of the accusation; to be confronted with the witnesses against him; to have compulsory process for obtaining witnesses in his favor, and to have the Assistance of Counsel for his defence.

AMENDMENT VII.

In Suits at common law, where the value in controversy shall exceed twenty dollars, the right of trial by jury shall be preserved, and no fact tried by a jury, shall be otherwise re-examined in any Court of the United States, than according to the rules of the common law.

AMENDMENT VIII.

Excessive bail shall not be required, nor excessive fines imposed, nor cruel and unusual punishments inflicted.

AMENDMENT IX.

The enumeration in the Constitution, of certain rights, shall not be construed to deny or disparage others retained by the people.

AMENDMENT X.

The powers not delegated to the United States by the Constitution, nor prohibited by it to the States, are reserved to the States respectively, or to the people.

AMENDMENT XI.
(Adopted Jan. 8, 1798)

The Judicial power of the United States shall not be construed to extend to any suit in law or equity, commenced or prosecuted against one of the United States by Citizens of another State, or by Citizens or Subjects of any Foreign State.

AMENDMENT XII.
(Adopted Sept. 25, 1804)

The Electors shall meet in their respective states and vote by ballot for President and Vice-President, one of whom, at least, shall not be an inhabitant of the same state with themselves; they shall name in their ballots the person voted for as President, and in distinct ballots the person voted for as Vice-President, and they shall make distinct lists of all persons voted for as President, and of all persons voted for as Vice-President, and of the number of votes for each, which lists they shall sign and certify, and transmit sealed to the seat of the government of the United States, directed to the President of the Senate;—The President of the Senate shall, in the presence of the Senate and House of Representatives, open all the certificates and the votes shall then be counted;—The person having the greatest number of votes for President, shall be the President, if such number be a majority of the whole number of Electors appointed; and if no person have such majority, then from the persons having the highest numbers not exceeding three on the list of those voted for as President, the House of Representatives shall choose immediately, by ballot, the President. But in choosing the President, the votes shall be taken by states, the representation from each state having one vote; a quorum for this purpose shall consist of a member or members from two-thirds of the states, and a majority of all the states shall be necessary to a choice. And if the House of Representatives shall not choose a President whenever the right of choice shall devolve upon them, before the fourth day of March next following, then the Vice-President shall act as President, as in the case of the death or other constitutional disability of the President—The person having the greatest number of votes as Vice-President, shall be the Vice-President, if such number be a majority of the whole number of Electors appointed, and if no person have a majority, then from the two highest numbers on the list, the Senate shall choose the Vice-President; a quorum for the purpose shall consist of two-thirds of the whole number of Senators, and a majority of the whole number shall be necessary to a choice. But no person constitutionally ineligible to the office of President shall be eligible to that of Vice-President of the United States.

AMENDMENT XIII.
(Adopted Dec. 18, 1865)

SECTION 1. Neither slavery nor involuntary servitude, except as a punishment for crime whereof the party shall have been duly convicted, shall exist within the United States, or any place subject to their jurisdiction.

SECTION 2. Congress shall have power to enforce this article by appropriate legislation.

AMENDMENT XIV.
(Adopted July 28, 1868)

SECTION 1. All persons born or naturalized in the United States and subject to the jurisdiction thereof, are citizens of the United States and of the State wherein they reside. No State shall make or enforce any law which shall abridge the privileges or immunities of citizens of the United States; nor shall any State deprive any person of life, liberty, or property, without due process of law; nor deny to any person within its jurisdiction the equal protection of the laws.

SECTION 2. Representatives shall be apportioned among the several States according to their respective numbers, counting the whole number of persons in each State, excluding Indians not taxed. But when the right to vote at any election for the choice of electors for President and Vice President of the United States, Representatives in Congress, the Executive and Judicial officers of a State, or the members of the Legislature thereof, is denied to any of the male inhabitants of such State, being twenty-one years of age, and citizens of the United States, or in any way abridged, except for participation in rebellion, or other crime, the basis of representation therein shall be reduced in the proportion which the number of such male citizens shall bear to the whole number of male citizens twenty-one years of age in such State.

SECTION 3. No person shall be a Senator or Representative in Congress, or elector of President and Vice President, or hold any office, civil or military, under the United States, or under any State, who, having previously taken an oath, as a member of Congress, or as an officer of the United States, or as a member of any State legislature, or as an executive or judicial officer of any State, to support the Constitution of the United States, shall have engaged in insurrection or rebellion against the same, or given aid or comfort to the enemies thereof. But Congress may by a vote of two-thirds of each House, remove such disability.

SECTION 4. The validity of the public debt of the United States, authorized by law, including debts incurred for payment of pensions and bounties for services in suppressing insurrection or rebellion, shall not be questioned. But neither the United States nor any State shall assume or pay any debt or obligation incurred in aid of insurrection or rebellion against the United States, or any claim for the loss or emancipation of any slave; but all such debts, obligations and claims shall be held illegal and void.

SECTION 5. The Congress shall have power to enforce, by appropriate legislation, the provisions of this article.

AMENDMENT XV.
(Adopted March 30, 1870)

SECTION 1. The right of citizens of the United States to vote shall not be denied or abridged by the United States or by any State on account of race, color, or previous condition of servitude.

SECTION 2. The Congress shall have power to enforce this article by appropriate legislation.

AMENDMENT XVI.
(Adopted Feb. 25, 1913)

The Congress shall have power to lay and collect taxes on incomes, from whatever source derived, without apportionment among the several States, and without regard to any census or enumeration.

AMENDMENT XVII.
(Adopted May 31, 1913)

The Senate of the United States shall be composed of two Senators from each State, elected by the people thereof, for six years; and each Senator shall have one vote. The electors in each State shall have the qualifications requisite for electors of the most numerous branch of the State legislatures.

When vacancies happen in the representation of any State in the Senate, the executive authority of such State shall issue writs of election to fill such vacancies: *Provided,* That the legislature of any State may empower the executive thereof to make temporary appointments until the people fill the vacancies by election as the legislature may direct.

This amendment shall not be so construed as to affect the election or term of any Senator chosen before it becomes valid as part of the Constitution.

AMENDMENT XVIII.
(Adopted Jan. 29, 1919)

SECTION 1. After one year from the ratification of this article the manufacture, sale, or transportation of intoxicating liquors within, the importation thereof into, or the exportation thereof from the United States and all territory subject to the jurisdiction thereof for beverage purposes is hereby prohibited.

SECTION 2. The Congress and the several States shall have concurrent power to enforce this article by appropriate legislation.

SECTION 3. This article shall be inoperative unless it shall have been ratified as an amendment to the Constitution by the legislatures of the several States, as provided in the Constitution, within seven years from the date of the submission hereof to the States by the Congress.

AMENDMENT XIX.
(Adopted Aug. 26, 1920)

The right of citizens of the United States to vote shall not be denied or abridged by the United States or by any State on account of sex.

Congress shall have power to enforce this article by appropriate legislation.

AMENDMENT XX.
(Adopted Feb. 6, 1933)

SECTION 1. The terms of the President and Vice President shall end at noon on the 20th day of January, and the terms of Senators and Representatives at noon on the 3d day of January, of the years in which such terms would have ended if this article had not been ratified; and the terms of their successors shall then begin.

SECTION 2. The Congress shall assemble at least once in every year, and such meeting shall begin at noon on the 3d day of January, unless they shall by law appoint a different day.

SECTION 3. If, at the time fixed for the beginning of the term of the President, the President elect shall have died, the Vice President elect shall become President. If a President shall not have been chosen before the time fixed for the beginning of his term, or if the President elect shall have failed to qualify, then the Vice President elect shall act as President until a President shall have qualified; and the Congress may by law provide for the case wherein neither a President elect nor a Vice President elect shall have qualified, declaring who shall then act as President, or the manner in which one who is to act shall be selected, and such person shall act accordingly until a President or Vice President shall have qualified.

SECTION 4. The Congress may by law provide for the case of the death of any of the persons from whom the House of Representatives may choose a President whenever the right of choice shall have devolved upon them, and for the case of the death of any of the persons from whom the Senate may choose a Vice President whenever the right of choice shall have devolved upon them.

SECTION 5. Sections 1 and 2 shall take effect on the 15th day of October following the ratification of this article.

SECTION 6. This article shall be inoperative unless it shall have been ratified as an amendment to the Constitution by the legislatures of three-fourths of the several States within seven years from the date of its submission.

AMENDMENT XXI.
(Adopted Dec. 5, 1933)

SECTION 1. The eighteenth article of amendment to the Constitution of the United States is hereby repealed.

SECTION 2. The transportation or importation into any State, Territory, or possession of the United States for delivery or use therein of intoxicating liquors, in violation of the laws thereof, is hereby prohibited.

SECTION 3. This article shall be inoperative unless it shall have been ratified as an amendment to the Constitution by conventions in the several States, as provided in the Constitution, within seven years from the date of the submission hereof to the States by the Congress.

AMENDMENT XXII.
(Adopted Feb. 27, 1951)

SECTION 1. No person shall be elected to the office of the President more than twice, and no person who has held the office of President, or acted as President, for more than two years of a term to which some other person was elected President shall be elected to the office of the President more than once. But this Article shall not apply to any person holding the office of President when this Article was proposed by the Congress, and shall not prevent any person who may be holding the office of President, or acting as President, during the term within which this Article becomes operative from holding the office of President or acting as President during the remainder of such term.

SECTION 2. This Article shall be inoperative unless it shall have been ratified as an amendment to the Constitution by the legislatures of three-fourths of the several States within seven years from the date of its submission to the States by the Congress.

AMENDMENT XXIII.
(Adopted Mar. 29, 1961)

SECTION 1. The District constituting the seat of Government of the United States shall appoint in such manner as the Congress may direct:

A number of electors of President and Vice President equal to the whole number of Senators and Representatives in Congress to which the District would be entitled if it were a State, but in no event more than the least populous State; they shall be in addition to those appointed by the States, but they shall be considered, for the purposes of the election of President and Vice President, to be electors appointed by a State; and they shall meet in the District and perform such duties as provided by the twelfth article of amendment.

SECTION 2. The Congress shall have power to enforce this article by appropriate legislation.

AMENDMENT XXIV.
(Adopted Jan. 23, 1964)

SECTION 1. The right of citizens of the United States to vote in any primary or other election for President or Vice President, for electors for President or Vice President, or for Senator or Representative in Congress, shall not be denied or abridged by the United States or any State by reason of failure to pay any poll tax or other tax.

SECTION 2. The Congress shall have the power to enforce this article by appropriate legislation.

AMENDMENT XXV.
(Adopted Feb. 10, 1967)

SECTION 1. In case of the removal of the President from office or of his death or resignation, the Vice President shall become President.

SECTION 2. Whenever there is a vacancy in the office of the Vice President, the President shall nominate a Vice President who shall take the office upon confirmation by a majority vote of both houses of Congress.

SECTION 3. Whenever the President transmits to the President pro tempore of the Senate and the Speaker of the House of Representatives his written declaration that he is unable to discharge the powers and duties of his office, and until he transmits to them a written declaration to the contrary, such powers and duties shall be discharged by the Vice President as Acting President.

SECTION 4. Whenever the Vice President and a majority of either the principal officers of the executive departments or of such other body as Congress may by law provide, transmit to the President pro tempore of the Senate and the Speaker of the House of Representatives their written declaration that the President is unable to discharge the powers and duties of his office, the Vice President shall immediately assume the powers and duties of the office as Acting President.

Thereafter, when the President transmits to the President pro tempore of the Senate and the Speaker of the House of Representatives his written declaration that no inability exists, he shall resume the powers and duties of his office unless the Vice President and a majority of either the principal officers of the executive department or of such other body as Congress may by law provide, transmit within four days to the President pro tempore of the Senate and the Speaker of the House of Representatives their written declaration that the President is unable to discharge the powers and duties of his office. Thereupon Congress shall decide the issue, assembling within forty-eight hours for that purpose if not in session. If the Congress within twenty-one days after receipt of the latter written declaration, or, if Congress is not in session, within twenty-one days after Congress is required to assemble, determines by two-thirds vote of both Houses that the President is unable to discharge the powers and duties of his office, the Vice President shall continue to discharge the same as Acting President; otherwise, the President shall resume the powers and duties of his office.

AMENDMENT XXVI.
(Adopted June 30, 1971)

SECTION 1. The right of citizens of the United States, who are 18 years of age or older, to vote shall not be denied or abridged by the United States or by any state on account of age.

SECTION 2. The Congress shall have power to enforce this article by appropriate legislation.

CONSTITUTION OF THE UNITED STATES

ORIGINS

MAGNA CHARTA
CONTINENTAL CONGRESS, FIRST (1774)
DECLARATION OF RIGHTS (1776)
DECLARATION OF INDEPENDENCE (1776)
    THOMAS JEFFERSON
    JOHN ADAMS
    JOHN HANCOCK
    ROBERT R. LIVINGSTON
REVOLUTIONARY WAR   (see Subject Map)
CONTINENTAL CONGRESS, SECOND
ARTICLES OF CONFEDERATION
    PARIS, TREATY OF (1783)
ANNAPOLIS CONVENTION (1786)

> The Subject Maps in the Encyclopedia illustrate the coverage of particular aspects of American History, showing the interrelationships among the articles in twelve critical areas of study. Entries in capital letters, except for titles, are subjects for which there are separate articles in the Encyclopedia.
>
> The Subject Maps are arranged alphabetically in the Encyclopedia under the following titles:
>
> American Wars
> Blacks in the United States
> Business Regulation and Industrialization
> Civil War and Reconstruction
> Constitution of the United States
> Exploration and Colonization
> Frontier in American History
> Indians
> Labor Movement
> New Deal and Depression
> Revolutionary War Era
> Slavery and Emancipation

MAKING OF THE CONSTITUTION

CONSTITUTIONAL CONVENTION (1787)
VIRGINIA PLAN
    EDMUND RANDOLPH
NEW JERSEY PLAN
CONNECTICUT COMPROMISE
    OLIVER ELLSWORTH

National Leaders
GEORGE WASHINGTON
BENJAMIN FRANKLIN
GEORGE MASON
ELBRIDGE GERRY
JAMES WILSON
GOUVERNEUR MORRIS

Issues
ANTI-FEDERALISM
    RICHARD HENRY LEE
    GEORGE CLINTON
FEDERALISM
    THE FEDERALIST
    ALEXANDER HAMILTON
    JOHN JAY
    JAMES MADISON
REPUBLICANISM

THE DOCUMENT

AMENDMENTS, CONSTITUTIONAL
BILL OF RIGHTS

SEPARATION OF POWERS

Executive
PRESIDENT OF THE UNITED STATES
    PRESIDENTIAL ELECTIONS
    ELECTORAL COLLEGE
VICE-PRESIDENT OF THE UNITED STATES

Legislative
HOUSE OF REPRESENTATIVES
    HENRY CLAY
    JAMES G. BLAINE
    JOSEPH G. CANNON
    SAM RAYBURN

SENATE
    JOHN C. CALHOUN
    DANIEL WEBSTER
    STEPHEN A. DOUGLAS
    ROBERT M. LA FOLLETTE
    ROBERT F. WAGNER
    LYNDON B. JOHNSON

Judicial
SUPREME COURT OF THE UNITED STATES
    JOHN MARSHALL
    EARL WARREN
JUDICIAL REVIEW
JUDICIARY ACT OF 1789

system of amendment to allow for future changes.

A Living Document. The U.S. Constitution has been enormously successful. Under it America has become the oldest and most stable country in the world to be governed by a written constitution. It has also become the most powerful and most prosperous.

Although written in the eighteenth century, the Constitution has proved to be extremely adaptable. There are many reasons for this, but perhaps the most important is that the Constitution is a very concisely written document (about 7,000 words) that provides only the basic framework of the government and some general principles. As a consequence, the meaning of the Constitution has been open to different interpretations. This has given the federal government great flexibility in dealing with changing social, economic, and psychological conditions.

Consult (III) Bowen, 1966; Corwin, 1958; Wood, 1971.

—Richard E. Ellis, *University of Virginia*

CONTINENTAL CONGRESS, FIRST (1774), first assembly of delegates from throughout the colonies. Responding to the Coercive Acts, Boston asked the colonies to cease importations from England, but at the suggestion of other cities a continental congress was called instead. On Sept. 5, 1774, delegates from 12 colonies convened in Philadelphia. On September 17, the Congress endorsed radical resolutions submitted by Suffolk County, Mass. The work of Dr. Joseph Warren, the Suffolk Resolves declared the Coercive Acts void, urged Massachusetts to form a government to collect and withhold taxes until the repeal of the acts, advised the people to arm, and recognized economic sanctions against Britain.

On September 28, Joseph Galloway of Pennsylvania proposed that Parliament establish in America an inferior branch of the British legislature consisting of a royally appointed governor general and a grand council elected by the colonial assemblies. The Congress rejected Galloway's Plan of Union, which would have required the consent of both legislatures for all bills affecting the colonies, and on October 14 passed its Declaration and Resolves, which claimed for the colonial assemblies exclusive power of legislation, subject only to royal veto. On October 18, the Congress established the Continental Association, which pledged to cease importing from Britain on Dec. 1, 1774, and to institute nonexportation on Sept. 1, 1775. The Congress adjourned on October 26, setting another meeting for May 1775.

See also Coercive Acts (1774); Continental Congress, Second.

Consult (II) Burnett, 1941.

CONTINENTAL CONGRESS, SECOND. The Second Continental Congress first met on May 10, 1775, in Philadelphia. Several conservatives, including Joseph Galloway of Pennsylvania, were conspicuously absent, and a number of new members, including Thomas Jefferson, joined the delegates from the First Continental Congress. The Congress was active. On May 15, it put the colonies in a state of defense and on May 25 invited Canada to send representatives. At the request of John Adams, the Congress took responsibility for the colonial troops that had surrounded Boston after Lexington and Concord and on June 15 appointed George Washington of Virginia to be commander in chief of the Continental Army.

Still hoping for peace, the Congress on July 5 adopted John Dickinson's Olive Branch Petition, which expressed the colonies' desire for reconciliation with Britain and asked George III to prevent further hostilities. But the Congress also saw fit to issue on July 6 "The Declaration of the Causes and Necessities of Taking Up Arms," which Thomas Jefferson wrote with Dickinson's assistance. On July 31 the Congress rejected Lord North's plan of reconciliation, by which Parliament agreed to refrain from taxing any colony that raised funds for defense and governmental costs.

The Congress took the final steps toward independence in 1776. On June 7, Richard Henry Lee of Virginia proposed that the colonies "are, and of right ought to be, free and independent States." The Congress on June 11 appointed a five-man committee to draft a Declaration of Independence and the next day established a committee to draw up a plan of colonial confederation. The delegates approved Lee's resolution on July 2 and adopted the Declaration of Independence on July 4. On Nov. 15, 1777, the Congress approved the Articles of Confederation.

Confederation Congress. The Second Continental Congress, known as the Confederation Congress after the final ratification of the Articles of Confederation in 1781, directed the fate of the nation until 1789. The delegates changed the site of their meetings several times before 1783 to escape entrapment by the British. Between 1775 and 1789 the Congress met at Philadelphia, Lancaster, and York, Pa., Princeton and Trenton, N.J., Annapolis, Md., and New York City.

See also Articles of Confederation; Declaration of Independence (1776).

Consult (II) Burnett, 1941.

—Thomas Archdeacon, *University of Wisconsin*

CONTRACT LABOR LAW (1885), federal legislation barring immigrants from coming to the United States under work contracts. The law applied only to laborers such as the Chinese and Irish who provided the cheap labor used to

First Continental Congress met in Philadelphia's Carpenters' Hall.

Calvin Coolidge, 30th President of the United States (1923-1929), throws out the first ball to start the baseball season in Washington, D.C.

James Fenimore Coopers' novels of frontier life made him one of the most popular U.S. authors.

build railroads and harvest crops. Professional, skilled, and domestic workers were exempted. Congress, convinced that the American labor market needed protection from foreign workers, had been encouraged by nationalists to pass the bill, which was modified in 1891, 1907, and 1917.

See also Chinese Exclusion.

CONTRERAS, BATTLE OF (1847), engagement during American advance on Mexico City. *See* Mexican War (1846-1848).

COOKE, JAY (1821-1905), American financier. Born on the Ohio frontier, he entered banking (1839) and by early 1861 had been successful enough to organize his Philadelphia firm, Jay Cooke and Company. He began to market government bonds in 1862, and through his new underwriting techniques and patriotic advertising he sold more than $2.5 billion in federal bonds (1862-1865). Although he received relatively little profit from these vast sales, the prestige he accumulated made him the most prominent American banker.

In the postwar years, Cooke continued his extraordinary success and opened branches in New York and London. His primary project became the financing of the Northern Pacific Railroad, which had advanced 500 miles westward by 1873. But Cooke had allowed enthusiasm for growth to influence his banking judgment. His firm, like most others, had extended too much credit and had ignored inflated stock prices and the most unfavorable balance of foreign trade. When the Panic of 1873 struck, 89 railroads defaulted on their bonds, and on Sept. 17, 1873, Jay Cooke and Company crashed. Although Cooke later paid his debts and rebuilt his personal fortune, banking prestige passed to other firms, notably that of J. P. Morgan.

See also Panics, Financial (Nineteenth Century); Railroads.

Consult (V) Oberholtzer, 1969.
—George Lankevich, *Bronx Community College of The City University of New York*

COOLIDGE, CALVIN (1872-1933), 30th President (1923-1929) of the United States.

Coolidge embodied in himself the contradiction between the increasing collectivism of business and the dedication of businessmen and many other Americans of his age to the nineteenth-century ideal of economic individualism. He was born in rural Plymouth Notch, Vt., on July 4, 1872, in a house attached to the general store kept by his father. The elder Coolidge was an old-fashioned Yankee trader from whom the son learned shrewdness, parsimony, and a great respect for successful businessmen.

Coolidge became a lawyer and politi-

cian in Northampton, Mass., and held virtually every type of local and state office, showing himself a conservative legislator and a budget-cutting administrator. Because of backing by conservative politicians and favorable publicity given his actions to crush the Boston police strike of 1919, Coolidge became vice-president in 1921. He succeeded to the presidency in 1923 upon the death of Warren G. Harding.

Presidency. From his taking the oath of office (by lamplight from his father, a justice of the peace) to his laconic statement in 1928 that he did "not choose to run" again, the public image of the taciturn, tight-fisted, honest Yankee charmed the public. He was, in fact, a calculating politician and an innocent echoer of the views of his rich friends and the U.S. Chamber of Commerce.

He continued the Harding policies of reducing taxes and encouraging peace both at home and abroad. Coolidge's Administrations were remarkable for the lack of legislation passed and the laxity in enforcing existing antibusiness and prohibition laws. His most notable actions were vetoes—of the McNary-Haugen Bill to help farmers and of the Muscle Shoals scheme to develop government power plants on the Tennessee River. In general, Coolidge exerted little influence on the course of history except to prevent vigorous actions such as those taken by his successors. He retired to Northampton, Mass., after the end of his term and died there on Jan. 5, 1933.

See also McNary-Haugen Bill.
Consult (VI) McCoy, 1967; White, 1938.
—John C. Burnham, *Ohio State University*

COOPER, JAMES FENIMORE (1789-1851), a prolific novelist, essayist, historian, and social critic. He grew up at Ostego Hall, Cooperstown, N.Y., a mansion on the edge of the frontier. From his earliest years Cooper was acquainted both with the life of the gentleman and with the wild frontier. After his expulsion from Yale University in 1806 he went to sea and was commissioned a navy midshipman; he resigned this post in 1810 to become a country gentleman.

His first novel, *Precaution* (1820), was a routine English social novel. His later novels dealt with settings Cooper knew personally—the frontier, the sea, and upper-class society. *The Spy* (1821), a Revolutionary War tale, clearly demonstrated Cooper's narrative skills. *The Pioneer* (1823) introduced the character Natty Bummpo (also called Hawkeye and Leather Stocking). Accompanied by Chingachgook, a Delaware Indian, Bummpo is Cooper's symbol of unspoiled nature. The frontiersman was the hero of four subsequent novels: *The Last of the Mohicans* (1826), *The Prairie* (1827), *The Pathfinder* (1840), and *The Deerslayer* (1841). These five novels, known as

The Leatherstocking Tales, represent the beginning of a favorite American literary genre, the Western, in which civilization is portrayed as corrupt and the savage and his wilderness as noble and natural.

Cooper lived extensively in Europe from 1826 to 1833 and became increasingly disenchanted with America. His later writing included a scholarly *History of the Navy of the United States* (1839), the two concluding Leatherstocking novels, and a significant trilogy of social novels, *The Littlepage Manuscripts,* comprising *Satanstoe* (1845), considered by many critics his best novel, *The Chainbearer* (1845), and *The Redskins* (1846).

See also Literature.

—Richard Collin, *Louisiana State University, New Orleans*

COPLEY, JOHN SINGLETON (1738–1815), American painter known for his portraits and historical scenes. Born in Boston, Copley received his early artistic education from his stepfather, Peter Pelham. Copley developed a successful career in Boston as portrait painter of elite New Englanders. His works display insight and the ability to capture the character of each subject. By European standards, however, his paintings were criticized for overly emphatic contours, improper use of colors, and abundant detailing. As a result, Copley, encouraged by Benjamin West, left Boston for Europe in 1774, a time when the Revolutionary conflict was imminent.

After a tour of the Continent, Copley sent for his family and settled permanently in London, where he became a noted historical painter who concentrated on realism rather than poetry or morality. His realistic emphasis was part of the then current academic canon. His most famous historical canvases include *Watson and the Shark* (1778), *The Death of the Earl of Chatham* (1780), and *The Death of Major Pierson* (1783).

Consult (III) Prown, 1966.

CORAL SEA, BATTLE OF (MAY 1942), halted Japanese advance on Australia. *See* World War II.

CORE. *See* Congress of Racial Equality.

CORRESPONDENCE COMMITTEES. *See* Committees of Correspondence.

CORRUPT BARGAIN ELECTION, presidential election of 1824, in which Henry Clay swung his electoral votes to John Quincy Adams. Clay later became Adams' secretary of state. *See* Presidential Elections.

CORRUPT PRACTICES ACTS, state and federal statutes aimed at eliminating campaign and election abuses. The movement to end these abuses, which were prevalent in the nineteenth century, began after the Civil War. New York's 1890 law against bribery, illegal registration, and ballot box stuffing was followed eventually by legislation in the other states.

The basis of modern federal legislation is the Corrupt Practices Act of 1925. It limited primary and general election expenses for congressional candidates, made disclosure of election expenses mandatory, outlawed fraudulent practices, and put controls on contributions by certain organizations, such as corporations. These acts were successful in ending many flagrant illegal election practices, but some restrictions, particularly on contributions, were often ineffective. Later, the scope of the federal act was widened and amended significantly, particularly in 1972, when campaign spending was put under tighter controls.

See also Hatch Act (1939); Taft-Hartley Act (1947).

CORTES, HERNAN (1485–1545), Spanish explorer and *conquistador* of Mexico. He made his first voyage to the New World in 1504 and had an important role in the conquest of Cuba in 1511. In 1518 he was appointed to lead an expedition to explore portions of Mexico.

On Feb. 10, 1519, with 11 vessels and 500 men, Cortés sailed from Cuba. He landed in Mexico in the spring and made contact with Montezuma, Emperor of the Aztecs. Cortés soon moved inland, where he received support from tribes suppressed by the Aztecs. Tactful treatment of early hostages and the acquisition of two interpreters, coupled with Montezuma's indecisiveness and an Aztec myth of the return of the light-skinned god Quetzalcoatl, gave Cortés a virtually insurmountable advantage. He entered Tenochtitlán (Mexico City) on Nov. 15, 1519. In June 1520 the Aztecs forced the Spaniards out of the city on the *noche triste* (sad night), but Cortés regained the city on Aug. 13, 1521.

On the basis of his conquest, Cortés was made governor of Mexico. Nevertheless, dissension and jealousy persisted in the New World, and Cortés was forced to return to Spain in 1528 to present his position. He was successful and returned to Mexico to devote his energies to development, Christianizing the Indians, and exploring new territory. In 1540, weary with the struggle, he once again returned to Spain, where he died.

See also Indians, North American.

Consult (I) Wright, 1970.

COTTON GIN, a machine that had a revolutionary effect on the output of cleaned cotton. It was patented by Eli Whitney in March 1794. Although exact estimates of its impact are difficult to calculate, Whitney himself claimed that the gin replaced the labor of 10 slaves if hand operated, 50 slaves if horse operated.

Portrait of Paul Revere by John Singleton Copley, who spent his later life in London. Courtesy, Museum of Fine Arts, Boston.

The gin was a wooden cylinder with wire teeth that revolved through slots in a bar. The raw cotton was pressed against the bar and the teeth tore away the lint. Brushes, revolving faster in the opposite direction, took the lint off the teeth. A hand crank operated the cylinder. This simple, easily made device separated the cotton fiber from the green seed of upland cotton.

The wider effects of the gin were seen in the vast increase in cotton output in the South and in that region's dependence thereafter on commercial agriculture for its way of life. Any hope of diversifying the economy or bringing in other industries vanished, and the South was tied to the plantation system and slavery.

See also Inventions; Mass Production; Whitney, Eli.

Consult (III) Green, 1956.

Father Charles Coughlin blamed national financial leaders for the Depression and became a vehement critic of President Roosevelt.

COUGHLIN, CHARLES E(DWARD) (1891–), Roman Catholic radio priest. As pastor of the Shrine of the Little Flower in suburban Detroit, he began broadcasting over the CBS network in 1926 but was dropped when his talks became heavily political. By 1930 he was inveighing against banks and banking and taking an inflationist position reminiscent of populism. In 1933 he considered himself a New Dealer but withdrew his support from Roosevelt's policies in 1935. Along with Huey Long and others, Coughlin helped turn Roosevelt leftward in anticipation of competition for New Deal votes in 1936. Coughlin's antibank tirades led him into anti-Semitism and from there to pro-Nazism by 1939, when he formed a fascist organization called the Christian Front.

See also Long, Huey.

Consult (VI) Tull, 1965.

COUNCIL OF NATIONAL DEFENSE. *See* National Defense Act (1916).

COUNTERVAILING POWER, doctrine holding that when political or economic organizations accumulate power and use it against other organizations or groups, the latter will react by creating counterpower. The concept was developed and used for economic analysis by John Kenneth Galbraith. Thus, according to Galbraith, labor unions develop in part as a reaction to the power exerted against the worker by business and corporation management. Or a retailer, in order to defend himself against producers, must unite with other retailers to exert power with respect to prices paid to producers, quality of goods, and so on. Exponents of the idea see it as a built-in regulator of the power relationships among political and economic associations.

Consult (VIII) Galbraith, 1955.

COUNTRY IDEOLOGY, a coherent set of assumptions and principles about government and history. It took shape in late seventeenth-century England, crossed the Atlantic to the colonies in the eighteenth century, and provided the language and basic concepts in which Americans debated their public issues from the Revolution through the War of 1812. Its progenitor was not John Locke, whose impact on American thought has been greatly exaggerated, but a radical republican theorist of the English interregnum (1649–1660), James Harrington, the author of *Oceana* (1656). For Harrington, political power was not really distinguishable from military power, and it rested ultimately upon the possession of land, which alone can make a man free and independent. Harrington believed that England had to be a republic, but both the monarchy and the House of Lords were restored in 1660.

Fifteen years later Harrington's ideas began to emerge in new forms emanating from the organizers of the early Whig Party, including William Penn. Instead of repudiating England's past these "country ideologues" (as modern scholars often call them) embraced and revered it. In particular they identified common law and England's ancient constitution with the balanced constitution of classical republican thinkers, finding in king, lords, and commons a perfect embodiment of monarchy, aristocracy, and democracy. They remained Harringtonian in their emphasis upon land as the basis of independence and in their strong preference for a militia of freeholders rather than a standing army. To these writers, who dominated the political scene by 1700, anything that threatened the ancient constitutional balance had to be resisted because change meant degeneration.

Role in Colonial Thought. Country ideology began to appear in the colonies in the 1730s. The trial of John Peter Zenger in New York (1735) gave extensive exposure to these concepts. Puritan New England was rather slow to adopt country ideology, the assumptions of which were starkly secular. But the plantation societies of the South completely accepted country ideology. At a time of crisis, its emphasis upon liberty as a function of land exerted wide appeal in a country with as many freeholders as early America contained.

To the extent that the Revolution was an intellectual event, it expressed itself through country ideology. Only country ideology seemed able to explain what was happening to America. Indeed, colonial resistance became revolutionary chiefly because most colonists believed that power tends to corrupt, and they had become convinced by 1774 that a hopelessly corrupt Parliament was consciously plotting against the colonies.

Independence forced Americans to ponder these questions in a new context, from which emerged a novel form of balanced constitution at the state level with elaborate safeguards to protect the legislature from executive corruption. Anti-Federalists opposed the Constitution, predicting that it would establish all the traditional engines of court corruption. Alexander Hamilton's fiscal policies of 1790–1791 confirmed the worst fears of Anti-Federalists, who reacted, however, not by rejecting the Constitution but by becoming strict constructionists.

To make their case, the Jeffersonian opposition had to deify the Constitution of 1787, which the Federalist Party was also pledged to upholding. The triumph of the Republican Party in 1800 and its continued success through the War of 1812 meant that the new republic would be governed by the principles of country ideology.

Consult (I) Bailyn, 1967; Buel, 1972; Wood, 1969.

—John M. Murrin, *Princeton University*

COURT PACKING, President Franklin Roosevelt's unsuccessful attempt to alter the composition of the Supreme Court. Fresh from his spectacular 1936 electoral victory, the President sought to reform a high court that had struck down New Deal measures such as the National Recovery Administration and the Agricultural Adjustment Administration.

No members of the Court seemed prepared to retire, and Roosevelt had made no appointments of his own. His Court-packing plan would have given him the authority to appoint up to six additional justices and would have presumably shifted the Court to a pro-New Deal orientation. However, Roosevelt badly misread his political strength, and opposition to his attack on the judiciary—even on the part of his Democratic colleagues—forced him to back down. Almost immediately the problem was resolved by other means. The Court, clearly frightened by the threat to its prestige, began turning out 5 to 4 decisions in favor of New Deal legislation. Older justices began retiring, and Roosevelt made his first appointments.

See also Agricultural Adjustment Act (1833); National Recovery Administration.

Consult (VI) Burns, 1956; Mason, 1958.

COVODE RESOLUTION. On Feb. 21, 1868, President Andrew Johnson removed Secretary of War Stanton. That same day Congressman John Covode introduced a resolution in the House declaring that the President "be impeached of high crimes and misdemeanors." Adopted on February 24, it became the basis for Johnson's trial before the Senate.

See also Johnson, Andrew.

COWBOYS. The romantic figure of the cowboy—dressed in hat, chaps, and boots and seated on a spirited horse—perhaps more than any other typifies the post-Civil War West to most Americans. According to myth these knights of the plains always carried six-guns, fought for justice, and then retired modestly from the scene. Reality found the cowboy less flamboyant. While doing his tedious and difficult chores, he labored in frequent isolation and lived with danger from weather, thieves, Indian raids, or even sickness and accident. From the hat atop his head to the boots on his feet, each portion of his clothing had a specific use and had been developed over the preceding century by the *vaqueros* of Mexico. In fact, many cowboys in the Southwest were Mexicans, Mexican-Americans, or blacks.

Most of the year cowboys spent their time line-riding—patrolling the ranch boundaries to keep their herds in. At the more well-known annual roundup each spring the men gathered, identified, and branded the cattle. Then they drove some of the herd to market. It was this long drive from Texas to the Kansas cow towns that brought the cowboy his most lasting fame, but by the mid-1880s the drive proved uneconomical and disappeared.

Despite the myths of adventure and violence that surround the cowboy, he was a skilled worker who labored under dangerous conditions for low wages. His well-publicized sprees in the cow towns were only brief flings after a year of isolation and hard work.

See also Frontier in American History.

Consult (V) Abbot and Smith, 1939; Frantz and Choate, 1955.

COWPENS, BATTLE OF (JAN. 17, 1781), rout of British in South Carolina. *See* Revolutionary War Battles.

COX, JAMES M(IDDLETON) (1870–1957), Ohio governor and Democratic presidential candidate. Beginning as a reporter, he became publisher of several Ohio newspapers by 1908. Elected to Congress in a heavily Republican district, Cox took part in the Insurgent-Democratic struggle against the Payne-Aldrich Tariff and House Speaker Joseph G. Cannon.

In 1912, Cox was elected governor of Ohio and managed one of the state's most productive legislative sessions. Although defeated for reelection in 1914, he regained the governor's office in 1916 and served until 1920. Under his prodding, the legislature enacted workmen's compensation, the regulation of child labor, a state industrial commission, the regulation of banking and utilities, and reorganization of the state's administrative and penal systems. This progressive record earned him the Democratic presidential nomination in 1920, but national dissatisfaction over World War I and the peace conference sent him down to overwhelming defeat by Warren G. Harding. Cox spent the remainder of his life building a newspaper and radio chain.

Consult (VI) Cox, 1946; Warner, 1962.

Arizona cowboy tries to control his rearing horse at range camp.

Cowhands move in to brand calf at 1909 roundup.

COXEY'S ARMY, group of unemployed men led by Jacob S. Coxey, an Ohio businessman, who marched on Washington, D.C., in the spring of 1894 to demand government relief. At the time, the country was in the throes of a deep depression, and bands of unemployed men roamed the country. Because the government provided no relief funds, Coxey, among others, advanced ideas to alleviate the mass unemployment. He wanted the federal government to establish a program of federal works with an appropriation of $500 million for road building. Local authorities could then exchange non interest-bearing bonds with the U.S. Treasury for paper money and use this money to hire the unemployed to build the roads.

Coxey and his two lieutenants set out with a group of about 500 to dramatize his plan; other armies of unemployed were to form across the country and merge in Washington. When they reached Washington, Coxey and his two leaders were arrested for stepping on the grass, and his army was dispersed by club-wielding policemen.

CRANE, STEPHEN (1871-1900), American novelist, poet, and short-story writer. Born in Newark, N.J., he moved to New York City in 1890 to write. His first novel, *Maggie: A Girl of the Streets* (1893), was a bitterly realistic portrayal of life in the slums drawn from his firsthand experience as an impoverished writer. Although not a commercial success, the work brought him to the attention of realist writers such as Hamlin Garland. Crane wrote for the New York *Herald* and the *Tribune* until the publication in 1895 of *The Black Rider and Other Lives,* a book of free verse, and *The Red Badge of Courage,* a remarkable account of the emotions and conflicts of a recruit during the Civil War, brought him fame. Crane called his Civil War novel "a psychological study of fear." On the strength of his reputation as a writer of war stories, Crane obtained work as a correspondent in Mexico, Cuba, and Greece.

Because of criticism of his work and malicious gossip about his personal life, Crane spent the years before his death from tuberculosis as an expatriate in Europe, where he won the friendship of Henry James and Joseph Conrad.

Crane combined vigor and realism in his writing with poetic symbolic use of language. In many of his tales, he shows skill in shaping colorful settings, dramatic action, and perceptive characterization into ironic explorations of human nature.

Consult (V) Stallman, 1972.

CREDIT MOBILIER, construction company controlled by managers of the Union Pacific (UP) Railroad. Congressional subsidies were misused when UP directors awarded contracts to Crédit Mobilier, then approved inflated charges that milked profits from the line and consumed about $23 million in government grants. To prevent disclosure, Rep. Oakes Ames made stock available on favorable terms to influential members of Congress, who could buy stock at half its market price and pay for it out of accumulated dividends. After the New York *Sun* exposed the fraud, the House censured Ames and James Brooks, but the Senate refused to expel James Patterson. Many reputations, including future President Garfield's, were tarnished, and the UP never attained true financial stability.

CREEK WAR (1813-1814), conflict that ended with the defeat of the Creek nation. From 1783 the Creeks had been under great pressure from American settlers, and many of them, called the Red Sticks, took the opportunity presented by the War of 1812 to attack outlying American settlements in what are now Alabama and Mississippi. On Aug. 30, 1813, a large party of Creeks attacked Fort Mims on the Alabama River north of Mobile. They took the fort after a bitter fight, and several hundred troops and settlers were killed.

Troops from Georgia, Mississippi Territory, and Tennessee, aided by friendly Creeks, retaliated for the attacks on Fort Mims and elsewhere. The main onslaught was carried out by Tennesseeans under the command of Andrew Jackson. In a series of battles, beginning at Tallassahatche (near the modern Jacksonville, Ala.) in early November 1813, hundreds of Creeks were killed. The climax of the war came on March 27, 1814 at Horseshoe Bend on the Tallapoosa River. There, where the river curved into the shape of a horseshoe, the Creeks were entrenched behind strong fortifications. Jackson's troops stormed the defenses, while Indians fighting with the Americans swam the river to the rear of the Creek position. A massacre ensued; about 550 Creeks were found dead on the field, and hundreds more died trying to flee across the river. In August 1814 at Fort Jackson, the Creeks were forced to cede more than half their land to the American government.

CRIME AGAINST KANSAS, THE, speech of Senator Charles Sumner in 1856 in which he attacked slavery's extension into Kansas. *See* Sumner, Charles.

CROCKETT, DAVY (DAVID) (1786-1836), frontiersman known as a fearless hunter, a narrator of tall tales, and a conscientious legislator determined to defend his constituents against land speculators and planter aristocrats.

Born in Greene County, Tenn., Crockett was a farmer and cattle driver as a youth. He served in the Creek War in 1813-1814 under General Andrew Jackson. In 1817 the Crockett family moved to southwestern Tennessee, where he became a justice of the peace and a

Stephen Crane's *Red Badge of Courage* detailed the horrors of the Civil War.

colonel. In 1821 and 1823 he was elected to the state legislature, where he supported bills favoring squatters and landholders.

Crockett served two terms in the U.S. House of Representatives. During his first term (1827-1831) he disagreed with Andrew Jackson about a land bill that Crockett believed should give land directly to squatters living in West Tennessee. His opposition to Jackson cost him the 1830 election, but he was returned to Congress for 2 more years in 1833. In February 1836, after losing his seat in Congress, Davy Crockett organized a band of Tennessee volunteers seeking to help Texas gain independence from Mexico. He joined the Texans in the fight for the Alamo, where he died heroically in April 1836.

See also Alamo.
Consult (III) Shackford, 1956.

CROP-LIEN SYSTEM, a characteristic feature of post-Civil War Southern agriculture that arose out of the region's capital scarcity. Local merchants extended credit to farmers for agricultural and personal supplies in return for a mortgage (lien) on the farmer's growing crop. At harvest time the farmer was obligated to turn over his entire crop to the merchant, who marketed it and returned to the farmer the amount in excess of his debt—if there was an excess. The contract frequently allowed the merchant to specify the crop to be grown, and he typically specified cotton, thus contributing to the one-crop dependency of the South.

See also Share-cropping.

CUBAN MISSILE CRISIS, U.S.-USSR confrontation (Oct. 22-28, 1962) over Soviet ballistic missiles in Cuba. On October 22, President Kennedy announced the presence of the missiles and the steps he was taking—a quarantine on military equipment shipped to Cuba; retaliation on the USSR if any Cuban missiles were launched at the United States; the alert of America's forces; action in the UN Security Council; and a demand to Premier Nikita Khrushchev to withdraw the missiles. To avoid a threatened air attack on the Cuban missile bases, Khrushchev agreed on October 28 to withdraw the Russian missiles and bombers stationed in Cuba.

The Soviets, hoping to change the international balance of power, had planned to announce in November 1962 the emplacement of missiles in Cuba. However, the Russians miscalculated the U.S. response, and the world found itself on the brink of nuclear war. Nevertheless, the favorable outcome of the crisis helped improve Kennedy's position, particularly in removing the onus of the 1961 Bay of Pigs debacle.

CULTURAL PLURALISM, condition in which two or more distinct cultures can develop and exist independently in the same political setting. Culture includes the knowledge, beliefs, art, morals, laws, customs, and habits acquired by man as a member of a group—that is, a way of life. For cultural pluralism to exist, each culture must be sufficiently strong to maintain its own ways, and each must receive equal treatment and tolerance by political and legal authorities. Cultural pluralism, therefore, can only exist in a society that stresses democracy and freedom.

An excellent example of cultural pluralism is provided by Switzerland, where French, Italian, and German cultural groups live in peace and harmony. In contrast, people of differing cultures entering the United States are generally subjected to pressures to integrate or assimilate into a common culture—to become Americanized. On the other hand, several cultural groups, such as black Americans, have maintained some distinct cultural traits, but they have never been accorded the equality and independence required by true cultural pluralism.

CUMBERLAND ROAD. *See* National Road.

CURRENCY ACT (1764), British legislation to prevent the colonies from paying creditors with depreciated money. Colonies lacking coined money sometimes resorted to paper currency as a temporary form of legal tender. When not properly funded, the paper declined in value, and after the French and Indian War, which prompted massive emissions of paper currency, Britain passed the Currency Act. It forbade further issues of paper and the extension of the recall dates of the bills in circulation and threatened colonial governors who assented to legislation contrary to its spirit with a £1,000 fine and permanent loss of crown offices.

CURRENCY ACT (1900) established the gold dollar as the unit of value and also provided for the enlargement of the U.S. Treasury gold reserve to $150 million. Several factors cleared the way for the establishment of the gold standard. The free-silver and cheap money advocates were defeated in the 1896 elections, and the free-silver faction's control of the Senate ended by 1900. Restored business confidence in the country, particularly as a result of the discovery of gold in Alaska, cleared the way for passage of the Currency Act.

See also Free Silver; Presidential Elections.

CURTISS, GLENN H., pioneer aviator. *See* Aviation.

CUSTER, GEORGE (ARMSTRONG) (1839-1876), American cavalry leader. He was born in Ohio and graduated from West Point in 1861 at the start of the Civil War. Although he gradu-

U.S. photographs revealed missile sites during Cuban Missile Crisis in 1962.

George Custer *(center)* hunting in Dakota Territory, where he was killed in 1876.

Clarence Darrow pores over mail at famous Scopes Trial (1925) in which he appeared in his customary role—for the defense.

ated last in his class, within 2 years he became at 23 the youngest brigadier general in the Union army. Custer, who was a popular figure, served ably during the war. He fought against Jeb Stuart at Gettysburg and led the charge at Yellow Tavern, where Stuart was killed.

After the war Custer became a lieutenant colonel in the 7th Cavalry and fought Indians under Generals W. S. Hancock and Philip Sheridan. In 1867 he was court-martialed for disobeying orders and was suspended for a year. Sheridan, however, requested his return, and Custer immediately won a victory over the Southern Cheyenne and their chief, Black Kettle, at Washita River (Oklahoma). Custer's troops guarded surveyors in the Northwest and fought at the Yellowstone River in 1873 and in the Black Hills in 1874. In 1876, Custer was sent to round up hostile Sioux and Cheyenne who were to meet with Sitting Bull. Custer and about 260 of his men rashly attacked a strong Indian encampment on June 25. Repulsed, they were forced into a poor defensive position and in "Custer's Last Stand" were overwhelmed by the Indians and wiped out at the Little Bighorn River.

See also Indian Wars, Western.
Consult (IV) Kinsley, 1967.

DANA, RICHARD HENRY (1815–1852), nineteenth-century author. See Two Years Before the Mast.

DANBURY HATTER'S CASE, popular name for Supreme Court decision dealing with boycotts. See Lowe v. Lawler (1908).

DANISH WEST INDIES, original name of part of Virgin Islands. See Virgin Islands.

DARROW, CLARENCE (SEWARD) (1857–1938), celebrated defense attorney. His early career was as law partner of Illinois governor John P. Altgeld. In 1894, however, his defense of Eugene V. Debs and the American Railway Union launched him on a vocation as defender of unpopular causes and minority rights.

As a labor lawyer, he represented, among others, the coal miners in the anthracite strike of 1902 and William Haywood and other Wobblies for their alleged murder of a former Idaho governor. An ardent opponent of capital punishment, he secured life imprisonment for Richard Loeb and Nathan Leopold in the infamous thrill slaying of a Chicago youth. In the Scopes trial of 1925 he engaged in a famous clash with William Jennings Bryan over the right of Tennessee to forbid the teaching of evolution in the public schools. The following year he defended 11 blacks accused of the murder of a Detroit Ku Klux Klansman. A lifelong Democrat, in 1934 Darrow was chosen by Franklin D. Roosevelt to head a commission

to study the operations of the National Recovery Administration.
Consult (VI) Darrow, 1932; Stone, 1943.

DARTMOUTH COLLEGE. See Colonial Colleges.

DARTMOUTH COLLEGE v. WOODWARD (1819), a Supreme Court decision protecting contracts that was of crucial importance to early business organizations. Dartmouth College was founded in 1769 by a charter granted by George III. The State of New Hampshire changed this charter in 1816 and established a new board of trustees, thus setting off a bitter struggle for control of the college. The old trustees brought suit on the grounds that the original charter was a contract, and therefore protected by the Constitution, and that New Hampshire had no right to change it by unilateral action. The case for the old trustees was argued by Daniel Webster, who considerably enhanced his reputation. The Court, led by Chief Justice John Marshall, decided that a charter did constitute a contract and that New Hampshire had no right to alter it. The scope of the decision was modified in later cases.

See also Charles River Bridge v. Warren Bridge (1837); Munn v. Illinois (1877).

DAVIS, BENJAMIN O(LIVER), JR. (1912–   ), the first black general in the U.S. Air Force. He was born in Washington, D.C., the son of the first black general in the U.S. Army. A graduate of the U.S. Military Academy in 1936, Davis spent 5 years in the infantry before transferring to the Army Air Corps in 1942. During the early years of World War II he commanded a fighter squadron manned by black pilots in North Africa and Sicily. Later, Davis commanded a fighter group that won distinction in operations over Germany, Czechoslovakia, and the Balkans.

After the establishment of the separate Air Force following the war, Davis advanced rapidly. In the Korean War he commanded a fighter-interceptor wing and later served on staffs in Japan, Europe, Washington, D.C., and Korea. In 1965 he was promoted to lieutenant general, becoming the first black to reach this rank in the U.S. armed services. In 1967 he assumed command of the 13th Air Force, based in the Philippines. After his retirement from the Air Force he became head of the Office of Civil Aviation Security with responsibility for antihijacking measures.

DAVIS, JEFFERSON (1808–1889), President of the Confederacy. Born in Kentucky, raised in Mississippi, and educated at West Point, he quit the army in 1835 to become a planter and politician in Mississippi. One of the most generous and patriarchal slaveholders, he bitterly resented abolitionists and reacted as an

Benjamin O. Davis, Jr. (left) confers with General Spaatz and Secretary of War Stimson in North Africa during World War II.

outspoken defender of slavery, the South, and states' rights.

In 1845, Davis entered the House and from 1847 to 1851 sat in the Senate, where he opposed the Compromise of 1850. As secretary of war under President Pierce (1853–1857), Davis tried to promote Southern economic interests. Returning to the Senate in 1857, he heatedly defended slavery and the South. At first lukewarm to secession after Lincoln's election, he was nevertheless chosen President of the Confederacy and inaugurated in February 1861.

Civil War. As president, Davis displayed great honesty, dedication, courage, energy, and dignity. Several qualities, however, made him less than a great leader. A poor administrator, he failed to delegate authority properly, spent far too much time on details, ran desultory meetings, and interfered in the affairs of his subordinates, especially military commanders.

A touchy egotist, Davis frequently quarreled with governors, generals, cabinet members, and the press. He showed no sensitivity to public opinion, and, although he tried, he was too cold to inspire his people. For all his flaws, Davis faced almost insuperable obstacles and met them as best he could. After the war he was imprisoned for 2 years but finally released without being tried for treason. He finished his days in quiet retirement.

See also Confederate States of America.
Consult (IV) Strode, 1955–1964.
—Michael Burlingame, *Connecticut College*

DAVIS RESOLUTIONS, introduced in the U.S. Senate by Jefferson Davis on Feb. 2, 1860, incorporated the Southern view on slavery. The resolutions declared that any attack on slavery was a violation of the Constitution and that the Senate had a duty to protect slavery in the territories. They also stated that neither Congress nor territorial legislatures could deny the right to hold slaves in the territories and that a decision on slavery should be withheld until a territory became a state.

The adamant and uncompromising principles of the Davis Resolutions, which went beyond the doctrine of popular sovereignty, discouraged any hope that the slave issue could be settled peaceably. The resolutions, adopted on May 24, touched off bitter debates in the Senate and widened the breach between proslavery and antislavery forces.

See also Popular Sovereignty; Secession.
Consult (IV) Craven, 1957.

DAWES PLAN (1924), plan devised by Charles G. Dawes, an American financier, to settle the World War I European reparations problem. Germany had been required to pay reparations to Britain, Italy, France, and other former enemies but had been unable to do so because of serious inflation. The question was whether Germany should continue to be compelled to do so, even at the expense of economic recovery and the restoration of amicable international relations, or whether a pragmatic scheme could be worked out to restabilize European economic and political conditions. Dawes' success in carrying out the second alternative by having the European governments agree to a new reparations schedule, coupled with a substantial loan to Germany, was evidence that the United States was playing an important role in European affairs even though it had not joined the League of Nations.

DAWES SEVERALTY ACT (1887), legislation affecting the Indian reservation system. *See* Indian Policy.

DAYS OF RAGE. When the Weatherman contingent of SDS (Students for a Democratic Society) left to "fight imperialism on the streets of America," it called for mobilization of militant young people in Chicago to demand the end of the Vietnam War, a cessation of political repression, and support for the Viet Cong and black liberation. During the Days of Rage (Oct. 8–11, 1969) that followed, a force of fewer than 400 Weatherpeople smashed cars and store windows in downtown Chicago before being arrested by the police.

D-DAY, the Allied invasion of France on June 6, 1944, deploying more than 1 million troops on five beaches along 60 miles of the Normandy coast from the Orne River to the east coast of the Cotentin Peninsula. The entire action, called Operation Overlord, was commanded by General Dwight D. Eisenhower as head of the Supreme Headquarters of the Allied Expeditionary Forces (SHAEF). To conceal the actual point of invasion along the 1,200-mile coast being guarded by the Nazis, elaborate diversionary schemes were developed. They worked, and when the actual invasion began, the Germans believed it to be a diversion.

A successful invasion depended in part on favorable tides and moonlight. Low tides were needed to clear paths through the mines and obstacles. Moonlight was needed to drop airborne units behind the German coastal lines. The weather on June 4 postponed the landing from the 5th to the 6th.

American troops landed on Utah and Omaha beaches, and the British and Canadian troops landed on Sword, Juno, and Gold beaches. Strong German defenses at Omaha caused very high casualties, but the Allies had driven 20 miles inland and had established an 80-mile front by June 13. Within a few weeks,

Jefferson Davis served as president of the Confederacy throughout the Civil War.

American troops wade ashore in Normandy, France, on D-Day—June 6, 1944.

KING DEBS.

His leadership of the American Railway Union brought Eugene V. Debs national attention, especially when the Pullman Strike (1894) halted Midwest rail traffic.

Patroit leaders gather in Philadelphia to approve Declaration of Independence on July 4, 1776.

1 million Allied troops were in France, and Paris was liberated from the German forces on August 15.

See also Eisenhower, Dwight D.; World War II.

DEBS, EUGENE V(ICTOR) (1855-1926), American socialist and labor leader. Born in Terre Haute, Ind., he began work on the railroads and soon became a leader of the railroad workers' craft union. The failure of the railroad brotherhoods to better the workers' conditions led Debs to create an industrial union for all railroad labor, the American Railway Union (ARU), in 1893.

When the Pullman Car Company initiated harsh wage cuts in 1894, Debs led the ARU in a bitter strike even though a federal court injunction prohibited strike activity. Debs was soon arrested and served 6 months in jail, during which he became educated in socialist theory. To create a decent society, Debs argued that private property had to be abolished. It encouraged competitiveness and forced men to be alienated from their own labor as well as from their fellowmen. "I am for socialism," Debs explained in 1897, "because I am for humanity." To further this goal, Debs ran for president on the Socialist Party ticket five times. The high point came in 1912, when Debs polled 6 percent of the vote.

When war broke out, Debs backed his party's plea for militant antiwar action. After a speech in 1918 that questioned the concept of "patriotic duty," he was tried under the Espionage Act and received a sentence of 10 years in prison that was upheld by the Supreme Court. After the war Woodrow Wilson refused to release Debs, who was not pardoned until 1921 by President Harding. During his imprisonment, Debs ran for president and polled 900,000 votes.

Debs came out of prison facing a socialist movement that was weak from postwar repression and internal splits developing in the new Communist parties. He spent the next few years unsuccessfully trying to rebuild the Socialist Party. In 1924, Debs endorsed the presidential candidacy of Progressive candidate Robert M. La Follette.

See also Espionage Act (1917); Presidential Elections; Pullman Strike (1894); Railroad Unions; United States v. Debs.

Consult (VI) Ginger, 1962.

—Ronald Radosh, *Queensborough Community College of The City University of New York*

DEBT, NATIONAL, the debt taken on by the central government to finance expenditures in the federal budget that cannot be met by money available. The public debt, which may sometimes be confused with the national debt,

is the national debt plus the local government debt.

The national debt has been carried by the U.S. government since the early days of the Republic. The Revolutionary War and the establishment of the new government produced a debt of $75 million. The deficit rose to $259 billion in 1945. Since then the debt has grown more slowly in comparison to the gross national product, but the debt is likely to keep rising. Since World War II, government revenues have decreased because of tax cuts, but increase in welfare payments, social security, and the like have continued to force government expenses up.

DECATUR, STEPHEN (1779-1820), American naval officer. He entered the navy in 1798 and first achieved prominence as a young lieutenant in the war with Tripoli when he led a small party to burn and destroy the frigate *Philadelphia,* which had run aground and had been captured on the North African coast.

In the War of 1812, Decatur added to his renown when in command of the frigate *United States.* Off Madeira on Oct. 25, 1812, the American ship forced the British frigate *Macedonian* to surrender. The *Macedonian* had about 100 seamen killed and wounded, while the Americans lost only 12. In January 1815, not knowing that a peace treaty had been signed in Europe, Decatur attempted to slip out of New York in the frigate *President* but after a running engagement with the British blockading squadron was obliged to surrender. Later in the year Decatur commanded an American squadron that forced Algiers to agree to peace. It was after his return from the Mediterranean that he gave the toast "Our Country! In her intercourse with foreign nations may she always be in the right; but our country, right or wrong." Decatur was killed in a duel with another naval officer in 1820.

See also War of 1812.

DECLARATION OF INDEPENDENCE (1776). By 1776 there had been a number of military engagements between British soldiers and American patriots, King George had declared the colonies in a state of rebellion, Thomas Paine had published *Common Sense,* and many Americans were convinced that separation from England was necessary to preserve their liberties. On April 12, North Carolina authorized its delegates to the Second Continental Congress to cooperate with others who might advocate independence.

On June 7, 1776, under instructions from his colony, Richard Henry Lee of Virginia proposed in the Congress "that these United Colonies are, and of right ought to be, free and independent States." Despite opposition from conservatives who thought independence ill

THE DECLARATION OF INDEPENDENCE

WHEN in the Course of human events, it becomes necessary for one people to dissolve the political bands which have connected them with another, and to assume among the powers of the earth, the separate and equal station to which the Laws of Nature and of Nature's God entitle them, a decent respect to the opinions of mankind requires that they should declare the causes which impel them to the separation.—We hold these truths to be self-evident, that all men are created equal, that they are endowed by their Creator with certain unalienable Rights, that among these are Life, Liberty and the pursuit of Happiness.—That to secure these rights, Governments are instituted among Men, deriving their just powers from the consent of the governed.—That whenever any Form of Government becomes destructive of these ends, it is the Right of the People to alter or to abolish it, and to institute new Government, laying its foundation on such principles and organizing its powers in such form, as to them shall seem most likely to effect their Safety and Happiness. Prudence, indeed, will dictate that Governments long established should not be changed for light and transient causes; and accordingly all experience hath shewn, that mankind are more disposed to suffer, while evils are sufferable, than to right themselves by abolishing the forms to which they are accustomed. But when a long train of abuses and usurpations, pursuing invariably the same Object evinces a design to reduce them under absolute Despotism, it is their right, it is their duty, to throw off such Government, and to provide new Guards for their future security.—Such has been the patient sufferance of these Colonies; and such is now the necessity which constrains them to alter their former Systems of Government. The history of the present King of Great Britain is a history of repeated injuries and usurpations, all having in direct object the establishment of an absolute Tyranny over these States. To prove this, let Facts be submitted to a candid world.—He has refused his Assent to Laws, the most wholesome and necessary for the public good.—He has forbidden his Governors to pass Laws of immediate and pressing importance, unless suspended in their operation till his Assent should be obtained; and when so suspended, he has utterly neglected to attend to them.—He has refused to pass other Laws for the accommodation of large districts of people, unless those people would relinquish the right of Representation in the Legislature, a right inestimable to them and formidable to tyrants only.—He has called together legislative bodies at places unusual, uncomfortable, and distant from the depository of their public Records, for the sole purpose of fatiguing them into compliance with his measures.—He has dissolved Representative Houses repeatedly, for opposing with manly firmness his invasions on the rights of the people.—He has refused for a long time, after such dissolutions, to cause others to be elected; whereby the Legislative powers, incapable of Annihilation, have returned to the People at large for their exercise; the State remaining in the meantime exposed to all the dangers of invasion from without, and convulsions within.—He has endeavoured to prevent the population of these States; for that purpose obstructing the Laws for Naturalization of Foreigners; refusing to pass others to encourage their migrations hither, and raising the conditions of new Appropriations of Lands.—He has obstructed the Administration of Justice, by refusing his Assent to Laws for establishing Judiciary powers.—He has made Judges dependent on his Will alone, for the tenure of their offices, and the amount and payment of their salaries.—He has erected a multitude of New Offices, and sent hither swarms of Officers to harass our people, and eat out their substance. He has kept among us, in times of peace, Standing Armies without the Consent of our legislatures.—He has affected to render the Military independent of and superior to the Civil power.—He has combined with others to subject us to a jurisdiction foreign to our constitution, and unacknowledged by our laws; giving his Assent to their Acts of pretended Legislation:—For quartering large bodies of armed troops among us:—For protecting them, by a mock Trial, from punishment for any Murders which they should commit on the Inhabitants of these States:—For cutting off our Trade with all parts of the world:—For imposing Taxes on us without our Consent:—For depriving us in many cases, of the benefits of Trial by Jury:—For transporting us beyond Seas to be tried for pretended offences:—For abolishing the free System of English Laws in a neighbouring Province, establishing therein an Arbitrary government, and enlarging its Boundaries so as to render it at once an example and fit instrument for introducing the same absolute rule into these Colonies:—For taking away our Charters, abolishing our most valuable Laws and altering fundamentally the Forms of our Governments:—For suspending our own Legislatures, and declaring themselves invested with power to legislate for us in all cases whatsoever.—He has abdicated Government here, by declaring us out of his Protection and waging War against us.—He has plundered our seas, ravaged our Coasts, burnt our towns, and destroyed the lives of our people.—He is at this time transporting large Armies of foreign Mercenaries to compleat the works of death, desolation and tyranny, already begun with circumstances of Cruelty & perfidy scarcely paralleled in the most barbarous ages, and totally unworthy the Head of a civilized nation.—He has constrained our fellow Citizens taken Captive on the high Seas to bear Arms gainst their Country, to become the executioners of their friends and Brethren, or to fall themselves by their Hands.—He has excited domestic insurrections amongst us, and has endeavoured to bring on the inhabitants of our frontiers, the merciless Indian Savages, whose known rule of warfare, is an undistinguished destruction of all ages, sexes and conditions. In every stage of these Oppressions We have Petitioned for Redress in the most humble terms: Our repeated Petitions have been answered only by repeated injury. A Prince, whose character is thus marked by every act which may define a Tyrant, is unfit to be the ruler of a free people. Nor have We been wanting in attentions to our British brethren. We have warned them from time to time of attempts by their legislature to extend an unwarrantable jurisdiction over us. We have reminded them of the circumstances of our emigration and settlement here. We have appealed to their native justice and magnanimity, and we have conjured them by the ties of our common kindred to disavow these usurpations, which would inevitably interrupt our connections and correspondence. They too have been deaf to the voice of justice and of consanguinity. We must, therefore, acquiesce in the necessity, which denounces our Separation, and hold them, as we hold the rest of mankind, Enemies in War, in Peace Friends.—

WE, THEREFORE, the Representatives of the UNITED STATES OF AMERICA, in General Congress, Assembled, appealing to the Supreme Judge of the world for the rectitude of our intentions, do, in the Name, and by Authority of the good People of these Colonies, solemnly publish and declare, That these United Colonies are, and of Right ought to be FREE AND INDEPENDENT STATES; that they are Absolved from all Allegiance to the British Crown, and that all political connection between them and the State of Great Britain, is and ought to be totally dissolved; and that as Free and Independent States, they have full Power to levy War, conclude Peace, contract Alliances, establish Commerce, and to do all other Acts and Things which Independent States may of right do.—And for the support of this Declaration, with a firm reliance on the protection of divine Providence, we mutually pledge to each other our Lives, our Fortunes and our sacred Honor.

DEFENSE SPENDING

Billions of Dollars

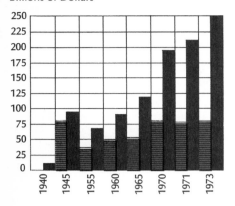

- Total Federal outlays
- Defense outlays

Democratic Party's top leaders of the 1950s—House Speaker Rayburn, Senate Majority Leader Johnson, and Adlai Stevenson—talk over political strategy at Johnson's Texas ranch.

advised or premature, the Congress on June 11 appointed John Adams, who had seconded Lee's resolution, Thomas Jefferson, Benjamin Franklin, Roger Sherman, and Robert R. Livingston to draft a declaration of independence. Jefferson's thoughts and style permeated the completed document. The introductory section justifies the Americans' decision in terms of the compact theory of government as explained by the English philosopher John Locke. The second portion is an indictment of King George that asserted he had violated his contract with his subjects and no longer could expect obedience. George III allegedly vetoed laws necessary for colonial well-being, attempted to destroy representative government, taxed without popular consent, and waged war on the colonies with illegal standing armies, foreign mercenaries, and cruel Indians. The Declaration concludes with an announcement of independence.

On July 2, Congress approved Lee's resolution and cleared the way for adoption of the Declaration. On July 4, after deleting Jefferson's passage denouncing King George for not ending the slave trade, 12 colonies approved the document. New York's delegates abstained but, after receiving further instructions, joined the other colonies on July 15. Beginning on August 2, 56 delegates signed the Declaration in its final form.

See also Continental Congress, Second; Jefferson, Thomas; Lee, Richard Henry.

Consult (II) Becker, 1922.

—Thomas Archdeacon, *University of Wisconsin*

DECLARATION OF RIGHTS (1776), basic legislation adopted by the Virginia Convention on June 12 that was intended to serve as the basis of government. Drafted by George Mason, the Declaration had a clear impact on the Declaration of Independence and the Bill of Rights of the U.S. Constitution.

The document avowed that all men are equal and have inherent rights to life, liberty, the acquisition of property, and the pursuit of happiness. It stated that the people are the source of political power and can establish, reform, and abolish governments in seeking their common benefit and protection. The Declaration affirmed that defendants in criminal cases had the right to confront their accusers, have quick impartial trials, and not to suffer cruel punishments. The Declaration also guaranteed freedom of the press, and, in a clause written by Patrick Henry, provided for freedom of religion.

See also Bill of Rights; Declaration of Independence (1776).

DECLARATION OF RIGHTS AND GRIEVANCES, protest against the Stamp Act. *See* Stamp Act (1765).

DECLARATION OF SENTIMENTS, landmark statement of women's rights. *See* Seneca Falls Convention (1848).

DECLARATORY ACT (1766), reasserted Parliament's right to legislate for the colonies "in all cases whatsoever" and was an attempt by the British government to secure the necessary support in the House of Commons for the repeal of the Stamp Act (1765). The measure mollified conservatives, who interpreted it as an affirmation of Parliament's authority to tax the colonies.

See also Stamp Act (1765).

DEFENSE, DEPARTMENT OF (DOD), executive department established in 1949 by an amendment to the National Security Act (1947) coordinating under civilian administration the policies and operation of the military departments of Army, Navy, and Air Force. Traditionally, the Army, established as the War Department in 1789, and the Navy, dating from 1798, dealt, respectively, with defense on land and water. Acquisition of overseas territories and worldwide commitments brought about conflicts and competition that were heightened by the growing role of the Air Corps, which was under the Army. Between the two world wars numerous unification measures were considered by Congress. The National Military Establishment (created by the National Security Act) and the cabinet post of Secretary of Defense provided overall direction; the Air Force became a coequal military department.

The top policy-making body within the military, the Joint Chiefs of Staff, is subordinate to the Secretary of Defense and to the civilian secretaries of each service.

DE GAULLE, CHARLES (1890-1970), French president and general. A native of Lille, he graduated from the Ecole Militaire of Saint-Cyr in 1912. De Gaulle served in the army during World War I until he was taken prisoner at the Battle of Verdun. During the 1930s De Gaulle taught at Saint-Cyr, served as Marshal Pétain's aide, and wrote several books on military ideas.

During World War II he opposed France's surrender to Germany and became head of the Free French. He came to be thought of as the symbol of the Resistance as well as its political leader. In 1944 he transformed the Committee of National Liberation into a provisional government and entered Paris in triumph in August.

De Gaulle was elected president in 1945 but resigned in 1946 because political reforms he thought necessary were not accepted. He remained in retirement and wrote until 1958 and the advent of the Algerian crisis, when he was elected president by an overwhelming majority.

As leader of France for the next 11 years,

De Gaulle was responsible for the Algerian cease-fire in 1962 and independence for all other French colonies in Africa during the early 1960s. He was instrumental in keeping the British from joining the European Common Market. He also successfully expelled the North Atlantic Treaty Organization and its troops from France. His Common Market and NATO policies were designed, in part, to reduce U.S. influence in Europe and to enhance France's position. De Gaulle resigned as president in 1969 after some political defeats. He retired to Colombey-les-Deux-Eglises, where he died. His books include *The Army of the Future* (1941), *The Call to Honor* (1955), *Unity* (1956), and *Salvation* (1960).

See also World War II.

Consult (VIII) La Couture, 1966.

DELAWARE, colony and state that took its name from Thomas West, Baron De La Warr, the governor of Virginia. First explored by Henry Hudson in 1609, the region was an object of contention between the colonies of the Dutch and English in the seventeenth century. In 1638 the Swedes established a fur-trading post, Fort Christiana, at the present site of Wilmington. The colony of New Sweden was settled by Swedes and Finns, who introduced the log cabin to America. Little more than a fortified outpost, the colony was annexed by the Dutch, led by Peter Stuyvesant, in 1655.

When the British assimilated New Netherlands in 1664, they thus swallowed both New Sweden and the Dutch colony. Delaware was part of the Duke of York's lands until 1682, when he gave the area to William Penn. Thereafter part of Pennsylvania, although with a separate representative assembly after 1704, Delaware did not become independent until 1776. It was the first state to ratify the U.S. Constitution (Dec. 7, 1787).

The capital is Dover; the legislature is bicameral. The population in 1970 was 548,104.

See also Pennsylvania; Stuyvesant, Peter.

DELAWARE AND RARITAN CANAL. *See* Canals.

DEMOCRATIC PARTY, one of two major political parties in the United States. The present Democratic Party traces its antecedents to the Democratic-Republican Party of the eighteenth century.

Democratic-Republican Party. Political opposition in the new nation started as strict constitutional constructionists (Jeffersonians) against loose constructionists (Hamiltonians) and became, by the election of 1800, Democratic-Republicans against Federalists. Thomas Jefferson won the election but had an inaugural message of conciliation: "We are all Republicans, we are all Federalists." The Federalist Party died out, but by the end of James Madison's presidency, Jefferson's party had come to accept the Hamiltonian program of tariff protection and the chartering of a Bank of the United States. The Jeffersonian party now encompassed clashing factions; the Era of Good Feelings was really a disintegration of party cohesion through rampant pluralism.

In the 1820s a largely legislative party became a constituency-based party as the states wiped out property-owning and tax-paying qualifications for the vote. After the 1824 election the party split into National Republicans (led by John Quincy Adams and Henry Clay) and Democrats (headed by Andrew Jackson). The polarization was over Jackson's personality as well as program. The parties and the sections competed for the allegiance of the West over such issues as the national bank, protective tariff, internal improvements, sale of public lands, territorial acquisition, and states' rights. While Jefferson emphasized minimal government, Jackson believed in the necessity of a strong federal government to curb predatory interests.

Jacksonian Democrats. With Jackson's election in 1828 a new Democratic-Republican Party was ascendant. Since the election of Jackson, this Democratic Party has been in control of the Senate for 38 of the 73 Congresses and of the House 45 times. It survived defections of anti-Jackson men to the Whig Party and post-Jackson bolts of antislavery Democrats to the Liberty, Free-Soil, and Republican parties.

Despite the Kansas-Nebraska Act (1854), the Democratic Party, although shaken to its foundations, managed to hold itself together for another half-dozen years. Its control of national patronage was a unifying influence. The breakdown of party ties in the 1850s, resulting from the polarizing effect of the slavery issue, was one of the factors leading the nation toward the "irrepressible conflict."

Modern Party. The campaign of 1860 was the last chance to head off disaster. Even those who foresaw the consequences were unable to bring the parties back from the brink of the abyss. The Southern Democratic bolters destroyed the instrument of their great power. The schism led to secession and gave the party a stigma of disloyalty. (As late as 1884 the party was vilified as one of "rum, romanism and rebellion.") The Democrats became a minority party. Except for interludes of recovery of the White House in 1884 and 1912, when the GOP split, they remained the minority until the Great Depression.

In the late nineteenth century there were factions within each party battling over the monetary system, control of big business, and imperialism. The Democratic left captured the party from the Grover Cleveland conservatives in 1896 but failed to forge a farmer-worker

Cartoonist Thomas Nast used donkey, which became Democratic Party symbol, in 1870 to characterize Democrats who criticized Secretary of War Stanton after his death.

DEMOCRATIC PARTY — Item Guide

The article on the DEMOCRATIC PARTY covers the highlights of the political party that has its roots in the DEMOCRATIC-REPUBLICANS of THOMAS JEFFERSON and, later, the DEMOCRATIC-REPUBLICANS of ANDREW JACKSON.

From 1800 until the Civil War it was the dominant party, led by presidents such as JAMES MADISON, JAMES MONROE, and Jackson, through the WAR OF 1812, the ERA OF GOOD FEELINGS, and the BANK WAR. After about 1840, the party gradually weakened, and the REPUBLICAN PARTY triumphed in 1860. The Republicans remained dominant until the Depression, with interruptions under GROVER CLEVELAND and WOODROW WILSON. WILLIAM JENNINGS BRYAN was unable to win the presidency, despite his eloquence on FREE SILVER and other issues. The election of FRANKLIN D. ROOSEVELT in 1932 began an era of Democratic hegemony that lasted through HARRY S TRUMAN's administration, despite Southern defections to the STATES' RIGHTS PARTY. Other leaders of the period were SAM RAYBURN and Adlai Stevenson of the highly political STEVENSON FAMILY. The party returned to power in the 1960s under JOHN F. KENNEDY and LYNDON B. JOHNSON.

The article on PRESIDENTIAL ELECTIONS details the Democrats in national elections, while POLITICAL PARTIES IN THE UNITED STATES charts the evolution of the modern party.

Unemployed in New York City stand in breadline to receive food in 1935.

alliance. It took the Depression to achieve this. Al Smith's urban ethnic support in 1928 foreshadowed the Democratic ascendancy of 1932. However, the Southern defections from a candidate who symbolized urban interests, Catholicism, and opposition to Prohibition was a harbinger of the breakup of the Solid South.

With Franklin Roosevelt's New Deal the Democrats abandoned (except in the South) their states' rights and small government philosophy. The FDR coalition survived the Dixiecrat and Wallace Progressive defections of 1948 but lost its generation-long hold on the White House in 1952. The Kennedy and Johnson forces returned the party to national leadership in 1960; however, defections in 1968 and 1972 cost it the White House although it still controlled both houses of Congress.

Consult (VIII) Chambers, 1964; Goldman, 1966.

—Martin Gruberg, University of Wisconsin, Oshkosh

DEMOCRATIC-REPUBLICANS (JACKSONIAN).
In the 1820s the Democratic-Republican Party that had originated with Thomas Jefferson and James Madison began to disintegrate. In the election of 1824, the main candidates were members of the Democratic-Republican Party, although they were divided on a variety of issues and along sectional lines. John Quincy Adams, after his election in 1824 and his alliance with Henry Clay, met bitter opposition from a coalition of the supporters of Andrew Jackson, John C. Calhoun, and William H. Crawford. This opposition called itself the Democratic-Republican Party and threw itself behind Jackson for the presidency in 1828. After Jackson's election the new Democratic Party, the forerunner of the modern Democratic Party, gradually came into being, but in the process Jackson lost some of his original supporters, including many who followed John C. Calhoun.

See also Democratic-Republicans (Jeffersonian); Jackson, Andrew.

DEMOCRATIC-REPUBLICANS (JEFFERSONIAN),
a party that formed in the 1790s in opposition to the administration policies of George Washington and the ideas of Alexander Hamilton. This opposition was led by James Madison and Thomas Jefferson. It objected particularly to Hamiltonian financial policies, to the extension of the power of the federal government, and after 1793 to the anti-French foreign policy. The signing of the controversial Jay's Treaty in November 1794 helped to increase local opposition to governmental policies.

In 1796 the party division extended to the presidential race with John Adams as the Federalist candidate and Jefferson as the Republican. Jefferson lost in 1796, but after his victory in 1800 the Democratic-Republicans dominated American politics. After they assumed power, the Democratic-Republicans proved willing to accept concepts of federal power that they had rejected in the 1790s. The party became fragmented in the 1820s and was defeated by the Democratic-Republicans (Jacksonian) in the election of 1828.

See also Democratic-Republicans (Jacksonian); Political Parties in the United States.

DEPENDENT PENSION ACTS (1887, 1890),
legislation approved by Congress awarding pensions to disabled Union veterans of the Civil War. Congressmen argued that pensions expressed America's gratitude to soldiers who had suffered for the Union, but they also recognized that pensions won votes from veterans' groups. President Cleveland vetoed the first bill, declaring it would foster "dishonesty and mendacity" among claimants. The veto stood, and veterans' anger helped elect Benjamin Harrison. The broader 1890 act granted pensions to disabled veterans unable to support themselves by manual labor, and the disability did not have to be service connected.

See also Cleveland, Grover; Harrison, Benjamin.

DEPRESSION,
a part of the business cycle normally following a period of prosperity, heavy (wartime) consumption, overextension of credit, overproduction, and speculation and usually accompanied by a financial panic or crash. Such a crash occurred in the United States for the first time in 1819, in part as a result of overextension during the Napoleonic wars. Crashes have occurred subsequently at fairly regular intervals: 1837, 1857, 1873, 1893, 1907, and 1929.

The Great Depression. In retrospect the first signs of the Great Depression can be seen in the postwar slump in agriculture prices that began in 1921. The construction industry went into decline in 1926, and inventories of new cars and other consumer goods were high by the summer of 1929. Bank failures were common throughout the decade. The stock market had risen steadily, however, since 1921 and precipitously after 1926, the prices on the market bearing little or no relation to corporate earnings. Market prices were the result of rampant speculation, which came to an abrupt end with the crash of October 1929.

As production increased through the postwar decade, profits did not go to those in the economy who might consume the product but to the wealthy few who often reinvested in plant and machinery to produce even more. Overseas markets were limited by the fact that most European nations were poverty stricken as a result of the war and were heavily in debt to the United States. Tariff barriers further inhibited the flow of American goods overseas.

Unemployment was the most striking effect of the Great Depression. Although marginal workers were always hit in hard times, unemployment was widespread after 1929. At one time nearly a fourth of the work force was unemployed. New Deal recovery programs tended to restore confidence and helped the unemployed, but full recovery did not come until the outbreak of World War II. New Deal legislation regulating the stock market, insuring bank deposits, and strengthening the Federal Reserve System has helped prevent a recurrence in the postwar period.

See also New Deal; Panics, Financial (Nineteenth Century).

Consult (VI) Galbraith, 1955; Mitchell, 1947; Wecter, 1948.

—Alan Kifer, *Skidmore College*

DESEGREGATION OF SCHOOLS. *See* Brown v. Board of Education of Topeka (1954).

DESERET, Mormon name for their settlement in what is now Utah. *See* Mormons; Young, Brigham.

DESERT LAND ACT (1877) authorized purchase of desert lands that were to be irrigated. *See* National Reclamation Act (1902).

DE SOTO, HERNAN (1500–1542), Spanish *conquistador* who explored the southeastern United States. Educated at the University of Salamanca, he sailed to Panama in 1519 under the guardianship of Governor Pedrarias Dávila. For 11 years De Soto worked for Pedrarias against rival Spaniards and discontented Indians. In 1530 he became a lieutenant of Francisco Pizarro and played a key role in the conquest of Peru. Although he was anxious to accumulate treasure, De Soto was a friend of the Indians and opposed the murder of the Inca ruler in 1533. Disillusioned with the intrigue of Pizarro's camp, De Soto left Peru in 1535 and returned to Spain with a fortune in gold.

Acclaimed as a hero, De Soto made an advantageous marriage and was soon appointed governor and captain general of Florida, which encompassed territory as far west as Texas. In 1538, De Soto again sailed for the New World. After establishing a supply base in Cuba, De Soto sailed for Florida, landing in May 1539. In general, the expedition followed the coastline from Tampa to Tallahassee, crossed to the Savannah River, traveled to Mobile Bay, and headed northward, a route that took him through most of what became the Southeastern states. On May 8, 1541, the party first saw the Mississippi River. Crossing to Arkansas, the expedition went west before returning to the Mississippi, where De Soto died on May 21, 1542. To prevent the Indians from learning of his death, he was buried in the

river. The remaining members of the expedition made their way to Mexico by September 1543.

See also Exploration and Discovery; Pizarro, Francisco.

DEWEY, GEORGE (1837–1917), one of the most highly honored figures in modern American naval history. After graduating from the U.S. Naval Academy, he was assigned to the *Mississippi*, which participated in the Battle of New Orleans in 1862. He served in a variety of midlevel posts until he was promoted to commodore and given command of the American Asiatic Squadron in November 1897. Thus, he was in a position to capitalize on the presence of his fleet in the Pacific at the outbreak of the Spanish-American War.

Having received advance warning from Assistant Secretary of the Navy Theodore Roosevelt, Dewey had taken his squadron to the Far East, and on the day he learned that war had been declared against Spain, Dewey pressed his fleet toward Manila in a dramatic 600-mile dash. Despite reports of floating mines, Dewey repeated the tactics of his mentor, David Farragut, and sailed boldly into Manila's harbor at dawn on May 1, 1898. In 7 hours of battle his squadron destroyed the Spanish fleet, giving apparent justification to Roosevelt's preparedness measures.

Dewey then remained within the harbor during a tense period when British and German warships arrived, the latter in particular being present to lend weight to German claims upon the Philippines if the United States chose not to retain them. He successfully avoided further conflict, and his victory gave the American Republic its first Far Eastern possession. Dewey returned to Washington a national hero, was voted the rank of Admiral of the Navy by a grateful Congress, and served until his death as president of the general board of the Navy Department.

See also Spanish-American War (1898).

—Robin W. Winks, *Yale University*

DEWEY, JOHN (1859–1952), philosopher and teacher whose ideas profoundly influenced philosophy, psychology, education, and social thought. He was born in Vermont. From 1894 to 1904 he taught at the University of Chicago, experimenting with ways of putting educational theory into practice and organizing a laboratory school. Then he moved to New York and taught at Columbia University until he retired in 1930. Among many other activities, he was president of the American Psychological Association (1899-1900), president of the American Philosophical Association (1905-1906), and first president of the American Association of University Professors (1915).

The scope of his thought can be suggested by a few examples. In philosophy he

Adm. George Dewey smashed the Spanish fleet in Manila Bay in Spanish-American War.

'THE INTERNATIONAL DERBY'

Missile competition between super powers overshadowed efforts to reach disarmament agreements in the post–World War II era.

Walt Disney's friendly cartoon characters were brought to life in Disneyland.

developed a form of pragmatism called "instrumentalism," which maintains that truth is not something fixed or discovered by metaphysical speculation but rather is known by the consequences that ideas have in the world. In education he stressed "learning by doing" and held that learning must have a practical outcome. His educational theories were picked up by the progressive movement, but many things done by his so-called followers did not have his approval. Some of his ideas, such as the value of individualized instruction and the role of experience in learning, came to the fore again in the late 1960s.

In psychology, Dewey's functionalist views helped turn American psychologists from abstract studies to practical concern for man in the environment.

Dewey's many books include *The School and Society* (1899), *How We Think* (1910), *Democracy and Education* (1916), *Human Nature and Conduct* (1922), *Reconstruction in Philosophy* (1920), *The Quest for Certainty* (1929), and *Experience and Education* (1938).

See also Education; Progressive Education.

Consult (V) Brickman and Lehrer, 1965.

DEWEY, THOMAS E(DMUND) (1902–1971), American lawyer and Republican political leader who ran unsuccessfully for the presidency in 1944 and 1948. He was born in Owosso, Mich., graduated from the University of Michigan in 1923, and received his law degree from Columbia University in 1925. From 1931 to 1933 he worked as a federal attorney and in 1935 was made a special prosecutor to investigate racketeering. Dewey gained national fame in 1938, when, as a New York City district attorney, he directed a sensational and successful prosecution of organized crime. In that year he also ran unsuccessfully for governor of New York but was elected to that office in 1942, 1946, and 1950. His achievements included a highway building program and the first state law prohibiting racial or religious discrimination in employment.

Dewey, who had sought in vain the Republican presidential nomination in 1940, was selected by the party in 1944. Although he lost to President Roosevelt, Dewey was renominated in 1948. He enjoyed wide leads in preelection polls but ran a poor campaign and lost to Harry S Truman. Dewey played an important part in securing the nomination of Dwight D. Eisenhower in the 1952 Republican convention. He reentered private law practice in 1955 at the end of his third term as governor.

See also Presidential Elections; Republican Party.

DICKINSON, EMILY (1830–1886), American poet. She was born and spent most of her life in Amherst, Mass. Dickinson, plain featured but vivacious, never married and, after a trip to Washington, D.C. and Philadelphia (1854), gradually withdrew from the world, scribbling verses on bits of paper and backs of envelopes and storing most of them in her bureau. Only 7 of her more than 1,000 poignant and beautiful poems appeared in print during her lifetime, all anonymously.

After 1870, letters, in which she often enclosed poems, became her sole means of maintaining contact with her friends. They included Ralph Waldo Emerson, Thomas Wentworth Higginson of the *Atlantic Monthly*, Samuel Bowles, publisher of the *Springfield Republican*, and poet and novelist Helen Hunt Jackson, the only contemporary who believed that Emily Dickinson was a poet of true distinction.

The distinguishing feature of the Dickinson poetry is its conciseness and intensity. Her brief lyrics, concerned primarily with the phenomena of nature, love, death, and immortality, break through nineteenth-century traditions to introduce new rhymes and metric forms.

Consult (V) Johnson, 1955.

DIES COMMITTEE, named after Chairman Martin Dies. *See* Un-American Activities Committee (House).

DISARMAMENT. As man's capacity to destroy himself has become more developed and complex, efforts to defuse this capacity through disarmament have become more numerous. Part of the difficulty has come in agreeing on first steps. Should disarmament be achieved by unilateral or multilateral action? Should it be partial, local, or general? Can effective disarmament precede solution of the outstanding differences among nations?

At the instigation of Russia, the nations of Europe went through the motions of discussing disarmament at the two Hague Conferences (1899, 1907). A more successful effort at arms reduction occurred at the 1921–1922 Washington Armament Conference. Follow-up meetings—the Geneva Naval Conference of 1927, the London Naval Conferences of 1930 and 1936, and the 1932 Geneva Disarmament Conferences—foundered on such difficulties as reconciling French demands for security with German demands for equality.

After 1945, disarmament was linked to a winding down of the Cold War. UN efforts have not been as effective as great-power deliberations outside the United Nations. Nuclear weapons have been banned by the United Nations from outer space, Africa, and Antarctica. Fourteen Latin American countries signed a treaty in 1967 outlawing such weapons within their jurisdiction. That same year a nuclear nonproliferation treaty was drafted. Big-power negotiations produced a ban in 1963 on atmospheric testing, but France and China have not gone along with the restriction.

The expense and hazards of nuclear stockpiling and continued development of ballistic missiles and antimissile systems led the United States and the USSR into extended Strategic Arms Limitation Talks (SALT), resulting in 1972 in a treaty to limit the deployment of antiballistic missiles and an executive agreement to limit the number of offensive weapons to those already under construction or deployed.

See also London Naval Conference (1930); Strategic Arms Limitation Talks; Washington Armament Conference (1921–1922).

Consult (VIII) Barnet, 1969; Roberts, 1970.

—Martin Gruberg, University of Wisconsin, Oshkosh

DISNEY, WALT (WALTER ELIAS) (1901–1966), American artist and film producer famous for his animated cartoons. After directing a number of silent and sound cartoons, Disney became a producer. The inventiveness and witty drawings of his cartoons, some tinged with the macabre as in Skeleton Dance (1930), and a gallery of such characters as Mickey Mouse, Donald Duck, and Pluto made him world famous. Disney was the first to use the improved three-strip technicolor process for one of his "Silly Symphonies," Flowers and Trees (1932), and achieved tremendous success with the color cartoon Three Little Pigs (1933). He developed synchronization of picture, music, and effects to such a degree that any close matching of visuals and sound became known as "Mickey Mousing." Disney's first full-length cartoon was Snow White and the Seven Dwarfs (1938), a perennial success, and was followed by Pinocchio (1940), Dumbo (1941), and Bambi (1942).

In 1948, Walt Disney began his true-life adventure series, including The Living Desert (1953), a brilliantly photographed wildlife documentary criticized for its sentimental commentaries and artificial synchronization of live action and music. During his last years, Disney concentrated on the development of family-entertainment parks—Disneyland and Disneyworld.

DISPLACED PERSONS, or refugees, people forced to leave their homelands because of the ravages of war, political upheaval, or persecution. "Displaced person" is usually used to refer to the millions of Europeans who were homeless following World War II and who were repatriated or resettled. Since that time, the office of UN high commissioner for refugees has come into existence to help provide protection and material assistance for displaced persons including Koreans, Vietnamese, Nigerians, and Pakistanis.

DISTRICT OF COLUMBIA, the nation's capital since 1800. The district was established by Congress in 1790 with territory ceded from Maryland and Virginia. Virginia's land was returned to the state in 1846. The site was chosen by George Washington, and the city was then designed by Pierre L'Enfant. The city was burned by the British during the War of 1812. Congress abolished the charter of the city in 1871 and instituted a territorial government. From 1878 until 1967, when a mayor-city council form of government was instituted, the district was governed by Congress. The city has a nonvoting representative in the House, and residents vote in presidential elections. The population in 1970 was 756,510.

DIX, DOROTHEA (LYNDE) (1802–1887), humanitarian and social reformer who devoted her career to improving the care of the mentally ill. A Boston schoolteacher, she undertook in 1841 to teach a Sunday school class for women in the East Cambridge jail. There she found insane inmates jailed in deplorable conditions with criminals, drunkards, and prostitutes. Turning her attention to the plight of the mentally ill, she surveyed every jail, prison, and almshouse in Massachusetts and in 1843 presented her findings in a Memorial to the Legislature of Massachusetts. When the legislature appropriated funds for the care of the mentally ill, Dix continued her crusade in other states, investigating conditions and issuing "Memorials" to state legislatures. She visited 18 state penitentiaries, 300 county jails and houses of correction, and more than 500 almshouses; her efforts were instrumental in the establishment of 32 state mental hospitals. Also interested in prison reform, she advocated such measures as prisoner education. Her primary goal was to obtain a federal land trust, the income of which could be used for the care of the insane. The measure finally passed Congress in 1857 but was vetoed by President Pierce.

In 1861, Dix was appointed superintendent of Army nurses, a new post created for the appointment and supervision of women nurses for the Union army. Less successful as an administrator than a reformer, she encountered friction with both subordinates and superiors. Her lasting achievement was to have directed attention to the plight of the mentally ill.

Consult (V) Marshall, 1937.

—Nancy Woloch, Hebrew Union College

DIXIECRATS, name applied to Southern

Washington Monument rises behind the White House in the nation's capital.

Reformer Dorothea Dix helped change inhumane conditions in the insane asylums.

Stephen Douglas, the Little Giant, whose doctrine of popular sovereignty widened sectional differences before the Civil War.

Democrats, particularly during the 1948 elections. *See* States' Rights Party.

DOLLAR DIPLOMACY, term first used by President Taft to describe American policies toward Latin America, where political and economic instabilities often threatened American economic investments. The United States asserted and sometimes acquired through treaties the right to intervene to protect American financial interests. Intervention included the landing of American troops in several Latin American countries. Taft described U.S. dollar diplomacy with pride, but it offended Latin Americans, and they used the concept to criticize American policy.

    See also Good Neighbor Policy; Taft, William Howard.

    Consult (V) Nearing and Freeman, 1970.

DOMESTIC SYSTEM. *See* Putting-Out System.

DONIPHAN'S EXPEDITION (1846–1847), early campaign, commanded by Col. Alexander W. Doniphan, in the Mexican War. *See* Mexican War.

DORR REBELLION (1842), revolt by citizens of Rhode Island who, by restrictions in the state constitution, were not allowed to vote. Since 1724, the franchise law in Rhode Island had restricted voting privileges to landholders and their eldest sons. As industry grew in Rhode Island and the population increased, the injustice of the voting system became a major issue.

    Thomas Wilson Dorr (1805–1854) led the rebellion of the suffragists. In early 1841, Dorr and his supporters held meetings to frame a new constitution and abolish the limited franchise. Dorr's adherents proclaimed a new state government with him as governor on April 18, 1842, but rival Governor Samuel W. King declared the Dorr party in a state of insurrection and instituted martial law. On May 18 the Dorrites unsuccessfully attempted to seize the state arsenal in Providence. The conservatives refused to make concessions, and Dorr eventually surrendered. Sentenced to life imprisonment, he was pardoned the next year, and, largely as a result of his efforts, suffrage reforms were made in the state constitution. In 1849 the Supreme Court decision in *Luther v. Borden,* which concerned the validity of rival state governments, ruled that it was an issue to be decided by Congress.

DOS PASSOS, JOHN (1896–1970), American author who was a member of the "Lost Generation." *See* Literature.

DOUGHBOYS, popular name for U.S. soldiers in World War I. *See* American Expeditionary Force.

DOUGLAS, STEPHEN A(RNOLD) (1813–1861), Illinois senator known as the "Little Giant," who was an advocate of popular sovereignty in the territories. Born in New England, he settled in Illinois at 20. The remainder of his life was devoted to his twin passions of politics and land speculation. His rapid rise in the Democratic Party culminated in his election to the U.S. Senate at the age of 35. During the same period, Douglas grew wealthy through timely land investments in the booming Chicago area.

    As chairman of the Senate committee on territories, Douglas squarely faced the North-South conflict over extending slavery into the developing territories. Even though Douglas had backed the Compromise of 1850, he reopened the slavery issue in 1854, when he sponsored the Kansas-Nebraska Act, which repealed the Missouri Compromise.

    In its place, Douglas endorsed the doctrine of popular sovereignty, which allowed the settlers of the territories to decide the slavery issue after they achieved statehood. This solution did not defuse the slavery issue, and Kansas was soon rent by conflict. The controversial role of Douglas in the debacle over Kansas was one of the factors that led the Democratic Party to nominate James Buchanan over Douglas in 1856.

    When President Buchanan backed the proslavery forces in Kansas in 1857, Douglas denounced this decision and accused Southern interests of controlling the Democratic Party. In a hard-fought senatorial campaign the following year, Douglas defeated the Republicans' nominee, Abraham Lincoln, but his inability to reconcile the Dred Scott decision (1857) with popular sovereignty damaged Douglas politically. Although Douglas received the nomination of the non-Southern wing of the Democratic Party in 1860, the party was fragmented, and Abraham Lincoln won an easy electoral victory. When the South seceded, Douglas rallied to Lincoln's support and seemed destined to play a crucial role as a Democratic unionist before he died suddenly of typhoid fever.

    See also Bleeding Kansas; Dred Scott Decision (1857); Kansas-Nebraska Act (1854); Lincoln-Douglas Debates (1858); Popular Sovereignty.

    Consult (IV) Capers, 1959.

    —Dan T. Carter, *University of Maryland*

DOUGLASS, FREDERICK (1817–1895), black leader and abolitionist. He was born Frederick Augustus Washington Bailey in Maryland the son of a slave woman and a white man. According to law, the child followed the condition of his mother and became a slave. His quick mind and proud spirit made his life as a laborer and house servant intolerable to him, and in 1838 he escaped to New York, later settling in Massachusetts.

As a reader of William Lloyd Garrison's *Liberator,* Douglass became well informed on abolitionist issues. In 1841 he stood up at a Garrison-sponsored meeting and made a powerful speech against slavery. He then embarked on a career as an abolitionist speaker and writer, describing his own life in *Narrative of the Life of Frederick Douglass* (1845). Douglass gave antislavery lectures in Britain (1845–1847) and collected enough money to buy his freedom. He then relocated in Rochester, N.Y., where in 1847 he founded *The North Star,* an abolitionist newspaper.

By 1851, Douglass had become convinced that his people could gain most by identifying with those who sought victory at the polls, a stand that lost him the support of Garrison's faction. During the Civil War, Douglass summoned all his eloquence to urge emancipation. He also called on blacks to serve the North.

After the war Douglass supported the Fourteenth and Fifteenth amendments and continued to seek practical programs to help blacks. He also held several government positions, including recorder of deeds (1881–1886) of the District of Columbia and U.S. consul general to Haiti (1889–1891). Although nationally famous, he was superseded before his death as leader of the black people by Booker T. Washington.

See also Abolitionism; Blacks in the United States; Garrison, William Lloyd; Slavery.
Consult (IX) Foner, 1950–1955; Quarles, 1948.

—Louis Filler, *Antioch College*

DOWNING, ANDREW JACKSON (1815–1852), architect whose use of landscape gardening and prolific writings transformed the face of American architecture. A landscape gardener, horticulturist, and architect, Downing became an authority on the new eclectic American architecture with his first book, *The Theory and Practice of Landscape Gardening* (1841). Americans built Gothic houses and Italian villas from plans contained in Downing's books. His *Cottage Residences* (1842) reproduced further plans for new houses suitable to the American countryside. He insisted that the place and type of house as well as the character of the owner must be considered in designing a house.

Downing advised President Fillmore on city plans when a revision of the original plan allowed the addition of irregular walks and parks to Washington's formal scheme. With Calvert Vaux and Frederick Law Olmsted, Downing helped plan Central Park in New York.

DRAFT. *See* Selective Service Act (1917).

DRAFT RIOTS, outbreaks protesting conscription during the Civil War. The Draft Act of March 3, 1863, provided that all physically fit men between the ages of 18 and 45 were eligible for conscription. Unmarried men from 18 to 45 and married men from 18 to 30 were to be called up first, then married men between 30 and 45. There were several exemptions, two of which angered many Northerners: draftees who procured a substitute or those who paid a $300 fee.

In New York City feeling against the draft ran high, and 2 days after the draft lottery began (July 11, 1863), riots erupted in Manhattan. Furious mobs demolished draft offices and armories, then turned on the city's black population, lynching and beating many blacks. After 3 days of mayhem, federal troops finally put down the rioters. Approximately 1,000 people were killed or wounded, and property losses totaled about $2 million.
Consult (IV) McCague, 1968.

DRED SCOTT DECISION (1857), a landmark case in the slavery controversy, the most significant after the *Prigg v. Pennsylvania* (1842) case. In 1834 Dred Scott, a slave, had been taken by his master from Missouri, a slave state, into Illinois, a free state, and then Wisconsin, a territory declared free under the Missouri Compromise. Back in Missouri, Scott sued for his freedom on the grounds that his residence in free territory erased his slave status. Ten years of litigation finally brought the case, known in full as *Dred Scott v. Sandford,* before the Supreme Court in 1854.

Involved in the decision were the questions of whether Scott, as a slave, was a citizen of Missouri with the right to make a federal appeal, whether his stay in free territory rendered him free, and whether the Missouri Compromise was constitutional. The Court could have rejected the case on the grounds that Missouri courts had held Scott was not a citizen and therefore could not sue in federal court. Instead, Chief Justice Taney decided to go beyond the narrow question involved and to pass judgment on the larger issues of slavery restriction.

Taney held that Scott was not a citizen, but he went on to assert that blacks had traditionally been held to be of an inferior order and that Congress had exceeded its authority in ruling that Northern territories were to exclude slavery under the Missouri Compromise. Thus, for the first time since *Marbury v. Madison* in 1803, the Court ruled that an act of Congress was unconstitutional, and, in addition, it said that slavery could not be excluded from federal territories.

It was widely held that Taney had deferred his decision until after the presidential election of 1856 in order to ensure a Democratic victory. Republicans used Taney's decision—especially his phrase declaring that

Born a slave, Frederick Douglass fled to freedom and became an abolitionist speaker.

Draft Riots in New York City in 1863 were far more violent than anti-draft demonstrations in the twentieth century.

Theodore Dreiser's realistic novels left a deep imprint on American fiction.

W. E. B. Du Bois, a militant spokesman for black rights, helped start the Niagra Movement (1905) and was a guiding force in NAACP.

blacks had been held "so far inferior that they had no rights which the white man was bound to respect"—as the basis of political charges. The decision raised a storm that made it certain that there could be no further accommodation between Northern and Southern interests.

See also Missouri Compromise (1820); Prigg v. Pennsylvania (1842); Slavery; Taney, Roger B.

Consult (IV) Nevins, 1950; Nichols, 1948.
—Louis Filler, *Antioch College*

DREISER, THEODORE (1871-1945), novelist known for his naturalistic view of American life. He was born into a poverty-stricken family in Terre Haute, Ind. Following a year at the University of Indiana, Dreiser became a newspaper reporter (1892-1894) in Chicago, St. Louis, and Pittsburgh. In 1894 he settled in New York and began a career as a magazine editor and free-lance writer. After 1910 Dreiser devoted all his time to writing. His novels bear the influence of deterministic philosophers, who influenced him to view life as a massive struggle for survival.

The main theme of most of his work is the conflict between the individual and society. His view of life as a welter of blind amoral forces was the underpinning of his first novel, *Sister Carrie* (1900), the tone of which brought on a long series of censorship battles and a great deal of hostile criticism. The novel was withdrawn by the publisher soon after publication.

Dreiser's naturalism permeated his other novels, including *Jennie Gerhardt* (1911) and a trilogy based on the unscrupulous career of a magnate: *The Financier* (1912), *The Titan* (1914), and *The Stoic* (1947). The novel that won Dreiser his widest audience was *An American Tragedy* (1925). Based on a 1906 murder case, the story traces the downfall of a young man trying to reach the American dream of success in a materialistic society.

DRUGS (HARD). No significant historical studies of American drug use have been done, but nineteenth-century patent medicines were laced with opium; morphine intake was widespread after the Civil War; and heroin was legally sold until 1914. No one knows what social classes or age groups were involved, but by the 1950s narcotics were largely confined to the poor, usually blacks, while barbiturates and amphetamines were the province of the adult white bourgeoisie.

During the 1960s these generational and class distinctions began breaking down, and young members of the white middle class experimented with various drugs. Initially the accent was on the nonaddictive psychedelic varieties—L.S.D., mescaline, hashish, marijuana. Gradually the emphasis shifted to addictive "hard" chemicals—barbiturates, narcotics, and amphetamines. By the 1970s depressants and stimulants probably took precedence over "soft" drugs except marijuana. The reasons are unknown, but the psychedelic hallucinogenic experience may have been more compatible with the rebellious, optimistic youth culture of the 1960s than with the more conventional generation of the 1970s.

See also Psychedelics.
Consult (VIII) King, 1972.

DU BOIS, W(ILLIAM) E(DWARD) B(URG-HARDT) (1868-1963), outspoken activist and propagandist against U.S. and European racism. Du Bois (pronounced Du Boyce) also made significant contributions in American history, sociology, and journalism.

Born in Great Barrington, Mass., he was the first black to receive a Ph.D. at Harvard (1895). While teaching at black Atlanta University, Du Bois wrote a major work on race relations, *The Souls of Black Folk* (1903), in which he criticized Booker T. Washington for accepting less than full citizenship rights for blacks. In 1905, Du Bois helped organize the Niagara movement, a black group that demanded an end to racial discrimination in education, public accommodations, voting, and employment. When the Niagara movement failed, Du Bois helped establish its successor, the National Association for the Advancement of Colored People (NAACP), in 1909 and became editor of its monthly journal, *The Crisis*. As editor, Du Bois advocated Pan-Africanism long before most NAACP leaders were interested in Africa.

During the Depression of the 1930s, Du Bois lost faith in integration and advocated a form of black self-segregation that resulted in his dismissal from the NAACP. For the next 20 years he was a race leader in limbo. After World War II, Du Bois, who had been a socialist, was indicted as a Soviet agent. The charges were dropped, but in 1961 the 93-year-old Du Bois, increasingly disillusioned with American society, joined the Communist Party, renounced his American citizenship, and joined African nationalist leader Kwame Nkrumah in Ghana. Du Bois is considered by black nationalists and black integrationists alike as one of their greatest leaders.

See also Blacks in the United States; National Association for the Advancement of Colored People; Washington, Booker T.

Consult (IX) Aptheker, 1968; Logan, 1971; Rudwick, 1968.
—Sheldon Avery, *The Johns Hopkins University*

DUKE, JAMES B(UCHANAN) (1856-1925), tobacco industrialist and philanthropist. He was the son of Washington Duke, who established a leaf tobacco firm at Durham, N.C., at the close of the Civil War. In 1881 the firm began making cigarettes, and Duke, who had joined the firm at 18, was instrumental in developing machinery for production and in establishing a national sales and marketing organization (1884). By 1889 the Duke firm accounted for 50 percent of national cigarette production.

Intense competition in the tobacco industry led to the merger of the five largest firms in 1890. Duke was named president of the newly formed American Tobacco Company, which, through subsequent mergers, was able to dominate the entire tobacco industry. The federal government was successful in prosecuting it under the Sherman Antitrust Act as a combination in restraint of trade, and in 1911 the trust was dissolved by order of the Supreme Court. Among the many beneficiaries of the Duke Endowment was Trinity College, subsequently renamed Duke University.

See also Antitrust Cases.
Consult (V) Heiman, 1960.

DULLES, JOHN FOSTER (1888-1959), international lawyer, diplomat, Eisenhower's secretary of state, and crusader against communism. Dulles was born in Washington, D.C., and educated at Princeton, the Sorbonne, and George Washington University. His family had a tradition of diplomatic and public service. He began law practice in New York in 1911 and was counsel to the American peace commission in 1918–1919 and U.S. representative at the war reparations conference in Berlin in 1933. Director of many large industrial and financial corporations conducting operations where he performed his diplomatic functions, Dulles was criticized for being partial to their interests.

Secretary of State. In 1945 he advised Senator Arthur Vanderberg at the UN Charter Conference and was a delegate to the General Assembly in 1946, 1947, and 1950. Author of the foreign policy platform of the Republican Party in 1952, he was appointed secretary of state by Eisenhower and held office from 1953 to 1959. In this capacity Dulles acted more as tactician than as policy maker, traveling extensively around the world to consolidate support for the United States during the Cold War.

He regarded communism as a moral evil with which there could be no honorable compromise. In the context of the confrontation between blocs of nations armed with nuclear weapons, his attitude of "brinkmanship" and threats of "massive relation" helped preserve America's decisiveness and credibility but were also widely criticized. His principal writings are *War, Peace and Change* (1939) and *War or Peace* (1950).

Consult (VI) Gerson, 1967.

DUMBARTON OAKS CONFERENCE, four-power meeting held at Dumbarton Oaks, an estate outside Washington, D.C., from Aug. 21 to Oct. 7, 1944, to draft proposals for an international organization. Delegates from the United States, the Soviet Union, Britain, and China quickly agreed that the United Nations should be composed of an assembly in which all members would be represented; an 11-member security council with primary responsibility for peace-keeping, in which the five great powers (including France) would have permanent seats; a social and economic council; and an international court of justice. The Dumbarton Oaks proposals formed the basis for the UN Charter , adopted in San Francisco on June 26, 1945.

See also United Nations.

DURAND, ASHER BROWN (1796-1886), painter who was a member of the Hudson River School. *See* Hudson River School; Painting.

DYLAN, BOB (ROBERT ZIMMERMAN) (1941-   ), folk singer, composer, and poet. An immensely popular figure during the 1960s, he has been characterized as a moralist, an angry young man with a guitar, and a social protest poet.

The son of a Minnesota appliance dealer, he was one of the important spirits behind the folk rock revolution in popular music that began in 1965. He taught himself to play the guitar and also mastered the piano, autoharp, and harmonica. His numerous compositions, songs, and ballads reflect the artistic influence of both blues and country music and the style of Woody Guthrie. He later lost some of his early intensity and power, but his writing gained a philosophic perspective on life and maturity. Dylan has been considered one of the twentieth century's popular culture heroes.

EAKINS, THOMAS (1844-1916), painter and art teacher who was the leading realist in nineteenth-century American art. He attended the Pennsylvania Academy of Fine Arts and studied painting with J. L. Gérôme and Léon Bonnat in Paris. After a visit to Spain in 1869, where he was impressed by Spanish painters, Eakins returned to Philadelphia and became an artist and a teacher (later dean) at the Academy of Fine Arts.

Eakins painted many portraits and eventually more elaborate compositions. His quest for realism in all his works led him to draw on his earlier study of anatomy at Jefferson Medical College. His medical scenes "The Gross Clinic" (1875) and "The Agnew Clinic" (1889) caused an uproar because of their scientific accuracy and realism.

Eakins experimented in other media, executing several sculptures and working with the photography of motion. His portraits and sporting subjects, such as "Max Schmitt in a Scull" (1871) and "The Swimming Hole" (1883),

John Foster Dulles, Eisenhower's secretary of state, firmly opposed spread of Communist influence.

Folk singer Bob Dylan *(left),* in concert on Britain's Isle of Wight.

Acrid smoke billows from industrial plant in Houston.

Mary Baker Eddy, founder of the Church of Christ, Scientist.

reveal a sculptural quality and an ability to paint uncompromising character analysis that often offended his sitters. In his last years, Eakins began to receive recognition, but his real stature was not appreciated until after his death.

EAST JERSEY. *See* New Jersey.

EATON AFFAIR (1831), social scandal during Andrew Jackson's first Administration that reflected a growing split between Vice-President John C. Calhoun and Secretary of State Martin Van Buren, both of whom hoped to succeed Jackson. The affair revolved around Peggy Eaton, the wife of John H. Eaton, a close friend of Jackson who had been appointed secretary of war in 1829. Peggy, the beautiful daughter of a Washington innkeeper, had been widowed shortly before marrying Eaton.

The status of the new Mrs. Eaton soon became a political issue. The women of Washington society, led by Mrs. Calhoun, consistently snubbed her, infuriating Jackson. Not only was he a personal friend of both Eatons, but he also remembered how his own late wife had been slandered in the campaign of 1828. Jackson defended Peggy's virtue and demanded that the members of his Administration do likewise. However, only Van Buren, himself a widower, came to the defense of Mrs. Eaton.

The Eaton affair dragged on until the spring of 1831, when Van Buren and Eaton resigned. Jackson then demanded and received the resignations of the remaining cabinet members. The cabinet reorganization that followed produced a stronger cabinet. The Eaton affair also sealed the enmity between Jackson and Calhoun and marked the ascendancy of Van Buren.

Consult (III) Schlesinger, 1945; Van Deusen, 1959.

ECOLOGY, the relationship of living organisms to the environment. The word was largely restricted to laboratory usage until Rachel Carson published *Silent Spring* in 1962 and Paul Ehrlich wrote *The Population Bomb* (1968). The impact of these two books was dramatically swift.

Starting in California, then sweeping across the United States, a movement of youthful "ecology-action" groups and middle-aged conservation societies was, by 1970, pressuring congressmen on a wide spectrum of issues ranging from the water pollution of phosphated detergents to the noise and air pollution of a proposed supersonic transport. The first nationwide Earth Day was held on April 22, 1970. Americans continued to be horrified by threats of ecological disaster—defoliants in Vietnam, pipelines in Alaska, and strip mining in West Virginia, and there were warnings of the com-

ing collision between ecology and capitalism. In response to public concern, President Nixon formed in 1970 the Environmental Protection Agency (EPA), which has tried to develop controls for industrial pollution. Ecologists have warned repeatedly that only 30 years remained to stop the pollution.

Consult (VIII) Commoner, 1971.

ECONOMIC AID. *See* Foreign Aid.

ECONOMIC OPPORTUNITY ACT (1964). The first major piece of legislation in President Johnson's war on poverty created the Job Corps and VISTA. Although opposed by Republicans as an election-year giveaway, it was passed by Congress.

The act created the Office of Economic Opportunity (OEO) to administer a coordinated attack on the various causes of poverty. The Job Corps, for youths between 16 and 21, was designed to provide educational, vocational, and on-the-job training. There was also federal aid for work-study and for state and local work training. VISTA, often called the domestic Peace Corps, authorized the recruiting and training of volunteers to help staff the antipoverty programs. Other sections of the act authorized federal grants for programs to provide better employment opportunities, education, small-business loans, and employment training for adults.

See also VISTA.

EDDY, MARY BAKER (1821–1910), founder of the practice of Christian Science and the Church of Christ, Scientist. Mary Morse Baker was born in Bow, near Concord, N.H. Her physical frailty as a youth forced her to receive her early education at home. Widowed at 22, a few months after her marriage to George W. Glover, she spent 9 years among relatives, teaching at times but often in ill health. In 1853 she married Daniel Patterson, a dentist who, unable to make a living, deserted her in 1861.

In an effort to regain her health, she began to practice a system of mental healing. She formulated the principles later associated with Christian Science after making, through "divine revelation, reason and demonstration," a remarkable recovery from a fall she had suffered. Setting up a spiritual healing practice at Lynn, Mass. (1870), she published *Science and Health with Key to the Scriptures,* in which she set forth the basic doctrines of Christian Science. In 1882 she married Asa Gilbert Eddy, one of her disciples.

The Christian Scientists' Association, which she established in 1876, was chartered as the Church of Christ, Scientist. In her last years, Eddy established the *Christian Science Monitor,* which became a leading newspaper.

EDISON, THOMAS (ALVA) (1847–1931),

American inventor, frequently cited as the country's greatest. Especially important are his invention of the phonograph, his discovery of the "Edison effect," which became the basis of the vacuum tube essential to modern radiotelephony, and his invention of the carbon telephone transmitter, still in general use. Edison also developed and perfected many items that others had discovered, including the incandescent electric bulb, the automatic telegraph, the motion picture projector, and the stock ticker.

He grew up in Lake Huron, Mich., in a prosperous family and was tutored by his mother. While a youth, he established a profitable newspaper, tobacco, and candy trade on long train runs, performed his laboratory experiments in baggage cars, made friends with telegraph operators, and examined electrical communications. In 1863 Edison became a telegraph operator and began inventing labor-saving telegraphic devices; he took out his first patents in 1868.

In 1869 Edison moved to New York and soon formed an electrical engineering partnership and sold some stock-ticker inventions for $40,000, which he used to set up his own laboratory in 1870. In 1876 he moved his laboratory to Menlo Park, N.J., and in 1886 to West Orange. Edison's chief aim in his inventions (resulting in more than 1,000 patents) was practicality. He sought inventions adaptable to large production, cheap sale, and wide commercial use. Money was important to him only as the means to continue his work. To manufacture and sell his products, Edison organized many commercial companies that ultimately became part of the General Electric Company.

Early in his career, Edison became the idol of the nation's press, which called him "Wizard," glorified all that he did, and credited him with inventions he had little to do with. He had a tremendous capacity for work, trained himself to dispense with regular sleep, and inspired others to follow his example. His life defined his saying, "Genius is two percent inspiration and ninety-eight perspiration."

See also Inventions.

Consult (V) Josephson, 1955.

—Ari Hoogenboom, *Brooklyn College of The City University of New York*

EDUCATION. Although education in America has its roots in the colonial era and although education developed significantly in the early nineteenth century, interest, coupled with public support, began its surge in the late nineteenth century.

Colonial Period (1607–1787). Initial provisions for schooling in America tended to reflect the various attitudes that the early settlers had toward education. The Puritans who settled in New England had strong religious motives for education. They believed that a knowledge of the Bible was essential for per-

sonal salvation, so the ability to read, "to search the Scriptures daily," was a major concern of the colonists. When voluntary home instruction and apprenticeship training proved unsatisfactory in Massachusetts, the colonial legislature enacted two laws of lasting importance. The Massachusetts Law of 1642 required that all children be taught to read, but it did not establish schools. It was followed by the Massachusetts Law of 1647, which required every town of 50 families to employ a teacher of reading and writing and every town of 100 families to establish a Latin grammar school. The laws of 1642 and 1647 were educational landmarks in the English-speaking world. They established the right of a legislative body of the state to make education mandatory and to require communities to provide and maintain schools.

The settlers of the Middle colonies, with various national and religious backgrounds, left education to private and parochial effort with no provision for tax support. Church control of schools became the practice, and instruction was generally rudimentary.

In the South, public education was considered a form of charity, and the more affluent families employed tutors or sent their children to private boarding schools. There were a few schools for orphans and children of the poor. Apprentices were taught to read and write by their masters.

Secondary Schools and Colleges. In 1635 a Latin Grammar School, limited to boys, was established in Boston. It was the first of what became the dominant type of secondary school during the colonial period. Modeled after similar schools in Europe, it offered preparation for college that stressed Latin and Greek.

In 1749 Benjamin Franklin wrote *Proposals Relating to the Education of Youth in Pennsylvania,* advocating a more practical secondary education than the Latin grammar schools. The Philadelphia Academy opened in 1751, offering instruction in accounting, English, and modern languages as well as in the classics. However, the academy soon became primarily a college preparatory institution. From the end of the Revolutionary War until the rise of the public high school in the late nineteenth century the academy was the dominant type of secondary school in America.

Harvard College was founded in 1636 with preparation for the ministry as its chief purpose. Other early colleges were William and Mary, 1693; Yale College, 1701; and the College of New Jersey (Princeton), 1746.

Early National Period (1787–1820). There was no mention of education in the U.S. Constitution, and the Tenth Amendment indicated that the responsibility for education was left to the states, but the Founding Fathers stressed the importance of education in a

Inventor Thomas A. Edison's development of a practical incandescent light bulb changed American life.

Early view of Yale College, one of the first colleges in colonial America.

EDUCATION — Item Guide

The article on EDUCATION describes the main trends in American education, from the colonial era to the present.

Religion was the impetus for much of colonial education especially among the PURITANS, who were responsible for the MASSACHUSETTS SCHOOL ACT. COLONIAL COLLEGES were generally started with a religious orientation. BENJAMIN FRANKLIN influenced educational development in Pennsylvania, also the home of the first LOG COLLEGE was established. EVENING SCHOOLS allowed young people to attend school after the work day had ended.

In the nineteenth century the founding of colleges was helped by the Supreme Court decision in DARTMOUTH COLLEGE V. WOODWARD (1819) and the MORRILL ACT (1862). HORACE MANN popularized the concept of free education, and CHARLES WILLIAM ELIOT influenced the course of higher education.

PROGRESSIVE EDUCATION, for which JOHN DEWEY was the primary spokesman, dominated much of educational theory and practice in the twentieth century. Interest in higher education was spurred by the NATIONAL DEFENSE EDUCATION ACT (1958) at the dawn of the space age. The most striking development in mid-twentieth century was the challenge to racial segregation in the schools, beginning with the BROWN V. BOARD OF EDUCATION OF TOPEKA decision (1954).

Village schoolhouse in 1860.

democracy. The Northwest Ordinances of 1785 and 1787 encouraged the establishment of schools and provided that the sixteenth lot of each township be set aside for educational use. The introduction of the Lancastrian system, by which teachers taught monitors, who in turn instructed large groups of students, gave added impetus to the establishment of schools, especially in the cities. By 1820, New York had 20 such schools.

In 1816 the New Hampshire legislature tried to transform Dartmouth College into a state institution. In 1819 the U.S. Supreme Court decided that the charter of a college was a contract that could not be impaired by the state. The result was not only to encourage the founding of other private colleges but also to stimulate the establishment of state universities.

Increased Interest in Education (1820–1860). As the new nation became stronger, the concern for education grew and school appropriations increased. In 1821 the English Classical School, later the English High School, was established in Boston. It offered a more practical curriculum than the academy or the Latin Grammar School. In time, the high school was to supersede both as the typical American secondary school.

In 1837 Massachusetts established the first state board of education, with Horace Mann as its secretary. His 12 annual reports aroused new enthusiasm for the common school as a free nonsectarian institution for elementary education. The need for trained teachers became apparent, and, largely through Mann, the first state-supported normal school was opened in Lexington, Mass., in 1839.

In 1839 Henry Barnard became the first secretary of the newly formed state board of education in Connecticut. Like Mann, Barnard had visited European schools. The journals that he had edited and his books and reports were instrumental in obtaining support for public education and for better teachers. When the U.S. Department (Office) of Education was established in 1867, Barnard became its first commissioner.

Educational Patterns (1860–1900). Although the ungraded one-room school still provided the basic elementary education in rural America in the nineteenth century, reports on elementary education in Prussia had led to the introduction of a system of grades in some American elementary schools before the Civil War. In the larger cities, schools were organized into seven or eight grades, and courses of study for each grade developed.

A four-year secondary school program based upon completion of the elementary grades and followed by four years of college became the pattern. This system contrasted with the European dual system of terminal elementary education for the masses and, for the elite, selective admission to secondary schools that prepared students for entrance into the university.

Morrill Act. In 1862 President Lincoln signed the historic Morrill Act, granting 30,000 acres of public land to each state for each senator and representative it had in Congress. The land was to endow a college of agriculture and mechanic arts, which would also teach military science.

Almost 70 colleges, many of them now state universities, resulted from this momentous legislation. The instruction they offered in agriculture and engineering and their extension services made a rich contribution to the development of America. The act also established the federal government's right to grant the states aid for specific educational purposes.

Kalamazoo Decision. In 1874 the Michigan Supreme Court upheld the right of the Kalamazoo school district to collect taxes for the support of a high school. Although the legality of taxes for common schools had been generally accepted, the legal basis for the public support of high school education had varied from state to state.

The Kalamazoo decision resulted in the acceptance of the high school as a valid part of a tax-supported public school system and paved the way for the extension of free secondary education.

Twentieth Century. The outstanding development in twentieth-century education has been the phenomenal growth of enrollment at all levels. Strong faith in the value of an education led to laws requiring attendance up to the age of 16 or 18; to the provision for schools, junior colleges, and four-year colleges and universities; and to unprecedented financial support of education.

John Dewey. America's most influential educational philosopher in the first half of the century was John Dewey. His *Democracy and Education* (1916) stressed that education should be useful and related to life. Pupil-teacher planning and pupil participation in meaningful learning experiences are basic tenets of Dewey's philosophy.

The progressive education movement, which grew out of the ideas of Dewey and his followers, did much to shift the emphasis in elementary education during the 1920s and 1930s from drill exercises and lesson-hearing to learning projects and creative self-expression. With the 1940s came a widespread public reaction against the movement because of its alleged failure to emphasize fundamental skills and knowledge.

The Federal Role. In 1917 President Wilson signed the Act for Vocational Education (Smith-Hughes Act), which marked the beginning of federal aid to schools below college level. In 1944 Congress passed the Serviceman's Readjustment Act, commonly known as the GI Bill, to provide education and training, mainly at the college level, for veterans of World War II. Later legislation provided similar funds for veterans of the Korean War and other conflicts.

A direct result of the Russian space explorations was the enactment by Congress in 1958 of a broad program of assistance to education known as the National Defense Education Act (NDEA). It provided federal funds for loans to college students and sought to improve the teaching of science, mathematics, and foreign languages.

The Higher Education Act (1965), providing funds for various collegiate purposes, was followed in 1972 by an omnibus bill authorizing a $1-billion annual program of nonrestricted grants. The Elementary and Secondary Education Act (1965) authorized federal aid to education on a large scale, including funds for children of low-income families, for school libraries, and for educational centers and research.

Racial Segregation. In a historic decision (*Brown v. Board of Education*) the U.S. Supreme Court on May 17, 1954, declared segregation in public schools on the basis of race to be illegal. Early attempts to enforce desegregation met with strong opposition in the Southern states. Federal troops were called out in Little Rock, Ark., and the National Guard at the University of Mississippi. Subsequent federal rulings and civil rights legislation have served to accelerate the integration process in schools at all levels, and equality of educational opportunity continued to be a goal of American education.

Consult (VIII) Johnson *et al.*, 1969; Schwartz, 1969; Tiedt, 1966.

—Edward Alvey, Jr., *Mary Washington College of the University of Virginia*

EDWARDS, JONATHAN (1703–1758), the greatest Puritan theologian of colonial America. A native of Connecticut, he was educated at Yale College and was a tutor there for several years. He served as minister of a Presbyterian church for a short time in 1722–1723, but his clerical career began in 1727 with his ordination and appointment as assistant to his grandfather, Solomon Stoddard, the pastor of the Northampton, Mass. Congregational church. On Stoddard's death, two years later, Edwards inherited that pulpit.

At Northampton, Edwards' preaching developed the religious revival that began the New England phase of the Great Awakening. His most famous sermon, "Sinners in the Hands of an Angry God," dates from this period. He preached a return to stricter Calvinist theology that included predestination and

emphasis on the experience of religious conversion, and he argued against the Arminian, or more liberal, church doctrines and practices that had developed in the New England churches. His analysis of the revival at Northampton, *A Faithful Narrative of the Surprising Work of God* (1737), was reprinted in 30 editions and became a classic manual on conversion.

Disputes over doctrine and congregational practices led to Edwards' dismissal from the Northampton church in 1750. He then moved to Stockbridge, Mass., where he lived until 1757 as pastor and as missionary to the Indians. During this period he wrote his most celebrated theological works, including his greatest intellectual achievement, *A Careful and Strict Enquiry into the Modern Prevailing Notions of Freedom of the Will* (1754). He was appointed the president of the College of New Jersey (later Princeton University) in 1757 but died of smallpox a few months after.

See also Colonial Religion; Great Awakening; Puritanism.

Consult (I) Winslow, 1940.

—Carl Ubbelohde, *Case Western Reserve University*

EISENHOWER, DWIGHT D(AVID) (1890–1969), 34th President of the United States (1953–1961). He was a political novice who appealed to a population that distrusted "politicians"—a conciliator and an accommodater.

He was born in Denison, Tex., on Oct. 14, 1890. Although the son of pacifist parents, he attended West Point and graduated in 1915. His brilliance in field maneuvers in the interwar period led to his assignment to planning operations. Eisenhower directed the North African invasion in 1943 and the Normandy landing in 1944, rising to the rank of five-star general. As commander in chief of SHAEF (Supreme Headquarters, Allied Expeditionary Forces), he handled with success political and diplomatic problems as well as military matters.

He was Army Chief of Staff from 1945 to 1948, retiring to become president of Columbia University. In 1948 he turned down efforts of many Democrats to draft him as their party's presidential candidate. In 1950 he returned to Europe as commander of SHAPE (Supreme Headquarters, Allied Powers in Europe) to coordinate military forces for the North Atlantic Treaty Organization (NATO). Once more he was sought out for a presidential candidacy, this time by Republicans. He wrestled the nomination from Senator Taft in 1952 and went on to win election and reelection handily.

As president, the popular Ike tried to combine liberalism in international affairs and human relations with conservatism in domestic affairs and economic relationships. He continued his predecessor's containment policy

THE READING CLASS. 21

MISS MILLS always took a great deal of pains with her pupils, who were learning to read. "The art of reading well," she often told them, "is only acquired by a few. Many persons learn to read in a monotonous tone, and with an indistinct pronunciation. Give every word its proper time and weight; and while you are reading, keep glancing forward to see if there are any difficulties in the way, that you may be ready to meet them."

Nineteenth-century pupils often learned their lessons by reading aloud.

General Eisenhower gives final instructions to paratroopers of the 101st Airborne on D-Day.

In 1954, during first term as president, Ike works on painting at Camp David, Md.

Numbers indicate the electoral vote of each state

toward communism, settled the Korean War, developed the Eisenhower Doctrine, and had summit conferences with his counterparts among the major powers. Domestically, he failed to impose his own brand of modern Republicanism on his party, was slow in cracking down on Senator Joseph McCarthy, established the Department of Health, Education and Welfare, and sent troops to Little Rock, Ark., to enforce school desegregation.

About midway through his 8-year tenure he suffered the first of three major illnesses that limited his activities. He retired in 1961 but continued to serve as patriarch of his party till his death in Washington, D.C., on March 28, 1969.

See also Eisenhower Doctrine; Presidential Elections; World War II.

Consult (VIII) Albertson, 1963; Eisenhower, 1963–1965.

—Martin Gruberg, *University of Wisconsin, Oshkosh*

EISENHOWER DOCTRINE, expression of the determination of the United States to defend its national interests in the Middle East, even by armed intervention. As a result of the Suez Canal crisis of 1956, Soviet influence and internal communist power were greatly increased in several Middle Eastern countries. In response to a request from President Eisenhower, Congress passed a resolution on March 9, 1957, declaring that "preservation of the independence and integrity of the nations of the Middle East" was vital to American security and giving the president the authority "to use armed forces to assist any such nation . . . requesting assistance against armed aggression from any country controlled by international communism."

Threatened by internal communist forces supported by Egypt, Syria, and Iraq, Lebanon asked for American help in the summer in 1958. The United States responded by landing several thousand Marines to bolster the Lebanon regime. Although similar direct action has not been taken since, the Eisenhower Doctrine remains a keystone of American policy in the Middle East.

EL ALAMEIN, battle on June 29, 1942, that halted the Axis advance into Egypt. *See* World War II.

ELECTORAL COLLEGE, the constitutionally required method for the selection of the president and vice-president.

Origin. The framers of the Constitution devised the electoral college (Article II and Amendment XII) so that the president and vice-president would be indirectly elected by the people through dispassionate reasonable men. Each state was assigned as many electors as it had senators and congressmen. In addi-

tion, the District of Columbia has three electors (Amendment XXIII). To be elected president and vice-president, the candidates must have a majority of the electoral votes.

Process. Electors are selected early in the presidential election year by the state laws and applicable political party apparatus. The electors are pledged to their respective party candidates. In November the voters in the 50 states choose one slate of electors, pledged to both candidates of each party, from among those on the state ballot. If the slate of electors wins a plurality in a state, all the electors so chosen then cast their ballots for the presidential and vice-presidential candidates of the winning party. Neither the Constitution nor federal law requires the electors to cast their ballots for the candidate of their party, although only rarely does an elector bolt his party's ticket.

If there is no majority for the president, the responsibility for selecting him from among the three top vote-getters falls on the House of Representatives, where each state has one vote and a majority of all the states is necessary to elect. If there is no majority cast for the vice-president, the Senate then chooses him from among the top two vote-getters. A majority of all the senators is required to elect.

The president and vice-president had to be chosen by Congress in 1801 (Jefferson and Burr), and John Quincy Adams was chosen president by the House in 1825. It is mathematically possible for a president to be elected by a majority of electoral votes without a majority of popular votes. In the twentieth century this paradox occurred in the elections of Democrats Woodrow Wilson (1912, 1916), Harry S Truman (1948), and John F. Kennedy (1960), and of Republican Richard M. Nixon (1968). Only once has a president lost the majority of the popular vote to one other candidate but won the electoral vote: in 1888 Benjamin Harrison defeated Grover Cleveland.

See also Presidential Elections.

Consult (VIII) Pierce, 1968.

ELEMENTARY AND SECONDARY EDUCATION ACT (1965). *See* Education.

ELIOT, CHARLES WILLIAM (1834–1924), president of Harvard for 40 years and a major influence on American education. He was born in Boston, graduated from Harvard in 1853, and taught mathematics and chemistry there (1854–1863). After two years of study in Europe, Eliot was appointed professor of chemistry at the Massachusetts Institute of Technology (1865). In 1869, at 35, he was made president of Harvard, a post he held until his retirement in 1909.

During his administration of the university, he effected changes that were responsible for making Harvard the pacemaker of American universities. He reformed the graduate and professional schools (especially law and medicine), enriched the curriculum, raised undergraduate standards, and introduced the sabbatical year and elective system. During his tenure the faculty increased tenfold and the student enrollment fourfold.

Eliot was also instrumental in securing a greater degree of uniformity in high school and college entrance requirements. He edited the famous 50-volume *Harvard Classics* (1910), the "five shelf" selection of world literature designed as a planned course of adult education.

ELIOT, T(HOMAS) S(TEARNS) (1888–1965), poet, playwright, and critic. He was born in St. Louis, Mo., and studied at Harvard, the Sorbonne, and Oxford. He took up residence in England in 1915 and became a British subject in 1927. Eliot was an Anglo-Catholic in religion, a classicist in literature, and a distinguished literary figure who exerted great influence on modern poetry through such poems as *The Waste Land* (1922). He received the Nobel Prize for Literature in 1940.

In several of his early works, Eliot expresses the anguish and barrenness of modern life. In 1920, with the publication of *The Sacred Wood*, a volume of essays, he attained stature as a critic. The publication of *The Waste Land*, a complex and difficult poem, marks Eliot's revolutionary break with tradition. Its imagery ranges from the rush hours of modern London to the symbolism of the Tarot and of Hinduism. Shortly after its publication, Eliot founded, and for many years (1923–1939) edited, the quarterly review *Criterion*.

In Eliot's later poetry, notably *Ash Wednesday* (1930) and the *Four Quartets* (1935–1942), he turned from skepticism to hope, strongly believing that writers should reflect not only their own society but also the consciousness of all ages.

Eliot tried to revitalize verse drama with *The Rock* (1934). *Murder in the Cathedral* (1935), based on the final hours and murder of Thomas à Becket, was Eliot's most successful play. Subsequent plays included *Family Reunion* (1939), *The Cocktail Party* (1949), and *The Confidential Clerk* (1953).

ELKINS ACT (1903), legislation passed to strengthen the Interstate Commerce Act of 1887 by defining more clearly the penalties for railroad rebates. The act said that only published rates were to be charged and that any attempt to deviate or to give rebates to favored shippers would be prosecuted.

The railroads favored the reform because they were suffering from disastrous rate wars and secret agreements, which had the effect of squeezing profit margins. The Elkins Act is thus a good example of how business regulation in the Progressive Era was often demanded by businessmen themselves. It was

followed by the Hepburn Act (1906) and the Mann-Elkins Act (1910).

See also Hepburn Act (1906); Interstate Commerce Commission; Mann-Elkins Act (1910); Railroad Legislation.

Consult (V) Thorelli, 1955.

ELLINGTON, DUKE (EDWARD KENNEDY) (1899–   ), jazz pianist, composer, arranger, and band leader who was an important representative of the big swing bands of the late 1920s and early 1930s. A native of Washington, D.C., Ellington had little formal music education beyond piano lessons, but at 17 he began his long professional career by playing in Harlem. In 1918 he was heading a small orchestra, which developed into the leading large ensemble for jazz.

The Duke's arrangements for his band were marked by rich and daring harmonies, subtle contrasts of color and timbre, and ingenious solo and ensemble relationships. Ellington wrote more than 2,000 compositions, many of which were recorded by his band. Several of his tunes became popular hits, among them "Solitude," "Sophisticated Lady," and "I Let a Song Go Out of My Heart." His longer works include "Concerto for Cootie," "Ko-Ko," and "Suite Thursday" (written with Billy Strayhorn).

ELLSWORTH, OLIVER (1745–1807), statesman and 2nd Chief Justice of the Supreme Court, respected by his contemporaries for his intelligence, common sense, diligence, and the major role he played in the Revolutionary period. A lawyer, Ellsworth represented Connecticut in the Continental Congress (1778–1783) and in the Constitutional Convention of 1787. He helped to frame the first draft of the Constitution and was instrumental in the adoption of the Connecticut Compromise.

Intimately familiar with organizational and administrative affairs, Ellsworth was prominent in the Senate from 1789 to 1796. He drafted the bill organizing the federal judiciary and defended Hamilton's plans for funding the national debt and for creating a Bank of the United States.

Appointed to the Supreme Court in 1796 by John Adams, Ellsworth did not excel as a justice. His decisions were marked by common sense, not great legal learning. In 1799 he reluctantly left the Supreme Court to become a member of the commission sent to improve relations with France. He and his colleagues were forced to accept terms that neither confirmed their hopes nor their instructions. Ellsworth felt, however, that a possible war with France had been avoided. In 1801 he returned to the United States.

EMANCIPATION MOVEMENTS derived from a tradition of protest and reform encouraged by frontier conditions and decentralized govern-

Poetry of T. S. Eliot was major influence on twentieth-century literature.

Oliver Ellsworth, 2nd Chief Justice of the Supreme Court.

mental authority. Leaders of the Revolution and philanthropists hoped that social conditions would make slavery obsolete or that manumissions (legal freeings) by slaveholders, court decisions, and state action would end slavery. Manumission societies in Pennsylvania, New York, and elsewhere in the North, plus similar organizations in the Border States and the upper South, sought the same end. They achieved modest results in laws, education, and other areas but were confronted with the fact that slaves multiplied faster than manumissions and that major efforts in Virginia (1831–1832) and in Kentucky as late as 1849 failed to abolish slavery.

The American Colonization Society, founded in 1816, seemed to promise an emancipation policy along with its program for sending American blacks to Liberia to build up the land and civilize its inhabitants. The Society received national approval and support that diminished as abolitionists became convinced that the Society's plan was less to encourage the freeing of slaves than to remove to Africa already free American blacks. The American Anti-Slavery Society labored to persuade Northerners to view slavery with moral disapproval and the Liberty and Free-Soil parties to gain power for emancipation at the polls. Abolitionists generally supported efforts to aid fugitives from slavery and in the process built up public sympathy in the North in their behalf.

The Civil War was undertaken in the North to save the Union rather than to end slavery. The Emancipation Proclamation (1863) was a war measure rather than a representative act of a movement opposing slavery. Yet it helped undermine the authority of slaveholders before the Thirteenth Amendment to the Constitution (1865) outlawed slavery.

See also Abolitionism; American Anti-Slavery Society; Emancipation Proclamation.
Consult (IV) Filler, 1960; Tyler, 1944.
—Louis Filler, *Antioch College*

EMANCIPATION PROCLAMATION (1863), declaration issued by President Lincoln on Jan. 1, 1863. For decades after its promulgation it was generally believed to have freed the slaves, a result actually achieved by the passage of the Thirteenth Amendment to the Constitution (Dec. 18, 1865). Later "realistic" criticism of Lincoln as having no personal regard for blacks and as having no more than issued a war measure intended to embarrass the rebel Confederacy contended that the proclamation had accomplished nothing.

Lincoln's true policy was first of all to save the Union at any cost, although he also underscored his personal desire that "all men, everywhere, could be free" (letter to Horace Greeley, Aug. 22, 1862). In pursuit of his main objective, he restrained Union generals from disturbing the slavery system in the Border States, which he considered the key to victory or defeat. He also made gestures, which were generally ignored, of penalizing Confederate forces for employing slaves for war purposes.

Lincoln was harassed by abolitionists who held that his reluctance to declare slaves free was prolonging the war. Partly in response to their criticism and partly in pursuit of his own egalitarian and war purposes, Lincoln issued a preliminary proclamation (Sept. 22, 1862), emphasizing once more that its purpose was to help save the Union. The Battle of Antietam, although not a clear Northern victory, enabled him to maintain that an emancipation policy would not be interpreted as the act of a desperate administration to raise a servile insurrection. In his 1863 proclamation, Lincoln carefully and specifically designated the territories in which slaves were to be considered free. These territories were actually in Confederate hands and therefore not subject to the proclamation's terms. The areas within Confederate states where federal troops were in control and the Border States were carefully excluded from the terms of emancipation.

On the basis of such exceptions, critics held that the proclamation was inadequate. However, most abolitionists found it expedient to hail the proclamation as a freedom measure, and Union military successes in Confederate territory resulted in the actual freeing of slaves. Many slaveholders in the exempted areas, notably in the Border States, interpreted the proclamation as making wholesale emancipations inevitable and voluntarily freed their slaves.

See also Abolitionism; Border States; Civil War: Causes; Emancipation Movements; Slavery.
Consult (IV) Donovan, 1964; Franklin, 1963.
—Louis Filler, *Antioch College*

EMBARGO ACTS (1807–1809), attempts to change British maritime policies by ending Anglo-American trade. The first Embargo Act, passed by Congress at the request of President Jefferson, went into effect on Dec. 22, 1807. It prohibited the departure of all American vessels for foreign ports, and foreign vessels were obliged to leave without cargo unless they were already loaded. The Embargo Act was accompanied by the enforcement of a limited Non-Importation Act against Britain.

In spite of later supplementary acts to help enforce the embargo, it was a failure. There was widespread evasion and opposition, particularly in New England, and the act did not achieve its primary object of changing British policy. On March 1, 1809, it was replaced by the Non-Intercourse Act, which for-

Lincoln's Emancipation Proclamation announced that slaves in rebel areas were free.

bade commercial relations with England, France, and their possessions but opened them with the rest of the world.

See also Macon's Bill No. 2; Non-Importation Act (1806).

EMERGENCY RAILROAD TRANSPORTATION ACT (1933), New Deal legislation on financial reorganization. *See* Railroad Legislation.

EMERSON, RALPH WALDO (1803–1882), minister, philosopher, poet, and lecturer who was one of the most influential writers of his age. He was born in Boston, graduated from Harvard in 1821, and became a Unitarian minister. Even the liberalism of Unitarianism could not satisfy Emerson's intellectual need to be free of organized religion; he resigned his pastorate at the Second Church of Boston in 1831. A period of personal illness and intellectual crisis then beset Emerson, but after a trip during which he met with most of Europe's leading intellectuals, he returned to Massachusetts, where he became a leader of the transcendental movement centered in Concord.

His first book, *Nature* (1836), outlined the new Emersonian transcendentalism, sounding a call for cultural and intellectual independence. He further attacked the establishment culture of New England in his *American Scholar* address at Harvard in 1837, when he called for an indigenous American culture. He expanded the Unitarian break from orthodox Calvinism with the "Divinity School Address" at Harvard in 1838.

Emerson became the most influential American man of letters, and in his work with the Transcendental Club and with *The Dial* (1840–1844) he inspired the New England writers around Concord and fellow writers elsewhere with the hope of a national American literature. He traveled widely and supported himself by extensive lecture tours. Many of his lectures served as the basis for his books, which included *Essays, First Series* (1841), *Essays, Second Series* (1844), *Representative Men* (1850), *English Traits* (1856), *Conduct of Life* (1860), and *Society and Solitude* (1870). Emerson's poetry ranged from the popular to the experimental. His interest inspired Walt Whitman and Emily Dickinson to continue their unconventional poetry.

See also Transcendentalism; Unitarianism.

Consult (III) Rusk, 1957.

ENCOMIENDA, Spanish system of land tenure in their New World colonies. From the Spanish word for "trust," it was basically a form of tribute imposed upon the Indians, who were allowed to commute the tribute by laboring on Spanish farms. The system originated in the colony of Hispaniola following the suppression of a native revolt in 1495. Soon Indian-cultivated lands were allotted to Spaniards, and Indians were forced to work on these allotments *(encomiendas)*.

In 1503 the system was expanded. Not only did the Spanish King order the Indians to be instructed in Catholicism and to be established in villages, but they were compelled to work in construction, mining, and farming. Although service in the mines at first lasted only from 6 to 8 months, there was a high mortality rate and a decrease in births. Besides causing population decrease, the system degenerated into virtual serfdom. The 1542 Code for the Indies prohibited any additional Indian enslavement, freed all Indians who had been abused, and provided for the gradual end of the *encomienda* system.

ENFORCEMENT ACTS, three laws passed in 1870 and 1871 to enforce the Fourteenth and Fifteenth amendments. The first (May 31, 1870) forbade the use of force, threats of violence, bribery, registration trickery, or economic coercion as tools to prevent eligible voters from exercising their franchise and set heavy penalties for violations. The first Enforcement Act also provided for strict federal supervision of congressional elections, a clause tightened by the second act (Feb. 28, 1871).

Congress passed the third Enforcement Act on April 20, 1871, to suppress the Ku Klux Klan and similar Southern organizations. It provided severe penalties for those guilty of terrorist activities and authorized the president to suspend the privilege of the writ of habeas corpus and to call out the army and militia to put down such violence.

See also Ku Klux Klan.

ENTAIL, restriction on dividing lands. *See* Colonial Agriculture.

ENUMERATED GOODS, articles produced in the colonies that, by the Navigation Act of 1660, could be shipped only to England or her colonies. Initially only tobacco, sugar, and indigo were enumerated, but by 1767 about 96 percent of colonial exports were similarly restricted. Through this procedure English control of the colonies' trade was assured.

See also Navigation Acts.

ENVIRONMENT. *See* Ecology.

EQUAL EMPLOYMENT OPPORTUNITIES COMMISSION. *See* Civil Rights Acts (1957, 1960, 1964).

ERA OF GOOD FEELINGS, phrase often used to describe the years from 1815 to 1825 or President James Monroe's two Administrations (1817–1825). The period began with a burst of

Ralph Waldo Emerson.

nationalistic enthusiasm, and in these years one party—the Democratic-Republican (Jeffersonian)—dominated politics. The phrase has often been condemned as inaccurate because these were also years of bitter sectional and personal quarrels.

ERICSSON, JOHN (1803-1889), Swedish-American inventor and marine engineer. Born in Sweden, he was technically educated from an early age. Before emigration to New York City in 1839, he lived for 12 years in London, where he designed the screw propulsion marine engine. He designed the U.S. warship *Princeton,* which had a vibrating or pendulum engine and which was the first warship to have all the machinery protected below the waterline. He is best known for his *Monitor* (launched 1862), a floating armored battery with a revolving turret (like a modern tank) and two large guns. The *Monitor,* the first of the ironclads that revolutionized naval warfare, was sheathed in iron plate, and its deck was only 8 inches above the water line. In the famous battle in 1862 between the *Monitor* and the *Merrimack* the result was a draw, although it is often claimed as a Union victory.

In 1862, in a message that forecast the nature of modern warfare, Ericsson cabled President Lincoln: "The time has come, Mr. President, when our cause will have to be sustained not by numbers, but by superior weapons. By a proper application of mechanical devices alone, will you be able with absolute certainty to destroy the enemies of the Union."

Ericsson's other devices included recoil mechanisms for gun carriages, a special leadline for sound depths, a telescopic smokestack, and heavy guns. He was interested also in solar physics.

ERIE CANAL, canal linking the Hudson River with the Great Lakes and thus, indirectly, New York City with the Midwest. Built in 1817–1825 by the state of New York and financed largely by loans from British investors, this great canal began the canal mania in the United States and had great impact on the economic development of the port of New York and of the near Midwest. The Erie was America's most outstanding technical achievement in transportation before the coming of the railroads. It cost more than $7 million, but tolls had paid off the interest charges on the original loans even before the canal was finished.

The Erie was the result of years of planning and proposals (dating back at least to 1777) to link the Hudson to the Great Lakes by water. The outcome gave New York a navigable waterway stretching into the heart of the Midwest. Travel time from Buffalo to New York City was cut from 20 to 6 days and freight charges fell from $100 to $5 a ton.

Locks of the Erie Canal at Lockport, N.Y. Construction of the Erie inaugurated the "canal mania" of early nineteenth century.

It took great courage to build the 364-mile canal through what was still wilderness. Its locks and aqueducts were engineering marvels. Political opposition was overwhelming, but Governor De Witt Clinton pushed the idea through. The manual labor involved was very strenuous, and the canal was built by immigrants, many from Ireland. When the canal was finished, it provided many more jobs in maintenance and use—an estimated 25,000 workers in the 1840s.

The Erie Canal was an early example of state capitalism—state enterprise for public benefit. It is doubtful if private enterprise could have built the canal in those days, although the venture did pay off handsomely.

See also Canals; Clinton, De Witt.
Consult (III) Shaw, 1966.
—Peter d'A. Jones, *University of Illinois, Chicago Circle*

ESCH-CUMMINS TRANSPORTATION ACT (1920), act enlarging the scope of federal regulation of railroads in many areas. *See* Railroad Legislation.

ESPIONAGE ACT (1917), bill limiting civil liberties passed as U.S. entry into World War I brought a wave of popular war hysteria and fear. The Espionage Act allowed up to 20 years imprisonment for disloyalty or opposition to the draft. The Sedition Act (1918) extended the charges to published writings. These federal laws were copied by the states, with some excesses. Almost 2,000 cases were tried under the acts, but many pardons were granted after war fears had subsided.

In three famous free-speech cases, the government's harsh actions against dissenters were upheld by the Supreme Court in 1919. The court was unanimous in *Schenck v. U.S.* that the conviction of Schenck for distributing leaflets urging draftees to oppose the war was no violation of Schenck's free speech rights under the First Amendment. Justice Holmes delivered his famous doctrine of "clear and present danger" in this case. Freedom of speech, he felt, must not endanger freedom of speech itself; the First Amendment did not protect a man who would falsely shout "Fire!" in a crowded theater. In Schenck's case the clear and present danger was the war.

In *U.S. v. Debs,* Holmes again upheld the government's case, believing again that there was a clear and present danger. Eugene V. Debs was the leader of the Socialist Party of America, which opposed the war. Debs' 10-year sentence was upheld, but he was released in 1921. The third case was *Abrams v. U.S.* in which both Holmes and Louis D. Brandeis dissented. In an eloquent argument, Holmes defended the free market in ideas and opposed the government's 20-year sentence of Abrams, a Russian émigré who had scattered leaflets in

New York urging workers not to produce arms that could be used to suppress the Bolshevik Revolution in Russia.

See also Debs, Eugene V.; Holmes, Oliver Wendell, Jr.

Consult (VI) Chafee, 1941.

—Peter d'A. Jones, *University of Illinois, Chicago Circle*

ETHNIC GROUP, group whose cultural habits, religious convictions, life style, and traditions are different from society at large. Members of an ethnic group may be bound together by common ties of race, nationality, religion, or culture. The existence of distinct ethnic and cultural groups within societies is widespread and exists at most cultural levels.

The term usually refers to peoples who have not been assimilated into the larger community in which they exist. One would not, for example, ordinarily refer to Americans of Scottish descent as an ethnic group. The lack of assimilation of an ethnic group may be by design, lack of social or economic mobility, or because the larger community, feeling threatened, rejects them. Perhaps the best-defined U.S. ethnic group is the Chinese-Americans, who have consistently remained apart from the greater community, usually settling in substantial enclaves in an area of the city that has come to be known as "Chinatown."

See also Acculturation; Assimilation; Immigration.

EUROPEAN RECOVERY PROGRAM. See Marshall Plan.

EVENING SCHOOLS, schools that generally met from October to March and offered courses in practical subjects such as reading, mathematics, bookkeeping, geography, and navigation. Many colonial indentures stipulated that as part of their training, apprentices were to receive a rudimentary education. Because masters often were unable to instruct their charges or were unwilling to devote working hours to such purposes, evening schools came into existence in many larger towns in the Northern and Middle colonies during the eighteenth century.

EXCLUSION, policy of prohibiting further U.S. immigration that received much support in the late nineteenth century. See Chinese Exclusion; Immigration.

EXECUTIVE REORGANIZATION ACT (1939). From 1936 to 1939 President Roosevelt sought legislation to enable him to reorganize the executive branch of the federal government in order to bring efficiency to the jumble of New Deal bureaus. A presidentially selected group of political scientists suggested that the many agencies, commissions, and boards be incorporated into the existing executive departments plus two new ones, a Department of Social Welfare and a Department of Public Works. They further recommended expanding the civil service and reorganizing the comptroller general's office.

To implement these and similar reforms, Roosevelt sought Congress' permission to make, by executive order, whatever changes were necessary. Adverse reaction from conservatives of all parties in Congress, who interpreted the proposal as a power grab by the President, prevented passage in 1937 and 1938. A much milder bill, exempting from reorganization all the independent regulatory agencies, the Civil Service Commission, and the comptroller general, was passed in 1939. It required the President to submit all reorganization plans to Congress. Under the new law Roosevelt reorganized the executive branch extensively, placing most New Deal projects under three superagencies: the Federal Security Agency, the Federal Works Board, and the Federal Loan Agency.

See also New Deal.

Consult (VI) Patterson, 1967.

—Allen F. Kifer, *Skidmore College*

EX PARTE MILLIGAN (1866), landmark civil liberties decision by the Supreme Court. During the Civil War, when Abraham Lincoln suspended the writ of habeas corpus and authorized military commissions to try Northern civilians accused of aiding the Confederacy, Lambdin P. Milligan was tried, convicted, and sentenced to be hanged by a military tribunal. The Supreme Court overruled this action, holding that no civilian could constitutionally be tried before a military court if the civil courts were open where the alleged crime was committed.

EXPEDITION ACT (1903), legislation to speed prosecution of antitrust cases. See Antitrust Cases.

EXPLORATION AND DISCOVERY. The development of the New World started gradually as Europe extended its contacts beyond the seas, eastward to Africa and Asia and westward to America. Much of the early story is obscured by legend and rumor, but there were two important "first times"—about 1000 the Vikings became the first Europeans to reach America, and in 1415 Prince Henry the Navigator began the long exploration around Africa to Asia. The climax came between 1492 and 1522, when knowledge of the world was expanded by the voyages of Christopher Columbus to America, of Vasco da Gama around the Cape of Good Hope to India, and of one of Ferdinand Magellan's ships around the world.

The First Voyages. The Atlantic voyages to America had their antecedents in the Viking

First friendly meeting between Spanish explorer Hernán Cortés and Aztec emperor Montezuma was shortly followed by Spanish conquest of Mexico.

Failing to find the mouth of the Mississippi, Sieur de La Salle landed in Texas in 1685.

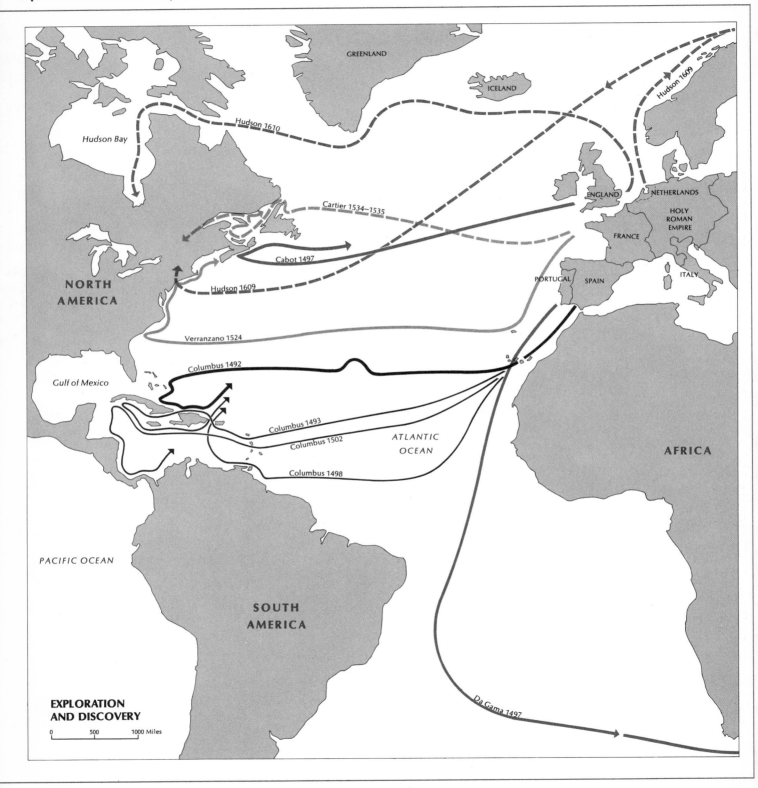

GREENLAND

ICELAND

Hudson Bay

Hudson 1610

Hudson 1609

Cartier 1534–1535

Cabot 1497

ENGLAND

NETHERLANDS

HOLY
ROMAN
EMPIRE

FRANCE

**NORTH
AMERICA**

Hudson 1609

ITALY

PORTUGAL   SPAIN

Verranzano 1524

Columbus 1492

Gulf of Mexico

Columbus 1493

Columbus 1502

*ATLANTIC
OCEAN*

AFRICA

Columbus 1498

PACIFIC OCEAN

**SOUTH
AMERICA**

**EXPLORATION
AND DISCOVERY**

Da Gama 1497

0   500   1000 Miles

EXPLORATION AND COLONIZATION

EXPLORATION

EXPLORATION AND DISCOVERY

Southern Exploration
CHRISTOPHER COLUMBUS
HERNÁN CORTÉS
HERNÁN DeSOTO
FRANCISCO PIZARRO
INDIANS, SOUTH AMERICAN
   ENCOMIENDA

Northern Exploration
VIKINGS
SAMUEL DE CHAMPLAIN
HENRY HUDSON
JESUITS
FATHER JACQUES MARQUETTE
SIEUR DE LA SALLE

NORTH AMERICAN COLONIZATION

First Efforts
JAMESTOWN SETTLEMENT
   JOHN SMITH
PILGRIMS
   WILLIAM BRADFORD
PURITANISM
PLYMOUTH
FRENCH COLONIES
SPANISH COLONIES, NORTH AMERICAN
HISTORICAL ARCHAEOLOGY (AMERICAN)
COLONIAL AGRICULTURE
   PATROONSHIPS
COLONIAL RELIGION

British Colonies
CONNECTICUT
DELAWARE
GEORGIA
MARYLAND
MASSACHUSETTS
NEW HAMPSHIRE
NEW JERSEY
NEW YORK
NORTH CAROLINA
PENNSYLVANIA
RHODE ISLAND
SOUTH CAROLINA
VIRGINIA

Leaders
CALVERT FAMILY
CARTERET FAMILY
FERDINANDO GORGES
ANNE HUTCHINSON
PETER MINUIT
JAMES E. OGLETHORPE
WILLIAM PENN
PETER STUYVESANT
ROGER WILLIAMS
WINTHROP FAMILY

Indian Contact
INDIAN WARS, COLONIAL
PEQUOT WAR (1637)
KING PHILIP'S WAR (1675–1676)
IROQUOIS CONFEDERACY

The Subject Maps in the Encyclopedia illustrate the coverage of particular aspects of American History, showing the interrelationships among the articles in twelve critical areas of study. Entries in capital letters, except for titles, are subjects for which there are separate articles in the Encyclopedia.

The Subject Maps are arranged alphabetically in the Encyclopedia under the following titles:

American Wars
Blacks in the United States
Business Regulation and Industrialization
Civil War and Reconstruction
Constitution of the United States
Exploration and Colonization
Frontier in American History
Indians
Labor Movement
New Deal and Depression
Revolutionary War Era
Slavery and Emancipation

settlement of Iceland (870) and Greenland (about 985). After the discovery of Vinland America about 1000, almost five centuries passed before Europeans visited North America again. The Italians played a major role in the renewed activity. Venice and Genoa had grown rich by supplying Europe with silks and spices, cargoes too valuable to be carried by any but skilled mariners. Consequently Italian captains were the best prepared—Columbus, the Cabots, Vespucci, and Verazzano took the lead under the flags of Spain, England, and France.

John Cabot was born in Genoa about the same time as Columbus but soon moved to Venice. In 1495 he and his son Sebastian settled in Bristol, the very active English port. In 1497, backed by Bristol merchants and with the blessing of King Henry VII, he reached the northwest corner of Newfoundland, close to the original Viking landing site. After skirting the Newfoundland coast and scooping up cod-fish on the Grand Banks, Cabot was back in Bristol in 11 weeks. Henry VII granted "£10 to him that found the new land," plus a pension. The significance of that brief voyage was that it became the basis of England's claim to North America. In 1498 with five ships, Cabot sailed again and was never heard from again. His son Sebastian, who apparently sailed on the first voyage, later became pilot general of Spain and eventually returned to direct English exploration, which had been dormant for a half century after the great Cabot voyage.

At the time of the 1497 Cabot voyage, Amerigo Vespucci, a Florentine aristocrat sailing under the Spanish flag, was actively exploring waters adjacent to South America. His accounts of his exploits, possibly exaggerated, so impressed a German geographer that he applied the name "America" to the whole region.

French Expeditions. While England did relatively little exploring in the early 1500s, France actively entered the field. The news of Magellan's discovery of a strait to the Pacific led France to hunt for a similar strait farther north as a shortcut to the Indies. This was the beginning of a centuries-long quest for the Northwest Passage—river after river was explored in the search.

Sailing under the French flag, Giovanni da Verazzano, another Florentine aristocrat, was the first to explore the American coast from the Carolinas to Maine. He missed Chesapeake and Delaware bays but did find the entrance to New York, anchoring in the Narrows, where a great bridge now bears his name. He named Rhode Island, called Maine "a land of bad people," and returned home by way of Newfoundland. He later explored Brazil and was eaten by cannibals in the Caribbean.

The French sent out another expedition in 1534, this time under Frenchman Jacques Cartier, who would become the "founder of New France." On the first of his three voyages, he stopped at the northwest tip of Newfoundland and found the St. Lawrence River. Back again on his very important second voyage, he ascended the St. Lawrence to the site of Quebec, which would become the capital of New France. Then he proceeded up the river to what is now Montreal, returning for a cold winter at Quebec. He returned home in 1536, and it was five years before he sailed on his uneventful third voyage. Cartier has been rated one of the "most expert seamen and careful explorers in the age of discovery." He definitely laid the foundations of future French colonization, work that Samuel de Champlain would carry on after 1604. During the half century from Columbus to Cartier, explorers had given Europe a fairly accurate idea of the coastline of North America and the Caribbean. Most subsequent explorers would operate on a more limited scale, filling in the details overlooked during the early voyages.

English Sailors. With the accession of Queen Elizabeth in 1558, England entered upon a remarkable maritime era with a brilliant group of "Sea Dogs" who raided the Spaniards, planned colonies, traded, and did some exploring. Humphrey Gilbert and his half brother Sir Walter Raleigh made pioneer colonial efforts. The two major British exploration voyages were those into the Arctic by Martin Frobisher in the 1570s and by John Davis in the 1580s, both of which were searches for the elusive Northwest Passage. One other Elizabethan Englishman, Richard Hakluyt, did not actually go to sea, but he was a tireless promoter of maritime effort and gathered several volumes of voyages and travels that are a rich record of exploration in the New World in the sixteenth century.

Consult (I) Debenham, 1960; Morison, 1971.

—Robert G. Albion, *Harvard University*

FAIR DEAL, President Truman's attempt to extend the New Deal, largely frustrated by Congress. *See* Truman, Harry S.

FAIRFAX RESOLVES (1774), statement of the colonies' attitude toward England. *See* Mason, George.

FAIR LABOR STANDARDS ACT (1938), major landmark in New Deal labor legislation—others were Social Security and the Wagner Act (also known as the "wages and hours" law). It set minimum wages and maximum working hours in interstate commerce—something the aborted National Recovery Administration had attempted to do. A minimum wage of 25 cents per hour and a maximum of 44 hours per week

Expedition of Father Marquette and Louis Joliet reaches the Mississippi River in 1673.

were set. The act also established time-and-a-half for overtime and forbade child labor on products shipped interstate. A special division was established in the Labor Department to enforce the law.

See also New Deal.
Consult (VI) Bernstein, 1970.

FALL, ALBERT B(ACON) (1861-1944), secretary of the interior who played a key role in the Teapot Dome scandal of the 1920s. See Teapot Dome.

FALLEN TIMBERS, BATTLE OF (1794), fought on August 20, 1794, in what is now northwestern Ohio between American forces under Gen. Anthony Wayne and Indians of the Old Northwest. Wayne's victory led to the Treaty of Greenville in August 1795, which ensured the rapid advance of American settlers across the Ohio River.

See also Greenville, Treaty of (1795); Wayne, Anthony.

FAREWELL ADDRESS. See Washington's Farewell Address.

FARM CREDIT ADMINISTRATION (FCA), agency organized during the first weeks of the New Deal to assume all the duties of existing farm loan agencies. Legislation during the Hundred Days of 1933—the Emergency Farm Mortgage Act and the Farm Credit Act—enabled the FCA under Henry Morgenthau, Jr., to provide emergency loans to farmers to stave off mortgage foreclosures. Farmers were encouraged to wire the White House for help when threatened with court action. In its first 2 years the FCA refinanced 20 percent of the farm mortgages in the country.

See also New Deal.
Consult (VI) Benedict, 1953.

FARMERS' ALLIANCES, a social, educational, economic, and political farmers' movement consisting of three separate organizations. The National Farmers' Alliance, or Northern Alliance, strongest in the upper Mississippi Valley, grew out of organizing efforts by Milton George, a Chicago publisher, in 1880. The National Farmers' Alliance and Industrial Union, or Southern Alliance, was strongest in the South. The Colored Farmers' National Alliance and Cooperative Union, founded in 1866 and strongest in the South, was organized because the Southern Alliance excluded blacks from membership.

Alliance activities included social gatherings, lectures on improved farming methods, and cooperative buying and selling ventures. Alliance study groups sought the causes of agrarian distress and posed radical solutions—including government ownership of the transportation, communication, and banking sys-

tems. Ostensibly nonpartisan, Alliancemen were expected to support sympathetic candidates regardless of party. Nonetheless, some Northern Alliancemen were active in the various radical agrarian parties of the 1880s. Southern Alliancemen were less prone to bolt the Democratic Party, the "white man's party," for fear of being charged with endangering white supremacy. An attempt to merge the Alliances in 1889 failed when Southerners refused to give up their secret rituals and exclusionary racial policies.

Northern Alliancemen in 1890 organized state-level independent parties that in 1892 formed the national People's Party. In 1890, Southern Alliancemen sought to capture the Democratic Party and had notable successes in some states; many Southern Alliancemen saw the People's Party in 1892. When the Populist Party absorbed the energies and enthusiasm of farm radicals, the Alliance lost members and soon died out.

See also Free Silver; Populists; Southern Alliance.
Consult (V) Hicks, 1961.
—Robert W. Cherny, California State University, San Francisco

FARM LOAN ACT (1916). See Federal Farm Loan Act (1916).

FARM SECURITY ADMINISTRATION (FSA), agency established to help poor farm laborers. See Bankhead-Jones Farm Tenant Act (1937).

FARM SUPPORTS. See Price Supports.

FARRAGUT, DAVID G(LASGOW) (1801-1870), leading Union admiral in the Civil War. Born in Tennessee and raised in New Orleans, he was adopted by Commodore David Porter, who had the boy appointed a Navy midshipman at nine. As a lad he performed nobly in the War of 1812 and saw active duty in the Mexican War.

Although a Southerner, Farragut stuck by the Union, and in December 1861 he was chosen to command the expedition against New Orleans. The battle began on April 18, 1862, when Farragut unsuccessfully assaulted two powerful strongholds 75 miles downriver. Farragut then boldly decided to run his 17 ships past the forts. Despite withering fire and the resistance of a Confederate fleet, he succeeded on April 24 with the loss of 3 ships and 184 men. He then took undefended New Orleans without further bloodshed. This magnificent victory was a tribute to Farragut's energy, audacity, and superior strategy.

In May and June 1862 he led an unsuccessful attack on Vicksburg, but his fleet managed to capture Memphis. The crowning achievement of Farragut's long career came in August 1864, when he seized the powerfully

Farmers Alliance saw itself as the effective voice of agrarian interests.

David Farragut's naval exploits helped break Confederate control of the Gulf of Mexico.

William Faulkner, at the University of Mississippi in his hometown of Oxford.

defended port of Mobile. After the war he continued to command the Navy.

See also Civil War Battles.

Consult (IV) Lewis, 1941–1943.

—Michael Burlingame, *Connecticut College*

FAULKNER, WILLIAM (HARRISON) (1897–1962), novelist and short-story writer who won the Nobel Prize (1949) and two Pulitzer Prizes (1955, 1963). He was born in Albany, Miss., and studied at the University of Mississippi. Faulkner's fiction deals chiefly with the American South, where he was born, lived, and died. Faulkner portrayed the South as a mythical, universal land, painfully suffering the turmoil, conflict, and corruption of twentieth-century humanity.

Many of Faulkner's volumes, some of which are humorous, show inventiveness of incident and character creation, and most are part of his historical treatment of fictional Yoknapatawpha County. His writings have been acclaimed for their technical virtuosity and brilliant stylistic effect. His complex method of presentation, his use of the extended sentence, and the moments of stasis in his action, however, repel some readers. Faulkner's mature writings began with the publication of *Sartoris* (1929). Other works include *The Sound and the Fury* (1929), *Absalom, Absalom* (1936), *The Hamlet* (1940), and *Intruder in the Dust* (1948). His most sensational novel, *Sanctuary* (1954), won the Pulitzer Prize, as did *The Reivers* (1962). *These Thirteen* (1931) and *Doctor Martino* (1934) contain some of Faulkner's most remarkable short stories.

See also Literature.

Consult (VIII) Brooks, 1963; Howe, 1962.

FEDERAL AID ROAD ACT (1916), pioneer highway legislation. *See* Highway System.

FEDERAL BUREAU OF INVESTIGATION, established in 1908, the fact-finding division of the Department of Justice. It investigates violations of all federal laws not specifically delegated to other agencies, including espionage, sabotage and other subversive activities, desertion and draft evasion, kidnapping across state lines, extortion, bank robbery, civil rights violations, and assassination of the president or a federal officer. J. Edgar Hoover, who served as director from 1924 to 1972, shaped the development of the FBI, which is known for outstanding investigative techniques. Following Hoover's death there was difficulty in finding a nonpartisan director. Agents' morale dropped sharply, and the bureau was implicated in the Watergate affair.

See also Hoover, J. Edgar; Justice, Department of.

FEDERAL COMMUNICATIONS COMMISSION. *See* Communications Act (1934).

FEDERAL CONVENTION. *See* Constitutional Convention (1787).

FEDERAL EMERGENCY RELIEF ACT (FERA) (1933), the New Deal's attempt to continue and expand federal participation in unemployment relief, reluctantly begun by President Hoover in 1932. Harry Hopkins, head of the New York Emergency Relief Administration, was brought to Washington as administrator. Federal funds were for the most part supplied on a matching basis with state and local governments. Many states, however, were unable to finance any relief functions, and FERA made direct grants for emergency doles. President Roosevelt thought of FERA as a temporary measure to be used only until an extensive public works program could take over the task of providing jobs for the unemployed. FERA was replaced in 1935 by the Works Progress (later, Projects) Administration (WPA).

See also Hundred Days; New Deal; Public Works Administration; Work Projects Administration.

Consult (VI) Charles, 1963; Mitchell, 1947.

FEDERAL FARM BOARD (FFB), attempt on the eve of the Depression to stabilize farm prices. *See* Agricultural Marketing Act (1929).

FEDERAL FARM LOAN ACT (1916), bill that was an essential part of President Wilson's New Freedom reform policy for agriculture, together with the Warehouse Act (1916). The goal was to give better credit facilities to farmers and to remove their heavy load of debt. The Farm Loan Act created 12 regional districts, each with a Farm Loan Board and a Farm Loan Bank that was authorized to extend loans to farmers for maintenance and improvement. Loans were made only through cooperative farmers' loan associations. This added complexity, plus legal opposition from private mortgage bankers, delayed use of the banks for some time. In 1921 the Supreme Court upheld the act. This was the start of the intricate system of farm credit that now exists.

The Warehouse Act provided for better federal control over warehouses through a licensing system. The act was a means of extending credit because the federal government issued receipts guaranteeing the amount of produce in the warehouse, and such receipts were acceptable as collateral for loans. Now, in addition to the land banks, the farmer could also deposit his crops and use them as a base for a farm loan.

Consult (VI) Benedict, 1967.

FEDERAL HOUSING ADMINISTRATION

(FHA), agency authorized by the National Housing Act (1934) and designed to stimulate the building and improvement of private homes. Long-term federally insured mortgages at low interest were provided, and between $3 and $4 billion in loans were insured prior to World War II. It differed from the Public Works Administration and the U.S. Housing Authority, which were established to provide slum clearance and public housing. The FHA brought significant prewar recovery to the house-building industry and survives as an important federal agency.

See also New Deal.

FEDERALISM, form of government in which powers are divided between a central government and local units so that both have some degree of autonomy. States having a federal form include the United States, Canada, and West Germany. Powers may be explicitly granted to the central government and reserved to the local units, as in the United States, or just the reverse, as in Canada. Two factors primarily account for the adoption of a federal system in the United States. There was general agreement that the powers of the central government had to be stronger than under the Articles of Confederation, but attachments to local rights prevented the granting of all powers to the central government. Also, a division of powers between the national and state governments was believed to be valuable as a safeguard against any abuse of power by a single faction or group.

To many Americans, the Constitution of 1787 gave too much power to the central government. Only with great effort and skill did the Founding Fathers persuade the various states to ratify the Constitution. Those supporting ratification were called Federalists and those opposing, Anti-Federalists. Historically, the powers of both the central and state governments have increased, and a high degree of integration and cooperation between the governments has developed.

See also Anti-Federalism; Constitutional Convention (1787); Separation of Powers.

Consult (III) White, 1971.

FEDERALIST, THE, a series of essays written by Alexander Hamilton, James Madison, and John Jay in support of the adoption of the U.S. Constitution. Eighty-five appeared serially in New York newspapers in 1787–1788 under the signature "Publius," and although the authorship of a few still remains controversial, it is now fairly certain that Hamilton wrote the majority, Madison about 28, and Jay 5 of the essays.

Written in response to Anti-Federalist condemnation of the proposed new national government under the Constitution, the main themes of *The Federalist Papers* are the inadequacies of the central government under the Articles of Confederation and the conformity of the Constitution with the republican values of the Revolution. Their underlying premise is that although man is capable of governing himself, he cannot be trusted always to do this properly, for man is also corruptible. What is needed, therefore, is an elaborate constitutional system to prevent rulers from acting in an arbitrary and willful manner and the ruled from unthinkingly responding to the passions of the moment.

The most famous of *The Federalist Papers* is the tenth essay, written by Madison. In it he brilliantly argues that a republican form of government can more effectively and fairly operate in a large and heterogeneous country than it can in a small and homogeneous one. It is one of the most important contributions made by an American to the general field of political theory.

See also Anti-Federalism; Federalism; Hamilton, Alexander; Jay, John; Madison, James.

Consult (III) Wright, 1961.
—Richard E. Ellis, *University of Virginia*

FEDERAL RESERVE ACT (1913), or Owen-Glass Act, the first major reform of American banking structure since the Civil War, established the Federal Reserve System. The National Monetary Commission set up by the Aldrich-Vreeland Act (1908) had recommended a central banking system for the United States able to control monetary fluctuations and influence the course of banking. After 1890 the U.S. Treasury had filled the gap, acting as a central bank and as a lender of last resort.

Under the act the nation was divided into 12 Federal Reserve districts, each with a Federal Reserve Bank to act as a bankers' bank and clearinghouse for member banks. All national banks were compelled to participate by subscribing to the capital fund of the system, and commercial banks were encouraged to do so. Overseeing the districts was the Federal Reserve Board, which could set the rediscount rate at the district banks, thus giving the board control of the nation's credit supply.

See also Aldrich-Vreeland Currency Act (1908); Federal Reserve System.

Consult (V) Studenski and Krooss, 1963.

FEDERAL RESERVE SYSTEM, central banking system of the United States that regulates credit and the total supply of dollars in circulation. The system is composed of 12 regional reserve banks coordinated by a central Board of Governors.

The Federal Reserve Act of 1913 was designed to insure individual banks against exhaustion of reserves resulting from periodic panic withdrawals by depositors. Member banks, which are required to deposit specified

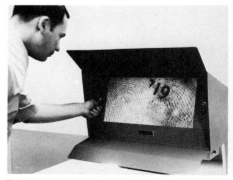

Technician tries to match fingerprints in FBI headquarters in Washington, D.C.

reserves, can obtain loans from reserve banks, whose assets consist of U.S. government securities bought on the open market.

Raising or lowering the rediscount rate (interest charged by the reserve banks for loans) and the extent of open market operations can curtail or encourage credit, thus influencing dollars in circulation and the pace of economic activity. The system has had severe weaknesses, including the contraction of Federal Reserve loans in times of economic recession and during the inflationary periods that resulted from stimulating credit to finance national wars. Numerous reforms were initiated, and since 1951 Federal Reserve policies have concentrated on domestic economic stablization.

See also Federal Reserve Act (1913).

FEDERAL THEATRE PROJECT, New Deal program. *See* Theater.

FEDERAL TRADE COMMISSION (FTC), federal agency created in 1914 by the Federal Trade Commission Act. The FTC, a crucial part of President Wilson's New Freedom program to control trusts, was established to administer the antitrust laws, to investigate cases, and to bring recommendations to the White House and Congress. It was given little power to punish firms that adopted monopolistic practices or shoddy labeling or selling methods, but it could issue cease-and-desist orders to recalcitrant corporations. Its power of exposure and publicity was often embarrassing to the firms investigated, and it had early successes in dealing with public utilities abuses.

Consult (VI) Wagner, 1971.

FEDERATION OF ORGANIZED TRADE AND LABOR UNIONS. Founded in 1881, it was forerunner of the American Federation of Labor. *See* American Federation of Labor; Gompers, Samuel.

FEKE, ROBERT (1705?–1750?) colonial portrait painter and sailor. His seafaring experience brought him to Newport, R.I., where he received several commissions. After that, he worked mainly in New York, Philadelphia, and Boston. His best paintings include those of the Bowdoin family, some of which hang at Bowdoin College in Maine. He is further represented by a portrait called "Unknown Lady" (Brooklyn Museum) and by portraits on display in Newport and Providence.

Feke's portraits, which reflected the influence of John Smibert and the conventions of the period, are characterized by their lifelike qualities and vivid use of color, particularly in the rich, elaborate costumes.

See also Painting; Smibert, John.

FEMININE MYSTIQUE, THE (1963), important statement of the feminist position. *See* Friedan, Betty.

"FIFTY-FOUR-FORTY OR FIGHT," the slogan in 1846 of American expansionists who believed that the United States should own the Oregon Territory all the way to the southern border of Alaska, or latitude 54° 40′. The United States had shared this territory with Britain since 1818.

When the dispute arose, the United States and Britain appointed representatives to arrange an agreement. A treaty was drawn up that divided the Oregon country at the forty-ninth parallel of latitude, a line that formed the United States–Canadian boundary westward from Minnesota. By the terms of the treaty, the British were given the northern part of the Oregon country, now British Columbia, and the United States was given the southern part, which included the Columbia River valley. This agreement, the Oregon Treaty, was signed in 1846, just as the Mexican War was beginning, and in 1848, after the war, Oregon was made a territory.

See also Oregon.

Consult (III) Billington, 1960; Pomeroy, 1957.

FILIBUSTERING EXPEDITIONS, private wars or attempts by one country to intervene in the affairs of another for adventure, power, or money. A number of expeditions of this type were organized in the United States against Latin American countries, mainly between 1850 and 1860.

Aaron Burr led an early filibustering expedition after his term as vice-president ended (1805). Having acquired title to more than 1 million acres of land in western Louisiana, he undertook to settle it in 1806, perhaps with the prospect of forming a separate nation centered in the Mississippi Valley. The success of Burr's scheme depended on the support of his old friend James Wilkinson, governor of Louisiana Territory. Unfortunately for Burr, Wilkinson instead wrote to President Jefferson calling for the arrest of Burr and his fellow "conspirators."

Narciso López, a Venezuelan-born revolutionist, led three filibustering expeditions to Cuba from the United States in 1849–1851 in an attempt to promote a revolt against Spain. None was successful, and López was captured by the Spanish in 1851 and executed.

William Walker led a notable filibuster in 1853 in the hope of annexing Sonora, Mexico. This effort ended in defeat, but two years later, with a group of adventurers from California, he landed in Nicaragua, joined a rebel faction, and captured Granada. Walker became president of Nicaragua in 1856 but was deposed in 1857, and, after organizing other abortive expeditions to Central America, he was executed in Honduras in 1860.

FILLMORE, MILLARD (1800–1874), 13th President (1850–1853) of the United States. He was born in Locke, N.Y., on Jan. 7, 1800. Fillmore began his career as a lawyer in western New York during the 1820s. His initial political allegiance was to the Anti-Masonic Party, but he became one of the early members of Henry Clay's Whig Party in the 1830s. He served three terms in the House of Representatives and unsuccessfully sought the New York governorship in 1844.

In the election of 1848, supporters of Henry Clay successfully backed Fillmore as their vice-presidential choice after the Whig convention had rejected Clay in favor of the popular military hero Zachary Taylor. At President Taylor's death the almost forgotten Fillmore assumed a crucial role in the dispute over slavery. In the summer of 1850, Congress was in the midst of debate on the measures, opposed by Taylor, that were ultimately enacted as the Compromise of 1850.

Once Fillmore became president, however, he reshaped the cabinet and supported the entire package of compromise measures; this was his most important accomplishment in the White House. In 1852, however, the Whigs bypassed Fillmore and nominated Gen. Winfield Scott in the mistaken belief that Scott's military record would repeat Taylor's 1848 victory. In 1856 Fillmore ran for the presidency on the ticket of the Know-Nothing, or American, Party, but he ran a poor third. He died in Buffalo, N.Y. on Mar. 8, 1874.

See also Compromise of 1850; Taylor, Zachary; Whig Party.

Consult (IV) Rayback, 1959.

—Dan T. Carter, *University of Maryland*

FIRESIDE CHATS, informal radio talks by President Franklin Roosevelt that were part of an attempt to reach the public in an attempt to make them understand his plans and programs. In addition to the more conventional messages to Congress and press conferences, Roosevelt used radio broadcasts, including these talks. He was the first president effectively to use radio, an art cultivated during his gubernatorial career. His warm and authoritative manner provided rapport with his listening audience. He gave eight fireside chats during his first term, half of them in the early months, the period in which emergency programs were being launched. He found the chats useful again during the months of the European war crisis.

FIRST BANK OF THE UNITED STATES. *See* Bank of the United States, First.

FISH, HAMILTON (1808–1893), one of the most distinguished secretaries of state of the late nineteenth century. Born in New York City,

Fish was an American aristocrat who was identified with the East and with the establishment of the time. A man of integrity, he was able to blunt the effects of President Grant's more errant adventures into foreign affairs and to modify the larger and less attainable claims of such aggressive senators as Charles Sumner of Massachusetts.

A graduate of Columbia College, Fish was admitted to the New York bar at 22. In 1842 he was elected to Congress as a Whig, and he served as lieutenant governor of New York from 1847 to 1848 and as governor in 1849–1850. After being elected to the Senate in 1851 (where he served until 1857), he became a Republican, and during the Civil War he was a powerful member of the Union Defense Committee for his state.

Chosen by Grant to be secretary of state, Fish settled the *Alabama* claims issue with Britain by concluding the Treaty of Washington in 1871; dealt with a series of crises engendered by Grant's expansionist desires; negotiated a key treaty for reciprocal trade with Hawaii in 1875, which in time led to the annexation of the islands; and in 1876 was able to come to a settlement with Spain over American claims in Cuba. Prudent and long suffering, Fish was a tower of good sense throughout the troubled 1870s.

See also Alabama Claims.

Consult (V) Nevins, 1936; Smith, 1941.

FITZGERALD, F(RANCIS) SCOTT (KEY) (1896–1940), novelist and short-story writer who became famous as spokesman for the jazz age of the 1920s. He was born in St. Paul, Minn., and educated at Princeton. Fitzgerald lived between poles of success and despair, much like the lost-rich characters in his novels. His first book, *This Side of Paradise* (1920), a semi-autobiographical novel of Princeton life depicting the younger generation of the jazz age, was an immediate success and gave him a reputation as a playboy. Fitzgerald married Zelda Sayre and began a life of desperate gaiety.

Fitzerald's second volume, *The Beautiful and the Damed* (1922), ultimately condemned the life of the rich that he and Zelda tended to emulate. In 1924 he and his family moved to Europe, where they hoped to live less expensively, and remained until 1930. Fitzgerald's life, however, was gradually becoming dominated by financial and spiritual crises. His wife suffered two mental breakdowns, and Fitzgerald began to drink heavily.

Fitzgerald's most brilliant book, *The Great Gatsby* (1925), a cynical portrait of the postwar Prohibition era, was a critical success but a financial failure. During his career much of his financial success came from his excellent short stories. His next novel, *Tender Is the Night* (1933), was a disappointment at the time

Millard Fillmore, 13th President of the United States (1850–1853).

Hamilton Fish, President Grant's secretary of state (1869–1877).

Novelist F. Scott Fitzgerald sits with wife Zelda and daughter Scottie.

Folksingers Joan Baez and Bob Dylan perform at the Newport (R.I.) Jazz Festival.

but later received critical acclaim. Fitzgerald's last works were *The Crack-Up,* recording Zelda's illness and his own collapse, and *The Last Tycoon,* inspired by his experiences as a Hollywood screenwriter.

FIVE NATIONS, collective name for tribes of the Iroquois Confederacy. *See* Iroquois Confederacy.

FLAG OF THE UNITED STATES. George Washington is said to have raised the first U.S. flag at Somerville, Mass., on Jan. 1, 1776, whereas other data indicate that the first stars and stripes were flown by John Paul Jones on the *Ranger* in 1778. The general form of the present flag, however, was delineated by order of the Continental Congress on June 14, 1777. According to folklore, Betsy Ross, a Philadelphia seamstress, was responsible for making the first stars and stripes, although there is no substantiation for this legend.

When Vermont and Kentucky were admitted to the Union in 1795, Congress provided for a flag of 15 stars and 15 stripes. As time passed, little uniformity was shown in the number of stripes, so that in 1818 President Monroe signed a bill providing that the flag would have alternating horizontal stripes of red and white, with 20 stars on a blue field, and that a new star would be added for each new state.

In 1912, New Mexico and Arizona were admitted to the Union, increasing the number of states (and stars) to 48. This flag remained the national emblem for more than 46 years until the admission of Alaska and Hawaii to the Union in 1959 made the 50-star banner the official flag.

FLETCHER V. PECK (1810), Supreme Court decision on contracts. *See* Yazoo Affair.

FLORIDA, the 27th state, admitted on March 3, 1845. In 1565 St. Augustine became the first permanent white settlement on the U.S. mainland. A group of French Huguenots had settled the area in 1564, but they were massacred by the Spanish. Florida had been claimed for Spain by Ponce de León in 1513. The territory was taken by England in 1763 but then returned to Spain 20 years later. In 1819, by the Adams-Onís Treaty, Florida was ceded to the United States for $5 million, and American settlement began 2 years later. Florida gained territorial recognition in 1822. It seceded from the Union during the Civil War.

The state legislature is bicameral; the capital is Tallahassee. The population in 1970 was 6,789,443.

See also Adams-Onís Treaty (1819).

FOLK MUSIC, songs handed down from generation to generation that represent a commu-

nity tradition and reflect the daily lives of the people who sing them.

Beginnings. The American folk song stems from two main traditions: English-language folk songs, characterized by solo-singing, tempered by the polyrhythms and polyphonics of black West African song brought to this country during the slave trade. The combination eventually resulted in British tunes performed in harmony with a strong beat and syncopation. American folk songs developed generally along regional and occupational lines so that there is no one national body of folk song.

Development. Eighteenth- and early nineteenth-century settlers in the mountains of Kentucky, Tennessee, the Carolinas, and Virginia brought traditional British ballads, lyric songs, and dance tunes. Because of the relative isolation of these mountain areas, many of these songs have been preserved to the present.

The songs of the North and the Southern mountains were carried west by traveling balladeers and the westward-moving pioneers, and it is these songs, molded by the hardships of the frontier, that form the main body of collected American folk music. Frontier hardships led to ironic songs, murder ballads, and romantic escapist songs. Cowboys, lumberjacks, trappers, and railroaders all produced distinctive occupational songs. Black folk music developed along its own lines to produce religious spirituals and prison and work songs.

Modern Themes. During the late nineteenth and early twentieth centuries industrialization and the fight for unionization produced protest songs such as "Which Side are You On?" The hard times of the 1930s also produced talking blues singers Woody Guthrie and Huddie Ledbetter (Leadbelly).

Folk songs enjoyed a new popularity during the 1950s and 1960s and were embraced by pop music singers. Old and new songs were adapted as protest songs by artists such as Joan Baez who were involved in the civil rights and antiwar movements. New songs in the folk idiom were produced by Bob Dylan and Arlo Guthrie, as well as numerous country and western artists.

See also Baez, Joan; Jazz; Music.

Consult (VIII) Lomax, 1960; Stambler and Landon, 1969.

FORAKER ACT (1900), legislation passed in the aftermath of the Spanish-American War that provided for a civil government for Puerto Rico, which Spain had ceded to the United States. By the act the island became an unorganized territory, with the U.S. president given the authority to appoint a governor and an executive council. The council was to be the upper chamber of a legislature; the lower chamber was to be elected by popular vote.

The executive and the council were given veto power. Puerto Rico's unusual status—as defined by the act it was neither a formally organized U.S. territory nor a foreign country—led to the Supreme Court decisions in the Insular Cases (1900–1901). The Court ruled that U.S. sovereignty over an area did not necessarily mean that the area was entitled to all the protections of the Constitution.

See also Puerto Rico.

FORCE ACT (1833), bill giving President Jackson authority to act against tariff opponents. *See* Nullification.

FORCE ACTS. *See* Enforcement Acts.

FORD, HENRY (1863–1947), pioneer automobile manufacturer. Born near Dearborn, Mich., he early displayed a knack for mastering mechanical logic and determined to develop something useful for the common man and to make it as mechanically perfect as possible. At 12 he set up a machine shop in his father's barn, and at 16 he became a steam engine apprentice in Detroit. In 1891 Ford joined the Detroit Edison Illuminating Co., and at night, with little encouragement, he worked on the internal combustion engine. In the spring of 1896 he drove his wife, Clara, and infant son, Edsel, on Detroit streets in his first automobile.

After venturing unsuccessfully in two automobile companies and building some famous racing cars, Ford organized the Ford Motor Company in June 1903. The company was plagued by patent difficulties for 8 years, but ultimately Ford was legally cleared.

In 1909 the Model T (called the flivver or the Tin Lizzie) came off the Ford assembly line, which was a revolutionary labor-saving device that made mass production possible and made Ford the largest independent automobile producer and one of the world's richest men. In 1914 Ford put his workers on an 8-hour day with a $5 minimum wage (then incredibly high) and inaugurated a profit-sharing plan. Hating the waste and horror of war, he chartered the *Oscar II* (the Ford Peace Ship) and went to Europe with a group of idealists hoping to stop World War I.

Ford was president of his company from its inception until 1919 and again from 1943 (when his son Edsel died) until 1945, when his grandson Henry Ford II took over. He collected artifacts, particularly those used by the common man, and displayed them in Greenfield Village in Dearborn. With his son, he established in 1936 the Ford Foundation, whose effect has been great in education, the arts, and other fields.

See also Automobile; Inventions.
Consult (VI) Burlingame, 1955; Nevins and Hill, 1954–1957.

—Ari Hoogenboom, *Brooklyn College of The City University of New York*

FOREIGN AID, general term for U.S. economic and military assistance to foreign countries. The American foreign aid policy dates to the Truman Doctrine announcement of March 1947. President Truman requested and received at this time an appropriation of $400 million for direct economic and military assistance to Turkey and Greece.

This was followed by the Marshall Plan, or European Recovery Program, under which the United States provided approximately $14 billion to assist the economic recovery of Western Europe from 1948 through 1952. In 1950, Congress appropriated the initial funds for the Point Four Program, developed to advance the economies of underdeveloped countries. Since then, four successive administrations have developed and continued American aid programs designed to strengthen the economies and military defenses of countries friendly to the United States.

American foreign aid has become sophisticated and diverse. Aside from direct economic and military assistance, the United States channels aid through the United Nations, supports international lending agencies such as the World Bank and the Export-Import Bank, and has provided direct grants of surplus agricultural products under Public Law 480. A variety of administrative agencies is involved in the aid programs, with the Agency for International Development (AID) assigned primary responsibility. Congress appropriates about $3.5 billion a year to finance foreign assistance programs.

See also Marshall Plan; Truman Doctrine.

Consult (VIII) Montgomery, 1967.
—Robert F. Smith, *Skidmore College*

FOREST RESERVE ACT (1891) gave the president the power to set aside forest areas. *See* Land Policy.

FORTEN, JAMES (1766–1842), a leading figure among blacks in the North. Born of free parents in Pennsylvania, he served in the navy during the American Revolution and settled in Philadelphia. Forten had a spectacular business career, primarily through an invention for handling sails. He became prominent not only in local black affairs but also in larger matters touching the city. During the War of 1812 he organized several thousand black volunteers to protect Philadelphia.

Forten was always alert to plans or legal actions that might endanger his people. Notable was his own protest, printed as *Letters from a Man of Colour* (1813), which helped defeat a bill that would have required blacks to carry certificates proving that they were free.

Forten, also seeing dangers in colonization plans, declared that the true intent of Liberian colonization was to drive free blacks

Children in Calcutta, India, line up to receive food under Food for Peace, one aspect of U.S. foreign aid program.

Automobile magnate Henry Ford.

out of the United States. He helped turn William Lloyd Garrison away from colonization, and when Garrison began the *Liberator* in 1831, Forten provided major financial aid. During the 1830s, a period of rapidly growing abolitionist sentiment in the North, Forten helped direct black plans and organization in support.

FORTS HENRY AND DONELSON, key river forts captured by General Grant in February 1862. *See* Civil War Battles.

FORT STANWIX, TREATY OF (1768), British treaty with the Iroquois. *See* Proclamation of 1763.

FORT SUMTER, CAPTURE OF (APRIL 14, 1862), opening engagement of the Civil War. *See* Civil War Battles.

FORTY-NINERS, those who emigrated to California in 1849 to search for gold. *See* Gold Rushes.

FOSTER, STEPHEN (1826–1864), one of the leading American composers of popular songs. He was born near Pittsburgh, and in his youth he studied music, played several instruments, and published his first song at age 16. While working as a bookkeeper in his brother's office, he kept up with his music, and after the publication of "Louisiana Belle," "Oh, Susanna," and "Away Down South" in *Songs of the Sable Harmonists* (1848), Foster devoted his full time to songwriting. His personal tastes favored nostalgic music rather than black tunes, but the popularity in the 1840s of minstrel shows made minstrel songwriting profitable, and Foster became a master at it.

In 1851 he gave to E. P. Christy of Christy's Minstrels the first singing rights to all his songs, but Foster retained publication rights. Foster composed about 400 songs during his lifetime, ranging from comic songs, popular ballads, war songs, and temperance songs to anything else that music publishers were willing to pay for. His best-known minstrel songs included "Swanee River," "Old Folks at Home," "Old Black Joe," "My Old Kentucky Home," "Camptown Races," "Massa's in de Cold, Cold Ground," and the sentimental ballads "Jeannie with the Light Brown Hair" and "Beautiful Dreamer." Foster's particular talents lay in melodies and lyrics that appealed to popular sentiment. His best work was done in the 1850s; his last years were lonely, and he died a poverty-stricken alcoholic.

FOURTEEN POINTS, President Woodrow Wilson's statement of U.S. aims in World War I. After the Russian Revolution in 1917, the Bolsheviks revealed a number of secret treaties embarrassing to the Allies. In a speech to Congress on Jan. 8, 1918, Wilson attempted to give some moral justification for World War I and to establish a fair basis for peace and future world harmony.

His most famous demand was for "open covenants openly arrived at," meaning the abandonment of the traditions of secret treaties and of the exclusion of the public from knowledge of foreign affairs. Other points were for freedom of the seas, free trade among nations, armaments reduction, and reform of colonialism (to take into account the wishes of the subjects). Several of the points dealt with the independence of regions and peoples engaged in the war and with various boundary settlements. The Fourteenth Point called for the creation of an association of nations after the war.

The Fourteen Points were not accepted by the Allies until after Germany had applied for an armistice. They were only accepted as the basis for peace negotiations with the provisions that Germany pay reparations and that the question of freedom of the seas remain open. Although many of the points were adopted in the Treaty of Versailles (1919), others had been compromised, and the United States repudiated the last point by refusing to join the League of Nations.

See also League of Nations; Versailles, Treaty of; Wilson, Woodrow; World War I: Causes.

FRAME OF GOVERNMENT, early constitution of Pennsylvania. In planning his ideal colony of Pennsylvania, William Penn went through 17 drafts before completing his First Frame of Government (1682), which envisioned an elective upper house of 72 men possessing sole powers to initiate legislation. A lower house of 200 representatives could only accept or reject what the upper house proposed. Viewed in traditional bicameral terms, the scheme seems conservative because of the restraints it imposed on the assembly, but Penn may have envisioned the upper house itself as almost a unicameral legislature whose decisions were subject to ratification by delegates of the people—a truly radical plan by seventeenth-century standards.

The settlers modified the proposal as soon as possible, reducing the upper house to 18 and the lower to 36, an arrangement usually called the Second Frame of Government (1683). In both plans the executive remained weak. A later Frame of Government was more commonly known as the Charter of Liberties.

See also Penn, William; Pennsylvania. *Consult* (I) Bronner, 1962.

FRANKFURTER, FELIX (1882–1965), associate justice of the Supreme Court and presidential adviser who was a leading liberal known as a champion of judicial restraint. An emigrant from Austria, he graduated from Harvard Law

Felix Frankfurter *(right)* appears with lawyer Dean Acheson at Senate hearings to confirm his appointment to the Supreme Court.

School with highest honors. In 1914 Frankfurter joined the faculty of Harvard Law School and remained a classroom teacher for a quarter century, with occasional leaves to carry out various advisory tasks.

In World War I, Frankfurter became a legal adviser at the Paris Peace Conference. While a law professor, Frankfurter was involved in many liberal causes. He helped to found the American Civil Liberties Union and the *New Republic* and tried to obtain a new trial for Sacco and Vanzetti.

In 1939 Frankfurter, an intimate adviser of President Roosevelt, was made an associate justice of the Supreme Court. During Frankfurter's long tenure he was said to have disappointed his liberal followers because he believed the judge's job was to decide cases not to influence the legislative function. Many of his opinions reflect his belief that government by judges is a poor substitute for government by the people. Frankfurter stepped down from the Court in 1962 because of poor health.

FRANKLIN, BENJAMIN (1706–1790), the most celebrated citizen of colonial America. Born in Boston, he attended school only two years. At 10 he began working in his father's soap and candle shop and then was apprenticed to learn printing from his brother James. By constant reading he educated himself culturally and scientifically.

He moved to Philadelphia in 1723, worked as a printer, and in 1729 became owner of *The Pennsylvania Gazette.* He also published annually (1723–1757) *Poor Richard's Almanack.* Philadelphia offered a rich arena for Franklin's "involved citizen" concept of social improvement. He formed a circulating library, a fire department, an academy from which the University of Pennsylvania later developed, and a debating club that became the American Philosophical Society. His scientific interests led to his famous kite experiment, confirming lightning as electricity, and his inventive talents were brilliantly demonstrated with the Franklin stove, bifocals, and lightning rods.

Public Career. Franklin's public career began with his appointment as clerk of the provincial assembly in 1736, and he was an elected representative to the assembly from 1751 to 1764. A delegate to the Albany Congress (1754), his Plan of Union for a federal system won approval but was rejected later in both Britain and the colonies. With William Hunter, Franklin was postmaster general for British North America from 1753 to 1774. In 1757 he left Philadelphia for England, where he lived for the next 18 years. Much of that time he was the agent for Pennsylvania and other colonies, including Georgia and Massachusetts Bay. His testimony before the House of Commons in 1766 was useful in the repeal of the Stamp Act. In 1774, following disclosure of his role in procuring some private letters of Thomas Hutchinson, Franklin was unceremoniously dismissed as postmaster general, and the following year he returned to an America already at war with Britain.

He immediately was named a delegate to the Second Continental Congress, where he aided in drafting and signed the Declaration of Independence. Congress then appointed him agent to France, where he went in 1776 to work for French aid in the Revolutionary War. After concluding a treaty of alliance in February 1778, Franklin became the first U.S. minister to France and one of the commissioners to negotiate the Treaty of Paris (1783), which ended the war. Now 80, Franklin returned to Pennsylvania and served as president of the state executive council and delegate to the Constitutional Convention in 1787.

See also Albany Congress (1754); Continental Congress, Second; Declaration of Independence (1776); Hutchinson Letters; Paris, Treaty of (1783).

Consult (II) Ketcham, 1965; Van Doren, 1938.

—Carl Ubbelohde, *Case Western Reserve University*

FRANKLIN, STATE OF, short-lived state (1784–1788) organized in eastern Tennessee by frontiersmen. Their effort at state making came when North Carolina ceded the region to the federal government, leaving the settlers without local government. What seemed worse, Congress had not yet devised a plan to create territories or new states, so the pioneers acted for themselves.

In late 1784 they held a convention and wrote a temporary constitution. The next year they accepted the document, created the state of Franklin, and elected John Sevier, a prominent militia leader and land speculator, as their first governor. The new state had a brief and troubled history. Not all the settlers supported it, and, more importantly, North Carolina had rescinded its cession of the region and now reimposed its laws on the citizens. The Franklin leaders then tried to extract land cessions from the Cherokee Indians, but Congress voided the resulting treaty. Consequently, when Sevier's term as governor expired in 1788, so did Franklin.

See also Frontier in American History.
Consult (III) Driver, 1932.

FREDERICKSBURG (DECEMBER 1862), bloody defeat of Union forces that repeatedly charged well-entrenched Confederates. *See* Civil War Battles.

FREEDMEN'S BUREAU, more formally the Bureau of Refugees, Freedmen, and Abandoned Lands, created on March 3, 1865, to unify and coordinate the many organizations that had

Medallion honoring Benjamin Franklin.

THE FREEDMAN'S BUREAU!

AN AGENCY TO KEEP THE **NEGRO** IN IDLENESS AT THE **EXPENSE** OF THE WHITE MAN.
TWICE VETOED BY THE **PRESIDENT**, AND MADE A LAW BY **CONGRESS.**
SUPPORT CONGRESS & YOU SUPPORT THE NEGRO. SUSTAIN THE PRESIDENT & YOU PROTECT THE WHITE MAN

Poster attacking the Freedmen's Bureau, which Radical Republicans had pushed through Congress over Andrew Johnson's veto.

sprung up during the Civil War to deal with the problems faced by freed slaves. Headed by Gen. O. O. Howard and staffed primarily by army officers, the bureau assumed a kind of overall guardianship of the emancipated slaves.

One of its most important functions was the regulation of labor relations. Agents defended the black man's right to select his own employer and to receive just compensation. To this end the bureau established courts and boards, which often handled civil and criminal cases as well as labor disputes. The bureau also founded schools and provided emergency rations for the hungry and medical care for the sick. In 1866 Congress overrode President Johnson's veto of a bill renewing the bureau, which finally ceased operations in 1872.

See also Reconstruction.
Consult (IV) Bentley, 1955.

FREEDOM DUES, goods received by indentured servants. *See* Indentured Servitude.

FREEDOM OF INFORMATION ACT (1967), a bill designed to give the public greater access to government records. The act, signed by President Johnson, superseded the Disclosure of Information Act (1966). Both these measures amended Section 3 of the Administrative Procedure Act.

The original Section 3 allowed agencies great discretion in the requirement that most federal proceedings and policies be made public, but the new act permitted exemptions in only nine specific areas. Among these areas were national defense, confidential financial information, law enforcement files, and certain personnel files, in addition to information whose disclosure was prohibited by statute. Critics soon charged that the act had had no visible effect, because agencies reclassified information under the permitted exemptions.

FREE ENTERPRISE, economic system in which all the means of production are privately owned and controlled and in which capital is invested in business and farming purely for private profit. The government does not interfere in any way with the working of private businessmen, and the forces of supply and demand in the market are allowed to determine price and quality of output.

This pure model, advocated by Adam Smith in his *Wealth of Nations* (1776), has never existed. Government has always intervened in one way or another; the *degree* of intervention is the question. For instance, a tariff is a form of interference in the free workings of the market system. Yet the supporters of free enterprise in nineteenth-century America usually wanted tariffs to protect American industries from foreign competition.

In truth the two principles that underlie free enterprise—laissez-faire and free competition—are at odds with each other. Laissez-faire means no government intervention. But if free competition is allowed to run its course, the superior or more unscrupulous firms will always try to establish monopolies to protect their positions—as John Jacob Astor did in the fur trade, for example. Monopoly destroys free competition, and so the government, as with antitrust acts, intervenes to prevent monopoly. But by intervening, the principle of laissez-faire is impaired. The free enterprise theorists never made up their minds about whether laissez-faire or free competition was more important.

In the nineteenth century large monopolies such as Standard Oil arose in the American economy. Meanwhile, the federal government was crippled in dealing with the problems of labor, immigrants, and poverty by the theory of laissez-faire.

See also Business Regulation; Free Trade; Mercantilism; Smith, Adam; Tariffs; Trusts.
Consult (III) Fine, 1964; Jones, 1965.
—Peter d'A. Jones, *University of Illinois, Chicago Circle*

FREEHOLD, system of land tenure. *See* Colonial Agriculture.

FREEPORT DOCTRINE, statement in support of popular sovereignty by Senator Stephen A. Douglas. *See* Lincoln-Douglas Debates (1858).

FREE SILVER, political movement seeking currency inflation through silver coinage, that reached its apogee in the presidential campaign of 1896.

Between 1792 and 1873, coinage laws had provided for the minting of all gold and silver brought to the mint—that is, for the free and unlimited coinage of silver and gold. In practice, few silver dollars had been coined because it was more profitable to sell silver on the open market than to have it coined at the silver-to-gold ratio established by Congress. In 1873 the silver dollar was dropped from the list of approved coins during a recodification of the currency laws. Almost simultaneously, the market price of silver dropped to where it was once again profitable for silver miners to have it minted.

Silver mineowners favoring the remonetization of silver were joined in their demands by currency inflationists. The period after the Civil War was one of currency deflation, in which prices fell and the purchasing power of money increased. Deflation is a special hardship on those in debt because it has the effect of increasing the debt by increasing the buying power of money. Debt-ridden farmers joined silver interests to demand an increased volume of circulating currency through coinage of all silver presented to the mint.

Currency inflation was one of the primary demands of farmer groups after the Civil War, including Populist supporters. The Democratic Party in 1896 joined this demand and nominated William Jennings Bryan, a prominent advocate of free silver, for president. Bryan's defeat by William McKinley, a gold standard supporter, together with increases in the quantity of gold coin, ended silver agitation.

See also Bryan, William Jennings; McKinley, William; Populists.

Consult (V) Hicks, 1961.

—Robert W. Cherny, *California State University, San Francisco*

FREE-SOIL PARTY, political party founded in 1848 by Salmon P. Chase and others to oppose the extension of slavery to new territories. The Wilmot Proviso had included such a proposal, but even after it was defeated in 1846–1847, the issue continued to provoke factionalism. The Free-Soilers were not moral abolitionists but were against slavery for economic reasons. They wanted free land from the government for homesteading, whereas Southern interests needed more land to perpetuate the slave-based plantation system.

In 1848 the first Free-Soil convention chose ex-President Martin Van Buren as the party's presidential candidate. The Free-Soil platform was an ambivalent document in which an initial antislavery plank was followed by the declaration that Congress had no right to interfere with slavery within a state. In the election, Van Buren helped to split the Democratic vote, which led to the election of Whig Zachary Taylor.

The Compromise of 1850 had the effect of weakening the Free-Soil cause, and after the 1852 election the party disbanded. Its members soon drifted into other political organizations, most notably the new Republican Party.

See also Chase, Salmon P.; Political Parties in the United States; Presidential Elections.

FREE SPEECH MOVEMENT, formed on Sept. 30, 1964, when University of California (Berkeley) students joined to occupy the administration building. It was a protest against a sudden ruling that denied them the right to recruit and raise funds for political organizations on a section of campus long used for that purpose.

FREE TRADE, economic theory that each nation will benefit more in the long run if all barriers to international trade are eliminated and if each specializes in producing what it is best at making. Sometimes a nation has an absolute advantage as a producer, as when it controls the supply of some rare natural resource. More often, a nation has a comparative advantage that can be exploited for a time by specialization; for example, the combination of rich soil and slave labor in the South created a comparative advantage for that region to specialize in growing cotton for the world market.

The problem with the theory of free trade is that it assumes that the world is in fact a free market, that national currencies are all easily exchangeable, and that large nations will not exploit their advantages over small nations. In the nineteenth century, most Americans favored protective tariffs, charges imposed on imported foreign goods. The British believed in free trade, but they were the world's workshop and had nothing to lose by the abolition of tariff barriers. From the start, Alexander Hamilton and economic nationalists like him opposed free trade and favored tariff protection and the stimulation of home industries to liberate the United States from dependence on Europe for its necessities.

See also Free Enterprise; Mercantilism; Tariffs.

Consult (III) Boulding, 1958.

FREMONT, JOHN C(HARLES) (1813–1890), explorer, Civil War general, and the first Republican candidate for the presidency. Born in Savannah, Ga., Frémont grew up in the South and in 1838 was named a second lieutenant in the U.S. Topographical Corps. In 1838–1841 Frémont accompanied J. M. Nicollet on an expedition to explore and map the region between the upper Mississippi and Missouri rivers, and soon after that he was commissioned to lead expeditions into the Oregon country. Frémont's reports and maps of these explorations to the Rocky Mountains, Oregon, and northern California stirred many people's interest in the West.

In the spring of 1845, Frémont was sent to California, where he defied the Mexicans by raising the U.S. flag. He became increasingly involved in U.S. expansion in California, including the Bear Flag Revolt, and later appointed Commodore Robert Stockton as commandant and governor of that new territory. A disagreement with Gen. Stephen Kearny, who succeeded Stockton, led to Frémont's recall to Washington and his dismissal from the service.

In 1848 and 1853, Frémont, supported by railroad entrepreneurs, led unsuccessful expeditions to the Pacific Coast. Despite the failure of these ventures, Frémont had gained a sufficiently good reputation to be elected U.S. senator from California (1850–1851) and to be nominated by the new Republican Party for president in 1856. His rival, James Buchanan, won the election by a relatively small margin of 60 electoral votes.

John C. Frémont served as a major general at the beginning of the Civil War.

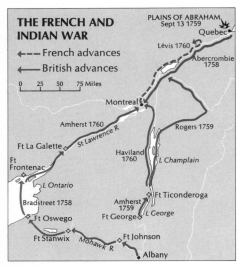

THE FRENCH AND INDIAN WAR

← - - French advances
← British advances

0   25   50   75 Miles

PLAINS OF ABRAHAM
Sept 13 1759
Quebec
Lévis 1760
Abercrombie 1758
Montreal
Amherst 1760
St Lawrence R
Rogers 1759
Ft La Galette
Haviland 1760
L Champlain
Ft Frontenac
L Ontario
Ft Ticonderoga
Bradstreet 1758
Amherst 1759
Ft George
L George
Ft Oswego
Ft Johnson
Ft Stanwix
Mohawk R
Albany

French and British forces battle on the Plains of Abraham outside Quebec on Sept. 13, 1759.

At the outbreak of the Civil War, Frémont was named a major general and commander of the Department of the West, but the severity of the measures he favored against the South aroused protest that led to his removal. In 1864 Frémont was backed by Radical Republicans for the presidency, but he withdrew his name. Frémont's later speculations in railroad projects ended in failure and cost him his fortune. He was saved from dire poverty at the end of his life by earnings from his wife's writings, by his appointment as governor of the Arizona Territory (1878–1883), and, shortly before his death, by the grant of a full military pension.

See also Bear Flag Revolt; Presidential Elections.

FRENCH ALLIANCE, Franco-American alliance that played a key role in the Revolutionary War. It was based on two treaties between the United States and France that were signed on February 6, 1778, after the American victory at the Battle of Saratoga in October 1777 convinced the French that the Americans posed a serious threat to the British. The first treaty dealt mostly with commercial matters, giving a generous interpretation of neutral rights. The second stated that neither France nor America would sign a separate peace with Britain and that France would fight until American independence was established. It was also agreed that the United States would have the right to conquer British possessions on the mainland of North America and that France would conquer British islands. The alliance collapsed in the 1790s.

FRENCH AND INDIAN WAR (1754–1763). Unlike earlier Anglo-French contests in North America, the Great War for the Empire began in the New World before it spread to the old—an indication of the growing importance of American possessions for the balance of both European and global power. The fighting began in 1754, when a Virginia expedition, led by youthful George Washington, tried to secure the colony's claim to the Forks of the Ohio (modern Pittsburgh). Discovering that the French had already erected Fort Duquesne on the spot, Washington opened fire on a French column only to be forced to retreat and then surrender.

London, determined to protect its Western claims, dispatched two regiments to Virginia under General Edward Braddock in 1755. Working closely with the expansionist governor of Massachusetts, William Shirley, Braddock sanctioned a four-pronged assault against New France. One force destroyed French resistance in Nova Scotia and, to prevent its recurrence, deported thousands of civilian Acadians, who were scattered through the English settlements. In New York one provincial expedition failed to take Crown Point despite an impressive early victory. Another, commanded by Shirley, tried to capture Fort Niagara but instead got bogged down at Oswego, where it had to surrender the following spring. Most dramatically of all, Braddock's regiments were annihilated in the Battle of the Wilderness, near Fort Duquesne, by a much smaller force of French and Indians.

British Victory. As the conflict widened into a global war in 1756, Britain found itself broadening the objectives of 1755 into a major effort to conquer all of New France. Eventually more than 30 regiments of redcoats served in America while the colonies raised perhaps 20,000 provincials per year in 1758–1760. New France simply lacked the resources to cope with this avalanche and began to crumble in 1758, when Fort Duquesne, Fort Frontenac on Lake Ontario, and Fortress Louisbourg all fell to British and provincial forces. The only British failure was a costly defeat at Ticonderoga, defended by Canada's commander in chief, Marquis de Montcalm. In 1759 provincials captured Fort Niagara to win control of the Great Lakes, while, in the most stunning engagement of the war, Gen. James Wolfe defeated Montcalm on the Plains of Abraham outside Quebec. Although both commanders died in this action, Quebec fell to the British, as did Montreal a year later.

The Peace of Paris, ending the war in 1763, reflected these victories on the mainland and others in the Caribbean. Britain acquired Canada from France and Florida from Spain, while France compensated Spain by ceding to it all of Louisiana west of the Mississippi plus the port city of New Orleans.

See also Shirley, William; Washington, George.

Consult (I) Fregault, 1969.
—John M. Murrin, *Princeton University*

FRENCH COLONIES. French claims on North America date back at least to the explorations of Jacques Cartier in Newfoundland and the Gaspé Peninsula region in 1534–1542. A French settlement at Quebec failed in 1542 and was not reestablished on a secure basis until Samuel de Champlain reached there in 1608. To the south, a small French Protestant settlement in Florida (Fort Caroline, near modern Jacksonville) was eliminated by the Spanish in 1563. Not until the seventeenth century did France begin American colonization in earnest.

Louis XIV and his finance minister, Jean Colbert, began a development plan for North America, and the colony of New France was created. Its basis was the Quebec region and Acadie (Acadia), later called Nova Scotia by the English. Colbert tried to encourage planned emigration, colonial defense, and state-controlled trade, but the French feudal system of land tenure in Canada discouraged the free emigration necessary to the growth of the colony.

French exploration was extensive. In 1682 Sieur de La Salle claimed the entire Mississippi Valley region for France and called it Louisiana. New Orleans was established at the mouth of the Mississippi in 1718. In the eighteenth century the French moved into the Northwest as far as the Black Hills of South Dakota and into the Southwest as far as New Mexico. They had theoretically hemmed in the English colonies on the East Coast. By the Treaty of Utrecht (1713), however, the French lost Newfoundland, Hudson's Bay Territory, and most of Acadia to the British.

Decline of French Influence. The great weakness of this French empire, however, was its vast size and tiny population. At the time of the last Anglo-French conflicts in North America, the French and Indian War (1754–1763), New France had a population of only about 65,000 French trappers and traders, aided by some Indian tribes. They faced a British population of slightly under 2 million, and the British were allied with the powerful Iroquois Confederacy.

The French fortified what was left of New France, but they lost the entire territory at the close of the French and Indian War through the Peace of Paris (1763). The French empire in North America had disappeared—although the vast territory of Louisiana, ceded to Spain in 1762, was eventually returned to French control. In British Canada, the French remained a distinct subculture.

See also Champlain, Samuel de; French and Indian War; La Salle, Sieur de; Louisiana Purchase (1803).

Consult (I) Brebner, 1970; Zoltvany, 1969.

—Peter d'A. Jones, *University of Illinois, Chicago Circle*

FRICK, HENRY CLAY (1849–1919), coke and steel manufacturer. Born in Pennsylvania, he began buying coal lands and operating coke ovens in the Connellsville coal district at 21 and achieved a youthful ambition—to be a millionaire at 30. In 1883 he joined forces with Andrew Carnegie, who recognized Frick's "positive genius for management" and in 1889 sold Frick an interest in his steel works. As general manager, Frick reorganized the firm, purchased his largest competitor, and overcame Carnegie's distaste for "pioneering" to achieve vertical integration of the company's operations.

Frick is most often criticized for his handling of the strike at the Carnegie steel works at Homestead, Pa., in 1892. Many were killed or wounded in the violence that followed Frick's attempts to break the strike with armed guards and to free the steel industry from the "tyranny" of organized labor. Public sentiment shifted from the strikers after an anarchist unconnected with the strike tried to assassinate Frick. After 5 months the workers returned to their jobs on the company's terms, having been taught a lesson, Frick wrote, "that they will never forget."

Although policy differences forced Frick's resignation in 1899, he subsequently played an important role in the negotiations leading to the sale of the Carnegie Steel Company and the consolidation of the major firms in the industry into the U.S. Steel Corporation. His New York City mansion and a large art collection, together with an endowment of $15 million, were willed to the public as the Frick Museum.

See also Carnegie, Andrew; Homestead Massacre (1892).

Consult (V) Josephson, 1934.

—Seddie Cogswell, *California State University, San Francisco*

FRIEDAN, BETTY (1921–   ) author, lecturer, and leading feminist who founded the National Organization for Women in 1966 and served as its first president (1966–1970). A 1942 graduate of Smith College, where she majored in psychology, Friedan gained prominence as author of a best-selling book, *The Feminine Mystique* (1963), that did much to inspire the growth of a new feminist movement in the late 1960s. She contended that the "mystique of feminine fulfillment"—an image to which women attempted to conform—relegated women to the roles of wife, mother, homemaker, and consumer. The mystique was perpetrated by business, advertising, the media, and educators; it derived scholarly support from Freudian thought and the writings of anthropologist Margaret Mead; and it caused uneasiness, frustration, and despair among its victims.

Friedan's impact as an author and her insight as a social critic carried her to a leadership role in the feminist campaign for legal and economic reform. "We are beginning to know," she wrote in 1970, "that no woman can achieve a breakthrough alone, as long as sex discrimination exists in employment, under the law, in education, in mores, and in denigration of the image of women."

See also National Organization for Women; Women's Liberation.

FRIENDS, SOCIETY OF. *See* Quakers.

FROMM, ERICH (1900–   ), German-American writer and psychoanalyst. Born in Frankfurt, Germany, he received his Ph.D. from the University of Heidelberg in 1922. In 1933, after receiving his early training in psychoanalysis in Berlin and Munich, he came to the United States, where he conducted a private practice for many years. He taught and lectured widely in the United States and Mexico.

Henry Clay Frick's opposition to unions was a key factor in the violence of the Homestead Massacre in 1892.

Feminist Betty Friedan urges women to participate actively in politics.

Fromm's major contribution to psychoanalytic thought was a fusion, as well as a reinterpretation, of the ideas of Freud and Marx. In forming his own theories, Fromm disagreed with Freud's ideas that self-realization and fulfillment are frustrated only by biological drives. Fromm, in his concern with the relationship between the individual and society, was influenced by Marx's concept that social character is also determined by cultural training.

In later years Fromm has been concerned with the creation of a sane society based on human needs as well as the establishment of harmony among nations in a nuclear age. To this end he helped to organize the National Committee for a Sane Nuclear Policy in 1957. Fromm's many works include *Escape from Freedom* (1941), *The Art of Loving* (1956), and *The Crisis of Psychoanalysis* (1970).

Consult (VIII) Schaar, 1961.

FRONTIER IN AMERICAN HISTORY. Most Americans find stories of the settling of the frontier fascinating, but the process of subduing the wilderness included far more than well-documented events such as the California gold rush, the cattle drives north from Texas, and the wars against the Plains Indians. Rather, the history of the American frontier encompasses nearly all early phases of the expansion and settlement of the nation from the colonial era to the end of the nineteenth century. Even the term "frontier" brings confusing ideas to mind. It means both a newly settled region and the process of turning the wilderness into a stable society.

Frontier Patterns. In 1893 historian Frederick Jackson Turner proposed the first framework for studying the frontier. He suggested that a procession of pioneer types could be noted. First he saw the frontier trader or trapper, far ahead of settlement. In their quest for furs these hardy individuals penetrated the Appalachians, crossed the Mississippi, moved into the Rockies, and finally reached the West Coast. Traveling alone or in small groups, they introduced the Indians to guns, steel knives, and liquor, and these contacts helped weaken the economic stability and social structures of tribal life.

Following the trapper, the miner hiked into the hills searching for gold, silver, or even lead. Greedy and determined, miners swept west, pushing aside all physical and human obstacles. At about the same time, pioneer herdsmen and ranchers sought to exploit free grass and water, whether in colonial Carolina or beyond the Mississippi.

Following these waves of migratory exploiters came the pioneer farmer. Equipped with a rifle, an axe, a crude plow, and a draft animal or two, this woodsman cleared tiny forest plots, built a log cabin, and planted some corn. When he had buildings and fences up and had cleared a few more acres for crops, he often sold out to a wealthier farmer and moved west to repeat the process. Finally, near the end of the procession came the would-be city dwellers. They supplied the farmer, miner, or rancher with goods and services. Printers, brewers, and blacksmiths, as well as lawyers, bankers, and physicians, hurried west. All hoped to find opportunity and profit, and the raw frontier towns offered opportunity to the competent and the greedy.

Not only did Turner see distinct waves of settlement, but also he suggested that civilization had to be recreated on each new frontier. That is, pioneers had a chance to build the kind of society they wanted in new communities because there was little form or structure when they arrived. As society started over on each new frontier the pioneers helped to mold and change their institutions.

Fur Frontier. In this process the fur traders certainly were among the first Anglo-Americans to enter many regions. In the late colonial era Pennsylvania and Virginia traders moved beyond the mountains to trade with the Ohio Valley tribes. Shortly after the United States acquired the Louisiana Purchase in 1803, traders pushed their boats up the Missouri. In fact, some of the men who had accompanied Lewis and Clark west were among the first Americans to trade there.

As early as 1810, John Jacob Astor organized the Pacific Fur Company to trade in the Pacific Northwest. His men built a trading post they called Astoria, but the British captured it during the War of 1812. In 1822 William H. Ashley led an expedition of young Americans up the Missouri to the Rocky Mountains. This group included some of the most famous mountain men; individuals such as Jim Bridger, Hugh Glass, and Jedediah Smith got their start under Ashley. Ashley's contribution was that his men were trappers, not mere traders. They spent most of the next 20 years trapping, exploring, and fighting with the Indians. By 1840 the fur business went into permanent decline because most of the beaver had been killed and also because fashions had changed. For the next few decades a few major trading centers such as Bent's Fort, Fort Laramie, and Fort Hall served as the centers for a much reduced regional fur trade.

Mining Frontier. Most Americans know little about the mining frontier except for the California gold rush and a few of the more famous strikes in the Far West. In the colonial era miners hunted bog iron in both Massachusetts and Virginia, but it was not until the early nineteenth century that mining rushes occurred. In the late 1820s and 1830s miners found gold in northern Georgia and Alabama, setting off small-scale rushes there. Even before that, discoveries of lead in Indiana, Missouri,

Miners in the depths of the Comstock Mine in Nevada. Discoveries of precious metals were major factor in westward expansion of the frontier.

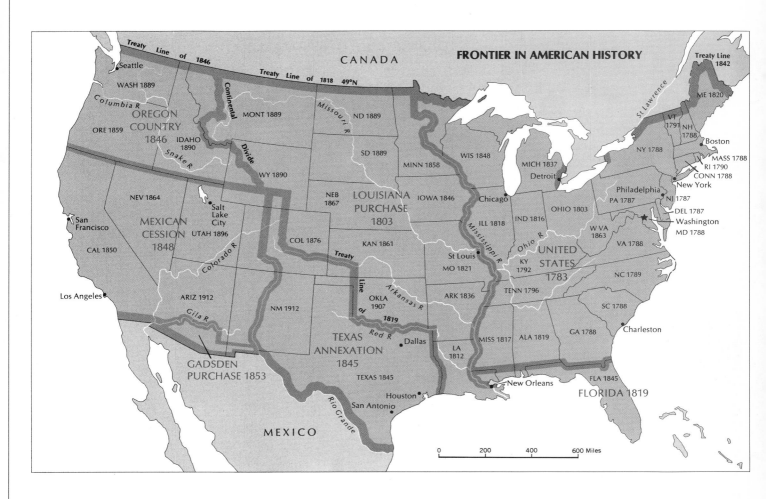

FRONTIER IN AMERICAN HISTORY

Treaty Line of 1846

CANADA

Treaty Line of 1818 49°N

Treaty Line 1842

Seattle

WASH 1889

Columbia R

OREGON
COUNTRY
1846

ORE 1859

IDAHO
1890

Snake R

Continental

Divide

Missouri R

MONT 1889

ND 1889

SD 1889

MINN 1858

WIS 1848

MICH 1837

Detroit

St Lawrence

ME 1820

VT
1791

NH
1788

Boston

NY 1788

MASS 1788

RI 1790

CONN 1788

New York

Philadelphia

PA 1787

NJ 1787

WY 1890

NEV 1864

Salt
Lake
City

San
Francisco

MEXICAN
CESSION
1848

UTAH 1896

COL 1876

NEB
1867

LOUISIANA
PURCHASE
1803

IOWA 1846

Chicago

ILL 1818

IND 1816

OHIO 1803

Washington

MD 1788

DEL 1787

W VA
1863

VA 1788

Ohio R

UNITED
STATES
1783

Mississippi R

KAN 1861

St Louis

MO 1821

KY
1792

CAL 1850

Colorado R

Treaty

Los Angeles

ARIZ 1912

NM 1912

Line

of

1819

Arkansas R

Red R

OKLA
1907

ARK 1836

TENN 1796

NC 1789

SC 1788

Charleston

Gila R

GADSDEN
PURCHASE 1853

TEXAS
ANNEXATION
1845

Dallas

MISS 1817

ALA 1819

GA 1788

TEXAS 1845

LA
1812

San Antonio

Houston

Rio Grande

New Orleans

FLA 1845

FLORIDA 1819

MEXICO

0   200   400   600 Miles

FRONTIER IN AMERICAN HISTORY

EXPLORATION AND COLONIZATION (see Subject Map)

EXPLORATION AND DISCOVERY
FRENCH COLONIES
SPANISH COLONIES, NORTH AMERICAN
CONNECTICUT
DELAWARE
GEORGIA
MARYLAND
MASSACHUSETTS
NEW HAMPSHIRE
NEW JERSEY
NEW YORK
NORTH CAROLINA
PENNSYLVANIA
RHODE ISLAND
SOUTH CAROLINA
VIRGINIA

BEYOND THE COLONIES

Institutions
FRANKLIN, STATE OF
NORTHWEST ORDINANCE
NORTHWEST TERRITORY
GREENVILLE, TREATY OF
LAND COMPANIES
    OHIO COMPANY
VANDALIA GRANT
CANALS
    ERIE CANAL
TURNPIKES, EARLY

Leaders
DANIEL BOONE
THOMAS JEFFERSON
JOHN QUINCY ADAMS
ANDREW JACKSON
    SEMINOLE WARS (1818–1819;
      1835–1842)
WILLIAM HENRY HARRISON

SOUTHWEST AND FAR WEST

Expansion
INDIAN WARS, WESTERN
INDIAN POLICY
MANIFEST DESTINY
ALAMO
SAN JACINTO, BATTLE OF
BEAR FLAG REVOLT
MEXICAN WAR (1846–1848)
    SLIDELL MISSION
    GUADALUPE-HIDALGO, TREATY OF
OREGON TRAIL
"FIFTY-FOUR-FORTY OR FIGHT"
PANAMA CANAL

Factors
FRONTIER IN AMERICAN HISTORY
FUR TRADE
    JOHN JACOB ASTOR
GOLD RUSHES
LAND POLICY
COWBOYS
RAILROADS
LOUISIANA PURCHASE (1803)
    LEWIS AND CLARK EXPEDITION
TERRITORIES AND POSSESSIONS
PONY EXPRESS
SANTA FE TRAIL

Leaders
STEPHEN F. AUSTIN
DAVY CROCKETT
JOHN C. FRÉMONT
SAM HOUSTON
ZEBULON PIKE
JAMES K. POLK
WINFIELD SCOTT
ZACHARY TAYLOR
BRIGHAM YOUNG

The Subject Maps in the Encyclopedia illustrate the coverage of particular aspects of American History, showing the interrelationships among the articles in twelve critical areas of study. Entries in capital letters, except for titles, are subjects for which there are separate articles in the Encyclopedia.

The Subject Maps are arranged alphabetically in the Encyclopedia under the following titles:

American Wars
Blacks in the United States
Business Regulation and Industrialization
Civil War and Reconstruction
Constitution of the United States
Exploration and Colonization
Frontier in American History
Indians
Labor Movement
New Deal and Depression
Revolutionary War Era
Slavery and Emancipation

Illinois, and Wisconsin brought hordes of miners to those regions. At one point before Illinois became a state in 1818, Galena was reputed to be the wickedest city in the West and was, in fact, the largest settlement in Illinois.

The discovery of gold on the American River in northern California in 1848 began the largest mineral rush in American history, with between 80,000 and 100,000 people pouring into that state within little more than a year. California was only a start for Western mining, however, as one discovery after another kept miners traveling from one mining camp to another. Mining activity poured millions of dollars into the national economy, stimulated better transportation facilities in the West, encouraged technological innovations, and lured thousands of people to the mountain West, an area where few might have settled without the mines.

Agriculture and Timber. As farmers hurried West, they found nearly unbroken forests from the Atlantic Coast to the Missouri Valley. Beyond they found a region that differed sharply from their homes in the East. On the plains, farmers had to work without enough water or timber and thus could not put up the typical log cabin. Using caves or temporary shelters built of sod blocks, the pioneers pushed out onto the plains. The sod house was snug for a season or even a year, but vermin, rain, and snow made it uncomfortable, so the successful farmer put his profits and effort into building a frame house as quickly as possible. Farming on the plains depended on good rain and an absence of grasshoppers. When the rain failed or the insects came, discouraged farmers retreated eastward. It took until nearly the end of the nineteenth century before new, drought-resistant strains of seed and dry farming techniques helped overcome natural disasters for the farmers.

While the homesteaders struggled with drought, the grazing frontier reached the Western plains and plateaus. Cattle raising had been a major agricultural industry for well over a century before it reached Texas. It was not until after the Civil War, however, that Western cattle growers could get their animals to market. As railroads inched their way west, the ranchers began driving their stock north to meet them. Such well-known paths as the Chisholm and Goodnight-Loving trails reached north from Texas to Kansas. During the 1870s and 1880s, Dodge City, Abilene, and Wichita, Kansas, all served as major cattle shipping points. By the mid-1880s an overstocking of the range, drought, and severe winters brought disaster. Since that time ranchers have raised most cattle near the railroads and have come to depend upon stored feed in addition to range grass for their animals.

Like ranching and mining, lumbering depended on a natural resource. Large-scale lumbering began in Maine and Mississippi during the 1820s. Within 10 years lumberjacks had moved into Michigan, and as the population grew in the upper Mississippi Valley lumbering operations moved into Wisconsin and Minnesota. By the 1880s Midwestern timber resources had begun to dwindle, so the lumbermen turned their attention to the Pacific Northwest, where much modern lumbering is done.

Frontier Missionaries. Most people went West to seek their fortune, but one group, frontier missionaries, sought souls instead. Missionary groups worked in two directions. Some tried to hurry the Americanization of the Indians, whereas others strove to build churches for the westward-moving population. The skills of frontier clergymen varied widely, but whether they were itinerant lay readers or college-trained ministers, all encountered hardship and difficulty in their work. By the midnineteenth century, missionary work among the Indians included not only churches but also model farms and schools. When successful, frontier missionaries helped to turn Indians into copies of the whites and nudged new settlements into peaceful reproductions of existing towns farther east.

See also Colonial Agriculture; Fur Trade; Gold Rushes; Indian Wars, Western.

Consult (V) Billington, 1967; Clark, 1969.

—Roger L. Nichols, *University of Arizona*

FRONTIER MISSIONARIES. *See* Frontier in American History.

FROST, ROBERT (LEE) (1874–1963), American poet who won four Pulitzer Prizes. He was born in San Francisco but at 10 was taken to New England, the family's home for generations. New England became Frost's home, and he considered himself a farmer-poet of that region.

Frost briefly attended Dartmouth College and then held a variety of jobs before entering Harvard, which he left after two years to try farming. In 1912 he went to England, where he first achieved recognition for two volumes of poetry about New England: *A Boy's Will* (1913) and *North of Boston* (1914). Returning to the United States a recognized poet, Frost settled down on a New Hampshire farm. During his long career, he intermittently left his farm to teach and lecture at colleges and universities.

Frost was awarded the Pulitzer Prize in poetry for *New Hampshire* (1923), *Collected Poems* (1931), *A Further Range* (1936), and *A Witness Tree* (1942).

In his later years, Frost was accorded honors seldom matched in the lifetime of an artist. The U.S. Senate gave him tributes on his

Robert Frost *(left)* welcomes Soviet poet Yevgheny Yevtushenko to the United States in 1962.

Captured fugitive slave is returned to the plantation.

75th and 85th birthdays, and he read a poem at the inauguration of President Kennedy in 1961.
See also Literature.
Consult (VIII) Thompson, 1966, 1970.

FUGITIVE SLAVE ACTS, legislation passed in 1793 and 1850 that was directed against runaway slaves seeking sanctuary in the North. The first act functioned weakly and irregularly because a relatively mild antislavery movement did not vigorously aid and encourage runaways and because the courts did not clearly distinguish federal from state authority in cases involving runaways.

The decision in *Prigg v. Pennsylvania* (1842) apparently settled the question of state versus federal authority, the Supreme Court ruling in favor of the latter. Northern states responded with personal liberty laws to protect their citizens and shelter blacks, and the Underground Railroad increased the number of fugitive slaves and made North-South differences more bitter.

As a result of the increase in runaways, a Fugitive Slave Act was passed as part of the Compromise of 1850. Northerners were increasingly outraged by such cases as that of James Hamlet, who was seized in New York and, although probably a free black, sent into slavery. Harriet Beecher Stowe's *Uncle Tom's Cabin* (1852) helped crystallize Northern opinion in favor of fugitive slaves.

Although some fugitives found themselves victimized by the act, its enforcement progressively declined. John Brown openly transported across the North slaves he had taken in Missouri. During the Civil War more and more runaways were given sanctuary by Federal troops, who also helped to undermine the slavery system.
See also Brown, John; Compromise of 1850; Personal Liberty Laws; Prigg v. Pennsylvania (1842); Slavery; Stowe, Harriet Beecher.
Consult (IX) Campbell, 1970.
—Louis Filler, *Antioch College*

FULBRIGHT, J(AMES) WILLIAM (1905–   ), chairman of the Senate Foreign Relations Committee from 1959, known for his defense of Senate prerogatives in foreign policy.

Born in Sumner, Mo., Fulbright grew up in Fayetteville, Arkansas. He graduated from the University of Arkansas in 1925 and then attended Oxford University as a Rhodes scholar. After George Washington University awarded him his LL.B. degree in 1934, he worked for the Justice Department for a short time. Following two years of teaching law, he became president of the University of Arkansas (1939). Elected to Congress as a Democrat in 1942, he won a Senate seat in 1944 and was reelected four times.

Committee Chairman. Senator Fulbright assumed the coveted chairmanship of the Foreign Relations Committee in 1959. An ardent internationalist, he strongly supported development of international cooperation among nations. He originated the Fulbright Scholarship plan, which awarded scholarships and fellowships to American students and teachers for study and teaching overseas in order to further international understanding.

Fulbright originally supported Kennedy's and Johnson's policies in Southeast Asia, leading the Senate in support of the Tonkin Gulf Resolution in 1964. However, in 1966, disenchanted with the rise of American military involvement and casualty rates, Fulbright chaired the Foreign Relations Committee in a long public hearing on American foreign policy in Southeast Asia. Recanting his former defense of American policy there, he continued as a formidable adversary to Johnson's and Nixon's alleged abuse of presidential power.
See also Vietnam War.
Consult (VIII) Coffin, 1966; Fulbright, 1964, 1967.

FULL EMPLOYMENT ACT (1946), effort to provide jobs for all who were able to work. *See* Welfare Legislation.

FULLER, MARGARET (1810–1850), author, journalist, teacher, feminist, and transcendentalist who achieved an international reputation as a literary critic. A precocious child, she received a rigorous classical education from her father and in her youth formed friendships with leading New England intellectuals, including Ralph Waldo Emerson and William Ellery Channing.

In 1836 she taught in a school run by utopian transcendentalist Bronson Alcott and then (1839–1844) conducted "conversations" attended by transcendental-minded Bostonians, including many women. She also served as editor of *The Dial* (1840–1842), a transcendentalist journal, along with Emerson and George Ripley, and from 1844 to 1846 worked as literary critic for Horace Greeley's New York *Tribune*. Her important feminist tract, *Woman in the Nineteenth Century* (1845), expressed in transcendental terms woman's claim to intellectual equality.

In 1846 Fuller went abroad as the *Tribune*'s foreign correspondent and supported the Italian patriot Guiseppe Mazzini in the Roman Revolution of 1848. In Italy, she married a young Roman nobleman, Giovanni Angelo, Marchese d'Ossoli, by whom she had had a child. The family died in a shipwreck while returning to the United States.
See also Transcendentalism.

FULLER, MELVILLE W(ESTON) (1833–1910), 7th Chief Justice of the Supreme Court

(1888–1910). Born in Augusta, Maine, Fuller was admitted to the bar in 1855 and in 1856 began private practice in Chicago, where he became noted for astute handling of difficult cases. He was soon involved with politics and was a delegate to the 1862 Illinois Constitutional Convention before becoming a member of the state legislature.

The appointment of Fuller as chief justice in 1888 by President Cleveland caused an uproar because Fuller lacked national prominence. During Fuller's term the Supreme Court's popular esteem rose through his skill in assigning cases for opinions, promoting compromises, and discouraging bitter dissents.

Fuller, a Democrat and a religious man, developed a deep friendship with Oliver Wendell Holmes, Jr., a Republican and skeptic. Fuller favored strict construction of the Constitution, whereas Holmes, in dissents, developed new interpretations. As chief justice, Fuller left no significant opinions of his own; his most important decision was rendered in *Pollock v. Farmers' Loan and Trust Company* (1895), which held the Income Tax Act of 1893 unconstitutional.

FULTON, ROBERT (1765–1815), American engineer, artist, and inventor of the steamboat. Born in Pennsylvania, Fulton was a gunsmith during the Revolutionary War and then settled in Philadelphia, where he worked as a portrait painter and draftsman (1782–1786). He went abroad to live for 20 years, studied painting with the leading American artist in London, Benjamin West, and got to know engineers such as James Watt, inventor of the steam engine, who stimulated his interest in machines.

Fulton moved to Paris in 1794, and Robert R. Livingston, the U.S. ambassador there, became his patron. It was Livingston who encouraged Fulton to experiment with a steamboat on the Seine River in 1802. Fulton had already invented a variety of mechanical devices, including the double inclined plane for lifting canal boats, the power shovel for digging canals, a flax spinner, a rope twister, a marble saw, and various designs for cast-iron aqueducts and bridges, several of which were built successfully in England. An enthusiast of canals, Fulton published a *Treatise on the Improvement of Canal Navigation* in 1796.

In 1801 in Paris, Fulton invented a submarine, the *Nautilus*, which submerged successfully to about 25 feet but was not purchased by either the French or British government. Neither was his self-propelled submarine torpedo, on which he spent nine years of research and development.

In 1805 Fulton returned home to continue his steamboat experiments. In August 1807 his *Clermont*, a 150-foot, two-side-paddled boat powered by his friend Watt's steam engine, chugged up the Hudson River from New York to Albany and back in 62 hours. The *Clermont* was the first successful commercial steamboat, although other Americans, including John Fitch and James Rumsey, had experimented with steamboats in the 1790s with some success. Uncertain economic conditions, owing to President Jefferson's Embargo of 1807 and the European wars, delayed the coming of general steam navigation in the United States until after the War of 1812.

Fulton and Livingston were also entrepreneurs, and they gained a monopoly on steamboat navigation of New York's harbors and the Hudson River. This tight monopoly retarded growth, but the Supreme Court finally overturned their rights in the case *Gibbons v. Ogden* (1824) with the case against the monopoly ably argued by Daniel Webster. A massive growth of steamboat transportation in the East and the West then followed.

See also Gibbons v. Ogden (1824).
Consult (III) Lane, 1943.
—Peter d'A. Jones, *University of Illinois, Chicago Circle*

FUNDAMENTALISM, a conservative religious movement that developed among Protestants during the early twentieth century. Its objective was to maintain literal interpretations of the Bible and traditional doctrines of Christian faith in the face of liberal theology. The main points of fundamentalist doctrine include infallibility of the Scriptures, the Virgin birth, physical resurrection of Christ, the physical Second Coming of Christ, and the bodily resurrection of men.

Aggressive fundamentalism was particularly strong in the South and in agricultural areas during the 1920s. Fundamentalists also tried to dominate nationwide churches, including the Presbyterian, but this drive failed.

Fundamentalists flatly opposed the teaching of evolutionary theories. This became a national issue in the Scopes trial at Dayton, Tenn., in 1925. Clarence Darrow defended J. T. Scopes, a public school teacher, who was tried for teaching Darwinian theory, contrary to Tennessee state statute. William Jennings Bryan, fundamentalist leader, orator, and Democratic presidential candidate, upheld the fundamentalist viewpoint and won the case. Although convicted, Scopes was later released on a technicality.

See also Bryan, William Jennings; Darrow, Clarence.

FUR FRONTIER. *See* Frontier in American History.

FUR TRADE, a major source of wealth and income in colonial America that grew from the

Robert Fulton, inventor of the steamboat.

very first contacts between whites and Indians. Europeans came to North America seeking gold, but when they did not find it, some developed the lucrative fur trade, with the French starting the trade in the St. Lawrence River area after 1534—especially in the 1580s. The New England trade died out in the late seventeenth century, and as European weapons and advancing settlement cleared the woods of beaver and deer, the growing demand for furs drove men farther inland. Thus, the fur trade speeded up the exploration of the hinterland and hastened the destruction of the Indians.

In Canada the fur trade was particularly important for settlement, and the British created two rival companies, the Hudson's Bay Company (1670) and the North West Fur Company (1787). Quebec, and later Montreal, were the headquarters of the fur trade for the whole of the St. Lawrence, Great Lakes, and upper Mississippi regions until challenged by John Jacob Astor's rival American Fur Company after 1808. This midcontinental area supported a flourishing trade in furs for almost 200 years, from the midseventeenth to the midnineteenth century.

The West. As the animals were depleted in the East and as the economic revolution and settlement brought more people, the center of the fur trade moved to the Rocky Mountains. The explorations of Lewis and Clark (completed in 1806) in the Far West encouraged hordes of trappers and traders in the great Northwest. St. Louis became the gateway for the trade and dominated its organization for more than 30 years. Among the great fur-trading families in the city were the descendants of R. A. Chouteau (1749–1829), who had moved from New Orleans. He was an early founder of the town of St. Louis and in 1809 became a member of the Missouri Fur Company. The most famous Chouteau was Pierre, a nephew of the founder, who became wealthy on the Rocky Mountain fur trade and was a leading Western financier.

Astor pushed the trade to the Pacific Northwest, where the Russians had been settled, particularly in Alaska, for some time. He established Astoria in 1811, the first U.S. settlement on the northern Pacific coast. Western furs were sold directly to China and thus helped to open up the whole of the Pacific, leading to multilateral trade and the American settlement of Hawaii. The Rockies' trade peaked around 1840 and then died away. It was replaced by the mining frontier.

The fur trade involved Americans in disputes and sometimes wars with several nations, including the French and British, the many Indian nations, the Dutch, the Russians, and the Spanish. It drew immigrants into the heart of the continent and opened up the wilderness for economic development. But by

the midnineteenth century the trade was no longer of major economic significance.

See also Astor, John Jacob; Frontier in American History.

Consult (III) Billington, 1956; De Voto, 1947.

—Peter d'A. Jones, *University of Illinois, Chicago Circle*

GABRIEL'S SLAVE PLOT (1800), an abortive attempt to organize a slave uprising. The key figure was a slave named Gabriel Prosser, who proposed to lead several thousand slaves in an assault on Richmond, Va. A combination of black informants and adverse weather stopped the attempt and revealed the ringleaders, some 20 or 30 of whom were executed. The plot was particularly distressing to such Virginia leaders as Thomas Jefferson and James Monroe because it contradicted the ideals they had recently asserted in the American Revolution. Jefferson felt that colonization rather than execution ought to be the lot of the insurgents.

See also Slavery.

Consult (IX) Aptheker, 1969.

GADSDEN PURCHASE (1853), territorial acquisition from Mexico that was the first concrete product of the expansionist policies of President Franklin Pierce. Pierce hoped to unify the Democratic Party behind a program of aggressive foreign expansion, and when General Santa Anna rose to power again in Mexico and needed money, Pierce instructed James Gadsden, his minister to Mexico and a South Carolinian, to try to buy a large area south of the Rio Grande. Rebuffed in this effort, Gadsden in December 1853 agreed to buy for $15 million a smaller strip of land south of the Gila River in present-day Arizona and New Mexico. The area provided a good route for a southern railroad to California, a route demanded by certain railroad and land speculators.

Already furious at the Kansas-Nebraska bill, which was under debate, and at the apparent Southern domination of the Pierce Administration, antislavery senators denounced the treaty as an effort by slaveholders to expand the area open to slavery and by speculators to protect their investments. Their opposition forced a reduction in the size of the purchase to 45,535 square miles and in its price to $10 million, but they were unable to prevent the treaty's ratification in June 1854.

GAG RULE, popular name among Northerners for a House of Representatives measure passed in 1836 at the insistence of Southern congressmen. It required that petitions demanding antislavery action of Congress be "laid upon the table," meaning ignored, which transgressed constitutional privileges given citizens by the First Amendment. It was on this ground that ex-President John Quincy Adams, now a congressman, began his fight to have the rule rescinded.

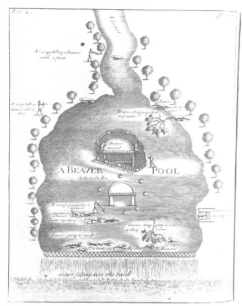

Fur trade stimulated interest in habits of beavers, as shown in this eighteenth-century illustration.

The gag rule was renewed at each session of Congress until 1840, when it became a standing rule (one that need not be renewed at each session). Adams' adroit and persistent challenge to it made it increasingly notorious. On Dec. 3, 1844, Adams' motion to end the gag rule won a House majority, which was considered a triumph for Northern opinion.

GALBRAITH, JOHN KENNETH (1908-), American economist. *See* Countervailing Power.

GALLATIN, ALBERT (1761-1849), Secretary of the Treasury under Presidents Jefferson and Madison. Born to a wealthy Swiss family, Gallatin was a young radical who left for America in 1780. A strong Jeffersonian, he entered politics and was elected to Congress in 1795. His brilliance was soon observed, and he became secretary of the treasury in 1801 and kept the job until he resigned in 1814 in order to go to Europe and negotiate the Treaty of Ghent that ended the War of 1812. Subsequently, Gallatin was U.S. ambassador to France (from 1816) and to Britain (from 1826).

In private life Gallatin was a successful land speculator and founder of a prominent New York bank. A cultured man, he pursued science and literary studies after his retirement from public life in 1827. He became the "father of American ethnology" through his major study of Indian linguistics and customs and his founding of the American Ethnological Society in 1842.

Evaluation. Gallatin's Treasury policies have sometimes been characterized as turning American policy away from Hamiltonian principles to those of Jefferson, but his policies did not differ from Hamilton's in any sharp way. In reality, he did as much to change the thinking of the Jeffersonians and to teach them the importance of the government's role in the economic life of a young, developing nation.

Gallatin is best known for his penetrating and forceful *Report on Roads and Canals* of 1808, which demanded large-scale and planned government intervention in the economy with federal aid for road and canal construction through land grants. It was a long-term plan for public investment unequaled in the United States until the twentieth century— but Congress did not go along with it.

Consult (III) Ferguson, 1967.
—Peter d'A. Jones, *University of Illinois, Chicago Circle*

GALLOWAY'S PLAN OF UNION, program to reform Britain's government of the colonies. *See* Continental Congress, First (1774).

GARFIELD, JAMES A(BRAM) (1831-1881), 20th President of the United States (1881). He was born in Cuyahoga County, Ohio, on Nov. 19, 1831. Garfield graduated from Williams College (1856), and when the Civil War broke out was an antislavery Republican serving in the Ohio senate. He raised a regiment and commanded it effectively, leaving the Union army with the rank of major general.

Elected to Congress in 1862, he served in the House (1863-1880), where his influence was rivaled only by that of James G. Blaine. Although touched several times by scandal, notably during the Crédit Mobilier revelations, Garfield was always reelected by his Republican district. Elected to the Senate early in 1880, he never served because of his dark horse nomination as Republican candidate for the presidency. Garfield had managed John Sherman's campaign through 35 fruitless ballots when the deadlocked convention drafted him.

Identified with Blaine's Half-Breeds, Garfield sought to ensure Republican unity by making Chester Arthur his running mate and by promising patronage to Roscoe Conkling's Stalwarts. The temporary allies defeated the Democrats' Winfield S. Hancock, but the appointment of Blaine as secretary of state, Garfield's desire for executive independence in appointments, and his intention of prosecuting the Star Route frauds led to party schism.

On July 2, 1881, Garfield was shot in Washington's railroad terminal by Charles Guiteau, a disappointed office seeker who shouted, "I am a Stalwart, and Arthur is President now." Garfield, the last president born in a log cabin, survived the summer but died of infection on Sept. 19, 1881, while recuperating in Elberon, N.J.

See also Arthur, Chester A.; Conkling, Roscoe; Crédit Mobilier; Stalwarts and Half-Breeds; Star Routes.

Consult (V) Smith, 1968.
—George Lankevich, *Bronx Community College of The City University of New York*

GARRISON, WILLIAM LLOYD (1805-1879), abolitionist leader responsible for introducing "immediatism"—the call for an immediate rather than a gradual end to slavery—into the emancipation movements. Born in Newburyport, Mass., Garrison entered journalism as a boy. By 1828, he was associated in the antislavery cause with Benjamin Lundy, but Garrison soon adopted a more radical stance toward slave owners, which caused him to be imprisoned for libel.

In 1831 Garrison founded the *Liberator*, a militant antislavery newspaper, to promote the abolitionist cause. The next year he set up the New England Anti-Slavery Society, which had few members initially but in time attracted such brilliant co-workers as Wendell Phillips, Lydia Maria Child, and Frederick Douglass.

Garrison was given no special position when the American Anti-Slavery Society was

Albert Gallatin, in 1805 portrait by Rembrandt Peale.

James A. Garfield, 20th President of the United States (1881), with daughter Mollie.

Crusader William Lloyd Garrison, one of the most prominent abolitionists in the North.

Marcus Garvey promoted black nationalism and pride in African heritage.

organized in 1833, and his followers tended to be more radical than those of Theodore D. Weld and Lewis Tappan. Increasingly through the 1830s, the Garrisonians were viewed with disapproval by other abolitionists because of their bitter criticism of institutional religion and of the federal government as proslavery and because of their insistence upon equal status for women in the abolitionist movement. In 1840 the moderates left to form the American and Foreign Anti-Slavery Society, and although Garrison remained the nominal head of the old society, it had little further influence.

Garrison was apparently overshadowed by leaders of the Liberty and Free-Soil parties in the 1840s, but in fact he continued to scandalize Northern audiences. In 1854 Garrison attained additional national notoriety when he burned a copy of the Constitution at a meeting in Framingham, Mass., on July 4.

The coming of the Civil War gave him the status of hero, but later historians and biographers continued to differ on his merits. After 1865, when the *Liberator* was discontinued, Garrison concerned himself with other reform movements, especially women's suffrage and temperance.

See also Abolitionism; American Anti-Slavery Society; Emancipation Movements.

Consult (IV) Nye, 1955.

—Louis Filler, *Antioch College*

GARVEY, MARCUS (1887-1940), black leader who is generally regarded as the father of modern black nationalism. From 1919 to 1925 he led more than 1 million blacks in a loosely organized international movement whose main purpose was the creation of an independent black nation in Africa.

Garvey, who believed that blacks and whites could not live together harmoniously, organized the Universal Negro Improvement Association (UNIA) in 1914 in his native (British) Jamaica. UNIA's slogan—"One Aim, One God, One Destiny"—symbolized the organization's goals of blacks' separation from whites, appreciation of their own racial heritage, and redemption of mother Africa from European colonialism.

In 1916 Garvey moved UNIA's headquarters to Harlem in New York City. The flamboyant and charismatic Garvey was particularly popular among poor urban blacks. Thousands of them bought shares in Garvey's most ambitious economic scheme, the Black Star Line, which was to provide a fleet of ships to carry blacks back to Africa, to establish triangular trade among blacks in the United States, the West Indies, and Africa, and to generate capital for other black enterprises. The Black Star Line's failure in 1922 contributed to Garvey's decline and UNIA's collapse. Most black leaders, led by the

NAACP's W. E. B. Du Bois, began calling Garvey a charlatan. In 1923 Garvey was convicted of mail fraud, and after his appeal failed (1925) he was imprisoned until he was pardoned by President Coolidge in 1927. He was then deported and never returned to the United States, although he continued to work for African independence. UNIA never regained its strength, and Garvey died in London without having seen Africa.

See also Blacks in the United States.

Consult (IX) Cronon, 1955; Vincent, 1971.

—Sheldon Avery, *The Johns Hopkins University*

GASPEE INCIDENT (1772), conflict indicative of the growing antagonism between the colonists and British authorities. On the night of June 9, 1772, a party of 64 men boarded the British customs schooner *Gaspee,* which had run aground at Namquit Point, near Providence, R.I. Led by the merchant John Brown, the attackers burned the vessel after putting ashore its commander and crew. On August 26, a royal proclamation offered a reward for information and established a five-man commission of inquiry to discover the culprits and send them to England for trial. Rhode Island's hostile population proved uncooperative, and the unsuccessful board adjourned in June 1773.

GATT. *See* General Agreement on Tariffs and Trade (GATT).

GAY LIBERATION, homosexual movement to gain legal equality. After confrontations between homosexuals and New York City police in 1969, two leading homosexual organizations (the Mattachine Society, for men, and the Daughters of Bilitis, for women) formed the Gay Liberation Front (GLF). They demanded complete equality in public and private hiring practices, the overthrow of state sodomy laws, the legalization of private sexual behavior between consenting adults, and an end to police harassment.

GEMINI SPACE FLIGHTS. *See* Space Exploration.

GENERAL AGREEMENT ON TARIFFS AND TRADE (GATT), accord negotiated in Geneva by 23 nations to lower customs tariffs and to reduce other restrictions. It went into effect in 1948. GATT members, which include the world's major noncommunist industrial nations, meet at least once a year at their headquarters in Geneva.

GATT calls for reciprocal rights and duties and sets rules for fair trading. It provides for equal treatment in the application of import and export taxes. Under GATT a country may protect domestic interests through customs tariffs but not through import quotas. Quotas can, however, be imposed for such purposes as redressing balance of payments.

GATT talks that began in 1963 and ended in 1967 led to a further reduction of trade barriers. Agreements were reached providing concessions valued at $40 billion over a period of five years. These talks, known as the "Kennedy Round," undertaken after the adoption of the U.S. Trade Expansion Act of 1962, enabled the president to reduce any existing tariff by as much as 50 percent.

GENERAL FEDERATION OF WOMEN'S CLUBS, organization of women's suffrage groups. *See* Suffrage, Women's.

GENERAL ORDER NO. 20 (1847), order issued by Gen. Winfield Scott to prevent war atrocities. *See* Mexican War.

GENERAL THEORY, principal statement of John Maynard Keynes' economic philosophy. *See* Keynes, John Maynard.

GENTLEMEN'S AGREEMENT (1907), tacit understanding between the United States and Japan to limit Japanese immigration into the United States. Anti-Japanese sentiment was running high, especially in California and the Western mine fields, when President Theodore Roosevelt proposed that the Japanese should voluntarily limit the emigration of laborers to the United States in exchange for his efforts to put an end to discrimination against the Japanese already in America. He personally felt that the racial feelings of the white majority on the Pacific Coast were "as foolish as if conceived by the mind of a Hottentot," and he honored the bargain through a series of diplomatic notes and by exertion of political pressure. The agreement was ended in 1924 by an act of Congress that prohibited Japanese immigration.

See also Immigration; Roosevelt, Theodore.

Consult (V) Bailey, 1934.

GEORGE, HENRY (1839–1897), journalist, economist, and reformer. Born in Philadelphia, his formal education ended at 14, and for the next several years he drifted from job to job—errand boy, sailor, typesetter, editor.

In 1865 George was converted to the cause of free trade, afterward a central tenet in his economic theories. Visiting New York in 1868, he was struck by the "shocking contrast between monstrous wealth and debasing want," by the seeming dictum that progress entailed poverty. He began to formulate his economic theory of land value in observing the effect of railroad expansion in California—increases in population brought increases in land value, raising rents for those who worked

the land and pushing them toward the poverty level. He published *Our Land and Land Policy* in 1871 and greatly expanded on the theory in *Progress and Poverty* (1879), which also included his solution, the Single Tax, to be based on land.

Progress and Poverty made George's reputation as a reformer. Single Tax Clubs, or Land Labor Clubs, were formed throughout the nation in support of his proposals. He moved to New York in 1880 and ran for mayor in 1886 as the candidate of labor and reformers and placed second; in 1897 he ran for mayor a second time but died five days before the election.

See also Single Tax.

—Robert W. Cherny, *California State University, San Francisco*

GEORGIA, colony and state first explored by the Spanish conquistador Hernán De Soto as early as 1540. Georgia was, nevertheless, a late British colony. The region was part of the Carolina grant of 1663, but in 1732 the Crown granted Georgia to a group of philanthropists and prison reformers in order to establish a refuge for debtors. It was hoped that the grant, which was for 21 years, would attract settlers, who would serve as a useful buffer against Indians and Spanish in the South.

James Oglethorpe, Viscount Perceval, and Dr. Thomas Bray were the principal organizers of Georgia, which was named after George II. Oglethorpe arrived at Charleston with 116 debtors in 1733 and founded Savannah. His settlement was open to all religions except Roman Catholicism, and it attracted Austrian Lutheran refugees, Germans, Moravians, and Scots. Oglethorpe was friendly to the local Creek Indians and honored his agreements with them. The utopian community was kept alive only by gifts and grants from Parliament, however.

Although the fear of Spanish attack subsided after the victory of the colonists at the Battle of Bloody Marsh (1742), Oglethorpe left the colony, and it did not thrive. It was organized as a benevolent despotism, and its paternalistic regulations did not encourage economic growth. Slavery was forbidden until 1750, as was the rich rum trade. When the charter expired in 1753, Georgia contained only about 3,000 settlers, 1,000 of them black. Georgia became a crown colony in 1753, and 10 years later its southern boundary with Florida was determined. Thereafter, the colony was no longer an open frontier area. Its present shape was fixed in 1802.

Pushed by the fear of Indian and Spanish attacks, Georgia was eager to accept the U.S. Constitution, and it was the first Southern state to ratify it (Jan. 2, 1788, by unanimous vote).

The legislature is bicameral, and the

Henry George

capital is Atlanta. The population in 1970 was 4,589,575.

See also Oglethorpe, James Edward.
—Peter d'A. Jones, University of Illinois, Chicago Circle

GERMANTOWN, BATTLE OF (1777), unsuccessful attempt by General Washington to drive General Howe away from Philadelphia. See Revolutionary War Battles.

GERRY, ELBRIDGE (1744-1814), an important Massachusetts statesman, politician, and 4th Vice-President of the United States. Elected to the General Court in 1772, he was committed to the patriot cause and became a close ally of Sam Adams. He was a member of the Second Continental Congress in 1776 and signed the Declaration of Independence.

He actively participated in the war effort, helping to set up prize courts, overseeing Continental finances, and obtaining supplies for the Army. Appointed a delegate to the Constitutional Convention of 1787, he played an important role in the proceedings but refused to sign the final document because he did not believe it was consistent with republican theory. He served as a representative to Congress for two terms (1789-1793) and then retired.

During the political battles of the 1790s he managed to stay on good terms with both Thomas Jefferson and John Adams, and in 1797 the latter sent him on the ill-fated mission, along with John Marshall and Charles Cotesworth Pinckney, that resulted in the XYZ Affair. Because he remained in France after the others left, he was denounced by the Federalists as excessively pro-French. He then moved into the Republican Party and several times ran unsuccessfully for governor of Massachusetts. He finally won in 1810 and was reelected in 1811.

His administrations have become famous for the changes that were made in the state's senatorial districts. The changes were designed to consolidate Federalist strength in a few areas, while making sure that the rest of the state would go to the Republicans. Because one of the newly designed districts looked liked a salamander, the procedure was dubbed "Gerrymander" by the Federalists. In 1812 he was elected vice-president on the Republican ticket with James Madison. He died in office two years later.

See also XYZ Affair.
—Richard E. Ellis, University of Virginia

GERRYMANDER, deliberate shaping of election districts in an unfair manner. See Gerry, Elbridge.

GETTYSBURG (JULY 1-3, 1863), pivotal battle

Elbridge Gerry's artful redistricting while governor of Massachusetts led to the coining of the term "gerrymander" for partisan political districting.

of the Civil War, resulting in Robert E. Lee's withdrawal to Virginia. See Civil War Battles.

GETTYSBURG ADDRESS, carefully prepared speech delivered by President Lincoln on Nov. 19, 1863, at a ceremony dedicating the Gettysburg National Cemetery.

"Four score and seven years ago, our fathers brought forth upon this continent, a new nation conceived in Liberty, and dedicated to the proposition that all men are created equal.

"Now we are engaged in a great civil war, testing whether that nation, or any nation so conceived, and so dedicated, can long endure. We are met on a great battlefield of that war. We have come to dedicate a portion of that field, as a final resting place for those who here gave their lives, that that nation might live. It is altogether fitting and proper that we should do this.

"But, in a larger sense, we cannot dedicate—we cannot consecrate—we cannot hallow this ground. The brave men, living and dead, who struggled here, have consecrated it far above our poor power to add or detract. The world will little note, nor long remember, what we say here, but it can never forget what they did here. It is for us, the living, rather, to be dedicated here to the unfinished work which they who fought here have thus far so nobly advanced. It is rather for us to be here dedicated to the great task remaining before us—that from these honored dead we take increased devotion to that cause for which they gave the last full measure of devotion—that we here highly resolve that these dead shall not have died in vain—that this nation, under God, shall have a new birth of freedom—and that government of the people, by the people, for the people, shall not perish from the earth."

This is Lincoln's most eloquent, succinct statement of the Northern cause and his most moving tribute to the Union dead. The President shunned any suggestion of vengeance, hatred, or vindictiveness.

Scholars consider this speech "one of the noblest prose-poems of the language," and contemporaries (legend to the contrary notwithstanding) also appreciated its remarkable qualities. Harper's Weekly called it "as simple, and felicitous, and earnest a word as was ever spoken."

See also Lincoln, Abraham.
Consult (IV) Nevins, 1964.

GHENT, TREATY OF (1814), agreement that ended the War of 1812. The final negotiations to end the war began at Ghent, Belgium, in August 1814. The negotiators for the United States were John Quincy Adams, James Bayard,

Henry Clay, Albert Gallatin, and Jonathan Russell and, for Britain, Admiral Lord Gambier, William Adams, and Henry Goulburn. The British hoped that successful invasions of the United States in 1814 would enable them to insist on major territorial concessions from the United States, but the failure of the attacks on Baltimore and from Canada convinced the British that they should agree to a settlement. On their part the Americans, with the country almost bankrupt and Washington in flames, were eager for peace.

The Treaty of Ghent was signed on Dec. 24, 1814. It was essentially an agreement to stop fighting because neither side made concessions. All territory taken during the war was restored, and there was no mention of the problem of neutral rights that had done so much to start the war. It was agreed that commissioners from each country would attempt to settle boundary problems along the Canadian-American border.

See also War of 1812.
Consult (III) Engelman, 1962.

GHETTO, a segregated section of a city inhabited by minority groups. Historically the term usually referred to the ghettos in European cities where the law forced Jews to live. In the United States the term has been applied to slums in which immigrants and now blacks and other minorities have been crowded by de facto segregation rather than by legal barriers.

Statistical investigations suggest that for many newcomers to the urban scene, especially prior to 1880, when the so-called new immigration from southern and eastern Europe took hold, the central cores of American cities never figured as an element in the formation of ghettos. Instead, immigrants often found themselves widely dispersed, many times settling in small clusters in peripheral locations. As for those whose lives were actually focused in the ghetto, the data point to relatively brief residence in the innermost neighborhoods before they moved outward to more desirable, less congested zones. Nor is it altogether accurate to conceive of largely homogeneous ghetto arrangements, inasmuch as those communities tended to attract diverse ethnic and racial mixtures. Much of the evidence, in fact, tends to belie the traditional sociological axiom of the urban ghetto's unique function in the assimilative process.

Black Ghettos. The black experience in the ghetto, of course, demands differentiation from that of the white population. Until the Civil War, urban blacks did not encounter highly concentrated residential arrangements in Northern cities. With the beginnings of the massive migration to urban centers in the late nineteenth century, the ensuing congestion further exacerbated city life. Ironically, as well as tragically, in modern times the black dominance of the urban cores has resulted in the suburbanization of society's cultural and economic institutions, thus serving to perpetuate "the enduring ghetto."

See also Blacks in the United States; City; Urbanization.
Consult (V) Osofsky, 1971; Ward, 1971; Woods and Kennedy, 1969.
—Michael H. Ebner, *City College of The City University of New York*

GI BILL provided educational benefits for servicemen after World War II. *See* Education.

GIBBONS V. OGDEN (1824), Supreme Court decision. Gibbons, a steamboat operator in New York, was sued by Ogden, who had succeeded to the steamboat monopoly originally granted to Robert Fulton and Robert Livingston. In ruling against Ogden the Court availed itself of an opportunity to enhance and consolidate national power over commerce. The Constitution had specifically granted Congress the power to regulate commerce, and Chief Justice Marshall interpreted "commerce" broadly and further held that there were no limitations on the commerce power other than those specifically found in the Constitution.

GILBERT, HUMPHREY, late sixteenth-century English explorer. *See* Exploration and Discovery.

GILDED AGE, THE (1873), novel by Mark Twain and Charles Dudley Warner that describes a vulgar generation of Americans obsessed with wealth and power. It implied that materialism was corrupting America's political, economic, and moral life. The term "Gilded Age" is now applied to that period of economic upheaval and political immorality following the Civil War.

GLASS-STEAGALL ACT (1933), also known as the Banking Act of 1933, legislation passed during the Hundred Days. President Roosevelt had closed all banks immediately upon assuming office and had obtained temporary legislation, the Emergency Banking Act, to permit the Treasury to assist in the judicious reopening of the most stable banking houses.

The Glass-Steagall Act was meant to prevent banking crises and lack of confidence in banks. It separated commercial banking from investment banking—banks could not use Federal Reserve resources and depositors' funds for speculation—and established the Federal Deposit Insurance Corporation to insure individual deposits. Glass-Steagall was only the first of a series of banking and investment reforms under the New Deal.

See also Hundred Days; Securities Exchange Act (1934).
Consult (VI) Pecora, 1939.

Arthur Goldberg's varied public career included cabinet officer, Supreme Court justice, and ambassador to the United Nations.

Solitary prospector searches for alluvial gold.

GOLDBERG, ARTHUR (JOSEPH) (1903–), American lawyer, associate justice of the Supreme Court, and diplomat. He was born in Chicago the youngest of eight children of Russian Jewish immigrants. He was admitted to the Illinois bar in 1923 and practiced law in Chicago. During World War II he served in the Office of Strategic Services.

In 1948 Goldberg became general counsel for the Congress of Industrial Organizations (CIO) and the United Steelworkers of America. He was an important figure in the AFL-CIO merger in 1955. He was appointed secretary of labor by President Kennedy in 1961. The next year Kennedy appointed him to the Supreme Court to succeed Justice Felix Frankfurter. Goldberg was identified with the more liberal members of the Court.

In 1965, President Johnson persuaded Goldberg to give up his Supreme Court seat and appointed him U.S. representative to the United Nations, succeeding Adlai Stevenson. At the United Nations, Goldberg was instrumental in solving monetary problems and, as president of the Security Council, helped to begin the negotiations that led to a cease-fire in the India-Pakistan War of 1965. He resigned his post in 1968 and entered a New York City law firm. In 1970 he was the unsuccessful Democratic candidate for governor of New York.

Consult (VIII) Moynihan, 1966.

GOLD CORNER (1869), attempt by Jay Gould and his associates to corner, or control, the gold market. *See* Black Friday; Gould, Jay.

GOLDEN HILL, BATTLE OF, clash in 1770 between British troops and New Yorkers protesting the Quartering Act. *See* Quartering Act (1765).

GOLD RUSHES, feverish races to find gold that began after gold was struck in the millrace of John A. Sutter's ranch in the Sacramento Valley of California in January 1848. President Polk brought public attention to the discovery in his farewell message of December 1848, and a mad gold rush followed in 1849. Thousands of Mexican War veterans and adventurers made their way to California. Ships were diverted off their courses to go to San Francisco; tall, unwieldy river steamboats made the perilous journey around the horn of South America; wives were abandoned and jobs deserted.

In one year about 80,000 gold-seekers moved to California, and the state entered the Union in 1850 with an estimated population of 100,000. The Forty-Niners were wild and unruly. Uncontrolled robbery, murder, and violence led the citizens to take the law into their own hands with lynch mobs and vigilante committees. Gamblers and prostitutes rushed in to live off the transient population, and

price-gouging for simple commodities such as eggs and bread produced hyperinflation. Few found gold, however, and the rush soon spent itself. Sutter, a Swiss-German immigrant who had previously built himself a small empire in the coastal trade and ranching, was totally ruined by the rapacity of the Forty-Niners, who trampled his land, looted, stole his cattle, and left him penniless. He died in 1880 in Pennsylvania a broken man.

Later Strikes. The California rush led to the opening up of the Rocky Mountain region to gold-, silver-, and other miners. The western Sierras were soon dotted with mining camps, and during the next 15 years various gold rushes came with new strikes in Colorado, Nevada, Arizona, and Idaho. Enough migrants stayed behind to form the Territory of Jefferson in 1859 with a population of about 35,000—admitted as the state of Colorado in 1876. Silver was also discovered in the Utah Territory in 1859. The richest of Western strikes, this Comstock Lode brought in sufficient settlers to establish Nevada as a state within five years (1864).

The life of the mining frontier was a repetition of the early experience of San Francisco, the richest strikes leading to the rapid growth of shanty towns with false fronts, sometimes an ornate "opera house," many bars, and gambling dens. They are the ghost towns now visited by tourists, and the former battlegrounds of characters such as Wild Bill Hickock and Calamity Jane, the crack horsewoman and sharpshooter.

The Black Hills gold rush of 1875 was one of the last in the American West, but in 1897–1898 Alaska reproduced the whole scene with the Klondike stampede. The Trail of 1898 can still be hiked from Skagway, Alaska, up to the Yukon Territory in northwestern Canada. Many men died on that trek and, as with the other gold rushes, few found wealth.

Consult (III) Paul, 1963.

—Peter d'A. Jones, *University of Illinois, Chicago Circle*

GOLDWATER, BARRY M(ORRIS) (1909–), a leader of the Republican conservatives, presidential candidate against Lyndon Johnson in 1964, and U.S. senator from Arizona. He was born in Phoenix and entered his family's department store business in 1929, becoming its president in 1937 and chairman of the board in 1953. He served in the Army Air Force from 1941 to 1945.

He entered state politics in 1950 and was elected to the Senate in 1953. In Washington, Goldwater became known as spokesman for the conservative wing of his party. Although he advanced no legislative program of his own, he established as his objectives total victory over world communism and the reduction of federal authority in all matters except military preparedness and control of trade unions. His *Conscience of a Conservative* (1960) , *Why Not Victory?* (1962), and *Where I Stand* (1964) reached millions of readers. He is a popular speaker and a successful fund raiser.

In the presidential campaign of 1964 he led many to believe that if elected he would swing the nation drastically to the right. Supported by some Southern Democrats but not by liberal Republicans, he lost to Johnson in a landslide. In 1968 he was reelected to the Senate.

GOMPERS, SAMUEL (1850-1924), labor leader. Born in London the son of a cigar maker, he migrated with his family to New York City in 1863. In 1864 he joined the Cigarmakers Union and became its president in 1874.

Believing that labor unity was necessary to counter the increasing power and aggressiveness of employers, Gompers, together with Adolph Strasser, was responsible for founding the Federation of Organized Trade and Labor Unions of the United States and Canada (1881), which was subsequently reorganized as the American Federation of Labor (AFL) (1886). Gompers was elected the first president of the new labor organization and, except for 1895, held the office until his death. Under his direction the AFL was committed to craft unionism and the autonomy of the national unions.

Although well read in the socialist school, Gompers adopted a completely pragmatic approach to labor's problems, believing that organized labor must first accept the capitalist system and then secure for itself as a legitimate reward a greater share of capitalism's profits. Direct political activity would be avoided, and labor would rely instead on its own moral and economic power to achieve its objectives through collective bargaining.
See also American Federation of Labor; Labor Movement.
Consult (V) Gompers, 1934; Mandell, 1963.
—*Seddie Cogswell, California State University, San Francisco*

GOOD FEELINGS, ERA OF. *See* Era of Good Feelings.

GOOD NEIGHBOR POLICY, new approach to Latin America formally inaugurated by President Franklin D. Roosevelt. It was aimed at reducing tension and mutual suspicion between the United States and its southern neighbors, conditions that were largely attributed to the policy of U.S. economic and political interventionism. FDR's Administration explicitly renounced the right of unilateral intervention. Instead, the United States was to employ peaceful means of settling disputes, to promote close economic ties, and to desist from the use of force to protect American

nationals. The Good Neighbor Policy was about the only distinguishable U.S. policy in the interwar years.
See also Latin American Conferences.
Consult (VI) Wood, 1961.

GORGES, SIR FERDINANDO (1566-1647), English soldier and colonial proprietor. He was knighted for his service against the French and was later made governor of Plymouth. His interest in American colonization began in 1605, and in 1606 he became a member of the Plymouth Company. Gorges was influential in outfitting three ships that sailed for Maine in May 1607. This settlement, known as the Popham Colony, was abandoned in 1608.

Gorges' interest persisted, and in 1620 the Plymouth Company obtained a grant to all the territory in North America lying between 40° and 49° north latitude. In 1623 Gorges and John Mason then procured a grant for the land lying between the Merrimac and Sagadahoc rivers, and further grants in 1629 and 1631 extended their territory into much of present-day New Hampshire and Maine. The two men expended considerable funds in establishing settlements, exploring the area, and developing the fur and fish industries.

These attempts at colonization and exploration brought disputes with the neighboring Massachusetts Bay Colony, but they were temporarily resolved in 1635 by a new division of the New England coastline by which Gorges acquired the province of Maine. Although Gorges placed his son Thomas as deputy governor of Maine, he lacked the finances to enforce obedience, and after his death Massachusetts seized his settlements in New Hampshire and Maine.
See also Maine; Massachusetts.

GOTTSCHALK, LOUIS MOREAU (1829-1869), American composer and musician. *See* Music.

GOULD, JAY (1836-1892), financier noted for his attempt to corner the gold market. While still in his teens, he entered the leather trade, and his success led him inevitably to Wall Street. A millionaire before he was 21, Gould lost his first fortune in the Panic of 1857 but learned the speculator's skills.

After the Civil War, Gould allied with James Fisk to win control of the Erie Railroad and then engaged Cornelius Vanderbilt's New York Central in "war." Both sides indulged in an orgy of bribery, stock market fraud, and judicial injunctions as they competed for control of the Hudson River Valley carrying trade. The attempt to corner the nation's gold supply on Black Friday 1869 was Gould's most notorious maneuver. After Fisk's murder in 1872, Gould was forced to resign as president of the Erie, leaving it a financial wreck.

In the 1870s, Gould's speculations in

Gold rushes created instant cities in the West but brought wealth to only a few.

AFL founder Samuel Gompers, head of the U.S. labor movement for 30 years.

Evangelist Billy Graham *(right)* receives congratulations from President Nixon in 1971.

Grangers worked secretly for farmers' interests.

Western railroads led Wall Street to avow, "His touch is death." Speculating in lines, such as the Union Pacific, that had been mismanaged, Gould showed genius at extracting millions from depleted stocks. He juggled control of half a dozen lines and by 1890 was reputed to own half the railroad mileage of the Southwest. He also owned most New York elevated lines and controlled Western Union. In his personal life, Gould was a devoted husband and an indulgent father of six. When he died of tuberculosis in 1892, this symbol of the evils of unrestricted capitalism left a fortune of more than $100 million.

See also Black Friday; Railroads; Vanderbilt, Cornelius.

Consult (V) Grodinsky, 1957.

—George Lankevich, *Bronx Community College of The City University of New York*

"GO WEST YOUNG MAN," phrase popularized by Horace Greeley. *See* Greeley, Horace.

GRAFLEY, CHARLES (1862-1929), American sculptor. *See* Sculpture.

GRAHAM, BILLY (WILLIAM FRANKLIN) (1918–), American evangelist. After his ordination as a minister of the Southern Baptist Church (1939) he graduated from Wheaton College (Illinois). During the next few years he turned to evangelism and, as he became known as a fiery speaker, began to attract large crowds.

He was thrust into national prominence in 1949 after having attracted an audience of more than 350,000 during an 8-week revival in Los Angeles. Through his organization he conducted evangelical crusades in most major U.S. cities, where the audiences were invited to "Decide for Christ." He has held revivals in Britain, Europe, the Far East, Australia and New Zealand, Africa, and the Holy Land. He was frequently invited by President Nixon to hold services at the White House. His books include *My Answer* (1960) and *World Aflame* (1965).

Consult (VIII) Pollock, 1966.

GRAND OHIO COMPANY. *See* Land Companies.

GRANGER MOVEMENT, a social, educational, economic, and political farmers' movement that grew out of the successes of the Patrons of Husbandry, a farm organization. The Patrons of Husbandry, popularly called "the Grange," was founded in 1867 as a social and educational organization for farmers. It grew rapidly in the early 1870s, feeding on agrarian economic distress. Grangers established cooperatives to buy or produce farm goods and to sell their crops.

Theoretically nonpartisan, the Grange provided a forum for political grievances, and

many Grangers became involved in local third parties seeking regulation of railroad rates and of businesses engaged in marketing farm products. Some Granger-related groups also endorsed currency inflation in the greenback debate. Their greatest political successes came in the upper Mississippi Valley.

Political activity bred dissension within the order, and bankruptcy of some cooperative enterprises brought the dissolution of local organizations, leading to a decline in Grange membership and activities in the late 1870s. The Greenback movement absorbed some state third parties. The Grange itself survived as a social, nonpolitical farmers' lodge.

See also Farmers' Alliances; Greenback Labor Party.

Consult (V) Buck, 1963.

GRANT, ULYSSES S(IMPSON) (1822-1885), General of the Armies and 18th President of the United States (1869-1877). The son of a tanner, Grant was born on April 27, 1822, in Point Pleasant, Ohio, and graduated from West Point in 1843. He served with distinction in the Mexican War and by 1853 was a captain, a rank then held by only five of his classmates. Lonely for his family, however, he began to drink.

Resigning from the Army (1854), Grant unsuccessfully tried a variety of endeavors, but when the Civil War erupted he was quickly appointed colonel, then brigadier general (1861). In February 1862, Grant captured Forts Henry and Donelson. Even near-disaster at Shiloh (April 1862) did not shake President Lincoln's confidence in Grant—"I can't spare this man, he fights." Lincoln's faith was rewarded when Grant took Vicksburg (July 1863), splitting the Confederacy. In late 1863 he was brought East as lieutenant general with orders to defeat Robert E. Lee. Grant's brilliant choice of subordinates and his tactics of attrition brought final victory at Appomattox (April 1865). Congress revived the rank of General of the Armies to honor him.

Grant supported Radical Reconstruction, and President Johnson believed Grant betrayed him in the controversy over Secretary of War Stanton's removal. The election of Grant as president in 1868 was probably inevitable once he agreed to nomination, and his plea "Let us have peace" swept the country. He easily defeated Horace Greeley to win reelection in 1872.

Presidency and Later Life. Grant believed that congressional actions represented the will of the people and that an executive's role was administrative—tenets that guaranteed a weak presidency. His Administration was run as an army headquarters, which led to autonomy, which in turn led to scandals such as Black Friday, Crédit Mobilier, and the Salary Grab. By defending friends who had abused his confidence, Grant's reputation suffered, although his own honesty was never questioned. His Administration ended inflation, funded the debt, resumed specie payments, and named the first Civil Service Commission.

After leaving Washington, Grant triumphantly toured the world (1877–1880). His last years were marred by business reverses and prolonged illness. Only his *Personal Memoirs* (1885) and a congressional pension saved his family from poverty. He died near Saratoga, N.Y., on July 23, 1885.

See also Black Friday; Civil War Battles; Crédit Mobilier; Salary Grab.
Consult (IV) Grant, 1894; Nevins, 1957.
—George Lankevich, *Bronx Community College of The City University of New York*

GREAT AWAKENING, revival of intense religious feeling that swept through the American colonies, reaching a peak in the 1740s. As early as 1726, Theodore J. Frelinghuysen stirred his Dutch Reform congregation to new spiritual fervor. In 1733 Jonathan Edwards, a brilliant and fiery theologian, inspired his congregation in Northampton, Mass., to believe ardently in the power of God and the depravity of man.

The religious fervor of the Great Awakening contrasted with the attitude of tolerance and skepticism that preceded it in most of the colonies in the early eighteenth century. Some Puritan churches taught Arminianism, which shifted the emphasis of religion from hell fire and predestination to the free will of the individual and the importance of a life of good works in order to assure salvation.

But under the leadership of Frelinghuysen, Edwards, and George Whitefield, who had great impact in the South and in frontier regions, the religious emotionalism of the Great Awakening spread rapidly. It continued into the Revolutionary period, taking various forms in different parts of the colonies and passing through many phases. It has been called a national movement in colonial history because it brought people from distant areas together to share, and frequently to dispute, new doctrines and concepts.

See also Colonial Religion; Edwards, Jonathan; Whitefield, George.
Consult (I) Ganstad, 1957; Sweet, 1942.

GREAT MIGRATION, influx of settlers into New England between 1629 and 1640. *See* Massachusetts.

GREAT NORTHERN RAILWAY. *See* Hill, James.

GREAT SWAMP FIGHT (1675), battle in which the colonists destroyed the effectiveness of the Narragansett Indians. *See* King Philip's War (1675–1676).

GREELEY, HORACE (1811–1872), newspaper editor and presidential candidate. Born in New Hampshire, Greeley came to New York as a young man intent on becoming a successful journalist. He gradually gained a following in New York during the late 1830s as editor of two Whig Party newspapers. When he established the New York *Tribune* in April 1841, it was an immediate success, and Greeley was on his way to becoming America's most influential midnineteenth-century journalist.

The *Tribune* set a new standard for journalism for the emerging, literate middle classes, emphasizing serious and reliable political reporting and thorough coverage of books and lectures. Restless and filled with energy, Greeley backed such assorted reforms as prohibition, labor unionization, women's rights (although not suffrage), and, ultimately, abolitionism. He immersed himself in a variety of projects and still found time to lecture and travel widely and edit his paper. His homespun wisdom ("Go West Young Man") won him a wide following in the North.

Greeley opposed any compromise on the slavery issue during the 1850s, and after the war began, he joined hands with the radical wing of the Republican Party to urge full emancipation and confiscation of Southern property. Although Greeley initially supported Ulysses S. Grant, a combination of political ambition and growing support for a liberal policy toward white Southerners led him to break with Grant in 1871. In the election of 1872, Greeley led a coalition of liberal Republicans and dispirited Democrats in a futile attempt to unseat Grant. Excoriated by Republicans as a turncoat, distrusted by Democrats for his earlier radicalism, Greeley went down in a smashing defeat. Within a month of the election, he was dead, discredited as a politician but mourned as one of the nation's greatest journalists.

See also Presidential Elections.
Consult (IV) Van Deusen, 1953.
—Dan T. Carter, *University of Maryland*

GREENBACK LABOR PARTY, political group that contested presidential elections between 1876 and 1888, drawing its strongest support from economically disadvantaged farmers.

The Greenbackers, known variously as the Independent or Independent National Party in 1876, as the Greenback Party in 1880, and as the Greenback, Greenback National, or Greenback-Labor Party in 1884, all had as their major policy proposal currency inflation through the medium of paper money (greenbacks). Debt-ridden farmers, hard hit by the deflation of the period, provided the bulk of

Ulysses S. Grant, 18th President of the United States (1869–1877), whose administration was marred by financial scandals.

Nathanael Green, one of the most successful patriot generals in the Revolutionary War.

Pioneer film maker D. W. Griffith interviews screen star Lillian Gish.

Greenback voters, who were never a significant force in national elections.

See also Farmers' Alliances; Free Silver; Populists.

GREENE, NATHANAEL (1742-1786), one of the most successful American generals in the Revolutionary War. A native of Rhode Island, he became the youngest brigadier general in the Continental Army in June 1775. Greene displayed logistical talent in gathering supplies for the siege of Boston and accompanied George Washington to New York in 1776. Fever forced him out of action before the Battle of Long Island in August 1776, but he soon assumed command of American troops in New Jersey. In this capacity Greene encouraged the retention of Fort Washington on Manhattan Island but his judgment proved incorrect, and on Nov. 16, 1776, the British captured the fort.

Greene redeemed himself by his able command of one of the two columns that attacked Trenton on Dec. 26, 1776. During Gen. William Howe's campaign against Philadelphia in 1777, Greene helped prevent the British from turning the Battle of Brandywine into a rout. In February 1778, Greene reluctantly accepted the post of quartermaster general; his strenuous efforts guaranteed that the Americans would not endure another experience such as Valley Forge.

Southern Actions. In October 1780, Washington sent Greene to command American operations in the South, a theater in which Greene exercised brilliant leadership. Together with Gen. Daniel Morgan, he inflicted heavy losses on General Cornwallis at Guilford Courthouse on March 15, 1781, and, despite a series of setbacks, by the fall of 1781 he managed to limit British control in South Carolina to the Charleston area. Greene returned to Rhode Island in triumph in 1783. He established a home near Savannah, Georgia, in 1785 on a confiscated estate that the state gave him. He died of sunstroke the next year.

See also Revolutionary War Battles.
Consult (II) Thayer, 1960.
—Thomas Archdeacon, *University of Wisconsin*

GREENVILLE, TREATY OF (1795), negotiated between the United States and the Indians of Ohio and Indiana, marked the temporary end of British and Indian efforts to keep American pioneers out of that area. Anticipating British aid against the Americans, the Indians fought intermittently with the frontiersmen from the late 1780s until 1794, when Gen. Anthony Wayne defeated them at the Battle of Fallen Timbers. In early 1795, Wayne dictated the Treaty of Greenville to the Indians. The accord stripped them of most of Ohio and much of Indiana, opened the region for settlement, and broke the alliance between the Indians and the British.

See also Fallen Timbers, Battle of (1794); Northwest Territory; Wayne, Anthony.

GREER, GERMAINE, militant feminist known for her pungent language; author of *The Female Eunuch* (1970). *See* Women's Liberation.

GRENVILLE, GEORGE (1712-1770), British official whose taxation policies angered the American colonies. He held a variety of political offices before being appointed first lord of the treasury and chancellor of the exchequer in April 1763. Anxious to relieve the burdened English taxpayer, Grenville decided that the Americans should pay the costs of maintaining British troops in North America to defend the colonies. In March 1764 he introduced the Sugar Act, which reduced the duties on West Indian products imported to America but also made more stringent the enforcement procedures, and in February 1765 he proposed the Stamp Act.

Grenville vigorously defended his policies against American attacks and voted against repeal of the Stamp Act in 1766. In 1767, Grenville again aided the British taxpayer by reducing the land tax, a maneuver that helped force Charles Townshend to propose his own program of colonial taxation.

See also Navigation Acts; Stamp Act (1765); Townshend Acts (1767).

GRIFFITH, D(AVID LEWELYN) W(ARK) (1857-1948), film producer and director who was the greatest pioneer in developing the movies. He had literary ambitions but drifted into the infant film industry, writing, acting, and later directing.

After considerable experimentation with new techniques of photography and production, Griffith brought out his masterpiece, *The Birth of A Nation* (1915). This film, more than three hours in length, combined all Griffith's technological innovations, including new uses of lighting and cutting. *Intolerance* (1916) was even longer and more daring. *Hearts of the World* (1918) incorporated war scenes actually filmed at the front. After these films, Griffith's projects became smaller and more sentimental, and the later reels were commercially unsuccessful.

Griffith led the way to modern filmmaking techniques with closer shots of actors and close-ups of faces; breaking the "one scene, one shot" tradition; and cutting away to simultaneous action, thus breaking the fixed audience viewpoint. In 1935 Griffith received a special Academy Award for his achievements as producer and director.

GRIMKE, SARAH (1792-1873) AND ANGELINA

(1805–1879), abolitionists and feminists. The sisters came from a prominent Anglican slave-owning South Carolina family. After leaving the South (Sarah moved to Philadelphia in 1821 and Angelina followed her in 1829), they joined the Quakers and soon turned their energies to the antislavery crusade. Both wrote abolitionist pamphlets in 1836, and Angelina became a worker for William Lloyd Garrison's American Anti-Slavery Society in New York.

Their abolitionist activism led the Grimké sisters to pioneer roles in the women's rights movement as well. Angelina gained notoriety by speaking against slavery to mixed audiences of men and women, an activity decried by the Massachusetts Congregationalist clergy in a "Pastoral Letter" of 1837. Sarah replied in a *Letter on the Equality of the Sexes and the Condition of Women* (1838), one of the first documents of the women's rights struggle. That same year, Angelina married abolitionist Theodore Weld, and the three noted abolitionists continued their antislavery work with petitions and publications and later became teachers. In 1868 the Grimké sisters acknowledged two mulatto nephews, then college students, and aided them in their careers.

See also Abolitionism; Weld, Theodore Dwight.

Consult (III) Lerner, 1967.

—Nancy Woloch, *Hebrew Union College*

GRISWOLD v. CONNECTICUT (1965), key birth control decision by the Supreme Court. *See* Abortion and Birth Control Laws.

GROVES, LESLIE R. (1896–1970), American general who directed the Manhattan Project. *See* Manhattan Project.

GUADALUPE HIDALGO, TREATY OF (1848), peace agreement that ended the Mexican War. Arranged by Nicholas P. Trist, chief clerk of the State Department, and Gen. Winfield Scott in February 1848, the treaty established the Rio Grande as the boundary of Texas and ceded New Mexico and Upper California to the United States. In return, the United States paid Mexico $15 million and agreed to assume Mexico's debts to American citizens (more than $3 million).

President Polk was displeased with the terms of the treaty, which did not bring the United States as much Mexican land as he believed it should have. Reluctantly, he submitted the treaty to the Senate for ratification, and it was accepted by a vote of 38 to 14.

See also Mexican War; Scott, Winfield.

Consult (III) Henry, 1950; Singletary, 1960.

GUILFORD COURTHOUSE, BATTLE OF (1781), American victory over British in North Carolina. *See* Revolutionary War Battles.

GULF OF TONKIN RESOLUTION, congressional resolution passed on Aug. 7, 1964, authorizing the president to "take all necessary measures to repel any armed attack against the forces of the United States" and "as the President determines to take all necessary steps, including the use of armed force, to assist any member or protocol state of the Southeast Asia Collective Defense Treaty requesting assistance in defense of freedom."

Requested by President Johnson, it marked a turning point in U.S. involvement in Vietnam. It came as a reaction to a report that North Vietnamese torpedo boats had attacked American ships on August 2 and 4, 1964, in the Gulf of Tonkin off the coast of Vietnam. Until the resolution, the United States had confined itself to an advisory role in South Vietnam, but using the resolution as evidence of congressional support, the U.S. role was expanded to include direct involvement by both ground and air forces.

See also Vietnam War.

Consult (VIII) Kahin and Lewis, 1969.

HAGUE PEACE CONFERENCES, held to limit the methods of warfare and to provide for the peaceful settlement of international disputes. The conferences were in The Hague, the Netherlands in 1899 and 1907. At the time, it was hoped that the conferences would make war unlikely—a hope shattered by the outbreak of World War I.

The first conference, called by Czar Nicholas II, was attended by 26 nations (including the United States); it prohibited the use of asphyxiating gases, expanding bullets, and bombing from balloons in warfare. In addition, it established the Hague Permanent Court of Arbitration, later replaced by the International Court of Justice, to settle international disputes. The second conference, attended by 44 countries, laid down rules for the humane treatment of prisoners of war. Other conventions included the need for a declaration of war before beginning hostilities, the rights and duties of neutral powers in war, and the nature of maritime warfare.

HALSEY, "BULL" (WILLIAM FREDERICK, JR.) (1882–1959), U.S. Navy admiral. He was born in Elizabeth, N.J., and graduated from the U.S. Naval Academy in 1904. By the end of World War I he had seen extensive service as a destroyer commander.

During World War II, Halsey served in the Pacific, where he took part in many important battles. As commander of the entire South Pacific area he led the forces that defeated the Japanese at the Battle of Guadalcanal. In No-

William F. Halsey, fleet admiral who played a vital role in Japanese defeat in the Pacific.

Secretary of the Treasury under George Washington, Alexander Hamilton was killed in a duel with Aaron Burr.

Patriot John Hancock, first man to sign the Declaration of Independence.

vember 1943 he was made a full admiral and was commander at the capture of Bougainville. He became fleet admiral in command of the Third Fleet in the Pacific in June 1944. The Japanese surrender was signed aboard Halsey's flagship, the *U.S.S. Missouri*, in Tokyo Bay on Sept. 7, 1945. Halsey retired from the Navy in April 1947 and became an airline vice-president.

See also World War II.
Consult (VII) Bryan, 1947.

HAMILTON, ALEXANDER (1755–1804), statesman, politician, economic theorist, and Founding Father of the first magnitude. Born and raised in the West Indies, he emigrated in 1773 to America, where he soon became involved in the Revolutionary movement. When fighting began, he formed an artillery company and so distinguished himself in the battle around New York City that he attracted George Washington's attention and became his aide-de-camp (1777–1781).

Although mainly a self-made man, Hamilton benefited greatly from the fact that he had married (1780) into the wealthy and influential Schuyler family. After the war he returned to New York City, where he rapidly established a reputation as a brilliant lawyer. He also entered politics, serving for a year (1782–1783) in the Continental Congress. During the 1780s he was a leader in the movement to create a strong central government, helping to organize and participating in the Annapolis Convention and the Constitutional Convention of 1787. Although he was critical of the Constitution because it left too much power with the states, he worked strenuously and successfully for its adoption and wrote most of *The Federalist Papers* in its behalf.

He was the first secretary of the treasury (1789–1795) under the new government and devised a fiscal policy for the country and an elaborate scheme of economic growth. This included the funding and assumption of national and state debts at face value (1790), a system of excise taxes, the establishment of the First Bank of the United States, and a *Report on Manufactures* (1791). These highly controversial measures were opposed by Jefferson and Madison, and during the 1790s Hamilton became a leader in the Federalist Party.

He resigned from the cabinet in 1795, returning to New York to practice law, but he still remained extremely active and influential in national politics. He openly broke with fellow Federalist President John Adams during the election of 1800, when Hamilton opposed making peace with France. He had begun work on rebuilding the Federalist Party when he died in New York City on July 12, 1804, from wounds suffered in a duel with Aaron Burr.

See also Annapolis Convention (1786); Bank of the United States, First; Constitutional Convention (1787); Federalist, The; Report on Manufactures (1791).
Consult (III) Miller, 1959; Stourzh, 1970.
—Richard E. Ellis, *University of Virginia*

HAMMER v. DAGENHART (1918), famous Supreme Court case often cited as typical of post-World War I federal government conservatism, in which the Court nullified a progressive era law passed by Congress to prevent child labor. The law prohibited from interstate commerce goods produced by children under 14 or by those 14 to 16 who worked excessive hours.

Federal action was necessary because Northern states that prohibited child labor suffered from competition with unregulated states. The Supreme Court asserted that if the federal government were permitted to legislate on purely state matters such as health, welfare, and police, our system of government would be "practically destroyed." By 1937, in a different era, the Supreme Court was reversing itself completely and permitting Congress to use the interstate commerce regulatory power to intervene in many "local" matters.

HAMPSHIRE COUNTY CONVENTION (1796), protest meeting that preceded Shays' Rebellion. *See* Shays' Rebellion (1786–1787).

HAMPTON ROADS CONFERENCE (1865), abortive Civil War peace conference held on Feb. 3, 1865, at Hampton Roads, Va. President Lincoln and Secretary of State Seward represented the North, while A. H. Stephens, R. M. T. Hunter, and John A. Campbell spoke for the South. Lincoln insisted that the Confederacy abandon the struggle, that the Union be restored, and that no retreat be made from the Emancipation Proclamation. The Southern delegates rejected this as "unconditional submission to the mercy of the conquerors."

The failure of the conference can in part be attributed to F. P. Blair, Sr., the mediator who had set it up. In preliminary discussions with Jefferson Davis, Blair had without authorization led the Confederate president to believe that the Union might agree to an armistice on terms short of surrender.

HANCOCK, JOHN (1737–1793), Massachusetts patriot leader. He became a prominent shipping merchant in Boston after his graduation from Harvard. A leader of the patriot cause, he was harassed by British officials, who illegally seized his sloop *Liberty* in 1768 for allegedly carrying smuggled wine.

Hancock won election to the Massachusetts General Court in 1769, became leader of the Boston town committee in 1770, assumed the presidency of the Provincial Congress in 1774, and also served as chairman of the Committee of Safety. General Thomas Gage, the British commander in America, excluded Hancock and Samuel Adams from his general amnesty offer on June 17, 1775. Hancock served as president of the Second Continental Congress from May 1775 until October 1777 and in this capacity signed his name to the Declaration of Independence large enough for George III to read without his eyeglasses. Hancock and Charles Thomson, the secretary of the Congress, were the only people who actually signed the document on July 4, 1776.

Hancock was a member of the Congress until 1780, when he was elected governor of Massachusetts, serving until 1785 and from 1789 until 1793. He was elected president of the Confederation Congress in November 1785, but illness prevented him from serving, and he resigned in May 1786. As president of the Massachusetts ratification convention in 1788, Hancock, at the suggestion of some Federalist associates, introduced a set of amendments that persuaded the delegates to accept the new U.S. Constitution.

See also Declaration of Independence (1776).

Consult (II) Allen, 1948.
—Thomas Archdeacon, *University of Wisconsin*

HAND, LEARNED (1872-1961), eminent jurist and long-term federal circuit judge noted for the clarity and perception of his opinions, which strengthened the development of public law. He was born in Albany, N.Y., to a family well known in the legal profession. An honor student at Harvard, he graduated in 1893 and obtained his degree at its law school in 1896. He began to practice in New York in 1897.

In 1909, Hand was made judge of the U.S. District Court for the Southern District of New York. In 1924 he was raised to the U.S. Circuit Court of Appeals. When he retired in 1951, he held a record of tenure for a federal judge. In addition to nearly 3,000 legal opinions his writings include *Bill of Rights* (1958) and *Spirit of Liberty* (1960). He was on the council of the American Law Institute. Although he never reached the Supreme Court and was limited in his jurisdiction, Hand was one of the best-known judges of his time, delivering important opinions on labor and maritime law, banking, and taxation. After his retirement he continued to sit on the bench and to write opinions.

HANNA, MARK (MARCUS A.) (1837-1904), Ohio businessman and political leader who had a major influence on President McKinley and also advised President Theodore Roosevelt. *See* McKinley, William; Roosevelt, Theodore.

HARD DRUGS. *See* Drugs (Hard).

HARDING, WARREN G(AMALIEL) (1865-1923), 29th President of the United States (1921-1923). He was born in Blooming Grove, Ohio, on Nov. 2, 1865. Harding, a newspaperman, was a product of Ohio small-town politics who rose to become president. He was nominated by the Republicans in 1920 and swept to victory on the dissatisfaction with Woodrow Wilson.

He has been dismissed as a handsome but dull-witted uncouth person, a passive tool of his wife's social ambitions and the manipulations of sleazy and corrupt businessmen and politicians who pretended to be his friends. Harding was, in fact, intelligent, and he exercised leadership. He succeeded in bringing an end to the agitations of the Wilson era and in laying a foundation for the business prosperity of the 1920s.

Adept in human relationships, he attempted (not too successfully) to mediate the industrial strife of the postwar era. His attorney general stopped federal government participation in the political persecution caused by the Red Scare. Harding ended American involvement in World War I and set up a relatively successful disarmament meeting, the Washington Armament Conference. His restorative and harmonizing efforts were what he had promised and what the voters seemed to want.

Most criticism of Harding was directed at the relations between business and his Administration. He stood for encouraging private investment by lowering government expenditures and reducing taxation, especially of the rich. By 1923 industrial prosperity was well launched, and the Republicans followed Harding's policies for many years. He was almost constantly in conflict with Congress, where progressive and farm representatives held a balance of power and wanted more governmental action.

Whatever Harding's abilities as a policy maker, as an administrator he had severe shortcomings. He and his appointees failed to enforce laws vigorously, from Prohibition to antitrust. He is perhaps best remembered for the series of scandals that marred his term in office, notably the Teapot Dome affair. His personal life was not unblemished either, and so he has not been considered a model president. Harding died of heart trouble in San Francisco on Aug. 2, 1923, probably mercifully spared criticism he could see coming.

See also Teapot Dome; Washington Disarmament Conference (1921-1922).

Consult (VI) Murray, 1969; Russell, 1968.
—John C. Burnham, *Ohio State University*

HARLAN, JOHN MARSHALL (1833-1911), an associate justice of the Supreme Court noted for his dissents in decisions upholding racial discrimination and segregation. He was named after the great Chief Justice, studied law, and

Warren G. Harding, 29th President of the United States (1921-1923), relaxes on the golf course.

was admitted to the Kentucky bar in 1858. Originally a Whig, he became active in the Know-Nothing Party and then moved over to the Unionist Party. Although he supported slavery and strict enforcement of fugitive slave laws, he joined the Union army when the Civil War broke out.

He returned to private practice in 1863 and entered local Kentucky politics, failing in gubernatorial bids in 1871 and 1875. His desire for black votes and his revulsion at terrorism helped to convert him to a pro-civil rights position.

Supreme Court. Harlan headed the Kentucky delegation to the 1876 Republican National convention, where his support for Rutherford B. Hayes led to Harlan's appointment to the Supreme Court in 1877. He served until his death and was the Court's outstanding liberal justice during his tenure. He was the only dissenter in the *Civil Rights Cases* (1883), which invalidated the Civil Rights Act (1875), and in the landmark *Plessy v. Ferguson* (1896), which established the separate-but-equal principle.

Harlan built his legal philosophy on an almost religious reverence for the Constitution and became known for his eloquent dissents. Aside from civil rights questions, Harlan was, for example, against weakening antitrust legislation. Harlan, considered one of the great justices, also influenced his grandson and namesake.

See also Harlan, John Marshall (1899-1971).

HARLAN, JOHN MARSHALL (1899-1971), an associate justice of the Supreme Court who was noted as the conservative conscience of an activist Court and for his strict adherence to prior judicial decision. Born into a distinguished legal family, Harlan was named for his grandfather, then an associate justice. He was admitted to the New York bar in 1925 and for more than 25 years enjoyed a successful Wall Street law practice.

Before his appointment to the Supreme Court, Harlan served briefly as an assistant U.S. attorney and was chief counsel to the New York State Crime Commission. However, his judicial views were mostly shaped while he was in a private practice that dealt primarily with corporate and antitrust cases. In 1954, President Eisenhower named Harlan to the U.S. Court of Appeals (Second Circuit) and less than a year later nominated him for the Supreme Court.

Supreme Court. Considered a "lawyer's judge," Harlan's opinions were extremely well researched and scholarly. In general, he dissented from the liberal philosophy of his colleagues although siding with the majority on civil rights issues. He also believed that the federal judiciary should not become involved in state and local problems. His conservative

Benjamin Harrison, 23rd President of the United States (1889–1893), in 1888 campaign poster.

philosophy was influential at a time when the majority would have been willing to assert judicial power over other branches of government.

HARLEM RENAISSANCE, also called the Black Renaissance and the New Negro Movement, a movement during the post-World War I period in Harlem (New York City), then the capital of black American intellectual life. Black artists—writers, poets, painters, and musicians—united to protest the quality of life for blacks in the United States. This was primarily a literary movement informally inaugurated by James Weldon Johnson with his publication *Fifty Years and Other Poems* (1917). The title poem commemorated the fiftieth anniversary of the Emancipation Proclamation. Other books soon followed—poems, novels, and essays—written by Langston Hughes, Countee Cullen, and others. *Crisis* and *Opportunity,* two periodicals, offered prizes to stimulate literary production among black writers and to encourage the younger ones.

Black musicians participated in the movement by turning to folk music as a source of material for composition and performance. The composers used poems by black poets in their songs. They employed the rhythms of black dances and the harmonies and melodies of the blues, as well as spirituals and jazz, in composed concert music.

HARPERS FERRY RAID (1859). *See* Brown, John.

HARRIS, JOEL CHANDLER (1848-1908), American author who was one of the local colorists. *See* Literature.

HARRISON, BENJAMIN (1833-1901), 23rd President of the United States (1889–1893). The grandson of President William Henry Harrison, he was born in North Bend, Ohio, on August 20, 1833. He moved to Indiana in 1854 and rapidly achieved success as a lawyer. He rose to brevet brigadier general during the Civil War. A staunch Republican, he supported Radical Reconstruction while building one of the most lucrative law practices in the Midwest.

Harrison's political career began in 1876, when he ran for governor of Indiana and lost. A majestic speaker, he was austere personally and never got along well with the Republican bosses. However, he became the titular leader of his state party, and in 1880 at a deadlocked national convention he led Indiana's switch to James A. Garfield. He refused a cabinet post in order to run for the Senate, where he supported civil service reform, conservation measures, and railroad regulation (1881–1887). He lost a reelection bid but was nominated for the presidency in 1888. He ran a front porch campaign, relying for victory on Republican machines, the veterans' vote, and business fear of Grover Cleveland's low tariff policy. After a vituperative and corrupt campaign, Cleveland won a popular majority, but Harrison won the electoral vote, 233 to 168.

Presidency and Later Life. Harrison's first Congress appropriated more than $1 billion, authorized a steel navy, purchased land for conservation, increased veterans' benefits, and passed the Silver Purchase Act and much pork barrel legislation. Harrison also signed the Sherman Antitrust Act. Yet by approving the prohibitive McKinley Tariff (1890), he reduced national income while increasing expenditures, thus bringing on the depression of 1893. He allowed Secretary of State Blaine complete freedom regarding Latin America and supported an imperialistic policy in the Pacific. Although renominated, he was defeated by Cleveland and resumed his successful law practice. He often spoke and wrote thereafter for humanitarian causes. He died in Indianapolis, Ind., on March 13, 1901.

See also Blaine, James G.; Cleveland, Grover; Presidential Elections; Tariffs.

Consult (V) Sievers, 1969.

—George Lankevich, *Bronx Community College of The City University of New York*

HARRISON, PETER (1716–1775), American architect. Born in England, he settled in 1740 in Newport, R.I., and joined his brother in farming and trade. With his brother, Peter moved in 1761 to New Haven, Conn., where he lived for the rest of his life.

It is not clear when or whether Peter Harrison received training in design and architecture. It is known that in 1745, during the war with France, he made maps of Cape Breton and of Newport, and in 1746 he assisted in the fortification of Newport. Between 1748 and 1763 he designed the Redwood Library in Newport, the basic structure of King's Chapel in Boston, the Brick Market in Newport, Christ Church in Cambridge, Mass., and the Touro synagogue in Newport. Except in the case of Christ Church, Harrison refused to take anything more than thanks for his services.

Harrison's buildings are considered exceptional for their purity of design and their monumental qualities. Critics have praised the manner in which he combined derivative elements with original details in a style that was highly distinctive in the colonial period.

See also Architecture.

HARRISON, WILLIAM HENRY (1773–1841), 9th President of the United States (1841). Born in Berkeley, Va., on Feb. 9, 1773, Harrison's career was associated primarily with the West. A veteran of various Indian wars in the 1790s, he was elected in 1799 as the Northwest Territory's delegate to Congress. He helped frame the land law of 1800, which reduced the minimum purchase of land from 640 to 320 acres and allowed payments to be spaced over a four-year period.

He resigned from Congress to serve as governor of Indiana Territory from 1800 to 1813. His most famous action as governor was to lead a militia force against an Indian encampment at Tippecanoe in 1811. Although the attack failed to destroy the Indian alliance under Tecumseh, Harrison gained lasting fame and a popular nickname, "Old Tippecanoe," from this battle. He was no more successful in the War of 1812 until he decisively defeated the British and their Indian allies on Oct. 5, 1813, at the Battle of the Thames, in which Tecumseh was killed. After the war Harrison moved to Ohio, which he represented in the House (1816–1819) and then the Senate (1825–1828).

Whig Politician. In the 1830s Harrison's political aspirations became entwined with the embryonic Whig Party. With little national cohesion, the Whigs ran three candidates for president in 1836, and, although he lost, Harrison, the favorite of various Western states as well as Whig–Anti-Masonic coalitions in Vermont and Pennsylvania, ran ahead of the other Whigs. Despite this showing, Henry Clay was initially the favorite for the Whig nomination in 1840, but various Whig politicians became convinced a general would be a more popular candidate than the congressional leader of the party. The backing of Pennsylvania's influential Anti-Masons, who balked at Clay (an old Mason), was especially crucial to Harrison's nomination.

The Whig "Log Cabin–Hard Cider" campaign of 1840 is famous because of the party's effort to arouse voters with populistic rhetoric, hoopla, free liquor, and catchy sloganeering such as "Tippecanoe and Tyler Too." They benefited just as much, however, from apparent Democratic responsibility for the Panic of 1837 and the subsequent depression. Moreover, the party was much better organized than in 1836. Harrison drubbed Van Buren 234 to 60 in the electoral vote, but the old general died of pneumonia on April 4, 1841, barely a month after his inauguration.

See also Presidential Elections; Tecumseh; War of 1812; Whig Party.

Consult (III) Green, 1941; Gunderson, 1957.

—Michael F. Holt, *Yale University*

HARTE, BRET (1836–1902), American author who was one of the local colorists. *See* Literature.

HARTFORD CONVENTION (1814–1815), convention to discuss national problems that met in Hartford, Conn., from Dec. 15, 1814, to Jan. 5,

William Henry Harrison, 9th President of the United States (1841) and grandfather of Benjamin Harrison.

Nathaniel Hawthorne, whose best-known work was *The Scarlet Letter.*

1815. The meeting grew out of the bitter opposition of many New Englanders to the War of 1812, which they considered a foolish conflict that ruined their commerce and aided Napoleonic France. At the suggestion of Massachusetts, delegates from Massachusetts, Rhode Island, and Connecticut, plus unofficial representatives from New Hampshire and Vermont, met in Hartford.

Although some delegates favored separation from the Union, the majority took a more 'moderate course and decided to recommend constitutional amendments to weaken the power of Southern states and the Democratic-Republican (Jeffersonian) Party. The suggested amendments were to allow Congress to make war, to restrict commerce, and to admit new states only when approved by two-thirds majorities in both houses of Congress. In addition, they wanted to make U.S. presidents ineligible for reelection, to abolish the three-fifths compromise by which slaves could be counted for congressional representation (which gave the South great influence), to prohibit embargoes of more than 60 days, and to forbid foreign-born citizens from being members of Congress or from holding civil office under federal authority. Any hope that the convention might have had of carrying out its desires collapsed with the news that the war had ended.

See also War of 1812.

HARVARD COLLEGE. *See* Colonial Colleges.

HAT ACT (1732). *See* Navigation Acts.

HATCH ACT (1939), legislation forbidding federal employees (or state employees in federally funded programs) from participating actively in political campaigns and from using their official positions to coerce voters. Primarily the law was an attempt on the part of conservatives of both parties to prevent Franklin Roosevelt's Administration from using relief monies to influence elections. It specifically outlawed "pernicious" political activity on the part of government workers, but the meaning of that word has never been fully clear.

HAVANA CONFERENCE (1940). *See* Latin American Conferences.

HAWAII, the 50th state, joined the Union on August 21, 1959. Originally settled by Polynesians in the eighth century, the Hawaiian Islands were discovered in 1778 by England's Capt. James Cook, who named the island group the Sandwich Islands. White settlers came to the islands in 1820. A constitutional monarchy was established in 1840 and was replaced in 1893 by a provisional government controlled by American planters. Hawaii was declared a republic in 1894 and annexed to the United States in 1898; two years later, Hawaii gained territorial status. The U.S. naval base at Pearl Harbor was the site of the Japanese attack that brought the United States into World War II.

Hawaii's legislature is bicameral; the capital is Honolulu. The population in 1970 was 769,913.

HAWTHORNE, NATHANIEL (1804–1864), novelist, short-story writer, and essayist who became one of the leading American writers of his century. He was born in Salem, Mass., and graduated from Bowdoin College. In 1837 a number of Hawthorne's tales and stories were collected in *Twice-Told Tales,* which gave evidence of his potential. Hawthorne supported himself by writing children's books and working in the Boston Customs House (1839–1841), which he left for a year to live at Brook Farm. One of the turning points in Hawthorne's life was his marriage to Sophia Peabody in 1842. Living in the Old Manse in Concord, Hawthorne wrote happily while maintaining contact with his famous literary neighbors, Ralph Waldo Emerson, Henry David Thoreau, and other transcendentalists.

After a brief political job in Salem as surveyor of the port, Hawthorne had to support himself solely through his writing. In the next three years he wrote the novels that marked the maturity of his art. *The Scarlet Letter* (1850) continued the main themes of his short stories, the contest between man's heart and mind within the moral symbolism of the old Puritan heritage. Critics generally consider this Hawthorne's most successful novel. His *House of the Seven Gables* (1851) also deals with the moral decadence of Puritan New England, while *The Blithedale Romance* (1852) described some of Hawthorne's disillusionment with Brook Farm.

Hawthorne's campaign biography of Franklin Pierce won him a political position as U.S. consul at Liverpool (1853–1857). After that he lived for two years in Rome, where he wrote *The Marble Faun* (1860), a novel with an Italian setting.

See also Brook Farm; Literature; Transcendentalism.

Consult (III) Van Doren, 1949.

—Richard Collin, *Louisiana State University, New Orleans*

HAY, JOHN M(ILTON) (1838–1905), distinguished diplomat and historian of the nineteenth century. A native of Indiana, he graduated from Brown University and later practiced law in Illinois, where he became a close friend of another Springfield lawyer, Abraham Lincoln. When Lincoln was elected president, Hay went with him to Washington as a private secretary and remained with Lincoln until his death. In the 1890s Hay wrote, with John G. Nicolay, the first multivolume life of Lincoln and edited Lincoln's speeches and other writings. As author of the first substantial biography of Lincoln, Hay helped set the mold in which the President appeared to later generations.

After Lincoln's death, Hay became a diplomat, serving in Paris, Madrid, and Vienna until 1868. For a few years he returned to private life to work as a journalist for the New York *Tribune,* but in 1879 he was appointed assistant secretary of state to William M. Evarts. In 1897-1898 he was President McKinley's ambassador to Britain and then served (1898-1905) as secretary of state to both McKinley and to Theodore Roosevelt. His major accomplishments—a series of notes to the Great Powers that helped inaugurate the Open Door Policy with respect to China, and the three treaties with Britain, Colombia, and Panama that helped assure possession of the Panama Canal—were diplomatic, but he thought his poetry and novels, as well as his work as a historian, to be equally important. A persistent expansionist, he sought to acquire the Galapagos Islands and Virgin Islands and to arbitrate the Alaskan boundary controversy for the United States.

See also Hay-Pauncefote Treaty (1901); Open Door Policy; Panama Canal.
Consult (V) Callcott, 1942; Dennett, 1933.
—Robin W. Winks, *Yale University*

HAYES, RUTHERFORD B(IRCHARD) (1822-1893),

19th President of the United States (1877-1881). He was born in Delaware, Ohio, on Oct. 4, 1822, and graduated from Kenyon College and Harvard Law School. During the Civil War he rose to brevet major general, although his military career was undistinguished. He was then twice elected to Congress (1864, 1866) as a Republican.

As governor of Ohio (1868-1872), Hayes in two terms induced the legislature to improve prison conditions, to revise railroad regulations, and to approve the creation of Ohio State University. He retired, avoided interparty strife, and was reelected governor in 1875. In 1876, when Republicans needed a candidate who could unite their Grant and reform wings, Hayes was not the dark horse some claim. He was named on the seventh ballot to oppose Samuel Tilden. After a bitter campaign, the results indicated Tilden's victory. However, disputed tallies from four states necessitated an electoral commission, which awarded the election to Hayes. Hayes never doubted he won, but to many Americans he became President "Rutherfraud."

During his White House years, Hayes completed the withdrawal of federal troops from the South and ended Reconstruction. He mobilized troops to suppress the railway strikes of 1877. As a sound money advocate, he vetoed the Bland-Allison Act (1878) although Congress passed it anyway. He also vetoed a Chinese Exclusion Act that would have compromised U.S. treaty obligations. His struggle with Roscoe Conkling's Stalwarts over New York patronage cost him political support but brought public acclaim. Although Hayes' presidency restored executive independence after a long period of congressional control, it remains one of America's most underrated administrations. Hayes would have accepted renomination, but his party turned to James Garfield in 1880. He died in Fremont, Ohio, on Jan. 17, 1893.

See also Bland-Allison Act (1878); Compromise of 1877; Conkling, Roscoe; Presidential Elections; Stalwarts and Half-Breeds.
Consult (V) Barnard, 1967; Bruce, 1970.
—George Lankevich, *Bronx Community College of The City University of New York*

HAYMARKET MASSACRE,

a bombing and shooting incident on May 4, 1886, following a labor gathering in Chicago. On May 3, striking workers at the McCormick Reaper works in Chicago attacked strikebreakers; police used guns and clubs to disperse the strikers. August Spies, editor of a German-language anarchist newspaper, called a protest meeting for Haymarket Square the following day.

Several anarchists spoke at a generally peaceful meeting. As the meeting was breaking up, a police officer at the head of 180 men ordered the crowd to disperse. A bomb was thrown among the police, and both sides opened fire with pistols. Seven policemen died, 60 or more were wounded, and a number of civilians were killed or wounded. Police arrested a number of prominent Chicago anarchists, including Spies, Albert Parsons (editor of an English-language anarchist newspaper), and Samuel Fielden (a teamster and anarchist leader). Seven men were sentenced to be hanged: four were hanged, one committed suicide, and two had their sentences commuted. In 1892, Governor John Peter Altgeld released the imprisoned survivors, claiming both judge and jury had shown extreme prejudice.

Although the identity of the bomb thrower never became known, the incident served to couple the labor movement to anarchic violence in the public mind and probably contributed to a decline in the membership of the Knights of Labor.

See also Anarchism; Knights of Labor; Labor Movement.

HAYNE, ROBERT Y.,

South Carolina senator who defended states' rights in a memorable debate with Daniel Webster. *See* Webster-Hayne Debate (1830).

HAY-PAUNCEFOTE TREATY (1901),

first of

GRAND NATIONAL REPUBLICAN BANNER.

Rutherford B. Hayes, 19th President of the United States (1877-1881), who won disputed 1876 election over Samuel J. Tilden.

Exponent of yellow journalism, William Randolph Hearst built publishing empire.

Ernest Hemingway in Madrid during the Spanish Civil War.

three international agreements that cleared the way for the United States to build and acquire the Panama Canal. It was concluded between Secretary of State John M. Hay and Lord Pauncefote, British ambassador to the United States, on Feb. 5, 1900.

Hay, fearful that Congress would authorize construction of a canal across the Nicaraguan isthmus in defiance of the earlier Clayton-Bulwer Treaty (1850) with Britain, found the Senate unwilling to accept the new agreement, which provided that the United States could construct and own an isthmian canal but could not fortify it. The jingoistic press, joined by anti-British Irish in America and by the Democrats, who depicted the treaty as a sellout to Britain, encouraged the Senate to reject the treaty—which it did early in 1901. Hay thereupon offered his resignation. Upon being persuaded to remain in office, he negotiated a second agreement with Britain that permitted fortification of the isthmian canal, and this treaty was signed on Nov. 18, 1901.

See also Clayton-Bulwer Treaty (1850); Panama Canal.

Consult (V) Gelber, 1938.

HEADRIGHT SYSTEM, method of granting land. *See* Colonial Agriculture.

HEALTH, EDUCATION AND WELFARE, DEPARTMENT OF (HEW), cabinet-level executive department created in 1953 to coordinate numerous social programs. It is concerned with the general welfare of U.S. citizens in the areas of health, education, social service, and social insurance. Among its branches are the Social Security Administration, the Office of Education, the Social and Rehabilitation Service, and the Public Health Service. The latter is composed of the Health Services and Mental Health Administration, National Institutes of Health and Consumer Protection, and the Environmental Health Service (including the Food and Drug Administration).

HEARST, WILLIAM RANDOLPH (1863–1951), American publisher and political figure. Born in San Francisco and educated at Harvard, Hearst took charge of a paper his father owned, the San Francisco *Examiner.* He experimented with flamboyant pictures, glaring typography, and earthy, mass-appeal news coverage.

In 1895 Hearst invaded New York, buying the unsuccessful *Morning Journal* and turning it into a profitable venture. Hearst began a long war with other papers—enticing employees of other papers with high salaries, buying distinguished talent, and using tactics called "yellow journalism" (battling for circulation with sensational articles).

Hearst made several unsuccessful bids to become mayor of New York City and served

two terms in the U.S. House of Representatives. He was disappointed in his hopes of winning a nomination for president, but he remained influential in politics. He supported Franklin D. Roosevelt in 1932 but later turned conservative.

He built up a publishing empire that included 18 newspapers in 12 cities; 9 magazines, including *Cosmopolitan, Good Housekeeping,* and *Harper's Bazaar;* the *American Weekly,* a syndicated supplement; and other news and photo services. He spent money lavishly on such projects as San Simeon, a castle he erected in California. There he placed part of his famous art collection and entertained friends from the motion picture industry, which he financed on a large scale.

Consult (VI) Swanberg, 1961.

HEMINGWAY, ERNEST (MILLER) (1899–1961), American short-story writer and novelist who won Pulitzer and Nobel prizes. He was born in Illinois the son of a doctor who took him on hunting and fishing trips through the Michigan woods. These trips provided the background for many of Hemingway's Nick Adams stories. After graduating from high school, Hemingway worked as a reporter on the Kansas City *Star* (1917). In 1918 he went to Italy as a Red Cross ambulance driver and was seriously wounded. This World War I experience became the material for one of his finest novels, *A Farewell to Arms* (1929). After the war, Hemingway lived for a time in Paris, socializing with expatriates such as Gertrude Stein and Ezra Pound. His European experiences were chronicled in the posthumous *A Moveable Feast* (1964).

His first major novel, *The Sun Also Rises* (1926), was a great success and was followed by a collection of stories, *Men Without Women,* in 1927. His enthusiasm for bullfighting was portrayed in *Death in the Afternoon* (1932), and after an African safari he wrote *The Green Hills of Africa* (1935). During the Spanish Civil War, Hemingway served as a newspaper correspondent (1937–1938) and used the experience in several works, particularly in the novel *For Whom the Bell Tolls* (1940).

After the war, Hemingway continued to write prolifically, first settling in Key West, Fla., then in Cuba, where he wrote *The Old Man and the Sea* (1952), which won the 1953 Pulitzer Prize and helped him to win the Nobel Prize for Literature in 1954. After intervals of hospitalization for a variety of mental and physical illnesses, Hemingway shot himself at his hunting and fishing lodge in Ketchum, Idaho.

Hemingway had a profound influence on American writers both as a storyteller and craftsman. His lean style and his themes of man's dignity in the losing battle of life have been widely admired and imitated. Some of his short stories, such as *The Killers* and *The Snows of Kilimanjaro,* are as well known as any other stories in English.

See also Literature.

Consult (VIII) Baker, 1969; Young, 1966.

HENRI, ROBERT (1865–1929), illustrator who was a leader of the Ashcan School. *See* Painting.

HENRY, PATRICK (1736–1799), Revolutionary War patriot and political leader. Born in Virginia, he became a lawyer in 1760. In 1763, as a defense attorney in the "Parsons Cause" case, Henry argued that the King, by disallowing a Virginia law, had violated the compact between ruler and ruled and had thereby forfeited all claim to obedience. Elected to the House of Burgesses in 1765, Henry attacked the Stamp Act by warning George III of the fate of Caesar and Charles I and by introducing seven radical resolutions, including the assertion that Virginia enjoyed complete legislative autonomy. He chided the less bold by advising: "If this be treason, make the most of it."

After Governor Dunmore dissolved the House of Burgesses, Henry in May 1774 led the call for a Virginia Convention and a Continental Congress and on March 23, 1775, declaring, "Give me liberty or give me death," urged armed resistance against the English. Outlawed by Dunmore on May 6, Henry took his seat in the Second Continental Congress on May 18. In August he returned to Virginia as a militia colonel, but his political opponents blocked his dreams of martial laurels. Henry resigned his commission, won election to the third Virginia revolutionary convention, and helped draft the state constitution of 1776. He served as governor of Virginia from 1776 to 1779 and from 1784 to 1786.

An Anti-Federalist, Henry opposed the U.S. Constitution as inimical to states' rights and was important in the successful movement for a Bill of Rights. Henry's political attitudes changed drastically in the 1790s. Although he declined George Washington's offers in 1795 of the offices of secretary of state and chief justice, he openly praised the Federalist President. In 1799 at Washington's request, Henry ran successfully as a Federalist for the Virginia House of Delegates, but he died before taking his seat.

Consult (II) Meade, 1957, 1969.

—Thomas Archdeacon, *University of Wisconsin*

HEPBURN ACT (1906), legislation that strengthened the powers of the Interstate Commerce Commission (ICC) to fix maximum railroad rates, determine through routings, decide fair division of rates among cooperating carriers, and establish uniform accounting systems. The ICC's decisions were now made binding without court action, so the railroads themselves had to take on the burden of appealing to the courts against a federal rule and of gathering evidence.

The law, a response to attacks on railroad abuses and a demand by President Roosevelt for tougher regulation, supplemented the Elkins Act (1903). A major flaw in the reform was its failure to provide for the proper assessment of railroad properties so that fair rates could be fixed. The Physical Valuation Act of 1913 gave the ICC this power, although little was done to use the authority until the 1920s.

See also Elkins Act (1903); Interstate Commerce Commission; Railroad Legislation.

Consult (V) Kolko, 1965.

HESSIANS, German mercenaries hired by the British during the Revolution to help subdue the colonial rebels. These Germans became known as Hessians, even though most did not come from the state of Hesse. They did not distinguish themselves in battle, and of the 30,000 who fought the patriots, approximately 7,700 were killed and 5,000 deserted.

HIGHER EDUCATION ACT (1965). *See* Education.

HIGHWAY SYSTEM. Early settlement in North America tended to follow waterways, and roads were slow to develop. Land transportation was so expensive that the major road-building efforts were military (Braddock's Road) or post roads, neither really worthy of the name. During the first half of the nineteenth century, however, demand for transportation became so great that roads were constructed for which users paid tolls—the turnpikes. The development of canals and then, after 1830, railroads soon reduced most roads to feeder status (farm-to-market). Such as they were, they were built and maintained locally only.

Growth of Modern Highways. The bicycle craze of the 1890s—each owned and operated independently, like a car—gave the first impetus to developing road systems, and the first Good Roads Convention met in 1892. Then automobile owners brought overwhelming pressure that culminated in the Federal Aid Road Act of 1916, which, by promising aid for state highway systems with interstate connections, forced every state to develop such a system, although many were already well advanced. The fact was that Americans bought and owned millions of cars before there were roads on which to operate them. The deficiency in highways was largely remedied in the 1920s, for by 1929 both national and state systems linking all major U.S. population centers by paved or very well improved thoroughfares had been completed.

By the 1940s, however, large parts of the

Patrick Henry helped mold revolutionary sentiment in Virginia and later served as its governor.

system were completely inadequate for the greatly increased traffic that developed, and new, limited access expressways, ultimately nationally planned and financed (the new interstate system was fully under way by 1956), seemed to offer the only hope for keeping traffic moving. But the highways led to further congestion in the cities, which increasingly came to resemble mere highway/parking lot complexes.

Cost of Highways. The economic impact of the new highway system built after 1918 would be difficult to overestimate. The cost of roads increased dramatically as graded, drained, and graveled ("improved") roadways of the best nineteenth-century technology gave way to concrete and asphalt paving in the twentieth century. Even costlier were the increases in size, quality, and traffic control necessitated by the increase in speed and the growth of motor truck traffic. Trucks destroyed such roads as there were during World War I, and building and rebuilding in 1921–1929 alone cost more than $15 billion. By 1965 the country was spending almost that much (in inflated dollars) on highways in a single year. These sums, incredible in both eras, came mostly from taxes on highway use: license fees and especially the gasoline tax, which metered highway use fairly accurately. So great was American demand for highways that not only were these taxes paid willingly, but also after World War II vehicle owners paid additional direct tolls to travel on through highways, again often called turnpikes.

See also Automobile; Canals; Railroads; Turnpikes, Early.

Consult (VIII) Rae, 1971.

—John C. Burnham, *Ohio State University*

Railroad builder James J. Hill *(center)* with William Howard Taft.

HILL, JAMES J(EROME) (1838–1916), railroad magnate and financier. He was born in Ontario, Canada, moved to the United States at age 18, settled in St. Paul, Minn., and quickly became an expert in the field of steamboat transportation. In 1872 he helped form the Red River Transportation Company, the basis of his fortune. In 1878, Hill and others purchased the St. Paul & Pacific Railroad, integrated its operations, and extended its lines to the Pacific. The railroad and several other Hill-controlled lines were consolidated in 1890 into the Great Northern Railway.

In 1895, Hill and his associates underwrote the financial stability of the Northern Pacific Railroad. Hill and J. P. Morgan (for the Northern Pacific) secured control of the Burlington lines in 1901. The same year Hill and Morgan emerged victorious in a battle for control of the Northern Pacific. Hill's success led him to attempt to ensure railroad stability in his operating area by organizing the Northern Securities Company to consolidate control of the Great Northern, Northern Pacific, Burlington, and other Hill-controlled properties. President Theodore Roosevelt opposed this move, and the company was ordered dissolved by the Supreme Court in 1904 as contrary to the Sherman Antitrust Act.

Under Hill's management, the Great Northern was the only transcontinental line to remain financially stable and prosperous, although most other lines received government aid and the Great Northern did not. The Great Northern sponsored extensive programs to develop the agricultural and commercial potential of its region, earning for Hill the title "empire-builder."

See also Morgan, J. Pierpont; Railroads.

—Robert W. Cherny, *California State University, San Francisco*

HILL-BURTON ACT (1946), or Hospital Survey and Construction Act, established a national hospital construction program. The act permitted the federal government to participate in financing and to set standards for hospital construction for the first time. Originally intended to fulfill the postwar need for small community hospitals, health centers, and related facilities, the act is now administered through HEW's U.S. Public Health Service. Initially funded at $3 million to aid the states in surveying their needs and $375 million to help finance construction for five years with federal participation in each project limited to one-third the cost, financing has been periodically extended and greatly increased since 1946.

HIPPIE, term, probably of Beat Generation origin ("hip" or hipster"), used to describe a person with a sophisticated sense of social reality. By the late 1960s, "hippie" denoted a genial, nonpolitical, long-haired youth wearing seemingly shabby clothing who was presumed to be a drug-user and school dropout.

HISS-CHAMBERS CASE developed in 1948 when Whittaker Chambers, a former Communist writer and an editor of *Time* magazine, appeared before the House Un-American Activities Committee and charged that Alger Hiss (a State Department official) had 10 years earlier given him classified information for transmission to Soviet agents. Hiss denied the accusations, and when Chambers repeated his charges on television, Hiss filed a libel suit. When Chambers came forward with documentation, the federal government prosecuted Hiss for testifying falsely that he had never turned over any State Department documents to Chambers and that he had not seen Chambers after January 1937.

It was a classic encounter between an admitted Communist and a distinguished State Department official. Hiss, a lawyer, had entered the State Department in 1936 and had advised

Roosevelt at Yalta. The first trial in 1949 ended in a deadlock, but the second convicted Hiss (1950), who was sentenced to five years in prison. The case continued to be debated, and the charges and countercharges were symbolic of the fear of communism during the era when Senator Joseph McCarthy was so influential.

Consult (VIII) Cooke, 1951.

HISTORICAL ARCHAEOLOGY (AMERICAN),

that aspect of archaeological research that deals with the remains of European and European-derived peoples who lived within the historic period beginning with the discovery of the New World and postmedieval Europe (about 1500) and extending to about 1900. Historical archaeology is an important segment of historical research, one that can throw significant light on the often dimly known past.

The primary objectives of historical archaeology are establishing the location of archaeological sites; securing, through excavation, detailed information about these sites both in terms of structures and artifacts; and analyzing and interpreting the information thus obtained in order to date the site and make meaningful interpretations about the life and times of the people who occupied it. Archaeological research can often reconstruct the story of the establishment, growth, and subsequent death of a site.

Sites investigated by archaeologists include historic houses, ranches, plantations, towns, churches, missions, forts, trading posts, and industrial establishments such as kilns, ironworks, glassworks, sawmills, and drydocks. Shipwrecks can be valuable sites to the archaeologist, especially when the year of destruction is known through historical documentation. In such a case, the ship becomes a sunken time capsule with an exactly dated cross section of life represented by its cargo.

Historical documents are sometimes a great aid to the historical archaeologist. However, more often than not, such records either have incomplete information or do not deal with the everyday life of the people. They do not indicate what the people built and where, what tools, pottery, and glassware they used and made. Often, written records are not available, in which case archaeology becomes the only means by which to discover the past.

Because of its concern with the tangible remains of the past, historical archaeology can build up a great body of otherwise unavailable historical data. Common finds include foundations of buildings; soil stains that represent the former locations of wooden structures such as walls and fences; a tremendous variety of artifacts or man-made objects such as nails, building hardware, weapons, glassware, ceramics, smoking pipes, buttons, spoons, coins; and animal and plant remains. Through careful study, the archaeologist is usually able to iden-

tify artifacts as to place of origin (France, Spain, England, China, Germany, or the United States), date of manufacture, and function. From this information, he is able to make inferences concerning architecture, trade relationships, technology, social organization, agricultural knowledge and techniques, and many other aspects of a culture.

North America. Archaeological research has significantly added to the knowledge about such North American sites as Jamestown, Williamsburg, the Moravian settlements of Bethabara and Bethlehem, the nineteenth-century Mormon town of Nauvoo in Illinois, Sutter's sawmill, Plymouth Plantation, Independence Square, and the Fortress of Louisbourg in Nova Scotia. Further examples of the value of historical archaeology are provided by research taking place at Flowerdew Hundred Plantation and the Yorktown Pottery Factory, both in Virginia. Established in 1618, Flowerdew Hundred was one of the many early settlements or villages along the James River. Historical records are almost nonexistent, but archaeology is revealing the size of the village, the characteristics of buildings and fortifications, the crafts and industries of the time, and thousands of artifacts, including early weapons and armor.

The knowledge of colonial crafts is very limited. The excavation of the Yorktown Pottery Factory in Yorktown, Va., has revealed substantial information about an eighteenth-century American potter: the size, shape, and characteristics of his factory and kiln; indications of how the kiln was fired and how pottery was loaded into it; and what pottery was manufactured.

See also Colonial Agriculture; Jamestown Settlement.

Consult (I) Hume, 1969.

—Norman F. Barka, *College of William and Mary*

Excavations at Flowerdew Hundred Plantation in Virginia uncovered stone foundation dating from 1620s.

HOFFA, JAMES R(IDDLE) (1913–),

controversial American labor leader. The son of a coal miner, he was born in Brazil, Ind. He dropped out of school in order to work. Hoffa's involvement with the labor movement began in the 1930s, when he headed a local union of the Teamsters. At the time, the Teamsters Union included a group of political radicals who, from their base in Minneapolis, realized the importance of the control of long-distance truck drivers. When this element was expelled, Hoffa seized their Central States Conference and took advantage of the opportunity to strengthen his own position in the union.

In 1957 Hoffa succeeded Dave Beck as president when Beck was jailed for stealing union funds. It was at this time that the Senate Committee headed by Senator John McClellan, with Robert F. Kennedy as chief counsel, began to investigate Hoffa's alleged connections with the underworld. As a result of these hearings

Caricature of Oliver Wendell Holmes, doctor and author.

the Teamsters were expelled from the AFL-CIO. In 1964 Hoffa was convicted of jury tampering in a 1962 trial. After losing several appeals, he entered prison in 1967 to begin an eight-year term. He was paroled by President Nixon in 1971.

Consult (VIII) James, 1965.

HOFFMAN, ABBIE (ABBOTT H.) (1936-   ), self-styled "revolutionary artist," author, and popular counterculture figure. He was expelled from high school but continued his education at Brandeis University and graduated in 1959. In 1966 he became an active civil rights worker for the Student Nonviolent Coordinating Committee (SNCC) in Mississippi, and in 1968 he founded the Youth International Party (YIP or "yippies").

The author of several books, the most popular works being *Woodstock Nation: A Talk Rock Album* and *Revolution for the Hell of It,* Hoffman was arrested more than 30 times for disruptive behavior. As a result of the "Chicago Seven" trial, he was convicted for his participation in activities connected with the 1968 Democratic Convention, but the conviction was reversed.

See also Chicago Seven; Yippies.

HOLDING COMPANIES, business organizations in which a corporation owns a controlling interest in other corporations. First legalized by New Jersey (1889), they hastened the general trend toward consolidation. Because 10- to 20-percent stock ownership will usually secure control, horizontal or vertical integration can be achieved with a relatively small investment. The federal government has sought to curb these combinations, which quite clearly eliminate competition in an industry. Successes were achieved with the dissolution of both the Standard Oil and American Tobacco companies (1911) and more recently in requiring the Dupont Company to sell its holdings of General Motors stock (1961).

See also Antitrust Cases; Business Regulation; Trusts.

HOLMES, OLIVER WENDELL (1809-1894), physician, teacher, essayist, poet, lecturer, and novelist born in Cambridge, Mass., he graduated from Harvard in 1829, studied law briefly, and then turned to medicine. Holmes graduated from Harvard Medical School in 1836. He was already known as a poet for "Old Ironsides" (1830), a work that saved the *U.S.S. Constitution* from being destroyed. Holmes' first edition of his collected *Poems* appeared in 1836.

Teaching rather than practicing medicine, Holmes was professor of anatomy at Dartmouth (1838-1840) until he moved to Harvard Medical School, where he served from 1847 to 1882. His essay "The Contagiousness of

Puerperal Fever" (1843) was one of the first medical theses on the dangers of contagion. In line with his dual career, Holmes initiated in his Lowell Institute Lectures of 1853 the practice of finishing each address with an original poem.

He continued his practice with his series *The Autocrat at the Breakfast Table,* which appeared serially in the *Atlantic Monthly* in 1857. Sequels to the *Autocrat,* published in book form in 1858, included *The Professor at the Breakfast Table* (1860) and *The Poet at the Breakfast Table* (1872). Holmes was a prolific poet who could turn from the serious to the lightest of after-dinner verse with scarcely a pause. One of his three psychological novels was *Elsie Venner* (1861); he also wrote serious biographies, *John L. Motley* (1879) and *Emerson* (1885).

Holmes was not only a significant medical scholar and an amusing minor writer; he was also a raconteur, wit, lecturer, and an eminent representative of the humane Boston society that rebelled against the severe Puritan background of early New England. His son Oliver Wendell Holmes, Jr., was famous as a Supreme Court justice.

Consult (V) Small, 1962.

—Richard Collin, *Louisiana State University, New Orleans*

HOLMES, OLIVER WENDELL, JR. (1841-1935). Appointed by President Theodore Roosevelt to the Supreme Court in 1902, Oliver Wendell Holmes, Jr., eventually ranked with John Marshall as one of the two greatest justices ever to sit on the Court. Born in Boston, the son of author Oliver Wendell Holmes, Holmes came to the Court already renowned. A veteran of the Civil War, he graduated from Harvard Law School in 1866, rapidly rose in the practice of law, and became a friend of many prominent scholars and philosophers. In 1881 he published *The Common Law.* The following year he was appointed to the faculty of Harvard Law School, largely through the influence of Louis D. Brandeis. A few months later, however, he accepted a justiceship on the Massachusetts Supreme Judicial Court and served almost 20 years, the last three as chief justice.

Supreme Court Justice. On the Supreme Court (1902-1931), Holmes became the most outspoken advocate of judicial self-restraint, dissenting time and again when the Court majority struck down federal and state legislative regulations of business (*Lochner v. New York,* 1905; *Hammer v. Dagenhart,* 1918). Skeptical of all absolutist philosophies, Holmes believed the Constitution allowed wide latitude in social experimentation by the states and by Congress.

When Holmes first came to the Court, battles were already raging over the meanings of the due process and the interstate com-

After World War II, Hoover toured war-torn Europe to make recommendations for avoiding famine.

stances. Born into a Quaker family in West Branch, Iowa, on August 10, 1874, he was orphaned at the age of seven. He then lived with relatives, earning his own living. Hoover worked his way through Stanford University and became a mining engineer who traveled all over the world and soon became a millionaire. When the United States entered World War I, Hoover became food administrator and by using persuasion was able to conserve supplies without rationing. This experience confirmed his belief that voluntary public action could solve many crises better than compulsory government interference. He later served as secretary of commerce under Republican presidents Harding and Coolidge. After Coolidge decided not to seek reelection, Hoover was easily nominated and triumphed over Democrat Alfred E. Smith in 1928.

Presidency. Hailed as a humanitarian and engineer who would keep and improve prosperity, Hoover began his term as president with the creation of the Federal Farm Board to increase farm income. He also inaugurated steps that would have led to a comprehensive social security system, largely through private, voluntary insurance programs.

When the Great Depression began, however, Hoover turned his energies to the economic crisis. Again and again Hoover tried to get Americans voluntarily to take actions to stop the downward spiral of economic activity, but when private capitalists failed to maintain credit, Hoover reluctantly called for a Reconstruction Finance Corporation, created in 1932, to bolster major capital institutions. He made imaginative use of government powers, such as controlling credit and expanding public works, all to little avail.

The Depression also hampered his foreign policy efforts, and although he backed the London Naval Conference, he was unwilling to take a firm stand against Japanese expansion in Manchuria in 1931.

Later Life. Turned out of office by the election of 1932, Hoover for years held to his ideal of voluntary cooperation of citizens and warned of the dangers of bureaucracy and big government. He died in New York City on Oct. 20, 1964.

See also Depression; Good Neighbor Policy; New Deal; Presidential Elections.

Consult (VI) Hoover, 1951–1952; Lyons, 1964.

—John C. Burnham, *Ohio State University*

HOOVER, J(OHN) EDGAR (1895–1972), American public official who served as director of the Federal Bureau of Investigation (FBI) for nearly 50 years. Hoover was born in Washington, D.C., and after high school he worked as a messenger in the Library of Congress. After receiving a law degree in 1917, he began work at the Department of Justice as a file reviewer. Within two years, however, he was named a special assistant to Attorney General Palmer. He became the director of the FBI in 1924.

During his long career, Hoover turned the FBI into a symbol of law enforcement, established the world's largest fingerprint file, and created the FBI National Academy, which trains police from all over the country.

From the late 1940s, Hoover was increasingly well known for his uncompromising attitude toward suspected communists and subversives. In addition, the FBI and Hoover came under fire for exceeding their authority. Prominent leaders such as Robert Kennedy called for his resignation, but he was stoutly defended by others, such as President Nixon. Despite criticism, Hoover continued in office until his death. Hoover's books included *Masters of Deceit* (1958) and *On Communism* (1969).

See also Federal Bureau of Investigation.

Consult (VIII) Mesnick, 1972.

HOPKINS, HARRY L(LOYD) (1890–1946), social worker and presidential adviser. Born in Sioux City, Iowa, he began a career in social work in New York City in 1912. He moved into government service in 1931, heading New York State's relief program, and when Governor Franklin D. Roosevelt became president in 1933, he brought Hopkins to Washington as federal relief administrator.

From 1933 to 1937, Hopkins, who ran the Work Progress Administration (WPA), dispensed billions of dollars and put thousands of people to work on projects ranging from the construction of airports to the compilation of bibliographies of local history. By 1937, Hopkins had become one of the most influential men in Washington. He combined a humanitarian zeal with a shrewd toughness, and Roosevelt particularly valued his ability to cut through to the heart of a problem and to get things done.

He served briefly as secretary of commerce (1939–1940), and from 1940 to 1945 was the President's most trusted adviser on foreign policy. An ardent supporter of aid to Britain, Hopkins visited London twice in 1941 and administered the early Lend-Lease program. His trip to Moscow in July 1941 helped to expedite Anglo-American assistance to the Soviet Union. Despite failing health, he undertook a last mission for President Truman, traveling to Moscow in May 1945 to discuss personally with Stalin the U.S.-USSR differences.

See also Federal Emergency Relief Act (1933); Work Projects Administration.

Consult (VI) Sherwood, 1948.

—George Herring, *University of Kentucky*

HORSESHOE BEND, BATTLE OF (1814), climaxing encounter of the Creek War. *See* Creek War.

HOSPITAL SURVEY AND CONSTRUCTION ACT, pioneer legislation for federal support of hospital construction. *See* Hill-Burton Act (1946).

HOUSE OF REPRESENTATIVES, UNITED STATES. The original democratic portion of the national government, the House has had to share its claim to have a popular mandate with the Senate and with the presidents. Despite periodic efforts at streamlining, it has been criticized for being a "house out of order."

The House, which evolved from the British House of Commons and the colonial assemblies, has the power to enact laws, vote appropriations, originate money bills and charges of impeachment, and elect the president if the electoral college fails to cast a majority (as in 1800 and 1824).

The first Congress had 65 members of the House. With the addition of new states and the growth of population, the House increased to 435 members after the 1910 census and was fixed at that number. As the House grew it had to delegate to its committees the real deliberative function. It exercises its influence in the twentieth century largely by responding to executive branch initiatives and monitoring executive performance through committee investigations and hearings.

Throughout its history it has been led by a series of powerful Speakers—leaders of the majority party in the House. The first was Henry Clay, who served six terms as Speaker starting in 1811. After his reign, though, the House became disorganized, and by the time James G. Blaine became Speaker after the Civil War, nearly 250 members were crammed into a tiny chamber, where tempers and factions flared. Blaine ruled that a party was obligated to ratify the candidate for Speaker chosen by the majority caucus (thereby ending the chaos of intraparty and coalition candidates).

The peak of the Speaker's authority came under Thomas B. Reed (1889–1891, and 1895–1899), who obtained absolute power over the legislative calendar. The "Reed Rules" ended House filibusters for all time. These rules were abused by Speaker Joseph G. Cannon (1903–1911), who was eventually stripped of his powers to select committee members and to set the agenda for debate. Other notable Speakers, who relied more on informal influence than formal authority, were Nicholas Longworth in the 1920s and Sam Rayburn (1949–1953, and 1955–1961).

In 1946, Congress made an effort to modernize by passing the Legislative Reorganization Act. It reduced the number of House committees through consolidation but did nothing to curb the abuses caused by an irresponsible Rules Committee (which has strict powers over the order of business) or by irresponsible committee chairmen (chosen by seniority).

Consult (VIII) Galloway, 1961; Green, Fallows, and Zwick, 1972.

—Martin Gruberg, *University of Wisconsin, Oshkosh*

HOUSING ACTS. There is a paradox in the government's role in the area of housing. Its aid is essential to reverse the deterioration of property, provide equal opportunity for housing, and finance low-income dwellings. Yet, governmental policies have fostered discriminatory renting and selling, crippled the housing financing market, prevented (through codes and zoning) breakthroughs in the use of modern construction materials, and inspired scandals in slum clearance and urban renewal programs. Only 4 percent of the housing built from 1935 to the early 1960s was publicly financed. Public housing has provided highrise slums for the poor, and urban renewal has replaced their homes with units they cannot afford.

The Housing Acts of 1949, 1954, and 1961 were intended to enable local governments to undertake slum clearance and urban renewal with federal funding. However, traditional urban renewal, emphasizing the physical factors, was not enough. In 1965 the Housing and Urban Development Act created a cabinet-level department to bring under a single agency the federal programs relating to housing and urban problems. The next year Congress approved the Demonstration Cities and Metropolitan Development Act, a massive coordinated attack on blight to treat the socioeconomic factors causing decay. However, "Model Cities" was inadequately funded for more than pilot projects.

In 1968 the Housing and Urban Development Act established a goal of 6 million units each year for 10 years of new or rehabilitated housing that would be available to the poor. However, far fewer units for low- and middle-income families were built than Congress had planned, and renovation also lagged badly.

See also City, Housing and Urban Development, Department of (HUD).

Consult (VIII) Friedman, 1968.

—Martin Gruberg, *University of Wisconsin, Oshkosh*

HOUSING AND HOME FINANCE AGENCY, forerunner of HUD. *See* Housing and Urban Development, Department of (HUD).

HOUSING AND URBAN DEVELOPMENT, DEPARTMENT OF (HUD), cabinet-level executive department that administers and coordinates a

HOUSE OF REPRESENTATIVES — Item Guide

The entry on the HOUSE OF REPRESENTATIVES covers its growth and most notable leaders. Its functions were outlined by the CONNECTICUT COMPROMISE and legally defined in the CONSTITUTION OF THE UNITED STATES. The House has played a role in PRESIDENTIAL ELECTIONS when the ELECTORAL COLLEGE was unable to elect a president. The House, as well as the SENATE, also has a part in the IMPEACHMENT process.

Numerous POLITICAL PARTIES IN THE UNITED STATES have been represented in the House, but the DEMOCRATIC PARTY and the REPUBLICAN PARTY have been dominant since the Civil War. Influential speakers of the House have included HENRY CLAY, JAMES G. BLAINE, JOSEPH G. CANNON, and SAM RAYBURN.

wide range of federal programs dealing with the availability of housing and the adequacy of city life. Established in 1965, HUD replaced the Housing and Home Finance Agency, a diffuse organization that embraced numerous agencies. The creation of HUD was another attempt to meet the growing problems of urban slums and suburban development and to coordinate the chaos of local, state, and federal programs.

The numerous agencies transferred from the Housing and Home Finance Agency to HUD included the Federal Housing Administration (created in 1934), the Public Housing Administration (1937), and the Federal National Mortgage Association (1938). Also included in the transfer were the Urban Renewal Administration, which stressed comprehensive community planning and housing rehabilitation, and the Community Facilities Administration, concerned with diverse public works.

See also Housing Acts.

HOUSTON, SAM(UEL) (1793-1863), the most commanding figure in early Texas history. Born in Virginia, he moved to Tennessee as a child and when he was 16 joined the Cherokee Indians for three years. He later served in the Creek War and then became a lawyer. He soon became a political power in Tennessee and in 1827 was elected governor. A disastrous and unhappy marriage in early 1829 caused Houston to resign as governor and head for the Cherokee country in Arkansas. He stayed six years, took an Indian wife, and represented the tribes in their conflicts with Washington.

In the early 1830s he made several trips to Texas and in November 1835, six weeks after the Texans revolted against Mexico, was elected commander of the Texas army. Houston began a policy of continual retreat, which led to considerable criticism. But on April 21, 1836, he surprised the Mexicans at San Jacinto, and in a battle that lasted only 18 minutes virtually annihilated the Mexican army. Houston was overwhelmingly elected president of the Republic of Texas (1836-1838) and later reelected (1841-1844). When annexation to the United States became the biggest question before Texans, Houston's stand was ambiguous, but he was probably trying to make annexation possible.

When Texas joined the Union in 1846, Houston was elected one of its first senators. He served until 1859, growing ever more isolated from his Southern colleagues because of his strong Union support. In 1859 he ran again for governor and was elected. Although Texas was decidedly pro-Southern and secessionist, Houston regularly denounced disunionists and predicted defeat for the South if it should secede. After Texas voted to secede on Feb. 23, 1861, the secession convention announced that his office was vacant. Houston quietly

Sam Houston, pioneer Texas leader, in early Matthew Brady photograph.

retired to his farm near Huntsville, where he died.

See also Austin, Stephen F.; San Jacinto, Battle of; Texas.

Consult (III) Friend, 1959; James, 1953.
—Joe B. Frantz, *The University of Texas, Austin*

HOWE, ELIAS (1819-1867), American inventor of the sewing machine. Howe, a mechanic in a Lowell, Mass. textile mill, invented a practical eye-pointed needle for his machine with an underthread shuttle. He received a patent for it in 1846, but when he could not sell it in the United States, he took it to England, where it was a big success. Howe returned to fight complex patent battles with other manufacturers such as Isaac Singer, which Howe won in 1854. He subsequently made a fortune from royalties and formed his own Howe Machine Company in 1865.

However, the home sewing machine was popularized not by Howe but by Isaac Singer (1811-1875), a Pittstown, N.Y. mechanic. His foot-treadle machine was patented in 1851, and Singer's factory soon led in the large-scale production of sewing machines. Civil War demand for uniforms boosted output, and the various sorts of sewing machines brought a revolution in the mass-produced clothing industry.

See also Sewing Machine.

HOWELLS, WILLIAM DEAN (1837-1920), critic, novelist, and journalist who became an important force and a champion of realism in American literature as editor of the *Atlantic Monthly*. Howell educated himself by incessant reading while working for his father, a small-town printer.

After a tour as U.S. consul in Venice (1861-1865), Howells gained recognition for his first travel books, *Venetian Life* (1866) and *Italian Journey* (1867). On his return to the United States, he began his long association with the *Atlantic Monthly* and later conducted the "Editor's Study" (1886-1891) and the "Easy Chair" (1900-1920) for *Harper's* magazine.

Howells was prolific, writing plays, critical works, reminiscences, novels, and many short stories. His works display a genuine concern for social problems. His realistic approach is seen in *The Rise of Silas Lapham* (1886), set among the *nouveau riche* of Boston. Although his works aged quickly, he prepared the way for a new breed of naturalistic novels.

Throughout his life, Howells encouraged young writers. His critical essays on the writings of such realistic Europeans as Tolstoy, Zola, and Ibsen helped to mold American literary taste. Howells was also a literary mentor of Mark Twain, Thorstein Veblen, and Stephen Crane.

HUCKLEBERRY FINN, THE ADVENTURES OF (1884). *See* Twain, Mark.

HUDSON, HENRY (died 1611), English navigator best known for discovering the Hudson River and Hudson Bay. Recognized as a competent navigator, Hudson was hired by the English Muscovy Company in 1607 to search for a route across the North Pole to China. By June, Hudson reached Greenland, but finding no northern passage he returned to England. He undertook a second unsuccessful expedition for the Muscovy Company in 1608.

In 1609 the Dutch East India Company hired Hudson to try to locate a northeastern route to the Far East. In April, Hudson sailed from Amsterdam on the *Half Moon* with a crew of 18. After encountering extremely bad weather off Norway and facing a mutiny, Hudson sailed west to America. By July he was exploring Chesapeake Bay. He then sailed north into lower New York Bay, where he found and investigated the river that bears his name, probably as far north as Albany, before returning to England.

Hudson, on a fourth and final voyage of exploration, left London in 1610 on the *Discovery,* hoping to find a northwest passage to the Pacific Ocean. In July he passed through the Hudson Strait and in August entered Hudson Bay, where the ship was frozen in for the winter. After the ice broke in June 1611, the crew mutinied, and Hudson, his son John, and seven others were cast adrift on Hudson Bay and were never seen again. The *Discovery* eventually returned to England with its crew thinned by starvation and Eskimo attacks.

See also Exploration and Discovery.

HUDSON RIVER SCHOOL, a group of nineteenth-century American artists who created large romantic landscapes of America's wilder countryside. So named by a derisive critic who wished to indicate their provincialism, the Hudson River painters adopted the name even though many of them painted scenes as far from the Hudson as South America. The group came together in 1827, when Thomas Cole founded his Greenwich Street Studio in New York City, and lasted until about 1875. Most of the painters did paint scenes of the Hudson Valley in New York and many lived near Catskill; however, the dozen painters who comprised the group differed widely in their style, their training, and even their subject matter. They had in common a new respect for man's relationship to nature as well as a fundamental need to express the wilder images of the American landscape before it became settled. In many ways the Hudson River painters shared the preoccupations of the transcendental writers in trying to unite in their art the boundless

optimism of the new American nation and an organic view of nature.

Thomas Cole was the spiritual leader of the school; on Cole's death in 1848 Asher Durand took his place. Also important in the movement were Thomas Doughty, Alwin Fisher, John Kensett, Worthington Wittridge, Frederick Church, John Casilear, William Hart, James Hart, Sanford Gifford, Jaspar Cropsey, and Thomas Rossiter.

See also Painting; Romanticism.

HUGHES, CHARLES EVANS (1862-1948), American jurist and political figure who was the 10th Chief Justice of the Supreme Court. Born in Glens Falls, N.Y., he took a law degree from Columbia University. He attracted public attention in 1906-1907, when he headed commissions investigating abuses in New York's gas utility and insurance industries. In 1906 he was elected governor of New York as a Republican and was reelected in 1908.

In 1910, Hughes was made an associate justice of the Supreme Court. Without his consent the Republicans nominated him for president in 1916, and he resigned from the Court to run against Woodrow Wilson. Political feuding in California between the Republicans and the Progressives, of whom he was also the candidate, cost Hughes the election, 277 to 254 electoral votes. He then returned to private law practice.

Secretary of State. After Harding became president in 1921, Hughes was made secretary of state. His attempt to bring the United States into the League of Nations was blocked by the Senate, but he did negotiate successfully to limit naval armaments, lessen tension in Asia, and improve U.S. relations in South America. Although he left government in 1925, he reentered public service in 1928 to sit on the Court of International Justice.

Chief Justice. President Hoover nominated Hughes for chief justice in 1930, and after opposition in the Senate he was confirmed. Hughes' rulings against the National Recovery Administration and other New Deal measures led to President Roosevelt's unsuccessful effort to "pack" the Supreme Court in 1937. Hughes retired from the court in 1941 and died in Osterville, Mass. Criticized and praised by both conservatives and liberals during his career, Hughes steered a middle course that emphasized constitutional liberties and curbed the power of administrative agencies.

Consult (VI) Pusey, 1963.

HUGHES, (JAMES MERCER) LANGSTON (1902-1967), writer noted for his portrayals in prose and poetry of the black in America. He was born in Joplin, Mo., and raised in the Midwest. Following his graduation from high school in Cleveland, he wrote one of his most

Alfred Bierstadt's *Discovery of the Hudson* romanticized adventures of explorer Henry Hudson.

Charles Evans Hughes, 10th Chief Justice of the Supreme Court, as governor of New York in 1906.

Langston Hughes, one of the main figures of the Harlem Renaissance.

famous poems, "The Negro Speaks of Rivers" (1921). Hughes attended Columbia University (1921-1923), leaving to explore Harlem, which he called the "great dark city." After a few months, he became a steward on a freighter and then traveled in Europe.

When Hughes returned to the United States, he began to publish the poems he had accumulated during his wanderings. Following his discovery as a poet by Vachel Lindsay, Hughes received a scholarship to Lincoln University in Pennsylvania, and, prior to graduation in 1929, his first two books were published: *The Weary Blues* (1926) and *Fine Clothes to the Jew* (1927). Launched on a career in letters, Hughes experimented with many literary forms—verse, prose fiction, biography, history, drama, articles, and children's books—leaving at his death 32 books in print. His newspaper columns featured a character he created, a young city black named Jesse B. Simple. Hughes' novel *Not Without Laughter* (1930) is a graphic account of a black boy growing up in America. Hughes wrote about his own life in *The Big Sea* (1940) and *I Wonder as I Wander* (1956).

HULL, CORDELL (1871-1955), secretary of state under Franklin D. Roosevelt. A representative from Tennessee for a quarter century and briefly chairman of the Democratic National Committee, Hull came to the New Deal as a representative of the Southern wing of the party.

A free-trade advocate and moralist-internationalist of the Wilsonian persuasion, Hull was primarily responsible for initiating and carrying out Roosevelt's Good Neighbor Policy and an elaborate program of reciprocal trade agreements through which tariffs could be systematically lowered.

Hull remained in the cabinet through 1944, actively participating in the establishment of the United Nations. Because Roosevelt often acted as his own State Department, it is difficult to sort out Hull's contributions, particularly in prewar relations with the belligerents and in wartime diplomacy.

See also Good Neighbor Policy.
Consult (VI) Hull, 1948; Langer and Gleason, 1952; Pratt, 1964.
—Allen F. Kifer, *Skidmore College*

HULL HOUSE, Chicago settlement house devoted to improving life in the city's slums. *See* Addams, Jane.

HULL-NOMURA DISCUSSIONS. Throughout 1941 Secretary of State Cordell Hull and Japanese Ambassador Nomura held a series of talks in Washington to try to avoid a serious crisis. The United States was opposed to Japanese military control over China, Japan's threat to create a new order in the rest of Asia, and

Japan's alliance with Germany. The Japanese hoped to obtain America's good offices in settling the war in China, to secure essential U.S. raw materials, and to assure America that the Axis Alliance would not be marshaled against the United States if the other two problems could be solved.

These two issues proved to be insurmountable obstacles, however. From Hull's point of view, no compromise was acceptable unless Japan renounced its aggression in China and pledged support of such principles as the Open Door and the integrity of China. He continued negotiations primarily to set the record straight and to delay a final rupture. But he was also convinced that by being firm the United States would be able to secure Japan's submission without a war, whereas any concession only invited further aggression. This policy of firmness without realistically facing the possibility of war proved a disaster for the United States.

See also Axis Alliance; Hull, Cordell. *Consult* (VII) Schroeder, 1958.

HUMPHREY, HUBERT H(ORATIO) (1911-   ), 38th Vice-President of the United States and Democratic candidate for president in 1968. He is known as a vigorous campaigner with a reputation for versatility, phenomenal memory, and volubility. He was born in South Dakota, but his political career is associated with Minnesota, where he was active in fusing the Democratic and Farmer-Labor parties. He was elected mayor of Minneapolis in 1945 on a reform ticket and was reelected in 1947.

A cofounder of Americans for Democratic Action (ADA), he made his appearance on the national stage in 1948 by championing a liberal civil rights plank at the Democratic National Convention. That year he won a race for the U.S. Senate, the first Democrat elected from his state. Serving in the Senate until 1964, he was a leading voice of liberalism, espousing medical care for the aged, Food for Peace, the Peace Corps, and nuclear arms limitation. Although at first his brashness alienated him from the inner circle of Senate leaders, his pragmatism and abilities as well as his ties with Lyndon Johnson, the Democratic Senate leader, helped him to be selected majority whip in 1961.

Known as the "happy warrior," he made unsuccessful efforts to get his party's vice-presidential nomination in 1956 and presidential nomination in 1960 before being selected as Johnson's running mate in 1964. As vice-president his background enabled him to be of service to city and state governments, labor, and minorities, but his loyalty to Johnson's Vietnam policies tarnished his liberal appeal. Johnson's sudden retirement announcement in 1968 gave Humphrey the coveted presidential nomination, but he lost a close election to Richard Nixon. In 1970 he returned to the

Senate and in 1972 unsuccessfully sought the presidential nomination.

See also Democratic Party; Presidential Elections.

Consult (VIII) Griffith, 1965; Sherrill and Ernst, 1968.

—Martin Gruberg, *University of Wisconsin, Oshkosh*

HUNDRED DAYS (MARCH 4–JUNE 16, 1933). For the hundred days immediately following Franklin Roosevelt's first inauguration, Congress in special session rubber-stamped presidential recovery measures. They included emergency banking legislation, legislation that took the country off the gold standard, the Federal Emergency Relief Act, the Civilian Conservation Corps, the Farm Credit Act, the Home Owners' Refinancing Act, the Agricultural Adjustment Act, and the National Recovery Administration. Long-range reforms that were instituted included the Tennessee Valley Authority, which provided electricity, flood control, and regional planning, and the Federal Deposit Insurance Corporation, which insured bank deposits.

See also New Deal; articles on specific acts and programs.

Consult (VI) Schlesinger, 1959.

HUTCHINSON, ANNE (1591–1643), colonial religious leader. Born Anne Marbury, the daughter of a minister in England, she married William Hutchinson, a merchant. Anne came to admire John Cotton, a vigorous Puritan minister, and when he fled to New England in 1633 to avoid imprisonment for nonconformity, she was greatly troubled. In 1634 the Hutchinsons followed Cotton to Boston. In Boston, where her husband was elected to the General Court, Anne served as a religious adviser to Boston women, holding weekly meetings where sermons were discussed. Her popularity grew rapidly, and soon she began to hold meetings for men as well.

Although everyone admitted she displayed genuine devotion to religion, her views ignited the most serious controversy of Massachusetts Bay Colony's early years. Anne denounced most of the colony's ministers, claiming they preached a false message that might lead men to believe that good deeds and outwardly holy lives were reliable signs of salvation, a notion antithetical to the orthodox Puritan belief in predestination. The controversy was complicated by her support of her brother-in-law, John Wheelwright, a Puritan convicted for criticizing the colony's ministers. Wheelwright's conviction spilled over into politics, and after the anti-Hutchinsonians won the election for governor, the General Court decided to ensure harmony in Massachusetts by banishing the leaders of the Hutchinsonian party.

However, the court found it difficult to convict Anne because she had not participated in the political disputes and proved quite able to parry her examiners' arguments. But when she admitted having received direct revelations from God, the court found a basis for her punishment. Banished in 1637, Anne went to Rhode Island, then to New York. In 1643 she and 12 members of her family were killed by Indians.

See also Colonial Religion; Puritanism.

Consult (I) Battis, 1962; Hall, 1968.

—Aaron M. Shatzman, *Washington University*

HUTCHINSON, THOMAS (1711–1780), loyalist colonial administrator. A Harvard graduate and the son of a wealthy Boston merchant, he entered public life in 1737 as a selectman and representative in the Massachusetts legislature. Early in his legislative career, his hard money policy made him unpopular with people who favored a paper currency. After serving for two years as Speaker of the House, Hutchinson was defeated for reelection in 1749. Soon afterward, however, he was appointed to the governor's council and to a judgeship. He was made lieutenant governor of Massachusetts in 1758 and chief justice of the colony in 1760.

As his Tory tendencies deepened during these years, so did his unpopularity. Hutchinson's attempt to enforce the Stamp Act (1765) so angered the people that a mob destroyed his house and valuable historical manuscripts. Hutchinson was appointed royal governor of Massachusetts in 1771. After four troubled years, marked by the publication in 1773 of some of his letters to the British cabinet, he was succeeded by Gen. Thomas Gage. Hutchinson traveled to England to give an account of his administration in 1775 and died there five years later.

See also Hutchinson Letters; Massachusetts.

HUTCHINSON LETTERS. In 1772 in London, Benjamin Franklin secretly sent to Massachusetts letters written by Governor Thomas Hutchinson and province secretary Andrew Oliver to the Grenville and North ministries. In 1773, against Franklin's wishes, Sam Adams published the letters, which showed how bad advice from America was partially responsible for Parliament's policies. The Massachusetts House of Representatives petitioned King George III to remove Hutchinson, and the Provincial Council called Franklin to testify. The Provincial Council rejected the Massachusetts petition, and Franklin, castigated as a thief without honor, lost his office as postmaster general for North America.

See also Franklin, Benjamin.

ICKES, HAROLD L. (1874–1952), New Deal

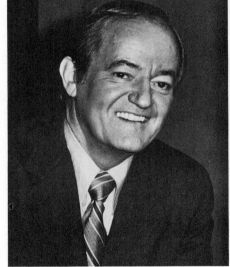

Zest for politics led to Hubert Humphrey's nickname of "The Happy Warrior."

IMMIGRATIONS:
10 YEAR TOTALS (1820-1970)

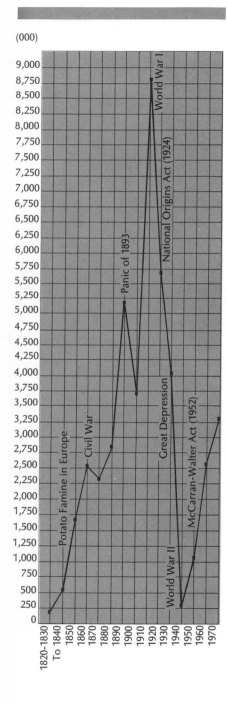

(000)

9,000
8,750
8,500
8,250
8,000
7,750
7,500
7,250
7,000
6,750
6,500
6,250
6,000
5,750
5,500
5,250
5,000
4,750
4,500
4,250
4,000
3,750
3,500
3,250
3,000
2,750
2,500
2,250
2,000
1,750
1,500
1,250
1,000
750
500
250
0

World War I

National Origins Act (1924)

Panic of 1893

Great Depression

McCarran-Walter Act (1952)

Potato Famine in Europe

Civil War

World War II

1820-1830
To 1840
1850
1860
1870
1880
1890
1900
1910
1920
1930
1940
1950
1960
1970

Secretary of the Interior who administered the PWA. *See* Public Works Administration.

IDAHO, the 43rd state, entered the Union on July 3, 1890. Although the Idaho area was surveyed in 1805 by the Lewis and Clark expedition, the first permanent white settlement was not made until 1860, when a group of Mormons founded Franklin. Gold was discovered in 1860; territorial status followed in 1863.

The state legislature is bicameral; the capital is Boise. The population in 1970 was 713,008.

ILLINOIS, the 21st state, admitted on Dec. 3, 1818. Father Marquette and Louis Joliet explored the Illinois area in the 1670s, and the first white settlement followed at Cahokia in 1699. The British took over the region in 1763, and in 1778, patriots captured the British forts at Kaskaskia and Cahokia. At first a part of Indiana Territory, Illinois gained territorial status in 1809.

The state legislature is bicameral; the capital is Springfield. The population in 1970 was 11,113,976.

ILLINOIS COMPANY. *See* Land Companies.

IMMIGRATION. Immigration to the United States represents the largest population movement in recorded history. Between 1820 and 1960 more than 40 million people entered the United States. The majority came from Europe, where a combination of factors ranging from economic to religious encouraged this outward movement. No one national or ethnic group dominated. Five groups did contribute the largest numbers—the Germans, British, Irish, Austro-Hungarians, and Italians—but people came from the farthest corners of the globe as well as neighboring Canada.

Push and Pull Factors. Across the world, people responded to stimuli called push and pull factors. Push factors related to the conditions in the place of birth that encouraged emigration. In Ireland and southern Germany in the 1840s, the potato famine acted as a prod to the discontented who chose to leave all behind and start anew in America. In Norway the lack of social and economic opportunities from 1850 through the 1870s created unrest. Greek peasants in the 1890s and early 1900s grew tired of political instability and agricultural depression. East European Jews fled religious persecution and violent pograms.

Leaving home did not always imply hardship and oppression. Some people migrated not because they found conditions unbearable but because they believed that emigration would improve their standard of living more rapidly. In the early nineteenth century, these circumstances influenced migrations from northern and western Europe. In the later

nineteenth century they affected the areas of southern and eastern Europe, and the ethnic composition of immigration changed.

Transportation routes were influenced by commercial and mercantile considerations. The fact that cotton shipped from New Orleans and grain shipped from Baltimore headed for the North German Baltic ports explains the flow of German immigrants through these cities. Once a colony of immigrants gathered in one location, letters, newspaper advertisements, and advice from repatriates directed prospective emigrants to the same place. Passenger traffic from Europe and Asia to the United States brought profits to the steamship companies, which engaged in price wars to attract patrons.

The newcomers in America responded to the pull factors, or conditions obtaining in the United States at the time of their migration. Nineteenth-century America offered them many challenges and opportunities. The Homestead Act of 1862 served as a beacon to farmers from Scandinavia. Northern Pacific Railroad agents in northern Europe tempted potential emigrants with land bargains along its right of way. American industry's call for workers echoed across the globe—Chinese, Irish, Hungarians, Poles, Italians, Greeks, and many others answered. American economic development reflected this human tide. The rate of immigration corresponded directly to the cycles of economic prosperity in the United States.

Effects of Immigration. The contribution of the foreign-born to economic development was crucial in many areas. For example, the Congressional Commission on Immigration in 1907 discovered that 75 percent of the workers in the garment industry were immigrants. Today, the ethnic characteristics of America's blue collar workers continue to be significant.

Immigration influenced every aspect of American life. Religion, politics, labor organization, urbanization, industry, commerce, the arts, education—all bear the stamp of this human tide. Native Americans differed in their attitudes toward the newcomers. Those who feared that foreigners would dilute the quality of American life emphasized their strange customs, religions, languages, and ideologies. These critics attributed many of America's problems—such as a fluctuating economy, labor unrest, a rise in crime rates, political corruption, and overcrowding and deterioration of New York, Chicago, Boston, Philadelphia, and other cities—to the foreign-born.

Restrictions on Immigration. Critics from the ranks of journalism, politics, labor, and academe supported various methods to control the numbers and activities of immigrants. These mechanisms ranged from attempts to increase restrictions on naturalization and denial of elective office to the foreign-born to numerical limitation and total exclusion. Restrictionists justified their policies by producing historical, cultural, and pseudoscientific data that "proved" the inferiority of the southern and eastern Europeans. The latter approach especially used racist doctrines that glorified Anglo-Saxon and Teutonic peoples. Unrestricted immigration, which had characterized America from colonial times, fell prey to attacks from restrictionists, who accomplished their objectives with the passage of the Johnson Act in 1924. This law established a national origins quota that favored prospective emigrants from northwestern Europe.

Proponents of unrestricted immigration ranged from industrialists motivated by self-interest to those who maintained that America's strength derived from its polyglot population. The latter group differed among themselves on the ultimate significance of this factor. Some stressed the melting pot concept, whereas others spoke of cultural pluralism or the existence of subcultures within the larger social structure. This disagreement concerning the role of ethnicity in American society clouded the issue. The presence of diverse cultures has offered a variety of life styles and values to the host community. And it has encouraged cultural borrowing, which adapts new concepts to the existing social system. The debate over the unmeltable ethnics continues as observers increasingly report the persistence of ethnicity in American life.

Consult (V) Handlin 1957; Hansen, 1940; Jones, 1960; Wittke, 1964.
—Jean Scarpaci, *Towson State College*

IMMIGRATION AND NATIONALITY ACT (1952). *See* McCarran-Walter Immigration Act.

IMMIGRATION AND NATIONALITY ACT (1965), legislation liberalizing U.S. immigration procedures by eliminating the national origins quota system and setting new ceilings and priorities. The act also repealed the "Asia-Pacific triangle" stipulation that an Asian applicant be charged to the quota of the country of his ancestry even though he was born outside the triangle, an area stretching from Pakistan and India to Japan and the Pacific islands. The bill set an annual quota of 170,000 immigrants from all nations not in the Western Hemisphere, with a limit of 20,000 from any single nation and an annual quota of 120,000 for the Western Hemisphere. It exempted parents, spouses, and children of U.S. citizens and granted top priorities to skilled workers and refugees.

See also McCarran-Walter Immigration Act (1952); Quota System.

IMPEACHMENT, the first part of a two-step process for removing a public official from office. When the House of Representatives presents and adopts formal charges against an official, he is impeached; the Senate then acts as a court to consider those charges. If the Senate convicts the accused, he is dismissed from office. The Constitution states that federal officials "shall be removed from Office on Impeachment for, and Conviction of, Treason, Bribery, or other high Crimes and Misdemeanors."

INCOME TAX. Demands for a federal income tax, based upon the "ability to pay," were made as soon as the emergency Civil War taxes were repealed in 1870. In 1894 the Democratic Congress, aided by Populists, enacted an income tax, only to have the Supreme Court overturn it on a highly questionable 5 to 4 decision (*Pollock v. Farmers Loan and Trust Co.,* 1895). In 1909 a coalition of Democrats and Insurgent Republicans had the votes to include the tax as part of the Payne-Aldrich Tariff, but Aldrich and President Taft substituted a constitutional amendment. The amendment was designed to remove the Supreme Court's objections and to shift the burden of voting on the controversial issue to the state legislatures. Taft was sincerely concerned about the tax's constitutionality, but Aldrich and his allies were confident that the regular Republicans who controlled the Northeastern legislatures would prevent ratification. However, the capture of crucial states by the Democrats provided the necessary votes for adoption of the Sixteenth Amendment by February 1913. The Democratic majority in Congress, prodded by the Insurgents, quickly enacted an income tax that provided for a 1-percent levy with a graduated surcharge up to 6 percent.

See also Amendments, Constitutional.
Consult (V) Studenski and Krooss, 1963.

INDENTURED SERVITUDE, system in which immigrants to the American colonies paid for their passage by selling their future labor. Indentured servitude brought penniless Europeans who desired to immigrate to America together with monied individuals who either needed laborers or wanted to obtain the 50-acre grants, or headrights, that a number of colonies offered for each servant brought within their jurisdictions.

In return for their trans-Atlantic passage, redemptioners before leaving Europe signed articles of indenture binding themselves to a period of service—usually 2 to 7 years. These indentures were sold to a ship captain, who transported the immigrants to a colonial port and there sold his human cargo to American buyers for the period of their indentures.

More than half the Europeans who came to America in the colonial period were redemptioners who could not have otherwise paid their passage. Most were purchased by inhabitants of Virginia, Maryland, Pennsylva-

IMMIGRATION — Item Guide

The article on IMMIGRATION covers the trends in the movement of people to the United States. The place of these people within American society is described in ACCULTURATION, ASSIMILATION, CITY, ETHNIC GROUP, and GHETTO.

The flood of nineteenth-century immigrants, many attracted by land acts such as the HOMESTEAD ACT (1862), caused resentment among established Americans. Anti-immigrant NATIVIST MOVEMENTS formed, expressed politically in such groups as the KNOW-NOTHING PARTY and the NATIVE AMERICAN PARTY. Opposition to Asiatic immigration was particularly intense and is detailed in the entries on CHINESE EXCLUSION, CONTRACT LABOR ACT, and GENTLEMAN'S AGREEMENT (1907).

Legislative restrictions on immigration in the twentieth century have included QUOTA LAWS, MC CARRAN-WALTER IMMIGRATION ACT (1952), REFUGEE RELIEF ACT (1953), AND IMMIGRATION AND NATIONALITY ACT (1965). Exceptions were made for DISPLACED PERSONS after World War II.

Newly arrived immigrants leave the docks at Ellis Island, N.Y.

Ticket to the impeachment trial of President Andrew Johnson.

Indian teenagers stand guard at Wounded Knee during 1973 takeover of the reservation town. Disgust with federal policies led to more militant demonstrations by disgruntled Indians in the early 1970s.

Indian agents such as John P. Clum of San Carlos Agency had broad authority on the reservations.

nia, and other colonies with the headright system. Redemptioners labored long hours and in return received only maintenance. At the end of their period of service, they were also given "freedom dues," which usually consisted of some tools and clothing. Beginning with only these few possessions, many former indentured servants eventually obtained land and gained a measure of prosperity.

But abuses were also common. Ships' agents were frequently accused of kidnapping impoverished persons from the streets of London and Bristol. They also used unscrupulous methods when they recruited in the areas of the Rhineland that had been devastated by the Thirty Years' War. And even when indentures were voluntarily made, conditions of the trans-Atlantic passage were wretched, families were destroyed when members were purchased by different owners, and in some instances masters mistreated their servants.

Consult (I) Morris, 1946.

—Thomas Archdeacon, *University of Wisconsin*

INDEPENDENT TREASURY ACT (1846), a revival of the Independent Treasury Act of 1840, served as the basis of the U.S. fiscal system until 1913, when the Federal Reserve Act was passed. The independent treasury system was originally proposed by President Van Buren and a group of Democrats who favored hard money, but Congress defeated this proposal several times. It was passed in 1840 but repealed in 1841 by a Whig majority who hoped to reestablish a national bank. For five years the Whigs defeated attempts by Democrats to reestablish subtreasuries.

With the defeat of the Whigs in 1844, Democrats in Congress were able to revive the act. The 1846 act, substantially the same as the 1840 version, proposed that the Treasury should hold all its fiscal revenues in treasury and subtreasury offices. Thus it could accept and pay out nothing but specie or treasury notes. Notes and checks drawn against money in state banks could not be used to pay government debts. The act also created subtreasuries, a system that existed until 1920, when it became clear that the Federal Reserve System had made the subtreasuries outdated.

See also Federal Reserve Act (1913).

INDIANA, the 19th state, joined the Union on Dec. 11, 1816. The French first settled Indiana in 1732 at Vincennes; the British acquired the territory in 1763. Indiana was part of the Northwest Territory, organized in 1787, and was granted territorial status in 1800. Indians in the region tried to unite under Tecumseh, but their hopes were ended by the Battle of Tippecanoe (1811).

The state legislature is bicameral; the

capital is Indianapolis. The population in 1970 was 5,193,669.

See also Tecumseh.

INDIANA COMPANY. *See* Land Companies; Vandalia Grant (1772).

INDIAN AFFAIRS, BUREAU OF (BIA), division of the Department of the Interior responsible for governing those Indian and Alaskan native peoples living on reservations. The Bureau's responsibilities include the fulfillment of the government's treaty obligations. Of the 650,000 Indians and native Alaskans (Indians, Eskimos, and Aleuts) in the United States, about 450,000 come under the bureau's jurisdiction. The bureau was established under the old War Department in 1824 and became part of Interior when it was created in 1849.

Until 1924, Indians were considered wards of the states in which they lived, and local field divisions of the bureau exercised ultimate control over reservation administration. Although Indians were made citizens in 1924, it was not until 1948 that they were granted full voting rights. Since that time the bureau, administered from the central office in Washington, D.C., has worked to promote greater self-management by using the resources of various other governmental and private agencies. The bureau coordinates these resources with those of the tribes to develop social and economic programs administered by the reservation population.

The bureau further works to reconcile its programs of modernization with tribal desires to retain some of the ancient traditions. Despite the bureau's announced policy of greater self-management, however, Indians and native Alaskans remain under a trust relationship with the federal government, which to a large extent retains control of their lands and funds. Militant Indian groups have protested against the bureau's actions with public actions, including a destructive take-over of the BIA's Washington offices in 1972 and the occupation of Wounded Knee, S.D., in 1973.

See also Indian Policy.

INDIAN CLAIMS COMMISSION ACT (1946) permitted Indians to sue the federal government when seeking redress for past damages. *See* Indian Policy.

INDIAN POLICY. For most of America's history federal Indian policy has failed. The basic problem resulted from the competition between peoples with two widely differing cultures for the same land area and natural resources. In the long run there were more white Americans than Indian Americans, and the technical superiority of the former carried the day. Despite frequent claims that genocide and planned extermination have been practiced against the Indians, the evidence fails to support such contentions. Certainly whites robbed and killed Indians, but usually this resulted from the disorganization and general impotence of the federal government rather than a calculated program.

Rather than employing a national policy of extermination, American leaders hoped to live at peace and to deal honestly with the tribesmen. Undoubtedly the whites expected their neighbors to share the vast tracts of land on which they hunted and farmed, and the authorities did hope that cooperation rather than warfare would result. From independence until the 1930s, federal Indian policies have had one underlying theme—Indians had to adopt at least some white American customs and economic practices in order for whites and Indians to live together in peace.

Early Policies. During the first decades of national independence the United States employed several policies toward the Indians. Beginning in the 1790s, Congress set up the so-called factory system. Government-owned and -operated factories offered the Indians fair prices and high quality goods for their furs, with the expectation that if the tribesmen were satisfied with the trade they would be more likely to remain at peace. At the same time the government allowed and even encouraged Christian missionary groups to build schools, model farms, and churches among the tribes if the Indians asked for them.

While the government supported these programs, a flood of settlers surged westward. Friction between the frontiersmen and tribesmen continued, so federal authorities worked to convince Indian leaders that their survival depended on becoming sedentary farmers. As such they would need less land, so the demands of the pioneers could be met more easily and the incidents of violence between the races might diminish. To do this, American negotiators tried to convince the Indians that they should sell their land and move beyond the frontier settlements.

Indian Removal. By the 1820s this idea came to be called Indian Removal, and during Andrew Jackson's first term as president it became the official federal policy. By presidential order he forced the major Southeastern tribes to the West. In spite of heated reaction in Congress and two decisions by the Supreme Court, the Indians were removed. During their trek to present-day Oklahoma many Indians caught diseases and died. The Cherokee still remember this with bitterness, recalling their march on the "Trail of Tears." A few tribes still resisted, and the Black Hawk War in Wisconsin and the Seminole Wars in Florida resulted.

These delayed but did not stop removal, because the government put the tribes on reservations gradually. The reservations were to be permanent, but whenever whites discovered valuable resources on tribal land the government retracted its promises, and the Indians had to sell their land or move again. One cynical Indian leader suggested that the whites put the tribesmen on wheels to make it easier for them to be moved from place to place. By the 1880s reformers had decided that the only way to keep the Indians from physical destruction was to dismember the tribes. So in 1887 Congress passed the Dawes Severalty Act, under which individual Indians and families got land of their own and citizenship. For the next 40 years Indian agents, government schools, and missionaries labored to destroy the tribes and to make the Indians copies of their white American rulers.

Twentieth Century. Demoralization swept through the tribes, and the Indian population plummeted, until by the 1920s a band of reformers demanded a complete policy reversal. They got their chance when President Franklin Roosevelt appointed John Collier as his new commissioner of Indian Affairs in 1933. Within a year he had steered the Indian Reorganization Act, sometimes called the Collier Act, into law. This encouraged the scattered tribesmen to regroup and organize tribal governments and aided the resurgent interest in Indian cultures that still continues.

The anti-Indian forces reemerged during the 1940s and since then have worked to merge all Indians into the general society. The Indian Claims Commission, established to repay tribes for lands taken unjustly, was a part of this drive. In the 1950s the termination policy carried this goal further by ending government support and programs for several tribes. At the same time relocation centers in major cities encouraged reservation dwellers to leave home and go to the cities for jobs. Many Indians moved to urban centers, but most returned to the reservation, and of those who remained many have low-paying jobs, poor housing, and difficulties related to low incomes.

At present the government seems undecided about its relationship with the Indians. Some bureaucrats want to get out of the Indian business, whereas others see a need to encourage pride in tribal cultural and religious practices. The Indians themselves share this ambivalence about their relationship with the government and with the rest of American society.

See also Subject Map on Indians.
Consult (X) Deloria, 1969; Hagan, 1961.
—Roger L. Nichols, *University of Arizona*

INDIAN REMOVAL, policy of resettling Indian tribes. *See* Indian Policy.

Indians gather at Pine Ridge Agency, S.D., in 1890 to receive supplies. Federal policies in late nineteenth century made Indians dependent on the government.

INDIAN REORGANIZATION ACT (1934), major attempt to restructure the federal government's treatment of the Indians. *See* Indian Policy.

INDIANS, NORTH AMERICAN. On the eve of the European intrusion, the North American Indians numbered perhaps 1.5 million and were grouped into more than 200 tribes speaking more than 50 languages. No tribe had a system of writing, although the Mayas and Aztecs of Mexico and Yucatan communicated with glyph symbols. Less advanced tribes used line drawings for communication. Delawares and other Algonkian-speaking tribes of the Atlantic Coast used belts and strings of wampum, tiny colored shells, to communicate war, peace, and other tribal intentions.

Religious Practices. The tribes of North America varied in culture but had some common practices. Most had a religious system that included a concept of life after death requiring elaborate mortuary (burial of weapons, tools, food, and personal effects with the deceased). They also believed in a common creator and lesser deities and in a variety of spirits, good and bad, that had to be placated with rituals and specific modes of behavior. Indians used their religion to explain lightning, thunder, and other natural phenomena.

Many tribes, notably the Natchez, Chickasaw, Cherokee, Maya, and Aztec, supported an elite class of priests. The hopoye, or holy men, presided at religious rites and served as healers because sickness was thought to be caused by spirits that inflitrated the body and had to be exorcised. Related to tribal religion were certain annual rites and festivals, ranging from the green corn festival of the Southeastern tribes to the water spirit fete of the Pacific Northwest tribes to the sun dance rite of the Plains Indians.

The purpose of the annual rite was a symbolic cleansing, personal purification, and national renewal. It required several days of fasting, dancing, and then feasting. In the case of the sun dance, which lasted several days, worshippers fasted, danced, and endured self-torture in order to reach a trance state wherein the communicant received guidance for the future. The Toltecs and certain other Mexican tribes practiced human sacrifice to propitiate deity wrath.

Social Organization. In social organization the tribes practiced a mix of matrilineal and patrilineal systems with the maternal line of descent dominating. Most of the tribes consisted of a collection of clans, in turn composed of a cluster of families. The clan provided education for youth, local government, identity for the individual, and marriage direction in that most tribes required marriage outside the clan. Mobility and status in the clan

Members of Iroquois Confederacy attack explorer Samuel de Champlain.

and the tribe were determined by talent in some art or craft, wisdom, and valor in battle.

Each tribe had a system of law based on custom that regulated behavior of tribal members and that protected life and personal property, clan and tribal integrity and honor. Clan elders served as a judicial body to pass judgment on offenses against the laws of the tribe, although punishment was often privately handled, particularly in cases of homicide.

Marriage customs varied, but most tribes practiced polygamy. One of the most unusual customs of the North American tribes was the potlatch practiced by the Pacific Northwest Indians. Tribal members gained the ultimate in prestige and stature by competitive giving, often during a marriage or name-giving ceremony. He who gave the most received the greatest glory.

Economy. Each family in the tribe was a self-sufficient economic unit. The Indians supported themselves by hunting, fishing, gathering, and agriculture. Corn was the principal crop of the agricultural tribes from the Atlantic seaboard to the Mississippi Valley. Many agricultural Indian communities of the desert Southwest produced corn with irrigation.

The buffalo was the focus of the economy of the Kiowas, Comanches, Cheyennes, Arapahos, and other tribes of the plains. Buffalo flesh provided the basic food; its thick hide was for shelter, clothing, and footwear; and its bones served as implements. The California tribes subsisted largely on the acorn, which was processed into flour. The Northwest tribes depended on fish, largely salmon, sturgeon, and eels, which were trapped in weirs and preserved by smoking over slow-burning fires.

Technology. The simple technology of the North American Indians yielded a wide range of articles essential to and adequate for their life. They had no wheeled vehicles and no domesticated animals except the dog. From nature they drew herbs, leaves, and roots to compound surprisingly effective medical cures. They fashioned household items from grasses, reeds, and other natural materials. Stone was sculptured into figures for worship, pipes, tools, and weapons. Clays were fashioned into bricks for building and into household utensils. Metalsmiths, particularly among the Mayan and Aztec communities, used gold, silver, and copper to fabricate exquisite ceremonial pieces and jewelry.

The North American Indians were town dwellers. Their shelters varied from the crude brush wickiups of California Indians to the earth-covered lodges of the Pawnees of the plains. The Algonkian-speaking tribes of the Atlantic Coast and north of the Ohio River constructed wigwams—dome shaped, framed with bent poles, and covered with woven mats.

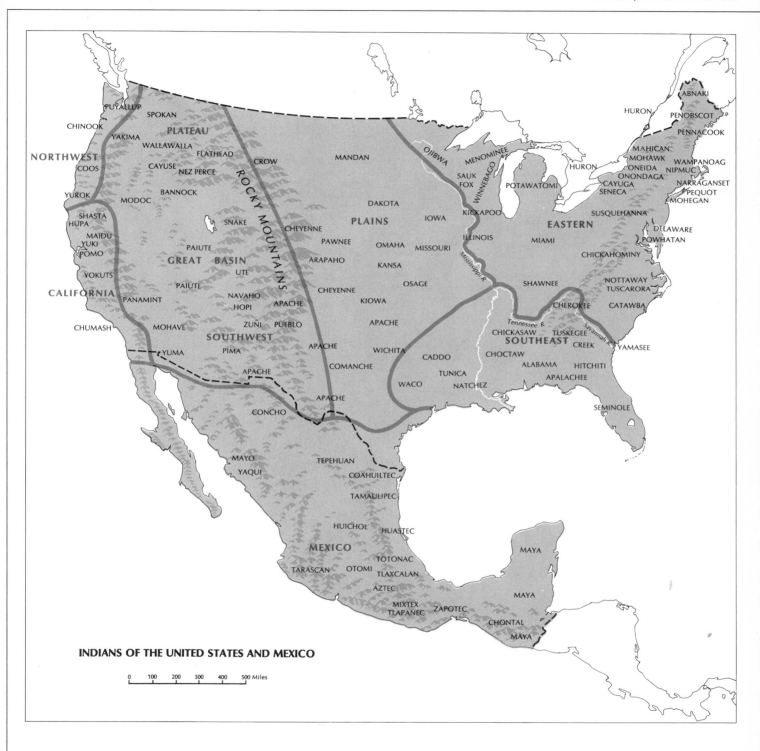

INDIANS OF THE UNITED STATES AND MEXICO

0   100   200   300   400   500 Miles

Encounter between colonists and Indians in King Philip's War (1675–1676).

Abenaki braves attack Deerfield, Mass., in 1704 during Queen Anne's War.

Most of the buffalo-hunting tribes of the desert Southwest constructed multifamily dwellings of stone and sun-dried brick.

The wonders of North American aboriginal advancement are the Indians of Mexico—Mayan, Toltec, and Aztec—and the Iroquois Confederacy—Seneca, Cayuga, Oneida, Mohawk, and Onondaga—situated in the upper Appalachian chain. Mayan preeminence was in architecture, engineering, and stone construction of temples and other public buildings; an incipient written form using glyph symbols; and a calendar rated more accurate than the Julian calendar. The Toltecs, conquerors of the Mayan, continued the tradition of Mexican Indian engineering excellence and added techniques of civil administration unparalleled for sophistication and effectiveness in aboriginal America. The Aztec successors to the Mayan-Toltec culture, supreme in Mexico by 1350, eclectically drew from their cultural predecessors and established a despotically ruled empire that endured until the Spanish conquest that began in 1519.

The Iroquois Confederacy functioned at the time of the European intrusion in the upper Hudson-Mohawk Valley. The five nations resided in large planned towns. Iroquois society focused on the "fireside," composed of the mother and her children. Collective firesides comprised clans. Women as mothers dominated the Confederacy because they headed the firesides and clans and named the male officials. Iroquois law, cohesiveness, and Confederacy pride made it the most awesome and successful North American Indian community outside of Mexico.

Consult (X) Boas, 1949; Driver, 1961; Hodge, 1910; Josephy, 1966; Thompson, 1954.

—Arrell M. Gibson, *University of Oklahoma*

INDIANS, SOUTH AMERICAN. In 1500, South America's Indian population numbered an estimated 10 million grouped in a number of tribes that have been classified into three language families—Macro-Chibchan, Ge-Pans-Carib, and Andean Equatorial. The first family was concentrated in the north, whereas tribes associated with the latter two language groups were scattered throughout the continent. The South American tribes ranged in cultural sophistication from the remarkably advanced Incan peoples of the northwest to the Yahgans, primal shellfish gatherers residing on the offshore islands of southern Chile.

Caribs, Arawaks, and Chibchas resided in Nicaragua, Costa Rica, Panama, Colombia, northern Venezuela, and the Caribbean islands. These Indians were largely sedentary, practicing an intensive agriculture with terraced fields and irrigation, and had an advanced technology. Commerce was extensive, and the economic as well as social life of each community centered on the marketplace. Most of the northern tribes practiced cannibalism and human sacrifice and were ruled by a militaristic caste system.

South of the Caribbean aboriginal community were the Rain Forest tribes, which included the Parintintins, Tupinambas, Guaranis, and Jivaros. They practiced slash-burn agriculture, a migratory style required by the excessive rainfall that leached the soil. Below the Rain Forest tribes extending through southern Paraguay, Uruguay, and Argentina were a number of hunting tribes that included the Zamucoans, Matacans, and Tehuelches. In Chile's southern Andes were the Atacameños, Diaguites, and Araucanians, who sustained themselves by agriculture and herding llamas. The Araucanians were particularly noteworthy for their intense pride and martial prowess.

Incan Civilization. The most advanced Indian civilization of South America evolved in the Andes of Ecuador, Peru, and northern Chile and centered on the Incas. The principal tribes were the Caran, Paltan, Chancan, Urun, and Incan. They had made a remarkable adjustment to the desert coastal strip and high, rugged Andes Mountains. By irrigation and mountain-side terracing and use of guano fertilizer, Incan farmers produced sufficient food to sustain a large population. They had domesticated alpacas and llamas, which they used as beasts of burden, food, and wool for textiles. Metalsmiths fashioned exquisite items from gold and copper alloy, and engineers constructed comprehensive public works from huge stone blocks.

Incan technology and administrative techniques made it possible for large towns to develop, some of them containing more than 1,000 dwellings. The components of this ethnic complex were ruled by militaristic societies dominated by warrior priests. One group in the Cuzco basin of the southern highlands—the Incan—integrated this community and by 1525 controlled a region extending over 2,000 miles along the Andean chain, with an estimated 7 million people.

Consult (X) Prescott, 1936; Steward, 1946–1950.

—Arrell M. Gibson, *University of Oklahoma*

INDIAN SLAVERY. *See* Slavery.

INDIAN WARS, COLONIAL. The earliest Indian wars, such as the Virginia massacre of 1622 or the Pequot War in New England, pitted vulnerable white settlements against a potentially far greater force of Indians. Indeed, much of the brutality of these conflicts stemmed from the colonists' awareness that they had to appear terrifying and invincible to avert the threat of annihilation. As late as King Philip's War in New England (1675–1676) and the

INDIANS

CULTURE

INDIANS, NORTH AMERICAN
IROQUOIS CONFEDERACY
INDIANS, SOUTH AMERICAN

First White Contacts
EXPLORATION AND DISCOVERY
SPANISH COLONIES, NORTH AMERICAN
HERNÁN CORTÉS
FRANCISCO PIZARRO
HERNÁN DeSOTO
FRENCH COLONIES
SAMUEL DE CHAMPLAIN
FATHER JACQUES MARQUETTE
SIEUR DE LA SALLE
JESUITS

RESISTANCE IN NORTH AMERICA

Colonial
INDIAN WARS, COLONIAL
PEQUOT WAR (1637)
KING PHILIP'S WAR (1675–1676)
    CONNECTICUT
    MASSACHUSETTS
    RHODE ISLAND
SCHENECTADY RAID (1690)
KING WILLIAM'S WAR (1689–1697)
QUEEN ANNE'S WAR (1702–1713)
TUSCARORA WAR (1711–1713)
FRENCH AND INDIAN WAR (1754–1763)
PONTIAC'S REBELLION (1763)
LORD DUNMORE'S WAR (1774)

Midwest and Southeast
FALLEN TIMBERS, BATTLE OF (1794)
    NORTHWEST TERRITORY
    GREENVILLE, TREATY OF (1795)
    ANTHONY WAYNE
TECUMSEH
    WILLIAM HENRY HARRISON
CREEK WAR
SEMINOLE WARS (1818–1819; 1835–1842)
BLACK HAWK WAR

Western
INDIAN WARS, WESTERN
    GEORGE ARMSTRONG CUSTER
GOLD RUSHES
FRONTIER IN AMERICAN HISTORY
    (see Subject Map)

Federal Programs
INDIAN POLICY
    ANDREW JACKSON
    CHEROKEE NATION V. GEORGIA (1831)
INDIAN AFFAIRS, BUREAU OF

The Subject Maps in the Encyclopedia illustrate the coverage of particular aspects of American History, showing the interrelationships among the articles in twelve critical areas of study. Entries in capital letters, except for titles, are subjects for which there are separate articles in the Encyclopedia.

The Subject Maps are arranged alphabetically in the Encyclopedia under the following titles:

American Wars
Blacks in the United States
Business Regulation and Industrialization
Civil War and Reconstruction
Constitution of the United States
Exploration and Colonization
Frontier in American History
Indians
Labor Movement
New Deal and Depression
Revolutionary War Era
Slavery and Emancipation

After Revolutionary War, British encouraged Indians of Old Northwest to resist American expansion on the frontier.

Apaches of Southwest were among last tribes to resist U.S. rule. Fierce warrior Geronimo sits in front row, third from right.

Yamasee War in South Carolina (1715), Indians could still raise fears for survival among the whites even though—as always—the Indians themselves absorbed more punishment than they inflicted.

In most areas the colonies were too well established by 1690 for Indians to challenge their existence. Instead white-Indian conflicts became border affairs with the fur trade and land encroachment as major issues. International rivalries among competing European powers added a new dimension to these relationships after 1689. New France won the allegiance of most tribes in northern New England and the Great Lakes area, whereas the British claimed support from the Iroquois Confederacy. On the south Atlantic frontier, a complex three-way rivalry emerged among the English, French, and Spanish, pitting particular tribes against one another or against the colony of a European opponent.

White Ascendancy. As white settlements continued to expand, while Indians continued to decline in absolute numbers, the military impact became quite evident. In King William's War (1689–1697), Indians provided New France with its main striking force. But in the final Anglo-French conflict of the period, the French and Indian War (1754–1763), they had been reduced to acting as auxiliaries to regular and provincial soldiers. Eastern North America had definitely become a white man's country, mostly for demographic reasons but also because Indians never developed adequate tactics for destroying white fortifications. By contrast, colonists aimed their principal blows at the Indian food supply in nearly every conflict between the two peoples. Because Indians lacked strong fortifications of their own, this strategy usually achieved devastating results.

See also Subject Map on Indians.

Consult (X) Fenton, 1957; Peckham, 1964.

—John M. Murrin, *Princeton University*

INDIAN WARS, WESTERN. When reference is made to "the Indian Wars," one normally is referring to the systematic attempt by the federal government, largely through the U.S. Cavalry, to press back and defeat in battle the Indian tribes of the prairies, high plains, and mountain West. These wars were only the final phase of a long confrontation between white settlers and native peoples in North America that began almost as soon as the first European stepped ashore in the New World. The wars in the West generally are seen to have been preceded by two other phases, the first beginning with the Indian war of 1622 in Virginia, including the Pequot War (1637) and King Philip's War (1675–1676), and running to the

mideighteenth century and a vicious war on the Pennsylvania frontier.

The second phase of the Indian wars was that in which the British and the French, and later the Americans, sought to form alliances with Indian groups in order to use them as collaborators in essentially European wars. This was markedly so during the French and Indian War (1754–1763), Pontiac's Rebellion (1763), the Revolution, and the rising of Tecumseh and the Prophet in the Old Northwest in 1811. This second phase ended with the Treaty of Greenville in 1814, by which the defeated Delaware, Miami, Seneca, Shawnee, and Wyandot Indians were obliged to declare war on Britain.

Development of Government Policy. In a sense, the final phase also began during the War of 1812, for it was in the Creek War in the Southeast that Andrew Jackson organized the frontier armies that became the prototype for the forces that made the final assault on the Eastern Woodlands Indians. Thereafter, the Indian was defeated, driven westward, or uprooted and forced to migrate to governmentally supplied and controlled lands.

Andrew Jackson's success in 1818 in the Seminole War, which brought all of East Florida under American military control, and his Indian policy as president, especially in 1832 when he declined to enforce the decision of Chief Justice Marshall in the case of *Cherokee Nation v. Georgia,* characterized the Indian policy until 1840—the federal government would be an instrument that sided with the encroaching settlers rather than with the Indians in any territorial disputes. When in 1835 the Cherokee surrendered to the United States all their lands east of the Mississippi in return for land in the Indian Territory, transportation costs, and $5 million, the process of displacement was given legitimacy.

Early Western Wars. Thereafter, wars with the Indians focused on the land west of the Mississippi. By 1846, having been defeated in the Black Hawk War of 1832, the Indians were removed from the Old Northwest. For decades a period of relative peace followed, before population movements once again pressed against the Indians. The new wars were to be fought with tribes that were more mobile and able to defend themselves, having horses and, until the systematic destruction of the Indians' hunting grounds (and especially of the buffalo), a dependable food supply. Beginning with the Cheyenne-Arapaho War of 1861–1864, caused by the movement of miners into the area now dominated by Denver and in which Colonel J. M. Chivington massacred 450 Indian men, women, and children, a savage series of set pieces occurred between the federal army, acting on behalf of the settlers, and the Indians.

The Civil War sped the demise of the

merce clauses. However, it was he who began the Supreme Court's initial involvement with freedom of speech and the meaning of the First Amendment. In a case testing the Espionage Act, he formulated the famous rule that an utterance could be punished only if there was a "clear and present danger" that it would lead to an evil that Congress or the states could legitimately prevent (*Schenck v. U.S.,* 1919).

Because of his distrust of all absolutes, this rule gave Congress somewhat less latitude in its ability to curb expressions than it had in economic regulations. At the same time, however, Holmes' rule consciously fell short of giving speech an absolute inviolability, especially in regard to the states. Holmes' belief in experimentation and his defense of state legislation on economics and free speech made him an ardent protector of federalism.

See also Espionage Act (1917); Hammer v. Dagenhart (1918).

Consult (VI) Bowen, 1944; Frankfurter, 1965; Howe, 1963; Lerner, 1948.

—David Forte, *Skidmore College*

HOLY EXPERIMENT, Quaker term for the policy of religious toleration in colonial Pennsylvania. *See* Colonial Religion; Pennsylvania; Quakers.

HOME DEPARTMENT, original name for the Interior Department, which was established in 1849. *See* Interior, Department of the.

HOME OWNERS' REFINANCING ACT (1933), New Deal emergency legislation passed during the Hundred Days to prevent foreclosures of home mortgages. It created the Home Owners' Loan Corporation (HOLC), which made direct loans of less than $14,000 to householders for the refinancing of homes threatened by foreclosure and for the recovery of many already lost. About 20 percent of all mortgaged homes in the country received some benefit from HOLC, which stimulated real estate and lending businesses as well. A companion act established the Farm Credit Administration.

See also Farm Credit Administration; Hundred Days.

Consult (VI) Harris, 1951.

HOMER, WINSLOW (1836–1910), American painter who was one of the most highly regarded artists of nineteenth-century America. Born in Boston, he was almost entirely self-taught and only slightly influenced by other artists, whether American or European; with a freshness and clarity of vision, he was a pioneer of naturalism. After two years in England and Paris, Homer settled in New York, where he earned a living as an illustrator and began to paint his first oils. During the Civil War he worked as a pictorial reporter for *Harper's Weekly*, recording the war with a sense of

actuality that became characteristic of his canvases.

Homer's early paintings were scenes of country life such as "Long Branch" (1869) and the rustic "Snap the Whip" (1870). Later he shifted to more dramatic settings of rugged Adirondack huntsmen and New England fishermen, as in "Huntsman and Dog" (1891) and "Herring Net" (1885).

In 1883 Homer moved permanently to Prout's Neck on the Maine coast, living almost as a recluse and leaving only to paint in different places where he found inspiration, such as the Adirondacks, Florida, and the British West Indies, the scene of some of his finest watercolors. His famous scenes of sea life include "The Life Line" (1884), "Eight Bells" (1886), and "The Gulf Stream" (1899). They mark him as one of the greatest painters of the sea.

See also Painting.

HOMESTEAD ACT (1862) provided 160 acres of free public land for those who would actually settle and improve it. Title to the land was to be granted after five years of settlement and cultivation. Although designed to help the laborer and small farmer and prevent speculators from grabbing huge tracts, the act was not entirely successful. Speculators found loopholes and snapped up great hunks of the available land. Workers looking for a new start in life often did not have the skills or money to establish a self-sufficient farm. Only about 11 percent of the 2 billion acres given out under the law actually went to truly needy pioneers.

HOMESTEAD MASSACRE (1892), a fight between strikers and company guards on July 6, 1892. Shooting occurred when Carnegie Steel Company's head manager, Henry Clay Frick, ordered 300 Pinkerton guards sent in to protect strikebreakers at the plant in Homestead, Pa. When striking workers forcibly resisted the arrival of the Pinkertons, 10 guards and strikers were killed. The state militia was sent in to maintain order and, incidentally, protect strikebreakers. Both the strike and the union were broken, and the steel industry remained unorganized until the 1930s.

See also Frick, Henry Clay; Labor Movement.

HOOKER, THOMAS, early settler of Connecticut. *See* Connecticut.

HOOVER, HERBERT (CLARK) (1874–1964), 31st President of the United States (1929–1933). A world hero as successful administrator of immense relief activities during World War I, this tall, complicated man became a devil to many Americans who associated his presidency with the Great Depression.

Hoover began ife in humble circum-

Oliver Wendell Holmes, Jr., served as associate justice of Supreme Court for 30 years.

President Hoover tried unsuccessfully to solve country's problems during early stages of Depression.

Indian because it increased the railroad technology that would bring thousands of settlers into the West; it enlarged the federal army and created a reservoir of trained fighting men; and it spurred the need for Western beef. While the Apache and Navajo Indians submitted in 1865 and were placed on reservations, the Sioux fought on until 1868, when they accepted a reservation in the Dakota Territory. However, a gold rush into their Black Hills reservation in 1875–1876—which again deprived the Sioux of their land—coupled with corruption in the Department of the Interior, led to a second war, in which Gen. George A. Custer and 264 of his men were massacred at the Battle of the Little Big Horn.

Last Stages. In the meantime, in 1871 the Apache war was renewed in New Mexico and Arizona with the massacre of more than 100 Indians at Camp Grant and the ultimate capture in 1886 of the great Apache leader, Geronimo. In the Pacific Northwest, the Nez Percé under Chief Joseph conducted a magnificent retreat in the face of white encroachments only to be defeated late in 1877 and assigned to land in Oklahoma.

The final war broke out among the Sioux once again in 1890, when a Paiute religious leader, Wovoka, inspired many Indians to accept the Ghost Dance faith by which they hoped to reject white values. The Battle of Wounded Knee, less a battle than a massacre of the defenseless by the cavalry, brought the period of the Indian wars to an end on December 29.

Evaluation. Neither side was without blame, and both had resorted to treachery on more than one occasion. The clash was the unhappy, and perhaps inevitable, result of contact between a questing, land-hungry, high-technology culture and a traditional, mobile, low-technology society. To the white settlers, most Indians were at best idle nuisances who stood in the way of "progress" and at worst heathen savages who brought death and destruction. Little effort was made to understand the Indian way of life or what the Indian could give to the white man.

Until recently in American fiction, in history texts, and in the mythology developed by the motion picture, the Indian was the villain, the U.S. Cavalry charging to the rescue of beleaguered whites in the nick of time. Beginning in the 1950s, however, many historians and writers, and in the 1960s and 1970s the motion picture industry and press, began to reexamine the Indian wars and to move increasingly toward an understanding of the wrongs done to the Indian. In this sense, the Indian wars are still with us, on the American conscience, a part of the constant reexamination of the American value system. Ironically, the Indian became the object of such attention (some of it no less romantic than the earlier glorification of the settler) only as the unique values he represented were also in danger of disappearing permanently from the American scene.

See also Subject Map on Indians.
Consult (X) Brown, 1966; Dunn, 1969; Finerty, 1961; Leckie, 1963.
—Robin W. Winks, *Yale University*

INDOCHINA WAR. *See* Vietnam War.

INDUSTRIAL WORKERS OF THE WORLD (IWW), labor organization founded in 1905 by an uneasy coalition of left-wing unionists and theorists. Ideologically committed to assaulting capitalism through direct action, the Wobblies (as they were called) eschewed the tools of political democracy in the quest of the working class' revolutionary goals. The IWW rejected the craft orientation of the American Federation of Labor, instead priding itself as "one big union" for unskilled and skilled alike.

Although its Western origins often are highlighted, the most dramatic successes achieved by the IWW were in Eastern industrial cities, such as Lawrence, Mass., in 1912, among unskilled workers from southern and eastern Europe who found themselves unwelcomed by the AFL. Despite occasional victories, the Wobblies never rivaled the older, more established union, which had accommodated itself into a mutually beneficial relationship with industry and government.

America's entry into World War I found the IWW incurring the wrath of the Wilson Administration, resulting in federal prosecution and conviction for many of its leaders as radicals, among them "Big Bill" Haywood. Although the IWW stills claims adherents among its surviving members as well as youthful disciples, its effectiveness waned less than 15 years after its formation.

See also Labor Movement.
Consult (V) Dubofsky, 1969.
—Michael H. Ebner, *City College of The City University of New York*

INFLUENCE OF SEA POWER UPON HISTORY, landmark book on naval strategy. *See* Mahan, Alfred T.

INSULAR CASES (1900–1901), Supreme Court decisions affecting the status of U.S. territories. *See* Foraker Act (1900); Territories and Possessions.

INSULL, SAMUEL (1859–1938), public utilities magnate. He was born in London, came to the United States in 1881, became Thomas Edison's private secretary that year, and was a vice-president of General Electric by 1892. He soon transferred his attention to the production of electricity and developed operating principles still commonly used in the industry.

Big Foot lies frozen in snow after massacre at Wounded Knee, S.D., (1890), an engagement known as the last battle of the Indian Wars.

By 1907, Insull had consolidated the electric business of Chicago and in 1912 began to expand his operations. By 1917, his systems served most of Illinois, but that year he became chairman of the Illinois State Council of Defense and devoted his full attention to war-related activities. At the end of the war, Insull inaugurated a "customer ownership" program based on the sale of securities to the general public and expanded his operations into natural gas and traction. His electrical interests expanded enormously, partly through use of the holding company.

The Depression brought the collapse of the Insull empire in 1932, and Insull moved to Europe. He was indicted for mail fraud, violation of bankruptcy laws, and embezzlement but was acquitted of all charges in 1934.

INSURGENTS, CONGRESSIONAL, group of Western and Midwestern Republicans who clashed with the party regulars or "standpatters" over a variety of issues between 1909 and 1916. Their numbers varied from 8 to 16 in the Senate and averaged about 40 in the House. Their most prominent leaders were Robert La Follette of Wisconsin, Albert Cummins of Iowa, William Borah of Idaho, George Norris of Nebraska, and Joseph Bristow of Kansas. During William Howard Taft's Administration (1909–1913), they pressed for tariff reduction, a federal income tax, liberalization of the House rules, and the protection of national resources. In the 1912 campaign they backed either Theodore Roosevelt or Woodrow Wilson or remained neutral, and during the Wilson years they strove for more stringent versions of reform legislation and forced higher income tax rates in 1913. By 1916 they were reunited with the Republican Party, and in 1919 many of them played a leading role in the defeat of the Versailles Treaty and the League of Nations charter.

See also La Follette, Robert; Norris, George W.; Progressive Party; Taft, William Howard.

INTERIOR, DEPARTMENT OF THE, cabinet-level executive department responsible for the management, development, and conservation of the nation's natural resources. Its divisions include those concerned with fish and wildlife, parks, public land, mineral resources, water quality, and water power development. The department is the trustee for the welfare of Indians, Aleuts, and Eskimos and the administrator of several U.S. territories.

Established in 1849 as the Home Department, it lumped together diverse government bureaus, including census, Indian affairs, and land, pension, and patent offices. Reaction in the early 1900s against the plundering of natural resources for private interests grew into the conservation movement, which was led by

Field worker in Interior Department's Geological Survey sets survey mark in mountain area.

Interstate Commerce Commission cowhands warily approach bucking iron horses. First efforts of ICC, established in 1887, were directed against abuses of railroad corporations.

men such as President Theodore Roosevelt, who set aside more than 148 million acres of national forest lands. Major legislation from the 1930s on expanded and supported the department's conservation activities.

INTERNAL SECURITY ACT, law passed in 1950, over President Truman's veto, to curb communist subversion. Also known as the McCarran Act and as the Subversive Activities Control Act, it provides for the registration of all communist and totalitarian action or front groups, revokes their members' passports, and requires public labeling of these organizations' broadcasts, publications, and mailings. Government or defense employees cannot contribute money or services to these organizations and must not conceal membership in them. Further, the act forbids the transmittal or receipt of classified information, regulates entry into defense plants, and strips infiltrated unions of their rights. The bill bans aliens who are connected in any way with communist or totalitarian organizations. Title II sanctions preventive detention during internal security emergencies where "reasonable grounds" exist for the belief that a person may engage in espionage or sabotage. To enforce the law, Congress established a five-man Subversive Activities Control Board.

The entire act raised distinct questions of constitutionality and was challenged several times. In 1964 the Supreme Court disallowed the ban on passports, and in 1965 the Court disallowed an order requiring individual Communist Party leaders to register.

See also Communist Control Act (1954).

INTERSTATE COMMERCE COMMISSION (ICC), first federal regulatory agency and model for all later ones, established by the Interstate Commerce Act (1887). The *Wabash Case* (1886) declared that states lacked the power to regulate interstate railroads, thus necessitating congressional action. Hearings led to bipartisan agreement on a bill that prohibited discriminatory railroad practices such as rebates and short-haul overcharges; "reasonable and just" rates were to be posted. Enforcement was vested in a five-man commission that would hear complaints, examine records, and order changes in railroad policy. Railroads did not oppose the ICC, because it could not fix rates and had to rely on federal courts for "cease and desist" orders. Leading businessmen were appointed to staff the commission, and the ICC was not effective until additional legislation was passed during the Progressive Era.

See also Railroad Legislation.

INTERSTATE HIGHWAY SYSTEM. *See* Highway System.

INTOLERABLE ACTS, alternate name for the Coercive Acts. *See* Coercive Acts (1774).

INVENTIONS, the organization of familiar elements to produce new results. To encourage inventions, the U.S. Patent Office was created in 1790 and had granted 36,000 patents by 1860. There is a lag between the issuing of a patent and its widespread use. Although John Fitch built the first steamboat (1787, patented 1791), it was two decades before Robert Fulton (1807) and John Stevens (1808) launched successful ones. John Stevens built the first multitubular boiler (1783) and used it in an experimental locomotive (1825), but Peter Cooper built the first commercially used U.S. steam locomotive (1830).

Agriculture was aided when Eli Whitney (who later pioneered the use of interchangeable parts in manufacturing) invented the cotton gin (1793) and when the reaper was invented by Cyrus H. McCormick (1831) and also developed independently by Obed Hussey.

Many inventions that brought changes after the Civil War had much earlier beginnings. Although Charles Thurber invented the typewriter (1843), Christopher L. Sholes and his collaborators made it practical (1867). Elias Howe invented the sewing machine (1846), and Isaac Singer popularized it (after 1860). Other examples are the electric telegraph invented by Samuel F. B. Morse (1844) and the airblast method of making steel developed by William Kelly (1851) independently of Henry Bessemer of England, who perfected the method (1856).

After the Civil War Alexander Graham Bell invented the telephone (1876), and Thomas A. Edison developed the first practical incandescent electric bulb (1879). Important to the development of the automobile was J. Frank Duryea, who built and operated the first gasoline-engined car (1895). A few years later Henry Ford applied mass production methods to automobile manufacturing. The high point in airplane development was when Orville and Wilbur Wright made the first heavier-than-air flight (1903). Because organized research hastens invention, most patents are now obtained by scientists and engineers connected with corporation laboratories, and each year's total greatly exceeds the number of patents granted from 1790 to 1860.

See also Automobile; Aviation; Cotton Gin; Sewing Machine; Typewriter; biographies of major inventors.

Consult (V) Burlingame, 1940.
—Ari Hoogenboom, *Brooklyn College of The City University of New York*

IOWA, the 29th state, entered the Union on Dec. 28, 1846. French trading posts were first established in the Iowa region in the seventeenth century, and the first permanent settlement was made by the French at Dubuque in 1788. Iowa became part of the United States in 1803 with the Louisiana Purchase. Settlers were harassed by Indians until the Black Hawk War of 1832. Territorial status came in 1838.

The state legislature is bicameral; the capital is Des Moines. The population in 1970 was 2,825,041.

See also Black Hawk War.

IRON ACT (1750). *See* Navigation Acts.

IRON CURTAIN, popular phrase for the line dividing Soviet-dominated Eastern Europe from the rest of the Continent. Speaking at Fulton, Mo., in early 1946, Winston Churchill declared that the Soviet Union had created "an iron curtain" across Europe from "Stettin in the Baltic to Trieste in the Adriatic." He also charged that the leaders of the Soviet Union wanted an indefinite "expansion of their power and doctrine" and that the British Commonwealth and the United States had to join together to stop this expansion.

Churchill's "iron curtain" address laid the foundation for the continuation of Anglo-American wartime cooperation to defend their common interests in postwar Europe. American policy makers were somewhat reluctant to accept Churchill's concept of an iron curtain, or impenetrable division of Europe, but before the year was out a change in the U.S. attitude toward the Soviet Union appeared. This was followed in early 1947 by the Truman Doctrine and the U.S. containment policy.

See also Marshall Plan; Truman Doctrine.

Consult (VIII) Lippmann, 1972.

IROQUOIS CONFEDERACY, a league of Iroquoian-speaking Indian tribes of North America. Originally there were five tribes—the Cayuga, Mohawk, Oneida, Onondaga, and Seneca—with a sixth, the Tuscarora, added in 1722. They lived in New York State between Lake Champlain and the Genesee River. Traditionally, the league was founded about 1570 by Dekanawida and his Mohawk disciple, Hiawatha. The Confederacy provided a sense of unity among the tribes and established agreements that ended serious conflicts among the tribes.

The most highly developed Indian confederation north of Mexico, the league was based on Iroquois political life, in which women held an important position. The "fireside," which was made up of the mother and her children, was the foundation of the organization. These firesides were part of a larger group of related women called the *ohwachira*. Two or more *ohwachiras* made up a clan, and the clans together made a nation. The women of the *ohwachiras* appointed male delegates and peace chiefs who made up the Confederacy's ruling council.

Isaac Singer's sewing machine brought great changes in clothing industry.

Alexander Graham Bell conducts aerodynamics experiment with unusual kite in 1903.

During the seventeenth century, when their Huron enemies allied with the French, the Iroquois sided with the British, an association they kept until the American Revolution. During the war, the Oneidas and Tuscaroras helped the Americans, while the rest fought with the British. After American independence was established, the Confederacy broke up as the Indians moved from their homelands.

See also Indians, North American; Indian Wars, Colonial.

IRVING, WASHINGTON (1783-1859), the first American professional man of letters. Born in New York, Irving was educated there and abroad and after a brief career in law began his work as a writer by contributing to his brother's newspapers. On his return from a trip to Europe, he helped write and edit the *Salmagundi*, a satirical social review. His first success occurred with the satire *A History of New York* (1809), written under the pseudonym Diedrich Knickerbocker.

Irving again left America, this time for an extended stay in Europe (1815-1832). His most important book, *The Sketch Book of Geoffrey Crayon, Gent.* (1819-1820), included his best-known stories, "Rip Van Winkle" and "The Legend of Sleepy Hollow," as well as sketches and essays. Irving's English novel, *Bracebridge Hall* (1822) earned him a solid European reputation. After traveling through Europe, Irving settled in Madrid as an aide at the U.S. consulate. Working in the Spanish archives, he wrote a popular *History of the Life and Voyages of Christopher Columbus* (1828), followed by *Chronicle of the Conquest of Granada* (1829) and *The Alhambra* (1832).

After serving as an attaché to the U.S. embassy in London, Irving returned to his Sunnyside home in Tarrytown, N.Y., a famous writer. He wrote extensively on a variety of subjects, from Western travels to biographies: *Oliver Goldsmith* (1849), *Mahomet* (1849-1850), and *George Washington* (1855-1859).

See also Literature.
Consult (III) Hedges, 1965.
—Richard Collin, *Louisiana State University, New Orleans*

ISOLATIONISM, a policy in diplomatic relations of maintaining a state's rights and interests without entering into alliances with other states. A country's geographical position sometimes enables it to avoid diplomatic alliances. Japan, an island empire, practiced isolationism for 1,000 years before it made a pact with Britain in 1902. The United States was intensely isolationist from 1800 to 1917 and, to a lesser extent, from the close of World War I to World War II.

American Isolationism. Due to their connection with Britain, the colonists were constantly involved in European wars. This was one factor in their demand for independence in 1776. The need for military aid led to the Franco-American alliance of 1778, but by 1796 George Washington, in his famous Farewell Address, was urging Americans to "avoid foreign entanglements." This attitude became more formalized in 1823, when President Monroe warned the European powers that the Americas were not to be considered prospective area for colonization and that European instrusions would be interpreted as threats to American security. Later known as the Monroe Doctrine, this policy remained the basis of U.S. foreign policy until World War I.

After World War I, the United States reentered diplomatic isolation by shunning the Treaty of Versailles and the Covenant of the League of Nations. For some Americans in the period between the World Wars, this attitude was a reflection of the overriding concern with domestic problems. Others thought that the United States should avoid foreign involvements. The approach of global war led to a change in feelings, and by 1940 a majority of Americans endorsed cooperation with Britain. Since the beginning of World War II, the United States has made numerous alliances that have taken it away from isolationism.

See also Monroe Doctrine; Lend-Lease; Washington's Farewell Address.
Consult (VI) Jonas, 1966.

IVES, CHARLES (1874-1954), American composer largely unappreciated until long after he had stopped composing. *See* Music.

JACKSON, ANDREW (1767-1845), 7th President of the United States (1829-1837). He was born in Waxhaw, S.C., on March 15, 1767, and served briefly in the American Revolution (1781), when he was taken prisoner by the British. He became a lawyer in 1787 and later settled in Nashville, Tenn. In 1791 Jackson married Mrs. Rachel Robards, who mistakenly believed that she had already been divorced (the divorce was granted two years later). Jackson served as the state's first U.S. congressman (1796-1797), as a senator (1797), and then as judge of the Tennessee Supreme Court (1798-1804).

Jackson later achieved great fame—and a measure of notoriety—in the military. He fought as a major general in the Creek War and on Jan. 8, 1815, became a national hero when he decisively defeated the British at the Battle of New Orleans. His toughness in the War of 1812 led to his nickname, "Old Hickory." Both the British and Indians were Jackson's target in 1818, when, commanding in the Seminole War, he invaded Florida. In 1821 he was appointed military governor of Florida.

Washington Irving, first American author to gain international recognition.

The Isolationist
Internationalists believed that U.S. isolationists before World War II were ignoring events in half of the world.

Returning to politics, Jackson again served as a senator from Tennessee (1823–1825). He sought the presidency in 1824 and received the largest number of electoral votes, although not a majority. The election went to the House of Representatives, which elected John Quincy Adams. Jackson organized for the 1828 election and had the satisfaction of defeating Adams. He was reelected over Henry Clay in 1832. He was succeeded by his choice, Martin Van Buren (elected in 1836), and retired to his plantation, "The Hermitage," near Nashville, where he died on June 8, 1845.

Administration. Jackson did a great deal to strengthen the power of the executive. This was achieved largely through negative acts. He used the veto more than all his predecessors combined; he also ignored his official cabinet, turning to a circle of political advisers, his Kitchen Cabinet, for assistance.

Jackson's Indian policy, announced in his 1829 inaugural address and codified by his Indian Removal Act (1830) and Indian Intercourse Act (1834), ordered all Indians in the states to move west to the Indian territories. He refused to enforce a Supreme Court ruling in favor of the Cherokee Nation; the Cherokee were forced to migrate at gunpoint.

Although Jackson has often been viewed as a symbol of the democratization of America, much belies this. In addition to his hatred of Indians, Jackson was a slaveholder who opposed abolitionists. Such extensions of democracy as the broadening of suffrage either preceded his presidency or had nothing to do with Jackson personally.

His veto of the Maysville Road ended the federal government's commitment to many internal improvements. He introduced the spoils system to national government, and he ended the Second Bank of the United States with an important veto.

See also Bank of the United States, Second; Creek War; Eaton Affair (1831); Maysville Road Veto (1830); New Orleans, Battle of (1815).

Consult (III) Parton, 1970; Schlesinger, 1945.

—Douglas Miller, *Michigan State University*

JACKSON, JESSE (LOUIS) (1941–), civil rights leader who was formerly head of Operation Breadbasket, the economic wing of the Southern Christian Leadership Conference (SCLC). He was born in Greenville, S.C., studied at North Carolina Agricultural and Technical College and Chicago Theological Seminary, and is an ordained Baptist minister. He helped Martin Luther King, Jr., found Operation Breadbasket and became head of its Chicago office in 1966 and national director in 1967. Through economic pressure, the organization induced businessmen to hire more blacks and to purchase more goods and services from black-owned enterprises.

Tensions developed between Jackson and the Southern-oriented leaders of SCLC, and he resigned as director of Operation Breadbasket in 1971. He shortly thereafter announced the founding of a more militant Operation PUSH (People United to Save Humanity).

JACKSON, MAHALIA (1911–1972), contralto called the "Queen of the Gospel Song." She took her gospel songs to the Newport Jazz Festival, concert halls, stadiums, and churches in the United States and abroad. Born and raised in New Orleans, Jackson sang in the choir of her father's church from age five and was exposed to the blues singing of Ida Cox and Bessie Smith. However, her interest remained with sacred music rather than blues.

At 16 she moved to Chicago, holding various jobs and singing with a quartet in churches. In 1934 she made her first recording, and in the 1940s her records became widely popular. Her song "Move Up a Little Higher" reached sales of more than 1 million. A successful concert at Carnegie Hall in New York in 1950 was followed by a concert tour of Europe. In later years she participated actively in the civil rights movement and was closely associated with Martin Luther King, Jr.

JACKSON, STONEWALL (THOMAS J.) (1824–1863), one of the most brilliant Confederate generals. He was born in Virginia and educated at West Point, but after six years in the army, including service in the Mexican War, he resigned to teach.

At the outbreak of the Civil War he became a brigadier general and fought at the First Battle of Bull Run (July 1861). At a critical moment a fellow general exclaimed, "There is Jackson, standing like a stone wall!" Jackson, by then a major general, first displayed his true genius in the Shenandoah Valley in spring 1862, when he maneuvered his small force so skillfully and daringly that thousands of Federal soldiers, who might otherwise have been transferred to join the assault on Richmond, were held back. In the Second Battle of Bull Run (August 1862) Jackson led his famed "foot cavalry" in a brilliant flanking movement swinging around and then falling on the Union lines. He achieved his final triumph during the Chancellorsville campaign (April–May 1863). He took his men on a long, swift flanking movement and routed the Union right. During the engagement Jackson was accidentally shot and killed by his own troops.

See also Civil War Battles.

Consult (IV) Vandiver, 1957.

JACKSONIAN DEMOCRATS. *See* Democratic-Republicans (Jacksonian).

Andrew Jackson, 7th President of the United States (1829–1837).

American author Henry James spent much of his later life in England.

NOVA BRITANNIA.

OFFERING MOST

Excellent fruites by Planting in
VIRGINIA.

Exciting all such as be well affected
to further the same.

LONDON
Printed for SAMVEL MACHAM, and are to be fold at
his Shop in Pauls Church-yard, at the
Signe of the Bul-head.
1 6 0 9.

Establishment of Jamestown Settlement led to advertisements extolling the virtues of Virginia.

JAMES, HENRY (1843–1916), major American author, brother of psychologist-philosopher William James. After schooling in Europe and America and after a "mysterious hurt" that kept him from the Civil War, James began in 1864 to write reviews and short fiction for major periodicals. Within a decade he was already being called "the best short story writer in America."

After assuming permanent residence in London, James created something of a scandal and a vogue with *Daisy Miller* (1878). Its international theme—American innocents confronting experienced Europeans—became his hallmark and contributed importantly to his first major masterpiece, *The Portrait of a Lady* (1881).

For the next 20 years James engaged in various formal experiments. From 1885 to 1890 he combined French naturalism with older Victorian techniques in three long novels of social commentary (*The Bostonians, The Princess Casamassima, The Tragic Muse*). After an unsuccessful flirtation with the stage, James used dramatic techniques to structure brilliant novels of mordant social criticism (*The Awkward Age, What Maisie Knew*).

Then, from 1903 to 1905, James entered what some critics call "the major phase" (*The Ambassadors, The Wings of the Dove, The Golden Bowl*). By presenting events through the "lucid reflector" of his characters' highly sophisticated consciousnesses, James dramatized his view that meaning resides not in events themselves but in their interpretation by the experiencing individual.

Besides novels, James mastered the novella form (*The Aspern Papers, The Spoils of Poynton, In the Cage*), wrote 12 volumes of short stories, and became a major critic of European and American literature, drama, and painting. His travel books and social commentary (especially *The American Scene*), his "Prefaces" to the New York edition of his collected works, and his unfinished autobiography are all masterpieces of their kind. *The Art of the Novel* stands as the first major defense of fiction as a serious art form.

See also Literature.

Consult (V) Dupee, 1956; Edel, 1953–1971.

—William Veeder, *University of Chicago*

JAMESTOWN SETTLEMENT, the first permanent settlement in America, founded on May 13, 1607, on Jamestown Island, Virginia, in the James River. Started as a trading post by the Virginia Company of London, it was the scene of disease, starvation, and strife during its first few years. The settlement was located near malarial swamps; the inhabitants were dependent on supplies from England and the Indians, and their leaders, who included strong-willed men such as John Smith, frequently quarreled among themselves. In 1612, John Rolfe, later the husband of Pocahontas, discovered that tobacco could be successfully grown. Tobacco production gave the colony economic stability, and the colony grew enough to withstand a savage Indian attack in 1622.

Jamestown was the capital of Virginia from 1607 until 1699 in spite of repeated fires. In 1676 it was burned to the ground during Bacon's Rebellion. Its population was already declining in 1698, when another fire destroyed the town. Williamsburg became the colony's capital in 1699, and Jamestown was deserted. Jamestown, which has been extensively excavated and restored, is now part of the Colonial National Historical Park.

See also Exploration and Discovery; Smith, John; Virginia.

JANE ROE v. HENRY WADE (1973), landmark Supreme Court decision that state laws prohibiting abortion during the first three months of pregnancy violate the constitutional "right of privacy" between a woman and her doctor under the Ninth and Fourteenth amendments. Under the decision, a state can prohibit abortion only during the last 10 weeks of pregnancy, when the fetus becomes "viable." However, the Court did not agree that a woman's right to abortion is absolute; they emphasized the legality of abortion as agreed upon by a woman and her doctor.

The Court agreed that during the first 3 months of pregnancy a doctor could recommend abortion "without regulation from the state." Following this period, the states can regulate abortion procedures "to the extent that the regulation reasonably relates to the preservation and protection of maternal health." Thus, for instance, a state could rule that abortions during this period must be performed in a hospital rather than a doctor's office. During the last 10 weeks of pregnancy, the state could take a legitimate interest in the potential life of the fetus. The decision states that, "with respect to the state's important and legitimate interest in potential life, the 'compelling' point is at viability." Thus the Court sidestepped the issue of when life begins. The majority decision remarked that "the unborn have never been recognized as persons in the whole sense" and so settled for the point at which the fetus could survive on its own outside the mother's body as the point at which the state could take a legal interest.

Impact. The decision affected the laws of 31 states where the laws permitted abortion only when it was necessary to save the life of the mother. Another decision at the same time on a case in Georgia invalidated the more modern abortion laws of 15 states, which permitted abortion under narrowly defined terms relating to the health of the mother. In this decision, the Court wrote that medical judgment in determining the abortion should cover "physical, emotional, psychological, familial factors" and "the woman's age."

While the *Jane Roe v. Henry Wade* decision was hailed by women's rights groups and population control advocates, the leaders of the Roman Catholic Church expressed shock and horror over the decision and vowed to work for a constitutional amendment outlawing abortion.

See also Abortion and Birth Control Laws.

JAPANESE-AMERICANS, WARTIME TREATMENT OF. In 1940 more than 126,000 Japanese-Americans were living in the United States, primarily in the three Pacific Coast states. Immediately after Pearl Harbor, about 3,000 were arrested by the FBI as enemy aliens. Deep-rooted anti-Japanese hostility soon manifested itself, with local prejudices quickly breeding rumors of espionage. National newspapers and magazines, as well as men in public office, joined in the attacks.

In February 1942, President Roosevelt signed an executive order delineating Western military areas from which all persons of Japanese ancestry were to be excluded and authorizing the construction of "relocation" camps to house them. Within six months 110,000 Japanese-Americans, two-thirds of them American citizens, were housed in 10 detention camps. Those considered to be loyal were allowed to leave for certain approved areas; about 35,000 evacuees resettled in the East and Midwest. A handful who had resisted evacuation were fined and jailed. Appeals led to a Supreme Court ruling (*Korematsu v. United States*) in support of the relocation. The mass exclusion orders were revoked in January 1945. Although many Japanese feared returning to their homes, prejudice began to ebb, largely due to the excellent war records of the 100th and 442d Japanese battalions.

The evacuees suffered great economic loss if not outright ruin. Their property, including farms, shops, homes, and personal possessions, was in many cases either stolen or confiscated. In 1948 President Truman signed into law the Japanese-American Evacuation Claims Act. Close to 24,000 claims were filed asking for $132 million, about one-third of estimated losses.

See also Korematsu v. United States (1944).

JAY, JOHN (1745–1829), political and diplomatic leader and first Chief Justice of the Supreme Court. He was born in New York City, graduated from King's College (Columbia) in 1764, and became a lawyer. As a delegate from New York to the First and Second Continental Congresses he adopted a conservative attitude, but he supported the Declaration of Independence. For a time he was chief justice of New York but in 1779 became minister to Spain. Along with John Adams and Benjamin Franklin he conducted the negotiations with Britain that led to the establishment of American independence.

Beginning in 1784 Jay served as secretary of foreign affairs in the government of the Confederation, a time when Britain in the Northwest and Spain in the Southwest ignored the official boundaries separating them from the United States. In 1785–1786 Jay negotiated with Spain's Diego de Gardoqui in an effort to obtain trading privileges and a settlement of Western problems. Jay suggested to Congress an agreement that would have secured trading rights within Spanish possessions but would have given up American rights to navigate the Mississippi for 30 years. This suggestion, which infuriated the West, was defeated mostly by Southern votes.

Jay was a strong supporter of the new Constitution and contributed five articles to what eventually became *The Federalist*. Jay became chief justice of the Supreme Court in 1789. The Court had fewer major decisions than later in its history, but in the case of *Chisholm v. Georgia* (1793) it declared that a citizen of one state had the right to sue another state in the federal courts. This decision was negated by the Eleventh Amendment.

Later Life. In 1794 Jay was sent as special envoy to Britain in an attempt to avoid war and to solve the outstanding maritime and frontier problems. Jay's Treaty, which was signed in November 1794, prevented war and secured a British agreement to evacuate posts within American territory, but it ignored basic maritime problems. The treaty was confirmed by the Senate after much controversy, but it stirred up considerable opposition both within Congress and the country at large, helping to create support for the new Democratic-Republican Party. On his return from England, Jay served two terms as governor of New York (1795–1800) and then retired from politics. He died in Bedford N.Y.

See also Amendments, Constitutional; Chisholm v. Georgia; Federalist, The; Jay's Treaty (1794).

Consult (III) Monaghan, 1935.

—Reginald Horsman, *University of Wisconsin, Milwaukee*

JAY-GARDOQUI NEGOTIATIONS. See Jay, John.

JAY'S TREATY (1794), an agreement designed to settle Anglo-American territorial and maritime disputes that continued after the Revolutionary War. In 1794 John Jay was sent to London to attempt to avoid war between the United States and England over British seizures of American shipping and border troubles in

Japanese-American child sits among her family's belongings before transportation to relocation center.

John Jay, patriot, diplomat, and 1st Chief Justice of the Supreme Court.

the Old Northwest. By the treaty signed on Nov. 19, 1794, England agreed that by June 1, 1796, she would evacuate her posts along the Great Lakes that were within American territory defined by the Treaty of Paris (1783) and that she would pay compensation for seizures of American shipping in 1793. The United States agreed to guarantee the payment of pre-Revolutionary private debts owed to British merchants, the amount to be decided by a joint commission. Joint commissions would also settle Canadian boundary problems, and the Mississippi River was declared open to both countries. Although England allowed American shipping into the East Indian trade, the concessions in the British West Indies were so limited that the Senate rejected that part of the treaty.

There was bitter opposition to the treaty in the United States, especially from the developing Democratic-Republican (Jeffersonian) Party, which claimed that American maritime rights had been ignored. The Senate ratified the treaty exactly by a two-thirds majority in June 1795.

See also Jay, John; Paris, Treaty of (1783).

Jazz greats Duke Ellington *(left)* and Louis Armstrong, at 1946 recording session.

JAZZ, popular twentieth-century American music characterized by improvisation and syncopation. The origin of the term "jazz" is uncertain; it may be derived from the French *jaser,* meaning to chat, because early jazz was much like a musical conversation.

Background. Jazz originated during the early 1900s in New Orleans' Storyville—the city's legalized brothel section, where early jazzmen (mainly blacks) were hired to entertain the customers. Their improvisatory music was a blending of earlier ragtime and blues. Ragtime was developed toward the end of the nineteenth century by performers such as Scott Joplin. Its main characteristics were binary meter and syncopation. Around 1909, with the composition of W. C. Handy's "Memphis Blues," the influence of the blues, an outgrowth of spirituals and folk songs, was added.

The Jazz Age. Ragtime syncopation plus a blues melody combined to form early jazz. Storyville musicians improvised countermelodies on the clarinet while a pianist or cornetist carried the tune. With the closing of Storyville in 1917, most jazzmen moved north to Kansas City and Chicago. Record companies began recording jazz, and this new music swept the country. However, popularization brought changes to jazz as white influences were added in the 1920s, leading to "sweet" jazz, a polished, nonimprovisational jazz, typified by Paul Whiteman's jazzed classics and George Gershwin's "Rhaposody in Blue."

But "hot" jazz—jazz in the true tradition—also continued to develop in the 1920s through jazz greats Louis Armstrong and Bix Beiderbecke—both horn men—and the compositions and arrangements of Fletcher Henderson and Duke Ellington. The hot jazz of the 1920s culminated in the swing music of the 1930s. Besides Ellington, Benny Goodman and the Dorsey Brothers performed and jazz singers such as Frank Sinatra, Ella Fitzgerald, and Billie Holiday became popular.

Progressive Jazz. During the 1940s boogie-woogie became a popular jazz form and was followed by progressive jazz, which was speculative and complex, using harmonic forms borrowed from modern composers. Small groups headed by Dizzy Gillespie, Charlie Parker, Thelonius Monk, and Dave Brubeck, among others, played the new jazz. A "West Coast" school of jazz was led by Gerry Mulligan, Miles Davis, and Dave Pell.

Progressive jazz began to splinter into subgroups during the 1950s. So-called chamber groups such as the Modern Jazz Quartet used classical form, while "hard" groups such as the Miles Davis Quintet used strong rhythms and unison melodic lines played between piano or horn solos. Experimental groups—John Coltrane, Ornette Coleman, Charles Mingus' Jazz Workshop—also surfaced during the late 1950s. Some of these groups continued into the 1960s and early 1970s when jazz continued quietly along the several paths of progressive jazz.

See also Armstrong, Louis; Ellington, Duke.

Consult (VIII) Dankworth, 1968; Hodeir, 1970; Williams, 1967.

JEFFERSON, THOMAS (1743–1826), 3rd President of the United States (1801–1809). He was born in Shadwell, Va., on April 13, 1743, attended the College of William and Mary, and was admitted to the bar in 1767. Before the Revolution he served in the Virginia House of Burgesses and through publication of his *Summary View of the Rights of British America* in 1774 became one of the Revolutionary leaders. He wrote the Declaration of Independence while a delegate to the Second Continental Congress.

During the years 1776–1781, Jefferson was engaged in Virginia politics, serving in the House of Delegates and as governor (1779–1781). In the House of Delegates he was ultimately responsible for great reforms: the revision of Virginia's code of laws and the establishment of religious freedom. His governorship, during which the British invaded the state, was a period of near disaster for him—he was at his worst as a war leader—but the years of the Confederation (1781–1789) enhanced his reputation. While in the Continental Congress in 1783–1784, he was responsible for the Ordinance of 1784 (a forerunner of the Northwest Ordinance), in 1785 his *Notes on Virginia* was published, and from 1785 to 1789 he served as minister to France.

Under the new Constitution, Jefferson became President Washington's secretary of state, and when the European wars broke out in 1792 and 1793 he supported a policy of American neutrality. The Washington cabinet had deep internal divisions, and as Washington increasingly leaned toward Alexander Hamilton's internal policies, Jefferson moved into opposition to the government. In December 1793 he resigned from the cabinet, and along with James Madison in the mid-1790s became the acknowledged leader of the new Democratic-Republican Party. In 1796 he ran for the presidency and lost by only 3 electoral votes to John Adams. Because this election preceded the Twelfth Amendment, Jefferson became vice-president. When the Alien and Sedition Acts were issued in 1798, he wrote the Kentucky Resolutions in opposition to them. These resolutions foreshadowed John C. Calhoun's later doctrine of nullification and strongly defended the rights of the states to resist federal power.

National Leader. In 1801 Jefferson became president at a time when his party also began to dominate American politics. His first term was a period of continual success: flourishing commerce, a reduction in taxes, and the Louisiana Purchase all helped to strengthen his position and to weaken the Federalists'. His second term was far more controversial. Relations with England deteriorated sharply, there were widespread maritime difficulties, and in December 1807 he introduced the embargo, an attempt to change European policies through economic coercion. This failed, and Jefferson left office in March 1809 at the time the embargo was removed.

In his long political retirement Jefferson continued his numerous intellectual pursuits. His major achievement in this period was the foundation of the University of Virginia. He died at his home, Monticello, on July 4, 1826, the fiftieth anniversary of the Declaration of Independence.

See also Declaration of Independence (1776); Democratic-Republicans (Jeffersonian); Embargo Acts; Louisiana Purchase (1803); Virginia and Kentucky Resolutions (1798).
Consult (III) Chinard, 1939; Peterson, 1970.
—Reginald Horsman, *University of Wisconsin, Milwaukee*

JEFFERSONIAN DEMOCRATS. *See* Democratic-Republicans (Jeffersonian).

JEHOVAH'S WITNESSES, religious sect whose doctrine centers around the Second Coming of Christ. The modern organization of the Witnesses dates from the work of Charles Taye

Russell in America in the 1870s. The Witnesses base their teachings on a literal reading of the Bible. They have no official ministers, because all Jehovah's Witnesses are considered ministers of the Gospel. They also have no churches as such but meet in buildings called Kingdom Halls. The views of the sect are circulated in *The Watchtower* and by zealous house-to-house canvassing by its members.

Witnesses refuse to salute the flag, to bear arms in war, and to participate in the affairs of government. Several Supreme Court cases arose in connection with the children of Jehovah's Witnesses members who refused to salute the flag and participate in school devotional exercises.

JESUITS, popular name for the members of the largest Roman Catholic religious order for men, the Society of Jesus. It was started by Saint Ignatius of Loyola in France in 1534. From its inception the society was active in missionary work, sending priests to all corners of the world. They played an important role in the early development of North America, especially on the East and West coasts, where they were sent to convert the Indians to Christianity. Spanish Jesuits were active in Florida as early as 1566.

In the early seventeenth century French Jesuits established a mission in Canada and reached Quebec in 1625. They went into Indian settlements, where they often suffered severe hardships and even death. Father Isaac Jogues and two helpers were captured and tortured to death by Mohawk Indians near Lake Champlain in the 1640s.

Following the natural waterway of the Great Lakes, the Jesuits established missions and explored much of the upper Midwest. Father Jacques Marquette left from the Mackinac Straits and explored the Mississippi River with Louis Joliet in 1673. From the Spanish Jesuit missions in California, trailblazers such as Eusebio Kino, who mapped the southwestern part of the United States in the late 1690s, fanned out from the coast. The first successful mission in lower California had been established by the Jesuit Juan María Salvatierra at Loreto in 1697.

See also Exploration and Discovery; Marquette, Father Jacques.

JESUS FREAKS, name given to followers of Christian nondenominational revivalist movement that began about 1967. Also known as the Jesus People Movement, it has a strong anti-drug orientation, and the believers shun attachment to any organized religion.

JEWS. *See* Colonial Religion.

JOB CORPS, agency that provides educational

Thomas Jefferson, 3rd President of the United States (1801–1809), in 1791 portrait by C. W. Peale.

Andrew Johnson, 17th President of the United States (1865–1869).

Lyndon Johnson, 36th President of the United States (1963–1969), mixes with enthusiastic crowds during 1964 campaign. After his election the Vietnam War's unpopularity led to hostile receptions.

opportunities and vocational training for disadvantaged youth. *See* Economic Opportunity Act (1964).

JOHN BIRCH SOCIETY, an ultraconservative, semisecret political organization founded in Belmont, Mass., in 1958 to fight communist subversion. Named for a Baptist missionary killed by Chinese communists at the close of World War II, the Society holds that communist influences have so deeply cut into American life that even high public officials have been affected. It has gone so far as to call for the impeachment of certain individuals, including former Chief Justice Earl Warren. The Society is opposed to the United Nations, North Atlantic Treaty Organization, foreign aid, and cultural or economic exchanges with communist nations and has sought the repeal of social security laws and the graduated income tax.

JOHN BROWN'S RAID (1859), attack on Harpers Ferry, Va. *See* Brown, John.

JOHNSON, ANDREW (1808–1875), 17th President of the United States (1865–1869). Born into a poor family in Raleigh, N.C., on Dec. 29, 1808, he left home at age 18 and settled in Greenville, Tenn. Self-educated, ambitious, and hardworking, he prospered and in 1835 entered politics as a Jacksonian Democrat. He served successively as a state legislator, U.S. representative, governor of Tennessee (1853–1857), and U.S. senator (1857–1862). In these posts he fought for many reforms, including homestead legislation, but he vigorously opposed the antislavery movement.

During the secession crisis of 1860–1861, he was the most prominent Southern loyalist, which led to his reappointment as governor of Tennessee in 1862. In 1864 Lincoln chose him as his vice-presidential running mate.

Presidency. Upon assuming the presidency after Lincoln's assassination, Johnson at first made radical statements but quickly changed and initiated a mild Reconstruction program. However, Congress was more radical and began to formulate its own plan. Always combative and quarrelsome, Johnson lashed out in early 1866 by vetoing two critical acts, the Freedmen's Bureau Bill and the Civil Rights Act. His unreasonable intransigence alienated most Republican moderates, who now sided with Radicals, and the vetoes were overridden.

Relations between Johnson and Congress continued to deteriorate, especially after the President's supporters were defeated in the 1866 elections. The battle reached a climax in 1868, when he removed Secretary of War Stanton in violation of the newly passed Tenure of Office Act. The House impeached him, but, by a one vote margin, the Senate exonerated him in the trial that followed.

After his return to Tennessee in 1869, he again entered state politics. In 1874 he won election to the U.S. Senate, but he died in Carter Station, Tenn., on July 31, 1875, soon after taking his seat.

See also Radical Republicans; Reconstruction; Stanton, Edwin M.; Tenure of Office Act (1867).

Consult (IV) McKitrick, 1960.
—Michael Burlingame, *Connecticut College*

JOHNSON, JAMES WELDON (1871–1938), black writer. *See* Harlem Renaissance.

JOHNSON, LYNDON B(AINES) (1908–1973), 37th President of the United States (1963–1969), who left an impressive legacy of legislation that would have justified an assessment of greatness had it not been for the devastating domestic consequences of the Vietnam War. He was born on August 27, 1908, in Stonewall, Texas, and began his political career in 1932 as secretary to a Texas congressman. From 1937 to 1949 he served in the U.S. House of Representatives.

Johnson moved to the Senate in 1949 and, being extraordinarily persuasive and skillful in effecting compromises, he was soon elected Democratic whip (1951) and party leader (1953). In 1960 John F. Kennedy selected him for the vice-presidential nomination. Kennedy had a high regard for Johnson's abilities and recognized that he needed the latter's influence in winning the South and getting his program through the Senate.

Administration. After the assassination of Kennedy, Johnson was able to get Congress to pass many of Kennedy's key measures that had been bottled up—the Civil Rights Act of 1964, a major education bill, a new tax plan, and an economic opportunity act.

Johnson won the election in 1964 by a landslide over Barry Goldwater that swept 71 freshmen Democrats into Congress. The result was that Johnson secured more significant legislation than any other president had obtained from a single session of Congress—Medicare, aid to education, a voting rights bill, a broad housing program, immigration reform, and antipollution measures.

However, the honeymoon period ended in late 1965, when the President chose to widen the war in Vietnam. At first he had the strong backing of Congress and the public, but continued escalation without victorious resolution made him the target of both hawks and doves. After Senator Eugene McCarthy's impressive challenge in the 1968 New Hampshire primary and with a repudiation impending in Wisconsin, Johnson announced that in the name of national unity he would not seek reelection. He retired to Johnson City, Tex., where he died on Jan. 22, 1973.

See also Civil Rights Acts (1957, 1960, 1964); Housing Acts; Medicare and Medicaid; Presidential Elections.
Consult (VIII) Goldman, 1969; Johnson, 1971.
—Martin Gruberg, *University of Wisconsin, Oshkosh*

JOHNSON ACT (1924), legislation that set immigration quotas. *See* Immigration.

JOHNSTON, JOSEPH E(GGLESTON) (1807–1891), one of the leading Confederate generals. A Virginian and a West Point graduate, he helped rout the Federals at the First Battle of Bull Run (July 1861). He presided over the defense of Richmond during George C. McClellan's peninsular campaign (March–July 1862) until, on May 31, he launched the Battle of Seven Pines, an indecisive engagement during which he was wounded and replaced by Robert E. Lee.

Upon recovery Johnston took part in the Vicksburg campaign (October 1862–July 1863), which ended with General Grant's capture of the city. In December, Johnston assumed command of the army facing William Sherman, whose turning maneuvers led Johnston to fall back all the way to Atlanta by July 1864. Jefferson Davis then relieved Johnston of command for failing to halt the enemy.

Johnston closed out the war in charge of forces in the Carolinas and after the war became a businessman. A small, courtly man, Johnston had an excellent intellect but bad luck. His superiors (especially Jefferson Davis) found him proud, petulant, and quarrelsome. Two great obstacles stood between Johnston and outstanding military success: his chronic defensive-mindedness and his antagonistic relationship with Jefferson Davis.

See also Civil War Battles.
Consult (IV) Govan and Livingood (1956).
—Michael Burlingame, *Connecticut College*

JOLIET, LOUIS (1648–1700), French explorer of the Mississippi Valley. *See* Marquette, Father Jacques.

JONES, JOHN PAUL (1747–1792), Revolutionary War naval hero. Born in Scotland, his actual name was John Paul. Before his twentieth birthday, Paul was first mate of a slave ship. He soon became master of a merchantman trading with the West Indies. In 1773 Paul was accused of murdering a mutinous crewman, and because he had previously been cleared of killing another mariner, Paul decided not to stand trial again and slipped away to America.

He assumed the name Jones and eventually was employed in fitting out the *Alfred*, the first ship bought by the Continental Congress.

Jones received a senior first lieutenancy on the *Alfred* in 1775 and gained command of the *Providence* in 1776. Promoted to captain with command of a small fleet, Jones took 16 prize ships in one cruise. He sailed to France as commander of the sloop *Ranger* in February 1777 and upon his arrival learned that the American commissioners in Paris had turned over to their hosts the frigate *Indian,* which he had been ordered to command. In April and May 1778, Jones harassed the English coast, capturing 7 prizes.

In 1779 the French gave Jones command of seven vessels, including his flagship the *Bonhomme Richard.* On August 14, 1779, Jones set sail with his flotilla and in a clockwise sweep around the British Isles captured 17 ships. On September 23, Jones defeated the 22-gun *Serapis,* although his flagship was sunk in the engagement. In this battle he answered a request for surrender with his famous "I have not yet begun to fight." Jones returned to America in December 1780. The Congress promised him command of the *America* but turned the vessel over to the French. In October 1787, the Congress granted Jones the only gold medal awarded to an officer of the Continental navy.

Consult (II) Morison, 1959.
—Thomas Archdeacon, *University of Wisconsin*

JUDICIAL REVIEW, the power of courts to determine the constitutionality of the acts of other branches of government and to declare unconstitutional acts null and void. In the United States, the concept is most often applied to the power of the national courts, especially the Supreme Court, to review acts of Congress, the national executive, and the state governments.

The U.S. Constitution does not explicitly grant this power to the national courts, and when the Supreme Court first began to review state actions, it aroused little controversy. But when it first declared a national law unconstitutional (*Marbury v. Madison,* 1803), opponents protested vigorously and threatened to impeach the justices. Although Thomas Jefferson and his party had won the presidency and Congress in the elections of 1800, Federalists still controlled the courts. The Jeffersonians therefore viewed the Supreme Court's actions as an effort to thwart the use of the power the Jeffersonians had won at the polls.

Chief Justice John Marshall, who wrote the decision in *Marbury v. Madison,* argued that both the Constitution and acts of Congress were laws of the land but that because the powers of Congress came from the Constitution, the Constitution was superior law. The Supreme Court was charged with upholding the law, and so when two laws clashed, it was the duty of the Court to uphold the superior

Confederate general Joseph E. Johnston could not stop General Sherman's drive into Georgia.

John Paul Jones, Revolutionary War naval hero.

law and to declare the inferior law void. Marshall's opinion did not end the controversy, and judicial review, although firmly established as a constitutional principle, often produces political conflict.

See also Marbury v. Madison (1803); Separation of Powers.

—Robert F. Smith, *Skidmore College*

JUDICIARY ACT (1789) established the framework of the American judicial system and helped extend the powers of the federal government. The act provided for a Supreme Court, composed of a chief justice and five associate justices; thirteen district courts; three circuit courts, each made up of two Supreme Court justices and a district judge; and an attorney general.

The act represented a compromise between two forces: one wanted a powerful judiciary to administer a uniform United States code of justice, and the other wanted existing state courts to enforce federal laws. Section 25 strengthened federal powers by permitting the Supreme Court to review judicially the states' highest courts when they upheld state laws that conflicted with federal statutes: the Constitution did not explicitly grant the Court these powers.

See also Supreme Court.

JUDICIARY ACTS (1801, 1802). The act of 1801 was passed by the Federalists after they had lost control of the presidency and Congress in the election of 1800 but before the new government had taken office. The act clearly would help to maintain a Federalist judiciary but it also introduced reforms that had become necessary in the 1790s. By this act the Supreme Court membership was to be reduced to five, a new set of circuit courts was to be created (with judgeships to be filled), and the number of district court judges was to be increased. This act led to last minute "midnight appointments" by President Adams and caused considerable bitterness among the Democratic-Republicans.

In 1802 the new Democratic-Republican Administration repealed the act of 1801. The second act restored the Supreme Court membership to six and established a lower number of circuit courts.

JUSTICE, DEPARTMENT OF, cabinet-level executive department headed by the attorney general, which represents the federal government in legal matters. It advises the president and other executive departments, investigates violations of federal laws, conducts all suits concerning the United States in the Supreme Court, and supervises the federal penal institutions.

The office of the attorney general, with

Firearms identification unit of FBI, an agency under the Department of Justice.

most of its present functions, was established by the Judiciary Act of 1789, which also set up the Supreme Court and the federal district and circuit courts. The attorney general was made head of the new Department of Justice in 1870. To promote uniformity in the trial and prosecution of cases, the attorney general was given direction over all counsel (including district attorneys) employed on behalf of the United States and supervisory power over officers of the federal courts. The Federal Bureau of Investigation, established in 1908, eventually gave the department extensive investigatory powers.

See also Federal Bureau of Investigation.

KAHN, LOUIS, influential modern architect. *See* Architecture.

KALAMAZOO DECISION (1874), Supreme Court decision upholding public support for high schools. *See* Education.

KANAGAWA, TREATY OF (1854) opened Japan to U.S. trade. *See* Perry, Matthew.

KANSAS, the 34th state, joined the Union on Jan. 29, 1861. Explored by Coronado in 1540, the area was claimed by the French during the 1600s, ceded to Spain in 1763, and then returned to France in 1800. Kansas became part of the United States in 1803 with the Louisiana Purchase and gained territorial status in 1854 by the Kansas-Nebraska Act. Slavery and abolitionist factions fought in Kansas for the next six years, and "Bleeding Kansas" and John Brown dominated the nation's headlines.

The state legislature is bicameral; its capital is Topeka. The population in 1970 was 2,249,071.

See also Kansas-Nebraska Act (1854).

KANSAS AND FREEDOM, a slogan of 1854 and after, illustrating Northern concern for the future of the American West. The Missouri Compromise of 1820 had set up a line of 36° 30′, limiting slavery to southern terrain in the West, but the Kansas-Nebraska Act of 1854 abrogated that agreement by stipulating that Kansas, although north of the 36° 30′ line, could obtain statehood with or without slavery. Free-Soilers, rallying around the cry "Kansas and Freedom," organized to resist the program of the proslavery partisans.

See also Bleeding Kansas; Kansas-Nebraska Act.

KANSAS-NEBRASKA ACT (1854), controversial legislation that repealed the Missouri Compromise of 1820. The Missouri Compromise prohibited slavery north of, and permitted slavery south of, a line drawn at the 36° 30′ parallel through the land obtained by the Louisiana Purchase. The original Kansas-Nebraska bill provided for the organization of Nebraska as a territory to facilitate the building of a transcontinental railroad. Southern congressmen agreed to support the bill only if it explicitly repealed the Missouri Compromise and incorporated the doctrine of popular sovereignty, permitting the people of the territories to decide the slave issue.

Some Northern congressional leaders, such as Senator Stephen A. Douglas of Illinois, argued that terrain and climate would decide the slave issue anyway and urged that the measure be adopted with the repeal proviso. As passed, the act divided the original Nebraska Territory into Kansas and Nebraska. Opponents of slavery denounced the act as a violation of a "sacred pledge" and "criminal." The acrimony of the congressional debates, the fighting that erupted in the Kansas and Nebraska territories, the strengthening of the newly formed Republican Party by antislavery forces, and the general effects of the act increased the division between the North and South and contributed to the coming of the Civil War.

See also Compromise of 1850; Douglas, Stephen A.; Missouri Compromise (1820); Popular Sovereignty.

Consult (IV) Ray, 1965.

KEATING-OWEN ACT (1916), a federal statute intended to restrict the employment of children in the nation's industrial system by prohibiting from interstate commerce the products of firms that employed child labor. This first attempt to regulate child labor at the national level was later ruled unconstitutional by the Supreme Court in *Hammer v. Dagenhart* (1918). The Court held that Congress exceeded its power to regulate interstate commerce by attempting to regulate local conditions of manufacture. This view was not reversed until 1941, when the Court upheld the Fair Labor Standards Act of 1938.

See also Hammer v. Dagenhart (1918).

KEFAUVER, (CAREY) ESTES (1903–1963), Democratic congressman who achieved national fame through televised Senate hearings on organized crime. He was born in Madisonville, Tenn. After receiving his law degree from Yale University in 1927, he began practicing law in Chattanooga. In 1939 he was appointed Tennessee tax and finance commissioner.

As a Democrat, he won a special election to the House of Representatives in 1939 and was reelected until 1948. In the House he was a staunch supporter of the New Deal and Fair Deal programs and showed concern about undue concentration of economic power. In 1948, defying the Tennessee political machine of boss Edward Crump, Kefauver entered the Democratic primary for the Senate. He won the bitter primary fight (during which he first wore

his distinctive coonskin cap) and the subsequent general election.

As chairman of the Senate Crime Investigating Committee probing crime syndicates and their involvement in politics, Kefauver won a reputation in 1950–1951 for hard-driving honesty. He campaigned for the Democratic presidential nomination in 1952, but he was defeated by Adlai Stevenson. He tried for the nomination again in 1956 but ended by accepting the vice-presidential candidacy. After the Stevenson-Kefauver ticket lost in an Eisenhower landslide, Kefauver concentrated on his Senate duties. In 1959 he chaired the Antitrust and Monopoly Subcommittee's head line-making investigations into professional sports and into pharmaceutical profiteering.

KELLOGG, FRANK (BILLINGS) (1856–1937), U.S. Senator and Secretary of State (1925–1929). Born in Potsdam, N.Y., he grew up in Minnesota, where his family moved when he was nine. Admitted to the bar in 1877, he served for three years as city attorney of Rochester, Minn., and for five years as a county attorney. In 1887 he moved to St. Paul, where he entered private law practice.

His first involvement in national affairs came when he served as counsel for the government in two antitrust actions and in a railroad investigation conducted by the Interstate Commerce Commission. He served from 1904 to 1912 as a Republican national committeeman from Minnesota and in 1917 was elected to the U.S. Senate from that state. In 1923, his Senate term completed, he represented the United States at the Fifth International Conference of American States at Santiago, Chile.

In March 1925 he became secretary of state in the cabinet of President Coolidge, a position he held until March 1929. He was acclaimed at the time for his role in the Kellogg-Briand Pact (1928), by which the major powers pledged to renounce war as an instrument of national policy although without creating any mechanisms for the enforcement of that pledge. A recipient of the Nobel Peace Prize in 1929, Kellogg sat from 1930 to 1935 as a judge of the permanent Court of International Justice at The Hague.

See also Kellogg-Briand Pact (1928).

—Paul S. Boyer, *University of Massachusetts*

KELLOGG-BRIAND PACT (1928), also known as the Pact of Paris, agreement to outlaw force in the settlement of international disputes. Secretary of State Frank B. Kellogg and French Foreign Minister Aristide Briand were the inspiration behind the treaty, which was essentially an innocuous statement of principle with no instrument of enforcement. But it embodied the spirit of the late 1920s—when it ap-

KANSAS-NEBRASKA ACT

Free states and territories

Slave states

Open to slavery by principle of popular sovereignty, Compromise of 1850

Open to slavery by principle of popular sovereignty, Kansas-Nebraska Act 1854

peared that the memories of the last war were receding and that mankind was at the threshold of building a stable era of peace—and was signed by most world powers.

Secretary of State Stimson invoked the pact in 1929, when China and the Soviet Union clashed in Manchuria, and in 1931, when Japan used force on a massive scale in the same region. By doing so, Secretary Stimson demonstrated that the United States was ready to act in the international community despite its abstention from membership in the League of Nations.

Consult (VI) Ferrell, 1952.

KELLY STEEL PROCESS. *See* Bessemer Steel Process (1856).

KENNEDY, JOHN F(ITZGERALD) (1917–1963), 35th President of the United States (1961–1963). He was born in Brookline, Mass., on May 29, 1917, graduated from Harvard in 1940, and served in the Navy (1941–1945).

In 1946 he was elected to the House of Representatives, holding the seat until his election to the Senate in 1952. During a convalescence he wrote *Profiles in Courage,* which won the Pulitzer Prize (1957). In 1956 he made a strong but unsuccessful bid for the Democratic vice-presidential nomination. This effort marked the beginning of a campaign by a well-oiled personal organization that resulted in his winning a first-ballot presidential nomination in 1960.

Presidency. Kennedy was elected president at 43, the youngest man and first Roman Catholic ever elected. He had triumphed over Richard Nixon by a narrow margin. Lacking an electoral mandate, his New Frontier Administration (modeled on the New Deal and Fair Deal) was thwarted by a bipartisan coalition of congressional conservatives.

Kennedy's major efforts went into foreign policy. After a shaky start—a confrontation with the Russians over Berlin and the unsuccessful invasion of Cuba by U.S.-aided refugees—Kennedy skillfully rode out the Cuban missile crisis. Kennedy also tried out strategies of counterinsurgency in Vietnam while embarking on such people-to-people aid programs as the Peace Corps and the Alliance for Progress. On the domestic scene Kennedy made the steel industry roll back a price increase, brought federal resources to bear in civil rights confrontations in Alabama and Mississippi, and took on a role as patron of the cultural arts. He was assassinated in Dallas, Tex., on Nov. 22, 1963.

See also Cuban Missile Crisis; Kennedy Family; Presidential Elections.

Consult (VIII) Schlesinger, 1965; Sorensen, 1965.

—Martin Gruberg, *University of Wisconsin, Oshkosh*

John F. Kennedy, 35th President of the United States (1961–1963), in the White House in 1962.

Attorney General Robert Kennedy *(left)* greets UN officials U Thant *(center)* and Ralph Bunche.

KENNEDY FAMILY. In 1848 Patrick Kennedy (1823–1868) arrived in America from Dunganstown, County Wexford, Ireland. He was the father of Patrick (1858–1929), who was influential in Boston politics and in constant conflict with John Francis Fitzgerald ("Honey Fitz"). The families, alternately political enemies and allies, were permanently united with the marriage in 1914 of Rose Fitzgerald to Joseph ("Joe") Patrick Kennedy (1888–1970).

Joe built a multimillion dollar empire and contributed lavishly to Franklin Roosevelt's campaign in 1936 and then became ambassador to Britain. Joe wanted his eldest son, Joseph Patrick (1915–1944), one of nine children, to have a career in politics, but he was killed during World War II. His second son, John (Jack) Fitzgerald (1917–1963), began his national political career in the House of Representatives, and rose to the presidency in 1961.

When the 83rd Congress convened in January 1953, there were two Kennedys present. Besides Jack, the new senator from Massachusetts, there was a new associate counsel of the Senate Permanent Investigation Subcommittee, Robert (Bobby) Francis (1925–1968), Joe's third son. He served as his brother's campaign manager during the 1960 presidential campaign and was appointed attorney general, a post he held until Jack's assassination in 1963. Bobby was elected to the Senate from New York in 1965 and served there until his assassination in Los Angeles while campaigning in California's presidential primary elections.

At the opening of the 89th Congress in 1966, there were two Kennedys in the Senate, Bobby and Edward (Ted) Moore (1932–   ), the youngest son of Rose and Joe. During the 1972 campaign Ted was considered as both a presidential and vice-presidential candidate but declined both. However, his sister's husband, Sargent Shriver, ran unsuccessfully as the Democratic vice-presidential candidate.

See also Kennedy, John F.

KENNEDY ROUND, negotiations to reduce tariffs. *See* General Agreement on Tariffs and Trade.

KENTUCKY, the 15th state, joined the Union on June 1, 1792, becoming the first state west of the Appalachian Mountains. The first white settlement was at Harrodsburg in 1774; the next year Boonesborough was established by Daniel Boone. In 1776 the Kentucky area was made Kentucky County by Virginia. A border state, Kentucky remained in the Union during the Civil War.

The legislature is bicameral; the capital is Frankfort. The population in 1970 was 3,219,-311.

See also Boone, Daniel.

KENTUCKY AND VIRGINIA RESOLUTIONS.
See Virginia and Kentucky Resolutions.

KEYNES, JOHN MAYNARD (1883–1946), British economist known for his General Theory, which had a great impact on U.S. economic policies. His great work, *General Theory of Employment, Interest, and Money* (1936), summed up the ideas he had been developing since about 1925. Keynes was primarily a problem solver, and his book was an attempt to solve the problems of world depression. Recognizing that capitalism was not what it had been in the nineteenth century, Keynes advocated salvaging it through government manipulation and control of money in circulation, interest rates, savings, and investment. He was, especially in the Depression period, interested in dealing with deflation and unemployment, against which he advocated monetary expansion (transferring money to those who will immediately put it into the economy) and deficit financing (which put money into the economy through government spending).

The New Deal. The New Deal could be said to have been accidentally Keynesian. When Keynes visited President Roosevelt in 1934, each man came away puzzled by the economic notions of the other. Certainly the early New Deal was inconsistent with any economic system or plan when it coupled revaluation of the currency (inflationary) with budget balancing (deflationary.) However, most New Deal relief programs were established on the principle of monetary expansion, as were social security and the Revenue Act of 1935. Deficit state and federal financing was common before the New Deal, but governments contracted such debts under pressure of great need and had no commitment to them on principle.

After the recession of 1938, government economists began talking openly in Keynesian terms, but they did not have the support of politicians, especially those in Congress. It was not until the Full Employment Act (1946) of the Truman Administration that the U.S. government took a clearly Keynesian position. Subsequent administrations, including President Nixon's, have implemented Keynesian theories.

See also New Deal; Revenue Act (1935); Roosevelt, Franklin D.

Consult (VI) Harris, 1947.

—Allen Kifer, *Skidmore College*

KING, MARTIN LUTHER, JR. (1929–1968), civil rights leader who won respect around the world by his nonviolent demonstrations and was awarded the Nobel Peace Prize in 1964.

Born in Atlanta, Ga., he studied at Morehouse College in Atlanta, Crozer Theological Seminary in Chester, Pa., and Boston University. He married Coretta Scott in Montgomery, Ala., and he soon drew national attention by leading a movement against segregation in buses. The 382-day Montgomery boycott in 1955–1956 was successful. Following this event, the Southern Christian Leadership Conference (SCLC) was formed to carry on the peaceful drive for the civil rights of black people.

King became president of SCLC and continued leading sit-ins and other forms of protest against discrimination. He was arrested many times for violating state segregation laws. The year 1963 saw two demonstrations that had nationwide effect. In the spring, King organized and shared in protests in Birmingham, Ala. Mass jailings and police use of dogs and fire hoses on peaceful pickets roused sympathy for the civil rights cause. In August, King was a leader of the March on Washington by as many as 250,000 supporters of equal rights. To this gathering he addressed his eloquent "I Have a Dream" speech. The efforts of King and his followers were a major force behind the passage by Congress of the Civil Rights Act of 1964, which has been called a Magna Charta for blacks.

King never wavered in his drive to win civil rights by nonviolent tactics, although some militant groups such as the Congress of Racial Equality began to advocate more radical action. He drew some censure by speaking out against the war in Vietnam.

In 1968 he went to Memphis, Tenn., to help striking garbage collectors. He was assassinated there on April 4.

See also Blacks in the United States; Civil Rights Movement.

Consult (IX) King, 1969; Lewis, 1970.

KING GEORGE'S WAR (1744–1748), the colonial name for the War of the Austrian Succession in Europe, pitted Britain against France. It merged with the War of Jenkin's Ear, an Anglo-Spanish conflict that had erupted in 1739 and that had already seen major British raids in the Caribbean and an unsuccessful Spanish attempt to conquer Georgia. French involvement shifted attention northward.

In 1744 Governor William Shirley of Massachusetts thwarted a French attempt to overrun Nova Scotia. A year later he astounded the British world by organizing an intercolonial force that reduced the supposedly impregnable French fortress of Louisbourg. Shirley tried to follow up this success with major invasions of Canada in 1746 and 1747, but he never obtained the necessary naval support from Britain. In the Treaty of Aix-la-Chapelle ending the war (1748), Britain disappointed New England by returning Louisbourg to France in order to offset French gains made in Europe at the expense of Britain's continental allies.

See also Shirley, William.

KING PHILIP'S WAR (1675–1676), the most

John Maynard Keynes, whose *General Theory of Employment, Interest and Money* was a milestone in the development of modern economics.

Civil rights leader Martin Luther King, Jr. urged followers to "overcome" by non-violence.

devastating Indian war in New England. It erupted in June 1675, when "King Philip," a sachem of the Wampanoag tribe, attacked Swansea in Plymouth Colony, thus ending nearly 40 years of peace since the Pequot War. Some tension over land did exist but probably not enough to lead to war. Equally disturbing may have been Puritan missionary activity among the Indians, which the more powerful tribes, such as the Wampanoags, resented as a threat to their cultural integrity.

Whatever the real grievances, New England settlers considered these attacks unprovoked aggression and responded with peculiar ferocity against the Wampanoags and their principal allies, the Nipmucs and the Narragansetts. Colonists killed more than 300 Indians, primarily Narragansetts and mostly women and children, in the Great Swamp Fight near modern Kingston, R.I., in November 1675. Indian counterattacks continued through the spring of 1676, but after several more defeats and the death of Philip in August they began to surrender in large numbers. When peace returned, New England had lost 12 towns and suffered damage to half the others. More than 5 percent of the adult males had been killed. Strong prejudices against Indians greatly weakened future missionary efforts. And, of course, the major tribes in Philip's coalition were either destroyed or weakened beyond the possibility of future serious military activity.

See also Indian Wars, Colonial; Massachusetts; Pequot War (1637).

Consult (I) Leach, 1958; Vaughan, 1965.

KING WILLIAM'S WAR (1689–1697), the colonial name for the War of the League of Augsburg (in Europe), marked the beginning of the Anglo-French struggle for the domination of North America. Early in 1690 an Indian expedition led by Frenchmen sacked Schenectady and captured or scattered its inhabitants. Later that year New York's Revolutionary leader, Jacob Leisler, called an intercolonial congress to organize for the conquest of Canada. Sir William Phips took Port Royal, Nova Scotia, and sailed up the St. Lawrence River to Quebec only to be bluffed into a hasty withdrawal by the French governor. A simultaneous invasion through northern New York achieved nothing, and in 1691 the French regained Port Royal. The war promptly evolved into a series of indecisive but brutal border skirmishes. The Treaty of Ryswick (1697) recognized the inconclusive nature of the struggle by affirming the prewar territorial status.

See also Schenectady Raid (1690).

KING'S COLLEGE (COLUMBIA COLLEGE). *See* Colonial Colleges.

KITCHEN CABINET, group of advisers on whom President Jackson relied. Jackson's offi-

cial cabinet was, with the exception of Martin Van Buren, composed of unexceptional men picked to placate sectional and factional interests of the Democratic Party. Soon after taking office in 1829, Jackson suspended cabinet meetings and relied for advice on a group of political confidants. Secretary of State Van Buren was the only "official" member of this group.

Many members of the Kitchen Cabinet were Democratic newspaper editors, including Francis P. Blair, Amos Kendall, Isaac Hill, and Duff Green. The Kitchen Cabinet was most influential from 1829 to 1831. In 1831, as a result of the Eaton Affair, Jackson reorganized and strengthened his official cabinet and subsequently relied on it.

KLONDIKE GOLD RUSH. *See* Gold Rushes.

KNICKERBOCKER SCHOOL, a group of writers centered in New York City. It drew its literary inspiration from the English writer Joseph Addison and its name from Washington Irving's satirical *A History of New York* (1809), which he wrote under the name Diedrich Knickerbocker. The association was primarily determined by geographical location and a common taste for the genteel styles popular in English writing. The major writers were Washington Irving, William Cullen Bryant, and James Kirke Paulding.

The influence of the school, which marked a transitional phase as American literature passed from its complete dependence on English literary styles, was slight. Edgar Allen Poe's "The Literati of New York City," a review published in *Godey's Lady's Book* (1846), offers a scathing view of the Knickerbockers. Their waning influence was kept alive in the *Knickerbocker Magazine* (1833–1865).

See also Literature.

KNIGHTS OF LABOR, labor organization open to skilled and unskilled workers that flourished between 1878 and 1893.

The order originated as a secret fraternity formed by Philadelphia garment cutters in 1869. Uriah S. Stephens served as Master Workman, highest office in the order, until 1879, when he was succeeded by Terence V. Powderly, who served until 1893. A national organization was formed in 1878.

Local assemblies were of two sorts, the trade assembly (consisting of workers in a single craft or trade) and the mixed assembly (open to all gainfully employed persons, even employers, and excluding only certain professionals). In admitting unskilled workers, farmers, and others not eligible for craft union membership, the Knights broke sharply with prevailing labor practices, thus becoming the first successful industrial union.

The Knights' greatest growth came be-

Knights of Labor leader Terence V. Powderly *(center)* rises to speak to delegates at 1886 convention.

tween 1878 and 1887, reaching a peak of more than 700,000 members and nearly 6,000 local assemblies. After the Haymarket Massacre in 1886, membership began to decline. By 1893, the order was dominated by farmers and died out soon after.

See also American Federation of Labor (AFL); Haymarket Massacre; Labor Movement.

KNOW-NOTHING PARTY, an antiforeign, anti-Catholic political party that mushroomed between 1853 and 1856 and then abruptly disappeared. In response to massive Irish and German immigration after 1846, the activities of the Catholic Church, and increased political participation by Catholic immigrants after 1851, a powerful nativist movement emerged that would politically proscribe all but native-born Protestants from public office and curtail immigrant voting by increasing the naturalization period from 5 to 21 years.

Organized initially in secret fraternal lodges whose members answered, "I know nothing" if asked about the exclusive native Protestant order, Know-Nothings secretly backed political candidates in 1854 and then campaigned openly as the American Party in 1855 and 1856. In 1854 and 1855, because of the extensiveness of prejudice, a widespread disgust with the old parties, and the breakdown of the Whigs, the Know-Nothings swept state and local elections, dominating lower New England and the Middle Atlantic states and showing strongly in the South. In 1856 Millard Fillmore, the American Party presidential candidate, garnered 21 percent of the popular vote, even though by then the party was badly divided over slavery and most of its Northern supporters had joined the Republicans. Indeed, by 1856 the party was more a conservative Unionist movement than a nativist organization, and after the campaign it rapidly disintegrated.

See also Fillmore, Millard; Political Parties in the United States.

Consult (IV) Billington, 1938; Holt, 1969.

KNOXVILLE ROAD. *See* Turnpikes, Early.

KOREAN WAR started on June 25, 1950, when troops from North Korea, allegedly repelling an invasion from the South, marched on Seoul, the South's capital. The stage for conflict had been set in 1945, when the Soviet Union had accepted the surrender of the Japanese north of the 38th parallel and the United States had accepted surrender south of the line. A UN commission established to conduct national elections was denied access to northern Korea, and in 1948 separate regimes had been proclaimed, each asserting authority over the entire country.

After the invasion, the UN Security Council (with Soviet delegates absent) urged member states to assist the Republic of (South)

Korea in repelling the attack, and President Truman authorized the use of U.S. air and naval forces. When this aid proved insufficient, U.S. ground forces were committed as part of a UN command under Gen. Douglas MacArthur.

By early August 1950 the UN forces had been pushed back to a narrow perimeter around the port of Pusan. Yet in mid-September an amphibious landing at Inchon, a port southwest of Seoul, and a simultaneous offensive from the Pusan area sent the North Koreans reeling north. After recapturing southern territory the UN army moved across the 38th parallel, and by the end of October 1950 some troops had reached the Yalu River. This came at a time when there were reports of possible Chinese intervention. MacArthur calculated that the Chinese would stay out, but on November 25 they struck in strength and the UN troops retreated to the 38th parallel.

A Chinese assault in January 1951 forced another UN withdrawal and resulted in the reconquest of Seoul. At this point the Chinese offensive died out, and a UN counteroffensive carried its forces in April to a strong position just north of the border. However, a fresh Chinese drive threw the UN troops back across the parallel. Finally in May another UN counterassault took the troops north of the 38th. Both sides suffered heavy casualties in the seesaw operations.

In April, MacArthur was dismissed by Truman in a dispute over extending the war beyond the Yalu; the UN allies feared the eruption of a world war. Although the war was limited, the UN forces eventually had a peak strength of about 800,000 men, including 400,000 from South Korea and 350,000 from the United States. The maximum communist strength was more than 1 million Chinese and 200,000 North Koreans.

Two years of armistice talks began in July 1951. Issues in dispute included the location of the truce line, repatriation of prisoners, and the composition of the supervisory commission that would enforce the provisions of the armistice. South Korea's President Rhee had to be persuaded not to obstruct the armistice, and in return he obtained a mutual defense treaty and long-term economic and military aid from the United States.

The impact of the war upon the United States was a major factor in the defeat of the Democrats and the election of Dwight D. Eisenhower in the presidential election of 1952.

See also MacArthur, Douglas.

Consult (VIII) Berger, 1957; Vatcher, 1958.

—Martin Gruberg, *University of Wisconsin, Oshkosh*

KOREMATSU v. UNITED STATES (1944), Supreme Court decision concerning the right of the military, under a presidential order, to

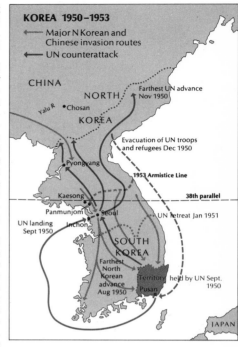

American bazooka team fires on North Korean positions.

Northern view of the Ku Klux Klan in 1874.

Monotony of assembly line work is a major area of concern in modern labor movement.

evacuate persons of Japanese ancestry from the West Coast during World War II. The petitioner, an American citizen of Japanese descent, was convicted for remaining in a "military area"—San Leandro, California—contrary to a military order. The Court held that Congress and the president, during time of war, had the power to order the military to exclude persons from a particular area, thus overriding the customary civil rights of such persons. In this case, the United States was at war with Japan, and the military feared an invasion. The Court emphasized that residents having ethnic affiliations with an invading enemy might be a greater source of danger than those of a different ancestry.

KU KLUX KLAN, secret organization that first flourished after the Civil War. Founded in Pulaski, Tenn., in May 1866, the Ku Klux Klan spread throughout the South until 1871. Its primary goal was political: the overthrow of Radical Republican governments established under the provisions of the Reconstruction Acts. The Klan also strove to maintain white social and economic supremacy. A terrorist organization usually operating at night, the Klan resorted to lynching, murder, arson, rape, whipping, mutilation, and economic coercion to achieve its ends.

To resist the Klan effectively was almost impossible because most Southern juries would never convict a Klansman. Therefore, in 1871 the federal government passed the Ku Klux Klan Act, which was designed to increase federal power in the South, and as a result the Klan collapsed in that same year. Shortly thereafter, however, white supremacists once again surfaced, and by 1877 they had helped oust all Radical governments in the South.

The Klan was revived in 1915, when the range of its enemies was broadened to include Jews, Catholics, and the foreign-born. The modern Klan employed the ritual and regalia of its predecessor and initiated the practice of cross-burning as a warning of impending violence, usually in the form of beatings, tarring and feathering, mutilation, or murder. In 1924 Klan membership peaked at 5 million, and the KKK gained political control in many local areas, but by the 1930s the Klan had essentially lost all national influence.

See also Enforcement Acts; Reconstruction Acts (1867–1868).

LABOR, DEPARTMENT OF, cabinet-level executive department that enforces federal legislation protecting the nation's workers and develops policies to improve working conditions and advance employment opportunities. The Bureau of Labor, created under the Department of the Interior in 1884, was made an independent agency four years later. From 1903 to 1913 it was part of the Department of

Commerce and Labor. In 1913 the Department of Labor was established as a separate cabinet agency.

Until 1932 strict judicial interpretation of the constitutional power of Congress to regulate interstate commerce confined national labor legislation to the railroad industry. However, a variety of New Deal measures considerably broadened areas in which the department had responsibilities, including hours, wages, and the rights of workers to organize.

See also New Deal.

LABOR MOVEMENT. The primary aim of the labor movement in America has been the improvement of the wage earner's economic position, but the U.S. labor movement has also been deeply involved in political and social developments. However, American workers have generally accepted the political-economic-social system, and only a small portion of the American movement has been devoted to an overthrow of the system.

Beginnings. The beginnings of the U.S. labor movement are, perhaps, lost forever. Almost any date from the arrival of the *Mayflower* may be cited as the first evidence of organized action by workers. Certainly, the movement was observable during the colonial period, and by the time of the Revolution, strikes had occurred. Toward the end of the eighteenth century, organizations of workers on a planned permanent basis were created. These early unions were generally found among the better-trained workers—the shoemakers, printers, carpenters, and tailors—who wanted better pay, shorter hours, and a right to jobs for members of the organization.

The employers responded with court actions, and the courts, bringing English common law to the cases, found the unions guilty of criminal conspiracy. From 1806 to 1842 any group of workers acting in concert to improve their condition of employment could well face fines or other punishment. The years were not totally wasted, however, for in several states the movement secured some concessions through political action. After the Supreme Court restricted the use of the criminal-conspiracy doctrine in 1842, organization continued.

Experiments. In the mid-1800s a number of experiments were tried. The unions were trying to organize on a larger scale, and the national union concept arose. The first such union failed, and others were attempted, but the national union was not really successful until late in the century. The movement tried other measures to attain its goals, but none worked, and it turned again to economic action.

In 1866 the National Labor Union was organized as a combination of labor groups,

LABOR MOVEMENT

NINETEENTH CENTURY

Factors
ANARCHISM
FREE ENTERPRISE
FREE TRADE
INVENTIONS
SWEATSHOPS
SOCIAL DARWINISM
PANICS, FINANCIAL (NINETEENTH CENTURY)
BUSINESS REGULATION (see Subject Map)

Unions and Leaders
LABOR MOVEMENT
    TEN-HOUR MOVEMENT
KNIGHTS OF LABOR
RAILROAD UNIONS
EUGENE V. DEBS
AMERICAN FEDERATION OF LABOR
SAMUEL GOMPERS
INDUSTRIAL WORKERS OF THE WORLD
MOLLY MAGUIRES

Strikes and Setbacks
HAYMARKET MASSACRE (1886)
HOMESTEAD MASSACRE (1892)
    HENRY CLAY FRICK
PULLMAN STRIKE (1894)

TWENTIETH CENTURY

Labor Legislation
RIGHT-TO-WORK LAWS
WORKMEN'S COMPENSATION
KEATING-OWEN ACT (1916)
NATIONAL LABOR RELATIONS ACT (1935)
    NATIONAL LABOR RELATIONS BOARD V. JONES
        AND LAUGHLIN STEEL CO. (1937)
SOCIAL SECURITY ACT (1935)
FAIR LABOR STANDARDS ACT (1938)
TAFT-HARTLEY ACT (1947)

Unions and Leaders
JOHN L. LEWIS
CONGRESS OF INDUSTRIAL ORGANIZATIONS
WALTER REUTHER
AMERICAN FEDERATION OF LABOR-CONGRESS
    OF INDUSTRIAL ORGANIZATIONS
GEORGE MEANY
JAMES R. HOFFA
CESAR CHAVEZ

The Subject Maps in the Encyclopedia illustrate the coverage of particular aspects of American History, showing the interrelationships among the articles in twelve critical areas of study. Entries in capital letters, except for titles, are subjects for which there are separate articles in the Encyclopedia.

The Subject Maps are arranged alphabetically in the Encyclopedia under the following titles:

American Wars
Blacks in the United States
Business Regulation and Industrialization
Civil War and Reconstruction
Constitution of the United States
Exploration and Colonization
Frontier in American History
Indians
Labor Movement
New Deal and Depression
Revolutionary War Era
Slavery and Emancipation

Unionized railroad workers attack strike breakers in Chicago in 1888.

Eight-hour day was long a goal of labor movement.

farmer organizations, suffragettes, and other reform movements. Described by one writer as labor leaders without members, farmers without land, and women without husbands, NLU turned to the eight-hour day as a goal. After some success it turned to monetary reform and cooperatives. The unions withdrew, and the movement failed.

As NLU was declining, the Knights of Labor (1869) was organized. The Knights turned to reform as well as economic action and admitted as members everyone except a few groups that were excluded because of occupation. After 1879 the organization grew very rapidly. Riding on a few successful strikes, membership rose to more than 1.5 million. Its decline was soon to follow, perhaps speeded by strike losses. However, the most important reason for its failure was its organizational framework. It took in too many members too fast with too few common interests and without a common philosophy. The trade unions could not accept the reform philosophy, and the division of interests broke the back of the movement.

The AFL. The most valuable contribution of these two organizations was negative—they showed what not to do in the labor movement. Samuel Gompers learned the lesson well, and in 1886, when he formed the American Federation of Labor, these negative contributions were very visible. Thus, the AFL was created as an economic union, not as a reform body. Based on the philosophy that unions are for skilled workers, that every skilled worker should be in a union with others of his trade, that the job of the union is to secure better conditions for its members, that the union is responsible and will honor its contracts, and that the proper role of the union is to bargain with employers, the AFL grew slowly and solidly.

The AFL was attacked from both sides. On the right the employers fought this rising union structure and in many ways were successful. On the left the Industrial Workers of the World, perhaps the only really radical movement in U.S. labor history, cursed the conservatism of the AFL.

These attacks may have resulted in some reduction of the growth rate, but the AFL continued to grow until 1920, when it had about 4 million members. In the 1920s the organized labor movement actually lost about 2 million members during a period of prosperity. The loss continued into the Depression of the 1930s.

New Deal. However, during the 1930s legislation made union organization easier. The most important gain was the National Labor Relations Act (1935), or Wagner Act, which granted to workers the right to be members of labor organizations and which placed a duty to bargain on the employer.

Perhaps the most significant result of the Wagner Act was the effect on those employees ignored by the AFL, the industrial workers. Under the rights granted by the act, workers in steel, automobiles, and other mass-production industries showed an interest in organization. A group of AFL leaders formed the Committee for Industrial Organization. Opposed by the AFL, in 1938 their unions were expelled from the federation, and a new labor group, the Congress of Industrial Organizations (CIO) was created. These two rival organizations dominated the labor movement until 1955, when they finally united. Another result of the Wagner Act was a rapid growth in union membership. From 1935 to 1945, membership grew from more than 3 million to over 14 million.

Postwar Problems. By the end of the war the favorable treatment of labor was attacked, and Congress again turned its attention to the movement. In 1947 the Taft-Hartley Act placed restrictions on the unions. Still the most important piece of labor legislation, the act proscribed a series of unfair labor practices for unions, abolished the closed shop, made state right-to-work laws legal, and set forth a procedure for national emergency strikes. Passed over President Truman's veto, the law was bitterly resented by labor leaders.

In the 1950s the progress of the labor movement abated, and membership grew very slowly. As a percentage of the labor force, membership actually declined. The major unorganized groups in the country remained unorganized—the Southern worker, the female worker, the white-collar worker, and the employees of small firms.

Also during the 1950s, Congress tried to reform what it considered flaws in union practices through the Labor-Management Reporting and Disclosure Act (1959), popularly known as the Landrum-Griffin Act. Financial practices, elections, officers, constitutions, member rights and other areas came under the law, and the unions were required to be more responsive to the membership. Thus, the unions entered the 1960s under fire. There was public as well as official suspicion, and the nonunionized worker was still hesitant to join a union.

Outlook. The problems the unions faced may have been related to the changing value system in the society, to the youth revolt on civil rights, and, later, to the attitudes toward the Vietnam War and pollution. In these areas, as the young groups often saw it, the labor movement was not relevant, and thus the younger worker was apt to view the union as part of the establishment.

It has been suggested that what future success the movement will have will depend on its ability to change. If it cannot adapt to the younger worker, the white-collar worker, the minority worker, or the female employee, it will continue to fade. Perhaps the most hopeful sign for the unions is the success the government employees' unions have had in the 1960s. Here all the groups just mentioned have joined to form a successful structure in a very difficult situation. In addition, farm workers have been the target of organizing drives by various groups.

Consult (III) Dulles, 1966.
—William D. Wagoner, *Louisiana State University*

LABOR-MANAGEMENT RELATIONS ACT (1947). *See* Taft-Hartley Act.

LAFAYETTE, MARQUIS DE (1757–1834), French nobleman who fought in the Revolutionary War. He found in the American Revolution an outlet for his desire for adventure and his hostility to England. Lafayette landed in America in June 1777, offered to serve without pay, and Congress commissioned him a major general without command. George Washington immediately took a strong liking to the young Frenchman.

On Washington's advice, the Continental Congress in December 1777 gave Lafayette command of Virginia light troops. Lafayette endured the hardships of Valley Forge and in 1778 participated ably in the actions around Monmouth, N.J., and Newport, R.I. In 1779 he went to France, where he received a hero's welcome and an appointment as colonel of dragoons. Lafayette returned to America in 1780, and a year later Washington sent him to Virginia to stop Benedict Arnold's raids. Lafayette showed considerable tactical ability in the Battle of Green Spring in July 1781. He was commander of the light infantry in the final defeat of Cornwallis at Yorktown.

Lafayette returned to France in 1781. He was not able to sustain a leadership position during the French Revolution and lost favor entirely when the Jacobins gained power. He remained away from politics until he won election to the Chamber of Deputies in 1818. In 1824 Lafayette made a triumphant tour of the United States.

See also Revolutionary War Battles.

LA FOLLETTE, ROBERT M(ARION) (1855–1925), U.S. senator from Wisconsin and presidential candidate who was a leader of the Progressives. A lawyer, "Fighting Bob" spent six years in the House of Representatives before being defeated for reelection in 1890.

Finding future progress through the state Republican ranks blocked by the old guard, La Follette spent a decade building his own reform organization, relying heavily on the University of Wisconsin faculty. Finally elected governor in 1900, he secured the passage of a progressive program that made the "Wisconsin Idea" a model for other states to emulate; it included a direct primary, a railroad commission, and major tax reform.

Elected to the Senate in 1905, La Follette quickly became the leader of a growing group of Midwestern insurgents and directed the fight on the Payne-Aldrich Tariff, the income tax, and other issues. In 1911 he founded the National Progressive Republican League and sought to be its standard-bearer in 1912 only to have Theodore Roosevelt capture the field. In foreign affairs La Follette led the Midwestern isolationist forces—opposing entry into World War I as well as membership in the League of Nations and the World Court. In 1924 he revived the Progressive Party and received about 5 million votes but carried only Wisconsin. He died in 1925 and was succeeded in the Senate by his son.

See also Presidential Elections; Progressive Party.

—John Buenker, *University of Wisconsin, Parkside*

LA GUARDIA, FIORELLO (1882–1947), U.S. congressman and mayor of New York City. He was a unique blend of elements in American politics during the period 1914–1945. Raised by immigrant parents—a Jewish mother and an Italian father who brought him up an Episcopalian—he spent his youth in Western army camps (his father was an army bandmaster) and was later a foreign service officer in Europe.

As a congressman from New York City (1917; 1923–1933) he served as a bridge between urban and rural elements among the Progressives, and as mayor of New York (1934–1945) he successfully combined ethnic politics with urban reform. An unorthodox Republican, he bolted to support La Follette in 1924 and Roosevelt in 1936. His own mayoral election came on a Fusion ticket, with support from Republicans, anti-Tammany Democrats, Socialists, and Independents.

In Congress he fought for social justice and against numerous trends and developments of the period between World War I and the New Deal: espionage laws, Prohibition, dollar diplomacy, business privilege, and immigration restriction. He supported public power, farm legislation, progressive taxation, and protection of labor. He is best remembered for the Norris-La Guardia Anti-Injunction Act of 1932, the intent of which was to prevent federal courts from interfering on the side of management in labor bargaining struggles.

Although La Guardia lost his congressional seat the same year Roosevelt was elected, he had close contacts with the new Administration. As mayor he was an exceptional municipal leader in his extensive and judicious use of New Deal funds. The "little

Wisconsin Governor Robert La Follette, a Progressive leader, later had distinguished career in U.S. Senate.

Fiorello La Guardia confers with Eleanor Roosevelt.

Oliver Hazard Perry transfers his command from the *Lawrence* to the *Niagra* during the Battle of Lake Erie.

LAND POLICY — Item Guide

The article on LAND POLICY describes the trends in government policy as the United States has grown.

Before the Revolution the British tried to control expansion through the PROCLAMATION OF 1763. After the war the NORTHWEST ORDINANCE (1787) organized the NORTHWEST TERRITORY in what is now the Midwest. The growth of the nation, facilitated by the LOUISIANA PURCHASE and other acquisitions and by the development of TURNPIKES, EARLY; CANALS; and RAILROADS, resulted in the formation of LAND COMPANIES, such as the OHIO COMPANY.

Westward movement of settlers, spurred by GOLD RUSHES, affected INDIAN POLICY and led to legislation such as the KANSAS-NEBRASKA ACT, MORRILL ACT (1862), and HOMESTEAD ACT (1862) for developing the West. FRONTIER IN AMERICAN HISTORY, which has a Subject Map, details the westward movement. Concern for the fate of U.S. lands resulted in a number of CONSERVATION ACTS and a growing interest in ECOLOGY.

New Deal" in New York used $250 million in federal monies to build bridges, tunnels, expressways, and subways and to provide employment. A flamboyant, honest, and popular mayor who removed many jobs from political patronage, he was reelected in 1937 and 1941.

Consult (VI) Mann, 1965.

LAKE ERIE, BATTLE OF (1813), naval engagement that gave America control of Lake Erie during the War of 1812. Lake Erie was strategically essential to the fighting in the Detriot region: if the Americans could control the lake, the British could not supply their troops in that region. Starting late in 1812 the Americans constructed a fleet on the lake, and in the summer of 1813 this fleet sailed under the command of Oliver Hazard Perry. On September 9 it met the weaker British fleet, commanded by Capt. Robert Barclay, near Put-in-Bay.

In the hotly fought engagement, Perry's flagship, the *Lawrence,* was totally disabled, and he had himself rowed to the *Niagara* to resume the command from that ship. The battle was a total victory for the Americans. Perry informed General William Henry Harrison in a famous dispatch that "We have met the enemy; and they are ours."

See also Perry, Oliver Hazard.

LAND COMPANIES, organizations that played a significant role in American economic development and settlement between 1750 and 1820. Most people were farmers, and land was the single most important natural resource of the time. Under these circumstances it was natural for investors and businessmen to consider Western land a major source of wealth and to organize land companies for speculation. In fact, many business and political leaders in the country took part in one or more land schemes, and the companies they established stimulated interest in western Pennsylvania and Virginia, as well as in Kentucky and Ohio, all prior to 1790.

Land speculation had occurred throughout the colonial era, but it was not until the late 1740s that powerful men started companies to get land. In 1747 the Grand Ohio Company was begun by Virginians, and two years later the British government granted the company 200,000 acres of land. During the French and Indian War (1754–1763), the speculators could only wait and dream, but when the fighting ended they resumed their efforts.

That year (1763) the Mississippi Company, led by George Washington, asked for 2.5 million acres of land, but renewed warfare with the Indians again halted the speculators. As a result of the fighting the British government issued the Proclamation of 1763, which closed the West to settlement, at least temporarily. However, the speculators and traders

who had lost goods during the Indian wars organized companies to compensate for their business losses. The Indian Company, organized in 1763 and involved with the Vandalia Grant, and the Illinois Company, which followed three years later, were two of the most important new companies. Few of their efforts produced much profit, but the companies' activities made it difficult for successful settlement because of conflicting and overlapping land claims.

During and after the Revolutionary War, land companies continued to exert their influence. Leaders of the Transylvania Company hired Daniel Boone to cut a trail west into Kentucky during the 1770s, and later that same decade the claims of major land companies delayed the ratification of the Articles of Confederation by some of the landless states. Ten years later the activities of a new Ohio Company helped to open the Old Northwest for settlement. Thus, the land companies had both negative and positive effects upon early American development.

See also Boone, Daniel; Ohio Company; Proclamation of 1763; Vandalia Grant (1772).

Consult (I) Livermore, 1939; Sosin, 1961.

—Roger L. Nichols, *University of Arizona*

LAND LAW OF 1800 reduced acreage pioneers were required to buy in Northwest Territory, stimulated settlement. *See* Harrison, William Henry.

LAND LAW OF 1820, effort to make it easier for pioneers to purchase land. *See* Land Policy.

LAND POLICY. As the United States expanded its boundaries and population, the problem of how to distribute land for farming, mining, and lumbering proved difficult. Throughout the colonial era and well into the nineteenth century, most Americans were farmers or had economic interests directly tied to agriculture. Therefore, one of the first questions facing the federal government was that of devising a workable land policy.

Land for the People. Prior to the ratification of the Constitution, Congress had no power to tax and found itself in desperate need of money. When the states grudgingly ceded their Western lands to Congress, its leaders decided to use the profits from land sales to finance the government. The Ordinance of 1785, often called the Land Ordinance, laid the foundation for future land policy and sales and was followed by the Northwest Ordinance of 1787. The law established a system for the regular survey and sale of land, set the price, and even reserved some land to support public schools. For the next 80 years the land system evolved from the plan to use land sale profits to pay government expenses to the idea that land

and other natural resources belonged to the people and that they should get them as easily and cheaply as possible.

Congress gradually reduced the number of acres an individual had to buy, as well as the purchase price. To begin with, plots had to be at least 1 square mile, or 640 acres—far too much land for the average farm family of that day. This requirement was lowered, and the Land Law of 1820 reduced the minimum to a mere 80 acres at a price of $1.25 per acre—the pioneer could buy his future farm for $100 if he had that much cash.

The original and subsequent early land laws forbade settlement before the federal survey crews had finished their work, but from the first, pioneers ignored this rule. As a result, when the land was first auctioned, the squatter, who was actually an illegal settler, had to bid first and then frighten others from trying to buy his land out from under him. Eventually the settlers formed claim clubs or pressure groups to control the public land sales and to petition Congress to change the laws. Their efforts succeeded in 1841, when the general Preemption Act passed. This law made settlement prior to survey legal and simplified land sales and property disputes considerably.

The trend away from viewing the public domain as a source of federal revenue began on a broad front during the first decade of the nineteenth century. In addition to reducing prices for farm land, Congress made frequent land grants to states to help them fund transportation projects such as roads and canals, as well as for public education. By 1862 the idea that the government should profit from selling land to the citizens had been discarded, and with the Homestead Act of that year land became essentially free. Although people could, and still did, buy federal land after 1862, the Homestead Act was the logical conclusion of an 80-year policy to get land and other resources into the hands of the citizens.

Natural Resource Programs. To begin with, the government had considered forest and mineral lands as another source of income, and policies toward them reflected that idea. Mineral-bearing land could not be bought. Miners were supposed to lease it, at least up to the 1840s. Lead miners in the Midwest paid a 10-percent rent payable in either cash or lead for the right to mine on federal land. Government officers found this impossible to enforce, and gradually the charges were eliminated. Forests were not for sale either, and it was illegal to cut timber on federal land. But the need for lumber was great and the government weak, so here too the laws had to be changed.

By the 1870s the idea of giving away or selling the national resources for a pittance was publicly challenged for the first time. In 1872 Yellowstone National Park was established, and a growing chorus of conservationists

spurred the eventual growth of the National Park Service. In 1891 the Forest Reserve Act slipped through Congress, and under it the next three presidents set aside more than 130 million acres of forest land.

As conservation became more popular, other laws were passed to preserve or develop carefully the resources still untouched. The Newlands Act of 1902 created the U.S. Reclamation Service, and Congress gave it funds for irrigation work in the arid West. Numerous dams, canals, and river improvement projects have been completed by this or other federal agencies during the twentieth century.

Consult (V) Nash, 1968; Robbins, 1942.
—Roger L. Nichols, *University of Arizona*

LANE REBELS, group of abolitionists at Lane Seminary in Cincinnati. *See* Oberlin College; Weld, Theodore.

LANGLEY, S. P., pioneer aviator. *See* Aviation.

LARGE-STATE PLAN. *See* Virginia Plan.

LA SALLE, SIEUR DE (1643–1687), French explorer who sailed to Canada in 1666 after losing his share of his father's estate. A few years later he embarked on his career as an explorer when he journeyed up the St. Lawrence River to Lake Ontario. Soon involved in the fur trade, his activities convinced him that the American interior was far more valuable than anyone realized. A trip to France in 1677–1678 won royal support for a bold effort to win the vast Mississippi River system with its tributaries for France. Sailing down the Mississippi in 1683, he named the region "Louisiana" and claimed it for King Louis XIV. A second expedition (1685), designed to reach the Mississippi through the Gulf of Mexico, failed. In a desperate attempt to march overland from Texas to Illinois, La - Salle was murdered by his rebellious men in 1687.

See also Exploration and Discovery; French Colonies.

LATIN AMERICAN CONFERENCES. During the 1930s the United States had a deliberate policy only with respect to the Western Hemisphere, where it took the initiative to create an improved atmosphere for understanding and cooperation. These attempts can best be summarized by the series of conferences attended by the United States and its southern neighbors.

In Montevideo, Uruguay (1933), Secretary of State Cordell Hull renounced America's right to use force in Latin American countries except where American lives were endangered. Even this qualification was removed at Buenos Aires, Argentina (1936), where President Franklin D. Roosevelt, attending a Latin American conference for the first time as president, un-

Open land attracted flocks of homesteaders to Oklahoma from 1884. Federal policy of offering low-cost land to settlers helped populate vast areas of the West.

William D. Leahy, Chief of Naval Operations before World War II, was key presidential adviser during the war.

Richard Henry Lee had many of his constitutional proposals incorporated in the Bill of Rights.

equivocally put an end to the policy of interventionism.

However, as the threat of Nazi Germany grew, the United States once again became interested in playing a leading role in the collective defense of the Western Hemisphere. The result was a series of conferences, including those held at Lima, Peru (1938) and Havana, Cuba (1940), in which the nations of the Western Hemisphere resolved to take joint measures for their security. It was inevitable, then, that countries such as Argentina that did not adhere to an explicitly anti-Axis stand would become an object of American concern.

Consult (VI) Bemis, 1943.
—Akira Iriye, University of Chicago

LATROBE, BENJAMIN (HENRY) (1764-1820), engineer and architect. He was born in England and emigrated to the United States, where he practiced both his professions. As an architect he popularized Greek Revival architecture, the vogue that began with his design for the Bank of Pennsylvania building in Philadelphia (1801). His pamphlet advocating a city water supply led to his commission to build for Philadelphia the first civic water supply system in America.

Latrobe was appointed surveyor of U.S. public buildings by President Jefferson in 1803. He designed many important public buildings, including parts of the new Capitol. In 1804 Latrobe was appointed engineer of the Navy Department. Latrobe's partnership with Robert Fulton and his associates, which was formed to build a steamboat that could navigate the Ohio River, ended in financial disaster. After another term as Capitol architect and after going bankrupt, Latrobe returned to private life. He died of yellow fever while attempting to finish the New Orleans water supply project in 1820.

See also Architecture.

LATTER-DAY SAINTS, CHURCH OF JESUS CHRIST OF, formal name of the Mormon Church. See Mormons.

LEAGUE OF AUGSBURG, WAR OF THE. See King William's War (1689-1697).

LEAGUE OF NATIONS, international association that was the forerunner of the United Nations. The Covenant of the League of Nations was adopted in 1919 as part of the Treaty of Versailles, which ended World War I, and began operations in January 1920.

Organization. The covenant provided for reduction of arms, collective security without resort to arms, and respect for the sovereignty of states. The covenant also provided for collective action—economic sanctions and military measures—against an aggressor.

The main organs of the league, which had its headquarters in Geneva, Switzerland,

were the assembly (of all members) and the council (of France, Italy, Japan, Britain, the United States, and nine other members elected by the assembly). Germany joined the council in 1927. The U.S. seat on the council was never occupied.

History. The covenant came into force on Jan. 10, 1920. Although President Woodrow Wilson had called for an association of nations to guarantee political independence, the Senate did not ratify the covenant, and the United States did not join the league. All states that were neutral in World War I joined the league, which by 1927 had 52 members. Germany became a member in 1927, but it withdrew in 1933. The Soviet Union joined the league in 1934.

After Japan annexed Manchuria in 1931, the league recommended that Manchuria be returned to China, but Japan responded by withdrawing from the league. When Italy invaded Ethiopia in 1935, the league imposed economic sanctions against Italy and continued to recognize Ethiopia as an independent state.

The league failed to contain the actions of Japan, Germany, and Italy and held no meetings during World War II. The league, however, settled disputes between Finland and Sweden over the Aland Islands, frontier disputes among Albania, Greece, and Yugoslavia, border problems between Germany and Poland and Czechoslovakia and Poland, and controversies between Britain and Turkey.

After the creation of the United Nations on Oct. 24, 1945, the league met for the last time in Geneva on April 19, 1946.

See also Versailles, Treaty of.

LEAGUE OF WOMEN VOTERS, an organization formed in 1920, the year that U.S. women won suffrage. It was started at the suggestion of Carrie Chapman Catt, president of the disbanding National American Woman Suffrage Association. The league's original purpose was to help newly enfranchised women carry out their responsibilities as voters. A nonpartisan organization, the league provides voter information and encourages the informed participation of all citizens in government and politics. It does not, however, support or oppose political parties or candidates for office.

See also Suffrage, Women's.

LEAHY, WILLIAM D(ANIEL) (1875-1959), naval officer, diplomat, and presidential adviser. He graduated from the Naval Academy in 1897 and saw action in the Spanish-American War. He advanced to the rank of captain during World War I and later headed the bureaus of ordnance and navigation. His old friend Franklin Roosevelt named him chief of naval operations in 1937 and governor of Puerto Rico in 1939.

In December 1940, Leahy accepted the

delicate and controversial appointment of ambassador to Vichy France. Critics then and later charged that the United States was tainted by doing business with the collaborationist regime of Marshal Pétain, but Leahy and his defenders have argued that he maintained a valuable listening post in Europe and helped keep the French fleet and French North Africa out of German hands.

Roosevelt promoted Leahy to admiral of the fleet and made him chief of staff to the commander in chief in July 1942. In this capacity he served as liaison man between the White House and the military. He remained one of the President's most trusted advisers throughout the war and attended most of the major conferences. A staunch nationalist and advocate of American military power, he was senior military adviser to President Truman from 1945 to 1949 and played a prominent part in the reassessment of U.S. policy toward Russia and the reorganization of the armed forces.

—George Herring, *University of Kentucky*

LEATHERSTOCKING TALES, five novels (*The Pioneers, The Last of the Mohicans, The Prairie, The Pathfinder,* and *The Deerslayer*) by James Fenimore Cooper that were the first American Westerns. *See* Cooper, James Fenimore; Literature.

LEAVES OF GRASS, major work of Walt Whitman. *See* Whitman, Walt.

LECOMPTON CONSTITUTION, constitution adopted by proslavery settlers in Kansas. *See* Bleeding Kansas.

LEE, RICHARD HENRY (1732-1794), Revolutionary statesman. A member of an aristocratic Virginia family, his political career began in 1758 as a member of the Virginia House of Burgesses. Here he became a close ally of Patrick Henry and worked with him to protest the taxes levied on the colonies. In 1773, he, Henry, and Thomas Jefferson developed a plan of intercolonial correspondence. In 1774 Lee was a Virginia delegate to the First Continental Congress; he and John Adams agreed at this time that the colonies should adopt their own governments. Lee thought that the colonies should declare their independence so they could form foreign alliances. After presenting the Virginia resolutions for independence at the Second Continental Congress in 1776, Lee worked for the Articles of Confederation.

He resigned his seat in 1779 but was reelected in 1784 and served as president of Congress. At this time he played an important role in the passage of the Northwest Ordinance. After the Constitutional Convention in 1787 he led the opposition to the new Constitution primarily because it lacked a bill of rights, which he urged in *Letters from a Federal Farmer.* Lee returned to Congress as a senator (1789-1792) and had many of his proposals for constitutional reform incorporated into the Bill of Rights. He retired in 1792 and died in Chantilly, Va.

See also Bill of Rights; Constitutional Convention (1787); Continental Congress, Second.

LEE, ROBERT E(DWARD) (1807-1870), commander of the Confederate forces. Son of a distinguished Revolutionary War officer, Lee was born and raised in Virginia and educated at West Point. During the secession crisis his loyalty to Virginia overrode his attachment to the Union.

On May 31, 1862, he assumed command of the Confederate troops defending Richmond and in the following month led them to a victory over George B. McClellan. In August he thrashed the federal forces at the Second Battle of Bull Run and decided to press his advantage by invading the North. At Antietam, Md., he fought a murderous draw with McClellan (September 1862), which forced Lee to abandon the offensive. At Fredericksburg, Va. (December 1862), Lee inflicted one of the worst defeats of the war on the Union army. The following spring Joseph Hooker led a well-planned offensive only to be outgeneraled and thoroughly defeated by Lee and Stonewall Jackson at Chancellorsville (May 1863), Lee's most brilliant triumph.

Once again Lee decided to penetrate the North, perhaps his greatest mistake. He had made many changes in command as a result of Jackson's death at Chancellorsville, thus causing a fatal lack of coordination during the battle of Gettysburg (July 1863), where Lee suffered a bad defeat. In May 1864 he inflicted heavy casualties on the enemy at Cold Harbor, Va. (June 1864). Grant, however, kept pushing south and besieged Lee at Petersburg, Va. By the spring of 1865, Lee was forced to abandon his lines and finally surrendered to Ulysses S. Grant on April 9 at Appomattox Courthouse.

After the war Lee served as president of Washington College. He died in 1870 as the best-loved man in Southern history, widely regarded as the embodiment of the best in that section's ideals: honor, courage, patience, dignity, and grace.

See also Civil War Battles; Lee Family.
Consult (IV) Freeman, 1934-1935.

—Michael Burlingame, *Connecticut College*

LEE FAMILY. Richard Lee (1613-1664) arrived in Virginia in 1640 and rose from a court clerk to attorney general of Virginia. By the time of the American Revolution, four generations of Lees had sat in the ruling councils of their colony, forming a powerful and talented political dy-

Robert E. Lee, commander in chief of the Confederate armies and a master of tactics and strategy.

United Mine Workers President John L. Lewis announces signing of new contract in 1951.

Sinclair Lewis, first American to receive Nobel Prize for Literature.

nasty. Richard Lee's principal heir, Richard (1646-1714), was a scholar who established the three family branches that produced American Revolutionary leaders: Stratford, Leesylvania, and Maryland.

The Stratford line began with Thomas Lee (1690-1750), Richard's fifth son. Thomas became acting governor of Virginia and the largest landowner in the family. His sons Francis Lightfoot (1734-1797) and Richard Henry (1732-1794) worked together for American independence in the Continental Congress. The best-known Lee from the Leesylvania branch of the family was Robert Edward (1807-1870). His father, Henry "Light Horse Harry" (1756-1818), was a member of the Continental Congress and the House of Representatives and instilled in his son a love of soldiering. It was natural for Robert E. to head for West Point. The Maryland line of the family, although less colorful, also produced several members who entered American politics.

See also Lee, Richard H.; Lee, Robert E.

LEND-LEASE, program to assist the victims of Axis aggression without directly involving America in war. The primary objective was to save Britain, which seemed on the verge of collapse in 1940-1941. Because Britain's cash reserves were running out, President Roosevelt decided on simply "lending and leasing" supplies to it.

It was not until March 1941 that the Lend-Lease Act passed Congress with a substantial majority, indicating that the American people supported all-out aid to Britain short of war. Winston Churchill called it a "most unsordid act" and attributed the survival of his country to the timely U.S. assistance. Later the program was extended to China and the Soviet Union.

See also World War II.

Consult (VII) Kimball, 1971.

LEOPARD AND CHESAPEAKE. *See* Chesapeake and Leopard (1807).

LETTERS FROM A FEDERAL FARMER. *See* Lee, Richard Henry.

LEWIS, (HARRY) SINCLAIR (1885-1951), American novelist and social critic who was the first American to win the Nobel Prize for Literature (1930).

Born in Sauk Centre, Minn., the son of a small-town doctor, Lewis was educated at Yale. After a period of writing, working, and wandering, Lewis produced several minor novels. In 1917 he penned his first distinguished work, *The Job,* a realistic novel about New York life. With the publication of *Main Street* (1920), an exposé of small-town Midwestern America, Lewis received wide recognition, and this work

became an outstanding success as did his other major volumes: *Babbitt* (1922); *Arrowsmith* (1925), for which he was offered the Pulitzer Prize and declined the honor; *Elmer Gantry* (1927); and *Dodsworth* (1929). Following these books, a long string of minor books marked Lewis' decline as an observer and social commentator.

Nevertheless, Lewis left his mark on American letters and on the American consciousness, particularly through *Babbitt.* This novel is a satiric, realistic, and yet sympathetic portrait of a prosperous Midwest businessman who tries but fails to get above the deadness of his life. The term "Babbitt" has become part of the language as a label for a conventional, limited middle-class person.

LEWIS, JOHN L(LEWELLYN) (1880-1969), labor leader. Born in Iowa of Welsh immigrant parents, he joined his father in the coal mines at 16 and later worked in mines in Colorado, Montana, and Illinois. In 1909 he was elected president of his local union in Illinois and became state legislative agent for the United Mine Workers (UMW) the same year. A field and legislative representative of the American Federation of Labor (AFL) from 1911 to 1916, he held various UMW offices from 1916 to 1919, when he became acting president. He was elected president in 1920 and served until 1960.

Lewis led his union on several highly publicized strikes in 1919, 1922, and 1925-1926, and by 1929 the UMW was the largest AFL affiliate. Throughout the 1920s and 1930s, Lewis aggressively promoted the cause of industrial unionism, of the organization of production-line workers and semiskilled and unskilled workers. He allied himself with President Franklin D. Roosevelt in 1933-1934 and embarked upon an extensive UMW organizing drive.

When the AFL balked at committing its full resources to industrial organizing, Lewis took the lead in forming the rival Congress of Industrial Organizations (CIO) from 1935 to 1938. He committed $500,000 to the reelection of Roosevelt in 1936 but broke with him in 1940 and resigned as CIO president when Roosevelt was reelected. In 1942 the UMW left the CIO, returned briefly to the AFL four years later, then became independent once more. The coal strike of 1946 led to temporary government seizure of the coal mines and helped to spur passage of the Taft-Hartley Act. Lewis retired as UMW president in 1960.

See also Congress of Industrial Organizations (CIO); Labor Movement.

Consult (VI) Alinsky, 1970.

—Robert W. Cherny, *California State University, San Francisco*

LEWIS AND CLARK EXPEDITION. In 1803, the year the United States bought Louisiana from

France, President Thomas Jefferson set into motion the Lewis and Clark Expedition. Between 1804 and 1806 this group of 27 men traveled up the Missouri River, crossed the northern Rocky Mountains, and followed tributaries of the Columbia River to the Pacific Ocean. Then they returned to St. Louis to complete one of the most successful explorations of American history.

When the expedition began, Meriwether Lewis, a 29-year-old army captain, had received a cram course in natural science to prepare him for his duties as an explorer. After the men returned from their journey in 1806, Jefferson appointed Lewis governor of Louisiana Territory. The captain fared badly in this job, however, and died mysteriously while traveling on the Natchez Trace in 1809.

His partner, 33-year-old William Clark, was another Virginia-born army officer. The younger brother of Revolutionary War hero George Rogers Clark, William had served with Meriwether Lewis in the army. In 1807, after the expedition, Jefferson appointed Clark superintendent of Indian affairs at St. Louis, a position he retained until his death in 1838. In 1813 he became the governor of Missouri Territory and served until 1821, when Missouri achieved statehood.

The Expedition. The two captains and their 25 men began their trek up the Missouri in the spring of 1804. They traveled up river as far as central North Dakota, where they spent the winter of 1804–1805 with the Mandan Indians. The next spring they continued west to the Pacific, and after spending the winter of 1805–1806 at the mouth of the Columbia River, they returned to St. Louis in 1806.

Jefferson had ordered them to record all interesting plants, animals, and rocks they saw, to map the major streams they used, and to establish friendly relations with the Indians. By keeping daily notes the explorers gathered a wealth of scientific data about the West. Unfortunately, most of their material lay unused until the 1890s.

See also Frontier in American History; Louisiana Purchase (1803).

Consult (III) Bakeless, 1947; Dillon, 1965.
—Roger L. Nichols, University of Arizona

LEXINGTON AND CONCORD (1775), opening engagement of the Revolutionary War. On the evening of April 18, 1775, Gen. Thomas Gage dispatched Lt. Col. Francis Smith from Boston with 700 British soldiers to destroy a patriot supply cache at Concord. The Boston Committee of Correspondence immediately sent Paul Revere and William Dawes to warn Lexington and Concord.

The next morning, Capt. John Parker and 70 Massachusetts Minutemen met the British on the Lexington Common. At the sound of shot, the British fired, killing 8 colonials. The Americans wounded only 1 soldier. Smith continued to Concord and accomplished his mission, but Americans inflicted 14 casualties on an English platoon at Concord Bridge. Militiamen hidden along the road harassed Smith's column on its return march to Boston. During the day the British lost 73 killed, 174 wounded, and 26 missing; total colonial casualties reached 93. The Americans then began a siege of Boston that lasted until the British evacuated the city in 1776.

See also Revere, Paul; Revolutionary War Battles.

LEYTE GULF, BATTLE OF (OCT. 23-25, 1944), gave the United States control of the waters around the Philippine Islands. See World War II.

LIBERAL REPUBLICANS, group of Republicans disenchanted with President Grant's Administration who decided in 1872 to bolt the regular party, which was clearly going to renominate Grant. Grant had alienated the Liberals by trying to annex Santo Domingo, ignoring appeals to end corruption through civil service reform, indulging in nepotism and cronyism, and refusing to reform the tariff.

Led by men such as Senators Carl Schurz and Lyman Trumbull, the dissidents gathered in Cincinnati in May and nominated Horace Greeley, the venerable, somewhat eccentric editor of the New York Tribune. Although subsequently endorsed by the Democratic Party, Greeley suffered an ignominious defeat at the polls in November.

LIBERATOR, abolitionist newspaper. See Garrison, William Lloyd.

LIBERIA, colony and later country in Africa established to provide a homeland for freed American slaves. The plan to settle American blacks near Sierra Leone on the west coast of Africa was endorsed by many prominent Americans, including Thomas Jefferson, James Monroe, and Henry Clay. Their interest culminated in the founding (1817) of the American Colonization Society. Colonization, it was thought, would encourage slaveholders to free their slaves.

In 1820 the Society sent out 88 free blacks along with several white associates. They organized a base on the African coast and in 1822 settled what became Monrovia. Nevertheless, colonization advanced slowly. American abolitionists, notably James G. Birney, concluded that the Society was more interested in ridding the United States of free blacks than in furthering emancipation. Some American blacks were sufficiently disheartened to urge a black exodus to Africa. In 1847 the settlers disassociated themselves from the American

Colonization Society. They set up a republic modeled on the United States and adopted the name of Liberia, with Joseph J. Roberts as president.

An outstanding colonist and liaison agent between American blacks and Liberians was Edward Wilmot Blyden, a West Indian. He first visited the United States in 1850 and the same year emigrated to Liberia, where he wrote, preached, and taught to promote black nationalism. Over the years, Blyden visited the United States eight times while attempting to inspire colonization projects.

Although Liberia was largely a creation of the United States, America initially offered Liberia relatively little aid as the new country struggled with tribal and domestic problems and with commercial difficulties. Later economic relations were better, and the United States extended help in meeting health, education, and other challenges.

See also Abolitionism; Slavery.

Consult (IX) Buell, 1947; Staudenraus, 1961.

—Louis Filler, Antioch College

LIBERTY LEAGUE, organization of conservative opponents of the New Deal. Beginning in 1934 business people from many industries supported Democratic spokesmen from the pre-New Deal era in lavishly expensive attacks on Franklin Roosevelt's programs. The most prominent League speaker was Alfred E. Smith, presidential candidate in 1928. The League fought nearly every aspect of the New Deal, primarily on the grounds of unconstitutional violation of private property rights. A part of the "thunder on the right" before the 1936 election, the League probably had little effect on the course of the New Deal.

Consult (VI) Schlesinger, 1960.

LIBERTY LOANS, five U.S. bond issues, the last called the Victory Loan, sold to help pay for World War I. As in most U.S. wars, the government did not finance the conflict through taxation, the most efficient and least inflationary method, but by use of government borrowing. Only about 30 percent of the war's cost was met by taxes.

Liberty Bonds were long-term loans sold with much publicity in great bond drives. In addition, the government also made frequent use of short-term borrowing through banks. This was a costly way to finance a major war, and taxation, by taking away consumer purchasing power, would have kept down prices. The four Liberty Loans yielded $17 billion, the final Victory Loan another $4.5 billion.

LIBERTY PARTY, political party organized in 1840 by abolitionists eager to establish their cause in politics. It was rejected by some abolitionists, who feared the new group would take away votes from antislavery Whigs. In 1840 the party received no more than 7,100 votes nationally for its presidential candidate, James G. Birney. Four years later, however, it created a sensation when Birney won enough votes in New York State to keep Henry Clay from winning the state and thus the presidency. The Liberty Party therefore had helped to elect a dedicated slaveholder, James K. Polk. By 1848 the Liberty Party had ceased to be a factor and was superseded by the Free-Soil Party.

See also Abolitionism; Birney, James G.; Free-Soil Party.

LIMA CONFERENCE (1938). See Latin American Conferences.

LINCOLN, ABRAHAM (1809–1865), 16th President of the United States (1861–1865), known as the "Great Emancipator." Born in Hardin, Ky., on Feb. 12, 1809, he grew up in Indiana and Illinois. He left home at 22 and spent six years working and reading law.

In 1834 he entered the Illinois legislature as a Clay Whig and served for eight years. In 1837 he cosponsored a resolution declaring that slavery was "founded on both injustice and bad policy." In 1846 he was elected to the House of Representatives, where he supported antislavery measures and denounced the Mexican War, which led to his defeat in 1848. He then resumed his law career in Springfield.

By 1858 Lincoln had emerged as one of the most prominent leaders of the new Republican Party and that year was nominated for Stephen A. Douglas' Senate seat. In a series of memorable debates these two thrashed out the issue of slavery expansion, with Lincoln arguing that the peculiar institution could and should be excluded from the territories. Although he lost the election, Lincoln won national recognition as an able spokesman for Republican principles and was made the party's presidential nominee in 1860.

Presidency. Upon Lincoln's election in November, states in the lower South seceded. Except for his adamant opposition to the extension of slavery, Lincoln was conciliatory toward the South and hoped that Southern moderates would rise up and defeat the radical secessionists. However, he could not surrender Fort Sumter, and when the South attacked it, the war began.

As a wartime president, Lincoln masterfully used his considerable powers of tact, persuasion, patience, and firmness to make all the disparate elements of the North work in harmony. Although cursed with inept generals early in the war, Lincoln showed a sound grasp of military strategy and eventually found men who could prosecute the war sensibly. On the slavery issue he proceeded cautiously and based the Emancipation Proclamation on the grounds of military necessity. On April 14,

Abraham Lincoln, 16th President of the United States (1861–1865), in 1859 photograph.

1865, in Washington, D.C., the crazed John Wilkes Booth assassinated the President, who died the next day.

See also Civil War: Causes; Emancipation Proclamation (1863); Gettysburg Address; Lincoln-Douglas Debates (1858).

Consult (IV) Randall, 1945-1955; Thomas, 1962.
—Michael Burlingame, *Connecticut College*

LINCOLN-DOUGLAS DEBATES (1858), series of seven confrontations between Democratic incumbent Stephen A. Douglas and Republican challenger Abraham Lincoln in the 1858 Illinois senatorial campaign. The occasion for the debates was itself significant because in an era when state legislatures, not voters, chose United States senators, the Republican nomination of Lincoln before the election was highly unusual. That is, the contestants were seeking votes for legislative candidates, not directly for themselves. The main issue was slavery and the most appropriate way to prevent its extension to territories. Early in 1858, Douglas, the champion of popular sovereignty (or territorial self-determination) on the issue, had joined the Republicans in the Senate against the Lecompton Constitution, by which Kansas would have been admitted as a slave state. Because his course effectively prevented slavery expansion, many Eastern Republicans urged his reelection.

To prevent free-soil defections to Douglas, Lincoln stressed slavery's immorality, castigated Douglas' amoral approach to the problem, and demanded congressional prohibition to put slavery on the road to "ultimate extinction." He also asked Douglas to reconcile his popular sovereignty doctrine with the Supreme Court's Dred Scott decision (1857) that congressional prohibition was unconstitutional.

In a reply at Freeport, Ill., Douglas repeated an earlier argument that a territory could bar slavery by not passing the codes necessary to protect it. By forcing this "Freeport Doctrine" from Douglas and thus turning the South against him, Lincoln supposedly helped elect himself president two years later. But it is more likely that Douglas' Lecompton stand had already permanently alienated the South. The debates, however, added to Lincoln's reputation outside Illinois and thereby facilitated his nomination in 1860. In the 1858 election the Republicans won more popular votes, but control of the legislature allowed the Democrats to reelect Douglas.

See also Douglas, Stephen A.; Dred Scott Decision (1857); Kansas-Nebraska Act (1854); Lincoln, Abraham; Popular Sovereignty.

Consult (IV) Fehrenbacker, 1962; Jaffa, 1959. Michael F. Holt, *Yale University*.

LINDBERGH, CHARLES A(UGUSTUS) (1902-), aviator who became a national symbol. He was born in Detroit, the son of Congressman Charles Lindbergh (1859-1924). He studied engineering at the University of Wisconsin but left to take up flying, and in 1926 he became one of the early airmail pilots.

On May 20-21, 1927, Lindbergh made the first nonstop New York to Paris flight. Immediately the lone pilot of the Ryan monoplane *Spirit of St. Louis* became the greatest hero of the decade. That his flight was one of the major events of the 1920s is a comment on the interests and values of the times. His clean-cut, boyish looks and modest deportment fit the national ideal. His use of technology confirmed national prejudices, and his stubborn independence in flying the Atlantic alone vindicated the faith of Americans in their nineteenth-century free enterprise ideals. The flyer was loaded with tributes and awards, including the Congressional Medal of Honor.

In 1929 Lindbergh married Anne Spencer Morrow. The couple made two extensive flights together, which she described in *North to the Orient* (1935) and *Listen: The Wind* (1938). The Lindberghs' first son was kidnapped and killed in 1932—a crime that shocked the world and led to one of the most sensational trials of the time, in which Bruno Hauptmann was convicted in 1935.

As World War II developed, Lindbergh became a leading spokesman for isolationism, opposing U.S. aid to Britain. He was accused of sympathy for Nazi Germany, but after the United States entered the war he served his country as a civilian technical expert. In 1954 he won the Pulitzer Prize for *The Spirit of St. Louis,* an account of his flight to Paris.

See also Aviation.

Charles Lindbergh stands by the *Spirit of St. Louis,* the plane he flew across the Atlantic.

LITERATURE. Literature in what has become the United States can be divided into six periods. The colonial period was succeeded by the Revolutionary and early national era. The Romanticism of the pre-Civil War period was followed by Realism after the war. The years before World War II form one natural period in the twentieth century, whereas the most recent is still unfinished.

Colonial America (1607-1765). Little of purely literary value survives from the colonial period. Michael Wigglesworth's once popular versification of *The Day of Doom* (1662) has become a literary curiosity, but the domestic verses of Anne Bradstreet and the religious musings of Edward Taylor have withstood the tests of time.

In prose, Roger Williams' *Bloody Tenet of Persecution* (1664) is remembered as a forceful plea for freedom of thought. Cotton Mather's *Magnalia Christi Americana* (1702) contains much of his increasingly impressive writings. Jonathan Edwards in *Freedom of the*

Poet Walt Whitman, author of *Leaves of Grass.*

Literature

LITERATURE — Item Guide

The article on LITERATURE surveys the broad spectrum of American letters.

Much of the early literature was written by clergymen such as COTTON MATHER and JONATHAN EDWARDS, but by the Revolution secular writings, such as BENJAMIN FRANKLIN's and THOMAS PAINE's were popular.

During the 1820s native authors such as WILLIAM CULLEN BRYANT, JAMES FENIMORE COOPER, and WASHINGTON IRVING began to publish. A period of ROMANTICISM followed, with poets JAMES RUSSELL LOWELL, HENRY WADSWORTH LONGFELLOW, and JOHN GREENLEAF WHITTIER becoming popular. Also writing before the Civil War were EMILY DICKINSON, RALPH WALDO EMERSON, NATHANIEL HAWTHORNE, HERMAN MELVILLE, EDGAR ALLAN POE, HENRY DAVID THOREAU, and WALT WHITMAN.

After the war, local colorists such as GEORGE WASHINGTON CABLE emerged, and REALISM developed. MARK TWAIN's work became immensely popular, and HENRY JAMES began to write in London. STEPHEN CRANE wrote just before the end of the century, when EDWIN ARLINGTON ROBINSON first published. NATURALISM, exemplified by THEODORE DREISER, was the next major literary movement.

America has produced many of the giants of twentieth-century literature. Among the poets have been T. S. ELIOT, ROBERT FROST, EZRA POUND, and WALLACE STEVENS. Novelists have included JAMES BALDWIN, WILLIAM FAULKNER, F. SCOTT FITZGERALD, ERNEST HEMINGWAY, SINCLAIR LEWIS, JOHN STEINBECK, THOMAS WOLFE, and RICHARD WRIGHT. EUGENE O'NEILL dominated drama.

"Little Eva reading the Bible to Uncle Tom in the arbor." Harriet Beecher Stowe's *Uncle Tom's Cabin* enjoyed world-wide popularity both as literature and as abolitionist propaganda.

Will (1754) formulated a view that influenced native thought for generations. Benjamin Franklin's posthumously published *Autobiography* (1867) has become an American classic.

Revolutionary and Early National Periods (1765-1830). During the Revolution much patriotic writing but little literature was produced. In verse, Francis Hopkinson's *Battle of the Kegs* (1778), John Trumbull's *M'Fingal* (1778-1783), and Philip Freneau's truculent lines—collected as *Poems Written during the American Revolution* (1786)—were popular favorites, as was Thomas Paine's *Common Sense* (1776) in prose. After the war, fervent epics, such as Timothy Dwight's *Conquest of Canaan* (1785) and Joel Barlow's *Vision of Columbus* (1787), appeared. William Hill Brown's *Power of Sympathy* (1789) is often called the first American novel, but better fiction was written by Charles Brockden Brown in *Wieland* (1798) and *Edgar Huntly* (1799).

Literature in the United States came of age in the 1820s. Washington Irving, already known for Knickerbocker's burlesque *History of New York* (1809), produced his *Sketch Book* (1820). The first of James Fenimore Cooper's "Leatherstocking Tales" appeared as *The Pioneers* (1823), followed two years later by *The Last of the Mohicans*. William Cullen Bryant emerged as a poet, and the early verses of Edgar Allan Poe began to appear.

Romanticism (1830-1865). During the 35 years preceding the Civil War, literature in the United States rose to its first great peak. Poe came to prominence with *The Raven* (1845) and his macabre *Tales* (1840, 1845), and Irving and Cooper continued to write voluminously. The poems of John Greenleaf Whittier and Henry Wadsworth Longfellow were popular favorites, followed closely by the lighter verse of Oliver Wendell Holmes and James Russell Lowell. The lectures of Ralph Waldo Emerson drew enraptured audiences, although his writings often seemed obscure.

Nathaniel Hawthorne was severely condemned in some quarters for *The Scarlet Letter* (1850), but it ushered in the "American Renaissance." *Moby Dick* (1851) by Herman Melville was also criticized as less readable than his earlier stories of South Sea adventure, but the story of the quest for the great white whale was later recognized as a prose masterwork. *Walden* (1854) by Henry David Thoreau was similarly misunderstood, and Walt Whitman's *Leaves of Grass* (1855) was thought by many to be versified barbarism. Later critics found important roots of the best in modern American literature in these four authors and in the observations of Emerson. Meanwhile, secluded in Amherst, Emily Dickinson wrote poems, most of which remained unpublished for many years.

Realism (1865-1900). Although many of the romantics wrote benignly on, almost to the

end of the century, new voices rose from new areas. Bret Harte revealed frontier California in *The Luck of the Roaring Camp* (1870), George Washington Cable pictured New Orleans in *Old Creole Days* (1879), and Joel Chandler Harris in Georgia gathered yarns of *Uncle Remus* (1880). These authors and many like them are remembered as local colorists. Closely allied to them were the colloquial humorists such as Charles Francis Brown, who wrote as "Artemus Ward," and George Washington Harris.

Combining traits of the local colorists and the colloquial humorists was Samuel Langhorne Clemens, who as "Mark Twain" was catapulted to instant popularity with *The Celebrated Jumping Frog of Calaveras County* (1867) and whose *Adventures of Tom Sawyer* (1876) and *Adventures of Huckleberry Finn* (1884) have made him the most widely read author of his time. His friend William Dean Howells in *The Rise of Silas Lapham* (1885) and *A Hazard of New Fortunes* (1899), together with his influential criticism, established a pattern of patient realism that was to have lasting effects. Their contemporary, Henry James, most of his adult life a resident abroad, from *The Portrait of a Lady* (1886) to *The Ambassadors* (1903) set standards for revelation of character that have not been surpassed.

Except for the later work of Whitman and the publication of Dickinson's *Poems* (1890), little verse of consequence appeared. *The Children of the Night* (1898) introduced the fresh voice of Edwin Arlington Robinson, but Stephen Crane's verse in *The Black Riders* (1895) is less often remembered than the imagistic prose of *Maggie: A Girl of the Streets* (1893) and *The Red Badge of Courage* (1895). Other fiction that receives continuing attention includes Sarah Orne Jewett's *Country of the Pointed Firs* (1896) and Frank Norris' naturalistic *McTeague* (1899).

Early Twentieth Century (1900-1946). Naturalism, dominated by the certainty that people were victims of environment, became an important element in American writing. Theodore Dreiser was its champion in novels from *Sister Carrie* (1900) to *An American Tragedy* (1925). Chief among his numerous disciples was James T. Farrell in *Studs Lonigan* (1932). However, other influences were at work. From *The House of Mirth* (1905) to *The Age of Innocence* (1925), Edith Wharton wrote as a social realist. Willa Cather in *My Antonia* (1918) added sympathetic knowledge of the Western frontier to Jamesian character insights.

In poetry, Robinson developed with *The Man against the Sky* (1916), and Robert Frost appeared with *A Boy's Will* (1913). Carl Sandburg's *Chicago Poems* (1916) introduced new perspectives, and Vachel Lindsay's *Congo* (1914) and Edgar Lee Master's *Spoon River Anthology* (1915) were harbingers of a rebirth of effective verse. T. S. Eliot's *Waste Land* (1922), together with Ezra Pound's *Cantos* (1925), had a tremendous influence on subsequent poetry in subject and techniques. Wallace Stevens, William Carlos Williams, and e. e. cummings, however, each spoke with a voice of his own.

The 1920s saw a second American Renaissance, ushered in by Eliot in poetry and in prose by Sherwood Anderson (*Winesburg, Ohio,* 1919), Sinclair Lewis, and Gertrude Stein. The disillusion of post-World War I writers, named by Stein the "Lost Generation," found expression in F. Scott Fitzgerald's *The Great Gatsby* (1925), Ernest Hemingway's *A Farewell to Arms* (1926), and John Dos Passos' trilogy, *U.S.A.* (1939). Influenced also by Anderson, William Faulkner developed a deeply probing style that enriched stories of aspiration and defeat such as *The Sound and the Fury* (1929), until he seemed to deserve a place beside Hawthorne, Melville, and James as one of America's major novelists.

The 1920s also saw the beginning of a resurgence in drama in the work of such playwrights as Eugene O'Neill and Maxwell Anderson. As the decade drew to a close, Thomas Wolfe in *Look Homeward Angel* (1929) introduced a new, expansively lyric prose style to fiction. But in the next decade, social criticism was in the ascendancy in the writings of Farrell, Dos Passos, Erskine Caldwell's *Tobacco Road* (1932), John Steinbeck's *The Grapes of Wrath* (1939), and Richard Wright's *Native Son* (1940). The Fugitive group in Tennessee, which included poets John Crowe Ransom and Allen Tate and novelist Robert Penn Warren, reacted against sociological literary orientation.

Post-World War II. More talented writers have appeared since World War II than in any other period, but few promise greatness comparable to that of some of their predecessors. In poetry, Robert Lowell and Theodore Roethke seem to overshadow the rest. In prose, Ralph Ellison's *Invisible Man* (1950) remains widely read, as does the fiction of Saul Bellow, Bernard Malamud, Philip Roth, William Styron, and John Updike. The large talents of James Baldwin and Norman Mailer seem in the 1970s to be in eclipse.

Consult (VIII) Foerster, 1962; Spiller *et al.,* 1948; Taylor, 1956.

—Lewis Leary, *University of North Carolina at Chapel Hill*

LIVINGSTON, ROBERT R. (1746–1816), early American political leader. A member of one of New York's most distinguished families, he graduated in 1765 from King's College (later Columbia) and gained admission to the bar in 1770. In 1775 Livingston won election to the Continental Congress. He was a member of the committee that drafted the Declaration of Independence but thought that the decision to separate from England was premature. Lacking instructions from his home state, he could neither vote for nor sign the Declaration. Livingston became a member of the committee that drafted the New York constitution in 1779. An indefatigable worker on committees, Livingston was appointed the nation's first secretary of foreign affairs in January 1781. He resigned from this post in June 1783 and returned to the Congress in 1784.

Livingston was a firm supporter of the proposed U.S. Constitution and in 1788 served as chairman of the New York ratifying convention. As chancellor of New York, a post which he held from 1777 until 1801, Livingston administered the presidential oath of office to George Washington in 1789. After a dispute over patronage, Livingston broke with the Federalists in 1791, became a Republican, and opposed Hamilton's financial policies and Jay's Treaty of 1794. His influence helped Aaron Burr defeat Philip Schuyler for the Senate, but Livingston himself was unable to win the governorship against Jay in 1795. In 1801 President Thomas Jefferson appointed Livingston minister to France, and he skillfully negotiated the Louisiana Purchase.

Livingston resigned as minister in 1804 and returned to New York. Assisting Robert Fulton, Livingston helped produce the first practical steamboat, the *Clermont,* by 1807. Livingston was also a patron of the arts and a founder of the American Academy of Fine Arts.

Consult (III) Dangerfield, 1952.

—Thomas Archdeacon, *University of Wisconsin*

LIVINGSTON, WILLIAM (1723–1790), first governor of New Jersey. A descendant of colonial proprietor Robert Livingston, he graduated from Yale College in 1741 and practiced law.

Livingston later moved from New York to New Jersey, where he was subsequently chosen to represent the state in the Continental Congress (1774–1776) and was elected the first governor of New Jersey (1776–1790) by the state legislature.

As governor, Livingston was confronted with the problems of the Revolutionary War (much of which was fought in New Jersey) and reconstruction. After the war he advocated moderation in dealing with the loyalists, opposed the cheapening of the currency, and recommended the abolition of slavery. Livingston was a delegate to the Constitutional Convention (1787), and he led the New Jersey state convention in the Constitution's ratification. Throughout his life Livingston wrote satirical verse and prose; his writings include *Philosophic Solitude* (1741) and *A Funeral Eulogium on the Reverend Aaron Burr* (1757).

LOBBY, a term used to describe an organiza-

Novelist Ernest Hemingway working on *For Whom the Bell Tolls.*

Robert Livingston helped negotiate the Louisiana Purchase.

Senator Henry Cabot Lodge *(left)* with President Taft in 1909.

Huey Long speaks to Democratic National Convention in 1932.

tion, special interest group (also known as pressure group), or individual that attempts to influence the passage of legislation and administrative decisions of government. The derivation of the term may be traced back more than a century to the habit of certain private citizens who regularly congregated in the lobby outside legislative chambers before a session.

The standard techniques employed by lobbyists are: (1) meeting privately with public officials to publicize the clients' interests, (2) monetary persuasion by contributions to campaign funds, (3) testifying before congressional committees, and (4) working to rally public opinion by organizing telegram and letter-writing campaigns and, in some cases, considerable advertising and public relations efforts.

History. Lobbying reached its peak in the late nineteenth century, when railroad and industrial interests openly bribed state legislators for the passage of beneficial legislation. Federal policy was in turn affected because at that time senators were not directly elected but were picked for office by state legislators.

The increased complexity and specialization of twentieth-century society has seen an upsurge of special interest groups and the creation of agencies and associations to present and promote their partisan views to the public and the government. Lobbyists may be full-time officials of companies, individuals representing paying clients, or private citizens with a special grievance or goal to press.

The Regulation of Lobbying Act (1946) requires all lobbyists to register annually with both House and Senate. They must also file quarterly reports listing their remuneration, clients' names, specific legislative interest, and expenditures. More than half the states require lobbyists to file financial reports open to the public. However, regulation of lobbying in an attempt to guard against corruption raises constitutional issues because the rights of free speech and petition are intimately involved. Curbing excesses is made all the more difficult by the prevalent, almost uncontrollable practice of indirect lobbying aimed at public opinion.

LOCHNER v. NEW YORK (1905), Supreme Court decision on contracts. *See* Holmes, Oliver Wendell, Jr.; Muller v. Oregon (1908).

LODGE FAMILY, aristocratic New England family. The first to become influential in politics was the aloof Henry Cabot Lodge (1850-1924). He began his political career as a Republican in the Massachusetts legislature. In 1886 he was elected to Congress, serving in the House until 1893, when he became a senator, an office he held until his death. He served as a powerful chairman of the Senate Foreign Affairs Committee, the judgments of which were highly valued by Theodore Roosevelt,

and was Senate majority leader (1918-1924). Lodge, a fervent isolationist, led the opposition to the Versailles Treaty and the League of Nations.

None of his three children entered politics, but his grandson, Henry Cabot (1902-   ), a son of poet George Cabot (1873-1909), was elected to the Senate in 1939. At the outset of his career, he was a moderate on domestic issues and a determined isolationist. Gradually, his horizons widened, and he became President Eisenhower's UN ambassador (1953-1960). He emerged from this experience a polished professional diplomat famous for providing the communists with instant rebuttals. He was an unsuccessful vice-presidential candidate with Richard Nixon in 1960 and twice served as ambassador to South Vietnam. His brother, John Davis (1930-   ), also entered national politics as a House member (1947-1951), governor of Connecticut (1951-1955), and ambassador to Spain and Argentina.

Henry's son, George Cabot (1927-   ), served as an assistant secretary of labor in the Kennedy Administration and ran unsuccessfully against Edward Kennedy for the Senate.

LOG CABIN-HARD CIDER CAMPAIGN, popular name for presidential campaign of 1840. *See* Harrison, William Henry; Presidential Elections.

LOG COLLEGE, a small log schoolhouse located in Neshaminy, Pa. The college was started in 1726 by William Tennent, an Irish Presbyterian minister who built the schoolhouse and taught in it until 1742, helped by others, including his son Gilbert. Tennent's students were candidates for the Presbyterian ministry. The simple schoolhouse served to emphasize the need for an institution to properly educate students for the ministry. In 1746 the charter for the organization of the College of New Jersey was issued to meet this need.

See also Colonial Colleges.

LONDON ECONOMIC CONFERENCE (1933), swan song of the interwar capitalist system of international economic relations. It was convened in order to see if the major capitalist countries could cope with the deepening world depression. Industrial countries were devaluing their currencies and erecting high tariff walls in order to stimulate exports and create jobs at home, a trend that spelled chaos unless it was checked. The United States, Britain, France, and other participants tried to restore stability by establishing new rates of currency exchange and by returning to the gold standard. However, President Roosevelt was not interested in sacrificing domestic recovery to international monetary stability and refused to agree to the new formula for rates of exchange. This "torpedoing," as it was called by his critics, all but put an end to international cooperation until 1944, when a stable system was reestablished.

LONDON NAVAL CONFERENCE (1930), follow-up to the successful Washington Armament Conference of 1921–1922. At that conference the major naval powers had agreed to limit the size of large (capital) ships, but nothing had been done about "auxiliary craft"— light cruisers, destroyers, and submarines. An unsuccessful conference in Geneva (1927) was followed in 1930 with a more successful meeting.

The overall tonnage of the auxiliary craft of Japan was set at 69.75 percent of that of the British and United States navies, an advance over its ratio of 60 percent for capital ships. The three countries were basically satisfied with the new arrangements: their security interests did not seem compromised, and the naval limitation program would save them money. Unfortunately, the London Naval Treaty came under attack in Japan and ultimately led to the downfall of a government committed to understanding with the West.

Consult (VI) Ferrell, 1957.

LONG, HUEY (1893–1935), Louisiana politician and U.S. congressman who rose to national prominence on an appeal to the "small" people. A lawyer, his career as an elected official began at 25. As the Louisiana public services commissioner he attacked the corporations, made a name for himself as a reformer, and, under the banner "Every Man a King," was elected governor in 1928.

He promised much, but unlike the typical demagogue, he delivered—regulating corporations, providing free school books, and constructing roads, bridges, and hospitals, while building a formidable political machine, a unique totalitarian organization with himself as "Kingfish." Running roughshod over his opposition and the state constitution, he survived an impeachment attempt in 1929 and gained nearly absolute control over the state.

The Depression. Long moved onto the national political scene with his election to the Senate in 1930, but he stayed on as governor—actually holding both offices—to ensure passage of his legislative program and control over his successor. At first he and Franklin Roosevelt worked together: both were Democratic liberals and New Dealers. But Long's ambitions put him on a collision course with Roosevelt. Critical of the New Deal's conservative banking legislation and the National Recovery Administration, Long loudly proclaimed that FDR's policies were inadequate to the nation's ills and proposed an alternative "Share Our Wealth" platform of income redistribution.

Fearing Long's potential as a third-party

candidate who would split the New Deal vote, Roosevelt moved to the left himself during 1935. Long was assassinated in September 1935, bringing an end to one of the most spectacular careers in American political history

Consult (VI) Sindler, 1956; Williams, 1969.

—Allen Kifer, *Skidmore College*

LONGFELLOW, HENRY WADSWORTH (1807–1882), poet who made immortal such figures as Hiawatha, John Alden, and Paul Revere. He was born in Portland, Me. and began writing poetry when he was 13. After graduating from Bowdoin College in 1825, he spent three years in Europe and then began his writing career while teaching at Bowdoin (1829–1833). His partly autobiographical romance, *Hyperion,* appeared in 1839, the same year as his first volume of poetry, *Voices in the Night.*

With the publication of *Ballads and Other Poems* (1841), Longfellow's reputation was solidly established; *Ballads* contained the famous "Excelsior," "The Village Blacksmith," and "The Wreck of the Hesperus." In 1842 Longfellow's first and only venture into social literature produced *Poems on Slavery,* but his destiny lay with less topical themes. *The Spanish Student* (1843), a poetic drama, *The Belfry of Bruges* (1845), *Evangeline* (1847), *The Seaside and the Fireside* (1849), and *Hiawatha* (1855) combined to make him America's most popular poet. He resigned the professorship he held at Harvard (1836–1854) to devote all his time to writing. *The Courtship of Miles Standish* (1858) sold more than 15,000 copies on the first day of its publication. In 1861 Longfellow lost his second wife tragically, as he had his first; his later works showed more serious tones. Most significant was his translation of Dante's *Divine Comedy* (1865–1867).

In his own time, Longfellow's reputation as a poet was unequaled in America and in Europe. His most memorable achievement in poetry was the fusion of European culture and American folk tales and the fact that he reached new audiences on both sides of the Atlantic.

See also Literature.

—Richard Collin, *Louisiana State University, New Orleans*

LONG ISLAND, BATTLE OF (AUGUST 1776), British victory that forced George Washington to withdraw from Long Island. *See* Revolutionary War Battles.

LONGSTREET, JAMES (1821–1904), leading Confederate general. Born in South Carolina and raised in Georgia, Longstreet was educated at West Point. Joining the Confederacy, he made an admirable showing at the First Battle of Bull Run (July 1861) and led a division in the

Henry Wadsworth Longfellow, most popular poet of late nineteenth century.

Confederate Gen. James Longstreet, one of Lee's principal lieutenants.

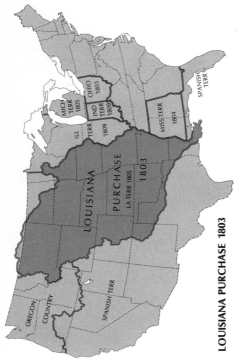

LOUISIANA PURCHASE 1803

Peninsular Campaign (March–July 1862). At the Second Battle of Bull Run (August 1862) he helped Stonewall Jackson rout the Union forces.

Longstreet did well in the Battles of Antietam (September 1862) and Fredericksburg (December 1862), but let Robert E. Lee down at Chancellorsville (May 1863) by failing to engage all his divisions. In Longstreet's last major campaign, Gettysburg (June–July 1863), he opposed Lee's plans and was slow and reluctant in carrying them out, thus significantly contributing to the Confederate defeat. After service in the Western theater, Longstreet closed out the war by helping Lee defend Richmond. After the war he became a prominent Republican and held various federal offices for the rest of his life.

See also Civil War Battles.
Consult (IV) Sanger and Hay, 1952.

LORD DUNMORE'S WAR, conflict in 1774 between the Shawnee Indians and pioneers trying to settle on their grounds. Sporadic fighting had broken out in 1773, when frontier whites attacked Shawnee hunting parties, but an uneasy peace prevailed. In 1774, when three surveying parties began marking land claims in Kentucky, the Shawnee of Ohio chose to fight, and Virginia Governor John Dunmore sent three militia armies west against them. In October 1774, troops under Col. Andrew Lewis defeated the warriors of Chief Cornstalk in a desperate battle at the Ohio and Kanawha rivers. Dunmore forced the defeated Shawnee to accept American occupation of Kentucky, thus opening that region for settlement.
Consult (II) Van Every, 1956.

LOST COLONY, settlement on Roanoke Island in 1585, which had disappeared by 1590. *See* Virginia.

LOUISIANA, the 18th state, joined the Union on April 30, 1812. Louisiana was first explored by Hernán de Soto in the sixteenth century, and in 1682 the area was claimed for France by Sieur de La Salle. Soon after, the first white settlements were made by fur traders and missionaries; New Orleans was founded in 1706. The eastern part of Louisiana was ceded to England in 1763; in 1803 the rest of it became part of the United States through the Louisiana Purchase. The Territory of Orleans was created in 1804 from land south of 33° north latitude; it joined the Union as the State of Louisiana.

Its state legislature is bicameral; the capital is Baton Rouge. Its population in 1970 was 3,643,180.
See also Louisiana Purchase.

LOUISIANA PURCHASE (1803), transaction by which the United States bought the region between the Mississippi River and the Rocky Mountains from France for about $15 million.

Adding more than 825,000 square miles of territory, the purchase nearly doubled the size of the nation. The area that now includes 13 of the 50 states had rich farm land, extensive forests, and vast mineral resources for Americans to exploit.

France had ceded the region beyond the Mississippi to Spain in 1762, and Spain held the area when the United States gained independence. Beset by internal and foreign difficulties, the new American government paid little attention unless the Spanish hindered American navigation on the Mississippi River. In the Treaty of San Lorenzo negotiated by Thomas Pinckney in 1795, the two nations seemed to have solved that issue, and as long as Spain held Louisiana, U.S. officials remained calm.

French Possession. The situation changed suddenly in 1801, however, when Napoleon pressured Spain to cede Louisiana back to France. When President Thomas Jefferson learned of this, he began immediate measures to buy some part of the region to ensure the continuing use of the Mississippi. He sent James Monroe to join Robert Livingston, the American minister to France, and with congressional approval instructed the two men to buy New Orleans and a part of the Gulf Coast as well.

By the time Monroe got to Paris, Napoleon had decided to abandon his territorial schemes in North America because of the continuing defeats of French soldiers in Santo Domingo. As a result, the French offered the American negotiators the entire Louisiana region for the equivalent of $15 million. Their decision to buy exceeded their instructions, but Jefferson welcomed their action and supported it when opponents in Congress objected.

Although the treaty of cession left some of the boundaries vague, it was approved in early 1803. When the United States took formal possession in December 1803, the men of the Lewis and Clark Expedition had already gone into their winter camp on the Illinois side of the Mississippi, and early the next spring they explored the vast region that the nation had acquired.

See also Lewis and Clark Expedition; Pinckney's Treaty (1795).
—Roger L. Nichols, *University of Arizona*

LOVEJOY, ELIJAH P., abolitionist newspaper editor. *See* Abolitionism.

LOWELL, JAMES RUSSELL (1819–1891), author, editor, professor, and diplomat who was the leader of the American literary establishment of his era. Born in Cambridge, Mass., Lowell's name is synonymous with New England's Brahmin culture. In 1844 he married Maria White, whose sympathies for the antislavery move-

Poet and editor James Russell Lowell also served as diplomat.

ment and for poetry were strong formative influences on young Lowell. Already known for *A Year's Life* (1841) and *Poems* (1844), Lowell launched his career as a literary critic with *Conversations with Some of the Old Poets* (1845). The high point of his writing career occurred in 1848, when he published four books: *Poems: Second Series; A Fable for Critics;* the satirical *Biglow Papers* (Vol. I); and *The Vision of Sir Launfal.*

After the unexpected death of his wife in 1853, Lowell succeeded Longfellow as Smith Professor of French at Harvard, a chair he held with several interruptions until 1886. He became editor first of the *Atlantic Monthly* (1857-1861) and then of *The North American Review* (1864-1872). His most significant poem, "Ode Recited at the Harvard Commencement, July 21, 1865," marked the end of his poetic creativity. In 1877 he turned to diplomacy as minister to Spain (1877-1880) and later to England (1880-1885).

See also Literature.
—Richard Collin, *Louisiana State University, New Orleans*

LOWE v. LAWLER (1908) (Danbury Hatters Case), a suit initiated by the Dietrich Lowe Co., a hat-making firm in Danbury, Conn., against the United Hatters Union. The company, which had resisted attempts of its employees to organize, charged that the boycott of its products initiated by the United Hatters was a violation of the Sherman Antitrust Act. The Supreme Court ruled that a secondary boycott by a labor union constituted a conspiracy in restraint of trade. The union was assessed more than $250,000 in damages, and the homes of 140 workers were eventually attached by the courts and sold to pay the fines.

LUCE, CLARE BOOTH (1903-   ), journalist, playwright, Republican congresswoman, and ambassador to Italy. Born in New York City, she worked in the 1930s as an editor on *Vogue* and *Vanity Fair* and as a newspaper columnist and playwright. Her five plays include *The Women* (1937) and *Kiss the Boys Goodbye* (1938), both satires about women.

In 1935 she married Henry R. Luce, editor, publisher, and founder of *Time, Life,* and *Fortune.* She was elected to Congress in 1942 from Connecticut and served until 1947. Appointed ambassador to Italy by President Eisenhower, she held the post from 1953 to 1956. With her husband she was an ardent supporter of Nationalist China.

LUMBER FRONTIER. *See* Frontier in American History.

LUNDY, BENJAMIN (1789-1839), abolitionist newspaper editor. *See* Abolitionism.

LUNDY'S LANE, BATTLE OF (1814), bloody battle on the New York-Canadian frontier. *See* War of 1812.

LUSITANIA, SINKING OF, ship torpedoing that inflamed U.S. opinion against Germany in World War I. The *Lusitania,* a passenger liner, was torpedoed without warning in the Atlantic by the German submarine U-20 on May 7, 1915. German warships had been patrolling in the Atlantic since the beginning of the war. Almost 1,100 passengers were killed, 128 of whom were Americans. U.S. reactions were very angry, but Germany never disavowed the act, and the United States did not enter the war for another two years. Later evidence (the U-20's logbook) seemed to show that the submarine torpedoed the liner for fear of being rammed.

See also World War I: Causes.

LUTHERANS. *See* Colonial Religion.

LUTHER v. BORDEN (1849), Supreme Court decision on jurisdiction. *See* Dorr Rebellion (1842).

LYNCHING. In American history two types of lynching were common. In frontier areas, with few courts and jails, vigilantes frequently took the law into their own hands and punished (often by death) those accused of crimes. In the South, especially after the Civil War, mobs lynched blacks in the name of white supremacy.

Although the practice dates from the eighteenth century, no statistics were kept before 1882. Since then about 5,000 people, four-fifths of them black, have been lynched. Ninety percent of lynchings were in the South with the remainder in bordering states, and most took place in poor rural areas. Frequently victims suffered torture and mutilation before being hanged, shot, or burned. Members of lynch mobs were almost never punished.

The alleged crimes committed by lynching victims were homicide (38%), rape (23%), theft (7%), felonious assault (6%), and "insults" to whites (2%). About one-quarter were for "miscellaneous offenses" such as a black's bringing suit (or testifying) against a white in court or a black's using "offensive" language, boasting, or refusing to pay a debt. Since 1940 lynching has disappeared.

MacARTHUR, DOUGLAS (1880-1964), war hero and controversial military leader. The son of a general who became military governor of the Philippines, MacArthur graduated first in his class from West Point in 1903. He became a brigadier general in 1918 and was named Army chief of staff in 1930. MacArthur's record was tarnished in 1932, when President Hoover had him drive out of the capital the Bonus Army of

Clare Booth Luce *(right)* on dais with Eleanor Roosevelt at awards dinner.

Douglas MacArthur, a five-star general in 1945, was relieved of command during the Korean War.

"We have evidence that this man is planning a trip to Moscow." Joseph McCarthy's accusations of Communist influence in government sometimes produced ridicule.

President Lincoln confers on the Antietam battlefield with General McClellan, who was soon removed from command.

unemployed veterans demanding payment of federal war bonuses. In 1935 he was appointed military adviser to the Philippine Commonwealth, and two years later he retired from the U.S. Army to become field marshal of the Philippine Army.

MacArthur was recalled to active duty in July 1941 to command U.S. army forces in the Southwest Pacific. When the Japanese overran the Philippines in March 1942, he left to participate in the defense of Australia. In April he was appointed commander of the Allied forces in the Southwest Pacific. He succeeded in halting the Japanese advance and devised an island-hopping strategy for bottling up enemy troops as the Allies counterattacked. MacArthur returned to the Philippines with the American Army in October 1944. As a five-star general he received the Japanese surrender on Sept. 2, 1945, and commanded the occupation forces.

In 1950 he was named commander of the UN troops fighting in Korea. MacArthur recommended enlarging the war by bombing Chinese supply centers in Manchuria and "unleashing" the Chinese Nationalists against the mainland, an open disagreement on presidential policy that led President Truman to relieve him of command in April 1951.

See also World War II; Korean War.
Consult (VII) James, 1970; MacArthur, 1964.

—Martin Gruberg, *University of Wisconsin, Oshkosh*

McCARRAN ACT. *See* Internal Security Act.

McCARRAN-WALTER IMMIGRATION ACT (1952), also known as the Immigration and Nationality Act. It essentially reaffirmed the national-origins quota system of 1924, under which quotas for admission were set in proportion to the number of former nationals of each country living in the United States at a given time. Under the act the annual quota for any quota area was "one-sixth of one percent of the population of the continental United States in 1920." People born in the Western Hemisphere and spouses and children of U.S. citizens were exempt from the quota, and certain racial restrictions were eliminated. But new categories of ineligibles were added, with emphasis on political reliability. It was passed over the veto of President Truman, who said that the bad parts far outweighed the acceptable ones.

See also Immigration; Immigration and Nationality Act (1965); Quota System.

McCARTHY, JOSEPH R(AYMOND) (1909–1957), American Senator who was renowned for his accusations against alleged Communist influence in the United States. Born in Grand

Chute, Wis., he worked his way through law school, was elected a circuit judge before and after serving in World War II, and was elected to the Senate in 1946 as a Republican.

In February 1950 he vaulted into national prominence with a speech in Wheeling, W. Va., in which he stated that he had a list of "card-carrying Communists" in the State Department. These charges remained unproved, and undocumented claims of "proof" became a trademark of later charges. McCarthy questioned the motives of those who doubted him and continued to accuse public figures of Communist associations and the Democratic Party of "twenty years of treason."

He was reelected to the Senate in 1952; in 1953, after his appointment as chairman of the Permanent Subcommittee on Investigations, he began probing Communism in the Army. The Army-McCarthy hearings, televised in 1954, gave him further national exposure, but his charges were not supported. His abrasive guilt-by-association tactics, which led to the coining of the word "McCarthyism," brought a Senate investigation that ended with his condemnation on Dec. 2, 1954. His political influence subsequently declined. He died in Bethesda, Md. Defended by some as a zealous patriot, McCarthy was criticized by most as demagogic and undemocratic.

Consult (VIII) Rovere, 1959.

McCLELLAN, GEORGE B(RINTON) (1826–1885), one of the principal Union generals in the Civil War and presidential candidate. He graduated from West Point in 1842 and served in the army until 1857. When the Civil War broke out he rejoined the service as a major general.

He cleared Confederate troops from western Virginia (June–July 1861) and soon thereafter became general in chief of the Union army. With great energy and skill he molded the demoralized troops into an excellent fighting force and sailed it to the Virginia peninsula to attack Richmond. This campaign, tardily launched in March 1862, brought McClellan to the outskirts of the Confederate capital, but Robert E. Lee then vanquished him, and by early July the Union commander abandoned his plan.

Deeply disappointed, Lincoln removed McClellan, but after the Union defeat at the Second Battle of Bull Run (August 1862) the President reinstated McClellan as Lee drove into Maryland. In the Antietam campaign (September 1862), McClellan fumbled opportunities to divide and conquer the Army of Northern Virginia but managed to fight Lee to a draw. Although Lincoln entreated him to pursue the retreating enemy, McClellan dallied so long that the President removed him once again

(November 1862), and McClellan never again held a field command.

A man of conservative political views, he was nominated for president by the Democrats in 1864, but Lincoln beat him by a wide margin. After the war he pursued an engineering career and served as governor of New Jersey (1878–1881). A gifted organizer and strategist, McClellan did poorly as a field commander because he lacked a fighter's instinct.

See also Civil War Battles.

Consult (IV) Hassler, 1957.

—Michael Burlingame, *Connecticut College*

McCORMICK REAPER, harvesting machine that helped to revolutionize agriculture in the United States. The reaper was invented in 1831 by Cyrus Hall McCormick (1809–1884), who patented it in 1834 and made many later improvements. McCormick was a Virginian, but in 1847 he established his factory in Chicago, the transportation center for farms of the Midwest. Salesmen were sent out to convert the farmers, and by 1851 his reaper was known in England (it won the grand prize at the London Exhibition of 1857) as well as throughout the United States.

McCormick sold 5,000 reapers within five years, the demand being stimulated by the Crimean War in Europe (1853–1856), which increased the need for grain. Later, the Civil War, the extension of railroads to the Midwest and West, and economic growth brought even greater calls for reaping machines. From this machine was eventually developed the combine harvester, which did all the operations at once: cutting, threshing, cleaning, and bagging grain. These combines were first used extensively on the broad, flat fields of California in the 1880s.

The McCormick reaper made possible the vast increase in grain output by American farmers in the nineteenth century despite the shortage of labor and the relative shrinking of the farm labor force. In addition, McCormick helped to develop assembly-line production and innovative marketing programs.

Consult (III) Gates, 1968.

McCULLOCH v. MARYLAND (1819), a key Supreme Court decision asserting the supremacy of the federal government over the state governments. The state of Maryland had placed a tax on the bank notes of all banks not chartered by the state. This was a direct attack on the Second Bank of the United States, which had a branch in Baltimore. The Baltimore branch refused to pay the tax, and Maryland sued the cashier, McCulloch.

Chief Justice John Marshall's decision dealt with two main points. He argued first that the United States had the power to charter a bank, even though this power was not expressly given in the Constitution and that the "necessary and proper" clause of the Constitution should not be construed narrowly. Marshall next considered whether it was constitutional for the state of Maryland to tax the Baltimore branch by pointing out that it was obvious that the power to tax was in this case the power to destroy. If the states could tax the bank, they could also tax the mail, the mint, and other functions of the federal government. Thus, the question was not simply one of taxation, it was also a question of supremacy. Marshall decided that the law taxing the Bank of the United States was unconstitutional.

McGOVERN, GEORGE S(TANLEY) (1922–), U.S. Senator (South Dakota) and Democratic presidential candidate. He began his career in state politics in the early 1950s while a professor of history and political science. He was elected to the House of Representatives in 1956 and 1958 and, after heading the Kennedy Administration's Food for Peace Program, won a Senate seat in 1962 and was reelected in 1968.

As early as 1963 McGovern announced his opposition to the Vietnam War. Although he voted for the 1964 Gulf of Tonkin Resolution, he emerged as one of the principal challengers to U.S. action in Vietnam and cosponsored the Vietnam Disengagement Amendment (Hatfield-McGovern) to set a deadline for U.S. troop withdrawal from Vietnam. After 1968 the Democratic Party turned to him to devise convention reforms for 1972.

In January 1971 McGovern made the earliest announcement of any presidential candidate in modern history. His presidential prospects were remote at the time, but he came to the Democratic Convention with the best organized presidential campaign and was easily nominated. He tried to broaden his support base beyond the antiwar movement by developing positions on other issues such as welfare reform. However, the alienation of many old-line Democrats and the shadow of Thomas Eagleton's withdrawal as his running mate cost McGovern any real chance of victory, and he lost to Richard Nixon in a landslide.

See also Democratic Party; Presidential Elections.

Consult (VIII) Anson, 1972.

—Martin Gruberg, *University of Wisconsin, Oshkosh*

McKINLEY, WILLIAM (1843–1901), 25th President of the United States (1897–1901). He was born in Niles, Ohio, on Jan. 29, 1843. Enlisting in the Union army as a private at 17, he rose through the ranks to brevet major. He was the last Civil War veteran to become president.

Elected to Congress as a Republican in 1876, he took the tariff as his specialty and rode

George McGovern, Democratic presidential candidate in 1972.

William McKinley, 25th President of the United States (1897–1901), campaigned from his front porch in 1896.

it to national prominence. Chairman of the House Ways and Means Committee in 1889–1891, he was largely responsible for drafting the tariff bill of 1890, the McKinley Tariff, which raised duties to the highest levels up to that time. Defeated for reelection in 1890, he was elected governor of Ohio in 1891 with the aid of Mark A. Hanna, an eminent businessman who backed McKinley's tariff views.

McKinley secured his party's presidential nomination in 1896, again with the aid of Hanna. McKinley had hoped to base his campaign on the tariff, but the rise of the silver crusade and the nomination of William Jennings Bryan by the Democrats and Populists dictated that silver would play a major role in the campaign. McKinley's previous position on silver was at best unclear, but he embraced the gold standard in 1896, defeated Bryan, and became the first presidential candidate in 26 years to win a majority of the popular vote.

Presidency. McKinley's Administration has been described as "orthodox in its Republicanism, with little distinction." True to his campaign commitments, he backed the passage of a higher protective tariff (1897) and an act officially putting the United States on the gold standard (1900). The most significant event of his Administration was the Spanish-American War. Personally opposed to war over Cuba, McKinley yielded to jingoists within his party and referred the matter to Congress, which in 1898 directed him to intervene to establish Cuban independence. McKinley's decision that the United States should take the Philippines, Puerto Rico, and other Spanish possessions gave the United States a colonial empire and guaranteed that the nation would henceforth be a major world power.

Reelected in 1900, McKinley was assassinated by an anarchist, Leon Czolgosz, in 1901. The President was shot in Buffalo, N.Y., on September 6 and died on September 14. He was succeeded by Theodore Roosevelt.

See also Bryan, William Jennings; Free Silver; Populists; Presidential Elections; Spanish-American War (1898).

Consult (V) Glad, 1964; Morgan, 1963.
—Robert W. Cherny, *California State University, San Francisco*

McKINLEY TARIFF, OR TARIFF OF 1890, a victory for protectionism, raised duties to almost 50 percent. *See* Tariffs.

McNAMARA, ROBERT S(TRANGE) (1916–), Secretary of Defense and World Bank president. He was a brilliant student and after service in World War II was part of a team of military "whiz kids" that went to work for the Ford Motor Company. McNamara rose to become president of Ford, the first person outside the Ford family to hold the position.

McNamara served only a month as president before becoming newly elected President Kennedy's secretary of defense. McNamara spent seven years in the Pentagon in a tug of war with the professional military and their congressional allies. He applied systems analysis techniques to decision making and consolidated and centralized the department's structures and processes. He shifted the defense emphasis from the threat of massive nuclear retaliation to a variety of strategies and weapons.

He was assailed for closing down bases and facilities that he considered uneconomical and for not spending appropriated money for weapons systems he opposed. The greatest storm came over his role in the expanding Vietnam War. McNamara resigned as defense secretary in late 1967 to accept the presidency of the World Bank (International Bank for Reconstruction and Development).

See also Vietnam War.
Consult (VIII) Trewhitt, 1971.

McNARY-HAUGEN BILL, the name given to several very similar bills debated in Congress in the 1920s. In general the measures were designed to increase the prices paid to American farmers for major cash crops that were oversupplied during the post-World War I period, such as wheat and cotton. The hope was to restore to the farmer his fair share of the national income. The proposals involved government purchase of commodities, which were then to be sold at cut-rate prices overseas.

A McNary-Haugen Bill twice passed Congress, in 1927 and 1928, only to be vetoed by President Coolidge. The passage symbolized the split between the business-oriented executive and Congress, in which rural legislators held a balance of power. Later attempts to help agriculture benefited from the McNary-Haugen debates, but in the 1930s not only subsidy but also crop restriction was included—something not included in the McNary-Haugen bills.

MACON'S BILL NO. 2, statute named after Representative Nathaniel Macon that was passed by Congress on May 1, 1810. It reopened trade with Britain and France, which had been embargoed by the Nonintercourse Act (1809) in an attempt to stop European interference with American commerce. The bill stipulated that if either Britain or France removed its trade restrictions before March 3, 1811, and the other country did not follow suit within three months, nonintercourse would be renewed against the latter nation.

In the summer of 1810, Napoleon announced falsely the end of restriction on American trade and by a trick brought about the renewal of nonintercourse against Britain,

Robert S. McNamara, Secretary of Defense during the escalation of the Vietnam War.

which did not remove its restrictions. These international trade problems were not resolved until the end of the War of 1812.

See also Embargo Acts (1807–1809); Nonimportation Act (1806).

MADISON, JAMES (1751–1836), 4th President of the United States (1809–1817). He was born in Port Conway, Va., on March 16, 1751, and graduated from the College of New Jersey (Princeton) in 1771. At the beginning of the Revolution he served in the Virginia Convention that drafted a new constitution for the state and issued a Declaration of Rights, and he later served both in the Virginia legislature and in the Continental Congress.

Madison played a particularly important part in the Constitutional Convention in Philadelphia in 1787. He attended as a delegate from Virginia and used his influence to argue in favor of a strong central government. Madison was also one of the most important figures in the fight for the adoption of the new Constitution. Along with Alexander Hamilton and John Jay he wrote a series of newspaper articles in support of the Constitution that were gathered together to form The Federalist Papers.

In the early 1790s Madison became one of the leading figures in the formation of the Democratic-Republican (Jeffersonian) Party in opposition to the Federalist Party of Washington and Hamilton. He temporarily retired from politics in 1797 but in 1799 again attacked Federalist policies when he wrote the Virginia Resolutions in opposition to the Alien and Sedition Acts of the Adams Administration. From 1801 to 1809 Madison served in Jefferson's Administrations as secretary of state. In the second Administration Madison played the key role in developing and writing the U.S. arguments against British maritime claims and policies.

Presidency. Madison became president in 1809, a time of deep crisis for the United States. His Administrations were dominated by the controversies with Britain and the War of 1812, called "Mr. Madison's War" by opponents. After first continuing Jeffersonian policies of economic coercion, Madison gradually reached the conclusion that war with England was necessary, and war was declared on June 18, 1812. Madison was not a dynamic war leader, and the country was ill prepared for the war it had entered. The low point of the conflict was reached in August 1814, when Madison had to flee from Washington before the advancing British forces.

In the two years after the war Madison helped to lead the burst of nationalistic feeling by supporting policies such as the Second Bank of the United States and a higher tariff, which would have been viewed as Federalist measures 20 years before. After his retirement from the presidency in 1817, he entered private life in Virginia, briefly emerging in 1829 to join in the Virginia Constitutional Convention. Madison died in Montpelier, Va., on June 28, 1836.

See also Constitutional Convention (1787); Federalist, The; Virginia and Kentucky Resolutions (1798); War of 1812.

Consult (III) Ketcham, 1971; Koch, 1950.
—Reginald Horsman, University of Wisconsin, Milwaukee

MAGNA CHARTA, or Great Charter, an English document that granted rights and privileges to some citizens. In the United States it influenced the first 10 amendments to the Constitution, the Bill of Rights.

The Magna Charta originally granted freedoms to barons and the church. It did, however, extend several rights to the common man. Pressured by his rebellious barons, King John issued the charter in 1215. It has, by liberal interpretations through the centuries, come to be thought of as the basis for constitutional government and as an impartial judicial system in English-speaking countries.

At the time that the settlement of the New World began, English common law provided that freeholders were guaranteed the protection of life, liberty, and property from arbitrary action. It was natural then that these guarantees would be incorporated into the laws of the U.S. Constitution. One of the most important of these rights was trial by jury. Additional liberties derived from English common law included prohibition of excessive fines and bails and the right of defendants against self-incrimination in criminal trials.

See also Bill of Rights; Constitution of the United States.

MAHAN, ALFRED T(HAYER) (1840–1914), U.S. Navy officer and historian. At the end of the nineteenth century, a number of scholars, publicists, and authors were introducing new principles of strategic thought to public debate. In the United States Mahan, a naval officer (since 1859) who had turned historian, had published the single most influential book on naval theory in modern time, The Influence of Sea Power upon History, 1660–1783. When his work appeared in 1890, Mahan had for some time been president of the Newport War College, and his position, combined with the cogent arguments he presented in two successive books, made him the master of the "large navy" school of thought. He argued for more naval bases (and thus the annexation of colonial territories), a larger navy, and an improved merchant marine, and his was the voice most often quoted in defense of America's participation in the developing naval arms race. Mahan died in December 1914 having lived to see the war he feared and predicted would engulf

James Madison, 4th President of the United States (1809–1813).

Europe. Ironically, while read and cited in America, Mahan was best known to naval officers in Germany and Japan, who used his historical volumes as their major justifications for their growing navies.

Consult (V) Puleston, 1939.

MAINE, the 23rd state, admitted to the Union on March 15, 1820. Settled by George Popham in 1607, Maine was purchased in 1677 by the Massachusetts Bay Colony and remained part of Massachusetts until the Revolutionary War. As part of the Missouri Compromise of 1820, Maine was brought into the Union as a free state to balance the entry of Missouri as a slave state.

The state legislature is bicameral; the capital is Augusta. The population in 1970 was 993,663.

See also Missouri Compromise (1820).

MAINE, SINKING OF, explosion of the battleship *Maine* in Havana harbor on Feb. 15, 1898, which triggered the Spanish-American War. "Remember the *Maine*" became a rallying cry for the war. *See* Spanish-American War (1898).

MAKEMIE, FRANCIS, colonial religious leader. *See* Presbyterians.

MALCOLM X (1925-1965), a leader of the black consciousness movement. He was born Malcolm Little in Omaha, Neb., and later lived in Michigan, Massachusetts, and New York. While serving a prison term to which he was sentenced in 1946, he joined the Black Muslims and took the name Malcolm X. After he was paroled from prison, Malcolm X had great success in expanding the Black Muslim movement, establishing a number of temples and lecturing to many audiences.

However, conflicts developed between Malcolm X and Elijah Muhammad, leader of the Black Muslims. In 1964, Malcolm X broke away to form his own black nationalist movement, the Organization of Afro-American Unity. In the same year he made a pilgrimage to Mecca. He was assassinated by black gunmen as he was about to make a speech to followers in the Audubon Ballroom in New York City on Feb. 21, 1965.

His autobiography has been described as an eloquent statement of the problems and desires of black people struggling for equality and dignity.

See also Black Muslims.

MALE CHAUVINISM, male behavior, according to women liberationists, that has led to women's oppression. *See* Women's Liberation.

MANHATTAN PROJECT, the supersecret effort to produce a transportable atomic bomb. Headed by Brig. Gen. Leslie R. Groves, the project got its name from the Manhattan District Engineers, who were designated as the bomb's builders at the end of summer 1942. Thousands of people were employed under the Manhattan Project, which developed the bomb for $2 billion.

The scientists did not know which of three methods was the best for separating U-235 to produce fissionable material, and all three methods had to be tried. A self-sustaining nuclear chain reaction was first produced by Enrico Fermi and his associates in December 1942. Plutonium was manufactured at Hanford, Wash., U-235 at Oak Ridge, Tenn., and the design and construction of a transportable bomb were carried out at Los Alamos, N.M., under the direction of J. Robert Oppenheimer. The first bomb was exploded near Alamogordo, N.M., on July 16, 1945. The huge blast was explained in the press as an exploding ammunition magazine at the Alamogordo Air Base. The order to use the A-bomb was issued by President Harry S Truman on July 25, and the first bomb was dropped on August 6.

See also Atom Bomb; Oppenheimer, J. Robert.

MANIFEST DESTINY, argument used by the United States in the nineteenth century to justify imperialism and its expansion across North America. To believers in Manifest Destiny, U.S. expansion westward and southward across the North American continent was inevitable, destined by Providence, and just. Those who stood in the way—Indians, Mexicans, Canadians, and the remnants of French and Spanish empires—did not view U.S. expansion in the same terms. The phrase "manifest destiny" appeared first in July 1845, when it was used by a Democratic editor, John L. O'Sullivan, who warned against foreign powers who wished to prevent the U.S. annexation of Texas. It was, he said, "the fulfillment of our manifest destiny to overspread the continent allotted by Providence for the free development of our yearly multiplying millions."

This useful idea was picked up by the New York *Morning News* in December 1845 and applied to the Oregon boundary dispute with Britain. After its use in Congress in 1846 the phrase became popular among all spread-eagle nationalist orators and writers. Some of the more extreme nationalists wanted to annex Canada. Most expansionists were less ambitious. Southern Democrats saw the opportunity to expand slavery into the Southwest and Cuba. But even antislavery Whigs and later Republicans supported the Manifest Destiny argument.

The major exponent of Manifest Destiny was President James K. Polk (1845-1849), whose Polk Doctrine extended the Monroe Doctrine. After the Civil War, Secretary of State William Seward bought Alaska (1867) and had

Malcolm X, Black Muslim leader, gestures during speech.

dreams of further territorial expansion. Manifest Destiny reappeared as an argument in the neoimperialist period of the 1880s and 1890s and in the Spanish-American War of 1898.

See also Monroe Doctrine; Mexican War; Polk, James K.; Spanish-American War (1898).

MANILA BAY, BATTLE OF, engagement on May 1, 1898, in which the U.S. fleet under George Dewey destroyed the Spanish fleet in the Philippines. *See* Dewey, George; Spanish-American War (1898).

MANN, HORACE (1796–1859), pioneer in the reform of the American public educational system. He was born in Franklin, Mass., graduated from Brown University in 1819, and practiced law successfully in Boston and Dedham starting in 1823. Moving into politics, Mann served in the Massachusetts House (1827–1833) and the Massachusetts Senate (1833–1837). As president of the Senate he signed the important Education Bill of 1837. Mann was active in his legislative years as a reformer of the school system. The 1837 bill called for a state board of education with a powerful secretary. Mann had enough political power to win appointment to this post, and from 1837 to 1848 he instituted widespread reforms in the Massachusetts school system.

Eliminating the chaos of the established decentralized school system, Mann brought about a minimum school year of six months, a doubling of educational appropriations, 50 additional schools, increased public support, higher teacher salaries, new curricula, new teaching methods based upon European models, professional training of teachers, and professional standards overseen by one central authority. Throughout the country he organized annual educational conventions that brought together leading intellectuals and educators. He helped establish the first American normal schools for training teachers.

See also Education.
—Richard Collin, *Lousiana State University, New Orleans*

MANN ACT (1910), also known as the White Slave Traffic Act, was passed after various lurid revelations of the growth of prostitution in the United States and in response to fears about the importing of European women for U.S. brothels. Nations had begun to cooperate against prostitution after an international congress on the problem held in London in 1899.

The act, upheld by the Supreme Court in 1913, forbade the transportation of women across state lines for immoral purposes and was so worded because of the federal government's authority over interstate commerce under the "commerce clause" of the Constitution. At the state level, every U.S. state government except Nevada and Arizona has outlawed houses of prostitution. At the international level, the trade still flourished despite efforts to suppress it.

MANN-ELKINS ACT (1910), measure to strengthen the power of the Interstate Commerce Commission, that followed passage of the Elkins Act (1903) and the Hepburn Act (1906). This new reform made the ICC a powerful government agency by giving it the power to regulate the growing communications industry. Telegraph, telephone, and cable corporations were now put under its jurisdiction. In addition the short-haul versus long-haul clauses of the ICC Act of 1887 were clarified to enable the ICC to regulate more effectively the rates charged by railroads.

See also Elkins Act (1903); Hepburn Act (1906); Interstate Commerce Commission; Railroad Legislation.

MANUFACTURES, REPORT ON (1791). *See* Report on Manufactures (1791).

MANUMISSION, the legal freeing of slaves by will and other methods and one of the means by which slavery was expected to fall in the South. In the North, a combination of economic, religious, legal, and other factors had brought about the gradual extinction of slavery. However, the plantation system in the South came to seem dependent on the use of slave labor. This made its abolition by state and national law more difficult and put increased emphasis on the individual slaveholder as the social element necessary to effect emancipation.

The American Revolution raised expectations that manumissions would spread enough to undermine slavery. This seemed especially possible because slaves were being granted their freedom by masters who were inspired by ideals embodied in the Declaration of Independence or who had reason to be grateful for slave services in the Revolutionary crisis. However, the invention of the cotton gin in 1793 made slave labor profitable, and the number of manumissions fell sharply. Some masters continued to free slaves for various reasons, but the increase in the birthrate of slaves far exceeded manumissions.

The founding of the American Colonization Society, with its plan for settling freed slaves in Liberia, was expected to inspire a wave of manumissions. The reality disappointed sincere slaveholders such as James G. Birney who felt that the Society was working to expel free blacks from the country rather than urging new manumissions.

Nat Turner's revolt also raised hopes that Virginians would end slavery by legal enactment or other means. However, the Virginia Convention of 1831–1832, which resulted from

Horace Mann's proposals for reform had profound effect on U.S. public education.

Francis Marion, the Swamp Fox, harassed British troops in the South during Revolutionary War.

General Marshall *(right)* tours French battlefields in 1944 with General Eisenhower.

the Turner attempt, defeated such hopes. The rise of an aggressive abolitionist movement in the North gave ardent proslavery advocates an additional reason to suppress liberal sentiment in the South and to pass laws limiting or forbidding manumissions.

See also Abolitionism; Birney, James G.; Liberia; Nat Turner's Revolt (1831); Virginia Convention (1831–1832).

Consult (IX) Eaton, 1940; Stampp, 1956.
—Louis Filler, *Antioch College*

MARBURY v. MADISON (1803), Supreme Court decision of Feb. 24, 1803, that arose from an appointment by President John Adams just before he left office in 1801. He appointed William Marbury as a justice of the peace, but although the commission was signed, it was not delivered. When Jefferson became president, his secretary of state, James Madison, did not send out the commission. Marbury sued, asking the courts to issue a writ of mandamus that would compel Madison to send the commission.

Chief Justice John Marshall used this case to expound the principle that the Supreme Court had the power to declare acts of Congress unconstitutional; in the 1790s the location of this power had been in some doubt. Marshall declared that, although Madison should not have withheld the commission, his Court had no power to issue a writ of mandamus to compel the secretary of state to act. Marshall's basis for this assertion was that the Judiciary Act of 1789 had been unconstitutional when it gave the Supreme Court the power to issue a writ of mandamus. This was the first time that the Supreme Court had declared an act of Congress unconstitutional.

MARCH TO THE SEA (1864), General Sherman's advance from Atlanta to the coast, which devastated and demoralized the South. *See* Civil War Battles.

MARINES, U.S., officially established on July 11, 1798, as part of the U.S. Navy to provide combined arms for land operations needed in a naval campaign. The commandant of the Marine Corps is coequal with the Joint Chiefs of Staff when discussing Marine matters.

The Marines have been active since the Continental Marines were organized by the Continental Congress on Nov. 10, 1775. Among the conflicts they have been engaged in are the War of 1812, the Seminole War (1835–1842), the Mexican War (1846–1848), the Spanish-American War (1898), the Boxer Rebellion (1900), World Wars I and II, Korea, and Vietnam.

MARION, FRANCIS (1732–1795), Revolutionary War military leader known as the "Swamp Fox." He grew up near Georgetown, and in 1775 he became a delegate to the South Carolina provincial congress and as a militia captain helped drive out the royal governor. Marion took part in the successful defense of Charleston in 1776 and two years later took command of the Second South Carolina Regiment.

Marion escaped capture when Charleston fell in May 1780, and he began to operate as a guerrilla. In September–October 1780, promoted to general, he audaciously attacked Tory troops at Blue Savannah, Black Mingo, and Tearcoat Swamp. General Cornwallis detached dragoons to hunt Marion, but their commander, Banastre Tarleton, complained that the devil could not catch the "damned old fox." Early in 1781, Marion cleared the enemy from his sector and occupied Georgetown on May 28. His adversary, Lt. Col. John W. T. Watson, complained that Marion "would not fight like a gentleman or a Christian." Marion cooperated with Gen. Nathanael Greene's operations, and on Sept. 8, 1781, he ably commanded the militias of North and South Carolina at Eutaw Springs. After the war he was elected to the South Carolina Senate three times.

See also Greene, Nathanael; Revolutionary War Battles.

Consult (II) Bass, 1959.

MARNE, SECOND BATTLE OF (JULY 18–AUGUST 6, 1918) ended the last great German offensive. *See* World War I Battles.

MARQUETTE, FATHER JACQUES (1637–1675), French Jesuit and explorer selected by the Canadian government in 1673 to investigate Indian rumors of a great Western river that emptied into the South Sea (or Pacific). Accompanied by Louis Joliet and five other men, he rowed down the Wisconsin River to the Mississippi, which he followed past the confluence with the Missouri and the Ohio. About 700 miles from its mouth, he concluded from information given him by Indians that the river actually flowed into the Gulf of Mexico, and the expedition turned back. A decade later, Sieur de La Salle completed the exploration that Marquette had begun.

See also Exploration and Discovery; French Colonies; La Salle, Sieur de.

MARSHALL, GEORGE (1880–1959), Army chief of staff during World War II and Secretary of State. His military education began at the Virginia Military Institute (not at West Point, a factor that may have impeded his advancement). He reached the rank of brigadier general in 1936 and in 1939 became Army chief of staff, a post he held throughout World War II. Starting with an army of fewer than 200,000, he eventually presided over a force of more than 8 million and coordinated the European and Pacific theaters. In December 1944 he became one of the first five-star generals of the army.

Marshall resigned as chief of staff in November 1945 and was sent by President Truman to China in an unsuccessful attempt to resolve differences between the Nationalists and Communists.

Marshall returned to the United States in 1947 to become secretary of state. His commencement address at Harvard in June 1947 unveiled what became known as the Marshall Plan, a program of economic assistance to rebuild Europe. He was awarded the Nobel Peace Prize in 1953 for his contributions to European recovery. Marshall left the State Department in 1949, but he returned to government during the Korean War and served as secretary of defense (1950–1951).

See also Marshall Plan; World War II.
—Martin Gruberg, *University of Wisconsin, Oshkosh*

MARSHALL, JOHN (1755–1835), 4th Chief Justice of the Supreme Court, called "the great Chief Justice" by Supreme Court Justice Benjamin Cardozo, a title that is hardly ever questioned. Appointed in the last days of President John Adams' Administration in 1801, Chief Justice Marshall battled with a series of presidents, nearly all of whom were vigorously opposed to Marshall's Federalist interpretation of the Constitution.

History. Marshall was born in Virginia. He joined the American Revolutionary forces at the first outbreak of hostilities and fought under George Washington until 1781, when he resigned his commission. After being admitted to the Virginia bar, he was elected to the Virginia House of Delegates, where he served intermittently until 1796, besides holding other state posts. In the Virginia Ratifying Convention he argued eloquently for the Constitution and afterward became a Federalist leader in that state.

Although utterly devoted to George Washington, Marshall refused federal appointments until 1797, when John Adams appointed him minister to France. There he became involved in the XYZ Affair, which led to the undeclared naval war with France and the subsequent passage of the Alien and Sedition Acts by Congress. When these acts were being debated in the Federalist-controlled Congress, Marshall was a member of the House of Representatives (1799–1800), and he strongly opposed the legislation. He served as secretary of state to John Adams in 1800 and was then appointed to the Supreme Court.

Significance. Although there are some disagreements, it is generally acknowledged that Marshall strengthened both the Supreme Court and the Federalist interpretation of the Constitution. During his 34 years as chief justice, he maintained dominance over those justices appointed by presidents opposed to his policies. Marshall's clear control of the Court seems to have slipped only during the last years of his term.

Marshall's expansion of the prestige of the Court was accomplished through formal changes, such as the establishment of a single opinion to express the Court's view. More important, he effected substantial changes in the law. He established the right of the Court to be the final arbiter of the Constitution and to declare congressional acts void (*Marbury v. Madison,* 1803). The Court also exercised the power to declare state laws invalid (*Fletcher v. Peck,* 1810) and to protect the right of contract (*Dartmouth College v. Woodward,* 1819). He established the supremacy of the federal government and expanded the power of Congress through broad interpretation of the "necessary and proper" clause (*McCulloch v. Maryland,* 1819). He also suggested a wide ranging definition of federal control over interstate commerce (*Gibbons v. Ogden,* 1824). He solidified the right of the Supreme Court over the judiciaries of the various states (*Martin v. Hunter's Lessee,* 1816; *Cohens v. Virginia,* 1821).

John Marshall helped structure a distribution of the powers of government that has lasted to the present. His work has strongly influenced the political history of the United States. He died in office still battling his adversaries in the other branches of government.

See also Dartmouth College v. Woodward (1819); McCulloch v. Maryland (1819).
Consult (III) Beveridge, 1919; Corwin, 1919; Jones, 1956.
—David Forte, *Skidmore College*

MARSHALL PLAN, basic program to funnel U.S. economic aid to Europe (1948–1952). Faced with an economic crisis and a rapid increase in the size of domestic Communist parties in major Western European countries, Secretary of State George Marshall proposed on June 5, 1947, that European countries create joint plans for economic recovery. In return, Marshall declared, the United States would provide direct economic assistance.

The Western European countries formed the Organization for European Economic Cooperation, and in early 1948 Congress passed the European Recovery Act, providing for economic assistance. During the four years of the Marshall Plan, also known as the European Recovery Program, the United States provided about $14 billion. The effort was highly successful—not only did Europe surpass its prewar economic production, but also the initial steps were laid for greater European economic unity, including the Common Market. Because the USSR and its satellites had withdrawn, the Marshall Plan was used as a cornerstone of the American containment policy during the Cold War.

See also Iron Curtain; Truman Doctrine.
Consult (VIII) Schmitt, 1962.

John Marshall, 3rd and most influential Chief Justice of the Supreme Court.

Marshall Plan was begun while George C. Marshall was secretary of state.

MARYLAND, colony and state given by Charles I to the Catholic convert George Calvert, first Lord Baltimore. He died and the grant went to his son, whose younger brother Leonard Calvert was sent out as first governor. St. Mary's, the chief settlement, was created as a Catholic refuge in 1634.

The land was divided into "manors" and given to large landholders in semifeudal fashion, and in theory the Calverts were the absolute rulers of Maryland. In practice, however, American frontier conditions and complex religious and boundary disputes in the area prevented this feudal system from taking hold. For example, the Calverts were forced to accede to a local assembly, and in 1649, under a Protestant lieutenant governor, the assembly voted for religious toleration. Border raids from Virginia and the influx of more Protestants into Maryland, together with the Puritan Revolution in England, made life difficult for the Catholic elite of the colony.

In 1654 the Puritan Parliament in England intervened in the religious struggles in Maryland, threw off Calvert authority, and denied civil rights to Catholics. Although the Puritans won the short Maryland civil war, the Calverts were restored in 1656. The colony developed large plantations that grew tobacco for export with the use of African slaves. Falling tobacco prices, as in the 1660s, always made tensions among Catholics and Protestants worse. The monarchy was restored in England in 1660, but anti-Catholic feeling remained and two revolts in Maryland had to be put down in 1676 and 1681.

When Calvert left the colony in 1684 and did not return and when the Whig Revolution was successful in England in 1688, the powerful Protestant Association took control of Maryland (1689-1691), governing through the assembly. Maryland became a crown colony for a time (1691-1716), but even when the Calverts were reinstated, their authority was restricted. Maryland adopted a new constitution in 1776 and eagerly ratified the U.S. Constitution on April 28, 1788.

The legislature is bicameral; the capital is Annapolis. The population in 1970 was 3,922,399.

See also Calvert Family.

MASON, GEORGE (1725-1792), a Virginia Revolutionary and important constitutional thinker. He was the son of a wealthy planter who died when Mason was 10 and left him a large estate. He participated widely in local affairs and was elected in 1759 to the House of Burgesses, where he became closely allied with George Washington. Suffering from continual ill-health and never comfortable in public life, he was a retiring figure. Nonetheless, he played a significant role in the Revolutionary movement in Virginia and wrote the Fairfax Resolves (1774), which stated the colonies' position on their relationship to the crown and were formally adopted by the Virginia Convention and by the Continental Congress.

His most significant achievement was the authorship of the Virginia Bill of Rights (June 1776). It served as a model for Thomas Jefferson's draft of the preamble to the Declaration of Independence and later as a basis for the first 10 amendments to the U.S. Constitution. He also drafted a major part of Virginia's constitution of 1776. He retired from public life in the 1780s but returned to serve as a member of Virginia's delegation to the Constitutional Convention of 1787. He refused to sign the completed document and unsuccessfully fought against ratification because he wanted a Bill of Rights included, feared the new government's consolidationist tendencies, and opposed the compromise that continued the slave trade until 1808, which he viewed as "disgraceful to mankind."

See also Bill of Rights.
Consult (III) Rutland, 1961.
—Richard E. Ellis, *University of Virginia*

MASON, JOHN (1600-1672), colonial commander during the Pequot War. *See* Pequot War (1637).

MASON-DIXON LINE, the southern boundary of Pennsylvania and therefore the northern boundary of Delaware, Maryland, and what is now West Virginia, which was regarded as the dividing line between the free and the slave states. The line is named after its English surveyors—Charles Mason and Jeremiah Dixon—who measured it (1763-1767) to settle a boundary claim between the Penn family of Pennsylvania and the Calvert family of Maryland. The border between the areas was fixed at 39° 43' 17.6" north latitude and was approved by the Crown in 1769. The Pennsylvania-Virginia extension was completed in 1784.

MASS PRODUCTION. Because of the relatively high cost of labor and the large consumer market in the United States, industrial developers have been unusually sensitive to techniques that increase productivity and reduce actual labor. Therefore, the core strategies of the industrial revolution, using machines instead of hand tools and using power to move the machines, were basic to early American factories. Another step was still necessary to establish the "American system" that became famous in the nineteenth century: development of interchangeable parts (most notably connected with the rise of machine tools and precision measurement in the small arms and clock industries).

The next development was the assembly line, in which the parts were added on as each unit moved past stationary workers (presum-

Mass production—with workers performing small parts of manufacturing process and with factories turning out thousands of identical products—revolutionized industry.

ably patterned after the way hog carcasses moved along a row of slaughterhouse workers on an overhead trolley). The assembly line proved its efficiency in Henry Ford's well-publicized Highland Park plant just before World War I.

During the 1920s especially, advanced industries greatly increased the extent to which mechanical action was substituted for repetitious human labor. The final development was the introduction of automatic controlling devices. The electric eye and other sensors, particularly when coupled with electrical relays and transfer devices, were already of immense importance by the era of the Great Depression. Hooking sensors to post-World War II computers completed the automation. Both technological unemployment in the 1920s and 1930s and displacement of workers by automation in the 1950s and 1960s created social problems and helped shift American employment predominantly production industries to service industries.

See also Automobile; Ford, Henry.

MASSACHUSETTS, colony and later state that embraced Massachusetts Bay Colony, Plymouth, and, for a time, Maine. Explored by Bartholomew Gosnold (1602) and mapped by John Smith (1614), Massachusetts was first settled by the Pilgrims of the Plymouth Colony (1620). However, the major group was the Puritans who formed the Massachusetts Bay Company, led by John Winthrop, Sir Richard Saltonstall, and Thomas Dudley and who received a charter from Charles I in 1629. A 17-ship fleet brought 1,000 Puritans to Salem in 1630. They established Boston and other towns, and their numbers were soon augmented by the Great Migration—20,000 emigrated to Massachusetts in the period from 1630 to 1640.

The Puritans of Massachusetts wished to create a "Bible commonwealth." Because they brought the company charter and all its officers with them, they were autonomous from the outset with no absentee authorities in England to bother them. Their form of government was modeled on the company, the stockholders becoming the freemen and making up the assembly, or General Court. Newer townships were established with democratic town meetings, which displayed a high degree of local self-government.

By May 1631 the original elite of company officers no longer held all the reins of power, and all church members were admitted to voting rights and some rights to hold office in Boston (the capital after 1632). Gradually, the General Court of church members won more rights, including that of electing the governor. After 1644 the court became a bicameral legislature. Members were elected from each local town meeting. The franchise was not extended to non-Congregationalists

until 1664, and the Congregational church was the official church of Massachusetts until 1833.

Early measures of the Bible commonwealth included the famous "Body of Liberties" (individual rights) drawn up by Nathaniel Ward in 1641 and the Massachusetts school law of 1647, the first such law to decree public education and establish a school system. Despite such enlightened and advanced ideas, the commonwealth was torn by religious disputes, and the elite fought hard to maintain purity of dogma. Dissidents such as Roger Williams and Anne Hutchinson could not be tolerated. Meanwhile, the economic growth of the colony brought secular influences, and many immigrants were not very pious.

The commonwealth reacted strongly to events in England, flourishing during Puritan triumphs there and languishing at other times. The restoration of the English monarchy in 1660 led eventually to a tightening of crown control. The jurisdiction of Massachusetts over the Maine region was revoked (1659), and in 1684 the Massachusetts Bay Company was dissolved and the original charter canceled.

A new royal charter of 1691 united Massachusetts Bay, Maine, and Plymouth into one royal colony, and the right to vote was no longer limited to church members. Economic growth continued, and the hold of the Congregational church weakened. Already in 1662, the Half-Way Covenant had eased the rules for full church membership. The witchcraft trials at Salem (1692) were the last gasp of superorthodoxy. Massachusetts flourished in trade, naval stores, and fish and fur exports and was a leading opponent of the crown in the late eighteenth century and the American Revolution. It ratified the U.S. Constitution on Feb. 6, 1788, by a fairly close vote. Maine did not enter the union as a separate state until 1820.

The legislature is bicameral, and the capital is Boston. The population in 1970 was 5,689,170.

See also Congregationalists; Pilgrims; Plymouth; Puritanism; Winthrop Family.

Consult (I) Morgan, 1958; Morison, 1930.
—Peter d'A. Jones, *University of Illinois, Chicago Circle*

MASSACHUSETTS GOVERNMENT ACT, one of the Coercive Acts, which dealt with the colony's judicial and legislative structure. *See* Coercive Acts (1774).

MASSACHUSETTS SCHOOL ACT, early legislation to increase literacy. Puritan insistence on individual Bible study necessitated a literate citizenry, and in 1642 the Massachusetts General Court set fines for towns that neglected to teach reading. In 1647 the court ordered towns with 50 families to hire a schoolmaster and those with 100 families to establish a Latin grammar school or be fined. Historians question whether the 1647 act was strictly enforced but agree that between 1640 and 1700 about 95 percent of New England males were literate.

MASTERS, EDGAR LEE (1869-1947), American poet, author of the *Spoon River Anthology*. *See* Literature.

MATHER, COTTON (1663-1728), a leading colonial Puritan clergyman. The son of Increase Mather, he was born in Boston and educated at Harvard. After ordination in 1685, he joined his father's ministry in the Second (North) Boston Church. When his father was in England and after his father's death, Cotton Mather served as pastor of that congregation. Although his reputation as a scholar rested principally on his work as a clergyman, Cotton Mather's interests, like his father's, extended to politics and science. During the 1689 uprising in Massachusetts against Governor Sir Edmund Andros and the Dominion of New England, Mather supported the insurgents and was the author of the manifesto issued to explain the revolt. His role in the Salem witch trials was somewhat ambiguous. He was concerned about hanging innocent people who were accused of the crime, but he was defensive about the judicial proceedings, particularly in his book *The Wonders of the Invisible World* (1693).

Mather published more than 450 books during his lifetime, a monumental record in any age. Of these, the most significant was *Magnalia Christi Americana, or The Ecclesiastical History of New England* (1702), in which he richly detailed the Puritan experience. Many of Mather's publications concerned science, especially *The Christian Philosopher* (1721). He was interested in astronomy, botany (he wrote an early description of plant hybridization), and medicine. Like his father, he was a staunch advocate of inoculation against smallpox. His accomplishments were recognized by his election as a fellow of the Royal Society of London, one of the few American colonists so honored.

See also Puritanism.
Consult (I) Middlekauff, 1971.
—Carl Ubbelohde, *Case Western Reserve University*

MATHER, INCREASE (1639-1723), Massachusetts Puritan clergyman and father of Cotton Mather. Increase was born in Dorchester, the son of the Reverend Richard Mather. He graduated from Harvard at 17, studied further at Trinity College, Dublin, and began his clerical career. In 1661, after the restoration of Charles II, Mather returned to America and in 1664 was named pastor of the Second (North) Church in Boston. His influence increased when he became president (rector) of Harvard in 1685, an office he held until 1701.

In 1688 Mather went to England as Massachusetts agent to plead for restoration of the

forfeited colony charter. He was not successful but did help select the first royal governor, Sir William Phips, appointed under the new (1691) charter. Mather returned to a colony embroiled in the Salem witch trials and ultimately argued for rules of evidence that ended the judicial proceedings against people accused of witchcraft. He was also interested in science, including the then unpopular inoculation against smallpox. A great pulpit orator, generally defending "orthodox" Puritanism against liberalizing influences, he published more than 100 books and pamphlets, most of them sermons, before his death in Boston.

See also Puritanism.
Consult (I) Middlekauff, 1971.

MAYFLOWER COMPACT (NOV. 21, 1620), agreement to establish civil government in Plymouth Colony. *See* Pilgrims; Plymouth.

MAYSVILLE ROAD VETO (1830), President Jackson's veto of the Maysville Road bill, which would have allowed the federal government to subsidize construction of a turnpike from Maysville to Lexington in Henry Clay's home state of Kentucky. Martin Van Buren's political desire to harm Clay led him to urge Jackson to stop federal financing of internal improvements. Jackson had spoken in his first annual address to Congress (1829) against such direct federal funding. Jackson said that he vetoed the bill because the turnpike was an intrastate, not interstate, project. Federal financing of internal improvements, he went on, should be sanctioned by a constitutional amendment. The Maysville veto was also a concession on Jackson's part to the South's states' rights position.

MEAD, MARGARET (1901-), anthropologist and author. She graduated from Barnard in 1923 and received her doctorate from Columbia in 1929. She was a curator of ethnology at the American Museum of Natural History (1926-1969), director of the Columbia University Research in Contemporary Culture Center, adjunct professor of anthropology at Columbia, and president of the American Anthropological Association (1960). Her research expeditions from 1925 on have taken her to Samoa, the Admiralty Islands, New Guinea, and Bali.

Mead is the author of more than a dozen books, including *Coming of Age in Samoa* (1928), *And Keep Your Powder Dry* (1942), *Male and Female* (1949), a study of sexual roles in seven South Sea Island cultures and in the United States, and *Culture and Commitment: A Study of the Generation Gap* (1970). Besides popularizing anthropological research and evoking interest in other cultures, she was a columnist for women's magazines.

MEANY, GEORGE (1894-), American labor

Anthropologist Margaret Mead stresses relationship between culture and psychology.

leader. He was born in New York City and became a plumber. Chosen as business representative of his local union in 1922, he was elected president of the New York State Federation of Labor in 1934. Six years later he was named secretary-treasurer of the American Federation of Labor (AFL). During World War II he served on the National Defense Mediation Board and the War Labor Board.

After his election as president of the AFL in 1952, Meany turned his attention to reunifying the U.S. labor movement. In 1955 Meany and Walter Reuther, president of the Congress of Industrial Organizations (CIO), signed a merger agreement. Meany was elected president of the combined AFL-CIO. Meany also served as vice-president of the International Conference of Free Trade Unions (1957–1958) and as a delegate to the UN General Assembly (1959–1960).

During his tenure as president, Meany attacked the problem of labor corruption and expelled three unions, including the Teamsters. As head of the huge labor organization Meany exerted a powerful influence on the American economy and was courted by political leaders.

See also American Federation of Labor-Congress of Industrial Organizations (AFL-CIO).

MEAT INSPECTION ACT (1906) aimed at improving sanitation in the meat industry. *See* Pure Food and Drug Act (1906).

MEDICARE AND MEDICAID, programs of government participation in financing health care instituted in 1965 as amendments to the Social Security Act. Medicare is a federal program of health and hospital insurance for the aged, and Medicaid is a federal-state program of health care assistance for low-income people of all ages. Medicare and Medicaid are administered by the U.S. Social Security Administration and by local social service departments, respectively. Medicare hospital insurance is a social security right for most people 65 and over; its health care plan is voluntary. Medicaid is available to recipients of public assistance and in some states to the medically indigent. Medicare benefits, uniform throughout the country, are limited (they exclude prescription drugs, eyeglasses, dental care, etc.); Medicaid programs, different in each state, can be very comprehensive.

The laws have no provisions for expansion of services or new health systems and have greatly increased demand for medical services, resulting in escalating costs and insufficient health facilities. Solutions frequently advocated are health maintenance organizations—already present in some states under Medicaid—and use of paramedical personnel.

MELVILLE, HERMAN (1819-1891), novelist and

poet whose *Moby Dick* is one of the classic novels of world literature. He was born in New York. After working as a bank clerk and in a store, Melville shipped out to sea as a cabin boy in 1837. Shortly after his return he went on a series of South Seas voyages. His 18-month trip on the Whaler *Acushnet* is probably the factual basis of *Moby Dick*. He jumped ship in July 1842 in the Marquesas Islands and spent an idyllic month with friendly natives, then escaped on an Australian ship to Tahiti. He returned home after serving in the U.S. Navy.

Melville then began setting down fictionalized accounts of his travels. *Typee* (1846) earned him enough popularity to convince him he had a genuine literary talent. With *Omoo* (1847), the second South Seas novel, Melville became famous. He married Elizabeth Shaw, the daughter of the Massachusetts chief justice, and settled down to a career of writing in New York. *Mardi* (1849), *Redburn* (1849), and *White-Jacket* (1850) were further accounts of sea adventures. After visiting Europe briefly he settled in Pittsfield, Mass., near Nathaniel Hawthorne, with whom he became close friends. *Moby Dick* (1851) marked the height of Melville's literary art.

In 1852 Melville published *Pierre*, a strange semiautobiographical novel that marked the beginning of the decline of his creative vigor. He published *Israel Potter* in 1855 and devoted himself chiefly to poetry afterward, also serving as a customs inspector from 1866 to 1885. *Billy Budd* was written shortly before his death in 1891 but was not published until 1924.

See also Literature; Moby Dick.
Consult (III) Mumford, 1962.
—Richard Collin, *Louisiana State University, New Orleans*

MENCKEN, H(ENRY) L(OUIS) (1880-1956), Baltimore newspaperman who became a literary critic whose acid-dipped pen exposed the foibles and hypocrisies of American culture during the Progressive Era and the 1920s. In 1924 he helped found and became editor of *The American Mercury*, which until the early 1930s was the most widely quoted journal of its day, specializing in witty denunciations of almost everything, many written by Mencken. He classified his fellow Americans as "homo boobiens". His favorite targets were Puritans and philistines.

He was, however, almost entirely negative: he attacked both conservatives and reformers ("Doing Good is in bad taste"), and he offered no constructive program except appreciation of good art (and even in that field he was often unfriendly to experiment). Mencken became the spokesman for a generation of disillusioned iconoclasts. He embodied both the negative attitudes of the 1920s and the increasing respect for individualistic, uncon-

George Meany, influential president of the AFL-CIO.

Baltimore journalist H. L. Mencken also had wide influence as literary critic.

ventional behavior that was one of the legacies of the era.

MENNONITES. *See* Colonial Religion.

MERCANTILISM, economic doctrine developed to defend the princely, centralized nation-state in Europe between the sixteenth and eighteenth centuries. It implied a policy of strict state regulation of the economy, specific standards of quality and output, high tariffs against foreign imports, and the acquisition of colonies as sources of raw materials and as markets for the finished goods of the mother country. The American colonies were in this category, although they managed to grow economically in any case and were left alone for long periods of time.

This system of state-managed economic life was what Adam Smith revolted against in his *Wealth of Nations* (1776). Smith tried to prove that economic growth was most encouraged by the government keeping its hands off (laissez-faire) and allowing private enterprise.

Few Americans were willing to let their government stand by and do nothing. They demanded high tariffs in the nineteenth century to protect the young textile industries and other ventures, and they expected to receive encouragement and aid in the form of land grants, government purchase of stock in railroad and canal companies, and federal surveying of Western territories. American economic policy was therefore one of neomercantilism, or economic nationalism. But Americans did accept some aspects of Smith's philosophy—his laissez-faire (as far as regulation of business was concerned) and his worship of the private businessman.

See also Free Enterprise; Free Trade; Smith, Adam; Tariffs.
Consult (III) Jones, 1965.

MERCHANT MARINE ACTS (1920, 1928, 1936), legislation passed by Congress to help develop a U.S. merchant marine fleet that could compete with foreign shipping and could be called upon in time of war.

The act of 1920 placed authority for the development of a fleet with the seven-man U.S. Shipping Board. Financial assistance was provided with extra mail payments and construction loans. The act of 1928 increased the construction loan fund set up in 1920 and provided for mail shipping routes for U.S. merchant marine vessels. However, neither of these acts was sufficient to improve the world position of the U.S. merchant marine, and it was not until the act of 1936, which granted both construction and operating subsidies, that substantial legislation was passed.

METHODISTS. *See* Colonial Religion.

Capture of the Chapultepec fortress on Sept. 13, 1847, was immediately followed by fall of Mexico City.

MEUSE-ARGONNE OFFENSIVE (Sept. 26–NOV. 11, 1918). American troops attacked in the Meuse-Argonne sector in the great Allied offensive that ended with Germany's defeat. *See* World War I Battles.

MEXICAN BORDER CAMPAIGN (1916-1917), skirmishes that almost led to war between Mexico and the United States. The Mexican government had been in turmoil since 1914 with warfare between Gen. Venustiano Carranza and Francisco "Pancho" Villa. President Woodrow Wilson recognized the Villa government and then turned about and recognized Carranza.

In 1916 Villa retaliated by stopping a train in Mexico and killing a group of American mining engineers; he then moved on to Columbus, N.M., where he burned the town, killing 17 people. His hope was to force American intervention in Mexico and so discredit Carranza. In March 1916, American troops led by Gen. John J. Pershing were sent across the border, thus intensifying anti-American feelings in Mexico as the U.S. forces were drawn further south by Villa. Finally, Wilson negotiated and withdrew the troops in early 1917. The Mexican constitutionalists under Carranza were soon able to establish a stable government.

MEXICAN WAR (1846-1848), war between Mexico and the United States that revolved around conflicting territorial claims and desires. Relations between Mexico and the United States, long strained, were finally broken after the United States annexed the Texas Republic in 1845. President James K. Polk, the embodiment of the spirit of American Manifest Destiny, wished to take the California-New Mexico region, although he was at first ready to buy it. The failure of the Slidell Mission led to Polk's command sending U.S. forces into disputed border territory between the Nueces River and the Rio Grande, which he claimed as American (although many Americans in Congress, such as Abraham Lincoln, disagreed). When bloodshed occurred, Polk claimed aggression by Mexico, and Congress declared war on May 13, 1846. Thousands of Westerners volunteered for battle, hoping for rich booty in Mexico; these untried and ill-disciplined Americans were later guilty of war atrocities.

The California-New Mexico region was rapidly Americanized in the early months of the war. Commander J. D. Sloat took a squadron to California and seized its major port cities. Stephen W. Kearny, a veteran of the War of 1812, commanded the Army of the West, and before the spring of 1847 he had taken Sante Fe, marched on to California, and joined up with John C. Frémont there. Serious problems of political command resulted, but

Kearny ended up as military governor of California for a time. By January 1847 the entire region was in U.S. hands.

Doniphan's expedition took the war into the northern Mexican province of Chihuahua. Colonel A. W. Doniphan led Missouri cavalry volunteers in a remarkable trek, 3,000 miles over mountains and waterless desert country. He occupied El Paso after the Battle of El Brazito (Christmas Day, 1846) and took the local capital city, Chihuahua, on March 1, 1847, after the Battle of the Sacramento.

Meanwhile, Gen. Zachary Taylor had defeated the Mexican leader, Santa Anna, at the battle near Buena Vista on Feb. 22–23, 1847, after disobeying orders to stay around Monterrey. Taylor had taken the northern town of Monterrey in September 1846, but he had then allowed the Mexicans an eight-week armistice, which President Polk did not like. He had lost confidence in Taylor and given major command to Gen. Winfield Scott. Although Taylor was reprimanded, he returned home a war hero and later became president.

Scott's Command. Scott's strategy was now followed: to invade central Mexico from the sea and take the Gulf of Mexico fortress of Veracruz. Like the original Spanish conquerors, Scott would then march inland and take Mexico City. Headquartered on the Gulf at Tampico, General Scott issued in February General Order No. 20, which condemned certain war crimes and aimed at winning over the local Mexican populace by better treatment than Taylor's men had doled out. His force landed on the beaches south of Veracruz and avoided a frontal assault on the fortress. Veracruz was then seized by land and sea bombardment and was occupied in late March. Turning inland for the march to the capital, on April 18 Scott fought the Battle of Cerro Gordo at a mountain pass. About 9,000 Americans met about 13,000 Mexicans led by Santa Anna, and the latter were routed in a final assault in hand-to-hand fighting. Scott headquartered and recouped for three months at Puebla, and on August 7 he entered the Valley of Mexico and waited at Ayotla for his final drive on Mexico City. Two preliminary battles were fought at Contreras and at Churubusco on August 19 and 20, bringing costly victories for the Americans but much greater losses for Santa Anna. From August 24 to September 7 an armistice was allowed while Santa Anna considered peace proposals. When this negotiation failed, Scott marched on the capital.

A gun foundry outside the city was attacked on September 8 in the Battle of Molino del Rey. The Americans retired temporarily, then stormed the fortified hill in the park of Chapultepec, which commanded the western approaches to the city. After artillery bombardment, his men assaulted the hill with axes and ladders and took the summit. Here Los Niños,

a group of young Mexican cadets, became heroes in the final resistance, and some threw themselves off the hill rather than surrender. Scott entered the city proper on the night of Sept. 13–14, 1847. After futile resistance by Santa Anna, the leader eventually fled to Jamaica on Oct. 7, 1897. Peace was signed in the suburb of Guadalupe Hidalgo on Feb. 2, 1848. By the treaty Mexico recognized U.S. claims to the territory north of the Rio Grande and ceded California and New Mexico in return for $15 million and other considerations.

See also Guadalupe Hidalgo, Treaty of (1848); Manifest Destiny; Scott, Winfield; Slidell Mission; Taylor, Zachary.

Consult (III) Ruiz, 1963; Singletary, 1960.
—Peter d'A. Jones, *University of Illinois, Chicago Circle*

MICHIGAN, the 26th state, joined the Union on Jan. 26, 1837. First settled in 1688 by French fur traders, the first major settlement was Detroit, established in 1701. Michigan was ceded to England in 1763 and was later part of the Northwest Territory. Michigan became a territory in 1805.

The state legislature is bicameral; the capital is Lansing. The population in 1970 was 8,875,083.

MIDDLE PASSAGE, term during the slave era that was used for the trip between Africa and the West Indies. *See* Triangular Trade.

MIDWAY, BATTLE OF (JUNE 1942), first significant defeat of Japanese Navy. *See* World War II.

MILITARY ASSISTANCE, often one of the components of foreign aid. *See* Foreign Aid.

MILLER, ARTHUR (1915–), American playwright, author of *Death of a Salesman*. *See* Theater.

MILLER-TYDINGS ENABLING ACT (1937), one of several laws salvaging usable parts of the National Recovery Administration—others were the Wagner Act, the Fair Labor Standards Act, and the Robinson-Patman Act—after the NRA was voided in the *Schechter v. U.S.* (1935) decision. Sponsored by the retail druggists' association, this anticompetition law permitted "fair-trade" pricing in interstate commerce, allowing manufacturers to set prices that had to be observed by retail stores.

See also National Recovery Administration; Schecter v. United States (1935).

MILLETT, KATE, radical feminist and author of *Sexual Politics* (1969). *See* Women's Liberation.

MINING FRONTIER. *See* Frontier in American History.

THE MEXICAN WAR 1846–1848

→ Mexican forces
↠ Mexican victory
→ United States forces
↠ United States victory
▨ Area of dispute between Texas and Mexico

Racists used whites' fear of miscegenation to arouse public sentiment against blacks.

MISSOURI COMPROMISE 1820

Slave state or territory

Free state or territory

MAINE 1820

MICHIGAN TERRITORY 1818

UNORGANIZED TERRITORY

MISSOURI 1821

ARKANSAS TERRITORY 1819

Free
Slave

36° 30'

MINNESOTA, the 32nd state, admitted to the Union on May 11, 1858. At first French territory, the Minnesota area was won by the British in 1763. The eastern part of the state was included in the Northwest Territory in 1787, and the remainder became U.S. territory with the Louisiana Purchase (1803). The first permanent settlements were at St. Paul in 1830 and Stillwater in 1843. Minnesota achieved territorial status in 1849.

The state legislature is bicameral; the capital is Saint Paul. The population in 1970 was 3,805,069.

MINOR v. HAPPERSETT (1875), case in which the Supreme Court affirmed that it was not unconstitutional for a state to deny women the vote. The case was brought against a registering officer by Virginia Minor of Missouri, who claimed that the state constitution, giving suffrage only to males, conflicted with the Constitution's Fourteenth Amendment. The Court ruled that voting was not a privilege of citizenship and that "the Constitution, when it conferred citizenship, did not necessarily confer the right of suffrage." The effect of the decision was nullified by the ratification of the Nineteenth Amendment in 1920.

See also Suffrage, Women's.

MINT ACT (1793) created a U.S. Mint. The mint was established in Philadelphia in 1793 under the directorship of David Rittenhouse, and it produced both silver (from 1794) and gold (from 1795) coins. In its early years it could not meet the demand for hard cash because of gold and silver shortages.

MINUIT, PETER (1580?-1638), Dutch colonial administrator and a Huguenot. In 1626 the Dutch West India Company sent him as director-general to New Amsterdam (New York City), which had been founded in 1625. The settlement was in disorder when Minuit arrived, but he soon added stability while maintaining good relations with the Indians, from whom he purchased all of Manhattan Island for goods valued at $24. However, his dictatorial manner was not popular with the colonists, and he was recalled in 1632 for favoring the powerful patroons.

A few years later Sweden, anxious to establish a colony, commissioned Peter Minuit, to the embarrassment of the Dutch, to lead a Swedish expedition to the New World in 1638. Minuit established Fort Christina on the Delaware River near modern Wilmington and served as governor of New Sweden in 1639-1641.

See also Patroonships.

MIRANDA v. ARIZONA (1966), important Supreme Court decision affecting the rights of defendants. In the Miranda case the Warren Court consolidated four criminal cases that each contained the use of a confession obtained from defendants who were not informed of their right to remain silent during interrogation by the police. Although in these cases, as in the earlier *Escobedo v. Illinois* (1964), the majority of the Court viewed the confessions as suspect, there was no showing of physical coercion or even psychological ploys.

The majority voted to reverse the convictions on the basis of the Fifth and Sixth amendments and declared that henceforth the suspect should be immediately informed of his right to a court-appointed lawyer, of his right to remain silent under questioning, and of the fact that anything he says may be used as evidence against him at the time of trial. The minority complained that the majority was distorting the Constitution by placing the rights of the individual criminal suspect above the rights of society as a whole.

MISCEGENATION, the mixture of races. Popularized by David G. Croly in *Miscegenation* (1864), the term has been used to characterize relationships between whites and blacks that resulted in children of mixed blood. White racists used the threat of miscegenation to heighten antagonism toward blacks and to justify the denial of social rights to blacks.

See also Slavery.

MISSISSIPPI, the 20th state, admitted to the Union on Dec. 10, 1817. First explored in 1540 by Hernán de Soto, the area was claimed for France in 1682 by Sieur de La Salle and ceded to the British in 1763. The first white settlement was made in 1699 near Biloxi Bay. It gained territorial status in 1798. A stronghold of the plantation system, Mississippi was a member of the Confederacy.

The state legislature is bicameral; the capital is Jackson. The population in 1970 was 2,216,912.

MISSISSIPPI COMPANY, colonial land company headed by George Washington. *See* Land Companies.

MISSOURI, the 24th state, joined the Union on Aug. 10, 1821. The first white men to reach the Missouri area were French—Marquette and Joliet—in 1673. The first permanent white settlement was in the early 1730s at St. Genevieve; St. Louis was founded in 1763. The Missouri area was ceded to Spain in 1763 but returned to France in 1800. The United States acquired Missouri as part of the Louisiana Purchase and granted it territorial status in 1812. Although Missouri was admitted as a slave state under the Missouri Compromise, slavery never really flourished. A border state, Missouri remained in the Union during the Civil War.

The state legislature is bicameral; the capital is Jefferson City. The population in 1970 was 4,677,399.

See also Missouri Compromise (1820).

MISSOURI COMPROMISE (1820), agreement that attempted to solve the sectional disputes between slave and nonslave states. After settlers in Missouri asked, beginning in 1817, for admission as a slave state, heated arguments developed. At this time the Senate was evenly divided between representatives of slave and nonslave states, a balance that would have been disrupted by Missouri's admission. The prospect of imbalance created fears in the North that political power would shift to the South and that more slave states would be admitted from the West. Bitter arguments about the status of slavery broke out in Congress in 1819, a year when Maine was petitioning for admission as a free state.

Henry Clay of Kentucky soon emerged as a compromiser, thus preventing further dissension. He persuaded Congress to grant Missouri statehood while accepting Maine as a free state. The Missouri Enabling Act of March 6, 1820, also stipulated no new slave states were to be permitted above the line 36° 30′ north latitude, a line that corresponds with the northern boundary of Arkansas. Missouri initially adopted a constitution excluding free blacks and mulattoes, but when this clause was challenged, Missouri agreed to respect the rights of all citizens and was admitted as a state on Aug. 10, 1821.

This compromise in effect permitted Congress to counteract Southerners and Northerners who were anxious to justify or denounce slavery. The Compromise of 1850 was held by some statesmen and abolitionists to have abrogated the Missouri Compromise because it permitted the capture of fugitive slaves in free territory. Others, such as Abraham Lincoln, insisted that the earlier compromise was still in force until 1854, when the Kansas-Nebraska Act opened to settlement that territory which lay north of 36° 30′.

See also Clay, Henry; Compromise of 1850; Kansas-Nebraska Act (1854).

Consult (IV) Moore, 1953.

—Louis Filler, *Antioch College*

MITCHELL, BILLY (WILLIAM LENDRUM) (1879–1936), was the spokesman for a group of strategists who advocated the use of the airplane in warfare in such a way as to revolutionize military techniques. As a young general during World War I he tried out mass bombing and aggressive use of air power on the western front. After the war he showed the threat of planes to battleships by sinking old ships with bombs in a demonstration. During the early 1920s, Mitchell found himself in conflict with conservative senior officers of the Army and Navy, who preferred the traditional ways of fighting. Mitchell advocated a separate air force that would not be hampered by the mossbacks.

In 1925, following the crash of the Navy dirigible *Shenandoah*, Mitchell made public charges of "incompetency" and "criminal negligence" and was convicted by court martial of insubordination. He resigned his commission and continued his crusade for air power, also warning of a possible Japanese attack on the United States.

He died before World War II tested his theories. On the one hand, the war could never have been won without air power. On the other hand, strategic bombing alone did not win in World War II, in Korea, or in Vietnam. One of Mitchell's aims was achieved in 1947, when the U.S. Air Force was made a separate part of the Department of Defense.

MOBILE BAY, BATTLE OF (AUGUST 1864), key Union naval victory in which David Farragut ended Confederate access to the Gulf of Mexico. *See* Civil War Battles; Farragut, David S.

MOBY DICK, novel by Herman Melville published in 1851. It is at once a realistic tale of a whaling voyage out of New England and a much deeper study of the confrontation between the *Pequod's* Captain Ahab and Moby Dick, the white whale. The story is told by Ishmael, a seaman who is the only survivor of the journey. The novel is filled with whaling lore, but the principal movement is toward the inevitable clash in which the whale is the victor, the *Pequod* is destroyed, and all its men but Ishmael perish.

Many interpretations of the novel exist, some critics seeing it as a symbolic representation of the struggle between good and evil. Others find a more complex metaphor—Ahab's search for order in the universe, an order that did not exist.

Moby Dick was not popular in its own time. It achieved its position as a classic during the revival of interest in Melville's work after World War I.

See also Melville, Herman.

MODEL CITIES, urban renewal program enacted in 1966. *See* Housing Acts.

MOLASSES ACT (1733). *See* Navigation Acts.

MOLEY, RAYMOND, member of the Brains Trust. *See* Brains Trust.

MOLINO DEL REY, BATTLE OF (1847), battle on the advance to Mexico City. *See* Mexican War.

MOLLY MAGUIRES, terrorist organization of Irish anthracite coal miners that flourished in

Billy Mitchell, who advocated a strong air force, was court-martialed for criticizing defense policies.

Molly Maguires meet secretly in the Pennsylvania coal country.

east-central Pennsylvania between 1843 and 1876. All members also belonged to the Ancient Order of Hibernians, an Irish benevolent group whose leaders had no connection with the Mollies.

The Mollies allegedly operated by terrorism—assaulting, even murdering, persons they found offensive. Many of the crimes attributed to the Mollies involved coal mine supervisory personnel. The group was eventually infiltrated by a Pinkerton detective who discovered information that led to the arrest of men alleged to be Mollies. Beginning in 1876, 19 of these men were hanged and others imprisoned.

Although the Mollies were not, strictly speaking, a labor organization, they were associated in the popular mind with the emerging labor movement and became a popular legend, especially among those sympathetic to labor.

See also Labor Movement.

MONITOR AND MERRIMACK, first engagement between ironclad ships (March 9, 1862). *See* Civil War Battles.

MONROE, JAMES (1758–1831), 5th President of the United States (1817–1825). He was born in Westmoreland County, Va., on April 28, 1758. After fighting in the Revolution, he studied law with Thomas Jefferson. Later in the 1780s he served in the Virginia legislature and in the Continental Congress, and after the adoption of the new Constitution he became U.S. senator from Virginia (1790–1794). Monroe had great sympathy for the French Revolution, and in 1794 he was appointed minister to France. It was not a happy appointment, because Federalist policies in the mid-1790s alienated the French and helped to make Monroe's position untenable. He was recalled in 1796 and then served as governor of Virginia (1799–1802). He returned to France in 1803 as Jefferson's special envoy and with Robert Livingston negotiated the Louisiana Purchase. In 1808 Monroe was a candidate for the Democratic-Republican nomination for president, and Madison's victory left Monroe politically weak. By 1811, however, he had returned to favor and became secretary of state. He continued in that position throughout the War of 1812 and in 1814–1815 was also secretary of war.

Monroe received the Democratic-Republican nomination for president in 1816 and won an easy victory over a demoralized Federalist Party. His reelection in 1820 was even easier because only one electoral vote was cast against him. Monroe, whose period in office was known as the Era of Good Feelings, was the last president of the so-called Virginia dynasty. In spite of his party's dominance, there were severe tensions in his Administrations with bitter sectional arguments over the tariff, internal improvements, and the expan-

James Monroe, 5th President of the United States (1817–1825), in portrait by John Vanderlyn.

sion of slavery, the last of which resulted in the Missouri Compromise (1820). In foreign policy Monroe was brilliantly served by Secretary of State John Quincy Adams, and it was Adams more than Monroe who was responsible for the famous Monroe Doctrine that formed a part of Monroe's annual message in December 1823.

After leaving the presidency in 1825, Monroe returned to private life in Virginia, emerging in 1829 to serve as president of the Virginia Constitutional Convention. He died in New York City on July 4, 1831.

See also Era of Good Feelings; Louisiana Purchase (1803); Missouri Compromise; Monroe Doctrine.

Consult (III) Ammon, 1971; Dangerfield, 1952.

—Reginald Horsman, *University of Wisconsin, Milwaukee*

MONROE DOCTRINE, a statement of U.S. foreign policy that evolved as a response to two specific problems—European claims to the Northwest Coast and the independence of Latin America. It epitomized attitudes about the position of the United States that had been developing throughout early American history. In the Adams-Onís Treaty of 1819 the United States had eliminated Spanish claims to the territory north of California, but both Russia and Britain still had ambitions on the Pacific Coast. In the early 1820s, Secretary of State John Quincy Adams made it clear to the British and the Russians that he considered the United States to have a natural right to the area.

Since 1808 the Spanish colonies in Latin America had been in revolt against Spain, and in the early 1820s a crisis developed because it appeared possible that other European powers would aid Spain in reconquering these colonies. Britain also feared such an intervention and suggested a joint Anglo-American declaration to resist such action.

The anxiety about South America became the occasion for the Monroe Doctrine. Adams urged the cabinet to reject the British request and to make a clear American statement of policy. President Monroe decided that this should be done in his annual message to Congress. He based much of his foreign policy message on Adams' ideas and even language, but he also shaped it to suit himself. What became known as the Monroe Doctrine consisted of two separate passages in Monroe's annual message of Dec. 2, 1823.

The first principle was that the American continents "are henceforth not to be considered as subjects for future colonization by any European powers." The second was that the United States would consider any attempt by the European powers to extend their system to the American continents as dangerous to American peace and safety: the United States would not interfere in Europe, and Europe should not interfere in the United States. The doctrine was revived by President Polk in the 1840s and gradually became an established principle of American foreign policy.

See also Adams-Onís Treaty (1819).
Consult (III) Perkins, 1955; Tatum, 1936.
—Reginald Horsman, *University of Wisconsin, Milwaukee*

MONTANA, the 41st state, entered the Union on Nov. 8, 1889. Montana came under U.S. jurisdiction as part of the Louisiana Purchase in 1803 and was explored by Lewis and Clark in 1805–1806. Gold strikes, which began in 1852 and lasted until about 1864, brought the first permanent settlers to the state; territorial recognition came in 1864. Indians, particularly the Sioux, dominated the area, but Indian resistance finally was put down in 1881.

The state legislature is bicameral; the capital is Helena. The population in 1970 was 694,409.

MONTEVIDEO CONFERENCE (1933). *See* Latin American Conferences.

MORAVIANS. *See* Colonial Religion.

MORGAN, J(OHN) PIERPONT (1837–1913), investment banker who became the leading U.S. symbol of finance capitalism. Born in Connecticut, he received his apprenticeship in finance in his father's London banking house and acted as its New York agent (1860–1864). He was a member of Dabney, Morgan & Company from 1864 to 1871 and in 1871 formed Drexel, Morgan & Company, which in 1895 became J. P. Morgan & Company. Under his leadership the firm became one of the world's leading banking houses.

Morgan, like other investment bankers, was committed to eliminating the chaotic, competitive business conditions that characterized the expansive economic environment of the late nineteenth century. In pursuit of stability, he first reorganized the major Eastern railroad lines. The results were both a more integrated railroad system and, because he always demanded centralized financial control, a vast concentration of power in Morgan's hands. Anticipating ruinous competition in the steel industry, he purchased the Carnegie Steel Company (1901) and reorganized the major competing firms into the U.S. Steel Corporation.

In 1895, during a financial panic, the federal government was forced to borrow $62 million in gold through Morgan's banking house in order to replenish the Treasury reserves. No event in Morgan's career demonstrated so vividly to the general public the power and influence that he exerted over the nation's economic life.

Renowned as an art collector, Morgan's collection, valued at more than $50 million at the time of his death, was one of the largest private collections ever assembled. It was given by his son, J. Pierpont Morgan, Jr., to the Metropolitan Museum of Art.

Consult (V) Allen, 1949; Josephson, 1934.
—Seddie Cogswell, *California State University, San Francisco*

MORGENTHAU, HENRY, JR. (1891–1969), Secretary of the Treasury (1934–1945). The son of Henry Morgenthau, a prominent Democrat and diplomat, he attended Cornell University and in 1913 began farming in Dutchess County, N.Y., where he became a close friend of Franklin D. Roosevelt. In the early days of the New Deal, Morgenthau headed the Farm Credit Administration.

In January 1934, Roosevelt appointed Morgenthau Treasury secretary. He retained the post longer than any of his predecessors except Albert Gallatin and spent more money than all of them combined. A nervous, irascible, suspicious man, Morgenthau was a tireless worker and a devoted servant of the President. He presided over the transfer of financial power from Wall Street to Washington, and his influence increasingly extended into foreign policy.

An uncompromising opponent of Nazi Germany, he coordinated British and French munitions purchases in the United States in 1939 and 1940 and played an important role in the early lend-lease program. He is best remembered for the Morgenthau Plan, devised in 1944, which would have stripped Germany of its industrial capacity and partitioned it into several weak agricultural states. At first sympathetic to the proposal, Roosevelt later dropped it and Morgenthau's influence declined. He did not get along with President Truman and resigned in July 1945. He subsequently devoted himself to philanthropies.

See also Lend-Lease.
Consult (VII) Blum, 1959–1968.
—George Herring, *University of Kentucky*

MORMONS, more properly, Church of Jesus Christ of Latter-Day Saints, religious group founded by Joseph Smith on April 6, 1830, at Fayette, New York. The religion is based on the *Book of Mormon*, which is believed by the Latter-Day Saints to be a lost section of the Bible describing a tribe of Israelites that lived in America. Prophet Smith claimed that an angel gave him a set of gold plates with the "true gospel" written in hieroglyphics on Sept. 22, 1827. It took Smith two years to translate the entire book, which was published as the *Book of Mormon* in 1830.

Smith, his brother, and some close friends gathered thousands of followers in the

J. Pierpont Morgan built one of the world's most powerful banking houses.

Mormon wagon train pushes west toward Utah, the one area in which Mormons were not persecuted.

229

Inventor of the telegraph Samuel F. B. Morse.

New York area. However, religious persecution followed them as they fled from New York and eventually settled at Nauvoo, Ill., where the industrious Mormons built prosperous farms, drilled their militia, and voted as a unit, thus exerting enormous political power. Moreover, there were rumors that the Mormons were practicing polygamy and that Smith himself had several wives. Non-Mormons resented all this; when Joseph Smith ordered the destruction of a critical newspaper, he was jailed. He escaped but returned and was lynched in 1844.

The Mormons fled Nauvoo, and Brigham Young assumed leadership. He organized a Western trek to found Zion, and Mormons spent the 1846–1847 winter in camps strung out across Nebraska and Iowa; the advance parties were to clear the way and plant crops. In 1848 the Mormons reached Utah, where they founded Salt Lake City. They formed a cooperative community and used irrigation to plant crops in the desert, and in two years the population grew to 11,000. Many of the settlers were European converts. Young sent settlers to other areas of the Great Basin, and the towns of Ogden and Provo were founded; he proclaimed the entire area the State of Deseret.

The area was granted territorial status in 1850 with Young as governor. His refusal to accept orders from Washington led to the intervention of federal troops, and the issue of polygamy delayed statehood. Young died in 1877, the Mormons renounced polygamy in 1890, and Utah statehood followed in 1896.

See also Utah; Young, Brigham.

MORRILL ACT (1862) established many technical and agricultural colleges through land grants in the Midwest and Far West. In response to long-term pressure for vocational training facilities, Representative Justin Morrill introduced a land-grant bill in 1857, but it was vetoed by President Buchanan. A similar bill signed by President Lincoln on July 2, 1862, has been called the Morrill Act.

Under the act, each state was endowed with 30,000 acres per representative and senator. In some states the land went to existing schools, while in other states it proved an impetus for founding new institutions. The act was amended in later years. Under the provisions of the act more than 13 million acres have been distributed and about 70 colleges have been founded.

MORRILL TARIFF (1861) raised tariff levels. *See* Tariffs.

MORRIS, GOUVERNEUR (1752–1816), Revolutionary War statesman and diplomat. Born into a wealthy and prominent New York land-owning family, Morris became a lawyer. Learned, intelligent, and witty, he was also very conservative. He was not enthusiastic about the Revolutionary movement, fearing in particular its democratic social and political implications, but he reluctantly supported independence.

During 1776 he served in New York's provincial congress, where he helped write the state's constitution. He also tried, without success, to bring about the abolition of slavery. Morris then served as a member of the Continental Congress (1777–1779). After failing to be reelected to Congress in 1779, he moved to Philadelphia and began practice as a lawyer. He quickly became involved in local politics and allied himself closely with Robert Morris (no relation), who was attempting to strengthen the Articles of Confederation. As a delegate from Pennsylvania to the Constitutional Convention of 1787, he played an extremely active role in the proceedings.

Following the convention he moved back to New York and two years later went to Europe, where he pursued business ventures and traveled for the next decade. Upon his return he became a senator from New York (1800–1803), but like many other outspoken members of the defeated Federalist Party he went into permanent political retirement during the first decade of the nineteenth century. He remained an eloquent but ineffective proponent of aristocratic privilege until his death.

See also Articles of Confederation.

Consult (III) Mintz, 1970.

—Richard E. Ellis, *University of Virginia*

MORRIS, ROBERT (1734–1806), superintendent of finance during the Revolutionary War. Born in England, he emigrated to America at 13 and by 1754 had become a partner in the business firm of Willing, Morris, and Company. Morris was a delegate to the First Continental Congress and a member of the Pennsylvania Committee of Safety in 1775.

Elected to the Second Continental Congress, Morris doubted the wisdom of breaking with England immediately but nevertheless signed the Declaration of Independence and served as chairman of the committee on finance. He used his talents to procure vessels, arms, and munitions for the patriots and, always aware of his personal economic interest, made large profits on these transactions as compensation for his risks. Morris returned to the Pennsylvania legislature in 1778 but suffered embarrassment when his company was charged with fraud. An investigation exonerated Morris, and after a defeat in 1779 he was again reelected in 1780.

On May 14, 1781, Morris accepted Congress' appointment as superintendent of finance. He planned to bring order to the chaotic state of American finances by putting government spending on a specie basis. In January 1783, Morris used a $200,000 loan from France to open the Bank of North America, which was to assist the government's fiscal operations. Lack of cooperation by the states hampered Morris' efforts, and he resigned in 1784.

Morris' experiences made him a staunch supporter of the U.S. Constitution, and he served as one of Pennsylvania's first senators (1789–1795). The economic fluctuations accompanying the Napoleonic wars ruined Morris, who spent more than three years (1798–1801) in debtors' prison and died a forgotten man.

Consult (II) Ver Steeg, 1954.
—Thomas Archdeacon, *University of Wisconsin*

MORSE, SAMUEL F(INLEY) B(REESE) (1791–1872), American painter and inventor, son of the New England geographer Jedidiah Morse (1761–1826). A well-known portrait painter, he studied art in London (under Benjamin West) and Paris and helped to establish the National Academy of Design in 1825. Morse gave up art because he thought there was no public for it in the United States.

His interest in electromagnetism (studied first at Yale) had been stimulated in Paris, and after his final return to the United States in 1832 Morse worked for many years trying to perfect his idea for an electric telegraph to transmit messages. He invented the Morse code for this purpose and in 1844 sent a message ("What hath God wrought!") from Baltimore to Washington.

The telegraph helped to unify the American nation. It made business deals possible at great speed and it enabled the railroads to communicate from station to station, thus increasing safety and therefore travel speeds (telegraph lines usually followed railroad lines). Later, Morse experimented with the New England entrepreneur Cyrus W. Field (1819–1892) in transmissions by undersea cable. Field laid the first transatlantic cable in 1858, but it broke and was not permanently secured until 1866.

Politically, Morse was very prejudiced. He was an outspoken nativist, who felt that immigrants and aliens were trying to overthrow American democracy. In 1835 he published *The Imminent Dangers to the Free Institutions of the U.S. through Foreign Immigration,* which attacked Catholics as "papal puppets" and spies. In the 1840s he was president of the American Protestant Union, a virulent Catholic-hating group, and in the 1850s he supported the Know-Nothing Party.

See also Inventions.

MOTT, LUCRETIA (1793–1880), Quaker minister who was led by her egalitarian beliefs to prominence in both the antislavery and women's rights movements. A teacher and mother of six, Mott was trained as a public speaker in the Quaker ministry, to which she was admitted in 1821. A lifelong opponent of slavery, she began in 1833 by supporting the American Anti-Slavery Society and helping to organize a women's counterparty, the Philadelphia Female Anti-Slavery Society. An active spokeswoman for immediate emancipation, Mott displayed great courage in the face of antiabolitionist mobs and harbored fugitive slaves in her home.

In 1840 she served as delegate to the World's Anti-Slavery Convention in London, where women were denied recognition. The experience inspired her, along with Elizabeth Cady Stanton, whom she met in London, to initiate the women's rights movement at the 1848 Seneca Falls Convention, of which her husband, James Mott, was chairman.

See also Seneca Falls Convention (1848).
Consult (III) Tolles, 1952.

Early women's rights leader Lucretia Mott.

MUCKRAKERS, American journalists, novelists, and critics who, during the early part of the twentieth century, attempted to expose abuses by big business and corruption in politics. The term was borrowed from John Bunyan's reference in *Pilgrim's Progress* to "the man with the Muckrake" and was first popularized by President Theodore Roosevelt in a speech in 1906 in which he agreed with many of the charges of the Muckrakers but criticized some of their methods as sensational and irresponsible.

Muckraking emerged in force with the January 1903 issue of *McClure's Magazine* with articles exposing abuses of government, labor, and trusts written by Lincoln Steffens, Ray Stannard Baker, and Ida Tarbell. Public demand for regulation of large combines was also generated by Charles Edward Russell's exposé of the beef trust, Thomas Lawson's of Amalgamated Copper, and Upton Sinclair's report on the meat packing industry, *The Jungle.*

See also Steffens, Lincoln; Tarbell, Ida.

MUGWUMPS, sneering term that regular Republicans used to describe the independents who refused to support James G. Blaine for president in 1884. The term derived from the Algonkian word for "big chief" and implied that Mugwumps acted as if they were above party loyalty. The spiritual heirs of the Liberal Republicans of 1872, Mugwumps believed in honest politics, civil service reform, and an end to excessive centralization in government. The Mugwumps considered Blaine corrupt, and most backed Grover Cleveland. They are often given credit for the Democratic victory.

MUHAMMAD, ELIJAH, Black Muslim leader. *See* Black Muslims.

MULLER v. OREGON (1908), crucial Supreme Court case both for women's history and for the evolution of "sociological jurisprudence."

Muckraker Upton Sinclair exposed conditions in meat industry in *The Jungle* (1906).

Following agreement in Munich, Prime Minister Chamberlain *(left)* and Adolf Hitler shake hands. The agreement came to symbolize the atmosphere of appeasement before World War II.

Works of Charles Ives were largely unrecognized until after he had stopped composing.

In *Lochner v. New York* (1905), the Court nullified a New York State law limiting hours for night work in bakeries on the grounds that the law interfered with the freedom of contract between the employer and his men.

In *Muller v. Oregon*, however, the Court upheld an Oregon law that limited women's work hours, on the grounds that women needed the protection of the police power of the state because they were the weaker sex. The case was won by Louis Brandeis. His argument presented medical, economic, and social data to support the notion of sexual inequality and noted "the widespread belief that woman's physical structure and . . . functions . . . justify special legislation restricting . . . the conditions under which she should be permitted to toil." Women's liberation leaders of the 1960s and 1970s often rejected this idea and sought to overturn the special laws that protect women's labor.

See also Brandeis, Louis D.
Consult (VI) Mason, 1956.

MUNICH CONFERENCE (SEPTEMBER 1938), meeting among Prime Ministers Neville Chamberlain of Britain and Edouard Daladier of France and Germany's Adolf Hitler. The agreement they signed on Czechoslovakia provided for the Czech evacuation of the Sudetenland in return for Hitler's declaration that Germany and Britain would "never go to war with one another again."

The Munich agreement amounted to an experiment in British-German understanding at the expense of Czechoslovakia. The United States expressed satisfaction that a serious crisis had been averted and a method worked out for peaceful settlement of boundary disputes. It was only after 1938, when Hitler annexed most of Czechoslovakia and attacked Poland, that the policy was discredited.

Consult (VII) Offner, 1969.

MUNN v. ILLINOIS (1877), one of the Granger cases, involved in 1873 Illinois law fixing rates that could be charged by grain warehousemen. The Granger movement of the early 1870s had secured laws in several Midwestern states regulating rates for railroads and other farm-related enterprises. Chicago grain warehousemen challenged the constitutionality of the 1873 law on the grounds that it infringed on the interstate commerce power of the federal government and violated the due process clause of the Fourteenth Amendment.

The Supreme Court ruled 7 to 2 that the Illinois law and similar acts were constitutional inasmuch as private property devoted to a public use is a fit subject for public regulation, and such regulation did not violate the due process clause. In dissent, Justice Stephen J. Field argued that procedural due process was insufficient protection for property rights, a

view that was to triumph before the end of the century.

See also Granger Movement.

MUSIC. American music stretches back to songs and dances from Indian tribal rituals, now being collected and studied, that can be traced to prehistoric times. The earliest European settlers brought music with them from their homeland so that the colonies had a wide-ranging musical culture. By 1700, Americans could support themselves by going into music as a career—choirmasters, teachers, performers, and composers. One of the most famous composers during these early years was William Billings (1746–1800), who wrote hymns and marching tunes.

It was not until fairly recently, however, that American music developed a real distinction of its own. Even though eighteenth- and nineteenth-century America was growing as a nation, music was still regarded as a luxury. An aspiring composer usually had to study in Europe; it was natural, therefore, that he would create music in the European manner. American composers in the nineteenth century—William Henry Fry, John Knowles Paine, George Wakefield Chatwick, and Edward MacDowell—were popular and frequently played, but most of their music was little more than skillful imitations of the great Europeans.

The Beginnings of American Music. The first native American to attempt a truly American music was Louis Moreau Gottschalk (1829–1869), a strange, flamboyant, near genius of part-Creole ancestry. Gottschalk took Creole and black folk tunes and fashioned them into large-scale works for piano, chorus, or orchestra. A piano virtuoso himself, he toured Europe with his own new American music and won great respect for this growing native art.

Gottschalk had no immediate successors, but 50 years later his techniques were imitated and much enlarged upon by another American individualist, Charles Ives. He, too, drew much of his material from native sources—the hymns he had played at his Connecticut church, popular songs, dances, and marches. He combined these tunes in symphonies and other large-scale compositions, often jamming them together in a fashion so highly dissonant and original that his music was dismissed in its time as utterly mad. Not until about 1960, nearly 50 years after Ives had retired, were his works rediscovered. By that time the world was more attuned to his daring practices, and he was widely hailed as a major innovator.

The Search for America. America's emergence as a world power in the early twentieth century was accompanied by a growing self-awareness by American composers. As if to make up for lost time, they applied themselves to the creation of a distinctly American music. To this end they continued the search for materials from popular and folk sources.

George Gershwin's "Rhapsody in Blue" and "Concerto in F for Piano" were attempts to give a symphonic status to jazz. A group of composers—among them Aaron Copland, Virgil Thomson, and Walter Piston—studied in Paris with the famous Nadia Boulanger in the 1920s and were sent home with the dictum to make America musically self-sufficient. The results of this can be found in such works as Copland's Wild West ballets *Rodeo* and *Billy the Kid,* Thomson's opera *Four Saints in Three Acts,* and a host of other works that pulled the whole expanse of popular American culture into the concert hall and the opera house.

Declarations of Independence. This "American" phase of American music ended more or less at the end of World War II, when America no longer needed self-conscious musical reminders of its status. The aim of Americans, instead, was to write important music in the mainstream of world culture. Older men such as Wallingford Riegger, Carl Ruggles, and Roger Sessions and younger composers such as Gunther Schuller, Andrew Imbrie, George Rochberg, and Salvatore Martirano expanded musical language by exploring the latest European currents—the twelve-tone techniques of Arnold Schoenberg, the hard clarity of Igor Stravinsky's attempts to revive classicism, and the efforts of men such as Paul Hindemith to keep alive the spirit of musical romanticism.

By the mid-1950s, an American avant-garde movement had gained dominance over the musical world. The experiments of John Cage to create music out of any available means (traffic noise, electronic sounds, even silence), the penetrating experiments of Milton Babbitt and Earle Brown with tape music and works produced by computer expanded the definition of a musical experience.

Performance. Musical life in America, like American music itself, began as a frank imitation of European methods. As early as 1820, groups of Italian singers came to New York, Boston, and Philadelphia to introduce the latest European works. By 1850 permanent grand-opera companies were established in most large American cities using primarily European singers and conductors. The first major American symphony orchestra, the New York Philharmonic, was established in 1842 and was followed by ensembles in Boston and St. Louis. As with the opera companies, the repertoire was largely European, although a few works by American composers were occasionally performed.

By 1900 most large American cities had an established musical life supported and patronized by the aristocracy. Famous musical artists—Ignace Paderewski, Fritz Kreisler, Enrico Caruso, and others—toured the country. But not until World War I, when soprano Rosa Ponselle and baritone Lawrence Tibbett triumphed at New York's Metropolitan Opera House, did the possibility that there could be distinguished American artists become clear. Even so, it was not until 1943, when Leonard Bernstein conducted for a nationwide radio audience, that American performing musicians really came into their own. Bernstein became in 1958 the first native regular conductor of a major orchestra. That same year, the American pianist Van Cliburn triumphed at the prestigious Tchaikovsky competition in Moscow.

Opera also accepted Americans slowly. During World War II, when travel to and from Europe was limited, several bright young Americans became established at the Metropolitan Opera and went on to distinguished careers. In 1944 New York got its second company, the New York City Opera, which specialized in American performers and composers.

See also Bernstein, Leonard; Folk Music; Jazz.

Consult (VIII) Cowell, 1962; Hitchcock, 1969; Mellers, 1965.

—Alan Rich, *Music Critic, New York Magazine*

NAACP. *See* National Association for the Advancement of Colored People.

NASHVILLE CONVENTION, meeting held by Southern political leaders in June 1850 to discuss slavery. The call for the meeting was issued in October 1849 to protest legislation providing for the admission of California and New Mexico as nonslave states. Before the Convention met, the Compromise of 1850, which provided that Congress would take no action toward slavery in these two states, was reached.

This solution satisfied the Southerners for the time being, so the Convention was held under relatively calm circumstances. Resolutions were passed denying Congress the right to exclude slavery from the territories, rejecting the Compromise of 1850, and demanding that the Missouri Compromise line be extended to the Pacific Ocean. Southern secession was postponed, but the Convention did increase sectional conflict and demonstrated the capacity of Southern leaders to take joint action on the slave issue.

See also Compromise of 1850; Missouri Compromise (1820).

Consult (IV) Cole, 1971.

NATIONAL AMERICAN WOMAN SUFFRAGE ASSOCIATION, group formed in 1890 by merger of National and American Woman Suffrage Associations. *See* Suffrage, Women's.

Composer George Gershwin used jazz forms in such works as *Porgy and Bess.*

Leonard Bernstein dramatically conducts the New York Philharmonic in 1965.

Opera singer Leontyne Price jokes with Rudolf Bing, General Manager of Metropolitan Opera.

NATIONAL ASSOCIATION FOR THE ADVANCEMENT OF COLORED PEOPLE (NAACP),

the oldest and largest U.S. civil rights group. Founded in 1910 by W. E. B. Du Bois, the black educator and writer, and seven white Americans, the organization devoted its earliest efforts to ending the widespread practice of lynching.

From its inception the NAACP has advocated nonviolence and eschewed extremist methods, working primarily through the courts to achieve black civil rights. Its Legal Defense and Educational Fund, which was for many years headed by Thurgood Marshall, brought to court cases involving discrimination in education, voting, travel, public facilities, and the racial composition of juries. Winning 29 of the 32 cases it argued before the Supreme Court, the NAACP's greatest legal victory came in 1954, when the Court, in *Brown v. Board of Education,* ruled segregation in the public schools to be unlawful.

The association has been criticized for being overly moderate. Having disavowed Black Power's separatism, the NAACP continues to seek legal compliance with federal civil rights laws.

See also Brown v. Board of Education of Topeka (1954).

NATIONAL ASSOCIATION OF MANUFACTURERS,

a powerful lobbying organization for business interests organized at Cincinnati in 1895. Its purpose has been to identify major problems and to inform both the government and the general public of its proposals. From its beginning the Association has expounded the doctrines of economic individualism and throughout most of its history has opposed organized labor as an impediment to free employment. However, its advocacy of economic individualism has never been consistent with a strict interpretation of laissez-faire, because the Association has always actively supported such probusiness governmental measures as the protective tariff, internal improvements, tax concessions, and direct subsidies.

Early activities of National Association of Manufacturers were directed against unions.

NATIONAL BANKING SYSTEM (1863–1864),

a national system of interlocking banks chartered by the federal government and subject to numerous federal controls and reserve rules. The National Currency Acts of 1863 and 1864 were passed in an attempt to bring order to the fragmented and sometimes unscrupulous banking industry, and they created a great many national banks. Beginning in 1865 the government taxed the notes of the state-chartered banks to drive them out of circulation, thus giving the field to national bank notes.

The supply of these notes did not vary enough to meet changing currency demands, a situation that, combined with the cash reserve system, contributed to the economic difficulties in the Panics of 1873, 1884, 1893, 1903, and 1907. The lack of a central bank that could act to help prevent crises was another serious fault, one that was not corrected until the formation of the Federal Reserve System in 1913. But by establishing many small banks, the National Banking System avoided the deep prejudice against central banking that had been created by the Bank of the United States in earlier years.

See also Federal Reserve System; Panics, Financial (Nineteenth Century).

Consult (III) Jones, 1965.

NATIONAL COLORED FARMERS' ALLIANCE,

a farmers' group organized during the 1880s, along with other farmers' alliances, to protest the plight of the farmer vis-à-vis big business. By 1891 the Colored Alliance had 700,000 members. It was particularly strong in the Southern states and was one of the farmers' alliances that met in St. Louis in December 1889 to consolidate the farmers' organization. However, the Colored Alliance, because of its black membership, was also the reason that this move toward unity failed; Southern white alliance groups refused to join a consolidation that included blacks.

See also Farmers' Alliances.

NATIONAL DEFENSE ACT (1916),

part of the preparedness legislation of 1916, created the Council of National Defense. The council had six cabinet members aided by an advisory commission of business, industry, and labor leaders. It inventoried the nation's industrial capacity and set up the Munitions Board, which was replaced by the crucial War Industries Board in 1917.

Meanwhile, the act, short of adopting national conscription (which Wilson wished to avoid) enlarged the regular army and the National Guard. In 1916, the hope was still alive that America could be defended by a purely volunteer army.

See also War Industries Board.

NATIONAL DEFENSE EDUCATION ACT (NDEA) (1958),

federal aid-to-education law administered by the Office of Education and conceived as an emergency measure to develop mental resources and technical skills, particularly in science, mathematics, and modern languages. Eligible college and university students were granted loans. Grants were made for new school laboratories, language training, and counselors of bright high school students, and national defense scholarships were made available to graduate students intending to teach at the college level.

NATIONAL FARMERS' ALLIANCE, also known

as the Northern Alliance, early farmers organization. *See* Farmers' Alliances.

NATIONAL INDUSTRIAL RECOVERY ACT (NIRA) (1933),

New Deal legislation passed during the Hundred Days. It granted the president broad discretionary power to establish and enforce codes of fair competition in industry. For over a year business groups had fostered a plan whereby the business community itself, through trade associations, could control production, wages, and prices and thus facilitate recovery from the Depression. They hoped to end destructive competition, limit production to permit price rises, and at the same time ensure that the government would refrain from initiating antitrust suits. President Roosevelt's Brains Trust drew up a bill that incorporated many of the features business and industry wanted plus some governmental controls and some protection for labor. The National Recovery Administration was set up, and one of the Brains Trust members, Hugh S. Johnson, was appointed administrator.

See also Brains Trust; Hundred Days; National Recovery Administration.

Consult (VI) Johnson, 1935; Schlesinger, 1959.

NATIONAL LABOR RELATIONS ACT (1935),

also known as the Wagner Act, outlawed unfair practices against unions and guaranteed organized labor the right to bargain collectively. In 1933 President Roosevelt had established a National Labor Board, chaired by Senator Robert F. Wagner, to carry out the intent of Section 7a of the National Industrial Recovery Act, that is, to settle labor disputes and uphold the right to bargain. In 1934 FDR replaced this relatively ineffective body with a National Labor Relations Board (NLRB), but Wagner and other congressional supporters of labor were still dissatisfied and sought more far-reaching legislation that would shift the federal government's role from the settlement of disputes to the ensuring of labor's rights.

Roosevelt was unenthusiastic about Wagner's bill, but he became convinced of the need for new legislation just before the Supreme Court declared the National Recovery Administration unconstitutional (*Schechter v. United States,* 1935), thus removing his authority for the first NLRB. The Wagner Act, in addition to establishing a permanent NLRB, outlawed employer interference in organization efforts, discrimination against union members, and blacklists. It made the establishment of company unions more difficult and reaffirmed the right of collective bargaining first put forth in Section 7a.

See also National Industrial Recovery Act; National Recovery Administration; Schechter v. United States (1935).

NATIONAL LABOR RELATIONS BOARD v. JONES AND LAUGHLIN STEEL CORPORATION (1937),

one of several decisions in which the Supreme Court upheld the National Labor Relations Act and thus the New Deal approach to labor-management relations. The case is indicative of the shift on the high court to a new position following President Roosevelt's Court-packing attempt. Ignoring the precedents of *Schechter v. United States* and other anti-New Deal decisions, the Court interpreted the commerce clause in broad terms—a manufacturer who draws raw materials from a variety of sources and ships to other parts of the country is engaged in interstate commerce.

See also Court Packing; National Labor Relations Act; Schechter v. United States (1935).

Consult (VI) Pritchett, 1948.

NATIONAL MILITARY ESTABLISHMENT,

umbrella department established in 1947 to coordinate the Army, Navy, and Air Force. *See* Defense, Department of; National Security Acts (1947, 1949).

NATIONAL MONETARY COMMISSION,

agency established (1908) to report on U.S. and European banking and currency systems. *See* Aldrich-Vreeland Currency Act (1908).

NATIONAL ORGANIZATION FOR WOMEN (NOW),

a civil rights pressure group formed in 1966 to campaign for legislative and economic reforms that will ensure equality for women. The organization, which admits men as well as women, has about 18,000 members. Since its inception, NOW has worked for a "fully equal partnership of the sexes" by promoting such measures as the proposed Equal Rights Amendment, equal employment opportunities, an end to abortion laws, free day-care centers, and an end to discriminatory educational quotas. NOW also seeks to revise state protective laws for women, social security laws, divorce and alimony laws, and to change the mass media's portrayal of women.

See also Women's Liberation.

NATIONAL ORIGINS SYSTEMS,

method of controlling immigration to the United States. *See* Quota System.

NATIONAL RECLAMATION ACT (1902),

or Newlands Act, a major part of President Theodore Roosevelt's conservation program. It decidedly changed federal irrigation policy, which was of great importance in the drier states. The Desert Land Act of 1877 had tried to stimulate private irrigation schemes by quadrupling (from 160 to 640 acres) the free land grants under the Homestead Act to settlers who would agree to water the land. However, fraudulent irrigation companies gained land

Members of the National Organization of Women demonstrate in front of the White House in February 1973.

under the act, and little real irrigation took place. In 1894 the Carey Act offered 1 million acres of federal land to each dry state if the state government would agree to irrigate the land. Again, the results were disappointing and in 1902 the Newlands Act took a more radical step.

The act used money from public land sales to create a revolving federal fund for reclamation costs—dam construction and canal building. Settlers on federal projects still received their homestead land free, but they were to repay (without interest) the cost of the reclamation work. Large irrigation schemes were begun in Arizona, Colorado, Utah, and California, and more than 2 million acres of former wasteland were made to bloom.

By 1915 the government had invested about $80 million in 25 projects, and within a decade these desert states were producing great quantities of fruit and grain. The great American dams were built under the act, the first being the Roosevelt Dam in Arizona.

See also Conservation Acts.
Consult (V) Nash, 1968.

NATIONAL RECOVERY ADMINISTRATION (NRA), agency that epitomized experimentation and innovation in the New Deal. For a time, because of an intense publicity campaign, the Blue Eagle of the NRA and the motto "We do our part" were symbolic of the whole New Deal. Under the NRA, directed by Hugh Johnson, industrial code authorities—one for each industry—were set up to represent management, workers, and consumers. In fact consumers never played an important part in the NRA, and labor's role was more often than not a secondary one. Labor did make one significant gain through the NRA, however. Secretary of Labor Frances Perkins insisted that the legislation include Section 7a, which gave for the first time a federal guarantee of organized labor's right to bargain collectively. This guarantee was later written into the National Labor Relations Act (1935). Before the NRA was declared unconstitutional by the Supreme Court in *Schechter v. United States* (1935), more than 500 industries had adopted codes and had begun to live under them.

See also National Industrial Recovery Act; National Labor Relations Act; Schechter v. United States (1935).
Consult (VI) Johnson, 1935.

NATIONAL REPUBLICANS, a party that arose out of the political restructuring that followed the election of Andrew Jackson as president in 1828. Its nucleus was the old John Quincy Adams-Henry Clay alliance that had given Adams the presidency in 1825. This was the main party of opposition to Jackson. The party was particularly strong in the Northeast and supported the Bank of the United States, a protec-

Employees of Paramount Pictures, including Mae West, proudly display their NRA Blue Eagle, awarded to firms that adhered to the fair competition codes of the National Recovery Administration.

tive tariff, and internal improvements. Among its main leaders were Henry Clay and Daniel Webster.

In the election of 1832, Clay ran for president on the National Republican ticket. He defended the Bank of the United States against the attack of Jackson, but Jackson won a decisive victory. After 1832 the party was expanded by the addition of Southern states' rights advocates and other opponents of Jackson, thus losing much of its philosophical coherence. By 1836 it had broadened to become the Whig Party.

See also Presidential Elections; Whig Party.

NATIONAL ROAD, the first major federally financed road. Originally called the Cumberland Road, it began at Cumberland, Md., and threaded its way west through modern West Virginia, Ohio, Indiana, and Illinois. Survey work began in 1806, but it took until 1811 for the construction contracts to be let. By 1818 it reached Wheeling, and despite President Monroe's veto of funds for repair the next year, work continued. By 1852 the road had inched its way west to Vandalia, Ill., where it stopped. It was well built, with stone bridges and wide shoulders, and quickly became the major east-west land route between the Ohio Valley and the East.

Consult (III) Jorday, 1948.

NATIONAL SECURITY ACTS (1947, 1949) reorganized defense agencies in the wake of World War II. The act of 1947 replaced the War and Navy departments with a National Military Establishment made up of separate Army, Navy, and Air Force departments under a civilian Secretary of Defense. There was no provision for a Defense Department. The secretary and the Joint Chiefs of Staff were named as the president's principal military advisers, and the National Security Council, with a Central Intelligence Agency under it, was created.

The 1949 amendment renamed the National Military Establishment the Department of Defense. The three military departments were incorporated into the new department but were to be separately administered by the secretaries. The law also provided for a nonvoting chairman of the Joint Chiefs of Staff. The service secretaries were removed from the National Security Council, and the vice-president was added.

See also Central Intelligence Agency (CIA); Defense, Department of.

NATIONAL SECURITY LEAGUE, military preparedness organization founded in 1914. *See* Preparedness Movement (1915–1916).

NATIONAL WOMAN SUFFRAGE ASSOCIATION, early feminist group. *See* Anthony,

Susan B.; Stanton, Elizabeth Cady; Suffrage, Women's.

NATIONAL WOMEN'S POLITICAL CAUCUS, a bipartisan political pressure group formed in Washington, D.C., in 1971 "to awaken, organize, and assert the vast political power represented by women." The national caucus, which had organized branches in 48 states by 1972, lobbies in Washington, backs measures such as day care and the proposed Equal Rights Amendment, and opposes legislation that discriminates against women. It supports women candidates and other candidates sensitive to the concerns of women, as well as the selection of women for high government positions and judgeships.

NATIONAL YOUTH ADMINISTRATION, New Deal agency established to serve those not covered by the CCC. *See* Civilian Conservation Corps (CCC).

NATION OF ISLAM, formal name for the Black Muslims. *See* Black Muslims.

NATIVE AMERICAN PARTY, political party formed in July 1845 to protect the interests of native Americans from the competition of millions of European immigrants, mainly Catholics. It paved the way for the rise of the Know-Nothing (American) Party in the 1850s.
See also Know-Nothing Party; Nativist Movements.

NATIVIST MOVEMENTS, efforts to halt the flow of immigrants and prevent the integration of their customs, religious beliefs, and traditions into American society. During the 1830s there was an influx of Irish and German immigrants, and the growth of Catholicism fostered anti-Catholic sentiment. By 1845, such concerns gave rise to the Native American Party and many secret nativist societies. Other nativist organizations were the Order of the Star Spangled Banner, formed in 1850, the Know-Nothing, or American, Party and the American Protective Association, a large, powerful, Republican, anti-Catholic, and antiforeigner force organized in 1887.
See also Immigration; Know-Nothing Party.

NAT TURNER'S REVOLT (1831), the most famous slave uprising. It took place in Southampton County in southern Virginia and acquired symbolic meanings that brought it greater attention than other uprisings. Turner, a slave who possessed high personal magnetism and intelligence, had visions that persuaded him that it was his duty to lead his followers on a mission to exterminate whites. During several days of action around the county seat of

Jerusalem, the insurrectionists, numbering about 70 slaves, killed 57 white men, women, and children. The counterattack by militia and others brought about the indiscriminate death of about 100 slaves, and an additional 20 were executed following trial.

The event resulted in the calling in 1831 of the Virginia Convention, which sought to determine what policy ought to be adopted toward slaves. Southern anxieties were heightened by the insurrection, and more attention was given to abolitionist William Lloyd Garrison. Turner's memory was kept alive by the stirring "confession" that he had made while in prison, and both friends and foes used it for their own purposes. It also inspired Harriet Beecher Stowe's novel *Dred* (1856) and William Styron's *The Confessions of Nat Turner* (1967), which retold the tale from limited sources but with intense imaginativeness.
See also Gabriel's Slave Plot (1800); Slavery; Vesey Slave Uprising; Virginia Convention (1831–1832).
Consult (IX) Styron, 1967; Tragle, 1971.

NATURALISM, a style of literary composition of the late nineteenth and early twentieth centuries stemming from nineteenth-century scientific thought and following in general the biological determinism of Darwin's theory or the economic determinism of Marx. The basic aim of the movement was a detached scientific objectivity in the treatment of natural man, making naturalism less selective but more inclusive than realism. Zola, Flaubert, and the Russian novelists influenced this trend in Europe. In the United States the leaders of the naturalistic movement included Stephen Crane, George Norris, Jack London, and, later, Theodore Dreiser, John Dos Passos, and James T. Farrell.
See also Crane, Stephen; Dreiser, Theodore; Literature.

NATURALIZATION ACT (1798). *See* Alien and Sedition Acts.

NAVAL STORES ACTS, English legislation designed to protect the supplies of raw material for marine industries that it obtained from the North American colonies. In 1705 naval stores were declared enumerated goods (they could be sent only to England or its colonies), and Britain began paying bounties on pitch, hemp, and similar articles. Legislation in 1727 further safeguarded England's maritime interests by limiting severely the cutting of white pines, which were used extensively in shipbuilding.
See also Enumerated Goods.

NAVIGATION ACTS. Parliament first tried to regulate colonial trade during the Interregnum following the execution of Charles I in 1649. Recognizing that the Dutch had established

Nat Turner's Revolt in 1831 alarmed slaveowners throughout the South.

control over most colonial commerce, Parliament in 1651 passed its first Navigation Act, aimed at excluding all but English ships (of which the master and at least half the crew also had to be English) from the colonial trade.

This legislation lapsed with the Restoration of Charles II in 1660, and in the next few years Parliament enunciated an even more comprehensive policy. The Navigation Act of 1660 barred non-English ships from the colonial trade, this time requiring three-fourths of the crews to be English. A new clause created a category of enumerated colonial products— tobacco, sugar, indigo, cotton, and a few others—that could be shipped only to England or to another English colony. The Staple Act of 1663 forced the colonies to obtain almost all Oriental and European imports through England. Evasions of the enumeration clause led to attempts to close loopholes through the Plantation Duty Act (1673) and the comprehensive Navigation Act of 1696. The 1696 act also extended the English customs service to North America and gave jurisdiction over violations to courts of vice-admiralty, which followed Roman rather than English common law and which did not use juries.

Eighteenth Century. Embodied in these measures was the principle that colonies should produce raw materials for the mother country and consume her manufactures in return. Parliament extended this idea through several measures—the Woollens Act (1699), the Hat Act (1732), and the Iron Act (1750), which restricted colonial manufacturing of finished goods in these areas. These restrictions were designed to stimulate colonial production of raw materials. Other legislation encouraged the production of certain items essential to the British, such as naval stores and indigo.

The Molasses Act of 1733 had a rather different purpose. It attempted to bolster the profits of one set of colonies, the West Indies, at the expense of another group, primarily New England. No regulation generated more smuggling than the Molasses Act, which was, in turn, the direct ancestor of the controversial Sugar Act of 1764. The former statute, the first to aim explicitly at taxing the colonies for revenue, cut the molasses duty in half, imposed duties on sugar and wine, and greatly strengthened the powers of the customs establishment. The hostility it aroused fed directly into the discontent that finally produced the Revolution.

Historians still debate the net impact of British mercantilism upon colonial economic development. Most now agree that it did little to discourage overall growth and definitely stimulated naval stores, indigo, iron production, and shipbuilding. But in certain local areas of the economy, such as tobacco culture, it did generate considerable resentment and a

demand for free trade that began to emerge in the pre-Revolutionary decade.

Consult (I) Dickerson, 1951.

—John M. Murrin, *Princeton University*

NAVY, U.S., officially established April 30, 1798, but active since the Revolutionary War. The Navy is part of the Department of Defense and is commanded by the chief of Naval Operations, who is a member of the Joint Chiefs of Staff.

The forerunner of the U.S. Navy won its first victories in the Revolutionary War; John Paul Jones was the best-known commander in the Continental Navy. With the creation of the Naval Department in 1798, the nation's three-ship navy was expanded and was soon fighting pirates off the North African coast (1801–1805). During the War of 1812, the U.S. Navy, bolstered by privateers, fought well, winning most of the single-ship duels but losing many ships.

Money for a modern steel navy was appropriated by Congress in 1883, and by the time of the Spanish-American War (1898) the U.S. Navy ranked fifth in the world; by 1917 it was second. The Navy entered World War I by sending six destroyers to Ireland for antisubmarine duty. During World War II the Navy was instrumental in winning the war in the Pacific, the turning point being the defeat of Japan at the Battle of Midway on June 3–6, 1942. The Navy maintained offshore firing positions and conducted mining and bombing operations in the Vietnam War.

See also articles on major wars and military leaders.

NDEA. *See* National Defense Education Act (NDEA) (1958).

NEBRASKA, the 37th state, admitted to the Union on March 1, 1867. Nebraska came to the United States as part of the Louisiana Purchase (1803), and for a time the Nebraska Territory extended north to the Canadian border. The first white men to enter the area were Lewis and Clark. Settlement in the area was spurred by the passage of the Homestead Act and the completion of the Union-Pacific Railroad. Nebraska gained territorial status in 1854 by the Kansas-Nebraska Act.

The state legislature is unicameral and nonpartisan; the capital is Lincoln. The population in 1970 was 1,483,791.

See also Kansas-Nebraska Act (1854).

NEOCOLONIALISM, condition that exists when any nation becomes heavily dependent on another for its major economic markets. Thus, several Latin American nations, although they gained their political independence in the 1820s, became economies that produced staple agricultural crops for sale to more industrially

British officials were often insensitive to American complaints about the Navigation Acts and then were shocked as violence mounted.

developed Europe and North America. Cuba depended entirely on the United States as its sugar market and for many years had to buy finished goods from the United States.

Within the United States, the South before the Civil War had become a "colony" of the North because it was an agricultural, staple-exporting region, whereas the Northeast was a manufacturing region. The South had to import all the finished goods and tools it needed because it overspecialized in cotton exports.

NEOMERCANTILISM. *See* Mercantilism.

NEUTRALITY ACT (1794). *See* Neutrality Proclamation.

NEUTRALITY ACTS, series of acts that clearly revealed the American people's determination to stay out of foreign complications in the 1930s. The act of 1935 provided for an arms embargo against all belligerents abroad, and in 1936 the embargo was extended to loans. The impetus for these acts was given by Senate hearings purportedly showing that the American sale of arms and munitions on long-term credits had inexorably involved the country in war in 1917. The 1937 neutrality act gave the president authority to apply a "cash and carry" principle to all trade. A foreign country could purchase commodities in the United States as long as it paid for them and carried them away in its own ships, thus keeping the United States free of entanglement.

However, President Roosevelt came to feel that neutrality acts were not really neutral; by failing to make a distinction between aggressor and victim, the United States was in reality siding with the former. It seemed that the only way to maintain neutrality was to enable victims of aggression to obtain arms and supplies in the United States. Thus in 1939, shortly after the outbreak of World War II, Congress passed a new neutrality act that placed arms exports under the cash and carry provision. This was a step toward American support of Britain, China, and other countries that was confirmed by the Lend-Lease Act of 1941.

See also Lend-Lease.
Consult (VI) Divine, 1962.
—Akira Iriye, *University of Chicago*

NEUTRALITY PROCLAMATION, statement issued by President Washington on April 22, 1793, in response to the news that France had declared war on Britain and that the European war had become general. The proclamation stated that the United States should pursue "a conduct friendly and impartial toward the belligerent powers" and that U.S. citizens were not to aid either side.

The proclamation meant that the United States was not construing the French Alliance of 1778 to mean that the United States had to offer aid to France in this new war against Britain. The Neutrality Act of June 5, 1794, gave legislative endorsement to Washington's proclamation and provided the necesssary regulations to prevent Americans from giving aid to the belligerents.

See also French Alliance.

NEVADA, the 36th state, admitted on Oct. 31, 1864. The first whites to explore the Nevada area, Jedediah Smith and Peter Ogden, came in the 1820s, and the first permanent settlement was Mormon Station (now Genoa) in 1851. The area was ceded to the United States by Mexico in 1848. Nevada became part of Utah Territory in 1850 and gained territorial status on its own in 1861. The Comstock lode strike in 1859 increased the flow of settlers but not enough to satisfy the population requirements for statehood; Nevada was admitted without the requisite population.

The state legislature is bicameral; the capital is Carson City. The population in 1970 was 488,738.

See also Gold Rushes; Mormons.

NEW DEAL, general label used by President Roosevelt to designate his programs of domestic relief and reform during the Great Depression. The New Deal was characterized by intense activity on the part of Congress and the executive branch, and after 1937, New Dealers served on the Supreme Court. President Roosevelt was an active legislator and was a principal author and sponsor of much New Deal legislation, although some items such as the Tennessee Valley Authority (TVA) and the National Labor Relations Act were primarily congressional in origin. New Deal legislation was often makeshift and contradictory—the product of many traditions and ideologies and political groups. New Dealers themselves came from a variety of backgrounds: there were progressive Republicans and Wilsonian idealists, professional politicians and social workers, agrarians and representatives of urban minorities, intellectuals from the great universities, and labor leaders.

The Hundred Days (March–June 1933). The early weeks of the New Deal saw the President and Congress busily attempting to restore confidence in the economy. A special session of Congress endorsed a presidential program taking the nation off the gold standard, closing all banks, and providing for the judicious reopening of only the strongest. It also passed an economy bill aimed at balancing the budget. For one hundred days Congress rubber-stamped Roosevelt's recovery measures as well as a number of long-range reforms such

"Doctor—'Maybe This Will Do the Trick.'"

NEW DEAL AND DEPRESSION

THE DEPRESSION

DEPRESSION
HERBERT CLARK HOOVER
LONDON ECONOMIC CONFERENCE
WELFARE STATE
WELFARE LEGISLATION

THE NEW DEAL

NEW DEAL

Major Figures

FRANKLIN D. ROOSEVELT
    BRAINS TRUST
    COURT PACKING
    EXECUTIVE REORGANIZATION
        ACT (1939)
    FIRESIDE CHATS
ELEANOR ROOSEVELT
FIORELLO LA GUARDIA
HARRY L. HOPKINS
HUEY LONG

HUNDRED DAYS

Legislation

Farm
AGRICULTURE ADJUSTMENT ACT (1933)
BANKHEAD-JONES FARM TENANT ACT (1937)
RESETTLEMENT ADMINISTRATION
RURAL ELECTRIFICATION ADMINISTRATION

General
FEDERAL EMERGENCY RELIEF ACT (1933)
FEDERAL HOUSING ADMINISTRATION
SOCIAL SECURITY ACT (1935)
WAGNER-STEAGALL ACT (1937)

Works Projects
CIVILIAN CONSERVATION CORPS
CIVIL WORKS ADMINISTRATION
PUBLIC WORKS ADMINISTRATION
TENNESSEE VALLEY AUTHORITY
WORK PROJECTS ADMINISTRATION

Labor and Business
COMMUNICATIONS ACT (1934)
FAIR LABOR STANDARDS ACT (1938)
NATIONAL INDUSTRIAL RECOVERY ACT (1933)
    NATIONAL RECOVERY ADMINISTRATION
    SCHECTER V. UNITED STATES (1935)
NATIONAL LABOR RELATIONS ACT (1935)
    NATIONAL LABOR RELATIONS BOARD V.
      JONES AND LAUGHLIN STEEL CO. (1937)
ROBINSON-PATMAN ACT (1936)
BUSINESS REGULATION (see Subject Map)

Financial
GLASS-STEAGALL ACT (1933)
REVENUE ACT (1935)
SECURITIES EXCHANGE ACT (1934)

The Subject Maps in the Encyclopedia illustrate the coverage of particular aspects of American History, showing the interrelationships among the articles in twelve critical areas of study. Entries in capital letters, except for titles, are subjects for which there are separate articles in the Encyclopedia.

The Subject Maps are arranged alphabetically in the Encyclopedia under the following titles:

American Wars
Blacks in the United States
Business Regulation and Industrialization
Civil War and Reconstruction
Constitution of the United States
Exploration and Colonization
Frontier in American History
Indians
Labor Movement
New Deal and Depression
Revolutionary War Era
Slavery and Emancipation

as the TVA and the Federal Deposit Insurance Corporation, which insured bank deposits. More far-reaching restrictions on banks, speculators, and the purveyors of securities followed. The Securities and Exchange Commission was established in 1934 to oversee many aspects of the stock market.

Relief to Reform. There was no clear-cut turn from relief to reform in the New Deal. Relief continued until World War II, much of it dependent on deficit spending. By 1935 relief programs were revamped to provide massive aid to the unemployed and the poor—the Work Projects Administration (WPA) aided millions of people through a variety of programs. The National Youth Administration was provided to assist the young who had not yet entered the labor market. The Farm Security Administration was established to help migrant workers and farm labor untouched by the benefits of the Agricultural Adjustment Act—and to sponsor experimental cooperative communities. Congress also recognized for the first time the right of unions to bargain collectively. Other permanent reforms—essentially a moderate welfare state—were legislated beginning in 1935: social security, an expanded progressive income tax, and federally financed public housing.

Consult (VI) Schlesinger, 1959, 1960.
—Allen Kifer, *Skidmore College*

NEW ENGLAND ANTI-SLAVERY SOCIETY. *See* Abolitionism; Garrison, William Lloyd.

NEW ENGLAND CONFEDERATION (1643), the first attempt in American history to unite some of the colonies in a federal organization. It was later a model for the Confederation of 1777. Four colonies—Massachusetts, Plymouth, Connecticut, and New Haven—combined and created a Board of Commissioners of eight men, two from each colony, selected by the legislatures. This board of the "United Colonies of New England" had authority to declare war, to supervise Indian affairs, and to mediate intercolonial disputes, particularly boundary questions.

The confederation grew out of colonial experience in fighting the Pequot War (1637); its greatest success was in King Philip's War (1675–1676). Generally the board was too weak and only advisory to the colonies, which jealously guarded their rights. Rhode Island was never allowed to join, because Massachusetts opposed it. In 1684 the revocation of the Massachusetts charter brought the confederation to its formal end.

See also King Philip's War.
Consult (I) Savelle and Middlekauff, 1964.

NEW ENGLAND RENAISSANCE, the cultural awakening that followed the intellectual activity generated by the Unitarian and Transcendental movements. The literary catalyst for this renaissance was Ralph Waldo Emerson, who, with many other New England writers, lived in the area around Boston. The movement received impetus from William Ellery Channing's break with orthodox Calvinism and his formation of the Unitarian church.

The movement's high point came in the period from 1850 to 1855, when writers such as Nathaniel Hawthorne (*Scarlet Letter*), Herman Melville (*Moby Dick*), Henry David Thoreau (*Walden*), and Emerson (*Representative Men*) published classic works. The Cambridge poets (Henry Wadsworth Longfellow, Oliver Wendell Holmes, and James Russell Lowell) also flourished in the 1850s and 1860s, as did a bard of rural New England, John Greenleaf Whittier.

See also Literature; biographies of individual figures.
Consult (IV) Brooks, 1936.

NEW FRANCE. *See* French Colonies.

NEW FREEDOM, program proposed by Woodrow Wilson during the 1912 presidential campaign. *See* Wilson, Woodrow.

NEW FRONTIER, phrase first used by John F. Kennedy in his acceptance of the Democratic presidential nomination in 1960. He was referring to the challenge of the 1960s, which he saw as a turning point in history.

It encompassed the application of intelligence to public affairs by the enactment of an agenda of reforms: federal aid to education, Medicare, equal opportunity in employment and public accommodations, tax reduction and reform, restoring world confidence in American leadership (Alliance for Progress, Kennedy Round of trade negotiations, arms limitation), tapping a wellspring of idealism and humanism (Peace Corps), and promoting advances in science.

The thousand days of Kennedy's Administration meant more than a New Frontier pattern of government—it also symbolized a vigorous, sophisticated way of life for Washington's "in" society.

See also Alliance for Progress; Kennedy, John F.; Peace Corps; Space Exploration.
Consult (VIII) Sorensen, 1969.

NEW HAMPSHIRE, colony and state that, like Maine, was essentially an offshoot of Massachusetts' colonization. New Hampshire had been sighted by Champlain in 1605 and mapped by John Smith in 1614. The Council for New England was given the area by royal grant in 1620, and Captain John Mason received rights to develop part of the region, which he named New Hampshire in 1629.

Although emigrants from southern England moved there in 1630 and founded the town of Portsmouth, most of the settlers came from Massachusetts and Connecticut. In fact, New Hampshire was virtually a part of Massachusetts for many years, and the region sent delegates to the Massachusetts General Court in 1641. Charles II created a separate crown colony out of New Hampshire in 1679.

The colony was poorly developed, and throughout the colonial period only the southern part was really settled. A long struggle with New York over lands to the west, which later became Vermont and which were known as the "New Hampshire Grants," was not settled until 1791. A dispute with Massachusetts over boundaries was settled in 1741. The northern border of the state was disputed with Canada, but this was resolved finally in 1842 by the Webster-Ashburton Treaty. New Hampshire was divided on the question of the U.S. Constitution, although its people had been the first to drive out their royal governor (1776). They ratified the Constitution on June 21, 1788, casting the deciding vote that established the new federal union.

The legislature is bicameral; the capital is Concord. The population in 1970 was 737,681.

See also Webster-Ashburton Treaty (1842).

Consult (I) Savelle and Middlekauff, 1964.

NEW HARMONY, Utopian town planned by Robert Owen. *See* Utopian Communities.

NEW HAVEN COLONY. *See* Connecticut.

NEW JERSEY, colony and state that was originally a part of New Netherlands. The land between the Hudson and Delaware rivers known as New Jersey was ceded to two of the noble proprietors of the Carolinas in 1664—Lord Berkeley and Sir George Carteret. New Jersey soon came under different control. West Jersey (the southern and western portion) was oriented economically toward Philadelphia and became controlled by wealthy, landed Quakers. East Jersey depended more on New York City and was settled mainly by Scotch Presbyterians and New England Calvinists, as well as some Catholics. West Jersey had the most liberal of all colonial constitutions, granting trial by jury, freedom of belief, freedom from arbitrary arrest, a representative assembly, and generous land grants.

In 1702, however, being unable to maintain order, the local powers asked for a royal government, and the two Jerseys were united as a crown colony with the proprietors maintaining their land rights and quitrents. In view of such difficulties, New Jersey was very much in favor of a stronger federal government at the end of the eighteenth century. Residents took

New Jersey's first college was in Princeton. Nassau Hall, the main structure, is still in use.

Battle of New Orleans, which made Andrew Jackson a national hero, was fought after peace was signed.

a strong anti-British stand in the Revolution, and their territory was a battlefield throughout the war. At the Constitutional Convention the state's delegates tried to preserve the power of the small states through the New Jersey Plan, but it was rejected. New Jersey ratified the Constitution unanimously on Dec. 18, 1787.

The legislature is bicameral; the capital is Trenton. The population in 1970 was 7,168,-164.

See also Carteret Family; New Jersey Plan.

NEW JERSEY PLAN, series of resolutions presented by William Paterson of New Jersey at the Constitutional Convention in 1787. Unlike the Virginia Plan, it was designed merely to amend the Articles of Confederation. A unicameral Congress with equal representation from each state would be retained, with the members chosen by the state legislatures. Additional powers would be granted to the Congress, including the authority to levy import duties and regulate commerce. A plural national executive with little power would be created along with a national Supreme Court. In general, however, the national government would still depend upon the states for funds and security.

The most important provision of the New Jersey Plan declared that "the authority of the United States shall be the supreme law of the land and the judges of the states bound thereby." This supremacy clause, incorporated into the Constitution, enabled the national government to assert its supremacy over the constitutions and the laws of the states, thus making possible a truly national government.

See also Connecticut Compromise; Constitutional Convention (1787); Federalism; Virginia Plan.

Consult (III) Hunt and Scott, 1920; Rossiter, 1953.

NEWLANDS ACT. *See* National Reclamation Act (1902).

NEW LIGHTS, or **NEW SIDE.** *See* Presbyterians.

NEW MEXICO, the 47th state, admitted to the Union on Jan. 6, 1912. The area was first explored and settled by the Spanish in the sixteenth century. Indian attacks plagued these early settlers, particularly in 1676 and 1680. The area became a Mexican province in 1821, and most of what is now New Mexico was ceded to the United States in 1848; the remainder was obtained through the Gadsden Purchase in 1853. It became a territory in 1850.

The legislature is bicameral; the capital is Santa Fe. The population in 1970 was 1,016,-000.

See also Gadsden Purchase (1853).

NEW NEGRO MOVEMENT. *See* Harlem Renaissance.

NEW ORLEANS, BATTLE OF (1815), climactic battle of the War of 1812. In 1814 the British planned to capture New Orleans and thereby force the United States to make large concessions in any peace treaty ending the war. The expedition formed in Jamaica in the fall, and British troops began to land near New Orleans just before Christmas. It was not known that peace had been signed in Ghent, Belgium, on December 24.

Preliminary engagements were fought over a two-week period, but the major battle took place on the morning of January 8. The American defenses had been organized by Andrew Jackson of Tennessee. He commanded about 4,500 men, while the British had nearly twice as many. The British attack was a disaster with over 2,000 casualties. Total American casualties were 71. The battle brought Andrew Jackson to national prominence and helped to produce a great outburst of nationalism in the United States.

See also Ghent, Treaty of (1814); Jackson, Andrew; War of 1812.

NEW SWEDEN. *See* Delaware.

NEWTON, HUEY P., Black Panther leader. *See* Black Panthers.

NEW YORK, colony and state that was probably sighted by John Cabot in 1498 and by Verrazano in 1524. The region was opened up by the explorations of Henry Hudson and Samuel de Champlain. Hudson sailed up the Hudson River to the present site of Albany in 1609, the same year that Champlain explored Lake Champlain. While French trappers and missionaries roamed the wild north and west of New York, the Dutch and English developed the southern area and the port of New York. In 1623 the Dutch established New Netherland with the town of New Amsterdam. Resenting Dutch intrusion, England's King Charles II granted to his brother James, Duke of York, all the land between the Connecticut and Delaware rivers—as if the Dutch were not already there. An English naval force in 1664 persuaded the Dutch, headed by Peter Stuyvesant, to surrender, and New Amsterdam was renamed New York. The Dutch recaptured it briefly in 1673–1674.

From 1674 to 1683 the governor of New York was the unpopular Sir Edmund Andros. The demand for local self-government grew, and a new governor, Thomas Dongan, was empowered to create a New York Assembly after 1683. The process was delayed by James becoming king and by the later Whig Revolution of 1688. The colony was deeply divided over that revolution, one result of which was Leisler's revolt of 1689. In 1691 the assembly was finally established. Although New York prospered, tension between the assembly and the colonial authorities was always present, as seen in the John Peter Zenger freedom of the press case of 1735.

An English alliance with the powerful Iroquois Confederacy opened up central New York for settlement, although the war with the French continued. New York was divided over its attitude toward the crown in the late eighteenth century. When the Revolutionary War came, much of it was fought on New York's soil, with the British occupying New York City throughout the war. Several leading American statesmen, including Alexander Hamilton, John Jay, and Gouverneur Morris, came from New York. After much debate, the state ratified the U.S. Constitution on July 26, 1788. New York City served as the first national capital in 1789–1790.

The legislature is bicameral; the capital is Albany. The population in 1970 was 18,241,266.

See also Anglo-Dutch Wars; Exploration and Discovery; Zenger, John Peter.

Consult (I) Savelle and Middlekauff, 1964.

—Peter d'A. Jones, *University of Illinois, Chicago Circle*

NEW YORK CENTRAL RAILROAD. *See* Railroads.

NEW YORK STOCK EXCHANGE, most important stock exchange in the United States. The exchange was begun in New York City in 1792 with an agreement among stock traders. The intent was to maintain one market for the buying and selling of stocks and to impose rules of conduct. Great amounts of business flowed from the new federal government's assumption of the states' debts and the refunding of the federal debt.

Exchanges grew up in other cities with the various booms in state government bonds, canal and railroad stock, Civil War bonds, insurance company stock, and later the stock of new industries such as oil and chemicals. After many panics, the stock market crash of 1929 finally led to federal regulation of the exchanges through the Securities and Exchange Commission (1934). Known as the Big Board, the New York exchange has maintained its preeminent position in the financial community.

See also Securities Exchange Act (1934).

Consult (III) Sobel, 1965.

NIAGARA MOVEMENT, drive for black equality organized in 1905. *See* Blacks in the United States; Du Bois, W. E. B.

NICARAGUA INTERVENTION. Because it

Typical bustling activity at N.Y. Stock Exchange.

straddles the strategically important Central American isthmus, Nicaragua has always been of interest to the United States. In the 1850s William Walker, a Southern filibusterer, set himself up as dictator of Nicaragua, perhaps with a view to increasing the power of the slaveholding states, only to die before a firing squad in 1860. In 1885 the United States sought to conclude a Nicaraguan treaty that would provide for joint ownership of an isthmian canal, and in 1901 Secretary of State John Hay finally negotiated the Hay-Pauncefote Treaty, which set aside the Clayton-Bulwer Treaty (1850) so the United States could build, possess, and fortify a canal through Nicaragua. No canal was built, however, because the Panamanian route was preferred.

Nonetheless, American interest in the tiny nation remained high, and under President William Howard Taft a vigorous Dollar Diplomacy practically reduced Nicaragua to an American colony with an American collector general of Nicaraguan customs in 1911. By treaty in 1916 the United States took a 99-year lease on Nicaragua's Great and Little Corn islands. During the 1920s, U.S. Marines policed Nicaragua in an effort to assure that only politicians favorable to the United States attained high office. In January 1933 the last Marines left.

See also Clayton-Bulwer Treaty (1850); Dollar Diplomacy; Filibustering Expeditions; Hay-Pauncefote Treaty (1901).
Consult (V) Bemis, 1943.

NIEBUHR, REINHOLD (1892–1971), American Protestant theologian, political philosopher, and social critic who pioneered in the "new theology" of neo-orthodoxy that strives to restate biblical Christian teachings in a form revelant to the great issues of contemporary life and history. Niebuhr developed a complex philosophy based on the fallibility of man, the absurdity of human pretensions, and the biblical precepts of life.

Niebuhr was born in Wright City, Mo., and educated at Elmhurst College, Eden Theological Seminary, and Yale Divinity School. He was a professor at New York's Union Theological Seminary from 1928 to 1960. His works include *The Nature and Destiny of Man* (2 vols., 1941–1943), an impressive statement of his fundamental theological position.

In his early writings, Niebuhr exhibited the quasi-humanistic religious liberalism and social idealism that pervaded the theological atmosphere of the times. In his later years, Niebuhr's thinking shifted to a concern with the problems of history and man's essential historicity, which is evident in such works as *Faith and History* (1949), *The Irony of American History* (1952), and *The Self and the Drama of History* (1955).

Richard M. Nixon, 37th President of the United States, mingles with public as Secret Service agents scan crowd.

NIMITZ, CHESTER W(ILLIAM) (1885–1966), American naval officer. He was born in Fredericksburg, Tex., and graduated from the U.S. Naval Academy in 1905. During World War I, he served as chief of staff to the head of the Atlantic Fleet's submarine force. After the war Nimitz held several posts and then served as assistant chief and later chief of the Bureau of Navigation until the attack on Pearl Harbor in 1941.

Nimitz was immediately named commander in chief of the Pacific Fleet and raised to the rank of admiral. Throughout the war he demonstrated his skill as a strategist and technician, especially as commander of all Allied naval, land, and air forces in the Southwest Pacific. It was under his direction that the Japanese navy was rendered ineffective and that the Gilbert, Marshall, Caroline, Mariana, and Bonin islands were successfully invaded. In 1945 he was named chief of naval operations and served until his retirement in 1947. In 1946 his rank of five-star admiral, received in 1944, was confirmed for life.

See also World War II.
Consult (VII) Hoyt, 1970.

NIXON, RICHARD M(ILHOUS) (1913–), 37th President of the United States (1969–), a centrist and pragmatist, a skillful politician with a reputation for learning from his crises and mistakes.

He was born on Jan. 9, 1913, in Yorba Linda, Cal. A lawyer, he served in the Navy from 1942 to 1946, emerging in time to enter a race for Congress. He won and served in the House until 1950, when he was elected to the Senate. His persistence in investigating Alger Hiss for the House Committee on Un-American Activities gave him a national reputation.

In 1952 Nixon was selected to run on the ticket with Dwight Eisenhower, thus becoming the second youngest vice-president in history. By 1960 he was the Republicans' heir apparent. However, he lost a close election to John Kennedy and suffered another defeat in 1962, when he tried for the governorship of California. He announced his retirement from politics and moved to New York to practice law and work for the Republican Party.

Presidency. His election as president in 1968 capped one of the most striking comebacks in U.S. political history. With the margin of victory over Hubert Humphrey narrow, Nixon encountered a Democratic Congress and a public that regarded him with respect but not affection. However, he was able to claim a number of achievements at the end of four years. In the international scene he achieved a phased withdrawal from Vietnam as well as the opening of dialogues with the Soviet Union and the People's Republic of China. Domestically, although locked in tugs of war with Congress over welfare reform, Supreme Court nominations, governmental reorganization, environmentalism, consumerism, and defense policy, he secured revenue sharing, a restructuring of the selective service, and law and order legislation. In 1971 he turned the tables on his critics by embracing Keynesian economics and a wage-price freeze.

His landslide victory over George McGovern in 1972 was interpreted by the Republicans as a mandate for Nixon's policies. In early 1973, however, the revelations of the Watergate affair diminished the effectiveness of the President and the executive branch.

See also Presidential Elections.
Consult (VIII) Nixon, 1962; Wills, 1970.
—Martin Gruberg, *University of Wisconsin, Oshkosh*

NONIMPORTATION, attempt by the American colonies during several crises to put pressure on Parliament by agreeing not to import British products. Massachusetts initiated the movement after the passage of the American Revenue Act in 1764. Nonimportation spread because of the introduction of the Stamp Act (1765) and helped bring about its repeal in 1766. Americans again resorted to the tactic in response to the Townshend Acts of 1767 and the Coercive Acts of 1774.

See also Stamp Act (1764); Townshend Acts (1767).

NONIMPORTATION ACT (1806), legislation passed in reaction to the economic policies of Britain and France, who were involved in a major war and had imposed restrictions on each other's trade. Napoleon's Continental System of 1806–1807 was a prohibition on British imports to Europe, and the British retaliated with their Orders in Council (1807) forbidding neutral ships to trade with the Continent. The Nonimportation Act banned the import into the United States of a list of English items, in this way trying to force the English to relax their regulations against neutrals. President Jefferson suspended the act in December 1806, but, when additional negotiations failed, he went one step further and imposed the Embargo of 1807, which hurt American businesses more than it did those in Britain or France.

See also Embargo Acts (1807–1809).

NONINTERCOURSE ACT (1809), legislation on the embargo of imports into the United States. *See* Embargo Acts (1807–1809); Macon's Bill No. 2.

NON-SEPARATISTS, those who wished to reform the Anglican church but not to leave it. *See* Pilgrims.

NORRIS, GEORGE W(ILLIAM) (1861–1944), U.S. Representative and Senator. Born in Ohio, he became a lawyer and in 1885 moved to Nebraska, where he served as a prosecuting attorney and district judge before being elected to the U.S. House of Representatives in 1902. During the next decade he became the acknowledged leader of the House insurgent Republicans, pressing for tariff revision, the income tax, the direct election of senators and organizing the successful revolt against House Speaker Joseph Cannon in 1910.

In 1913 Norris was elected to the Senate and for the next 30 years championed a wide variety of progressive causes. He was the father of the so-called lame duck Twentieth Amendment to the Constitution (1933) and coauthor of the Norris-LaGuardia Act (1932), which outlawed yellow dog contracts. He fought against the sale of the Muscle Shoals region to private industry in the 1920s and for its evolution into the Tennessee Valley Authority. Norris also sponsored legislation to aid farmers and was a pioneer in the movement to abolish the poll tax. A maverick Republican, he supported the Progressive ticket in both 1912 and 1924, the Democratic from 1928 on, and ran unsuccessfully as an Independent in 1943 after party regulars had denied him the nomination.

See also Tennessee Valley Authority.
Consult (VI) Zucker, 1966.

NORSEMEN. *See* Vikings.

NORTH ATLANTIC TREATY ORGANIZATION (NATO). Formed in 1949 to deter possible aggression by the Soviet Union against Western Europe, NATO's original members included Belgium, Britain, Canada, Denmark, France, Iceland, Italy, Luxembourg, the Netherlands, Norway, Portugal, and the United States. In 1952 Greece and Turkey joined, to be followed by West Germany in 1955. The major organs of NATO are the North Atlantic Council (composed of the foreign ministers), a staff secretariat, and the military committee.

History. NATO's early policy of relying on American nuclear power changed during the Korean War to an emphasis on meeting a conventional Soviet attack. A European reluctance to meet the manpower demands of this strategy, plus President Eisenhower's espousal of nuclear weapons, led in 1954 to a series of agreements emphasizing tactical nuclear weaponry.

Under President Kennedy, the United States sought to expand the European conventional force contributions so that an immediate nuclear response to a Soviet attack would not be necessary. The U.S. policy of maintaining total control of the alliance's nuclear capability failed with France's development of a nuclear force and with French withdrawal from military involvement with NATO in 1965. By the late 1960s and early 1970s a combination of

Secretary of State Acheson signs North Atlantic Treaty Organization Pact in 1949 as President Truman *(standing, right)* and Vice-President Barkley watch.

factors that indicated a lessening of East-West tension led to proposals for an all-European security conference to reduce military forces.

NORTH CAROLINA, colony and state settled chiefly by colonists moving from within America rather than by new settlers from England. Verrazano explored Carolina in 1524, and in the 1580s Raleigh's colonial experiments centered on Roanoke Island.

By the midseventeenth century, squatters from Virginia had settled along Albemarle Sound, growing tobacco and corn and raising livestock. The region was called Carolina, after Charles I, who gave it to Sir Robert Heath. In 1663, Charles II reassigned the territory to the Carolina proprietors, who appointed a governor for Albemarle. Beginning in 1691 this northern section became known separately as North Carolina and had a governor different from that of South Carolina.

While South Carolina became relatively rich on rice cultivation and trade, North Carolina remained a backward, poor, frontier society of small farmers, radical and difficult to govern. For example, they revolted in 1676, and although North Carolina became a royal colony in 1729, the deepest political unrest persisted there. The sectional tension between the prosperous Tidewater and the poorer backcountry was marked, as seen in the violent Regulator movement (1765–1771). Population increased after 1729 from a low of 13,000 to about 300,000 just before the Revolution. North Carolina strongly resisted the British but, jealous of its own states' rights, it did not ratify the Constitution until Nov. 21, 1789. The state created in 1789 the nation's first state university at Chapel Hill.

The legislature is bicameral; the capital is Raleigh. The population in 1970 was 5,082,059.

See also South Carolina.

NORTH DAKOTA, the 39th state, admitted to the Union simultaneously with South Dakota on Nov. 2, 1889. The western part of North Dakota was obtained by the United States in the Louisiana Purchase (1803); the remainder was received from England in 1818. The earliest settlers in the area were fur traders of the Hudson's Bay and Northwest companies. The completion of the Northern Pacific Railroad encouraged more settlers to come to the area, and North Dakota became a territory in 1861.

The state legislature is bicameral; the capital is Bismarck. The population in 1970 was 617,761.

NORTHERN SECURITIES CO. v. UNITED STATES (1904), Supreme Court decision that revitalized the Sherman Antitrust Act. *See* Antitrust Cases.

NORTHMEN. *See* Vikings.

NORTH STAR, abolitionist newspaper. *See* Douglass, Frederick.

NORTHWEST ORDINANCE (1787), legislation to organize the territory in what is now known as the Midwest. The Congress, which had received control of Western lands under the Articles of Confederation, appointed Thomas Jefferson chairman of a committee to devise a plan of government for the territory.

In April 1784 the Congress adopted Jefferson's report except for a proposed ban on slavery in the territory. Administrative problems impeded implementation, and conservatives used the delay to seek limitations on democratic aspects of Jefferson's program. The conservatives wanted to grant the territorial governor an absolute veto, restrict the franchise to property holders, and require a minimum population of 5,000 for the establishment of a legislature.

In 1787 the Congress achieved its greatest success under the Articles of Confederation with the passage of a revised land ordinance, which was based primarily on Jefferson's modified proposal. The Northwest Ordinance, passed on July 13, 1787, provided that a governor, secretary, and three judges appointed by the Congress would administer the territory. When the population reached 5,000 free adult males, the inhabitants could establish a bicameral legislature. Ultimately the Congress would create three to five states from the territory, each of which would have a population of at least 60,000 people.

The Northwest Ordinance stated that the new states would be the equals of the old in all respects and guaranteed freedom of worship, trial by jury, and publicly supported education. The measure also restored Jefferson's original proposal that involuntary servitude, except as punishment for crime, be banned from the territory.

Consult (III) Philbrick, 1965.

—Thomas Archdeacon, *University of Wisconsin*

NORTHWEST TERRITORY, region north of the Ohio River organized by the Northwest Ordinance of 1787. The territory included the present states of Ohio, Indiana, Illinois, Michigan, and Wisconsin and was the first effort by the federal government to provide local government for the pioneers. Residents of the territory faced a three-stage evolutionary process leading to statehood on equal terms with the original 13 states. During the first stage Congress appointed the governor, territorial secretary, and judges. Once the adult male population reached 5,000, the settlers entered the second stage. They could elect the members of the lower house of the legislature and send a nonvoting delegate to Congress. Finally, when the population grew to 60,000, the people could prepare a constitution and apply for statehood. This plan assured the pioneers that eventually they would be on the same legal footing as those who remained in the East.

Despite the extension of democratic principles into the area, settlers still faced danger from the Indians, and intermittent fighting continued until Gen. Anthony Wayne's campaign in 1794 and the Treaty of Greenville that followed. After this the confusing efforts of land speculators inhibited settlement temporarily. Nevertheless, the flow of pioneers continued, and by 1800 Indiana Territory had been created in the western part of the Northwest Territory. Only three years later, in 1803, Ohio entered the union as a state, and the Northwest Territory disappeared from the map.

See also Greenville, Treaty of (1795); Land Companies; Land Policy; Northwest Ordinance (1787); Ohio Company.

Consult (III) Eblen, 1968; Van Every, 1963.

—Roger L. Nichols, *University of Arizona*

NOTES ON VIRGINIA (1785). *See* Jefferson, Thomas.

NULLIFICATION, doctrine that a state has the right within its territory to overrule, or "nullify," federal legislation. It developed after the Tariff of 1828, which satisfied almost no one, was passed. South Carolina politicians quickly blamed the tariff for the state's economic problems, and on Dec. 19, 1828, the South Carolina legislature adopted a set of resolutions declaring the tariff unconstitutional, oppressive, and unjust. This was accompanied by the "South Carolina Exposition and Protest," an unsigned essay by John C. Calhoun expounding the doctrine of state nullification.

Rather than implementing nullification, the South Carolinians waited to see what action Jackson's Administration would take. When they were denied relief by the Tariff of 1832, they called a state convention that promptly nullified the tariff acts of 1828 and 1832 and set Feb. 1, 1833, for formal nullification.

President Jackson responded to this state challenge of federal authority by attacking the "absurdity" of nullification and asserting the sovereignty and indivisibility of the federal government. In January 1833, Jackson asked Congress for authority to uphold the revenue laws—by military force if necessary. This so-called Force Act passed Congress on March 1, but that same day a lower Compromise Tariff sponsored by Senator Henry Clay

was also approved. On March 15, the South Carolina convention reassembled and rescinded its ordinance of nullification. To save face, however, the convention adopted a new ordinance nullifying the Force Act.

See also Calhoun, John C.; Jackson, Andrew; Tariff of 1828.

Consult (III) Freehling, 1966.

—Douglas Miller, *Michigan State University*

OBERLIN COLLEGE, pioneer institution in unsegregated coeducation. It was opened in northern Ohio in 1833 by Rev. John Jay Shipherd in order to bring the Protestant Christian message to the West. After a debate on abolitionism organized by Theodore Weld in 1834 turned the students of Lane Seminary in Cincinnati against the trustees, a group of theological students left Lane for Oberlin. Supported by funds from the abolitionist New York businessmen Arthur and Lewis Tappan, Oberlin accepted the Lane rebels.

At this point the college began its long career of socially conscious education. Lucy Stone was one of its graduates, as was the black leader John M. Langston. Oberlin was uncompromisingly opposed to the Fugitive Slave Act, and students and faculty showed their opposition to it during the "Oberlin-Wellington Rescue" of 1858, one of the notable acts of abolitionist resistance to federal authority.

See also Abolitionism; Weld, Theodore.

OFFICE OF ECONOMIC OPPORTUNITY. *See* Economic Opportunity Act (1964).

OFFICE OF PRICE ADMINISTRATION. *See* Price Administration, Office of (OPA).

OGLETHORPE, JAMES EDWARD (1696-1785), the principal founder of Georgia. He was a soldier and a member of Parliament interested in reform causes—naval impressment, black slavery, penal reform and others. His humanitarian concerns, reinforced by his military convictions, involved him in a vast project to establish a buffer colony between South Carolina and Spanish Florida.

Chartered in 1732 and lavishly supported by parliamentary grants, the new colony of Georgia gave Oglethorpe the chance to create an overseas refuge for imprisoned English debtors of demonstrable moral character, to build a society free of slavery and rum, and to strengthen imperial defenses against Spain. But his programs antagonized the settlers (who liked rum and demanded slaves), the home government (which grew alarmed at the expenses he accrued), and South Carolina (which resented his interference in the Indian trade).

When Britain attacked Spain in the War of Jenkin's Ear (1739), Oglethorpe tried without

James Oglethorpe, who organized the settlement of Georgia, negotiates with Indians.

success to storm St. Augustine in 1740 but cleverly defended the outpost of Frederica against a much larger Spanish force two years later. Criticism following another failure in 1743 to take St. Augustine led to his recall and to his acquittal after a court martial. Oglethorpe never returned to Georgia but instead spent his last 40 years in literary and reform circles. Meanwhile Georgia rapidly deviated from his master plan and became a near twin of South Carolina, complete with rice, slaves, and rum.

See also Georgia.
Consult (I) Ettinger, 1936.
—John M. Murrin, *Princeton University*

OHIO, the 17th state, joined the Union on March 1, 1803. Disputes between French and British fur traders in the Ohio area helped trigger the French and Indian War. When Britain obtained the area in 1763, it forbade settlement west of the Appalachians, and this issue was one of the many that led to the Revolutionary War. The United States gained the Ohio area in 1783, and the first permanent settlement was made in 1788 at Marietta. Ohio gained territorial status in 1799.

The state legislature is bicameral; Columbus is the capital. The population in 1970 was 10,652,017.

OHIO COMPANY, land company, not to be confused with the Grand Ohio Company of Virginia, that originated in Boston in 1786. Former army generals Rufus Putnam and Benjamin Tupper formed the group to use depreciated government bonds to buy Western lands. After a brief survey of the upper Ohio Valley, they chose the Muskingum Valley in Ohio and hired the Reverend Manasseh Cutler to negotiate with Congress.

Cutler proposed that Congress sell the company land at much less than the set price, and after some haggling leaders there agreed to an illegal scheme. The Ohio Company got 1.5 million acres at just over 8 cents an acre. To provide government and make the new land attractive to pioneers, Cutler encouraged his congressional allies to pass the Northwest Ordinance of 1787. Thus, the Ohio Company played an important role in opening the region north of the Ohio River for American settlement.

See also Land Companies; Northwest Ordinance (1787); Northwest Territory.
Consult (III) Eblen, 1968.

OKLAHOMA, the 46th state, admitted to the Union on Nov. 16, 1907. The United States acquired the Oklahoma area as part of the Louisiana Purchase (1803). In 1819 the eastern part of the present state was organized as Indian Territory, and the Indians deported

Nobel Prize winner Eugene O'Neill, whose plays started new trends in American drama.

from the Southern United States were resettled there. Oklahoma Territory was established in 1890, one year after it had been opened to white settlers.

The state legislature is bicameral; Oklahoma City is the capital. The population in 1970 was 2,559,253.

OLD LIGHTS, or **OLD SIDE.** *See* Presbyterians.

OLD NORTHWEST, area north of the Ohio River between Pennsylvania and the Mississippi River. *See* Northwest Territory.

OLIVE BRANCH PETITION (1775), last attempt by the Continental Congress to become reconciled with Britain. *See* Continental Congress, Second.

OMNIBUS ACT (1868), legislation that paved the way for the readmission of representatives and senators from South Carolina, North Carolina, Louisiana, Georgia, Alabama, and Florida. After noting that these states had fully complied with the Reconstruction Acts, the statute declared that, as soon as the legislatures of those six states had ratified the Fourteenth Amendment, they would be allowed to resume their seats in Congress, provided only that the state constitutions would never be amended so as to deprive anyone of the vote. By the end of July 1868 five of the six states had complied with the law's provision (only Georgia balked) and were readmitted to Congress.

See also Reconstruction; Reconstruction Acts (1867–1868).

O'NEILL, EUGENE (GLADSTONE) (1888–1953), American playwright who was the first American dramatist to win the Nobel Prize for literature (1936). He was born in New York, attended Princeton for one year (1906–1907), and then spent several years traveling. He shipped to sea as a merchant seaman, after which he worked briefly as a reporter for the New London *Telegraph.* Shortly thereafter, O'Neill contracted tuberculosis and spent 6 months in a sanitorium in Connecticut, where he began to write plays.

His first efforts were awkward melodramas, but in 1916, after he had studied with George Pierce Baker at his workshop at Harvard, O'Neill's first one-act sea play, *Bound East for Cardiff,* was produced at Provincetown, Mass. This work was followed by other one-act plays based on his seagoing experiences. In 1920 *Beyond the Horizon,* his first full-length play, won the Pulitzer Prize. The work impressed audiences and critics alike with its tragic realism and sensitivity, earning him recognition as an important American playwright.

From 1920 to 1943, when forced by

Parkinson's disease to give up writing, O'Neill completed more than 20 plays of varying lengths. They cover a great variety of subjects, all from an intensely personal viewpoint, and they present an astonishing array of psychological and sociological relationships.

His most celebrated plays are *Anna Christie* (1921), *Desire Under the Elms* (1924), *Strange Interlude* (1928), *Mourning Becomes Electra* (1931), *The Iceman Cometh* (1946), and *Long Day's Journey into Night.* The latter work, completed in 1941 but not produced until 1956, is rather clearly an autobiographical tragedy of his parents, brother, and self.

See also Literature.

OPA. *See* Price Administration, Office of (OPA).

OPEN DOOR POLICY, policy toward China developed to ensure that Americans would not be excluded by other great powers from equal trade in China, which was weak and divided. At this time the great powers—Britain, France, Russia, Japan, and some others—had carved China into "spheres of influence," commercial enclaves where their nationals lived and enjoyed special privileges and immunity from Chinese laws, a status that angered the Chinese.

Growing rivalry in the Far East among great powers anxious to benefit from the China trade led Secretary of State John Hay to issue in 1899–1900 the "Open Door" notes. They demanded that China open its doors equally to all the powers and that China's territorial integrity be safeguarded against a take-over by any one power. Hay sent his notes to all the powers who were involved, demanding equal treatment for all the great powers in China. Some of the answers were noncommittal, but early in 1900 Hay announced that the policy was firmly accepted.

The foreign enclaves in China were seriously threatened in 1900 by the nationalist Boxer Rebellion. About 250 "foreign devils" were murdered, and U.S. troops took part in a combined international force that put down the rebellion. The major disturbance of the Far East equilibrium, however, was not weak Chinese resistance but the growing confrontation between Russia and Japan. This led in 1904 to the outbreak of the Russo-Japanese War. Through the efforts of President Theodore Roosevelt the war was ended in 1905 at the Portsmouth Peace Conference. Roosevelt had been anxious to end the war because he feared that the complete victory of either belligerent would disturb the Open Door.

In a secret agreement preceding the Treaty of Portsmouth, the United States recognized Japanese power in Korea (and implicitly in Manchuria), while the Japanese promised to respect U.S. rights in the Philippines. In 1908, during the successful goodwill tour of the U.S. fleet to Japan and then around the world, the Root-Takahira Agreement was signed. The two nations agreed upon a comprehensive equilibrium policy for the Far East, including the Open Door in China.

Alienation of Japan. American investors were encouraged to take advantage of the Open Door by an aggressive expansionist in the State Department, Willard Straight. When President Taft replaced Roosevelt and pushed a policy of Dollar Diplomacy, Straight emerged as a leader of such politics and as agent for American bankers in the Far East. Arguments over railroad construction in China and Manchuria soon strained relations between Japan and the Occidental powers active in the Far East. Further tension with Japan was caused by racist state policies in California, which denied citizenship and landholding rights to Japanese immigrants and almost brought war between the two nations in 1913–1914.

World War I gave Japan the opportunity to menace China in 1915 in violation of the Open Door agreement. Anglo-American pressure brought Japanese retraction, but the settlement was ambiguous. In 1922 the Washington Armament Conference reiterated the Open Door principle, but in 1931 the Japanese invaded and annexed Manchuria. The Open Door was now fully rejected by Japan.

"Open Door imperialism," as it is called by critics of this big power policy, thus lay behind the complex U.S. relationship with Japan. It helped to produce the breakdown of understanding that led to World War II.

See also Dollar Diplomacy; Hay, John; Portsmouth Peace Conference (1905); Russo-Japanese War; Taft, William Howard.

Consult (VI) Iriye, 1967.

—Peter d'A. Jones, *University of Illinois, Chicago Circle*

OPERATION BREADBASKET, black economic program. *See* Jackson, Jesse.

OPERATION OVERLORD, code name for the D-Day invasion on June 6, 1944. *See* D-Day; Eisenhower, Dwight D.

OPPENHEIMER, J. ROBERT (1904–1967), American nuclear physicist who directed the production of the first atom bomb. Oppenheimer was born in New York City, graduated from Harvard in 1925, and received his Ph.D. in Germany. From 1929 to 1947 he taught at the University of California and the California Institute of Technology, where he applied the methods of quantum mechanics to problems involving the nucleus of the atom. On leave from university work from 1943 to 1945, Oppenheimer successfully directed the atom

Japanese intervention in Manchuria before World War II signaled the end of the Open Door Policy in China.

Nuclear physicist J. Robert Oppenheimer, the father of the atom bomb, was later considered a security risk because of his political associations.

bomb project at Los Alamos, N.M. From 1947 to 1966 he was director of the Institute of Advanced Study at Princeton University.

In 1954, during the period when extreme efforts were being made to hunt out communists in government, Oppenheimer's security clearance was taken from him because of his alleged past political allegiances and opinions. His opposition to the hydrogen bomb may also have influenced those who questioned his loyalty. Although his investigators considered him a "loyal citizen," his clearance was never restored. His case aroused much controversy because of the issue of infringement on the rights of personal freedom. Oppenheimer was, however, presented the Enrico Fermi Award in 1963, the highest honor of the Atomic Energy Committee.

See also Atom Bomb.

Consult (VIII) Michaelmore, 1969.

ORDERS IN COUNCIL (1807), British commercial regulations, issued during the Napoleonic Wars, that hindered American shipping. The year's first Order in Council, on January 7, prohibited neutrals from trading with ports that were held by enemies of Britain. The main Orders in Council were issued on November 11 and were supported by supplementary orders issued later in the month. In general, they stated that neutrals could only trade with countries from which the British were excluded if the neutrals first called at British ports, paid certain duties, and obtained British approval.

ORDINANCE OF 1785. *See* Land Policy.

OREGON, the 33rd state, admitted to the Union on Feb. 14, 1859. While searching for the Northwest Passage in 1778, Britain's Capt. James Cook claimed the Oregon area for the British. At that time, Oregon stretched from California north to Russian Alaska. The first permanent white settlement was in 1811 at Astoria—a fur trading post established by John Jacob Astor. By 1820 the area was under the control of the Hudson's Bay Company.

In the 1840s many pioneers made the western trek over the Oregon Trail to settle the area. The United States and England both claimed the area, and in 1846 they agreed to divide the territory along the 49th parallel, despite the cries of "54° 40' or fight" in the United States. Two years later the area gained territorial status.

The state legislature is bicameral; Salem is the capital. The population in 1970 was 2,091,385.

See also Oregon Trail.

OREGON QUESTION, Anglo-American dispute over the Oregon boundary. *See* "Fifty-Four-Forty or Fight."

Patriot Thomas Paine advocated American independence in *Common Sense* and supported the French Revolution in *Rights of Man.*

OREGON TRAIL, the route from Independence, Mo., to the mouth of the Columbia River on the Pacific coast, a distance of about 2,000 miles. Originally traveled by fur traders, by 1842 it was the highway for pioneers who moved west into the Oregon Territory mainly in search of fertile farmland. The Lewis and Clark Expedition followed part of the Oregon Trail in 1805.

Missionaries and emigrants, many under the leadership of Rev. Marcus Whitman and Jesse Applegate, traveled along the trail to the West in the 1830s and 1840s. In 1845 about 3,000 emigrants used the trail. The diaries of the travelers note in grim detail such obstacles as prairie fires, hostile Indians, impassable mountains, and other conditions that plagued them on the way. Later pioneers used improved equipment and oxen rather than horses. Good routes were established after years of experience, but the trail was always a route of hardship and danger.

ORISKANY, BATTLE OF (AUG. 6, 1777), American victory that halted a British drive into central New York. *See* Revolutionary War Battles.

OSCEOLA (1800–1838), Seminole Indian leader who doggedly resisted the American advance into Florida. *See* Seminole Wars.

OSTEND MANIFESTO, secret report on Cuba prepared in part in Ostend, Belgium, by James Buchanan, American minister to Britain; John Y. Mason, minister to France; and Pierre Soulé, minister to Spain. It was sent to the American secretary of state, William Marcy, in October 1854.

The immediate occasion for the manifesto was the seizure of an American ship's cargo by Spanish authorities in Cuba, but it reflected long-standing American ambitions to annex Cuba. Southern leaders were especially interested in the Spanish-held island as a territory for the extension of slavery. The report repeated the often stated political and economic advantages of adding the island to the United States, but it also expressed fear that Spain would free the slaves in Cuba and that the island would become "Africanized." Under these circumstances, the dispatch declared, "By every law, human and divine, we shall be justified in wresting it [Cuba] from Spain, if we possess the power." News of the meeting and dispatch leaked, and the critical publicity led Marcy to repudiate the manifesto.

OWEN-GLASS ACT (1913). *See* Federal Reserve Act (1913).

PACIFIC FUR COMPANY. *See* Astor, John Jacob.

PACIFIC RAILWAY ACT (1862), legislation to stimulate construction of a transcontinental railroad. *See* Railroad Legislation.

PAINE, THOMAS (1737–1809), articulate advocate of American independence. Born in England, he was dismissed from a government post in 1772, when he led a movement for higher wages. The affair brought Paine into contact with Benjamin Franklin, who was in England as a colonial agent. Franklin sent Paine to America, and the immigrant met Dr. Benjamin Rush, who encouraged him to write an essay calling for American independence.

Paine's pamphlet *Common Sense,* which appeared anonymously in Philadelphia on Jan. 10, 1776, savagely attacked monarchy. If the institution were useful, asked Paine, why would nature ridicule it "by giving mankind an ass for a lion [symbol of the British monarchy]" on the throne? Paine's central theme, the necessity of independence, caught the American imagination in 1776. "The blood of the slain, the weeping voice of nature cries," said Paine, " 'Tis time to part.' " During the Revolutionary War, Paine published a series of exhortatory tracts called "Crisis." Congress appointed Paine as secretary to the committee on foreign affairs in 1777, and in 1779 he became clerk to the Pennsylvania assembly.

After the war, Paine lived modestly in New Jersey and New York. In the hope of finding a producer for his favorite invention, an iron bridge, Paine went to France in 1787. His *Rights of Man* defended the French Revolution against the writings of Edmund Burke. The French Assembly made Paine an honorary citizen in 1792, but the Jacobins later imprisoned him. In 1794 James Monroe, the American minister to France, obtained his release, and Paine returned to the United States in 1802. Unfortunately, Paine's *Age of Reason,* which attacked organized religion, and his *Letter to George Washington* (1796), which criticized the great man, irritated many Americans, and the radical spent the years before his death in poverty.

Consult (II) Aldridge, 1959.
—Thomas Archdeacon, *University of Wisconsin*

PAINTING. From its beginnings, when it depended on European traditions for guidance, American painting has developed into a distinctive force in the art world.

The Colonial Period. American art has always reflected its rich European heritage, although early colonists were confronted with a region far different from their homeland. There was little need for art in the daily life of people struggling for survival. The patronage that had generally supported the arts in Europe was not a part of colonial America, and the

new churches, which were essentially Puritan at first, had little need for religious art.

The only kind of art that attained any real popularity was portrait painting, which was also the dominant aspect of painting in England, so the colonial limners—anonymous, self-taught folk painters who traveled the countryside making primitive likenesses of settlers and their families in return for food or shelter—were continuing a long tradition of English provincial painting.

As the United States established itself as a nation, American art became more sophisticated and its relation to European tradition more complex. It was an elusive blend of the primitive craft and vision of a young frontier civilization and the rich traditions of European mother countries. A neoclassical humanism emerged, much influenced by Thomas Jefferson's admiration of Roman art and architecture. As in the classical world, man was the center of things, and quite logically the portrait remained dominant in painting. Gilbert Stuart's portrait of "Mrs. Yates" and Ralph Earl's of "Roger Sherman" are indicative of the dual nature of American art in the late eighteenth century. Earl's work is simple and provincial whereas Stuart's painting is more elegant and sophisticated, reflecting Stuart's years of training in England and Ireland.

Early Nineteenth Century. The nineteenth century brought a new consciousness to America, an awareness of the vast scope and potential of the new country. Westward expansion carried with it a new romanticism, a celebration of the American wilderness. Landscape replaced portraiture as the dominant theme of American painting. The new romantic vision brought with it an appreciation of picturesque scenery from the Hudson River to the Rocky Mountains. While some artists were essentially realists, others were more idealistic, attempting to show to man a more grandiose creation than he actually knew. Writers such as Washington Irving, William Cullen Bryant, and Ralph Waldo Emerson embraced this idealism.

The Hudson River School, a group of landscape painters, typifies the idealistic approach to landscape. Thomas Cole's "The Oxbow" reflects a vast scope and grandeur. Asher Durand's "Kindred Spirits," showing Thomas Cole and William Cullen Bryant in a mountain landscape, was painted a year after Cole's death as a memorial to his and Bryant's mutual friend. This same tranquility is visible in other facets of nineteenth-century American painting. Scenes of westward expansion seldom recorded the conflicts or hardships of the frontier—rather they depicted the peaceful solitude seen in George Caleb Bingham's painting of "Fur Traders Descending the Missouri."

Late Nineteenth Century. The realistic

Alice Mason portrait is characteristic of work of colonial limners.

Romantic landscape painting of Hudson River School was popular in early nineteenth century. Asher B. Durand showed his friends William Cullen Bryant and painter Thomas Cole in *Kindred Spirits* (1849).

and romantic qualities in American painting between 1800 and 1865 did not reflect any real break from European traditions and influences but rather paralleled their trends. The close of the Civil War marked the beginning of a tremendous period of expansion and change in America: a growth in industry, wealth, and, most of all, cultural sophistication.

The emphasis of art shifted from the idea of painting as real or ideal representation to a greater concern for visual sensations and personal attitudes. Many influences contributed to the change. The increasing popularity of the camera and its mechanical ability to reproduce exact images had a major effect. But again, the trends dominant in America had strong roots in Europe, in the French Impressionists' parallel concern with light and visual effects and in the overall quality of design.

Most American artists visited Europe with some frequency, a great many still turned to the Continent for training, and some became expatriates. Notable among them were John Singer Sargent, Mary Cassatt, a significant member of French Impressionist and Post-Impressionist groups, and James Whistler. Whistler's "Nocturne in Black and Gold" suggests a concern for light and atmosphere similar to that of the French Impressionists, and his portrait of his mother is indicative of a dominant concern for flat pattern and overall design.

Others—including Winslow Homer, Thomas Eakins, and Albert Pinkham Ryder—were comparatively solitary and isolated, influenced less by new ideas from Europe and relying more on a personal interpretation of realism and romanticism. Homer's "Fox Hunt" and his seascape "West Point, Prout's Neck" reveal nature with more vitality and intimacy than Cole or Durand had done previously. Ryder, in "Toilers of the Sea," presents a romantic image that is completely original, the product of a highly personal imaginary world in which forms are simplified to enhance their visual effect. Eakins drew largely on the daily life of the urban middle class for his subjects.

The Twentieth Century: A Personal Search. The beginning of the century brought no major change in the essentially conservative nature of American painting despite the virtual explosion in European culture. The turning point came as a result of a series of independent exhibitions of young artists returning from Europe and culminated in the Armory Show of 1913, which signaled the end of the isolation and provincialism that had always been characteristic of much American painting.

The impact of this exhibit on the American public was confusing at best; they were ill-prepared for its radical ideas. Total abstraction, the absence of any recognizable subject matter in favor of pure form and color, was a promi-

Winslow Homer's Maine coast seascape *West Point, Prout's Neck* (1900). Sterling and Francine Clark Art Institute.

Christina's World (1948), haunting painting by Andrew Wyeth. Collection, The Museum of Modern Art, New York.

nent part of the Cubist concepts of painting that prevailed in contemporary Europe. Young American painters used those concepts as points of departure to evolve primarily personal images.

Prior to the Armory Show, the only coherent direction apparent in twentieth-century American painting was the work of "The Eight." This group of painters, led by the illustrator Robert Henri, sought a new realism. Their primary concern for life in an urban environment—the streets, the people—earned them the label of the "Ashcan School." John Sloan's paintings of "Backyards, Greenwich Village" and "The Hairdresser's Window" are indicative of this representation of the commonplace realities of life in the city.

Following the Armory Show, a more personal abstract quality emerged. Charles Demuth and Charles Sheeler, using Cubist abstraction as a basis, generated a more precise view of the American industrial scene. Often called the "precisionists" or the "immaculates" because of the clarity and geometric precision of their images, they reduced the industrial landscape to its essence, a precise, ordered design. Georgia O'Keefe, in a similarly "immaculate" personal abstraction, most frequently turned to nature for subject matter. "Black Iris" is a reduction of the flower to a pure, simple motif, an almost rhythmic pattern.

The Regionalism of the 1930s. The Depression of the 1930s turned American painting inward not toward a purer abstraction but toward a more conservative view of the American scene. Artists returned again to a nostalgic, culturally isolated realism, rejecting urban and contemporary values. Three Midwestern painters, Thomas Hart Benton, John Steuart Curry, and Grant Wood, championed this regionalism, and Wood's "American Gothic" is representative in its attempt to present old-time virtues. Some of the qualities of solitary isolation evoked by regional self-consciousness have persisted. The inherent loneliness and solitude projected by Edward Hopper's "House by the Railroad" and the nostalgia of Andrew Wyeth's "Christina's World" have become a permanent part of the character of American painting.

The International Style. Following the brief introspection of the 1930s, American nationalism began to evolve into internationalism with the United States becoming a world center for artistic activity. The resurgence of abstraction was reinforced by a new generation of American painters and by the arrival of a number of prominent European artists seeking a more liberal artistic climate than Hitler's Europe provided. Abstraction as a concept was no longer new; now its various aspects were explored, and artists became more and more occupied with the actual materials of painting and the physical act of manipulating them.

Jackson Pollock's "Blue Poles" is indicative of his method of painting—pouring pigment from cans with wide-swinging arm movements. The art of painting became as much process as final product.

The Abstract Expressionism of the 1950s, the action painting that sought to record not only abstract forms and color relationships but also the act of painting itself, became the dominant style in American and European art. "Woman I" and "Gotham News," paintings by Willem de Kooning in which the subject matter is secondary to the expression of the physical act of manipulating paint, are excellent examples of this new direction in painting.

Although Abstract Expressionism has dominated postwar painting, there have been attempts to explore other directions such as Pop Art. One was the reintroduction of recognizable images, sometimes in the form of actual objects. Robert Rauschenberg's "Third Time Painting" actually combines a functioning clock with a conventionally painted canvas. It has also resulted in the use of many commonly recognizable objects of daily life—soup cans, soft drink bottles, newspaper photographs, or, in the case of Jasper Johns' "Three Flags," the American flag—to produce an imagery that will have significant meaning for an increasingly broader and more fragmented society.

The reintroduction of tangible subject matter has not hindered the frequent use of more abstract forms in a continuation of the search for an art form appropriate to the contemporary world. Such minimal and hard edge explorations as Kenneth Noland's "Via Blues" and "Chamfer" are both a reexamination of the "immaculate" concepts of the 1920s and an attempt to reach a purer, more universal level of expression.

Consult (VIII) Baur, 1957; Goodrich, 1966; Hunter, 1959; Larkin, 1964; McCoubrey, 1963.

—Philip C. Homes, *Franconia College*

PANAMA CANAL. In the days of naval competition between major powers and when the American business community hoped to expand trade to the Far East, some means of access across Central America at its narrowest point seemed essential because the journey by sea around the tip of South America was too long, and a railroad meant transshipment of goods. A canal across the Isthmus of Panama was the obvious answer, and the building of one was the dream of all empire builders.

Ultimately the United States gained exclusive rights to a route across the isthmus, first by the Clayton-Bulwer Treaty of 1850 with Britain; then by the Hay-Pauncefote Treaty of 1901, which transferred this right exclusively to the United States; and later by two Latin American treaties. The first of the latter treaties, the

Hay-Herran Convention with Colombia, provided that, in return for a payment of $10 million and an annual rental of $250,000, the United States would be granted a 99-year lease over a zone 6 miles wide in which a canal could be constructed. The second, or Hay-Bunau-Varilla Treaty, was concluded with newly independent Panama. It gave the United States control of a canal zone 10 miles wide for all time in exchange for the same fees that were to have been paid to Colombia. Both agreements, concluded in 1903—the latter immediately after Panama's revolt against Colombia—were taken in Latin America to be representative of President Theodore Roosevelt's "Big Stick Diplomacy," the more so because the United States was closely implicated in the Panamanian revolution.

The canal, one of modern man's most magnificent engineering achievements, was opened to traffic on Aug. 15, 1914. It was 40.3 miles long, and it cost in excess of $365 million. A by-product of its construction was a series of major advances in bacteriology over malaria and yellow fever under the direction of Col. William C. Gorgas.

See also Clayton-Bulwer Treaty; Hay, John; Hay-Pauncefote Treaty.

Consult (V) Mack, 1944.

—Robin W. Winks, *Yale University*

PANAMA DEBATE, Senate controversy over the confirmation of delegates to a congress of Latin American states. In 1824 Simón Bolivar called for the congress to meet in Panama, and the United States was invited to attend. President John Quincy Adams and Secretary of State Henry Adams wanted to accept, and Adams nominated Richard C. Anderson and John Sergeant as delegates.

These nominations encountered considerable resistance in the Senate, partly because of partisan politics but also because there was opposition to the prospect of foreign entanglements. The delegates were finally confirmed in March 1826, but by then it was too late. One died on the way to Panama, the other never attended, because the congress was over before he was ready to go. The Senate made it clear in approving the delegates that commercial connection with foreign nations was not to include any political connection. The congress was unsuccessful in producing greater unity in Latin America.

PANICS, FINANCIAL (NINETEENTH CENTURY), name given to various financial, industrial, and agrarian economic disorders. The United States suffered the ups and downs of most capitalist societies in the nineteenth century, but it also had other elements that made the fluctuations more pronounced. The westward movement was erratic and jerky, largely

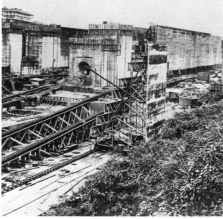

Mammoth Gatun Upper Locks of Panama Canal under construction in 1910.

because of land booms; the banking structure was poorly regulated; the currency system was confused; the growing transport network made the effects of local collapses felt all over the nation.

In 1819 the boom in Western lands and the trade expansion after the War of 1812 suddenly collapsed. European demand for American foodstuffs fell off, prices dropped, and the Bank of the United States suddenly contracted its loans and credits. The West suffered the most, although urban workers were also unemployed. Banks closed and stopped paying out cash. By 1823 the depression had gone, and Nicholas Biddle took over at the Bank of the United States to expand credit.

In 1837 another boom collapsed after President Andrew Jackson, through the Specie Circular of 1836, had barred the federal land agencies from accepting paper bills for land. This destroyed public confidence in paper money. Meanwhile, the state governments had overinvested in canal and railroad ventures, and they defaulted on their debts to foreign lenders. Too many small banks, no longer regulated by the now defunct Bank of the United States, had given too many easy loans, which were recalled hastily. The depression lasted five years and was felt worst in the South and West.

The Panic of 1857 was primarily financial rather than industrial or agrarian, although the land boom in the Southwest and West did collapse briefly. The main cause was over-speculation in railroad stocks, and banks failed all over the nation, ruining many depositors. But the depression did not last, and European demand for cotton and American foodstuffs soon picked up again. The South suffered the least this time, the financial Northeast the worst.

Post-Civil War Panics. The expansion that preceded the Panic of 1873 was fueled by over-investment in railroads and unstable financing. The post-Civil War transcontinental railroad-building mania had doubled total mileage since 1865 and had stimulated the steel industry and farming too. The failure of Jay Cooke and Company, which went bankrupt on Northern Pacific Railroad investments, triggered a general collapse of confidence. Banks failed, and the New York Stock Exchange closed. The nation suffered a five-year depression consisting of unemployment, wage cuts, strikes, factory closings, and falling farm prices. Crop failures abroad then brought increased American exports, and the economy picked up again. A brief financial crisis in 1884 produced a one-year depression. By the late 1880s the boom in Western lands had regenerated itself, and foreign loans and investment flowed in again.

Critics blamed fiscal policies of Grant administration for Panic of 1873.

The Panic of 1893 brought the failure of more than 600 banks, especially in the West. Three times as many businesses failed as in 1873, and all railroad building stopped. The panic was brought on partly by lack of confidence in the nation's financial policies, which had surfaced in the debate over the gold standard and the Sherman Silver Purchase Act. The depression that ensued was the worst of the century, almost as bad as that of the 1930s. Three million men were unemployed in 1894, and hard times produced bitter strikes, such as the Pullman Strike of 1894. Farmers suffered severely from falling agricultural prices. The economic picture did not improve until after 1897. Years of prosperity followed, interrupted by a financial crisis in 1907, until World War I.

See also Bank of the United States, Second; Cook, Jay; Pullman Strike (1894); Sherman Silver Purchase Act (1890).

Consult (III) Sobel, 1972.

—Peter d'A. Jones, *University of Illinois, Chicago Circle*

PARIS, TREATY OF (1783), agreement between the United States and Britain that ended the Revolutionary War. In June 1781 five American commissioners were empowered to conduct negotiations to end the war and establish American independence. These commissioners were John Adams, Benjamin Franklin, John Jay, Thomas Jefferson, and Henry Laurens. Jefferson took no part in the negotiations, and Laurens played only a slight role. The commissioners were ordered to cooperate with the French and consider their advice, and negotiations began in the summer of 1782. The American commission, believing that the French would not support them in all their demands, acted alone. A preliminary peace treaty between Britain and the United States was signed on Nov. 30, 1782, and the official treaty on Sept. 3, 1783.

By the treaty the United States obtained its independence and was given boundaries along the Great Lakes in the north, the Mississippi River on the west, and on the south along the 31st parallel to the Apalachicola River, to the St. Mary's River, and down the St. Mary's to the Atlantic. This last boundary was a cause of dispute with the Spanish, who claimed they owned territory north of the 31st parallel. The Americans were also given fishing rights in their traditional areas off Canada. There were to be no legal impediments to the collection of debts contracted before the Revolution, Congress was to urge the states to restore the confiscated property of loyalists, and there were to be no future property confiscations from those who took part in the war. The navigation of the Mississippi was declared free and open to citizens of both America and Britain. Many of the treaty's articles were to cause future controversy—particularly those relating to the boundaries, the recovery of debts, and the treatment of loyalists—and were settled by later treaties.

See also Adams-Onís Treaty (1819); Ghent, Treaty of (1814); Jay's Treaty (1794). —Reginald Horsman, *University of Wisconsin, Milwaukee*

PARKER, THEODORE (1810–1860), controversial clergyman and reformer. A Unitarian, he graduated from Harvard Divinity School and became a minister in West Roxbury, Mass. In many ways the successor of William Ellery Channing, Parker was a Transcendentalist and admired aspects of many religions. In addition, his social politics were radical and sympathetic to labor and the poor. His vivid and impassioned prose disturbed conventional thinkers and brought criticism that caused Parker to resign his pulpit in 1852 and become the leader of a large congregation in Boston that loyally supported him.

Parker's most dramatic cause was abolitionism. The Compromise of 1850, with its fugitive slave provision, seemed an intolerable affront to him and co-workers such as Wendell Phillips. Parker headed the Boston Committee of Vigilance, which denounced and defied government efforts to return runaways to slavery, especially in the Anthony Burns affair in 1854. Parker's eloquence in this case and on the issue of Kansas, where slavery and antislavery forces fought, influenced many in their attitudes toward abolitionism.

Parker was familiar with John Brown's plans for carrying the war against slavery into the South, but a severe illness took Parker to Europe before Brown's raid on Harpers Ferry in 1859. Parker died in Florence, Italy.

See also Abolitionism; Phillips, Wendell; Transcendentalism.

Consult (IV) Commager, 1960.

PATRONS OF HUSBANDRY, farmers' social and educational organization. *See* Granger Movement.

PATROONSHIPS, system of land colonization used by the Dutch in settling New Netherlands (New York). When the inhabitants of the Netherlands were reluctant to emigrate to the New World, the Dutch West India Company supported a proposal to grant large estates to men (patroons) who would pay the cost of settling and cultivating the land. Starting in 1629 under a Charter of Freedom and Exemptions, patroons were allowed four years to settle 50 colonists over age 15. The territory occupied had to lie along a navigable river for 16 miles on one side or for 8 miles on both sides. The patroons could dispose of their grants and were free to trade in all commodities except furs, which were reserved for the Dutch West

India Company. Colonists were bound to a patroon for a certain number of years, and it was illegal for a colonist to enter the service of another patroon during this time.

The most famous and successful patroonship belonged to Kiliaen Van Rensselaer, an Amsterdam jeweler who never visited the New World. In his name, a territory known as Rensselaerswyck was settled on both sides of the Hudson River. The power of the patroons quickly grew so great that it challenged that of the Dutch West India Company. When the director-general of New Amsterdam, Peter Minuit, favored the patroons' interest, he was replaced by the company in 1631. Although the patroonships established the Dutch in New York, they suffered from absentee management, quarrels with the company, and conflict with the Indians. By 1664, when the English took control of New York, only two remained.

See also Minuit, Peter; New York.

PATTON, GEORGE S(MITH), JR. (1885–1945), American army officer. Born in San Gabriel, Cal., he attended the Virginia Military Institute and U.S. Military Academy, where he received his commission in 1909. Patton served with Gen. John J. Pershing in Mexico and then in France during World War I, where he became interested in the use of tanks and where he established a tank training school.

During World War II he became famous for his command of the 2nd Armored Division and the I Armored Corps in North Africa. As head of the newly formed U.S. Seventh Army, he swept rapidly through Sicily in 1943. He then led the Third Army from the invasion of France in 1944 through the defeat of Germany in 1945. Called "old blood and guts," Patton was a controversial figure because of his quick temper and frank comments on military and political matters. He died in Heidelberg, Germany, after an automobile accident.

See also World War II.

Consult (VII) Patton, 1947.

PAUPER SCHOOLS, schools at which poor white children, Indians, and blacks could learn to read and write and become thoroughly acquainted with Anglican religious doctrines. From 1701 until the end of the American Revolution, the Anglican Society for the Propagation of the Gospel operated pauper schools throughout the colonies. The religious aspect of the Society's educational program aroused considerable antagonism among many colonists, who believed that it was more interested in converting religious dissenters to Anglicanism than in educating the indigent and heathen.

PAYNE-ALDRICH TARIFF ACT (1909), controversial tariff act supported by President Taft. Spurred by farmer and consumer discontent

George S. Patton, Jr., one of the most successful American commanders in World War II, was master of armored warfare.

Many U.S. ships were caught at anchor by Japanese attack on Pearl Harbor.

William Penn concludes a treaty with the Indians.

and the platform pledges of both parties, the House of Representatives proposed a tariff bill in 1909 that made substantial rate reductions and placed several items on the free list. The Senate Finance Committee, chaired by Nelson Aldrich of Rhode Island, made more than 8,000 amendments, most of which raised rates and removed items from the free list. The Republican Insurgents, led by Robert La Follette of Wisconsin, led an unsuccessful attempt to undo Aldrich's work. Although the Insurgents lost, the debate was the beginning of the Republican split of 1912.

PEACE CORPS, created by President Kennedy in 1961 to promote world peace and friendship by sending volunteer men and women abroad to help developing nations fill their critical need for skilled manpower. Formerly under the Department of State, the Peace Corps is now under ACTION, an independent agency established in 1971 to bring all federal voluntary action programs together.

Peace Corps volunteers, who are carefully selected and trained, serve for periods of 2 years. Volunteers live in the communities to which they are sent to work. The Peace Corps is headed by a director appointed by the president with the advice and consent of the Senate. Each of the corps' four geographical regions—Africa; East Asia and the Pacific; Latin America; and North Africa, the Near East, and South Asia—is headed by a director whose responsibilities include the operation of the region and the training of volunteers.

PEARL HARBOR, U.S. naval base on Oahu in the Hawaiian Islands. Japan's surprise air attack on it on Dec. 7, 1941, was one of the most successful tactical moves in military history and brought the United States into World War II. American forces were caught completely unprepared and suffered heavy losses: 8 battleships, 3 cruisers, and 3 destroyers were sunk, disabled, or heavily damaged; 149 planes were destroyed; 2,403 civilian and military personnel were killed and another 1,178 wounded. Designed to cripple U.S. naval power in the Pacific and force the United States to accept Japanese domination of the Far East, the attack instead galvanized American opinion behind the war and stimulated a fierce determination to avenge the humiliating defeat at Pearl Harbor.

See also World War II.

PENDLETON ACT (1883), enacted because of public pressure and political expediency, established the federal Civil Service. President Garfield's assassination (1881) by a disappointed office seeker caused his successor, Chester Arthur, to demand a merit system that would eliminate patronage struggles. After the Democrats carried the 1882 elections, the lame

duck Republican Congress became convinced that merit laws could protect incumbent Republican appointees. A bill written by the Civil Service Reform Association and sponsored by Senator George Pendleton won bipartisan approval in January 1883. Arthur appointed a three-man commission to prepare and administer competitive examinations for government positions. The Pendleton Act outlawed political assessments on federal employees, apportioned new appointments among the states, and gave presidents the power to widen coverage. Although the act originally covered only 10 percent of federal employees, almost all presidents have expanded its scope, and the merit system now covers about 85 percent of government jobs.

See also Arthur, Chester A.

PENN, WILLIAM (1644–1718), English Quaker who organized settlement of Pennsylvania. Son of a parliamentary admiral during the English Civil Wars, Penn enraged his father by joining the Quakers a few years after the Restoration of 1660, but he also retained important contacts at court, including the King's brother James, Duke of York. In 1681 Penn accepted a proprietary charter for "Pennsylvania" in payment of an old Crown debt to his family. He then worked hard to organize his claim as a Holy Experiment, a truly utopian society where Quakers in particular (although others were welcome too) could live together in peace, toleration, love, and prosperity.

He probably expected to spend the rest of his life in Pennsylvania when he arrived there in 1682, but conflicting boundary claims with Maryland forced his return to England in 1684. He again sailed to his colony in 1699, only to be recalled two years later to defend his charter against parliamentary attack. Back in England, he discovered that his trusted steward had embezzled most of his family fortune over the years. After spending some time in debtors' prison, he was released only to suffer a severe stroke in 1712. He was seldom lucid thereafter.

Penn believed that his distinct roles as feudal proprietor of a large colony and Quaker pacifist were compatible, but events were disillusioning. While in his colony, he normally placed its interests above his own and was able to arrange fairly satisfactory compromises on divisive issues. As a distant absentee, his demands became more strident, and the settlers less respectful and less cooperative. Only under his children, Thomas and John Penn, would the province begin to make the family rich.

See also Pennsylvania.

Consult (I) Bronner, 1962; Tolles and Alderfer, 1957.

—John M. Murrin, *Princeton University*

PENNSYLVANIA, colony and state that was first effectively settled by William Penn. It was named in honor of Penn's father, an admiral who had served the English royal family. His son received the colony in 1681 in payment of a debt to his father, and being a Quaker, he determined to make Pennsylvania a haven for religious refugees of all kinds. He openly advertised for them, and the colony grew rapidly. In 1682 Penn wrote a Frame of Government for his Holy Experiment, a most liberal system that allowed religious freedom, generous land grants, and a unicameral assembly. Penn's famous treaty of friendship with the Indians did not last, but his aim was to treat them fairly. He laid out the City of Brotherly Love (Philadelphia), and it soon became second in size in the British Empire only to London.

The emigrants to Pennsylvania made it a plural society—English and Welsh Quakers, who dominated the economy and society of eastern Pennsylvania; Pennsylvania Dutch (southwestern Germans and Swiss), who farmed the rich soils of southeast Pennsylvania; Scotch-Irish in the Cumberland Valley and the west. The colony remained under proprietary control until the Revolution, surviving the French and Indian wars of the eighteenth century and producing leading American patriots such as Robert Morris and Benjamin Franklin. Philadelphia was a Revolutionary headquarters and served as the U.S. capital from 1790 to 1800. Pennsylvania ratified the Constitution on Dec. 12, 1787, the second state to do so. By that date the Holy Experiment phase was long since gone, and the state was a leading commercial, farming, and intellectual center.

The legislature is bicameral; the capital is Harrisburg. The population in 1970 was 11,793,909.

See also Penn, William; Quakers.
Consult (I) Bronner, 1962.

PENNSYLVANIA, UNIVERSITY OF. *See* Colonial Colleges.

PEOPLE'S PARTY, political party with an agrarian base, usually called the Populist Party. *See* Populists.

PEQUOT WAR (1637), violent clash between New England colonists and the Pequot Indians that resulted in the virtual annihilation of the Pequots. The Pequots, a Connecticut tribe, had had poor relations with the white men, but in 1634, threatened by the Narragansetts and the Dutch, they concluded a pact with Massachusetts Bay Colony. In return for its protection, the colony exacted a stiff annual tribute. When John Oldham, collector of the Pequot tribute, was murdered in July 1636, Massachusetts used his death as a pretext for sending a punitive expedition against the Pequots.

Although little damage was done, the Pequots, as predicted by Connecticut colonists, began preparing for a war on the settlers.

They attempted to enlist their Narragansett enemies, but the influence of Roger Williams kept the Narragansetts on the side of the colonists. War broke out in spring 1637. By May, 30 settlers were dead. Connecticut raised 90 men under Capt. John Mason, who without waiting for Massachusetts aid, sailed to the Indians' stronghold on the Pequot River. With 80 Mohegan and 200 Narragansett allies, he surprised the Pequots, and slaughtered almost all the 400 inhabitants in the Indian village.

After repelling another party of 300 Indians, Mason gathered reinforcements and pursued the remaining Pequots, who were caught in a swamp near New Haven. Most of the Indians were captured or killed, with the captives enslaved in New England or the West Indies. Not more than 200 free Pequots remained in Connecticut. On Sept. 21, 1638, the Connecticut settlers concluded a treaty with the Mohegans and Narragansetts that gave the Pequot property to the Connecticut towns and divided the remaining Pequots between the two tribes.

See also Connecticut; Williams, Roger.

PERRY, MATTHEW (CALBRAITH) (1794–1858), American naval officer who opened up Japan to world trade. Born in Rhode Island, Perry served in the War of 1812, including a tour under his brother, Oliver Hazard Perry.

In later years he held a variety of posts and was responsible for several innovative navy programs. Promoted to captain in 1837, he took command of the *Fulton,* one of the first steam warships in the U.S. Navy, named after Robert Fulton. He had supervised its building and turned it into the first naval gunnery training vessel. During the Mexican War, Perry commanded a squadron that worked with Gen. Winfield Scott in the capture of Veracruz.

In 1852 President Fillmore gave Perry the mission of establishing diplomatic and trade relations with Japan, which had previously rebuffed efforts by Western nations to make contact. Perry arrived in Japan in 1853 with an impressive armed squadron. After delivering the U.S. messages, Perry went to China for several months. He returned to Japan in 1854 and negotiated the famous Treaty of Kanagawa (1854), by which the United States was permitted to open a consulate in Japan and to use certain Japanese ports.

PERRY, OLIVER HAZARD (1785–1819), American naval officer. He entered the navy as a midshipman in 1799 and served in the naval war against France. He saw further service in the war against Tripoli but achieved his greatest fame in the War of 1812 as commander of the American naval forces on Lake Erie.

He assumed his command there in March 1813 and hurried along the completion of the American ships for the lake. In spite of a

Japanese block print of Matthew Perry, whose expedition to Japan opened the island empire to western trade.

Oliver Hazard Perry, naval hero of the War of 1812.

John J. Pershing, Commander of the American Expeditionary Force in World War I.

British blockade he managed to get his vessels out of Presque Isle in the summer of 1813, and on Sept. 10, 1813, was engaged by the British fleet at the decisive Battle of Lake Erie. Perry showed great bravery and initiative in this victorious engagement, which made him a national hero. Although his force was superior in armament and men, there was a point in the battle when all could have been lost. When his flagship, the *Lawrence,* was shattered by British fire he had himself rowed to the *Niagara.* This was the decisive point in the battle. After the engagement he sent a terse and famous dispatch to Gen. William Henry Harrison: "We have met the enemy; and they are ours." He died while on a diplomatic mission to Venezuela.

See also Lake Erie, Battle of (1813).
Consult (III) Dutton, 1935.

PERSHING, JOHN J(OSEPH) (1860–1948), Army general who commanded the American Expeditionary Force (AEF) in World War I. A stern West Pointer, he had served in Indian wars, the Spanish-American War, the military occupation of the Philippines, and as a military teacher. In 1916 he led the expedition into Mexico seeking the raiders led by Pancho Villa. The expedition was a failure and was soon withdrawn, but in 1917 President Wilson deliberately passed over the popular Gen. Leonard Wood and gave command of the AEF to Pershing, who was made a full general.

In Europe, Pershing insisted that the American forces should not merge with Allied armies but maintain their own separate and distinct identity. He resisted sending half-trained men into battle. However, German advances forced him to relax and to allow some use of Americans in various positions on the front. A good administrator, Pershing developed well-organized and tough American combat forces in a very short time. In 1919 he was promoted to the rank of General of the Armies, a unique position created for him. He was Army chief of staff from 1921 until his retirement in 1924.

See also American Expeditionary Force; World War I.

PERSONAL LIBERTY LAWS, legislation passed by Northern states to shield their citizens from false arrest and possible conveyance into slavery. They were enacted in response to the Supreme Court's decision in *Prigg v. Pennsylvania* (1842). The demand for individual protection from arbitrary actions by federal marshals was intensified after the Fugitive Slave Act was passed in 1850. Thus, the Massachusetts Personal Liberty Act (1855) made it all but impossible for an alleged fugitive to be seized or held by a state officer. One section of the act made any officer who did so liable to a fine and imprisonment.

See also Fugitive Slave Acts; Prigg v. Pennsylvania (1842).

PHILLIPS, WENDELL (1811–1884), orator and abolitionist. Born in Boston to a patrician family, Phillips began a career in law, but his life was abruptly changed in 1837, when he attended a meeting at Faneuil Hall in Boston. He spoke out brilliantly against the killing of Rev. Elijah P. Lovejoy, an abolitionist editor.

Phillips became a radical who denounced churches and the Constitution as honoring slavery. Dissatisfied with Abraham Lincoln's record as president, Phillips declared in 1864 that he would rather cut off his hand than vote again for Lincoln. With slavery outlawed in 1865, Garrison deemed his work completed. Phillips, who succeeded Garrison as president of the American Anti-Slavery Society, went on to fight for women's rights and civil rights for blacks. He then turned his attention to "wage slavery," working with unionists and others for the eight-hour work day, equal pay for women for equal labor, antimonopoly laws, and other reforms.

Phillips revolutionized oratory and debate, using an easy, colloquial style and an abundance of wit and irony. He was an exceptionally popular speaker even among those who condemned his principles. Phillips drew large audiences on noncontroversial topics, which he then gave libertarian overtones. His speech on "The Lost Arts" was delivered before approximately 2,000 audiences.

See also Abolitionism.
Consult (IV) Filler, 1965; Sherwin, 1956.
—Louis Filler, *Antioch College*

PHYSICAL VALUATION ACT (1913), bill that gave the Interstate Commerce Commission additional powers. *See* Hepburn Act (1906).

PIERCE, FRANKLIN (1804–1869), 14th President of the United States (1853–1857). He was born in Hillsboro, N.H., on Nov. 23, 1804. Although he served as a Democratic representative and senator from his state from 1833 to 1842, Pierce compiled an undistinguished record and was known primarily for his party regularity and his skill in leading the New Hampshire Democratic Party.

When the Democratic convention of 1852 deadlocked, shrewd New England politicians put forth Pierce as a compromise candidate. He was a New Englander and an ardent nationalist, but he was also respected in the South for his opposition to abolitionism. In the election of 1852 he won an easy victory over Whig candidate Winfield Scott and Free-Soiler John P. Hale.

Presidency. Once in office, Pierce tried

unsuccessfully to maintain harmony between the Northern and Southern wings of his party. Preoccupied with his grandiose expansion plans, he supported the Kansas-Nebraska Act (1854), which reopened the complex problem of slavery in the territories. Pierce's support of the proslavery forces in Kansas and his abortive attempt to purchase Cuba from Spain convinced many Northern Democrats and Independents that he was too pro-Southern. In 1856 the Democratic Party turned away from Pierce and drafted James Buchanan.

After 1860 Pierce retreated into social and political obscurity, becoming increasingly alienated from Northern political opinion because of his strident opposition to Abraham Lincoln's wartime policies. He was an inexperienced man who had little training or temperamental fitness for the tremendous task of reconciling regional differences. He died in Concord, N.H. on Oct. 8, 1869.

See also Bleeding Kansas; Buchanan, James; Kansas-Nebraska Act (1854).

Consult (IV) Nichols, 1958.

—Dan T. Carter, *University of Maryland*

PIKE, ZEBULON M(ONTGOMERY) (1779–1813), American army officer and explorer. The son of an army officer, he became a cadet in his father's company at age 15 and was commissioned a lieutenant in 1799. In 1805 Pike was assigned to find the source of the Mississippi River, and, although unable to do so, he explored its upper course. From St. Louis in 1806, Pike led an expedition to the headwaters of the Red and Arkansas rivers and scouted Spanish settlements in New Mexico. During this trip Pike discovered the peak named for him in Colorado and explored the country around Leadville. Pike was arrested in January 1807 by Spanish authorities for taking military possession of Spanish territory, but he was released in July.

After the War of 1812 began, Pike was promoted to the rank of brigadier general. He led the attack on York (now Toronto), Canada, where he was fatally injured by an exploding powder magazine.

PILGRIMS, the first colonists of New England. By the end of the sixteenth century many Englishmen had come to believe that the established Anglican church employed practices that at best stood in the way of pure religion as defined in the Bible and at worst were openly corrupt. Those who called for reforms were labeled Puritans because their goal was the purification of religion in England. Puritans split into two general groups. Those who believed that needed changes could be accomplished within the Church of England were known as Non-Separatists. Others openly separated from the established church, and these Separatists frequently suffered persecution at the hands of the English government.

One group of Separatists was located in the village of Scrooby, where they met at the manor house of William Brewster. These Puritans, having renounced the Anglican church, sought no reforms in it and wanted only to be left alone to practice religion in their own way. But the Anglicans in Scrooby harassed them, and in 1607, 125 of them left for Holland, which tolerated a variety of Protestant sects.

But life in Holland did not prove agreeable to the dissenters, and they eventually decided to leave. In February 1620 they secured from the London Company a patent for a settlement in Virginia. Because they could not finance such an undertaking, they agreed to work for seven years in Virginia, then divide the profits and property with a group of English merchants who would pay for their journey.

Voyage to the New World. In early September, 102 settlers left England for Virginia aboard the *Mayflower*. Fewer than half were Puritans, for they had been joined by men such as Miles Standish (whom they chose as military officer), whose motives in emigrating to America were not religious. After a two-month journey the *Mayflower* came within sight of Cape Cod, far to the north of its intended destination, but the Pilgrims (as the group has come to be named) decided to stay. Because the area was outside the jurisdiction of the Virginia Company, the settlers met aboard ship and drafted the Mayflower Compact, a document that established the principles and rules by which their community would be governed. The Pilgrims then elected John Carver, the wealthiest member of the group, to serve as their first governor.

Settlement. After landing at Plymouth on Dec. 21, 1620, the Pilgrims faced terrible hardships. Few of the settlers had any experience in colonization. Worse still, they had come to America without adequate food supplies, and they could not begin to plant crops until spring. By then more than half the Pilgrims, including Governor Carver, had died. Carver was replaced by William Bradford, who supervised the Pilgrims' struggle with the wilderness during a long tenure in office (he was reelected nearly every year until his death in 1657) and wrote a famous history of the colony.

Having received help from Squanto, an Indian who taught them how to plant corn, showed them where to fish, and negotiated on their behalf with neighboring tribes, the Pilgrims celebrated their harvest in October 1621. The same year the Pilgrims secured a charter for Plymouth Colony from the Council for New England.

See also Bradford, William; Massachusetts; Plymouth; Puritanism.

Consult (I) Demos, 1970; Langdon, 1966.

—Aaron M. Shatzman, *Washington University.*

Franklin Pierce, 14th President of the United States (1853–1857).

The *Mayflower* brought the Pilgrims to Plymouth in 1620.

PINCHOT, GIFFORD (1865-1946). A graduate of Yale University, he studied forestry in England and France and in 1898 was appointed chief of forestry in the Department of Agriculture. In 1905 he became the first chief forester of the United States after a departmental reorganization. His conservation efforts during the Roosevelt Administration were so outstanding that the President dubbed him "the man to whom the nation owes most for what has been accomplished as regards the preservation of the natural resources of our country."

During the Taft Administration, Pinchot sparked a controversy by accusing Secretary of the Interior Richard Ballinger of making public lands available to private business interests. Taft fired Pinchot, and the resulting furor sharply divided the Conservative and Insurgent wings of the Republican Party. Pinchot played a major role in forming the Progressive Party and in inducing Roosevelt to be its standard bearer. In 1922 Pinchot became governor of Pennsylvania after leading a revolt against the Republican "Old Guard" and was reelected in 1930, achieving national prominence for his accomplishments in conservation, business regulation, and labor legislation.

Consult (VI) McGeary, 1960; Pinkett, 1970.

PINCKNEY'S TREATY (1795), attempt to settle disputes between Spain and the United States in North America. After the Revolutionary War there was constant tension between the two countries, particularly over American shipping on the Mississippi River, which Spain could control because it owned New Orleans; over the boundary in the south; and over Spanish support for the Indians. Negotiations between John Jay and Diego de Gardoqui in 1785-1786 resulted in failure.

Agreement between the two countries was made possible by the European wars of the 1790s. Troubled by her position between France and England, Spain was ready to reach an agreement with the United States. Thomas Pinckney was sent as special envoy to Spain, and a treaty was signed at San Lorenzo on Oct. 27, 1795. Spain agreed on the 31st parallel as a boundary, promised not to incite the Indians, gave Americans full navigation rights to the Mississippi, and agreed that for three years (renewable) the Americans could deposit goods at New Orleans before sending them on ocean-going ships.

See also Jay, John.

PIZARRO, FRANCISCO (1475?-1541), Spanish explorer and *conquistador* of Peru. Born illegitimately, Pizarro left Spain for the New World driven by dreams of glory. As early as 1509, he was a member of an expedition from Hispaniola to the Colombian coast, and he later accompanied Balboa on the trek across Central America to the Pacific Ocean. Pizarro then formed a partnership to explore the western coastline of South America, openly acknowledging his greed for gold and making no pretense of converting the Indians to Christianity.

Learning of the Inca Empire, he eventually obtained a commission in Spain for an expedition into inland South America. Pizarro outfitted 3 ships and with 183 men set sail from Spain in January 1531. He landed on the coast of Peru and was welcomed as a friend by the Indians until the Spanish plundered a village. The Inca Empire was ruled by a wealthy, highly cultured elite known as the "People of the Sun," who closely regulated the lives of their subjects. Pizarro arrived at a time when this elite was split into factions, and he was also able to take advantage of an Inca legend that the sons of the white demigod Viracaclu, with whom the Spanish were confused, would return.

Pizarro met Atahualpa, the Inca leader, in November 1532 under the guise of friendship but soon made him a prisoner. Pizarro demanded and received a huge gold and silver ransom but then had Atahualpa strangled in August 1533. Without substantial opposition, Pizarro entered Cuzco, the Inca capital, in November 1533. Not content with his success, Pizarro founded a new capital at Lima and was exploring Bolivia and Chile by 1535. Pizarro and one of his partners, Diego de Almagro, quarreled over territorial jurisdiction, and Pizarro ordered him executed in 1538. In retribution, Almagro's followers assassinated Pizarro on June 26, 1541, in Lima.

See also Indians, South American.

Consult (I) Wright, 1970.

PLAINS OF ABRAHAM, battleground outside Quebec on which British forces defeated the city's French defenders. *See* French and Indian War (1754-1763).

PLANTATION DUTY ACT (1673). *See* Navigation Acts.

PLANTATION SYSTEM, vast tracts dedicated to a single crop and worked by gangs of slaves under foremen and overseers. It became identified with the South, even though the word referred originally to a colony, as in "Plymouth Plantation." Although there were a number of Southern estates that used thousands of acres and hundreds of slaves, they represented a small proportion of actual holdings. Perhaps two-thirds of all white Southerners were not associated with plantations. Yet few of the nonslaveholding class expressed active antagonism toward slaveholders, and those who did became social outcasts.

The Plantation Economy. The Virginia colony, precariously initiated in 1607, had liter-

Idyllic view of plantation life in Alabama before the Civil War.

ally been saved by tobacco: a hardy weed, easily grown, and readily marketed. Tobacco became the first of the cash crops to which the South was committed. Later, rice was grown in South Carolina and sugar in Louisiana, employing slaves who had to endure excessive heat and swamp conditions. Cotton, following the invention of the cotton gin in 1793, became the greatest Southern staple, making the region dependent for manufactured goods and other necessities on British mill owners and on New York and other Northern merchants and money lenders.

The simple tasks of seeding, picking, and carrying these staples caused their masters to maintain slaves in strictly limited working and living conditions. Although many slaves found ways and means of maintaining their dignity and even ambition, they were weighed down by circumstances that abolitionists criticized and that slaveholders felt more and more compelled to defend as preferable to freedom. Whether the slave economy was profitable, and in what sense, has been argued. Southern apologists declared that it was and that, in addition, theirs was a unique culture, a patriarchal system comparable to that of ancient Greece, with its own traditions and achievements.

The Old South, with which the plantation system was identified, was destroyed by the Civil War and the emancipation of the slaves. The resurgence of white supremacy in the South in 1877 and after, with its sharecropping and lend-lease systems of farming, differed notably from the earlier plantation system.

See also Sharecropping; Slavery.
Consult (IV) Phillips, 1969; Woodman, 1966.
—Louis Filler, *Antioch College*

PLATT AMENDMENT, legislation incorporated into the Army Appropriations Bill of 1901 by Senator Orville H. Platt of Connecticut. Its purpose was to assure that Cuba, newly freed from Spain by American intervention, and at the time under U.S. military occupation, would not permit any foreign power to take control of the island, incur any foreign indebtedness that would encourage foreign intervention, or otherwise compromise its independence. However, because the amendment also gave the United States full liberty to intervene in Cuban affairs for the purpose of maintaining that independence and because Cuba was forced to agree to sell or lease to the United States sites for naval and coaling stations, the island in effect became an American protectorate. When American troops left the island, the amendment was incorporated into the Cuban-American Treaty of 1903. It was abrogated in May 1934.
Consult (V) Dozer, 1959.

PLATTSBURG BAY, BATTLE OF. *See* War of 1812.

PLATTSBURG IDEA, concept of military training camps for civilians. *See* Preparedness Movement (1915–1916).

PLESSY v. FERGUSON (1896), controversial Supreme Court decision involving "separate but equal" treatment of blacks. In an 8 to 1 decision, the Court upheld a Louisiana statute that required railroad accommodations to be segregated. The majority held that the Fourteenth Amendment was intended "to enforce the absolute equality of the two races before the law," but not "to abolish distinctions based upon color, or to enforce social, as opposed to political, equality . . . " As long as the statute required equal treatment, it did not violate the equal protection of the law clause of the Fourteenth Amendment. The majority went on to say the separation does not mean that one of the races is thereby stamped as inferior. Justice Harlan, in dissent, said that the Constitution contains an absolute prohibition against legislation discriminating between the races in their public or civil relations.

The majority decision in this case allowed for further state legislation in public schools, in transportation, and in public accommodations based on the separate but equal standard. The decision was overruled by *Brown v. Board of Education of Topeka* (1954).
See also Brown v. Board of Education of Topeka (1954); Education.

PLYMOUTH, the colony of the Pilgrim Fathers, later incorporated into Massachusetts. Plymouth, sometimes known as New Plymouth, was settled in 1620 on the coast of Massachusetts by those who came on the *Mayflower*. Some of the group were Separatists, who had quit the Church of England and gone to live in Holland in 1607. They were the congregation from the village of Scrooby, who used to meet in the house of William Brewster and whose number included the young William Bradford and the preacher John Robinson.

After almost 13 years in Holland, these Pilgrims wanted to leave and live elsewhere, under the English flag but not in England. Thus some of them, joined by Puritans and several non-Puritans from England, set sail for America in 1620 under a patent issued by the Virginia Company. The capital was provided by a group of London merchants, led by Thomas Weston, who expected profits—the Puritans were to provide lumber, fish, and furs.

After a rough crossing, the *Mayflower* made landfall far north of the jurisdiction of the Virginia Company. Non-Puritans were now ready to revolt and seek their freedom in this unclaimed area, but the *Mayflower* Compact was drawn up on board ship, off Provincetown,

Pilgrims landed at Plymouth in December 1620.

Cape Cod, and signed on Nov. 11, 1620. The Compact was an unprecedented agreement for a form of self-government, although modeled on a "company" structure with a governor and assistants. In June 1621, Sir Ferdinando Gorges received a new charter from the King for a Council for New England. This new council awarded the Pilgrims their Bradford patent of January 1630, which legalized their landholdings and settlement in the Plymouth region.

Led by William Bradford, the Pilgrims survived very harsh beginnings and labored hard to provide lumber and furs for export. Until 1623 everything was held in common, but after that date private property was introduced, and productivity increased. Many difficulties with the London merchants led eventually to the capitalists selling their title in the colony to the settlers in 1626 for £1,800. Profits from the fur trade helped the Pilgrims to pay off their debt.

The Bradford patent confirmed their land titles and boundaries within which new towns now grew up, besides Plymouth itself. Gradually, a form of representative government came into being, each township being locally self-governed and sending representatives from town meetings to a general court in Plymouth. The first code of laws, the Great Fundamentals, appeared in 1636. Plymouth joined the New England Confederation in 1643 and, after much internal religious dissension, was finally assimilated by Massachusetts Bay Colony when the latter received a royal charter in 1691.

See also Bradford, William; Massachusetts; New England Confederation; Pilgrims.
Consult (I) Demos, 1970; Langdon, 1966.
—Peter d'A. Jones, *University of Illinois, Chicago Circle*

POE, EDGAR ALLAN (1809–1849), poet, critic, and short story writer who in a short and troubled life produced some of the most original literature of his century. Born in Boston, he was orphaned at three. Raised by a Richmond tobacco dealer, John Allan, Poe broke with his mentor during his first term at the University of Virginia in 1826. The ultimate pattern of Poe's life was already beginning to emerge. His literary gifts became apparent in *Tamerlane and Other Poems* (1827), but gambling debts and alcoholism clouded his future.

Under an assumed name Poe enlisted in the U.S. Army and was appointed to West Point but was released for gross neglect of duty in 1831. *Poems of Edgar A. Poe* (1831) failed to arouse literary notice, although it contained three of Poe's best known poems, "To Helen," "The Doomed City," and "Israfel." His first popular success came with the publication in a Baltimore periodical of "MS. Found in a Bottle," which won him a prize and also a friend

and patron who arranged for Poe to write for *The Southern Literary Messenger.* Poe joined the *Messenger's* staff and helped to increase circulation several times over with his writings and editing.

Poe married his 14-year-old cousin, Virginia Clemm, in 1836, and they moved to New York looking for broader literary horizons. He supported himself with free-lance writing and editing and published *Tales of the Grotesque and Arabesque* (1840), winning a prize for the story "The Gold Bug." Still troubled by gambling and drinking, Poe went from one position to another, writing prolifically in order to support himself.

He received great critical acclaim for "The Raven," published in the *New York Evening Mirror* in 1845, and the same year he became sole editor of the *Broadway Journal.* His wife, Virginia, died of tuberculosis, and Poe's private life became even more chaotic. In 1849 he was found in a Baltimore saloon semiconscious and died four days later. A talented poet, an inventor of the detective story, and original literary critic, Poe always had a greater reputation abroad, where his bizarre poems greatly influenced the French symbolist movement.

See also Literature.
Consult (III) Davidson, 1957; Wagenknecht, 1963.
—Richard Collin, *Louisiana State University, New Orleans*

POETRY. *See* Literature.

POLIO VACCINE. *See* Salk, Jonas.

POLITICAL MACHINE, a vote-gathering organization that acts with mechanical consistency and precision. Its hierarchy has clearly defined authority and responsibility. The term, like political boss, is generally negative in its connotation and implies manipulation of unthinking automatons by unscrupulous politicians. In the rural and small towns of the North, machines have often served to defend the populace against the aspirations of the immigrant working class of the cities and in the South have performed the same service for those who feared black resurgence.

Most common, however, was the urban political machine, which delivered the immigrant-working-class vote by filling a variety of needs that were largely unmet by the prevailing system. The machine dispensed jobs, providing a career ladder for minority groups, and a wide variety of other welfare benefits (rent, food, and clothing) at a time when public programs were virtually nonexistent. It intervened with the law, provided fellowship through picnics and dances, and gave the lower class some personal day-to-day contact with city govern-

Author Edgar Allan Poe, poet and master of the Gothic short story.

ment. Finally, it was careful to treat the cultural and religious traditions of urban minorities with respect and deference.

At the other end of the social scale, the machine politician also helped the entrepreneur to buy his city contractor franchise (for a consideration) without the necessity of meeting all the legal requirements. This system of informal government provided ample opportunity for graft and corruption and allowed vice and crime to operate with official connivance. Reformers who railed against such evils rarely appreciated the necessity of the machine's services or made provision for alternative solutions. Many even sought to solve the problem by removing the immigrant working class from effective political participation. The most successful urban reformers, such as Tom Johnson in Cleveland and Hazen Pingree in Detroit, did recognize these realities and built their own reform machines. The machines themselves began to produce much more enlightened representatives, such as Robert F. Wagner, Sr., and Alfred E. Smith in New York, David I. Walsh in Massachusetts, and Joseph P. Tumulty in New Jersey, who saw the need to reduce graft, vice, and crime and find more effective ways of serving their constituents.

Ironically, the federalization of welfare removed one of the major functions of the machine, while political reforms such as civil service and city-wide elections restricted its ability to operate. Much of its constituency became assimilated and dispersed in the suburbs. By 1970 the Daley machine in Chicago appeared to be the last vestige of the political organizations that once controlled the nation's major cities.

Consult (VI) Stave, 1972.

—John Buenker, *University of Wisconsin, Parkside*

POLITICAL PARTIES IN THE UNITED STATES.

American political party development has gone through three stages. The first is the period from the creation of parties in the 1790s and again in the 1820s, following a time of one-party rule, through the presidencies of James Monroe and John Quincy Adams. The second stage lasted from Andrew Jackson's presidency until the Civil War. During this period two national parties—the Democrats and the Whigs—were solidly established. The third period, following 1860, has featured competition between the modern Democratic and Republican parties.

For convenience, this third period is usually subdivided into the post-Civil War period, which ended in 1896, the Progressive movement, which was vigorous until 1921, and the current phase, which began with the New Deal.

Federalists and Republicans. The initial partisan divisions occurred over the adoption of the Constitution with the Federalists proposing adoption and the Anti-Federalists opposing ratification. These factions gradually developed into political parties. The Federalists lost the election of 1800 to Thomas Jefferson's party (by then called the Republicans) and never returned to national power.

Democrats and Whigs. From 1816 to 1828 most voters considered themselves Jeffersonian Republicans, and two-party competition gave way to intraparty rivalry, but this balance proved to be unstable, and the followers of Henry Clay and of John Quincy Adams split with Andrew Jackson in the elections of 1824 and 1828. The factions rapidly became separate parties under the names of Democrats and Whigs. During this period the parties became institutionalized, for instance, in developing and using national nominating conventions to select the presidential and vice-presidential candidates.

From Lincoln to McKinley. The election of 1860 shattered the existing party system. With four major candidates in the presidential competition, Abraham Lincoln, as the candidate of the recently formed Republican Party, received a majority of the electoral vote but only 39.9 percent of the popular vote. A new alignment grew up after the war, when the South became heavily Democratic and the North heavily Republican. One result of the disputed Hayes-Tilden election of 1876, in which Samuel J. Tilden won the popular vote but lost in the electoral college to Rutherford B. Hayes, was the end of Reconstruction in the South. The Democrats then consolidated their hold on the Southern political apparatus. The next crucial election of the period was that of 1896, in which the Republicans under William McKinley severely defeated the Democratic and Populist candidate, William Jennings Bryan. The Democrats were not able to recoup their losses significantly until Wilson's reelection in 1916.

The Progressive Era. The Progressive movement of the last part of the nineteenth and early part of the twentieth centuries had a direct influence on national party politics. In 1912 Theodore Roosevelt, in a major schism within the Republican Party, ran as a Progressive against Republican William Taft and Democrat Woodrow Wilson. This division of the Republican vote made Wilson's victory possible. The Wilson Administration enacted into law much of the Progressive Party's platform, and the party rapidly disintegrated.

Republican Hegemony. From the Republican presidential victory under Warren Harding in 1920 through the election of Herbert Hoover in 1928, the Republicans were the dominant national party. In 1924 Robert La Follette broke with the Republican Party and ran as a Progressive. Four years later Alfred Smith, a Catholic and a "wet," ran unsuccessfully against Herbert Hoover. It was the Great Depression and the failure of the Hoover Administration to deal with it that ended Republican hegemony in the critical realigning election of 1932.

The New Deal. The impact of Franklin Roosevelt's electoral victories in 1932, 1936, 1940, and 1944 was profound. In terms of policy the New Deal began an era of positive government. Roosevelt used his position to give personal leadership to the Democrats. His fireside chats over the radio established a new form of direct communication between president and electorate. In the 1944 election Thomas Dewey, the Republican candidate, succeeded in reducing the proportion of the popular vote for Roosevelt.

Truman and Eisenhower. In April 1945 Vice-President Harry Truman assumed the presidency on the death of Roosevelt. Truman won election in his own right in 1948, largely through keeping the labor, big-city, and minority votes. For the time being, the New Deal coalition persisted. It was shattered, however, in the election of 1952 and the triumph of Republican Dwight Eisenhower. The deterioration of Democratic strength was general, being reflected in congressional and gubernatorial races. Eisenhower was reelected in 1956 by a larger electoral vote than in 1952.

Kennedy and Johnson. The Democratic candidate in 1960, John Kennedy, narrowly defeated his Republican opponent, Richard Nixon. Kennedy received only a plurality of the popular vote. Following the latter's assassination, Lyndon Johnson assumed the presidency. In the 1964 election Johnson crushed the Republican Barry Goldwater in the most lopsided contest of modern times. The vote amounted to popular approval of positive government. Because of difficulties stemming from his conduct of the unpopular war in Vietnam, Johnson declined to stand for reelection in 1968.

The Nixon Victory. After an interval of eight years Richard Nixon again ran for the presidency on the Republican ticket in 1968. His main opponent was Hubert Humphrey, Johnson's vice-president. George Wallace, who ran as the candidate of the American Independent Party, took five Southern states with a combined electoral vote of 46. Nixon carried 32 states with a total of 301 electoral votes and received 31.7 million popular votes. Humphrey carried 14 states with 191 electoral votes and received 31.2 million popular votes. In 1972 Nixon ran for reelection against Senator George McGovern, whose liberal programs alienated many traditional Democrats such as the blue-collar workers. Nixon won an overwhelming victory with only Massachusetts and the District of Columbia giving McGovern a majority. Nixon's triumph deepened the divisions in the Democratic Party, which had been torn by open discord since 1968.

The National Two-Party System
The Political Environment. The national party system operates within a political environment that affects what the parties do and how they do it. One constraint is the attitude of the public toward parties. Another constraint is the constitutional framework. The separation of powers among executive, legislative, and judicial branches of government renders impossible in the United States the cabinet type of government found in parliamentary systems. Federalism, by dividing power between the federal government and the states, makes for a diffused governing system. This decentralization of political power has been accompanied by the decentralization of party power.

Causes of a Two-Party System. There are several reasons for the dominance of two major parties to the detriment or even exclusion of minor parties. The first is the electoral system itself. The use of a single-member district in choosing congressional representation means that whoever receives a plurality of the vote wins the contested seat. This system tends to work against smaller parties. The same principle is visible in the election of presidents, where the electoral college also has a bipolarizing effect. There are additional historical, cultural, and psychological factors that support a two-party system. The relative absence of ideology in American politics also tends to sustain a two-party system.

Minor Parties. Although the national parties receive the lion's share of the popular and electoral vote, there usually are minor parties that enter into national, state, and local contests. When these parties are secessions from a major party—such as the Progressives in 1912—they may be formidable, if temporary, contestants. Where the parties are more interested in propaganda than in winning an election—such as the Prohibition Party—the results must be judged by changes in public law; the function of such parties is to raise issues that are eventually taken over by one of the major parties.

See also Presidential Elections; articles on individual political parties.

Consult (VIII) Binckley, 1963; Chambers, 1963; Schattschneider, 1942; Stedman and Stedman, 1967.

—Murray S. Stedman, *Temple University*

Glossary of Political Parties
American Independent Party. George Wallace headed a third-party ticket under the label of the American Independent Party in the 1968 presidential election. His followers were essentially Democrats who opposed the national administration of President Johnson. The emphasis was on race and nationalism. He

received 9.89 million popular and 46 electoral votes. After Wallace was shot and withdrew from the presidential race in 1972, the party's appeal was greatly diminished.

Anti-Federalists. This name was given to those elements opposing the ratification of the Constitution. Eventually most of them became Jeffersonian Republicans.

Communist Party. *See* Marxist Parties.

Democratic Republicans. *See* Democrats; Whigs.

Democrats. The Democratic Party had its origins in the Jeffersonian Republicans, who often called themselves Democratic Republicans. Under Jackson's leadership, the party changed its name to the Democratic Party. This party is the oldest continuing party in the Western world. Modern Democratic leaders have included Woodrow Wilson, Franklin Roosevelt, Harry Truman, John Kennedy, and Lyndon Johnson. The party normally controls a substantial number of state governments and is dominant in the largest cities.

Farmer-Labor Parties. Various individual parties active in 1870–1900 are included in this term. The most prominent on the national scene were the Greenback Party and the People's Party, or Populists. The parties were generally reformist and in favor of government intervention. Many of the specific demands of such parties have subsequently been adopted by a major party and have become public law.

Federalists. The proponents of the Constitution were termed Federalists because they favored the proposed federal Union. Subsequently they became a political party. Under the leadership of George Washington, Alexander Hamilton, and John Adams, they controlled the presidency and Congress during the first three administrations. The Federalists gave shape, direction, and vigor to the new government.

Greenback Party. *See* Farmer-Labor Parties.

Jacksonian Democrats. *See* Jeffersonian Republicans.

Jeffersonian Republicans. The origins of the first Republican Party go back to the divisions in Congress between the followers of Alexander Hamilton and those of Thomas Jefferson. By 1800 the Republicans had become a national party and won the presidential election of that year under the leadership of Jefferson. From 1816 to 1828 most Americans were Jeffersonian Republicans. Distinctions eventually developed inside the party, with followers of John Quincy Adams and Henry Clay calling themselves National Republicans and followers of Andrew Jackson calling themselves Democratic Republicans. Under Jackson the organization became simply the Democratic Party, whence the terms "Jacksonian Democrats" and "Jacksonian Democracy."

National Republicans. *See* Jeffersonian Republicans; Whigs.

People's Party. *See* Farmer-Labor Parties; Populists.

Populists. The Populist, or People's, Party was active in national and state politics during the 1880s and early 1890s. Its base was agrarian, and the party's program was reformist. The party fused with the Democrats in 1896, when it endorsed the Democratic presidential candidate, William Jennings Bryan. The party's best showing was in 1892, when its presidential candidate, James Weaver, received more than 1 million popular votes and 22 electoral votes.

Progressives (1912). In a major schism with the Republican Party, former president Theodore Roosevelt ran for the presidency in 1912 as a Progressive. A three-way contest developed among Democratic candidate Woodrow Wilson, regular Republican candidate William Taft, and Roosevelt. The Progressive candidate took enough votes away from Taft so that Wilson was elected. Roosevelt received more popular and more electoral votes than Taft.

Progressives (1924). Robert La Follette of Wisconsin ran as a Progressive candidate for the presidency in 1924. He was endorsed by the Socialists, who did not run a candidate of their own. He received 4.8 million popular votes but only 13 electoral votes.

Progressives (1948). Former vice-president Henry Wallace ran for the presidency as a Progressive in 1948. His followers were essentially Democrats who refused to support the Democratic candidate, Harry Truman. The primary emphasis was opposition to Truman's foreign policy. Wallace received 1.15 million popular votes but no electoral votes. The party did not survive the election.

Republicans (GOP). The second Republican Party, sometimes abbreviated GOP (Grand Old Party), was created in the mid-1850s from various groups seeking to fill the vacuum created by the collapse of the Whigs as a national party. The Republicans' first national convention was held in 1856, at which time they nominated John C. Frémont as their presidential candidate. Four years later, under the banner of Abraham Lincoln, the party won the presidency. From 1860 to 1932 the Republicans were in the ascendancy, particularly in presidential elections. During that time only Cleveland and Wilson broke the string of Republican victories. Modern party leaders include Dwight Eisenhower, elected to the presidency in 1952 and again in 1956, and Richard Nixon, elected in 1968 and 1972. The Republicans normally control numerous state governments and are especially strong in the more prosperous suburbs of the large central cities.

Socialist Parties. The oldest Socialist

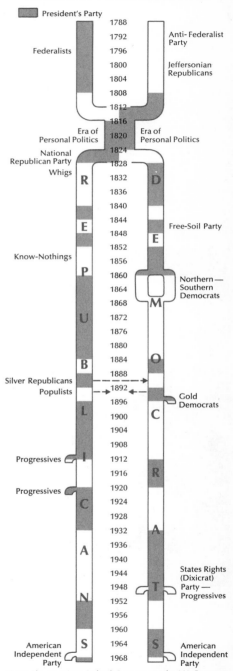

DEVELOPMENT OF
AMERICAN POLITICAL PARTIES

"From *The American Federal Government*, by J.H. Ferguson and D.E. McHenry. Copyright 1969, McGraw-Hill Book Co. Used with permission of McGraw-Hill Book Company.

265

party is the Socialist Labor Party, which was founded in the 1870s by German immigrants. Its chief theoretician was Daniel De Leon, a one-time Columbia University instructor. The program of the party calls for a syndicalist organization of society.

The Socialist Party was officially founded in 1901 by persons who would not accept the leadership of De Leon. The Party's most famous leaders were Eugene Debs and Norman Thomas. In three presidential elections between 1900 and 1948 the party polled nearly 1 million votes. In recent years the Party has shrunk to a fraction of its former electoral importance.

The Communist Party was formed as a result of a split in the Socialists following the victory of the Bolsheviks in Russia. The Communist Party has not been important as an electoral force, although it has at times been influential in certain unions. In 1928 the Communists expelled the Trotskyites in their midst, who became the Socialist Workers Party. This party regularly nominates presidential and other candidates.

States' Rights Party (1948). In 1948 Strom Thurmond of South Carolina headed the States' Rights Party, which was essentially a regional spinoff of Southern Democrats dissatisfied with the Truman Administration. Emphasis was placed on the contention that civil rights problems should be solved at the state, not the national, level. Thurmond received 1.69 million popular and 39 electoral votes.

Whigs. The Jeffersonian Republicans eventually split into two separate groups—the National Republicans under Henry Clay and Daniel Webster and the Democratic Republicans under Andrew Jackson. In opposition to Jackson, the National Republicans formed a new party, the Whigs. At the national level, the Whigs were able to elect only two presidents—William Harrison in 1840 and Zachary Taylor in 1848. Unable to maintain their unity over the slavery issue, the Whigs disintegrated as a national party during the 1850s.

POLK, JAMES K(NOX) (1795–1849), 11th President of the United States (1845–1849). He was born in Mecklenburg County, North Carolina on Nov. 2, 1795, and lived in Tennessee. He was a lawyer in Tennessee and served in the state legislature before moving to Congress (1825–1839), where be became Speaker in 1835 and a Democratic leader. Polk was governor of Tennessee from 1839 to 1841 and in 1844 was nominated as presidential candidate by the Democrats.

Coming out strongly for Manifest Destiny and territorial expansion, Polk won the election. He was an orthodox Jacksonian Democrat, and his Administration added more lands to the United States than that of any

James K. Polk, 11th President of the United States (1845–1849), promoted western expansion.

president but Jefferson. The four great issues he promised to face were: tariff reductions, reestablishment of the independent treasury system, settlement of the Oregon question, and territorial expansion in the West. At first Polk demanded all of Oregon ("Fifty-Four-Forty or Fight" had been a campaign slogan), but in the end he agreed with the British to compromise and divide the region along the 49th parallel. He was most aggressive with Mexico, trying through the Slidell Mission to buy New Mexico and California and then taking the first opportunity to initiate the Mexican War (1846–1848).

The Polk Doctrine expanded the Monroe Doctrine by warning European powers still more clearly that their legitimate interests had nothing to do with Western Hemisphere affairs and by decreeing that any independent Western Hemisphere state could unite with the United States if it so wished (December 1845). Polk refused to run for reelection and retired to his Nashville home, where he died on June 15, 1849.

See also "Fifty-Four-Forty or Fight"; Mexican War; Monroe Doctrine; Slidell Mission.

Consult (III) Sellers, 1957.
—Peter d'A. Jones, *University of Illinois, Chicago Circle*

POLLOCK, JACKSON (1912–1956), an Abstract Expressionist painter and chief American exponent of action painting (splashing and dribbling paint on canvas). Pollock executed his works on continuous lengths of canvas tacked to the floor and later cut up with selective care.

After a period of realism in the style of Thomas Hart Benton, Pollock began to paint in his new action style, mingling energetic linear invention with imagery derived from the surrealists of the 1920s. In 1947 he abandoned the use of brushes to pour, drip, and spatter paint directly onto the canvas.

His radical technique brought him unfavorable publicity but helped him to become an exponent of free, unarranged pictorial effects. This was the foremost principle of Abstract Expressionism, which became one of the dominant international trends after World War II. Pollock has become identified in the minds of many young American artists as the most revolutionary artist of an older generation of innovators who assumed that the unconscious mind could take over and produce a work.

See also Painting.

POLLOCK v. FARMERS' LOAN AND TRUST COMPANY (1895), Supreme Court decision that declared the Income Tax Act (1893) unconstitutional. *See* Fuller, Melville W.; Income Tax.

PONTIAC'S REBELLION (1763), Indian uprising against the British during the French and Indian War. Unlike their French predecessors, the British who occupied the Old Northwest after 1760 were not able to conciliate the Indians. Their inflexibility angered the Indians, and a visionary, the Delaware Prophet, encouraged the tribes to seek spiritual regeneration by driving out the whites.

His disciple, Pontiac, chief of the Ottawa, soon took command, and in May and June 1763 the Indians destroyed every British fort west of Niagara except Forts Pitt and Detroit. The British regained the offensive, and on August 6 at Bushy Run, Col. Henry Bouquet routed the Indians harassing Fort Pitt. At Detroit, Maj. Henry Gladwin withstood a siege by Pontiac, whose men badly mauled a force that attempted a sortie from the fort on July 31. Pontiac lifted the siege in November 1763 after learning of the peace ending the war, and he finally signed a peace treaty with Sir William Johnson on July 24, 1766.

See also Indian Wars, Colonial.

PONY EXPRESS, a relay system for carrying mail on horseback, as fast as possible, the 2,000 miles from St. Joseph, Mo., to Sacramento, Cal. It lasted for only 18 months, April 1860 to October 1861. The idea arose out of rivalry between the Butterfield Overland Mail and the freighting firm of Russell, Majors, and Waddell. The Overland Mail held the federal contract for taking mail to California by a Southern route, from St. Louis and Memphis via Texas and Arizona to Los Angeles and San Francisco. W. H. Russell wished to prove the viability of the *central* route for mails, via Wyoming, South Pass, and Utah to Sacramento.

The Pony Express was therefore an experiment but it greatly speeded up mail service to the coast. The 75 relay riders could deliver the mail in 12 days (sometimes less) by riding hard between stations and allowing only minutes to change horses or riders. They carried the news to California of Lincoln's election, Southern secession, and the outbreak of the Civil War and probably helped to keep California in the Union. Financially, the venture was a failure for Russell, Majors, and Waddell, and worse, the central route contract was given to their rivals. In any case the new electric telegraph system, which reached California in October 1861, made the Pony Express obsolete for fast messages.

POOLS, any agreements among several railroads in the same operating area to divide the business among themselves. Such arrangements were justified in the name of efficiency and economy. Railroad spokesmen argued that cutthroat competition would eventually result in destruction of the competitors and losses for

shippers. The first widely publicized pool was the Iowa Pool, formed in 1870, among lines operating between Omaha and Chicago. Pooling contributed to public demands for state and federal regulation.

See also Munn v. Illinois (1877); Railroad Legislation.

POOR RICHARD'S ALMANACK. *See* Franklin, Benjamin.

POPULAR SOVEREIGNTY, concept popularized in the pre-Civil War debates over slavery. It stressed sovereignty, or possession of ultimate power, by the people. Its advocates insisted that not Congress but the people living in Western territories should decide whether or not they would possess slaves. The principle was incorporated into the Compromise of 1850 for the territory acquired from Mexico and was later included in the Kansas-Nebraska Act of 1854, thus extending the principle to all Western territories.

See also Compromise of 1850; Kansas-Nebraska Act (1854).

POPULISTS, a third party of the 1890s that drew most of its support from the farmers and miners of the West and South.

Throughout the 1870s and 1880s, farmers felt exploited by high railroad freight rates, high interest rates on farm loans, currency deflation, and, in the South, the crop-lien and sharecropping systems. In the late 1880s these grievances contributed to the rapid growth of the Farmers' Alliances. In a number of North Central states in 1890, the Alliance fostered independent parties, the most successful of which were in Kansas and Nebraska. Southern Alliancemen in 1890 sought to take over the Democratic Party in their states and scored several apparent successes.

A national party, the People's Party—quickly dubbed "Populists"—was formed in 1892 and nominated James B. Weaver, a veteran of Greenback agitation, for president. The Populists proposed national ownership of the transportation, communication, and banking systems and currency inflation to counteract the existing deflation. Receiving about 8.5 percent of the vote, Weaver ran most strongly among disadvantaged farmers in the Southern and North Central states and among miners in the Rocky Mountain states.

In 1896 the Democratic Party nominated William Jennings Bryan for president and accepted the Populist program of silver coinage to counteract deflation. After considerable discussion, the Populists also nominated Bryan. Bryan's defeat by William McKinley and a rise in farm prices contributed to a decline in Populist strength, and the party disappeared soon after. Since then, a political leader or

Pontiac meets with Major Robert Rogers, one of the Indians' main opponents in Pontiac's Rebellion.

Populists considered William Jennings Bryan, a Democrat, one of their most effective spokesmen.

movement seeking to replace established leaders by going outside traditional and established channels and appealing directly to the people has sometimes been called populist.

See also Bryan, William Jennings; Farmers' Alliances; Free Silver; McKinley, William; Political Parties in the United States.

Consult (V) Hackney, 1971; Hicks, 1961.
—Robert W. Cherny, *California State University, San Francisco*

PORTAGE DES SIOUX, TREATIES OF (1815), peace agreements between the United States and Indian tribes that had been allies of the British during the War of 1812. The treaties concluded at Portage des Sioux on the west bank of the Mississippi, slightly north of its confluence with the Missouri, were signed with 13 tribes of the region during the late summer of 1815. Despite these agreements, the Sac, Fox, and Winnebago tribes remained dissatisfied, and the War Department began building new forts in the upper Mississippi Valley to maintain peace there.

See also Ghent, Treaty of (1814).
Consult (III) Prucha, 1962.

PORTSMOUTH PEACE CONFERENCE (1905), peace talks mediated by President Theodore Roosevelt to settle the Russo-Japanese War. In 1905 the Japanese attacked Russia over the Manchurian question and won substantial land and sea victories. However, the Japanese did not want to become involved in a long war, and they secretly informed Roosevelt that they would accept his offer to mediate. Roosevelt agreed to do so if Japan would respect the Open Door in China. Russia and Japan began their meetings on Aug. 9, 1905, in Portsmouth, N.H. Japan's demands included a free hand in Korea, Russia's Sakhalin Island, title to the Russian sphere of interest at Port Arthur, and a large cash settlement to offset the costs of the war. The first two demands were met, but Japan had to settle for only the southern half of Sakhalin Island; no cash settlement was made. The Treaty of Portsmouth was signed on Sept. 5, 1905, and President Roosevelt received the 1906 Nobel Peace Prize for his role in the settlement. The Portsmouth settlement established Japan as overlord in Manchuria and as the major naval power in the Pacific—a status the United States would regret during World War II.

See also Open Door Policy; Roosevelt, Theodore; Russo-Japanese War.

POSTAL SERVICE, UNITED STATES, an independent establishment within the executive branch responsible for the delivery of billions of pieces of mail each year. The world's largest mail system with nearly 32,000 post offices and more that 700,000 employees, the Postal Service

Automation is key to increased efficiency of Postal Service.

is also the largest civilian agency in the most important communications organization.

The Colonies. The U.S. postal system has its origins in the colonial mail service, first established on a rudimentary basis in the seventeenth century. In 1707 the British government assumed control over the American postal service.

In 1753 Benjamin Franklin and William Hunter were appointed by the Crown as joint postmasters general in the colonies. Franklin effected many lasting improvements in the colonial posts, most notably extending the mail service throughout the colonies and facilitating communications with the mother country. Dismissed by the Crown in 1774, Franklin was named by the Continental Congress as head of the American postal system the next year.

Early America. The Articles of Confederation (1778) gave Congress exclusive control over the mail service. In 1789, Congress established a post office and created the office of postmaster general under the Treasury Department.

In 1792, Congress passed legislation detailing provisions for the Post Office Department. Subsequent laws enlarged the duties of the department. In 1829 President Jackson's postmaster general became the first head of the Postal Service to sit as a member of the cabinet, but it was not until 1872 that the Post Office Department officially became an executive department.

Modern America. In 1970 the Postal Reorganization Act—which removed the postmaster general from the cabinet and provided for the conversion of the department to an independent agency within the executive—took effect. The agency, known as the U.S. Postal Service, was to be managed by a presidentially appointed, bipartisan Board of Governors and by a postmaster general and deputy postmaster general selected by the Board. The new Postal Service officially began operations in 1971. Since postal reform took effect, the Postal Service has embarked on a program of reorganization, modernization, and mechanization.

POTSDAM CONFERENCE (JULY 17–AUGUST 2, 1945), the final Big Three conference of World War II, held in Potsdam, a suburb of Berlin. There Joseph Stalin, Harry Truman, and Clement Atlee, who succeeded Winston Churchill as British prime minister during the conference, attempted to make arrangements for peace in Europe. But the Soviet Union and the Western Allies disagreed profoundly on most major issues, and they were able to do little more than defer some matters for future discussion and settle others with statements of general principle. A Council of Foreign Ministers was established to draft peace treaties for the Balkan allies of the Axis. The Big Three agreed that Germany should be demilitarized and de-Nazified, without spelling out the means, and worked out a compromise by which each occupying nation would take reparations from its own zone in Germany. The Potsdam agreements proved unworkable in many instances, and the issues left unresolved by the conference increased East-West tensions in the months that followed.

See also World War II.

POUND, EZRA (LOOMIS) (1885–1972), American poet, critic, and noted expatriate. He was born in Hailey, Idaho, and educated at the University of Pennsylvania and Hamilton College. Pound first traveled in Europe as a graduate student in Romance literature and in 1908 made Europe his home. He lived in London from 1908 to 1920, then Paris (1920–1924), and finally in Italy (1924–1945, and after 1958). From 1946 to 1958, Pound was confined in St. Elizabeth's Hospital, Washington, D.C., having been adjudged mentally unfit to answer indictments for treason arising from his short-wave broadcasts critical of American policy beamed to the United States from Rome during World War II. During his confinement, Pound continued to write, and his reputation as an influential poet remained undiminished. On his release, he returned to Italy.

Exultations (1909) and *Personae* (1909) began his reputation as a poet, while *The Spirit of Romance* (1910), a study of Renaissance literature, was his first prose work. As a critic he influenced T. S. Eliot, noticeably in Eliot's *The Waste Land.*

Pound's *Cantos* has been called the most ambitious poetic project in English in the twentieth century, the first appearing in 1917 and the latest in 1959. The *Cantos* deal, by analogy to the voyage of man's spirit in Dante's *Divine Comedy,* with fragments of history from ancient, Renaissance, and modern times (particularly in the United States).

POWERS, SEPARATION OF. *See* Separation of Powers.

PREEMPTION ACT (1841). *See* Land Policy.

PREPAREDNESS MOVEMENT (1915–1916), movement to prepare the United States for war that followed the outbreak of World War I in Europe. Leaders such as Theodore Roosevelt and Henry L. Stimson demanded American armament and said that the nation must be prepared for any eventuality. As early as 1914 the Navy League, the Army League, and the National Security League had the full support of military men. The National Security League was headed by Roosevelt's friend Gen. Leonard

Wood. In 1915 other groups formed, such as the American Defense Society, the League to Enforce Peace, and the American Rights Committee.

President Wilson for some time resisted the preparedness agitators. He wanted to avoid armament, the draft, and war. The sinking of the *Lusitania,* German submarine warfare, and political considerations made him change his view. Characteristically, Wilson then stumped the nation in 1916, demanding in strong, moral terms what he had previously opposed—a comprehensive national defense posture. The original "Plattsburg Idea" of August 1915 (that civilians could train themselves in hastily constructed military camps) was now long past; the nation was all set for full-scale professional militarization.

See also Lusitania, Sinking of; World War I.

PRESBYTERIANS, a religious group that believes, basically, that the Christian church consists of those who profess the Christian faith and is therefore universal, transcending denominations and national boundaries. Presbyterianism functions as a system of representative church government administered by presbyters, that is, courts composed of clerical and lay elders equal in status.

Presbyterianism was introduced in America in the early seventeenth century by a small number of French Huguenots, by Dutch Reformed settlers in New Netherlands, by English Puritans in New England, and by German Reformed immigrants in the Middle Atlantic colonies. A large increase in membership occurred with the migration of the Scotch and Scotch-Irish who came to Maryland, Delaware, Pennsylvania, and other colonies during the late seventeenth century.

The first American presbytery was organized in 1706 in Philadelphia by Francis Makemie (1658–1708), a missionary from Ireland. By the mideighteenth century, during the Great Awakening, American Presbyterians became divided between those who rejected evangelism (called Old Lights or Old Side) and those who espoused it (New Lights or New Side).

In the 1770s, after Congregationalists, Presbyterians were the most numerous religious body in the colonies. They vigorously supported the American Revolution, and one of their ministers, John Witherspoon (1723–1724), was a signer of the Declaration of Independence. Presbyterians were active in frontier missions in the West and in the founding of educational institutions, including the College of New Jersey (Princeton University).

Between 1837 and 1869, Presbyterians suffered another schism, this time between Old School and New School adherents over slavery, theology, and church government is-

Poet Ezra Pound's work, especially his *Cantos,* had widespread influence on twentieth-century literature.

sues. In 1906 the largest Presbyterian body, the Presbyterian Church in the United States, merged with many other churches to form a united group eventually consisting of more than 4 million members.

See also Colonial Religion; Congregationalists; Great Awakening.

Consult (I) Slosser, 1955.

PRESIDENTIAL ELECTIONS. Article II of the Constitution established the election procedure for president and vice-president. Each state was to choose, in any way its legislature determined, electors equal to the number of its members in Congress. These electors, meeting in their respective states, would cast ballots for two individuals. The results would be sent to the national government, where in the presence of Congress, they would be opened and counted. If there was a tie or if no candidate received a majority of the votes cast, the House of Representatives would decide, with each state acting as a unit having one vote. Where no candidate had a majority, the House would choose from the five leading contenders.

After the 1800 election tie between Jefferson and Burr, the Twelfth Amendment, providing separate voting for president and vice-president, was enacted. If no presidential candidate receives a majority, the House selects from among the three highest candidates. Similarly, if no vice-presidential candidate secures a majority, the Senate chooses from between the two highest.

1789. The last Congress under the Articles of Confederation set the first Wednesday in January as the date for choosing state electors. They were to meet and vote on the first Wednesday in February; and the new Congress would assemble and tabulate the vote on the first Wednesday in March. Of the original states, North Carolina and Rhode Island had not yet ratified the Constitution and could not vote, and the N.Y. legislature could not agree on procedure for selecting electors within the specified time. Most state legislatures determined their electors; only in Pennsylvania, Virginia, and Maryland were they directly selected by the voters.

As had been expected, George Washington, military hero and chairman of the Constitutional Convention, was unanimously elected first president. He received all 69 electoral votes, including those of the 3 Anti-Federalists; John Adams led more than 10 other candidates with 34 votes to become vice-president. The election was clearly a Federalist triumph.

1792. Congress decided that state electors were to be chosen within 34 days of the first Wednesday in December, the day presidential electors would cast their votes. On the second Wednesday in February, Congress would tabulate the results. There were now 15 states.

This election saw the emergence of a strong opposition party among the Anti-Federalists (Democratic-Republicans, as they were later called). Led by Secretary of State Thomas Jefferson, they accused the Administration of monarchist tendencies and capitalist interests. The party was an alliance of Southern agrarian interests and town mechanics in New York (particularly Aaron Burr and the Sons of St. Tammany of New York City).

A reluctant Washington was again unanimously chosen president with an electoral vote of 132, but the contest for vice-president reflected the increasing party solidarity. Adams received 77 votes; New York governor Clinton, Anti-Federalist, 50; Jefferson, Anti-Federalist, 4; Aaron Burr, Anti-Federalist, 1.

1796. The French Revolution was in progress, and France had declared war with Spain and Britain. Washington's Administration tried to maintain U.S. neutrality, but reactions were divided between Federalists (Monocrats), accused of English sympathy, and Democratic-Republicans (Jacobins), felt to be pro-French. Reaction to the Jay Treaty with Britain, the Citizen Genêt affair, the Whiskey Rebellion in 1794, and the Administration's use of militia to curb the defiant taxpayers—all helped solidify party lines.

Washington refused to accept the nomination and thereby established a precedent for two successive terms that lasted until 1940. At a meeting of congressmen and senators (the first congressional caucus), John Adams and Thomas Pinckney (S.C.) were informally selected for president and vice-president. Thomas Jefferson, leader of the opposition, and New York governor Aaron Burr were chosen by the Democratic-Republicans. There were 16 states, but only 6 had a popular vote of electors. John Adams became president with a narrow majority of 71 votes, and Thomas Jefferson became vice-president with 68, the only instance when president and vice-president were not of the same party. Thomas Pinckney had 59 votes; Aaron Burr, 30; and nine other candidates received a total of 48 electoral votes.

1800. Through Adams' Administration, there was the constant threat of war with France, which culminated in the XYZ affair, an attempted bribe by members of the French Directory to ensure peace between the two nations. War fever ran high. Preparations for war were in earnest, and the slogan "Millions for defense but not one cent for tribute" was coined. Dissension among the Federalists, particularly Adams and Hamilton, gave Jefferson, Madison, Gallatin, and Burr the opportunity to consolidate a powerful alliance against the Administration. Charging the Federalists with

Year	Candidates	Parties	Popular Vote	Electoral Vote
1789	George Washington (Va.)			69
	John Adams			34
	Others			35
1792	George Washington (Va.)			132
	John Adams			77
	George Clinton			50
	Others			5
1796	John Adams (Mass.)	Federalist		71
	Thomas Jefferson	Dem.-Rep.		68
	Thomas Pinckney	Federalist		59
	Aaron Burr	Dem.-Rep.		30
	Others			48
1800	Thomas Jefferson (Va.)	Dem.-Rep.		73
	Aaron Burr	Dem.-Rep.		73
	John Adams	Federalist		65
	C. C. Pinckney	Federalist		64
	John Jay	Federalist		1
1804	Thomas Jefferson (Va.)	Dem.-Rep.		162
	C. C. Pinckney	Federalist		14
1808	James Madison (Va.)	Dem.-Rep.		122
	C. C. Pinckney	Federalist		47
	George Clinton	Dem.-Rep.		6
1812	James Madison (Va.)	Dem.-Rep.		128
	DeWitt Clinton	Federalist		89
1816	James Monroe (Va.)	Dem.-Rep.		183
	Rufus King	Federalist		34
1820	James Monroe (Va.)	Dem.-Rep.		231
	John Qunicy Adams	Dem.-Rep.		1
1824	John Quincy Adams (Mass.)	Dem.-Rep.	108,740	84
	Andrew Jackson	Dem.-Rep.	153,544	99
	William H. Crawford	Dem.-Rep.	46,618	41
	Henry Clay	Dem.-Rep.	47,136	37
1828	Andrew Jackson (Tenn.)	Democrat	647,286	178
	John Quincy Adams	Nat. Rep.	508,064	83
1832	Andrew Jackson (Tenn.)	Democrat	687,502	219
	Henry Clay	Nat. Rep.	530,189	49
	John Floyd	Whig		11
	William Wirt	Anti-Masonic		7
1836	Martin Van Buren (N.Y.)	Democrat	765,483	170
	William H. Harrison	Anti-Masonic		73
	Daniel Webster	Whig		14
	W. P. Mangum	Whig		11
	Hugh L. White	Whig		26
1840	William H. Harrison (Ohio)	Whig	1,274,624	234
	Martin Van Buren	Democrat	1,127,781	60
	J. G. Birney	Liberty	7,059	
1844	James K. Polk (Tenn.)	Democrat	1,338,464	170
	Henry Clay	Whig	1,300,097	105
	J. G. Birney	Liberty	62,300	
1848	Zachary Taylor (La.)	Whig	1,360,967	163
	Lewis Cass	Democrat	1,222,342	127
	Martin Van Buren	Free-Soil	291,263	
1852	Franklin Pierce (N.H.)	Democrat	1,601,117	254
	Winfield Scott	Whig	1,385,453	42
	John P. Hale	Free-Soil	155,825	
1856	James Buchanan (Pa.)	Democrat	1,832,955	174
	John C. Frémont	Republican	1,339,932	114
	Millard Fillmore	American	871,731	8
1860	Abraham Lincoln (Ill.)	Republican	1,865,593	180
	Stephen A. Douglas	Democrat	1,382,713	12
	John C. Breckinridge	Democrat	848,356	72
	John Bell	Constitutional Union	592,906	39
1864	Abraham Lincoln (Ill.)	Republican	2,206,938	212
	George B. McClellan	Democrat	1,803,787	21
1868	Ulysses S. Grant (Ill.)	Republican	3,013,421	214
	Horatio Seymour	Democrat	2,706,829	80
1872	Ulysses S. Grant (Ill.)	Republican	3,596,745	286
	Horace Greeley	Dem., Lib. Rep.	2,843,446	66
1876	Rutherford B. Hayes (Ohio)	Republican	4,036,572	185
	Samuel J. Tilden	Democrat	4,284,020	184
1880	james A. Garfield (Ohio)	Republican	4,453,295	214
	Winfield S. Hancock	Democrat	4,414,082	155
1884	Grover Cleveland (N.Y.)	Democrat	4,879,507	219
	James G. Blaine	Republican	4,850,293	182
1888	Benjamin Harrison (Ohio)	Republican	5,447,129	233
	Grover Cleveland	Democrat	5,537,857	168
1892	Grover Cleveland (N.Y.)	Democrat	5,555,426	277
	Benjamin Harrison	Republican	5,182,690	145
	James B. Weaver	People's	1,029,846	22
1896	William McKinley (Ohio)	Republican	7,102,246	271
	William J. Bryan	Democrat, People's	6,492,559	176
1900	William McKinley (Ohio)	Republican	7,218,491	292
	William J. Bryan	Dem., Fusion Populists	6,356,734	155
1904	Theodore Roosevelt (N.Y.)	Republican	7,628,461	336
	Alton B. Parker	Democrat	5,084,223	140
	Eugene V. Debs	Socialist	402,283	
1908	William H. Taft (Ohio)	Republican	7,675,320	321
	William J. Bryan	Democrat	6,412,294	162
	Eugene V. Debs	Socialist	420,793	
1912	Woodrow Wilson (N.J.)	Democrat	6,296,547	435
	Theodore Roosevelt	Progressive	4,118,571	88
	William H. Taft	Republican	3,486,720	8
	Eugene V. Debs	Socialist	900,672	
1916	Woodrow Wilson (N.J.)	Democrat	9,127,695	277
	Charles E. Hughes	Republican	8,533,507	254
	A. L. Benson	Socialist	585,113	
1920	Warren G. Harding (Ohio)	Republican	16,143,407	404
	James M. Cox	Democrat	9,130,328	127
	Eugene V. Debs	Socialist	919,799	
1924	Calvin Coolidge (Mass.)	Republican	15,718,211	382
	John W. Davis	Democrat	8,385,283	136
	Robert M. La Follette	Progressive	4,831,289	13
1928	Herbert Hoover (Calif.)	Republican	21,391,993	444
	Alfred E. Smith	Democrat	15,016,169	87
	Norman Thomas	Socialist	267,835	
1932	Franklin D. Roosevelt (N.Y.)	Democrat	22,809,638	472
	Herbert Hoover	Republican	15,758,901	59
	Norman Thomas	Socialist	881,951	
1936	Franklin D. Roosevelt (N.Y.)	Democrat	27,752,869	523
	Alfred M. Landon	Republican	16,674,665	8
	William Lemke	Union and Others	882,479	
1940	Franklin D. Roosevelt (N.Y.)	Democrat	27,307,819	449
	Wendell L. Willkie	Republican	22,321,018	82
1944	Franklin D. Roosevelt (N.Y.)	Democrat	25,606,585	432
	Thomas E. Dewey	Republican	22,014,745	99
1948	Harry S Truman (Mo.)	Democrat	24,105,812	303
	Thomas E. Dewey	Republican	21,970,065	189
	J. Strom Thurmond	States-Rights Democrat	1,169,063	39
	Henry A. Wallace	Progressive	1,157,172	
1952	Dwight D. Eisenhower (Kans.)	Republican	33,936,234	442
	Adlai E. Stevenson	Democrat	27,314,992	89
1956	Dwight D. Eisenhower (Kans.)	Republican	35,590,472	457
	Adlai E. Stevenson	Democrat	26,022,752	73
1960	John F. Kennedy (Mass.)	Democrat	34,227,096	303
	Richard M. Nixon	Republican	34,108,546	219
	Harry F. Byrd	Democrat		15
1964	Lyndon B. Johnson (Tex.)	Democrat	43,129,484	486
	Barry M. Goldwater	Republican	27,178,188	52
1968	Richard M. Nixon (N.Y.)	Republican	31,785,480	301
	Hubert H. Humphrey	Democrat	31,275,165	191
	George C. Wallace	Independent	9,906,473	46
1972	Richard M. Nixon	Republican	47,168,963	517
	George S. McGovern	Democrat	29,169,615	17
	John G. Schmitz	Am. Indep.	1,080,541	0

excessive taxation, they blamed the Jay Treaty with Britain for friction between the United States and France. They denounced the Alien and Sedition Acts as unconstitutional. The Federalists accused Jefferson of being a fanatic, a revolutionary, and an atheist.

Of the 16 states taking part in the election, only 4 chose their electors by popular vote. The Democratic-Republicans won. Adams was defeated (and with his defeat the Federalist era ended), but Jefferson and Burr were tied with 73 electoral votes; Adams had 65; C. C. Pinckney had 1. The choice went to the House of Representatives, where after 35 ballots a majority was still not reached. Although it was understood that Jefferson was the intended Republican presidential candidate, the Federalists controlling the House decided to support Burr as the lesser of two evils. However, Burr did nothing to gain the necessary support. Bayard, a Delaware Federalist, was then instrumental in an arrangement that broke the deadlock. The Federalist electors of Vermont and Maryland went to Jefferson, and Federalists from South Carolina and Delaware abstained. Jefferson was elected by 10 out of 16 states. This election proved that with the advent of political parties this method of electoral voting was inoperable. Before the next presidential election the Twelfth Amendment was passed.

1804. The Jefferson Administration was popular. The country was prosperous, the Alien and Sedition Acts had expired, taxes were repealed, the national debt had been reduced, agriculture and land migration were encouraged, and the Louisiana Territory was acquired. The election was an easy victory for Jefferson and his vice-presidential nominee, George Clinton (N.Y.). Only in New England was there any opposition. The Federalists informally named C. C. Pinckney (S.C.) for president and Senator Rufus King (N.Y.) for vice-president. Jefferson and Clinton received 162 of the 176 electoral votes.

1808. Jefferson, declining to run for a third term, named James Madison (Va.) his successor. George Clinton was renominated for vice-president. Dissatisfaction with Administration policies caused John Randolph and John Taylor of Virginia, leaders of a splinter group advocating stronger states' rights, to put forth James Monroe as Republican presidential candidate. Both France and England were harassing American shipping, and Britain in particular ignored neutral rights. The Jefferson Administration had passed the Embargo Act, bringing trade with Europe to a stop and seriously jeopardizing the economy. The embargo became the major campaign issue, and Federalists, enjoying a brief revival, again named C. C. Pinckney and Rufus King as their candidates. The Federalists regained control of

New England, but Madison and Clinton, nonetheless, were elected by a substantial majority.

1812. Relations with Great Britain were deteriorating rapidly. American vessels were boarded, cargo was taken, and U.S. seamen were pressed into British service. Southern and Western expansionists urged war, hoping to end the English-Indian alliance and to annex more land in the West and Canada and ultimately gain Florida from the Spanish. On June 19, 1812, war was declared with Great Britain, and it became the single most important issue of the presidential campaign.

The congressional caucus renominated James Madison; Elbridge Gerry (Mass.) was chosen as the vice-presidential nominee. Those New York Democratic-Republicans opposed to the war held a separate caucus at Albany, nominating De Witt Clinton for president and Charles Jared Ingersoll (Pa.) for vice-president. They gained the endorsement of anti-war Federalists.

The results of the election were largely sectional. New England and the Middle states except Vermont, Pennsylvania, and part of Maryland voted for Clinton. Madison was reelected president with 128 electoral votes to Clinton's 89.

1816. The peace treaty between the United States and England was signed on Dec. 24, 1814. There were no strong political issues at stake, and the Republicans' only opposition came from those Federalist New England merchants who had been against the war and had even considered secession. The congressional caucus nominated James Monroe, another of the "Virginia Dynasty" and Madison's choice for president. New York governor Daniel Tompkins was selected for vice-president. Federalists unofficially supported Rufus King (N.Y.) for president and John E. Howard (Md.) as his running mate. The Republicans carried the election with 183 electoral votes, and King received only the 34 electoral votes of Massachusetts, Connecticut, and Delaware.

1820. Domestic, rather than foreign, issues were now in the forefront, and differences were less party than sectional. Controversies were over slavery, a tariff, and internal improvements. Despite the financial panic of 1819 and the bitter struggle over admission of Missouri as a slave state (which led to the Missouri Compromise), Monroe was intensely popular, and his Administration became known as the Era of Good Feelings. Monroe was reelected with only one dissenting vote, cast for John Quincy Adams, son of John Adams. Daniel D. Tompkins was again elected vice-president.

1824. The Democratic-Republicans lost all semblance of party solidarity, and attention focused on six sectional candidates. New England favored John Quincy Adams (Mass.), Secretary of State; the South, John C. Calhoun (S.C.), Secretary of War, and William H. Crawford (Ga.), Secretary of the Treasury; the West, Henry Clay (Ky.), House Speaker, Andrew Jackson (Tenn.), War of 1812 hero, and New York governor De Witt Clinton. Adams and Jackson favored a tariff and internal improvements. Clay, in addition, advocated Western expansion, the U.S. Bank, and recognition of the South American republics. Crawford, a states' rightist, opposed the tariff. In what proved to be the last congressional caucus, Crawford was nominated for president and Albert Gallatin (Pa.) for vice-president. State legislatures had chosen Jackson and Clay; Adams was nominated at a Boston party; and Calhoun, who had announced his candidacy in 1821, withdrew to become vice-presidential candidate on the Adams and Jackson ticket. A paralytic stroke eliminated Crawford as a serious contender. Gallatin withdrew because Crawford's followers asked Clay to form a Crawford-Clay ticket, but Clay refused.

Jackson led the total popular vote, receiving 99 electoral votes; Adams, 84; Crawford, 41; and Clay, 37. Because no one received a majority, the vote went to the House, where the choice was among the three leading candidates. Clay, eliminated but wielding considerable power, released his votes to Adams, giving him the required 13 states for the presidency. Jackson received 7 states' votes; Crawford, 4. Jackson men claimed a corrupt bargain had been made between Clay and Adams and became more enraged when Clay was selected secretary of state. John C. Calhoun was chosen vice-president by electoral vote. John Quincy Adams was the first president to take office with a popular vote minority.

1828. The Democratic-Republicans split into two rival parties. Supporters of Adams and Clay became National Republicans, and Jackson's followers formed the Democrats. In October 1825 the Tennessee legislature nominated Andrew Jackson for president. John C. Calhoun, vice-president under Adams, became Jackson's running mate. The National Republicans renominated John Quincy Adams and chose Secretary of State Richard Rush for vice-president.

Adams, advocating internal improvements and a high tariff, appealed to New England and Midwestern manufacturing interests, conservative Federalists, and those Westerners favoring internal improvements. He also had support of the Anti-Masons, the first organized third party. Adams was identified with the aristocracy, and Jackson was the people's candidate, supported by Western farmers, Eastern laborers, and the South. William Crawford and John C. Calhoun allied with Old Hickory, and, through efforts of Martin Van Buren (N.Y.), the diverse anti-Adams factions were

consolidated. Jackson supporters still maintained the charge of a corrupt bargain between Adams and Clay. Racial, religious, and class prejudices played a major role in this campaign.

There was an unprecedentedly large popular vote. Jackson won with 647,276 votes against Adams' 508,064.

1832. The major issue of the 1832 campaign was the Bank of the United States. President Jackson, opposed to the renewal of its charter, vetoed it and rallied the sentiments of the people against it. The National Republicans allied with Nicholas Biddle, director of the Bank, to defend it. The Anti-Masons held their first national convention of elected delegates to choose candidates for president and vice-president; the other parties quickly followed suit. The Anti-Masons nominated William Wirt (Md.) for president and Amos Ellmaker (Pa.) for vice-president. The National Republicans nominated Henry Clay for president and John Sargeant (Pa.), a chief legal and political adviser of the Bank, as his running mate. Jackson easily won the Democratic renomination, and Martin Van Buren, minister to Great Britain and Jackson's choice for vice-president, became his running mate. Jackson was reelected with 219 electoral votes; Clay received 49 from six states.

1836. President Jackson had tangled with the Senate over withdrawal of government funds from the Bank of the United States and was accused of assuming autocratic powers. His opponents rallied together as Whigs to try to defeat Martin Van Buren, his chosen successor. At the Democratic National Convention, Van Buren secured the presidential nomination and Richard M. Johnson (Ky.), soldier and congressman, the vice-presidential. The Whigs, disagreeing among themselves, were unable to hold a national convention and left the choice of candidates to state legislatures in the hope that the voting of favorite sons would divide the vote and throw the election to the House.

Martin Van Buren won with 170 votes against William Harrison (Ohio-Whig), who emerged as the only serious rival with 73; Hugh L. White (Tenn.-Whig), 14; William P. Mangum, (N.C., a Calhoun man), 11. Lacking a majority, the vice-presidential election, for the first and only time, went to the Senate, where Richard M. Johnson was chosen vice-president with 33 votes against 16 votes for Francis Granger (N.Y.-Whig).

1840. The campaign of 1840 was notable for its exuberance, its introduction of processions and rallies, and its party songs, banners, and emblems. The Democrats renominated Van Buren but could not agree on a vice-presidential nominee. The first Whig national convention nominated William Henry Harrison for president. Harrison, a former soldier

Music sheet for song in William Henry Harrison's Log Cabin campaign of 1840.

who had won the Battle of Tippecanoe (1811), had an ambiguous stance on all issues, which made him an acceptable candidate for the diverse Whig factions. He won over Henry Clay, whose long political career was felt to be a liability. John Tyler (Va.) was chosen for vice-president. The Liberty Party, or Abolitionists, held its first national convention and named James G. Birney and Thomas Earl for president and vice-president, respectively.

"Tippecanoe and Tyler, too" became one of the popular Whig slogans. The log cabin, hard cider, and coonskin cap became Harrison's symbols and helped create his image of a man of the people, while Van Buren represented the aristocracy. Harrison won by a very close popular vote but received 234 electoral votes against Van Buren's 60.

1844. The annexation of Texas and the controversy over the Oregon boundary were the most important issues of this election. Expansionism led the Democrats and the country onward to its Manifest Destiny. Van Buren's attitude toward annexation was unfavorable to the South, and thus the Democratic National Convention finally selected James K. Polk (Tenn.) as the compromise and first dark horse candidate for president. George M. Dallas (Pa.) was the vice-presidential candidate. "All Oregon or none" and "Fifty-Four Forty or Fight" were the Democratic slogans. The Whigs nominated Henry Clay, 1824 and 1832 presidential candidate, for president and Theodore Frelinghuysen (N.J.) for vice-president. John Tyler, who had succeeded to the presidency after Harrison's death in 1841, was the first president not to receive a nomination for a second term. James G. Birney, renominated by the Liberty Party with Thomas Morris (Ohio) as his running mate, took enough votes from Clay to make Polk president. Polk had 170 electoral votes against Clay's 105 but only a slim margin in the popular vote.

1848. The acquisition of Texas, New Mexico, Arizona, and California made slavery the leading issue. Zachary Taylor (La.), Mexican War hero, was the Whig candidate for president; Millard Fillmore (N.Y.) was the vice-presidential candidate. Polk did not run for reelection, and the Democratic convention chose Gen. Lewis Cass, Michigan expansionist, for president and William O. Butler (Ky.), a slaveholder, as his running mate. The antislavery "Conscience" Whigs of New England, supported by the Barnburners of New York (antislavery Democrats) and Liberty Party members, selected Martin Van Buren (N.Y.) and Charles Francis Adams (Mass.) as their candidates. "Free soil, free speech, free labor and free men" became their slogan, and its proponents, Free-Soilers.

The New York Democratic split between Cass and Van Buren gave Taylor New York's 36

AN AVAILABLE CANDIDATE.
THE ONE QUALIFICATION FOR A WHIG PRESIDENT.

Opponents criticized Zachary Taylor's Mexican War record in 1848 campaign, but the Whig candidate won a close election.

electoral votes, making him president. In 1845 Congress passed a law designating "the Tuesday next after the first Monday in the month of November" as election day, and for the first time all 30 states appointed their presidential electors on the same day.

1852. After President Taylor's death in 1850, Millard Fillmore, succeeding to the presidency, promptly endorsed Clay's Compromise of 1850. It established that California would be a free state and that all other territories acquired from Mexico would have no slavery restrictions; it contained a stringent fugitive slave law, and abolished slave trade within the District of Columbia.

After extended balloting the Democratic convention selected the dark horse candidate Senator Franklin Pierce (N.H.) and Senator William R. D. King (Ala.), Minister to France, as their choices for president and vice-president, respectively. Pledging to support all aspects of the Compromise of 1850, Pierce and King promised to resist efforts to renew agitation on this question. Overcoming sectional differences, the Whigs selected Winfield Scott (N.J.), Mexican War hero (over Webster and Fillmore), and William A. Graham (N.C.), Secretary of the Navy, as their candidates. They acquiesced on the Compromise and vowed to maintain it until further legislation proved necessary. The dissatisfied Northern Whigs broke from the party to join the Free-Soilers, who nominated John P. Hale (N.H.) for president and George W. Julien (Ind.) for vice-president. They condemned both slavery and the Compromise. Franklin Pierce won the presidency with a large electoral majority.

1856. The Kansas-Nebraska Act (1854) repealed the Missouri Compromise (1820), thus intensifying the slavery conflict. James Buchanan (Pa.), Minister to England during the Kansas-Nebraska debates, was the least controversial candidate and became the Democratic nominee for president, winning over Franklin Pierce, Stephen A. Douglas, and Lewis Cass. John C. Breckinridge (Ky.) was Buchanan's running mate. The Democrats promised to avoid agitating the slavery question and condemned the Native Americans (or Know-Nothings), whose policies were directed against the foreign-born and Roman Catholics. The Know-Nothings chose former president Millard Fillmore for president and A. J. Donelson (Tenn.) for vice-president. The Republican Party, comprised of antislavery Democrats and Whigs and of Free-Soilers, was formed in 1854. At their first national convention they chose John C. Frémont, explorer and soldier, as their candidate for president; William L. Dayton (N.J.) was his running mate. They argued that Congress should prohibit slavery in the territories. Their campaign was characterized by "Bleeding Kansas," and their slogan was "Free Soil, Free Speech and Frémont."

The remnants of the Whig Party endorsed the candidates, but not the political principles, of the Know-Nothings. Buchanan was elected by all the slave states except Maryland, which went to Fillmore, and the free states of Pennsylvania, Indiana, New Jersey, California, and Illinois. Eleven free states voted for Frémont.

1860. The central figure of the Democratic convention, which met in Charleston, S.C., on April 23, was Stephen A. Douglas (Ill.), a firm believer in popular sovereignty and the Compromise of 1850. The convention adopted a platform reflecting Douglas' beliefs, and eight Southern states, demanding a repudiation of popular sovereignty and a guarantee of slavery in the territories, withdrew. After 57 ineffective ballots the convention adjourned to meet in Baltimore on June 18. There Douglas was nominated for president and Herschel V. Johnson (Ga.) for vice-president but not before another Southern withdrawal. The Southern Democratic delegates then assembled and chose John C. Breckinridge (Ky.) and Joseph Lane (Ore.) as running mates. Their platform repeated their demands for protection of slavery in all territories and threatened secession.

The Constitutional Union Party, a remnant of the Whigs and Know-Nothings, nominated John Bell (Tenn.) and Edward Everett (Mass.). They advocated preservation of the Union. Republicans, meeting in Chicago, chose Abraham Lincoln (Ill.) as their candidate, passing over party favorite William H. Seward. Hannibal Hamlin (Me.) was their choice for vice-president. The Republicans proposed slavery prohibition in the territories, river and harbor improvements, a higher tariff, a homestead law, and a railroad to the Pacific. After his nomination, the Rail-Splitter did not actively campaign; his election was almost assured by the Democratic split. The campaign was primarily a two-party fight with Lincoln against Douglas in the North and Bell against Breckinridge in the South. Lincoln carried the free states for 180 electoral votes; Douglas, 12; Breckinridge, 72 from 11 slave states; and Bell, 39.

1864. Casualties mounted as the war dragged on. The Radical, or anti-Lincoln, Republicans named John C. Frémont (Cal.) for president and General John Cochrane (N.Y.) for vice-president. The regular Republican convention renominated Lincoln on the first ballot and chose Andrew Johnson (Tenn.), a war Democrat, as his running mate. The Democratic convention adopted a stop-the-war platform with George B. McClellan (N.J.), former commander-in-chief of the Union army, as presidential candidate and George Pendleton, Ohio Senator, as his running mate. McClellan accepted the nomination but not the platform. With the Northern victories of General Sherman and Admiral Farragut, Frémont withdrew

from the race, Lincoln's popularity heightened, and he was easily reelected.

1868. Four days after Andrew Johnson's acquittal on the impeachment charges levied by the Radical Republicans, the Republican convention met and unanimously selected Gen. Ulysses S. Grant as its presidential candidate; Schuyler Colfax (Ind.), House Speaker, was chosen for vice-president. Reconstruction policy was the main issue of the campaign. The Republican platform called for equal suffrage and the payment of the public debt in gold rather than paper money. Horatio Seymour (N.Y.), the "Great Decliner," reluctantly accepted the Democratic nomination for president; Francis P. Blair (Mo.) was his running mate. The Democrats advocated the greenback policy, the repayment of government bonds in paper currency rather than gold. Grant won the election because of the Southern vote and the widespread popular confidence he inspired.

1872. The Liberal Republicans, a reform movement of the Republican Party against the corrupt practices of the Grant Administration, united the advocates of women's suffrage, tariff reduction, and civil service reforms. The platform condemned the spoils system and the harsh policies toward the South but was evasive about a tariff. Horace Greeley, New York *Tribune* editor, and Missouri governor B. Gratz Brown were the nominees. The Republicans renominated Grant and voted Senator Henry Wilson (Mass.) his running mate. The Democrats endorsed Greeley and Brown, but a group of dissatisfied Straight-out Democrats held a separate convention and nominated Charles O'Connor (N.Y.) and John Quincy Adams II (Mass.). Both men refused the nomination but their names were still used.

For the first time all 37 states held their elections by popular vote. Grant was easily reelected. Greeley died before the electoral vote was counted, and his votes were scattered among other Democratic and Liberal Republican candidates.

1876. In December 1875 Congress passed a resolution upholding the two-successive-term precedent and ending any hope Grant may have had for a third term. The Republican convention nominated Ohio governor Rutherford B. Hayes for president over former House Speaker James G. Blaine. William A. Wheeler (N.Y.) was Hayes' running mate. Samuel J. Tilden (N.Y.), a millionaire corporation lawyer, was elected the Democratic presidential nominee, and Thomas A. Hendricks (Ind.) was the vice-presidential candidate. The Prohibition Reform Party nominated Gen. Green Clay Smith (Ky.). The Independent National Convention (Greenback successor to the Labor Reform and Granger movements) chose Peter Cooper (N.Y.).

The country was tired of the corruption of the Grant Administration, the severity of the

Conservative tone of 1856 campaign ad reflects style, stance of successful candidate Buchanan.

Seven years after Lincoln's assassination, his image invokes support for party candidates.

Reconstruction policies, and the high unemployment since 1873. Both major parties wanted reform, and there appeared to be little difference between the candidates. Tilden received the popular-vote majority but lacked one disputed vote to secure the electoral majority. In January, fearing the deadlock would leave the nation without a president, Congress submitted the problem to a Republican-dominated commission. The commission's vote was strictly partisan, and Hayes received 185 electoral votes against Tilden's 184. The Democrats accepted the commission's results rather than face the possibility of civil war, but only after a Southerner was placed in the cabinet and federal troops were withdrawn from the South.

1880. President Hayes did not seek reelection. Republicans were divided into two factions: Stalwarts, conservatives against reform, led by New York senator Roscoe Conkling, and Half-Breeds, who were more liberal, under James G. Blaine of Maine. The Republican Party nominated James A. Garfield (Ohio) for president on the 36th ballot when former president Grant (backed by Stalwarts) and Blaine supporters were deadlocked. Chester A. Arthur, "Gentleman boss" of New York, was nominated as vice-president as an appeasement to the Conkling faction. Democrats chose Winfield S. Hancock (Pa.) and William H. English (Ind.). James B. Weaver (Iowa) was the candidate of the National Greenback Labor Party, and Neal Dow, a Maine Quaker, was the Prohibition candidate. No real political issues existed, and the campaign concentrated on the candidates' personalities. Garfield won the presidency with a very slim majority. Had any of the minor-party candidates supported Hancock, the Democrats could have won.

1884. The Republicans chose James G. Blaine, the "Plumed Knight," as their presidential candidate and Gen. John A. Logan (Ill.) as his running mate. The Republican reform movement, later called Mugwumps, rebelled against Blaine's nomination and met with Democrats to back a reform ticket. New York governor Grover Cleveland and Thomas A. Hendricks (Ind.) were the Democratic candidates. Gen. Benjamin F. Butler (Mass.), a former Radical Republican and the Tammany candidate, became the Greenback candidate; John P. St. John (Kans.) became the Prohibition candidate. The campaign deteriorated into personal abuse of the candidates. Compromising business letters of Blaine were published, and Democrats and Mugwumps chanted: "Blaine! Blaine! James G. Blaine! The con-tin-nen-tal liar from the state of Maine." Republicans accused Cleveland of fathering an illegitimate child and sang: "Ma! Ma! Where's my Pa?" The Democrats retorted, "Gone to the White House. Ha! Ha! Ha!" Grover Cleveland won the election by a very small majority. Blaine lost the important New York Irish-American vote when

he did not immediately repudiate a supporter's reference to Democrats as the party of rum, Romanism, and rebellion.

1888. Cleveland's annual message to Congress in December 1887 advocated serious tariff reductions. The tariff became the major campaign issue, with Democrats urging lower rates and Republicans opposing them. Cleveland was renominated by acclamation at the Democratic convention; Allen G. Thurman (Ohio) was named for vice-president. The Republicans nominated Blaine's choice, Benjamin Harrison (Ind.) and Levi P. Morton (N.Y.). Clinton B. Fisk was the Prohibitionist candidate, and Alson J. Streeter ran for the Union Labor Party. Enormous contributions from businessmen afraid of losing the protective tariffs poured into Republican coffers. Vote buying and deal making were flagrant, and Harrison was elected president, although he lost the popular vote by 100,000.

1892. Republicans renominated President Harrison; Whitlaw Reid (N.Y.) was his running mate. Harrison's only possible rival, James G. Blaine, refused to run. Democrats nominated Grover Cleveland for the third successive time. Adlai E. Stevenson (Ill.) was their vice-presidential choice. The two parties differed only on the tariff: Democrats again advocated a tariff for revenue only, denouncing the Republican protective policy and the McKinley Tariff passed by the 51st Republican Congress.

The People's Party, or Populists, formed in 1891 from rebelling farmers of the South and West, nominated James B. Weaver (Iowa) for president and James G. Field (Va.) for vice-president. The party's radical platform blamed Republican monopolists for economic hardships and labor problems and advocated free coinage of silver and gold and government ownership of the railroad, telegraph, and telephone systems. The Populists won 8 percent of the vote to make an impressive showing in the election. Cleveland easily won the presidency.

1896. The country suffered a severe depression. The free-silver coinage issue dominated the campaign, pitting the agrarian South and West against the financial East, the people against the privileged classes. The Republicans chose Ohio governor William McKinley, whose campaign was managed by millionaire Mark Hanna. Garret A. Hobart (N.J.) was the vice-presidential nominee. A minority group led by Henry M. Teller (Col.), opposed to the gold standard and protective tariff of the Republican platform, left the convention and later backed William Jennings Bryan. Bryan's cross-of-gold speech earned him the Democratic candidacy; Arthur Sewall, rich Maine shipbuilder, was the vice-presidential nominee. Democrats advocated free and unlimited gold and silver coinage and a tariff for revenue only. Backing Bryan but not Sewall, Populists nominated Thomas E. Watson (Ga.) for vice-

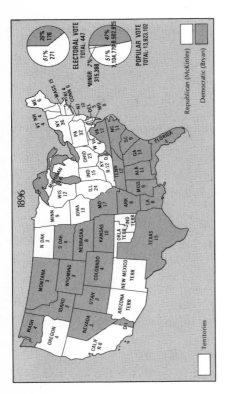

president. Prohibitionists split over the silver issue: Narrow Gaugers, opposing free coinage, nominated Charles E. Bentley; Broad Gaugers (or National Party), favoring free silver, chose Joshua Levering. The National Democratic Party (Democrats for the gold standard) nominated John M. Palmer (Ill.) for president.

Bryan, denounced as an anarchist and revolutionary, toured the country making speeches, while McKinley spoke to delegations brought to his home. In a record turnout of 14 million, McKinley won the presidency by 95 electoral votes.

1900. The economy revived, and the main concern of the campaign was imperialism. The United States, after the Spanish American War of 1898, acquired Cuba, the Philippines, and Puerto Rico. Interest centered on annexation of Hawaii and the construction of an isthmian canal. Republicans renominated William McKinley; N.Y. governor Theodore Roosevelt was the vice-presidential nominee. William Jennings Bryan was again the Democratic choice for president; Adlai E. Stevenson, former vice-president under Cleveland, was Bryan's running mate. Middle-of-the-road Populists backed Wharton Barker (Pa.). The Social Democratic Party, holding its first national convention, nominated Eugene V. Debs and Ignatius Donelly. The United Christian, Socialist Labor, Union Reform, and National Prohibition parties also named candidates. The Democrats denounced McKinley and the Republicans for their imperialist policies, but the promise of "Four Years More of a Full Dinner Pail" was effective, and McKinley was easily returned to the White House.

1904. After McKinley's assassination in 1901, Theodore Roosevelt became at 43 the youngest president. He unanimously won the Republican nomination; Indiana senator Charles Warren Fairbanks was nominated vice-president by acclamation. Democrats passed over twice-defeated Bryan, choosing Judge Alton B. Parker (N.Y.); millionaire Henry G. Davis (W.Va.) was his running mate. Democrats advocated a "safe and sane" platform and accepted the gold standard. Eugene V. Debs was again the Socialist candidate, running with Benjamin Hanford (N.Y.). Big business and progressive reformers endorsed Roosevelt, and he won the election by an overwhelming majority.

1908. Roosevelt's "Imperial Years" were exciting; foreign affairs, vigorous and successful. Domestically, many progressive laws were enacted. The Panama Canal was begun, and Roosevelt continued his crusade against trusts. Roosevelt did not seek a third term and chose William Howard Taft, Secretary of War, as his successor. James S. Sherman (N.Y.) was the candidate for vice-president. The Democrats nominated Bryan for the third time; John W. Kern (Ind.) was their vice-presidential choice.

Eugene V. Debs was Socialist candidate for the third time; Prohibitionists selected Eugene W. Chafin and Aaron Watkins; Populists nominated Thomas E. Watson; Socialist Laborites, August Gilhaus; and Independents, Thomas E. Hisgen. Taft easily won the election.

1912. Taft, instead of carrying on Roosevelt's policies, became more conservative. Before the Republican convention, Roosevelt and Taft battled for the nomination. Party bosses favored Taft, and after a credentials battle most of the contested seats went to Taft. Republicans renominated him and James S. Sherman. Roosevelt left the convention to become the presidential nominee of the Progressive Party; Hiram Johnson (Cal.) was his running mate on the Bull Moose ticket, which endorsed most of the current reform proposals. New Jersey governor Woodrow Wilson won the Democratic nomination on the 46th ballot over House Speaker Champ Clark (Mo.). Bryan refused to support anyone with Tammany connections and turned to Wilson. Indiana governor Thomas R. Marshall was the Democratic vice-presidential choice. Wilson's New Freedom did not differ much from Roosevelt's New Nationalism. Eugene V. Debs again ran for the Socialists. Because of the split in the Republican Party, Wilson easily won the election with 435 electoral votes over Theodore Roosevelt's 88, and President Taft's 8.

1916. War in Europe and American involvement were the primary issues. Wilson and Marshall were renominated in line with the Democrats' antiwar campaign slogan "He kept us out of war." Republicans chose Justice Charles Evans Hughes (Mass.) and Charles W. Fairbanks, Vice-President under Roosevelt, as their candidates. Roosevelt, refusing to run under the Progressive Party banner, later supported Hughes and unsuccessfully tried to prod Hughes into a stronger war position. Wilson's peace attitude and progressive record won him the presidency by a slight majority. Republicans on election eve believed that they had won and learned of their defeat the next morning, when the California votes came in. Hughes had not asked for the support of California's governor Hiram Johnson.

1920. Senator Warren G. Harding (Ohio) and Governor Calvin Coolidge (Mass.) ran for the Republicans. His health failing, Wilson did not run for reelection. Democrats nominated Governor James M. Cox (Ohio) and Assistant Secretary of the Navy Franklin D. Roosevelt (N.Y.). The Socialist candidates—Eugene V. Debs, serving a federal sentence for violating the Espionage Act, and Seymour Stedman—attained their greatest vote in this election. The Nineteenth Amendment had passed, and women voted for the first time. The Republicans promised a "return to normalcy" and advocated nationalism, isolationism, and opposition to the League of Nations. The Demo-

Poster extolling virtues of Democratic candidate Bryan in 1900 election.

Bringing Home the Captive.

Theodore Roosevelt was reluctant vice-presidential nominee in 1900, when McKinley won reelection.

Coolidge wooed 1924 voter with "common sense," won reelection over rivals Davis and LaFollette.

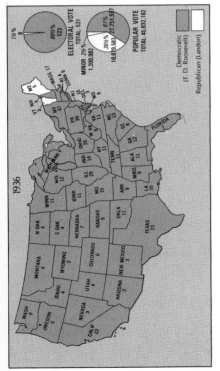

1936 Election

As Republicans attacked the New Deal, Franklin D. Roosevelt pointed persuasively to economic gains and rode to a landslide victory over Alf Landon, who won in Vermont and Maine.

crats favored ratification of the Treaty of Versailles and endorsed the League. The country, suffering from high prices, labor disputes, and anti-Red hysteria, swept in Harding as president, a conservative reaction to Wilson's progressive policies.

1924. Calvin Coolidge, succeeding to the presidency on the death of Harding in 1923, easily won the Republican nomination. Charles G. Dawes (Ill.) was his running mate. The Democratic convention, setting a record for the longest convention in history, was split on the issue of the Ku Klux Klan. Anti-Klan delegates, largely from the East and large cities, fought Klan advocates from the South and West. Anti-Klan leader Governor Alfred Smith (N.Y.), whose liberalism and Catholicism were intolerable to the Klan, was pitted against pro-Klan William Gibbs McAdoo (Cal.). On the 103rd ballot, John W. Davis (W.Va.) was chosen by the Democrats as a compromise candidate. Governor Charles W. Bryan (Neb.), brother of William Jennings Bryan, ran as vice-president.

A new third party, the Progressives, nominated Robert M. La Follette (Wis.) for president and Senator Burton K. Wheeler (Mont.). Progressives attempted to merge farmers and laborers in one party to attack monopolies. Republican strategy identified Coolidge with prosperity and stressed economy. It was "Keep Cool and Keep Coolidge!" Republicans won a decisive victory; the Democratic vote was greatly reduced by the Progressives.

1928. Coolidge did "not choose to run for president," and the Republicans selected Secretary of Commerce Herbert Hoover as their candidate; Charles Curtis, Senate majority leader, was his running mate. New York governor Alfred E. Smith was the Democratic choice for president. Senator J. Taylor Robinson (Ark.) received the vice-presidential nomination. The Socialist candidate was Norman Thomas, former clergyman, pacifist, and editor of *The Nation.*

Republicans capitalized on the nation's continued prosperity. Prohibition was a major issue: Hoover advocated full enforcement, and Smith wanted modification of the laws. Religious bigotry directed against Smith, a Roman Catholic, played a large part in what became one of the most virulent campaigns. Although Smith, the "Happy Warrior," polled the largest vote ever given a Democratic candidate, he lost the election to Hoover by 357 electoral votes.

1932. Seven months after Hoover took office the great crash occurred, and despite his optimism the Depression deepened. Republicans renominated Hoover and Charles Curtis. Governor Franklin D. Roosevelt (N.Y.) was the Democratic presidential nominee; John Nance Garner (Tex.), House Speaker, was his running mate. Norman Thomas and James H. Maurer were the Socialist candidates, William Z. Foster and James W. Ford the Communist candidates.

Republicans had no specific plans for combating the Depression and advocated a protective tariff, sound money, a balanced budget, and self-determination by states on Prohibition. Democrats promised relief for the unemployed and the elderly, aid for farmers, conservation, development of power resources, regulation of securities exchanges, a balanced budget, sound currency, and repeal of the Eighteenth, or Prohibition, Amendment. Roosevelt pledged himself to a "New Deal" to aid the "forgotten man," believing it the duty of government to regulate economic controls if private means failed. To Roosevelt's benefit, major speeches of candidates were heard over radio for the first time. Democrats won 42 states, Republicans, 6, placing Roosevelt in office.

1936. The nation was on the way to economic recovery. Democrats renominated Roosevelt and Garner without opposition. The President drafted the Democratic platform, which incorporated continuation of the New Deal. Republicans promised goals similar to the New Deal's, but by "constitutional" means and with a balanced budget. Kansas governor Alfred M. Landon and W. Franklin Know, Illinois newspaper publisher, were the Republican candidates. The Union Party denounced the New Deal and ran William Lemke (N.D.) and Thomas C. O'Brien (Mass.). They were supported by Father Coughlin's National Union for Social Justice and Dr. Francis E. Townsend, advocate of federal pensions for the aged. The Socialists nominated Norman Thomas; the Communists, Earl Browder. The Liberty League attracted Republican and Democratic anti-Roosevelts and tacitly endorsed the Republican ticket. Roosevelt had the endorsement of Senator La Follette and Labor's Nonpartisan League, formed by labor leaders siding with John L. Lewis.

Landon could not compete with growing evidence of economic recuperation nor with Roosevelt's eloquence and personality. It was a landslide. Roosevelt won all but 8 electoral votes.

1940. World War II had begun in Europe and domestic issues were overshadowed by foreign affairs. Roosevelt ran for a precedent-breaking third term. Henry A. Wallace (Iowa), Secretary of Agriculture, was Roosevelt's choice for vice-president. Wendell L. Wilkie, New York lawyer and utilities executive, received the Republican nomination over party favorites Thomas Dewey, Arthur Vandenberg, and Robert Taft. Wilkie, voting Democratic until 1938, had never held a political post; he was backed by big business and amateurs in a highly organized campaign. Charles L. McNary (Ore.), Senate minority leader and an extreme isolationist, was the Republican vice-presidential candidate.

Wilkie barnstormed the country in a battle against the concentration of power in one man. Many Democratic conservatives and isolationists turned to Wilkie. Although an internationalist, Wilkie attracted the isolationist vote. Both sides favored British aid, national defense programs, and hemispheric defense. Domestically, Wilkie agreed with New Deal goals but not their implementation. Roosevelt carried 38 states with 449 electoral votes to become the first third-term president.

1944. The war was drawing to a victorious finish. Roosevelt was the Democratic candidate for the fourth time. Senator Harry S Truman (Mo.) was his running mate, following a battle for the nomination in which Vice-President Wallace's radical policies proved unacceptable to the conservatives. Republicans nominated New York governor Thomas E. Dewey and John W. Bricker, conservative Ohio governor.

Democrats conducted their campaign primarily by radio because of newspaper hostility. There was little policy difference between the two parties. Dewey assailed the Administration of "tired old men" with unpreparedness and mismanagement of the war and charged Roosevelt with Communist support. Rumors of Roosevelt's ill health were spread. Sidney Hillman, chairman of the Political Action Committee of the CIO, who campaigned vigorously for Roosevelt, was the target of an assault in thinly disguised Ku Klux Klan terms, which boomeranged and brought out the labor vote. Because of the war, many voters did not wish to "change horses," and Roosevelt was easily reelected.

1948. The 1946 midterm election gave Republicans control of Congress. Harry S Truman, succeeding to the presidency on Roosevelt's death in 1945, was the Democratic choice for president; Alben W. Barkley (Ky.) was the vice-presidential nominee. In opposition to a strong civil rights plank, the Mississippi delegation formed the States' Rights (Dixiecrat) Party with Governors J. Strom Thurmond (S.C.) and Fielding L. Wright (Miss.) as candidates. Before the convention, Henry A. Wallace left the Democrats to be the Progressive Party candidate; Senator Glen H. Taylor (Idaho) was his running mate. Advocating greater domestic reforms and diplomatic negotiations with Russia, the Progressives lost strength when their large Communist following became known. Republicans renominated Thomas E. Dewey for president; Governor Earl Warren (Cal.) was his running mate.

Truman stressed the inaction of the "do-nothing" Congress and compared Dewey's liberal campaign promises with the record of the 81st Congress. Barnstorming across the country, he won the Northern minority, labor, and farm votes as he spoke to the common man on specific issues. Truman's Fair Deal advocated social welfare measures, repeal of the Taft-Hartley law, civil rights legislation, and anti-inflation proposals. Although mass media and public opinion polls were confident of a Republican victory, Truman won the election with a comfortable majority.

1952. Effects of Communist control of China and the start of the Korean War in 1950, plus rising prices and taxes and disclosures of governmental corruption and Communism, justified Republican hopes for a presidential victory. Senator Robert A. Taft (Ohio), "Mr. Republican," in a third attempt to gain the Republican nomination, appealed to the conservatives. Liberal Republicans, led by Governor Dewey, favored Gen. Dwight D. Eisenhower. After a credentials fight, Eisenhower became the presidential nominee; Senator Richard M. Nixon (Cal.) was his running mate. The Republicans approved extension of social security and the Taft-Hartley law, stressed states' rights, and promised an early end to the Korean War.

Truman declined to run. Senator Estes Kefauver (Tenn.) actively campaigned but lacked organizational approval, and Governor Adlai E. Stevenson (Ill.), liberal and intellectual, was drafted as the Democratic presidential nominee. Senator John J. Sparkman (Ala.) was vice-presidential candidate. Stevenson was hampered by the Democratic Administration's record and a hostile press. He upheld the civil rights platform and advocated federal control of offshore lands, losing the Southern conservative and states' rightists to Eisenhower. It was an Eisenhower sweep, but Republicans barely gained control of Congress.

1956. Adlai Stevenson, Democratic presidential nominee, left the choice of vice-presidential candidate to convention delegates. Estes Kefauver became the nominee, but the suprisingly large vote for Senator John F. Kennedy ensured him future presidential consideration. Republicans renominated Eisenhower and Nixon. There was little policy difference between the two major parties. School segregation was not stressed. Only Stevenson's proposal for an agreement with Russia for a ban on nuclear-bomb testing stirred any controversy.

Democrats stressed the uncertainty of Eisenhower's health following his recovery from a heart attack. Republicans cried, "We like Ike," pointing to the end of the Korean War and a stabilized prosperity. Democrats countered that Eisenhower's ability to work with congressional Democrats caused prosperity. It was a personal victory for Eisenhower: he

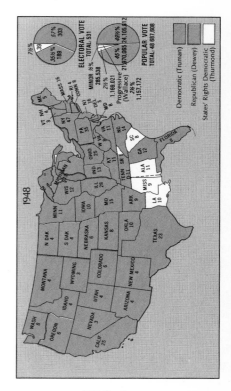

1948 Election
Despite opposition from dissident Democrats who formed the States Rights party and predictions that Republican Thomas E. Dewey would win, Harry Truman triumphed.

was reelected by an overwhelming majority, but the country chose a Democratic Congress.

1960. Eisenhower remained popular, but the Twenty-second Amendment (1951) had barred any president from a third term. The Republicans nominated Vice-President Richard M. Nixon for president after New York governor Nelson A. Rockefeller withdrew from competition; UN ambassador Henry Cabot Lodge (Mass.) was his running mate. Democrats nominated Senator John F. Kennedy (Mass.) following his skillfully run preconvention campaign. Senator Lyndon B. Johnson (Tex.) was Kennedy's choice for vice-president in a maneuver to gain Southern acceptance of a strong civil rights platform. Both candidates conducted intensive campaigns. Kennedy stressed a decline in the U.S. economy and in foreign prestige and presented the challenge of a "New Frontier" for the 1960s. The campaign climaxed in a series of four nationwide television debates. Kennedy was elected in one of the closest popular contests in U.S. history with 34,226,731 votes to Nixon's 34,108,157 to become the first Catholic and the youngest elected president. Senator Harry F. Byrd (Va.) received 15 electoral votes.

1964. Lyndon B. Johnson, serving as president following Kennedy's assassination, was chosen by acclamation as Democratic presidential nominee. Minnesota senator Hubert H. Humphrey was Johnson's choice for vice-president to gain the support of liberals and labor. Republican conservatives, led by Arizona senator Barry M. Goldwater, engaged in a power struggle with moderates before the Republican convention met. Attempts by the moderate-liberal wing, led by Governors Nelson A. Rockefeller (N.Y.) and William W. Scranton (Pa.), to pass a more liberal platform failed. Goldwater was nominated on the first ballot; Representative William E. Miller (N.Y.) was his running mate.

Goldwater denounced encroachment of the individual's freedom by "big government," voted against civil rights, and urged acceleration of the Vietnam War, including the possible use of nuclear weapons. Johnson's Great Society program advocated additional government aid to help high-school dropouts, and worker retraining, support of the civil rights law, and responsibility in international affairs, especially in control of nuclear weapons. It was a Johnson landslide, and he carried every state except Arizona and five Southern states.

1968. Vietnam and violence were the major issues of the 1968 campaign. There was nationwide rioting after the assassination of Martin Luther King, Jr., an advocate of nonviolence, and a sense of shock enveloped the country after the killing of Robert Kennedy, leading Democratic candidate. Former vice-

president Nixon was the Republican candidate; Governor Spiro T. Agnew (Md.) was Nixon's choice for vice-president. Following Johnson's decision not to run for reelection so that he could intensify his efforts to bring peace to Vietnam, Vice-President Humphrey received the Democratic presidential nomination, winning over peace candidate Senator Eugene McCarthy. Senator Edmund S. Muskie (Me.) was Humphrey's running mate.

Former Alabama governor George C. Wallace ran for president on the American Independent Party ticket with Air Force Gen. Curtis LeMay as his running mate. Wallace's "law and order" campaign had strong racial overtones. Nixon's was a middle-of-the-road campaign. Humphrey tried to rally the support of the Kennedy and McCarthy liberals without denying support of the Administration's Vietnam policies. Nixon, in an extremely close race, won the presidency with 43.4 percent of the popular vote; Humphrey received 42.7 percent, and Wallace 13.5 percent from five deep South states. A Democratic Congress was reelected.

1972. In a sense, the campaign of 1972 can be said to have begun with the conclusion of the 1968 contest. Nixon and the Republicans had a challenge and an opportunity. The .5-percent margin of presidential victory (500,000 votes) was the product of defections from the Democrats by doves and Wallaceites. If the Democrats engaged in a renewed bloodletting, Nixon had the opportunity to convert his razor-thin success into a working majority.

The President, like his immediate predecessor, was on the firing line with respect to the issues of Vietnam (victory or withdrawal?), race relations (accommodation or strife?), and the economy (inflation or recession?). Would Nixon move to the left (welfare programs, civil rights enforcement, foreign policy disengagements) or the right (tax reductions, defense spending increases, law and order emphases), or would he, like Lyndon Johnson, try to achieve consensus?

Events were going the President's way. The campuses quieted as such measures as draft reform, troop reduction in Vietnam, and the 18-year-old vote coincided with the passing of a militant student generation and the job recession. The U.S. economy began turning upward as the Vietnam War subsided. The summit meetings in Peking, Moscow, and elsewhere established the President as an architect of peace.

As 1972 opened, the leading Democratic candidate was Senator Edmund Muskie, but he faltered in the primaries as, virtually unnoticed by the public or the political pros, Senator George McGovern and his men put together an organization that far surpassed any other. Hu-

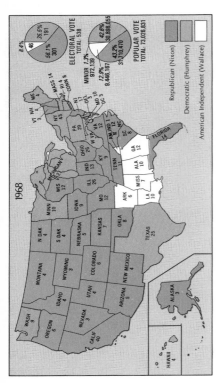

1968 Election

Opposition to Democrats' Vietnam War policy was a major factor in defeat of Hubert Humphrey and victory of Republican Richard Nixon. Third-party candidate George Wallace took five states.

bert Humphrey and a host of other candidates also tried for the nomination. McGovern's bandwagon gathered more supporters as he won the key primaries in California, New York, and other large states, and he easily won the nomination.

McGovern's campaign ran into roadblock after roadblock. There was the expected friction between his own staff and Democratic party officialdom. Then came the controversial decision to replace Thomas Eagleton as his running mate. The Missouri senator was succeeded by Sargent Shriver, former director of the Peace Corps and the War on Poverty. Neither had been the first choice, yet both had the virtues of being handsome campaigners who were Roman Catholic.

McGovern flailed around on several fronts—courting party leaders such as Mayor Richard Daley and Lyndon Johnson, wooing Jewish voters with pledges regarding Israel, trying to capitalize on the bungled break-in of Democratic national headquarters, reconstructing his welfare proposal, reacting to Republican charges that he and his lieutenants were undercutting the disengagement from Vietnam.

The Republican convention had few surprises but was a well-produced showcase. In the nominating speeches and in the President's acceptance address was a bipartisan electoral appeal. Nixon called for establishing the GOP as a new all-American party.

Polls indicated that Nixon could capture 30 to 40 percent of the Democratic votes. The Nixon strategy was to woo Wallace supporters, conservative Catholics, organized labor, senior citizens, and other traditionalists. While McGovern stressed things in American life that he wanted to change, Nixon and Agnew concentrated on what should be preserved.

With disaster apparently approaching, Democratic state and local party organizations sought to dissociate their efforts from that of the presidential ticket. There was concern that 1972 would be like 1896, ushering in a period of national decline for the party.

Some of the Democratic fears were realized with Nixon's landslide victory—McGovern won only Massachusetts and the District of Columbia—but they retained control of Congress. The Nixon triumph, plus the end of the conflict in Vietnam, left the Democrats floundering at the national level.

See also Political Parties in the United States; President of the United States; articles on presidents and prominent candidates.

Consult (VIII) Campbell *et al.,* 1960; Lorant, 1951; Roseboom, 1970; Schlesinger and Israel, 1971; White, 1961, 1965, 1969.

—Martin Gruberg, *University of Wisconsin, Oshkosh*

PRESIDENTIAL SUCCESSION, the constitutional provision for a successor to the president in the event of his death, incapacitation, or resignation. Article II, Section 1 of the Constitution names the vice-president as his first successor and delegates choice of further successors to Congress. In 1947, Congress passed the Presidential Succession Act, which specified that the Speaker of the House would be next in line for the presidential succession, followed by the president pro tempore of the Senate, the secretary of state, and the other members of the cabinet. Cabinet members serve only temporarily—until a speaker or president pro tempore is selected.

The Twenty-fifth Amendment (1967) provides that the president may voluntarily transfer the powers of his office to the vice-president by sending to the Speaker and the president pro tempore written notification of inability to perform the functions of his office. The amendment also establishes that the president may be removed if he is held incapacitated by the vice-president, sundry officials, and Congress. Although eight presidents have died in office, none has ever been declared unable to fulfill the functions of office.

See also Vice-President of the United States.

PRESIDENT OF THE UNITED STATES. The president of the United States is elected for a four-year term by the people of the 50 states through the electoral college and is limited to two terms by Article II, Section 1 of the Constitution and Amendments XII and XXII. He is the chief executive officer of the United States and derives his authority, duties, and powers from Article II.

Constitutional Authority is both explicit (such as the appointment power, the command of the armed forces, and the power to grant reprieves and pardons) and ambiguous (such as guarding "that the laws are faithfully executed"). From both the explicit and ambiguous sections of Article II the president draws "resultant" powers. For example, as commander in chief of the armed forces he can order the deployment of the military anywhere in the world, without having Congress officially declare war, as long as Congress has authorized enough military forces and money. The clause that he shall oversee the faithful execution of laws gives the president much leeway in enforcing or not enforcing them as he sees fit. If a bill becomes law, there is nothing Congress can do to require the president to enforce some provision he deems unconstitutional. Nor is there any effective way for Congress to force a president to spend all the money it has appropriated.

The president's authority to make treaties with the approval of two-thirds of the

Exuberant Democratic candidates George McGovern *(right)* and Sargent Shriver join hands in 1972.

President Nixon *(right)* and Vice-President Agnew acknowledge cheers following their renomination at Miami Beach in 1972.

President of the United States

1. George Washington (1732-99)
President (Fed) 1789-97
Commander in chief Continental
Army 1775-81; presided
Const. Convention 1787-89

2. John Adams (1735-1826)
President (Fed) 1797-1801
Min. to Netherlands 1780-82
1st U.S. Min. to Britain
1785-88; Vice Pres. 1789-97

3. Thomas Jefferson (1743-1826)
President (Dem-Rep) 1801-09
Gov. of Virginia 1779-81
Secretary of State 1789-93
Vice President 1797-1801

4. James Madison (1751-1836)
President (Dem-Rep) 1809-17
Called "Father of Constitution"
House of Rep. 1789-97
Secretary of State 1801-09

5. James Monroe (1758-1831)
President (Dem-Rep) 1817-25
Gov. of Va. 1799-1802, 1811
Secretary of State 1811-16
Secretary of War 1814-15

6. John Quincy Adams (1767-
1848); Pres. (Dem-Rep) 1825-29
Senate 1803-08
Minister to Russia 1809-14
Secretary of State 1817-25

7. Andrew Jackson (1767-1845)
President (Dem) 1829-37
House of Rep. 1796-97
Senate 1797-98, 1823-25
Tenn. Supreme Ct. 1798-1804

8. Martin Van Buren (1782-
1862); Pres. (Dem) 1837-41
Governor of New York 1829
Secretary of State 1829-31
Vice President 1833-37

9. William Henry Harrison
(1773-1841); Pres. (Whig)
1841; Gov. of Indiana Terr.
1800-12; House of Rep. 1816-
19; Senate, elected 1825

10. John Tyler (1790-1862)
President (Whig) 1841-45
Gov. of Virginia 1825-27
Senate 1827-29, 1830-36
Vice President 1841

11. James Knox Polk (1795-
1849); Pres. (Dem) 1845-49
Tenn. House of Rep. 1823-25
U.S. House of Rep. 1825-39
Gov. of Tennessee 1839-41

12. Zachary Taylor (1784-1850)
President (Whig) 1849-50
Served 40 years in the Army
where he gained the name of
"Old Rough and Ready"

13. Millard Fillmore (1800-74)
President (Whig) 1850-53
N.Y. State assembly 1829-31
House of Rep. 1833-35, 37-43
Vice President 1849-50

14. Franklin Pierce (1804-69)
President (Dem) 1853-57
N.H. House of Rep. 1829-33
House of Rep. 1833-37
Senate 1837-42

15. James Buchanan (1791-
1868); Pres. (Dem) 1857-61
Senate 1834-45
Secretary of State 1845-49
Min. to Gr. Britain 1853-56

16. Abraham Lincoln (1809-65)
President (Rep) 1861-65
Kentucky legislature 1835-43
House of Rep. 1847-49
Emancipation Proc. 1863

17. Andrew Johnson (1808-75)
President (Rep) 1865-69
Gov. of Tennessee 1853-57
Senate 1857-62
Vice President 1865

18. Ulysses Simpson Grant
(1822-85); Pres. (Rep) 1869-77
Commander in chief of all
Union forces in the Civil
War 1864-65

19. Rutherford Birchard Hayes (1822-93); Pres. (Rep) 1877-81; maj. general, Civil War House of Rep. 1865-67 Gov. of Ohio 1867-77

20. James Abram Garfield (1831-81); Pres. (Rep) 1881 maj. general in Civil War House of Rep. 1863-80 Elected to Senate 1880

21. Chester Alan Arthur (1830-86); Pres. (Rep) 1881-85; quartermaster of N.Y. State in Civil War Vice President 1881

22 & 24. Grover Cleveland (1837-1908); Pres. (Dem) 1885-89, 1893-97; elected mayor of New York 1881; elected gov. of New York State 1882

23. Benjamin Harrison (1833-1901); Pres. (Rep) 1889-93 brig. gen. in Civil War candidate for gov. of Ind. 1876; Senate 1881-87

25. William McKinley (1843-1901); Pres. (Rep) 1897-1901 major in the Civil War House of Rep. 1877-83, 85-91 Gov. of Ohio 1892-96

26. Theodore Roosevelt (1858-1919); Pres. (Rep) 1901-09 N.Y. state leg. 1882-84 Asst. Sec. of Navy 1897-98 Vice President 1901

27. William Howard Taft (1857-1930); Pres. (Rep) 1909-13; 1st civil Gov. of Philippines; Chief Justice U.S. Supreme Court 1921-30

28. (Thomas) Woodrow Wilson (1856-1924); Pres. (Dem) 1913-21; Pres. Princeton 1902-10 Gov. of New Jersey 1911-13 Nobel Peace Prize 1919

29. Warren Gamaliel Harding (1865-1923); Pres. (Rep) 1921-23; Ohio senate 1899-1903 Lt. Gov. of Ohio 1904-06 Senate 1915-20

30. (John) Calvin Coolidge (1872-1933); Pres. (Rep) 1923-29; Mass. lt. gov. 1915-18 Mass.gov. 1918-21 Vice President 1921-23

31. Herbert Clark Hoover (1874-1964); Pres. (Rep) 1929-33; Sec. of Commerce 1921-29 Hoover Commission on Executive reorganization 1947-49, 1953-55

32. Franklin Delano Roosevelt (1882-1945); Pres. (Dem) 1933-45 N.Y. State Senate 1911-13 Asst. Sec. of Navy 1913-20 Gov. of New York 1929-33

33. Harry S. Truman (1884–1972) President (Dem) 1945-53 Jackson Co., Mo., judge 1926-34 Senate 1935-45 Vice President 1945

34. Dwight David Eisenhower (1890-1969); Pres. (Rep) 1953-61; Comm. Europe invasion, Army chief of staff 1944-48; SCAPE 1950-52

35. John Fitzgerald Kennedy (1917-63); Pres. (Dem) 1961-63 House of Rep. 1947-53 Senate 1953-61 Pulitzer Prize 1957

36. Lyndon Baines Johnson (1908-1973); Pres. (Dem.) 1963–69 Senate 1949-61 Senate Dem. leader 1953-61 Vice President 1961-63

37. Richard Milhous Nixon (1913-   ); Pres. (Rep) 1969-House of Rep. 1947-51 Senate 1951-53 Vice President 1953-61

Senate, his authority to make executive agreements with other nations simply as the executive head, and his authority to recognize the legitimacy of other nations make him the ultimate spokesman for the United States on foreign policy. The Constitution makes the foreign policy of the president the foreign policy of the nation.

Statutory authority is created for the president by Congress acting within the domain of its legislative function and role (see Article I). When Congress creates and funds a new independent agency to carry out some national function, Congress is adding authority to the presidency. When Congress empowers him to freeze wages and prices when he deems it economically necessary (such as in the Economic Stabilization Act of 1970 and 1971), Congress is again increasing the president's overall authority by act of Congress. Numerous examples could be given to show the expansion of presidential power by legislative action.

Political Power is an extremely important facet of presidential authority. Particularly in this century, presidents have developed a myriad of techniques to persuade and induce Congress to act as they suggest. By taking the constitutional duty to give Congress information on "the state of the Union" and "recommend to their consideration such measures as he shall judge necessary and expedient" (Article II, Section 3), twentieth-century presidents have assumed an all-important political position of establishing the president's legislative program at the beginning of each session of Congress. Thus, the president has indeed become the chief legislator because he sets legislative priorities through his State of the Union address, budget and economic messages, and follow-up measures introduced in Congress for him by his own party's congressional leaders.

Political power can also be enhanced through his power of appointment. Furthermore, as modern legislation has become more and more tied to financial considerations and needs, the presidential Office of Management and the Budget has become the chief executive's focal point for gathering even more political authority unto himself. The president's skill with the press, his television performances, and his personal rapport with other political leaders and the people also contribute to his political power.

The president is, then, the chief administrator of a large establishment, the head in essence of his political party, and formulator of public opinion. His is the most public of the three branches of government, with his daily routine, schedule, and policies the subject of much scrutiny by the press, radio, TV, Congress, and the public. The vigor of a one-man office with its singleness of purpose, the fixed

Opera star Leontyne Price sings in *Madame Butterfly* at Milan's La Scala theater.

presidential term that keeps him in office for at least four years without danger of being replaced suddenly because of a controversial decision, and his having the only national constituency of the three branches of government establish for the president the indispensable platform from which to educate, persuade, and lead the nation.

See also Presidential Elections; Presidential Succession; articles on individual presidents.

Consult (VIII) Burns, 1966; Kallenbach, 1966; Koenig, 1968; Rossiter, 1960; Wildavsky, 1969.

—Erwin L. Levine, *Skidmore College*

PRESSURE GROUP. *See* Lobby.

PRICE, LEONTYNE (1927–), prominent soprano. She was born in Laurel, Miss., and was trained at the Juilliard School of Music in New York and studied with Florence Page Kimball.

In 1950, Price made her debut as a concert singer and in 1951 her stage debut. In 1954 she greatly moved her audience in New York's Town Hall with her spectacular performance. In the years to follow, she successfully toured in Europe, triumphing in *Aida* at La Scala and in *Don Giovanni* at the Salzburg Festival in 1960. In 1961 Price made her debut as Leonora in *Il Trovatore* with the Metropolitan Opera Company. She created the role of Cleopatra in *Antony and Cleopatra,* which was the opening production at the Metropolitan Opera Company's new home in Lincoln Center.

PRICE ADMINISTRATION, OFFICE OF (OPA), agency created by President Franklin Roosevelt on April 11, 1941, to stop profiteering and hoarding and to control inflation during World War II. He combined the price and consumer divisions of the National Defense Advisory Commission and then by executive order on August 28, 1941, named this division the OPA. The OPA rationed consumer goods such as sugar, meat, and coffee, established price ceilings, and stabilized rents. The OPA's authority lapsed on July 1, 1946.

PRICE SUPPORTS, a complex economic system used by governments to prohibit market prices from falling below a certain level. Governments regulate the prices in particular industries in order to guarantee a standard of living for those who produce certain commodities, thus ensuring that the industry will continue to operate. Price supports are most frequently applicable to the agriculture industry.

Farmers have little or no control over prices and production because of variables such as weather conditions and crop diseases.

This means that prices vary greatly and are subject to rapid change. The U.S. government makes guarantees to farmers by limitation of crop production in order to cut supplies and raise prices, by purchase-loan storage programs that guarantee to keep prices at a set level, by purchase and resale plans, and by payments to divert land to conservation projects. To arrive at a price support standard, the government chooses a base period during which the members of the industry have had a good standard of living. It then tries to maintain this standard through the price supports.

PRIGG v. PENNSYLVANIA (1842), a milestone Supreme Court decision dealing with the status of fugitive slaves. The Fugitive Slave Act of 1793 had committed the federal government to return runaway slaves to their masters. However, the law had not been strongly enforced, and Northern state courts had maintained their right to judge cases on their own merits. This point of view was intended to preserve states' rights as much as to ensure justice for alleged runaways. The abolitionist drive in the 1830s widened differences between North and South and raised Southern anxiety for the security of its slave "property."

After Edward Prigg seized a runaway slave in Pennsylvania and returned her to Maryland in 1837, he was indicted for kidnapping under a Pennsylvania statute—which brought up questions of jurisdiction that were appealed to the Supreme Court. It ruled in 1842 that the Fugitive Slave Act of 1793 had a higher authority than that of any state statute. This decision satisfied neither the North nor the South. The South feared for its own states' rights. The North, pushed by its civil liberties advocates, enacted personal liberty laws that were intended to protect its citizens from slave "kidnappers" supported by federal authorities.

See also Fugitive Slave Acts; Personal Liberty Laws.

PRIMOGENITURE, in land tenure, restriction of inheritance to the eldest son. *See* Colonial Agriculture.

PRINCETON, BATTLE OF (JAN. 3, 1777), patriot victory that drove the British from central New Jersey. *See* Revolutionary War Battles.

PRINCETON UNIVERSITY. *See* Colonial Colleges.

PRIVATEERS, privately owned armed vessels that attack and seize enemy ships. American privateers operated under letters of marque issued by the colonial governments. During the series of wars in which England and France and their respective American provinces engaged between 1689 and the time of the Revolution, the colonists reaped vast riches from privateering. According to maritime law such captured vessels were considered prizes, and "prize courts" generally awarded the proceeds from the sale of captured ships to the privateersmen. The profits to be gained from privateering were immense, and during the French and Indian War alone approximately 11,000 colonists engaged in such operations.

Privateers also were active during the American Revolution. Between 1775 and 1783, American privateers captured about 600 English vessels and won prize money estimated at $18 million. Yet the contribution of privateering to the patriot cause is questionable because the opportunity of winning riches attracted many mariners to privateering and thereby hindered the growth of the Continental Navy.

PROCLAMATION OF NEUTRALITY. *See* Neutrality Proclamation.

PROCLAMATION OF 1763 temporarily forbade further migration into the Ohio country and ordered settlers already there to retreat across the mountains. England's victory in the French and Indian War brought it control of Canada and, except for the city of New Orleans, all American territory east of the Mississippi River. Lord Shelburne, as head of the Board of Trade, took responsibility for devising a plan to administer the new acquisition without antagonizing the resident Indians.

In June 1763, Shelburne proposed the establishment of three new colonies—Quebec, East Florida, and West Florida—and the prohibition of further American settlement west of the Appalachian Mountains. In August 1763 news of Pontiac's Rebellion reached England, and the government realized the urgency of the American situation. The less experienced Earl of Hillsborough replaced Shelburne in September and hastily issued in the Proclamation of 1763 a modified version of his predecessor's plan.

Treaties with the Indians subsequently altered the limits of expansion. The Cherokees in treaties of October 1768 and October 1770 agreed to the westward extension of Virginia's border. The Iroquois in November 1768 by the Treaty of Fort Stanwix negotiated by William Johnson secured for the British much of western New York, the lands between the branches of the Susquehanna River, and the area west of the Big Kanawha. In November 1768, Creeks allowed South Carolina to enlarge its territory to the west, and Georgia did the same.

Consult (II) Sosin, 1961.
—Thomas Archdeacon, *University of Wisconsin*

"Teacher's pet." Critics of federal price-support programs saw them as handouts to farmers.

John Dewey, foremost exponent of progressive education.

PROGRESSIVE EDUCATION

PROGRESSIVE EDUCATION, a liberal movement in American education that began at the end of the nineteenth century and influenced schooling for several generations. Some of the ideas of the movement can be traced back to Jean Jacques Rousseau, Johann Pertalozzi, and Friedrich Froebell—for example, the "child-centered school" and the advantage of observation over verbal learning. These and other ideas were organized and put into practice by John Dewey, the greatest intellectual force in progressivism. He stressed such themes as that modes of behavior are most readily learned by actual performance and that children learn best when they have a strong interest in what they are doing.

Dewey's ideas were picked up and often misapplied by many educators. Some schools went all out for progressive teaching, and most schools felt some influence. Many traditionally inclined critics attacked progressive education for destroying discipline, letting the children do what they wanted, and failing to teach basic subjects. Dewey was blamed for many things that he never advocated. He never meant, for example, that following interests meant avoiding hard work. By the 1950s the movement had lost favor and force.

See also Education.
Consult (V) Cremin, 1961.

PROGRESSIVE PARTY, political party that split off from the Republicans and ran Theodore Roosevelt for president in 1912. Conflict between the Republicans' progressive and conservative elements during William Howard Taft's Administration spurred the formation of the National Progressive Republican League in 1911. Dissatisfaction with Taft led to primary victories for Robert La Follette and Roosevelt, but Taft's control of the convention assured his renomination. Roosevelt, who frequently equated the bull moose with strength and vigor, then presided over the foundation of the new "Bull Moose" Party.

Its leadership was recruited largely from the urban middle class and took a very advanced position on social and industrial legislation. It was bankrolled by businessmen who favored federal regulation rather than trust-busting. In some states progressive forces captured the regular Republican machinery, in some they ran separate tickets, in others they fused. Campaigning on this New Nationalism, Roosevelt captured nearly 30 percent of the popular vote and 88 electoral votes, but the Republican split led to the election of Woodrow Wilson. In 1914 the Progressive Party suffered disastrous setbacks, and in 1916 Roosevelt declined its presidential nomination, endorsing Republican Charles Evans Hughes.

La Follette revived the party name on a far different base in 1924 and polled 17 percent of the vote. Henry Wallace, running an unsuccessful third-party campaign in the presidential election of 1948, also used the party name.

See also La Follette, Robert; Political Parties in the United States; Roosevelt, Theodore; Taft, William Howard.
Consult (VI) Mowry, 1951; Nye, 1951.
—John Buenker, *University of Wisconsin, Parkside*

PROHIBITION. Attempts to prohibit either the sale or manufacture of alcoholic beverages by state law in the 1850s and 1880s proved largely unsuccessful, but during the Progressive Era many would-be reformers came to regard alcohol and the saloon as the major source of social evils. For them Prohibition became a panacea without which other reforms would be ineffective. Such arguments were particularly compelling to old stock, middle-class men and women, whose fervor expressed itself in the Anti-Saloon League and the Women's Christian Temperance Union. Opposition was centered in the urban, new-stock, non-Protestant working class, whose religious and cultural traditions stressed personal temperance rather than legislated abstinence.

Statewide and local-option Prohibition made great strides in the South and West after 1900. By April 1917 there were 26 Prohibition states, and more than 50 percent of the people lived in dry territory. By early 1919, saloons were illegal in 90 percent of the nation, in which two-thirds of the population lived. The prohibitionists sought federal action in the form of the Webb-Kenyon Act (1913), which forbade interstate traffic in liquor, and, after several unsuccessful efforts, they finally got the necessary two-thirds of Congress to propose the Eighteenth Amendment in 1917. The ratification struggle was closely contested in the major industrial states, with Connecticut and Rhode Island rejecting and New Jersey holding out until 1922. The amendment swept the South and West, however, and Prohibition became law on Jan. 16, 1920.

The debate continued throughout the 1920s as it became clear that enforcement was nearly impossible and that bootlegging was threatening to destroy the entire law enforcement system. In both 1928 and 1932 the Democratic presidential candidates committed themselves to repeal, and Franklin Roosevelt's victory lead to the introduction of the repeal amendment in February 1933. It was ratified before the year was out.

See also Amendments, Constitutional; Anti-Saloon League; Webb-Kenyon Act (1913); Willard, Frances.
—John Buenker, *University of Wisconsin, Parkside*

Temperance movement assailed alleged degenerating effects of saloons.

PROVIDENCE PLANTATIONS, name for the four Rhode Island towns—Providence, Portsmouth, Newport, and Warwick—that were granted a patent in 1644. In 1663 the patent was superseded by a royal charter incorporating the Colony of Rhode Island and Providence Plantation.

See also Rhode Island.

PSYCHEDELICS, term first proposed in 1957 to distinguish lysergic acid diethylamide (LSD), mescaline, and peyote (and later psilocybin) from depressant drugs (alcohol, barbiturates, and opium derivatives) and stimulant drugs (amphetamines and caffeine). It was believed that psychedelics produced in the user a mystical experience that enhanced his capacity to experience. Although psychedelics were thought to be nonaddictive, users were warned against psychological dependence and possible bizarre alterations of sensory perception. Marijuana and hashish, milder types of psychedelics, came into widespread use beginning around 1965.

See also Drugs (Hard).

PUBLIC BROADCASTING ACT (1967), legislation that created the Corporation for Public Broadcasting (CPB) as an agency charged with the task of channeling funds to local and national noncommercial programming efforts. It was passed after a report recommended that the federal government subsidize a fourth live national noncommercial cultural and informational network. The recipient of most of this money was the Public Broadcasting System (PBS), which selects, schedules, and promotes programs but distributes no money and produces no programs. The law had safeguards against political or governmental control. The CPB has a chairman appointed by the president with the advice of the Senate, as well as a presidentially named 15-member board. PBS has its board drawn from public TV management.

The CPB began operations in 1969 with funds provided by Congress, the Ford and Carnegie foundations, and the Columbia Broadcasting System. In 1972 President Nixon vetoed a bill providing long-term expanded funding for CPB. There had been conservative criticism of the public affairs and cultural programming as well as of the high salaries of some educational broadcasters. The President also preferred greater local programming.

PUBLIC HOUSING. See Housing Acts.

PUBLIC LAW 480 established Food for Peace program. See Foreign Aid.

PUBLIC WORKS ADMINISTRATION (PWA), agency established by the National Industrial Recovery Act (1933) and designed to pour large sums of money into the nation's economy through construction projects. Placed by President Roosevelt under the control of Harold L. Ickes, Secretary of the Interior, PWA provided little immediate economic stimulation. Ickes was so cautious and scrupulous, so concerned that the public receive its money's worth, that agency resources went into planning rather than into providing assistance to the unemployed. However, the long-range results were significant. The PWA built roads, power plants, sewage systems, school buildings, hospitals, dams, bridges, airports, and even some naval vessels. Some badly needed public housing—22,000 units in 50 projects—were constructed by the PWA before the U.S. Housing Authority was set up in 1937.

See also Civil Works Administration.
Consult (VI) Ickes, 1953.

PUERTO RICO. Annexed as an unincorporated U.S. territory in 1898, it became, while still part of the United States, a self-governing commonwealth in 1952. Discovered by Columbus in 1493, the island, claimed for Spain, was called San Juan Bautista. The first settlers came with Ponce de León, who dubbed the island un puerto rico, a rich port. In 1521 the city of San Juan was founded. El Morro castle, the oldest fort on U.S. territory, was begun in 1539 to protect the port, which was attacked many times by the British and Dutch.

In 1898 Puerto Rico was occupied by U.S. troops during the Spanish-American War; later that year Spain ceded Puerto Rico to the United States. U.S. citizenship was granted to Puerto Rican citizens in 1917, and in 1947 the island was granted local self-government. The statehood movement on the island has not been strong enough to produce a favorable vote on statehood.

The legislature is bicameral; San Juan is the capital. Puerto Rico's population in 1970 was 2,712,033.

PULITZER, JOSEPH (1847-1911), newspaper editor and publisher. Born in Hungary, he emigrated to the United States in 1864 to join the Union army. Discharged from the army in 1865, he went to work as a journalist in St. Louis under Carl Schurz. In 1878 Pulitzer bought the St. Louis *Post* and merged it with the *Dispatch,* laying the cornerstone of his publishing empire. As owner and publisher, he successfully dominated the St. Louis evening newspaper field.

In 1883 he bought the New York *World* from Jay Gould for $346,000. Pulitzer used aggressive techniques often characterized as yellow journalism, including numerous illustrations, news stunts, crusades against corrup-

Settlements in Puerto Rico, one of first islands colonized by the Spanish.

tion, and cartoons, as well as in-depth news coverage, to build up the *World*. In 1895 William Randolph Hearst established his New York *Journal* to vie with Pulitzer's papers in sensationalism and circulation.

After 1890, Pulitzer's partial blindness kept him from the editorial offices, but this did not lessen the paper's tradition of independent liberalism. Pulitzer served briefly in the U.S. House of Representatives in 1885. He endowed the Columbia University School of Journalism, which opened in 1912. He also established the Pulitzer prizes, awarded annually for achievements in fiction, drama, history, biography, poetry, music, and various categories of newspaper work.

PULLMAN STRIKE (1894), one of the most significant strikes in labor history. It began in May 1894, when the Pullman Palace Car Co. cut wages without reducing workers' rents in the company town of Pullman, Ill. When the company refused to discuss grievances or arbitrate, Eugene Debs' American Railway Union joined the strike, and rail transportation in 27 states was paralyzed. The government used the Sherman Antitrust Act to obtain a blanket injunction against the union. Violence followed, and President Cleveland sent federal troops to crush the strike. The strike demonstrated that government was not a neutral arbiter in the confrontation between labor and capital, and it was demonstrated that the Sherman Antitrust Act was more effective against labor than trusts. The injunction became a widely used device against labor, and Debs emerged from jail a dedicated foe of American capitalism.

See also Debs, Eugene V.; Railroad Unions; Sherman Antitrust Act (1890).

PURE FOOD AND DRUG ACT (1906), legislation supported by President Theodore Roosevelt in response to mounting criticism of the food preparation industries. It was passed in conjunction with the Meat Inspection Act. The food and drug act barred the sale or manufacture of adulterated or falsely labeled drugs and food involved in interstate commerce, while the meat act required federal inspection of meat plants engaged in interstate commerce.

The campaign for the Pure Food and Drug Act had attacked the use of dyes and artificial preservatives in foods sold to the public. As early as 1898, public health officials had banded together in the National Association of State Dairy and Food Departments to agitate for federal food controls, and in the Spanish-American War a huge public scandal over the "embalmed beef" supplied for U.S. troops aroused public opinion. However, the most effective propaganda came in 1906 with

Upton Sinclair's shocking novel about the Chicago stockyards, *The Jungle*.

Later amendments strengthened these reforms, and in 1938 the Wheeler-Lea Act required clearer labeling of food, drugs, and cosmetics and provided for prosecution of false advertisers. Weaknesses remain in the U.S. laws, and the growth in the 1960s of the conservation-ecology movement, which expressed fear about the use of insecticides and chemicals, produced strong demands for further stiffening of laws against adulterated and mislabeled products. Women's cosmetics were the least protected and least labeled of the whole range of consumer products.

See also Ecology.
Consult (V) Benedict, 1967.

PURITANISM, a movement within England's established Anglican church that originated in the late sixteenth century. Its adherents argued that religion in England had been corrupted by practices for which there was no biblical sanction. Puritanism embraced a variety of groups. Congregationalists believed that Protestants should organize themselves in small autonomous churches that could limit their memberships and select their own officers and ministers. Presbyterians believed individual congregations should be subject to control by a central supervisory body. In spite of differences over church structure, Puritans shared a common theology that was basically Calvinist.

Puritan Faith. Puritans believed in predestination—that God knew even before the Creation which men He would save later. The problem for men was that they could never be sure just who was predestined for salvation—Puritans lived in uncertainty. Men might, however, achieve a measure of understanding about God and their fate because God usually saved those who led decent lives, attended church, and strove for goodness.

In spite of nagging uncertainties, Puritans believed their churches could approach purity. Thus they frequently required that in order to attain church membership prospective applicants had to demonstrate that they led decent lives. Moreover, Puritans knew that God rewarded men, communities, and entire nations for following His laws. All men, even those predestined to damnation, could follow those laws because God had given all the ability to think—to understand His word. Thus governments, in enforcing rules of behavior, protected not only the good from the evil but also the community from God's anger.

Emigration. Despairing of reform of church and state in England, Puritans began emigrating to the New World, where they hoped to form perfect communities. The Pilgrims were the first group to arrive (1620), but the great migration of Puritans did not begin until 1629-1630. By 1640 some 20,000 people had settled in New England. The colonies in Massachusetts and Connecticut were ruled along Puritan lines, and Puritanism survived in America long after it had ceased to be a powerful force in England.

See also Congregationalists; Connecticut; Massachusetts; Pilgrims; Presbyterians.

Consult (I) Miller, 1956; Morgan, 1958, 1963.

—Aaron M. Shatzman, *Washington University*

PUTTING-OUT SYSTEM, manufacturing process in which colonial entrepreneurs furnished materials and at times necessary tools to workers who made finished products in their own households. Also called the domestic system, it had importance in the economic life of the colonies on the eve of the American Revolution. The system was particularly suited to the textile and shoe industries. Women and children working at home looms wove tens of thousands of yards of cloth, while household laborers in Lynn and other Massachusetts towns produced vast quantities of shoes for wholesale trade.

QUAKERS, religious group founded in 1647 by the English religious leader George Fox (1624-1691), who rejected clergymen and churches in favor of a direct and personal experience of God for every man. The formal name of the group is the Society of Friends. Quaker missionaries first began arriving in the American colonies during the 1650s. New England Puritans harassed them mercilessly for their refusal to conform and their insistence on passive resistance. In this period all the colonies except Rhode Island passed several laws against Quakers.

By 1674 the Quakers had acquired proprietary rights in West New Jersey, where they were able to practice their religion in peace. In 1681 William Penn, in a "Holy Experiment," opened up his huge colony of Pennsylvania to all who sought religious liberty, and by 1685 there were almost 9,000 settlers in Pennsylvania. Persecution in the colonies gradually subsided in the eighteenth century.

Beliefs. The fundamental beliefs of the Quakers have changed little over the years. As in the seventeenth century, they trust to an "Inward Light" to lead them—without intermediary rites, church, creed, or priesthood—to their own experience of God. They gather at meetings held in silence unless someone is moved to speech or prayer. They are ardent humanitarians supporting all forms of social betterment and education. Among the institutions of higher learning founded by them are Haverford, Swarthmore, and Bryn Mawr colleges.

See also Colonial Religion; Penn, William; Pennsylvania.

QUARTERING ACT (1765), act of Parliament that required colonial legislatures to supply barracks and provisions for British troops. A supplementary act in 1766 authorized billeting in inns, alehouses, and unoccupied dwellings. The colonies condemned the measures as taxation without consent, and New York's assembly was so uncooperative that Parliament in June 1767 empowered Governor Henry Moore to suspend its sessions.

When the New York legislature in December 1769 finally appropriated money to comply with the act, Alexander McDougall of the Sons of Liberty denounced the delegates. Civilians and soldiers clashed in New York City as tensions increased. On Jan. 19, 1770, in the Battle of Golden Hill, soldiers used bayonets against citizens armed with swords and clubs; several participants were wounded, but none died. Parliament in 1774 passed a stronger Quartering Act, which permitted the billeting of soldiers in occupied private houses in the colonies.

QUEBEC, BATTLE OF (1775), attack in which American forces failed to capture Quebec. *See* Revolutionary War Battles.

QUEBEC ACT (1774), British legislation that provided Canada with a civil government. Parliament retained the power to levy all but local taxes, vested legislative authority in a council appointed by the crown, and granted the Catholic population religious toleration and civil rights. The American colonists disliked these provisions, but they especially opposed the extension of Canada's boundary to the Ohio River, an area in which Virginia, Connecticut, and Massachusetts had claims.

QUEEN ANNE'S WAR (1702-1713), the colonial name for the War of the Spanish Succession, a conflict that to a large extent began over American interests. Britain, the Netherlands, and the Holy Roman Empire all declared war on France to prevent Louis XIV from inheriting the Spanish Empire, whose childless king had just died. In 1702 a South Carolina force failed to conquer the fort at St. Augustine after plundering and burning the town. New England forces twice faltered before Port Royal in Nova Scotia (1704-1707), while the French and Indians destroyed a few outlying villages. Canada proved far more vulnerable to English assault (Port Royal was taken in 1710) than New England was to French attack. The Treaty of

Philadelphia: Quäkerkirche.

Print of early Quaker meeting in Philadelphia.

Utrecht, which ended the conflict in 1713, awarded Nova Scotia, Hudson's Bay, and Newfoundland to Britain. From Spain the British extracted the *asiento,* a contract for supplying slaves to New Spain on an annual basis.

Consult (I) Peckham, 1964.

QUEEN'S COLLEGE. *See* Colonial Colleges.

QUITRENTS, payments for use of land. *See* Colonial Agriculture.

QUOTA SYSTEM, policy of setting immigration quotas by nationality. In 1921 Congress enacted a bill designed to restrict immigration to 3 percent of the foreign-born from that country residing in the United States in 1910 and limiting overall immigration to 357,000. In the Immigration Act of 1924, the limit was cut in half, and the percentage was reduced from 3 to 2, based on the 1890 rather than the 1910 census. In 1929 the national origin law fixed maximum immigration at 150,000. Each nationality's immigrants were fixed through a complicated ratio system based on the nationality's representation in the 1920 U.S. census. It remained the basis of U.S. immigration laws until the 1950s.

See also Immigration and Nationality Act (1965); McCarran-Walter Immigration Act (1952).

RADICAL DEMOCRATS. *See* Barnburners.

RADICAL REPUBLICANS, Republicans of the 1850s, 1860s, and 1870s who differed from their moderate and conservative colleagues in several ways. Before the Civil War the Radicals took an uncompromising stand on slavery expansion, bluntly declaring that the institution was wrong and must be put on the road to extinction. In the secession crisis they insisted that no compromise be made with proslavery forces, and during the war they championed complete emancipation and a vigorous prosecution of the conflict. After the South surrendered, they demanded that it not be restored to the Union until full civil and political rights had been granted to the freedmen.

Their greatest legislative achievements were the Thirteenth, Fourteenth, and Fifteenth amendments, the Reconstruction Acts, the Enforcement Acts, and the Civil Rights Acts. The unsuccessful attempt to remove President Johnson was their most conspicuous blunder, and the most serious shortcoming in their program was the failure to provide a solid economic foundation for the freed slaves.

The leading Radicals in the U.S. Senate were Charles Sumner and Henry Wilson of Massachusetts, Benjamin F. Wade of Ohio, and Zachariah Chandler of Michigan. In the House

prominent Radicals included Thaddeus Stevens and William D. Kelley of Pennsylvania, Joshua Reed Giddings and James M. Ashley of Ohio, Henry Winter Davis of Maryland, and George S. Boutwell and Benjamin F. Butler of Massachusetts.

See also Amendments, Constitutional; Civil Rights Acts (1866–1875); Reconstruction; Reconstruction Acts (1867–1868); Stevens, Thaddeus; Sumner, Charles.

Consult (IV) Hyman, 1967; Trefousse, 1969.

—Michael Burlingame, *Connecticut College*

RAGTIME. *See* Jazz.

RAIL PASSENGER ACT (1970), legislation creating AMTRAK. *See* Railroad Legislation.

RAILROAD LEGISLATION has run the gamut from promotion to regulation and finally to consolidation. Significant federal support began with the first Pacific Railway Act (1862), which provided for a transcontinental railroad to connect the West Coast to the rest of the nation. To subsidize building this link, the government pledged alternate sections of public lands to the depth of 10 miles (later increased to 20) on either side of the track and provided for loans ranging from $16,000 to $48,000 for each mile completed. Grants to build other railroads followed, with the federal government giving railroads more than 130 million acres of land and lending more than $64 million.

Early Regulation. In the 1870s many Midwestern states attempted to regulate railroads with Granger laws. Although the Supreme Court initially upheld these laws, it reversed itself in *Wabash v. Illinois* (1886) by insisting that Congress rather than the states had the power to regulate interstate commerce. Congress responded with the Interstate Commerce Act (ICA) (1887) creating the prototype of future regulatory bodies, the five-man Interstate Commerce Commission (ICC). The ICA required that rates be reasonable, that the abuses be eliminated, and that if the commission were not obeyed it would have recourse to the courts. Although hampered by adverse judicial decisions, the ICC signified a shift from promoting to restraining railroads.

The Progressive Era brought more railroad regulation. The Elkins Act (1903) attempted to stop rebates. The Hepburn Act (1906) empowered the ICC to determine and prescribe maximum rates. Railroads could appeal, but the burden of proof now rested with them. The ICC's authority was also extended to cover storage, refrigeration, and terminal facilities, as well as sleeping cars, and express and pipeline companies. The Mann-Elkins Act (1910) gave the ICC the undisputed right to fix rates charged by carriers.

Since World War I. Federal support for consolidation began when the wartime Railroad Control Act (1918) established the U.S. Railroad Administration to run railroads regionally. The Esch-Cummins Transportation Act (1920) returned railroads to private control but encouraged them to consolidate into approximately 20 competition groups, gave the ICC complete jurisdiction over financial operations of railroads to protect the investing public clause and stockholders, established the Railroad Labor Board to mediate wage disputes, and sought to benefit low-income railroads. The Emergency Railroad Transportation Act (1933) promoted financial reorganization of carriers to improve rail transportation and avoid duplication of services and placed railroad holding companies under the ICC. The Rail Passenger Act (1970) created a National Railroad Passenger Corporation (AMTRAK) to manage and operate a national railroad network. AMTRAK was to provide modern, efficient intercity rail passenger service on a profit basis by operating trains through contracts with existing railroads. The corporation was to be supervised by a president and a 15-member board of directors with member railroads contributing money or equipment and receiving stock or tax reductions in return.

Consult (VI) Cochran and Miller, 1961.
—Ari Hoogenboom, *Brooklyn College of The City University of New York*

RAILROADS. The first commercial railroad in the United States, the Baltimore and Ohio, was built to protect Baltimore's competitive position in the race for Western connections. Its 13 miles of track in 1830 was worked by an American steam locomotive, Peter Cooper's *Tom Thumb*. Experiments with horse and sail-traction on rails now ended, and the age of steam began. In South Carolina, the Charleston and Hamburg, with its 136 miles of track, was the longest line in the world when it was completed in 1833.

Early Growth. From the mid-1830s rail building became common all over the North and East, and the main cities were connected. Boston had three railroads and was linked to the Hudson River. Philadelphia had four lines by 1849 and by 1850 was linked to the South at Charleston, S.C. The 700-mile trip took about 60 hours—a triumph of progress. New York surpassed other states in mileage by 1850, and the New York Central system, with its interconnections, joined the Northeast and Middle Atlantic states. By 1850 it had a through connection to the Great Lakes, by 1853 to Chicago, and by 1854 to the Mississippi River. In 1860 the United States had 30,000 miles of track, and

several lines had reached the very edge of the Western frontier. From then on, lines sometimes went ahead of the pioneers.

The 1850s saw the growth of rail connections in the Midwest—Ohio, Indiana, and Illinois. Chicago was linked to New Orleans, and the Gulf of Mexico to the Great Lakes. Southern ports fought desperately to keep the Western trade, but the railroads and canals in the North, running east to west, cut the South off from this trade and linked the North and West. Before the Civil War, various cities on the frontier—Chicago, St. Louis, Memphis, New Orleans—vied to become the jumping-off place for the projected transcontinental railroad to the Pacific Ocean. The war ensured the defeat of the South in this area.

Transcontinental Lines. After the war, railroad building was even more enthusiastic, averaging about 4,000 miles a year until 1917. The Civil War destroyed much of the South's track network but stimulated growth in the North and West. More than 250,000 miles had been built by World War I—one-third of the world's total. The first transcontinental line was chartered by Congress in 1862: the Union Pacific was to build westward from Nebraska, and the Central Pacific was to build eastward from Sacramento, Cal. The two eventually met at Promontory Point, Utah, and were symbolically joined by a gold spike on May 10, 1869. Their combined 1,700 miles of track brought the Atlantic and Pacific oceans within a week of each other.

Congress also chartered several other companies. The Northern Pacific linked Puget Sound (Seattle) with the Great Lakes. The Atlantic and Pacific, which was to build westward from Springfield, Mo., was a failure and merged into the well-known Atchison, Topeka, and Santa Fe—a line extending across New Mexico and Arizona to California—which was finished in 1881. In the Southwest the Texas and Pacific were chartered to join Texas to southern California at San Diego.

These long lines were a great engineering feat, but they were financed in seamy fashion. The federal government gave land from the public domain to each company, a precedent set by Congress in 1850, when it gave alternate strips of land 6 miles wide, on each side of the track, in order to encourage the building of the Illinois Central line from Mobile, Ala., to Chicago. Before the Civil War, the federal government had donated 18 million acres to railroads, and the individual state governments had donated even more. After the war this figure was dwarfed: by 1884 the federal government had given out 155 million acres.

Corruption came with this system. The rival lines built hastily in order to get more land; bridges and tracks were weak, and accidents were frequent. The Union Pacific and

Eastern and western sections of the first transcontinental railroad meet at Promontory Point, Utah, in 1869.

Rail crew lays track across the western plains.

Central Pacific engaged in open warfare with each other. The wild scramble for franchises and land led to the construction of unnecessary lines accompanied by wild financial speculation. The construction company that built the Union Pacific, called the Crédit Mobilier, got the contract through Oakes Ames, a congressman who was a member of both the Union Pacific and the Crédit Mobilier company. Having other common directors also, Crédit Mobilier charged the railroad as it pleased for the construction job. The public and the government had to foot the bill, which amounted to $73 million for work worth about $50 million. Ames gave shares in the companies to influential politicians to smooth the path of approval and even lent them money to buy the stock. The Crocker Company, which built the Central Pacific, used the same tactics and charged at least twice the actual cost.

Railroad Competition. The most infamous railroad magnate was Jay Gould, who was a financier and gambler rather than a railroad builder. He made a fortune out of the Erie railroad before being forced out and then assumed temporary control of the Union Pacific in 1873. Later, in opposition to the same line, he tried to encircle it and bought up rival railroads. He built a large network in the Southwest and then allied himself with the Southern Pacific to try to ruin the Atchison, Topeka, and Santa Fe. Gould fought ruinous, undercutting rate wars. He paid out dividends that were unearned and created panics and rumors to get rid of rivals or to unload worthless stock on the market.

More creative was James J. Hill, who rescued the Northern Pacific from financial disaster in 1893 and began to build up the Great Northern system. By 1890 he controlled nearly 3,000 miles of track and was allied with Canadian railroad interests. Minnesota, North Dakota, and Montana were virtually Hill states; the entire economic life of the Northwest was tied up in his system. Hill established communities and built schools, churches, and homes. He encouraged farming, bred cattle, created banks, and built his own fleet of ships to trade directly with the Far East. The Great Northern was a good example of the "colonization" work of railroads—building ahead of settlement.

End of the Railway Age. World War I halted railroad building abruptly, and in the 1920s and 1930s more lines went out of use than were added. By then, America's railroads, like those of other nations, were in chronic insolvency—almost bankrupt. They had overbuilt; they had built too quickly and faster than population growth; and they had built shoddily but expensively.

The railroad market was saturated, just when new competition appeared—automobiles, buses, and trucks. Later came the airplane. All over the world, railroads could no longer return a profit on passenger traffic, and in many nations they were nationalized and run by the government as a public service. Freight trains, however, were still useful for transporting bulky goods and continued to be a good source of revenue.

See also Crédit Mobilier; Gould, Jay; Hill, James J.; Railroad Legislation; Railroad Unions.

Consult (V) Chandler, 1965; Stover, 1961.
—Peter d'A. Jones, *University of Illinois, Chicago Circle*

RAILROAD UNIONS. The first railroad union was the Brotherhood of the Footboard (later Brotherhood of Locomotive Engineers) organized in 1863 in Detroit to create a mutual life insurance association. In 1868 the Order of Railway Conductors was formed, and in 1873 the Brotherhood of Locomotive Firemen organized. Finally in 1883 the Brotherhood of Railroad Brakemen (later the Brotherhood of Railroad Trainmen) was established. These four groups became known as the Big Four.

After the militant strike activity of the 1850s, many railroad workers joined the Knights of Labor, with whom there were later conflicts. A railroad union for all railroad workers, whether skilled or unskilled, was organized in 1893. Called the American Railway Union (ARU), it was headed by Eugene Debs and soon had a membership of 150,000, more than the combined membership of the Big Four. However, the power of the fledgling ARU was soon dissipated by the disastrous Pullman Strike (1894). Black railroad workers, often limited to working in the sleeping cars, were organized by A. Philip Randolph in the Brotherhood of Sleeping Car Porters in the 1920s.

After providing insurance for their workers, the railway unions turned to working conditions and wages. In the 1890s they succeeded in having railway wages standardized. The 8-hour day was won in 1917, and in 1926 the Railway Labor Executive Association was formed. Made up of the unions in the AFL and the independent trainmen brotherhoods, this is a policy-making body that has functioned effectively in negotiating and striking to achieve benefits.

See also Debs, Eugene V.; Pullman Strike (1894).

RANDOLPH, A(SA) PHILIP (1889-), American labor leader who was a major force in the struggle for civil rights.

Randolph was born in Florida the son of a Methodist clergyman. He migrated to New York as a young man, doing odd jobs while attending the City College of New York. In 1917 Randolph, attracted to the socialism of Eugene

V. Debs, launched the *Messenger,* a radical journal in which he urged blacks to join labor unions, advocated solidarity between white and black workers, and concerned himself with the plight of blacks in ghettos.

In 1925 he organized the Brotherhood of Sleeping Car Porters (AFL) and became its president. During the 1930s, he was president of the National Negro Congress, a coalition of black labor groups. In 1957 he became the first black vice-president of the AFL-CIO.

In 1941, when industry refused to hire blacks for defense jobs, Randolph organized a mass march on Washington as a protest. To forestall the march, President Roosevelt issued a fair employment practices executive order. Randolph also led a movement in 1947 to press for the abolition of segregation in the armed forces.

During the 1963 March on Washington for Jobs and Freedom, for which 250,000 people converged, Randolph and other principal speakers endorsed the policy of nonviolent direct action in their fight for civil rights. In 1966 he was named honorary chairman of, and became an active participant in, the White House Conference on Civil Rights.

See also Blacks in the United States; Labor Movement.

RANDOLPH, EDMUND (1752-1813), a prominent Revolutionary War statesman, politician, and lawyer. Born into an important family, Randolph received all the benefits of being part of Virginia's ruling class: a secure place in society, an education at the College of William and Mary, and a position of political leadership. Although his father was a loyalist, Randolph was a firm patriot, serving for a while as George Washington's aide-de-camp. He participated in the framing of Virginia's first state constitution, was elected a delegate to the Second Continental Congress, and served as attorney general of Virginia.

He became governor in 1786 and was a member of the delegations to the Annapolis Convention in 1786 and the Constitutional Convention of 1787. It was Randolph who introduced the Virginia Plan, around which most of the debate of the Constitutional Convention took place. It was a revised version of the Virginia Plan that became the U.S. Constitution. However, Randolph refused to sign the document because he felt it was not republican enough in form; he preferred the calling of a second convention to draft another constitution. But when it became clear that this was not going to happen and that the choice was between adopting the Constitution or retaining the Articles of Confederation, he supported adoption in the Virginia ratifying convention.

Shortly thereafter President Washington appointed him the first U.S. attorney general under the new Constitution. He held this post

until he succeeded Thomas Jefferson as secretary of state in 1794. The next 18 months were a stormy period because he constantly fought with Alexander Hamilton over diplomatic affairs and was eventually forced to resign in a highly controversial and unpleasant episode when the Federalists claimed that he was in the employ of the French and had made a number of indiscreet disclosures to them. Immediately following his retirement, Randolph wrote an elaborate vindication of himself, returned to Richmond to practice law, and wrote a history of Virginia, which was not published until 1970.

See also Annapolis Convention (1786); Bill of Rights; Constitutional Convention (1787); Virginia Plan.

RANKIN, JEANNETTE (1880-1973), a pacifist and suffragist who became the first woman member of Congress when she served in the House of Representatives from 1917 to 1919. Born on a Montana ranch, she graduated from the University of Montana in 1902 and became active in women's suffrage campaigns in Washington, California, and her home state. She worked as a field secretary of the National American Woman Suffrage Association and as chairman of the Montana State Suffrage Committee.

In 1914, Montana women gained the vote, and two years later Miss Rankin was elected to Congress. There she introduced the Nineteenth Amendment in the House of Representatives and opposed U.S. entry into World War I. Her pacifism cost Rankin her reelection. She returned to Congress for a second term in 1941 and was the only member to vote against U.S. entry into World War II.

RAPP, GEORGE (1757-1847), religious leader who was the founder of New Harmony, Ind. *See* Utopian Communities.

RAYBURN, SAM(UEL) (TALIAFERRO) (1882-1961), Democratic congressman known for his understanding of the mood of the House of Representatives. He was born near Kingston, Tenn., and moved to north Texas when he was five. After working his way through college, he was elected to the Texas House of Representatives (1906) before his graduation from law school (1908). He was chosen Speaker of the Texas House in 1911 and successfully ran for the U.S. House in 1912. He served without interruption until his death.

During his first term he was named to the Interstate and Foreign Commerce Committee and from 1931 to 1937 was its chairman, responsible for shepherding through the House many of President Roosevelt's New Deal regulatory measures. In 1937 he was chosen House majority leader and in 1940 became Speaker of the House. He served as Speaker

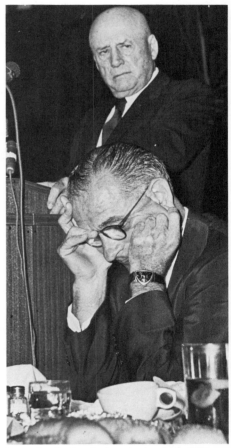

House Speaker Sam Rayburn lauds presidential hopeful Lyndon Johnson *(foreground)* during 1960 fundraising dinner.

until his death, except from 1947 to 1949 and 1953 to 1955, when he was minority leader.

A master of procedure, Rayburn exerted his power decisively in 1941, when he first pressed for passage of an extension of the Selective Service Act and then gaveled down opponents calling for its reconsideration. Although generally a supporter of Democratic presidents, he opposed federal price regulation of the natural gas industry and most civil rights bills.

Sam Rayburn served the longest term in history as Speaker of the House. He spoke rarely, but he wielded enormous power behind the scenes by utilizing his comprehensive knowledge of politics and of the members of the House.

REALISM, a term applied to a creative work that aims at an interpretation of the actualities of any aspect of life free from objective prejudice, idealism, or romantic color. No chronological point may be indicated as the beginning of realism, but the nineteenth century is considered to mark its origin as a literary movement, specifically with the works of Flaubert and Balzac.

Realism, in both art and literature, has been chiefly concerned with the commonplaces of everyday life and with life among the middle and lower classes. In American painting, realism is identified with John Singleton Copley, Winslow Homer, and Thomas Eakins. In drama, realism has been associated with the works of Ibsen and O'Neill. The writings of Mark Twain are frequently considered realistic in their observation of detail, whereas the descriptive poems of Walt Whitman are a primary source of modern realism.

RECONSTRUCTION (1864–1877), the era after the Civil War, in which the United States tried to deal with the problems of the reintegration of the Confederate states into the Union and the place of the freed blacks in the American society and economy.

Among the issues debated during Reconstruction were whether the Confederate states should be automatically readmitted or whether conditions should be imposed. Those who agreed that there should be conditions were divided as to whether the legislative or the executive branch should dictate them— and there were serious disagreements about what the conditions should be.

The extent of the federal government's involvement in the Reconstruction process and its commitment to the rights of the freed slaves was hotly debated. The Radical Republican governments installed in the South created great controversy, as did the violence directed against them.

The following chronology lists the major events during Reconstruction, and the Subject

Thomas Nast cartoon satirizing President Johnson's Reconstruction program.

Map that accompanies the Civil War: Causes article lists encyclopedia entries related to Reconstruction.

Chronology

1865 April 11. Lincoln deals with Reconstruction in his last public address.

1865 April 15. Lincoln dies from assassin's bullet and is succeeded by Johnson.

1865 May 29. Johnson sets forth Reconstruction policies.

1865 July 13. Johnson completes naming of provisional governors for Confederate states.

1865 November 22. Mississippi passes first part of its Black Code; most Confederate states follow suit by spring 1866.

1865 December 4. Congress refuses to seat senators and representatives elected from Confederate states.

1865 December 18. Thirteenth Amendment formally proclaimed in effect.

1866 April 9. Congress overrides Johnson's March veto of the Civil Rights Bill.

1866 May. Ku Klux Klan founded.

1866 June 13. Congress approves the Fourteenth Amendment.

1866 June 22. Johnson issues message objecting to the Fourteenth Amendment.

1866 June 25. Pro-Johnson forces call for a bipartisan National Union Convention to endorse his Reconstruction policies.

1866 July 16. Congress overrides Johnson's February veto of Freedmen's Bureau Bill.

1866 July 30. Race riot in New Orleans leaves 37 blacks dead, 119 wounded; 3 white radicals killed, 17 wounded.

1866 August 14. Pro-Johnson National Union Convention meets in Philadelphia.

1866 November 6. Anti-Johnson Republicans sweep congressional elections.

1867 January 8. Congress overrides Johnson's veto of bill enfranchising blacks in Washington, D.C.

1867 January 14. Supreme Court rules (*Cummings v. Missouri; Ex Parte Garland*) that state and federal governments cannot keep people from practicing their professions on grounds of disloyalty.

1867 March 2. Johnson vetoes First Reconstruction Act; Congress overrides veto and passes Tenure of Office Act and Command of the Army Act.

1867 March 23. Second Reconstruction Act passed.

1867 May 16. In *Georgia v. Stanton* the Supreme Court dismisses Georgia's appeal to have the Reconstruction Acts enjoined.

1867 July 19. Third Reconstruction Act passed.

1867 November–December. Alabama, Louisiana, Virginia, and Georgia constitutional conventions meet.

1868 January. Mississippi, North and South Carolina, and Florida constitutional conventions meet.

1868 February. Alabama ratifies new state constitution.

1868 February 21. Johnson tests Tenure of Office Act by removing Secretary of War Stanton.

1868 February 24. House passes Covode Resolution, impeaching Johnson.

1868 March 11. Fourth Reconstruction Act passed.

1868 March 13. Arkansas ratifies new state constitution.

1868 March 30. Senate trial of Johnson begins.

1868 April. South Carolina, Louisiana, Georgia, and North Carolina ratify new state constitutions.

1868 May. Florida ratifies new state constitution.

1868 May 26. President Johnson acquitted.

1868 June. Mississippi ratifies new state constitution.

1868 June 24. Arkansas delegation seated in Congress.

1868 June 25. Congress passes the Omnibus Act, paving the way for the readmission of Florida, North Carolina, South Carolina, Louisiana, and Georgia.

1868 July 28. Official ratification of the Fourteenth Amendment is announced.

1868 November 3. Republican U. S. Grant elected president.

1869 February 26. Congress passes the Fifteenth Amendment.

1869 April 12. Supreme Court rules (*Texas v. White*) that Congress has the power to reconstruct states that had seceded.

1870 January 26. Congress readmits Virginia.

1870 February 17. Congress readmits Mississippi.

1870 March 30. Congress readmits Texas; official ratification of the Fifteenth Amendment is announced.

1870 May 31. First Enforcement Act passed.

1870 July 15. Congress readmits Georgia.

1871 February 28. Second Enforcement Act passed.

1871 April 20. Third Enforcement Act (Ku Klux Klan Act) passed.

1872 May 22. General Amnesty Act passed.

1872 November 5. Grant reelected president.

1875 March 1. Civil Rights Act bans racial discrimination in public places.

1877 March 4. Hayes sworn in as president after Electoral Commission awards him states contested.

1877 April. Hayes removes federal troops from South Carolina and Louisiana.

Consult (IV) Stampp, 1965; Stampp and Litwack, 1969.

—Michael Burlingame, *Connecticut College*

RECONSTRUCTION ACTS (1867-1868). On March 2, 1867, Congress passed the Reconstruction Act over President Johnson's veto. In the next 12 months, three supplementary acts were adopted to clarify the intent of the original legislation and to plug loopholes in the law.

The first act provided that the ex-Confederate states be ruled temporarily by martial law. Five military districts were created, each under the control of a federal commander. Elections were to be held for a constitutional convention; blacks were eligible to vote, while all whites disqualified from office holding under Section 3 of the proposed Fourteenth Amendment were ineligible. Black suffrage and disqualification of Confederate leaders had to be incorporated into the new state constitutions, which then had to be ratified by a majority of the voters. The new state legislatures then had to ratify the Fourteenth Amendment, after which a state could resume its place in Congress.

The white South tried to thwart the law by refusing to call constitutional conventions. Congress responded on March 23, 1867, by requiring the military commanders in the South to initiate the proceedings. On July 19, 1867, Congress passed the third Reconstruction Act, a complicated statute that elaborated on the intent of the previous measures. Among other things, it provided that obstructionist state officials were to be removed, and voter registration boards were empowered to deny the franchise to those suspected of taking the loyalty oath in bad faith.

The failure of Southern white conservatives to vote in the elections for the ratification of the new constitutions necessitated the fourth and final Reconstruction Act. Because earlier legislation had specified that a majority of registered voters was needed for ratification, this tactic successfully prevented the adoption of the new constitutions. On March 11, 1868, Congress amended the law to allow ratification by a simple majority of the votes cast.

See also Amendments, Constitutional; Civil Rights Acts (1866-1875); Reconstruction.

Consult (IV) Brock, 1963; Donald, 1965.

—Michael Burlingame, *Connecticut College*

RED BADGE OF COURAGE, THE (1895), novel about the Civil War. *See* Crane, Stephen.

REFUGEE RELIEF ACT (1953), emergency immigration bill authorizing entry of European refugees into the United States in addition to previously fixed immigration quotas. The bill, supported by President Eisenhower at a high point in the Cold War, was a significant change in U.S. foreign policy. It was designed to relieve criticism from European neutralists who felt that the United States, by not admitting refugees from Eastern Europe, was acting as badly as countries on the other side of the Cold War. A major opponent to the bill was Senator McCarran, who had been initially responsible

SOUTH RETURNS

Reconstruction governments established under Lincoln

Arkansas	Tennessee
Louisiana	Virginia

Reconstruction governments established after Lincoln

Alabama	Mississippi
Florida	North Carolina
Georgia	South Carolina
	Texas

Alabama b.-1868 c.-1874	**North Carolina** b.-1868 c.-1870
Arkansas a.-1864 b.-1868 c.-1874	**South Carolina** b.-1868 c.-1876
Florida b.-1868 c.-1877	**Tennessee** a.-1865 b.-1866 c.-1869
Georgia b.-1870 c.-1872	**Texas** b.-1870 c.-1873
Louisiana a.-1864 b.-1868 c.-1877	**Virginia** a.-1861 b.-1870 c.-1869
Mississippi b.-1870 c.-1876	

a.-Dates of establishment of Reconstruction Governments

b.-Dates of readmission to the Union

c.-Dates of establishment of Conservative Governments

Republican elephant first appeared in 1874. Thomas Nast cartoon depicting the party blundering on the edge of chaos after Democrats charged that President Grant wanted a third term in office.

REPUBLICAN PARTY — Item Guide

The article on the REPUBLICAN PARTY covers the highlights of the political party that emerged as a coalition of antislavery forces—members of the WHIG PARTY, FREE-SOIL PARTY, DEMOCRATIC PARTY, KNOW-NOTHING PARTY, BARNBURNERS, and supporters of ABOLITIONISM.

JOHN C. FRÉMONT was the first Republican presidential candidate, and ABRAHAM LINCOLN won the election of 1860. Party divisions led to the confrontation between ANDREW JOHNSON and RADICAL REPUBLICANS. Scandals that began in ULYSSES S. GRANT's administration and internal strife between STALWARTS AND HALFBREEDS weakened the party, although it remained strong enough to secure the presidency for RUTHERFORD B. HAYES in the disputed election of 1876.

The rise to the presidency of THEODORE ROOSEVELT, after WILLIAM McKINLEY's death, rejuvenated the party. Roosevelt's bolt to the PROGRESSIVE PARTY in 1912, however, allowed the Democrats to enter the White House. After World War I the Republicans controlled the presidency—under WARREN G. HARDING, CALVIN COOLIDGE, and HERBERT HOOVER—until 1933.

Since the Depression the Republicans have been a minority party but enjoyed presidential successes with DWIGHT D. EISENHOWER and RICHARD M. NIXON.

The article on PRESIDENTIAL ELECTIONS details the Republicans in national elections, while POLITICAL PARTIES IN THE UNITED STATES traces the development of the modern party.

for the restrictive McCarran-Walter Immigration Act (1952).

See also Displaced Persons; McCarran-Walter Immigration Act (1952).

REGULATION OF LOBBYING ACT (1946), legislation to control lobbying abuses. *See* Lobby.

RELIGION, COLONIAL. *See* Colonial Religion.

RELOCATION, method used to defuse "threat" of U.S. Japanese to World War II effort. *See* Japanese-Americans, Wartime Treatment of.

REMINGTON, FREDERICK (1861-1909), painter and sculptor, particularly of the American West. *See* Painting; Sculpture.

RENSSELAERSWYCK, patroonship in New York. *See* Patroonships.

REPORT ON MANUFACTURES (1791), a report submitted to Congress in December 1791 by Secretary of the Treasury Alexander Hamilton. In it he outlined the advantages of promoting industry, the development of which he considered to be so vital to the United States that it should be given special governmental aid, including protective tariffs and special bounties for new industries. In the early 1790s these ideas were extremely controversial because agrarian interests were opposed to protective tariffs and saw industry as harmful to agriculture. The opposition prevented the main outlines of Hamilton's plan from being adopted.

REPUBLICANISM, form of government in which laws are made and executed by officials elected by and representative of those obeying the laws. In American history, it refers to the political movement that developed in the 1790s in opposition to the Federalists, who controlled the first national government. A major charge the republicans brought against the Federalists was that they did not represent the generality of the people. This charge was also made in the struggle over ratification of the Constitution, and to some extent, republicanism as a political movement was a continuation of that struggle. A Democratic-Republican political party, formed in 1796, supported Thomas Jefferson for president. John Adams won, but he was defeated by Jefferson in 1800.

The Jeffersonian Republicans opposed the national program developed by Alexander Hamilton, Secretary of the Treasury under George Washington. The party advocated decentralization of government, expansion of the electorate, and national protection of civil rights. It created a national party composed of state parties and it united behind a single presidential candidate. Its organization served as a model for later parties, and its national

campaign created a greater sense of public unity and participation in government. The party's victory at the polls in 1800, combined with the acceptance of the election results by the Federalists, helped to legitimize the American democratic process.

See also Anti-Federalism; Democratic-Republicans (Jeffersonian); Federalism; Jefferson, Thomas.

Consult (III) Bassett, 1968; Bowers, 1972.

REPUBLICAN PARTY, major national party that developed as the antislavery debate grew bitter before the Civil War.

In 1854 every Northern Whig in both houses of Congress voted against the Kansas-Nebraska bill; every Southern Whig voted for it. The fissure never healed, and 30 members of Congress—Whigs, Democrats, and others—led by Representative Israel Washburn, Jr., of Maine, announced that a new party was needed and declared themselves Republicans. The new party included Free-Soilers, Independent Democrats, Conscience Whigs, Know-Nothings, Barnburners, and abolitionists.

The party's presidential candidate in 1856 was John C. Frémont, who had been elected to the Senate in 1850 as a Democrat, and half the delegates that nominated Lincoln in 1860 were former Democrats. Lincoln ran on a platform that opposed the extension of slavery and favored Western railroads, homesteads, protective tariffs, and internal improvements. Despite gaining an electoral college victory, the Republicans won slightly less than 40 percent of the popular vote.

Republican Dominance. Only Reconstruction gave the Grand Old Party a majority. The Radical Republicans and President Johnson engaged in a bitter feud for control of the party and country. As a result of the Radicals' victory, the GOP became identified as a congressional party. The South was treated as a conquered province, which produced short-term benefits for the Republicans in controlling Congress and the White House but also a long-term disability for the party in the South.

The occupation of the South came to an end after the disputed election of 1876, in which Rutherford B. Hayes was accepted as president by the Democrats in return for troop withdrawal and federal public works funds for the South. Although the Republicans remained the majority party, there was a series of close contests from 1876 to 1896. Within the Republican fold, there were battles between the Stalwart faction (Roscoe Conkling and Ulysses S. Grant) and their Half-Breed rivals (Hayes and James G. Blaine). Insurgents who could not find a home in either faction bolted in 1872, 1884, and 1896. Many of the dissidents had allied with the Republicans in the crusade against slavery and in the effort to win the war.

They were inclined to vote for and against candidates rather than parties and were disgusted with inefficiency and corruption in government.

Twentieth Century. The elections following 1896 focused on class issues (monetary system, labor unrest, and trusts) rather than on sectional politics. The reform movement found its champion in Theodore Roosevelt, the first strong Republican president since Lincoln. The 1912 clash between the Roosevelt progressive wing and the Taft standpat wing gave the Democrats a chance to govern, and for the first time since the Civil War the Republicans lost both houses of Congress.

After Woodrow Wilson's two terms, the nation returned to the normalcy of conservative Republican ascendancy. The GOP became the minority party with the onset of the Depression, and since 1930 the Republicans have controlled Congress for only four years (1947–1949, 1953–1955).

The Republicans have been less inclined than the Democrats to apply governmental powers to economic problems. The party's long-term hope of once more becoming the majority party depends on a Southern-Western-Midwestern alliance. In 1952 Eisenhower scored what was essentially a personal victory. For six of his eight years of modern Republicanism, he had to work with a Democratic Congress. The GOP bounced back from the disastrous showing of Barry Goldwater in 1964, and in 1968 Richard Nixon achieved an amazing comeback, capitalizing on Democratic failure to end or win the Vietnam War, domestic unrest, and inflation. Yet, he also had a Democratic Congress, even after his landslide reelection in 1972. In more than a century of existence (1856–1972), the Republicans could claim victory in 18 out of 30 presidential races, including the election of five of their candidates to second terms.

Consult (VIII) Jones, 1965; Benkley, 1962.
—Martin Gruberg, *University of Wisconsin, Oshkosh*

RESETTLEMENT ADMINISTRATION (RA), New Deal agency established by President Roosevelt in 1935 to take over the rural rehabilitation and subsistence homestead programs started earlier by the Federal Emergency Relief Act (FERA), the Interior Department, and the states. RA systematically purchased submarginal acreage to take it out of production—and establish homestead communities on good land for tenants and sharecroppers. RA took over a dozen existing homesteads and added another 20, thus settling about 4,000 farm families on new lands. All RA's functions were continued and significantly expanded after 1937 under the provisions of the Bankhead-Jones Farm Tenant Act.

See also Bankhead-Jones Farm Tenant Act (1937).

Consult (VI) Conkin, 1959.

REUTHER, WALTER (PHILIP) (1907–1970), American automobile union official noted for his innovative practices. He was born in Wheeling, W. Va., the son of a union supporter. In 1926 he went to Detroit, soon joining Ford Motor Company.

In 1933 he was fired for union organizing and left on a tour of European automobile factories, returning to Detroit in 1935. He became active in the newly founded United Automobile Workers (UAW) and helped gain union recognition at the major companies. Reuther received national attention before Pearl Harbor with a plan for converting the automobile plants to wartime airplane production.

After the war Reuther led the precedent-setting General Motors strike of 1945–1946, which sought "wage increases without price increases." In 1946 he was elected president of the UAW and began purging the union of communists. Subsequent negotiations and strikes brought the auto workers higher wages tied to cost-of-living increases, pensions, and valuable fringe benefits. He became president of the CIO in 1952 and urged its merger with the AFL (1955). His dissatisfaction with the AFL-CIO's commitment to social reform caused him to lead the UAW out of the federation in 1968 and into an affiliation with the Teamsters Union in 1969. He died in an airplane crash near Pellston, Mich. Reuther's advocacy of racial and social justice brought him respect and influence far beyond the huge and powerful union that he had been instrumental in creating.

Consult (VIII) Gould, 1971.

United Auto Workers President Walter Reuther urged merger of CIO and AFL.

REVENUE ACT (1935), developed from a far-reaching progressive tax plan that originated in the Treasury Department in 1934, was temporarily abandoned, and then resuscitated by President Roosevelt in response to Huey Long's "Share Our Wealth" income redistribution plan. Enacted after stormy hearings and rancorous public debate, the act contained provisions for estate taxes, a surtax on the highest personal incomes, and a graduated corporate income tax. It had started out as an administration tax program with a social purpose—taxes on the wealthy through inheritance and gift taxes, taxes on high personal and corporation incomes, and reduction of depletion allowances to finance New Deal reforms—and ended up a congressional revenue bill aimed at balancing the budget. Roosevelt's support for the bill was a modest step in the direction of a

REVOLUTIONARY WAR ERA

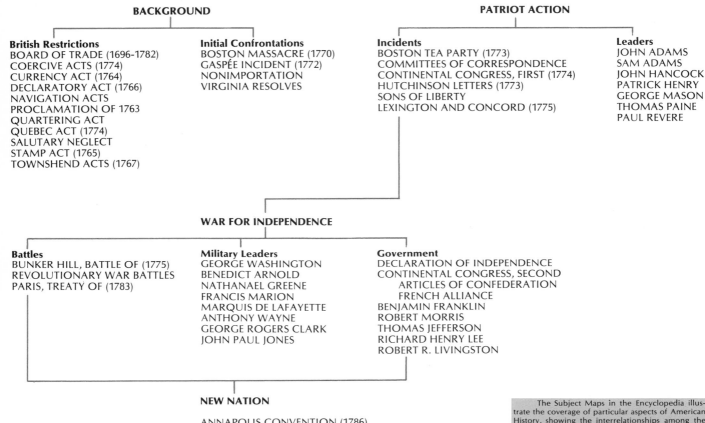

BACKGROUND

PATRIOT ACTION

British Restrictions
BOARD OF TRADE (1696-1782)
COERCIVE ACTS (1774)
CURRENCY ACT (1764)
DECLARATORY ACT (1766)
NAVIGATION ACTS
PROCLAMATION OF 1763
QUARTERING ACT
QUEBEC ACT (1774)
SALUTARY NEGLECT
STAMP ACT (1765)
TOWNSHEND ACTS (1767)

Initial Confrontations
BOSTON MASSACRE (1770)
GASPÉE INCIDENT (1772)
NONIMPORTATION
VIRGINIA RESOLVES

Incidents
BOSTON TEA PARTY (1773)
COMMITTEES OF CORRESPONDENCE
CONTINENTAL CONGRESS, FIRST (1774)
HUTCHINSON LETTERS (1773)
SONS OF LIBERTY
LEXINGTON AND CONCORD (1775)

Leaders
JOHN ADAMS
SAM ADAMS
JOHN HANCOCK
PATRICK HENRY
GEORGE MASON
THOMAS PAINE
PAUL REVERE

WAR FOR INDEPENDENCE

Battles
BUNKER HILL, BATTLE OF (1775)
REVOLUTIONARY WAR BATTLES
PARIS, TREATY OF (1783)

Military Leaders
GEORGE WASHINGTON
BENEDICT ARNOLD
NATHANAEL GREENE
FRANCIS MARION
MARQUIS DE LAFAYETTE
ANTHONY WAYNE
GEORGE ROGERS CLARK
JOHN PAUL JONES

Government
DECLARATION OF INDEPENDENCE
CONTINENTAL CONGRESS, SECOND
    ARTICLES OF CONFEDERATION
    FRENCH ALLIANCE
BENJAMIN FRANKLIN
ROBERT MORRIS
THOMAS JEFFERSON
RICHARD HENRY LEE
ROBERT R. LIVINGSTON

NEW NATION

ANNAPOLIS CONVENTION (1786)
CONSTITUTIONAL CONVENTION (1787)
ALEXANDER HAMILTON
JAMES MADISON
GOUVERNEUR MORRIS
OLIVER ELLSWORTH
NEW JERSEY PLAN
VIRGINIA PLAN
CONNECTICUT COMPROMISE
CONSTITUTION OF THE UNITED STATES
(see Subject Map)

The Subject Maps in the Encyclopedia illustrate the coverage of particular aspects of American History, showing the interrelationships among the articles in twelve critical areas of study. Entries in capital letters, except for titles, are subjects for which there are separate articles in the Encyclopedia.

The Subject Maps are arranged alphabetically in the Encyclopedia under the following titles:

American Wars
Blacks in the United States
Business Regulation and Industrialization
Civil War and Reconstruction
Constitution of the United States
Exploration and Colonization
Frontier in American History
Indians
Labor Movement
New Deal and Depression
Revolutionary War Era
Slavery and Emancipation

welfare state and toward Keynesian economics.

See also Keynes, John Maynard; Long, Huey.

REVENUE CUTTER SERVICE, early name for the Coast Guard. See Coast Guard, U.S.

REVERE, PAUL (1735-1818), Revolutionary War patriot and silversmith. The son of a Huguenot immigrant, he became a silversmith and used his talents to produce an engraving of the Boston Massacre that depicted the British as murderers of innocent colonials. Revere helped plan the Boston Tea Party and was the official courier of the Massachusetts Provincial Congress to the Second Continental Congress.

On April 18, 1775, Revere made his famous night ride to warn the people of Lexington and Concord of the British advance. The British temporarily detained Revere as he left Lexington, but Dr. Samuel Prescott carried the message to Concord. Revere designed the first official seal for the colonies, printed the first Continental currency, and manufactured gunpowder for the rebels. After the war, Revere's foundry helped outfit *Old Ironsides* and provided the copper boilers for Robert Fulton's experimental steamboat. In 1861 poet Henry Wadsworth Longfellow immortalized his famous ride to Lexington in "Paul Revere's Ride."

REVOLUTIONARY WAR BATTLES. Preliminary engagements fought at Lexington and Concord and at Bunker Hill in spring 1775 were followed by war in the summer. Although Gen. George Washington, whom the Continental Congress appointed commander in chief on June 15, 1775, personally commanded the patriot forces that surrounded Boston after Bunker Hill, the focus of action in summer 1775 was Canada. Late in June, Congress ordered Gen. Philip Schuyler to interdict Canadian Governor Carleton's planned invasion of New York. On August 28, Schuyler left Fort Ticonderoga on Lake Champlain, which Ethan Allen and Benedict Arnold had captured on May 10. Brig. Gen. Richard Montgomery replaced the ill Schuyler on September 13, accepted the surrender of the garrison at St. Johns, Canada, on November 2, and entered Montreal on November 13. Montgomery arrived at Quebec on December 3 and combined forces with Benedict Arnold, who had arrived from Massachusetts. In a disastrous joint attack on December 31, Montgomery was killed and Arnold wounded. The Americans withdrew south early in 1776.

Opening Campaigns. Meanwhile, Americans achieved a decisive advantage in Boston. On the night of March 4-5, 1776, Gen. John Thomas placed artillery on top of Dorchester Heights and thereby gained control of the harbor. Gen. William Howe, who had replaced Thomas Gage as the British commander, wisely evacuated the city by sea on March 17 and made New York his new base. Beginning on August 22, Howe moved 20,000 troops to Long Island, where on August 27 they inflicted 1,500 casualties on 5,000 men Washington had moved there from Boston. On the night of August 29-30, Washington withdrew to Manhattan, and on September 15, Howe followed. The retreating Americans repulsed the British at Harlem Heights on September 16 and at White Plains on October 28. Washington then joined forces with Gen. Nathanael Greene at Hackensack, fled across New Jersey, and entered Pennsylvania on December 11.

The American situation was grave, but Washington restored morale with daring attacks on British encampments in western New Jersey. On Christmas night, Washington crossed the Delaware River, captured a garrison of Hessians at Trenton the next morning, and attacked Princeton on January 3. The British then withdrew to eastern New Jersey, and the Americans went to winter quarters at Morristown.

1777. British plans for 1777 focused on a three-pronged campaign to isolate New England. Gen. John Burgoyne was to push south down Lake Champlain; Col. Barry St. Leger was to move east from Oswego; Gen. William Howe was to proceed north from New York City. Howe became involved in operations against Philadelphia and never completed his part of the mission. Gen. Nicholas Herkimer halted St. Leger at the Battle of Oriskany on August 6, and the British withdrew to Oswego on August 22.

Burgoyne forced the Americans to evacuate Fort Ticonderoga on July 5, but thereafter General Schuyler's forces slowed his advance. Gen. John Stark defeated a detachment from Burgoyne's force on August 16 at Bennington, Vt., and Gen. Horatio Gates, who replaced Schuyler, repulsed Burgoyne's advance at Freeman's Farm on September 19 and at Bemis Heights on October 7. Burgoyne retreated to Saratoga and surrendered on October 17.

General Howe decided to attack the rebel capital at Philadelphia but did not complete the operation in time to help Burgoyne. After Howe defeated Washington at Brandywine Creek on September 11 and Gen. Anthony Wayne at Paoli on September 21, he moved into Philadelphia unopposed on September 26. Washington unsuccessfully attacked Howe's encampment at Germantown on October 3 and then went into winter quarters at Valley Forge, Pa.

1778-1779. The British surrender at Saratoga convinced the French to offer the rebels military support. Count d'Estaing's fleet sailed for New York, and Gen. Henry Clinton, who replaced Howe, withdrew from Philadelphia to meet the challenge. On June 28, 1778, Gen.

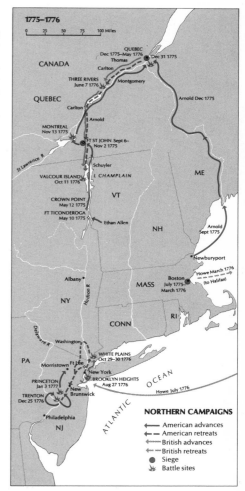

NORTHERN CAMPAIGNS

← American advances
←- - American retreats
← British advances
←-- British retreats
● Siege
※ Battle sites

Battle of Bunker Hill as seen from Boston Harbor.

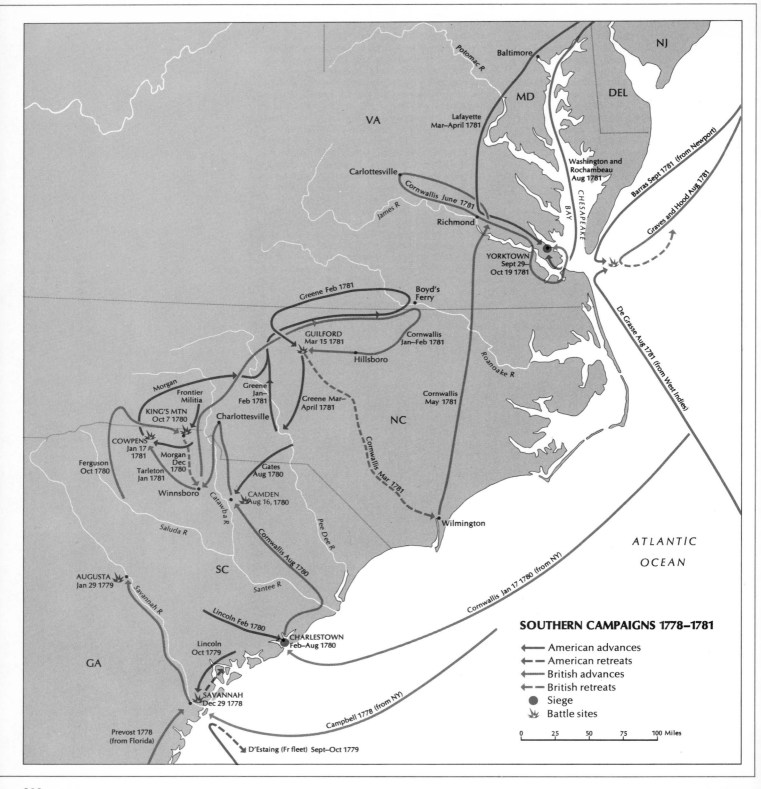

SOUTHERN CAMPAIGNS 1778–1781

⟵ American advances
⟵ - - American retreats
⟵ British advances
⟵ - - British retreats
● Siege
🔥 Battle sites

0 25 50 75 100 Miles

NJ

MD
Baltimore
Potomac R

DEL

Barras Sept 1781 (from Newport)

VA
Lafayette
Mar–April 1781

Carlottesville

Washington and
Rochambeau
Aug 1781

Graves and Hood Aug 1781

James R

Cornwallis June 1781

Richmond

CHESAPEAKE
BAY

YORKTOWN
Sept 29–
Oct 19 1781

De Grasse Aug 1781 (from West Indies)

Greene Feb 1781

Boyd's
Ferry

GUILFORD
Mar 15 1781

Cornwallis
Jan–Feb 1781

Hillsboro

Roanoake R

Morgan

Frontier
Militia

Greene
Jan–
Feb 1781

Greene Mar–
April 1781

Cornwallis
May 1781

KING'S MTN
Oct 7 1780

Charlottesville

NC

COWPENS
Jan 17
1781

Morgan
Dec
1780

Cornwallis Mar 1781

Ferguson
Oct 1780

Tarleton
Jan 1781

Gates
Aug 1780

Winnsboro

Catawba R

CAMDEN
Aug 16, 1780

Wilmington

Saluda R

SC

Pee Dee R

Santee R

Cornwallis Aug 1780

**ATLANTIC
OCEAN**

AUGUSTA
Jan 29 1779

Savannah R

Lincoln Feb 1780

Cornwallis Jan 17 1780 (from NY)

Lincoln
Oct 1779

CHARLESTOWN
Feb–Aug 1780

GA

SAVANNAH
Dec 29 1778

Campbell 1778 (from NY)

Prevost 1778
(from Florida)

D'Estaing (Fr fleet) Sept–Oct 1779

Charles Lee ineptly led an attack against the British column at Monmouth Courthouse, N.J., but Washington saved the day. Clinton reached New York, and Washington waited for d'Estaing at White Plains. However, the French admiral found the New York harbor unsuitable for a sea-land assault and soon sailed back to the West Indies.

At the end of 1778, Clinton shifted his attention to the South. On December 29, Lt. Col. Campbell defeated the rebel militia near Savannah and occupied it. Campbell seized Augusta on January 29, 1779, and repulsed American attempts to recapture the city. Count d'Estaing later joined Gen. Benjamin Lincoln in besieging Savannah, but a coordinated assault on the city on October 9 failed, and d'Estaing withdrew.

1780. British forces again took the offensive in the South in 1780. Clinton arrived off Carolina on February 1 and forced General Lincoln to surrender Charleston on May 12. Clinton returned to New York, leaving General Cornwallis in command. Andrew Pickens, Francis Marion, and Thomas Sumter, leading guerrilla forces, harassed the British, and Congress on June 13 dispatched Gen. Horatio Gates to lead an army against Cornwallis. Gates attacked Cornwallis' supply base at Camden, S.C., on August 16, but Cornwallis badly defeated him and began an invasion of North Carolina. Frontiersmen under Col. Isaac Shelby and Col. William Campbell defeated a loyalist force at King's Mountain on October 7, and the British retreated to South Carolina.

Last Campaigns: 1781. Gen. Nathanael Greene took over Gates' command in December 1780. He dispatched Gen. Daniel Morgan, who gained a smashing victory over Col. Banastre Tarleton's dragoons on Jan. 17, 1781, at Cowpens, S.C. Cornwallis then chased the Americans into North Carolina, where Morgan joined with Greene at Guilford Courthouse. The rebels retreated into Virginia but returned to Guilford Courthouse to inflict heavy losses on the British on March 15.

Cornwallis, convinced that he had to destroy the rebels' supply and training bases in Virginia, left North Carolina on April 25 and joined the traitor Benedict Arnold's force in Virginia. Cornwallis raided deep into Virginia, but on August 1 he withdrew to the coastal town of Yorktown to maintain communication with Clinton in New York.

The Continental forces had been strengthened in July 1780 by the arrival of the Comte de Rochambeau with a French army at Newport, R.I. In May 1781 Washington and Rochambeau laid plans for an attack on New York to be supported by Admiral de Grasse's fleet from the West Indies, but when de Grasse announced that he would operate in the Chesapeake Bay area from mid-August until

mid-October, they decided to move against Cornwallis in Virginia.

By September 10, de Grasse had cleared the British fleet under Adm. Thomas Graves from the Yorktown area. Washington and Rochambeau arrived between September 14 and 24 and joined forces with the Marquis de Lafayette, General Wayne, and Baron von Steuben. On October 9 the allied artillery began firing on Cornwallis' fortifications, and on October 17 the British general opened negotiations. The British surrender on October 19 ended the last major battle of the war. Sir Guy Carleton replaced General Clinton and withdrew the British troops from their remaining strongholds (such as Charleston), to New York, where they awaited the end of the war (1783). Peace negotiations began in Paris in April 1782, and articles of peace were signed in November. The War officially ended early in 1783.

Consult (II) Alden, 1954.

—Thomas Archdeacon, *University of Wisconsin*

RHODE ISLAND, the smallest colony and state, first settled by religious radicals who left Massachusetts Bay Colony. In the dead of winter in January 1636, Roger Williams went to live among the Narragansett Indians near what is now Providence. A dissident individualist, Williams opposed the close links between church and state in orthodox Puritan Massachusetts and the power wielded by the clergy, who were not separatist enough for his taste.

When other radicals joined him, Williams found himself at the head of a small township. Meanwhile, others had left Massachusetts. Anne Hutchinson settled on Narragansett Bay at Portsmouth in 1638; William Coddington, Williams' disciple, founded Newport in 1639; and a little earlier Samuel Gorton had created Warwick in 1634. The four settlements did not agree with one another, but they were forced into unity by defense needs and for fear of expansion by the newly created New England Confederation of 1643, which excluded them.

Williams was a powerful figure, and his friendliness with some Indians and trading with the Dutch upset the Massachusetts authorities almost as much as his unorthodoxy. So he went to England and negotiated a charter from Parliament in 1644. This united the four towns as "Providence Plantations." They continued to squabble over lands and frontiers, but the new charter of 1663 that Charles II gave them produced years of relative harmony. Quakers and Jews also came to Rhode Island, which enjoyed a large measure of local self-government, a broad franchise (heads of families), and total religious freedom. Newport was a noted Jewish center in the seventeenth century, and Touro Synagogue, built in 1763, is

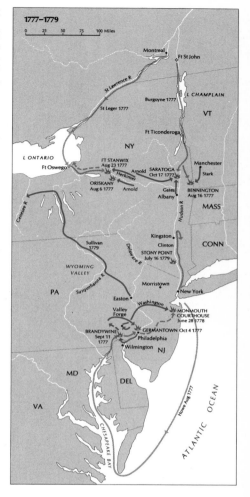

Epic sea battle between John Paul Jones' *Bonhomme Richard* and British ship *Serapis* in February 1779.

Matthew B. Ridgway succeeded Douglas MacArthur as commander of UN forces in Korea.

now a historic landmark. The town thrived on foreign trade until British occupation during the Revolution. After 1783 Samuel Slater brought textile manufacturing to the state from England.

Rhode Island, as a small state, was suspicious of the U.S. Constitution and protective of its own rights. It finally ratified the Constitution on May 29, 1790—when the United States had already been in existence for 15 months.

The legislature is bicameral; the capital is Providence. The population in 1970 was 949,723.

See also Hutchinson, Anne; New England Confederation; Slater, Samuel; Williams, Roger.

—Peter d'A. Jones, *University of Illinois, Chicago Circle*

RHODE ISLAND COLLEGE (BROWN UNIVERSITY). *See* Colonial Colleges.

RICHARDSON, HENRY HOBSON (1838-1886), American architect. *See* Architecture.

RIDGWAY, MATTHEW B(UNKER) (1895-), U.S. Army general. He was born in Fort Monroe, Va., graduated from West Point in 1917, and after serving in the infantry for a year, he returned to West Point as an instructor. Before World War II he served in China, Nicaragua, the Panama Canal Zone, the Philippines, and Brazil. From 1939 to 1942 he was a colonel in the War Plans Division of the War Department.

In March 1942 he was given command of the newly formed 82nd Airborne Division, with the rank of major general. During the invasion of Sicily, he led his troops in the first large-scale American airborne operation. They went on to jump at Salerno and at Normandy on D-Day. He subsequently directed major operations as head of the 18th Airborne Corps in Europe.

In 1950 he was named commander of the U.S. Eighth Army in Korea and succeeded Gen. MacArthur as commander in chief of the Far East after MacArthur had been relieved of command by President Truman in 1951. General Ridgway then succeeded Eisenhower as Supreme Allied Commander of NATO forces in 1952. He was appointed chief of staff of the Army in 1953 and retired in 1955.

See also Korean War.

Consult (VIII) Ridgway, 1956.

RIGHTS, BILL OF. *See* Bill of Rights.

RIGHT-TO-WORK LAWS, state laws that prohibit labor unions and employers from requiring a worker to belong to a union in order to get or keep a job. In effect, the provisions outlaw the closed shop and the union shop. The Taft-Hartley Act of 1947 outlawed the closed shop but permitted a union shop agreement with safeguards. The Taft-Hartley Act also specified that states could pass more stringent legislation regulating the union shop arrangements.

See also Labor Movement; Taft-Hartley Act (1947).

RIPLEY, GEORGE (1807-1880), moving spirit of the utopian community at Brook Farm. *See* Brook Farm.

RITTENHOUSE, DAVID (1732-1796), colonial clockmaker, mathematician, and astronomer born near Germantown, Pa. Using books and tools inherited from his uncle, Rittenhouse learned to make clocks and mathematical instruments, and by the age of 19 he had acquired a reputation for excellent workmanship and knowledge of astronomy. He constructed two precisely detailed orreries (working models of the solar system), and in 1769 he accurately calculated the movements of the planet Venus.

Rittenhouse moved to Philadelphia in 1770. There, his contributions to science paved the way for his participation in politics. After the war with Britain began, he was asked to serve as engineer of the Committee of Safety. He supervised the manufacture of major weapons and became president of the Safety Committee. In 1775 Rittenhouse was elected to the provincial legislature and helped to draw up the Pennsylvania state constitution. He was named state treasurer in 1777 and served as director of the U.S. Mint from 1792 until a year before his death.

ROBINSON, EDWIN ARLINGTON (1869-1935), American poet whose somber, introspective work bears the stamp of his Puritan New England ancestry. Robinson's psychological development was influenced by a neurotic family background. He always saw himself as a pathetically buffeted figure, and his philosophy derives from that state of mind. Robinson attended Harvard for two years and later settled in New York, where he spent most of his mature life, often living in near poverty. One of his best works was a verse novel, *Captain Craig* (1902). Prior to that time, he had written two volumes of poetry, *The Torrent and the Night Before* (privately printed, 1896) and *The Children of the Night* (1897).

To give Robinson an opportunity to develop as a poet, President Theodore Roosevelt aided him financially by appointing him to the New York Custom House (1905-1910).

Recognition of his creative talent was achieved with the publication of *The Man against the Sky* (1916). He was awarded three Pulitzer prizes—for his *Collected Poems* (1921), *The Man Who Died Twice* (1924), and

Tristram (1927), a verse novel that was based on the Arthurian legend and that became a best seller.

ROBINSON, JACKIE (JACK ROOSEVELT) (1919–1972),
black baseball player who broke the color barrier in organized baseball.

Born in Georgia and raised in Pasadena, Cal., Robinson first gained notice in sports as an All-American halfback for UCLA. After serving in the army during World War II, Robinson joined the Montreal Royals. In 1947 Branch Rickey purchased Robinson's contract for the Brooklyn Dodgers. Fiercely competitive, he won the National League's rookie of the year award in 1948, its most valuable player award in 1949, played on six National League pennant winners as well as one world championship team, and was named to the Baseball Hall of Fame in 1962. Robinson was active in politics, business, the civil rights movement, and the fund-raising activities of the NAACP and the Southern Christian Leadership Conference.

ROBINSON-PATMAN ACT (1936),
legislation to discourage competition in wholesale and retail trade. Very much in the spirit of the National Recovery Administration (NRA)—and designed to provide protections for business—Robinson-Patman attempted to outlaw "differential pricing." The wholesale grocers' association, where the bill originated, sought to prevent chain stores and others who could afford to buy in quantity from receiving rebates or special prices that would allow them to lower prices. Enforcement, which was to be the responsibility of the Federal Trade Commission, proved very difficult. The Miller-Tydings Enabling Act, passed the next year, had similar aims.

See also Miller-Tydings Enabling Act (1937).

ROCKEFELLER, JOHN D(AVISON) (1839–1937),
industrialist and philanthropist who became America's first billionaire. He had several clerical jobs before establishing his own produce company in 1859. In 1863, four years after the discovery of oil at Titusville, Pa., Rockefeller entered the oil business, and by 1870 his Standard Oil of Ohio was refining 14 percent of U.S. oil.

Standard soon outdistanced all competitors and made Cleveland the center of the refining industry. Rockefeller used the South Improvement Company to receive rebates from railroads and pioneered the techniques of cutthroat competition. He created a national distribution network to market Standard's products and by 1879 was refining more than 90 percent of America's oil. A vertically organized company, Standard produced its own barrels, bungs, freight cars, ships, pipeline, and so on. Rockefeller's first trust attempt failed

(1879), but in 1882 he merged 77 companies into a monolithic organization. Adverse decisions by Ohio's Supreme Court (1892–1899) forced the "mother of trusts" to move to New Jersey, where it remained until dissolved by the U.S. Supreme Court (1911).

Rockefeller retired from active business in the 1890s to devote himself to philanthropy, dispersing about $550 million before his death. The University of Chicago alone received more than $34 million, and four foundations were established to distribute monies for "the well being of mankind."

See also Antitrust Cases; Rockefeller Family; Trusts.

Consult (V) Nevins, 1953; Williamson and Daun, 1959.

—George Lankevich, *Bronx Community College of The City University of New York*

ROCKEFELLER FAMILY.
The Rockefeller dynasty began with John D. Rockefeller (1839–1937), industrialist, philanthropist, and founder of the Standard Oil Company. Over the years, Rockefeller amassed an immense fortune that he systematically and liberally used for a wide range of philanthropic causes. John D., Jr. (1874–1960) worked closely with his father in the family's business, philanthropic, and civic enterprises. Together, he and his father donated more than $1 billion to a great variety of educational, environmental, cultural, religious, and medical philanthropies. In 1901 they founded the Rockefeller Institute of Medical Research.

A deeply religious man and a fervent environmental protectionist, John D. Jr. devoted his life principally to social and civic responsibilities associated with the vast wealth that he inherited, and he imbued his children, John D. III, Nelson, Laurence, Winthrop, and David, with the same sense of responsibility. He personally contributed more than $50 million to the Rockefeller Brothers Fund, which his sons formed in 1940 to channel their philanthropies. After graduating from Princeton, John D. III (1906–) entered into many of the family's business activities and became chairman of the Rockefeller Foundation. He was also actively interested in Far Eastern affairs, was instrumental in the development of Asia House, and helped to create Lincoln Center in New York City.

Nelson Aldrich (1908–), an executive and politician, graduated from Dartmouth College in 1930 and joined the family organization. One of his most notable projects was the organization of Rockefeller Center, constructed during the Depression. In 1958 Nelson, a Republican, was elected governor of New York, an office to which he was reelected three times. He was also the founder of the Museum of Primitive Art in New York and

Known for his daring base running, baseball's Jackie Robinson endured racist slurs as first black to play in major leagues.

John D. Rockefeller amassed enormous fortune through his control of the oil industry.

New York Governor Nelson Rockefeller campaigned hard for presidential nominations but was considered too liberal by many Republicans.

Eleanor Roosevelt devoted much of her later life to humanitarian causes.

served as a trustee of the Museum of Modern Art.

Laurence Spelman (1910–   ), a noted environmentalist, was chairman of Rockefeller Brothers Fund. Winthrop (1912–1973) spent several years in the oil business before settling in Arkansas, where he developed Winrock Farms, noted for its prize herd of Santa Gertrudis breeding stock, and in 1966 was elected the state's first Republican governor since Reconstruction. David (1915–   ) was chairman of the Chase Manhattan Bank and the Rockefeller Institute. He also served as a trustee of the Museum of Modern Art.

John D. Rockefeller IV (1938–   ), the great-grandson of John D., distinguished himself in the Action for Appalachian Youth poverty program and was elected as a Democrat to the West Virginia House of Delegates in 1966. He was subsequently elected secretary of state but was defeated in his gubernatorial bid in 1972.

See also Trusts.

ROMAN CATHOLICS, a religious group that first entered the United States in Florida as part of the settlement of San Augustin (St. Augustine) in 1565. The Spanish Franciscans founded missions along the Georgia coastal islands and westward across the Florida peninsula, but they were destroyed by the English in 1702–1704 and were never successfully revived. After 1598, Franciscan and Jesuit missions were founded in New Mexico, Arizona, and Texas. Missionaries from Canada were active in the northeast corner of America, preaching to the Hurons and the Iroquois, in the seventeenth century.

Roman Catholics formed a small and frequently unpopular minority in the British colonies, and the only colony where Catholics were truly welcome was Maryland, founded as a refuge for Catholics in 1632. The colony became officially Protestant in 1688, but the Roman Catholic church remained strong. In 1784 John Carroll of Baltimore was named superior of the American missions. In 1790 he was made bishop of Baltimore, and sees were established at Boston, New York, Philadelphia, and Bardstown, Ky.

Later History. In the following century the membership of the church grew at a rate unparalleled in the history of any other nation. The peaks of growth, coinciding with the heavy waves of immigration from Catholic countries between 1840 and 1910, caused many problems. One particular problem was nativism, which included opposition to Catholic immigrants on the grounds of religion and which gave impetus to an anti-Catholic movement led by the Know-Nothing Party in the 1850s. Organized anti-Catholicism reappeared in the 1880s and again after World War I in the form of the Ku Klux Klan. The election of John

F. Kennedy as president in 1960 indicated that anti-Catholic feeling was no longer as significant as it had been.

See also Colonial Religion; Know-Nothing Party; Nativist Movements.

ROMANTICISM, a movement in early nineteenth-century America that sprang from and paralleled a similar movement in Europe. Romanticism as an imaginative movement replaced classicism as the artist's principal inspiration. Instead of regularity of form, dependence upon reason, and the ideals of harmony—which were characteristic of the classic movement—the romantics relied on a boundless sense of freedom and optimism and an emphasis on emotions rather than reason.

Romanticism triumphed politically in the American and French revolutions. The belief in personal freedom and the importance of the individual led to greater political democracy, an emphasis on environment rather than heredity as the main factor determining an individual's growth, and an optimistic exuberance that was a factor in the development of the New World. John Locke, the English philosopher, Jean Jacques Rousseau, the French writer and thinker, and Immanuel Kant, the German philosopher, were instrumental in establishing the intellectual foundations of the romantic sensibility. Samuel Taylor Coleridge, Eugène Delacroix, Goethe, and Sir Walter Scott were some of the important early European romantic artists who influenced American writers and artists.

U.S. Romantics. American Romanticism, although drawing upon European sources, was nourished by American ideals of democracy, political and economic independence, the frontier, the unsettled wilderness, and the American belief in equality. William Ellery Channing and Ralph Waldo Emerson spearheaded the theological and literary break with the past. The Hudson River painters emphasized the wilder vision of the American landscape, and the Gothic architects led the Romantic revival in American building styles. Ralph Waldo Emerson, Henry David Thoreau, Herman Melville, Nathaniel Hawthorne, and Walt Whitman were the most significant New York and New England Romantic writers. Transcendentalism was the most influential American intellectual manifestation of Romanticism.

See also Hudson River School; Literature; Painting; Transcendentalism; biographies of major figures.

—Richard Collin, *Louisiana State University, New Orleans*

ROOSEVELT, (ANNA) ELEANOR (1884–1962), social reformer and wife of Franklin Roosevelt. She married her distant cousin Franklin in 1905 and spent the next two decades raising a large family and assisting her husband in his developing political career. When FDR was struck down by polio in 1921, she encouraged his rehabilitation and his return to political life. Her political activities crested in 1928 with her vigorous role in her husband's gubernatorial campaign and in the presidential campaign of Alfred E. Smith.

Public Life. As first lady in Albany and Washington (1929-1945), she assumed a responsible role—writing, speaking, and serving as a liaison between her husband and the public. She was particularly committed to the special needs of young people and blacks in the Depression, and she took an active part in the planning and administration of several New Deal programs.

With the war she turned, with the President, to an interest in foreign affairs, where her concern with the survival of democracy was predominant. After Franklin's death she pursued an active public career on her own. She was appointed a member of the U.S. delegation to the United Nations by President Truman, she continued to be active in party politics, and she was a founder of Americans for Democratic Action—a group that sought to perpetuate the New Deal. She spoke out on housing, labor, civil liberties, and other domestic issues while she worked in the United Nations and with its relief affiliates.

See also Roosevelt, Franklin D.

Consult (VIII) Hareven, 1968; Lash, 1972.

—Allen Kifer, *Skidmore College*

ROOSEVELT, FRANKLIN D(ELANO) (1882-1945),

32nd President of the United States (1933-1945). He was born in Hyde Park, N.Y., on Jan. 30, 1882, the son of a railroad president and country squire. He married his distant cousin Eleanor—niece of Theodore Roosevelt (1905)—and took a job with a New York City law firm. He entered politics in 1910 and followed a path similar to his cousin Theodore— the New York legislature, the Navy Department, and the governorship of New York. In 1920 his success as assistant secretary led to his selection as the running mate of Democratic presidential candidate James M. Cox. Temporarily frustrated by polio in 1921, which left him unable to walk, he returned to the political arena as a protégé of, and successor to, Governor Alfred E. Smith.

Depression Decade. As Depression governor of New York (1929-1933), FDR instituted relief and reform measures that served as a rehearsal for parts of the New Deal. Edging Smith out of the presidential nomination in 1932, FDR went on to an easy electoral victory over Herbert Hoover. Roosevelt's New Deal was characterized by improvisation, opportunism, and eclecticism in social experimentation and political action. Increasingly hedged about by conservative resistance, he was nevertheless reelected to unprecedented third and fourth

terms and built a coalition of interest groups and ideologies that persisted through the domestic programs of Presidents Truman, Kennedy, and Johnson. Most of his early programs were aimed at the Depression emergency, but in time he embraced Keynesian economics, supported collective bargaining, and built the foundations of a modest welfare state. Like the presidents he most admired (Theodore Roosevelt and Woodrow Wilson), FDR believed in a strong and active executive branch and worked to extend its power.

World War II. In foreign affairs Roosevelt was at first an isolationist emphasizing hemispheric solidarity and discretionary neutrality until 1939, when he actively sought to aid the democracies against the Axis. In 1941 he strove to commit the country as an "arsenal of democracy" to supply war materiel to the British and met with Winston Churchill to discuss goals.

After the Japanese attacked Pearl Harbor in December, Roosevelt was an active commander in chief and diplomat. He expected the United Nations to assume much of the Allies' job in maintaining a power balance in the postwar world, but he did not live to attend its first meeting in San Francisco, dying in Warm Springs, Ga., on April 12, 1945.

See also New Deal; Roosevelt, Eleanor; World War II.

Consult (VII) Burns, 1956; Freidel, 1952-1956; Leuchtenburg, 1963; Schlesinger, 1959-1960.

—Allen Kifer, *Skidmore College*

ROOSEVELT, THEODORE (1858-1919),

26th President of the United States (1901-1909). He was born in New York City on Oct. 27, 1858, into a socially prominent family. After graduating from Harvard in 1880, he briefly attended law school and then wrote *The Winning of the West* and several biographies. He served as a New York State assemblyman, failed in a bid to become mayor of New York City (1886), in 1889 was appointed U.S. civil service commissioner, and in 1895 became president of the New York City Board of Police Commissioners.

President McKinley made him assistant navy secretary in 1897, but he resigned in 1898 to lead the Rough Riders during the Spanish-American War. Roosevelt parlayed his military record into election as governor of New York (1898) and was nominated by the Republicans as vice-president in 1900. Roosevelt became president in 1901, when McKinley was assassinated.

Presidency. As chief executive, Roosevelt popularized many progressive causes but achieved a spotty record as a reformer. He worked hard for conservation of natural resources, took labor's side in the anthracite coal strike of 1902, and established the Department of Commerce and Labor. Roosevelt's support

FDR on boating trip to Campobello Island, a favorite vacation retreat, in 1933.

Franklin Roosevelt, 32nd President of the United States (1933-1945), campaigns in 1940.

An avid sportsman, Roosevelt often vacationed in the West.

Theodore Roosevelt, 26th President of the United States (1901–1909), speaks in Brattleboro, Vt., in 1902.

also led to the passage of federal pure food and drug and meat inspection legislation. On the other hand, he failed to take a clear-cut stand on such vital issues as tariff reduction, child labor, the income tax, and railroad regulation. Despite his popular reputation as a trust-buster and some spectacular prosecutions, Roosevelt did not believe that bigness in itself was a danger. Internationally, Roosevelt pursued a vigorous foreign policy—intervening unilaterally and frequently in Latin American affairs, building the Panama Canal, and sending the Great White Fleet around the world. In 1905 he received the Nobel Peace Prize for his role in ending the Russo-Japanese War.

Later Life. Roosevelt stepped down in 1909 after picking William Howard Taft to succeed him, but Taft's difficulties with Republican progressives brought Roosevelt back to politics. He bested Taft in several primaries, but he was unable to win the Republican nomination. After this rebuff Roosevelt became a leader in the formation of the Progressive, or Bull Moose, Party and proclaimed his program of New Nationalism, an amalgamation of the ideas of businessmen and social reformers. He won almost 30 percent of the popular vote and 88 electoral votes, but his presence served mainly to elect Democrat Woodrow Wilson, who later espoused many Progressive programs.

In 1916 Roosevelt rejected another bid from the Progressive Party and campaigned for Republican Charles Evans Hughes. When the United States finally entered World War I, Roosevelt was bitterly disappointed at Wilson's refusal to give him a commission and severely criticized the President for his conduct of the war. He died on Jan. 6, 1919, in Oyster Bay, N.Y.

See also Antitrust Cases; Presidential Elections; Progressive Party; Spanish-American War (1898); Taft, William Howard.

Consult (V) Blum, 1954; Harbaugh, 1961; Mowry, 1956.

—John Buenker, *University of Wisconsin, Parkside*

ROOT, ELIHU (1845–1937), Secretary of War and of State. He graduated from law school in 1867 and soon became the nation's foremost corporation lawyer, serving as personal counsel to such men as Jay Gould, Thomas Fortune Ryan, and E. H. Harriman. This orientation carried over to his political career, where he seemed inured to the social evils of the day. In 1899 he was appointed secretary of war, as which he became known as the "father of the modern army" because of his reorganization policies. He also revamped the colonial system of the United States, especially concerning the Philippines.

In 1905 Root became secretary of state and negotiated a series of arbitration treaties that anticipated the Good Neighbor Policy in Latin America. The Root-Takahira Agreement (1908) with Japan had an important effect on the Open Door Policy in China. He resigned his post in 1909 to take a seat in the Senate, where he became part of the regular Republican bloc but did not seek reelection in 1914. In 1912 he had been awarded the Nobel Peace Prize. In 1920 he joined with Herbert Hoover and William Howard Taft to rally Republican support for the League of Nations and the World Court, and he continued to interest himself in national and international affairs until his death.

See also Open Door Policy.

ROOT-TAKAHIRA AGREEMENT (1908), Japanese-American executive agreement on Asia. *See* Open Door Policy.

ROUGH RIDERS, volunteer cavalry group that fought under Leonard Wood and Theodore Roosevelt in Cuba. *See* Spanish-American War (1898).

RUFFIN, EDMUND (1794–1865), agricultural reformer and pioneer in solid chemisty. Ruffin, a Virginia planter and student of agricultural chemistry, was aware of the European work in this area and also experimented on his own lands. In 1832 he published his *Essay on Calcareous Manures,* a pioneer breakthrough in soil chemistry that began an era of reform in farming methods in the South and that helped to rejuvenate the upper South, whose soil had been depleted. He edited the influential *Farmer's Register* (1833–1842), although he filled it with fiery pro-Southern, states' rights propaganda.

The originality of Ruffin's scientific findings lay in his insistence that plant and animal-manure fertilizers alone were inadequate. Some soils needed additional minerals. Organic manures could only restore land to its original level of fertility, but in order to improve land, mineral composition had to be checked and, if necessary, altered. He found vegetable acids in his own soil and a lack of calcium carbonate, so he plowed in calcareous manures—manures with calcium carbonate—to neutralize the acids. This change increased his corn yields 40 percent.

Ruffin, a Southern extremist, emigrated to South Carolina before the Civil War. As a member of the state's Palmetto Guard he was given the honor of firing the first shot of the Civil War on Fort Sumter on April 21, 1861. When Gen. Robert E. Lee surrendered in 1865, Ruffin shot himself in despair.

RUNAWAY SLAVES. *See* Fugitive Slave Acts.

RURAL ELECTRIFICATION ADMINISTRATION (REA), one of the numerous programs and services initiated under the emergency relief umbrella of the New Deal. Established by presidential order in 1935, REA used Work Projects Administration labor and Reconstruction Finance Corporation loans to local cooperatives to extend electricity into areas that had never been served by the private companies (only 11 percent of American farms had had access to electricity before 1935). Complaints from the privately owned utilities failed to prevent enlargement of REA after 1936 under legislation sponsored by George W. Norris. One of the most popular New Deal programs, REA was made permanent under Department of Agriculture jurisdiction in 1939. The program was an important impetus to the almost total electrification of rural America by 1960.

Consult (VI) Schlesinger, 1960.

RUSH-BAGOT AGREEMENT (1817), Anglo-American agreement to remove military ships from the Great Lakes. It was achieved by an exchange of notes between Richard Rush, acting secretary of state, and Charles Bagot, Britain's minister in Washington, on April 28 and 29, 1817. The two powers agreed that they would not maintain military naval forces on the Great Lakes, merely the vessels necessary for customs and routine duties. The agreement aimed to prevent the type of naval race that had taken place on the Great Lakes in the War of 1812, although it did not eliminate land fortifications, armaments, and troops along the U.S.-Canadian border.

In order to satisfy British qualms and to give this exchange of notes a more formal treaty status, President Monroe submitted it to the Senate. The agreement was approved on April 16, 1818.

RUSSO-JAPANESE WAR (1905), dispute over Manchuria. Both Japan and Russia regarded Manchuria as a frontier area for development, and Russia had built the Chinese Eastern Railroad across Northern Manchuria with the consent of China and sought to extend its control into Southern Manchuria.

Japan's interest in the area led it to attack Russia in 1905 and defeat its fleet and armies. The Japanese asked President Theodore Roosevelt to mediate a settlement, and the Treaty of Portsmouth was signed on Sept. 5, 1905, with Japan obtaining substantial concessions. Essentially, Russia was replaced by Japan as the dominant power, although China still retained sovereignty in the area.

See also Portsmouth Peace Conference (1905).

SACCO-VANZETTI CASE, celebrated trial and execution that has been considered a microcosm of the social, political, and economic issues of the 1920s. On April 15, 1920, two men were murdered in South Braintree, Mass., in the course of a payroll robbery. On May 5, Nicola Sacco, a fish peddler, and Bartolomeo Vanzetti, a factory worker, were arrested for the crime. Both were Italian immigrants who had come to the United States in 1908, and both were well known for their anarchist views and activities. They were tried before Judge Webster Thayer and convicted on July 14, 1921. From that time until their execution on August 23, 1927, the question of the justice of the trial, conviction, and execution of Sacco and Vanzetti agitated the country and helped discredit American justice. To this day the case can arouse the most heated passions because the issues are still very much alive, particularly the issue of whether or not members of unpopular minority groups can get a fair trial.

The defenders of Sacco and Vanzetti were, at first, political leftists who wanted to use the case to discredit capitalism. But the substance of their charges soon attracted many fair-minded citizens. It was never clear whether upholders of the verdict were defending the jury system and respect for courts or just the social status quo. The trial was badly conducted and conviction appeared to be based on bias rather than investigation. From evidence presented at the trial, a professional writer as late as 1962 deduced that Sacco may very well have been guilty but Vanzetti almost certainly not.

The question of the guilt or innocence of the two anarchists, who went to their deaths bravely and mouthing noble sentiments, is quite separate from the fairness of the trial. The real question was, "Could someone else—not belonging to an unpopular group—have been convicted from the same evidence?" The answer is almost certainly, "No." In the 1920s, no procedural concessions were made to the defense, and the trial did involve prejudices—against the foreign-born and "non-Teutonic," against leftist political agitators, against the poor. The whole incident symbolized the Red Scare and anti-immigration feelings of the early 1920s, plus the rigidity of conservatives of that day in the face of facts.

Consult (VI) Russell, 1962.

—John C. Burnham, *Ohio State University*

SAINT MIHIEL SALIENT, BATTLE OF (SEPT. 12–16, 1918), American operation under General Pershing that eliminated a dangerous German threat. *See* World War I Battles.

SALARY GRAB, popular name for a bill signed by President Grant in 1873 that doubled the President's salary for his next term and also raised the salaries of congressmen from $5,000 to $7,500. A provision for two years' retroactivity in effect legislated a $5,000 gift for each member of Congress. Outraged national protest forced repeal of the congressional increases, but the Salary Grab was typical of the moral failings of the Grant era.

Sacco and Vanzetti *(second, third from right)*, shortly before their controversial execution in 1927.

Polio vaccine developer Dr. Jonas Salk in 1954, when the vaccine was tested nationally.

Birth control advocate Margaret Sanger appears before Senate subcommittee in 1931 to urge changes in federal birth control information laws.

SALK, JONAS (EDWARD) (1914-), American research scientist who developed the immunization vaccine against poliomyelitis. He was born in New York City and received his medical degree from New York University in 1939. Following his internship, he served first at the University of Michigan and in 1945 moved to the University of Pittsburgh's School of Medicine, where he became professor of preventive medicine.

During World War II, Salk and his teacher, Dr. Thomas Francis, Jr., had worked for the Army in developing a vaccine against influenza. In 1949 Salk began his research to develop a vaccine to immunize the public against polio. His success in 1954 helped to eradicate the crippling disease and brought him world fame. He subsequently continued his research at the Salk Institute for Biological Studies in La Jolla, Cal.

SALUTARY NEGLECT, English policy, during most of the colonial period, of not exerting strict control over its American colonies. Robert Walpole, England's leading politician from 1721 until 1742, thought that this "salutary neglect" encouraged colonial development beneficial to both the provinces and the mother country, and he raised the practice to the level of official policy.

SAN FRANCISCO CONFERENCE ON INTERNATIONAL ORGANIZATION, meeting held in San Francisco, April 25-June 26, 1945, to draft the UN Charter. Attended by 282 delegates representing 46 nations, the conference produced sharp conflict between large nations and small and among the great powers. After much wrangling, the delegates adopted a charter based on the Dumbarton Oaks proposals but with important additions and modifications. A Trusteeship Council was created to administer the former colonies held by Italy and Japan. The assembly was given the authority to make recommendations to the Security Council. Article 51, adopted at the insistence of the American nations, allowed regional security organizations to function within the scope of the charter. The most controversial question, the inclusiveness of the permanent members' veto in the Security Council, was finally resolved when Stalin agreed not to insist upon a veto to block discussion of issues. The UN Charter went into effect on Oct. 24, 1945.

See also Dumbarton Oaks Conference; United Nations.

SANGER, MARGARET (1883-1966), birth control crusader. She herself was one of 11 children. As a public health nurse in New York City slums she observed the "ill effects of childbearing on the women of the poor" and began to seek and propagate information on contraception. After her publication *Women Rebel* advocated legalization of birth control (a term she coined), it was confiscated by the post office, and Sanger was indicted for publishing obscenity. In 1915 she embarked on a campaign for the dissemination of contraceptive information and devices by physicians, an activity then prohibited by law. In 1916, with her sister, Sanger established the first U.S. birth control clinic in the Brooklyn slums. Both sisters were convicted of violating the Comstock Law of 1873, which prohibited the dissemination of birth control information, and they were sentenced to a month in prison, after which Sanger resumed her campaign.

In *Women and the New Race* (1920), she proclaimed women's right to "voluntary motherhood" and birth control's potential contribution to women's emancipation. In 1921 the first American Birth Control Conference was held, and thereafter the movement gained international recognition. Finally in 1937, dissemination of birth control information by physicians was legalized. Sanger recorded her experiences in *My Fight for Birth Control* (1931) and *Margaret Sanger: An Autobiography* (1938).

See also Abortion and Birth Control Laws.

Consult (VII) Kennedy, 1970.
—Nancy Woloch, *Hebrew Union College*

SAN JACINTO, BATTLE OF, the last important battle of the war for Texas independence. It was won on April 21, 1836, by Gen. Sam Houston and about 800 Texans fighting more than 1,500 Mexicans under General Santa Anna.

Inspired by Houston's urging to "Remember the Alamo," the Texans met the Mexicans in a skirmish on April 20 but were forced to withdraw. Santa Anna and his men established their defenses within a mile of Houston's camp and took time to rest after their recent long march. Houston, who drew up his army behind a screen of trees, attacked at 4 A.M., and the fighting was virtually over within half an hour. The Texans claimed to have killed 630 Mexicans, wounded 208, and taken 730 prisoners. Among the Mexican prisoners was Santa Anna, who signed a treaty with the Texans granting their independence and establishing terms for ending the war.

See also Houston, Sam; Texas.

SAN JUAN HILL, BATTLE OF, one of the pivotal battles in Cuba. *See* Spanish-American War (1898).

SAN LORENZO TREATY (1795). *See* Pinckney's Treaty.

SANTA ANNA, ANTONIO LOPEZ DE (1795?-1876), Mexican general and president. *See* Alamo; Mexican War; San Jacinto, Battle of.

SANTA CLARA COUNTY v. SOUTHERN PACIFIC RAILROAD (1886), unanimous decision by the Supreme Court that a corporation was a legal person. In the San Mateo case (1882), Roscoe Conkling had argued that the equal protection and due process clauses of the Fourteenth Amendment were drafted to protect the legal rights not only of black citizens but also those of corporations. In *Santa Clara* the Court accepted this doctrine before deciding the specific litigation. The rights guaranteed to "persons" became a legal shield protecting capitalist enterprise. Historians do not accept Conkling's testimony regarding the intent of the amendment, but the Court did.
See also Conkling, Roscoe.

SANTA FE TRAIL, route to the West that stretched southwest from Franklin and Independence, Mo., to Santa Fe, N.M. It was started in 1821 by Missouri trader William Becknell, and for 25 years annual caravans of American traders drove wagons loaded with hardware and cotton cloth west to trade for silver bullion, furs, and mules. The trade averaged about $130,000 a year and brought a solid profit to Missouri merchants.
    The trail itself led Americans 800 miles from Missouri—south and west across the Arkansas and Cimarron rivers, through the Cimarron Desert, and then on to Santa Fe. A longer, but safer route, the Mountain Branch, followed the Arkansas west to Bent's Fort in southeastern Colorado. Then it turned south through Raton Pass to Taos and Santa Fe. Using these routes, American traders learned much about the region, and during the Mexican War U.S. troops used the trail on their way to California.

SARATOGA, scene of surrender of General Burgoyne's forces on Oct. 17, 1777. *See* Revolutionary War Battles.

SARGENT, JOHN SINGER (1856-1925), American painter noted for his portraits of leading figures of his time. Born in Florence, Italy, to American expatriate parents, Sargent studied in Florence and Paris, visited the United States frequently, and traveled to Spain during the 1880s.
    Sargent is best known for his portraits and brilliant watercolors. His technical skill and the simple color schemes of most of his canvases reflect the influence of Velázquez. This technique is illustrated in "Madame Gautreau," or "Madame X" (1884). The work was a *succès de scandale,* and was one of the causes of his departure from Paris, where his work was critized as eccentric and erotic. He then moved to London and became increasingly involved with portraiture. His portraits were conceived in the formal tradition, always elegant and decisive but neither intimate nor psychologically profound.
    Sargent gradually grew bored with portraits and, with a few exceptions, refused to paint them. He devoted the rest of his life to decorative work, watercolors, and landscapes in oil. However, his portrait-painting career left the world likenesses of Henry James, Robert Louis Stevenson, Theodore Roosevelt, Woodrow Wilson, John D. Rockefeller, and other eminent men.

SCALAWAGS name given by Southern white conservatives to fellow native whites who supported Reconstruction and the Republicans after the Civil War. Scalawags came from two sources: the hill country where slavery had never taken firm root and where pro-Union and antislavery sentiments were strong and from the ranks of former Whigs, often members of the Southern elite, who had never liked Democrats.

SCARLET LETTER, THE (1850), Nathaniel Hawthorne's major novel. *See* Hawthorne, Nathaniel.

SCHECHTER v. UNITED STATES (1935), one of the Supreme Court's many anti-New Deal decisions in the spring of 1935. The case arose out of an attempt on the part of the Live Poultry Code Authority of the National Recovery Administration (NRA) to enforce its standards on a member of the industry. The Court ruled unanimously that the NRA was unconstitutional because Congress had no right to delegate its legislative power to the code authorities. The Court gratuitously ruled that Schechter Brothers, a kosher poultry concern, was not engaged in interstate commerce—a position which forced Chief Justice Hughes to reach back to the nineteenth century for an antiquated definition of commerce. The Schechter decision was one of those that led Franklin Roosevelt to seek Court reform. The NRA itself was controversial and unworkable enough that no attempt was made to revive the experiment through new legislation.
    See also Court Packing; National Recovery Administration.
    Consult (VI) Schlesinger, 1960.

SCHENCK v. UNITED STATES (1919), Supreme Court decision upholding the Espionage Act. *See* Espionage Act (1917).

SCHENECTADY RAID (1690), attack on Schenectady, N.Y., by a force of French Canadians and Indians. As part of a three-pronged attack against northern English settlements during King William's War (1689-1697), French Canada sent a 210-man party composed almost

Joseph Pulitzer, whose newspapers used sensationalism to build circulation, in portrait by John Singer Sargent.

Winfield Scott directed the advance on Mexico City in the Mexican War.

equally of French Canadians and Christianized Indians into New York in the winter of 1690.

The French and their Indian allies planned to attack well-fortified Albany, but they reconsidered and struck about 15 miles away at Schenectady. Shortly before midnight on Feb. 8, 1690, the attackers entered the open gates of the stockade and within two hours killed 60 inhabitants. Suffering only 2 casualties, the Canadians returned north with 22 white and 5 black captives, while 60 survivors fled to Albany.

See also King William's War.

SCOPES TRIAL (1925), test case that involved the public-school teaching of evolution, a concept that offended Fundamentalists. It attracted national publicity and led to a courtroom confrontation between William Jennings Bryan and trial lawyer Clarence Darrow. Teacher John Scopes was convicted of teaching evolutionary theories.

See also Bryan, William Jennings; Darrow, Clarence; Fundamentalism.

SCOTT, DRED. *See* Dred Scott Decision (1857).

SCOTT, WINFIELD (1786–1866), soldier and statesman. Born near Petersburg, Va., he briefly practiced law before joining the Army in 1808 as a captain. Scott's military career began in earnest during the War of 1812. As a colonel he led the attack on Fort George (May 27, 1813) and, promoted to brigadier general, became the hero of the Battles of Chippewa and Lundy's Lane in July 1814.

After the War of 1812, Scott traveled to Europe on a military and diplomatic mission. He also participated in the Black Hawk War (1832), supervised the removal of the Cherokee Indians to the Southwest, skillfully managed the *Caroline* affair (1837), and negotiated the truce following the Aroostook War (1839).

Scott was made general in chief of the Army in 1841. In the Mexican War (1846–1848) he led the march from Veracruz to Mexico City, returning home a national hero and receiving his second congressional gold medal. In 1852 he won the Whig nomination for president but lost the election to Franklin Pierce. Scott then continued his military career by rendering distinguished service in settling a dispute with Britain over San Juan Island, on the Oregon-Canada border, in 1859. Although a Southerner by birth, Scott remained loyal to the Union in the Civil War. Still supreme commander of the Army, he provided for the defense of the Capitol and opposed the action that led to the First Battle of Bull Run. He yielded his command to George B. McClellan in November 1861. He was appointed superintendent of West Point, a post he held until his death.

Standing Woman (1932), monumental bronze by French-American sculptor Gaston La Chaise. Collection, The Museum of Modern Art, New York. Mrs. Simon Guggenheim Fund.

Although Scott's pompous bearing had won him the nickname of Old Fuss and Feathers, he was highly regarded and is frequently called the foremost U.S. military figure between George Washington and Robert E. Lee.

See also Aroostook War; Caroline Affair; Mexican War.

SCULPTURE. American sculpture began as simple embellishment of functional colonial necessities such as gravestones and Bible boxes. Religious suspicion of art, the lack of cultural models, and the pressures of building a country out of wilderness inhibited artistic expression.

The First Sculptors. Patience Lovell Wright (1725–1785), America's first recorded sculptor, was forced to move to London to earn a living as a wax medallion portraitist. The sons of carpenters Joseph Rush and Simeon Skillen added art to craft as the colonies prospered in the late 1700s, carving widely admired ships' figureheads and ornamenting their wooden furniture with figurines representing Agriculture, Liberty, and Plenty.

After the Revolutionary War, when the young nation had cause to celebrate and immortalize its achievement, sculptors found a public market, and monumental sculpture was begun. The first major commission was awarded to Jean-Antoine Houdon, a leading French sculptor, to honor George Washington. Houdon was imported at great expense to do life sketches of Washington in 1785; the plaster model was done in Paris, the marble worked in Italy; and the completed piece was erected in the State House in Richmond, Va., in 1796. The promise of large-scale commissions lured Italian marble carvers such as Giuseppe Ceracchi to America at the end of the century, but the lack of marble quarries and trained artisans soon sent them home. However, young Americans followed to study and to serve as apprentices in Italy. Although an American naturalism marked the work of men such as John Frazee, Horatio Greenough, and Hiram Powers, the influence of the French and Italian style of neoclassicism dominated as long as American sculptors were forced to send their plaster originals to the Italian marble quarries for replication.

As industrialization progressed, sculptors sought to free themselves from the necessity of sending models to Italy. In the midnineteenth century, bronze casting became the favored technique, allowing sculptors to work on a grander scale and to guide fabrication more closely. Bronze generals on horseback proliferated in town squares, one of the earliest being Henry K. Brown's "George Washington on Horse" (1853).

Beginnings of Expressionism. As the nation's centennial celebration of 1876 approached, public sculpture became a big business supported by government. The pressure to create commemorative statues dissipated much of the vitality of earlier monuments. Meanwhile, seeds were being sown for the twentieth-century transformation of sculpture from a public statement to the expression of a personal vision. Influenced perhaps by the competition of the camera, men such as Frederick Remington (1861–1909) and Charles Grafley (1862–1929) added a more candid, dynamic quality to their sculpture. Grafley pursued social realism with tableaus of street scenes and character studies, while Remington translated his reportorial illustrations of the Wild West into bronze and did much to create American myths about the cowboy and the Indian. Ann Whitney (1821–1915) took another tack, sculpting subjects such as Indians not from life but from her personal, idealized vision of what they represented to America's culture.

William Rimmer (1816–1879) presaged the twentieth century more dramatically than any other American sculptor. Some 40 years before Auguste Rodin, he was exploring the emotional content of himself and his subjects. He worked with a direct, abstract touch and, although scorned in his own time, he is now recognized as the first expressionist sculptor.

A New Century. At the turn of the century, artists of every country were rejecting Realism and seeking new vocabularies of expression in Impressionism, Fauvism, Cubism, Futurism, and Constructivism. The American public was introduced to these varied efforts at the Armory Show held in New York City in 1913, and the center of Western art began to shift from Europe's capitals to New York. As two world wars and a depression plunged Europe into turmoil, artists such as Elie Nadelman, Walter Gropius, Marcel Duchamp, Gaston La Chaise, and Alexander Archipenko fled to America to teach and to continue their experiments. They made key contributions to Dadaism, Surrealism, the Bauhaus, German Expressionism, and the New York school of Abstract Expressionism.

Sculpture was changing from public monument to personal statement; its environment from town square to museum and the private collector; its materials from bronze and marble to the nearly limitless variety produced by a highly industrialized and inventive society. The generation of American sculptors developing in the years between the wars—Isamu Noguchi, Alexander Calder, Louise Nevelson, David Smith—no longer needed to seek the center of creative activity abroad—it had shifted to America.

From 1940 to 1950, sculptural expression took a back seat to war. Work progressed (David Smith used skills acquired as a tank welder to create massive assemblages of welded steel), but the emphasis was on teaching a new and very large number of artists who burst on the scene as postwar prosperity set in.

The Art Boom. A new explosion of experimentation followed World War II, accompanied by a burgeoning art market in which a work of art became a speculative financial investment. Distinctions between disciplines blurred as painters sought sculptured canvases, sculptors painted their works or integrated them into music, dance, and theater presentations; architects sculpted entire buildings; and artists declared as art such phenomena as mathematical equations, ditches, and dye dispersion in a river. Names to categorize what was happening proliferated: kinetic art, pop art, earthworks, conceptual art, minimal art, concrete art, junk art, environments, soft sculpture, assemblage, formalism.

Sculptors have worked on an increasingly monumental scale, exploring the relationships of man to his environment. The more innovative and talented figures of the postwar scene include Claes Oldenburg, Kenneth Snelson, Robert Rauschenberg, Ronald Balden, Joseph Cornell, José De Rivera, and Carl Andre. Collaborations have developed among artists and also between the artist and the new artisans of a technological society.

See also Painting.

Consult (VIII) Craven, 1968; Davidson, 1966; Ritchie, 1952; Tuchman, 1967.

—Merle Steir, *Designer-Sculptor*

SDS. *See* Students for a Democratic Society.

SEALE, BOBBY, Black Panther leader. *See* Black Panthers.

SEATO. *See* Southeast Asia Treaty Organization.

SECESSION, the withdrawal from the Union of 11 Southern states before and at the beginning of the Civil War. South Carolina seceded on Dec. 20, 1860, and was soon followed by Mississippi (Jan. 9, 1861), Florida (January 10), Alabama (January 11), Georgia (January 19), and Louisiana (January 26). Texas withdrew on February 1. After the fall of Fort Sumter in April, four other states quickly seceded: Virginia (April 17), Arkansas (May 6), Tennessee (May 7), and North Carolina (May 20).

In most states, the process followed this pattern: the governor recommended to the legislature that it call a convention to sever ties with the Union; the legislature then complied, delegates were elected, and the convention met and adopted a secession ordinance. There were some variations. In Texas, Virginia, and Tennessee the secession ordinance was submitted for popular ratification. There were no conventions in Arkansas and Tennessee; the state legislatures themselves passed secession

Horatio Greenough's statue of George Washington reflects neoclassical influence in American sculpture.

Frederick Remington's bronzes, such as *The Bronco Buster,* helped to create a romantic image of the West. The Metropolitan Museum of Art, Bequest of Jacob Ruppert, 1939.

ordinances. One state (South Carolina) went so far as to issue a declaration of causes impelling it to secede.

See also Civil War: Causes.
Consult (IV) Wooster, 1962.

SECOND BANK OF THE UNITED STATES. See Bank of the United States, Second.

SECOND FRONT, the proposal for an Anglo-American invasion of France, one of the most divisive strategic issues within the Grand Alliance from 1941 to 1944. British reluctance to undertake the invasion, originally scheduled for 1942, forced postponement until 1944 and deeply annoyed the Russians, who felt that their Allies had betrayed them.

SECRET SERVICE, branch of the Treasury charged with protecting the president and other officials. See Treasury, Department of the.

SECURITIES EXCHANGE ACT (1934), New Deal legislation designed to regulate the nation's stock exchanges. It was one in a complex of laws reforming the financial structure so that no crash such as that of 1929 could recur. The Securities and Exchange Commission (SEC) was set up to protect investors from the manipulations of insiders and from misrepresentation in the sale of securities and to reduce speculation by the regulation of margin buying. Established despite concerted opposition from the financial community, the SEC became a part of the financial structure bringing stability to the exchanges. Its first chairman was Joseph P. Kennedy, who had made a fortune in the market, sometimes using the methods now outlawed. During his brief tenure Kennedy administered the SEC with vigor, helping to establish it as a workable institution.

SEDITION ACT (1918), amendment to the Espionage Act extending its scope. See Espionage Act (1917).

SELECTIVE SERVICE ACT (1917) introduced the registration and classification for military service of all American men between the ages of 21 and 30 (later broadened). President Woodrow Wilson had tried to avoid establishing the draft, but the volunteer response was simply not great enough to meet America's projected needs for men in Europe. Although the act was administered by local civilian draft boards and although antidraft riots and demonstrations were common, opposition was never so violent as it had been during the Civil War. Almost 24 million men were registered, of whom nearly 3 million were drafted.

SEMINOLE WARS (1818–1819; 1835–1842), series of conflicts between the United States and the Seminole Indians, who were mainly established in Florida and who clashed with American settlers in Georgia. In 1818 Andrew Jackson was given the command of an expedition against the Seminoles, and he invaded Spanish East Florida in March 1818. This incident caused a dispute in Congress over Jackson's conduct and also occasioned an international quarrel with Britain because Jackson had executed two British subjects. Secretary of State John Quincy Adams used the incident to help convince the Spanish that they should cede the Floridas.

The wars with the Seminoles in the late 1830s and early 1840s were precipitated by the government's desire to drive the Indians out of Florida to land west of the Mississippi. Most of the Seminoles refused to leave, and they engaged in a long struggle with the U.S. Army. The most famous Seminole leader in this struggle was Osceola, who was captured in 1837 while traveling under a flag of truce and who subsequently died in prison. The Seminoles put up stiff resistance, and a treaty signed in 1842 permitted some to remain in Florida. Many others had been killed or compelled to move west in the previous 10 years.

See also Adams-Onís Treaty; Jackson, Andrew.

SENATE, UNITED STATES, upper house of Congress. The framers of the Constitution regarded the Senate as representative of the semisovereign states rather than the people. The document they drafted prevents denial of equal representation without the consent of every state (it is the only portion of the Constitution that cannot be changed by the regular amendment process). It was not till 1913 that the Seventeenth Amendment replaced selection of senators by state legislatures with direct election by the people.

The growth of House membership in the early nineteenth century meant that for the popular branch to function there had to be restrictions on debate. Even today, with 100 members, the Senate enjoys free debate; it takes a two-thirds vote, which is rarely achieved, to end a filibuster.

Their 6-year term gives senators greater independence and prestige than representatives. In addition, the Senate has special powers—to give advice and consent on treaties (by a two-thirds vote), to approve appointments (by a majority vote), to try cases of impeachment, and to elect the vice-president in the event the electoral college fails to give a majority to a candidate.

The vice-president of the United States is president of the Senate but votes only in case of a tie. In his absence, a president pro tempore selected by the Senate (usually the senior senator of the majority party) presides or else someone designated by him.

Party leadership in the Senate is usually

SENATE — Item Guide

The article on the SENATE covers its legal functions, which were established by the CONSTITUTION OF THE UNITED STATES; the method of electing senators has been changed by AMENDMENTS, CONSTITUTIONAL. When there is no majority in the ELECTORAL COLLEGE, the Senate elects the VICE-PRESIDENT OF THE UNITED STATES. It also tries IMPEACHMENT cases.

Nearly half of the PRESIDENTS OF THE UNITED STATES have sat in the Senate, ranging from JOHN QUINCY ADAMS, the first, to JOHN F. KENNEDY, LYNDON B. JOHNSON, and RICHARD M. NIXON. In the nineteenth century powerful senators included HENRY CLAY, JOHN C. CALHOUN, DANIEL WEBSTER, STEPHEN A. DOUGLAS, and CHARLES SUMNER. In the twentieth century influential members have been ROBERT M. LA FOLLETTE, ROBERT F. WAGNER, JOSEPH McCARTHY, J. WILLIAM FULBRIGHT, BARRY GOLDWATER, and members of the TAFT FAMILY, KENNEDY FAMILY, and BYRD FAMILY.

decentralized. In the 1950s, Lyndon Johnson augmented the authority of majority leader and made himself the center of Senate activity. However, after his assumption of the vice-presidency, the power slipped back to the individual senators and the standing committees.

Consult (VIII) Harris, 1953; Ripley, 1969.
—Martin Gruberg, *University of Wisconsin, Oshkosh*

SENECA FALLS CONVENTION (1848), the first women's rights convention, called by Elizabeth Cady Stanton and Lucretia Mott to "discuss the social, civil, and religious condition and rights of women." Almost 300 persons, including 40 men, gathered at a chapel in Seneca Falls, N.Y., on July 19, 1848, to hear addresses by the organizers and a "Declaration of Sentiments" modeled on the Declaration of Independence. Resolutions concerning women's rights to their wages, persons, and children and to educational and economic opportunities were unanimously approved, although a suffrage resolution was controversial; it was passed only through the efforts of black abolitionist Frederick Douglass, who attended the convention. The Seneca Falls meeting began the women's rights movement in the United States.

SEPARATION OF POWERS, the distribution of political and legal powers among governmental institutions. It was developed most thoroughly in the political theories of John Locke and Baron de Montesquieu. The basic assumption underlying the separation of powers principle is that men tend to abuse power given to them and to use it to oppress others. The solution is to construct governmental institutions with checks and balances so that no one person or group has all the power. The proper distribution or separation would give each office sufficient power to perform its duties well but not enough for it to become oppressive. In this way, private interest expressed as ambition or the desire for power can be channeled to serve a public or common good.

The U.S. Constitution incorporates the principle of separation of powers by dividing power among the executive, legislative, and judicial branches. No person can hold office in more than one branch, and each branch can in some way check the other two. For example, the president can veto acts of Congress, Congress can impeach the president, the president and Congress together appoint members of the courts, and the courts can declare acts of Congress and the president to be unconstitutional.

See also Constitution of the United States; Judicial Review.

SEPARATISTS, reformers who separated from the Anglican church. *See* Pilgrims.

SEVIER, JOHN (1745–1815), frontier leader who helped settle what is now Tennessee. *See* Franklin, State of.

SEWARD, WILLIAM H(ENRY) (1801–1872), Secretary of State during the Civil War. He was born in upstate New York, where he established a successful legal practice and became a state senator. In 1838, as a Whig, he became governor of New York and promoted internal improvements, public support for Catholic schools, and the antislavery cause. He also displayed considerable skill as a political manipulator with the aid of his alter ego, Thurlow Weed. In 1848 he entered the U.S. Senate. During the debates over the Compromise of 1850 he appealed to a "higher law than the Constitution" as a basis for opposing slavery.

By 1860, Seward was the most conspicuous antislavery politician in the country. Deeply disappointed that he was not nominated at the Republican convention, he nevertheless campaigned for Lincoln, who chose him as secretary of state. In the secession crisis Seward disillusioned his former supporters by backing compromises with the South. He deviously tried to avoid sectional conflict, but he later redeemed himself by skillfully persuading European nations not to intervene in the war.

After Appomattox he continued as secretary of state, pursuing an expansionist foreign policy that culminated in the acquisition of Alaska. In domestic affairs Seward urged caution on Presidents Lincoln and Johnson and thus became anathema to Radical Republicans. A cheerful, cultivated man, Seward is one of the most puzzling figures in American history, a peculiar blend of idealism, political opportunism, and conservatism.

See also Alaska Purchase (1867); Radical Republicans.

Consult (IV) Van Deusen, 1967.
—Michael Burlingame, *Connecticut College*

SEWARD'S FOLLY, derisive nickname given to U.S. purchase of Alaska. *See* Alaska Purchase (1867).

SEWING MACHINE, invention that revolutionized the apparel industry. The first practical sewing machine was developed by Elias Howe of Massachusetts (1846). Howe's patent was improved upon by other Americans, including Allen B. Wilson (1824–1888) and Isaac Singer (1811–1875), who added a treadle operation, thus freeing both hands to guide the cloth (1851).

Singer's improvement made the home sewing machine possible, although the real revolution produced by the sewing machine was in industry—it speeded the passing of homespun and the coming of cheap, mass-

An expansionist, Secretary of State William Seward negotiated purchase of Alaska and urged annexation of Hawaii.

First Singer sewing machine, patented in 1850.

produced ready-made clothing. It also created the first of a whole series of consumer goods that made light engineering a major branch of industry. Led by the great showman and publicity expert, Singer, the sewing-machine industry pioneered such sales techniques as installment purchasing and customer service. With Edmund Clark, Singer opened a factory in New York in 1853; by 1860 his agents were selling more machines abroad (as far away as Japan) than within the United States.

The sewing machine not only created the mass-clothing industry with its sweatshops, it also affected other industries—gloves and hats, hosiery, carpets, lace, and especially boots and shoes. The tough Singer machine could sew leather, and in 1858 it was adapted to sew the soles of shoes to the uppers.

An improved patent by Gordon MacKay (1821-1903), granted in 1861, brought a much faster machine. By 1880 McKay had joined with rubber pioneer Charles Goodyear (1853-1896). In 1899, United Shoe Manufacturing Company, a monopoly controlling most machinery patents, was established and has continued to be dominant. The sewing machine was one of the chief American inventions of the pre-Civil War years and a major American contribution to the history of mass technology.

See also Howe, Elias; Inventions.
—Peter d'A. Jones, *University of Illinois, Chicago Circle*

SHARECROPPING, a characteristic feature of post-Civil War Southern agriculture. It resulted from the problems of the postwar period, when capital was scarce, some men had large landholdings but no capital to hire laborers, and many men wished to engage in farming but had no capital to invest in land, tools, or supplies. The result was a system of tenant farming whereby the tenant agreed to turn over to the landowner, as rent, a portion (share) of the crop. The amount was typically half the crop if the landowner supplied tools, mules, and seed, less if the tenant had his own. Landowners frequently were also merchants and held crops in that capacity.

See also Crop-Lien system.

SHARE OUR WEALTH PROGRAM, Huey Long's income redistribution plan. *See* Long, Huey.

SHAYS' REBELLION (1786-1787), protest by Massachusetts farmers against the refusal of the state legislature to issue paper money that would make it easier to pay debts or to delay foreclosures during the hard times that followed the Revolution. Angry farmers at the Hampshire County Convention (August 22-25, 1786) demanded relief. Armed bands soon forced courts to close, and on September 26, 600 men under Daniel Shays confronted 500

Philip Sheridan ably led Army of the Potomac's cavalry and then commanded the Union's Army of the Shenandoah in the Civil War.

militiamen under Gen. William Shepherd and prevented the court from sitting at Springfield.

Shays attempted to seize the Springfield arsenal on Jan. 25, 1787, but Shepherd repulsed the assault. Shays' forces were pursued, and on February 4 the insurgents were routed at Petersham, N.H. The rebellion convinced the legislature not to levy a direct tax and to exempt certain necessities from debt procedures and persuaded others that the Articles of Confederation did not provide an adequate government. Massachusetts immediately pardoned almost all the rebels and even extended clemency to Shays in June 1788.

SHENANDOAH VALLEY CAMPAIGN (1862), brilliant harassing campaign conducted by Stonewall Jackson against superior Union forces. *See* Civil War Battles.

SHERIDAN, PHILIP H(ENRY) (1831-1888), Union cavalry leader in the Civil War. He grew up in Ohio and graduated from West Point in 1853. After serving with distinction early in the Civil War, he received a corps command and led his men so well at Chattanooga (November 1863) that Grant put him in charge of the 10,000 cavalry attached to the Army of the Potomac. In May 1864 he led a daring and destructive raid behind Lee's army that boosted Union morale.

In August 1864 Grant ordered Sheridan to repulse Jubal Early, whose army was rampaging in the Shenandoah Valley. After a series of pitched battles, he forced Early to retire. At Cedar Creek (Oct. 19, 1864), Sheridan, who was 20 miles away when the fighting began, rushed to his men, regrouped their broken lines, and transformed a rout into victory. During the fall and winter Sheridan laid waste to the Shenandoah, denying the Confederacy valuable food resources and guerrilla bases. In the final Union offensive (February–April 1865) he turned Lee's flank, forced him to evacuate Petersburg, and cut off his escape route, leaving the Confederate general no option but surrender.

During Reconstruction, Sheridan commanded the Texas-Louisiana department. Later he led the army in the Indian wars, and from 1884 to 1888 was commander in chief of the army.

See also Civil War Battles.
Consult (IV) O'Connor, 1953.
—Michael Burlingame, *Connecticut College*

SHERMAN, WILLIAM T(ECUMSEH) (1820-1891), one of the most distinguished Union commanders in the Civil War. Born and raised in Ohio, Sherman graduated from West Point in 1840, resigned from the army in 1855, but rejoined at the outbreak of the Civil War. He had little success early in the war but played a key role in the capture of Vicksburg (July

1863) as a corps commander under General Grant. In November 1863 Sherman, commanding the Army of the Tennessee, helped win the critical battle of Chattanooga. He took charge of the western armies in spring 1864 and with a series of brilliant maneuvers and marches forced the Confederates to fall back all the way to Atlanta. The Union army promptly besieged the city, and on September 1 captured it.

In November, Sherman began one of the most dramatic actions of the war, the march to the sea, which was designed to cut off Confederate supplies and break Southern morale. As his 60,000 men drove toward Savannah, they lived off the land and destroyed everything in their path. Discipline among the troops broke down and pillaging and looting soon became widespread. This irregular campaign, marred by excesses as it was, achieved its aims and shortened the war. After capturing Savannah (December 21) Sherman pressed north, cutting a swath through the Carolinas. On April 17, 1865, Sherman accepted Joseph E. Johnston's surrender on exceedingly generous peace terms, which Washington promptly vetoed.

After the war Sherman served as general in chief of the army for 14 years and firmly refused to enter politics. A fierce, iron-willed, restless man, Sherman disliked fighting and killing but fully realized that the war had to be prosecuted relentlessly. He has aptly been termed "the first modern soldier."

See also Civil War Battles.
—Michael Burlingame, *Connecticut College*

SHERMAN ANTITRUST ACT (1890), passed with only one dissenting congressional vote, sought "to protect trade and commerce against unlawful restraints and monopolies." Although 27 states had legislated against trust abuses, these combinations controlled entire sections of the economy and circumvented state regulation of their activities. The law made federal courts arbiters of the terms "restraint" and "monopoly" and provided for triple damage fines. Prosecutions were to be determined by the attorney general, but three successive administrations virtually ignored the antimonopoly intentions. However, the law was invoked against labor, notably in the Pullman Strike (1894).

President Theodore Roosevelt was the first to use the act effectively against monopolies. In 1911 the Supreme Court imposed a "rule of reason": size alone was not a violation of the Sherman Act but rather the use of predatory methods. New legislation explicitly listed business activities that constituted restraint, while court decisions freed labor from prosecution.

See also Antitrust Cases; Pullman Strike (1894); Trusts.

SHERMAN SILVER PURCHASE ACT (1890) provided for the purchase of 4.5 million ounces of silver each month by the secretary of the Treasury; for the silver, the Treasury issued notes that could be redeemed either in gold or silver coin.

The Sherman Act was an attempt, like the Bland-Allison Act (1878), by the Western silver Republicans to hold up the price of silver and to produce more abundant currency for the rural West and South. Despite the act, the price of silver continued to fall, and the Treasury had to pay less and less per ounce for the silver. But the act had a more serious effect because it permitted silver certificates to be exchanged for gold. Silver notes were redeemed in gold at a rapid rate, and by June 1893 the gold reserves fell below the "safe" limit of $100 million. Because of the already existing business depression, there was too much money in circulation; the result was a severe financial crisis—the Panic of 1893. A special session of Congress was called, and the Sherman Silver Act was repealed. The Populists, who viewed gold as the coin of the rich and silver as the coin of the people, labeled the repeal as the "Crime of '93."

See also Bland-Allison Act (1878); Free Silver; Panics, Financial (Nineteenth Century).

SHILOH (APRIL 1862), battle in Tennessee that led to a Confederate withdrawal into Mississippi. See Civil War Battles.

SHIRLEY, WILLIAM (1694–1771), English governor of Massachusetts (1741–1756). Although Massachusetts had seemed all but ungovernable throughout the eighteenth century, Shirley soon built a remarkably effective political coalition that drew heavily upon country towns for support.

When King George's War with France erupted in 1744, Shirley moved energetically to save Nova Scotia, and then in 1745 he organized the intercolonial expedition that conquered the fortress of Louisbourg. He tried without success to launch an even greater force to conquer Canada in 1746 and 1747 and by the end of the war commanded his own regiment. When the French and Indian War broke out in 1754, he helped to organize the Albany Congress, encouraged the military union of the colonies, revived his own regiment, and persuaded Gen. Edward Braddock to authorize a four-pronged assault upon New France in 1755 with Shirley attacking Fort Niagara. After Braddock's death, Shirley served as British commander in chief, but his civilian background left him vulnerable to criticism, especially among professional soldiers who needed someone to blame for Britain's military reverses of 1755–1756. Not long after the surrender of his regiment at Oswego in 1756,

Union general William T. Sherman near Atlanta in 1864.

Shirley's opponents got him removed from both his military command and his governorship. After a brief term as governor of Bermuda, Shirley retired to Massachusetts.

See also Albany Congress (1754); French and Indian War (1754–1763).

Consult (I) Schutz, 1961.

SHOLES, CHRISTOPHER LATHAM (1819–1890) developed first practical typewriter. *See* Typewriter.

SIEMENS PROCESS. *See* Bessemer Steel Process.

SINGER, ISAAC M. (1811–1875), popularizer of the sewing machine. *See* Sewing Machine.

SINGLE TAX, a tax reform propounded by Henry George and elaborated in his book *Progress and Poverty.* George's solution to the paradox of poverty in the midst of economic growth was to confine all taxes to the unearned increment in land values that accompanied growth. The community would thus benefit from what its growth had created. Monopoly, based on land values, would disappear, and the economic system—freed from monopoly and all other government taxes—would function smoothly and for the benefit of all. George's theories were popular with some reformers and radicals throughout the 1880s and early 1890s.

See also George, Henry.

SIOUX WARS. *See* Indian Wars, Western.

SIT-INS. For nearly 100 years after Reconstruction, white Southerners denied black people access to public eating facilities. On Feb. 2, 1960, a group of well-dressed black college students filed into Greensboro, N.C., lunch counters, sat down, and refused to move until they had been served. This marked the expansion of the "Nonviolent Coercion" policy enunciated by Dr. Martin Luther King, Jr. Despite repeated intimidation, beatings, and the imprisonment of those engaged in the sit-ins, their nonviolent but determined behavior began to win mass support, thus leading to the slow desegregation of the Southern way of life. So successful were the sit-ins of 1960–1962 that the tactic was often used during subsequent protests.

See also King, Martin Luther, Jr.

SIX NATIONS. *See* Iroquois Confederacy.

SKINNER, B(URRHUS) F(REDERIC) (1904–   ), American psychologist and author. He was born in Susquehanna, Pa., and graduated from Hamilton College in 1926. After trying unsuccessfully to be a poet, Skinner in 1928 began his graduate work in psychology at Harvard, where he spent most of his academic career.

A member of the behaviorist school of psychology, Skinner has been a controversial figure. In the 1940s he developed the Air Crib, a box designed to provide the best environment for an infant, who could live in it without clothing for nearly two years. He also invented the Skinner Box, an environment for observing laboratory animals. In recent years he has been deeply involved with the concept of programmed instruction and teaching machines, which he feels will revolutionize current methods of education. Skinner's many books include *Walden Two* (1948), *Science and Human Behavior* (1953), and *Beyond Freedom and Dignity* (1971).

SLATER, SAMUEL (1768–1835), textile pioneer in the United States. Slater was a textile mechanic from Derbyshire, England, who worked under Richard Arkwright in developing textile machinery. At this time the British, in order to protect their textile industry, barred both the export of textile machinery and the emigration of textile workers. Slater, however, memorized the plans for textile machines and emigrated secretly to the United States.

Financed by the Quaker merchant Moses Brown of Providence, R.I., Slater built from memory a cotton spinning mill at Pawtucket in 1790, a building that still stands. This was the first textile factory in the United States. Other mills quickly followed, and an American textile industry was soon established. Slater built other mills over the years and went through various partnerships. In 1827 he erected the first steam mill at Providence.

SLAUGHTERHOUSE CASES (1873), Supreme Court decision on the Fourteenth Amendment. In 1869 the Louisiana legislature granted a monopoly to a slaughterhouse company in New Orleans. Independent butchers filed suit, claiming that their property rights had been denied in violation of the Fourteenth Amendment. The Supreme Court in a 5 to 4 decision ruled against the butchers, contending that the amendment did little to protect American citizens from abuses at the hands of state governments. The Court declared that every citizen was both a U.S. citizen and a citizen of his state and that most liberties, privileges, and immunities, including the right to acquire and possess property, stemmed from one's state citizenship. The Fourteenth Amendment's privileges-and-immunities clause, therefore, did not apply.

See also Amendments, Constitutional.

SLAVE CODES. *See* Black Codes; Slavery.

SLAVE REVOLTS, COLONIAL. Blacks fre-

Advertisement for eighteenth-century slave auction.

quently committed isolated acts of violence during the colonial period, but the number of plots involving more than a handful of slaves was relatively small. The first serious conspiracy occurred in Gloucester County, Va., in 1663, when white indentured servants and black slaves determined to gain their freedom by force. Betrayed by an indentured servant, the rebels were executed on Sept. 13, 1663. In 1687 blacks planned to murder all whites living in the Northern Neck region of Virginia before their plot was discovered and ended.

In 1709, Indians as well as blacks were involved in the conspiracy that was unearthed in Surry, James City, and Isle of Wight counties, Va. In April 1712, slaves actually put their plans into operation when about 30 blacks and 2 Indians set a building on fire in New York City and then killed 9 whites as they extinguished the blaze. For the offense 21 slaves were executed. Black conspiracies were disclosed in South Carolina in 1720 and in Virginia in 1722 and 1723. In 1730 Virginia, South Carolina, and Louisiana blocked planned slave uprisings.

The promise of freedom in Spanish Florida caused several instances of slave violence in South Carolina in 1739, the most serious of which was the Cato Conspiracy, during which approximately 50 blacks and 25 whites died. In 1740 a plot was discovered in Charleston, S.C., and 50 blacks were hanged.

Also in 1740, slaves were accused of poisoning New York City's water supply, and in 1741 a series of fires convinced the city's white populace that blacks and poor whites were planning a revolution. In the wave of hysteria that followed, 101 Negroes were convicted on scanty evidence; 31 were executed and 70 banished. Other slave conspiracies were uncovered in South Carolina in 1759 and 1765; in Virginia in 1767; in Savannah, Ga., in 1772; and in Perth Amboy, N.J., in 1772.

See also Cato Conspiracy; Slavery.
Consult (IX) Jordan, 1968.
—Thomas Archdeacon, *University of Wisconsin*

SLAVERY, an ancient system of labor and property relationships. It was originally a by-product of war and conquest requiring whips and chains for organization. Civil law and religion reduced part of its inhumanity, allowing the emergence, among slaves, of teachers, skilled workers, entertainers, and favorite servants, who although slaves often received honor and respect in families and from the community. From their ranks, also, developed classes of freed men and women who influenced Greek and, later, Roman civilization. Muslim nations also teemed with white, African, and native slaves and continued to maintain slavery even after Europe had transformed its slaves into semifree serfs.

Africa and the Slave Trade. The systematic exploitation of the West African coast as a source of slaves accompanied the naval explorations of Spain, Portugal, the Netherlands, and Britain. In the fifteenth and later centuries they created a slave trade that brought thousands of blacks in chains to South and North America and the Caribbean Islands.

The first blacks in the colonies, who were brought by a Dutch ship to Jamestown in 1619, were not slaves, because no laws in Virginia covered such a condition. As servants, blacks experienced different fates. Some early blacks themselves became masters of slaves. The stigma of color remained, however, and it created a caste of slaves, as court cases and local laws in Northern and Southern colonies separated blacks from white indentured servants, who had bound themselves to masters for periods of four to seven years. However, the freeing of some blacks and the mixing of others with whites, produced "blacks" with every gradation of color. This permitted some of them to "pass" into white society over the generations.

Indians as Slaves. A lost chapter in the early history of slavery in the colonies was the attempt made throughout the New World to enslave Indians. They did not respond well to slave conditions except in their own tribal wars and family relations. By the end of the seventeenth century in the Spanish colonies, many of them had been wiped out by disease and hard work. In the North American colonies, they were succeeded by blacks and by a flood of toughened English, Scotch-Irish, and German servants, who themselves eventually became freeholders of land, especially on the frontier.

Slavery in the Eighteenth Century. Black slaves continued to have an uncertain future in the colonial labor system, and enslavement proceeded without a plan. A few humanitarian voices, especially among the Quakers, singled out slaves for special concern. The vigor of the free white labor force and the fact that free blacks promised to increase in numbers raised expectations that slave labor would disappear in time.

Slavery did not flourish in the North, although it seemed fairly well established in New York, as well as in Rhode Island, where a plantation type of slave farming became traditional. Otherwise, black slaves tended to be mainly household servants.

Slavery in the South. Virginia became the largest Southern slave colony and the foundation of Southern culture and economics. It produced an outstanding aristocracy that was highly educated and showed keen understanding. Such leaders as Thomas Jefferson and George Mason owned slaves. However, they studied history and searched for ways to increase free government. Virginians long remembered their efforts to end the foreign slave

Critical view of South Carolina slave sale, which is separating members of a family.

SLAVERY AND EMANCIPATION

ORIGINS AND INSTITUTIONS

TRIANGULAR TRADE
SLAVE REVOLTS, COLONIAL ——————————— GABRIEL'S SLAVE PLOT (1800)
PLANTATION SYSTEM   VESEY SLAVE UPRISING (1822)
COTTON GIN   NAT TURNER'S REVOLT (1831)
   ELI WHITNEY   VIRGINIA CONVENTION

CONTROVERSY

NORTHWEST ORDINANCE (1787)
MISSOURI COMPROMISE (1820)
   HENRY CLAY
COMPROMISE OF 1850
FUGITIVE SLAVE ACTS
   PRIGG V. PENNSYLVANIA (1842)
KANSAS-NEBRASKA ACT (1854)
   KANSAS AND FREEDOM
   STEPHEN A. DOUGLAS
   POPULAR SOVEREIGNTY
   LINCON-DOUGLAS DEBATES
DRED SCOTT DECISION (1857)
   ROGER B. TANEY

EMANCIPATION MOVEMENTS

Freedom
ABRAHAM LINCOLN
EMANCIPATION PROCLAMATION (1863)
AMENDMENTS, CONSTITUTIONAL
BLACKS IN THE UNITED STATES
   (see Subject Map)

ABOLITIONISM
   WILLIAM LLOYD GARRISON
   JOHN GREENLEAF WHITTIER
   JAMES G. BLAINE
   THEODORE DWIGHT WELD
   THEODORE PARKER
   JOHN BROWN
AMERICAN ANTI-SLAVERY SOCIETY
AMERICAN AND FOREIGN ANTI-SLAVERY
   SOCIETY
LIBERIA
FREDERICK DOUGLASS
UNDERGROUND RAILROAD
   HARRIET TUBMAN

POSTWAR CONDITIONS

The South
RECONSTRUCTION
FREEDMAN'S BUREAU
UNION LEAGUE CLUBS
BLACK CODES
KU KLUX KLAN
LYNCHING

The North
ANDREW JOHNSON
RADICAL REPUBLICANS
   CHARLES SUMNER
   THADDEUS STEVENS
LIBERAL REPUBLICANS
ULYSSES S. GRANT

Politics
LIBERTY PARTY
FREE-SOIL PARTY
   MARTIN VAN BUREN
REPUBLICAN PARTY
   JOHN C. FRÉMONT
DEMOCRATIC PARTY
   FRANKLIN PIERCE
   JAMES BUCHANAN
PRESIDENTIAL ELECTIONS
CIVIL WAR: CAUSES

Legislation
CIVIL RIGHTS ACTS (1866–1875)
RECONSTRUCTION ACTS (1867–1868)
OMNIBUS ACT (1868)
ENFORCEMENT ACTS (1870–1871)

> The Subject Maps in the Encyclopedia illustrate the coverage of particular aspects of American History, showing the interrelationships among the articles in twelve critical areas of study. Entries in capital letters, except for titles, are subjects for which there are separate articles in the Encyclopedia.
>
> The Subject Maps are arranged alphabetically in the Encyclopedia under the following titles:
>
> American Wars
> Blacks in the United States
> Business Regulation and Industrialization
> Civil War and Reconstruction
> Constitution of the United States
> Exploration and Colonization
> Frontier in American History
> Indians
> Labor Movement
> New Deal and Depression
> Revolutionary War Era
> Slavery and Emancipation

trade. They passed measures in their legislature that were disallowed by the British Board of Trade. The "Tidewater aristocrats"—those whose plantations lay along the Atlantic seaboard—were resented by their fellow Virginians in the hilly, western counties, where they were unable to use large numbers of slaves on their land, as in the plantation system of eastern Virginia. The inhabitants of what would later be West Virginia thus felt little commitment to slavery.

The American Revolution. Such facts, coupled with the rise of libertarian thought, combined to raise questions about the right and wrong of enslavement. Americans South and North were excited by expectations during the Revolution that slavery would crumble as a system. They foresaw a torrent of manumissions (voluntary freeings of slaves). The loyal services of many slaves during hostilities with the British did indeed increase the rate of emancipation.

Also inspiring was the fact that Northern states began processes of gradual emancipation, setting dates when slavery must end. In 1783 the Massachusetts Supreme Court ruled that under its new state constitution, which became law in 1780, slavery was outlawed. In 1787 the Jefferson-sponsored Northwest Ordinance stipulated that slavery was not to be permitted in what became the states of Ohio, Indiana, Illinois, Michigan, Wisconsin, and Minnesota.

Effect of the Cotton Gin. Thus, slavery seemed on the road to extinction in the new United States. In 1807, under constitutional provisions, the foreign slave trade was officially ended. (It continued, and even grew, as an outlawed occupation.) The fateful event was Eli Whitney's invention in 1793 of the cotton gin. This machine efficiently separated the cotton from its seeds and made cotton a sensationally profitable crop. Cotton became king of the Southern economy. Manumissions of slaves fell precipitously. Although there were relatively few large plantations, their success, combined with the low status of blacks (slave and free), permitted Southern intellectuals to refer to what they termed their "Peculiar Institution" in ways that suggested slavery was a permanent feature in their lives. Nevertheless, slavery was criticized on grounds of religion and humanity.

Slave Revolts. The battle over the entrance of Missouri into the Union as a slave state revealed in 1820 that North and South did not agree on the future of slavery. In addition, the peace of the white South was shattered by rumors of slave conspiracies and uprisings. As early as 1801, Gabriel's Plot in the Richmond area frightened Virginians. In 1822, South Carolinians were shaken by the Denmark Vesey Conspiracy, and as a result they passed rigid state laws suppressing slaves. They also defied

national laws against ill treatment of black visitors. Nat Turner's Revolt (1831) was a turning point. Although relatively small, it revealed the fears at the base of Virginia society. A crucial debate in the House of Delegates (1831–1832) on the proposition that slaves be freed or colonized elsewhere resulted in the complete victory of the proslavery forces.

Thereafter, slaveholders in Virginia gave up the old idea that slavery was a burden and a problem to be solved. Slavery was now in Virginia—and therefore throughout the Southern states—held to be a "Positive Good." In the Border States, slavery was less aggressively defended. Slaveholders were little threatened in their legal rights in Kentucky, Tennessee, Maryland, Delaware, and Missouri. However, their "Southern feeling" and loyalty to the institution of slavery—compared with their loyalty to the Union—remained a major encouragement to Southern secessionists.

Fugitive Slaves. The constitutional compromise of 1787 had permitted the return of fugitive slaves. It had granted apportionment in representation to Congress on the basis of a slave equaling three-fifths of a white person. (Slaves were in the category of "all other persons" in the Constitution.) The Constitution now became the basis for Southerners' demands that they be secure in their "property."

While free-soil and abolitionist sentiment now flourished in the North, suppression of black attitudes and ambitions was firmly pursued in the South. The most spirited slaves sought freedom. They were carried to safety by the Underground Railroad, a network of Northern antislavery workers and their sympathizers. Once fugitives were in the North, they created constitutional debates over how they were to be received. They helped abolitionize the North because otherwise law-abiding white citizens refused to help catch fugitives.

Frederick Douglass, an exslave and runaway, became a living argument against the idea that blacks were naturally inferior or were satisfied to be slaves. Douglass, lecturing openly in defiance of slave-catchers, helped persuade many Northerners that their own civil liberties, as well as his, were in danger.

The Compromise of 1850 completely politicized the slavery question by giving Northerners a choice of obeying its strict Fugitive Slave Law or breaking it. The compromise ended the slave trade in Washington, D.C., but it did not end slavery there. It angered Northerners who wished to keep slavery out of the government domain by permitting slavery to move to the Southwest.

End of Slavery. It now seemed to the sensitive North that slaveholders had turned the South into an armed camp. Southern leaders retorted that abolitionist agitation had forced them to end black education, meetings of slaves for religious services, and other tradi-

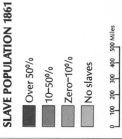

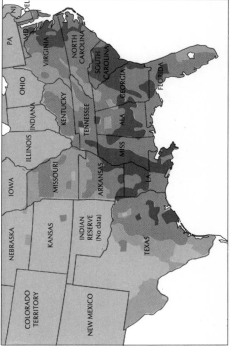

SLAVE POPULATION 1861

Over 50%
10–50%
Zero–10%
No slaves

0 100 200 300 400 500 Miles

UNITED STATES SLAVE TRADE. 1830.

Harsh conditions of slavery had led to organized abolitionist movement by 1830.

Slave family spanning several generations on Beaufort, S.C., plantation in Civil War.

tions. The opening of Kansas to settlement began a border war that separated Free-Soilers and proslavery groups still more. John Brown in Kansas became an extreme case of a Northerner determined to free the slaves by any means. The Dred Scott decision (1857) by the Supreme Court in effect made it clear that slavery had a legal right to exist anywhere in the Union. The North, outraged, rallied to defend its way of life.

The assault by John Brown and his men on Harpers Ferry, Va., in 1859 was based on his faith that slaves would join him in a guerrilla war on their masters. Slaves failed to support him in his effort. The determination of Virginia authorities to hang Brown, rather than treat him as insane, persuaded Northerners that the South was guilt-ridden and insecure. The Civil War failed to produce slave uprisings, but slaves increasingly gave aid to federal troops. President Abraham Lincoln's Emancipation Proclamation (Jan. 1, 1863) was a war measure and did not free slaves in great numbers. Slavery in the United States was outlawed by passage of the Thirteenth Amendment to the Constitution (Dec. 18, 1865).

Consult (IX) Elkins, 1968.

—Louis Filler, *Antioch College*

SLIDELL, JOHN (1793–1871), politician and diplomat who played an important role in the Mexican War and was a Confederate diplomat during the Civil War. *See* Slidell Mission; Trent Affair.

SLIDELL MISSION, attempt in 1845 to negotiate the American purchase of New Mexico and California and to settle the boundary dispute between Mexico and Texas.

John Slidell (1793–1871), a successful New Orleans attorney and member of Congress (1843–1845), was sent by President Polk to Mexico, but the Mexican government was not interested in Slidell's offer of $5 million for New Mexico and $25 million for California. The Mexicans would not officially receive Slidell after he arrived in Mexico City in December 1845, and even after the Senate confirmed Slidell's appointment in January 1846, the Mexicans would talk only about the Texas boundary issue. Slidell thought the Mexican position was based on their belief that the United States would soon be involved in a war with Britain over Oregon. He left Mexico in March 1846, and the Mexican War soon started.

Slidell later became an important Southern senator (1853–1861). During the Civil War he was sent by the Confederacy to gain diplomatic recognition and aid from Britain. He failed but is remembered for being captured by the Union in the *Trent* Affair.

See also Mexican War; Polk, James K.; Trent Affair.

SMIBERT, JOHN (1688–1751), Scottish-born colonial painter who worked mainly as a portraitist in Newport, R.I., and later in Boston. He came to America at 41, after having studied painting in Europe and having gained a minor reputation as a portraitist in London and Edinburgh.

During the years that Smibert lived in America, he painted some of the most notable people in New England. He completed about 200 portraits, many of which have been lost. A large group portrait of Bishop Berkeley—Smibert's patron—with his family and friends (including Smibert) and a painting of Sir William Pepperrell, done about 1745, are among Smibert's most ambitious pieces.

In addition to painting, Smibert operated a profitable business selling prints and reproductions of the great European masters. He also did some work in architecture and provided the designs for Faneuil Hall (1742) in Boston. Although his portraits are not considered distinguished, his work had considerable influence on other American painters, including Robert Feke and John Singleton Copley.

See also Copley, John Singleton; Feke, Robert; Painting.

SMITH, ADAM (1723–1790), Scotch economist and father of classical economics. His *Enquiry into the Nature and Causes of the Wealth of Nations* (1776) tried to explain the perennial problem of economic growth—why some nations are rich and others poor. In the course of this essay he explained the workings of economic systems and suggested what he regarded as optimum conditions for growth. Smith stood for free trade, although he was not totally inflexible on the principle; laissez-faire, or nonintervention by government in economic life; and free enterprise. He accepted the labor theory of value and said that division of labor (specialization and therefore growth) is limited by the extent of the market.

Smith detested mercantilism and close economic supervision by the state. However, he was in many ways a precursor of modern welfare economics and in a later era would probably not have opposed state intervention to prevent monopolies and to safeguard welfare. Yet his name is forever associated with the market economy—the central concept that the neutral workings of the forces of supply and demand in the free market are the best safeguards of economic growth and individual liberty. His theories were widely studied in the United States, and efforts were made to apply them to the American economy. However, they were modified by practical economic and political demands.

See also Free Enterprise; Free Trade; Mercantilism.

Consult (III) Heilbroner, 1967.

SMITH, ALFRED E(MANUEL) (1873–1944), Democratic presidential candidate. Born in New York City, he worked at a variety of jobs and entered politics at the ward level as a member of the Tammany Hall machine. In 1903 he was elected to the state assembly, where he established an outstanding record in labor and welfare legislation, civil rights, and political and administrative reform. In 1911 he served as vice-chairman of the Triangle Fire Commission and guided its recommendations through the assembly. In 1913 he was elected speaker and presided over the passage of progressive legislation.

Smith was elected governor of New York in 1918 and held the post for 8 of the next 10 years. Under his leadership, New York made tremendous strides in welfare and regulatory legislation as well as administrative reorganization. In 1924 Smith and William Gibbs McAdoo dueled for 100 ballots over the Democratic presidential nomination before a compromise candidate, John W. Davis, was chosen. The convention was torn by disagreements over Prohibition, immigration restriction, and the Ku Klux Klan. In 1928 Smith received the nomination but lost to Herbert Hoover in an election that saw the Republicans crack even the Solid South because of opposition to Smith's Catholicism, his big-city origins, and his stand against Prohibition. These same qualities, however, brought millions from the urban minorities into the Democratic Party, thus paving the way for the electoral victories of Franklin D. Roosevelt. Denied renomination in 1932, Smith became bitter and alienated from the New Deal.

Consult (VI) Handlin, 1958; O'Connor, 1970.

SMITH, JOHN (1580–1631), English explorer who had a central role in the settlement of Jamestown, Va. After an adventuresome youth as a soldier of fortune in Europe, Smith returned to England in 1604. He became interested in the Virginia venture, and when a charter was approved in 1606 he was named one of the colony's seven councillors. On Dec. 19, 1606, Smith sailed for Virginia. He was criticized for his conduct on the voyage, but efforts to unseat him as a councillor were ultimately unsuccessful.

After the colonists landed at Jamestown in May 1607, Smith made exploratory trips in search of supplies. On the second journey, he was captured and eventually carried to the main town of Powhatan, the leader of a powerful Indian confederation. There, after many religious ceremonies and discussions, Smith faced what he considered certain death, although it may have been only an initiation rite. However, Powhatan's favorite daughter, Pocahontas, intervened and saved Smith, who was adopted by Powhatan as his son. He returned to Jamestown, where, because two men in the original party had been killed, he was convicted of murder. Smith was saved through the intervention of another councillor and took his seat on the council. When other councillors died in the winter of 1609, Smith became the sole administrator of the colony. During this time, he issued his famous proclamation: "He that will not worke shall not eat, except by sickness he be disabled." Through Smith's activity and example, the colony survived the winter.

A new supply ship arrived in May 1609 with a new charter and additional colonists, which eroded the absolute power of Smith. Seriously burned by a gunpowder explosion, he returned to England in October 1609. There in 1612 Smith published his second book on Virginia; the first had appeared in 1608.

Following a voyage to New England in 1614, Smith published a very accurate map of the region in his *Description of New England.* Although Smith made other trips to the New World, his role was unimportant. A practical administrator with a sincere interest in the Indians of the New World, Smith did not receive the respect he desired during his lifetime.

See also Exploration and Discovery; Jamestown Settlement; Virginia.

Consult (I) Barbour, 1964; Smith, 1953.

SMITH, JOSEPH (1805–1844), founder of the Mormon religion. *See* Mormons.

SMITH, MARGARET CHASE (1897–   ), Republican Senator from Maine from 1948 to 1973. Born in Maine a barber's daughter, she graduated from high school in 1916 and worked as a teacher, telephone operator, and office manager. In 1930 she became a member of Maine's Republican State Committee and married Clyde H. Smith, for whom she worked as secretary when he became a congressman in 1936. In 1940, when her husband died, she became congresswoman, serving until 1948, when she was elected to the Senate.

A moderate Republican, Smith became known in the Senate for never missing a roll call vote, for not announcing her position until she voted, and for her political independence, which won her the title "Conscience of the Senate." In 1950 she was the first senator to denounce the tactics of Senator Joseph R. McCarthy. In later years she ignored Republican Party policy and opposed new missile systems and the Haynsworth and Carswell nominations to the Supreme Court. Smith served as a member of the Senate's GOP Policy Committee, chairman of the GOP Senate Conference, and a ranking member of the Armed Services and Appropriations Committee. For a decade she was the only woman in the Senate.

Consult (VIII) Smith, 1972.

Alfred E. Smith, a "wet" (opposed to Prohibition), represented urban interests among Democrats and was opposed by agrarian sector of party, led by William Jennings Bryan.

John Smith, guiding force during early years of Jamestown Settlement.

SMITH-CONNALLY ANTISTRIKE ACT (1943), also called the War Labor Disputes Act, legislation passed to prevent disruption of industry during World War II. Passage of the bill was precipitated by the United Mine Workers' May 1943 strike, in which the government seized the coal mines.

Sponsored by Senator Tom Connally and Representative Howard W. Smith, the bill was bitterly opposed by labor unions and was passed over President Roosevelt's veto. Under the act the government could seize control of a struck plant or mine if the strike impeded the war effort and operate it until productive efficiency was restored for 60 days. Strike action while the government was in control was illegal; the War Labor Board was to settle disputes; and 30 days' notice had to be given before a strike. The antistrike act was to be in force only during wartime, and it automatically expired in 1947. Under the law, both Presidents Roosevelt and Truman acted several times, including the seizure of the coal mines in 1946.

SMITH-HUGHES ACT (1917), first legislation to provide federal aid to schools below the college level. *See* Education.

SMOOT-HAWLEY TARIFF (1931), the highest tariff in American history. Signed by President Herbert Hoover on June 17, 1931, it placed an average duty rate of 41 percent on imports and included Canadian goods. In addition, the Smoot-Hawley tariff gave the President the power to make tariff changes on the recommendation of the tariff commission.

The bill originally was intended to give more protection to U.S. agricultural products, but manufacturing interests also succeeded in gaining increased protection. The tariff's results were disastrous. Canada took retaliatory action, and U.S. exports to Canada decreased sharply, thus deepening the Depression. Other nations also enacted tariff reprisals, and world trade was stifled because European nations could not afford the exorbitant U.S. tariffs, and they were unable to earn U.S. dollars to make payments on World War I debts.

See also Tariffs.

SNCC. *See* Student Nonviolent Coordinating Committee.

SOCIAL DARWINISM, the application to human society of the biological theories of evolution and natural selection advanced by Charles Darwin. English philosopher Herbert Spencer used Darwin's scientific hypothesis to buttress the theory of "social selection," which he had applied to England's industrial society. The world was a jungle in which the strong and the most fit inevitably triumphed; it now seemed that science and sociology agreed. This philosophy suited the materialistic age of the late

nineteenth and early twentieth centuries, for it justified the power of industrial leaders as the end product of a natural process; individuals whom God or Nature had endowed with exceptional talents would win the competition for wealth.

Social Darwinists believed that a society of "perfection and the most complete happiness" would result from rugged individualism. Darwinists defended monopoly, abhorred government regulation, accepted slums and low wages as inevitable, and held wealth a sign of innate superiority. Critics charged that social Darwinism represented only a sophisticated defense of greed, but the theory remained a cardinal tenet of the business credo.

SOCIAL SECURITY ACT (1935), New Deal legislation that was the product of a careful study by a cabinet-level Committee on Economic Security. It was a limited and hesitant program covering only a minority of the working population, but President Roosevelt and its other sponsors, recognizing its inadequacies, expected it to be expanded and improved over the years. And since 1939, when the first major changes were made, the law has been progressively liberalized.

As a welfare-state measure, the first social security law was modest indeed. It provided unemployment compensation through an extremely complex but workable tax relationship with the states and retirement insurance for workers in jobs outside agriculture, domestic service, the merchant marine, governments, and charitable and educational institutions. There were other provisions for financial assistance to the indigent aged, the handicapped, widows, and dependent children. In a spectacular defense of the federal taxing power, the Supreme Court upheld social security in *Steward Machine Co. v. Davis* (1937) shortly after FDR's Court-packing attempt.

Consult (VI) Witte, 1962.

SOCIETY OF JESUS. *See* Jesuits.

SOD-HOUSE FRONTIER. *See* Frontier in American History.

SOLDIERS BONUS ACT (1924), also known as the Adjusted Compensation Act, in effect a "soldiers' bonus" to make up in part to World War I veterans what they had sacrificed by not being at home enjoying war profits (about which many had heard rumors at the front). The act was first passed in 1922, but President Harding vetoed it. In 1924 the act was passed over President Coolidge's veto. It provided a 20-year endowment life insurance policy that could be cashed in for each veteran in an amount proportional to his time of service.

During the depths of the Great Depression of the 1930s pressure mounted to have the government pay the entire amount out at once, and so a second bonus crisis troubled both the Hoover and Roosevelt administrations. The act was politically popular, but it went counter to the efforts of all presidents in the 1920s and 1930s to limit federal expenditures and taxes. The repeated passage of the original act was a symptom of how much trouble Harding and Coolidge had with Congress in the early 1920s.

SOLID SOUTH, term used to describe the Democratic bloc voting of the Southern states in local, state, and federal elections. Southern allegiance to the Democratic Party dates from the influence of Thomas Jefferson of Virginia, who founded the forerunner of the present party. After the Civil War the Radical Republican Reconstruction program alienated the South, which voted Democratic until the candidacy of Dwight D. Eisenhower in 1952, when Republicans began to make significant inroads even into the deepest Southern states. The demise of the Solid South has become more apparent with each succeeding election.

See also Democratic Party.

SOMME OFFENSIVE (AUGUST 8, 1918), first stage in the Allied offensive that ended World War I. *See* World War I Battles.

SONS OF LIBERTY, one of the patriot organizations formed to oppose the Stamp Act (1765). Borrowing a phrase used in Parliament to describe the colonists in a denunciation of the proposed Stamp Act, the members called themselves "Sons of Liberty." The societies appeared primarily in the colonial port cities, where the act was to have its greatest effect, and attracted men who followed almost exclusively urban occupations. Often influential citizens who had previously associated with one another in social, civil, and religious clubs provided the leadership of the groups. The Sons of Liberty actively sought to broaden the base of opposition and encouraged ordinary citizens to show their hostility to the Stamp Act. They resorted to intimidation to force Stamp Act distributors to resign and on some occasions were behind violent demonstrations.

SOULE, PIERRE (1802-1870), U.S. diplomat. *See* Ostend Manifesto.

SOUL ON ICE (1968), examination of the problems confronting blacks in America. *See* Cleaver, Eldridge.

SOUTH CAROLINA, colony and state that, like North Carolina, was largely a product of native American expansion. Few settlers went there from England, although the colony did attract foreigners. However, whereas North Carolina

was poor and radical, South Carolina, because of black slavery, rice culture (introduced in 1693), and indigo, became a colony of wealthy aristocrats. It was dominated by the city of Charleston, a cosmopolitan center.

The first settlers sent out by the Carolina proprietors reached the Charleston area in April 1670. English Protestants were joined by French Protestants escaping the persecution of Louis XIV and later by people from Barbados, as well as Scots and Germans. Its population grew faster than North Carolina's: in 1721 there were about 9,000 whites and 12,000 black slaves; by 1775, 70,000 whites and 100,000 blacks.

South Carolina was controlled by the proprietors until 1719, but they were strongly disliked, and the colonists constantly disputed with them over the questions of land policy, adequate defense against the Indian raiders and the Spanish, and local rights. The Crown encouraged the colonists, and in 1719, after a major disagreement, South Carolina was made a royal colony. Under royal control and with royal aid, the economy grew—exporting hides, rice, and indigo. Despite their deep sectional divisions (back-country farmers opposed rich Tidewater planters, as in North Carolina), the colonists were united against England. They wrote their own state constitution in 1776 and ratified the U.S. Constitution on May 23, 1788.

The state legislature is bicameral; the capital is Columbia. The population in 1970 was 2,590,516.

See also North Carolina.

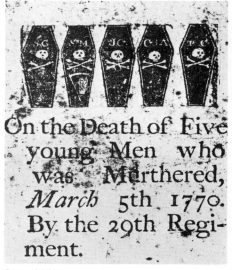

Sons of Liberty reacted angrily to Boston Massacre.

SOUTH DAKOTA, the 40th state, was admitted to the Union simultaneously with North Dakota on Nov. 2, 1889. The United States acquired the South Dakota area in the Louisiana Purchase (1803), but permanent settlement of the area did not begin until 1858, when a peace agreement was signed with the Sioux Indians. The area gained territorial status in 1861, and the discovery of gold further increased the population.

The state legislature is bicameral; Pierre is the capital. The population in 1970 was 665,507.

SOUTHEAST ASIA TREATY ORGANIZATION (SEATO). Formed in 1955 on the initiative of U.S. Secretary of State John Foster Dulles, SEATO was designed to fill the vacuum caused by the evacuation of Indochina by the French in 1954. SEATO's members are Australia, Britain, France, New Zealand, Pakistan, the Philippines, Thailand, and the United States. SEATO provided the means for the United States to extend its power to Southeast Asia in order to contain the Communist bloc. By a protocol attached to the treaty, SEATO extended its protection to Laos, Cambodia, and South Vietnam.

Nursemaid John Foster Dulles tries to put Asian nations in SEATO carriage as Communist China's Chou en-Lai attempts to lure them away.

Although there have been no joint military undertakings, the council has passed resolutions of support for the South Vietnamese government, and individual states in SEATO have provided military assistance to Saigon. The military infrastructure that SEATO developed was primarily designed to counter a conventional invasion from Communist China. By 1971, with the American policy of withdrawal from Vietnam established and with many Southeast Asian states signing a pact pledging "independence and neutrality," SEATO redefined its primary goal to provide each member with an individual counterinsurgency capability.

See also Vietnam War.
Consult (VIII) Fifield, 1968.

SOUTHERN ALLIANCE, the variant of the Farmers' Alliance movement that existed in the Southern United States. For whites only, it was the outgrowth of a Texas group incorporated in 1880 that began to expand into other Southern states in 1887.

See also Farmers' Alliances; Populists.

SOUTHERN CHRISTIAN LEADERSHIP CONFERENCE (SCLC), civil rights organization. *See* Civil Rights Movement; King, Martin Luther, Jr.

SOUTHWEST TERRITORY. *See* Territories and Possessions.

SOVEREIGNTY, POPULAR. *See* Popular Sovereignty.

SPACE EXPLORATION. The United States did not develop rockets large enough to send objects into space until the midtwentieth century. Robert L. Goddard, the American pioneer in practical rocketry, had suggested the possibility of moon flights as early as 1919, but Germany led in the large-rocket field through World War II.

In the immediate postwar years, American rocket research was devoted mainly to short-range missiles, aircraft, and sounding rockets, but interest in space exploration was spurred by the arrival of Wernher von Braun and members of his team of rocket scientists from Germany. By the early 1950s his workers had developed the Army's Redstone rocket, the basis of some of the first launch vehicles. They had also proposed a satellite program, but it was the Navy's Vanguard that gained official support for a launch attempt during the 1957–1958 International Geophysical Year.

Before the launch took place, however, the Soviet Union surprised the world by orbiting Sputnik 1 on Oct. 4, 1957. American public opinion was aroused over a supposedly serious technology lag, although the Army's Jupiter rocket soon launched a small satellite, Explorer 1. On Oct. 1, 1958, the government centralized its nonmilitary space efforts by creating the National Aeronautics and Space Administration (NASA). The growth of NASA's facilities in its first decade reflected the technological orientation of the times as the well-budgeted agency advanced a host of scientific and technological programs. The most ambitious program was announced by President Kennedy in 1961, when he proposed that men be landed on the moon by the end of the decade—a goal attained on July 20, 1969, when Neil Armstrong and Edwin Aldrin of Apollo 11 set foot on the lunar surface.

In the meantime American and Soviet probes were sent to neighboring planets, complex scientific observatories were orbited, and meteorological and communications satellites were proving their worth. Numerous military satellites also were sent into space. Before the final Apollo mission in 1972, however, public enthusiasm for space exploration had begun to ebb, a change in mood aggravated by the national turbulence of the late 1960s. Objections were raised in particular to the costliness of manned space flights. As the flow of funds into NASA diminished, the American space program appeared to be settling into a pattern of limited manned orbital ventures, occasional research satellites and probes, and the launching of applied technology spacecraft on a fairly regular basis.

The following selective list mentions some of the most scientifically important or historically significant of the hundreds of space flights.

Significant Space Flights

Oct. 4, 1957. The space age began when the Soviet Union launched Sputnik 1, an earth satellite weighing 184 pounds. The achievement drew worldwide attention to space flight.

Nov. 3, 1957. Sputnik 2 and its passenger, a dog named Laika, increased U.S. public concern over its apparent lag in space efforts.

Jan. 31, 1958. Explorer 1, an 18-pound satellite hurriedly launched by the U.S. Army on a modified Jupiter, discovered what became known as the Van Allen radiation belt.

March 17, 1958. The U.S. Navy's space program finally got under way with the launch of Vanguard 1, an 8-pound geodetic satellite.

Oct. 11, 1958. Pioneer 1, the first successful launch by the newly formed NASA, failed to reach the moon as intended.

August 7, 1959. Explorer 6 investigated the space environment and returned the first TV picture of Earth's cloud cover.

Sept. 12, 1959. The USSR's Luna 2 was launched and two days later became the first man-made object to crash into the surface of the moon.

Oct. 4, 1959. Luna 3 was sent on a trajectory behind the moon and sent back the first photographs of the side facing away from Earth.

Apollo 11 astronaut Edwin E. Aldrin stands on the moon during the first expedition to the lunar surface.

April 1, 1960. Tiros 1 became the first of many U.S. meteorological satellites to provide information for weather study and prediction.

August 10, 1960. A capsule ejected by U.S. Discoverer 12 in orbit was the first object to be recovered successfully back on Earth.

August 19, 1960. Sputnik 5 was launched with two dogs, Belka and Strelka, that returned alive to Earth on the following day.

April 12, 1961. Soviet pilot Yuri A. Gagarin, in Vostok 1, became the first man to orbit the earth. After one orbit the capsule landed safely inside the Soviet Union.

May 5, 1961. Alan B. Shepard, Jr., the first American to be launched in a rocket, made a 15-minute suborbital flight from Cape Canaveral aboard "Freedom 7," a Mercury capsule.

August 6, 1961. Gherman G. Titov achieved 17 orbits of the earth in Vostok 2, a Soviet craft weighing approximately 10,400 pounds.

Nov. 29, 1961. For the first time the United States orbited and recovered an animal, the chimpanzee Enos, launched in Mercury-Atlas 5.

Feb. 20, 1962. John H. Glenn, Jr., carried out the first U.S. manned orbital flight, making 3 orbits in his "Friendship 7" Mercury.

March 7, 1962. OSO 1 was launched, the first in a highly successful series of U.S. Orbiting Solar Observatories for studying the sun.

July 10, 1962. U.S. Telstar 1, the first commercially financed communications satellite, relayed messages across the Atlantic Ocean.

August 26, 1962. The United States launched a Venus probe, Mariner 2. Mariner passed within 22,000 miles of the planet on December 14 and relayed back temperature data.

June 16, 1963. Valentina V. Tereshkova, in the USSR's sixth and last Vostok, became the first woman to enter space.

July 26, 1963. U.S. communications satellite Syncom 2 was placed in an orbit 22,300 miles high, synchronous with the earth's rate of revolution—the first such comsat orbit.

July 28, 1964. The United States launched its first successful Ranger probe toward the moon. It transmitted more than 4,000 photographs before crashing into the moon on July 31.

Sept. 4, 1964. OGO 1, the first U.S. Orbiting Geophysical Observatory, was sent into space to study the earth and its environment.

Oct. 12, 1964. The first three-man spacecraft, Voskhod 1, was launched by the USSR. The crew made a day-long flight of 16 orbits.

Nov. 28, 1964. U.S. Mariner was sent toward Mars. Passing close to the planet on July 15, 1965, it transmitted photographs revealing that Mars has a cratered surface.

March 18, 1965. Voskhod 2 was launched, and cosmonaut Aleksei A. Leonov became the first man to "walk" in space.

March 23, 1965. Gemini 3, piloted by Virgil Grissom and John W. Young, made the first in a series of 10 flights by the two-man Gemini craft in preparation for Apollo missions.

June 3, 1965. Gemini 4 was launched, and astronaut Edward H. White II became the first American to perform a spacewalk.

Nov. 26, 1965. With the launch of A 1, France became the first nation to orbit a satellite without either Soviet or American vehicles.

Dec. 15, 1965. Gemini 6 carried out the first close rendezvous with another spacecraft by moving to within 1 foot of Gemini 7.

Jan. 31, 1966. The USSR's Luna 9 was launched toward the moon and in 79 hours made the first soft landing there. It transmitted pictures of the surface for three days.

March 31, 1966. Luna 10 was launched and became the first craft to establish a lunar orbit.

May 30, 1966. Surveyor 1 was sent toward the moon. On June 2 it soft-landed and transmitted thousands of photographs, the first of several successful Surveyor missions.

August 10, 1966. The United States launched the first of its Lunar Orbiters, which photographed landing sites for future Apollo missions.

April 23, 1967. Cosmonaut Vladimir Komarov flew the first Soyuz craft but was killed the following day during reentry.

June 12, 1967. The USSR's Venera 4 was sent toward Venus. On October 18 the craft ejected a capsule that transmitted data as it descended through the planet's atmosphere.

Oct. 30, 1967. Soviet Cosmos 188 was launched as target vehicle for Cosmos 186 in the first automatic rendezvous and docking.

July 4, 1968. Explorer 38, the first in a series of radio astronomy satellites, was launched to monitor radio waves from space.

Oct. 11, 1968. The three-man Apollo spacecraft was test-flown in Earth orbit.

Dec. 21, 1968. Intelsat 3 F-2, of International Telecommunications Satellite Consortium, became the first global commercial satellite.

Dec. 21, 1968. Frank Borman, James A. Lovell, Jr., and William A. Anders were launched toward the moon in Apollo 8. They flew 10 lunar orbits and returned on December 27.

Feb. 24 and March 27, 1968. Mariners 6 and 7 were sent toward Mars. They returned pictures on July 31 and August 5, respectively.

July 16, 1969. Neil A. Armstrong, Edwin E. Aldrin, Jr., nd Michael Collins were launched in Apollo 11. On July 20, Armstrong and Aldrin became the first men to land and walk on he moon.

Nov. 14, 1969. Apollo 12 carried Charles Conrad, Jr., Alan L. Bean, and Richard F. Gordon, Jr., to the moon. On November 19–20, Conrad and Bean explored the lunar surface.

Feb. 11, 1970. Japan launched a 50-pound satellite, Rising Sun 1, on its own booster.

April 24, 1970. Communist China launched its first satellite, which weighed 381 pounds.

Astronaut tests new tools under simulated space conditions in preparation for Skylab mission.

Mysterious explosion of U.S. battleship *Maine* in Havana harbor on Feb. 15, 1898, triggered Spanish-American War.

Rough Riders storm San Juan Hill on July 1, 1898.

August 17, 1970. USSR probe Venera 7 traveled toward Venus. On December 15 it returned data from the planet's surface for the first time.

Sept. 12, 1970. Luna 16 entered a moon trajectory. It landed on September 20, collected samples, drilled into the moon, and returned a capsule with the samples on September 24.

Jan. 31, 1971. Alan B. Shepard, Jr., Edgar D. Mitchell, and Stuart A. Roosa were orbited in Apollo 14. Shepard and Mitchell spent more than 200 hours on the surface of the moon.

May 19 and May 28, 1971. Soviet Mars 2 and Mars 3 were launched, photographed the surface, and sent two capsules down to the planet.

June 6, 1971. Soyuz 11 was launched with Georgi Dobrovolsky, Vladislav Volkov, and Viktor Patsayev aboard. Crew docked with orbiting Salyut laboratory and spent almost 24 days there, but the men were killed during reentry.

July 26, 1971. Apollo 15 took David R. Scott, James B. Irwin, and Alfred M. Worden toward the moon. Scott and Irwin used a Lunar Rover vehicle to travel over the moon's surface.

April 16, 1972. Apollo 16 was launched with John W. Young, Charles M. Duke, Jr., and Thomas K. Mattingly II aboard. Young and Duke traveled nearly 17 miles on the moon in their Rover.

July 23, 1972. ERTS-1, the first in a series of U.S. Earth Resources Technology Satellites, was orbited to provide data for the better management of the earth's resources.

August 21, 1972. Copernicus, last and most complex of the series of U.S. Orbiting Astronomical Observatories, carried a 32-inch telescope and other instruments into space.

Dec. 7, 1972. Apollo 17 took Eugene A. Cernan, Harrison H. Schmitt, and Ronald E. Evans toward the moon, where Cernan and Schmitt spent more than 22 hours in lunar surface excursions. The flight, last of the Apollo missions, marked the end of an era in space.

May–June 1973. Skylab 1, unmanned orbiting laboratory, was launched May 14. Initial difficulties were overcome, and astronauts Charles Conrad, Joseph Kerwin, and Paul Weitz flew spaceship to Skylab and successfully carried out a 28-day scientific mission.

Consult (VIII) Von Braun and Ordway, 1969.

SPANISH-AMERICAN WAR (1898), a short, decisive encounter between the oldest European empire in the New World and the United States. Many Americans had been interested in the future of Cuba in particular, beginning soon after the American Revolution—an interest made explicit in the Ostend Manifesto (1854). The Southern slaveholding states coveted Cuba as a possible counterbalance to the growing power of the free-soil North, and as long as slavery existed in the United States, the nation could not be united in hoping to acquire the island.

Background. By 1868 Cuban discontent with Spanish rule broke into rebellion, and for 10 years a revolution was waged throughout the island. At the end of the war, Spanish promises of reform were not kept, and sporadic fighting broke out thereafter. In 1895 rebellion erupted again, and to combat Cuban guerrillas the Spanish authorities herded large groups of people from the countryside into urban *reconcentrado,* or concentration, camps, where lack of food and shelter and a high disease rate led to many deaths. Many Americans felt sympathy for the rebels; others saw the strategic value to the United States of an island athwart the two main passages to the Caribbean; still others were disturbed by the loss to American investments caused by the recurrent fighting in Cuba. When the jingoistic yellow press led by William Randolph Hearst and Joseph Pulitzer clamored for war, Americans were prepared to put the worst possible interpretation upon the sudden destruction of the American battleship *Maine* in Havana's harbor. Earlier, Hearst had released an intercepted letter from the Spanish minister to Washington, Depuy de Lôme, to an aristocratic Cuban friend that showed contempt for President William McKinley.

When McKinley suggested to the Spanish that they observe an armistice in Cuba, he received no reply, and he decided on war with Spain. The day before he addressed Congress on the Cuban crisis, McKinley learned that the Queen of Spain had personally ordered hostilities suspended; nonetheless, he asked Congress to grant him authority to intervene in Cuba. Congress resolved that Spain must abandon the island, authorized potential intervention, and pledged to withdraw American troops once independence was achieved. On April 22 Congress called for the enlistment of a volunteer army, and two days later Spain declared war upon the United States. On April 25, Congress declared that a state of war had existed since April 21.

The War. The war was one sided, dramatic, and destructive. On May 1 an American squadron under George Dewey swept into Manila harbor in the Philippines and destroyed the Spanish vessels there. On May 19 the Spanish fleet off Cuba sought refuge in the harbor of Santiago de Cuba, where it was blockaded by Commodore W. S. Schley and Rear Admiral W. T. Sampson. The Spanish fleet attempted to escape from the harbor on July 3 and was totally destroyed.

In the meantime, American troops under W. S. Shafter had landed on Cuba, and after heavy encounters with the Spanish at Siboney, El Caney, and San Juan Hill—where the Rough Riders under Theodore Roosevelt, the assistant secretary of the Navy who had ordered Dewey to sail toward the Philippines, won popular affection and fame—took possession of the island. An armistice was signed on August 12, while Puerto Rico was still under attack from troops led by Gen. Nelson A. Miles.

Results. Peace was concluded through the Treaty of Paris, signed on Dec. 10, 1898, and ratified by the U.S. Senate on Feb. 6, 1899, after much heated debate over imperialist and anti-imperialist positions. Cuba became independent but subject to American intervention through the Platt Amendment (1901). As indemnity the United States received Puerto Rico and Guam. In exchange for a payment of $20 million the Philippines also were ceded to the United States. With these acquisitions, the United States became a colonial power, found itself drawn ever more deeply into Far Eastern affairs, was placed in a position of clear hegemony in the New World, and was itself divided by domestic debate over the retention of its colonies and the purposes of empire.

Consult (V) Friedel, 1957; Millis, 1931.
—Robin W. Winks, *Yale University*

SPANISH COLONIES, NORTH AMERICAN. The Spanish began to establish colonies in the Caribbean, Central and South America, and parts of North America in the sixteenth century. In Central and South America they confronted ancient Indian civilizations and millions of natives: the Aztecs, Chibchas, and Incas. In the Caribbean they met fewer Indians and, through disease and forced labor, totally wiped them out and had to replace their labor with imported African slaves. In North America the Spanish mainly explored the Southwest and Florida, although they did push up the Pacific coast to the Northwest.

New Spain, the viceroyalty of the Spanish crown in North America, was created in 1535 with Mexico City as its center. For almost 300 years Spanish laws and customs ruled over a vast area that included Florida, the Gulf Coast, the Southwest, and southern California. Starting in 1769, Spanish missions, Franciscan seminaries, and *presidios* (seats of government) spread into California from San Diego north to San Francisco (established in 1776). Spanish control declined after the Mexican war of independence from Spain (1822). In the 1840s the U.S. annexation of Texas and the Mexican War (1846–1848) transferred Mexico's North American possessions to the United States. The Spanish colonization of North America never approached the cultural and economic significance of the Spanish colonial civilizations that were established in Central and South America.

See also Cortés, Hernán de; Exploration and Discovery; Indians, South American; Mexican War; Pizarro, Francisco.
Consult (I) Gibson, 1966.

SPANISH SUCCESSION, WAR OF THE. *See* Queen Anne's War (1702–1713).

SPECIAL INTEREST GROUP. *See* Lobby.

SPECIE CIRCULAR (1836), effort by President Jackson to check inflation and land speculation by requiring that certain land payments be made in hard currency. *See* Panics, Financial (Nineteenth Century).

SPOILS SYSTEM, practice by which political party loyalists are rewarded for their support with government offices. When Andrew Jackson became president in 1829, many appointed federal officeholders had held their posts for nearly a generation. To Jackson, such entrenched officeholders violated the principles of democracy. Although clothed in democratic rhetoric, Jackson's policy served partisan political purposes: his appointees were loyal Democrats. As the Jacksonian senator William Marcy of New York proclaimed in 1831, "To the victor belongs the spoils."

Jackson's celebration of the spoils system firmly established it in national politics, but he was not the first to use it, and he did not abuse it, as critics have charged. Jefferson was the first president to use patronage for party purposes, and by 1829 this was established political practice in several states, including New York and Pennsylvania. During his Administrations (1829–1837), Jackson removed no more than 20 percent of the officeholders.

Consult (III) Aronson, 1964.

SQUARE DEAL, Theodore Roosevelt's platform for reelection in 1904. The term arose from his promise to give both labor and capital a "square deal" during the anthracite coal strike and was later expanded to include farmers, ethnic minorities, and other socioeconomic groups. It was not so much a systematic program of specific reforms as it was a promise to play fair with all groups, although Roosevelt later talked of such measures as business regulation, income and inheritance taxes, tariff revisions, and aid to farmers and laborers in connection with it. He briefly revived the term in his 1912 campaign but eventually replaced it with New Nationalism.

STALIN, JOSEPH (1879–1953), Soviet dictator. The man who during his underground days took the name of Stalin (man of steel) was born Iosif Dzhugashvili in the Caucasus region of Georgia. He was educated for the priesthood but left it for the revolutionary movement. Stalin first met Lenin in 1905 at a Communist Party conference. Loyal to Lenin, he became a power in the party, and after Lenin's death in 1924, Stalin gradually consolidated his position, emerging as Russia's undisputed leader in 1929.

Admiral Dewey oversees Battle of Manila Bay from platform. The battle destroyed Spain's naval effectiveness in the Pacific.

**SPANISH-AMERICAN WAR (1898) —
Item Guide**

The article on SPANISH-AMERICAN WAR (1898) has several related entries. OSTEND MANIFESTO (1854) indicates early U.S. interest in Cuba.

Public opinion was swayed by journalists WILLIAM RANDOLPH HEARST and JOSEPH PULITZER, and helped to influence President WILLIAM McKINLEY's decision to go to war. American victory was swift, as GEORGE DEWEY took the Philippines, and Cuba was overrun. THEODORE ROOSEVELT's war service furthered his political career. The United States received PUERTO RICO after the war and, despite the TELLER RESOLUTION (1898), supporting Cuban independence, gave itself the right to intervene in Cuba through the PLATT AMENDMENT (1901).

Joseph Stalin *(left)* with President Roosevelt and Prime Minister Churchill at Teheran Conference in 1943.

He transformed Russia into a great industrial state using an authoritarian bureaucratic governmental system and institutionalized terror. Forced collectivization and industrialization led to serious resistance to Stalin's policies within the party, but Stalin directed a purge of a vast number of political and military figures in the late 1930s.

The threat from Nazi Germany caused him to seek popular front alliances with the West. In August 1939 he came to terms with Hitler in a nonaggression treaty that was an effort to buy peace. This did not prevent a German attack in June 1941, and Stalin took personal command of the war effort. During the war there were Big Three conferences at Tehran, Potsdam, and Yalta. Churchill was apprehensive of Stalin's intentions, while Roosevelt believed that the Soviet leader could be handled by face-to-face negotiations. After the defeat of the Axis, Stalin directed the establishment of Communist governments throughout Eastern Europe. He died on the eve of another purge of alleged state enemies.

See also Potsdam Conference; Tehran Conference; Yalta Conference.

Consult (VIII) Deutscher, 1967; McNeal, 1963.

—Martin Gruberg, *University of Wisconsin, Oshkosh*

STALINGRAD, Russian city entered by the Germans in September 1942 and retaken by the Russians in February 1943. *See* World War II.

STALWARTS AND HALF-BREEDS, competing factions within the Republican Party. The main issue between the Stalwarts, led by Roscoe Conkling, and the Half-Breeds, under James G. Blaine, concerned the proper division of federal patronage.

When President Hayes attacked Conkling's control of the New York Customs House, he fostered a Stalwart attempt to renominate Ulysses S. Grant for president in 1880. However, that election became a Half-Breed triumph when James Garfield was elected and then named Blaine his secretary of state. Most Stalwarts were appeased by the choice of Chester Arthur as vice-president and a promise of fair patronage. When Garfield reneged on the alleged agreement, Conkling resigned from the Senate, a gesture that miscarried when he was not reappointed. Conkling's enforced retirement and the assassination of Garfield by a Stalwart aroused public opinion against both groups, and the terms soon fell from common usage.

See also Arthur, Chester A., Blaine, James G.; Conkling, Roscoe.

STAMP ACT (1765), British taxation measure that created an uproar among American colonists. Parliament, hoping to have the colonies

Leland Stanford, railroad magnate, Governor of California, and U.S. Senator.

help pay for maintaining British armies in America, imposed a stamp tax on the colonies in March 1765. Colonials were required to affix revenue stamps to almost all documents, and violators could be prosecuted in juryless vice-admiralty courts.

Americans denounced the Stamp Act as an internal tax unconstitutionally levied without their consent. Adopting Patrick Henry's resolutions, the Virginia House of Burgesses claimed that only their elected representatives could tax the colonies. Delegates from nine colonies met in New York City in October 1765 and issued a Declaration of Rights and Grievances that reiterated Virginia's position and agreed that Americans were not and could not be represented in Parliament. After this Stamp Act Congress, colonial merchants agreed not to import from England, and when the tax became effective in November 1765, Americans either ceased business or conducted their affairs without using stamps. Groups such as the Sons of Liberty sometimes intimidated those who used the stamps. Confronted with American recalcitrance and recognizing the hardships being suffered by English merchants due to the boycott, Parliament repealed the Stamp Act in 1766.

See also Sons of Liberty.
Consult (II) Morgan, 1953.

STAMP ACT CONGRESS. *See* Stamp Act (1765).

STANDARD OIL TRUST. *See* Rockefeller, John D.; Trusts.

STANDISH, MILES (1584–1656), military leader who accompanied the Pilgrims. *See* Pilgrims.

STANFORD, LELAND (1824–1893), railroad builder, governor of California, and U.S. senator. He began his law practice in Wisconsin in 1846, joined his brothers' mercantile business in California in 1852, and in 1861 was elected governor. In the same year Stanford became interested in the transcontinental railroad project and joined with several others to organize the Central Pacific Railroad. He did not hesitate to use the power of his office to secure substantial financial aid for the railroad from the state and municipal governments. After 1863 he devoted himself entirely to the railroad business, serving as lifelong president of the Central Pacific, which joined the Union Pacific at Promontory Point, Utah, in 1869 to form the nation's first transcontinental line. He later organized the Southern Pacific Company and served both as director and president (1885–1890). Stanford served without distinction as a U.S. senator from 1885 to 1893. He founded and endowed Stanford University (1885) in memory of his only son, Leland Stanford, Jr.

Like many other railroad entrepreneurs

in the nineteenth century, Stanford amassed a large part of his fortune with profits obtained through his connections with construction firms that were organized by the parent companies to build the railroads. The results of such dual business arrangements were usually railroads shoddily built at exorbitant cost both to the public and to the general stockholders in the parent companies.

—Seddie Cogswell, *California State University, San Francisco*

STANTON, EDWIN M(cMASTERS) (1814-1869), Secretary of War during the Civil War, whose removal in 1868 sparked the impeachment of President Johnson. Born in Ohio, he overcame the poverty of his youth and won fame as a lawyer. President Buchanan appointed him attorney general in December 1860. A firm Unionist, Stanton opposed the surrender of Fort Sumter and worked to undermine secessionist moves.

In January 1862 Lincoln named Stanton secretary of war. He promptly reorganized the department and urged a vigorous prosecution of the war. With extraordinary single-mindedness, he organized and supplied armies and mobilized the railroad and telegraph as highly effective adjuncts of war. Stanton's most spectacular move came in September 1863, when he managed to rush 23,000 troops from the Virginia front to Chattanooga within a week, thus saving William Rosecrans' army.

Although his quick temper, vindictiveness, and often tyrannical behavior alienated many subordinates, Stanton enjoyed Lincoln's utmost trust and confidence. "He was not a great man," concludes Stanton's biographer, but "he *was* the man for those extraordinary times, and he did a titanic job in the face of immense difficulties."

After Appomattox, Stanton continued to serve as secretary of war, although he opposed President Johnson's Reconstruction policy. When Johnson replaced him in 1868, Stanton resisted, and Congress impeached the President. Resigning after the Senate failed to convict Johnson, Stanton was nominated for the Supreme Court by President Grant but died before he could take his seat.

See also Civil War Battles; Johnson, Andrew.

Consult (IV) Thomas and Hyman, 1962.
—Michael Burlingame, *Connecticut College*

STANTON, ELIZABETH CADY (1815-1902), women's rights leader, reformer, suffragist, and the leading spokeswoman for nineteenth-century feminism. She graduated from Troy Female Seminary in 1832 and then became involved in the antislavery and temperance movements.

After her marriage to reformer Henry B.

Stanton in 1840, she attended the World's Anti-Slavery Convention in London, where women were denied recognition. One of those excluded was Quaker minister Lucretia Mott, who joined Stanton eight years later in summoning the first women's rights convention at Seneca Falls, N.Y. Stanton drafted the "Declaration of Sentiments" adopted at the convention and proposed a controversial women's suffrage resolution. In 1851 she began a lifetime collaboration with Quaker schoolteacher Susan B. Anthony, involving five decades of agitation for the women's cause.

In 1863 she organized the Women's National Loyal League; in 1868 she became coeditor with Anthony of the suffragist journal *The Revolution;* and in 1869 she was elected president of the National Woman Suffrage Association, an office she held for 21 years. During this period she gained national prominence lecturing for the New York Lyceum Bureau. She secured the introduction of a federal women's suffrage amendment in 1878, spoke at annual woman suffrage conventions, and attempted unsuccessfully to vote in 1888. Stanton also participated in preparing the *History of Woman Suffrage* (1881-1922) and, when the suffrage movement united, served as president of the National-American Woman Suffrage Association from 1890 to 1892.

See also Anthony, Susan B.; Mott, Lucretia; Seneca Falls Convention (1848); Suffrage, Women's.

—Nancy Woloch, *Hebrew Union College*

STAPLE ACT (1663). *See* Navigation Acts.

STAR ROUTES, rural postal routes where mail was carried by private contractors. Post Office officials conspired with bidders to defraud the government by approving high payments for useless or fictitious routes. Some conspirators contributed heavily to James Garfield's campaign. President Arthur ordered prosecutions, but the verdict "Not guilty as indicted" cost the government approximately $4 million.

STAR SPANGLED BANNER, THE, national anthem of the United States, written by Francis Scott Key and set to the tune of "Anacreon in Heaven."

Key, a successful Washington lawyer, was enlisted to aid his intimate friend, Dr. William Beanes, who, for unclear reasons, found himself confined aboard a British vessel of war in 1814. Key and Col. John Skinner went aboard the ship to arrange for Dr. Beanes' release. In so doing, Key learned of impending British plans for an attack on Baltimore and was confined to the ship until after the attack. Thus, Key witnessed the bombardment of Fort McHenry during the night of Sept. 13-14, 1814. In "the dawn's early light," the cannonading

Edwin Stanton, Secretary of War under President Lincoln.

Pioneer feminist Elizabeth Cady Stanton, who worked closely with Susan B. Anthony.

British shelling of Fort McHenry in 1814 inspired Francis Scott Key to write "The Star-Spangled Banner."

State	Order of Admission to Union	Organized as Territory	Admitted to Union
Delaware	1	....	Dec. 7, 1787
Pennsylvania	2	....	Dec. 12, 1787
New Jersey	3	....	Dec. 18, 1787
Georgia	4	....	Jan. 2, 1788
Connecticut	5	....	Jan. 9, 1788
Massachusetts	6	....	Feb. 6, 1788
Maryland	7	....	April 28, 1788
South Carolina	8	....	May 23, 1788
New Hampshire	9	....	June 21, 1788
Virginia	10	....	June 25, 1788
New York	11	....	July 26, 1788
North Carolina	12	....	Nov. 21, 1789
Rhode Island	13	....	May 29, 1790
Vermont	14	....	March 4, 1791
Kentucky	15	....	June 1, 1792
Tennessee	16	....	June 1, 1796
Ohio	17	....	March 1, 1803
Louisiana	18	March 24, 1804	April 30, 1812
Indiana	19	May 7, 1800	Dec. 11, 1816
Mississippi	20	April 17, 1798	Dec. 10, 1817
Illinois	21	Feb. 3, 1809	Dec. 3, 1818
Alabama	22	March 3, 1817	Dec. 14, 1819
Maine	23	....	March 15, 1820
Missouri	24	June 4, 1812	Aug. 10, 1821
Arkansas	25	March 2, 1819	June 15, 1836
Michigan	26	Jan. 11, 1805	Jan. 26, 1837
Florida	27	March 30, 1822	March 3, 1845
Texas	28	....	Dec. 29, 1845
Iowa	29	June 12, 1838	Dec. 28, 1846
Wisconsin	30	April 20, 1836	May 29, 1848
California	31	....	Sept. 9, 1850
Minnesota	32	March 3, 1849	May 11, 1858
Oregon	33	Aug. 14, 1848	Feb. 14, 1859
Kansas	34	May 30, 1854	Jan. 29, 1861
West Virginia	35	....	June 20, 1863
Nevada	36	March 2, 1861	Oct. 31, 1864
Nebraska	37	May 30, 1854	March 1, 1867
Colorado	38	Feb. 28, 1861	Aug. 1, 1876
North Dakota	39	March 2, 1861	Nov. 2, 1889
South Dakota	40	March 2, 1861	Nov. 2, 1889
Montana	41	May 26, 1864	Nov. 8, 1889
Washington	42	March 2, 1853	Nov. 11, 1889
Idaho	43	March 3, 1863	July 3, 1890
Wyoming	44	July 25, 1868	July 10, 1890
Utah	45	Sept. 9, 1850	Jan. 4, 1896
Oklahoma	46	May 2, 1890	Nov. 16, 1907
New Mexico	47	Sept. 9, 1850	Jan. 6, 1912
Arizona	48	Feb. 24, 1863	Feb. 14, 1912
Alaska	49	Aug. 24, 1912	Jan. 3, 1959
Hawaii	50	June 14, 1900	Aug. 21, 1959

ceased, and Key, Skinner, and Beanes were returned to shore. It is said that the sight of the flag over the fort inspired Key's verses, which were almost immediately published in the Baltimore *Patriot*. In 1931, "The Star Spangled Banner" became the national anthem by act of Congress, although it had been used for decades.

STATE, U.S. DEPARTMENT OF, a cabinet department that advises the president on the creation and implementation of foreign policy.

History. The department, the oldest in the executive branch, was established during Washington's first Administration. Its antecedents, however, date from the Continental Congress, which executed U.S. foreign policy both during the Revolution and under the Articles of Confederation until 1781. A separate Department of Foreign Affairs set up at that time was succeeded by the newly named Department of State in 1789. Although the earlier versions dealt also with certain domestic concerns, including the census, patents, and territorial affairs, the department's current responsibilities are exclusively in foreign policy.

Organization and Functions. The department is organized under a secretary of state appointed by the president with the advice and consent of the Senate. The secretary is assisted by an undersecretary, who is second in overall command, and an undersecretary for political affairs. In addition to its advisory and policy-making functions, the State Department acts as the nation's spokesman in the United Nations and in more than 50 major international organizations and 500 annual international conferences. The department negotiates treaties and agreements with foreign countries. It is aided in these tasks by the National Security Council.

Although many state departments remain anonymous executors of presidentially inspired policy, some secretaries, such as Thomas Jefferson, John Hay, Elihu Root, Cordell Hull, and John Foster Dulles, have stamped that policy with their own unique outlook. Nevertheless, although the makeup of the department varies with each changing administration, sudden radical policy changes have been few.

STATES. Each state has a separate entry, with the 13 colonies receiving fuller treatment. *See* individual articles.

STATES' RIGHTS PARTY, or **DIXIECRATS,** a states' rights party organized by dissident Democrats in 1948. Angered by the passage at the Democratic National Convention of a civil rights plank, the Southerners convened a States' Rights Democratic Convention in Birmingham, Ala., on July 17. Amidst the waving

of Confederate flags and bitter denunciations of Truman, Governor Strom Thurmond of South Carolina was nominated for president.

The Dixiecrats soon found themselves at odds with loyal Democratic regulars over the choice of presidential electors in the Southern states. Although the States' Rights supporters hoped to prove that the loss of the South would cost Truman the election, Thurmond carried only four Southern states—South Carolina, Alabama, Mississippi, and Louisiana—for a total of 39 electoral votes and 1,168,000 popular votes.

In the North, the movement benefited Truman and contributed to the subsequent enactment of his "Fair Deal" program, which included federal antilynching laws, the abolition of poll taxes, and the establishment of the Fair Employment Practices Commission.

See also Political Parties in the United States; Presidential Elections.

STATUTE FOR RELIGIOUS FREEDOM. *See* Virginia Statute for Religious Freedom (1786).

STEEL TRUST. *See* Trusts.

STEFFENS, (JOSEPH) LINCOLN (1866–1936), American journalist, lecturer, and political philosopher. He was born in San Francisco and graduated from the University of California in 1889. After three years of studies abroad, Steffens entered journalism in New York, where he became a leading figure among the writers whom Theodore Roosevelt called "muckrakers." Steffens' well-documented sociological case studies on corrupt business practices were more than yellow journalism or sensational exposés; they provided abundant evidence of corruption of politicians by businessmen seeking special privileges. As managing editor of *McClure's Magazine* (1902–1906) and thereafter as an associate editor of the *American Magazine* and *Everybody's*, Steffens wrote—and encouraged other writers, including Ida M. Tarbell, to write—articles exposing municipal corruption.

Although his nationwide lecture tours won him popular recognition, his unorthodoxy concerning reform and revolution (developed after a trip to Russia in 1914) lost him his American audience during the 1920s. His studies of revolutionary politics and his support of many Communist activities gained him a following of young expatriates, and his *Autobiography* (1931) was well received. As a writer and lecturer, Steffens was responsible for persuading great masses of people to examine the character of contemporary civilization.

STEIN, GERTRUDE (1874–1946), American author remembered primarily for her influence on other authors. *See* Literature.

STEINBECK, JOHN (ERNST) (1902–1968), American writer born in Salinas, Cal., who achieved fame in the 1930s for his powerful novels about agricultural workers in California. In 1962 Steinbeck became the seventh American to receive the Nobel Prize for Literature. He had already been awarded the Pulitzer Prize (1940) for *Grapes of Wrath*.

In his writings, Steinbeck developed an early reputation as a proletarian naturalistic writer with keen sociological observations who combined realism and romance in an often uneasy juxtaposition. His books include commentary on poverty-stricken Oklahoma migrants in *Grapes of Wrath* (1939), corrupted morals in *The Winter of Our Discontent* (1961), oppressed fish-canning factory workers in *Cannery Row* (1945), and well-loved land, but sick society in *Travels with Charley* (1962). *Of Mice and Men* (1937), which is about two migrant laborers and is one of Steinbeck's most powerful novels, was adapted for the stage and received the New York Drama Critics' Circle award. *The Moon Is Down* (1942), a play set in a Nazi-occupied country during World War II, was also well received. Other books include the novels *The Wayward Bus* (1947) and *East of Eden* (1952).

See also Literature.

STEINEM, GLORIA, articulate exponent of women's rights and a founder of *Ms.* magazine. *See* Women's Liberation.

STEPHENS, ALEXANDER H(AMILTON) (1812–1883), Vice-President of the Confederacy. He was born in Georgia, where he became a leading lawyer. In 1843 he entered the U.S. House as a Whig and outspokenly opposed the Mexican War and antislavery measures. A devoted Unionist, he helped persuade Georgians to accept the Compromise of 1850, but he continued to defend slavery until his retirement from Congress in 1859.

Despite his lack of enthusiasm for secession, Stephens was chosen vice-president of the Confederacy in February 1861. The following month he declared, "Our new government is founded upon exactly the opposite idea (from the Declaration of Independence); its foundations are laid, its corner-stone rests upon the great truth that the negro is not equal to the white man; that slavery . . . is his natural and normal condition."

During the war Stephens sharply disagreed with many of Jefferson Davis' policies and publicly denounced conscription and the suspension of habeas corpus as violations of states' rights and civil liberty, going so far as to urge Georgia to secede from the Confederacy. In February 1865 he served as a delegate to the abortive peace conference at Hampton Roads. After the war Stephens resumed his law practice and dabbled in journalism before once again taking a seat in the U.S. House (1873–1882).

See also Confederate States of America; Hampton Roads Conference.

Consult (IV) Von Abele, 1946.

—Michael Burlingame, *Connecticut College*

STEVENS, THADDEUS (1792–1868), leading Radical Republican in the House of Representatives during Reconstruction. Born in Vermont, he was lame and poor and developed an intense hostility toward aristocracy and a profound sympathy for the underdog. As a lawyer in Pennsylvania he defended fugitive slaves. Stevens entered Pennsylvania politics in 1831, and his personality, extraordinary talent as a speaker, and grasp of parliamentary procedure made him one of the strongest figures in state politics.

In 1848 he won election to the U.S. House as a Whig. There he vigorously opposed proslavery measures. In 1855 he helped found the Republican Party in Pennsylvania and in 1858 as a Republican was returned to the House seat he had quit in 1852. During the Civil War he became chairman of the powerful Ways and Means Committee. He demanded a stern prosecution of the war, confiscation of rebel property, and liberation of the slaves.

Stevens made his greatest mark as an advocate of Reconstruction policies designed to protect freedmen and Southern white Unionists and also to punish Confederates. He denounced presidential Reconstruction programs, arguing that the South had, by rebelling, reverted to a territorial condition and was thus subject to the will of Congress. He shepherded the Freedmen's Bureau Bill and Civil Rights Act through Congress and led the fight against Andrew Johnson's vetoes. Appointed to the Joint Congressional Committee on Reconstruction, he helped frame the Fourteenth Amendment and paved the way for the passage of the Reconstruction Act (1867). He closed his career as an architect of the impeachment of Johnson. Deeply disappointed by the failure of Congress to remove the President, he died shortly after Johnson's acquittal.

See also Civil Rights Acts (1866–1875); Johnson, Andrew; Radical Republicans; Reconstruction Acts (1867–1868).

Consult (IV) Brodie, 1959.

—Michael Burlingame, *Connecticut College*

STEVENS, WALLACE (1879–1955), American poet who was born in Reading, Pa. After studying at Harvard (1897–1900), where he became acquainted with George Santayana—the model for much of his philosophical poetry—Stevens attended New York University Law School and was admitted to the bar in 1904. He practiced law until he joined the Hartford

Author John Steinbeck, whose *Grapes of Wrath* (1939) evoked the tragedies of the Depression.

Alexander H. Stephens, served as vice-president of the Confederacy.

Adlai Stevenson, while UN ambassador, addresses the Security Council in 1964.

Henry L. Stimson served as secretary of state and twice as secretary of war.

Accident Indemnity Company (1916), serving as its vice-president from 1934 until his death.

Stevens began his career as a poet with contributions to *Poetry Magazine* (1914). His first book, *Harmonium* (1923), which contains one of his best known poems, "Sunday Morning," was well received by the critics. Other major volumes include *Ideas of Order* (1935), *Parts of the World* (1942), *The Auroras of Autumn* (1950), and his *Collected Poems* (1954), for which he was awarded the Pulitzer Prize.

Stevens penned imaginative, romantic, pictorial, and musical verse that ranged from descriptive and narrative lyrics to meditative discourse. He felt that mankind, through verse, could escape from troubled reality into a world of serene imagination. A volume of critical essays, *The Necessary Angel* (1951), was devoted to the chief concern of his poetry, the relationship between imagination and reality.

STEVENSON FAMILY. The first Stevenson to enter the American political scene was Adlai Ewing (1835–1914). Born in Kentucky, he moved to Illinois with his parents at an early age and became a lawyer. The Lincoln-Douglas debates in 1858 stimulated his interest in politics, and he soon became active in local and national politics. During the first Administration of Grover Cleveland (1885–1889), Stevenson served as first assistant postmaster general. In 1892 he was elected vice-president on the Democratic ticket. He unsuccessfully ran for vice-president on the ticket with William Jennings Bryan in 1900 and for governor of Illinois in 1908.

His grandson, also named Adlai Ewing (1900–1965), came to national prominence when he ran as the Democratic presidential candidate in 1952 and 1956. The son of Louis Green Stevenson, a newspaper executive, Adlai, like his grandfather, was raised in Illinois. After serving as an apprentice seaman during World War I, he entered Princeton, graduating in 1922, and went on to study law at Harvard and Northwestern University, where he graduated in 1926.

Stevenson began his legal practice in Chicago, but it was often interrupted by periods of public service. In 1948 he was elected governor of Illinois, a post in which he distinguished himself with far-reaching legal and administrative reforms.

During the presidential campaign of 1952, Stevenson waged a strong and intelligent, although unsuccessful, fight against Dwight D. Eisenhower. In 1956 Stevenson was also defeated by Eisenhower. In 1961 President Kennedy appointed him U.S. ambassador to the United Nations, a position he held until his death. Among Stevenson's published works, most of which reflect his public service, are *Call to Greatness* (1954), *The New America*

(1957), and *Looking Outward: Years of Crisis at the United Nations* (1963).

Adlai Ewing III (1930–   ), the third of Adlai's sons, like his father and great-grandfather, became active in Illinois politics. In 1970 he entered the national scene when he won a seat in the Senate by a large majority.

STEWARD MACHINE CO. v. DAVIS (1937), Supreme Court decision upholding the constitutionality of the Social Security Act. *See* Social Security Act (1935).

STIMSON, HENRY L(EWIS) (1867–1950), American statesman. Born in New York City, he was an undergraduate at Yale and did graduate work at Harvard before beginning law practice in New York City in 1893.

Stimson's long career in government began under President Theodore Roosevelt with a term (1906–1909) as U.S. attorney for the southern district of New York. In May 1911, having been defeated as the Republican candidate for governor of New York, he joined the cabinet of President Taft as secretary of war, serving until Taft left office in March 1913. After service with the field artillery in France during World War I, he returned to private law practice in New York. However, he returned to government in 1927 for a two-year term as governor general of the Philippines.

In 1929 he became secretary of state in the cabinet of President Hoover. In this capacity he chaired the American delegations to the London Naval Conference (1930) and the Geneva Disarmament Conference (1932). Although Stimson was deeply troubled by Japanese expansion, he limited his response (under Hoover's direction) to moral sanctions, particularly in the policy of not recognizing territories acquired by aggression. After 1933, once more in private legal practice, he urged an adamantly anti-Fascist foreign policy.

In July 1940 he once again became secretary of war, this time in the Democratic Administration of Franklin Roosevelt, an act for which he was read out of the Republican Party at its 1940 convention. Stimson served in this demanding position throughout World War II, retiring in September 1945 at 78.

See also London Naval Conference; World War II.

Consult (VII) Stimson, 1948.

—Paul S. Boyer, *University of Massachusetts*

STOCK EXCHANGE. *See* New York Stock Exchange.

STONE, HARLAN FISKE (1872–1945), 11th Chief Justice of the Supreme Court. He began his law practice in New York City in 1899 and for the next 25 years divided his time between teaching at Columbia Law School and his private practice.

Supreme Court. In 1924 President Coolidge appointed Stone attorney general, and in 1925 he became an associate justice of the Supreme Court. In 1941 President Roosevelt, ignoring partisan politics and Stone's basically Republican philosophy, selected him to succeed Charles Evans Hughes as chief justice.

During the first part of Stone's Supreme Court tenure, he was deeply involved with decisions that affected the role of government in shaping the nation's economic and legal structure. While he was chief justice, there was a great debate over the government's power to control matters touching affairs of conscience and expression. As chief justice during World War II he presided over cases of martial law, military courts, and treason, many of which involved constitutional matters presented to the Court for the first time.

Stone wrote more than 600 opinions covering a wide range of judicial problems. One of his more famous dissents (1935) involved the constitutionality of the first Agricultural Adjustment Act of the New Deal. Stone wrote that "while unconstitutional exercise of power by the executive and legislative branches of the government is subject to judicial restraint, the only check upon our exercise of power is our own sense of restraint."

See also Agricultural Adjustment Act (1933).

STONE, LUCY (1818–1893), feminist, abolitionist, and suffragist. She graduated from Oberlin College in 1847 and then became a lecture agent for the American Anti-Slavery Society and an agitator for women's rights. Married to abolitionist Henry B. Blackwell in 1855 in a ceremony that protested current marriage laws, she insisted upon keeping her maiden name and was called "Mrs. Stone." After the Civil War, she participated in the American Equal Rights Association and in 1869 became a leader of the American Woman Suffrage Association (AWSA). Beginning in 1872 Stone and her husband served as editors of the AWSA newspaper, *The Woman's Journal,* and in 1890, when the suffrage movement united, she served on the executive committee of the National-American Woman Suffrage Association.

STORY, JOSEPH (1779–1845), an associate justice on the Supreme Court and educator who was a confirmed nationalist and supporter of the Federalist views of Chief Justice John Marshall.

Born in Marblehead, Mass., he practiced law in Salem and became a prominent Jeffersonian Republican. He served in state offices before becoming speaker of the state House of Representatives in 1811. During that year, he was appointed to the Supreme Court by James Madison.

At the time of Story's appointment, each justice was assigned to a circuit, and Story's consisted of the New England region north of Connecticut. His circuit decisions in admiralty, prize, patent, and copyright law helped to make a significant body of law on these subjects. While serving on the Court, Story was also a Harvard law professor and had an important influence in shaping jurisprudence and legal education in the United States.

On the Court, Story served primarily under Chief Justice Marshall, with whom he concurred in most opinions. Story was on the bench for nearly 34 years, although he almost resigned when Roger B. Taney became chief justice in 1836. Under Taney, Story became silent on the constitutional issues.

STOWE, HARRIET BEECHER (1811–1896), the author of *Uncle Tom's Cabin.* The daughter of Lyman Beecher and the sister of Henry Ward Beecher, she was born in Litchfield, Conn. After her early education in Litchfield and Hartford, she moved to Cincinnati in 1832. There she was exposed to the intellectual atmosphere of the Lane Theological Seminary, where discussions of slavery inspired her first writings. In 1836 she married Calvin E. Stowe, a professor of biblical literature, and when he became a professor at Bowdoin in 1850, she moved back to New England.

She began writing *Uncle Tom's Cabin, or, Life Among the Lowly* while debate raged over the Fugitive Slave Law in 1850. The novel appeared serially in the *National Era,* an antislavery periodical, from June 5, 1851, to April 1, 1852. In book form *Uncle Tom's Cabin* sold more than 300,000 copies in the first year, and Tom, Eliza, and Simon Legree became known throughout America and Europe. In 1853 Stowe answered her critics with *The Key To Uncle Tom's Cabin,* a collection of documents designed to dispel charges of inaccuracy. Seldom has a work of fiction had as much political impact as *Uncle Tom's Cabin,* which made the antislavery cause known throughout the world and turned public opinion in favor of President Lincoln and the North when the Civil War broke out.

An international celebrity and a popular writer of wide appeal, Stowe continued to write prolifically, travel widely, and speak out against slavery. Her second antislavery novel, *Dred* (1856), *Oldtown Folks* (1859, a mature but neglected work), and many literary reminiscences of European travels and childhood memories followed. After the Civil War, Stowe moved to Florida, where she spent most of the rest of her life.

—Richard Collin, *Louisiana State University, New Orleans*

Lucy Stone, abolitionist speaker and women's suffrage leader.

Uncle Tom's Cabin brought author Harriet Beecher Stowe international fame.

STRAIGHT, WILLARD, financial agent who influenced U.S. role in the Far East. *See* Open Door Policy.

STRATEGIC ARMS LIMITATION TALKS (SALT), discussions between the United States and the USSR to stablize nuclear arms competition between the two countries. These discussions were initially proposed in 1964 by President Lyndon Johnson. With the continuation of the buildup of antiballistic missile (ABM) systems and intercontinental ballistics missile (ICBM) systems, the United States again approached the USSR on discussions to limit ABMs in 1966 and 1967.

After delays, during which both countries began developing costly new systems, preliminary talks began in 1969 in Helsinki, Finland, were resumed in 1970, and then were held alternately in Vienna and Helsinki. An agreement was signed by both nations during President Nixon's May 1972 visit to Moscow, limiting ABM installations to 200 and freezing the number of offensive missile sites on land and sea. It was hoped that further talks would lead to additional limitations on offensive weapons.

STRICT CONSTRUCTION, doctrine that the Constitution should have only its traditional literal meaning and that constitutional changes should be made through the amendment process. Paradoxically, strict constructionist positions have been used to support both conservative and liberal political and economic doctrines. For example, Justice Black argued that provisions of the First Amendment are absolute prohibitions against governmental actions. President Nixon, on the other hand, contended that Supreme Court judges should exercise restraint in expanding defendants' rights through application of provisions of the Bill of Rights.

What is now taken as strict construction would have seemed to Thomas Jefferson the loosest possible. Jeffersonians stood for a narrow construction so as to retain as much power as possible for the states, but the Louisiana Purchase was contrary to this precept.

In *McCulloch v. Maryland* (1819) the issue with respect to chartering a bank was whether the national government had only those powers expressly delegated to it or whether it had implied powers. In the Social Security Act cases (1937), the question was whether the general welfare clause gave Congress an unlimited taxing and spending power. In both cases strict constructionists argued unsuccessfully that Congress has only those powers that were explicitly set forth in the Constitution.

See also McCulloch v. Maryland (1819).
Consult (VIII) Sutherland, 1965.

Jeb Stuart, outstanding Confederate cavalry leader.

STUART, J(AMES) E(WELL) B(ROWN) (1833–1864), Confederate cavalry leader called "the greatest cavalry officer ever foaled in America" by an opposing general. Born in Virginia and educated at West Point, he left the U.S. cavalry to join the Confederacy in 1861. After the First Battle of Bull Run (July 1861), Stuart was given command of the cavalry in the Army of Northern Virginia. In that post he became, as Lee put it, "the eyes of the army." Against the Union forces under McClellan, Stuart made two extraordinary raids (June and October 1862), going completely around the enemy's army, that thrilled the South. At the Second Battle of Bull Run (August 1862) and Chancellorsville (April–May 1863) he ably screened the infantry. In the Gettysburg campaign (June–July 1863), however, he got separated from the main army, which committed important mistakes, in part because it lacked its "eyes." In May 1864 he thwarted a Union cavalry drive on Richmond at the Battle of Yellow Tavern, during which he was mortally wounded.

A natural, exuberant, and bold fighter, Stuart was not reckless. He carefully prepared his moves and was loved by his men. His superiors shared the feeling. Lee said, "A more zealous, ardent, brave and devoted soldier than Stuart the Confederacy cannot have."

See also Civil War Battles.
Consult (IV) Davis, 1957.

STUDENT NONVIOLENT COORDINATING COMMITTEE (SNCC), civil rights group founded in 1960 by a group of Southern black and white college students who felt that Martin Luther King, Jr.'s leadership of the civil rights movement was not sufficiently dynamic. SNCC initiated voter registration drives in the South and later advocated the formation of a national black political party with the black panther as its symbol.

The organization adopted the slogan and concept of Black Power and became increasingly militant when Stokely Carmichael replaced John Lewis as its chairman in 1966. Although white members were welcome in the early years, they were discouraged after 1966. In 1969 it was renamed the Student National Coordinating Committee.

STUDENTS FOR A DEMOCRATIC SOCIETY (SDS), student organization that was influential during the 1960s. It evolved from a small radical study group of socialists who attracted liberal and idealistic students disenchanted with the American establishment. SDS grew into the largest, most powerful national white leftist organization, which had, at its peak, an estimated 70,000 to 100,000 members. SDS became a major national force when it led white students to take action (mostly sit-ins and a few violent incidents) against racism, poverty, and war on major college campuses across the nation in the spring and summer of 1968.

Due in large part to factionalism, SDS had declined in power and influence by summer 1969, at which time a small, tightly organized, revolutionary fighting force of white youth, called Weatherman, emerged. They engaged in bombings, street fighting, and other offensive action. They were the first organization in recent years to stress publicly the importance of armed struggle in the United States. In 1970 the Weatherman moved underground.

STUYVESANT, PETER (1592–1672), autocratic soldier who governed the Dutch colony of New Netherlands from 1647 to 1664. He had previously been governor of Curaçao (1643–1644) in the West Indies—where he lost a leg fighting the French. Thereafter Stuyvesant wore a fancy silver false leg.

For 17 years his rule in New Netherlands was stormy and violent, marked by disputes with his elected advisers in which the Dutch government generally supported him. Stuyvesant was made to allow a measure of city government to New Amsterdam in 1652 and to other settlements the following year. In 1655 he captured several forts on the Delaware River and absorbed the Finnish-Swedish colony of New Sweden. With the English colonies to the north he tried to settle boundary disputes by the Treaty of Hartford (1650), but the English government in London did not ratify Stuyvesant's agreement. In 1664 an English naval expedition captured the Dutch colony by sailing up the Hudson. Stuyvesant had no means of opposing them, so he simply surrendered. He retired to his farm in what is now New York.

See also Anglo-Dutch Wars; Delaware; New York.

SUBTREASURIES. *See* Independent Treasury Act (1846).

SUBVERSIVE ACTIVITIES CONTROL ACT. *See* Internal Security Act (1951).

SUFFOLK RESOLVES (1774), radical resolutions adopted by the First Continental Congress. *See* Continental Congress, First (1774).

SUFFOLK SYSTEM, an early bankers' clearinghouse in Boston for cashing the notes of out-of-town banks. By 1825 the Suffolk Bank (Boston) had agreed to act as the one bank to accept the notes of country banks and cash them. This put an end to the need for each Boston bank to return notes by messenger to the country banks and bring back cash. The country banks began to put deposits in the Suffolk Bank to cover their notes, and the Suffolk Bank could thus use the money and make enough profit to more than cover its costs. Today, bankers' clearinghouses are essential for the speedy and efficient clearing of checks and paper, and the financial system could not work without them.

SUFFRAGE, WOMEN'S. The struggle for women's suffrage, which lasted more than 70 years, was started at the Seneca Falls Convention for women's rights in 1848, where the "inalienable right to the elective franchise" was among many demands for the social, legal, and economic equality of women. Suffrage resolutions were repeated at women's rights conventions throughout the pre-Civil War period, and when feminism reemerged after the war, the vote became the main goal of women activists. In 1866, women from the prewar movement joined the American Equal Rights Association, which supported suffrage for women and blacks. In 1869, however, after the Fourteenth and Fifteenth Amendments granted suffrage to black men (but not to women), the feminist movement suffered a major schism, caused partly by personal conflicts among its leaders and partly by disagreement over issues and tactics.

Rival Associations: NWSA and AWSA. The more radical, New York-based faction, led by Elizabeth Cady Stanton and Susan B. Anthony, formed the National Woman Suffrage Association (NWSA), which refused to support the Fifteenth Amendment, agitated for a federal women's suffrage amendment, and advocated more liberal divorce legislation. It also allied itself briefly with a number of eccentrics, such as George Francis Train, a wealthy Democrat who financed Anthony's radical publication, the *The Revolution*, and Victoria Woodhull, a notorious exponent of free love.

Such connections, as well as the NWSA's interest in unpopular causes, alienated more conservative feminists, who formed the Boston-based American Woman Suffrage Association (AWSA). Led by the prominent reformers Julia Ward Howe, Lucy Stone, Henry Blackwell, and Thomas Wentworth Higginson, the AWSA supported the Fifteenth Amendment and campaigned at the state level for the passage of state suffrage laws. For the next two decades, suffragists agitated across the country with speeches, petitions, and conventions and attempted to influence congressmen and state legislators. Opposition was widespread. In 1875 the Supreme Court ruled that suffrage was not a privilege of citizenship (*Minor v. Happersett*), and the women's suffrage amendment, proposed in 1878 at the instigation of NWSA leaders, was repeatedly defeated.

Women's Clubs. A parallel development during these early years of the suffrage movement was the rapid growth of women's clubs. Organized at first for cultural and educational purposes, the clubs provided a means of drawing middle-class women out of the home. In

Women's suffrage leaders Susan B. Anthony *(standing)* and Elizabeth Cady Stanton.

Union of rival organizations into National-American Woman Suffrage Association strengthened the movement.

Women voting in Wyoming, first territory to grant women suffrage in territorial elections.

Abolitionist Charles Sumner was brutally beaten in Senate after antislavery speech in 1856.

1890 the General Federation of Women's Clubs (GFWC) was formed; their membership grew to 1 million or more during the Progressive Era.

Soon after the turn of the century, the clubs turned their efforts from self-improvement to civic action. They promoted such measures as public libraries, the Pure Food and Drug Act, child labor bills, and civil service reform. Not only did the women's clubs involve a large number of otherwise conservative women in public affairs but also taught them to exercise political pressure, which in 1914 was turned to the benefit of the suffrage campaign.

United Effort by NAWSA. Meanwhile, in 1890 the two branches of suffrage organizations overcame their differences and formed the National-American Woman Suffrage Association (NAWSA). Stanton, former NWSA president, served as president (1892–1900) and was followed by Carrie Champman Catt (1900–1904; 1915–1920) and Dr. Anna Howard Shaw (1904–1915). Suffragists now worked for both a federal women's suffrage amendment and the achievement of women's suffrage state by state. They were successful in Colorado (1893) and Idaho (1896). Wyoming, the first to grant women's suffrage in territorial elections in 1869, was admitted to the Union in 1890; Utah, which gave women the vote in 1870, was admitted in 1896. By 1912, nine states, all in the West, allowed women to vote. That year Theodore Roosevelt's Progressive Party endorsed women's suffrage, and two years later the support of the GFWC lent respectability to the cause. The proposed federal amendment made no progress, however, and many state campaigns failed.

During World War I, NAWSA supported the war effort and continued its battle for the vote, but schism had again occurred in the ranks. In 1916, activists of the National Women's Party, led by Alice Paul, left NAWSA. The National Women's Party held the party in power (the Democrats) responsible for the failure of the women's suffrage amendment. In 1917, members hanged President Wilson in effigy, burned his speeches, picketed the White House, were arrested, and held hunger strikes. Such tactics were not favored by NAWSA, which proceeded with its political campaign, but the new activism won sympathy for the cause.

Victory. In 1917 women's suffrage gained a crucial victory in New York State. In 1918 the women's suffrage amendment passed the House of Representatives, and in June 1919, after several tries, the amendment was approved by the Senate. Suffragists now concentrated their efforts in the states, and on August 26, 1920, Tennessee became the thirty-sixth state to ratify the amendment, thus ensuring its adoption. The Nineteenth Amendment enabled women to vote in the 1920 national election.

Victorious in its long campaign, NAWSA came to an end. Its membership was partially absorbed by the League of Women Voters, formed in 1920, and in 1921 by the New National Woman's Party, which campaigned for an Equal Rights Amendment. Women's clubs turned their attention to Prohibition and film censorship. The struggle for the vote had united massive organizations of women in a common cause; once it was won, the feminist impulse was temporarily spent.

See also Anthony, Susan B.; Minor v. Happersett (1875); Seneca Falls Convention (1848); Stanton, Elizabeth Cady; Women's Rights (Item Guide).

Consult (VI) Flexner, 1959; O'Neill, 1969.
—Nancy Woloch, *Hebrew Union College*

SUGAR ACT (1764). *See* Navigation Acts.

SUGAR TRUST. *See* Trusts.

SULLIVAN, LOUIS (HENRI) (1856–1924), American architect and pioneer of the modern movement in architecture, was born in Boston and studied in Paris. His most productive designing period began after he formed a partnership with Dankmar Adler in Chicago in 1881. Sullivan's experimental, functional, skeletal constructions of skyscrapers and office blocks were designed to harmonize with the purpose of the structure and to be appropriate to the new building materials then being developed. This technique is seen particularly in the Gage Building and the stock exchange in Chicago. The works earned him the title "Father of Modernism." He greatly influenced Frank Lloyd Wright, who entered Sullivan's office at 18 and became an ardent disciple.

Sullivan's philosophy of architectural design, however, was more influential than his buildings. He fervently attacked the imitation of historic styles and called for a modern style expressive of twentieth-century reality and spirit.

See also Architecture; Wright, Frank Lloyd.

SUMNER, CHARLES (1811–1874), Radical Republican Senator. Born and raised in Boston, Sumner became a follower of Rev. William Ellery Channing and involved himself in a number of social causes, notably prison reform, education, and peace. Sumner learned some of his libertarian principles from the abolitionist *Liberator,* but he differed from its dedicated partisan readers by adhering to the Constitution and the federal Union, which they repudiated. In addition, although Sumner expressed contempt for slavery, he believed that blacks were inferior to whites.

Sumner was drawn into politics by the dissatisfaction of Northerners with Southern plans to expand slavery in the West, and he helped to organize the Free-Soil Party in 1848. In 1851 he was elected to the Senate.

The fugitive slave provision of the Compromise of 1850 had aroused the country, and Sumner made himself a principal spokesman against it. In 1854 he fought against the Kansas-Nebraska Act, and on May 20, 1856, he denounced "The Crime against Kansas" in a Senate speech, in the course of which he disparaged South Carolina senator Andrew P. Butler. Two days later he was beaten with a walking stick and severely injured by Butler's nephew, Representative Preston S. Brooks. It took Sumner three years to recover from his injuries, but he was reelected to his Senate seat in 1857 and continued to hold it until his death.

Radical Republican. During the Civil War he was a staunch advocate of slave emancipation and became a leader of the Radical Republicans. His theory that the South, by rebelling, had committed "state suicide" made the task of Reconstruction more difficult. His long record of bitter, personal denunciations continued in his rhetorical condemnation of President Andrew Johnson, against whom he helped to institute impeachment proceedings.

During the Grant Administration, Sumner charged Britain with aiding the Confederacy, which embarrassed efforts to advance peace between the nations. More distinguished was his successful campaign against the Administration's attempt to annex Santo Domingo. In revenge, Grant had Sumner removed from his chairmanship of the Foreign Relations Committee in 1872.

See also Compromise of 1850; Kansas-Nebraska Act (1854); Radical Republicans.

Consult (IV) Donald, 1960, 1970.

—Louis Filler, *Antioch College*

SUPREME COURT OF THE UNITED STATES

heads the judicial branch of the American government and is the nation's highest law court. It also performs a political function of tremendous importance as the official interpreter and expounder of the Constitution. Because many of the most important provisions of the Constitution are extremely broad and offer much room for difference of interpretation (for example, "due process of law" or "equal protection of the laws"), the Court's role in the political development of the American Republic has been very great, often exceeding that of the president or Congress. The Supreme Court was created by Article III of the Constitution and is headed by the chief justice of the United States. The size of the Court is determined by Congress; since 1869 the Court has been composed of nine justices appointed by the president with the advice and consent of the Senate. They serve during good behavior and are removable only by impeachment.

Jurisdiction. The Supreme Court is pri-

marily an appellate court. It reviews decisions of the lower federal courts by writ of certiorari, a discretionary writ granted on the affirmative vote of four of the nine justices. In general the Court grants certiorari only in cases presenting novel or significant legal issues. The Court also hears appeals against decisions of state supreme courts that involve a federal question, that is, an interpretation of the U.S. Constitution, federal laws, or treaties. The supremacy clause (Article VI) makes the Constitution, laws, and treaties of the United States the "supreme law of the land" and binding on state judges; review by the Supreme Court enforces this obligation. In addition, a few types of cases, principally suits between states, can be filed directly in the original jurisdiction of the Supreme Court without having gone through any other court.

Limitations. As final interpreter of the Constitution, the Supreme Court has the power to invalidate presidential actions or congressional statutes that it regards as unconstitutional. For this reason the American system is sometimes referred to as one of judicial supremacy. However, this nomenclature is misleading because the Court is, in fact, limited by the countervailing powers of the other two branches. The president can arouse public opinion against Court decisions to which he objects, but his greatest influence is through the appointment of justices to fill vacancies. He must, of course, keep in mind the necessity of securing Senate confirmation; two of President Nixon's nominees were rejected by the Senate.

Congress exercises pressure on the Court principally by initiating legislation or constitutional amendments to reverse judicial interpretations. Congress can also threaten impeachment, but no Supreme Court justice has ever been removed in this way. The Constitution provides that the appellate jurisdiction of the Court is subject to "such regulations as the Congress shall make." Court critics in Congress have occasionally threatened to use this authority to punish the Court, but the power has been used only once.

History

First Period. From the founding to the Civil War (1789–1865) the major influence was John Marshall, Chief Justice from 1801 to 1835. His strong leadership lifted the Court out of the obscurity of its first decade, and in the monumental case of *Marbury v. Madison* (1803) he successfully claimed the power to declare acts of Congress unconstitutional. He was a strong nationalist, and his basic strategy was to strengthen the power of the national government by such methods as broad interpretation of the congressional power to regulate commerce (*Gibbons v. Ogden* [1824]) and extension of federal protection to property rights under the contract clause (*Dartmouth College v. Woodward* [1819]).

SUPREME COURT — Item Guide

The article on the SUPREME COURT outlines its functions as set by the CONSTITUTION OF THE UNITED STATES and the main points in its history.

JOHN JAY, the first chief justice, was followed by OLIVER ELLSWORTH, architect of the Connecticut Compromise. JOHN MARSHALL's epic tenure spanned the decisions of MARBURY V. MADISON (1803), DARTMOUTH COLLEGE V. WOODWARD (1819), and GIBBONS V. OGDEN (1824). ROGER B. TANEY's term was clouded by the DRED SCOTT DECISION (1857). After the Civil War, chief justices included SALMON P. CHASE, MORRISON R. WAITE, MELVILLE W. FULLER, and EDWARD D. WHITE.

WILLIAM HOWARD TAFT then became the only man to serve both as president and chief justice. During the Depression, when CHARLES EVANS HUGHES was chief justice, FRANKLIN D. ROOSEVELT's attempt at COURT PACKING was thwarted. HARLAN FISKE STONE and FRED M. VINSON followed Hughes. EARL WARREN's tenure was marked by numerous landmark decisions, including BROWN V. BOARD OF EDUCATION OF TOPEKA (1954) and MIRANDA V. ARIZONA (1966). WARREN BURGER became chief justice in 1969.

In addition, there are entries on prominent associate justices, such as HUGO BLACK, BENJAMIN CARDOZO, LOUIS D. BRANDEIS, FELIX FRANKFURTER, JOHN M. HARLAN, JOHN MARSHALL HARLAN, and OLIVER WENDELL HOLMES, JR.

Marshall's successor, Roger B. Taney (1836–1864), was a spokesman for states' rights and for agrarian property in land and slaves rather than for the Eastern commercial-creditor class, as Marshall had been. Taney sought to maintain the Court's authoritative position, but his decision in *Dred Scott v. Sanford* (1857), denying the power of Congress to control slavery in the territories and the right of blacks to be citizens, destroyed the standing of the Court for almost a generation and helped bring on the Civil War.

Second Period. From the Civil War to the New Deal (1865–1937) the Court increased its stature by allying itself with the forces of an emergent capitalism and by implementing the nation's industrial development. After some initial reluctance, the Court concluded that the provision in the Fourteenth Amendment (adopted in 1868) protecting property from being taken without due process of law was a directive to the courts to protect business enterprises from legislative regulation. The Court's resistance to governmental interference with free enterprise was demonstrated by decisions invalidating a New York 10-hour law for bakers (*Lochner v. New York* [1905]), holding unconstitutional the federal Child Labor Act (*Hammer v. Dagenhart* [1918]), and voiding the District of Columbia minimum wage law for women (*Adkins v. Childrens Hospital* [1923]).

The economic Depression of the 1930s brought the Court's conservative views into head-on conflict with the liberalism of Franklin Roosevelt's New Deal. In 1935–1936 the Court declred unconstitutional a number of key statutes in the Roosevelt economic recovery program, in several cases by votes of 5 to 4. Roosevelt sharply attacked the Court's horse-and-buggy thinking and, after his overwhelming reelection in 1936, sought to reform the Court by increasing its size from 9 to 15. This effort failed in Congress, but beginning in 1937, vacancies on the Court enabled him to appoint new members who fully accepted the principle of governmental responsibility for the state of the economy.

Third Period (1937–1969). The liberal orientation resulting from Roosevelt's appointments was generally maintained throughout the Truman, Eisenhower, Kennedy, and Johnson administrations. Particularly under Earl Warren (1953–1969) the Court took advanced positions in a number of constitutional policy areas. Emphasis was transferred from property rights to civil rights, and the justices gave primary consideration to promoting equality and enforcing the protections of the Bill of Rights.

The Court's major constitutional rulings during this period fall into four areas. First, the Court gave greatly increased protection to the First Amendment rights of speech, press, as-

sembly, and religious freedom. Newspapers were assured against libel prosecutions unless malicious falsehoods were published (*New York Times v. Sullivan* [1964]). Obscenity was defined so broadly as to permit much greater freedom of expression than formerly (*Roth v. United States* [1963]). Individuals or organizations charged with subversion could be punished or denied privileges only for illegal acts, not for mere advocacy, teaching, or membership (*Aptheker v. Secretary of State* [1964]). Civil rights organizations were protected from official harassment (*NAACP v. Alabama* [1958]). Bible reading and prayers in the public schools were declared unconstitutional as state-imposed exercises amounting to an establishment of religion (*Engel v. Vitale* [1962]).

A second major judicial concern was with the fair-trial rights of individuals accused of crime. The provisions of the Fourth through the Eighth Amendments, which spell out procedures in federal criminal prosecutions, were extended to the states (*Mapp v. Ohio* [1961]). Representation by counsel was made mandatory in all criminal cases (*Gideon v. Wainwright* [1963]) and was extended to the pretrial period (*Escobedo v. Illinois* [1964]). A code of conduct for police in their interrogation of suspects was announced in *Miranda v. Arizona* (1966). The standards for permissible searches and seizures were tightened (*Katz v. United States* [1967]).

Third, the Court endeavored to make the equal protection clause of the Constitution a reality. The famous case of *Brown v. Board of Education of Topeka* (1954) declared racial segregation in the public schools unconstitutional. Subsequent decisions outlawed all racial classifications or discriminatory provisions affecting access to public services. Equal protection was extended to other disadvantaged groups such as the poor, who were guaranteed against denial of access to the courts because of their poverty (*Griffin v. Illinois* [1956]).

Finally, the Court undertook to implement the principles of representative government by its decision in *Baker v. Carr* (1962) and subsequent cases requiring that the districts from which legislators are elected be approximately equal in population. Enforcing the principle of "one person, one vote" involved the nation's courts in an unprecedented degree of supervision over the process of legislative apportionment.

Outlook. Rulings in all these fields aroused great opposition, made the Court a major target of political controversy, and stimulated efforts to reverse the decisions or limit the Court's powers. Constitutional amendments to nullify the public-school-prayer and one-person–one-vote decisions failed in Congress. However, Richard Nixon in his 1968 presidential campaign attacked the Warren Court's decisions, particularly those on

William Howard Taft, 27th President of the United States (1909–1913) and 9th Chief Justice of the Supreme Court (1921–1930), as Republican presidential nominee in 1908.

criminal trials, and promised that if elected he would change the Court's thinking by appointing "strict constructionists" and judicial conservatives to the Court. To succeed Chief Justice Warren he appointed Warren Burger, who as a federal appeals court judge had been critical of the Supreme Court's decisions. Furthermore, during Nixon's first term three additional vacancies occurred on the Court, all of which he filled with judicial conservatives. Thus it appeared that with the Nixon Court a fourth period in the history of the Supreme Court was beginning.

Consult (VIII) Lewis, 1964; McCloskey, 1960; Murphy, 1972; Swindler, 1970.
—C. Herman Pritchett, *University of California, Santa Barbara*

SUTTER, JOHN A. (1803-1880), California mill owner on whose property gold was discovered in 1848. *See* Gold Rushes.

"SWAMP FOX," popular name for Francis Marion. *See* Marion, Francis.

SWEATSHOPS, businesses in which adults and children worked long hours at low wages under appalling conditions of health and safety, were commonplace in America's urban centers during the period of industrialization. Most notorious in the garment industry, they were usually located in tenement areas and attracted large numbers of immigrant workers.

SWIFT AND CO. v. UNITED STATES (1905), Supreme Court decision upholding prosecution of beef trust. *See* Antitrust Cases.

TAFT, WILLIAM HOWARD (1857-1930), 27th President (1909-1913) of the United States and 9th Chief Justice of the Supreme Court. He was born in Cincinnati on Sept. 15, 1857. His father, Alphonso, was one of the founders of the Republican Party in Ohio, and both his son and grandson became U.S. senators. He became a lawyer, was appointed assistant county prosecutor in 1882, and in 1887 became a judge of the Ohio superior court, where his decisions often had an antilabor cast, earning him the lifelong enmity of organized labor.

In 1890 he became solicitor general of the United States, followed by an eight-year stint on the bench of the Sixth Federal Circuit Court. In 1900 he resigned to become governor general of the Philippines, where he remained until Theodore Roosevelt appointed him secretary of war in 1904. He quickly earned Roosevelt's confidence as the Administration's troubleshooter, and when Roosevelt retired in 1908 he engineered the selection of Taft as his successor.

Presidency. Taft evidently had little desire or taste for the presidency, and his Administration had one crisis after another due to the split in his own party. The Insurgents pressed hard for tariff reduction, a federal income tax, and liberalization of the House rules. Taft instituted far more antitrust suits than Roosevelt and backed the income tax and direct election of senators, but he invariably ended up the captive of the conservatives. He reluctantly agreed to the Payne-Aldrich Tariff (1909), vacillated when the Insurgents moved against House Speaker Joseph Cannon, and frustrated the advocates of an immediate income tax by his amendment scheme. He incurred the Insurgents' wrath by proposing to let farm products from Canada be imported without tariff duties.

Taft so alienated the progressive wing of his party that Robert La Follette and Roosevelt were able to beat him in nearly all the primaries. He was able to arrange his renomination in 1912 but ran a poor third nearly everywhere, getting only 25 percent of the vote.

Supreme Court. After his term as president, Taft taught constitutional law at Yale, served as joint chairman of the National War Labor Board, and was appointed chief justice of the Supreme Court in 1921. In the next nine years, the happiest of his life, Taft reorganized the federal court system and wrote a famous dissent upholding a minimum wage law for women. True to his earlier conservative views, however, he wrote opinions that struck down the federal child labor law and held the United Mine Workers liable for damages done during a strike. He died in Washington, D.C., on March 8, 1930, and was buried in Arlington National Cemetery.

See also Insurgents, Congressional; Presidential Elections; Progressive Party; Roosevelt, Theodore; Taft Family.

Consult (VI) Mowry, 1958; Pringle, 1939.
—John Buenker, *University of Wisconsin, Parkside*

TAFT FAMILY, prominent Ohio clan whose ancestors were New England tradesmen and farmers. Within a century after Alphonso Taft's (1810-1891) arrival in Cincinnati, several members of the family had become nationally prominent. Alphonso, the first of his family to graduate from college, moved to Cincinnati in 1839. A humorless Baptist, he was a lawyer and a Republican who served as secretary of war, attorney general, and minister to Austria and Russia. A disciplinarian and the epitome of a stern Yankee, he produced four sons who became leaders in publishing, politics, law, and education.

Charles Phelps (1843-1929), his eldest, served in the House of Representatives. Imbued with a sense of public service and buoyed by his wife's money, Charles bought the Cincinnati *Times* and later merged it with the *Cincinnati Evening Star*. William Howard (1857-1930), Alphonso's second son, helped by his brother's bankroll, rose to the presidency

Robert A. Taft, known as Mr. Republican, was powerful senator and presidential hopeful.

Following in his father's footsteps, Robert A. Taft, Jr., entered politics and won a seat in the Senate.

Roger B. Taney, 4th Chief Justice of the Supreme Court, was severely criticized for his role in Dred Scott Decision (1857).

Muckraker Ida Tarbell attacked practices of Standard Oil Company.

and later served as chief justice of the Supreme Court. Henry Waters (1859-1954) was a leading lawyer in New York City. Horace Dutton (1861-1943), Alphonso's youngest son, founded the Taft School, much against his father's wishes. Horace wanted to teach boys, and his school in Watertown, Conn., at which he served as headmaster for 46 years, stood for public service and an old-fashioned disciplinary-style education.

Of the later Tafts, most have been committed to public service. William Howard's son, Robert Alphonso (1889-1953), made a name for himself in the Senate, where he urged the passage of the Taft-Hartley Act and where he served from 1944 until his death. Known as "Mr. Republican," he was a four-time candidate for the Republican presidential nomination. His son, Robert A., Jr. (1917–   ), served in the House of Representatives and the Senate.

See also Taft, William Howard; Taft-Hartley Act (1947).

TAFT-HARTLEY ACT (1947), or Labor-Management Relations Act, a law regulating numerous labor activities in which interstate commerce is concerned. Passed over President Truman's veto but endorsed by business leaders, the act reflected the antilabor sentiment aroused by such strikes as John L. Lewis' 1946 coal walkout and by fear of Communist influence in unions.

The act refined the Wagner Act (1935) by defining employers' unfair labor practices; led many states to enact right-to-work laws by limiting the closed shop; and ended the check-off system, by which employers had collected union dues. The most controversial section required unions to abide by an 80-day cooling-off period in strikes involving national emergencies. In addition, union leaders had to swear that they were not Communists. The Landrum-Griffin Act (1959) amended some Taft-Hartley sections.

See also Labor Movement.

TANEY, ROGER B(ROOKE) (1777-1864), 4th Chief Justice of the Supreme Court, whose decision in the Dred Scott case in 1857 became a violently controversial issue. Taney, who was descended from a prominent Maryland Tidewater family, studied law for three years in Annapolis. He later served in the Maryland House of Delegates and built a successful practice. During the 1820s, Taney allied himself with the Jacksonian Democrats. He gained national recognition when, as Andrew Jackson's attorney general, he persuaded the President to veto a bill to renew the charter of the Bank of the United States.

In 1836, as a reward for Taney's political loyalty, Jackson appointed him chief justice, succeeding John Marshall. Taney held the position for nearly three decades despite a political furor among nationalists who felt the Taney

Court would dismantle Marshall's work. In retrospect, however, it is seen to have refined Marshall's concepts of national judicial power although without extending them.

Slavery Issue. Until the mid-1850s, the Court avoided the slavery question, which was becoming increasingly important. By 1856, however, the prestige and reputation of the Court were thought great enough for it to consider the issue. Although Taney did not believe in slavery, he wrote the opinion of the Court in the Dred Scott decision (1857), which maintained that blacks did not possess rights of citizenship entitling them to sue in federal courts.

With this decision, the prestige of the Court fell to its lowest point, and, with it, the reputation of Taney, a position from which he never recovered. Although unpopular at his death, today Taney is considered one of the great justices by conservatives and liberals alike.

See also Dred Scott Decision (1857).

TAPPAN, ARTHUR AND LEWIS, brothers who were prominent abolitionists. *See* American and Foreign Anti-Slavery Society; American Anti-Slavery Society.

TARBELL, IDA (MINERVA) (1857-1944), American author and editor who became known as a leader of the muckraking movement. Her *History of the Standard Oil Company* (1904) was a sensational and influential revelation of savage competition and exploitation of natural resources.

After editing and writing for *McClure's Magazine* she joined Lincoln Steffens and others in founding the *American Magazine*. Muckraking was only one of many interests in her life. She wrote on many topics, including nine books on Abraham Lincoln.

See also Muckrakers.

TARIFF OF 1828, known as the Tariff of Abominations, was a political maneuver that misfired. It angered the South and produced a serious threat of disunion and the nullification of a federal law by South Carolina. Antitariff men who supported Andrew Jackson introduced a bill with exceptionally high tariffs, hoping that the bill would be defeated and that President Adams would be blamed. This in turn would help swing protectionist states into the Jackson column. The act was more concerned with the "manufacture of a president," said John Randolph of Virginia, than with the manufacture of products.

The tariff passed, however, and one of the chief sponsors, John C. Calhoun of South Carolina, subsequently led the Southern battle against the act—called the Tariff of Abominations not only for its high levels of protection but also for the political trickery behind it.

South Carolina nullified the act in 1832 and threatened to leave the Union. President Jackson stood firm, made the counterthreat of using the army, and a compromise was hammered out in 1833.

See also Calhoun, John C.; Jackson, Andrew; Nullification; Tariffs.

Consult (III) Freehling, 1967; Remini, 1969.

TARIFFS, the taxes placed on goods imported into a country, have played a significant role in U.S. economic policies. After independence, many Americans followed Alexander Hamilton's lead in demanding high tariffs against foreign imports to protect native American producers from competition. Others, especially farmers and exporters (such as cotton planters), hated tariffs because a tariff made foreign goods more expensive for them to buy, made it harder for foreigners to sell goods in America, and therefore probably cut down the amount of exports the same foreigners could afford to buy from Americans.

From the antitariff or free trade point of view, an import duty is really a tax imposed by the government on the American consumer. It raises the price he must pay for the foreign product, and because it benefits the native producers of that same product, the tariff in essence takes money from the general consumer and transfers it to the native producer. It redistributes income in favor of certain privileged and protected businessmen and the workers in the protected industries.

Early Tariffs. The first tariff, introduced by Hamilton in 1789, was mainly for revenue, which was desperately needed by the new government, but it also gave slight protection to certain industries. Hamilton was not pleased with it and demanded much higher levels, openly for protection, in his *Report on Manufactures* (1791). An act of 1792 raised tariff levels, and New England and Pennsylvania supported the act, while the South and West opposed it.

The beginnings of an infant textile industry in New England created more general support. The new nationalism of the West, expressed by spokesmen such as Henry Clay of Kentucky, made farmers in the new Midwestern settlements see the value of tariffs. The revenues from them would finance the internal improvement—roads, canals, and later railroads—that the West needed. The stimulus to Eastern industry would lead to city growth and the expansion of a home market for farm products.

Clay's American System could not attract the Southern cotton planters—their major market was still in England. New England was at first split over the tariff: shippers did not like it, because it could reduce their flow of business; manufacturers wanted it. However, after

about 1830, the Northeast supported tariffs, while the South consolidated itself against them. The issue was thus a major source of conflict between North and South.

The Tariff of Abominations of 1828 was most hated by Southerners, and when the Tariff of 1832 failed to mollify the South, South Carolina nullified the act, and there was a threat of secession. After that, the tariff level decreased until the Civil War. The Republicans passed the Morrill Tariff of 1861 and increased rates again in 1864, to an average level of more than 47 percent of value.

Era of High Tariffs. After the war, business interests were in control, and tariffs increased so much that the federal government had an embarrassing surplus of funds—$145 million in 1882. A tariff commission suggested cuts of up to 25 percent in levels, but the 1883 act that followed did very little to lower rates. Since the days of President Polk the Democrats had stood for lower tariffs, and President Cleveland, another Democrat, tried to reduce the duties. He fought for reelection in 1888 on that plank, and after his defeat the Republicans' McKinley Tariff of 1890 raised levels still further, to an average of almost 50 percent. Protection was even extended to foodstuffs.

The free traders took heart with the second Administration of Cleveland, who was elected in 1892. But his Wilson-Gorman Tariff Reform Act of 1894 was another fiasco because the Senate hacked the reductions out of the bill. When McKinley, for whom protection and Americanism were the same thing, became president in 1896, upward revisions were inevitable. The Dingley Tariff of 1897 raised tariffs to 57 percent, the highest level of the nineteenth century.

No serious inroad was made in tariff protection in the United States until the act of 1913 under President Woodrow Wilson. The 1920s saw higher rates again, and the Smoot-Hawley Tariff of 1931 brought such levels that it made it impossible for Europe to repay World War I debts to the United States. The act was a factor in the breakdown of the European economy in the 1930s and had disastrous political results.

Postwar Tariffs. Modern economists are not fully agreed on what impact tariffs actually have on economic growth. Do they really protect? Do they speed up growth? It seems agreed that U.S. tariffs did not have much effect on the overall shape, content, or course of trade or industrial development. Nevertheless, they must have affected the rate of manufacturing growth by accelerating it to some degree.

Since World War II, the U.S. attitude toward tariffs has softened considerably, as seen by its participation in such programs as the General Agreement on Tariffs and Trade

TARIFFS, 1861–1931

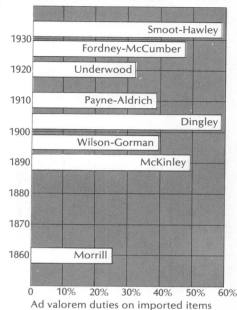

Ad valorem duties on imported items

TARIFFS — Item Guide

The main article TARIFFS has several related entries. Economic concepts are discussed in FREE TRADE and FREE ENTERPRISE.

ALEXANDER HAMILTON was one of the early tariff defenders in his REPORT ON MANUFACTURES (1791). Regionally, the South came to oppose trade barriers and reacted strongly to the TARIFF OF 1828. To reassert state sovereignty, JOHN C. CALHOUN developed the doctrine of NULLIFICATION to oppose federal tariffs.

After the Civil War tariffs were high, although President GROVER CLEVELAND tried to lower them. President WILLIAM McKINLEY was the foremost exponent of high levels. WOODROW WILSON reduced tariffs, but the SMOOT-HAWLEY TARIFF (1931) restored high duties. Since World War II the GENERAL AGREEMENT ON TARIFFS AND TRADE has brought general reductions.

(GATT). Weaknesses in the U.S. trade position, such as the imbalance in U.S.-Japanese trade, bring demands for protection of native industries. But the vehemence of tariff disputes throughout U.S. history has been out of proportion to the relatively small economic significance of tariffs. They were a red herring in political life.

Consult (V) Bolino, 1966; Bunke, 1970; Hacker, 1970.

—Peter d'A. Jones, *University of Illinois, Chicago Circle*

TAYLOR, ZACHARY (1784–1850), 12th President of the United States (1849–1850). Also a frontier Indian fighter and military hero, he was the last Whig elected to the White House. Born in Montebello, Va., on Nov. 24, 1784, Taylor spent his youth in Kentucky. At 22 he volunteered for military service and spent most of the next 30 years in campaigns against Indians in the Midwest and Florida. It was his 1837 victory over the Seminoles that won him promotion to brigadier general.

In 1846 and 1847 he achieved a national reputation in the Mexican War when his outnumbered forces won major victories at the battles of Monterrey and Buena Vista. Despite his success, he was soon embroiled in a bitter dispute with his superior officer, Gen. Winfield Scott, and with President Polk. Part of Taylor's difficulties stemmed from his headstrong refusal to obey the orders of Scott and Polk, but he also became convinced he was a victim of the President's political jealousy and envy— Polk was a Democrat, Taylor a Whig.

Presidency. Taylor's national reputation and his vague position on key issues made him the Whig candidate for president in 1848. He won over Democrat Lewis Cass and ex-President Van Buren, the Free-Soil candidate. Taylor began his term as president with noncommittal platitudes and a promise to appoint a nonpartisan cabinet, but his nonpartisan cabinet was soon rocked by scandal, and Taylor found himself in the middle of the growing dispute over the extension of slavery into the territories. In the summer of 1849, it became apparent that California and New Mexico would request admission as nonslave states and upset the precarious balance between slave and nonslave states. Taylor himself was a slaveholder, but he supported the admission of California and New Mexico, thus defying Southern Whigs and Democrats.

When Henry Clay brought forth a series of compromise measures to settle the issue, Taylor denounced them as concessions to Southern sentiment. Because of his political ineptness, Taylor had little success in shaping congressional action on these issues. In the midst of the debates that ultimately resulted in the Compromise of 1850, Taylor was stricken ill and died in Washington, D.C., on July 9. His successor, Millard Fillmore, successfully supported Clay's measures.

See also Compromise of 1850; Fillmore, Millard; Mexican War.

Consult (III) Hamilton, 1951.

—Dan T. Carter, *University of Maryland*

TEA ACT, British legislation that levied tax on tea and led to Boston Tea Party. *See* Boston Tea Party (1773).

TEAPOT DOME, a U.S. Navy oil reserve in Wyoming that became the symbol for a series of governmental scandals in Warren G. Harding's Administration of the early 1920s. The most flagrant scandals involved, besides Teapot Dome, another oil reserve (Elk Hills), the Veteran's Bureau, the Alien Property Custodian, and the attorney general's office.

In the Teapot Dome-Elk Hills case, the Secretary of the Navy turned control of the reserves over to Secretary of the Interior Albert B. Fall of New Mexico. Fall in turn traded the oil-rich property to some sleazy oil operators in exchange for above-ground petroleum storage. The arrangement was advantageous for the government because the reserves were being drained by nearby private wells. Unfortunately the oilmen made a lot of money, and Fall even more unfortunately took money from them, for which he went to prison.

Senator Walsh of Montana, who led the congressional investigation uncovering the scandal, was persecuted by the press and FBI agents. Indeed, perhaps the most significant aspect of Teapot Dome and the other scandals was how little they upset the voting public. A large part of the population apparently agreed with journalists who asserted that such incidents involving get-rich-quick businessmen were a necessary by-product of maintaining prosperity. On the other hand, critics said that materialism was bad enough but that corrupt materialism was unforgivable.

See also Harding, Warren G.

Consult (VI) Bates, 1966.

TECUMSEH (1768?–1813), Shawnee Indian war leader who opposed the land-grabbing tactics of Indiana governor William Henry Harrison before the War of 1812. While Harrison extracted more than 3 million acres of land in central and northern Indiana, Tecumseh and his brother, the Prophet, had begun a confederacy of tribes that they hoped would block American expansion. Preaching a return to the old practices, the Prophet led a religious revival movement among the tribesmen, while Tecumseh strove to weld a political and military alliance among tribes from the Great Lakes to the Gulf of Mexico. Gradually, the abilities of these two leaders convinced many of the northern tribes to join in a desperate effort to halt the flood of pioneers into their homeland.

Zachary Taylor, 12th President of the United States (1849–1850), won election of 1848 as Mexican War hero.

In 1808 the Indians founded the village of Prophetstown near the confluence of the Wabash River and Tippecanoe Creek in Indiana. When the Indians visited the British at Fort Malden near Detroit, officials there warned them not to start any fighting, but raids on frontier settlements began by 1810.

In July 1811 Tecumseh went south to enlist the large tribes there in the confederacy, but he had little success. When Tecumseh left Indiana, Governor Harrison led a militia army against Prophetstown, meeting the Indians in November at the Battle of Tippecanoe. Although the fighting was inconclusive, it scattered the confederacy, made Harrison a national hero, and touched off the northwestern phase of the War of 1812. Tecumseh returned to Indiana, rallied the dispersed warriors, and fought beside the British for the next year and a half. He died while fighting against Harrison's troops at the Battle of the Thames (October 1813) in Canada.

See also Harrison, William Henry; War of 1812.

Consult (III) Klinck, 1961; Tucker, 1956.
—Roger L. Nichols, *University of Arizona*

TEHERAN CONFERENCE, the first Big Three conference of World War II, held in Teheran, Iran, Nov. 28–Dec. 1, 1943. Franklin Roosevelt, Winston Churchill, and Joseph Stalin concentrated on grand strategy for the last phase of the European war and reached important decisions. The United States and Britain made a firm commitment to open a second front in France in May 1944, and the Russians agreed to time their spring offensive with the cross-channel invasion. Stalin also reaffirmed an earlier promise to enter the war against Japan after Germany had been defeated. Although no political agreements were concluded, the Big Three also discussed postwar questions, and Roosevelt and Stalin in particular seemed to be in agreement on such general matters as the need for an international organization to keep the peace and for severe treatment of Germany. The meetings were often tense, but the conference ended harmoniously and brought the Allies closer together than at any previous time in the war.

See also Churchill, Winston S.; Stalin, Joseph.

TELEGRAPH. *See* Inventions; Morse, Samuel F. B.

TELEPHONE. *See* Bell, Alexander Graham; Inventions.

TELLER RESOLUTION (1898), passed by Congress in April 1898 as part of the war resolution that preceded the Spanish-American War. Proposed by Senator Henry Teller of Colorado, it put the United States on record as having no intention of exercising any "sovereignty, jurisdiction, or control" over Cuba when it was liberated from Spanish rule. Once the war was over, however, the United States feared that U.S. strategic and financial interests would be compromised, and a stronger U.S.-Cuban relationship was established by the Platt Amendment in 1901.

See also Platt Amendment (1901).

TEMPORARY NATIONAL ECONOMIC COMMITTEE, group established in 1938 to investigate the growth of monopolies. *See* Business Regulation.

TEN-HOUR MOVEMENT, effort by laborers to reduce the normal working day to 10 hours. American urban workers began to push for the 10-hour day by the 1830s, when the average was 12 or 13 hours. Agitation for shorter hours began under President Jackson and increased until President Van Buren decreed a 10-hour day for all labor on federal contracts (1840). A New England convention demanded in October 1844 the extension of this rule to the private sector.

Labor strikes and agitation continued through the radical 1840s, and local pressures made some states pass laws—eight states having the 10-hour day by 1855. These laws were loose, and there were no inspection provisions. After the Civil War the movement for shorter hours continued, but as late as the 1890s many workers were still laboring a 9-hour day, and 10 hours was not at all unusual.

Consult (III) Dulles, 1966.

TENNENT, GILBERT (1703–1764), American Presbyterian minister. Born in Ireland, he came to America with his family about 1717. With his three brothers, he was trained for the Presbyterian ministry by his father, William Tennent, founder of the Log College.

In his early sermons in the Middle Atlantic colonies Tennent stressed dramatically the need for repentance and conscious inner change by sinners. During this period (1726–1740) Tennent helped his father with the Log College, and he came to know George Whitefield and other leaders of the Great Awakening, many of whom lived in the vicinity of the Log College.

Between 1741 and 1748, Tennent became deeply involved in the split in the Presbyterian church in the colonies. He was the acknowledged leader of the New Light faction, although in subsequent years Tennent worked to heal the breach. Tennent traveled to England in 1753 to raise funds for the newly formed College of New Jersey (now Princeton University), of which he was a trustee. Soon after that

Tennessee Valley Authority supported land reclamation projects to improve watershed protection and commercial timber potential.

Less than 20 years later the badly eroded hillside had been transformed into a productive, forested area.

he returned to Philadelphia, where he lived until his death.

See also Log College; Presbyterians.

TENNESSEE, the 16th state, admitted to the Union on June 1, 1796. It was the first state created from national territory. Hunters from Virginia were the first settlers in the area, coming to the Watauga River Valley in 1769. Part of eastern Tennessee was included in the short-lived state of Franklin. Tennessee gained territorial status in 1794. A Confederate state during the Civil War, Tennessee was the first to be readmitted to the Union (March 1866).

The state legislature is bicameral; Nashville is the capital. The population in 1970 was 3,924,164.

See also Franklin, State of.

TENNESSEE VALLEY AUTHORITY (TVA), long-range regional planning project established in 1933 in the midst of the emergency legislation of the Hundred Days. It was the result of a long-term crusade by Senator George W. Norris, a leading proponent of the public ownership of utilities, who enlisted President-elect Roosevelt to support the legislation. An immediate result was 40,000 new construction jobs in the Tennessee River Valley. A long-range result was rehabilitation of the depleted and underdeveloped region.

For a generation after 1933 the Authority—in the form of a three-man directorate—added 20 dams to existing facilities, providing the region with flood control, an extensive inland waterway, electric power for industrial development, and soil conservation. TVA's sponsors saw it as a model for additional regional authorities. In the late 1930s, Norris advocated six others like it, but TVA's critics viewed it as a socialistic experiment, and Congress would not follow his lead.

See also Hundred Days; New Deal; Norris, George W.

Consult (VI) Lilienthal, 1965; Lowitt, 1971.

TENURE OF OFFICE ACT (1867), legislation passed to reduce President Johnson's power over federal patronage. It provided that no federal officeholder whose appointment was made with the advice and consent of the Senate could be removed by the president without senatorial approval. Johnson tested the constitutionality of the law on Feb. 21, 1868, by removing Secretary of War Stanton from office. The Senate refused to concur, and the House promptly passed the Covode Resolution impeaching the President.

During Johnson's Senate trial (March–May 1868), his lawyers argued that the President, like any citizen, had a right to violate what he thought an unconstitutional law in

order to test it; that Johnson had therefore no criminal intent and could not be considered guilty; that presidents had customarily had the power to remove cabinet officers; that the act did not cover Stanton's case, because Lincoln, not Johnson, had appointed him in the first place, an opinion supported by influential senators. These arguments swayed enough senators so that Johnson escaped conviction by the margin of one vote. On March 5, 1887, the act was officially repealed.

See also Covode Resolution; Johnson, Andrew.

TERMINATION POLICY, program to end government support for certain Indian tribes. *See* Indian Policy.

TERRITORIES AND POSSESSIONS. Since 1783 the United States has held land organized as either territories or possessions. The Treaty of Paris (1783), which recognized American independence, granted the new nation a vast land area between the Appalachians and the Mississippi River. Only a few thousand whites lived there, and although some of the original 13 states claimed portions of the West, no effective government existed there. During the summer of 1787 the Reverend Mannaseh Cutler and his associates in the Ohio Company urged Congress to set up some plan of government for the West, a request that resulted in the Northwest Ordinance (1787), which laid the foundation for the American territorial system.

Northwest Territory Model. This legislation created the first territory and provided guidelines for the peaceful evolution of government in the West. The first step in the process came when Congress passed an organic act, which created the territory, establishing its name and boundaries as well as an outline of what future steps had to be taken to gain statehood. The Northwest Territory faced a three-step process. First the federal government appointed all territorial officials. Then, when the free adult male population reached 5,000 the citizens elected one of the two legislative houses and sent a nonvoting delegate to Congress. The third step came when the territory had a population of 60,000. When territorial leaders petitioned for statehood, it was assumed that Congress would pass an enabling act authorizing a territorial constitutional convention. After the constitution had been written and approved by the citizens, it went to Congress. If it was accepted, the territory became a state.

Usually this general outline was followed, although the history of the territories varies widely. During the first few decades after the passage of the Northwest Ordinance, the territories achieved statehood quickly and with little opposition. For example, the Southwest

Territory, created in 1790, became the state of Tennessee only six years later. In addition to Tennessee, Ohio, Louisiana, Indiana, Mississippi, Illinois, and Alabama had passed through the territorial process to achieve statehood by 1820.

Development of the West. After 1820, however, political and economic considerations became more significant, and prior to the Civil War each new application for statehood drew Congress and the nation more deeply into the slavery controversy. For example, Missouri's 1820 application caused enormous debate, resulted in the Missouri Compromise, and introduced a sense of division and bitterness that had not been evident in earlier decisions to grant statehood.

Despite the increasing debate over creating new states, the Wisconsin Organic Act of 1836 eased the path somewhat by eliminating the first stage of federal rule. After that, all territories began their climb toward statehood at the second stage with an elected legislature and a congressional delegate in Washington.

Once the Civil War had ended debate over slavery, other considerations complicated and delayed territorial political evolution. The voting habits of territorial citizens were used to support or oppose statehood. However, politics was not the only reason to ignore Western demands for statehood. Strong anti-Mormon feelings and a recurring fight between church and federal officials combined to keep Utah a territory for decades. New Mexico suffered from anti-Catholic and anti-Mexican views that delayed its admission as a state until 1912. Frequently, the small and mobile Western population was cited as the reason for congressional inaction, but in several instances territorial citizens themselves opposed statehood because they would then have to pay the cost of their own government. In spite of these deviations from the system, the pattern of development from unsettled area to state assured American pioneers that they would have their basic civil rights.

Beyond the 48 States. While the last of the contiguous parts of the nation moved toward statehood, the United States embarked on an era of overseas expansion that differed markedly from earlier continental territorial growth. On several occasions during the nineteenth century, Americans discussed annexing neighboring islands and even countries. Mexico, Santo Domingo, Cuba, and Canada all attracted American attention, but good sense overcame such ideas. Nevertheless, well before the Spanish-American War the nation stepped beyond its continental borders to buy Alaska and the nearby islands from Russia in 1867.

At the end of the Spanish-American War, however, the nation suddenly found itself occupying Spanish-held islands in both the Pacific and the Caribbean. The easy victory over Spain and an unwillingness to part with these territories created an American overseas empire. A short but bitter debate over whether America should keep the captured regions ended with the decision to do just that. By World War I the United States held islands stretching from the Philippines and Hawaii in the Pacific to the Virgin Islands and Puerto Rico in the Caribbean. Arguments over taxation, citizenship, and constitutional freedoms for the inhabitants of these possessions led to the Insular Cases. In three decisions handed down in 1901 the Supreme Court ruled that the Constitution did not always follow the flag and that Congress could give or withhold whatever rights it chose from those living in the possessions. U.S. interest in overseas territories waned after World War I as Americans discovered their high cost and low value. Although the Philippines gained its independence in 1946 and Hawaii became the fiftieth state in 1959, the nation still retains other overseas possessions.

See also Alaska Purchase (1867); Land Companies; Northwest Ordinance; Northwest Territory; Spanish-American War (1898).

—Roger L. Nichols, *University of Arizona*

TEXAS, 28th state, entered the Union on Dec. 29, 1845. Initial white settlement of the area was by the Spanish in 1681 at Ysleta, now part of El Paso. Although John Quincy Adams offered $1 million and Andrew Jackson $5 million for the purchase of Texas, Spanish and then Mexican domination of the area continued until 1836, when Texas declared its independence. Although the Texans were defeated at the Alamo in March, the next month they were victorious at San Jacinto under the leadership of Sam Houston. The independent Republic of Texas existed until 1845, when it was annexed by the United States. Texas joined the Confederacy during the Civil War.

The state legislature is bicameral; the capital is Austin. The population in 1970 was 11,196,730.

See also Mexican War.

THAMES, BATTLE OF THE (1813), American victory over British and Indian allies on the Canadian border. *See* War of 1812.

THEATER. The beginnings of American theater were in Mexico and Canada rather than what is now the United States. As early as 1534, there are fragmentary records of religious plays being performed in Mexico. In 1606 in Port Royal (now Annapolis Royal, Nova Scotia), a play called *Neptune's Folly* was performed as part of a regular entertainment called "The Order of the Good Time."

Perhaps it was somewhat prophetic that this early performance was produced by The

Eugene O'Neill's work helped to transform twentieth-century drama.

Dance scene from *Oklahoma!*, one of the most successful American musicals.

Order of the Good Time because in American theater it was not until well after 1900 that the theater was to be regarded as more than a medium of entertainment. With the plays of Eugene O'Neill in the 1920s, the theater became a forum of ideas and a place of innovative experiment.

Colonial Period (1700–1800). From 1700 to 1750, a few small rudimentary theaters were built, first in Williamsburg, Va., and then in Charleston, S.C. Their existence showed an enthusiasm and a desire for theater in the colonies except for New England, where there was opposition to "play-acting and similar lewd diversions." By the 1750s several theaters had been built in New York and Philadelphia, and an English professional company, under the leadership of Lewis Hallam, came to the colonies. The Hallam family, father and son, were to be the leading figures in American theater of this colonial period.

After the Revolutionary War, Lewis Hallam, Jr., started the American Company, which for some years had almost a complete monopoly on the theater of the Eastern seaboard. It was this company that produced *The Contrast* by Royall Tyler in 1787—the first play written by an American on an American theme for an American audience.

Two large theaters were built about 1800—the Chestnut Street Theatre in Philadelphia and the Park Theatre in New York. The Park Theatre was headed by William Dunlap, who, inspired by a performance of *The Contrast,* became a playwright and wrote 53 plays. Dunlap has been called "the father of American drama" even though modern criticism does not usually rank him as an important playwright.

Nineteenth Century. With the opening of the Western frontier, theaters were built soon after the towns sprang up. New Orleans, Cincinnati, and St. Louis had substantial theaters by the 1820s. This activity in the cities was mirrored in small towns all over the country. Showboats plied the waters of the Mississippi and its tributaries.

During this period of expansion, the plays were mostly sheer entertainment—melodramas, comedies, romances. Before 1850, there was a mixture of farces, burlesques, importations from England, and an occasional Shakespearean revival. From 1850 to 1900, the fortunes of the American commercial theater were built mainly on four plays: *Uncle Tom's Cabin, Camille* (a European import), *East Lynne* (a melodrama), and *The Black Crook* (a musical melodrama). The "Tommers" (as the *Uncle Tom's Cabin* companies were called) played almost every local theater and "opera house."

The nineteenth century was also the age of American actors, who perhaps enjoyed a fame even greater than at present, when the competition of film and television stars tends to overshadow theater actors. The great actors of the century included Edwin Booth (whose brother shot Lincoln), Edwin Forrest, William Gillette, James H. Hackett, Robert Mantell, Richard Mansfield, Minnie Maddern Fiske, and Maude Adams. Foreign actors included Sir Henry Irving, Ellen Terry, and Mrs. Patrick Campbell from England and Sarah Bernhardt and the great Coquelin from France.

Early Twentieth Century. Society comedies, revivals, burlesques, Weber and Fields, and Maude Adams in *Peter Pan* were about the sum of the regular and rather bland diet provided by the American theater in the first two decades of the twentieth century. Always in the background was the gray eminence of David Belasco, a producer-director who insisted on detailed realism on stage but actually did little to advance the American theater artistically.

These two decades were a time of furious theater-building. Theater had become "show business," and there were a number of businessmen, such as the three Shubert brothers, who were happy to turn producer to reap some of the financial rewards. In 1900 there were 43 theaters in New York, and by 1928 the number had nearly doubled.

The Dynamic Period (1920–1950). In 1920 the American theater was rescued from mediocrity by Eugene O'Neill, certainly one of the most provocative and contradictory playwrights. His plays, for which he received the Nobel Prize (1936), included *The Emperor Jones* (1920), *Anna Christie* (1921), *The Hairy Ape* (1922), *Strange Interlude* (1928), *Mourning Becomes Electra* (1931), *The Iceman Cometh* (1946), and the posthumously produced *Long Day's Journey Into Night* (1956). Possessed of an essentially tragic view of life, he startled the American theater by writing plays of deep emotion and considerable thought and by cutting deep into the complacency and conventions of the period.

O'Neill was followed by Thornton Wilder's *Our Town* (1938). Beneath its sentimental surface picture of small-town New England life it digs deep into the eternal values of birth, love, marriage, and death. Wilder also wrote *The Skin of Our Teeth* (1942) and *The Matchmaker* (1954), which was turned into the long-running musical *Hello Dolly.*

During the 1930s the U.S. government tried its first and rather brief experiment in national theater, the Federal Theatre Project. It was conceived as a public works project to give employment to out-of-work actors, but it became a political football that destroyed the possibility of its becoming a national theater.

Whereas Thornton Wilder had written with great humanity about life in New England, Tennessee Williams wrote sensitively about the South, its decadence, and the broken dreams of some of its people. His most famous and successful play was *A Streetcar Named Desire* (1947), but some of his other plays, notably *The Glass Menagerie* (1944), *Summer and Smoke* (1945), and *Camino Real* (1953), show different facets and aspects of his sensitive and varied talents. Arthur Miller brought something of Ibsen's anger and passion for reform into his plays: *All My Sons* (1947), *The Crucible* (1952), and *Death of a Salesman* (1949). In *Death of a Salesman,* Miller came close to writing the tragedy of modern America—the overwhelming tragedy of a devotion to false ideals.

American musical comedy also came into its own in the period from 1920 to 1950, starting with the Jerome Kern-Oscar Hammerstein production of *Showboat* in 1927. The team of Richard Rogers and Hammerstein was especially successful: *Oklahoma* (1943), *Carousel* (1945), *South Pacific* (1949), and *The King and I* (1951).

Scarcely less important and popular are the gay, sophisticated musicals of Cole Porter—especially *Kiss Me Kate* (1948). Irving Berlin wrote the music for *Annie Get Your Gun* (1946), and George Gershwin wrote the score for *Porgy and Bess* (1935).

Modern Theater. Since about 1950 the American theater has been desperately "searching"—trying to find meaning in absurdity and new ways of saying familiar things while confronted with the massive competition of television and films.

Certainly this period includes the extraordinary success of *Who's Afraid of Virginia Woolf* by Edward Albee, but Albee has written nothing to equal it since. Other writers, such as Arthur Miller and Tennessee Williams, have not produced important plays since the mid-1950s. There have been some interesting imports from abroad, which were influenced by the Absurdist School started by Eugene Ionesco and Samuel Beckett, whose *Waiting for Godot* is probably the best of them. Significant American plays include Lorraine Hansberry's *A Raisin in the Sun* (1959) and, in the musical field, *West Side Story*, with a brilliant score by Leonard Bernstein, and *Godspell,* a modern rock version of a medieval mystery play. The light comedies of Neil Simon have been extremely popular.

See also Albee, Edward; Berlin, Irving; O'Neill, Eugene; Williams, Tennessee.

Consult (VIII) Atkinson, 1970; Engel, 1967; Mathews, 1967; Meserve, 1965.

—A. Munroe Wade, *Westminster Choir College*

THEORY OF THE LEISURE CLASS, THE (1899). *See* Veblen, Thorstein.

THOREAU, HENRY DAVID (1817-1862). The most individualistic Transcendentalist, Thoreau was by temperament an iconoclast whose life seems especially relevant today. He was born in Concord, Mass., and lived there virtually all his life. Graduating from Harvard in 1837, he taught in the Concord schools and tried in vain to carry on the family pencil-making business. Thoreau opened his own small school with his brother in Concord and ran it from 1839 to 1841. From an early age Thoreau loved to roam the wilderness and record his personal observations in journals.

In September 1839, Thoreau and his brother undertook a two-week river journey that became the subject of his first book, *A Week on the Concord and Merrimack Rivers* (1849). He lived with Ralph Waldo Emerson for two years and was associated with the Transcendental group active in Concord. On July 4, 1845, he took up residence at Walden Pond on Emerson's land and for two years used this as a retreat from civilization. In 1845 he spent a night in jail for refusal to pay the poll tax in a protest against slavery and the Mexican War. His essay justifying his actions, "On Civil Disobedience," has become one of the leading twentieth-century texts on civil passive resistance and has been quoted by Ghandi as well as by many Americans and Europeans.

Thoreau's major book, *Walden*, appeared in 1854. In it he sums up his individualistic philosophy and his love of nature; the volume distills a lifetime of journal notes. Thoreau's objections to the encroachment of a new industrialized, urbanized civilization have made *Walden* his most influential work. After *Walden*, Thoreau devoted himself to lecturing on the antislavery movement and to further explorations into natural history.

See also Emerson, Ralph Waldo; Transcendentalism.

Consult (III) Anderson, 1968.

—Richard Collin, *Louisiana State University, New Orleans*

Daguerreotype of Henry David Thoreau, author of *Walden.*

THURMOND, (JAMES) STROM (1902-), American political leader. He was born in Edgefield, S.C., graduated from Clemson College in 1923, and was admitted to the bar. He entered politics in 1929 and became a Democratic state senator in 1938. During World War II he served in the army.

Thurmond was elected governor of South Carolina in 1946. In 1948 he disagreed strongly with President Truman and the national Democratic Party over their civil rights program and ran for president as the States' Rights, or Dixiecrat, nominee. He won four Southern states and received 39 electoral votes. In 1954 he became the only successful write-in candidate for the U.S. Senate in the history of the country.

In 1964 Thurmond became a Republican. He helped to swing South Carolina into the Republican column in 1964 and in 1968 was influential in keeping several key states committed to Richard Nixon at the convention. Although his party influence declined somewhat after 1968, Thurmond retained his influence in his home state.

See also Presidential Elections; States' Rights Party.

Consult (VIII) Lachicolte, 1966.

TILDEN, SAMUEL J(ONES) (1814–1886), presidential candidate and lawyer. He was admitted to the New York bar (1841) and entered politics as a Free-Soil Democrat, or Barnburner. Physically frail and secretive, Tilden displayed legal genius at railroad finance and wisely invested his fees to build a vast fortune. He supported the Union in the Civil War, although he disliked President Lincoln and feared centralized government.

Tilden, as chairman of the New York State Democratic Committee (1866–1871), cooperated with Boss Tweed to rebuild Democratic power. When the Tweed Ring was exposed, Tilden turned on Tweed and led the prosecution that broke the ring. Public acclaim carried Tilden to a gubernatorial victory (1874), which enabled him to reduce taxes, revamp the judicial structure, and destroy the Republican-dominated Canal Ring. Tilden inevitably became the Democrats' presidential choice to run against Republican corruption.

The campaign of 1876, marred by fraud in both parties, saw Tilden win the popular vote and apparently the electoral vote also. However, challenged votes in four states forced the creation of an electoral commission that, by a partisan vote, awarded the victory to Rutherford B. Hayes. Tilden displayed irresolution during the controversy and finally accepted the verdict, stating it would prevent renewed civil strife and guarantee the election of a Democrat in 1880. He assumed he would be renominated and vindicated, but his poor health led the Democrats to another candidate. Tilden never married and willed the bulk of his fortune for a free library, a bequest that helped create the New York Public Library.

See also Hayes, Rutherford B.; Presidential Elections; Tweed, Boss.

Consult (V) Woodward, 1966.

—George Lankevich, *Bronx Community College of The City University of New York*

TIPPECANOE, BATTLE OF (1811), battle with Indians that Americans acclaimed as a victory. *See* Tecumseh.

TONKIN RESOLUTION. *See* Gulf of Tonkin Resolution.

TOWNSHEND ACTS (1767), taxes levied by Parliament on the colonies at the suggestion of Chancellor of the Exchequer Charles Townshend. The taxes were supposed to raise money to pay both royal troops stationed there and Crown officials in the provinces, who had been dependent on the colonial legislatures for support. Designed to meet objections to the Stamp Act, the Townshend Acts taxed only imports, including glass, paper, paints, lead, and tea.

Parliament established the American Board of Customs Commissioners, headquartered in Boston, to enforce the laws and set up juryless vice-admiralty courts with original and appellate jurisdiction over cases involving violations of the Acts. Angered by the Townshend program, Americans argued that Parliament could levy import duties only to control trade and not to raise revenue and denounced as hostile to the rights of Englishmen the establishment of courts that did not have jury trials.

TRADE EXPANSION ACT (1962) gave the president wide authority to cut tariffs. *See* General Agreement on Tariffs and Trade.

TRAIL OF TEARS, name given to route Cherokees took on their removal to Oklahoma. *See* Indian Policy.

TRANSCENDENTALISM, system of beliefs that maintains that faith and imagination are more important than reason, which deals solely with material things. American Transcendentalism formally began with the founding of the Transcendental Club in Concord, Mass., in 1836. Ralph Waldo Emerson and Bronson Alcott were the mainstays of the club and the movement, which included among its members virtually all the New England literary establishment—Theodore Parker, Margaret Fuller, Orestes Brownson, Elizabeth and Sophia Peabody, William Ellery Channing, and Henry David Thoreau. The Transcendentalists were influenced by Immanuel Kant's *Critique of Pure Reason* (1788), which challenged scientific rationalism's predominance in intellectual matters. Transcendentalism, with its ideals of individual ability and an inward relationship to God and the Universe, was well suited to American beliefs of political equality as well as to the development of American Protestant theology.

The Dial (1840–1844), with Margaret Fuller as editor, became the semiofficial organ of the group. Important statements of Transcendental beliefs are in Emerson's *Nature* and his essay "Over-Soul," which sets forth the Emersonian metaphor of Transcendental belief. Also important are Emerson's "Compensation," "Self Reliance," and "Divinity School Address" and Thoreau's *Walden*.

Transcendentalism's multiple sources make difficult any identification of direct influences by specific European writers on the New

England movement. However, Kant's influence on other German philosophers, on Goethe, and also on the English Romantic writers was profound, and many of Kant's ideas came to America in second- or third-hand versions. More a state of mind than a consistent philosophical system, Transcendentalism maintained that God was immanent throughout the world and that everyone shared in this divinity; each man was therefore a microcosm of all the world's inherent potentialities. Man fulfilled his divine potential by contact with God directly or by contact with nature, which contained the divine truth, wisdom, and beauty of the Over-Soul, or the unity of all man and nature with God.

See also Emerson, Ralph Waldo; Thoreau, Henry David.

—Richard Collin, *Louisiana State University, New Orleans*

TRANSPORTATION, DEPARTMENT OF (DOT), cabinet-level executive department charged with developing and coordinating federal transportation policies and programs.

An outgrowth of the U.S. trend toward comprehensive planning, DOT was established in 1966. DOT combined about 30 existing agencies and bureaus, including the Bureau of Public Roads, the Great Lakes Pilotage Administration, and the St. Lawrence Seaway Development Corporation, all formerly in the Commerce Department; the U.S. Coast Guard from the Treasury Department; and the safety functions of the Civil Aeronautics Board and the Interstate Commerce Commission.

TRANSYLVANIA COMPANY. *See* Land Companies.

TRAVIS, W. B., commander of the Alamo defenders. *See* Alamo.

TREASURY, DEPARTMENT OF THE, cabinet-level executive department concerned with national fiscal policy. Established in 1789, it is responsible for the collection of revenue and the manufacture of coin and currency. The first official U.S. mint was set up in Philadelphia in 1792, but paper currency was privately printed in varying designs until the 1860s, when Congress authorized the issuance of official U.S. and national bank notes. The Secret Service, whose duties include protecting the president, was established by the Treasury in 1865 to prevent counterfeiting of the new paper currency.

Alexander Hamilton, the first secretary of the treasury, used financial policies to develop the strength and credibility of the new national government, but the power of his successors was considerably reduced. Until the Civil War, the government depended primarily upon customs duties (tariffs) and public land sale for income. The personal income tax, collected by the Treasury's Internal Revenue Service and the chief source of revenue today, was not initiated until 1913. The Coast Guard, long an arm of the Treasury, was transferred to the Department of Transportation, created in 1966.

See also Coast Guard, U.S.; Hamilton, Alexander; Income Tax.

TREATY OF . . . *See* second part of the name.

TRENT AFFAIR, diplomatic controversy during the Civil War that nearly plunged the United States and Britain into war. It began on Nov. 8, 1861, when Federal Capt. Charles Wilkes stopped the British merchant ship *Trent* and removed the Confederate ambassadors to England (James M. Mason) and France (John Slidell). The North rejoiced wildy over the capture of such notable political prisoners, while the British fumed at such a blatant violation of international laws of neutrality. Britain felt that its national honor had been insulted and began to prepare for war. The common sense of President Lincoln, Secretary of State Seward, Ambassador to Britain C. F. Adams, and Senator Charles Sumner, combined with the restraint of the English cabinet, prevailed and led to an amicable settlement. In late December the United States released the prisoners, and the British accepted the American explanation that Wilkes had acted without authority.

TRENTON, BATTLE OF (DEC. 26, 1776), battle in which Washington crossed the Delaware River to capture Trenton, N.J. *See* Revolutionary War Battles.

TRIANGULAR TRADE, system of international trade with Africa, the West Indies, and New England as its focal points. It involved many products but became notorious because it depended on the manufacture and export of New England rum and its barter on the African Gold Coast for slaves, who were then transported to the West Indies. In the West Indies they were exchanged for sugar or molasses, basic components in the production of rum. The New England vessel then returned with the rum ingredients to its home port, there to refit for another voyage.

Triangular arrangements began early in the North American colonies. Rum gained ascendancy in such transactions because of its exchange value and durability, and slaves became important because the slave trade opened up after the monopoly held by the Royal African Company ended in 1697. Accordingly, rum distilleries multiplied in New England.

The outlawing of the foreign slave trade

Harry S Truman, 33rd President of the United States (1945-1953), waves to crowd during whistlestop campaign of 1948.

"Composer: 'It's A Duet—I Can't Play It Alone.'" President Truman's attempts to secure Congressional cooperation in passing Fair Deal legislation failed.

Reformers urged voters to fight business combinations by electing candidates opposed to trusts.

in 1808 helped to diminish the traffic. Abolitionists who painted the horrors of the Middle Passage—the inhumane ways by which slave traders had conveyed slaves across the Atlantic from Africa to the West Indies and the mainland—were also instrumental in discrediting the triangular trade.

See also Slavery.

TRIPOLITAN WAR. *See* Barbary Coast Wars (to 1815).

TRUAX v. CORRIGAN (1921), Supreme Court decision on due process and equal protection. *See* Brandeis, Louis D.

TRUMAN, HARRY S (1884-1972), 33rd President of the United States (1945-1953). The successor of the popular and influential Franklin Roosevelt, Truman wound up one major war and fought another.

He was born on May 8, 1884, in Lamar, Mo. He served in World War I, entered Missouri Democratic politics after the war, and in 1922 was elected to a county judgeship. Truman was elected to the U.S. Senate in 1934, and he achieved brief renown during World War II for heading a Senate watchdog committee investigating graft in military contracts, which led to his selection in 1944 as Roosevelt's running mate.

Presidency. Truman was ill prepared for assuming the presidency when Roosevelt died on April 12, 1945, but he learned fast. He immediately made a number of major decisions, including backing the formation of the United Nations, using the atom bomb on Japan, and adopting occupation policies for Germany and Japan.

The history of Truman's Administration is largely the record of the early stages of the Cold War: the unsuccessful Big Power conferences, the Truman Doctrine of foreign aid to blunt communist aggression, the Marshall Plan, the Berlin airlift, and NATO.

Truman's domestic accomplishments, with the exception of housing, were quite limited. His Fair Deal program was blocked by conservatives in Congress. He made this an issue in the election of 1948 and pulled a political upset in winning. Despite this vindication, he still was unable to get his program through Congress.

Much of the difficulty in his second term came from the inconclusive war in Korea. In June 1950 he sent in U.S. troops under UN auspices to repulse the North Korean invaders. Although this was accomplished, the Chinese Communist intervention threatened to widen the war. Truman fired his popular field commander, General MacArthur, for insubordination when the latter publicized his disagreements with Truman over strategy.

Although his image was tarnished when he left office in 1953, Truman came to be regarded as the senior statesman of his party. He died in Independence, Mo., on Dec. 26, 1972.

See also Korean War; Marshall Plan; Presidential Elections; Truman Doctrine; World War II.

Consult (VIII) Steinberg, 1962; Truman, 1955-1956.

—Martin Gruberg, *University of Wisconsin, Oshkosh*

TRUMAN DOCTRINE, plan often regarded as the basis for the U.S. position in the Cold War with the Soviet Union. In early 1947 the pro-American governments in Turkey and Greece were seriously threatened with subversion, and Britain had just announced that it could no longer be responsible for maintaining these governments. In response, President Truman asked Congress on March 12, 1947, to provide $400 million in economic and military assistance to bolster the Greek and Turkish governments.

His overall message, however, was more far-reaching. He declared that there existed a struggle between "two ways of life," one free and the other totalitarian. The United States, he declared, should "help free people to maintain their free institutions and their national integrity against aggressive movements that seek to impose upon them totalitarian regimes" in order to maintain international peace and U.S. security. Truman's declaration of America's determination to resist communism provided the ground for the U.S. containment policy in Europe and elsewhere.

See also Marshall Plan.
Consult (VIII) Acheson, 1971.

TRUSTS, combinations in which stockholders of affiliated companies agree that their securities be administered by a common board of trustees. However, the term "trust" soon came to refer to any monopolistic enterprise whether or not it used the trust device. The trust movement grew in the period of stiff competition and falling prices that followed the Civil War. Trusts replaced unenforceable agreements (or pools) between rivals to maintain prices and divide business.

The Standard Oil trust, the first of many trusts, was organized by S. C. T. Dodd in 1882 (a less comprehensive trust agreement had been formed in 1879). What Dodd sought to create was a legal "corporation of corporations." Numerous other trusts followed, controlling among other things cottonseed oil (1884) and whiskey, sugar, and lead (1887). The trust device proved vulnerable; the New York Court of Appeals dissolved the sugar trust (1890), and the Ohio supreme court ordered the breakup of the Standard Oil trust (1892). Undaunted, the sugar trust reorganized as the American Sugar Refining Company (1891), and Standard Oil also reorganized (1899). Both were New Jersey holding companies (preferring that state's lax incorporation laws) that produced no goods directly but owned a controlling portion of the stock of affiliated companies. J. P. Morgan spectacularly merged mergers in 1901 by creating the U.S. Steel Corporation, known to the public as the steel trust.

Attacks on Trusts. Trusts came under early attack. Between 1889 and 1893, 16 states and territories enacted antitrust laws. Federal legislation came with the Sherman Antitrust Act (1890), but it was ineffective until Theodore Roosevelt resolved to abolish trust abuses. Antitrust prosecutions by Roosevelt and his successor, William Howard Taft, did not halt trusts; between 1901 and 1912 the number of trusts expanded sixfold, while their capital expanded fourfold.

Trusts that were broken (such as Standard Oil in 1911) proved resilient. By using such devices as interlocking directorates, unwritten understandings, and price leadership, the various Standard Oil companies continued to cooperate. Woodrow Wilson's efforts to regulate competition were also ineffective. Neither the Clayton Antitrust Act (1914) nor the Federal Trade Commission Act (1914) arrested the concentration of industry, while World War I encouraged the growth of big business.

After 1920 the term "trust" gradually fell into disuse, but monopolies continued. They flourished in the prosperous 1920s and were strong enough to cope with the Great Depression of the 1930s. Although some New Deal legislation curbed combinations, other legislation proved beneficial. The mobilization of the economy in World War II and postwar economic expansion further encouraged the growth of industrial giants, which no longer were called trusts but oligopolies.

See also Antitrust Cases; Business Regulation.

Consult (V) Cochran, 1957; Cochran and Miller, 1961.

—Ari Hoogenboom, *Brooklyn College of The City University of New York*

TRUTH, SOJOURNER (1797–1883), black speaker whose life story contributed to Northern appreciation of abolitionism. Born a slave in New York State, she was named Isabella. She became free in 1827 under a state law providing for gradual abolition, but she had to flee for her freedom because of her master's reluctance to let her go and had to obtain a court order for the return of one of her children.

A mystic, she fell under the influence of a false religious prophet for a time but overcame this influence with the aid of sympa-

thetic white people. She resumed her travels, adopting the name Sojourner Truth in the process, and became a speaker at abolitionist, and later at women's rights, meetings. During the Civil War, Sojourner Truth served as an intermediary between government officials and blacks in Washington and elsewhere. Afterward, she returned to work on religious and libertarian causes.

See also Abolitionism.

Consult (IX) Bernard, 1967.

TUBMAN, HARRIET (1821?–1913), most famous black conductor on the Underground Railroad, was known as "the Moses of her people." She was born and raised in slavery in Maryland. Overworked and cruelly treated, she escaped to freedom in 1849.

After the Fugitive Slave Act of 1850 caused wide resentment in the North and multiplied active friends of escaped slaves, she made daring raids into slave territory—possibly as many as 19—to bring out fugitives, including several of her relatives. In the process, she met many abolitionists and stirred antislavery gatherings with her testimony. Her most famous exploit was her bold and public rescue of the fugitive slave Charles Nalle from the police in Troy, N.Y., in April 1860. She also planned to join John Brown in his Harpers Ferry raid but was stopped by illness. During the Civil War she acted as a scout and nurse. Her reputation was augmented by Sarah H. Bradford's publication in 1869 of *Scenes in the Life of Harriet Tubman,* largely comprised of Tubman's memories.

See also Underground Railroad.

Consult (IX) Conrad, 1943.

TUGWELL, REXFORD G., member of the Brains Trust. *See* Brains Trust.

TURNER, FREDERICK JACKSON (1861–1932), historian noted for his interpretation of the effect of the frontier on American life. *See* Frontier in American History.

TURNER, NAT. *See* Nat Turner's Revolt.

TURNPIKES, EARLY. Although most American transportation before 1820 depended on rivers and crudely marked trails, the first major roads, or turnpikes, had been built by the 1790s. Whether begun by private road companies or state and local governments, turnpikes differed from most existing roads in two ways. They charged travelers for using the road, and, more importantly, they showed that quality roads could be built with the existing technology. The first commercially successful turnpike, constructed in the 1790s, connected Philadelphia and Lancaster, Pa. Promoters soon built similar roads in New England and the Middle Atlantic states. For pioneers moving west, the

Oil trust assembled by John D. Rockefeller was frequent target of critics of monopoly.

Harriet Tubman, born a slave, was most famous conductor of the Underground Railroad.

Tuskegee Institute pioneered in providing education and opportunities for young blacks.

Mark Twain stands outside his boyhood home in Hannibal, Mo., on the Mississippi River.

Knoxville Road and the Old Walton Road opened the way as far as Nashville.

Major roadbuilding slowed for the next two decades, although work on the National Road began just before the War of 1812. This road extended from Maryland to central Illinois. Paved with several layers of crushed rock and flanked with broad, sloping shoulders, it provided travelers and freight haulers with solid stone bridges across the troublesome streams in its path. Between the end of the War of 1812 and the early 1820s a turnpike craze swept the country, and by 1821 more than 4,000 miles of turnpikes had been completed. Growing enthusiasm for canals and, later, railroads combined to cut interest in improving roads until the end of the nineteenth century.

See also National Road.

TUSCARORA WAR (1711–1713), campaign against North Carolina's Tuscarora Indians, who had been aroused by the encroachment of white settlers onto their lands, especially the establishment of a new colony at New Bern. In September 1711 the Tuscaroras killed about 130 colonists. Commanded by Col. John Barnwell, a force of 33 militiamen and 500 Yamasee and Catawba Indians subdued the Tuscaroras, but within a short time the tribe resumed fighting.

Hostilities continued until March 1713, when Col. James Moore, Jr., of South Carolina led 100 militiamen and 800 Cherokee, Catawba, and Creeks against the unruly Indians. The colonists and their native allies overwhelmed the Tuscaroras. After losing 800 warriors and surrendering their fort on the Neuse River, the remaining Tuscaroras left North Carolina for New York, where they found protection among their kinsmen, the Oneidas, and became the sixth Iroquois Nation.

See also Iroquois Confederacy.

TUSKEGEE INSTITUTE, a coeducational, private institution in Tuskegee, Ala., founded by Booker T. Washington as a school of vocational training for Southern blacks. Originally emphasizing farming and crafts in the tradition of the Hampton Institute, Tuskegee now offers degree-granting undergraduate courses and graduate courses and hospital dietetics certification. The school has grown from a student body of 30 to nearly 3,000 undergraduate and graduate students.

Tuskegee was established by an act of the Alabama General Assembly on Feb. 12, 1881, with an annual appropriation of $2,000 for teachers' salaries. The school opened on July 4, 1881, with Booker T. Washington as first principal. George Washington Carver was active as a researcher and teacher at Tuskegee from 1896 until his death.

See also Carver, George Washington; Washington, Booker T.

TWAIN, MARK (1835–1910), pseudonym of Samuel Langhorne Clemens, American humorist, short story writer, and novelist. He grew up in Hannibal, Mo., on the banks of the Mississippi River. As a young man he was successively a journeyman printer, writer of humorous sketches, and wandering journalist. In 1857 he became a riverboat pilot, later recording his experiences on the river in *Life on the Mississippi* (1883). His pseudonym is the river call for a water depth of two fathoms ("mark twain").

The Civil War ended river traffic, and after failing in several get-rich-quick schemes, Twain became a journalist for the Virginia City, Nev., *Territorial Enterprise* and later worked in California. He became famous after the publication of *The Innocents Abroad* (or *The New Pilgrim's Progress*) (1869), a collection of articles about his newspaper-financed trip to Europe and the Holy Land. In 1870 Twain married Olivia Langdon and, after a brief period as an editor in Buffalo, N.Y., settled in Hartford, Conn.

In Hartford he wrote *The Adventures of Tom Sawyer* (1876), a tale of boyish exploits that drew scenes and feelings from the author's early years in Hannibal. His masterpiece, *The Adventures of Huckleberry Finn* (1884), told of a white boy's flight down the Mississippi with Jim, an escaped slave. Ernest Hemingway called this the first and best book in American literature. This judgment is supported by the fact that Twain not only wrote on American themes but also wrote without condescension in the American vernacular. Moreover, he took frontier styles of humor and worked them up to the level of art.

Twain was a popular success as a writer, but misguided business ventures threw him into bankruptcy. While he was on a round-the-world lecture tour to raise money to pay his creditors, he heard of the death of his favorite daughter. A period of extreme depression lasted from 1896 to 1904, marked by the writing of the philosophically pessimistic *The Mysterious Stranger*. In his final years Twain dictated his autobiography.

See also Literature.
Consult (V) Cox, 1966.

TWEED, BOSS (WILLIAM MARCY) (1823–1878), New York political leader who came to symbolize the corruption of political bosses. Born on the Manhattan Island he came to dominate, he rose to political power in classic fashion, holding a variety of increasingly powerful offices. He was one of the New York City aldermen known as the "Forty Thieves," a congressman, and finally Grand Sachem of Tammany Hall (1863). Tweed was first called "Boss" during the Civil War, as he laid the foundations for his "ring."

The Tweed Ring's thievery was possible because it monopolized all parts of the government. Contracts submitted to the city were approved only after payments, from 10 to 85 percent, went to the ring. In 1867 Tweed, as a state senator, broadened his system to include the legislature. When John Hoffman, Tweed's protégé, was elected governor in 1868, the ring's power encompassed all New York State.

Outraged citizens alerted by Thomas Nast's anti-Tammany cartoons and the editorials of the New York *Times* demanded an investigation, but only when disgruntled ring members made documentary evidence available was a "Committee of Seventy," led by Samuel Tilden, able to break the ring. Tweed served a short jail term, then fled to Spain to avoid a trial to recover the stolen money. After extradition, he died in jail. Only Tweed of all the ring was punished, although it is estimated that New York was looted of between $30 and $200 million.

See also Tilden, Samuel J.
Consult (V) Callow, 1969.
—George Lankevich, *Bronx Community College of The City University of New York*

TWO-THIRDS RULE (1832), rule requiring that "two-thirds of the whole number of votes in the convention shall be necessary to constitute a choice." The first national nominating convention of the Democratic Party (1832) adopted the two-thirds rule, which remained in force until 1936.

TWO YEARS BEFORE THE MAST (1840), a lively, realistic, personal narrative of sea life by Richard Henry Dana (1815–1852). Written in the form of an extended journal, it was an instant success and became a classic in sea-story literature. Its publication marked a break from the romanticism of the early nineteenth century.

The book was written from notes Dana made during his two-year voyage from Boston around Cape Horn to California. Dana, much to his father's consternation, interrupted his studies at Harvard to become a seaman aboard the brig *Pilgrim*. His adventures aboard ship seem to convey the same spirit that his forebears might have felt when they first set sail for North America.

TYLER, JOHN (1790–1862), 10th President of the United States (1841–1845). He was born in Greenway, Va., on March 29, 1790. He served the Jeffersonian and then the Jacksonian Democrats of his native state as a U.S. representative (1816–1821), governor (1825–1827), and U.S. senator (1827–1836). An adamant strict constructionist, he broke with Jackson over nullification and the removal of the deposits from the Bank of the United States. In the mid-1830s he joined the state's rights wing of the Southern Whig Party.

In 1840, to appease supporters of Henry Clay and Southern Whigs in general, Tyler was given the Whig vice-presidential nomination after William Henry Harrison won the top spot. Thus emerged the Whig slogan "Tippecanoe and Tyler Too." Tyler assumed the presidency upon Harrison's death in April 1841, but he quickly broke with the Whigs' nationalistic congressional wing by vetoing bills for a new national bank and by frustrating schemes to distribute the proceeds of land sales to the states while simultaneously raising the tariff.

Isolated from the Whigs, who scorned him as "His Accidency," Tyler maneuvered unsuccessfully in 1843 and 1844 to obtain the Democratic nomination for the next election. Hoping to woo Democrats with the scheme to annex Texas or build a third party based on that issue, Tyler was primarily important for injecting the carefully avoided slavery issue back into the national political arena. When his secretary of state, John C. Calhoun, defended annexation as a proslavery measure, Northern opposition was aroused. Consequently, Tyler's treaty with Texas was defeated in the Senate in the summer of 1844, but in February 1845, in one of his last acts as president, he acted on a joint resolution of Congress to annex the proslavery republic. Tyler emerged from retirement in 1861 to help organize the "Old Gentlemen's Convention," which tried to compromise the secession crisis. When this effort failed, he represented Virginia in the Confederate provisional congress before his death in Richmond on Jan. 18, 1862.

See also Bank War; Harrison, William Henry; Whig Party.
Consult (III) Seager, 1963.
—Michael F. Holt, *Yale University*

TYPEWRITER, invention that revolutionized office work. The father of the typewriter was an American printer, editor, and inventor, Christopher Latham Sholes (1819–1890) of Milwaukee. Sholes built his first working model, which he called a "typewriter" in 1867 (patented 1868), although writing machines had been invented many years before, perhaps the first being that of the English engineer Henry Mill (1714). W. A. Burt, a Detroit inventor, patented an unsuccessful "typographer" in 1829, and Charles Thurber of Connecticut made another in 1843. The major difficulty that Sholes faced was the clashing of the type bars. Without rapid fingering, no machine would be commercially successful. The first words he printed were: C. LATHAM SHOLES, SEPTEMBER 1867. Not until 1878 did he perfect a machine for lower case as well as capital letters.

In 1873 Sholes' patent rights were sold to the New York arms and sewing machine firm of E. Remington and Sons. Sholes went through 30 models with the encouragement of an oilman who spent most of his fortune on the

Thomas Nast's biting cartoons were major factor in exposure and dissolution of Tweed Ring.

John Tyler, 10th President of the United States (1841–1845).

experiments, James Densmore. Eventually, Sholes and Densmore found the model that worked well enough for mass production by Remington, and the typewriter became popular in the 1880s and 1890s. It was no longer a plaything of famous writers [such as Mark Twain, whose *Adventures of Tom Sawyer* (1876) is said to be the first typed manuscript to go to press]. By 1890 about 30 U.S. firms were manufacturing typewriters, and thousands of young women were now finding jobs available for them in the world of business at the lower clerical levels. The typewriter was also a factor in the enlargement of the white-collar class.

See also Inventions.
Consult (V) Oliver, 1956.

UN-AMERICAN ACTIVITIES, HOUSE COMMITTEE ON (HUAC), investigative committee known for its probes into alleged subversive activities. Established in 1938 as the Special Committee on Un-American Activities, it evolved into HUAC. Its first chairman was Martin Dies.

When Dies began conducting hearings in 1938, it was ostensibly to look at all totalitarian and "un-American" influences, including fascism. However, members exerted most of their energies in looking leftward, which to Dies and J. Parnell Thomas, who later became chairman (1947–1948), meant toward organized labor, civil rights advocates, and liberal programs in general. Harold Ickes, Harry Hopkins, and Frances Perkins all came under attack as did the Federal Theatre and Writers' Projects of the Work Projects Administration. The committee went into eclipse during World War II, but reemerged as an instrument of cold war politics in the late 1940s and early 1950s, investigating alleged communists including movie actors and writers. Although the committee's influence subsequently declined, its hearings were often opposed, as in San Francisco in 1960. The committee was renamed the House Internal Security Committee in the late 1960s.
Consult (VI) Latham, 1966.

UNCLE TOM'S CABIN, novel by Harriet Beecher Stowe that heightened antislavery sentiment throughout the world. *See* Stowe, Harriet Beecher.

UNDERGROUND RAILROAD, an informal series of networks that aided fugitive slaves to evade slave-catchers and to either disappear anonymously in Northern states or escape to Canada. Such "railroads" had nothing to do with actual railroads. They were composed of local "stations" and employed abolitionists and their sympathizers to receive fugitives and pass them on secretly to others along the "line." The underground railroad became one

means for stirring the compassion and winning the aid of Northerners who were unwilling to join the abolitionist movement but who responded to appeals in behalf of harassed fugitives.

The Underground Railroad passed along its fugitive "cargo" in northern directions that took in all the states above the Mason-Dixon Line. Famous workers in the movement included Levi Coffin, whose *Reminiscences* (1876) described work that won him the title of "president" of the Underground Railroad. Rev. Charles T. Torrey was a pioneer in developing the system. He was caught, tried, imprisoned, and died a martyr to the cause of slave emancipation. Thomas Garrett of Delaware, the model for the character Simeon Halliday in *Uncle Tom's Cabin,* was said to have aided 2,700 fugitives to escape north. Perhaps as many as 50,000 slaves were helped to freedom by the Underground Railroad.

Blacks throughout the North had an "underground railroad" of their own, hiding fugitives and maintaining correspondence and connections on the subject. However, their relatively limited means made the problem of aiding runaways complex; the movement required substantial legal, financial, and human assistance. Although such figures as Frederick Douglass, Harriet Tubman, and William Wells Brown were effective, their efforts were necessarily small compared with that of the network of white workers.

See also Douglass, Frederick; Slavery; Tubman, Harriet.
—Louis Filler, *Antioch College*

UNION LEAGUE CLUBS, organizations formed in the North during the Civil War to propagandize the Union cause. During Reconstruction the Union League became an arm of the Republican Party in the South. Local clubs scattered throughout the South engaged in political education among the freed slaves and were particularly important in 1867 and 1868, when Congress enfranchised Southern blacks. The League urged blacks to support the Republicans and assisted them in registering to vote and in voting. White Southerners greatly feared the League. The Ku Klux Klan selected it as a prime target and by 1870 had significantly disrupted the League's activities.

UNION PACIFIC RAILROAD. *See* Railroads.

UNITARIANS, an association that became influential beyond its numbers in American life and thought, particularly in New England. The movement developed in a time of questioning of Calvinist doctrines such as predestination, total depravity, and the infallibility of the Bible. Unitarians also reject the doctrine of the Trin-

Leeds Anti-slavery Series. No. 35.

SINGULAR ESCAPES FROM SLAVERY.

THE MYSTERIOUS BOX.

Tʜᴇʀᴇ are many remarkable incidents in the history of fugitive slaves, which at once mark their ingenuity and the desperate determination of the victims of this cruel system to escape from it.

Underground Railroad used variety of ingenious methods to help slaves escape from the South.

ity. Taking as their watchword "deeds not creeds," they have no code of doctrine and welcome anyone to membership, believing in a universal brotherhood of God and man.

The ideas of Unitarianism had roots in Europe. American Unitarianism formally began in 1825 with the formation of the American Unitarian Association, under the leadership of William Ellery Channing. A number of transcendentalists, including Ralph Waldo Emerson, became Unitarians. Emerson was a Unitarian minister but resigned in 1832. Under his influence some members of the association began to call themselves theists rather than Christians, and Theodore Parker and others hoped to found a universal religion.

In 1961 the Unitarians merged with the Universalists to form the Unitarian Universalist Association.

See also Channing, William Ellery; Emerson, Ralph Waldo; Transcendentalism.

Consult (III) Cheetham, 1962; Parke, 1957.

UNITED COLONIES OF NEW ENGLAND. *See* New England Confederation.

UNITED FARM WORKERS ORGANIZATION, labor union. *See* Chavez, Cesar.

UNITED MINE WORKERS, labor union concentrated in the coal industry, which for 40 years was led by John L. Lewis. *See* Lewis, John L.

UNITED NATIONS, international organization designed to maintain peace. The successor of the League of Nations, the United Nations was established in 1945. As victors of World War II, the original 50 members were automatically eligible for admission to the ranks of "peace-loving" states. Five powers—the United States, the USSR, Britain, France, and China—were made permanent members of the Security Council, in which they had veto power. By 1950, 10 new members had been admitted to the United Nations.

A second phase in its history started in 1950. Until a Russian boycott of the Security Council, which coincided with the invasion of South Korea, the Council had been immobilized by its veto. In the Russian absence a resolution was passed by the General Assembly giving that body authority to take over peacekeeping if the Security Council was stymied by the veto. The United Nations then became more active in attempting to maintain peace, but this phase came to an end about 1964 as a result of a number of factors. Major members, such as the USSR and France, failed to pay their share of the cost of UN peacekeeping forces, and membership doubled as Third World and excolonial nations were admitted.

Since then, the United Nations has been in a third stage. Bloc politics (Afro-Asians, Latin Americans, NATO and Commonwealth, Communists, Arabs) affect its structure, finances, and exercise of powers and threaten its survival. The organization is near financial bankruptcy, and its political resolutions are ignored. Major matters are negotiated outside the UN framework.

The UN has had a number of successes to its credit, primarily through its specialized social and economic agencies. Its peacekeeping record is spotty, but it kept South Korea free and stabilized the Congo and Cyprus. However, when India invaded Goa, the United Nations was mute, and the withdrawal of UN truce supervisors contributed to the outbreak of the 1967 Israeli-Arab war. There is no machinery whereby the organization can mount a military deterrent to a strong power, and it failed to curtail violence in Hungary, Tibet, and Czechoslovakia.

See also Korean War; League of Nations.
Consult (VIII) Claude, 1971; Coyle, 1969.
—Martin Gruberg, *University of Wisconsin, Oshkosh*

Soviet Premier Khrushchev gestures angrily during 1960 UN debate.

UNITED STATES CONSTITUTION. *See* Constitution of the United States.

UNITED STATES HOUSING AUTHORITY. *See* Wagner-Steagall Act (1937).

UNITED STATES v. AMERICAN TOBACCO CO. (1911), Supreme Court decision against the Tobacco Trust. *See* Antitrust Cases.

UNITED STATES v. BUTLER (1936), Supreme Court decision declaring the AAA unconstitutional. *See* Agricultural Adjustment Act (1933).

UNITED STATES v. DEBS (1895), appeal to the Supreme Court in which the federal court injunction was legalized for use against strikers. During the Pullman Strike (1894), a federal court injunction was obtained against Eugene Debs as leader of the American Railway Union's boycott of Pullman cars for impeding the government mails. Debs was sentenced to 6 months in jail for contempt of court when he defied the injunction. He appealed this sentence to the Supreme Court. The court's decision held that the power to regulate interstate commerce and the transport of the mail was the federal government's by virtue of the Constitution; thus, in the absence of statutory law, the federal courts had the jurisdiction to prevent obstruction.

See also Debs, Eugene V.; Pullman Strike (1894).

UNESCO, an agency of the United Nations, sponsors work-oriented adult literacy pilot project in Ecuador.

UNITED STATES v. E. C. KNIGHT CO. (1895), first Supreme Court decision affecting the Sher-

Increasing urbanization caused crowded conditions in early twentieth century, and summer heat often drove apartment dwellers to the roofs to sleep.

Planned, new cities, such as Reston, Va., are one solution to problems posed by urbanization.

man Antitrust Act (1890). The American Sugar Refining Co., after purchasing the E. C. Knight Co. and several other producers, held 98 percent of the nation's refining capacity. The government argued that the company was a monopolistic combination in violation of the Sherman act and asked that the acquisitions be disallowed. The Court ruled against the government, holding that the company was engaged in manufacturing whereas the Sherman act was directed only against restraint of trade or commerce. "Manufacture and commerce," said the court, "are two different and very distinct things." The importance of the case in shaping antitrust policy has been greatly overstated because within a few years the Court reversed itself (*Addyston Pipe and Steel Co. v. United States,* 1899), and it subsequently interpreted the Sherman act to include manufacturing firms.

See also Antitrust cases; Sherman Antitrust Act (1890); Trusts.

Consult (V) Letwin, 1965.

UNIVERSAL NEGRO IMPROVEMENT ASSOCIATION (UNIA), black separatist group organized by Marcus Garvey. *See* Garvey, Marcus.

URBANIZATION. The process of urbanization has been a force throughout American history, but the way in which it operates has changed.

Growth of Cities. From the earliest days immigrants, supplies, and news came through the seaports, which thus served as the source of civilization. The first concentrations of population sprang up around port areas and were associated with transportation and merchandising. Most of the great cities developed around transshipment points where there were breaks in transportation units whether ocean (Boston), canal (Buffalo), or railroad (Omaha). Only later did industry alone draw large numbers of people so as to create an urban area. Typically, industry concentrated around transshipment areas and reinforced the attractive force of transportation (as in Chicago). Ultimately, factories, which grouped large numbers of people working together, became the chief factor in concentrating population into urban centers. The process was often hastened by aggressive local leaders who had a strong sense of the influence and advantage of urbanization.

At the time of the American Revolution, only about 5 percent of the population lived in urban areas. By 1970, about 80 percent did, and the half-way point had been reached early in the twentieth century.

Adjustments to City Life. Urbanization involved more than merely living in city areas; the process came to mean having the benefits of technology and the services and social life available to concentrations of population. Typically in American society, the farm boy did not go directly to the big city, but rather to the village or small town; yet the move involved a great change in way of life—stores, social activities outside the family, regular working hours. The great exceptions were late nineteenth- and early twentieth-century peasants from abroad, and midtwentieth-century blacks and mountain whites, all of whom tended to move directly from rural life to the great metropolitan areas. Their problems of adjustment created many of the so-called urban problems.

The basic impact of urbanization upon people was compelling them to coordinate their activities with those of their interdependent neighbors. No longer self-sufficient, the city dweller had to find some specialized way to earn a living, that is, to get various types of life support. Insofar as concentrating population intensified the difficulties of managing to get the necessities of life and to avoid disease and violence associated with crowding, the demands upon the individual to surrender his independence of action far surpassed those of a looser, rural existence.

On the farm one was supposed to adjust to natural forces, from which there was no relief. On the new frontier in the cities one had to trust to one's fellow man rather than nature. The fact that large parts of the urban population came from authoritarian and paternalistic cultures made it easier for the new immigrants to adapt to the external controls of city life and in turn, then, reinforced the paternalistic influence of cities in American life, especially in the development of the so-called bureaucratic society of the twentieth century.

The Image of the City. In national imagery the city has become more and more dominant. The critical change occurred sometime around the election of 1896, when William Jennings Bryan made a frankly antiurban plea and was beaten. The United States at that point developed the "farm problem," a new phrase that would not have been meaningful earlier, for the farm had been America. The city was no longer a center of alluring wickedness but rather came to mean comfort and good living.

Then in the mid-1950s the image turned negative, for smog and factory pollution and overpopulation were particularly visible in the cities. Violence, and crime, which had for so long been tolerated there, became unacceptable when they spread into middle-class areas. The suburbanization movement, which had begun with rapid transit in the late nineteenth century and intensified in the 1920s and post-World War II period, represented an attempt to escape the crowds, dangers, and minority groups of the core city and still have urban conveniences.

See also City; Ghetto.

Consult (V) Jackson and Schultz, 1972.

—John C. Burnham, *Ohio State University*

URBAN RENEWAL. *See* Housing Acts.

UTAH, the 45th state, admitted to the Union on Jan. 4, 1896. Originally inhabited by the Paiute, Ute, and Shoshone Indians, the area was first explored by the Spanish, who claimed it in 1819. The first permanent white settlement was by the Mormons at Salt Lake City in 1848. The same year the area was ceded to the United States by Mexico. Utah Territory was created in 1850 with Brigham Young, the Mormon leader, as its governor, but the Mormon issue of polygamy soon had federal troops in the area, and the matter of statehood was postponed until the church formally renounced polygamy. Mining interest developed in the state with the coming of the railroad in 1869.

The state legislature is bicameral; Salt Lake City is the capital. The population in 1970 was 1,059,273.

See also Mormons.

UTOPIAN COMMUNITIES. A number of high-minded experiments in communal living were tried in nineteenth-century America. Some were founded by religious or socialist groups from Europe, who hoped that the frontier would give them both the space and the freedom to develop cooperative, productive, and peaceful societies. Other communities were founded by Americans influenced by European idealists.

A pioneer in the movement was George Rapp (1757-1847), a Protestant leader who left Germany with his followers to escape religious persecution and founded the town of Harmony near Pittsburgh, Pa., in 1804. The Harmony Society was organized around principles of work by all, sharing of produce by all, equality, and celibacy. The group moved to Indiana in 1815 but later sold their settlement to Robert Owen and returned to Pennsylvania, where the colony died out because of the rule of celibacy.

Robert Owen (1771-1858), British mill owner, philanthropist, and socialist, established a famous experiment in cooperative living on the land he purchased from Rapp's followers. Plans for the new socialist community, named New Harmony in 1825, were ambitious, and Owen invested heavily and had elaborate plans for ideal towns drawn up, but the project failed by 1828.

In American life and letters, the most famous Utopian community was Brook Farm, established on 200 acres at West Roxbury, Mass., in 1841. The founder was a Transcendentalist, George Ripley, who hoped that collective living would solve economic problems. He wanted intellectuals and workers to join in plain living and high thinking. The development of the community was influenced by the teachings of French socialist Charles Fourier.

Although the farm closed in 1847, it attracted famous people during its brief existence. Ralph Waldo Emerson, Amos Bronson Alcott, and other Transcendentalists lectured at the community. Nathaniel Hawthorne was a member but did not find the communal life congenial. He drew on his experiences for a novel he wrote later, *The Blithedale Romance* (1852).

Less famous but more enduring was the Amana Society, a cooperative of seven villages in Iowa. This society was founded by German Pietists who settled first in New York and then moved to the banks of the Iowa River in 1855. The settlement, run by church elders, followed strictly communal principles until reorganized in 1932.

Some of the ideals and experiments of the nineteenth-century communities have been tried again by communes established in the 1960s and 1970s. These have stressed such concepts as living simply from farming and handicrafts and sharing in the products of the group.

See also Brook Farm; Transcendentalism.

VAN BUREN, MARTIN (1782-1862), 8th President of the United States (1837-1841). Of Dutch ancestry, he was born in the village of Kinderhook, N.Y., on Dec. 6, 1782. The son of a tavern keeper, Van Buren studied law and was admitted to the bar (1803). He entered local politics and then served as a state senator (1812-1820) and attorney general (1815-1819). By 1820, Van Buren had become the leader of the Albany Regency, the Democratic Party machine of New York. That year he was sent to the U.S. Senate, where he served until 1828.

Although supporting William H. Crawford for the presidency in 1824, Van Buren soon became one of Andrew Jackson's most ardent supporters. In 1828 he helped carry New York for Jackson, while winning its governorship—a post he resigned to become Jackson's secretary of state (1829-1831). In 1832 he was elected vice-president for Jackson's second term, and in 1836 as Jackson's choice on the Democratic ticket he achieved the presidency.

Short and slight, with reddish hair, bushy sideburns, and a kindly face, Van Buren was a shrewd professional politician. Known

Martin Van Buren, 8th President of the United States (1837-1841), opposed the extension of slavery.

variously as "The Sage of Kinderhook," "The Little Magician," and "The Red Fox," he seldom gave or took offense. The years of his presidency, 1837–1841, coincided with a major depression, and although renominated in 1840, the depression had undermined his popularity, and he was easily defeated by William Henry Harrison, a Whig. In 1844, the Democrats bypassed Van Buren, choosing instead the expansionist James K. Polk.

During the 1840s, Van Buren opposed the extension of slavery, and he was the Free-Soil Party nominee for president in 1848. Shortly thereafter, Van Buren retired from active politics and settled near his birthplace on a country estate, where he died on July 24, 1862.

See also Free-Soil Party.
Consult (III) Remini, 1959.
—Douglas Miller, *Michigan State University*

VANDALIA GRANT (1772), land grant made by the British government to a group of American and British speculators who proposed establishing a new colony beyond the Appalachians named Vandalia. It included 20 million acres in western Pennsylvania and Virginia and eastern Kentucky. Following the French and Indian War, American business and political leaders looked to the west for land and profits, and when the Proclamation of 1763 temporarily closed that area for settlement they worked to register their claims and then to have the boundary line moved so that they could sell the land. The Indiana Company and its British allies were most successful and in late 1772 received the Vandalia Grant. Plans for the new colony never materialized because of the American Revolution.

See also Land Companies; Proclamation of 1763.

VANDERBILT, CORNELIUS (1794–1877), self-made steamship and railroad promoter and financier. He worked in harbor transport in New York City as a boy, and at 19 he married his cousin, who became the mother of his 13 children.

A large, loud, hard-working, and hard-fighting man of courage, Vanderbilt began making his fortune and reputation during the War of 1812 by provisioning forts around New York harbor. In 1818 he became involved with steamboats, and after 1829 he established steamboat lines of his own on the Hudson River and Long Island Sound. Insisting that his boats be strong, fast, handsome, and comfortable, he was responsible for many advances in steamboat construction. When the California gold rush came, Vanderbilt, whom everyone

called "Commodore," started a new line via Nicaragua. He shortened the California trip by two days, greatly reduced the fare, got most of the traffic, and then sold out.

As he neared 70, Vanderbilt turned to railroads, using his son William Henry as his lieutenant. In 1862 he gained control of the New York & Harlem Railroad and soon secured the Hudson River Railroad. He also controlled by 1867 the New York Central, running from Albany to Buffalo, but failed in 1868 to win the Erie after a spectacular fight with Daniel Drew, James Fisk, Jr., and Jay Gould. By 1870, however, his system extended from New York to Chicago, and before his death he had created one of America's greatest transportation systems. Basically, Vanderbilt did not construct new lines; he gained control of rundown roads, which he improved and linked with his other roads. Not noted for his philanthropy, he gave Vanderbilt University $1 million and left his heirs a fortune of more than $100 million.

See also Railroads.
Consult (V) Josephson, 1934.
—Ari Hoogenboom, *Brooklyn College of The City University of New York*

VANZETTI, BARTOLOMEO, Italian immigrant whose trial and execution were a major issue in the 1920s. *See* Sacco-Vanzetti Case.

VAUDEVILLE, a form of stage entertainment popular in the United States from the 1880s to the late 1920s, when its techniques and performers were gradually absorbed by other media, principally radio and films. Vaudeville, originally derived from English and American variety theater, featuring continuous performances of songs, comedy skits, acrobatics, and playlets. This form of popular theater was introduced in Boston by B. F. Keith in 1883, who in partnership with E. F. Albee organized a nationwide vaudeville circuit. Among the most famous vaudevillians were such song and dance performers and comedians as Weber and Fields, the Marx Brothers, Fannie Brice, Al Jolson, and Eddie Cantor.

VEBLEN, THORSTEIN (1857–1929). A pessimistic American critic of society and its economic system, he was the founder of the institutionalist school of economic theory. His most important book, *The Theory of the Leisure Class* (1899), approached economics from a broad evolutionary perspective and introduced such terms as leisure class and conspicuous consumption. Veblen felt that the structure of society and the economy could be best viewed as the outcome of a process of natural selection of institutions. However, institutions do not change as rapidly as society, thus creating a continual state of conflict.

In the *Leisure Class* and other works, Veblen attacked conventional economics on a number of grounds. He felt that the view of the entrepreneur as a risk bearer was basically incorrect and that marginalist theory supported the present income and wealth distribution. Veblen, who was a university professor, wished to replace conventional theory with an exposure of the business system and its effect upon man.

While much was wrong with Veblen's work, it did confront economics with questions and problems that conventional theory had generally ignored until that time.

VENERABLE SOCIETY FOR THE PROPAGATION OF THE GOSPEL IN FOREIGN PARTS. *See* Colonial Religion.

VERACRUZ, SIEGE OF (1847), led to capture of Mexican city by Americans under Winfield Scott. *See* Mexican War.

VERMONT, the 14th state, joined the Union on March 4, 1791. First known as the New Hampshire grants, the Vermont area was disputed by New York and New Hampshire. Ethan Allen and his Green Mountain Boys fought New York authority, and, in 1777, Vermont declared its independence. New York agreed to this claim in 1789, and statehood soon followed.

The state legislature is bicameral; the capital is Montpelier. The population in 1970 was 444,732.

VERRAZANO, GIOVANNI DE, Italian navigator who explored the New World for France. *See* Exploration and Discovery.

VERSAILLES, TREATY OF, peace treaty of World War I. The American peace program was first outlined by President Wilson in his Fourteen Points speech, which he delivered before Congress on Jan. 8, 1918, and which included formulas for national self-determination and a league of nations. Germany agreed to peace on the basis of the Fourteen Points, but the Allies, who had made a number of secret treaties among themselves to divide the spoils of war, refused to give up their claims for reparations and annexations. Only after Wilson had twice threatened to negotiate a separate peace were they willing to accept the Fourteen Points as the basis for negotiation.

The treaty fell short of Wilson's Fourteen Points. Article 231, the "war guilt" clause, assigned to Germany sole responsibility for causing the war. It alone was disarmed and saddled with a reparations bill that was subsequently set at $33 billion. The transfer of the Chinese province of Shantung to Japan, which had entered the war in 1915 on the Allied side, was a violation of the principle of self-determination. On the other hand, Wilson blocked French attempts to dismember Germany, secured the adoption of the mandate system to administer Germany's former colonies under League of Nations supervision, and established the League of Nations.

When Wilson returned from Paris, he submitted the treaty to the Senate for ratification. Although most Americans favored a league organization of some kind, the treaty was voted down in November 1919 and again in March 1920. Personal and political partisanship, isolationist sentiment, and Wilson's uncompromising attitude all contributed to the defeat. By failing to ratify the treaty, the United States repudiated its involvement in the war and betrayed its ideals and national interests. It also weakened the League of Nations and contributed to an unstable postwar world.

See also Fourteen Points; League of Nations; Wilson, Woodrow.

Consult (VI) Bailey, 1944; Birdsall, 1941; Smith, 1965.

—Alexander W. Knott, *University of Northern Colorado*

VESEY SLAVE UPRISING (1822), a controversial episode in the history of slave insurrectionary efforts. Denmark Vesey, a former West Indian slave who had bought his freedom and settled in Charleston, S.C., was accused of having master-minded a conspiracy to lead a revolt among local slaves. Alleged information given by a slave resulted in arrests, trials, deportations, and 35 executions. The scope and character of the "plot" have been questioned. It resulted in a Negro Seamen's Act intended to prevent the entrance into Charleston of sailors from abroad who might stir unrest among South Carolina slaves. The law was harshly enforced against Northern black seamen and even against British subjects, transgressing international treaties.

See also Gabriel's Slave Plot (1800); Nat Turner's Revolt.

VESPUCCI, AMERIGO, Italian sailor who explored extensively the New World. *See* Exploration and Discovery.

VETO. When the president rejects a bill sent to him by both houses of Congress, he writes "veto" (Latin, "I forbid") across it. Then the bill returns to the house of its origin. Both houses must pass the rejected bill by a two-thirds majority if it is to become law. The president can also refrain from either signing or vetoing a bill (pocket veto). In this case, the bill automatically becomes law after 10 congressional working days, unless Congress adjourns before the period has elapsed. If Congress adjourns, the pocket veto stands, and the bill is dead. The

Big Four representatives chat at Versailles Peace Conference. From left, Prime Minister Lloyd George of Britain, Premier Orlando of Italy, Premier Clemenceau of France, and U.S. President Wilson.

Vice President	Term	President
1. John Adams	1789–97	Washington
2. Thomas Jefferson	1797–1801	J. Adams
3. Aaron Burr	1801–05	Jefferson
4. George Clinton	1805–09	Jefferson
George Clinton [A]	1809–12	Madison
5. Elbridge Gerry [B]	1813–14	Madison
6. Daniel D. Tompkins	1817–25	Monroe
7. John C. Calhoun	1825–29	J. Q. Adams
John C. Calhoun [C]	1829–32	Jackson
8. Martin Van Buren	1833–37	Jackson
9. Richard M. Johnson	1837–41	Van Buren
10. John Tyler [D]	1841	W. H. Harrison
11. George M. Dallas	1845–49	Polk
12. Millard Fillmore [E]	1849–50	Taylor
13. William R. D. King [F]	1853	Pierce
14. John C. Breckinridge	1857–61	Buchanan
15. Hannibal Hamlin	1861–65	Lincoln
16. Andrew Johnson [G]	1865	Lincoln
17. Schuyler Colfax	1869–73	Grant
18. Henry Wilson [H]	1873–75	Grant
19. William A. Wheeler	1877–81	Hayes
20. Chester A. Arthur [I]	1881	Garfield
21. Thomas A. Hendricks [J]	1885	Cleveland
22. Levi P. Morton	1889–93	B. Harrison
23. Adlai E. Stevenson	1893–97	Cleveland
24. Garret A. Hobart [K]	1897–99	McKinley
25. Theodore Roosevelt [L]	1901	McKinley
26. Charles W. Fairbanks	1905–09	T. Roosevelt
27. James S. Sherman [M]	1909–12	Taft
28. Thomas R. Marshall	1913–21	Wilson
29. Calvin Coolidge [N]	1921–23	Harding
30. Charles G. Dawes	1925–29	Coolidge
31. Charles Curtis	1929–33	Hoover
32. John N. Garner	1933–41	F. Roosevelt
33. Henry A. Wallace	1941–45	F. Roosevelt
34. Harry S. Truman [O]	1945	F. Roosevelt
35. Alben W. Barkley	1949–53	Truman
36. Richard M. Nixon	1953–61	Eisenhower
37. Lyndon B. Johnson [P]	1961–63	Kennedy
38. Hubert H. Humphrey	1965–69	Johnson
39. Spiro T. Agnew	1969–	Nixon

(A) Died April 20, 1812.
(B) Died Nov. 23, 1814.
(C) Resigned Dec. 28, 1832, to become United States Senator.
(D) Succeeded to presidency April 6, 1841, following the death of William Henry Harrison.
(E) Succeeded to presidency July 10, 1850, following death of Zachary Taylor.
(F) Died April 18, 1853.
(G) Succeeded to presidency April 15, 1865, following the assassination of Abraham Lincoln.
(H) Died Nov. 22, 1875.
(I) Succeeded to presidency Sept. 20, 1881, following the assassination of James A. Garfield.
(J) Died Nov. 25, 1885.
(K) Died Nov. 21, 1899.
(L) Succeeded to presidency Sept. 14, 1901, following the assassination of William McKinley.
(M) Died Oct. 30, 1912.
(N) Succeeded to presidency Aug. 3, 1923, following the death of Warren G. Harding.
(O) Succeeded to presidency April 12, 1945, following the death of Franklin D. Roosevelt.
(P) Succeeded to presidency Nov. 22, 1963, following the assassination of John F. Kennedy.

president is obligated to give a reason for vetoing a bill. The pocket veto carries no such obligation. The president often uses the pocket veto at the end of a legislative session, when Congress is likely to adjourn before the 10-day period had ended.

The veto provides the president with considerable power over legislative programs. It is relatively rare for Congress to override a presidential veto, owing to the difficulty of procuring a two-thirds majority.

VICE-PRESIDENT OF THE UNITED STATES, the second highest official of the U.S. federal government, first in line to succeed the president in case of his death, resignation, removal, or incapacitation. The vice-president is also the president of the Senate, but as presiding officer he is not allowed to vote, except to break a tie. He has no other specific constitutional functions; he is not a member of the Senate, does not participate in debates or committee work, and has little actual power beyond his own personal influence and the prestige of his office. He is totally dependent on the president for extraconstitutional responsibilities.

Historically, the vice-president was chosen to balance a ticket or heal a split in the party and not for any conspicuous talent. As a result, the office was considered insignificant and a dead end for an ambitious politician. The office has been upgraded recently, largely because energetic men have filled it. The last four vice-presidents, Richard Nixon, Lyndon Johnson, Hubert Humphrey, and Spiro Agnew, were major national figures. They attended cabinet meetings, traveled abroad, and conveyed the president's wishes to Congress. Both Nixon and Johnson ascended to the presidency, and Hubert Humphrey became the presidential candidate of his party. The Twenty-fifth Amendment (1967) allows the president, with the consent of Congress, to choose another vice-president if the office becomes vacant.

See also Presidential Succession.

VICKSBURG, SIEGE OF (MAY–JULY 1863), led to capture of city by General Grant on July 4. Its fall gave the Union control of the Mississippi and split the Confederacy. *See* Civil War Battles.

VICTORY LOAN, popular name for the last bond loan of World War I. *See* Liberty Loans.

VIETNAM WAR, conflict in Southeast Asia whose roots reached back at least to the Japanese conquest of the 1930s, which was followed by an anticolonial war against the returning French. The French defeat at Dien Bien Phu in 1954 was followed by an armistice signed at Geneva on July 21, 1954, ending the Indochina War with a recognition of the independence of Vietnam (temporarily split in half along the 17th parallel), Laos, and Cambodia. Ngo Dinh Diem took over as premier in southern Vietnam, suppressed the Communist Party, and in 1955 was declared president of a new republic.

South Vietnam under the Diem regime was racked with corruption and oppression. In 1958, Communist-led guerrillas (including non-Communist foes of Diem) launched their campaign. By 1960 the United States, which had also been providing substantial aid, had sent in about 2,000 military advisers to prop up the southern state. Diem's repressive measures and inability to win the civil war led to his overthrow in 1963 in a military coup, followed by four years of instability and military rule. In 1967, Gen. Nguyen Van Thieu was elected president over 10 civilian candidates.

Escalation and Negotiation. A sudden deterioration of the military situation in 1965 led to an escalation of U.S. involvement, including air attacks on the north and the commitment of ground troops. By the end of 1968 about 550,000 American servicemen, commanded by General Westmoreland, were in the country. With each escalation there was debate in America among the hawks (who advocated the use of U.S. military might to win the war), the doves (who urged prompt U.S. disengagement), and the owls (who urged support of an independent South Vietnam until a peaceful disengagement could be accomplished).

U.S. aid was matched, however, by continued North Vietnamese infiltration and determined attacks, such as the Tet Offensive of February 1968. Vietnamization, a plan for U.S. provision of matériel and advisement to the South Vietnamese military, who would bear the brunt of the country's defense, was advocated as a face-saving device to explain American withdrawal. From 1968 to 1973 efforts were made to find a diplomatic end to the fighting. Finally, on Jan. 23, 1973, an agreement was announced in Paris. U.S. troops were withdrawn, and U.S. prisoners were released.

It was America's longest war, claiming 350,000 U.S. casualties. It was also a war that created bitter divisions at home, that brought down President Johnson, and that caused soul-searching over possible U.S. war crimes, such as the My Lai Massacre (March 1968), and over the wisdom of saturation bombing of both Vietnams.

See also Westmoreland, William C.

Consult (VIII) Buttinger, 1967; Halberstam, 1972; Sheehan and Kenworthy, 1972.

—Martin Gruberg, *University of Wisconsin, Oshkosh*

VIKINGS, seagoing Scandinavians, also known

as Norsemen, who ranged throughout Europe and the Atlantic Ocean between 800 and 1000. They became Normans in France, Danes in England and Ireland, and Varangians in Russia. Their voyages into the Atlantic led to the settlement of Iceland around 870 and Greenland around 985 and the discovery of North America about 1000. Their story comes partly from written sagas, partly from runes carved on stones, and partly from maps they made. These tell some things definitely, but leave much to speculation.

Contact with North America. Most important historically was the work of Erik the Red and his family. To escape murder charges, Erik fled from Norway and then from Iceland. About 985 he started a colony in southwest Greenland. Another Viking, Bjorni, inadvertently sailed past Greenland to Labrador—the first European to see America—but did not land. In 1001 Erik's son Leif sailed west from Greenland with 35 men and actually settled in a region he called Vinland.

This name later became a source of misunderstanding, as grapes do not grow well north of New England, and it was assumed that Leif's Vinland was in Maine, Cape Cod, or even further south. Later scholarship showed that the Norse "wine-berry" could mean not only grapes but also cranberries and other hardy fruit that could grow in Newfoundland and Labrador. In 1960 a Norwegian archaeologist found the presumed remains of Leif's two houses on the northwestern tip of Newfoundland. Some of Leif's relatives stopped there briefly and then went to the nearby Labrador mainland for a short time. There is no tangible evidence of further Norse settlements there or elsewhere in North America. Even the inhabitants of Greenland had died out by 1400.

There have been constant rumors to the contrary, however. Furthest afield was the "Kensington Stone," dug up in northern Minnesota in 1898, which told of Vikings who came overland and had a bloody fight with the Indians. Runes were found in Maine in 1970 but were also generally discredited. A "Vinland Map," possibly made around 1440, showed the supposed region in outline and was published in 1965 with the suggestion that Columbus might have learned of North America from it. Although it seems that Leif Ericson reached America in 1001, his voyage was not followed up, whereas Columbus' discovery in 1492 led to immediate settlement.

See also Exploration and Discovery.
Consult (I) Jones, 1968; Morison, 1971; Skelton, 1965.
—Robert G. Albion, *Harvard University*

VINLAND. *See* Vikings.

VINSON, FREDERICK M(OORE) (1890-1953), 12th Chief Justice of the Supreme Court, who was noted for his support of the broad interpretation of the powers of the federal government.

He began his law practice in 1911 in his hometown of Louisa, Ky. He also became active in politics and from 1923 until 1938, except for one two-year term, served in the House of Representatives. He became an influential congressman, supporting Franklin Roosevelt's New Deal. In 1938, President Roosevelt rewarded Vinson with an appointment to the U.S. Circuit Court of Appeals for the District of Columbia. In 1943, he moved to the executive branch, serving in several posts, including secretary of the treasury (1945-1946).

Chief Justice. Vinson was a close friend of Truman, and his experience and point of view regarding the power of the federal government influenced his appointment in 1946 to the Supreme Court. As chief justice, Vinson's judicial philosophy often led him to reject claims of individual rights asserted in opposition to the exercise of governmental authority.

Vinson's failure to unite a faction-ridden court and make it a major force in American life led critics to consider him one of the less successful justices. He did, however, help to improve the legal status of blacks by upholding the rights of members of racial minorities under the equal protection clause of the Fourteenth Amendment (*Shelley v. Kraemer*, 1948).

VIRGINIA, colony and state, named by Sir Walter Raleigh after Elizabeth, the "Virgin Queen." The area was first successfully colonized by the Virginia Company of London, which sent colonists to Jamestown in 1607. Raleigh had himself sent out a number of expeditions to Roanoke Island (N.C.) in the 1580s. These schemes were undercapitalized, but the Virginia Company in 1607 was backed by wealthy speculators. Despite the efforts of leaders such as John Smith, conditions were terrible in the first years, especially in the "starving time" in 1609-1610.

Once tobacco was developed as a cash crop by John Rolfe about 1612, the colony improved rapidly. Blacks were imported from 1619 onward, and a "tobacco aristocracy" grew up along the Tidewater. In 1619, Governor Thomas Yeardley began the first representative assembly in North America, the Virginia House of Burgesses, elected with wide suffrage. An Indian massacre in 1622 and the bankruptcy of the company, which had made no profits from Virginia, led in 1624 to Virginia becoming England's first crown colony. The House of Burgesses was allowed to continue, and it later split into two chambers. Future leaders, including George Washington and Thomas Jefferson, were trained here, and Virginia would produce four of the first six U.S. presidents.

The wealthy Tidewater gentry controlled Virginia politics for over 100 years. Economic

U.S. IN VIETNAM, 1961-1973
Build-up and Withdrawal

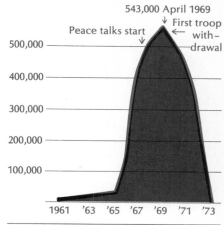

543,000 April 1969

Peace talks start ↓ First troop ← withdrawal

Casualties – Jan. 28, 1973 cease-fire

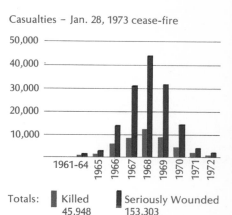

Totals: ■ Killed 45,948   ■ Seriously Wounded 153,303

Vietnam War leaders meet in Hawaii in 1966. President Johnson walks with South Vietnam's Premier Ky *(left)* and President Thieu. Behind them are *(from left)* Secretary of State Rusk, Ambassador Lodge, and Defense Secretary McNamara.

depression produced tension with the smaller farmers and in the back-country, as in Bacon's Rebellion of 1676. In the eighteenth century new immigrants moved mainly into the Shenandoah Valley and the Piedmont plateau regions rather than the coastal lands. Land speculators, such as the Ohio Company of 1749, hastened the sale of western lands. Virginia's population increased from about 72,000 whites and 23,000 blacks (1721) to about half a million people, 60 percent of them white (1775). The westerners began to outnumber the easterners, and the Anglican Tidewater oligarchs were fighting a losing battle of numbers.

The colony played a major role in the Revolution, and much of the leadership during the war and afterward came from Virginia. The state ratified the U.S. Constitution on June 25, 1788, although leaders such as Jefferson had grave misgivings about it. In May 1861, Virginia seceded and joined the Confederate States of America.

The legislature is bicameral; the capital is Richmond. The population in 1970 was 4,648,494.

See also Bacon's Rebellion (1676); Jamestown Settlement; Smith, John.

—Peter d'A. Jones, *University of Illinois, Chicago Circle*

VIRGINIA AND KENTUCKY RESOLUTIONS (1798), issued in response to the Alien and Sedition Acts by which the Federalist administration of President John Adams attempted to curb internal criticism. James Madison wrote the Virginia Resolutions and Thomas Jefferson the Kentucky; they were then passed by the two state legislatures. These resolutions presented the idea that the state should have the right to decide when acts of Congress were unconstitutional. Jefferson's Kentucky Resolutions were the most strongly worded; he asked the other states to declare the Alien and Sedition Acts void. The states' replies to the Resolutions were generally unfavorable. Most of the Northern states asserted that the courts, not the states, should decide on the constitutionality of acts of Congress. This authority was in fact asserted by the Supreme Court in the case of *Marbury v. Madison* in 1803.

Although Jefferson and Madison were unsuccessful in securing general state support for their assertions, their firm stance against the Alien and Sedition Acts helped the Democratic-Republican Party in the election of 1800.

See also Alien and Sedition Acts; Marbury v. Madison (1803); Nullification.

VIRGINIA BILL OF RIGHTS (1776), model for the Declaration of Independence and the U.S. Constitution's Bill of Rights. *See* Mason, George.

VIRGINIA CONVENTION (1831–1832), a turn-ing point in the Southern attitude toward slavery and its future. Fears for the safety of their families after Nat Turner's Revolt (1831) impelled Virginians to review their situation. In addition, poor whites and others in hilly western Virginia resented both slavery and its more aristocratic supporters in the eastern part of the state.

Proslavery and antislavery factions convened in Richmond to debate the issues. Although antislavery opinion was not strongly affected by humanitarian concern for blacks, it was touched by religious and democratic ideals. The main hope of antislavery proponents at the convention was that they could agree on a colonization scheme that would free the state of all blacks. However, the determination of proslavery forces, coupled with confusion in the antislavery ranks, brought the defeat of emancipation proposals.

See also Nat Turner's Revolt; Slavery.

VIRGINIA PLAN, one of the two comprehensive programs for creating a new American government presented to the Constitutional Convention in 1787. Also known as the "large-state plan," it consisted of 15 resolutions proposed by the Virginia delegation.

The most important provisions called for a strong central government with power "to legislate in all cases in which the separate states are incompetent." It provided for a national executive, legislature, and judicial system. The legislature would consist of two chambers, the members of the lower house to be elected by the people and the upper house to be chosen by the lower house from nominees submitted by the state legislatures. Representation in both houses would be based on wealth and numbers, thus giving the more populous and wealthy states greater representation. The national executive would be chosen by the legislature, and the legislature could disallow state legislation in conflict with the national constitution. The executive and the Supreme Court could veto acts of Congress. Through a series of compromises, primarily the Connecticut Compromise, the Virginia Plan was combined with the New Jersey Plan to provide the major provisions of the U.S. Constitution.

See also Connecticut Compromise; Constitutional Convention (1787); New Jersey Plan.

Consult (III) Hunt and Scott, 1920; Rossiter, 1953.

VIRGINIA RESOLVES, a series of resolutions drafted by George Mason and introduced in the Virginia House of Burgesses by George Washington on May 16, 1769. Adopted without dissent, the Virginia Resolves claimed that the governor and assembly had the sole authority to tax, chided the British for their denunciation of the Massachusetts Circular Letter, and condemned a proposal in Parliament to bring American radicals to trial in England. Patrick Henry and Richard Henry Lee drew up an address to the King. Angered by these activities, Governor Botetourt dissolved the Burgesses on May 17. The next day the delegates met informally and adopted the Virginia Association, which banned the importation of most British goods, of slaves, and of many European luxury goods.

VIRGINIA STATUTE FOR RELIGIOUS FREEDOM (1786), pioneer legislation for religious freedom in the United States. Virginia's Bill of Rights of 1776 had avowed the principle of religious liberty, and in 1779 the state had disestablished the Anglican Church, but the debate over church-state relationships continued. Some leaders, including George Washington and Patrick Henry, favored the support of religion through impartially distributed taxes. Others, led by Thomas Jefferson, wanted to separate religion entirely from politics.

In 1785, James Madison, George Mason, and other legislators proposed a bill guaranteeing absolute freedom of religion and forbidding use of public funds to support churches. Written by Jefferson, the measure became law in January 1786, and, according to Madison, "Thus in Virginia was extinguished forever the hope of making laws for the human mind." Jefferson included the statute, which became the basis for the First Amendment to the U.S. Constitution, among his greatest accomplishments.

VIRGIN ISLANDS, group of islands, formerly known as the Danish West Indies, that the United States bought from Denmark in 1917 for $25 million. The U.S. islands are part of a larger group, the rest of which are British possessions. Americans had seen the islands as a potential Caribbean naval base since the midnineteenth century. Secretary of State Seward almost completed the purchase, but in 1870 the Senate refused to ratify the agreement.

By 1917, fears for protection of the seaways to the Panama Canal (completed in 1915) and anxiety about German aggression ended dissension, and the islands were purchased. They are neither a territory nor a state, but their residents have been U.S. citizens since 1927. The governor is a direct appointee of the president. The three chief islands are St. Thomas, with a superb harbor, St. John, and St. Croix.

VISTA (VOLUNTEERS IN SERVICE TO AMERICA), "the domestic Peace Corps," established in 1964 under the Economic Opportunity Act. Part of the War on Poverty, its basic objectives were to raise the health and educational levels of poor people and to eradicate causes of poverty. VISTA workers serve for one year in rural and urban community action programs, Job Corps and migrant worker camps, Indian reservations, hospitals, and schools. Through community welfare projects they help minority group members develop technical skills and administration experience. They are paid only a subsistence allowance. VISTA is part of the Action agency, established in 1971 to consolidate a number of government-sponsored volunteer groups.

VOLUNTEERS IN SERVICE TO AMERICA. See VISTA.

WABASH AND ERIE CANAL. See Canals.

WABASH v. ILLINOIS (1886), Supreme Court decision invalidating state laws regulating railroads. See Railroad Legislation.

WADE-DAVIS BILL (1864), Reconstruction bill passed by congressional Radicals. It stated that provisional governors, appointed for the Confederate states by the president, were to enroll all white male citizens. When a majority had sworn allegiance to the Constitution, a state constitutional convention would be called. Only those who had been loyal to the Union throughout the war could participate in the election of delegates and the framing of the new constitutions, which must abolish slavery, repudiate the Confederate debt, and disfranchise Confederate leaders. The bill was pocket-vetoed by President Lincoln.

WAGES AND HOURS LAW. See Fair Labor Standards Act (1938).

WAGNER, ROBERT F(ERDINAND) (1877-1953), progressive U.S. Senator who was called the "father of the welfare state." Born in Germany, he emigrated to the United States in 1885 and eventually became a lawyer. He practiced law for 5 years, was elected to the state assembly, and in 1909 rose to the state senate, where he served as Democratic floor leader from 1911 to 1918. He was chairman of the Triangle Fire Commission and, along with Alfred E. Smith, was primarily responsible for the passage of the state's extremely enlightened factory codes as well as numerous other laws dealing with labor and welfare, civil rights, and business regulation. In 1918 he was elected to the state supreme court, where he rendered decisions in favor of organized labor, government responsibility for welfare, and minority rights.

In 1926 he became a U.S. senator and in the next 22 years made what is probably the most productive record in that body's history. Among the measures that he sponsored wholly or in part are the Reconstruction Finance Corporation, Federal Emergency Relief Act, Civilian Conservation Corps, National Industrial

VISTAs lend architectural advice on designs for Baltimore community development project.

Robert F. Wagner, influential senator who sponsored many New Deal reform measures.

Morrison R. Waite, 6th Chief Justice of the Supreme Court.

George Wallace campaigned for 1972 Democratic presidential nomination before he was struck down by paralyzing gunshot wounds.

Recovery Act, National Labor Relations (Wagner) Act, Social Security Act, the U.S. Housing Authority, and a federal antilynching law. Wagner, who retired from the Senate in 1949, has been called by one observer the "pilot of the New Deal."

Wagner's son Robert F. Wagner, Jr. (1910-   ) was a three-term mayor of New York City (1953-1965).

See also National Labor Relations Act (1935); New Deal; Social Security Act (1935); Wagner-Steagall Act (1937).

Consult (VI) Huthmacher, 1971.

WAGNER ACT. *See* National Labor Relations Act (1935).

WAGNER-STEAGALL ACT (1937) established the U.S. Housing Authority (USHA) with power to make long-term loans and grants to meet the interest on those loans to local housing authorities—a new departure advocated by Senator Robert F. Wagner of New York. In effect it provided federal subsidies to encourage slum clearance and public housing rather than direct involvement in construction, as in the case of the earlier Public Works Administration (PWA). The USHA replaced the public housing division of PWA, and over Wagner's objections the new agency was lodged within the Interior Department. Between 1937 and 1941, when it became a separate agency, the USHA lent $750 million to local authorities for the construction of 162,000 units in 500 projects, a spectacular acceleration over the PWA's record.

See also Public Works Administration.
Consult (VI) Huthmacher, 1971.

WAITE, MORRISON (REMICK) (1816-1888), 6th Chief Justice of the Supreme Court (1874-1888), who is generally regarded as a chief justice of only fair capabilities. Born in Connecticut, Waite was educated at Yale. He moved to Ohio to practice law and soon became successful as a bank and railroad lawyer. In 1856 he joined the new Republican Party. Waite was loyal to Lincoln and the Union and supported emancipation, although he was not enthusiastic about other measures aiding blacks.

Waite came to national notice in 1871, when he was appointed one of the American counsels to argue the *Alabama* case against Great Britain, which he helped win. In 1874, after his return to the United States, he was appointed chief justice by President Grant.

Chief Justice. The Court in 1874 was just beginning to recover from the shocks of Dred Scott, the Civil War, and Reconstruction. Striving to return the Court to a position of honor, Waite refused to run for president, lest the office of chief justice seem an inferior post.

Although Waite had been a Unionist, once on the Court he vigorously supported the states' ability to legislate economic regulation and civil rights. Waite found the interest of the state superior to that of businesses "affected with a public interest." However, his opinions in this area were based not on the absolute right of a state to regulate for the public welfare but on the reasonableness of the regulation.

Waite's Court heard many cases concerning black civil rights. In the most famous (the *Civil Rights Cases,* 1883) the Court struck down the Civil Rights Act of 1875, which had prohibited discrimination in public accommodations. Waite believed that the states had the primary authority in defining the social relations among its citizenry. It was not until the 1950s that the black's fate was taken out of the hands of the states. Waite died in office.

See also Civil Rights Cases (1883).
—David Forte, *Skidmore College*

WALDEN (1854), Thoreau's summation of his individualistic philosophy. *See* Thoreau, Henry David.

WALLACE, GEORGE C(ORLEY) (1919-   ), American political leader and presidential candidate. He was born in and grew up in rural Alabama. He graduated from the University of Alabama Law School in 1942 and entered private practice after serving in World War II. His political career began in 1948, when he was an Alabama delegate to the Democratic National Convention. In 1952 he was elected a state district court judge. In 1958 he made an unsuccessful bid for the governorship but was elected to that office in 1962. As governor he had nationwide publicity for his opposition to federal civil rights legislation, and in 1964 he had considerable support in Democratic state primaries as a presidential candidate.

In 1966, when the Alabama state legislature refused to abolish a law forbidding two consecutive terms as governor, Wallace's wife, Lurleen, ran and was elected. George played a major role in his wife's administration before she died in 1968, and he was reelected in 1970. During the 1968 presidential campaign, Wallace ran as the candidate of his American Independent Party. An outspoken supporter of states' rights, his platform advocated "law and order" and condemned urban riots and protest demonstrations. He received about 13 percent of the vote and won five states.

On May 15, 1972, while making another bid for the presidency, Wallace was the victim of an unsuccessful assassination attempt. He was paralyzed from the waist down and was forced to withdraw from the race, although he continued as governor of Alabama.

Consult (VIII) Frady, 1969.

WALTHAM SYSTEM, early effort to introduce efficiency into factory production. *See* Boston Associates.

WAR, DEPARTMENT OF, established in 1789 as one of the first cabinet-level posts to be organized. It was headed by a civilian secretary and had authority over the military establishment. The War Department was the predecessor of the Department of the Army (established 1947). Efforts to unify the military establishment led to the formation of the Department of Defense as the supervisory agency over the Army, Navy, and Air Force. The war secretary was replaced by the defense secretary as a member of the cabinet.

See also Defense, Department of.

WAREHOUSE ACT (1916). *See* Federal Farm Loan Act (1916).

WAR HAWKS, name used to describe the group of young Democratic-Republican congressmen who from 1810 to 1812 urged the United States to protect the national honor and fight the British rather than submit to further indignities. The most famous of them, and their leader, was Henry Clay of Kentucky.

See also War of 1812.

WAR INDUSTRIES BOARD (WIB), chief agency created by the federal government to plan and control the war effort in World War I. First created by the Council of National Defense, the WIB had too little authority, so President Wilson made it independent of the council and gave it executive authority to coordinate the national industrial, agricultural, and financial effort. In March 1918 he placed the brilliant Wall Street financier and philanthropist Bernard Baruch in charge.

Baruch made himself a sort of economic supreme commander in a short space of time. He created "war service committees" for each industry—an idea later copied by the New Deal's code authorities in the 1930s. The four main powers of the WIB were establishing priorities in production, enforcing good standardization and conservation procedures in industry, fixing prices, and outright commandeering of goods or industries when necessary. Baruch never used the last, most drastic, authority. The WIB accelerated war production, but it was less successful in controlling inflation.

See also Baruch, Bernard M.; National Defense Act (1916).

Consult (VI) Jones, 1965.

WAR LABOR DISPUTES ACT. *See* Smith-Connally Anti-Strike Act (1943).

WAR OF 1812, war between Britain and the United States over various issues that had festered since the Treaty of Paris ended the Revolutionary War in 1783. After 1783 the United States and Britain quarreled over fulfilling the details of the peace settlement, but it was not until after the outbreak of general European war in 1793 that their relations deteriorated sharply. The Revolutionary and Napoleonic wars lasted, with minor breaks, from 1793 to 1814, and during these years England severely restricted Franco-American trade and also impressed seamen, including Americans, from American merchant ships. After 1803 British maritime blockades and seizures increased in intensity. At first the United States tried to change British policy by restricting trade, but after 1810 an increasing number of Americans, led by the War Hawks, called for war to protect American shipping and seamen and to preserve national honor. These arguments were opposed by the Federalist Party, chiefly centered in New England, but on June 18, 1812, the United States declared war on Britain.

War Begins. America was ill prepared for war: the U.S. army had fewer than 10,000 men, the navy fewer than 20 ships, and the country was divided over the war. The American strategy was to conquer Canada to force a change in British maritime policies while harassing British shipping by means of privateers and the few ships of the regular American navy. The attack on Canada failed dismally. General William Hull surrendered his army and his stronghold at Detroit in the West in August 1812, and attacks across the Niagara frontier and along Lake Champlain were unsuccessful later in the year.

The surprise of the war was the success of the American navy in defeating the British in single-ship engagements. In August the *Constitution* defeated the *Guerrière;* in October Capt. Stephen Decatur led the *United States* to a victory over the *Macedonian;* and in December, off the coast of Brazil, the *Constitution* beat the *Java.* At the same time American privateers had great success in raiding British commerce. This privateering success continued throughout the war, but in 1813 and 1814 the British navy established superiority along the coasts of the United States. American commerce was paralyzed, and the American coasts lay open to attacks by British forces.

In 1813 there were renewed efforts along the Canadian frontier, but campaigns on the Niagara front and along Lake Champlain were again complete failures. There was a little more success in the West. Although the year began with a defeat at Frenchtown in January, Oliver Hazard Perry's naval victory at the Battle of Lake Erie on September 10 forced the British to retreat from the Detroit region. General William Henry Harrison pursued them and won a crushing victory on October 5 at the Battle of the Thames, in which the great Indian chief

WAR OF 1812 — Item Guide

The main entry WAR OF 1812 covers the primary events of the conflict. Deteriorating relations before the war, during the administrations of THOMAS JEFFERSON and the first of JAMES MADISON's are described in ORDERS IN COUNCIL and EMBARGO ACTS. American anger at British policies was most intense among the WAR HAWKS, such as HENRY CLAY.

Prominent American naval commanders included STEPHEN DECATUR and OLIVER HAZARD PERRY, hero of LAKE ERIE, BATTLE OF. On land, WILLIAM HENRY HARRISON played an important role in the west, and ANDREW JACKSON defeated the British at NEW ORLEANS, BATTLE OF, in the south. Opposition to the war surfaced in the HARTFORD CONVENTION, but was defused by GHENT, TREATY OF, which ended the war.

U.S.S. *Constitution,* most famous American ship in War of 1812, was at sea when peace was signed and captured Britain's *Cyane* and *Levant* after war had ended.

Tecumseh was killed. However, the most populous parts of Canada remained firmly in the hands of the British.

1814 and Peace. In 1814 the nature of the war changed. Napoleon was defeated in the spring, and England could transfer ships and troops from Europe for an invasion of the United States. The United States seemed ill prepared to meet this threat. Federalist opposition was becoming more intense, American commerce was ruined, and the country was near bankruptcy. The British wanted to invade across the Niagara frontier, down Lake Champlain, in Chesapeake Bay, and at New Orleans. At Niagara the British were unable to advance after bitterly fought battles at Chippewa on July 5 and Lundy's Lane on July 15 ended in standoffs. More importantly, the major British attack along Lake Champlain ended in failure when American naval forces under Thomas Macdonough defeated the British ships at Plattsburgh Bay, threatened to cut the invasion force's supply lines, and forced the British to retreat.

In Chesapeake Bay the British were able to land an army, defeat the Americans at Bladensburg, Md., on August 24, and burn the public buildings in Washington, but they were repulsed at Baltimore. At New Orleans the British expedition did not arrive until December, and the decisive battle was not fought until Jan. 8, 1815, when an army of regulars, volunteers, and Western militia under Maj. Gen. Andrew Jackson inflicted on the troops under Sir Edward Pakenham the most severe defeat Britain suffered during the war. It was an unnecessary battle because peace had already been agreed on in Europe.

Negotiations at Ghent, Belgium, to end the war had been successful on Dec. 24, 1814. With the war in Europe over, the menace to American shipping had ended, and the two countries agreed to restore any conquered territory. Peace also took the main political issue from the Federalist opposition in the United States. Although the opposition discussed disunion at the Hartford Convention (December 1814–January 1815), Ghent and the Battle of New Orleans brought a great burst of national enthusiasm that swamped any opposition to the government.

Consult (III) Coles, 1965; Horsman, 1969.
—Reginald Horsman, *University of Wisconsin, Milwaukee*

WAR PRODUCTION BOARD (WPB), a government agency established in 1942 by President Roosevelt to regulate the use of the nation's raw materials. The WPB halted nonessential residential and highway construction to conserve resources for the war effort. In October 1945, the board was terminated and its function absorbed by the Civilian Production Administration.

Earl Warren, 13th Chief Justice of the Supreme Court, dons robe on his first day in office, Oct. 5, 1953.

WARREN, EARL (1891–   ), 14th Chief Justice of the Supreme Court (1953–1969). Not since John Marshall has a chief justice been credited with engendering as many social and political changes as Earl Warren, who was appointed by President Eisenhower. Born in Los Angeles, he graduated from the University of California Law School at Berkeley. From 1920 on, Earl Warren spent his entire career in appointive and elective political offices: deputy district attorney, district attorney, attorney general, and governor of California. He was also the Republican candidate for vice-president in 1948.

President Eisenhower, hoping Warren would be a moderate, unifying force on the Court, was very surprised by the subsequent behavior of his chief justice, although Warren's background indicated future judicial activism rather than restraint. "The Warren Revolution" began almost immediately in 1954, when Warren argued that state-imposed segregation of public schools was unconstitutional because it fostered feelings of inferiority (*Brown v. Board of Education of Topeka*).

By the 1960s—with a secure majority behind him—Warren led the Court to establish a strict one-man–one-vote standard in the apportionment of legislative districts (*Reynolds v. Sims,* 1964). The Warren Court also expanded First Amendment freedoms and the requirements for counsel for defendants (*Gideon v. Wainwright,* 1963) and ruled on the necessity of informing defendants of particular rights (*Miranda v. Arizona,* 1966), the invalidation of illegally seized evidence at trial (*Mapp v. Ohio,* 1961), and the outlawing of prayers in public schools (*Engel v. Vitale,* 1962).

Always concerned with the immediate social issue before him, Warren's opinions are more often filled with justifications for a certain policy than with legal precedents. He rarely referred back to one of his own opinions, preferring to approach each case as a new problem in need of a practical rather than legalistic solution. Warren became the personal symbol of the Court's expanded role and was the object of both the highest praise and the deepest criticism. He retired in 1969.

See also Brown v. Board of Education of Topeka (1954); Miranda v. Arizona (1966).
Consult (VIII) Christman, 1966.
—David Forte, Skidmore College

WASHINGTON, the 42nd state, admitted to the Union on Nov. 11, 1889. The search for the Northwest Passage in the 1770s brought British traders and then Russian trappers to the area. In 1792 Capt. Robert Gray claimed the area for the United States. The Northwest Company's Spokane House was established in 1810, and the next year Astor's Pacific Fur Company settled in the area. America and Britain agreed to joint occupation of the area, but by 1846 they were almost at war over the issue; finally the 49th parallel was agreed upon as the dividing line. Washington gained territorial status in 1853.

The state legislature is bicameral; Olympia is the capital. The population in 1970 was 3,409,169.

WASHINGTON, BOOKER T(ALIAFERRO), (1856?-1915).

No black man in American history was more controversial or had more personal power and influence than Booker T. Washington, principal of Tuskegee Institute (Alabama). By 1895 Washington, who was born a slave, had built Tuskegee into a nationally known black industrial, vocational, and agricultural college.

Washington gained national prominence with his Atlanta Exposition speech (1895), in which he told a white audience that blacks would accept social segregation and disenfranchisement in exchange for educational and economic opportunities. Whites hailed Washington's "compromise" as the race problem's solution. From 1895 to 1905 he was recognized by most whites and blacks as the "spokesman of his race."

Washington's power was further enhanced by his close ties with Northern industrialist-philanthropists, such as Andrew Carnegie and John D. Rockefeller, who gave large sums of money to Tuskegee and (through Washington) to other Southern black schools. Washington also had close political ties with the White House, especially during Theodore Roosevelt's Administrations (1901-1909). Washington established the National Negro Business League, dominated the Afro-American Council on race relations, controlled black educational, agricultural, and political organizations, and influenced most black newspapers. He used these power levers to crush the Niagara Movement (1905-1908), organized by black integrationists such as W. E. B. Du Bois, who opposed his accommodationist policies.

Although Washington worked behind the scenes against segregation, disenfranchisement, and lynching, he publicly exhorted blacks to work together to turn adversity to their advantage. He held firm in his belief that blacks would progress only by winning support from the "better sort" of whites and by working hard, living frugal and moral lives, and developing and supporting black enterprises. Today blacks are divided in their estimates of Washington, some calling him an Uncle Tom and others calling him an early advocate of black power.

See also Blacks in the United States; Du Bois, W. E. B.; Tuskegee Institute.

Consult (IX) Harlan, 1972; Thornbrough, 1969; Washington, 1901.

—Sheldon Avery, *The Johns Hopkins University*

WASHINGTON, GEORGE (1732-1799),

Revolutionary War leader and 1st President of the United States (1789-1797). He was born in Bridges Creek, Va., on Feb. 22, 1732. As a young man he served as a county surveyor, but he first achieved more than local attention in 1753-1754. In the former year he was sent by Virginia to demand that the French withdraw from an area around the forks of the Ohio River claimed by Virginia. The French refused to yield to this ultimatum, and in the spring of 1754 Washington again journeyed to the Ohio country, this time to reinforce a Virginia fortification at the forks. The French had already taken it, and in May 1754 Washington skirmished with them at Great Meadow. In 1755 Washington accompanied the disastrous expedition of Britain's General Braddock, which was overwhelmed by the French and Indians while approaching the forks of the Ohio. Washington escaped safely, and later that year he was appointed commander in chief of all the Virginia forces and had the responsibility of protecting a long frontier line.

Revolutionary War. In June 1775 Washington, who had been a delegate to the First and Second Continental Congresses, was chosen to command the American armies in the struggle against Britain. He took command of the army at Cambridge, Mass., in July and eventually forced the British to withdraw from Boston by occupying Dorchester Heights. He then went to New York, where he was defeated but conducted a masterly withdrawal. In these early years of the Revolution, Washington was successful in avoiding the British destruction of his army, which would have been disastrous for the Revolutionary cause. Although he frequently, as at Valley Forge in 1777, led a very small army desperately short of supplies, Washington managed to sustain resistance to the British. His long struggle culminated at Yorktown in 1781 with the surrender of Britain's General Cornwallis.

Presidency. In the 1780s, Washington retired to private life, but he threw his influence in support of plans for a more powerful central government. When the new Constitution was at last adopted in 1788, he was the obvious and popular choice for president. As president he proved himself to be an able administrator who leaned toward a conservative position. In the struggle between Alexander Hamilton and Thomas Jefferson he increasingly favored the former and by his second term was clearly within the new Federalist Party. When war broke out in Europe, he strove to keep the United States neutral and to maintain friendship with Britain in spite of British provocations. He was less successful with the French. They resented his bias in favor of the British, and the French alliance began to collapse in these years. Washington retired from

General Washington as commander of the Continental Army in the Revolutionary War.

George Washington, 1st President of the United States (1789-1797) in portrait by Rembrandt Peale.

the presidency in 1797. After his death at Mount Vernon, Va., on Dec. 14, 1799, he was eulogized as "first in war, first in peace, and first in the hearts of his countrymen."

Consult (III) Flexner, 1968–1972; Freeman, 1948–1957; Stephenson and Dunn, 1940.

—Reginald Horsman, *University of Wisconsin, Milwaukee*

WASHINGTON ARMAMENT CONFERENCE (1921–1922), a high point of post-World War I international cooperation that focused on China and naval armament. It also testified to the fact that the United States, while refusing to participate in the League of Nations, was actively interested in playing an international role. Japan had made vast inroads in China, and both Japan and the United States were engaged in ambitious naval expansion programs. The two countries' mutual suspicion was aggravated by the continued existence of the Anglo-Japanese alliance.

The Washington Conference did not solve all issues, but it succeeded in reducing tension in Asia and the Pacific. The Anglo-Japanese alliance was abrogated, a disarmament treaty fixed the ratios of capital (large) ships of the United States, Britain, and Japan at 5:5:3, and a nine-power treaty reaffirmed support for the integrity of China.

These agreements revealed that both the United States and Japan were anxious to avoid trouble and curtail an expensive arms race. The abrogation of the Anglo-Japanese alliance meant that the two countries would not combine politically or militarily in Asia and the Pacific and that together with the United States they would each engage in peaceful economic competition.

See also London Naval Conference (1930).

Consult (VI) Iriye, 1965.

—Akira Iriye, *University of Chicago*

WASHINGTON'S FAREWELL ADDRESS, dated Sept. 17, 1796, was never delivered orally and first appeared in American newspapers in September. Washington wrote it with the help of Alexander Hamilton and John Jay and in it expressed his intention not to seek a third term. Washington used his Farewell Address to give his views on the internal and foreign problems then besetting the United States and to provide guidelines for the proper conduct of American domestic and foreign policy.

Although the Farewell Address is best known for its discussion of foreign policy, much of it is devoted to the domestic scene. Washington warned of the dangers of sectionalism and of extreme party divisions, and he asked for internal unity. Concerning foreign policy he argued for impartiality toward foreign nations and for commercial, not political, ties. He also foreshadowed the Monroe Doctrine in his argument that Europe had a set of primary interests separate from those of the United States. His warning that the United States should avoid permanent alliances with foreign nations was particularly influential in later American thinking. Later politicians were able to use Washington's arguments to defend a policy of isolationism.

See also Isolationism; Washington, George.

WATERGATE AFFAIR, most sensational political scandal of the twentieth century, involving numerous prominent Republicans. During the 1972 presidential campaign, the Democrats had their party headquarters in the Watergate Complex in Washington, D.C. In June 1972, burglars, originally thought to be anti-Castro Cuban refugees who opposed George McGovern, were caught in the Watergate headquarters.

The Nixon Administration and the Republican campaign organization at first denied complicity, but following President Nixon's landslide reelection and the conviction of the burglars, more revealing details began to emerge. In addition to wide-ranging financial irregularities, the affair involved the use of independent government agencies for partisan political purposes and widened the gulf between the executive and Congress, which held its own investigation into Watergate. Maurice Stans, ex-Secretary of Commerce, and John N. Mitchell, ex-Attorney General, as well as John Ehrlichman and H. R. Haldeman, the President's top White House advisers, and the President's personal lawyer and his White House counsel were all implicated. A host of lesser Republican Administration and campaign officials were also caught up in the controversy, which continued to widen.

WAYNE, ANTHONY (1745–1796), Revolutionary War general whose daring earned him the nickname "Mad Anthony." As a militia colonel, he participated in the unsuccessful attack on Trois Rivières, Canada, in June 1775. Promoted to brigadier general in February 1777, Wayne joined George Washington's forces in the spring and commanded the Pennsylvania Line in the unsuccessful defense of Philadelphia in the fall.

Wayne achieved his most memorable victory in an exceedingly well-planned action at Stony Point, N.Y., in July 1779. In 1780 he conducted raids in the lower Hudson River Valley but was repulsed in an attack at Bulls Ferry, N.J., in July. At winter quarters in Morristown, N.J., in January 1781, Wayne prudently dealt with mutineers in the Pennsylvania Line until delegates from the state arrived to negotiate a settlement. Wayne's reorganized forces took part in the final campaign against General Cornwallis and then went to Georgia, where they forced the Cherokee and Creek Indians to sign treaties of submission.

Wayne left the army in 1783 but returned to active service in 1792 as a major general with the mission of pacifying the tribes of the Old Northwest. His American Legion defeated the Indians in a decisive battle at Fallen Timbers, near modern Toledo, Ohio, on August 20, 1794. In 1795 the Indians agreed to a complete submission by the Treaty of Greenville.

See also Fallen Timbers, Battle of; Revolutionary War Battles.

WEALTH OF NATIONS (1776), book that strongly influenced early U.S. economic policy. *See* Smith, Adam.

WEATHERMAN, radical faction of SDS. *See* Students for a Democratic Society.

WEBB-KENYON ACT (1913), first federal attempt to control the liquor traffic. It was passed by Congress in 1912, vetoed by President Taft, and overridden by both houses on a vote that saw the West and South triumph over the Northeast. The law forbade the importation of intoxicating liquor into any state where its possession or use was prohibited. In effect, it stated that liquor lost its status as interstate commerce once it passed into a dry state, and its opponents argued that this represented unconstitutional delegation of congressional power to the state. Only three states took advantage of the law before 1917, but a favorable Supreme Court ruling that year motivated seven others to follow suit. The passage of the Eighteenth (Prohibition) Amendment (1919) removed the need for further action.

WEBSTER, DANIEL (1782–1852), noted nationalist orator and Senator from Massachusetts. He graduated from Dartmouth (1801) and was admitted to the Boston bar in 1805. Settling in Portsmouth, N.H., he entered politics as a Federalist, opposing Jefferson's Embargo Act (1807). In 1812 he was elected to Congress, where he opposed the War of 1812 and later the protectionist tariff of 1816.

After two terms in Congress he returned to Boston, where he built up a lucrative law practice and helped to impose a broad interpretation of the Constitution through his successful appearances before the Supreme Court in such cases as *Dartmouth College v. Woodward* (1819), *McCulloch v. Maryland* (1819), and *Gibbons v. Ogden* (1824). In 1823 he was again elected to Congress, and in 1827 entered the Senate. Although he had opposed protective tariffs in 1816 and 1824, Webster had shifted with his constituency by 1828 to become a staunch protectionist and nationalist.

His new position was clearly revealed in his 1830 debate with Senator Robert Hayne and in the leading role he took in supporting the Second Bank of the United States.

In 1836 and 1840, Webster was an unsuccessful contender for the Whig nomination for the presidency. He served as secretary of state under Presidents Harrison and Tyler (1841–1843), negotiating the Webster-Ashburton Treaty (1842). Reelected to the Senate in 1844, his eloquent support of the Compromise of 1850 outraged New England abolitionists. From 1850 until his death Webster served as Millard Fillmore's secretary of state.

With John C. Calhoun and Clay, Webster was part of a great senatorial triumvirate and was viewed by most of his contemporaries as an outstanding statesman and the foremost orator of the age.

See also Dartmouth College v. Woodward (1819); Webster-Ashburton Treaty (1842); Webster-Hayne Debate (1830).

Consult (III) Brown, 1969; Current, 1955.
—Douglas Miller, *Michigan State University*

Daniel Webster, famed orator and one of most powerful senators before the Civil War.

WEBSTER, NOAH (1758–1849), lexicographer whose books did much to set standards for American English. He was born in West Hartford, Conn., graduated from Yale in 1778, and practiced law from 1789 to 1793. His speller, *Grammatical Institute of the English Language, Part I* (1783), followed by a grammar (1784) and a reader (1785), were declarations of independence of American language from its English heritage. Based upon actual American usage, the Webster blue-backed speller sold more than 35 million copies in the next 100 years.

Webster was disturbed by the piracy of his work and fought for an American copyright law. This fight propelled him into politics in favor of the strong centralized Federalist policies. He edited two Federalist newspapers (1793–1803), wrote many pamphlets, and traveled throughout the country before turning exclusively to lexicography. In 1806 he published *A Compendious Dictionary of the English Language*. More scholarly was his *American Dictionary of the English Language* (1828), in which he first recorded American usage as distinct from the original English and attempted to define words used in the vernacular as well as in literature. Webster's work was not as polished, especially in etymology, as that of his English predecessors, but his books expressed an important phase of America's cultural independence and offered scholars and teachers an invaluable canon of a newly developing language on the eve of American mass education.

WEBSTER-ASHBURTON TREATY (1842) fixed the present northeastern Maine-Canada

Noah Webster's dictionary and his spelling book helped standardize American language.

boundary and settled several issues of long-standing dispute between Britain and the United States. These conflicts had brought the two nations near armed conflict in the Aroostook War (1839). The treaty was negotiated by Secretary of State Daniel Webster and Britain's ,Alexander Baring, first Lord Ashburton. With this agreement, the controversial provisions of the Treaty of 1783 were replaced by new terms regarding 12,000 square miles of territory. The United States received about 7,000 square miles of the disputed land, and the British were allowed to retain their military route between New Brunswick and Quebec. Maine and Massachusetts accepted these terms on condition that Britain pay each of them $150,000 and that the United States reimburse them for expenses incurred defending the area against encroachment.

The treaty also gave the United States navigation rights on the St. John River and adjusted the northern frontiers of Vermont and New York so that the United States retained military works on northern Lake Champlain. The treaty allowed free navigation on the St. Lawrence, Detroit, and St. Clair rivers and Lake St. Clair and established a frontier between Lake Superior and the Lake of the Woods that gave the United States the valuable Mesabi iron deposits.

See also Aroostook War.

WEBSTER-HAYNE DEBATE (1830), Senate debate between Daniel Webster of Massachusetts and Robert Hayne of South Carolina. Hayne, who sought Western support for the South's lower-tariff drive, spoke on Jan. 19, 1830, of the need for self-defense on the part of the West and South in an affirmation of states' rights over federal (and presumably Northeast) encroachment.

Daniel Webster challenged Hayne's stand, and a debate on the nature of the federal Union soon developed. In an eloquent two-day speech, Webster ultimately spoke not just to Haynes but to Vice-President John C. Calhoun, who presided over the Senate. "I go for the Constitution as it is, and the Union as it is," he declared. The "true principles" of the Constitution insist on national power: "Liberty *and* Union, now and forever, one and inseparable!"

Both the Northeast and South considered their respective debaters triumphant but knew that Jackson's opinion would decide the issue. At a Democratic banquet in April 1830, Jackson showed his belief by toasting, "Our Federal Union—it must be preserved."

WELD, THEODORE DWIGHT (1803–1895), one of the outstanding abolitionists of the 1830s. He began his career as an evangelist preaching temperance reform and, eventually, abolition of slavery. Early in 1834, Weld organized at Lane Seminary in Cincinnati a debate on slav-

ery that not only divided the institution, with a majority of the "Lane rebels" leaving to attend Oberlin College, but also affected opinion in all Northern antislavery circles.

Within the American Anti-Slavery Society, which he had helped to found in New York in 1833, he brought together about 70 clergymen and sent them out to propagandize in behalf of abolition. He lost his voice and could no longer conduct his own remarkable work in this area. His most important pamphlet, *American Slavery As It Is* (1839), influenced the writing of Harriet Beecher Stowe and Charles Dickens among others. Weld married Angelina Grimké, pioneer advocate of women's participation in public affairs. Disillusioned by factional struggles among abolitionists, Weld retired to private life early in the 1840s.

See also Abolitionism; Grimké, Sarah and Angelina; Oberlin College.

WELFARE LEGISLATION, legislation that is the result of society's assuming a share of the obligation for such social ills of urban industrial life as poverty, long working hours, poor conditions of labor, child and female labor, unemployment, old age, and industrial accidents. It represents an effort to correct some of the inequalities created by the private ownership of the means of production and to guarantee every human being the right to minimal standards of decency.

Background. Although many European states began to develop comprehensive national programs to meet these needs as early as the 1880s, the United States lagged behind for a variety of reasons. American devotion to the ideal of individual responsibility made it difficult to persuade people that society bore any responsibility for these conditions. The abundance of free land, the relative shortage of labor, and the constant expansion of industry during the nineteenth century prevented conditions from becoming as serious as they were in Europe. Prior to 1900 the care of the unfortunate was left to private charities, churches, machine politicians, fraternal organizations, or to poor houses and poor farms, which threw together the unfortunate with the insane and the retarded.

First Efforts. The Progressive Era brought increased demands for relief from the lower classes and new theories of social responsibility from economists and social scientists. For the most part the problems were attacked at the state level. Illinois enacted a mother's pension law in 1911, and other states followed suit; Alabama and Massachusetts pioneered in the field of old age pensions for state employees; comprehensive pension systems were common by 1933. Conditions of labor, especially for women and children, were closely regulated by nearly every state, and 21 states created industrial commissions to oversee work conditions. New York produced the nation's first comprehensive workmen's compensation law in 1910, and all but four states had adopted some form of it by 1935. The maximum number of hours was slowly whittled down, particularly for women and children, with Massachusetts achieving a 48-hour week by 1920. Several states experimented with minimum wage laws during the Progressive Era. Railroad workers were limited to an 8-hour day, and merchant seamen were guaranteed better conditions of labor. The U.S. Employment Service and the Department of Labor were established, and bills were introduced for minimum wage legislation and old age pensions. The biggest struggle, however, came over attempts to bar the products of child labor from interstate commerce. The first Keating-Owen Act (1916) was declared unconstitutional (1918), and a second (1919) lasted only until 1922 before the Supreme Court struck it down. A federal child labor amendment was then submitted to the states but was not ratified.

New Deal Programs. Although many states expanded their programs during the 1920s, the Great Depression demonstrated the need for much greater federal involvement. For the first time direct relief to the unemployed was provided through public works projects and the efforts of the Federal Emergency Relief Agency, the Work Projects Administration, and the Civilian Conservation Corps. Most significantly, the Social Security Act of 1935 provided for federal old age pensions and a joint federal-state system of unemployment compensation.

Modern Legislation. Since 1940 attempts to expand the federal welfare state have produced only spotty results. The minimum wage has been raised several times and its coverage extended to many formerly excluded occupations. Social Security benefits and coverage have expanded and been augmented: survivor's benefits (1939), disability insurance (1954), and medical care for the aged (1965). Other efforts have been much less fruitful. Although the Full Employment Act of 1946 theoretically committed the federal government to providing jobs for all who were able to work, it was riddled with exemptions and shorn of enforcement machinery.

The Department of Housing and Urban Development was created in the 1960s but has been rarely funded sufficiently to provide for the nation's housing needs. The Department of Health, Education and Welfare, created in the 1950s, has suffered from a lack of money and the complexity of the welfare system. Proposals to provide for a national system of medical care have been delayed for almost three decades by the opposition of health insurance firms and the American Medical Association.

Evaluation. Despite more than 70 years of effort, America's welfare legislation has failed to meet the ideal of providing a decent standard of living for everyone. The amount of money invested, relative to the defense budget, has been woefully insufficient. Millions of Americans fail to qualify for the existing programs and remain "beyond the welfare state." The large numbers of hidden subsidies to the well-to-do seem at times to justify the charge that the United States provides "socialism for the rich and free enterprise for the poor."

The bewildering complexity of state, local, and federal programs produces widely varying benefits and multiplies administrative costs and delays. The private interest groups and notions of rugged individualism still impair efforts to provide satisfactory solutions. Most importantly, the requirements for receiving assistance often serve to penalize those who try to better themselves and to make it difficult for them to retain their dignity and self-respect.

See also Keating-Owen Act (1916); Medicare and Medicaid; New Deal; Social Security Act (1935).

Consult (VIII) Chambers, 1963; Lubove, 1968; Wilcox, 1969.

—John Buenker, *University of Wisconsin, Parkside*

WELFARE STATE, one in which the government assumes primary responsibility for the economic and social well-being of its citizens. In capitalist countries that have adopted the welfare state, governments provide unemployment compensation, retirement benefits, and assistance to the handicapped, the indigent, and the helpless. These governments provide health services, public housing, and education for all. Such programs are accompanied and supported by schemes for income redistribution.

In the United States a full-blown welfare state has not developed, although there has been some government involvement with education. Such development has been hindered by a strong capitalist-individualist tradition and by decentralization built into the federal system. In public medical care the United States has lagged behind most other capitalist nations. Under the New Deal the federal government assumed primary responsibility for emergency relief and then set up a moderate and piecemeal welfare state, which has been expanded in subsequent years.

See also New Deal; Social Security Act (1935); Tennessee Valley Authority; Welfare Legislation.

WELLAND CANAL. *See* Canals.

WESTINGHOUSE, GEORGE (1846–1914), inventor and manufacturer. After serving the Union during the Civil War, he joined his father's farm implement shop in Schenectady,

Inventor and industrialist George Westinghouse.

N.Y., in 1865. Within the year he obtained a patent for a rotary steam engine—the first of more than 400 patents issued to him. His invention of the compressed air brake in 1869 made safe high-speed rail transportation possible by giving complete control of the train to the engineer. The Westinghouse Air Brake Co., the first firm of his future worldwide industrial empire, was organized the same year.

After developing a system of electrical railroad signals and switches, as well as a pipeline pressure system for transmitting natural gas over long distances, Westinghouse turned his attention to the problems of electrical power transmission and utilization. Under his direction and within only a few months after taking up the problem, power transformers were developed that made possible the introduction of a high voltage, alternating-current single-phase system for the distribution of electricity in the United States. Having acquired the patents of Nikola Tesla, Westinghouse modified the distribution system so that it could be used for running electric motors as well as lighting lamps. These discoveries were followed by the organization of the Westinghouse Electric Co. in 1886.

See also Inventions.
Consult (V) Garbedian, 1946.

WEST JERSEY. *See* New Jersey.

WESTMORELAND, WILLIAM C(HILDS) (1914-), American Army officer who commanded U.S. forces during the height of the Vietnam War. A native of South Carolina, he studied at The Citadel in 1931–1932 and graduated from the U.S. Military Academy in 1936. In World War II he participated in the North African and Sicilian campaigns and the occupation of Germany. During the Korean War he commanded the 187th Airborne Regimental Combat Team in Korea. He was made a major general in 1956 and in 1958 was given command of the Army's elite 101st Airborne Division.

In May 1960 President Eisenhower named him superintendent of the U.S. Military Academy, a prestigious assignment he held until taking command of the XVIII Airborne Corps in 1963. From 1964 to 1968, Westmoreland, as a full general, commanded the U.S. forces in Vietnam, overseeing a buildup of American troops from fewer than 100,000 to more than 500,000. As protest against the war mounted in the United States, he was faulted by war critics for his optimistic assessment of the course of the war. Westmoreland served as Army chief of staff from 1968 until his retirement in 1972.

See also Vietnam War.
Consult (VIII) Furguson, 1968.

WEST VIRGINIA, the 35th state, admitted to the

Whig Party banner of 1844, when Henry Clay was its presidential candidate.

Union on June 20, 1863. The Virginia area was claimed for the British in 1716 by Alexander Spotswood, while the French claimed the Ohio Valley region. Colonists began to settle the area in the 1730s. It was originally part of Virginia but the development of coal mining made the area quite different from the eastern part, and when Virginia seceded from the Union in 1861, western Virginia opposed the action by setting up its own government.

The state legislature is bicameral; Charleston is the capital. The population in 1970 was 1,744,237.

WHARTON, EDITH (1862–1937), author of *Ethan Frome* (1911) and other works. *See* Literature.

WHEELER-LEA ACT (1938), comprehensive measure that superseded the Pure Food and Drug Act. *See* Pure Food and Drug Act (1906).

WHIG PARTY, political party that developed out of factions regrouped from the defunct Federalist Party. The future Whigs first appeared in 1832 as National Republicans supporting Henry Clay for the presidency. Formally organized in 1834, they had learned from Jacksonians the art of popular campaigning and elected Gen. William Henry Harrison in the spectacular "Tippecanoe and Tyler too" presidential race in 1840. The Whig Party sought to develop a national program (as in its cooperation with John Tyler, who was essentially a Virginia Democrat), but the increasing firmness of the Democrats in defending slavery made the Whigs a magnet for antislavery Northerners.

The Whigs won the 1848 election with Gen. Zachary Taylor, like Harrison a national military hero, but they found it more and more difficult to straddle the slavery-antislavery issue. The Whigs' last hero, Gen. Winfield Scott, was severely defeated in 1852, the last election in which the party played an important role. In 1856 Millard Fillmore ran far behind the candidate of the new Republican Party, John C. Frémont, who was himself decisively defeated by Democrat James Buchanan.

See also Harrison, William Henry; National Republicans; Presidential Elections.

WHISKEY REBELLION, an uprising in western Pennsylvania in 1794. As part of Alexander Hamilton's financial program, Congress had put an excise tax on whiskey. This tax was particularly annoying to the Western areas of the country because in many regions, owing to the extremely poor communications, it was easier to send grain to market after it had been converted to whiskey because there was far less bulk. Also, with a shortage of hard cash, whiskey was used as a medium of exchange. General Western dissatisfaction erupted in western Pennsylvania in the summer of 1794. Excise officers were attacked, and the disaffected threatened further military action. President Washington asked the states for militia to quell the disturbance, and their favorable response demonstrated the advance that had been made since the 1780s in the creation of an effective central government. A force was quickly provided, and the rebels dispersed before any real fighting was necessary.

WHISTLER, JAMES ABBOTT McNEILL (1834–1903), American painter and etcher. He was born in Lowell, Mass. After failing to graduate from West Point, he worked as a cartographer and learned the technique of etching. In 1855 Whistler left America, never to return, and went to Paris to study art. In 1863 London became the center of his activities. He became celebrated as a witty and argumentative personality, somewhat theatrical in dress and manner.

Whistler conceived of his portraits as experiments in color harmony and tonal effect, and he emphasized the aesthetic nature of his works. Among his most important canvases are "Thomas Carlyle" (1873) and "Miss Cicely Alexander" (1873). His most famous work is "Arrangement in Grey and Black No. 1" (Whistler's Mother). His individual style of painting did not evoke wide imitation, but his spontaneous and charming etchings were emulated by many artists.

Some of Whistler's works show the influence of Japanese mannerism, then popular on the Continent. In both "Gold Screen" (1863) and "Little White Girl" (1863), certain qualities of Japanese art, composition, and line are blended with draftsmanship and tonal interest. Whistler was the author of some astute critical essays, including *Ten O'Clock* (1888) and *The Gentle Art of Making Enemies* (1890). Earlier he was involved in a famous lawsuit with John Ruskin, whose critical comments on a painting caused the artist to sue for slander. Whistler won damages of one farthing and wore the coin on his watch chain.

WHITE, EDWARD DOUGLASS (1845–1921), 8th Chief Justice of the Supreme Court. He is noted for opinions reflecting a conservative and nationalistic viewpoint.

Born in Louisiana, he served in the Confederate army and afterward resumed his studies in the office of a New Orleans lawyer. White, who was admitted to the bar in 1868, developed a successful private practice and also participated in local politics as a Democrat. In 1874 he was elected to the state senate and served on the Louisiana Supreme Court (1879–1880) before his election to the U.S. Senate in 1890. Then, in 1894, President Cleveland, thwarted by his efforts to appoint two

close associates to the U.S. Supreme Court, nominated White, who was more likely to receive Senate confirmation.

White served as an associate justice from 1894 to 1910, when he was elevated to chief justice by President Taft. During his 27 years on the Court, White developed a somewhat uneven and, in the opinion of some critics, very poor and inconsistent legal style. His chief distinction lies in his dissenting opinion in the Income Tax Cases and his concurring and dissenting opinions in the Insular Cases, in which he was chiefly responsible for formulating the doctrine of incorporated and unincorporated territories. White's writings concerning the Interstate Commerce Act are considered his greatest contribution to law.

See also Antitrust Cases.

WHITEFIELD, GEORGE (1715–1770), English clergyman who played a major role in America's Great Awakening in the 1740s. In England Whitefield was associated with John and Charles Wesley and the Methodist movement. He undertook to teach the importance of "oneness with God" wherever the opportunity arose and did so with fiery zeal and rare dramatic ability.

Whitefield, who had first visited America in 1738, landed in 1739 in Savannah, Ga., where he began construction of an orphanage. He traveled widely in the colonies preaching the revival of religious zeal and raising money for his orphanage. In 1741 Whitefield returned to England. He had become a rigid Calvinist, and during this period in England he broke with the Wesleys and assumed leadership of the Calvinistic Methodist movement. He subsequently made trips to America to preach and write. He died in Newburyport, Mass., during one of these visits.

See also Colonial Religion; Great Awakening.

WHITE PLAINS, BATTLE OF (OCT. 28, 1776), British attack repulsed by George Washington. *See* Revolutionary War Battles.

WHITE SLAVERY. *See* Mann Act (1910).

WHITMAN, WALT(ER) (1819–1892), one of the most individual voices in American poetry. Whitman was born in Huntington, N.Y., and spent his youth partly in New York City and partly at the sea and countryside. Whitman began his long association with newspapers at 13, when he went to work as a printer's devil for the *Long Island Patriot*.

He wrote stories for the *Democratic Review* in the 1840s and served as editor of the *Brooklyn Eagle* from 1846 to 1848. Little of his early writing survives. His verse was conventional, and his temperance novel, *Franklin Ev-*

Poet Walt Whitman celebrated the dignity and freedom of the common man.

ans or the Inebriate, was routine. His editorial work on behalf of social reforms and free soil led to his dismissal from the *Eagle.*

Leaves of Grass. Whitman's life began to change in 1848 as he began work on *Leaves of Grass,* which transformed him from a traveling journalist into a major poet. The first edition of *Leaves of Grass* contained 12 poems, including pieces later titled "Song of Myself," "There was a Child Went Forth," "I Sing the Body Electric," and a preface, omitted from later editions, in which Whitman set forth the ideals of the great poet. In this preface Whitman asserted that the poet must be in harmony with the universe as well as with the common people; his verse should be plain and contain no unnecessary ornamentation.

By 1860, *Leaves of Grass* had grown to 456 pages with 122 new poems. Whitman continued to add to *Leaves of Grass,* which went through nine successively enlarged editions, the final one appearing in 1892, the year of his death.

Later Life. Whitman served as a volunteer nurse in the Civil War; his *Drum Taps* (1865) recorded in verse his Civil War experiences. *Democratic Vistas* (1871) was a significant prose work containing Whitman's fears of the developing materialism in American society. After suffering a stroke in 1873 he lived until his death in Camden, N.J.

See also Literature.
Consult (V) Allen, 1955.
—Richard Collin, Louisiana State University, New Orleans

WHITNEY, ELI (1761–1825), American inventor. Whitney graduated from Yale and went south to teach. Instead, while staying on a friend's plantation near Savannah, Ga., in 1793, he invented the cotton gin. Just one year out of college, Whitney revolutionized the cotton business and created enormous wealth in the South. Patent infringements prevented him from benefiting, and he made little money out of the gin.

In 1798, however, he began firearms production under federal contract for 10,000 muskets. At his factory near New Haven, Conn., he adopted a mass production system of interchangeable parts. Prefabricated parts of rifles could be readily assembled by relatively unskilled workers. He is thus credited with introducing the "American system" of manufacture. However, others had preceded him, and the system was later made more sophisticated by another firearms manufacturer, Samuel Colt.

See also Cotton Gin; Inventions; Mass Production.

WHITNEY v. CALIFORNIA (1927), Supreme Court decision that extended the protection of the Fourteenth Amendment. *See* Brandeis, Louis D.

WHITTIER, JOHN GREENLEAF (1807–1892), New England poet. He was born in Haverhill, Mass. and as a youth was encouraged to write by William Lloyd Garrison, who also influenced Whittier's interest in abolitionism. Whittier served in the Massachusetts legislature in 1835 and edited various publications, among them the *Pennsylvania Freeman* (1838–1840). Although grateful to Garrison, Whittier was a Quaker and therefore unwilling to speak harshly in controversy. He was distressed by the bitter rhetoric that Garrisonians employed against slave owners, government figures, and churchmen and was one of the moderates who left the American Anti-Slavery Society to form the American and Foreign Anti-Slavery Society in 1840.

His literary prestige aided Northern antislavery forces as North-South differences became sharper, and several of his poems, such as "Massachusetts to Virginia" and especially "Ichabod," which condemned Daniel Webster's support of the Compromise of 1850, had outstanding popularity. As an editor and contributor to the antislavery *National Era,* Whittier was close to the development of the Republican Party.

After the Civil War, Whittier returned to his earlier interests in personal and descriptive verse and prose. Poems such as "Maud Muller," "The Barefoot Boy," and "Barbara Frietchie" became standard recitation pieces; the volume *Snowbound* was widely recognized as Whittier's masterpiece. His prominence as a national poet lost him much of his place in U.S. political history.

Consult (IV) Bennett, 1941.
—Louis Filler, *Antioch College*

WILDER, THORNTON (1897–   ), American novelist and playwright. *See* Theater.

WILDERNESS, BATTLE OF THE (1755), engagement in which French and Indian forces slaughtered troops commanded by Edward Braddock. *See* Braddock, Edward.

WILDERNESS, BATTLE OF THE (MAY 5–6, 1864), engagement in which Robert E. Lee inflicted heavy losses on General Grant. *See* Civil War Battles.

WILDERNESS ROAD, route through the Appalachian Mountains to Kentucky. *See* Boone, Daniel.

WILLARD, EMMA (1787–1870), teacher who advocated equal educational rights for women. Born Emma Hart, she began teaching after an education at the Berlin (Connecticut) Academy and for two years was head of the Middlebury (Vermont) Female Academy before leaving to marry John Willard. In 1814 she opened her own school for girls.

She believed that women were entitled to the same educational privileges as men, and she carried out these ideals by teaching mathematics, philosophy, and allied subjects to her students. She proposed that the New York State legislature act on her views of educational equality for women but was turned down. In 1821, at the invitation of the community, she established at Troy, N.Y., the Troy Female Seminary, which offered the first college level instruction for women in the United States.

Her influence was widespread, and her textbooks on history and geography were as influential as her innovative teaching techniques and her training of teachers. She retired from teaching in 1838 to devote herself to the enlargement and improvement of common schools. Her writings included a volume of mediocre poetry, which included her best-known poem, "Rocked in the Cradle of the Deep."

WILLARD, FRANCES (1839–1898), temperance leader, suffragist, and social reformer who became nationally known through the Woman's Christian Temperance Union (WCTU), of which she was president for 20 years. Originally a teacher, she became active in Illinois temperance reform in 1874 and in the National Woman's Christian Temperance Union.

The WCTU was formed in 1874 for the abolition of use, manufacture, and sale of alcoholic beverages. After Willard became president of the union in 1879, she transformed it into the most influential women's pressure group of her day and used it as an instrument for leading women into public affairs. Under her direction, the union became international in scope, and by its 1897 convention, the world's WCTU had almost 2 million members. Following Willard's "Do Everything" slogan, the WCTU broadened its interests to include other reforms besides prohibition. By 1889, 39 departments were devoted to such causes as labor reform, prison reform, pacifism, welfare, "social purity," and, after 1882, women's suffrage, a particular interest of Willard's.

Attempting to turn the WCTU into a force in party politics, she helped to organize the Prohibition Party, which under her influence supported women's suffrage from 1882 to 1884. At the end of her life, she endorsed socialism and favored education rather than prohibition as a temperance tool. After her death the WCTU lost interest in all but one of her goals and returned to a strict prohibitionist policy.

See also Prohibition; Suffrage, Women's.
—Nancy Woloch, *Hebrew Union College*

WILLIAM AND MARY, COLLEGE OF. *See* Colonial Colleges.

WILLIAMS, ROGER (1603–1683), colonial religious leader and founder of Providence, R.I. He was born in England and, after being exposed to Puritanism in the 1620s, sought a career in the ministry. But Williams had adopted Separatist views, and life in England could be unpleasant for those who openly renounced the Anglican church. In 1630 he left England for Massachusetts Bay Colony.

Soon after arriving in America, Williams was offered a post in Boston's church. He rejected the offer because he did not wish to minister to Non-Separatists and soon settled in Plymouth, a community founded by Separatists. In Plymouth, Williams came to know Indians, and he began to argue that because America belonged to them, the King of England had no right to grant land or charter colonies in the New World. By this reasoning, the Puritans' authority to rule their communities was invalid.

If such ideas angered many New Englanders, Williams proceeded to come up with other, equally disturbing notions. He asserted that to preserve the purity of the church, church and state must be completely separated and, even worse, he challenged the basic idea of a Puritan commonwealth by asserting that a variety of sects ought to be tolerated.

Although Williams' thought was logical and based on the orthodox Puritan concept of God as all powerful and beyond human comprehension, his ideas threatened the stability, indeed the very existence, of the Puritan experiment in America. The magistrates did not want to punish him—nearly everyone liked him immensely—so they tried repeatedly to convince him either to alter his views or keep quiet.

Williams refused, and in 1635 he was banished. He went to Rhode Island, bought land from the Indians, and in 1636 named his settlement Providence. There he and those who joined him could worship as they wished. He was also instrumental in the political life of the new colony, making trips to England to obtain a charter (1644) and in the 1650s to secure approval of the union of the Rhode Island towns. After his return he was governor of the colony in 1654–1657.

See also Colonial Religion; Rhode Island.

Consult (I) Morgan, 1967; Winslow, 1957.

—Aaron M. Shatzman, *Stanford University*

WILLIAMS, TENNESSEE (THOMAS LANIER) (1911–), American dramatist, twice winner of the Pulitzer Prize. He was born in Columbus, Miss., and began to write as a child, experi-

Author Tennessee Williams won Pulitzer Prize for *A Streetcar Named Desire* (1947).

menting with fiction, poetry, and drama. His successful long-run Broadway production of *The Glass Menagerie* (1945–1946) brought him critical acclaim and public recognition. Williams won the New York Drama Critics' Circle Award on four occasions: for *The Glass Menagerie*, *A Streetcar Named Desire* (1947), *Cat on a Hot Tin Roof* (1955), and *The Night of the Iguana* (1962). He was twice awarded the Pulitzer Prize: for *A Streetcar Named Desire* and *Cat on a Hot Tin Roof*.

Through his plays, Williams, one of the most influential and controversial contemporary playwrights, deftly and compassionately examines human emotions in theatrically exciting settings. His characters range from poor to rich, from pretentiously genteel to crude and ruthless.

Williams' other full-length plays include *Summer and Smoke* (1948), *The Rose Tattoo* (1951), *Camino Real* (1951), *Orpheus Descending* (1957), and *The Milk Train Doesn't Stop Here Anymore* (1963). He has also written short plays, poems, stories, and a novel, *The Roman Spring of Mrs. Stone* (1950).

WILMOT PROVISO, attempt by a dissident Democratic congressman, David Wilmot (1814–1868), to attach an amendment to an appropriations bill to pay for negotiations with Mexico over possible acquisition of Mexican territory. The Wilmot Proviso would have denied the funds unless "as an express and fundamental condition" of any agreement, "neither slavery nor involuntary servitude shall ever exist in any part of said territory" acquired from Mexico. The amendment passed the House twice (in 1846 and 1847) but was defeated in the Senate. The fear of a struggle over the status of slavery in the lands ceded by Mexico hung over the Polk Administration and was a factor in the election of 1848. Wilmot himself left the Democratic Party and joined the new Free-Soil Party. His proviso helped to polarize opinion on the question of slavery extension before the Civil War.

WILSON, JAMES (1742–1798), Revolutionary statesman and legal figure. Born and educated in Scotland, Wilson emigrated to America in 1765. He settled in Pennsylvania, where he studied law under John Dickinson and soon established a lucrative practice. He then embarked upon a lifelong interest in land speculation. He was a patriot during the movement for independence. In 1774 he moved to Carlisle, where he headed the Committee of Correspondence and wrote an important, widely read pamphlet, *Considerations on the Nature and Extent of the Legislative Authority of the British Parliament*, which denied Parliament's right to legislate for the colonies.

He served as a member of the Second Continental Congress and signed the Declara-

tion of Independence. But after the break with England, he became increasingly conservative, opposing the radical Pennsylvania Constitution of 1776 and subsequently working hard to increase the powers of the national government at the expense of the states. He was a member of the Constitutional Convention of 1787 and played a leading role both in the proceedings and in the battle over its adoption. He served as an associate justice of the Supreme Court (1789–1798) and wrote a noted decision in *Chisholm v. Georgia*. It predated John Marshall's judicial nationalism in many ways, but it was overturned by the Eleventh Amendment. Business failures forced him to flee his home state in 1797 in order to avoid arrest for debt, and he died in North Carolina amidst demands for his impeachment.

See also Amendments, Constitutional; Chisholm v. Georgia (1793); Committees of Correspondence.
Consult (III) Smith, 1956.
—Richard E. Ellis, *University of Virginia*

WILSON, (THOMAS) WOODROW (1856–1924), 28th President of the United States (1913–1921). He was born in Staunton, Va., on Dec. 28, 1856, and grew up in Georgia. After graduating from Princeton in 1879, he took a law degree, briefly practiced law, and returned to school for a Ph.D. in history and government (1886), which he then taught. Wilson authored numerous scholarly books, including *Congressional Government* and *The State*.

In 1902 Wilson was elected president of Princeton and almost immediately became embroiled in conflicts with the trustees and other administrators over his plans for reforms. At the height of the controversy in 1910, New Jersey Democratic leaders urged Wilson to run for governor, and he accepted. As governor he gained nationwide fame by enacting laws for a direct primary, public utilities regulation, employer liability, corrupt practices control, and business regulation. Wilson received the Democratic presidential nomination in 1912 and defeated Theodore Roosevelt and William Howard Taft in a three-way race.

Domestic Policies. Although he campaigned on a New Freedom program that promised a return to competition and small government, Wilson proceeded to enact a good portion of the Progressive Party platform. The Clayton Antitrust Act and the Federal Trade Act inaugurated federal regulation of business, while the Federal Reserve Act did the same for banking. Labor benefited by provisions for an eight-hour day for railroad workers, the regulation of seamen's working conditions, and the Keating-Owen Act, which affected child labor. The tariff was lowered for the first time in 20 years, and farmers benefited from the Federal Farm Loan Act. In 1916 Wilson narrowly won

Woodrow Wilson, 28th President of the United States (1913–1921), greets public in 1913.

reelection over Charles Evans Hughes and the reunited Republicans and spent most of his second Administration trying to prevent Prohibition and immigration restriction after reluctantly agreeing to women's suffrage.

Role in World War I. When World War I broke out, Wilson proclaimed American neutrality and sought to negotiate a "peace without victory." He proposed his Fourteen Points as a basis for peace and campaigned in 1916 on the slogan "He kept us out of war." However, in April 1917 Wilson, citing German violations of American neutrality, asked Congress for a declaration of war.

After the armistice, Wilson led the American delegation to Versailles to press for a just peace and the creation of the League of Nations. Although neither the treaty nor the League charter was all that he had hoped for, Wilson refused to compromise with his Senate opponents, who rejected his handiwork twice (in 1919 and 1920). Bitterly disappointed and partially paralyzed by a stroke, Wilson died in Washington on Feb. 3, 1924.

See also Federal Farm Loan Act (1916); Fourteen Points; League of Nations; Presidential Elections; Versailles, Treaty of; World War I: Causes.

Consult (VI) Blum, 1956; Link, 1947–1965; Smith, 1964.

—John Buenker, *University of Wisconsin, Parkside*

WINTHROP, JOHN, IV (1714–1779), scholar, scientist, astronomer, and member of a New England family prominent in politics and science. He was born in Boston, was educated at the Boston Latin School and Harvard, and was elected Hollis Professor of Mathematics and Natural Philosophy at Harvard in 1738. Winthrop established at Harvard the first laboratory for experimental physics in America. There he introduced the study of Newtonian fluxions, now known as differential and integral calculus.

Through Winthrop's observations in astronomy and his papers to England's Royal Society, of which he became a member in 1766, and the American Philosophical Society, he gained an international reputation. He calculated the movement of Mercury across the sun in 1740 and made accurate observations of earthquakes, comets, eclipses, and the aberration of light. John Winthrop was an ardent supporter of the patriot cause during the American Revolution. Although he died at the height of it, he influenced through his friendship and advice such founders of the republic as George Washington and Benjamin Franklin.

WINTHROP FAMILY, influential family of colonial New England. John Winthrop (1588–1647), the governor of Massachusetts Bay Colony for many years, was a Suffolk gentleman farmer who studied law at the Inner Temple in London and became a successful attorney. A Puritan, he despaired of England and emigrated to America as a leader of the Massachusetts Bay Company in 1630. For most of the rest of his life he dominated the colony, fighting to keep it pure in doctrine and character and opposing dissidents such as Roger Williams and Anne Hutchinson. Nevertheless, Winthrop was a moderate man who sought the middle course in all things. His *Journal,* kept from 1630 to his death, is a vital historical source.

Winthrop's son John Winthrop, Jr. (1606–1676) was the founder of industrial chemistry in America and an initiator of the important Saugus Iron Works, begun in Massachusetts in 1644. A practicing physician and a wide reader in scientific literature, Winthrop was well known abroad and was the first American elected to the Royal Society in England (1663). He collected a large scientific library. Born in England, he had been educated at Trinity College, Dublin, and by travels in Europe. He founded New London, Conn., in 1646 and was the governor of Connecticut Colony in 1657 and from 1659 to 1676, being reelected each year. John Jr.'s son Fitz-John Winthrop (1638–1707) was also governor of Connecticut (1698–1707).

See also Massachusetts.
Consult (I) Dunn, 1962.

WISCONSIN, the 30th state, was admitted to the Union on May 29, 1848. Jean Nicolet explored the Wisconsin area in 1634; soon after, fur trade sprang up in the area; France claimed it in 1686 and then ceded it to Britain in 1763. Although Britain left the area after the Revolution, it reclaimed the land for a time during the War of 1812. The area then became part of the Illinois Territory and in 1818 part of Michigan Territory. Wisconsin gained territorial status in 1836.

The state legislature is bicameral; Madison is the capital. The population in 1970 was 4,417,933.

WISCONSIN IDEA, name given to progressive program initiated by Robert M. La Follette while he was governor of Wisconsin. *See* La - Follette, Robert M.

WITHERSPOON, JOHN (1723–1794), religious leader who headed the College of New Jersey (Princeton) and signed the Declaration of Independence. *See* Presbyterians.

WOBBLIES, popular name for members of the Industrial Workers of the World. *See* Industrial Workers of the World.

WOLFE, THOMAS (CLAYTON) (1900–1938), Southern writer born and brought up in Ashe-

WOMEN'S RIGHTS — Item Guide

The struggle for women's rights at first centered on SUFFRAGE, WOMEN's, with the SENECA FALLS CONVENTION (1848) one of the earliest organized meetings. SUSAN B. ANTHONY, ELIZABETH CADY STANTON, and LUCY STONE were forceful leaders, but the Supreme Court ruled in MINOR V. HAPPERSETT (1875) that suffrage was not a constitutional right. Women's suffrage finally came with the XIX Amendment (1920), (AMENDMENTS, CONSTITUTIONAL), and many suffragist leaders joined the LEAGUE OF WOMEN VOTERS.

The women's movement subsequently concentrated on full equality with men. ABORTION AND BIRTH CONTROL LAWS were a primary target for change, and pioneers such as MARGARET SANGER were eventually vindicated in the Supreme Court's decision in JANE ROE V. HENRY WADE (1973). Supporters of WOMEN's LIBERATION, such as BETTY FRIEDAN, formed groups such as NATIONAL ORGANIZATION FOR WOMEN. Liberationists and politicians such as BELLA ABZUG and SHIRLEY CHISHOLM lobbied for the Equal Rights Amendment.

Women liberationists surge down New York City's Fifth Avenue during August 1970 march demanding equality for women.

ville, N.C. (the "Altamont, Old Catawba" of his fiction). Educated first at the University of North Carolina (1920), Wolfe then studied playwriting at Harvard under G. P. Baker. Realizing that the theater was not his medium, Wolfe, after a trip to Europe, worked intermittently as an English instructor at New York University.

Wolfe published two successful novels based on his own life, *Look Homeward, Angel: A Story of the Buried Life* (1929) and *Of Time and the River* (1935). He was helped by Scribner's Maxwell Perkins, who persuaded and aided Wolfe in the cutting, editing, and reorganizing of lengthy manuscripts. *Look Homeward, Angel*, although generally well received, stirred local animosities in Asheville, causing Wolfe not to return to his hometown until a year prior to his death. *Of Time and the River* was equally autobiographical, but the scenes were removed to New York, Boston, and Europe.

Several of his works, including his third and fourth novels, which enhanced his position as a major writer, were published posthumously: *The Web and the Rock* (1939), *You Can't Go Home Again* (1940), *The Hills Beyond* (1941), and a collection of stories and studies.

WOMEN IN THE NINETEENTH CENTURY (1845), tract by Margaret Fuller calling for equality for women. *See* Fuller, Margaret.

WOMEN'S CHRISTIAN TEMPERANCE UNION. *See* Willard, Frances.

WOMEN'S CLUBS, important force in the women's suffrage movement. *See* Suffrage, Women's.

WOMEN'S LIBERATION, general label for the activities of the current feminist movement, which was initiated by the formation of the National Organization for Women (NOW) in 1966. More specifically, it refers to women's groups that began to form in the larger cities in the late 1960s and subsequently proliferated around the United States. Varied in tactics and convictions, unstructured and informal in organization, these groups attempt to achieve a psychological reorientation and sense of sisterhood through the innovative technique of "consciousness-raising." Although the movement is opposed to leaders or spokeswomen, public attention has often focused on articulate advocates of women's rights such as Betty Friedan, Gloria Steinem, Kate Millett, and Germaine Greer.

Liberationists gained attention through publicity stunts, confrontations, and protests. They demonstrated at the Miss America Beauty Pageant, government agencies, marriage license bureaus, publishing offices, welfare centers, and legislative hearings. They also sup-

ported campaigns for day care, abortion, and equal rights and attempted to welcome all types of women, including minority group members and lesbians.

The women's liberation camp, encompassing the more radical wing of the new feminist movement, has developed an ideology and issued a call for radical alteration of our society. The source of women's oppression, according to radical feminists, is not merely in laws but in attitudes: both men and women must be liberated from rigid conventional conceptions of male and female roles. The campaign against sexism and male chauvinism has led to attacks on marriage and the family as oppressive sexist institutions. Viewing women as an oppressed class, radical feminists find their oppression to be a political problem, not merely a personal one.

See also Friedan, Betty; National Organization for Women.

Consult (VIII) Firestone, 1970; Greer, 1971; Millett, 1970; Morgan, 1970.

—Nancy Woloch, *Hebrew Union College*

WOMEN'S RIGHTS MOVEMENT. *See* Suffrage, Women's; Women's Liberation.

WOOLLENS ACT (1699). *See* Navigation Act.

WORCESTER v. GEORGIA (1831), Supreme Court decision holding that federal, rather than state, legislation applied to the Cherokee Indians. *See* Cherokee Nation v. Georgia (1831).

WORKMEN'S COMPENSATION, state laws that protect injured workers and their families from some of the costs of work-connected diseases and accidents. The oldest type of social insurance program in the United States, workmen's compensation is state administered and state supervised. These laws specify that employers guarantee their employees certain cash and medical benefits. Railroad workers and most domestic and farm laborers are excluded.

WORKS PROJECTS ADMINISTRATION (WPA). Known as the Works Progress Administration until 1939, this New Deal agency provided massive and direct aid to the unemployed. The average monthly enrollment on work relief was approximately 2 million. The agency expended $11 billion, nearly half of which was budgeted for the first year (no government had ever before made so large an appropriation at one time). Its purpose when established by Congress in 1935 was to replace and enlarge the Federal Emergency Relief Administration (FERA) as the major unemployment relief agency.

At the outset there was a struggle for control of the new program between the parsimonious Harold Ickes of the Public Works Administration (PWA) and Harry Hopkins of FERA, who were willing to spend. President Roosevelt chose Hopkins as administrator. Most of the recipients were unskilled, but WPA also provided imaginative and innovative jobs for unemployed teachers, musicians, theater people, and artists. This largest and most influential (conservative congressmen were most concerned about its impact on votes) of all New Deal programs assisted and influenced others: The Civilian Conservation Corps used WPA teachers as educational advisers; the Rural Electrification Administration used WPA labor; the National Youth Administration was an adjunct to WPA designed to keep students and other young people off the labor market.

See also Federal Emergency Relief Act; New Deal; Public Works Administration.

Consult (VI) Charles, 1963.

WORLD COURT, permanent court of international arbitration, officially known as the Permanent Court of International Justice, was established by the League of Nations in 1921. The court's impartiality was to be safeguarded by distinguished jurists drawn from all parts of the world. There was a strong movement for U.S. participation, even though it had refused to join the League of Nations. But the Senate wished to retain the right to decide which questions the nation should present for arbitration, so the United States never joined. Before the court's demise in 1945, however, several Americans, including Charles Evans Hughes and Frank B. Kellogg, served as judges.

WORLD'S COLUMBIA EXPOSITION, world's fair held in 1893 to commemorate the discovery of America by Columbus. The fair was held in Chicago from May to October at a cost of $60 million and was attended by about 21 million people. There were more than 65,000 foreign and domestic exhibits.

The plan for the exposition was introduced in Congress in 1889. Washington, St. Louis, and New York wanted the fair, but Congress gave it to Chicago, and the city raised the necessary 10 million dollars to construct the fairgrounds. After the fairgrounds were designed by Frederick Law Olmsted, the "White City"—a plaster of Paris building designed by Richard Morris Hunt and the firm of McKim, Mead, and White—rose on the shores of Lake Michigan as a pillared tribute to classicism. The lack of originality in the building design and in the fair exhibits was offset by the resourceful management of the city. People were moved efficiently by electrified railways and electric-powered boats. The design of the fair influenced the construction of public buildings for years to come, as pillared banks, railroad stations, and city halls began to appear across the country.

WORLD WAR I: CAUSES. On June 28, 1914, Gavrilo Princip, an ardent Serbian nationalist, assassinated Archduke Franz Ferdinand, heir to the Austro-Hungarian throne. The Austrian government, blaming Serbian authorities for the political murder and determined to crush Serbian nationalism, presented Serbia with a 48-hour ultimatum. When Serbia failed to comply fully, Austria-Hungary declared war on July 28. Two days later, Russia, Serbia's ally, entered the conflict. The other nations of Europe quickly followed, pulled in by the alliance system and the political-economic rivalry underlying it. By the middle of August, the Entente, or Allied Powers of France, Britain, and Russia, were at war with the Central Powers of Germany, Austria-Hungary, and Italy. The war eventually involved most of the world.

America and the War. Americans emerging from an era of progress, hope, and relative peace were shocked and stunned by the outbreak of the war. In accordance with past American policy and traditions of isolationism, President Wilson proclaimed official neutrality on August 4 and two weeks later urged the American people to be neutral in thought as well. Despite Wilson's appeal, the American public was never neutral. Many "hyphenated-Americans," such as German-Americans and Irish-Americans, sympathized with the cause of the Central Powers, while the majority of Americans, including prominent government leaders, were pro-Ally, reflecting cultural and economic bonds with England and traditional Franco-American friendship.

This pro-Ally disposition was strengthened by growing economic ties with the Allies. When war broke out, the United States opened its markets to both sides in accordance with its traditional policy and with international practice. Because the Allies controlled the seas, the bulk of the war trade flowed to the Entente countries. They began purchasing vast quantities of war materials, which turned the United States into a war production center for the Allies. By 1917 the sale of munitions alone reached $1 billion, while Allied borrowing to finance the war trade amounted to $2.25 billion.

Relations with the Belligerents. Difficulties with the belligerents soon arose over neutral rights. The objective of the United States was to maintain legitimate trade in noncontraband goods with Germany and the neutral states of Europe. British policy, on the other hand, was designed to cut Germany off completely by regulating neutral trade. When the British steadily expanded the contraband lists, censored neutral mails, and illegally blockaded Germany, the United States protested these violations of international law but generally acquiesced in British policy. In contrast, President Wilson held Germany fully accountable

WORLD WAR I — Item Guide

The articles on WORLD WAR I: CAUSES and WORLD WAR I BATTLES concentrate on the American involvement in the conflict, which started almost three years before the United States went to war. American public opinion supported the Allies, particularly after the LUSITANIA, SINKING OF, in 1915. U.S. relations with the Central Powers deteriorated, and President WOODROW WILSON led the nation into war in 1917.

The AMERICAN EXPEDITIONARY FORCE, commanded by JOHN J. PERSHING, was quickly formed, in part through the provisions of the SELECTIVE SERVICE ACT (1917). Funds for the war were raised through LIBERTY LOANS, and the economy was supervised by the WAR INDUSTRIES BOARD, headed by BERNARD BARUCH. Domestic criticism of U.S. participation was stifled by the ESPIONAGE ACT (1917).

The Allies' victory was followed by VERSAILLES, TREATY OF, into which Wilson attempted to have his FOURTEEN POINTS incorporated. U.S. membership in the LEAGUE OF NATIONS was rejected by the Senate, led by WILLIAM E. BORAH and Henry Cabot Lodge of the LODGE FAMILY.

Allied troops in the trenches at Verdun.

NORWAY

SWEDEN

FINLAND

0 100 200 300 400 500 Miles

NORTH
SEA

• Petrograd

• Moscow

GREAT
BRITAIN

DENMARK

RUSSIA

• Hamburg

• Danzig

• Berlin

• Tannenberg

March~Nov 1918

London •

NETH

GERMANY

• Warsaw
POLAND

• Brest Litovsk

BELGIUM

LUX

Sept 1914

UKRAINE

ATLANTIC
OCEAN

Paris •

• Strasbourg
Munich •

• Prague

• Vienna

• Budapest

FRANCE

Berne •
SWITZ

Nov
1917

• Trieste

AUSTRIA-HUNGARY

RUMANIA

PORTUGAL

• Madrid

ITALY

• Belgrade

• Bucharest

Nov 1915
Sept 1918

• Bucharest

Constantinople

SPAIN

• Rome

SERBIA

MONTENEGRO

BULGARIA

• Sofia

ALBANIA

OTTOMAN EMPIRE

GREECE

Athens •

SPANISH
MOROCCO

ALGERIA

TUNISIA

MOROCCO

CYPRUS

CRETE

WORLD WAR I

Central Powers

Allied Powers

Neutral nations

Farthest extent of Central Powers

Armistice Line Nov 11 1918

for any losses of American lives from submarine attacks.

After the sinking of the *Lusitania* in May 1915, with the loss of 128 American lives, and the *Sussex* in March 1916, Germany complied with American demands. It promised not to attack unresisting belligerent merchant and passenger vessels without warning and without providing for the safety of those on board. Germany feared war with the United States and still hoped President Wilson could end the war by peace offers and mediation. When his efforts to end the war failed, Germany resumed unrestricted submarine warfare in February 1917. The United States responded first by breaking diplomatic relations and then by declaring war in April.

Consult (VI) Seymour, 1935; Smith, 1965; Tansill, 1938.

—Alexander W. Knott, *University of Northern Colorado*

WORLD WAR I BATTLES. German strategy during World War I was based on the Schlieffen Plan, named after Count von Schlieffen, Germany's former chief of staff. The goal of the Schlieffen Plan was to encircle Paris by a huge wheeling movement through Belgium. The speed with which the Russian army mobilized, however, forced the Germans to shift many troops to the eastern front. After losing the critical Battle of the Marne in France in September 1914, they were forced to withdraw to defensive positions behind the Aisne River. The result was a stalemate on the western front that lasted until 1918.

Battle of Belleau Wood (June 6–July 1, 1918). In March 1918, following the withdrawal of Russia from the war, the Germans began a series of great spring offensives designed to end the war before American troops arrived in force. The first three drove the British back in the Somme Valley and the French to the Marne. By the end of May the Germans had reached Château-Thierry, less than 40 miles from Paris. They were checked there in a series of local actions that culminated in an American attack that recaptured Belleau Wood and the villages of Vaux and Bouresches. Although the U.S. Marines suffered heavy casualties (55 percent of the 27,500 troops engaged), they stabilized the line and bolstered sagging Allied morale.

Second Battle of the Marne (July 18–August 6, 1918). The fourth German offensive, known as the Second Battle of the Marne, was the turning point of the war. On July 15 the Germans attacked simultaneously on both sides of Rheims, hoping to roll down the Marne Valley to Paris. The German drive was repelled with the help of about 85,000 American troops. Three days later, the Allies began a counteroffensive with 270,000 Americans participating to eliminate the German salient on the Marne River. By August 6 it had been flattened.

Somme Offensive (August 8, 1918). After the Marne, the initiative passed to the Allies. Allied strategy was designed to reduce the two main German salients at Amiens and Saint Mihiel and set the stage for a general offensive. On August 8, the British, with the aid of 54,000 American troops, struck the Amiens salient south of the Somme River. At comparatively slight cost, the Somme offensive eliminated the Amiens salient and forced the Germans back to their original positions.

Saint Mihiel Salient (Sept. 12–16, 1918). The first distinctively American offensive was the reduction of the Saint Mihiel salient, a deep extension of the German lines southeast of Verdun. It was strategically important because it commanded the Mézières-Sedan-Metz railway and the great Briey iron basin. On September 12, the American army of more than 500,000 men attacked under the command of Gen. John J. Pershing. In two days it wiped out the salient, captured 16,000 prisoners, and suffered only 7,000 casualties.

Meuse-Argonne Offensive (Sept. 26–Nov. 11, 1918). After the Saint Mihiel victory, the United States and the Allies launched a grand offensive all along the front from Ypres to Verdun to push the Germans back. The American First Army was assigned the sector between the Meuse River and the Argonne Forest. The assault, begun on September 26, was the greatest American engagement of the war. It involved 1.2 million troops and cost 120,000 casualties. By early November, the Americans were advancing east of the Meuse River, while in the north they had reached the outskirts of Sedan. Before the operation could be completed, however, Germany sued for peace. The armistice was eventually signed on November 11.

Consult (VI) Coffman, 1968; De Weerd, 1968; Pershing, 1931.

—Alexander W. Knott, *University of Northern Colorado*

WORLD WAR II, struggle for mastery in Europe and Asia that began on Sept. 1, 1939, and ended on Sept. 2, 1945.

Background. In 1933 Adolf Hitler, dedicated to redressing grievances arising from the Treaty of Versailles and to restoring Germany to a position of power in Europe, came to power. He took Germany out of the League of Nations, began rearming, and occupied the Rhineland. In 1938 he annexed Austria and at the Munich Conference secured British and French agreement to German acquisition of the Sudeten region of Czechoslovakia. In violation of the Munich agreement, he then occupied the remainder of Czechoslovakia.

Paralyzed by the fear of war and by the Great Depression, Britain and France at first

Soldiers pick their way through blasted forest in March 1918.

Capt. Eddie Rickenbacker was leading U.S. flier in World War I, destroying 21 enemy aircraft.

Ball of flame erupts from U.S. destroyer *Shaw* during attack on Pearl Harbor.

WORLD WAR II — Item Guide

The article on WORLD WAR II outlines the main events of the war. Worsening relations in the Pacific had been indicated by the collapse of the OPEN DOOR POLICY and the lack of success in HULL-NOMURA DISCUSSION in the 1930s and in Europe by the MUNICH CONFERENCE (1938). American sympathy for the British was indicated by the LEND-LEASE program.

U.S. entry into the war came after the Japanese attack on PEARL HARBOR in 1941 and did not end until the ATOM BOMB was dropped in 1945. President Roosevelt's advisers included Admiral WILLIAM D. LEAHY and GEORGE C. MARSHALL, who directed military operations. Outstanding American commanders were DOUGLAS MacARTHUR, BULL HALSEY, and CHESTER W. NIMITZ in the Pacific and DWIGHT D. EISENHOWER, OMAR BRADLEY, and GEORGE S. PATTON in Europe. Americans participated in the D-DAY invasion of France, whose leader-in-exile was CHARLES DeGAULLE.

Allied leaders FRANKLIN D. ROOSEVELT and WINSTON S. CHURCHILL met at the CASABLANCA CONFERENCE and convened with JOSEPH STALIN at the TEHERAN CONFERENCE and YALTA CONFERENCE. Near the end of the war the SAN FRANCISCO CONFERENCE ON INTERNATIONAL RELATIONS was held, followed by the founding of the UNITED NATIONS.

acquiesced to German expansion, but after Munich they concluded that Hitler could not be appeased. The British signed a defense pact with Poland, and when Hitler invaded Poland on Sept. 1, 1939, Britain and France declared war on Germany.

German Advance in Europe. The initial phase of the European struggle—the so-called phony war—was uneventful, but in the spring of 1940 Hitler's mechanized armies took the offensive. In April the Nazi blitzkrieg swept through Denmark and Norway and in May struck at France through the Low Countries. British and French forces were cut in half. On June 22, France agreed to an armistice in the same railway car at Compiègne in which the Allies had accepted Germany's surrender in 1918.

Britain was now the major obstacle to German ambitions. Hitler hoped to lure Britain into a settlement or bomb it into submission. But Prime Minister Winston Churchill inspired a fierce determination to resist, and the Royal Air Force fought valiantly in the Battle of Britain (August–September 1940). Using radar to great advantage, British pilots inflicted heavy losses on the Luftwaffe, and by winter Britain was saved.

Hitler next turned eastward. Tempted by the rich natural resources and confident that he could win an easy victory, he invaded Russia on June 22, 1941. The Germans enjoyed amazing successes at first. The Red Army offered little resistance, and by October, Nazi forces had taken the Ukraine, besieged Leningrad, and advanced on Moscow.

Hitler's position appeared unchallengeable in the autumn of 1941, but appearances were deceptive. Britain fought on, and Russian defenses stiffened—Moscow and Leningrad refused to fall. The United States, neutral at the outbreak of the war, was on the brink of intervention. Americans increasingly distrusted Hitler after Munich and feared for the security of the Western Hemisphere after the fall of France. In March 1941 the United States committed itself to aid Britain short of entering the war. In the summer it extended help to Russia and began to escort British merchant vessels. Incidents with German U-boats followed, and by November an undeclared naval war had begun.

Global War, 1942-1943. American intervention came on Dec. 7, 1941, but in the Far East, where the United States and Japan had long been on a collision course. Japan had also been dissatisfied with the post-Versailles status quo. In 1931 it had seized Manchuria, and in 1937 it launched a full-scale war against China. After concluding an alliance with Germany and Italy, the Japanese in 1940 began to move into the vacuum left in Southeast Asia by the defeat of France and the preoccupation of

Britain. The United States sympathized with China and refused to accept Japanese domination of Asia. Japan saw no alternative but war and gambled that a surprise attack on the American base at Pearl Harbor would force the United States to terms. The attack was enormously successful but brought a declaration of war instead of an appeal for peace. Germany and Italy then declared war on the United States.

In the first months of 1942 the Axis won a series of stunning victories. The Japanese navy ruled the seas from Wake Island to the Bay of Bengal, and the army overran the Philippines and swept through Southeast Asia to the gates of India. Germany's "desert fox," Marshal Erwin Rommel, broke through British lines into Egypt and threatened the Suez Canal. In June the Germans aimed another major offensive at the rich oil fields of southern Russia.

In the second half of 1942, however, the Allies began to check Axis advances and take the offensive. The United States and Britain agreed that in a two-front war they would concentrate major force against the more powerful enemy, Germany, and hold Japan in defensive operations. The U.S. Navy effectively implemented this strategy. In the battles of the Coral Sea and Midway (May and June 1942) the navy inflicted severe losses on the Japanese and prevented possible operations against Australia and Hawaii.

In the meantime, the Allies had taken the offensive in the Mediterranean. Bernard Montgomery's British Eighth Army stopped Rommel's drive into Egypt at El Alamein in June. In October Montgomery counterattacked, and within a month had pushed the Germans out of Egypt. On November 8, Anglo-American armies under Dwight D. Eisenhower landed in Algeria and Morocco. After six months of intensive combat, Montgomery and Eisenhower forced the surrender of German armies in North Africa.

During the same period, the Red Army was winning perhaps the most decisive land battle of the war. The German offensive had reached Stalingrad by mid-September, but the Russians savagely defended every inch of the city, even in hand-to-hand combat. In November Stalin launched a daring counterattack and encircled German forces inside Stalingrad. By February 1943, the victory was secured. The campaign cost the Nazis heavily in men and equipment and deprived them of desperately needed oil. Hitler tried one more offensive in Russia in the summer of 1943, but his overextended armies were no match for the resurgent Red Army. Soviet forces quickly blunted the attack and began the long march to Berlin.

Defeat of the Axis. The Allies now began the assault on Hitler's Fortress Europe. Anglo-American forces took Sicily in August and

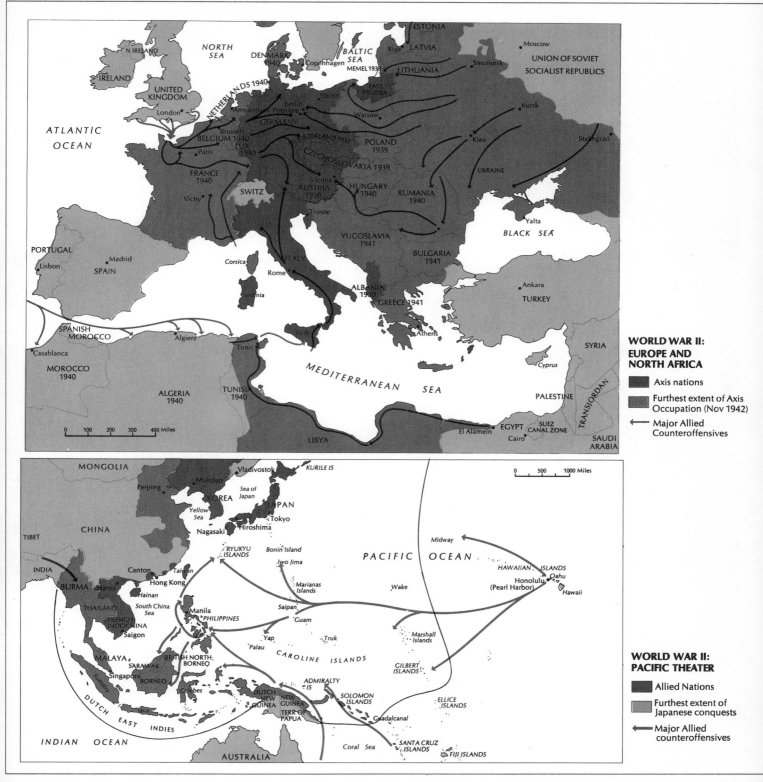

WORLD WAR II: EUROPE AND NORTH AFRICA

- Axis nations
- Furthest extent of Axis Occupation (Nov 1942)
- → Major Allied Counteroffensives

WORLD WAR II: PACIFIC THEATER

- Allied Nations
- Furthest extent of Japanese conquests
- → Major Allied counteroffensives

American convoy winds through bombed out French town in 1944.

Mushroom cloud from atom bomb rises over Nagasaki, Japan, on Aug. 9, 1945. The Japanese made their first offer to surrender the next day.

invaded Italy in September. The Italian government quickly surrendered, but a long and frustrating campaign to take German-held points on the peninsula ensued. From January to May 1944, U.S. and British air forces conducted heavy bombing raids on France and Germany. Then on June 6, 1944, in the greatest amphibious operation in military history, the Western Allies landed 176,000 troops on the Normandy beaches. Within a month, Allied strength in France totaled 1 million men. Meanwhile, the Russians had started a massive offensive along an 800-mile front south of Leningrad.

Allied forces moved so rapidly in the summer of 1944 that it appeared the war might end before the year was out. On September 12, U.S. forces crossed into Germany. The Red Army penetrated deep into Central Europe, advancing to Warsaw in August, forcing the capitulation of Bulgaria and Rumania in September, and entering East Prussia on October 20.

A last desperate German offensive slowed the drive to Berlin. Gambling that they could split the Anglo-American armies, the Germans attacked overextended U.S. forces in the Ardennes in mid-December. They were stopped after advancing 50 miles, but the Battle of the Bulge cost 77,000 American casualties, strained supplies and manpower, and set back the strategic timetable by months.

The Allies regained the initiative in January 1945 and began to close the vise on Germany. The Red Army mounted an offensive in Poland in January and by late April was preparing to assault Berlin, and the British reached Bremen by late April. U.S. armies enveloped the Ruhr, took Frankfurt and Nuremberg, and joined hands with the Russians at Torgau on April 25. On May 1 a provisional German government announced Hitler's suicide, and on the following day, Berlin fell. On May 7, 1945, the Germans surrendered.

By the end of the war in Europe, Allied forces had established naval supremacy in the Pacific and had advanced to within 350 miles of Tokyo. Abandoning earlier plans to strike at Japan through China, strategists in 1943 determined upon an island-hopping campaign across the Pacific. In some of the bloodiest fighting of the war, naval and amphibious units advanced from Australia to New Guinea to the Philippines and "up the ladder" from the Gilbert Islands to the Marshalls and Marianas. The decisive naval battle of Leyte Gulf, Oct. 23–25, 1944, crippled Japanese sea power. U.S. forces landed on the Philippines in December 1944 and liberated Manila in February 1945. They invaded Okinawa in April and took it in June after losing 11,000 killed and 33,000 wounded.

Stalin declared war on the Japanese on August 8, and Soviet troops poured into Manchuria. On August 6, American aircraft dropped the first atom bomb on Hiroshima, causing death or injury to more than 160,000 people; three days later a second nuclear bomb leveled Nagasaki. The Japanese accepted Allied terms on August 14 and signed the formal document of surrender on September 2 aboard the U.S.S. *Missouri* in Tokyo Bay.

Consult (VII) Hoyle, 1970; McNeill, 1953; Morison, 1963; Werth, 1964.

—George Herring, *University of Kentucky*

WOUNDED KNEE, BATTLE OF (1890), slaughter of Sioux in South Dakota, considered the last "battle" of the Indian Wars. *See* Indian Wars, Western.

WRIGHT, FRANK LLOYD (1869–1959), American architect, one of the great innovators in his field. He studied civil engineering at the University of Wisconsin, where the collapse of a newly built wing sparked his determination to apply engineering principles to architecture. Wright worked under Louis Sullivan from 1888 to 1893 and was encouraged to shun stylistic revivals and to evolve unorthodox forms suited to modern living and new structural methods and materials. He became known for his low-built prairie-style homes but soon launched out into more daring and controversial designs.

By 1900 Wright was regarded as an outstanding designer of modern private dwellings planned in conformity with the natural features of the land. Wright also pioneered in commercial buildings, such as the earthquake-proof Imperial Hotel in Tokyo (built in 1916) and the Guggenheim Museum in New York (designed in 1943, opened in 1959), in which the exhibits line the walls of a continuous spiral ramp.

A pioneer in the field of open planning, or organic architecture, Wright used ornamental details, earthy colors, and rich textures throughout his career. His sensitive employment of materials helped to perfect and control his dynamic use of space, which he called "the reality of building."

His period of greatest fulfillment began in 1936 and included such important works as the residence Fallingwater at Bear Run, Pa. (1936), his own winter quarters and workshop, Taliesin West, near Phoenix, Ariz. (1938), and the First Unitarian Church, Madison, Wis. (1951).

See also Architecture; Sullivan, Louis.

WRIGHT, RICHARD (1908–1960). American novelist, born on a plantation near Natchez, Miss., he drew on his personal experience to dramatize the issue of racial injustice and its brutalizing effect. Through his writings, particularly in the 1940s, Wright set the standard for a generation of black prose writers, including Ralph Ellison and James Baldwin.

In 1938, under the auspices of the Works Projects Administration (WPA), Wright published *Uncle Tom's Children,* a collection of stories based on his Mississippi boyhood. The book won an award for the best work of fiction by a WPA writer and helped Wright to receive a Guggenheim Fellowship. The publication of *Native Son* (1940) further enhanced his reputation. A dramatization of the novel was produced on Broadway and filmed in South America with Wright himself in the role of Bigger Thomas. In 1945 Wright's largely autobiographical *Black Boy* became his second best seller.

In the early 1950s Wright moved to Paris, where he continued to write both fiction and nonfiction, including *The Outsider* (1953), *Black Power* (1954), *The Color Curtain* (1956), and *The Long Dream* (1958).

WRIGHT, WILBUR AND ORVILLE, inventors of the first plane to make a manned, powered flight. Wilbur Wright (1867–1912) and Orville (1871–1948) grew up in Dayton, Ohio, the sons of a bishop of the Church of the United Brethren in Christ. Neither brother completed high school. They established a bicycle shop in Dayton in 1892 and three years later began to manufacture bicycles.

They began seriously to consider the problems of aviation in 1896, read the existing studies in the field, and began to experiment—first with kites, then with captive, manned gliders. In 1900–1903 they experimented with gliders near Kitty Hawk, N.C., a location they selected after consultation with the U.S. Weather Bureau. They discovered certain errors in their calculations that were based in part on errors in existing data. In order to improve their design, they invented the wind tunnel and tested more than 200 possible structures.

By early 1903 they had arrived at a satisfactory glider design, and, in the fall of that year (on December 17), they successfully tested a gasoline-engine-powered device. The first flight, manned by Orville, lasted 12 seconds and covered 120 feet. A flight later in the day by Wilbur lasted 59 seconds and covered 852 feet.

Despite the derision of friends and relatives, the Wrights, upon returning to Dayton, sought to improve their now successful design. By late 1905, they had succeeded in making a 24-mile circular flight; they patented their machine the following year. In 1907–1909 the Wrights demonstrated their device to various European governments; in 1907 they received a U.S. government contract to construct a flying machine, and their plane was accepted by the Army in 1909. After 1909 Wilbur took the lead in conducting negotiations with various European governments, and commercial development and manufacture were begun that year with the organization of the Wright Company.

See also Aviation; Inventions.

Consult (V) Kelly, 1951.

—Robert W. Cherny, *California State University, San Francisco*

WYETH FAMILTY, three generations of American artists. N(ewell) C(onvers) Wyeth (1882–1945) was born in Needham, Mass., but lived most of his life on the Brandywine River at Chadds Ford, Pa. He studied illustration with Howard Pyle and became a prolific and admired illustrator, doing vigorous oils for such books as Stevenson's *Treasure Island,* James Boyd's *Drums,* Marjorie Kinnan Rawlings' *The Yearling,* and *Tales of Robin Hood.* N. C. Wyeth also painted murals in New York, Boston, Washington, and other cities. He taught numerous students, including his son Andrew.

Andrew Wyeth (1917–   ) was trained in his father's studio, working first in water color but coming to prefer egg tempera. His first show, an exhibition of his water colors when he was 20, was sold out, and he became one of the best-selling artists of his generation. Many of his works show scenes and people around his winter home at Chadds Ford or his summer home on the Maine coast. His most famous pictures include "Ground Hog Day," "Corner in a Barn," "Wind from the Sea," and "Christina's World." Andrew Wyeth trained his son, James Browning (1946–   ), who also paints the Brandywine Valley countryside.

WYOMING, the 44th state, was admitted on July 10, 1890. Originally inhabited by a variety of Indian tribes, including the Crow, Cheyenne, and Blackfeet, the area was first explored by the American John Cotter in 1807. The first settlement was at Fort Laramie in 1834. Gold was discovered in 1867, and Wyoming gained territorial status the next year.

The state legislature is bicameral; Cheyenne is the capital. The population in 1970 was 332,416.

XYZ AFFAIR, diplomatic controversy between the United States and France in 1797–1798. A crisis had developed in Franco-American relations, when France, resenting what it considered a pro-British Federalist policy, began to interfere with American shipping. When John Adams became president in 1797, he attempted to solve this problem by sending a special mission to France. Charles Cotesworth Pinckney, John Marshall, and Elbridge Gerry, the three commissioners, arrived in Paris in October 1797. They discovered that Talleyrand, the French foreign minister, expected a bribe of $250,000 as well as an American "loan" of several million dollars to France before he would begin negotiations. The agents who asked for the bribes became known as X, Y, and

American novelist Richard Wright talks with Italian intellectuals in Rome in 1948.

Orville and Wilbur Wright, who built and flew the first successful airplane.

Z. Refusing to open the negotiations in this way, the Americans made no progress, and the mission was a failure. A report on the affair, made in April 1798, aroused the American public and allowed Adams and Congress to begin preparations for war.

The whole affair is well known for the famous slogan it produced. In one of the encounters with the agents seeking bribes, Pinckney replied, "No, No, not a sixpence." Later, in a toast, this refusal to give money was memorialized in the words "Millions for defense, but not a cent for tribute."

YALE COLLEGE. *See* Colonial Colleges.

YALTA CONFERENCE, the last meeting among Winston Churchill, Franklin Roosevelt, and Joseph Stalin, held at Yalta in the Crimea, Feb. 4–11, 1945. In a secret protocol, Stalin pledged to declare war on Japan, and Roosevelt agreed to a restoration of Russia's pre-1905 status in the Far East. The United Nations moved closer to existence when the USSR accepted 3 votes in the assembly and agreed to allow the Security Council to make procedural decisions with 7 out of 11 votes. Major European problems proved less susceptible to agreement. German reparations had to be referred to a commission for further study. The most divisive question—the establishment of governments for Poland and the other liberated nations of Eastern Europe—was settled by vague and unworkable statements of general principle. These latter agreements broke down within weeks after the conference ended and formed central issues in the early stages of the Cold War.

See also Churchill, Winston S.; Stalin, Joseph; World War II.

YAMASEE WAR (1715), Indian war in South Carolina. *See* Indian Wars, Colonial.

YAZOO AFFAIR, a long and complicated controversy that originated in 1795, when the Georgia legislature, extensively bribed, sold huge tracts of land in the present Alabama-Mississippi region to four land companies. The next Georgia legislature rescinded the action.

A famous court case arose out of the affair because the speculators had quickly sold some of the land to third parties. The Georgia cancellation left these purchasers without recompense, and they sought a remedy in the courts. In the case of *Fletcher v. Peck* (1810), the Supreme Court decided that the Georgia legislature had violated a contract when it rescinded the sale. Congress later gave compensation to those who had suffered.

YELLOW JOURNALISM, sensational type of newspaper reporting. *See* Hearst, William Randolph; Pulitzer, Joseph.

Brigham Young, dynamic Mormon leader, who played crucial role in development of Mormon settlement in Utah into prosperous community.

YIPPIES, popular name for the Youth International Party (YIP), founded in 1968 by Abbie Hoffman and later led by Jerry Rubin. The Yippies are a loosely organized group who were particularly disruptive during the 1968 Democratic Convention in Chicago. The life style, attitudes, and antiestablishment behavior of the Yippies have led to numerous spontaneous demonstrations featuring outrageous behavior.

YORKTOWN CAMPAIGN (SEPTEMBER-OCTOBER 1781), last major engagement of the Revolutionary War, ending with the surrender of Lord Cornwallis. *See* Revolutionary War Battles.

YOUNG, BRIGHAM (1801–1877), 2nd president of the Mormon church, generally considered its greatest practical leader and second only to Joseph Smith as a spiritual leader. Born in Vermont, he grew up in western New York in frontier poverty. In January 1832 he visited a Mormon colony in Pennsylvania, shortly after which he was baptized into the Mormon church. After the death of his wife in September, Young and his two daughters moved to the Mormon colony in Kirtland, Ohio.

Young quickly became one of the leaders of the Kirtland colony and in 1835 became one of the Ten Apostles in the church. When Kirtland had to be disbanded because of financial difficulties and non-Mormon opposition, Young moved westward and helped the Mormons establish a new home in Nauvoo, Ill. In 1844, after a mob in Nauvoo murdered Joseph Smith, Young used the theme of Gentile (non-Mormon) persecution to good effect, stiffened the will of the dispirited Mormons, and even obtained converts. He also believed that the Mormons had to move westward and establish their own community, removed from both official and unofficial harassment.

In the winter of 1846 the Mormons began the long trek to Utah. Against frightful hazards, a vanguard persevered until July 1847, when it arrived in the valley of the Great Salt Lake, or Deseret, as they originally called it. The transformation of the desert into a fertile valley rivals biblical miracles except that it was in large part the result of hard work and good planning. In 1849 the Mormons organized the provisional state of Deseret with Young, who was also president of the church, as governor. An attempt to gain statehood was rejected, undoubtedly because of the practice of polygamy. In 1850 President Fillmore officially named Utah a territory with Young as governor. The discovery of gold in California in 1848 stimulated overland travel, and Utah began to fill with non-Mormon settlers, which led to conflict. Young was removed as governor in 1857 by the federal government, but the Mormons still considered Young their leader until his death.

Because of the opposition to Young as a symbol of Mormonism and polygamy it is doubtful that Utah could have achieved statehood while he was still alive. He married 53 women whose wedding dates are known, and the number of wives may have exceeded 70. He was survived by at least 56 children. Few men in American history have performed a more magnificent colonization feat, and Mormons look on him as a true prophet.

See also Mormons; Utah.

Consult (III) Hirshson, 1969; Stegner, 1964.

—Joe B. Frantz, *University of Texas at Austin*

YOUNG, WHITNEY MOORE, JR. (1921–1971), prominent civil rights leader who was born in Lincoln Ridge, Ky. In 1961, during a time when the fight for integration and equal rights was approaching its peak, Young was appointed executive director of the National Urban League. Young was an organizer of the greatest nonviolent demonstration in American history, the historic March on Washington in 1963, during which more than 250,000 persons demanded jobs and freedom.

Unemployment and underemployment were urgent concerns to Young, who campaigned for a domestic Marshall Plan to provide opportunities and employment for minorities. He died while swimming in the surf near Lagos, Nigeria, while attending the African-American Dialogue, the third in a series of conferences to improve understanding between Americans and Africans.

ZENGER, JOHN PETER (1697–1746), printer whose trial set a standard for a free press. Zenger was a German-born printer who migrated to New York via England in 1710 with a large group of Palatine refugees. After an undistinguished printing career in Philadelphia, Maryland, and New York, he agreed in 1733 to print the New York *Weekly Journal,* an antiadministration newspaper. The *Weekly Journal* emphasized the "corruption" of Governor William Cosby and his supporters. Finally, Cosby had Zenger arrested and tried in 1735 on the charge of publishing seditious libels, which in the eighteenth century meant anything likely to lower the esteem of the government in the eyes of the people.

Andrew Hamilton, Zenger's lawyer, won over the jury with a famous oration suggesting that truth ought to be a sufficient defense against such a charge. When the court refused to let Hamilton introduce witnesses to validate the *Journal's* claim, he persuaded the jury to make up its own mind on the question, and it returned a general verdict of not guilty. Although the legal impact of the case was slight in its own day, two Zengerian principles—that truth is an adequate defense and that juries should determine general guilt or innocence—have since been embodied in the public law of most states.

Consult (I) Levy, 1960.

ZIMMERMANN NOTE, telegram sent in January 1917 from the German Secretary for Foreign affairs, Alfred Zimmermann, to his ambassador in Mexico. The telegram was intercepted by British intelligence and served to escalate tension between the United States and Germany before the U.S. entry into World War I.

Zimmermann told the ambassador to expect unrestricted submarine warfare to begin on Sept. 1, 1917, and tried to ensure Mexican support for the Germans by offering a military alliance. Mexico would invade the United States, take back Texas, New Mexico, Arizona, and parts of California, thus keeping the Americans occupied while Germany advanced in Europe. This imaginative plot backfired, and Americans were further enraged against Germany.

See also World War I: Causes.

Consult (VI) Tuchman, 1966.

Civil rights leader Whitney Young, executive director of National Urban League.

Bibliography

This comprehensive bibliography lists all the works cited in the Encyclopedia. Bibliographic references following articles direct the student to the appropriate section of the bibliography. For example, a citation of *"Consult* (V) Bruce, 1973" directs the reader to the 1973 book by Robert V. Bruce listed in Section V of the bibliography. If more than one book by an author is listed in a section, the publication date identifies the specific title.

The titles are grouped in 10 sections; the first eight cover American history chronologically, from the first explorers to the most recent events. Materials dealing with American blacks and Indians are collected in sections nine and ten, but many references to works in the first eight sections are also books that discuss blacks and Indians in the context of the events of a particular era.

The sections of the bibliography are

I.   Exploration and Colonization (circa 1000–1763)
II.   Revolutionary America (1763–1787)
III.   The New Nation (1787–circa 1850)
IV.   Civil War and Reconstruction (circa 1850–1877)
V.   Growth and Empire (1877–1914)
VI.   World War I to World War II (1914–1941)
VII.   World War II and Postwar America (1941–1948)
VIII.   Modern America (1948–Present)
IX.   Blacks in the United States
X.   Indians in America

I. EXPLORATION AND COLONIZATION (circa 1000–1763)

Bailyn, Bernard, *The Ideological Origins of the American Revolution* (1967).

Barbour, Philip L., *The Three Worlds of Captain John Smith* (1964).

Barker, Charles A., *The Background of the Revolution in Maryland* (1940).

Battis, Emery, *Saints and Sectaries* (1962).

Bishop, Morris, *Champlain: The Life of Fortitude* (1948).

Bradford, William, *Of Plymouth Plantation* (1952).

Brebner, John B., *Canada* (1970).

Bronner, Edwin B., *William Penn's "Holy Experiment": The Founding of Pennsylvania, 1681–1701* (1962).

Buel, Richard, *Securing the Revolution: Ideology in American Politics, 1789–1815* (1972).

Cremin, Lawrence A., *American Education: The Colonial Experience 1607–1783* (1970).

Debenham, Frank, *Discovery and Exploration* (1960).

Demos, John, *A Little Commonwealth: Family Life in Plymouth Colony* (1970).

Dickerson, Oliver M., *The Navigation Acts and the American Revolution* (1951).

Dunn, Richard S., *Puritans and Yankees: Winthrop Dynasty of New England, 1630–1717* (1962).

Ettinger, Amos A., *James Edward Oglethorpe, Imperial Idealist* (1936).

Fregault, Guy, *Canada: The War of the Conquest* (1969).

Ganstad, Edwin S., *The Great Awakening in New England* (1957).

Gibson, Charles, *Spain in America* (1966).

Hall, David D., *The Antinomian Controversy, 1636–1638* (1968).

Hume, Ivor N., *Historical Archaeology* (1969).

Jernegan, Marcus W., *Laboring and Dependent Classes in Colonial America 1607–1783* (1931).

Jones, Gwyn, *A History of the Vikings* (1968).

Langdon, George D., Jr., *Pilgrim Colony: A History of New Plymouth 1620–1691* (1966).

Leach, Douglas E., *Flintlock and Tomahawk: New England in King Philip's War* (1958).

Levy, Leonard W., *Freedom of Speech and Press in Early American History: Legacy of Suppression* (1960).

Livermore, Shaw, *Early American Land Companies* (1939; reprinted 1968).

Middlekauff, Robert, *The Mathers: Three Generations of Puritan Intellectuals, 1596–1728* (1971).

Miller, Perry, *Errand into the Wilderness* (1956).

Morgan, Edmund S., *The Puritan Dilemma, The Story of John Winthrop* (1958).

Morgan, Edmund S., *Roger Williams: The Church and the State* (1967).

Morgan, Edmund S., *Visible Saints, The History of a Puritan Idea* (1963).

Morison, Samuel Eliot, *Builders of the Bay Colony* (1930; reprinted 1963).

Morison, Samuel Eliot, *The European Discovery of America: The Northern Voyages, 500–1600* (1971).

Morris, Richard B., *Government and Labor in Early America* (1946).

Morris, Richard B., *Studies in the History of Early American Law* (1930).

Olmstead, C. E., *Religion in America: Past and Present* (1961).

Peckham, Howard H., *The Colonial Wars, 1689–1762* (1964).

Savelle, Max, and Middlekauff, Robert, *History of Colonial America* (1964).

Schutz, John A., *William Shirley, King's Governor of Massachusetts* (1961).

Skelton, R. A., *The Vineland Map and the Tartar Relation* (1965).

Slosser, G. J., *They Seek a Country* (1955).

Smith, Abbott E., *Colonists in Bondage* (1947).

Smith, Bradford, *Captain John Smith* (1953).

Smith, James Morton, *Seventeenth-Century America: Essays in Colonial History* (1959).

Sosin, Jack M., *Whitehall and The Wilderness* (1961).

Steele, I. K., *Politics of Colonial Policy: The Board of Trade in Colonial Administration, 1696–1720* (1968).

Sweet, W. W., *Religion in Colonial America* (1942).

Tolles, Frederick B., and Alderfer, E. Gordon, *The Witness of William Penn* (1957).

Vaughan, Alden T., *New England Frontier: Puritans and Indians, 1620–1675* (1965).

Washburn, Wilcomb E., *The Governor and the Rebel: A History of Bacon's Rebellion in Virginia* (1957).

Winslow, Ola E., *Jonathan Edwards 1703–1758* (1940).

Wood, Gordon, *The Creation of the American Republic, 1776–1787* (1969).

Wright, Louis B., *Gold, Glory, and the Gospel: The Adventurous Lives and Times of the Renaissance Explorers* (1970).

Zoltvany, Yves F., *The French Tradition in America* (1969).

II. REVOLUTIONARY AMERICA (1763–1787)

Alden, John R., *The American Revolution 1775–1783* (1954).

Aldridge, Alfred O., *Man of Reason: The Life of Thomas Paine* (1959).

Allen, Herbert L., *John Hancock: Patriot in Purple* (1948).

Bakeless, John E., *Background to Glory: The Life of George Rogers Clark* (1957).

Bakeless, John E., *Daniel Boone* (1965).

Bass, Robert D., *Swamp Fox* (1959).

Becker, Carl, *The Declaration of Independence: A Study of the History of a Political Idea* (1922).

Burnett, Edmund C., *The Continental Congress* (1941).

Farrand, Max (ed.), *The Records of the Federal Convention of 1787* (1966).

Jensen, Merrill, *The Articles of Confederation* (1940).

Ketcham, Ralph, *Benjamin Franklin* (1965).

Kincaid, Robert L., *The Wilderness Road* (1949).

Meade, Robert Douthat, *Patrick Henry* (1957–1969).

Miller, John C., *Sam Adams: Pioneer in Propaganda* (1936).

Morgan, Edmund S., and Morgan, Helen M., *The Stamp Act Crisis: Prologue To Revolution* (1953).

Morison, Samuel Eliot, *John Paul Jones: A Sailor's Biography* (1959).

Sosin, Jack M., *Whitehall and the Wilderness* (1961).

Thayer, Theodore, *Nathanael Greene: Strategist of the American Revolution* (1960).

Van Doren, Carl, *Benjamin Franklin* (1938).

Van Every, Dale, *Men of the Western Waters* (1956).

Ver Steeg, Clarence, *Robert Morris: Revolutionary Financier* (1954).

Wallace, Willard M., *Traitorous Hero: The Life and Fortunes of Benedict Arnold* (1953).

Warren, Charles, *The Making of the Constitution* (1967).

III. THE NEW NATION (1787–circa 1850)

Abernethy, Thomas P., *The Burr Conspiracy* (1954).

Ammon, Harry, *James Monroe: The Quest for Identity* (1971).

Anderson, Charles R., *The Magic Circle of Walden* (1968).

Aronson, Sidney H., *Status and Kinship in the Higher Civil Service* (1964).

Bakeless, John E., *Lewis and Clark: Partners in Discoveries* (1947).

Barker, Eugene C., *The Life of Stephen F. Austin* (1968).

Bassett, J. S., *The Federalist System, 1789–1801* (1968).

Bemis, Samuel F., *John Quincy Adams and the Foundations of American Foreign Policy* (1949).

Bemis, Samuel F., *John Quincy Adams and the Union* (1956).

Beveridge Albert J., *The Life of John Marshall* (4 vols., 1919).

Billington, Ray A., *The Far Western Frontier* (1956).

Billington, Ray A., *Westward Expansion* (1960).

Boulding, Kenneth, *Principles of Economic Policy* (1958).

Bowen, Catherine Drinker, *Miracle at Philadelphia: The Story of the Constitutional Convention, May to September, 1787* (1966).

Bowers, Claude G., *Jefferson and Hamilton* (1972).

Brant, Irving, *The Bill of Rights: Its Origins and Meanings* (1967).

Brown, Norman D., *Daniel Webster and the Politics of Availability* (1969).

Capers, Gerald M., *John C. Calhoun, Opportunist* (1960).

Cheetham, H. H., *Unitarianism and Universalism* (1962).

Chinard, Gilbert, *Thomas Jefferson: The Apostle of Americanism* (1939).

Coles, Harry L., *The War of 1812* (1965).

Corwin, Edward S., *John Marshall and the Constitution* (1919).

Corwin, Edward S., *The Constitution and What It Means Today* (1958).

Current, Richard N., *Daniel Webster and the Rise of National Conservatism* (1955).

Curris, James C., *The Fox at Bay: Martin Van Buren and the Presidency, 1837–1841* (1970).

Dangerfield, George, *The Era of Good Feelings* (1952).

Davidson, Edward H., *Poe: A Critical Study* (1957).

De Voto, Bernard, *Across the Wide Missouri* (1947).

Dillon, Richard, *Meriwether Lewis* (1965).

Driver, Carl S., *John Sevier* (1932).

Dulles, Foster R., *Labor in America* (1966).

Dumond, Dwight L., *Antislavery* (1961).

Dutton, Charles J., *Oliver Hazard Perry* (1935).

Eaton, Clement, *Henry Clay and the Art of American Politics* (1957).

Eblen, Jack E., *The First and Second United States Empires* (1968).

Engleman, Fred L., *The Peace of Christmas Eve* (1962).

Ferguson, E. James (ed.), *Selected Writings of Albert Gallatin* (1967).

Fine, Sidney, *Laissez-Faire and the General Welfare-State* (1964).

Flexner, James T., *George Washington* (4 vols., 1968–1972).

Freehling, William W., *The Nullification Era* (1967).

Freehling, William W., *Prelude to Civil War: The Nullification Controversy in South Carolina, 1816–1836* (1966).

Freeman, Douglas Southall, *George Washington: A Biography* (1948–1957).

Friend, Llerena B., *Sam Houston: The Great Designer* (1959).

Gates, Paul W., *The Farmer's Age* (1968).

Govan, Thomas, *Nicholas Biddle* (1959).

Green, Constance M., *Eli Whitney and the Birth of American Technology* (1956).

Green, James A., *William Henry Harrison, His Life and Times* (1941).

Gunderson, Robert G., *The Log-Cabin Campaign* (1957).

Hamilton, Holman, *Zachary Taylor: Soldier in the White House* (1951).

Hedges, William L., *Washington Irving: An American Study 1802-1832* (1965).

Heibroner, Robert L., *The Worldly Philosophers* (1967).

Henry, R. S., *The Story of the Mexican War* (1950).

Hirshson, Stanley P., *The Lion of the Lord* (1969).

Horsman, Reginald, *The War of 1812,* (1969).

Hunt, G., and Scott, J. B., *Debates in the Federal Convention of 1787* (1920).

James, Marquis, *The Raven: A Biography of Sam Houston* (1953).

Jones, Peter d'A., *The Consumer Society: A History of American Capitalism* (1965).

Jones, William M. (ed.), *Chief Justice John Marshall: A Reappraisal* (1956).

Jorday, Philip D., *The National Road* (1948).

Ketcham, Ralph L., *James Madison: A Biography* (1971).

Klinck, Carl F., *Tecumseh: Fact and Fiction in Early Records* (1961).

Koch, Adrienne, *Jefferson and Madison: The Great Collaboration* (1950).

Kurtz, Stephen G., *The Presidency of John Adams: The College of Federalism, 1795-1800* (1957).

Lane, D. C., *American Paddle Steamboats* (1943).

Lerner, Gerda, *The Grimké Sisters from South Carolina: Rebels Against Slavery* (1967).

Marshall, Helen E., *Dorothea Dix: Forgotten Samaritan* (1967).

Miller, John C., *Alexander Hamilton: Portrait in Paradox* (1959).

Mintz, Max M., *Gouverneur Morris and the American Revolution* (1970).

Monaghan, Frank, *John Jay: A Defender of Liberty* (1935).

Mumford, Lewis, *Herman Melville: A Study of His Life and Vision* (1962).

Nevins, Allan, *Ordeal of the Union: Fruits of Manifest Destiny, 1847-1852* (1947).

Nichols, Roger L., *General Henry Atkinson* (1965).

Parke, D. B., *The Epic of Unitarianism* (1957).

Parton, James, *The Presidency of Andrew Jackson* (1970).

Paul, Rodman W., *Mining Frontiers of the Far West 1848-1880* (1963).

Perkins, Dexter, *A History of the Monroe Doctrine* (rev. ed., 1955).

Peterson, Merrill D., *Thomas Jefferson and the New Nation: A Biography* (1970).

Philbrick, Francis S., *The Rise of the West 1754-1830* (1965).

Pomeroy, Earl S., *In Search of the Golden West* (1957).

Porter, K. W., *John Jacob Astor, Businessman* (1931).

Prown, Jules D., *John Singleton Copley* (1966).

Prucha, Francis P., *American Indian Policy in the Formative Years* (1962).

Prucha, Francis P., *Sword of the Republic* (1969).

Remini, Robert V., *Andrew Jackson* (1969).

Remini, Robert V., *Andrew Jackson and the Bank War* (1968).

Remini, Robert V., *Martin Van Buren and the Making of the Democratic Party* (1959).

Rossiter, Clinton, *Seedtime of the Republic* (1953).

Ruiz, Ramon E., *The Mexican War: Was It Manifest Destiny?* (1963).

Rusk, Ralph L., *The Life of Ralph Waldo Emerson* (1957).

Rutland, Robert A., *George Mason, Reluctant Statesman* (1961).

Schachner, Nathan, *Aaron Burr: A Biography* (1937).

Schlesinger, Arthur M., Jr., *The Age of Jackson* (1945).

Seager, Robert, *And Tyler Too: A Biography of John and Julia Gardiner Tyler* (1963).

Sellers, Charles, *James K. Polk* (1957).

Shackford, James A., *David Crockett: The Man and the Legend* (1956).

Shaw, Ronald E., *Erie Water West: A History of the Erie Canal, 1792-1854* (1966).

Singletary, Otis A., *The Mexican War* (1960).

Smith, C. Page, *James Wilson: Founding Father, 1742-1798* (1956).

Smith, C. Page, *John Adams* (1962).

Sobel, Robert, *The Big Board: A History of the New York Stock Market* (1965).

Sobel, Robert, *Panic on Wall Street* (1972).

Spaulding, E. Wilder, *His Excellency, George Clinton* (1938).

Stegner, Wallace, *The Gathering of Zion* (1964).

Stephenson, Nathaniel W., and Dunn, Waldo H., *George Washington* (1940).

Stourzh, Gerald, *Alexander Hamilton and the Idea of Republican Government* (1970).

Tatum, Edward H., *The United States and Europe, 1815-1823: A Study in the Background of the Monroe Doctrine* (1936).

Taylor, George R., *The Transportation Revolution, 1815-1860* (1968).

Tolles, Frederick B., *Slavery and "The Woman" Question* (1952).

Tucker, Glenn, *Tecumseh: Vision of Glory* (1956; reprinted, 1973).

Van Deusen, Glyndon G., *The Jacksonian Era, 1828-1848* (1959).

Van Deusen, Glyndon G., *The Life of Henry Clay* (1937).

Van Doren, Mark, *Nathaniel Hawthorne* (1949).

Van Every, Dale, *The Ark of Empire* (1963).

Wagenknecht, E. C., *Edgar Allan Poe: The Man Behind the Legend* (1963).

Warren, Charles, *The Making of the Constitution* (1967).

Wiltse, Charles M., *John C. Calhoun* (1944–1949).

Wood, Gordon S., *The Creation of the American Republic, 1776–1787* (1972).

White, Leonard D., *The States and the Nation* (1971).

Wright, B. F., *The Federalist* (1961).

Wyatt-Brown, Bertram, *Lewis Tappan and the Evangelical War Against Slavery* (1969).

IV. CIVIL WAR AND RECONSTRUCTION (circa 1850–1877)

Abels, Jules, *Man on Fire* (1971).

Basler, Roy P., *A Short History of the American Civil War* (1967).

Bennett, Whitman, *Whittier, Bard of Freedom* (1971).

Bentley, George R., *A History of the Freedman's Bureau* (1955).

Billington, Ray A., *The Protestant Crusade 1800–1860* (1938).

Brock, W. R., *An American Crisis: Congress and Reconstruction, 1865–1867* (1963).

Brodie, Fawn M., *Thaddeus Stevens: Scourge of the South* (1959).

Brooks, Van Wyck, *The Flowering of New England* (1936).

Capers, Gerald M., *Stephen A. Douglas: Defender of the Union* (1959).

Catton, Bruce, *The Centennial History of the Civil War* (1961–1965).

Cole, A. C., *The Irrepressible Conflict* (1971).

Commager, Henry S., *Theodore Parker* (1960).

Cox, LaWanda, and Cox, John H., *Politics, Principle, and Prejudice, 1865–1866* (1963).

Craven, Avery, *The Coming of the Civil War* (1957).

Davis, Burke, *Jeb Stuart, The Last Cavalier* (1957).

Donald, David, *Charles Sumner and the Coming of the Civil War* (1960).

Donald, David, *Charles Sumner and the Rights of Man* (1970).

Donald, David, *The Politics of Reconstruction* (1965).

Donovan, Frank, *Mr. Lincoln's Proclamation* (1964).

Dorris, Jonathan T., *Pardon and Amnesty under Lincoln and Johnson* (1953).

Dumond, Dwight L., *The Secession Movement, 1860–1861* (1931).

Eaton, Clement, *The Confederate States of America* (1954).

Fehrenbacher, Don E., *Prelude to Greatness: Lincoln in the 1850s* (1962).

Filler, Louis, *The Crusade Against Slavery, 1830–1860* (1960).

Filler, Louis (ed.), *Wendell Phillips on Civil Rights and Freedom* (1965).

Franklin, John H., *The Emancipation Proclamation* (1963).

Freeman, Douglas S., *R. E. Lee: A Biography* (4 vols., 1934–1935).

Govan, Gilbert E., and Livingood, James W., *A Different Valor: The Story of General Joseph E. Johnston, C.S.A.* (1956).

Grant, Ulysses S., *Personal Memoirs* (1894).

Hamilton, Holman, *Prologue to Conflict* (1964).

Hassler, Warren W., Jr., *General George B. McClellan: Shield of the Union* (1957).

Holt, Michael F., *Forging a Majority: The Formation of the Republican Party in Pittsburgh, 1848–1860* (1969).

Hyman, Harold, *The Radical Republicans and Reconstruction, 1861–1870* (1967).

Jaffa, Harry V., *Crisis of the House Divided: An Interpretation of the Issues in the Lincoln-Douglas Debates* (1959).

Kinsley, D. A., *Favor the Bold: Custer* (1967).

Klein, Philip S., *President James Buchanan* (1962).

Lewis, Charles L., *David Glasgow Farragut* (2 vols., 1941–1943).

Lewis, Lloyd, *Sherman, Fighting Prophet* (1932).

McCague, James, *The Second Rebellion* (1968).

McKitrick, Eric L., *Andrew Johnson and Reconstruction* (1960).

McWhiney, Grady. (ed.), *Grant, Lee, Lincoln, and the Radicals* (1964).

Meade, Robert D., *Judah P. Benjamin: Confederate Statesman* (1943).

Moore, Glover, *The Missouri Controversy, 1819–1821* (1953).

Nevins, Allan, *The Emergence of Lincoln* (1950).

Nevins, Allan, *Hamilton Fish: The Inner History of the Grant Administration* (1957).

Nevins, Allan, *Lincoln and the Gettysburg Address* (1964).

Nevins, Allan, *The Ordeal of the Union* (8 vols., 1947–1971).

Nichols, Roy F., *The Disruption of American Democracy* (1967).

Nichols, Roy, *Franklin Pierce, Young Hickory of the Granite Hills* (1958).

Nye, Russel B., *William Lloyd Garrison and the Humanitarian Reformers* (1955).

Oates, Stephen B., *To Purge This Land with Blood* (1970).

O'Connor, Richard, *Sheridan the Inevitable* (1953).

Phillips, Ulrich B. *Plantation and Frontier* (1969).

Pressley, Thomas J., *Americans Interpret Their Civil War* (1965).

Randall, J. G., *Lincoln the President* (4 vols., 1945–1955).

Rawley, James A., *Race and Politics: "Bleeding Kansas" and the Coming of the Civil War* (1969).

Ray, P. O., *The Repeal of the Missouri Compromise: Its Origins and Authorship* (1965).

Rayback, Robert, *Millard Fillmore* (1959).

Robert, Joseph C., *The Road from Monticello* (1970).

Rozwenc, Edwin C., *Compromise of 1850* (1957).

Sanger, Donald B., and Hay, Thomas R., *James Longstreet* (1952).

Sherwin, Oscar, *Wendell Phillips* (1956).

Stampp, Kenneth M., *The Causes of the Civil War* (1965).

Stampp, Kenneth, M., *The Era of Reconstruction* (1965).

Stampp, Kenneth M., and Litwack, Leon, *Reconstruction: An Anthology of Revisionist Writings* (1969).

Strode, Hudson, *Jefferson Davis* (3 vols., 1955-1964).

Thomas, Benjamin P., *Abraham Lincoln* (1952).

Thomas, Benjamin P., and Hyman, Harold, *Stanton: The Life and Times of Lincoln's Secretary of War* (1962).

Trefousse, Hans L., *The Radical Republicans: Lincoln's Vanguard for Racial Justice* (1969).

Tyler, Alice F., *Freedom's Ferment* (1944).

Van Deusen, Glyndon G., *Horace Greeley: Nineteenth-Century Crusader* (1953).

Van Deusen, Glyndon G., *William Henry Seward* (1967).

Vandiver, Frank E., *Mighty Stonewall* (1957).

Von Abele, Rudolph, *Alexander H. Stephens: A Biography* (1946).

Wiley, Bell I., and Milhollen, Hirst D., *Embattled Confederates* (1964).

Williams, T. Harry, *P. G. T. Beauregard: Napoleon in Gray* (1955).

Wilson, Theodore B., *The Black Codes of The South* (1966).

Woodman, Harold D., *Slavery and the Southern Economy* (1966).

Woodward, C. Vann, *Reunion and Reaction: The Compromise of 1877 and the End of Reconstruction* (1951).

Wooster, Ralph A., *The Secession Conventions of the South* (1962).

V. GROWTH AND EMPIRE (1877-1914)

Abbott, Edward C., and Smith, Helena H. *We Pointed Them North* (1939; reprinted, 1966).

Allen, Frederick Lewis, *The Great Pierpont Morgan* (1949).

Allen, Gay Wilson, *The Solitary Singer: A Critical Biography of Walt Whitman* (1955).

Bailey, Thomas A., *Theodore Roosevelt and the Japanese-American Crises* (1934).

Barnard, Harry, *Rutherford B. Hayes and His America* (1967).

Bemis, Samuel F., *The Latin American Policy of the United States* (1943).

Benedict, Murray R., *Farm Policies of the U.S.* (1967).

Billington, Ray A., *Westward Expansion* (1967).

Bolino, August, *Development of the American Economy* (2nd ed., 1966).

Bolles, Blair, *Tryant from Illinois* (1951).

Brickman, William W., and Lehrer, Stanley, *John Dewey: Master Educator* (1965).

Bruce, Robert V., *Alexander Graham Bell and the Conquest of Solitude* (1973).

Bruce, Robert V., *1877: Year of Violence* (1970).

Buck, Solon Justus, *The Granger Movement* (1963).

Bunke, Harvey C., *Primer on American Economic History* (1970).

Burlingame, Roger, *Engines of Democracy* (1940).

Burlingame, Roger, *Out of Silence into Sound: The Life of Alexander Graham Bell* (1964).

Callcott, W. H., *The Caribean Policy of the United States, 1890-1920* (1942).

Callow, Alexander, *The Tweed Ring* (1969).

Chandler, A. D., *The Railroads: The Nation's First Big Business* (1965).

Clark, Thomas D., *Frontier America* (1969).

Cochran, Thomas C., *The American Business System: A Historical Perspective, 1900-1955* (1957).

Cochran, Thomas C., and Miller, William, *The Age of Enterprise: A Social History of Industrial America* (1961).

Coletta, Paolo E., *William Jennings Bryan* (1964-1969).

Cox, James M., *Mark Twain: The Fate of Humor* (1966).

Cremin, Lawrence, A., *The Transformation of the School: Progressivism in American Education 1876-1957* (1961).

Dennett, Tyler, *John Hay* (1933).

Dozer, Donald M., *Are We Good Neighbors?* (1959).

Dubofsky, Melvyn, *We Shall Be All: A History of the Industrial Workers of the World* (1969).

Dupee, Frederick W., *Henry James* (1956).

Edel, Leon, *Henry James* (5 vols., 1953-1971).

Frantz, Joe B., and Choate, J. E., *The American Cowboy* (1955; reprinted 1968).

Freidel, Frank, *A Splendid Little War* (1957).

Garbedian, H. Gordon, *George Westinghouse* (1946).

Gelber, Lionel M., *The Rise of Anglo-American Friendship* (1938).

Glad, Paul W., *McKinley, Bryan, and the People* (1964).

Glad, Paul W., *The Trumpet Soundeth: William Jennings Bryan and His Democracy 1896-1912* (1960).

Gompers, Samuel, *Seventy Years of Life and Labor* (1934).

Grodinsky, Julius, *Jay Gould* (1957).

Hacker, Louis M., *Course of American Economic Growth and Development* (1970).

Hackney, Sheldon, *Populism: The Critical Issues* (1971).

Handlin, Oscar, *Race and Nationality in American Life* (1957).

Hansen, Marcus Lee, *The Immigrant in American History* (1940).

Heiman, Robert K., *Tobacco and Americans* (1960).

Hicks, John D., *The Populist Revolt: A History of the Farmers' Alliance and the People's Party* (1961).

Howe, George Frederick, *Chester A. Arthur* (1934; reprinted 1957).

Jackson, Kenneth T., and Schultz, Stanley K., *Cities in American History* (1972).

Johnson, T. H., *Emily Dickinson: An Interpretive Biography* (1955).

Jones, Maldwyn Allen, *American Immigration* (1960).

Jones, Peter d'A., *The Consumer Society: A History of American Capitalism* (1965).

Josephson, Matthew, *Edison: A Biography* (1955).

Josephson, Matthew, *The Politicos* (1938).

Josephson, Matthew, *The Robber Barons* (1934).

Kelly, Fred C. (ed.), *Miracle at Kitty Hawk, The Letters of Wilbur and Orville Wright* (1951; reprinted 1971).

Kelly, Fred C., *Wright Brothers* (1951).

Kolko, Gabriel, *Railroads and Regulation, 1877–1916* (1965).

Letwin, William, *Law and Economic Policy in America: The Evolution of the Sherman Anti-Trust Act* (1965).

Levine, Lawrence W., *Defender of the Faith: William Jennings Bryan, The Last Decade, 1914–1925* (1965).

Mack, Gerstle, *The Land Divided* (1944).

Mandell, Bernard, *Samuel Gompers, A Biography* (1963).

Marshall, Helen E., *Dorothea Dix: Forgotten Samaritan* (1937).

Merrill, Horace, *Bourbon Leader: Grover Cleveland and the Democratic Party* (1957).

Millis, Walter, *The Martial Spirit* (1931).

Morgan, H. Wayne, *William McKinley and His America* (1963).

Nash, Roderick, *The American Environment: Readings in the History of Conservation* (1968).

Nearing, Scott, and Freeman, Joseph, *Dollar Diplomacy: A Study in American Imperialism* (1970).

Nevins, Allan, *Grover Cleveland: A Study in Courage* (1932).

Nevins, Allan, *Hamilton Fish* (1936).

Nevins, Allan, *Study in Power: John D. Rockefeller* (2 vols., 1953).

Oberholtzer, Ellis, *Jay Cooke, Financier of the Civil War* (2 vols., 1969).

Oliver, J. W., *History of American Technology* (1956).

Osofsky, Gilbert, *Harlem: The Making of a Ghetto, 1890–1930* (1971).

Puleston, W. D., *Mahan* (1939).

Robbins, Roy, M., *Our Landed Heritage* (1942).

Siever, Harry L., *Benjamin Harrison* (1969).

Small, Miriam R., *Oliver Wendell Holmes* (1962).

Smith, Goldwin, *The Treaty of Washington, 1871: A Study in Imperial History* (1941).

Smith, Theodore Clark, *Life and Letters of James Abram Garfield* (1968).

Stallman, Robert W., *Stephen Crane* (1972).

Stover, John F., *American Railroads* (1961).

Studenski, Paul, and Krooss, H., *Financial History of the United States* (1963).

Thorelli, Hans B., *Federal Antitrust Policy* (1955).

Wall, Joseph F., *Andrew Carnegie* (1970).

Wallace, Irving, *The Fabulous Showman* (1959).

Ward, David, *Cities and Immigrants, A Geography of Change in Nineteenth-Century America* (1971).

Williamson, Harold, and Daun, Arnold, *The American Petroleum Industry, 1859–1899* (1959).

Wittke, Carl, *We Who Built America* (1964).

Woods, Robert A., and Kennedy, Albert J., *The Zone of Emergence* (1969).

Woodward, C. Vann, *Reunion and Reaction* (1966).

VI. WORLD WAR I TO WORLD WAR II (1914–1941)

Addams, Jane, *Twenty Years at Hull House* (1966).

Alinsky, Saul D., *John L. Lewis, An Unauthorized Biography* (1970).

Bailey, Thomas A., *Woodrow Wilson and the Lost Peace* (1944).

Baldwin, Sidney, *Poverty and Politics: The Rise and Decline of the Farm Security Administration* (1968).

Baruch, Bernard, *Baruch: My Own Story* (1957).

Bates, J. Leonard, *The Origins of Teapot Dome* (1966).

Bemis, S. F., *The Latin American Policy of the United States* (1943).

Benedict, Murray R., *Farm Policies of the United States, 1790–1950* (1967).

Bernstein, Irving, *New Deal Collective Bargaining Policy* (1950).

Bernstein, Irving, *Turbulent Years: A History of the American Worker, 1933–1941* (1970).

Bickel, Alexander M., *The Unpublished Opinions of Mr. Justice Brandeis: The Supreme Court at Work* (1967).

Birdsall, Paul, *Versailles Twenty Years After* (1941).

Blum, John M., *The Republican Roosevelt* (1954).

Blum, John M., *Woodrow Wilson and the Politics of Morality* (1956).

Bowen, C. D., *Yankee from Olympus* (1944).

Burlingame, Roger, *Henry Ford: A Great Life In Brief* (1955).

Burns, James M. *Roosevelt: The Lion and the Fox* (1956).

Chafee, Zechariah, Jr., *Free Speech in the United States* (1941).

Chambers, Clarke, *Seedtime of Reform: American Social Service and Social Action 1918-1933* (1963).

Charles, Searle F., *Minister of Relief: Harry Hopkins and the Depression* (1963).

Cochran, Thomas C., *The American Business System: A Historical Perspective, 1900-1955* (1957).

Cochran, Thomas C., and Miller, William, *The Age of Enterprise: A Social History of Industrial America* (1961).

Coffman, Edward M., *The War to End All Wars, The American Military Experience in World War I* (1968).

Conkin, Paul K., *Tomorrow a New World: The New Deal Community Program* (1959).

Conrad, David E., *The Forgotten Farmers* (1965).

Cox, James M., *Journey Through My Years* (1946).

Darrow, Clarence, *The Story of My Life* (1932).

De Weerd, Harvey A., *President Wilson Fights His War, World War I and the American Intervention* (1968).

Divine, Robert, *The Illusion of Neutrality* (1962).

Ferrell, Robert H., *American Diplomacy in the Great Depression* (1957).

Ferrell, Robert H., *Peace in Their Time* (1952).

Flexner, Eleanor, *Century of Struggle: The Woman's Rights Movement in the United States* (1959).

Frankfurter, Felix (ed.), *Mr. Justice Brandeis* (1932).

Frankfurter, Felix, *Mr. Justice Holmes and the Supreme Court* (2nd ed., 1965).

Galbraith, John K., *The Great Crash* (1955).

Gerson, L. L., *John Foster Dulles* (1967).

Ginger, Ray, *Eugene V. Debs* (1962).

Gusfield, Joseph R., *Symbolic Crusade: Status Politics and the American Temperance Movement* (1963).

Handlin, Oscar, *Al Smith and His America* (1958).

Harbaugh, William, *Power and Responsibility: The Life and Times of Theodore Roosevelt* (1961).

Harris, C. L., *History and Policies of the Home Owners' Loan Corporation* (1951).

Harris, Seymour E., *The New Economics: Keynes' Influence on Theory and Public Policy* (1947).

Hoover, Herbert C., *Memoirs* (1952).

Howe, Mark D., *Justice Oliver Wendell Holmes* (2 vols., 1957-1963).

Hull, Cordell, *Memoirs* (2 vols., 1948).

Huthmacher, J. Joseph, *Senator Robert F. Wagner and the Rise of Urban Liberalism* (1971).

Ickes, Harold L., *The First Thousand Days* (1953).

Iriye, Akira, *Across the Pacific: An Inner History of American-East Asian Relations* (1967).

Iriye, Akira, *After Imperialism* (1965).

Johnson, Hugh S., *The Blue Eagle From Egg to Earth* (1935).

Jonas, Manfred, *Isolationism in America* (1966).

Jones, Peter d'A. *The Consumer Society: A History of American Capitalism* (1965).

Langer, William L., and Gleason, Sarell E., *Challenge to Isolation, 1937-1940* (1952).

Lash, Joseph P., *Eleanor and Franklin* (1971).

Latham, Earl, *The Communist Controversy in Washington* (1966).

Leopold, Richard William, *Elihu Root and the Conservative Tradition* (1954).

Lerner, Max, *The Mind and Faith of Justice Holmes* (1948).

Lief, Alfred, *Brandeis: The Personal History of an American Ideal* (1936).

Lilienthal, David E., *The Journals of David E. Lilienthal: The TVA Years* (1965).

Link, Arthur S., *Wilson* (1947-1965).

Lowitt, Richard, *George W. Norris: The Persistence of a Progressive* (1971).

Lubove, Roy, *The Struggle for Social Security, 1900-1935* (1968).

Lyons, Eugene, *Herbert Hoover: A Biography* (1964).

McCoy, Donald R., *Calvin Coolidge: The Quiet President* (1967).

McGeary, Martin Nelson, *Gifford Pinchot, Forester-Politician* (1960).

Mann, Arthur, *La Guardia Comes to Power: 1933* (1965).

Mann, Arthur, *La Guardia: A Fighter Against His Times* (1959).

Mason, Alpheus T., *Brandeis: A Free Man's Life* (1956).

Mason, Alpheus T., *Brandeis: Lawyer and Judge in the Modern State* (1933).

Mason, Alpheus T., *The Supreme Court from Taft to Warren* (1958).

Mitchell, Broadus, *Depression Decade, From New Era Through New Deal 1929-1941* (1947).

Mowry, George, *The California Progressives* (1951).

Mowry, George, *The Era of Theodore Roosevelt and the Birth of Modern America, 1900-1912* (1958).

Mowry, George, *Theodore Roosevelt and the Progressive Movement* (1956).

Murray, Robert K., *The Harding Era: Warren G. Harding and His Administration* (1969).

Nevins, Allan, and Hill, Frank Ernest, *Ford* (2 vols., 1954-1957).

Bibliography

Nye, Russell B., *Midwestern Progressive Politics* (1951).

O'Connor, Richard, *The First Hurrah: A Biography* (1970).

O'Neill, William L., *Everyone Was Brave: The Rise and Fall of Feminism in America* (1969).

Patterson, James T., *Congressional Conservatism and the New Deal* (1967).

Pecora, Ferdinand, *Wall Street Under Oath* (1939).

Pershing, John J., *My Experiences in the World War* (2 vols., 1931).

Pinkett, Harold T., *Gifford Pinchot, Private and Public Forester* (1970).

Pratt, Julius W., *Cordell Hull, 1933–1944* (1964).

Pringle, Henry, *The Life and Times of William Howard Taft* (1939).

Pritchett, C. Herman, *The Roosevelt Court* (1948).

Pusey, Merlo J., *Charles Evans Hughes* (2 vols., 1963).

Russell, Francis, *The Shadow of Blooming Grove* (1968).

Russell, Francis, *Tragedy in Dedham, The Story of the Sacco-Vanzetti Case* (1962).

Salmond, John A., *The Civilian Conservation Corps* (1967).

Schlesinger, Arthur M., Jr., *The Coming of the New Deal* (1959).

Schlesinger, Arthur M., Jr., *The Politics of Upheaval* (1960).

Seymour, Charles, *American Diplomacy During the World War* (1935).

Sherwood, Robert, *Roosevelt and Hopkins: An Intimate History* (1948).

Sindler, Allan P., *Huey Long's Louisiana* (1956).

Smith, Daniel M., *The Great Departure: The United States and World War I, 1914–1920* (1965).

Smith, Gene, *When the Cheering Stopped* (1964).

Stallings, Laurence, *Doughboys* (1963).

Stave, Bruce M., *Urban Bosses, Machines and Progressive Reformers* (1972).

Stone, Irving, *Clarence Darrow for the Defense* (1943).

Swanberg, W. A., *Citizen Hearst* (1961).

Tansill, Charles C., *America Goes to War* (1938).

Tuchman, Barbara, *The Zimmermann Telegram* (1966).

Tull, Charles J., *Father Coughlin and the New Deal* (1965).

Turnbull, Andrew W., *Scott Fitzgerald* (1962).

Wagner, Susan, *The Federal Trade Commission* (1971).

Warner, Hoyt L., *Progressivism in Ohio, 1897–1917* (1962).

Wecter, Dixon, *Age of the Great Depression 1929–1941* (1948).

White, William A., *A Puritan in Babylon* (1938).

Wilcox, Clair, *Toward Social Welfare* (1969).

Williams, T. Harry, *Huey Long* (1969).

Witte, Edwin, E., *The Development of the Social Security Act* (1962).

Wood, Bryce, *The Making of the Good Neighbor Policy* (1961).

Zucker, Norman L., *George W. Norris: Gentle Knight of American Democracy* (1966).

VII. WORLD WAR II AND POSTWAR AMERICA (1941-1948)

Blum, John M., *From the Morgenthau Diaries* (1959-1968).

Burns, James M., *Roosevelt: The Lion and The Fox* (1956).

Bryan, Joseph, *Admiral Halsey's Story* (1947).

Churchill, Randolph S., *Winston S. Churchill* (3 vols., 1966-1971).

Freidel, Frank, *Franklin D. Roosevelt* (3 vols., 1952-1956).

Hoyle, Martha Byrd, *A World in Flames: A History of World War II* (1970).

Hoyt, Edwin P., *How They Won the War in the Pacific* (1970).

James, Dorris C., *The Years of MacArthur* (1970).

Kennedy, David M., *Birth Control in America: The Career of Margaret Sanger* (1970).

Kimball, Warren, *The Most Unsordid Act* (1971).

Leuchtenburg, William E., *Franklin D. Roosevelt and the New Deal* (1963).

MacArthur, Douglas, *Reminiscences* (1964).

McNeill, William H., *America, Britain and Russia: Their Cooperation and Conflict* (1953).

Morison, Samuel Eliot, *The Two-Ocean War* (1963).

Offner, Arnold, *American Appeasement* (1969).

Patton, George S., *War As I Knew It* (1947).

Poque, Forrest C., *George C. Marshall* (3 vols., 1963-1972).

Schlesinger, Arthur M., Jr., *The Politics of Upheaval* (1960).

Schroeder, Paul W., *The Axis Alliance and Japanese-American Relations* (1958).

Stimson, Henry L., *On Active Service in Peace and War* (1948).

Werth, Alexander, *Russia at War, 1941-1945* (1964).

Wilson, Theodore, *The First Summit* (1969).

VIII. MODERN AMERICA (1948-Present)

Abzug, Bella, *Bella—Ms. Abzug Goes to Washington* (1972).

Acheson, Dean, *Present at the Creation* (1971).

Albertson, Dean, *Eisenhower as President,* (1963).

American Heritage History of Flight (1962).

Anson, Robert S., *McGovern: A Biography* (1972).

Atkinson, Brooks, *Broadway* (1970).

Baker, Carlos, *Ernest Hemingway: A Life Story* (1969).

Barnet, Richard J., *The Economy of Death* (1969).

Baur, John I. H. (ed.), *New Art in America* (1957).

Berger, Carl, *The Korea Knot: A Military-Political History* (1957).

Binkley, Wilfred E., *American Political Parties: Their Natural History* (1962).

Bradley, Omar, *A Soldier's Story* (1951).

Brooks, Cleanth, *William Faulkner: The Yoknapatawpha Country* (1963).

Brooks, Thomas R., *Toil and Trouble: A History of American Labor* (1964).

Buckley, William F., *Inveighing We Will Go* (1972).

Burns, James M., *Presidential Government: Crucible of Leadership* (1966).

Buttinger, Joseph, *Vietnam: A Dragon Embattled* (1967).

Callow, Alexander B., *American Urban History: An Interpretive Reader with Commentaries* (1969).

Campbell, Angus, *et. al., The American Voter* (1960).

Chambers, William N., *The Democrats: 1789-1964* (1964).

Christman, Henry M. (ed.), *The Public Papers of Chief Justice Earl Warren* (1966).

Claude, Inis L., Jr., *Swords Into Plowshares: The Problems and Progress of International Organization* (1971).

Coffin, Tristram, *Senator Fulbright: Portrait of a Public Philosopher* (1966).

Commoner, Barry, *The Closing Circle* (1971).

Cooke, Alistair, *A Generation on Trial* (1951).

Cowell, Henry, *American Composers on American Music* (1962).

Coyle, David Cushman, *The United Nations and How It Works* (1969).

Craven, Wayne, *Sculpture in America* (1968).

Dankworth, Avril, *Jazz: An Introduction to Its Musical Basis* (1968).

Davidson, Jean, *Alexander Calder, An Autobiography with Pictures* (1966).

Davidson, Walter P., *The Berlin Blockade: A Study in Cold War Politics* (1958).

Deutscher, Isaac, *Stalin: A Political Biography* (1967).

Eisenhower, Dwight D., *The White House Years* (2 vols., 1963-1965).

Engel, Lehman, *The American Musical Theatre* (1967).

Fifield, Russell, *The Diplomacy of Southeast Asia 1945-1958* (1968).

Firestone, Shulamith, *The Dialectic of Sex* (1970).

Foerster, Norman, *Image of America: Our Literature from Puritanism to the Space Age* (1962).

Frady, Marshall, *Wallace* (1969).

Friedman, Lawrence M., *Government and Slum Housing: A Century of Frustration* (1968).

Fulbright, J. W., *The Arrogance of Power* (1967).

Fulbright, J. W., *Old Myths and New Realities* (1964).

Furgurson, Ernest B., *Westmoreland, The Inevitable General* (1968).

Galbraith, John K., *American Capitalism: The Concept of Countervailing Power* (1956).

Galloway, George B., *History of the House of Representatives* (1961).

Gans, Herbert, *People and Plan: Essays on Urban Problems and Solutions* (1968).

Gist, Noel, and Fava, Sylvia, *Urban Society* (5th ed., 1954).

Goldman, Eric F., *The Tragedy of Lyndon Johnson* (1969).

Goldman, Ralph M., *The Democratic Party in American Politics* (1966).

Goodrich, Lloyd, *Three Centuries of American Art* (1966).

Gould, Jean, *Walter Reuther* (1971).

Graebner, Norman A., *An Uncertain Tradition: American Secretaries of State in the 20th Century* (1961).

Green, Constance M., *The Rise of Urban America* (1965).

Green, Mark J., Fallows, James M., and Zwick, David R., *Who Runs Congress?* (1972).

Greer, Germaine, *The Female Eunuch* (1971).

Griffith, Winthrop, *Humphrey, A Candid Biography* (1965).

Halberstam, David, *The Best and the Brightest* (1972).

Hareven, Tamara K., *Eleanor Roosevelt: An American Conscience* (1968).

Harris, Joseph P., *The Advice and Consent of the Senate* (1953).

Havens, Murray Clark, *et al., The Politics of Assassination* (1970).

Hitchcock, H. Wiley, *Music in the United States: A Historical Introduction* (1969).

Hodeir, Andrew, *Worlds of Jazz* (1970).

Howe, Irving, *William Faulkner: A Critical Study* (1962).

Hunter, Sam, *Modern American Painting and Sculpture* (1959).

James, Ralph C., *Hoffa and The Teamsters: A Study of Union Power* (1965).

Johnson, James A., *et al., Introduction to the Foundations of American Education* (1969).

Johnson, Lyndon B., *The Vantage Point* (1971).

Jones, Charles O., *The Republican Party in American Politics* (1965).

Kahin, George M., and Lewis, John W., *The United States in Vietnam* (1969).

Kallenbach, Joseph, *The American Chief Executive: The Presidency and the Governorship* (1966).

Bibliography

Kaufman, Edgar, Jr., *The Rise of an American Architecture* (1970).

King, Rufus, *The Drug Hangup: America's Fifty Year Folly* (1972).

Koenig, Louis, *The Chief Executive* (1968).

Lachicolte, Alberta, *Rebel Senator* (1966).

La Couture, Jean, *DeGaulle* (1966).

Larkin, Oliver W., *Art and Life in America* (1964).

Lash, Joseph P., *Eleanor: The Years Alone* (1972).

Lewis, Anthony, *Gideon's Trumpet* (1964).

Lewis, Richard S., and Wilson, Jane, *Alamagordo plus Twenty-Five Years* (1971).

Lippmann, Walter, *The Cold War* (1972).

Lomax, Alan, *Folk Songs of North America* (1960).

Lorant, Stefan, *The Presidency: A Political History of Presidential Elections from Washington to Truman* (1951).

McCloskey, Robert G., *The American Supreme Court* (1960).

McCoubrey, John W., *American Tradition in Painting* (1963).

McNeal, Robert H., *The Bolshevik Tradition: Lenin, Stalin, Krushchev* (1963).

Major, Reginald, *A Panther is a Black Cat* (1971).

Manson, Grant, *Frank Lloyd Wright, 1869–1959* (1958).

Mathews, Jane DeHart, *The Federal Theatre 1935–1939* (1967).

Mayer, George H., *The Republican Party: 1854–1964* (1964).

Mellers, Wilfred, *Music in a New Found Land* (1965).

Meserve, Walter J., *An Outline History of American Drama* (1965).

Mesnick, Hank, *John Edgar Hoover* (1972).

Michaelmore, Peter, *The Swift Years* (1969).

Millett, Kate, *Sexual Politics* (1970).

Moholy-Nagy, Sibyl, *Native Genius in Anonymous Architecture* (1957).

Montgomery, John D., *Foreign Aid in International Relations* (1967).

Morgan, Robin, *Sisterhood is Powerful: An Anthology of Writings from the Women's Liberation Movement* (1970).

Moynihan, Daniel P., *The Defense of Freedom: The Public Papers of Arthur J. Goldberg* (1966).

Murphy, Paul L., *The Constitution in Crises Times, 1918–1969* (1972).

Nash, Roderick, *Wilderness and the American Mind* (1970).

Nixon, Richard, *Six Crises* (1962).

Pierce, N. R., *The People's President* (1968).

Pollock, John, *Billy Graham* (1966).

Preis, Art, *Labor's Giant Step: Twenty Years of the CIO* (1964).

Rae, John B., *The Road and the Car in American Life* (1971).

Ridgway, Matthew, *Soldier* (1956).

Ripley, Randall B., *Power in the Senate* (1969).

Ritchie, Andrew, *Sculpture of the Twentieth Century* (1952).

Roberts, Chalmers M., *The Nuclear Years: The Arms Race and Arms Control, 1945–1970* (1970).

Roseboom, Eugene H., *History of Presidential Elections* (rev. ed., 1970).

Rossiter, Clinton, *The American Presidency* (1960).

Rovere, Richard H., *Senator Joe McCarthy* (1959).

Schaar, John, *Escape from Authority, The Perspectives of Erich Fromm* (1961).

Schattschneider, Elmer E., *Party Government* (1942).

Schlesinger, Arthur M., Jr., *A Thousand Days: John F. Kennedy in the White House* (1965).

Schlesinger, Arthur M., Jr., and Israel, F. L. (eds.), *History of American Presidential Elections 1789–1968* (1971).

Schmitt, H. A., *The Path to European Union: From the Marshall Plan to the Common Market* (1962).

Schwartz, Lita L., *American Education: A Problem-Centered Approach* (1969).

Scully, Vincent, *American Architecture and Urbanism* (1969).

Seale, Bobby, *Seize the Time* (1970).

Sheehan, Neil, and Kenworthy, E. W., *The Pentagon Papers* (1972).

Sherrill, Robert, and Ernst, Harry W., *Drugstore Liberal* (1968).

Singer, Charles, et al., *History of Technology* (1958).

Smith, Margaret Chase, and Lewis, William C., *Declaration of Conscience* (1972).

Sorensen, Theodore C., *Kennedy* (1965).

Sorensen, Theodore C., *The Kennedy Legacy* (1969).

Spiller, Robert E., et al., *Literary History of the United States* (1948).

Stambler, Irwin, and Landon, Grelun, *Encyclopedia of Folk, Country and Western Music* (1969).

Stedman, Murray S., and Stedman, Susan W., *Discontent at the Polls, A Study of Farmers and Labor Parties 1827–1948* (1967).

Steinberg, Alfred, *The Man from Missouri: The Life and Times of Harry S Truman* (1962).

Sutherland, Arthur E., *Constitutionalism in America: Origin and Evolution of Its Fundamental Ideas* (1965).

Swindler, William F., *Court and Constitution in the Twentieth Century* (1970).

Taylor, Walter Fuller, *The Story of American Literature* (1956).

Thompson, Lawrance, *Robert Frost: The Early Years, 1874–1915* (1966).

Thompson, Lawrance, *Robert Frost: The Years of Triumph, 1915–1938* (1970).

Tiedt, Sidney W., *The Role of the Federal Government in Education* (1966).

Trewhitt, Henry L., *McNamara* (1971).

Truman, Harry S, *Memoirs* (2 vols., 1955–1956).

Tuchman, Maurice, *American Sculpture of the Sixties* (1967).

Udall, Stewart L., *The Quiet Crisis* (1963).

Vatcher, William H., *Panmunjom: The Story of the Korean Military Armistice Negotiations* (1958).

Von Braun, Wernher, and Ordway, Frederick, *History of Rocketry and Space Travel* (1969).

White, Theodore H., *The Making of the President, 1960* (1961); *1964* (1965); *1968* (1969); *1972* (1973).

Wildavsky, Aaron, *The Presidency* (1969).

Williams, Martin, *Jazz Masters of New Orleans* (1967).

Wills, Gary, *Nixon Agonistes: The Crisis of the Self-Made Man* (1970).

Witcover, Jules, *White Knight: The Rise of Spiro T. Agnew* (1972).

Young, Philip, *Ernest Hemingway: Reconsideration* (1966).

IX. BLACKS IN THE UNITED STATES

Aptheker, Herbert, *American Negro Slave Revolts* (1969).

Aptheker, Herbert (ed.), *The Autobiography of W. E. B. Du Bois* (1968).

Bemis, Samuel F., *John Quincy Adams and the Union* (1956).

Bernard, Jacqueline, *Journey Toward Freedom* (1967).

Bontemps, Arna, *The Story of George Washington Carver* (1954).

Butcher, Margaret, J., *The Negro in American Culture* (1956).

Buell, Raymond L., *Liberia* (1947).

Campbell, Stanley W., *The Slave Catchers* (1970).

Chisholm, Shirley, *Unbought and Unbossed* (1971).

Conrad, Earl, *Harriet Tubman* (1942).

Cronon, Edmund D., *Black Moses: The Story of Marcus Garvey and the Universal Negro Improvement Association* (1955).

Eaton, Clement, *Freedom of Thought in The Old South* (1940).

Elkins, Stanley M., *Slavery: A Problem in American Institutional and Intellectual Life* (1968).

Elliott, Lawrence, *George Washington Carver: The Man Who Overcame* (1966).

Foner, Philip S., *The Life and Writings of Frederick Douglass* (1950–1955).

Foner, Philip S., *The Voice of Black America* (1972).

Frazier, E. Franklin, *The Negro in the United States* (1957).

Harlan, Louis, *Booker T. Washington: The Making of a Black Leader, 1856–1901* (1972).

Holt, Rackham, *George Washington Carver: An American Biography* (1943).

Jordan, Winthrop, *White Over Black* (1968).

King, Coretta S., *My Life With Martin Luther King, Jr.,* (1969).

Lewis, David, *King: A Critical Biography* (1970).

Lincoln, C. Eric, *The Black Muslims in America* (1961).

Logan, Rayford, *W. E. B. Du Bois: A Profile* (1971).

Meier, August, *Negro Thought in America, 1889–1915* (1963).

Myrdal, Gunnar, *An American Dilemma: The Negro Problem and Modern Democracy* (1962).

Quarles, Benjamin, *Frederick Douglass* (1948; reprinted 1968).

Rudwick, Elliott, *W. E. B. Du Bois: Propagandist of the Negro Protest* (1968).

Stampp, Kenneth M., *The Peculiar Institution* (1956).

Staudenraus, P. J., *The African Colonization Movement, 1816–1947* (1961).

Styron, William, *The Confessions of Nat Turner* (1967).

Thornbrough, Emma Lou, *Booker T. Washington* (1969).

Tragle, Henry I., *The Southampton Slave Revolt of 1831* (1971).

Vincent, Theodore G., *Black Power and the Garvey Movement* (1971).

Washington, Booker T., *Up From Slavery: An Autobiography* (1901).

X. INDIANS IN AMERICA

Boas, Franz, *Race, Language and Culture* (1949).

Brown, Mark H., *The Flight of the Nez Perce* (1966).

De Young, C. A., and Wynn, Richard, *American Education* (1968).

Deloria, Vine, Jr., *Custer Died for Your Sins* (1969).

Driver, Harold E., *Indians of North America* (1961).

Dunn, J. P., Jr., *Massacres of the Mountains: A History of the Indian Wars of the Far West 1815–1875* (1969).

Fenton, William N., *American Indian and White Relations to 1830: Needs and Opportunities for Study* (1957).

Finerty, John F., *War Path and Bivouac, Or the Conquest of the Sioux* (1961).

Hagan, William T., *American Indians* (1961).

Hodge, Frederick W., *Handbook of American Indians North of Mexico* (1910).

Josephy, Alvin M., Jr., *The Indian Heritage of America* (1966).

Leckie, William H., *Conquest of the Southern Plains* (1963).

Peckham, Howard H., *The Colonial Wars, 1689–1762* (1964).

Prescott, William H., *History of the Conquest of Peru* (1936).

Steward, Julian H., *Handbook of South American Indians* (1946–1950).

Thompson, J. Eric, *The Rise and Fall of Maya Civilization* (1954).

Credits

Credits

1. Wide World Photos
2. Library of Congress, Brady Collection
3. Jean Wolcott; Courtesy of the Department of State
4. National Portrait Gallery, Smithsonian Institution; National Portrait Gallery, Smithsonian Institution
5. National Portrait Gallery, Smithsonian Institution
6. Culver Pictures; White House Photo
7. U.S.D.A. Photo by Jim Strawser
8. Culver Pictures; Library of Congress
9. Culver Pictures; Wide World Photos
11. AFL-CIO
14. Library of Congress
15. Library of Congress; Culver Pictures
16. Library of Congress; Culver Pictures
17. Seagram's, N.Y.C.
19. Library of Congress
21. Los Alamos Scientific Laboratory; Los Alamos Scientific Laboratory
22. Los Alamos Scientific Laboratory; Library of Congress
23. Educational Affairs Department, Ford Motor Company; Smithsonian Institution
24. Library of Congress
25. Wide World Photos; Mottke Weissman
27. Library of Congress
28. Library of Congress; Wide World Photos
29. Culver Pictures; AT&T Company Photo Center
30. Wide World Photos; U.S. Information Agency
33. Wide World Photos; Library of Congress
35. Wide World Photos; Editorial Cartoon by Pat Oliphant, copyright The Denver Post. Reprinted with permission of Los Angeles Times Syndicate; Wide World Photos
36. National Portrait Gallery, Smithsonian Institution
37. Library of Congress
38. Library of Congress; Dwight D. Eisenhower Library
39. Culver Pictures
40. Library of Congress
41. Library of Congress; Library of Congress
42. Wide World Photos; United Nations
43. Library of Congress; Herblock, *The Washington Post*
44. Fred O. Seibel in the Richmond *Times Dispatch;* Senator H. F. Byrd, Jr.
47. Library of Congress; Culver Pictures
48. Library of Congress; Library of Congress
49. Culver Pictures; Wide World Photos
51. Library of Congress; Library of Congress
52. Library of Congress; Wide World Photos
53. Culver Pictures; Shirley Chisholm
54. Library of Congress; Culver Pictures
55. U.S. Signal Corps
56. Roy Justus in the Minneapolis *Star;* Bruce Shanks in the Buffalo *Evening News*
58. Library of Congress
61. Library of Congress; Library of Congress
63. Library of Congress; Library of Congress
64. National Portrait Gallery, Smithsonian Institution; National Portrait Gallery, Smithsonian Institution
65. Wide World Photos
66. National Portrait Gallery
68. Library of Congress
69. Courtesy, Museum of Fine Arts, Boston

70. Library of Congress; Department of Commerce
72. IBM
73. Culver Pictures
74. U.S.D.A. Photo by Joe Bednorz
85. Culver Pictures
86. Library of Congress; National Portrait Gallery, Smithsonian Institution
87. Courtesy, Museum of Fine Arts, Boston: Gift of Joseph W., William B. and Edward H. R. Revere
88. Wide World Photos
89. Library of Congress; Library of Congress
90. Culver Pictures
91. U.S. Air Force Photo; Library of Congress
92. Culver Pictures; U.S. Air Force Photo
93. National Portrait Gallery, Smithsonian Institution; U.S. Office of War Information
94. Library of Congress; Library of Congress
96. Wide World Photos
97. Thomas Nast, *Harper's Weekly* of Jan. 15, 1870
98. Culver Pictures
99. U.S. Navy Photo
100. White in the Akron *Beacon-Journal;* ©Walt Disney Productions
101. White House Historical Association; Library of Congress
102. Library of Congress
103. Library of Congress; Library of Congress
104. Culver Pictures; Library of Congress
105. Courtesy, Department of State; Wide World Photos
106. E. P. H. Documerica-Marc St. Gil; Library of Congress
107. Courtesy General Electric Company; Library of Congress
108. Library of Congress
109. Library of Congress; Library of Congress
110. Dwight D. Eisenhower Library
111. Angus MacBean & Faber & Faber LTD; Independence National Historical Park Collection
112. Library of Congress
113. Culver Pictures
114. Culver Pictures
115. Library of Congress; Library of Congress
118. Culver Pictures
119. New York Public Library Picture Collection; U.S. Navy Photo
120. Ralph Thompson
121. FBI
123. Library of Congress; Courtesy of the Department of State
124. Culver Pictures; Wide World Photos
125. Wide World Photos; Educational Affairs Department, Ford Motor Company
126. Wide World Photos
127. National Portrait Gallery, Smithsonian Institution
128. Library of Congress
129. Culver Pictures
130. Library of Congress
131. Associated Photographers, Pittsburgh, Pa. Wide World Photos
132. RG 77-Naval Observatory
135. Wide World Photos
136. Library of Congress
137. National Portrait Gallery, Smithsonian Institution
138. Library of Congress

139. Independence National Historical Park Collection; Library of Congress
140. Library of Congress; Culver Pictures
141. The Bettmann Archive
144. United States Mission to the UN; Geological Survey (Photo no. 57-HS-910 in the National Archives)
145. U.S. War Dept. General Staff (Photo no. 165-FF-3C-10 in the National Archives); Courtesy of the AFL-CIO
146. Wide World Photos; Library of Congress
147. Library of Congress
148. Independence National Historical Park Collection; Culver Pictures
149. U.S. Navy Photograph
150. National Portrait Gallery, Smithsonian Institution
151. Library of Congress
152. Library of Congress
153. National Portrait Gallery, Smithsonian Institution
154. Library of Congress
155. Library of Congress
156. Courtesy of the Hearst Corporation; Courtesy of Charles Scribner's Sons
157. National Portrait Gallery, Smithsonian Institution
158. Culver Pictures
159. Courtesy of Norman F. Barka
160. Library of Congress
161. Library of Congress
162. Library of Congress
164. Library of Congress
165. Library of Congress
166. Library of Congress
167. Courtesy of Hubert Humphrey
169. Culver Pictures; Library of Congress
170. Wide World Photos; U.S. Signal Corps (Photo no. 111-SC-94849 in the National Archives)
171. U.S. Signal Corps (Photo no. 111-SC-82522 in the National Archives)
172. Library of Congress
174. Library of Congress
176. Library of Congress; RG 106-Smithsonian Institution, in the National Archives
177. U.S. Signal Corps (Photo no. 111-SC-82412 in the National Archives)
178. U.S. Department of the Interior Geological Survey; Library of Congress
179. Courtesy of Singer, Co.; Library of Congress
180. National Portrait Gallery, Smithsonian Institution; Courtesy of Al Hirschfeld
181. National Art Gallery, Smithsonian Institution
182. Culver Pictures; Rare Book Division, The New York Public Library, Astor, Lenox, and Tilden Foundation
183. Library of Congress; National Portrait Gallery, Smithsonian Institution
184. Wide World Photos
185. Independence National Historical Park Collection
186. Library of Congress; The Lyndon Baines Johnson Library
187. Library of Congress; National Portrait Gallery, Smithsonian Institution
188. Justice Department
190. Wide World Photos
191. Brown Brothers; Wide World Photos

192. Library of Congress
193. U.S. Information Agency (Photo no. 306-PS.50.15199 in the National Archives)
194. Library of Congress; UAW Solidarity Photo
196. Library of Congress; Library of Congress
197. Culver Pictures; Library of Congress
198. Library of Congress
199. Land Management (Photo no. 49-AR-19B in the National Archives)
200. Navy Photograph; Independence National Historical Park Collection
201. Library of Congress
202. Wide World Photos; Library of Congress
204. Library of Congress
205. Library of Congress; Library of Congress
206. Library of Congress
207. Wide World Photos; National Art Gallery, Smithsonian Institution
208. Library of Congress; Wide World Photos
209. Library of Congress; Library of Congress
210. Library of Congress
211. Wide World Photos; U.S. Army Photograph
212. Herblock, *The Washington Post;* Library of Congress
213. George McGovern; Library of Congress
214. U.S. Army Photographic Agency, Photo by Oscar Porter
215. National Portrait Gallery, Smithsonian Institution
216. Courtesy of Grove Press
217. Culver Pictures
218. National Portrait Gallery, Smithsonian Institution; Dwight D. Eisenhower Library
219. National Portrait Gallery, Smithsonian Institution; Courtesy of the Department of State
220. Solidarity Photo
222. Margaret Mead
223. AFL-CIO; Culver Pictures
224. Library of Congress
226. Library of Congress
227. U.S. Army Photographer
228. Library of Congress; National Portrait Gallery
229. Courtesy of Morgan Guaranty Trust Company; U.S. War Department General Staff (Photo no. 165-X5-7 in the National Archives)
230. Library of Congress
231. Library of Congress; Culver Pictures
232. Wide World Photos; Culver Pictures
233. Culver Pictures; Wide World Photos; Wide World Photos
234. Library of Congress
235. Wide World Photos
236. Culver Pictures
237. Library of Congress
238. Library of Congress
239. New York Picture Library
242. Library of Congress; Library of Congress
243. New York Stock Exchange
244. Courtesy of U.S. Secret Service
245. Wide World Photos
247. Library of Congress
248. Wide World Photos
249. New York Public Library; Courtesy of the Institute For Advanced Studies, by Alan W. Richards
250. Library of Congress
251. Fasch Studio; New York Public Library

252. Sterling and Francine Clark Art Institute; The Museum of Modern Art, New York
253. U.S. Army Photograph
254. Culver Pictures
255. U.S. Army Photograph
256. Courtesy of the U.S. Navy; Library of Congress
257. Library of Congress
258. Courtesy of U.S. Navy, U.S. Army Photograph
259. Library of Congress; Library of Congress
260. Culver Pictures
261. Library of Congress
262. Library of Congress
266. Library of Congress
267. Library of Congress; Library of Congress
268. Courtesy of U.S. Postal Service
269. Boris De Rachewiltz, Courtesy of New Directions Publishing Corp.
273. Library of Congress
274. Library of Congress
275. Brown Brothers; Brown Brothers
277. Library of Congress; Library of Congress
278. Brown Brothers
281. United Press International; United Press International
284. Wide World Photos
285. Mergen in the *Atlantic Journal*
286. Wide World Photos
287. Library of Congress
289. Library of Congress
291. Secretary of Agriculture (Photo no. 16-C-95 in the National Archives); Quartermaster General (Photo no. 92-F-79B-21 in the National Archives)
293. Wide World Photos
294. Library of Congress
296. New York Public Library
297. Chase Ltd., Washington
299. Library of Congress
301. Library of Congress
302. U.S. Army Photograph
303. Wide World Photos; An Exxon Photo
304. Bob Wands; Library of Congress
305. Franklin D. Roosevelt Library; Franklin D. Roosevelt Library
306. Library of Congress; Library of Congress
307. Wide World Photos
308. Wide World Photos; Wide World Photos
309. Columbia University
310. U.S. Army Photograph; Museum of Modern Art New York, Mrs. Simon Guggenheim Fund
312. Courtesy of Department of State; Singer Sewing Co.
313. Courtesy of the Department of State; Singer Sewing Co.
314. Library of Congress; Library of Congress
315. Library of Congress
316. Library of Congress
317. Library of Congress
319. Library of Congress
320. Library of Congress, Brady Collection
321. Library of Congress; Library of Congress
323. Library of Congress; Estate of David Low
324. NASA
325. NASA
326. Library of Congress; Library of Congress
328. Library of Congress; Stanford University
329. Library of Congress; Library of Congress
330. Library of Congress

331. Paul Farber; Library of Congress
332. Wide World Photos; U.S. Army Photograph
333. Library of Congress; Library of Congress
334. Library of Congress
335. Library of Congress; Library of Congress
336. Library of Congress; Library of Congress
338. Library of Congress
339. Wide World Photos; Taft Family
340. Library of Congress; Library of Congress
342. Library of Congress
344. TVA; TVA
346. Culver Pictures; Inc., Culver Pictures, Inc.
347. National Portrait Gallery, Smithsonian Institution
350. National Park Service Photograph; New York Public Library; Library of Congress
351. Culver Pictures; Library of Congress
352. Library of Congress; Library of Congress
353. Library of Congress; Library of Congress
354. Library of Congress
355. United Nations; UNESCO/Dominique Roger
356. Library of Congress; Houston Park, Inc.
357. Library of Congress
359. Library of Congress
361. Wide World Photos
363. VISTA; Wide World Photos
364. Library of Congress; Wide World Photos
365. Library of Congress
366. Wide World Photos; National Portrait Gallery, Smithsonian Institution; National Portrait Gallery, Smithsonian Institution
369. National Portrait Gallery, Smithsonian Institution; National Portrait Gallery, Smithsonian Institution
371. Westinghouse Electric Co.
372. Library of Congress
373. Library of Congress
375. Photo by Bruce Paulson, Courtesy of New Directions Publishing Company
376. Library of Congress
378. Wide World Photos
379. U.S. Signal Corps (Photo no. 111-SC-23056 in the National Archives)
381. U.S. Signal Corps (Photo no. 111-SC-8364 in the National Archives); U.S. Signal Corps, (Photo no. 111-SC-50126 in the National Archives)
382. U.S. Navy Photograph
384. U.S. Office of War Information (Photo no. 208-YE-122 in the National Archives); U.S. Office of War Information (Photo no. 208-OX-43888)
385. Wide World Photos; Library of Congress
386. Library of Congress
387. Wide World Photos

Contributing Artists; Francis & Shaw, Nathalie Van Buren, Louise Emmons Merriman

Encyclopedia of
American History Staff

Publisher	**Stephen P. Elliott**
Associate Publisher	**Gayle Johnson**
Editor	**Ernest Kohlmetz**
Designer	**Louise Emmons Merriman**
Photo Researcher	**Margaretta Barton**
Production Supervisor	**Joseph J. Corlett**
Administrative Assistant	**Diane Bell**

This book was set in Optima on the Fototronic CRT by
Rocappi/Lehigh, Pennsauken, New Jersey

The text was printed in web offset lithography and bound by
Kingsport Press, Inc., Kingsport, Tennessee.

Text paper is Finch Title '94,' furnished by Pratt Paper Company,
Boston, Massachusetts.

The cover material is Lexotone, furnished by The Holliston Mills,
Inc., Norwood, Massachusetts.

Covers were printed in offset lithography by The Lehigh
Press/Lithographers, Pennsauken, New Jersey.